Critics across America acclaim "A People's History"

"This People's History is a celebration."　　—*The New York Times Book Review*

"Readers are sure to be rewarded. . . . Smith's multi-volume story of who we Americans are and how we came to be is an admirable project."
　　—*The Washington Post Book World*

"Engrossing narrative history . . . bound to invigorate and instruct . . . Amazing in its sweep and scope"　　—*Chicago Sun-Times*

"Popular history set down with the candor of a maturing New Journalism"
　　—*Publishers Weekly*

"Smith's achievement is truly remarkable. No American historian since Charles Beard has produced anything comparable in length, scope, or readability. To find standards with which to judge this work we must go back to 19th-century masters like George Bancroft, Francis Parkman, and Henry Adams."　　—*San Francisco Chronicle Book Review*

"A remarkable achievement in the writing of popular history"
　　—*Dallas Times Herald*

"The individual characters' lives Smith dramatizes truly live."　—*Miami Herald*

"Distinguished . . . Belongs on the shelves of anyone who wants to understand where we've been, so he can form a more educated opinion on where we're going."　　—*Milwaukee Journal*

"Smith brings to his work not only a clear and thorough knowledge of his subject, but a literary elegance rarely found among today's scholars."
　　—*The Boston Sunday Globe*

"The author's great gift lies in his unerring eye for the evocative or perceptive quotation that opens for the reader a view of the times as seen by the women and men living in them."　　—*The Philadelphia Inquirer*

"Smith writes as a lover loves—from the heart. . . . Not since the 19th century has an American historian written so extensively and passionately about his country."　　—*Los Angeles Times Book Review*

PENGUIN BOOKS

AMERICA ENTERS THE WORLD

Page Smith was educated at the Gilman School in Baltimore, Dartmouth College, and Harvard University. He has served as research associate at the Institute of Early American History and Culture, and has taught at the University of California at Los Angeles and at Santa Cruz, where he makes his home. Dr. Smith is the author of numerous books, including the highly acclaimed two-volume biography *John Adams*, which was a Main Selection of the Book-of-the-Month Club, a National Book Award Nominee, and a Bancroft winner; *The Historian and History*; *The Constitution: A Documentary and Narrative History*; *Daughters of the Promised Land: Women in American History*; and *Jefferson: A Revealing Biography*. His People's History series consists of the following volumes: *A New Age Now Begins: A People's History of the American Revolution* (two volumes); *The Shaping of America: A People's History of the Young Republic* (an American Book Award nominee); *The Nation Comes of Age: A People's History of the Ante-Bellum Years*; *Trial by Fire: A People's History of the Civil War and Reconstruction*; *The Rise of Industrial America: A People's History of the Post-Reconstruction Era*; *America Enters the World: A People's History of the Progressive Era and World War I*; and *Redeeming the Time: A People's History of the 1920s and The New Deal*. He is also coauthor, with Charles Daniel, of *The Chicken Book*.

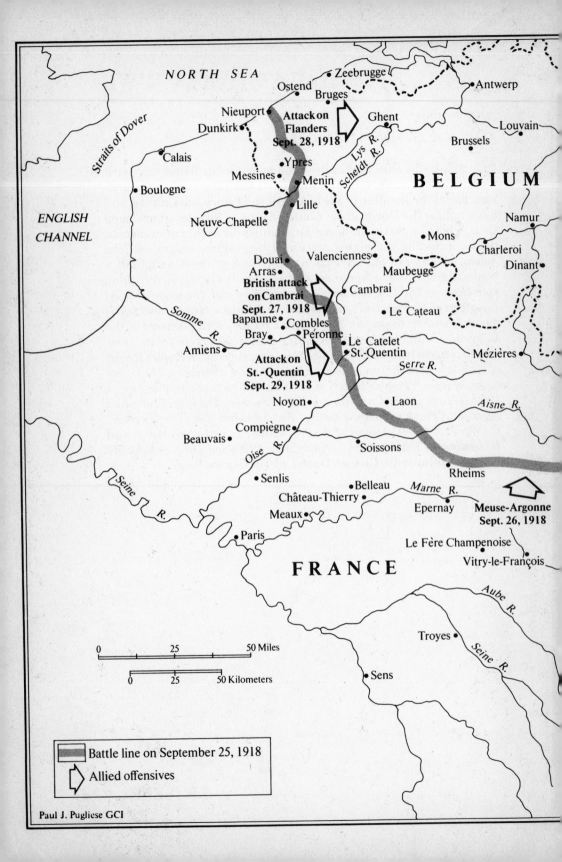

NORTH SEA

ENGLISH
CHANNEL

Straits of Dover

• Zeebrugge
Ostend •
• Bruges • Antwerp
Nieuport •
**Attack on
Flanders
Sept. 28, 1918** • Ghent
Dunkirk •

• Calais

• Boulogne

• Ypres
Messines • • Menin

Neuve-Chapelle • • Lille

Lys R.
Scheldt R.

BELGIUM

• Louvain
• Brussels

Douai • Valenciennes • • Mons

• Namur

• Maubeuge
Arras •
**British attack
on Cambrai
Sept. 27, 1918** • Cambrai

• Charleroi
• Dinant

Somme R.
Bapaume •
Bray • • Combles
• Péronne
Amiens • • Le Catelet
St.-Quentin •
**Attack on
St.-Quentin
Sept. 29, 1918**

• Le Cateau

• Mézières

Serre R.

Noyon • • Laon

Aisne R.

Compiègne •
Beauvais • • Soissons

Oise R.

• Rheims

• Senlis
• Belleau
Château-Thierry •
Meaux • *Marne R.*
• Epernay

**Meuse-Argonne
Sept. 26, 1918**

Seine R.

• Paris

FRANCE

• Le Fère Champenoise
• Vitry-le-François

Aube R.

0   25   50 Miles

0   25   50 Kilometers

Troyes •

Seine R.

• Sens

▓▓ Battle line on September 25, 1918

⬜▷ Allied offensives

Paul J. Pugliese GCI

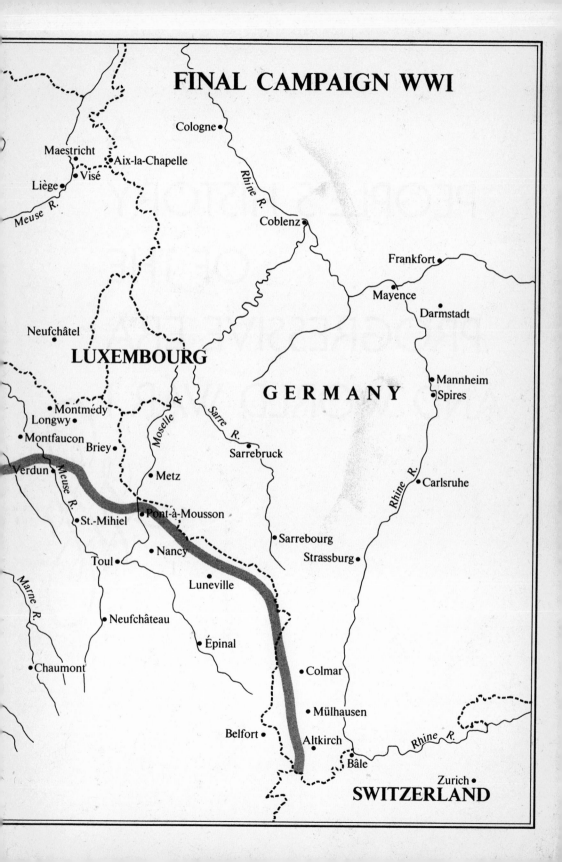

A
PEOPLE'S HISTORY
OF THE
PROGRESSIVE ERA
AND WORLD WAR I

AMERICA ENTERS THE WORLD

Page Smith

VOLUME SEVEN

PENGUIN BOOKS

PENGUIN BOOKS
Published by the Penguin Group
Viking Penguin, a division of Penguin Books USA Inc.,
375 Hudson Street, New York, New York 10014, U.S.A.
Penguin Books Ltd, 27 Wrights Lane,
London W8 5TZ, England
Penguin Books Australia Ltd, Ringwood,
Victoria, Australia
Penguin Books Canada Ltd, 2801 John Street,
Markham, Ontario, Canada L3R 1B4
Penguin Books (N.Z.) Ltd, 182–190 Wairau Road,
Auckland 10, New Zealand

Penguin Books Ltd, Registered Offices:
Harmondsworth, Middlesex, England

First published in the United States of America by
McGraw-Hill Book Company 1985
Reprinted by arrangement with McGraw-Hill, Inc.
Published in Penguin Books 1991

10 9 8 7 6 5 4 3 2 1

LIBRARY OF CONGRESS CATALOGING IN PUBLICATION DATA
Smith, Page.
America enters the world: a people's history of the Progressive
Era and World War I/Page Smith.
p. cm.
Reprint. Originally published: New York: McGraw-Hill, c1985.
Includes index.
ISBN 0 14 01.2263 X
1. United States—Politics and government—1865–1933.
2. Progressivism (United States politics)   3. World War, 1914–1918–
United States.   I. Title.
E743.S58   1991
973—dc20   90–43646

Printed in the United States of America

Contents

For Frances Rydell,
with gratitude and affection

Introduction

In the preceding volume I focused particularly on what was called by contemporaries the war between capital and labor, the bitter and bloody struggle between mine and factory owners and their ruthlessly exploited workers. Two other major themes were the effect of Darwinism on traditional American notions about man and his relation to the natural and "transnatural" world and, finally, the emergence of the West as a major factor in American life. There were, of course, numerous other themes and trends, some new and some going back several generations, but these were, in my opinion, subservient to the major developments listed above. In this volume the same three themes continue to dominate. The war between capital and labor becomes, if possible, more bitter and unrelenting than ever. Most thoughtful individuals with social consciences are socialists or anarchists of one denomination or another and continue to anticipate a revolution, hopefully peaceful but probably violent, which will lead to a more just social and economic order.

The Populists, having been absorbed into the Bryan-led Democratic Party, having become Socialists under the leadership of Eugene V. Debs, or, attracted by the dynamic and "Progressive" leadership of

Robert La Follette, having returned to the Republican fold, disappear from the political scene as quickly as they appeared, the most extraordinary political phenomenon in our history, their brief ascendancy leaving historians with a bone they seem never to tire of gnawing.

The principal drama of the first decade of the new century involves that brilliant and indefatigable actor Theodore Roosevelt, who gives the intoxicating illusion that he is capable, almost single-handedly, of taming predatory capitalists and militant workers alike while at the same time making the United States a power to be reckoned with in the world of international diplomacy.

Meanwhile, a final vast wave of immigration rounds out, so to speak, the multinational character of the United States and in the process adds substantially to the radicalism and the rancor of the war between capital and labor. Perhaps most important of all in the long run, a new consciousness continues to struggle to be born or, having been born, fights for life and, indeed, for domination. Art becomes a talismanic word for the new consciousness which manifests itself most strikingly in the visual arts.

Finally, the outbreak of the European War, which, with the entry of the United States, becomes the World War, combines with the Russian Revolution to sound the death knell of the old world order and mark the beginning of a new age—or perhaps mark the end of the beginning of that new age ushered in by the American Revolution. In this perspective the American Revolution is simply the beginning of that "age of democratic revolutions" which had in view the "emancipation of a world." The Russian Revolution, however perverted, and its companion, the Chinese Revolution, mark the end of ideological revolution (though not, of course, the end of revolutionary upheavals in various third world countries) and, at the same time, the end of the utopian expectation—i.e., that there is a particular social/economic/political system that can ensure both justice and freedom. This is not, certainly, clear by the end of the period covered by this volume. The proponents of the Russian Revolution argue that it is still in its infancy and that its horrid tyrannies and "liquidations" are simply the growing pains of the new world order. The true believers, perhaps conscious that it was their last hope, believed more devoutly than ever. But the seed of doubt had been sown, and with it the seeds of that contest for world domination between the United States and the Soviet Union that was to overshadow every other issue in the second half of the twentieth century.

The story begins simply enough with Theodore Roosevelt, the exuberant "cowboy," as Mark Hanna called him derisively, ensconced in the White House—"living above the store," as his wife put it.

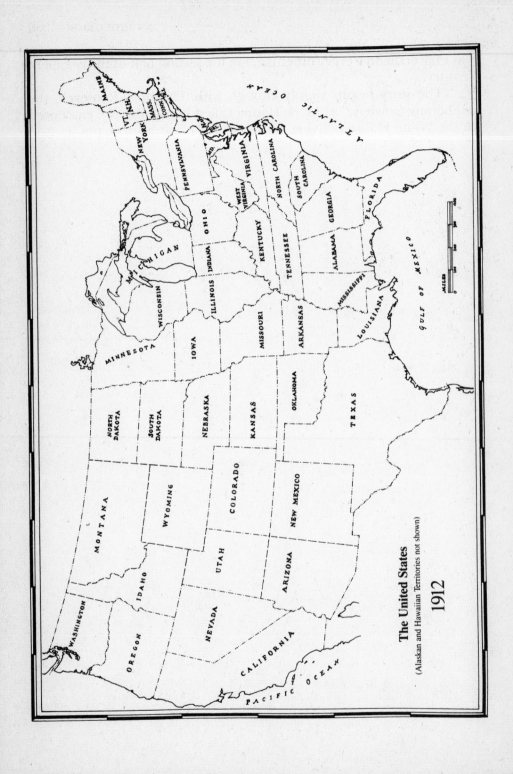

The United States

(Alaskan and Hawaiian Territories not shown)

1912

AMERICA
ENTERS
THE
WORLD

A New Hand at the Helm

The man who became the twenty-sixth president of the United States by virtue of an anarchist's bullet had been, as every schoolchild knows, a frail and sickly child who as an adult became the exemplar of masculine strength and energy.

Theodore Roosevelt was convinced that he literally owed his life as well as his robust good health to the loving care of his father. Theodore, Sr., was a model of upper-class noblesse oblige. A large, imposing man, with a hearty laugh and an irrepressible penchant for good works, he helped establish the Newsboys' Lodging House, where several hundred boys were given a bed each night for five cents, the Children's Aid Society, and the New York Orthopedic Dispensary and Hospital for children with diseases of the spine. He was also one of the founders of the Metropolitan Museum of Art and the Museum of Natural History. It was he who organized the Bureau of Charities to coordinate the activities of all the city's charitable associations. A friend called him "the model of Christian manhood." His precepts were simple, old-fashioned ones: "I always believe in showing affection by doing what will please the one we love, not by talking. . . . I have often thought that unselfishness combined in one word more of the teachings of the Bible than any other in the language." His sister-in-law called him

1

Greatheart, comparing him to the Puritan warrior in *The Pilgrim's Progress:* "Come now, and follow me, and no hurt shall happen to you from the lions. . . ."

"Take care of your morals first, your health next, and finally your studies," the elder Roosevelt advised the younger Theodore on his departure for Harvard. From there Theodore, or Teedie or Thee, as he was called in the family, wrote: "I do not think there is a fellow in college who has a family that love him as much as you all do me, and I am *sure* that there is no one who has a father who is also his best and most intimate friend as you are mine. . . . I do not find it nearly so hard as I expected not to drink and smoke. . . ."

When the senior Roosevelt died during his eldest son's junior year at Harvard, he was universally eulogized. George William Curtis, alumnus of Brook Farm and editor of *Harper's Weekly,* called him "an American citizen of the best type. . . ." After his father's death Theodore felt that he might go "mad" with grief, reflecting, "I am as much inferior to Father morally and mentally as physically. . . . He did everything for me, and I nothing for him. I remember so well how, years ago, when I was a very weak, asthmatic child, he used to walk up and down with me in his arms. . . ." When his father picked him up, "I could breathe, I could sleep, when he had me in his arms, my father— he got me breath, he got me lungs, strength—life," he told Lincoln Steffens.

If the relationship with his father did more than anything else to shape his character, the role of class—in some ways, of course, inseparable from that of the family—was also crucial. Class gives an assurance that is often not far from arrogance, but as we have seen in numerous other instances, it also commonly frees its members from deference to "mere" wealth. While money was essential to maintain the prerogatives of class, it was vulgar to think and certainly to talk about it. And those who made it by rapacious methods of dubious legality were beneath contempt. So, in addition to the spirit of noblesse oblige that he inherited from his charitably disposed father, Teddy Roosevelt acquired, as naturally as his accent and his clothes, the attitudes of his class toward new wealth, which was, in the main, the wealth that bore most oppressively on the country.

We have already taken note of Roosevelt's infatuation with outdoor life. It was a class attitude in large part, and it was distinct from the earlier Emerson-Thoreau love of nature. It was, rather, an all-out assault on nature, a constant contest and competition with nature that was related directly to the American male's notion of maleness.

In addition to his passion for outdoor life, Roosevelt had an infinite capacity for play—for romps, as he called them—an impulse plainly derived from his father. On one occasion, when Gifford Pinchot and Grant La Farge arrived at the Governor's Mansion at Albany during Roosevelt's regime, they found the state's chief executive fighting off an attack of hypothetical Indians and helping the children in the house escape by lowering them by a rope from a second-story window. After a discussion of the desirability of applying proper forest management to the state-owned forests of New York, Pinchot and the governor engaged in wrestling and boxing matches.

As an addict of the strenuous life the new President soon incorporated it as a principle of government, devising a kind of survival training for members of his administration and foreign diplomats assigned to Washington. When a newly appointed assistant secretary of state appeared at the White House in a cutaway coat, striped trousers, patent leather shoes, and a handsome silk necktie, Roosevelt took him on one of his famous walks. As they reached the Potomac, after (in Pinchot's words) "sloshing through mud and water for the better part of an hour," the skiff on which the President usually crossed was missing. After a moment's pause Roosevelt removed his hat, put his watches and other valuables in it, replaced it on his head, and waded into the frigid river. Pinchot and the unhappy secretary followed suit, up to their waists and then to their shoulders before they reached the opposite bank.

The President had a "tennis and riding cabinet" made up of athletic young men. Wrestling and boxing were also de rigueur. Pinchot, who was seven years Roosevelt's junior, seems to have borne the brunt of the President's strenuousness. He recalled that he often returned home from some jaunt or tussle with "the boss" too tired to eat.

The President learned " 'Juido'—as they now seem to call Jiu Jitsu . . ." from a Professor Yamashita. The Japanese naval attaché, Commander Takashita, visited Roosevelt with a young friend, Kitgaki, who was entering the Naval Academy at Annapolis, and the President wrestled with both of them. He was curious about whether an American wrestler could hold his own with a judo master, and he arranged to match a young man named Grant, "the champion middleweight wrestler of the United States," against Yamashita. "Inside of a minute Yamashita had choked Grant, and inside of two minutes more he got an elbow hold on him that would have enabled him to break his arm; so that there was no question that he could have put Grant out," Roosevelt wrote to his son Kermit.

All of which was engaging but also somewhat pathological. The President turned every boxing or wrestling match into a competition and every walk or ride into a race, often a dangerous one. He so frequently seemed to be bent on killing or seriously injuring himself that even his most devoted admirers sensed something demonic in his headlong dash at life. The pathology seemed to spring from an inner doubt, a gnawing lack of confidence, a need to reaffirm daily his fearlessness, his certitude.

Life in the Roosevelt White House was both lively and informal. The liberal journalist Oswald Garrison Villard recalled discussing some important international issue with Roosevelt and Secretary of War Elihu Root at the Roosevelt breakfast table when young Ted appeared, carrying a fierce-looking macaw. When the President saw the bird, he ordered it taken away, whereupon little Alice set up a chant: "Father's afraid, father's afraid, father's afraid, father's afraid." Roosevelt jumped up, took the bird from his son and, "showing his teeth, turned upon his offspring and said: 'Now who's afraid, now who's afraid, now who's afraid?'" Then he resumed his seat, and the conversation continued as though there had never been an interruption.

When journalist Finley Peter Dunne, the famous "Mr. Dooley" and an old friend of the Colonel's, visited the Roosevelts at Sagamore Hill in Oyster Bay, on Long Island, with his young son Philip, Roosevelt instructed the child to hit him in his ample stomach as hard as he could, and when Philip skinned his knuckles on the Colonel's watch chain, Roosevelt carried him off to the bathroom and applied first aid.

Roosevelt was indeed at his most appealing in his relations with children. "I am really touched," he wrote a friend, "at the way in which your children as well as my own treat me as a friend and playmate." He read James Fenimore Cooper's *The Last of the Mohicans* and *The Deerslayer* to his sons Archie and Quentin. He wrote that there had been "skating and sleigh-riding all the week." His letters to his sons were filled with the kind of information important to children. He wrote "Archikins" that he had seen his lizard—"Bill the lizard—your lizard that you brought home from Mount Vernon"—in the honeysuckle. Games, horseback rides, romps, and "scrambles" were enumerated.

When Florence Harriman, a friend of the Roosevelts, dined at the White House, the President made a point of drawing her into conversation about her social work with immigrant children. "What do you think is best," he asked, to "send children to day-nurseries as we do, or ought we to try the German scheme of mothers' pensions?" Before she could answer, Roosevelt's aide, Colonel Archie Butts, came in with a waterproof suit that the President had ordered for his African safari. Harriman recalled that like a small boy with a new toy, Roosevelt gave a whoop of delight, climbed into the new garment, "grabbed a cane, ran up and down the hall shouting, pretending to shoot aides, ushers and any old thing handy, as imaginary lions. He even ran up the stairs and down again testing the suit to see whether he could have free play for his arms and legs."

Harriman wrote: "All the Roosevelts have a delightfully mad enthusiasm for each other and one can't be fond of one of them without presently acquiring a contagious affection for all. . . ."

Roosevelt's most striking quality was his remarkable energy. Hutchins Hapgood, the reformer-journalist, recalled his first impression of Roosevelt as governor of New York State: "He wore a tall black hat and he strode along the platform with the physical power of a landslide. Never before or since have I been so much impressed by the physical impact of a human being." It was, in the last analysis, the energy and its by-product enthusiasm which made the "Colonel" irresistible to most of those who came within the orbit of his remarkable personality. In the words of William Allen White, the Topeka editor, "the squeaking falsetto in which he gently clowned himself was most disarming. . . . When he came into a room, he changed all the relations in the room because . . . all minds and hearts turned to him. . . . I felt the joy and delight of his presence and, knowing his weakness, still gave him my loyalty—the great rumbling, roaring, jocund tornado of a man, all masculine save sometimes a catlike glint, hardly a twinkle, in his merry eyes."

The new journalist Ray Stannard Baker never forgot his first visit with the President. He was ushered into Roosevelt's library. On his desk were a gold miner's pan, a silver dagger, and piles of books. The skins of animals decorated the walls and covered the floors. Roosevelt soon appeared—"robust, hearty, wholesome, like a gust of wind," clad "in knickerbockers, a worn coat, and a disreputable pair of tramping shoes."

The variety of guests to the White House, invariably reported in the papers, was a constant source of wonder to the public. In addition to journalists, Rough Riders, and reformers, there were humorists, novelists, gunfighters, and poets. As a friend of letters the President invited Edwin Arlington Robinson, "a rather forlorn little poet and his nice wife," as he wrote Kermit, to lunch. "What a queer, mystical creature he is!" Roosevelt added. ". . . But he certainly has the real spirit of poetry in him."

When William Allen White and his wife, Sallie, were invited to the White House, the guests included Justice Oliver Wendell Holmes, Elihu Root, and General Leonard Wood. "Roosevelt fished the table like a fly fisherman," White wrote, "throwing to each guest." He "baited Holmes with a professor fly and got him to talking about his father, the poet." The irrepressible Roosevelt children were at the lunch table. They joined freely in the conversation, and when someone asked them who their father's favorite Cabinet members were, they replied in chorus, drumming on the table with their knives and forks for emphasis, "Mr. Root and Mr. Knox." The story was soon all over the Capitol.

Roosevelt exemplified the classic American view that a day spent without shooting something was a day misspent; a buffalo was preferable, but a squirrel would do. Farther West human varmints were fair game—rustlers, Indians, greasers, bandits. Roosevelt doted on Bat Masterson, who had been a law officer in Dodge City, Tombstone, and Deadwood and had shot any number of men. Masterson ended up a sportswriter for the *New York Morning Telegraph,* an appropriate, if somewhat ignominious, end. The humorist Opie Read, on a lecture tour, was a guest at a White House breakfast with Bat Masterson. Read had received a letter from the President which read: "Out west I have lain with my head on a saddle reading your yarns. The next time you are in Washington come over and snack with me." When Read was in Washington, the telephone rang early in the morning in his hotel room. He answered, "Hello, who is this?"

"Roosevelt . . . Come over about ten o'clock and break bread with me." *Slam!*

At the White House Roosevelt greeted Read with reminiscences about his visits to the Press Club, of which Read was a prominent member, and then hailed Masterson: "Well, if here isn't old Bat Masterson. Hello, Bat! Haven't seen you since you said you didn't know how many men you had killed, counting Greasers." Alexander Graham Bell was a guest, as was James Mann, Congressman from Illinois and enemy of prostitution. "Masterson," Read noted, "received the major part of Roosevelt's attention." Was it true, Roosevelt asked, that after a revivalist's sermon Masterson had placed his famous six-shooter in the collection plate—"Surely not the gun with all the notches in it." Masterson denied the allegation. Had he offered to shoot a nearby Indian to distract a bawling child? No.

This, according to Read, led the President to reflections on the nature of history. The difference between myth and history, he declared, "is that history lies in a more dignified way. The first writer of a lie is ever thereafter accepted as authority. If actual history should be written, mankind would blush in shame for itself. And yet we must have history for without it the world would be like a man without a memory." There was certainly an element of truth in the specific events of history, "but what brought about those events lies for the most part in mysticism." History's principal shortcoming, Roosevelt declared, was in the failure of historians to reveal fully the character of historical figures. "No statesman has been a saint and no tyrant without some color of virtue."

The conversation then turned to the recently proposed Mann Act, forbidding the transportation of women across state borders for immoral purposes, and Bat Masterson expressed his opinion that it was a "damned bad law. Nature's law is that women are sometimes as willin' as men."

"Shame on you, Bat," the President replied, grinning his famous grin.

When the story circulated that Roosevelt drank to excess and took dope, the President consulted Lincoln Steffens for advice on how to counter the rumors. Should he fight them or ignore them? Steffens replied that he would "follow your good old rule in all such matters."

"Old rule?"

"Never deny anything unless it is true." Steffens added: "He was himself strong drink. His vice was eating; it was not bad enough to be called gluttony, but he was a fast and enormous eater. A good big dinner and a lively company would make him almost drunk."

Roosevelt could be as disarming in his candor as he was captivating in his enthusiasms. He told John Hay, "I in my soul know I am but an average man, and that only marvelous good fortune has brought me where I am."

To a people noted for restraint, inhibitions, and indeed repression, this completely uninhibited leader suggested a new range of human potentialities, a kind of total engagement with the world. Often maniacal in their intensity, his enthusiasms nonetheless made the world a more interesting place to live in. As childish and absurd as his behavior often was—his high-pitched cries of "Bully!," his upper-class prejudices, his random bellicosity, his innately reactionary view of the world—all these faded into comparative insignificance beside the new image of the presidency that he created. In the words of William Allen White, "The gift of the gods to Theodore Roosevelt was joy, joy in life. He took joy in everything he did, in hunting, camping, and ranching, in politics, in reforming the police or the civil service, in organizing and commanding the Rough Riders." A British politician and journalist, John Morley, wrote: "The two things in America which seem to me extraordinary are Niagara Falls and President Roosevelt." Again in White's words, "Roosevelt bit me and I went mad." The Colonel gave "young men in their twenties, thirties, and early forties, a quickening sense of the inequities, injustice, and fundamental wrong of the political and economic overlay on our democracy, which was keeping too large a per cent of its citizens below average participation in the blessings of our democracy."

One early visitor to the White House whose visit stirred up a hornet's nest of bitter protest was the black leader, Booker T. Washington. The whole South shuddered at such villainy; Southern newspapers exploded with wrath. (A Southern Congressman, who was also a guest, solved the dilemma of how to address Washington—"boy" and "nigger" were clearly inappropriate, and he could not bring himself to call a black man mister—by addressing Washington as Professor.)

Roosevelt assured Senator Henry Cabot Lodge that the hue and cry raised over Washington's visit to the White House only confirmed "the continued existence of that combination of Bourbon intellect and intolerant truculence of spirit . . . which brought on the Civil War." The Southerners could not bluff him. "They can't even make me abandon my policy of appointing decent men to office in their own localities," he added, referring apparently to his appointments of blacks to Federal posts in the South. When officials in Indianola, Mississippi, ousted the black postmistress there, Roosevelt abolished the post office.

Not surprisingly the White House became the focus of the nation's fascinated attention. It was like a stage on which a continuous drama was being enacted. The projectors of this drama were the nation's journalists. Most of them adored the President in part because he was such inexhaustibly good "copy" and perhaps more because he considered himself "one of them," knew (or knew of) their wives and children, and showed a lively interest in them personally. A popular cartoon showed a husband putting aside the morning paper. "My dear," says his startled wife, surprised to see her husband's face emerge, "the paper must be dull today."

"It is," her husband replies. "Not a thing doing in the White House."

The President had hardly taken up residence in the White House before he began running for reelection. His anxiety about that relatively remote event was a measure of his self-doubt and insecurity.

By the midsummer of 1901 Roosevelt met with Western political supporters at Colorado Springs to lay the foundations for his presidential candidacy. William Allen White was among those politicians and "opinion-makers" who pledged their "political lives as hostages . . . to return Roosevelt delegates to the Republican Presidential Convention from Colorado, Wyoming, Kansas, Nebraska, and Missouri . . ." and, it was hoped, Iowa.

The President also began a highly publicized attack on those he termed "the malefactors of great wealth." The phrase was inspired. It took its place at once with such great utterances as "Don't fire till you see the whites of their eyes," "Don't give up the ship," and "Damn the torpedoes. Full speed ahead," utterances so dear to the American heart.

The war between capital and labor (of which Roosevelt aspired to be no more than a referee) raged on unabated, with capital clearly in the ascendant. One of the favorite pastimes of journals and journalists came to be millionaire counting. By 1892 the *New York Tribune* had counted up 4,047, the majority of whom had made their money in transportation, most typically the railroads, and in "trade." Merchandising counted 986, banking only 294—most of them in New York, Boston, and Philadelphia; a number in Chicago, St. Louis, Denver, and San Francisco. There were estimated to be 84 millionaires in agriculture, half of them Western cattlemen. There were 65 corporation lawyer millionaires. The concentration of wealth went on decade by decade. By 1900 there were 67 millionaires in Pittsburgh alone and 63 in Cleveland with an aggregate wealth of $300,000,000. In three "villages" in New York State 60 millionaires had a combined wealth, it was calculated, of $500,000,000, and the average *annual income* of 100 of the richest Americans was estimated at $1,500,000. Some 250,000 persons, or 0.35 percent of the population, owned three-fourths of the wealth of a country the population of which totaled 70,000,000, and between 25,000 and 40,000 families owned one-half of the country's wealth, or $31,000,000,000.

Of all the anthracite coal in the United States 87 percent was owned or controlled by eleven railroads—63 percent by the Philadelphia & Reading alone. By the same token Judge Elbert Gary, chairman of United States Steel, testified that his company owned 75 percent of all the iron ore in the Michigan-Minnesota region. The meat-packinghouse of Armour owned $11,000,000 worth of private railroad boxcars through which it controlled the movement of cattle from the range to the packinghouse.

Brooks Adams made an "in-depth" analysis of the character type of the American capitalist—the malefactor of great wealth. In Adams's view, the highest human attribute was the power of generalization (which he also called administration). Modern capitalists, he noted, "appear to have evolved under the stress of an environment which demanded excessive specialization in the direction of a genius adapted to money-making under highly complex industrial conditions. To this money-making attribute all else has been sacrificed. . . . The modern capitalist looks upon life as a financial combat of a very specialized kind, regulated by a code which he understands and has indeed concocted, but which is recognized by no one else in the world. He conceives sovereign powers to be for sale. He may, he thinks, buy them; and if he buys them, he may use them as he pleases. He believes, for instance . . . that it is the constitutional right of the citizens to buy the national highways [i.e., the railroads] and, having bought them, to use them as a common carrier might use a horse and cart upon a public road. He may sell his service to whom he pleases at what price may suit, and if by doing so he ruins men and cities, it is nothing to him. He is not responsible, for he is not a trustee for the public. If he be restrained by legislation, that legislation is an outrage, to be annulled or eluded by any means which will not lead to the penitentiary." To Brooks Adams, the capitalist, who profited from his manipulation of the legal system, was the most lawless man in America. He was dependent upon the law to uphold his privileges; nonetheless, "in spite of his vulnerability, he is of all citizens the most lawless." He assumed that the law would be upheld when it served his purposes. When it did not, he used all the expensive legal talent at his disposal to evade it. "He . . . looks upon the evasion of a law devised for public protection, but inimical to him, as innocent or even meritorious." It was this type, in whose ranks he had, to be sure, many friends and some political supporters, that Roosevelt undertook to chasten.

We have already noted the enthusiasm with which reformers of all varieties and persuasions reacted to Roosevelt's ascension. As Lincoln Steffens put it, "they rose into the air and made a beeline for Washington." There was, for a certainty, a considerable degree of naïveté in that response. Roosevelt, as police commissioner of New York City and as governor of the state, had been a tireless enemy of corruption and the champion of modest reforms, but the notion that he had any general or comprehensive view of radical social change (or even modest social change) was far off the mark. The cure for the ills of capitalism, Roosevelt believed, was the steadfast enforcement on wayward capitalists and thievish corporations of the Ten Commandments, especially the eighth. He wrote to Ray Stannard Baker: "I believe in corporations; I believe in trade unions. Both have come to stay, and are necessities in our present industrial system. But where, in either one or the other, there develops corruption or mere brutal indifference to the rights of others, and short-lived refusal to look beyond the moment's gain, then the offender, whether union or corporation, must be fought. . . ." The President conceived of himself as a kind of moral policeman whose principal task was punishing transgressors. He believed the people to be inherently good and the "system," such as it was, to be benign. If erring individuals, corporations, or unions were forced back into line, all should be well with the Republic. His inclination, Baker wrote, "was to cuff the radical on one ear and the conservative on the other, without enlightening either. . . . But what energy and gusto he had, what wholesome enthusiasms, what common human goodness and courtesies!" Baker added.

In Lincoln Steffens's opinion, Roosevelt "was a politician much more than he was a reformer; in the phraseology of the radicals, he was a careerist, an opportunist with no deep insight into issues, but he was interesting, picturesque." "You don't stand for anything fundamental," Steffens told him. Then, mustering all his scorn, the journalist declared, "All you represent is the square deal."

" 'That's it,' Roosevelt shouted, and rising to his feet, he banged the desk with his hands. 'That's my slogan: the square deal. I'll throw that out in my next statement. The square deal.' . . . 'A square deal,' a phrase shot at him in reproach and criticism, he seized upon and published it as his war cry; and a good one as it proved."

Roosevelt's "Square Deal" called for an income tax amendment, postal savings bank, parcel post, railroad regulation, taming the trusts, a pure food and drug act reinforced by strong state laws and stiff penalties, the promotion of public health, collective bargaining, shorter hours for labor, primary elections in place of party caucuses, workmen's compensation for injury or death in the work place, the extension of civil service, the building of an adequate system of roads, and the regulation of insurance companies, banks, and savings institutions.

The idol of the reformers, Roosevelt prided himself on his ability to get along with political bosses. "I am on excellent terms with Senator Platt," he wrote Henry Cabot Lodge in April, 1899, while he was governor of New York. "He has treated me admirably in every way and is I believe equally satisfied with the way I have treated him, except that I have not been able to back up some of his views about corporations." This was the same Thomas Platt whom William Allen White found in "a frowzy little cubbyhole" full of "mildewed junk." Platt himself looked like "a little old mangy rat in his nest . . . his face . . . blotched with brown spots, his bleary eyes . . . rummy. . . ."

Another of Roosevelt's political pals was Matthew Quay. Quay, the boss of Pennsylvania, was one of the nation's masters of political manipulation and the management of corruption just this side of the law. Roosevelt was with Quay when he was dying, and the boss said, "That's all right, dying, only I hate to be dying here on a bed like this. What I would like would be to crawl off on a rock in the sun and die like a wolf." It was a great exit line by any measure and one peculiarly calculated to move the President. Quay was part Indian, and he had been the titular chief of the old Five Nations. Dying, he asked Roosevelt to take his place, "as the chief and the protector of the Five Nations." Roosevelt said, telling Steffens of Quay's death, "I promised Quay to take and fill his place, and I will." And then turned angrily on Steffens, denouncing him for attacking men like Quay and other "really great men." Steffens could see that Roosevelt was tormented by the paradoxical nature of his relations with such "bad" politicians: his secret affection and admiration for them and his dislike of many of the reformers in their self-righteousness. What most galled the President and bemused Steffens was the fact that the middle- and upper-class reformers, in their rectitude, failed to understand the degree to which the system that provided them with their stock dividends and comfortable style of living was dependent on the "corruption" that oiled the wheels and kept the political (and economic) machinery running.

Roosevelt's remedy for the misdeeds of tycoons was publicity. In a speech at Providence, Rhode Island, in 1902, he declared, "Such publicity would by itself tend to cure the evils of which there is just complaint; it would show us if evils existed, and where the evils were imaginary, and it would show us what next ought to be done."

One of the first practical problems Roosevelt had to confront as President was the anthracite coal strike that broke out in Pennsylvania in the late spring of 1902. Encouraged by a successful strike a year earlier, John Mitchell, the organizer and president of the United Mine Workers, called on the operators to recognize the union and adopt an eight-hour day.

Mitchell was ambitious, vain, and basically subservient in his attitude toward business. He saw himself less as the champion of the overworked and underpaid miners than as a skillful mediator between capitalists and workingmen and as a loyal lieutenant of Ohio's Senator Mark Hanna. But whatever his ideological bent, he was an excellent organizer. It was largely through his efforts that the United Mine Workers had grown from a few thousand to 115,000 by 1900.

Hanna, incidentally, took the line that labor should be encouraged to organize, seeing unions as an alternative to socialism and communism. Unions would help secure higher wages and better working conditions for their members, thus lessening the dangers of class warfare. Hanna was a strong supporter of the National Civic Federation, which had helped negotiate a settlement in the conflict between United States Steel and the Amalgamated Association of Iron, Steel, and Tin Workers in 1901, a settlement, incidentally, that was very disadvantageous to the union.

Having won important concessions in the bituminous coalfields of Ohio largely through Hanna's assistance, Mitchell once more looked to the Senator for help in winning management's acceptance of unions in the anthracite mines of Pennsylvania. The National Civic Federation, of which Hanna was now president, was called on to act as mediator. But the owners, determined to break the union, were obdurate: no recognition for the union, no wage increase. The miners walked out, and Mitchell found himself virtually abandoned by his Federation friends, with Hanna powerless to help him.

In contrast to the Pullman strike, a decade earlier, the liberal sentiment of the country was clearly on the side of the strikers. George Baer, president of the mineowners' association, was as fiercely unreconstructed in his social attitudes as George Pullman, but Mitchell, radiating Irish charm, was careful to eschew any Socialist opinions. He placed himself carefully on the Samuel Gompers end of the labor spectrum and proved far more adept at creating public support for his miners than Eugene Debs had been in the Pullman strike. The tireless efforts of the battalions of reformers in the intervening decade had had a substantial effect in helping create that "new conscience" that Henry Demarest Lloyd had proclaimed so persistently. Joseph Pulitzer's *World* and the papers of William Randolph Hearst were outspoken in criticism of the mineowners and in support of the strikers. Baer's obduracy, his refusal to negotiate with the strikers or to enter into arbitration, and his rebuff of Mark Hanna's offer to help resolve the points at issue, seemed to many people to symbolize the arrogance of capitalists and their disregard of public opinion. "Anthracite mining," Baer declared to a committee of clerics who appealed to him to submit the dispute to arbitration, "is a business, and not a religious, sentimental, or academic proposition." Former President Grover Cleveland, whose handling of the Pullman strike had aroused such hostility in liberal and radical circles, called for prosecution of the anthracite mineowners and carriers under the terms of the Sherman Act. Many reformers joined Lloyd and Jacob Riis in a demand for the nationalization of the mines and the railroads that carried their coal.

Ray Stannard Baker, back from Europe and assigned to write a series of articles on labor and capital, hurried to the strike headquarters at Wilkes-Barre, Pennsylvania, to join "quite a group of writers and students, to say nothing of radical leaders in other fields who sensed the historic importance of what was happening. . . ." There, "in dingy hotel bedrooms filled with tobacco smoke . . . the issues were discussed with a passionate certitude not warranted," in Baker's opinion, "by any real or deep knowledge of the facts." Baker was disturbed by the refusal of some 17,000 miners to support the strike. The bitterest warfare, it seemed, was between the striking miners and their nonstriking fellows. He wrote an article entitled, rather prophetically, "The Right to Work." It appeared in *McClure's* in January, 1903, along with "The Shame of Minneapolis," one of Steffens's first exposés of municipal corruption, and the third installment of what became Ida Tarbell's book, *History of the Standard Oil Company*. All three articles had to do, in Baker's opinion, with the issue of lawlessness—lawless capital and lawless labor. The public response was, in Baker's word, "astonishing." He wrote: "I doubt whether any other magazine published in America ever achieved such sudden and overwhelming recognition. . . . [We] had put our fingers upon the sorest spots in American life."

As the coal strike dragged on week after week, with the coal operators "exceptionally obdurate," Washington Gladden, the reform-minded minister, consulted with the editor of the *Cincinnati Post*, a newspaper with a predominantly working-class circulation, to frame a petition asking the President to intervene. It read in part: "Some of us are men and women who work with our hands; some of us are earning our livelihood in other ways; many of us are losers now by this conflict; all of us are appalled by the prospect of the suffering before the country if [the strike] be not speedily terminated; and we feel that we have a right to call upon you as our representative to see what you can do to make peace. . . . You can speak as no one else can speak for the plain people of this country. Every workingman knows you are his friend; no capitalist of common sense can imagine that you are his enemy. The fact that others have spoken without effect does not shake our faith that your words of counsel and persuasion would be heeded. . . . This is not business, Mr. President, it is not politics; it is something much higher and finer. May God help you to render this great service to your country, and crown you with the blessing that belongs to the peacemakers." Gladden's petition was signed by thousands and found its way, with similar documents, to the White House.

Roosevelt was beset by the right and the left. The right exhorted him to call out the U.S. Army to drive the strikers back to work, while the left urged him to seize the mines and have them operated under the aegis of the Federal government. He was also under heavy pressure from Lodge to take steps to end the strike. Lodge was concerned that in the upcoming election the Republicans would lose ground if the strike continued. "The coal business is getting rapidly worse," he wrote Roosevelt. "School houses are closing for lack of fuel. Prices are enormous and rising. . . . If no settlement is reached it means political disaster in New England and especially in this State [Massachusetts]. . . . Is there any thing we can appear to do?" Lodge added. "Is there any form of pressure we can put on the operators who are driving us to ruin? The unions are just as obstinate but the rising public wrath makes for them and they stand all the firmer."

In reply the same day Roosevelt expressed a sense of helplessness, noting that while he was "genuinely independent of the big monied men in all matters where I think the interests of the public are concerned" and was "probably . . . the first President of recent times of whom this could be truthfully said," he still had no notion of how he could constitutionally intervene. Lodge continued to bombard the President with warnings and admonitions. He was furious with the mine operators. "Such insolence and arrogance coupled with stupidity I have never seen," Lodge wrote to the President. The consequence of their intractability was that "the Socialistic feeling is growing apace and the demand that the government take over the mines—one of the greatest disasters that could befall us." Lodge was convinced that J. Pierpont Morgan was behind the operators.

As winter approached, various soothsayers began to warn of a freezing nation immobilized by the scarcity of coal, although in practical fact the coalfields in West Virginia, Ohio, and Illinois could have provided a large part of the country's winter needs. Roosevelt did his bit by calling the paralysis of the Pennsylvania coalfields a crisis "only less serious than that of the Civil War." In October, with clamor growing for a settlement and the owners in distinctly bad odor, Roosevelt summoned Mitchell and his lieutenants and the operators, including Baer and Morgan, to the White House. The owners were furious, believing that the meeting itself gave legitimacy to the union. They refused to speak directly to Mitchell and referred to him as the man "whom you [the President] invited to meet *you*." It was clearly the wrong tack. When the operators assured the President that the majority of miners wanted to mine coal but were kept from doing so by fear of violence from the minority of strikers, Roosevelt agreed to allow more troops into the fields. But the majority of the miners preserved their solidarity.

The President increased pressure for a settlement by having a plan prepared for a government takeover of the mines. His proposal was to appoint a presidential commission but, when he undertook to get the operators' agreement to abide by the recommendations of the "fact-finding" commission, he found their representatives "literally almost crazy." They would not cooperate, they insisted, unless the commission had on it a majority that could be assumed friendly to the operators' cause. They grew "more and more hysterical," Roosevelt reported to Lodge, while admitting that failure to come to an agreement on the composition of the commission "meant probable violence and possible social war." The President finally realized that the operators would accept the appointment of a man favorable to labor if he were appointed under the category of "an eminent sociologist." Roosevelt readily agreed, and in his words, "at this utterly unimportant price, we [have] come out of as dangerous a situation as I ever dealt with."

Meanwhile, the friends of the workingman, the idealists, the visionaries, the Fabian socialists and the "Red" socialists, the trade unionists, the Nationalists, the single taxers, the various and assorted enemies of capitalism, or at least of George Baer and his fellow capitalists, rallied. Clarence Darrow was prevailed upon to act as counsel for the United Mine Workers. Henry Demarest Lloyd became an unofficial aide to John Mitchell, writing news articles, giving speeches, advising on grand strategy. Reams of material were turned out, describing the conditions in the mines. Children maimed in the mines were produced for newspaper interviews. Although he had no legal training, Lloyd called his involvement "my first case," and when Charles William Eliot, president of Harvard, declared that "the strike breaker is a good type of American hero," Lloyd wrote: "Men like President Eliot . . . however honest they may be are holding the hands of the defenceless masses while capitalism robs them of the only thing they have left—union." Eliot made partial amends by observing that "the operators are in an inhuman state of mind."

The "hearings" conducted by the commission were high drama. Twenty-five high-powered corporation lawyers represented Baer and the independent mineowners. Darrow, for his part, called 241 witnesses, who recited hair-raising stories of poverty and of callous indifference on the part of the owners to every grim aspect of their living and working conditions. Lloyd helped choose "some of the miners' wives to tell how the wife & mother holds her family together, brings up the children, always has something for the man's dinner pail on $35 a month." To those Americans who sympathized with the miners' cause, John Mitchell, handsome and imposing, witty and articulate, emerged as the hero of the commission's hearings. (It must be noted that Mother Jones and many of the miners felt that he had sold out to the politicians.)

Mitchell declared, "For more than twenty years the anthracite miners have groaned under intolerable and inhuman conditions. In a brotherhood of labor they seek to remedy their wrongs." Lloyd wrote home to his wife: "Mitchell is a wonder. He was cross-examined today by Wayne MacVeagh [the principal counsel for the owners], and he . . . threw him . . . down time after time. Even the Commission sometimes so far forgot themselves to join in the laugh."

Perhaps the most damaging witness from the point of view of the operators was nine-year-old Andrew Chippie, looking small and stunted for his age, who recounted how he had been charged for his father's back rent in a company house after his father's death in the mine. The father had owed Markle & Company $88.17 back rent, and Chippie, working as a breaker boy although he was below the age set by state law, had the rent deducted from his wages. The high point of the boy's testimony came when he exhibited to the commissioners "the statement of the balance owed with his wages of 40 cents for his first fortnight's work deducted from the delinquent rent." Many in the hearing room wept. Henry Demarest Lloyd had pictures taken of Chippie with his bill and sold copies for the boy's benefit.

In addition to the parade of union officials and miners and their wives and children, as well as their parish priests, Darrow produced piles of evidence to demonstrate the virulence of the owners' antiunion practices and doctors and health officials to testify to the occupational diseases suffered by the miners.

When George Baer announced that "the rights and interests of the laboring man will be protected not by the labor agitator but by the Christian men and women to whom God in His infinite wisdom has given control of the property interests of this country," Clarence Darrow answered him: "These agents of the Almighty have seen men killed daily; have seen men crippled, blinded and maimed and turned out to almshouses and on the roadsides with no compensation. They have seen the anthracite region dotted with silk mills because the wages of the miner make it necessary for him to send his little girls to work twelve hours a day, a night in the factory . . . at a child's wages. President Baer sheds tears because boys are taken into the union but he has no tears because they are taken into the breakers. . . . This contest is one of the important contests which have marked the progress of human liberty since the world began. Every advantage that the human race has won has been at fearful cost. Some men must die that others may live. It has come to these poor miners to bear this cross, not for themselves alone but that the human race may be lifted up to a higher and broader plane."

After five and a half weeks of hearings Darrow concluded the union's case with a brilliant summary, and the nation awaited the commission's report. At a mass meeting in Chicago on February 16, 1903, held to honor those who had managed the case for the miners—principally Darrow and Lloyd—5,000 supporters of the cause of labor heard Darrow eulogized as "that rare bird, a lawyer whose first love is love of justice." Roosevelt received his share of praise for "the most novel, the boldest, the greatest stroke of recent statesmanship" in his appointing the commission.

Five weeks later the commission's findings were announced. The *United Mine Workers Journal* called it "a good decision," but many miners and many of the union rank and file, including Mother Jones, believed it a betrayal. The union had not been recognized, nor had the principle of collective bargaining been accepted. An angry Darrow denounced it as "a most cowardly document." Roosevelt, not surprisingly, declared that "no Government document of recent years marks a more important piece of work better done."

The miners received a 10 percent increase in pay and a reduction of their hours of labor to nine per day. A number of minor grievances were accommodated, but the stipulation that no one could be refused employment on the basis of being a union or nonunion man was decidedly double-edged and was the part of the "award" most resented by union men.

The importance of the strike and the mode of settlement lay, of course, far beyond the specifics of the commission's award. There was much truth in the verdict of the editor of the *Review of Reviews,* who wrote that "while it fell short of being all that was expected the award is the greatest step forward that has been made in my recollection," and the *Outlook* called it "the most important event in the industrial history of the past quarter century." It was certainly of considerable significance on two levels. It established the principle that the government, as the agent of the electorate, had a direct and paramount interest in large-scale strikes that threatened the nation's economy. That notion is so commonplace today as not to warrant comment. In 1902 it was novel to the point of being, at least in the minds of many Americans, revolutionary. Men like Lloyd had already raised the cry: that "that government governs best which governs most." Roosevelt's intervention in the anthracite strike was a step in the direction of acceptance by the government of its responsibility to "govern more."

John Mitchell had graduated from a plain sack suit to a frock coat. To Mother Jones it was the final sign of his corruption. She said to Florence Harriman, "Oh, it was a pity, he was a fine fellow, but he had his head turned by feasting with the plutocrats, and so he lost his influence with the workers." While he had had the heady experience of hobnobbing with some of the most powerful political and business leaders in the country, he lost the confidence and support of the miners, was ousted from the leadership of the United Mine Workers in 1908, and became thereafter a minor functionary of the National Civic Federation. An alcoholic, he died at the age of forty-nine.

One of the principal beneficiaries of the settlement was, of course, Roosevelt. Despite his reluctance to intervene, despite his doubts and hesitations, he appeared by an unprecedented use of the powers of his office to have saved the nation from a coalless winter, to have aided labor (very modestly, to be sure), and to have chastened capital.

Some observers believed that the effect of the anthracite strike on public opinion could be seen in the fall elections in the increased Socialist vote, more than 200 percent in Massachusetts, comparably in a number of other states, and an increase of 400,000 nationwide. On the other hand, the fact that the operators and their allies profited from the strike settlement is suggested by the comment of George Baer, no admirer of Roosevelt, that "the best thing he ever did was to appoint the Coal Strike Commission."

2

Other Battlefields

If the anthracite strike drew the principal attention of the public, there were many other skirmishes and battles in the war between capital and labor. In a strike in the soft coal mines of Holly Grove, West Virginia, the miners, many of them ousted from their company-owned houses, camped out with their families in tents. The mineowners procured an armored train, filled it with "deputies" armed with rifles and machine guns, and dispatched it to the strikers' tent colony. There, unprovoked, the deputies opened fire on the tents, killing and wounding a number of miners and members of their families. The Associated Press account of the incident read: "The first serious outbreak in over a month occurred Friday when a passenger train was fired on . . . and a number of persons [were] shot down."

The same month—February, 1903—that Darrow, Lloyd, and others who had rallied to the support of the United Mine Workers were feted in Chicago, another devastating miners' strike began in Colorado City and spread in a few weeks to the large Guggenheim-owned copper mines in Cripple Creek. This time the Western Federation of Miners, far more militant than the United Mine Workers, was the representative of the strikers. The stronghold of the Western miners' union was Colorado, where the legislature had passed a law setting an eight-hour day for miners. The Western miners' union owned substantial property in the state. Union officials held public offices in mining towns and could count on the support of a number of state legislators.

The most colorful of the union leaders was William "Big Bill" Haywood. Haywood was a big, roughhewn man of English and Scotch-Irish ancestry. His father had been a rider with the pony express and had settled in Salt Lake City after the Civil War. Haywood was born there and grew up in the nearby mining town of Ophir. At the age of nine, Haywood went to work in the Treasure Mine. Later a job in Salt Lake City as usher in a theater introduced young Haywood to Shakespeare and launched him on a lifelong passion for literature. Successively a store clerk and a messenger boy, Haywood observed everything and learned much. The job as messenger, he recalled, "put me in touch with all the leading citizens of Salt Lake City. People were not guarded in what they said before a young boy, and I heard their business plans, their scandals and their political schemes." It was a highly practical education for a precocious boy. Haywood saw a black man lynched and heard a touring Southern Senator, Ben Tillman of South Carolina, speak. From him, Haywood got his first taste of Southern bigotry. When a black man in the audience asked the Senator a question, Tillman cursed him as a "saddle-colored son of Satan." The expression on the black man's face caused Haywood "forever after to feel that he and his kind were the same as myself and other people. I saw him suffer the same resentment and anger that I should have suffered in his place." At the age of fifteen, threatened with being apprenticed to a boilermaker, Haywood decided to try mining and headed for Humboldt County, Nevada, with "overalls, jumper, blue shirt, miners boots, two pairs of blankets, a set of chessmen, and a pair of boxing gloves." The town closest to the mine was Winnemucca, sixty miles away. With little diversion many of the miners were, by Haywood's testimony, "great readers." Among the volumes Haywood found in their possession was Darwin's *Origin of Species* and works by Voltaire, Shakespeare, Byron, Burns, and Milton.

Forsaking mining after several years, Haywood married his childhood sweetheart, Nevada Jane Minor, and went to work as a cowhand. "According to the season," he wrote, "sheep-shearing, breaking horses, handling the cattle, or haying kept us on the go." Next came a stint of surveying and then mining once more and homesteading with his wife and infant girl. In the midst of hard times, Haywood was informed that the land he had homesteaded on was to be part of an Indian reservation. Out of work and penniless, he felt "as if a black curtain had been pulled down on the future; there was no ray of hope. . . . There was nothing left; no compensation for the work I had put into the homestead, for the house I had built, the fences I had run, the trees I had set out." Leaving his wife in the care of her father, Haywood joined Charles Kelly's industrial army, one of the groups of unemployed workers that marched on Washington in 1892. After the breakup of the army, Haywood found a job as a miner and was soon active as a union organizer.

The Colorado Supreme Court found the eight-hour law unconstitutional, causing one bitter miner to declare that "if I could have my way with them I would kill them all and see if that would be considered unconstitutional." The prolabor forces in the state responded with a constitutional amendment permitting the eight-hour day for any industry in which shorter hours might lessen the danger of accidents, an amendment that was passed by a margin of three to one. The mineowners then put pressure on the legislature, and an eight-hour bill was turned back by the Republicans. Again the response of the miners was one of anger and bitterness. They had been urged to trust in the "democratic process" for redress of their most serious grievances. The miners decided to strike despite the warning of the governor "that if the miners of this State should go out on strike, every agitator and every man who went on strike would be driven out of the State." In the words of the president of the Western Federation of Miners, Charles Moyer, "Ever since the eight-hour strike of 1899 it has been preached to the men that legislation was the only proper means to secure relief. They were led to believe that they could win at the ballot box, and they believed that they did win, but the legislature threw them down. The men now realize that they will never get relief by legislation, and that they must get it through their own action. . . . After waiting four years, patiently enduring the hardships and the injustices of a twelve-hour system, is it surprising that at last they have arisen in their power to assert their rights?"

Governor James H. Peabody committed himself wholeheartedly to breaking the strike. He joined the Denver Citizens' Alliance, an openly antilabor group, and attended a "Law and Order" banquet put on for him at the Brown Palace by Simon Guggenheim. At a meeting called by the Colorado State Federation of Labor a speaker declared, " 'The land of the free and the home of the brave' has been converted into a Siberia . . . where military might rides rampant over Constitution and law. . . . Civil authority has been strangled, and a free press and free speech have been suppressed."

In Telluride the Citizens' Alliance imposed a form of martial law on the town, invading miners' homes to search for firearms and arresting miners on charges of trespassing on company property. Just as negotiations between the mineowners and the union seemed about to reach a successful conclusion, the Citizens' Alliance appealed to Governor Peabody for militia, and the governor at once complied. Supported by the presence of the soldiers, the Citizens' Alliance began arresting union officials and strikers on the charge of vagrancy, thirty-eight "at one swoop." The town was placed under martial law, the press was censored, and the telephone and telegraph lines were cut. Many miners were shipped out of town, their families left behind to fend for themselves. Some of those arrested were given eight hours to pay their fines and either leave the county or go back to work in the mines. One miner who refused to work or to leave was handcuffed to a telephone pole and left standing in the cold. A judge, sympathetic to the strike and finding his orders ignored by the Citizens' Alliance, closed his court, declaring "it would simply be a farce to attempt to enforce civil law in this county." Fifteen months after the strike had started, the operators agreed to the union demands, but their compliance was fitful, and many miners were driven out of the district by threats against them or their families.

With the partial victory at Telluride, the Western miners union decided to strike the Cripple Creek mines for an eight-hour day. The Cripple Creek strike soon became one of the bitterest and most violent in the history of Western mining. When the Citizens' Alliance prevailed on the town's merchants to refuse credit to the miners, the union opened its own stores, stocked them with food bought in bulk in Denver, and sold it at minimum prices to the strikers and their families. A commission, sent to Cripple Creek by Governor Peabody, wired him that its members were "of the opinion that the lives of the citizens of the district are in imminent danger and personal rights are in jeopardy. . . . We find that a reign of terror exists in the district." The report was made in spite of the fact that one of the struck mines—the Portland—had already agreed to the miners' demand and reopened. Soon 1,000 militiamen arrived (they were paid by the mineowners) and established themselves at strategic points around the town. Residents had to have passes issued by the military to traverse the streets of Cripple

Creek. Their commanding officer, Adjutant General Sherman Bell, received $3,200 from the mineowners in addition to his military pay.

As the strike at Cripple Creek dragged on, the original militia, mostly clerks, businessmen, and lawyers, were gradually replaced by strong-arm men from Denver and as far east as Chicago. Sherman Bell meanwhile announced that he would pay no attention to the civil authorities of Cripple Creek. From Denver, Haywood cranked out a stream of publicity, dispatched to papers all over the country, describing the abuses of the law committed by Bell and the militia.

One of the owners of a Cripple Creek mine was a West Virginia Senator who denounced the Western Federation of Miners as a promoter of "riot, arson, blood shed and general disorder," which imposed its will on the miners of the Cripple Creek district by "intimidation and even murder."

Union officers wired the headquarters of the Western Federation of Miners in Denver asking for help. "The rights of property have supplanted the rights of the individual," they declared, "and a lawless mob militia are arresting citizens without authority and at their pleasure. Please arouse the citizens of the state and save us from the anarchism, militarism, unAmerican blatherskitism and Bellism." In nearby Victor the Grand Army post of Civil War veterans added their voices to the growing chorus of protest.

In the strike at Westmoreland, Colorado, Mother Jones organized the miners' wives, instructing them to bring their children with them to the mines. When a judge told the women that he was going to fine them $30 each for disturbing the peace, Mother Jones told them to refuse to pay the fines and insist on keeping their children with them when they were jailed: "God Almighty gave you the babies, and you keep them until they are taken away from you." The judge ordered the women and children taken by train to the jail at nearby Greensburg. On the way to the station the wives encountered a group of scabs and, in Mother Jones's words, "I took care of the babies until they licked the scabs." At the Greensburg jail, Mother Jones told the women, " 'You sing all night, and sing all day if you want to but sing all night, and don't stop for anybody' . . . they sang the whole night, and the people complained about the singing, and the women would not shut up, and they turned them all out."

When Mother Jones turned up at Trinidad to help the striking miners there, she was arrested as an outside agitator and taken to the

Sisters of Mercy Hospital, which was transformed into a prison for her, with three military guards. For nine weeks she was confined there without formal charges or a trial.

Everywhere there were reports of beatings and shootings, of reprisals by miners, of dynamitings and evictions of miners' families from houses owned by the mining companies. The Denver convention of the Colorado Federation of Labor adopted resolutions declaring that "organized labor in the State of Colorado is fighting a deathless battle for the right to organize and live" and denouncing the smelting trust and the Citizens' Alliance. The state militia, one resolution declared, "has become corporate hirelings and resolved themselves into a military mob to annihilate organized labor, to train gatling guns upon the temple of justice, to defy the courts, to invade the sanctity of homes, to arrest without warrant or process of law, to incarcerate in a prison known as a military 'bull-pen,' men who have committed no crime save to clasp hands under the banner of unionism. . . ."

The bloodiest event of the Cripple Creek strike was the blowing up of the Independence Depot, resulting in the death of twelve miners and the wounding of many others. The federation blamed the Citizens' Alliance, which in turn charged the federation with the atrocity. When a union meeing was held at Victor to condemn the act, a riot that broke out ended in the arrest of a number of union men. Meanwhile, the stores opened by the union at Anaconda, Victor, and Cripple Creek to supply food for the strikers were broken into, and flour, sugar, meat, and other foodstuffs destroyed. The printing press of the *Victor Record,* which had been sympathetic to the strikers, was also demolished. About 1,600 men were arrested, and 42 tried on criminal charges. None was convicted. Some 250 men were deported; among them were a number of prominent residents of Cripple Creek whose only crime was that they had espoused the cause of the miners.

The anthracite coal strike in Pennsylvania and the violence at Cripple Creek and Telluride were only the most sensational strikes. Thousands of others, large and small, flared across the country. When the wretchedly underpaid coal miners of Oklahoma went out on strike, the governor of the state called for Federal troops. They evicted the strikers from the company shacks and shipped whole families off to Arkansas or Texas.

As the strikes dragged on, Haywood and some of his allies decided to call a conference to be held in Chicago to lay plans for a more militant and revolutionary union movement. The call to the secret meeting asserted the confidence of its conveners "in the ability of the working class, if correctly organized in both political and industrial lines, to take possession of and operate successfully . . . the industries of the country." The proposed conference would "discuss ways and means of uniting the working people of America in correct revolutionary principles, regardless of any general labor organization of past or present."

In June several hundred radical labor leaders, many of them veterans, like Haywood, of the Western Federation of Miners, gathered in Chicago to launch an unabashedly Marxist-Socialist labor movement. One of the more prominent figures was Daniel De Leon, ex–Columbia University professor and creator of the Socialist Labor Party (to be distinguished from the Socialist Party), already notorious for his disruptive ways. Lucy Parsons, the wife of Albert Parsons, the executed anarchist of the Haymarket Affair, was a guest of the convention, as were Eugene V. Debs, Algie Simons, a leading Socialist, and Mother Jones.

The most exotic figure was Father Thomas J. Hagerty, a Roman Catholic priest. An assistant to the rector of Our Lady of Sorrows Church in Las Vegas, New Mexico, Hagerty had taken up the cause of Mexican railroad workers, urging them to organize and fight for their rights. He had been conspicuous at the 1902 convention of the Western Federation of Miners, pressing the case for the Socialist Party. To him Marxism and Catholicism were, if not entirely compatible, at least reconcilable, a view not shared by his superiors. He had been suspended from his duties, whereupon he had declared, "I am a Catholic priest, as much a Catholic as the Pope himself." More than six feet tall with a powerful voice, he was much in demand as a speaker and organizer.

It was Haywood who called the meeting to order. "The aims and objects of this organization," he told the 200 delegates, "shall be to put the working-class in possession of the economic power, the means of life, in control of the machinery of production and distribution, without regard to capitalist masters. . . ." Greetings were read from the labor movements of a number of European countries.

Debs followed Haywood to the podium and, like him, denounced the American Federation of Labor (AFL) as being "under control of the capitalist class . . . preaching capitalist economics . . . serving capitalist purposes."

After numerous speeches predicting the demise of capitalism, the delegates, dominated by the Western Federation of Miners, adopted a constitution, the preamble of which read: "The working class and the employing class have nothing in common. . . . Between these two classes a struggle must go on, until all the toilers come together on the political as well as the industrial field, and take and hold that which they produce by their labor. . . ."

Much in the minds of the delegates was the news from Russia, where the workers of Odessa had seized the city and raised the red flag before they had been ruthlessly suppressed. The delegates passed a resolution urging "our Russian fellow-workmen on in their struggle" and promising "financial assistance as much as lies within our power, to our persecuted, struggling and suffering comrades in far-off Russia" and issued a militant manifesto which began: "Social relations and groupings only reflect mechanical and industrial groupings. The great facts of present industry are the displacement of human skill by machines and the increase of capitalist power through concentration in the possession of the tools with which labor is produced and distributed." The consequence of these developments was that "trade divisions among laborers and competition among capitalists alike are disappearing. Class divisions grow ever more fixed and antagonisms more sharp. . . . The worker, wholly separated from the land and the tools, with his skill of craftsmanship rendered useless, is sunk in the uniform mass of wage slaves. . . . The worn out and corrupt system offers no promise of improvement and adaptation. There is no silver lining to the clouds of darkness and despair settling down upon the world of labor." Much of the manifesto was an attack upon the craft union movement, indirectly upon the American Federation of Labor. The "universal economic evils" which afflicted the working class could be eradicated only "by a universal working-class movement . . . one great industrial union embracing all industries . . . founded on the class struggle," recognizing "the irrepressible conflict between the capitalist class and the working class." Haywood was elected "permanent chairman"; the means of achieving "a Workers' Co-operative Republic" would be an organization called the Industrial Workers of the World (IWW). Two hundred thousand copies of the manifesto (which, it must be said, was far too long for a manifesto) were printed for distribution throughout the country.

If Big Bill Haywood was the most compelling figure in the IWW, Joe Hill was the writer of its songs. The most famous, of course, was

"Hallelujah, I'm a Bum," with its irreverence and self-mockery. But there were a dozen others that raised the spirits of weary strikers on the picket lines at scores of mills and mines. "There Is Power in a Union" had a rousing chorus:

> There is pow'r, there is pow'r
> In a band of workingmen,
> When they stand hand in hand,
> That's a pow'r, that's a pow'r
> That must rule in every land—
> One Industrial Union Grand.

In addition to the unionized miners—coal and silver primarily—there was a vast Western migratory labor force, the core of it Irish. It lived, much of the time, in "camps"—mining camps, which might turn into towns; lumber camps, which seldom did; and construction camps, perhaps the grimmest life of all. The Western railroads were constantly extending or repairing lines, and they depended on labor agents to recruit workmen on what was largely a seasonal basis. The construction laborers lived in the camps with the minimum of sanitary facilities, crowded together in tents or hastily constructed shacks, often sleeping in boxcars on sidings and eating in the open air. The workers paid the labor agents for the jobs, and the railroads transported them to the site. Most of the construction laborers were floaters, men who worked long enough to earn a few dollars and then headed for the nearest town or city saloon to drown their miseries in cheap booze. A labor agent defined floaters as "men who have no intention or desire to remain upon a given job until its completion. . . . I would say that the percentage of floaters among unskilled laborers is considerably over 99 per cent." The superintendents of construction jobs did all in their power to hold their workers. Just as many of the lumber camps in the South distributed drugs at the companies' stores to hold their workers by addiction, construction camps sold liquor on the sly. The construction camps were usually without toilets or facilities for bathing. Although most Western states had laws requiring such facilities, the excuse of the contractors was invariably that the men would not use them. Another excuse for not providing toilets was that they would simply serve to transmit venereal diseases, which one employer insisted afflicted 60 percent of the workers. At one construction camp in the Northwest the average length of time a worker stayed on the job was fourteen days out of a month. In some it was no more than nine. One labor contractor declared he had to hire 8,000 men to have a steady work force of 3,000 available. The standard fee charged by a labor agent to the laborer for providing the job was $2.

The contractors typically charged the laborers for food, lodging, and health insurance, in addition, of course, to items, such as tobacco, purchased from the company store at inflated prices. A kind of perpetual contest took place, with the contractor trying to keep the worker on the job as long as possible by whittling away the pay that would, when it had sufficiently accumulated, allow him freedom. Usually he could be kept several additional days waiting for his company scrip or check to be converted into money. The work itself was desperately hard, the grossest forms of physical labor. Accidents were frequent, and medical attention ranged from absent to inadequate so that in every large labor camp established for any length of time many men died from disease and epidemics as well as from accidents.

Not infrequently in the larger towns and cities employment offices were run in conjunction with saloons. When a man had drunk up all his money, the saloonkeeper would pass him along to the labor contractor. In a city like San Francisco employed workmen could live in pestilent flophouses for ten or fifteen cents a night. "As for eating," one witness testified, "I had in mind that during the time the men are in town they spend most of their money for liquor and very little for food, and they rarely eat more than two meals a day. And a meal for a laborer usually consists of . . . a cup of coffee and a heavy meat and possibly a pie or something of that kind." Such meals seldom cost more than fifteen or twenty cents.

Fraud against the construction workers was so common as to be taken for granted. Witnesses before a presidential Commission on Industrial Relations told horrendous stories of men who worked for months under the most hazardous conditions only to be told at the end of that time that they owed the company $100 or more. Twelve men in an Oregon camp, working on contract, were told after four months' work that they had run up charges for material and equipment, so that their pay was $6.14 apiece.

Floaters were described by one of their number as "the men who build the country's railroads and aqueducts, its power plants and pipe lines. You will find us in the lumber woods and on ranches—in fact, anywhere where there is demand or might possibly be demand for surplus labor. As we lack organization, our condition is the most miserable of all the working class. You will find that many in our ranks are above the average in intelligence and education, our misfortune being due generally to the fact that we lacked the opportunity to learn a trade or specialize in some subject." After working for twelve or fourteen hours thrashing in a bean field, men often slept in the open, exposed to heavy dew. "If one has worked two or three months in some railroad camp, sleeping perhaps in the second floor of a two or three story bunk in company with a lot of Mexicans, debarred during that time from even the sight of a woman, one can't expect to be very conventional. When one carries his bed on his back, over country roads and through towns, is looked at askance, perhaps sneered at as a tramp, do you wonder at one becoming radical? . . . It is said that revolutions start from the bottom; and there is no doubt but that there are many embryo revolutionists in the lower ranks of labor; and it will be only by removing causes as indicated above, besides many others, . . . that radicalism will be eliminated."

A government commission described the floaters as "young men full of ambition and high hopes for the future, [who] start life as workers, but meeting failure after failure in establishing themselves in some trade or calling, their ambitions and hopes go to pieces, and gradually they sink into the ranks of migratory and casual workers." Many of these in turn acquired "certain negative habits"—such as drinking and begging—and "losing all self-control and self-respect, and desire to work, they become . . . tramps, bums, vagabonds, gamblers, pickpockets, yeggmen, and other petty criminals—in short public parasites. . . ."

In Portland, Oregon, the Gypsy Smith Tabernacle fed and lodged thousands of floaters. Denouncing the tabernacle as a magnet for undesirables, city officials closed it down and turned the men out on a cold, rainy night. Hoboes, as some floaters preferred to call themselves, collected in "hobo jungles" on the outskirts of cities and larger towns, where they could hop freights when the spirit moved them or the police harassed them. In the hobo jungles they developed their own culture with its language and mores. They organized the International Hoboes of America and elected a "king." In Seattle they founded the Hotel De Gink, which also ran an employment agency that boasted it had found 20,000 jobs. As many as 2,000 men at a time could be provided with lodging.

A hobo official told the Commission on Industrial Relations "that the majority of the men on the road are not there of their own free will. They are placed there through false representations by the employment office that ships them out to the different work." Yet there was clearly more to the matter than that. The "road" had a compelling sound to it; the "open road" drew bold and restless spirits. To be "on the road" was to be ranging far beyond the conventions and constraints of civilization; it was to be "free as a breeze," your own boss and no man's servant. The road was a kind of by-product of the disintegrative effects of American life. The tramps and hoboes were only the most visible and dramatic manifestations of American rootlessness, the human atoms that ricocheted around in the vast vacuum chamber of America.

To move perpetually in space across the enormous landscape was a peculiarly American experience. A whole genre of popular culture developed to celebrate that movement over road and railroad. It rejected all the sacred objects of middle-class culture, all the patient amassing of "things" so precious to Americans. Inserted into the interstices of the larger society, it used two of its most valued artifacts— roads and railroads—for its own purposes and in its own mode of life. It was to men like these that the IWW had the strongest appeal.

The most enterprising and indefatigable champion of the oppressed may well have been Mother Jones. In the spring of 1903, 75,000 textile workers in Kensington, Pennsylvania, went out on strike for higher pay and shorter hours. Of the strikers, 10,000 were small children. Mother Jones was called upon to assist the strikers. "Every day," she recalled, "little children came into Union Headquarters, some with their hands off, some with the thumb missing, some with their fingers off at the knuckle. They were stooped little things, round shouldered and skinny. Many were not over ten years of age." The mothers of many of the children, when questioned by Mother Jones about why they let their children work in the mills, explained it was a matter of work or starve; the fathers of the children had been killed or maimed in the mines. When Mother Jones asked the newspapermen who had gathered to report the strike why they did not publish the facts about child labor in Pennsylvania, they replied that they could not do so because the millowners had stock in the papers. "Well, I've got stock in these little children," Mother Jones replied, "and I'll arrange a little publicity." The publicity was a parade of the child workers with the maimed children leading. Mother Jones "held up their mutilated hands and showed them to the crowd." She cried, "Philadelphia's mansions were built on the broken bones, the quivering hearts and drooping heads of these children," and "neither state nor city officials paid any attention to these wrongs. They did not care that these children were to be the future citizens of the nation."

At this point Mother Jones noticed that city officials in a building across the street were watching the meeting. "I called upon the millionaire manufacturers to cease their moral murders," she wrote, "and I cried to the officials in the open windows opposite, 'Some day the workers will take possession of your city hall, and when we do, no child will be sacrificed on the altar of profit.' " The windows were promptly closed. The reporters took note of the parade and meeting, and Mother Jones got the attention that she sought for the plight of the children. Professors debated the question; preachers preached on it. Mother Jones decided to expand the field. She got permission from the parents of a number of the children to take them on a tour, an "army" of children on strike. Each child carried a knapsack with a knife, fork, and plate. One had a drum, and another a fife. Some carried banners that read: "We want more schools and hospitals"; "We want time to play"; "Prosperity is here. Where is ours?" After a mass meeting in Philadelphia Mother Jones decided to take her "army" to see President Roosevelt in his summer retreat at Oyster Bay, on Long Island. "All along the line of march the farmers drove out to meet us with wagon loads of fruit and vegetables." Jones wrote: "Their wives brought the children clothes and money. The interurban trainmen would stop their trains and give us free rides." At Trenton, New Jersey, the police sent by the millowners to turn the marchers back were invited to lunch and became instant converts to the cause. That night, after a large public meeting, the wives of many of the policemen took children home to spend the night.

The strange procession went on, sometimes walking, sometimes getting rides. At Princeton they slept in the big cool barn on Grover Cleveland's estate, and the next day Mother Jones addressed the townspeople, and the professors and the students of the university on the iniquities of the capitalist system. "Here's a text book on economics," she declared, pointing to a boy ten years old who was stooped like an old man. "He gets three dollars a week and his sister who is fourteen gets six dollars. They work in a carpet factory ten hours a day while the children of the rich are getting their higher education."

New York City was Mother Jones's objective, but uneasy officials tried to bar her and her troop from entering the city or holding a rally. She addressed herself to Seth Low, mayor of New York, and His Honor

finally yielded to her determination. They could march up Fourth
Avenue, but they could not hold their meeting at Madison Square, the
traditional forum for outdoor public meetings. Why? They did not
have enough police to control the crowd that might be attracted. So
Mother Jones and the children were confined to Twentieth Street,
where, it was hoped, their audience would be neither so large nor so
unruly as might have been anticipated at Madison Square. It was,
nonetheless, an immense crowd that gathered to hear her tale of the
horrors of child labor in the mills of the anthracite region. Money was
raised in substantial amounts, and many members of the audience were
recruited to the cause. The next day the children were invited to Coney
Island to enjoy the rides and see the trained animals. Again there was
a speech. "We want President Roosevelt to hear the wail of the children
who never have a chance to go to school but work eleven and twelve
hours a day . . . who weave the carpets you walk upon; and the lace
curtains in your windows, and the clothes of the people. Fifty years
ago there was a cry against slavery and men gave up their lives to stop
the selling of black children on the block. Today the white child is sold
for two dollars a week to the manufacturers. Fifty years ago the black
babies were sold C.O.D. Today the white baby is sold on the installment
plan. . . . The trouble is that no one in Washington cares. I saw our
legislators in one hour pass three bills for the relief of the railroads
but when labor cries for aid for the children they will not listen. . . . You
see those monkeys in those cages over there," Mother Jones called out
to her audience. "The professors are trying to teach them to talk. The
monkeys are too wise for they fear that the manufacturers would buy
them for slaves in their factories."

Senator Thomas Platt of New York had agreed to meet the children at a Manhattan Beach hotel, but he lost his nerve and skedaddled
when he saw them coming. The President refused to greet the army
or answer Mother Jones's letters, but fresh impetus had been given to
the movement to ban child labor. The Kensington strike was lost, but
the Pennsylvania legislature soon after passed a child labor law, setting
the age of fourteen as the earliest a child might work in a factory.

Some of the worst conditions of labor were in the South, where
unions were ruthlessly suppressed. At Lattimer, Tennessee, twenty-
three striking miners were shot in the back by the sheriff and his
deputies.

Mother Jones took a job in a Southern textile mill to find out at
first hand what conditions were like. There she met a fellow worker

who had a three-day-old infant with her at the factory. "The boss was good and saved my place," she told Mother Jones.

"When did you leave?"

"The boss was good; he let me off early the night the baby was born."

"What do you do with the baby while you work?"

"Oh, the boss . . . lets me have a little box with a pillow in it beside the loom. The baby sleeps there and when it cries I nurse it."

Recounting the story, Mother Jones added, "So this baby, like hundreds of others, listened to the whiz and whir of machinery before it came into the world. From its first weeks, it heard the incessant racket raining down upon its ears, like iron rain. It crawled upon the linty floor. It toddled between forests of spindles. In a few brief years it took its place in the line. It renounced childhood and childish things and became a man of six, a wage earner, a snuff sniffer, a personage upon whose young-old shoulders fortunes were built.

"And who is responsible for this appalling child slavery? Everyone," Mother Jones declared. Alabama had passed a child labor law, but capitalists from Massachusetts and Rhode Island had it repealed. Whenever a Southern state attempted reform, the millowners threatened to close the mills. "They reach legislatures, they send lobbies to work against child labor reform, and money, northern money for the most part, secures the nullification of reform laws through control of the courts." Mother Jones returned to New York, "burdened with the terrible things I had seen. . . . For a long time after my Southern experience, I could scarcely eat. Not alone my clothes, but my food, too, at times seemed bought with the price of the toil of children."

As these accounts indicate, the succession of Theodore Roosevelt to the presidency, coinciding with the beginning of the new century, did not bring any substantial change in the war between capital and labor. The conflict continued as bitterly and relentlessly as ever. A survey revealed that more than 1,500,000 children worked for as little as 25 cents a day in 1900, while the average adult yearly wage was $490 a year, the highest in any industrial nation. Capital became, if anything, more resistant to labor's demands, and labor more radical in its denunciation of capital. The most conspicuous exception was Samuel Gompers, who year after year fought off the efforts of the Socialists to take over the American Federation of Labor. He told the delegates at an AFL convention in Boston in 1903: "I want to say to you, socialists, that . . . I have kept close watch upon your doctrines for thirty years;

have closely associated with many of you, and know how you think and what you propose . . . and I want to say that I am entirely at variance with your philosophy. Economically, you are unsound; socially you are wrong; industrially, you are an impossibility."

At the same time more and more middle- and upper-class Americans gave their support to what might be called rather vaguely the labor movement. In the words of Washington Gladden, "To the support of the militant and aggressive propaganda of organized labor has come, within recent years, a small but rapidly increasing host of ministers of the gospel, college professors, writers, journalists, and others of the professional classes, distinguished . . . by exceptional talent which they devote with no hope of material reward, and a devotion that can be explained only in the light of the fervid religious spirit which animates the organized industrial unrest."

Walter Lippmann was one of the young radicals who made the cause of labor his own. "The effort to build up unions," he wrote, "is as much the work of pioneers as the extension of civilization into the wilderness. The unions are the first feeble effort to conquer the industrial jungle for democratic life. . . . Men are fighting for the beginnings of industrial self-government."

3

Roosevelt Takes Charge

Indignant over the obduracy of the mineowners during the course of the coal strike, Roosevelt was anxious to ensure the passage of a bill that would give him more leverage in dealing with recalcitrant corporations, and Senator Knute Nelson of Minnesota was glad to oblige. The Nelson amendment to a bill to establish a Department of Commerce and Labor gave the Bureau of Corporations wider powers and the president the authority to publicize information on corporate wrongdoing (or rightdoing) collected by the bureau. Democrats were alarmed by the degree of presidential discretion. An Alabama Congressman, William Richardson, declared that the amendment would enable the President to "suppress all data, every scintilla of information. He can hold it secret and can stand pat and do nothing, and no law can move him. Is that publicity?" On the question of what were "good" and what were "bad" trusts, surely there should be some other judgment involved than that of the President. "It should be the law," Richardson insisted, "under the rules and regulations prescribed for eliciting the truth."

When John D. Rockefeller, Jr., sent telegrams to six Senators opposing the Nelson amendment, Roosevelt used that inappropriate intervention to rally support for it. On February 10, 1903, the House passed the amended Department of Commerce and Labor bill by a vote of 252 to 10, and a triumphant Roosevelt declared, "The enactment of this law is one of the most significant contributions which have been made in our time toward a proper solution of the problem of the relations to the people of the great corporations and corporate combinations." The President pledged that the law would be administered in "a spirit of absolute fairness and justice and of entire fearlessness."

The first test of the efficacy of the new bureau involved the beef trust, against which a suit had already been filed by the Department of Justice. Delaying until after the presidential election of 1904, Roosevelt then directed the bureau to cooperate fully with the Department of Justice in bringing to light any skulduggery. Charles Edward Russell's series of articles on the beef trust, later published as a book entitled *The Greatest Trust in the World,* had stirred up a storm of public outrage. When the report of the bureau proved far milder, there were widespread charges of a government cover-up. That, of course, was hardly what the President had had in mind when he had had the bureau created as an agent of his will. The *New York Press* expressed the view that the commissioner of corporations, James Garfield, son of the former President, was incompetent. He "should not wait for the Beef Trust officials to go to jail" before he goes out of office, the paper editorialized: "he should get out now." The *New York Sun* noted: "The public is not interested in tedious and voluminous reports. It wants to know why its steaks and its roasts cost more than they did a short time ago."

One of the most significant pieces of legislation passed during Roosevelt's first term was the Newlands Act, proposed by Senator Francis Newlands of Nevada. The act set aside the proceeds of public land sales to finance construction of irrigation projects in arid states. Visionary champions of the arid lands like William Smythe viewed the act as the beginning of a new era of small-scale farming and democracy in the West. Along with an act establishing a licensing system for the use of waterpower on public lands, the Newlands Act marked the extension of the range of Federal action, particularly in the area of land use and management.

The Elkins Act and the bill creating the Department of Commerce and Labor, which was initially headed by the New York Republican George Cortelyou, attacked the issue of railroad rebates by strengthening the definition of unfair discrimination between shippers engaged in interstate commerce. Fines were specified for offending shippers and railroad officials, and the Federal courts were given the power to issue injunctions to violators.

The most notable case that came before the Supreme Court during Roosevelt's first term was that of *Northern Securities* v. *U.S.* The Northern Securities Company, in Roosevelt's view, represented the inclination of huge corporations to form mergers not in the public interest. When Congress ignored the President's exhortations to pass legislation prohibiting such mergers, Roosevelt directed Attorney General Philander Knox to file a suit for the dissolution of the company under the provisions of the Sherman Antitrust Act. He felt confident of a favorable decision, for he had just appointed as an associate justice to the Court his old friend Oliver Wendell Holmes, a jurist of well-known liberal disposition. The Court's verdict was indeed in favor of the government, but Holmes dissented, and Henry Adams wrote: "Poor Wendell Holmes is the immediate victim. Theodore brought him here to do his dirty work, and flattered and cooed over him; but when Wendell saw what the job was, his gorge rose, and he kicked like a Congressman." Roosevelt had "gone wild" at Holmes's opinion and denounced him "in the most forcible terms of his sputtering vocabulary."

At the same time the President aroused the indignation of labor leaders by rescinding an order firing a government clerk for refusing to join a union. He fretted about its effect on the labor vote but congratulated himself on doing what he thought right despite the political consequences. When he agreed to meet with a delegation of labor men that included John Mitchell and Samuel Gompers, the news "caused one of those curious panics habitual among our friends of the wealthy and cultivated classes. . . . They immediately fell into a panic and screamed that I *had* weakened."

Roosevelt told the delegation, "I am President of all of the people of the United States, without regard to creed, color, birthplace, occupation, or condition. My aim is to do equal and exact justice as among them all. In the employment and dismissal of men in the government service I can no more recognize the fact that a man does or does not belong to a union as being for or against him than I can recognize the fact that he is a Protestant or a Catholic, a Jew or a Gentile, as being for or against him." The labor delegates expressed themselves as "satisfied"; "overawed" might have been the more accurate word.

If the President was inherently conservative in domestic matters, he was hardly less so in the field of foreign policy. He believed that beyond question or cavil it was the destiny of the United States to be a dominant force in world affairs and that to be such a force required above all a formidable Pacific fleet and a substantial army.

Although his ideas were conventional in the field of international power politics, Roosevelt's instinct and tactics were brilliant. John Hay described a typical foreign policy strategy session with the President. "It was a curious sight," he wrote. "I have often seen it, and it never ceases to surprise me. He storms up and down the room, dictating in a loud and oratorical tone, often stopping, recasting a sentence, striking out and filling in, hospitable to every suggestion, not in the least disturbed by interruption, holding on stoutly to his purpose, and producing finally, out of these most unpromising conditions, a clear and logical statement. . . ."

The European nations were engaged in those fierce struggles for empire which had been productive of so much evil and misery in the world and would shortly create very much more, exacting from the imperialistic powers themselves a terrible price for their disposition to gobble up the world.

Like all members of his class, Roosevelt began his term of office with a strong bias toward Great Britain. Anglo-American friendship had indeed been the cornerstone of the McKinley-Hay foreign policy. Roosevelt had no disposition to disturb that relatively new but promising understanding. The British, anxious to curry favor with Roosevelt, made much of the fact that they had prevented the intervention of the European powers in the Spanish-American War.

The Germans, however, revealed a dispatch that indicated that Lord Pauncefote had really urged intervention. Henry Adams wrote his friend Elizabeth Cameron: "Poor old Pauncefote is almost broken up by a question of veracity forced on him by the German government. . . . The Kaiser is running the details of every movement directly by telephone. Theodore is much bothered."

The German campaign, carefully orchestrated by the kaiser, reached a climax when the German ruler invited seventeen-year-old Alice Roosevelt to christen a royal yacht built in American shipyards and sent his brother, Prince Henry, to participate in the ceremony. Thousands of German-Americans turned out for the occasion, supplemented by large numbers of Irish, pleased to have an opportunity to irritate the British.

Roosevelt had hardly succeeded to the presidency when he wrote Cecil Spring-Rice, the British diplomat: "Just a line to say how much I have thought of you. I do wish you could come over now and be my guest at the White House. Is there any chance of it?" Spring-Rice had been best man at Roosevelt's wedding, although they had met only a few weeks earlier. While Spring-Rice was too junior to be eligible as ambassador, the British government, well aware of the advantage of exploiting the President's capacity for friendship, sent another friend, Sir Michael Herbert, whom Roosevelt had taught to play baseball. "It is not recalled," the *New York Tribune* noted, "that ever before has so intimate a personal friendship existed between a President and a foreign diplomat as that between President Roosevelt and Ambassador Herbert."

Another diplomatic pal was Baron Hermann Speck von Sternburg. Roosevelt wrote to the baron urging him also to visit the United States, adding, "I am very fond of you, as you know, and I should so like to have . . . you at the White House." Like a schoolboy who had a new clubhouse, he wanted all his chums to visit him and share his pleasure in his astonishing new eminence.

One of Speck's earlier assignments had been to "get up" for the German government a report "as to America's strengths and weaknesses in the event of his Government finding it necessary to take a smash at us," Roosevelt had written to Spring-Rice in 1896. He added that "he was going about it and discussed it with me, with his usual delightfully cold-blooded impartiality."

The President soon had occasion to make clear that he was determined to uphold the Monroe Doctrine. The only gobbling up in the Western Hemisphere would be done by the United States. When Venezuela, in the midst of one of its periodic upheavals, defaulted on debts owed to German, British, and Italian creditors, the kaiser made known his intention of seizing certain ports to ensure the payment of the German portion of that unhappy country's debts. To accomplish this bit of piracy, the emperor sought the support or at least compliance of Great Britain, a country grown old and wise in the strategies of territorial aggrandizement. An allied fleet was sent into Venezuelan waters to institute what was called a "pacific blockade." This blockade Roosevelt and Secretary of State John Hay undertook to thwart. When Britain and Germany severed diplomatic relations with the South American nation on December 2, 1902, and indicated their intention of bombarding its seaport towns and occupying its territory, Roosevelt invoked the Monroe Doctrine. Britain and Italy reluctantly agreed to arbitration. Only Germany remained obdurate. Roosevelt thereupon summoned the German ambassador (Speck's predecessor, Baron Theodor von Holleben) and asked him to inform the kaiser that if Germany did not consent to arbitration within ten days, he would order the United States fleet under Admiral George Dewey to sail to the Venezuelan coast to protect that nation from any act of German aggression. A week passed without a response. Holleben requested an audience with the President but said nothing about the ultimatum. Before the ambassador left, the President asked him if he had received an answer to the message. Holleben replied in the negative. In that case, Roosevelt is said to have replied, Dewey would be ordered to sail for Venezuela a day earlier than scheduled. Now there were forty-eight hours left for the emperor to respond. Wilhelm yielded, and Roosevelt at once publicly praised the kaiser's desire to find a peaceful solution to the crisis which he had, in fact, created. The claims against Venezuela were carried to the International Court at The Hague.

Holleben was soon summoned home by the kaiser with instructions to feign illness. "The ways of the German Foreign Office have always been abrupt toward its agents, not to say ruthless," Henry Adams noted, "and yet commonly some discontent has been shown as an excuse; but, in Holleben's case, no cause was guessed for Holleben's disgrace except the Kaiser's wish to have a personal representative in Washington." Holleben's replacement was Roosevelt's friend Speck von Sternburg. In the words of the *Washington Times*, "Emperor William has chosen a chum of President Roosevelt to represent Germany at Washington."

The British ambassador, Sir Michael Herbert, wrote the British foreign secretary: "The explosion of feeling against Germany here is somewhat remarkable. I confess to regarding it with malevolent satisfaction, especially when I think of the German efforts to discredit us and to flatter America during the past year."

Roosevelt was delighted by Speck's appointment. The German was a fine rider and hiker and almost as dedicated to the strenuous life as Teddy himself. It was much the same with the kaiser. Wilhelm was, in practical fact, very much a kind of German counterpart to Roosevelt. He was a devoted family man; he loved to hunt large animals; he was an excellent shot—all qualities that ranked high in the President's inventory of desirable characteristics. He was "manly" and highly military. The German chancellor, Prince Bernhard von Bülow, told the kaiser, not entirely inaccurately, that President Roosevelt "is a great admirer of Your Majesty and would like to rule the world hand in hand with Your Majesty, regarding himself as something in the nature of an American counterpart to Your Majesty," news which pleased Wilhelm's simple heart.

Henry Cabot Lodge, sensing Roosevelt's temperamental affinity for the kaiser, judged the German ruler more severely. "He seems to me easily understood," he wrote Roosevelt. "He is unstable, crazy for notoriety—not to be trusted. Not a man to rely on at all—with a saving sense of the danger of war and a strong inclination to bully up to the verge of war." Roosevelt rejected indignantly the suggestion that he was, in the slightest degree, "under the influence of the Kaiser." He wrote Lodge: "The heavy witted creatures [the British] do not understand that nothing could persuade me to follow the lead of or enter into close alliance with a man who is so jumpy, so little capable of continuity of action, and therefore so little capable of loyalty to his friends or steadfastly hostile to an enemy."

The Venezuela affair had far-reaching consequences. If the United States was to fend off intrusions by foreign nations into the affairs of the Americas, it seemed to Roosevelt to follow inevitably that the United States must assume responsibility for the behavior of its neighbors to the south.

The European powers were soon clamoring for the bankrupt Dominican Republic to pay its international bills. If Roosevelt would not permit them to use their gunboats to collect, then the United States must become, if not precisely the collection agent, at least the policeman who accompanied the aggrieved creditor. Roosevelt said as much, thus making an alarming extension—it was called the Roosevelt Corollary—to the Monroe Doctrine.

Another touchy issue was that of the Alaska boundary. Canada claimed the Alaskan panhandle—the strip of coastline running from the area of Juneau to that of Ketchikan. The dispute centered on the question of whether Canada's claim ran only to the heads of the bays and inlets (the U.S. position) or, as the Canadians insisted, to the headlands.

Great Britain and the United States accepted an arbitration commission of three Americans, two Canadians, and the lord chief justice of England, and the President hinted tactfully that if the commission decided in favor of Canada, he would simply seize the disputed area. "I have always," he had declared several years earlier, "been fond of the West African proverb: Speak softly and carry a big stick, you will go far."

The competition of foreign powers for presidential favor reached comic proportions with the arrival of a new French ambassador, obviously chosen to be one of Roosevelt's ambassadorial suitors. Jean Jules Jusserand arrived close on the heels of Speck von Sternburg. "He is a nice little man," the President wrote to his son Kermit, "very dark & dapper, and is really a fine scholar. Having diplomats presented to me is an awful bore as a rule. But this was a different matter. I kept him talking half an hour." Jusserand was the author of an impeccably scholarly work, *English Wayfaring Life in the Middle Ages* (still a highly regarded study). His wife, Elise Richards, was from an old New England family and a scholar in her own right. Roosevelt was delighted. "In the smoking room," Jusserand recalled in his memoirs, "the talk was about present-day politics. The President, exuberant, full-blooded, joyful, shrewd, 'enfant terrible,' accompanying his talk with forceful gesticulation, was a delight to look at and listen to. In a burst of joy he had a sonorous laugh; he struck the table, exclaiming Hoo! Hoo!"

Roosevelt gave Jusserand the Rock Creek test, and the Frenchman passed with flying colors. It was important, Jusserand soon perceived, to "walk straight into a river, or a mud-hole and avoid with a feeling of horror paths and bridges." The Frenchman, who had been something of a mountain climber in his youth, crossed over a stone ledge stretched out on his stomach, moving along "as seals do." The final test was a swim in the Potomac. Stripped to the buff, the President and the ambassador were about to plunge in when Roosevelt shouted, "Eh, Mr. Ambassador, have you forgotten your gloves?"

Jusserand shouted back, "We might meet ladies."

Jusserand soon discovered that Roosevelt shared his countrymen's conviction that the French in general were an effeminate and decadent lot, strong in skepticism and weak in religious conviction. He promptly undertook to change the President's view of the French people (at one point he countered Roosevelt's enthusiasm for the legend of the *Nibelungenlied* by lending him the almost equally gory French classic *Chanson de Roland*).

Among the topics Roosevelt discussed with Jusserand was that of a possible war between France and Germany. Such a war, the two speculated, might well start with an invasion of Holland. In that case, Roosevelt assured Jusserand, he would dispatch American warships to the Caribbean to protect Dutch islands from German warships. Such an act, Roosevelt must have known, would in all probability have meant war with Germany.

After the sudden death of Ambassador Herbert, Roosevelt hoped that Spring-Rice might be sent to replace him, but the British Foreign Office decided otherwise, and Roosevelt wrote to his British friend: "I am very, very sorry, we all of us are that you are not coming. . . . I have a strong desire during the period I am 'up,' to have people I am fond of around me . . . here are fifty matters that come up that I would like to discuss with you, notably about affairs in the Far East. . . ." Roosevelt wrote to Henry White, who had replaced Whitelaw Reid as ambassador to Great Britain, urging him to arrange for a visit from Spring-Rice. "I do not have much faith," he added, "in the tenacity of purpose or willingness to stand punishment of either the English Government or the English people, and as it is impossible to foretell what conditions will arise, and therefore what position our people will be willing to take, I think that all that can be done at present is to try to get a clear idea of the prospective mental attitudes of the two governments." But that was not to be.

Spring-Rice wrote to Mrs. Henry Cabot Lodge, another close friend, to assure her and her husband that the new ambassador, Sir Mortimer Durand, was a capital fellow and a great admirer of the President. He thought "Teddy R. the greatest man in the world and has treated me with immense respect since I let on that I correspond with Teddy. I tell him stories and he listens open-mouthed." But Durand failed the entrance exams to Roosevelt's inner circle. He was not durable enough. As the Briton described it, the President put him through a kind of obstacle course to test his suitability: "We drove out to Rock Creek, a wooded valley with streams running through it, and he then plunged down the *khud,* and made me struggle through bushes and over rocks for two hours and a half, at an impossible speed, till I was so done that I could hardly stand. His great delight is rock climbing, which is my weak point. I disgraced myself completely, and my arms and shoulders are still stiff with dragging myself up by roots and ledges. At one place I fairly stuck, and could not get over the top till he caught me by the collar and hauled at me. . . . He did almost all the talking to my great relief, for I had no breath to spare."

On the diplomatic front the President's passion for personal connections rather than formal ones bore fruit when King Edward VII, who, like the kaiser, was fascinated by Roosevelt and expressed his admiration to Spring-Rice for the President's legendary heroism at San

Juan Hill, where he had "fought like a tiger," wrote to him and sent him a valuable miniature portrait of John Hampden, the Puritan leader and enemy of the monarchy in the days of the Long Parliament. When Durand delivered the letter and the accompanying gift, which the king, strictly speaking, had no right to give, nor the President to receive, Roosevelt assured Durand that he was favorably disposed to the British and, despite his close friendship with Speck, was not unduly influenced by the kaiser. "I like the Emperor very much in a way," he declared, "but I don't trust him, and am not in the least affected by the ridiculous messages he makes 'Specky' bring me. . . . I have told 'Specky' his fears of an attack by England are utter nonsense, and Specky is half ashamed of them himself. You need never be the least afraid that I shall take the Kaiser seriously."

It was clear to Roosevelt that the kaiser was paranoid about the British. "The Kaiser has become a monomaniac about getting into communication with me every time he drinks three pen'orth of conspiracy against his life and power." It seemed to the President that his hopes of achieving some kind of reconciliation between Britain and Germany were doomed. "It is perfectly hopeless to try to bring about a better understanding between England and Germany," he wrote to his friend George von Meyer.

As the months passed, Roosevelt grew increasingly concerned over the possibility of war between the European powers. The doomsday predictions of the Adamses, Brooks and Henry, affected him, as did John Hay's unabashedly pro-British warnings of German perfidy.

Roosevelt's old teacher Henry Adams was a fascinated student of his pupil's diplomatic maneuverings, but he shared Henry Cabot Lodge's devotion to the British. It was all very well for "Theodore" to "play with Kings . . . but Kings are bad partners," Adams wrote to Elizabeth Cameron. "We have got to support France against Germany, and fortify an Atlantic system beyond attack; for if Germany breaks down England or France, she becomes the centre of a military world, and we are lost. The course of concentration must be decided by force,— whether military or industrial matters not much to the end, but to us it is the whole game for we are industrial." And to the same correspondent Adams wrote a few weeks later: "To me who still lives in the eighteenth century, it is weird to see France, England, Germany and Russia stand humbly aside to let Theodore Roosevelt dictate their fate. . . . Only forty years ago Europe walked over us roughshod." To Roosevelt himself Adams wrote: "You have established a record as the best herder of Emperors since Napoleon. . . . I need your views about the relative docility of Kings, Presidents of South American Republics, Railway Presidents and Senators. . . ."

Following the teachings of Admiral Alfred Thayer Mahan, Roosevelt was committed to a two-ocean navy. In this scheme an American-controlled Philippines was an essential element. At the same time there was a constant barrage of criticism over U.S. possession of the islands. Even the journalist Herbert Croly, so confident of the benign effects of American imperialism, was critical of the continued American occupation of the Philippines. "But," he added, "even though from the military point of view the Philippines may constitute a source of weakness and danger, their possession will have the political advantage of keeping the American people alive to their interests in the grave problems which will be raised in the Far East by the future development of China and Japan." Lodge and Roosevelt had no misgivings. Lodge especially had no patience with those who opposed the continued occupation of the Philippines. "One turns sick," he wrote Roosevelt, "to think that there are such creatures crawling between Heaven and Earth in America."

Roosevelt took the line that the acquisition of new islands, whether in the Caribbean or in the Pacific, was at best a painful necessity, and when someone inquired if he wished to annex some additional ones, he was said to have replied, "About as much as a gorged anaconda wants to swallow a porcupine wrong end to."

Cuba remained a troublesome issue. The joint resolution of Congress in April, 1898, which authorized military action against the Spanish occupiers of that island, had been headed "For the recognition of the independence of the people of Cuba, demanding that the Government of Spain relinquish its authority and government in the island of Cuba, and to withdraw its land and naval forces from Cuba and Cuban waters, and directing the President of the United States to use the land and naval forces of the United States to carry these resolutions into effect." The President was further "authorized" to "leave the government and control of the island of Cuba to its people so soon as a government shall have been established in said island. . . ."

Three years later, with a United States army of occupation firmly in control of the island, the Platt Amendment, attached, appropriately enough, to the army appropriations bill, laid down the conditions that the Cubans must satisfy in order to be given their independence *by the United States*. They must, among other things, agree "never to enter into any treaty or other compact with any other foreign power or powers which will impair or tend to impair the independence of Cuba." Cuba must not "assume or contract any public debt . . . for the ultimate discharge of which, the ordinary revenues of the island . . . shall be inadequate."

It must, moreover, agree that the United States was free to intervene "for the preservation of Cuban independence." Perhaps most galling of all to Cubans was the stipulation that they provide for sanitation in the towns and cities of their island, to prevent infectious diseases and thereby protect "the commerce of Cuba, as well as . . . the commerce of the southern ports of the United States and the people residing therein." Finally, Cuba was required to "sell or lease to the United States lands necessary for coaling or naval stations at certain specified points. . . ." To many Cubans it seemed that the United States had an odd notion of "independence." Numerous incidents involving United States soldiers and Cuban "insurgents" made it increasingly clear that some Cubans at least bitterly resented the continued presence of American troops and the highhanded edicts of the island's American governor. Roosevelt had urged McKinley to appoint General Leonard Wood "in immediate command of all Cuba, with complete liberty to do what he deems wisest in shaping our policy for the island, and with complete control over every other military and civil officer." As for the Philippine insurgents, the proper policy, in Roosevelt's view, was "to harass and smash [them] in every way until they are literally beaten into peace; entertaining no proposition whatever from them save that of unconditional surrender." Wood's policy, incidentally, was not to "promise or give the Cubans independence" but to "govern them justly and equitably, giving them all possible opportunities for civic and military advancement," with the result that "in two or three years they will insist on being part of us." But the Cubans remained curiously obdurate, and Roosevelt expressed his disgust in a letter to Lodge. "Nobody wants to annex them," he wrote, "but the general feeling is that they ought to be taken by the neck and shaken until they behave themselves." A common Roosevelt prescription for recalcitrant nations was "taking by the neck and shaking." It was a kind of complement to "carrying a big stick." But in fact, Roosevelt was seldom hasty to act. Albert Beveridge, the Indiana Senator, urged him to "take the island at once" in September, 1906, while Ohio's Senator Joseph Foraker wired him that the authority to intervene lay with Congress, not with the President. "I should be ashamed to look anybody in the face,"

Roosevelt wrote Lodge, "if I hesitated to take important measures to try to secure peace, if necessary by landing sailors and marines or even troops, so as to try to reestablish some government in Cuba and keep the Island as far as possible in decent condition until Congress meets. . . . I hope that, Beveridge to the contrary notwithstanding, we shall not have to intervene in any permanent form at present, and that we can simply make temporary arrangements to keep order until an election can be held and a new government or modified government started." He was determined, he added, to "do all that I can to avoid" taking possession of the island, even temporarily. A crisis was avoided when the incumbent Cuban president insisted that the United States must take over a provisional government and the insurgent leaders thereupon agreed to disband their forces.

The most momentous event of Roosevelt's first term was the complex and somewhat dubious negotiation that cleared the way for the construction of the Panama Canal. The idea of a canal across the Isthmus of Panama was not, of course, new. It had been in the air at least since gold rush days, and the Clayton-Bulwer Treaty of 1850 between Great Britain and the United States had provided that any canal that might be built should be jointly controlled and should serve all nations without discrimination. When sentiment for a canal revived in the wake of the Spanish-American War, the conquest of the Philippines, and talk of a two-ocean navy, the United States was reluctant to accept the notion of joint control, and John Hay turned his considerable diplomatic talents to negotiating an agreement more favorable to it. The result was the first Hay-Pauncefote Treaty, concluded in February, 1900. It was rejected by Parliament, and the second Hay-Pauncefote Treaty provided for U.S. construction and control with the promise of accessibility to all nations.

On January 8, 1902, the House accepted the treaty, but it was almost six months and a number of amendments later before the Senate passed its own version, which was accepted by the House and signed into law by the President on June 28. The accompanying Spooner bill provided for the purchase, for $40,000,000, of the rights of the New Panama Canal Company, a French-based corporation which had begun construction of a canal and then, overwhelmed by the technical and human problems involved, had abandoned it. The government was also authorized to buy from the republic of Colombia a strip of territory six miles wide reaching from the Gulf of Mexico to the Pacific Ocean. It was soon apparent that "fair price" was a dangerously vague term.

Moreover, the Colombian government was hardly more "republican" or stable than its Central American neighbors to the north and south. When it procrastinated, Hay began issuing a series of threats: If negotiations failed, the President would be forced to take whatever steps were necessary to give effect to the determination of the American people that a canal should be built. There was already substantial sentiment in the Senate, led by John T. Morgan of Alabama, for simply annexing the Colombian province of Panama to the United States as "the simplest way to assure the political safety of the Isthmian Canal." Panama had, to be sure, once been independent and might well be again if the Colombians dragged their feet. The president of Colombia, it was pointed out, had crushed a revolt of "liberals" in 1900 and was frequently denounced as a dictator.

The terms offered by the United States were $10,000,000 (one-fourth of the sum given the virtually defunct New Panama Canal Company for its "rights") and, after nine years, an annual "bonus" of $250,000. This was the Hay-Herrán Treaty, which was ratified by the Senate on March 17, 1903, and shipped off to Bogotá for ratification by the Colombian legislature. It was hardly surprising that the Bogotá politicians quickly came to the conclusion that $10,000,000 was not enough.

Meanwhile, the New Panama Canal Company, anxious to ensure the consummation of the plan, contributed $60,000 to the Republican campaign fund with the understanding that the party's platform would include a plank calling for the construction of the canal, preferably in Panama.

The treaty arrived in Bogotá in March. The Colombian Senate met on June 20. A month later it was still considering the treaty despite a barrage of increasingly threatening notes from the State Department to the Colombian foreign minister. On August 12, the Colombian Senate rejected the treaty, but the government asked for two more weeks of grace to put forward a counterproposal. Colombia's agreement with the New Panama Canal Company would expire in 1904. If the government could delay any action on the canal until then, Colombia could lay claim to the sum that the United States was prepared to pay to the company.

There now appeared on the scene a new actor, Philippe Bunau-Varilla, a Frenchman and a veteran of the old De Lesseps company, which had originally planned to build the canal. He represented himself as a friend of the Panamanians, who, he assured Hay and Roosevelt, wished the canal built at all costs, who resented the government in

Bogotá and, in fact, wished for independence. With a little encouragement from the United States—a few gunboats off the coast to protect the "revolution" and discourage attempts from Bogotá to suppress it—all the American aims might be accomplished.

The appearance of Bunau-Varilla seemed to Hay and Roosevelt heaven-sent, another instance of the truth of the words on the Great Seal of the United States: *Annuit coeptis* ("He [God] favors our undertakings"). The recalcitrant Colombians would get their comeuppance. Events now moved with reassuring speed. Bunau-Varilla saw the President on October 9. A week later he conferred with Secretary Hay, who reported that American warships, in anticipation of the "revolution," were already on their way to the Isthmus. Splendid, said Bunau-Varilla; then the revolution would occur on November 9, coincident with the arrival of the warships sent "to protect American interests and the lives of American citizens if a revolutionary outbreak should occur," with instructions to "prevent landing of any armed force, either government or insurgent, at any point within fifty miles of Panama." The revolution took place on schedule with one Chinese resident and one dog accidentally killed. The republic of Panama was proclaimed the next day, and two days later the United States recognized the new independent republic. Shortly thereafter Bunau-Varilla reappeared in Washington—he had hurried back to Panama to arrange the revolution—as the envoy of the republic, "with full powers to conclude a treaty." A few hours sufficed to explain the terms to him, and by evening "the momentous document" was signed "in the little blue drawing-room, out of Abraham Lincoln's inkstand. . . . So the great job is ended," Hay wrote his daughter Helen Hay Whitney, wife of Payne Whitney, heir to the Whitney fortune. When news of the maneuverings incident to the "independence" of Panama got about, there was a scandal in liberal circles. It was evident once again that the United States, with all its pose of moral rectitude, did not hesitate, when it served its interests, to behave as immorally or "piratically," to use a word much employed by the opposition press, as any other world power. There was a congressional investigation which infuriated the President and much pious talk about "freeing" the Panamanians.

The canal itself was as much a technical marvel in its own way as the Erie Canal eighty years earlier, but both the country's temper and the larger significance of the achievement were very different. William James, the grandfather of the philosopher, one of the principal contractors for the canal, and a featured speaker at its dedication, had declared, "We . . . rejoice this day for the extension of the population, liberty, and happiness of man. . . . At this moment," he added, "I feel an indescribable emotion, something like a renewal of life." No orator or journalist was apt to see in the Panama Canal, as splendid an engineering achievement as it undoubtedly was, a "renewal" of anything except perhaps the impulse to lay claim to what belonged to other people. At the same time it must be said that the Bogotá government was far from a model of republican virtue and that strictly from the point of view of the Panamanians themselves it was a reasonably good bargain. They enjoyed a degree of prosperity and stability unknown to their sister republics albeit at the price of being, for all practical purposes, a colony of the United States. As for Colombia, that nation, which had once been part of Simón Bolívar's dream of a grand federation, remained, for the most part, firmly in the hands of the Conservative Party and doubtlessly benefited from being free of the frictions that must have resulted from an unequal and uneasy relationship with the United States. None of which is to condone the means by which the way was cleared for the building of the canal, but only to remind the reader that dubious means sometimes achieve better ends than they deserve.

One result of the hanky-panky that resulted in the independence of Panama from Colombia and its dependence on the United States was the fall from power of General Rafael Reyes, the Colombian head of state, who hurried to Washington to try to prevail on President Roosevelt to reconsider. His arrival in Washington provided Root with the opportunity for a notorious pun. "I have a complaint to make of Root," Hay wrote the President. When Hay told the secretary of war that he had consented to see Reyes, Elihu Root replied, "Better look out. Ex-Reyes are dangerous." Hay wrote the President: "Do you think that on my salary, I can afford to bear such things?"

John Hay's biographer William Roscoe Thayer had an engaging euphemism for the canal affair. He referred to it as "the dynamic solution of the Panama Question," but it was clear that Thayer was troubled by the moral problems inherent in the acquisition of Panama. "We must ask," he wrote, "whether blackmailers have no rights, even when they deny the rights of others. Must we not keep faith with the faithless? . . . How shall we escape from justifying the shockingly cynical treatment of Inferior by Superior peoples?" (The capitalizations are significant; they are what we might call Darwinian capitals.) "Morally, the Colombians were Cretins, but with the rapacity of wild Indians." (Like the Indians, they resented being swindled by pious and "Superior" North Americans.) "The Canal which the American Government planned," Thayer wrote, concluding his debate on a positive note, "was for the benefit of the entire world. Should the blackmailing greed of the Bogotá ring stand in the way of civilization? I believe there is only one answer to this question—blackmailers must not be tolerated. . . ." Thayer's principal criticism of the Panama takeover was that it should have been done boldly and openly instead of letting it appear that the United States was "conniving at a conspiracy." Furthermore, morally murky as our actions in Panama may have been, "they had nothing in common" with the "international crimes" committed by the Germans.

The *Nation* and the *New York Evening Post* were relentless in exposing and denouncing the "trickery and falsity of our Panama aggression," as Oswald Garrison Villard wrote. When a member of the Yale faculty denounced the arrangement as the "rape of Panama," Hay, obviously touched on a tender nerve, replied that the "only alternative would have been an infinite duration of bloodshed and devastation through the whole extent of the Isthmus." Roosevelt's own views were expressed in a letter to William Roscoe Thayer written more than ten years later. "To talk of Colombia as a responsible Power to be dealt with as we would deal with Holland or Belgium or Switzerland or Denmark is a mere absurdity. The analogy is with a group of Sicilian or Calabrian bandits. . . . You could no more make an agreement with the Colombian rulers than you could nail currant jelly to a wall. . . . The people of Panama were as a unit in desiring the Canal and in wishing to overthrow the rule of Colombia. If they had not revolted, I should have recommended Congress to take possession of the Isthmus by force of arms; and . . . I had actually written the first draft of my Message to this effect." The responsibility for the decision was his alone, Roosevelt declared. He did not even discuss the matter with Root or Hay "or any one else . . . because a council of war does not fight; and I intended to do the job once for all." Such arguments could, of course, be used to justify interference in the affairs of any nation in political turmoil or unable to defend itself against greedy "friends." (And such arguments were, of course, used constantly by the United States and other powers to justify gobbling up a substantial part of the world in the last decades of the nineteenth and first decades of the twentieth centuries.)

Felix Frankfurter, the future Supreme Court justice, who was becoming an authority on the legal aspects of American relations with Latin American countries, had no doubts about the Panama Canal. It was just the sort of issue he felt his more soft-headed liberal friends flunked on. "We're doing a great big job at Panama—" he wrote in his diary in November, 1911, "will revolutionize trade movement of the world and add tremendously to military advantages of U.S. I haven't a particle of doubt that there would still be no Panama if T.R. hadn't been President at the time. The more I study his administration . . . the bigger his statesmanship."

Even staunch liberals like Ray Stannard Baker were proud of the canal. Baker considered it "a kind of symbol of the American gift of imagination, American inventiveness, American willingness to gamble on . . . vast and costly enterprises."

Whatever reformers, professors, and journalists might have to say about the Panama Canal deal, there was little doubt about the public's sentiments. The effort of Senator Arthur Pue Gorman, the Maryland Democrat, to rally his fellow Democrats to oppose the Panama Canal Treaty may well have cost him his party's nomination in the 1904 presidential election. In the words of the *Atlanta Constitution* of December 20, 1903, "The simplest observer of popular temper in this country cannot mistake how the American people feel about this matter. They approve what has been done to date, they want and mean to have that canal, and they will visit their wrath upon whatever man or party may defeat their wishes. The defeat of the treaty would simply delay the canal and enrage the people. That defeat would be fatuous and fatal to the popularity of the party producing it."

Of the period of what might be properly called American imperialism Hay wrote with a disarming lack of self-consciousness: "The briefest expression of our rule of conduct is, perhaps, the *Monroe Doctrine and the Golden Rule*." How the insurgent Filipinos responded to that declaration if it ever reached them is not recorded. Thayer, however, had no trouble with it. To him Hay was "the Statesman of the Golden Rule." However many opponents might call the Panama Canal strategy immoral, piratical, and treacherous, many others, Thayer among them, were convinced that if John Hay approved of it (or helped devise it), the negotiations "could not have been dishonorable." What can be said with some confidence is that in the dark rolls of international hanky-panky the Panama Canal deal, if not exactly "square," was a comparatively modest bit of chicanery.

The Election of 1904

In May, 1903, Roosevelt took a combination vacation/political tour through the West. He had, he wrote Lodge, "some splendid rides" and was entranced by "the utterly new sights of New Mexico, Arizona and Southern California." The Grand Canyon was just his cup-of-enthusiasm-tea. It defied description. "It impresses one as some wonderful and terrible sunset impresses one; with awe and sense of grandeur and sublimity, a sense of the majesty of the work of the ages." Nicholas Murray Butler, president of Columbia University, accompanied him and Benjamin Ide Wheeler, president of the University of California—"a first rate man"—joined the party in California.

At the Presidio in San Francisco the President reviewed the detachment of U.S. soldiers under the command of General Arthur MacArthur and delighted the general by "riding the line." From San Francisco Roosevelt went on to Yosemite to spend four days with John Muir.

Everywhere that he appeared "officially" Roosevelt was greeted by wildly enthusiastic crowds. In San Francisco, Seattle, and Tacoma, Washington, the streets were jammed with cheering throngs, but the President was indignant at the newspaper report in the last city that he had kissed babies in the manner of a common politician. He denounced the "outrageous lie" in a letter to Lodge, adding, "There are certain things, which are not matters of morals but of good taste, which I ought not even to be asked to deny."

When he heard in Ohio that Hanna had stated he would not support him for election in 1904, Roosevelt wrote Lodge that he was prepared for "a knockdown and dragout fight with Hanna and the whole Wall Street crowd." At the same time he would make clear to "the labor people . . . that I set my face like flint against violence and lawlessness of any kind on their part, just as much as against the arrogant greed of the rich, and that I would be as quick to move against one as the other. . . . The big New York and Chicago capitalists—and both the criminal rich and the fool rich—will do all they can to beat me."

As the election year approached, an alarmed Lodge wrote to Roosevelt that his capitalist enemies were giving "out the idea that you are entirely given over to the labor side and that you are wholly prepared to make war on capital and you will not treat the labor men in the same way you would capital if they violate the law. Our Wall Street friends are at great pains to spread this idea. . . ." Roosevelt himself was apprehensive over the depressed state of the economy, caused, in his view, by "the speculators, the promoters who have over-capitalized the great trusts, and the reckless, greedy and over-sanguine men generally. . . ." But they all would nonetheless try to place the blame on his administration.

Indeed, the fearless fighter and hunter showed a disconcerting disposition to panic at the slightest indication of opposition anywhere in the country. A gloomy letter from a Republican county chairman in Illinois would produce an instant reaction, often in the form of an alarmed communiqué to Lodge. "There has been really a great gust of popular anger against me," he wrote his faithful correspondent, apropos of some misunderstanding with the leaders of the Civil War veterans' association, the Grand Army of the Republic. Lodge's principal task in the months preceding the election was to reassure an apprehensive President that the country still loved him and that he was bound to be reelected. But despite the enormous and wildly enthusiastic crowds that greeted him everywhere, Roosevelt was consumed by doubts and anxieties. "You will, of course, be renominated with hearty acclamation," Lodge wrote in September, 1903, a full year before the election. "You entered the White House with extreme popularity, both personally and politically," Lodge reminded him. "That popularity increased until it may be said to have been universal. I have certainly never seen anything like it for any President in my time. . . ." It was inevitable that there should be criticism from individuals and factions that had suffered from the President's reforms. Then Lodge added a significant sentence: "You are always so buoyant and fearless that everyone thinks that you are one of the most sanguine of men. I am one of the two or three people in the world who know better. I know that you are, and always have been, a pessimist in regard to yourself and your prospects, and though this does not in the least affect your spirit or your courage it does make you see things sometimes too darkly."

Henry Adams wrote to an English friend in 1904: "I can laugh at all my friends who are running what they call a government. They are droll like most men who run governments." The nation, he added, "is terribly interesting. It has no character but prodigious force,—at least twenty million horsepower constant; about as much as all the rest of the world together, by coal output. . . . All the same, our great managers of industry are dead scared."

As the election of 1904 approached, Roosevelt could think or talk of little else. Despite the evidence on every hand of his overwhelming popularity, he was prey to unsettling doubts. "That he is still a bore as big as a buffalo I do not deny," Henry Adams wrote to Elizabeth Cameron of the President, "but at least he is a different sort." A few weeks later he noted, "Of all the Presidents that ever lived, Theodore thinks of nothing, talks of nothing, and lives for nothing but his political interests. If you remark to him that God is Great, he asks naïvely at once how that will affect his election. He is flying every day into fits about speeches in Congress, and writing letters by the ream to catch half a dozen votes anywhere out West. . . . Theodore writes like a centipede. . . . Theodore could win best by holding his tongue now, and buying Democrats to bolt."

In the spring, a few months prior to the party nominating convention, Congress began to express its restiveness under the President's imperious rule. It was, in practical fact, a new experience for that body to be so dominated by a president. It had not happened since Lincoln. "One after another," Adams wrote to Cameron, "all his friends in the House had been getting up on the floor in a frenzy of passion, and yelling 'liar' and 'scoundrel' at him all day. . . . No such scene had ever taken place in Congress. All the wounded vanity of the Congressmen, two years in arrears, broke out . . . and lashed itself into fits." They had seen themselves, as they thought, "sacrificed to [Roosevelt's] selfishness and trampled on by his contempt, till they were mad for his blood." Adams added, "Apparently, he had no suspicion of the hatred they feel for him. . . . He will override Congress, no doubt, and crush the life out of it at the election . . . but he will do it without intending it, or understanding it. . . ."

Still fretting over the possibility of defeat, Roosevelt wrote to Lodge in May: "If I win at all this year it will be because the bulk of the people believe I am a straight-forward, decent and efficient man, upon whose courage and common sense no less than upon whose honesty and energy they can depend." Although many of the electorate doubtless regarded the President highly because of one or another of the virtues he so unselfconsciously enumerated, it is to be doubted that any combination of them appealed to them nearly as strongly as his remarkable gift for self-dramatization, a gift which was certainly more instinctive than deliberate.

Roosevelt worried about the effects of a butchers' strike and the cotton mill strike. There were also serious strikes in Chicago, and the Colorado mines strike dragged on, producing a litany of horrifying stories of violence and oppression. Labor leaders appealed to Roosevelt to take some action to end the strikes, but he insisted that any such action would give the impression that he was an ally of labor against capital rather than an impartial arbiter.

Roosevelt had a disconcerting habit of casting every issue in simple moral terms. He and his supporters were invariably not just on one side or the other of an issue; they were on the *right* side and his opponents were on the *wrong*, or evil and immoral, side. In the months before the presidential election of 1904 he wrote Lodge that "this contest [is] essentially one between sincerity and trickiness."

"Theodore," Henry Adams wrote, "is beginning to be scared about Hearst who is buying the Democratic nomination like a string of bananas. He and Bryan, it is calculated, can carry the whole hoodlum vote in the critical cities . . . with an immense sweep, and through them may well carry the states." Adams was confident that Roosevelt could defeat any older man, "but Hearst," he wrote, "is five years younger than he and quite as mad. Theodore bid as low as he could for the hoodlum vote, but Hearst easily takes it from him."

The Socialist National Convention met in Chicago on May 1 and nominated Eugene Debs as its candidate for president and Benjamin

Hanford of New York for vice-president. Debs delivered a speech that was both a party platform and a manifesto for the cause. The party's appeal, he declared, was "to the exploited class, the workers in all useful trades and professions, all honest occupations, from the most menial service to the highest skill. . . ." It had been issued a challenge to "put an end to the last of the barbarous class struggles by conquering the capitalist government, taking possession of the means of production and making them common property of all, abolishing wage-slavery and establishing the cooperative commonwealth." The first step must be "to sever all relations with capitalist parties. They are precisely alike and I challenge the most discriminating partisans to tell them apart in relation to labor. . . . Read the national platform of the Republican party and see if there is in all its bombast a crumb of comfort for labor. The convention that adopted it was a capitalist convention and the only thought it had for labor was how to abstract its vote without waking it up."

The Prohibition Party, meeting in Indianapolis at the end of June, nominated Silas C. Swallow as its candidate. The Socialist Labor Party nominated Charles Corregan of New York, while the People's Party, sadly shrunken in numbers since its heyday in the 1890s, convened at Springfield, Illinois, on July 4 and nominated Tom Watson for president and Thomas Tibbles, an adopted member of the Omaha tribe and crusader for Indian rights, for vice-president. Its platform affirmed the "basic truths of the Omaha platform of 1892" and renewed its "allegiance to the old-fashioned American spirit that gave this nation existence, and made it distinctive among the peoples of the earth." The ills that America suffered from were the consequence of its departure from the principles of the Declaration of Independence. Special privileges having been given to the few, they had been enabled "to dominate the many, thereby tending to destroy the political equality which is the corner-stone of democratic government." Abolition of child labor, the right to organize unions, the eight-hour day, the control of monopolies, the initiative, referendum, and recall, and a Federal monetary system—all were included, but they had almost an archaic air about them. A number of these once radical notions were embedded in the platforms of the two major parties. The People's Party was plainly expiring. The momentum of radical reform had shifted to the Socialists.

As the date of the Republican nominating convention approached, Roosevelt engaged in a feverish correspondence with Lodge, who had been appointed chairman of the Platform Committee at the President's behest.

The tariff continued to be a volatile political issue. There was widespread demand for tariff reform, with which the President had little sympathy. He suggested to Lodge that the requisite tariff plank in the platform be as vaguely worded as possible and contain a clause to the effect that "the minimum duty must always be that which will cover the difference in labor costs here and abroad, because under no circumstances must the standard of living of the American working men be brought down." That, of course, was the difficulty with any extensive tariff reform. It was one of the few issues on which capital and labor joined forces. The fact was that time and experience made it evident that in many protected industries the difference in "labor costs"—i.e., wages—was heavily in favor of the American worker because advanced technology gave him a far higher rate of productivity than his foreign counterpart.

On June 21 the Republicans convened in Chicago. An odd atmosphere pervaded the convention. The majority of the delegates were soldiers of the old guard, reactionary to their deepest souls. They distrusted and, in many instances, hated the man whom they had met to nominate as the candidate of their party. An Indiana Republican, at a dinner of that state's delegation, proposed a toast to Roosevelt, "whom nobody wants," nobody, of course, but the great rank and file of Republicans and uncounted thousands of Democrats. Where the delegates' hearts lay was suggested by a portrait of Mark Hanna, hanging in the convention hall, five times as large as the portrait of the President.

Roosevelt's control of the convention extended even to telling Elihu Root, his choice for chairman of the convention, what to say about him in his keynote address. The *New York Sun* proposed an abbreviated Republican platform: "RESOLVED: That we emphatically endorse and affirm Theodore Roosevelt. Whatever Theodore Roosevelt thinks, says, does, or wants is right. Roosevelt and Stir 'Em Up. Now and Forever; One and Inseparable." Mr. Dooley summed up the proceedings: "Th' raypublican convintion labored . . . like a cach reigester. It listened to three canned speeches, adopted a predigested platform, nommynated a cold storage vice presidint, gave three expecially prepared cheers and wint home. Th' convintion's mind was made up f't befure it met."

The Democratic Convention met at St. Louis on July 6. Senator Arthur Pue Gorman had been the candidate of the conservative or Cleveland wing of the Democratic Party, which put him forward "to repress the Wild People," the Midwestern Bryanites, but Gorman had made himself a political liability by his opposition to the Panama Canal Treaty. The conservative Cleveland "Wall Street" Democrats turned up a somewhat reluctant anti-Bryan candidate, Alton B. Parker. Born in Cortland, New York, in 1852, Parker had been a schoolteacher before he became a lawyer. The office of chief justice of the New York Supreme Court was an elective office, and Parker had won it in 1897 by a large margin. To importunings from Democratic leaders to run for the Senate as a preliminary to challenging Bryan for the Democratic nomination in 1904, Parker, a realist, had replied, "There is no more chance for a sound money Democrat being elected to the Presidency two years hence than there is to go to Heaven without dying." Nonetheless, he was prevailed upon to oppose Bryan.

Bryan, in his struggle to maintain his control of the party, denounced Parker's candidacy and called the judge "the muzzled candidate of Wall Street." The various Democrats whom Bryan pushed forward as alternatives to Parker were dismissed by conservative Democratic newspapers as "Bryan's Little Unknowns from Nowhere."

Parker's most serious rival was Hearst. His backers chanted:

> Boom, boom, boom;
> First, first, first;
> California, California
> Hearst, Hearst, Hearst.

The *Nation*'s attack on Hearst under the title "Unthinkable Hearst," published on March 1, 1904, was credited by many people with killing the Hearst boomlet for president. "It is not simply that we revolt at Hearst's huge vulgarity," Rollo Ogden, Edwin Godkin's successor as editor of the *Evening Post*, wrote; "at his front of bronze; at his shrieking unfitness mentally, for the office which he sets out to buy. All this goes without saying. There never has been a case of a man of such slender intellectual equipment, absolutely without experience in office, impudently flaunting his wealth before the eyes of the people and saying, 'Make me President.' This is folly. This is to degrade public life. . . . An agitator we can endure; an honest radical we can respect; a fanatic we can tolerate; but a low voluptuary trying to sting his jaded senses to a fresh thrill by turning from private to public corruption is a new horror in American politics."

The real battle in the Democratic Convention centered on Bryan's bargaining his support for Parker (Parker's nomination seemed inevitable but would mean little without Bryan's backing) for substantial liberalization of the Democratic platform. The income tax, direct election of Senators, antitrust legislation, and anti-imperialism were the sticking points. Bryan won them all except for the income tax plank.

The delegates revealed their true colors when they cheered enthusiastically at Mississippi Senator John Sharp Williams's statement that the party "will not hypocritically pretend to sympathize with those who desire . . . the Africanization or Mongolization of any State or community within the bounds of the American Republic." Parker was put into nomination on Friday night, July 8. At four-thirty the next morning Bryan nominated Francis Cockrell of Missouri. Twice defeated as his party's presidential nominee, hated by the Eastern, predominantly Cleveland wing of the party, facing a crushing defeat in the prospective nomination of Parker, Bryan revealed that he had lost little of his old magic, his power to touch men's hearts and exalt their spirits. To the Western delegates he was still an untarnished hero. When he rose to speak, he was greeted with an emotional outburst ten minutes long, the longest ovation afforded anyone during the course of the convention, and he was interrupted forty-seven times by applause.

Bryan was particularly severe on Roosevelt's militarism. "Must we choose between a god of war and a god of gold?" he asked, referring to Parker's progold views. ". . . Give us a pilot who will guide the Democratic ship away from the Scylla of militarism without wrecking her upon the Charybdis of commercialism." Even Bryan's enemies confessed themselves moved by his eloquence, but soon afterward Parker was nominated by 679 votes to 181 for Hearst and 42 for Cockrell.

The Democrats, having nominated Parker and provided him with an eighty-one-year-old running mate, Henry Gassaway Davis of West Virginia, a famous old relic of the Populist days, had the demoralizing experience of having Parker immediately declare his support of the gold standard, the classic Republican issue, winning thereby, in Henry Adams's words, "the hysterical adulation of the large neurotic class typified by the *Evening Post*." Parker's declaration was, in the words of the *Post,* a "calmly heroic act," so "bold in conception, so triumphant in execution" that it must finally spell the end of free silver. The *Nation* was equally enthusiastic over Parker's acceptance speech, in which he denounced the American occupation of the Philippines and called for lower tariffs. Parker's luster for anti-Roosevelt liberals was soon dimmed by his close association with financiers Thomas Ryan and August Belmont, who, by generous applications of money—Belmont contributed $250,000, the equivalent of several million today—came to play an increasingly prominent role in his campaign.

The campaign itself was a ho-hummer. Parker proved a colorless and ineffective campaigner who stuck to tired political bromides. Roosevelt's advisers, convinced that he could lose only by some ill-advised outburst, counseled silence. They urged him to speak and write as little as possible. "From the moment Theodore submitted to be choked," Henry Adams wrote, "the tide went his way; but he must be nearly suffocated by suppressed loquacity."

The principal charge leveled against the President by the Democrats was that he was a "nationalizer," an enemy of states' rights, and a despot. The *Evening Post* was hostile to Roosevelt on the alleged ground of his disposition to lie when it seemed expedient to do so.

Henry Watterson, the Democratic editor of the *Louisville Courier*, declared Roosevelt "altogether the most startling figure who has appeared in the world since Napoleon Bonaparte...." Watterson went on to suggest that if, as many people thought, the government of the United States was a failure, it might be time for "a strong man having the courage to take all the bulls of corruption by the horns...." If that was the case, Roosevelt was clearly the man for the job.

Although all the indications were that Roosevelt would win a decisive victory over his colorless opponent, the President, in a panic, decided that his campaign needed large infusions of money. To secure it, he secretly summoned a gaggle of tycoons. Edward Harriman, then president of the Union Pacific, Henry Frick, and Daniel Lamont were among those called on for emergency contributions to the campaign. Henry Frick, not necessarily the most unimpeachable of witnesses, later told Oswald Garrison Villard of the meeting with the President. "He got down on his knees to us," Frick declared. "We bought the son of a bitch and then he did not stay bought." E. H. Harriman told the same story. Harriman, who contributed a last-minute $250,000 to Roosevelt's campaign, claimed that the President had promised in return for the contribution to appoint old Chauncey Depew ambassador to France. The evidence that Roosevelt was following Steffens's advice in the Harriman case (to deny only what was true) is inconclusive. What is certain is that Roosevelt appealed to some of the most prominent malefactors of great wealth to bail out his boat, which certainly was far from sinking. When the story came out after the election, the *New York World* took the President severely to task. "It should never be possible," the editors declared, "even to suspect that a secret partnership existed between the campaign managers of a candidate for President and great corporations liable to punishment for violations of federal statutes."

When the votes were counted in November, it turned out that all of Roosevelt's fears and anxieties had been groundless. As the patient Lodge had continually assured him he must, the President triumphed by a great margin. "Your place in history was already safe," Lodge wrote, "but it has now been signed and sealed by the verdict of your contemporaries—by men of your own time—and you have four years in which to add to the fame you have won and the great work you have done."

In the popular vote Roosevelt polled 7,628,834; Parker 5,084,401; Debs 402,460; Swallow that irreducible 259,000 or so Prohibition votes; Tom Watson 114,753. In electoral votes Roosevelt had 336; Parker, 140. An elated Roosevelt wrote his son: "I am stunned by the overwhelming victory we have won. I have the greatest popular majority and the greatest electoral majority ever given to a candidate for President."

With the election out of the way, Roosevelt and an ailing John Hay were free to push their global strategies. War between Russia and Japan had broken out in February, 1904, and the Russians suffered an almost uninterrupted succession of disastrous defeats. The shock waves from this unexpected turn of events was worldwide. There were as well alarming domestic consequences in Russia. The entry of the Far East into the calculations of European diplomacy had been very recent and most strikingly evident in the ruthless dismemberment of a prostrate China.

When John Hay suggested to the Russian ambassador, Count Cassini, that "the inevitable result of [Russia's] present course of aggression would be the seizure by different Powers of different provinces in China, and the accomplishment of the dismemberment of the Empire," Cassini shouted, "This is already done. China is dismembered and we are entitled to our share." Hay observed to Henry White that "the poor devils of Chinks" fear that the "raised club" of Germany would have more effect on their future than the "open hand" of the United States.

Russia from its geographical proximity, its large army and navy, and its imperial ambitions was the dominant power in the region. It was, above all, a European power. Thus, while it was clear that its economy was chaotic, and its autocratic and repressive government inefficient and decadent, it had occurred to very few observers of the international scene that its hegemony could be seriously challenged by that militant upstart of the Pacific, Japan. Moreover, the consequences of Japan's achievement of Great Power status and the humbling of Russia were alarming. The whole house-of-cards balance of power in the world was imperiled. "Whatever the result of the war," Henry Adams wrote to John Hay, "Russia has fifty years of reorganization before her. . . . My blood curdles to think of what will happen there if society breaks up; and there is nothing to hold it together except the ridiculous Tsar and the preposterous Church."

The Russian defeats gave fresh impetus to the internal enemies of the czar. A congress of liberals met at St. Petersburg in November, 1904, to demand a representative assembly and broader civil liberties, and a few months later on Bloody Sunday, January 22, 1905, a vast crowd of workingmen marching to the palace to place their demands before the czar were fired upon by royal guards; 70 were killed, and 240 wounded. A few months later the now thoroughly alarmed czar announced a number of concessions, among them an edict calling for religious toleration, but the unrest continued as strikes and demonstrations spread all over the country. Radicals the world over hailed what they believed were the opening acts of the anticipated world revolution. The news of the Russian upheaval was to Emma Goldman "electrifying." It carried her "to ecstatic heights." The massacre of January 22 had been followed by a general strike in which even the prostitutes joined. "The radical East Side," Goldman wrote, "lived in a delirium, spending almost all of its time at monster meetings and discussing these matters in cafés, forgetting political differences and brought into close comradeship by the glorious events happening in the fatherland."

The moment proved short-lived. The hated Cossacks quenched the revolutionary fires. Again, in Emma Goldman's words, "Cossack terror stalked through the land, torture, prison, and the gallows doing their deadly work. Our bright hopes turned to blackest despair. The whole East Side profoundly felt the tragedy of the crushed masses." Goldman decided "to use whatever ability I possessed to plead the heroic cause of revolutionary Russia." She found herself much in demand as a speaker by liberal and even conservative groups. The Honorable William Dudley Foulke, a devoted follower of Roosevelt, was president of the Society of the Friends of Russian Freedom. Alice Stone Blackwell, daughter of Lucy Stone, was another ardent advocate of the revolution. Jane Addams, Charles Edward Russell, and Lillian Wald were also prominent members of the society.

In the immediate aftermath of the revolutionary outbreak, Catherine Breshkovskaya—known as Babushka—heroine of the long struggle against the czar, arrived in the United States to rally support for the revolutionaries in her homeland. When Emma Goldman met her, "her simplicity, the tenderness of her voice, and her gestures" affected Goldman "like the balm of a spring day."

Breshkovskaya's first appearance was at Cooper Union, where her impassioned eloquence entranced the huge crowd that turned out to hear her. Upper-class liberals and radicals pledged their support to the cause. Emma Goldman and "Babushka" began a month-long lecture tour to acquaint the public with the conditions in Russia that had given rise to the revolutionary protests.

"Russia," Henry Adams wrote to Elizabeth Cameron, "is dropping to pieces. The Tsar is almost literally Louis XVI over again. The country is, or is near, being bankrupt. . . . Revolution is inevitable. War is a gambler's chance. This conviction has turned me into a Russian. I don't want to see Russia go to pieces. Such a disaster would be worse than the collapse of France in 1870. It might throw all of us into one big heap of broken crockery. Germany and France would have to scuttle like crabs. . . . Yet I doubt whether any action can save RUSSIA. . . . Japan has already lanced her as if she were a sick whale." Adams added, "If Russia breaks down, France must be isolated, and a victim. Either she must annex herself to Germany or to us. Either way she is sunk. If China goes to pieces, we are in the full maelstrom."

"Russia seems to be lapsing into anarchy," Roosevelt wrote Lodge. There were also "signs of disintegration . . . in Austria and Sweden and Norway."

William James, writing to Henri Bergson to congratulate him on his *Creative Evolution* (praising it for inflicting "an irrecoverable death-wound upon Intellectualism. It can never resuscitate!"), noted that he was grateful to have lived to witness the Russo-Japanese War and the publication of *Creative Evolution*—"the two great modern turning points of history and of thought!"—and Henry Adams wrote to Hay: "To

America [the war] is all profit. Japan has become the first power in the East. Germany alone is very cold."

The Japanese victories pointed up an awkward and possibly dangerous development on the western fringe of the continent. There state legislatures were busy passing discriminatory legislation against the Japanese, as they had done earlier against their fellow Asians the Chinese. "I am utterly disgusted," Roosevelt wrote to Lodge in May, 1905, "at the manifestations which have begun to appear on the Pacific slope in favor of excluding the Japanese exactly as the Chinese are excluded. The California State Legislature and various other bodies have acted in the worst possible taste in the offensive manner to Japan."

Roosevelt's indignation at the behavior of the Californians in regard to the Japanese—he called it "as foolish as if conceived by the mind of a Hottentot"—was based less on distaste of racist attitudes than on his concern that the Japanese might be moved to take military action against the United States, such as seizing the Philippines and/ or Hawaii. "These Pacific Coast people," he wrote, rather as though he were writing of a foreign land, "wish grossly to insult the Japanese and to keep out Japanese immigrants on the ground that they are an immoral, degraded and worthless race . . . and at the same time . . . they expect to be given advantages in Oriental markets. . . . The Japanese soldiers and sailors have shown themselves to be terrible foes. There can be none more dangerous in the world . . . [and] if, as Brooks Adams says, we show ourselves 'opulent, aggressive and unarmed,' the Japanese may some time work us an injury."

It was, in a substantial measure, Roosevelt's respect for the fighting qualities of the Japanese and the formidable character of their navy that made him the ideal person to undertake to negotiate the end of the Russo-Japanese War. The Japanese were well aware of the President's friendly disposition and thus felt free to approach him, in the utmost secrecy, to initiate peace talks with the Russians. The fact was that the Japanese economy was feeling the effects of the pressure imposed on it by the war. There was, moreover, a small but vociferous peace party in Japan opposed to imperial ventures. The Japanese had gained a series of spectacular victories which had immeasurably enhanced their international prestige, indeed marked their unquestioned emergence as the dominant military and naval power in the Pacific. They were ready for peace.

Roosevelt and Hay began a series of skillful moves in the spring of 1905 designed to bring Russia to the conference table. The negotiations showed the President at his best: shrewd, tactful, firm, and even threatening when he judged it propitious to be so.

When he pressed Count Cassini, the Russian ambassador replied with, in Roosevelt's words, "his usual rigmarole, to the effect that Russia was fighting the battles of the white race . . . ; that Russia was too great to admit defeat and so forth, and so forth."

Roosevelt opened negotiations with a similar dispatch to both governments which read in part: "The President feels that the time has come when in the interest of all mankind he must endeavor to see if it is not possible to bring to an end the terrible and lamentable conflict now being waged. With both Russia and Japan the United States has inherited ties of friendship and good will. It hopes for the prosperity and welfare of each, and it feels that the progress of the world is set back by the war between these two great nations." Peace between them was "in the interest of the whole civilized world. . . ."

Roosevelt wrote to Henry Cabot Lodge, giving a detailed account of the diplomatic moves that led up to the treaty conference. In the course of the negotiations he had reached the conclusion that "Russia is so corrupt, so treacherous and shifty, and so incompetent, that I am utterly unable to say whether or not it will make peace, or break off the negotiations at any moment." The President felt that a Russian triumph would have been "a blow to civilization," but "her destruction as an eastern Asiatic power would also . . . be unfortunate. . . . As for Japan, she has risen with simply marvelous rapidity, and she is as formidable from the industrial as from the military standpoint. She is a great civilized nation. . . . There are some things she can teach us, and some things she can learn from us. She will be as formidable an industrial competitor as, for instance, Germany, and in a dozen years I think she will be the leading industrial nation of the Pacific." There remained the problem, of course, of Japan's warlike spirit. "Whether her tremendous growth in industrialism will in course of time modify and perhaps soften the wonderful military spirit she has inherited from the days of the Samurai supremacy it is hard to say," he added. "Personally, I think it will; but the effect will hardly be felt for a generation to come. Still, her growing industrial wealth will be to a certain extent a hostage for keeping the peace." Roosevelt's principal concern was for the Philippines, but he did not think that Japan would cast possessive eyes on those islands until it had settled affairs with mainland China.

As a kind of dramatic conclusion to the treaty negotiations, John Hay died a few weeks after the treaty had been signed. The last entry in his diary, two weeks before his death, read: "I say to myself that I should not rebel at the thought of my life ending at this time. I have lived to be old, something I never expected in my youth. I have had many blessings, domestic happiness being the greatest of all. I have lived my life. I have been a success beyond all dreams of my boyhood. My name is printed in the journals of the world. . . . If I were to live several years more I should probably add nothing to my existing reputation. . . . I know that death is the common lot, and what is universal ought not to be deemed a misfortune; and yet—instead of confronting it with dignity and philosophy, I cling instinctively to life and the things of life, as eagerly as if I had not had my chance at happiness and gained nearly all the great prizes."

Hay "in his eight years of office . . . had solved nearly every old problem of American statesmanship, and left little or nothing to annoy his successor," in the opinion of Henry Adams. "He had brought the great Atlantic powers into a working system, and even Russia seemed about to be dragged into a combine of intelligent equilibrium based on an intelligent allotment of activities. For the first time in fifteen hundred years a true Roman *pax* was in sight, and would, if it succeeded, owe its virtues to him . . . and if the worst should happen, setting continent against continent in arms—the only apparent alternative to his scheme—he need not repine at missing the catastrophe. . . . Always unselfish, generous, easy, patient, and loyal, Hay had treated the world as something to be taken in block without pulling it to pieces to get rid of its defects; he liked it all; he laughed and accepted. . . ." It had been a remarkable life, a link between the greatest of presidents—Lincoln—with whom the lighthearted young Hay and his friend John Nicolay had shared confidences, more like Lincoln's sons than his aides, and the modern world. After years of political exile Hay had returned to guide American foreign policy in the era of the nation's emergence as a world power.

Roosevelt, in his negotiations with the Russians and the Japanese, showed himself at his best. The fact that his perpetual bellicosity and his prating about the redemptive character of war are uncongenial to most of us today should not blind us to his remarkable grasp of what has come to be called geopolitics. He was thoroughly unsentimental in his assessment of the realities of international power politics, and it is hard to imagine that his prescription of firmness, restraint, courtesy, and tact in dealing with foreign powers can be improved upon.

The fact that Roosevelt had acted as an impartial arbiter of a dangerous conflict between major powers changed the chemistry of international politics and at once elevated the United States to a new level of importance in world affairs. The widely publicized language of the initial appeal to the two belligerents struck an irresistible note. The action of the United States, with no ax to grind and no advantage to gain, was undertaken "in the interest of the whole civilized world." There was a breath-taking presumption about the words and the conception behind them. Benjamin Franklin had startled Europe by suggesting, during the negotiations in Paris that concluded the war for American independence, that the United States might now act as disinterested arbiter between the great (and, he thought, though he did not say so, decadent) powers of Europe. The suggestion was too presumptuous to merit notice, but now, 124 years later, an American president had acted in precisely that spirit.

The success of the negotiations made Roosevelt a figure of exceptional potency in that "civilized world" he so confidently evoked. It symbolized, as no declaration or state paper could have done, the reality of American power and American influence. More important, it did so in a manner that suggested that United States intervention in world affairs would be benign, not on the side of international-politics-as-usual but in a new spirit of justice and humanity. Roosevelt, it is true, had not originated the idea of a peace conference; that had been Japan. But that nation would not have broached the subject if its leaders had not perceived Roosevelt as both a friend and a person whose feeling for the dangerous waters of international diplomacy was akin to their own. The point to be stressed is that his personality and his principles created the opportunity, and he had the wit and skill to make brilliant use of it. There was truth in Henry Cabot Lodge's comment "It has been a service to humanity."

Old Carl Schurz, hero of the Civil War and Republican bellwether through many political campaigns, wrote Roosevelt that his "interposition between Japan and Russia" was "one of the most meritorious and brilliant achievements of our age, not only bold and noble in conception, but most admirable for the exquisite skill and tact with which it was carried through. . . ." Schurz, whom Roosevelt commonly spoke of with scorn for his pacifist views, urged the President to use the prestige that he had acquired as a consequence of his "interposition" to call an international conference on disarmament. Roosevelt's response was hardly generous. He wrote an essay on the importance of military strength, pointing out that it was in large part his evident determination to uphold the honor of the United States by force of arms if necessary that had enabled him to be an effective advocate of peace. Typically, he wrote, "Peace has only come as the sequel to the armed interference of a civilized power, which relative to its opponent, was a just and beneficent power. . . . Unjust war is dreadful; a just war may be the highest duty. To have the best nations, the free and civilized nations, disarm and leave the despotisms and barbarisms with great military force, would be a calamity. . . ." And Roosevelt wrote to Root that he hoped his role in the Russo-Japanese treaty would not give him the appearance of "a professional peace advocate—a kind of sublimated being of the Godkin or Schurz variety. . . ."

5

Municipal Reform

The focus of reform remained in the city and its most powerful instrument, the new journalism. The great era of investigative reporting had begun almost inadvertently with Ida Tarbell's *History of the Standard Oil Company*. As Sam McClure told the story, he set out with the idea of doing a series of articles "on the greatest American business achievements." Standard Oil seemed a good place to start. The talk of trusts was in the air, so it seemed appropriate to start with the mother of trusts, Standard Oil. John D. Rockefeller, the genius of American finance, was the central figure. Standard Oil, moreover, was eager to assist in the project. Ida Tarbell was assigned to the story. Three years of patient research preceded the appearance of the first article. It seems safe to say that no aspect of American social or economic life had received such detailed and careful treatment. The result was a shocking story of the ruthlessness of economic power, of indifference to the public good, and of the buying and selling of compliant politicians.

Oddly enough, the case was similar with Lincoln Steffens, who was certainly no novice with regard to municipal corruption. Acting on a suggestion by Tarbell, Steffens had set out to do an article on aspects of municipal reform in Cleveland. Diverted to St. Louis, he turned up a rock, so to speak, and found under it a variety of forms of civic evil, normally hidden from the light of day or simply ignored. The result was a sensational exposé of corruption in that city. It was followed by similar excursions to other cities and a series that grew into a book, *The Shame of the Cities*. Steffens found a common pattern in virtually all cities. Bosses, typically Democrats, with large immigrant constituencies, were hand in glove with capitalists, usually owners of or applicants for municipal utilities—gas, water, electricity, garbage disposal, public transportation, etc. (in San Francisco it was the labor leaders who were in bed with the politicians). The politicians—the bosses—were, in the words of the reformer Frederic Howe, the "scavengers, stokers, shovellers, who kept the machine going for the captains on the bridge." The captains were "bankers, clubmen, gentlemen, whose influence was so powerful that it protected them from exposure through the press. . . . An oligarchy of business bosses strangled Cleveland and every other city in Ohio," Howe wrote.

In each city where there was a boss, there was a dedicated reformer ready to pour into Steffens's ear tales of wrongdoing supported by facts and figures that no one wished to hear and no newspaper dared publish. In St. Louis the boss was the agreeable, smiling Ed Butler, and the reformer was Joseph W. Folk; "a small man, small-boned, with a white face sharpened by thin black hair and dark eyes . . . he came of the race of southern Puritans who have the hard, righteous traits of their New England cousins, and chivalry besides. . . . Folk's hardest virtue was duty. He had had all the world pictured for him in the schools of Tennessee and in his law studies. The Bible, the English common law, the Constitution of the United States, and the charter of the City of St. Louis described things as they were. . . ." Or so he had assumed when he arrived from Tennessee to begin a career as a corporation lawyer. Drafted by Boss Butler as a "safe" man for district attorney, Folk had been appalled to find out what was really going on in St. Louis. His Puritan sensibilities deeply offended, he had become a reformer.

In Minneapolis the boss and the mayor were the same, Dr. A. A. Ames, and the reformer was a man named Hovey Clarke. In Pittsburgh it was Nut Brown who ran the town. Brown had "started as a newsboy, missed school, and learned life as it happened to him. He . . . never suffered ideals. He was a success as a politician, as a reporter, as a business man. He played the game, beat it, and was not cynical." Like Dick Croker in New York, he told Steffens, "I'll give you the dope."

Brown's reformer-nemesis was Oliver McClintock, a "merchant reformer who was the spoilsport of Pittsburgh." From McClintock, Steffens heard "the American reformer's story, a modern tragedy of defeat,
humiliation, martyrdom." McClintock was a successful businessman
"who, somehow, had kept apart the child's picture of a noble world of
brave men and good women, the picture of romance and the school
histories." He had accumulated all the evidence "to show the regular,
outrageous grafting of the ring in all public business. He offered it for
publication; he showed it privately to friends. . . . He knew and could
prove what was going on in little business but no one wanted his demonstrations. He was shunned. . . ."

In Philadelphia the graft was old and ivy-covered like the ancient
buildings in the park. In the City of Brotherly Love there was a kind
of jolly, good-natured swindle. Multiple voters cast ballots in the names
of the signers of the Declaration of Independence, thereby displaying
their knowledge of the past, if not their respect for it. "This joyous
defiance of the holy of holies," Steffens wrote, "was only a sign of the
novelty I saw in this fine old city." The city was run by Israel Durham,
"a slight figure . . . his eyes were quick; they were kind, inquiring." He
was friendly, as candid and as unabashed as the other bosses Steffens
had quizzed. In Philadelphia Steffens took his postgraduate work in
municipal corruption under the professional, one might almost say
professorial, direction of Iz Durham. The old pols had broken the
hearts of the reformers by taking the reform legislation that they had
passed and demonstrating that under its aegis graft and corruption
could flourish as never before. When Durham finished his recital,
Steffens said, "Political corruption is, then, a process. It is not a temporary evil, not an accidental wickedness, not a passing symptom of
the youth of a people. It is a natural process by which democracy is
made gradually over into a plutocracy. Treason, in brief, is not a bad
act; it is an inevitable, successful policy, and the cities differ one from
another according to age. Philadelphia is worse than St. Louis because
it is older—in experience."

Back and forth they went, the old (it turned out dying) boss and
the young journalist, soon fast friends, trying to define the nature of
the American city and its relation to "business," to "capitalism." Steffens
wrote: "I repeated again and again that political corruption was a
process, and I repeated because I could not accept it myself. If that
were so, then Nature, God, was on the side of the bribers. In a country

where business is dominant, business men must and will corrupt a government which can pass laws to help or hinder business."

Durham indignantly rejected Steffens's proposition. "It ought to be stopped; it mustn't go on," he kept repeating. There must be men with the "power, imagination, and courage" to set things right. "The reformers can't," Steffens declared; "they lack the knowledge, the tools and the honesty."

Durham reflected and agreed: "Yes, they ain't straight, and they haven't got the nerve."

So, Steffens concluded, Iz Durham, despised by the good citizens of Philadelphia, was "the best man I met in that town, the best for mental grasp, for knowledge of life and facts in his line, and—he had one other advantage which is something akin to honesty but must be described in other terms. The New Testament puts it the most clearly and briefly. Jesus said that He could save sinners; the righteous He could not save."

In Chicago Lincoln Steffens looked up Clarence Darrow, "the philosopher and attorney who defended criminals and must therefore know his city from the underworld up." Darrow received the exposé-writing journalist with a great burst of laughter. "Oh, I know. You are the man that believes in honesty!" He laughed Steffens out of countenance and waved him away. Chicago was in the midst of one of its periodic reforms. Hinkey Dink and Bathouse John, two of the old ward heeler standbys, had been ousted, and a tough businessman, George Cole, was the new broom. Cole, elected mayor through the efforts of the Voters' League, and his reform successors "did not see or touch sources of privilege." All they used their power for "was to persuade, or, if need be, force the business interests that had to come . . . to get their privileges, to make open terms with and render some service to [the] city."

The problem was, Steffens finally concluded, that the voters really didn't want good government and could be only intermittently shamed into voting for it. Perhaps even more basic was the fact that most businesses didn't want good government. Bad government had the great virtue of being predictable. You wanted a franchise; you paid either the going rate or somewhat more to close out your rivals. You wanted an easement; you paid for it. But with reformers in office everything became extremely personal. It often came down to no more than the question of whether a reform official liked the way you parted your hair or the shoes you wore. The "good" official introduced a bewildering element of uncertainty into routine negotiations. And this was bad for business. Another kind of bribery, far more subtle and difficult to define, came into operation; a sort of emotional currency circulated in place of hard money. Chicago and New York, Steffens observed, "were alike in that their governments, their laws, customs, practices, represented business generally and big or privileged business especially." Additionally, "the people do not like good men and good government, or, let us say, professionally good men in office and un-yielding good government. They both [business interests and the "people"] prefer 'bad government.' "

It was hard to argue with John Jay Chapman's reflections on the subject. "By the way and historically speaking," he wrote a friend, "do you know that there has never before been such wickedness on the globe as today in big American cities? It's a new record. Poor old darling little Antioch—and its fountains built by the prostitutes. . . . Poor harmless little middle ages with just a few sharp pinches of Inquisition—or a murder or two . . . chiefly the necessary discipline of church govern-ment. But in America we have constructed various machines—as big as the nation—seventy million soul-power machines—for destruction of humanity. The most heartless people in history—that's what we are. But I think we are changing for the better."

As Steffens came to see it, the bosses were, in a sense, the real heroes of the impossible cities; they were the "convinced sinners" who saw through all the hypocrisy, the petty subterfuges, the double-entry moral bookkeeping by means of which "honest" men and reputable citizens kept their hands clean while lining their pockets. The politician was allowed his graft in order that the businessman might make his profits. Thus the dirty hand washed the clean. Steffens was the un-sparing moralist of American municipal politics; state and national politics rested, of course, in large degree, upon municipal politics. He never resolved the dilemma or found an answer to the riddle. He was a kind of modern Machiavelli, a student, like the Florentine, of the uses and abuses of political power.

Encouraged by the success of *McClure's*, magazines devoted to "investigative journalism" proliferated. *McClure's* gave rise to the *American Magazine; Collier's* entered the field along with the *Survey*. Among the contributors to the *Survey* were Lillian Wald, Jacob Riis, and Jane Addams. One of its editors was Edward Devine, professor of social economics at Columbia, called the dean of social welfare. "Misery, as we say of tuberculosis," Devine wrote, "is communicable, curable, and preventable. It lies not in the unalterable nature of things but in our particular human institutions." John Fitch was an economist on the faculty of the New York School of Social Work. Paul Kellogg, another of the new breed of journalists, had been reared in Michigan. "The old frontiers of my grandfathers were gone," he wrote. "The new frontiers were the cities. So I came to New York." He noted, "For eighty-five years, we have suffered from the over-hang of institutions and patterns out of gear with American ideals of freedom and equality."

The popularity of muckraking was indicated by the history of a faltering magazine called *Broadway,* which had a circulation of some 12,000 in 1901. Bought by an enterprising journalist and turned into an exposé magazine, it found its circulation soaring to 480,000.

An important recruit to the ranks of the new journalists was Charles Edward Russell, the son of the editor of the *Davenport* (Iowa) *Gazette,* a four-page journal "about the size of a bed quilt." The radicalization of young Russell began when his father, a staunch Republican and sometime abolitionist, dispatched him to a boy's academy at St. Johnsbury, Vermont, to add polish to his education. Russell had already been reading in secret the atheistic thunderings of Robert Ingersoll. In St. Johnsbury he encountered a rigid Puritanism, long gone sour, and a social hierarchy that graveled his Midwestern soul. For the first time he had encountered "the Problem of Accumulated Wealth." The Fairbanks family, owners of the Fairbanks Scale Manufacturing Company, which employed most of the citizens of the town, ran St. Johnsbury and set its moral, social, and political standards. This was done in the name of what Russell called "The great Trickle and Filter Theory of Social Existence," which held that it was "well that a few men should have all the wealth in the nation because through them the rest of us had a chance. They spent it and we got some of the spending. It reached and enriched in this way the lower strata that otherwise would have been but barren." Russell was assured by those to whom he addressed his unsettling questions that the well-to-do and wealthy of St. Johnsbury were good and pious men who richly deserved the material good that had fallen to their lot. But Russell was persistently skeptical. "These men," he reflected, "might be so good that they were blue in the face and still the fact remained that in a so-called democracy they were clothed with autocratic power; without mandate from the people they were the government."

At this point a friend introduced Russell to Henry George's *Prog-*

ress and Poverty and to the writings of Wendell Phillips. Phillips, in Russell's words, "grew to be the god of my idolatry." He pored over his speeches and memorized his favorites, among them Phillips's address on Harpers Ferry and "his still unequalled classic among all elegies, his speech at the grave of John Brown." "I thought then," Russell wrote years later, "that he was the greatest of Americans; I think so still. By so much as service for an ideal is above service for a man's own fortune or glory he towers above all others we have elected to call great."

Russell found a job with *Everybody's Magazine* and wrote an exposé first of the refrigerator car scandal and then of the machinations of the beef trust. The champion of the beef trust in Congress was William Lorimer of Illinois. One of the packinghouses had contributed $200,000 to Roosevelt's campaign. The President, according to Russell, asked Lorimer if Russell's charges were true and, being reassured by Lorimer that they were a tissue of falsehood, pursued the matter no further. Nonetheless, Russell's revelations, soon reinforced by Upton Sinclair's *The Jungle,* stirred up a hornet's nest of public indignation. Samuel Hopkins Adams checked in with hair-raising accounts of the patent medicine shenanigans. Every month brought some new disclosure of adulterated products and criminal conspiracies to defraud the public. John Mathews exposed the waterpower trust.

To Thomas Lawson, businessman and yachting enthusiast, there came the conviction that having made a fortune, he could use part of it to reveal the nefarious activities of his fellow capitalists. In the July, 1904, issue of *Everybody's Magazine,* he announced his intention to tell all. "I think nothing stranger has happened in our national life," Charles Edward Russell wrote. Lawson "told a story that for lurid details exceeded the imaginations of the wildest shocker writers and in its disclosures of reckless viciousness seemed to show new capacities in the human spirit for the cruel and avaricious. . . . The country gasped and wondered and gasped again. For a time it talked of nothing else. Then it seemed tacitly to agree that the whole thing was part of the helterskelter and insanity of modern life and turned to something else."

These successive and apparently interminable revelations of a substantial element of criminality in most, if not indeed in all, big business activity brought forth howls of glee from socialists of all persuasions. It was just what they had been saying for decades. Now magazines published by corporations that could by no stretch of the imagination be called radical were vindicating the most radical charges against capitalism, thereby giving aid and comfort to that system's avowed enemies.

John Jay Chapman noted that in some countries satire was an effective political weapon but that in the United States "one might as well feed bon-bons to a hippopotamus as expend wit upon the American business man." He added, "Sharp abusiveness" might sting him a bit, but only if "you beat him half to death," metaphorically speaking, could you get his undivided attention. That, in Chapman's view, was "the philosophy of agitation" and, it might be added, the rationale of the new journalism.

Even the unions and "Big Labor" were not immune to the journalists' pursuit of truth. Ray Stannard Baker set himself the particular task of investigating labor racketeering and the startling new phenomenon of businessmen and union leaders joining forces to squeeze out competition. Increasingly businesses found that they could accept union shops and then bribe or otherwise prevail upon leaders to strike rival businesses that were not unionized. Such tactics were accepted by some union officials as a powerful stimulus to unionization. For others it was simply a conspiracy in corruption. One such was Sam Parks, a delegate of the New York City Housesmiths' and Bridgemen's union with 4,500 members. Parks rode in taxicabs, wore diamonds, sported a fighting bulldog, bet on the horses, and rode a handsome white horse in union parades. He had served time in Sing Sing, but no building was done in the city without his approval and without a suitable payoff. Baker heard a carpenter say, "Sam Parks is good-hearted all right; if he takes graft he spends it with the boys." Parks's partner in crime was the Fuller Company, which turned out to be owned by Standard Oil, United States Steel, and a number of large railroad corporations. The Fuller Company, which had originated in Chicago, brought Sam Parks with it, when it expanded its operations into New York, to manage the union side of things. "There was evidence," Baker wrote, "that he was on their payroll long after he became a leader of the union; that all the while he was drawing money from the Fuller Company to look out for *its* interests."

Writing of the Parks-Fuller link, Baker quoted the district attorney of New York City: "This corruption in the labor unions is simply a reflection of what we find in public life. Everyone who has studied our public life is appalled by the corruption that confronts him on every side. It goes through every department of the national, state and local government." Baker added, "And this corruption in public life is a mere reflection of the sordidness of private life." These were not "sporadic evils, they were deliberately organized and generously financed; *they actually represented the American way of life in many of its most important activities.*"

Sam McClure's editors had grown restive under his volatile leadership. He appeared to them increasingly dictatorial and arbitrary. Tarbell, Baker, and Steffens resigned from *McClure's* and joined forces with William Allen White, Finley Peter Dunne (Mr. Dooley), and the scholarly Alfred Jay Nock to start the *American Magazine*. Nock, after twelve years as an Episcopalian minister (more and more clergymen were leaving their ministries to take up the cause of reform or become liberal professors of sociology and economics), abandoned his wife and family and became a journalist. He was a disciple of Matthew Arnold, a Darwinian with classical, agrarian, pacifist inclinations. Steffens recalled the early days of the *American Magazine* as a "feast of fun." Dunne, a dilatory writer, was the wit of the group. "I never knew a writer who made such a labor of writing; he seemed to hate it," Steffens wrote. The initial issue promised that "We shall not only make this new *American Magazine* interesting and important in a public way, but we shall make it the most stirring and delightful monthly book of fiction, humor, sentiment, and joyous reading that is anywhere published. It will reflect a happy, struggling, fighting world, in which, as we believe, good people are coming out on top. There is no field of human activity in which we are not interested. Our magazine will be wholesome, hopeful, stimulating, uplifting, and above all, it will have human interest on every page, whether expressed in fiction or articles or comment or editorials." A bold prospectus! And one that might be read as a kind of index of American aspirations. The "happy, struggling, fighting world" in which good people were "coming out on top" gave no hint of the widespread corruption which the editors had made their names exposing in *McClure's*. There was no mention of reform or reformers, of predatory capitalists and exploited workers. The magazine would be "wholesome"—that is to say, no sordid or unpleasant subjects, nothing in "bad taste"—and uplifting. Whatever the state of the world might be, "uplift" was dear to the hearts of Americans. The exhilarating days of "exposure" were over; "exposure" would be an important element in the new journal, but "humor," "sentiment," "joyous reading," and "human interest" would predominate.

The *American Magazine* was soon a smashing success. Each of its founders had the prospect of making a substantial amount of money.

"I noticed, with some pain, shame, and lying denials to myself," Steffens wrote, "that I was going easy. All by myself, without any outside influence, I was being bought off by my own money, by the prospect of earning money." Dismayed, he resigned from the *American Magazine* and began a period of free-lance journalism.

The brilliant successes of the exposé journalism stirred the business community into counteraction. What worked for the reformers— a deluge of articles and books critical of the actions of big business— could presumably work as well for the capitalists. More and more of the great industries and industrial associations subvented or outright employed writers who wrote in praise of the glorious achievements of the business world. Ray Stannard Baker began to clip out articles that he was sure had been inspired by business interests. One such declared that Roosevelt was heartily tired of "his venture into the railroad regulation field and wishes he had kept out of it." The writer quoted a Senator as declaring, "If we adopt his recommendation and pass the legislation he asks for we shall throw the country into a panic and he will have to take the responsibility for it—he and the Republican party together. . . . We will save the President from that blunder."

To the investigative journalists were added the "globe-trotting" journalists, whose prototype was Richard Harding Davis. Davis's jaw was much admired, as were the dashing journalist costumes devised for him by Brooks Brothers. Wherever his journeys took him he reported faithfully to his remarkable mother, Rebecca Harding Davis, a highly successful novelist in her own right, and she in turn urged him to keep alive "the Love of Christ," which would make him "more social and cheerful and alive" and warned him above all to avoid "hack work for money." It would be "the beginning of decadence both in work and in reputation for you," she warned.

Richard Harding Davis was, Booth Tarkington wrote, the "beau ideal of *jeunesse doré*" to the college boys of the day. Tarkington and his college friends were in the Palm Room of the newly completed Waldorf Hotel in New York when Davis entered. "Then, oh, then, our day was radiant!" Tarkington wrote. "That was the top of our fortune; we never could have hoped for so much. Of all the great people of every continent, this was the one we most desired to see."

A friendly rival of Davis was Stephen Bonsal. Bonsal was an upper-class Marylander, a gentleman jockey, a rider to hounds, a linguist, a student of European politics, a classic *bon vivant*. As a correspondent for *The New York Times* Bonsal was said to have "surveyed" all the countries of Europe, South America, and Asia (with the exception of Persia). He had been Davis's friendly rival in the Spanish-American War and undoubtedly the most cosmopolitan of all the journalists of his day.

The new journalists were not satisfied with simply writing about municipal wickedness and corruption. They participated actively in the practical tasks of reform. The Liberal Club of New York City included Lincoln Steffens, Hutchins Hapgood, and a number of other radical reformers. Hapgood leaned to the anarchist side, but he was careful to make a distinction between an anarchist and a revolutionist. "A revolutionist," he wrote, "believes in force, an anarchist does not. One of the cardinal doctrines of anarchism is non-resistance to evil." The Free Speech League was another organization in which both Steffens and Hapgood were active along with their friend Theodore Schroeder, whose liberalism failed him on the subject of religion. "I believe," said the exasperated Steffens, "in Free Speech for everybody except Schroeder."

The Good Government Clubs—the goo-goos—brought together "college graduates, rich men, even society leaders and the wealthy curled darlings of our nation," Charles Edward Russell wrote, ". . . until the city was covered with these pious and alphabetical sodalities and many an elegant social favorite found himself near to touch elbows with persons he would not otherwise have recognized. It was a lovely and inspiring sight. . . ." The citizens of German descent were termed Garoos, and those of Latin descent who formed their own Good Government Clubs, Laroos.

"The under dog bothered us all," William Allen White wrote. "We were environmentalists. We believed faithfully that if we could change the environment of the under dog, give him a decent kennel, wholesome food, regular baths, properly directed exercise, cure his mange and abolish his fleas and put him in the blue-ribbon class, all would be well. We reformers who unconsciously were sucking at the pablum of the Old Greenbackers and Grangers and Populists were intent upon making wholesome biscuits for the under dog. We did not know we were merely treating the symptoms. . . . So reform magazines and reform books made towering piles every month at the corner bookstore of Emporia. And the boss-busters arose and the devil was to pay . . . , all across this lovely land of the free, the home of the brave. . . . We were—all of us in New York, in Washington, in Kansas, in the forty-eight states—doing and thinking what men all over Christendom were doing and thinking; we were trying to establish all over the civilized world more equitable human relations. We were trying to distribute the economic surplus of the machine age, and curiously, we thought that if we took the surplus away from the rich and gave it to the poor, we would be achieving our aims."

If the consequence of Ida Tarbell's *History of the Standard Oil Company* was a whole genre of big business exposés, the consequence of Lincoln Steffens's *The Shame of the Cities* was a new wave of municipal reform. The shock troops of reform in a particular city often included a reformed tycoon plus assorted visiting journalists and a newly aroused regiment of middle- and upper-class goo-goos.

One of the readers of Henry Demarest Lloyd's *Wealth Against Commonwealth* was Samuel Jones, president of the Acme Sucker Rod Company of Toledo, Ohio, and president of the Western Oil Men's Association. Inspired by Lloyd, Jones rented an empty factory and hired unemployed men and women to run it with the Golden Rule as the shop's only regulation. The eight-hour day, free lunches, company picnics, and a week's vacation with pay, a Golden Rule park for his employees, and a company band were among his innovations. Jones soon extended his reform inclinations to "municipal democracy" and won election as mayor on a Golden Rule platform. "I am elected in spite of six hundred saloons, the traction company [the extension of whose franchise he had opposed] and the devil," he wired Lloyd. "Big, bluff, strong, warm-hearted" Golden-Rule Jones established an eight-hour day for municipal employees, cleaned up the police department, and wrote a book entitled *Letters of Love and Labor.*

Brand Whitlock was Jones's secretary and successor mayor. Whitlock gave Jones a copy of Walt Whitman's *Leaves of Grass,* and that book and Henry George helped convert Jones to a kind of Tolstoyan anarchist. Jones's office, Frederic Howe noted, "was filled with vagrants. People in trouble came to him freely. He went to the workhouses and talked with the prisoners, released them wholesale if they had been committed for drunkenness or vagrancy and were unable to pay their fines. . . . It was the same with prostitutes; we had them because we wanted them. If they were to be punished, men should be punished as well."

Howe wrote: "Jones rejected organized charity and capital punishment. . . . Good people shunned him. His quotations from Christ were a scandal to the churches. Preachers denounced him. The Chamber of Commerce opposed him. Every one was against him except the workers and the underworld. 'I don't want to rule anybody,' Jones declared, 'nobody has a right to rule anybody else. Each individual must rule himself.' . . . The immigrants and the poor had heard a gospel. It offered them nothing in particular, but it was free of cant."

The most dramatic story of municipal reform was undoubtedly that which involved Tom Johnson and the city of Cleveland. Johnson, the czar of the Cleveland transportation system, was persuaded by the candy butcher on one of his streetcars to buy and read Henry George's *Social Problems*. The book so disturbed Johnson that he instructed his lawyer to compose an answer to it, saying that "if that book is right I am all wrong and I'll have to get out of my business." Not satisfied with the lawyer's answer, Johnson traveled to New York, called his "rich friends" together, "and put it up to them." They read Henry George, then met one night and debated it until dawn. Not only did his friends fail to persuade Johnson of the falsity of George's single tax theory, but they themselves became converts. "They all saw what Henry George pointed out: that excessive riches came unearned to individuals and companies owning land, natural resources, like water, coal, oil, etc., and franchises, such as steam and street railways, which being common wealth to start with, became more and more valuable as the growing population increased the need and value of these natural monopolies." The government, George argued, should recover that value "by taxing nothing but the values of the land, natural resources, and monopolies."

Johnson went back to Cleveland, sold out his transportation monopoly, and ran for Congress as a single taxer. Frustrated in Washington, he returned to Cleveland and joined forces with George, determined to make the city a model of single tax principles. There he was denounced for "going back on his class."

"Honesty is not enough," Steffens wrote; "it takes intelligence, some knowledge of theory of economics, courage, strength, will power, humor, leadership—it takes intellectual integrity to solve our political problems. And these Tom Johnson had above all the politicians of my day. His courage was the laughing sort; his humor was the kind that saved him tears. . . . He could pick and lead a team; men loved to follow him; he made it fun." It was Tom Johnson who completed Lincoln Steffens's education. "He cleared my head of a lot of rubbish, left there from my academic education and reform associations," Steffens wrote. It was Johnson who taught him that it was "privilege that causes evil in the world, not wickedness; and not men." It was to Steffens "more like a flash of light than a speech." Perhaps most endearing of all of Johnson's qualities to Steffens and what set him off from the great mass of reformers was that in addition to running the city well, he enjoyed running it so much. "It's fun," he declared, "running the business of the city of Cleveland; it's the biggest, most complicated, most difficult, and most satisfying business in Cleveland."

Tom Johnson knew John Winthrop's "A Model of Christian Charity," written on board the *Arabella,* carrying the Puritans to New England to establish a Bible Commonwealth and redeem Christendom. Like John Winthrop, he wished to make Cleveland a model city so "that all who came after might say, 'Let us be as a city upon a hill.' " (The words are Winthrop's.) Johnson knew cities too well, their ingrained habits and the stubborn resistance to change, to have any illusions about the task at hand. His estimate was that it would take at least ten years to make Cleveland a single tax haven. In Howe's words, "the struggle involved the banks, the press, the Chamber of Commerce, the clubs, and the social life of the city. It divided families and destroyed friendships. . . . If you were for [Johnson] you were a disturber of business, a Socialist, to some an anarchist."

But to Howe and the other young men and women who rallied around Johnson, the "possibility of a[n] . . . orderly, beautiful city became . . . an absorbing passion. Here were all of the elements necessary to a great experiment in democracy." Howe traveled to Germany to observe the German cities. Munich especially charmed him; there was "orderliness, . . . concern for architecture, provision for parks, for gardens and museums, for the rich popular life of the people." Howe studied cities "as one might study art," he wrote. "I was interested in curbs, in sewers, in sky-lines. I wrote about cities. . . . I dreamed about them. The city was the enthusiasm of my life. . . . And I saw cities as social agencies that would make life easier for people, full of pleasure, beauty, and opportunity." Howe added, "My passion for the city was also a passion for Tom Johnson. And I had come to love him as fervently as I loved the things he promised to achieve."

Howe wrote: "The single tax was the passion of his [Johnson's] life—a passion for freedom, for a world of equal opportunity for all. . . . He had a vision of a new civilization free from poverty, free from fear, free from vice and crime, of a new society that would be born when the strangle-hold of special privilege was loosened."

While Henry Demarest Lloyd, the Populists, and the Socialists wished to see the Federal government exert the powers that they were convinced had been given it under the Constitution to fashion a more just and humane society, Johnson believed that the new order must be born in the cities, must grow out of local and state initiatives rather than descend from a central authority.

"If one city should adopt the single tax," Johnson told his audiences, made up largely of steelworkers, all stout Democrats, "other cities would have to follow suit. If we are the first to take taxes off houses, factories, and machinery, we will have a tremendous advantage. Factories will be attracted to Cleveland; it will be a cheap city to do business in, cheap to live in. Untaxing the things people use will cheapen them, it will encourage production." Johnson taught his disciples that the corporation was unresting in its greed. The corps of lawyers at its command had to find only one loophole in a law while the government had to block every one. He had attended midnight meetings on Wall Street at which men, distrusting one another, "swapped securities behind locked doors."

The fight for reform centered initially on the public ownership of utilities, particularly the street railways and electricity, and the reduction of trolley fares to three cents. "On one side there were men of property and influence; on the other the politicians, immigrants, workers, and persons of small means," in Frederic Howe's words. Fifty injunctions were obtained by Johnson's enemies to prevent the city from setting cheaper streetcar fares and building a municipal electric lighting plant.

At Johnson's instance the city's chief of police instituted a policy of treating the city's poor with restraint, even with consideration. He freed hundreds of prisoners who had not been able to pay small fines on the ground that they had been "imprisoned for debt," rather than for crime. The prisons were reformed as well. A workhouse with an infirmary was built on a 2,000-acre park; a boys' farm school, outdoor work for prisoners, and an honor system for the less serious offenders were other innovations that were widely imitated.

Johnson seemed, in Howe's words, "not to have a high opinion of the kind of men on whom I counted to save democracy. He held a cigar in his hand while he spoke and went away with a crowd of riotous politicians." He was short and fat and jolly, the very prototype of the big-city boss. The difference was that he was committed to remaking Cleveland for all the people of the city rather than to pillaging it. Undoubtedly a major factor in his success was that he looked so reassuringly like a run-of-the-mill boss rather than the kind of high-minded, rather prim upper-class reformer of whom lower-class citizens of the city were instinctively suspicious.

Everywhere Tom Johnson preached his doctrines. Society could not be changed by getting "good" men—that was to say, cultivated, educated, upper-class men—into office but only "by making it possible for all men to be good." Most men would be good if they were given a chance. Even a company of angels would be corrupted by the American system. At the root of the trouble lay poverty. "Poverty was the cause of vice and crime. It was social conditions that were bad rather than people." The social system must be changed through democratic politics.

Johnson, in Frederic Howe's words, "judged no man, and so far as I can recall had no hatreds. He saw men and institutions like a detached scientist; he was ready to learn from any one and to get what pleasure he could from every experience." His mind "was a garden rather than a safe-deposit vault. . . . He had as much time for affection as he had for work, and he was greedy for both. . . . A great part of his strength was in his loveableness. He was open, frank, and joyous, like a big boy in his enthusiasms and in depressions which he rarely showed." Johnson's luxurious house on fashionable Euclid Avenue was the headquarters of the young reformers enlisted in his army. "We went there for breakfast, for luncheon, for dinner, as we chose," Howe wrote. "Sunday evenings found us around the big fireplace discussing politics, economics, philosophy, literature." There were differences of opinion in the little band but "no jealousies and no friction. . . . We were never disillusioned; there were no disaffections, and for nearly ten years we worked and lived together in this way."

The Johnson house was also a center for visiting reformers. Brand Whitlock, Samuel Jones's aide from Toledo, was often there. Lincoln Steffens, Jones himself, and Clarence Darrow also visited, along with "party leaders, political bosses, magazine writers, and business men."

Not only was Johnson a brilliant politician, but he had, in addition, a remarkably fertile and original mind. In the basement of his Euclid Avenue home he had workmen construct an abbreviated railroad line on which cars would be moved by electromagnetic force suspended above the rails. Friction would thus be eliminated, and trains could move at tremendous speeds. When the officials of General Electric, Charles Steinmetz among them, were consulted, they agreed that the notion was scientifically sound. General Electric expressed an interest in proceeding with the experiments but demanded control of the pat-

ents, which Johnson would not give it. Howe was convinced that Johnson could have made a second fortune out of inventions if he had
devoted as much time to them as he did to his efforts at political reform.

Howe ran for the Cleveland City Council and gave his allegiance
to "the dream of a free city, with a master mind and a great idealist
as its directing genius." One of the first things he discovered was that
the "interests" had supported his campaign with the assumption that
they could thereby control his vote. When he failed to vote as the better
people of the city expected him to, when he voted for "playgrounds
for children . . . public baths and dance-halls" for the purpose of "providing recreation for the poor," he found himself cut by his friends
and excluded from the city's higher social circles. The Chamber of
Commerce denounced public baths as socialistic, and there was a general protest against "the wider use of the parks," especially against
taking down the keep-off-the-grass signs. But gradually Johnson and
his allies prevailed. Soon there was a citywide system of parks, playgrounds, and public baths. In Howe's words, "On Saturday and Sunday
the whole population played baseball in the hundreds of parks laid
out for that purpose. Cleveland became a play city. . . ."

But there was a price to pay, he discovered. It was as though a
posted sign read: "Reformers beware!" Howe was most disturbed at
the loss of friendships. "I wanted to live with my class," he wrote, "to
enjoy its approval, to exhibit the things I had learned at the university
among the people who lived in fine houses, who made the social and
club life of the city." But the doors of this world were closed to him.

Having served on the Cleveland City Council, Frederic Howe ran
for the State Senate on a reform ticket, which was swept into office.
In the Senate, with a comfortable majority, with good leadership and
the support of the liberal press, Howe anticipated that much could be
done. "Our programme," he wrote, "had been approved by the people.
It should have been enacted into law." But things turned out differently. "Bosses remained unshaken in their power; measures were buried in committees or crippled by amendment. . . . The supreme
court . . . interfered to block inquiry and investigation. We could only
win a skirmish, never a battle." No one listened to discussions. During
debates members fled to the cloakrooms and reappeared to vote as
they had been instructed. "Business men and bosses," Howe wrote,
"showed no respect for the Constitution that I had been taught to
revere. It had no sanctity in their eyes. The laws they wanted could be
driven through it with a coach and four. It was only referred to when

some labor measure was to be defeated. Liberal laws for the protection of women and children in industry were always discovered to be unconstitutional, while fifty-year grants to street-railways were upheld." The Constitution, it seemed, "was an instrument that worked easily and well for one class and interest only."

If the Constitution failed Howe, his "class" also failed him, in his view. The men who held or aspired to social position, who owned the businesses and banks and confessed to having a civic conscience and a sense of responsibility were the ones who were always to be found blocking reform and, in the crucial moments, supporting the alliance of rapacious capitalists and corrupt politicians. However piously they might affirm their devotion to reform, when the chips were down, they displayed their true colors. They could not, in the last analysis, separate their own economic interests from the broader needs of the society. Time and again it turned out that they acted as though the two were the same.

Three times Johnson won election against the combined forces of the city's business interests. He proved a brilliant campaigner, setting up circus tents in various vacant lots around the city and rushing from tent to tent in his car, known popularly as the Red Devil, to give speeches describing his program of reform and exhorting his listeners to help turn out the vote.

In the end Johnson was defeated, and many of his hopes with him. When he was beaten by a few thousand votes, Cleveland still had not inaugurated the single tax. The courts ruled that the city had no right to run its own street railway system, and the lines were returned to the old companies. "A great movement was ended," Howe wrote. "The dream of municipal ownership, of a free and sovereign city was set back indefinitely." Johnson did not long outlive his defeat. "For eight years he had given every bit of intelligence, every ounce of energy he possessed to the city. When victory was in his hand the people turned against him. His health failed, his fortune was dissipated. . . ." He died doubting the value of his long struggle—"whether any good had come of it all." Good there had certainly been. There was good in the struggle and in the modest residue of reform that it left behind: good in the public baths, the parks, and playgrounds; good in the sense on the part of the poorer citizens of the city that it was their city as much as it was the city of the wealthy old families who lived along Euclid Avenue; and perhaps above all, good in the company of reformers like Frederic Howe, Newton D. Baker, Brand Whitlock, and Sam Jones.

The legend of Tom Johnson lingered as a reminder of the possibilities of urban reform, desperately difficult as it might be.

Although Tom Johnson is not exactly a household name (we know by now that posterity is a fickle mistress), there was more than a modicum of truth in Frederic Howe's statement that he was "one of the greatest statesmen America has produced." His field of operations was small—primarily the state of Ohio and the city of Cleveland—and in the end he failed, but his influence was vast: It spread to every corner of the continent where idealistic men and women worked for the new order.

In Missouri, St. Louis and Kansas City were notorious centers of graft and corruption. Joseph Folk was elected governor of Missouri on a reform ticket, but his efforts to clean up Kansas City were frustrated until a notorious pickpocket, one Dawson, broke his leg jumping from a moving train. It was discovered that a police surgeon had set his leg and various police officers had given him aid and comfort, including flowers and fruit, during his period of convalescence. It further developed that police gave refuge to bank robbers, fenced loot, and, when threatened with exposure, beat and intimidated prospective witnesses.

George Creel, a native of Missouri, was one of a growing company of reformers who joined forces with Frank Walsh to clean up the city. Walsh got the ex-governor of the state, William Stone, on the witness stand and exposed him as the lobbyist for the schoolbook trust and the baking powder trust as well as for other "interests." Stone was known thereafter as Gumshoe Bill. (Emma Goldman described Frank Walsh as "the most vital person" she met in Kansas City. "He did not flaunt his radicalism in public, but he could always be depended upon to aid an unpopular cause," she wrote. "By nature he was a fighter; his sympathies were with the persecuted.")

Creel and Walsh went over the Kansas City court records for the preceding twenty-five years and turned up 244 cases against the railroads that had been taken away from the state courts and carried into the Federal courts, where corrupt judges had decided them in favor of the railroads or summarily dismissed them. The two men decided that spasms of reform were not enough; they must build "a people's machine that would function just as effectively as that of the gangs." Having elected to the state legislature candidates who ran on the reform ticket, the reformers found that they had been bought up or diverted by lobbyists. At the next session of the legislature a contingent of reformers established themselves at Jefferson City with the legislators, determined to *"stay on guard"* until their program was enacted into law. Out of the session came the direct primary, a child labor law, the initiative and referendum, restrictions on railroads carrying cases to the Federal courts, factory inspection, and the registration of lobbyists.

When Ben Lindsey, the reforming judge in Denver, had attempted to reform the system of juvenile justice, he ran head-on into the defenders of the status quo. "Not much bigger than a boy and as naïvely logical as a child," Lincoln Steffens wrote of him, "his idea was to abolish the conditions which made . . . boys and girls do bad things. . . . Lindsey's purpose was so sensible that sensible men and women rallied to his support. . . . But this fight . . . disturbed things as they were in Denver; the party machines and bosses felt threatened. . . . The cleaning up of the slums and the Tenderloin would take away from the political bosses the shifting vote which, as they bought and placed it, gave them the decision as between the nearly equally balanced votes of the good citizens who were loyal to their parties." Hence the opposition of the bosses. Lindsey "could deal with the children after they had done evil, but he must not interfere with the conditions which led them into evil. Those conditions were part of the conditions that made business good and paid dividends."

Lindsey, whom William Allen White described as a "trim, slim, sawed-off dynamo in a Prince Albert coat . . . ," became world-famous for his creation of juvenile courts. While his efforts won the applause of reformers around the country, the criminal-police alliance threatened his life. From the reform of the courts, Lindsey turned to battles against the utilities, specifically the powerful Denver Gas and Electric Company. An investigation, launched by Lindsey's supporters, revealed a long record of graft and bribes to public officials passed out by the company's president, Henry Doherty. Escaping from the state one jump ahead of the bailiff, Doherty went on to form the Cities Service Company and became a famous philanthropist.

Lindsey, meanwhile, aroused further hostility among the power brokers of the state by denouncing the state legislature for sending Simon Guggenheim to the Senate despite his notorious antilabor record in Colorado and by espousing "companionate marriage"—a prenuptial trial period.

Having made substantial inroads into Kansas City corruption, Creel was lured to Denver to assume the editorship of the *Post* and aid Lindsey and his supporters in cleaning up that notoriously corrupt city. Creel committed the *Post* to the fight for "a free state, a free city," free of the manipulations and pillage of Eastern investors and their political chore boys. Creel exhorted his readers to throw the rascals out. "The ballot," he wrote, "becomes a gleaming sword. . . . It is an adventure—this fight for equal justice—the Great Adventure which has ever enlisted all that was best and truest in the American heart. For the People! Say that word over. People! *People!* Why, it grows electric! It thrills! Not this banker, not that bricklayer, but all who toil in patience or impatience, courage or despair, sorrow or happiness, struggling that tomorrow may be better than today."

Josephine Roche, just out of Vassar, joined Creel and Lindsey in the effort to break the machine in Denver. Their reform candidate was elected mayor, and he in turn appointed Creel as police commissioner to clean up the police force and drive organized crime out of the city, particularly the prostitutes, who solicited from their "cribs" and were protected by the police. Creel's plan for reform called for closing restaurants which were simply fronts for prostitution, "massage parlors," and notorious "houses" in the residential section of the city, while barring minors from the crib district and abolishing the system of prostitutes advertising their phone numbers on "outcalls." When Creel began his reforms, it was estimated that there were in Denver 700 professional prostitutes as well as a substantial number of amateurs and part-timers. Six months later the number had shrunk to some 250. The health authorities of the city believed that two-thirds of the professional prostitutes were infected with venereal diseases. According to Creel, if each infected woman had on the average twenty customers a night, the rate of infection could be readily calculated. The incidence of school students who had contracted venereal diseases was rising at an alarming rate. Under Creel's reform administration, prostitutes were taken to nearby hospitals and given medical examinations. Out of one group of 144, 95 had syphilis, gonorrhea, or both. These were detained for treatment. With the help of Josephine Roche many were given a new start in life or sent back to their families.

The *Denver Republican* ran a poem which read:

> George Lochinvar Creel came out of the West.
> His ideas were naked, his reforms undressed,
> And save his good nerve, he weapons had none,
> But he boomed into office like a 13 inch gun.

So erratic in politics, abnormal by far,
There n'er was a reformer like Creel Lochinvar.

In the winter of 1903, while the controversy over the doctrine of companionate marriage was in full flower, the combative judge visited New York to address the Churchmen's Association, a society of liberal Episcopal ministers. When William Manning, the notoriously reactionary bishop of the diocese of New York, learned of the proposed meeting, he ordered it canceled, and when the clergy refused, he announced that he would deliver a "chastisement sermon" at the Cathedral of St. John the Divine, a structure which was, in a manner of speaking, his own creation. The judge insisted on attending to hear the bishop's denunciation, promising George Creel that he would refrain from any act or statement that would attract unfavorable attention to him. But when Manning called companionate marriage "a foul and wicked thing, a filthy propaganda for lewdness, promiscuity, adultery and unrestrained sexual gratification," Lindsey forgot his resolution and, jumping up, shouted, "Bishop Manning, you have falsely represented me. If this is not a house of justice it is not a house of God. I ask for five minutes to answer your unfair attack." The cathedral was immediately in an uproar. Lindsey, belabored by canes and umbrellas, was rescued from the furious congregation by the police.

Disbarred from practicing law in Colorado, the state he had done so much to clean up and to "put on the map" of reform, Lindsey and his wife made their home in liberal San Francisco, where, championed by the influential William McAdoo, he was admitted to the California bar.

San Francisco, with its long tradition of municipal corruption, intrigued the English Fabian socialist Beatrice Webb. She found there none of "that extreme sensitiveness of Eastern opinion that one notices in cities west of Chicago; neither is there any desire or effort to declare its independence of the East. It seems isolated from and unconcerned with any other part of America. It is out and out the most cosmopolitan city I have yet come across. It has no standards, no common customs; no common ideals of excellence, of intellect or manners—only one universal anarchy, each race living according to its own lights, or rather according to its own impulses, seeing that all alike are free from their own racial public opinion. To the person who wishes to live unto himself without any pressure of law, custom or public opinion, San Francisco must be a Haven. If he combines with this 'individualism' a Bohemian liking for variety of costume, manners, morals and opinions, San Francisco must be a veritable paradise." When Webb asked a Scottish merchant if he missed his homeland, he confessed to longing for the moors, "but the shackled life of Glasgow, Edinburgh or London— I could na return to it."

For all its charm, San Francisco was a thoroughly corrupt city. When Lincoln Steffens arrived to report on the campaign to clean it up, his guide was "a New Englander and a Swedenborgian," Joseph Forester, "an exquisite, very shy old bachelor gentleman." Looking out over the city from his cottage on Russian Hill, he whispered, "Beautiful. But wicked. It is very wicked. And do you know, I think that that is why I love it so, this wicked, beautiful city."

The possibilities of graft created by the necessity of rebuilding San Francisco after the earthquake proved highly demoralizing. The City Council waxed fat on the take from contractors and public utility corporations. Many of the "best families," the most prominent businessmen in the city, were exposed by Fremont Older and the *San Francisco Bulletin* as having been involved in pillage of the public treasury. Capital and labor had joined forces to pillage the city. The "Labor administration of San Francisco was . . . bought over and owned by big businesses; and the Labor leaders and the Labor mayor, boss, and officials," Steffens wrote, "had been demoralized by the easy money that they were getting in large sums." Patrick Calhoun, president of the street railroad company, and Abraham "Abe" Ruef, the Republican boss of the city, became the special targets of Older's investigative journalism. Older calculated that to press his investigation into the corrupt practices of Ruef, he would need a fund of $100,000. James Phelan, a former mayor of San Francisco, and Rudolph Spreckels, a banker and an heir to a great sugar fortune, pledged their support. Steffens described Calhoun as "a man of the world . . . an expert in modern ways," adding, "He was a New Southerner. . . . He was a tall, straight, handsome man, with the eyes of a lion, the grace of a tiger-cat, and the strength of a serpent. He was . . . unbeaten and unbeatable."

Steffens formed an alliance with Francis "Frank" Heney, the "fighting prosecutor" who had got the conviction of an Oregon Senator for the theft of public lands. Older, with the financial support of Spreckels, had imported Heney to prosecute, among others, Abe Ruef. He and Heney found a congenial spirit in Spreckels, "a smiling, young, personally powerful millionaire, who had made and won some very revealing fights against graft and corruption in corporations. . . . He did not think that business was good and politics bad. This young man had learned at first hand that capital also 'throws bricks,' 'destroys property,' 'hurts business,' . . . pads payrolls, and bribes men not only in politics but in business. . . . He was the surest fighter I had ever met. . . ." For a time, with Spreckels's sponsorship, Steffens and Heney were cordially received in the higher circles of San Francisco society: the Pacific Union Club and the Bohemian Club. They were asked to lecture at the University of California, Berkeley, and the president, Benjamin Ide Wheeler, told Steffens that he and Heney were to receive honorary degrees. When Steffens passed on the news to Heney, he added a cautionary note: If Heney's prosecution of municipal corruption reached the higher levels of the corporate and financial world, "we would not be doctors; we would get no more bids to dine and speak, and I would be excluded from the clubs." And so it turned out. "The business leaders who give out the bribe money control honors, too," Steffens noted. Heney and Steffens got no honorary degrees, and Spreckels was asked to stop bringing Steffens to his club. When the list of honorary-degree recipients was published, Heney passed it to Steffens with a grin. If Steffens was curious about why the two had been omitted, he need only read the list of the names of the regents of the university. Included among them were a number of rich and powerful men soon to be named in Heney's indictments.

Frederic Howe, visiting San Francisco during the investigations, described it as an "armed camp." Men walked cautiously on the streets, armed for self-protection. Spreckels told him it was unsafe to stand in the open. When Howe visited Older, the editor pulled him away from a window; a sniper might fire at him, mistaking him for Older. In Howe's words, "Arson, murder, dynamiting, abduction—all were traceable to the attempt of a few men to secure and hold a street-railway franchise which they had gotten by bribery. . . . And well-to-do people were almost a unit in protesting against the criminal prosecutions which followed." Graft from the disorderly houses alone was estimated at more than $7,000,000 a year.

After several murder attempts, including a plan to blow up Older's house with dynamite, had been abandoned or proved abortive, the newspaperman was kidnapped on the streets of San Francisco and hustled onto the night train for Los Angeles. The plan was to leave the train at some inconspicuous stop, kill Older, and dispose of his body. A young lawyer on the train, observing Older and his kidnappers, sensed that something was wrong. He found out who Older was, slipped off the train at the next station, and called the offices of the *Bulletin* in San Francisco. The police were alerted, and Older was rescued at Santa Barbara. The men who did the kidnapping were agents of Calhoun's railway company. They were indicted, but the witnesses against them were bribed or frightened away, and the men were never convicted.

The mayor, Eugene E. Schmitz, a labor racketeer, was indicted for bribery and sentenced to five years' imprisonment. With Francis Heney conducting the prosecution of Ruef the prospects of conviction seemed good when an ex-convict entered the courtroom and shot Heney in the neck. While the prosecutor was still in the hospital recovering from his wound, Hiram Johnson, another reform-minded lawyer, took his place. Ruef was convicted and sentenced to fourteen years in prison. Johnson parlayed his role as prosecutor into leadership of the California Progressives.

Lincoln Steffens continued to brood about municipal corruption. His conclusions were not encouraging. He stated his convictions at a dinner given for a group of influential Los Angelenos: "You cannot build or operate a railroad, or a street railway, gas, water or power company, develop and operate a mine, or get forests and cut timber on a large scale, or run any privileged business [in the United States], without corrupting or joining in the corruption of government." At the heart of the matter lay "the absolute control of credit: political power and business power and money were only phases of this business man's control of the function of money-lending, of credit-lending."

Fremont Older's reflections were along much the same lines. Abraham Ruef was a graduate of the University of California with high honors, an able and intelligent young man who was ambitious for a career in politics. "In those days," Older wrote in his autobiography, "there was only one kind of politics, and that was corrupt politics. It didn't matter whether a man was a Republican or a Democrat. The Southern Pacific Railroad controlled both parties, and he either had to stay out of the game altogether or play it with the railroad. He didn't create this situation. We created it. He didn't create the standard of success, which is possession. We created it. He came out of college and found those things that we have fixed through all those years. He entered our civilization, and went ahead." It came to seem to Older wrong to send a man to prison "for being caught in our system." He visited Ruef in jail and expressed his ambivalence at having been, as a reforming journalist, an agent of Ruef's misfortune.

When Lincoln Steffens extended his travels abroad, he came to some interesting conclusions about Britain and France. The British accepted a class government. A Member of Parliament was expected to represent "an interest"—mines, railroads, banks. What Americans called graft, the English called privilege. "An Englishman," Steffens wrote, "will stand up for his privileges, wherever he is, with the same sense of virtue that an American will defend his rights." Steffens believed that Americans must give up their notion that the British government was better than its American counterpart. Indeed, to Steffens "the skeletons of all the governments of Europe that I saw were as alike one another as the boney structures of human beings are alike." He came back to the question to which he had set out years before to find an answer: "Wasn't political corruption the very essence of the life of a state, the necessary accompaniment of its development? Industry with its machinery, coming into an agricultural organization, finds the constitution, laws, customs, and the culture of a community of farmers a hindrance to the new breath of life; so it must make changes in the old order to admit the new. . . . Captains of industry have to lick the southern planters, 'get' the government, 'give' to the schools, colleges, and churches, and buy the newspapers. And they do so, and that makes the changes historians describe as progress." The new men were not interested in "ruling" in the formal sense; they, as practical men, were far more concerned with the fact than with the trappings of power (just as Tocqueville had predicted more than a half century earlier). Steffens predicted as the final outcome of all the reform activity a "better class" of politician. He wrote from his vantage point in Britain: "My prophecy . . . is that we shall also have a government of the people by gentlemen for the business men."

Slowly and laboriously the worst municipal abuses and corruptions were ameliorated, if not eradicated. The city remained the vessel of hope, the symbol of a better order.

To American radicals it often seemed that all their efforts went for naught, but sympathetic European visitors reacted differently. One visiting German writer and journalist, Arthur Holitscher, told Hutchins Hapgood, "The strongest impression I have formed from my visit to America is the fact that what may be called the middle-classes in America—well-to-do people, but not the great multi-millionaires . . . are deeply interested in social reform. I have gone to many meetings and clubs, and always somebody says something serious and earnest about social matters—about child labor, about strikes, about insurgency—something. And I never pick up a magazine without finding at least one muckraking article in it. All this astounded me. There is nothing like it in Germany. People of corresponding condition merely amuse themselves in Germany. . . ." The fact was that every impulse toward reform became, in short order, a "movement." There was, thus, the "playground movement," to provide urban schools with playgrounds, and the "small parks movement," to create neighborhood parks in ghetto areas. There was even "the greater-classroom-use movement," dedicated to opening public school classrooms to adult evening courses in such subjects as basketry, bench work, Venetian ironwork, elementary sewing, dressmaking, millinery, and drama and to free lectures. This movement also urged the utilization of school facilities in the vacation periods, especially the summers.

Perhaps the spirit of municipal reform is best suggested by the "ephebic oath," taken by the 1913 graduating class of the College of the City of New York. The oath, modeled on that of Athenian youth "when entering citizenship," read: "We, men of the class of February, 1913, to-day receiving the arms of the city as a symbol of her faith in us, take this oath of devotion to her: We will never bring disgrace to these [the city's] arms by an act of dishonesty or cowardice. We will never desert our suffering comrades in the ranks. We will fight for the ideals and sacred things of the city, both alone and with many. We will revere and obey the city's laws and do our best to incite a like respect and reverence in those about us who are prone to set them at naught. We will strive ever to do our whole duty as citizens, and thus in all these ways to transmit this city not only not less but greater, better, and more beautiful than it was transmitted to us." Of the seventy-seven graduates, half were Jews, most of them from the homes of immigrants.

6

1906

By the spring of 1906 Roosevelt, the principal beneficiary, it might be argued, of the new journalism, decided that its revelations had gone far enough. In April, at the Gridiron Club, a society of Washington correspondents, he denounced the muckrakers (the word came from John Bunyan's *The Pilgrim's Progress* and had a decidedly negative connotation) "who raked the mud of society and never looked up." Steffens's response the next day was, "Well, you have put an end to all these journalistic investigations that have made you." Despite the President's disclaimer of any such intention, it was obvious to Steffens that Roosevelt *had* "called the close of a chapter."

The speech was widely and favorably quoted, but the President did not let it rest there. Lest anyone might have missed the point, he repeated it a few weeks later at a ceremony to lay the cornerstone of the new office building for the House of Representatives.

Certainly exposé journalism became a mania, a fad, a form of literary expression. As we have seen, Americans were always of two minds (and spirits) about entrepreneurial activity. From wooden nutmegs to watered stock they had displayed a sometimes grudging, sometimes uninhibited admiration for the sharp operator. Isabella Lucy Bird, the English traveler, had been startled to hear Americans boast of their fast deals and unscrupulous practices, and the German journalist Moritz Busch, noting the almost universal nature of such traits, had called the United States Slick and Smart Incorporated. Clearly the Protestant ethic was often stretched to its limits and beyond by pious Christians who believed that morality stopped at the church door. There were tens of thousands of small-business men whose proudest boast was their integrity, but the nagging question remained whether success with a capital *S*, the success that most Americans sought ardently and admired inordinately when achieved by others—business success on a large scale—did not require sharp dealing that often verged on outright criminality. It was this question, above all others, that tantalized, fascinated, and alarmed Americans, and it was this question that, it was increasingly apparent, lay behind the fascination with exposé journalists. The President in his schoolmasterish way undoubtedly sensed this. The probing of the secret life of American capitalism had gone far enough. It was one thing to attack police corruption and clean up Democratic Tammany Hall, to close saloons and suppress vice; it was quite another matter to erode the public's confidence in the business leaders of the nation. Finally, there was the fact that many of the bribe takers and givers in municipal government were "foreigners," typically Irish with a mixture of Germans. The business leaders, on the other hand, were predominantly Anglo-Saxon, and many of them were leaders in society and even in philanthropy. The dean of capitalists, John D. Rockefeller, had, after all, following the lead of Andrew Carnegie, established a great philanthropic foundation which dispensed, among other infinite numbers of good causes, generous grants to professors.

Ray Stannard Baker was doing an exposé of the Armour meat-packing empire when Roosevelt made his muckraking speech. Armour threatened to sue *McClure's*. The magazine had been threatened before and indeed had lost suits, but this time it rejected Baker's article, and he felt, as he put it, "that the very earth was dropping out from under me." He wrote: "I met the President many times afterward and there were numerous exchanges of letters, but while I could wonder at his remarkable versatility of mind, and admire his many robust human qualities, I could never again give him my full confidence, nor follow his leadership." After Roosevelt's attack, editors, in George Creel's words, went "off the raw-meat diet, convinced that T.R.'s speech reflected a more conservative public opinion."

David Graham Phillips, the novelist, had been given the assignment by William Randolph Hearst to investigate the relationship between Congress and big business. The result was another popular shocker, *The Treason of the Senate*. When Phillips got too close to the President's friends and supporters, the famous Roosevelt temper was unleashed. Things had gone far enough.

Phillips and his articles were savagely attacked in *Collier's*, and when Charles Edward Russell, his fellow muckraker, encountered him on the street soon afterward, he found Phillips "terribly cut up." But Phillips had his own vindication. Most of the individuals named by him, the "butlers" of the tycoons and corporations, were removed by the voters, and impetus was given to the crusade to have Senators elected by the voters rather than chosen by state legislators.

Russell himself was philosophical about Roosevelt's attack. While he conceded that "one word so applied did more to discredit reform and assist financial buccaneering than the whole mass of newspaper and other literature published in defense of the buccaneers," he was also ready to recognize the fact that the country could tolerate only a certain amount of truth about the "system." The system rested, after all, on a kind of consensus of more or less manageable dishonesty, or so, at least, it seemed to many Americans.

It would be a mistake to suggest that Roosevelt's attack marked the end of the new journalism, but it was certainly dampened. A British writer, summarizing its accomplishments, declared in 1910, "Muckraking provided the basis for the entire movement toward Social Democracy that came to its head in the first Wilson administration."

It can, I think, hardly be doubted that Roosevelt's attack on exposé journalism was prompted in large part by fear and hatred of his fellow New Yorker William Randolph Hearst; it may simply have been the misfortune of the new journalists to have been standing in the line of fire.

In a discussion of the shortcomings of reform, Herbert Croly described Hearst's principles as "an ingenious adaptation of Jefferson to the needs of 'yellow journalism.'. . . He approves expansion, but abhors imperialism. He welcomes the opportunity for war, but execrates militarism. He wants the Federal government to crush the trusts by the most drastic legislation, but is opposed to centralization. . . . Hearst and Hearstism," Croly added, are "a living menace to the orderly process of reform and to American national integrity."

Lincoln Steffens, assigned to do a hatchet job on Hearst, rather typically found he liked him. He decided he was "a great man, able, self-dependent, self-educated (though he had been to Harvard) and clear-headed; he had no moral illusions; he saw straight as far as he saw, and he saw pretty far, further than I did then. . . ." His goal, Steffens believed was "to establish some measure of democracy."

Hearst, an unsuccessful aspirant for the presidential nomination in 1904, had won the Democratic nomination for governor of New York in 1906. As Oswald Garrison Villard put it, "The people wanted redress, knew that the time was ripe for it, and turned to Hearst because his newspapers had been so outspoken in their attacks upon great evildoers. . . ." An alarmed Roosevelt wrote to Lodge that Hearst's nomination was "a very, very bad thing . . . and yet," he added, "I cannot blind myself to his extraordinary popularity among the 'have-nots,' and the chance there is for him because of the great agitation and unrest which we have witnessed during the last eighteen months— an agitation and unrest in large part due simply to the evil preaching of men like himself, but also due to the veritable atrocities committed by some wealthy men and by the attitude of the Bourbon reactionaries who endeavor to prevent any remedy of evils due to the lack of supervision of wealth. . . . I am horrified at the information I receive on every side as to Hearst's strength on the East Side among laborers; and also even among farmers. It is a very serious proposition." Roosevelt was convinced that people were so prosperous that they felt at liberty to indulge themselves in experiments. "There has been during the last six or eight years," he wrote, "a great growth of socialistic and radical spirit among the workingmen, and the leaders are obliged to play to this or lose their leadership." Roosevelt took comfort from the thought that the high-minded and moderately reformist Charles Evans Hughes was bound to counterbalance Hearst's strength in New York City by the votes of rural and upstate New York.

Henry Cabot Lodge was delighted with Roosevelt's attack on the muckrakers. It was just what was needed to reassure the more conservative members of the party. It was, he wrote Roosevelt, a "very brilliant" speech. But Lodge felt that the President could do still more to reassure the capitalists. He recounted the observations of a labor leader who believed "that there was great danger . . . from the socialistic movement led by men of some education who made incendiary appeals to all laboring men. . . . I think that Hearst and his papers and Moran [John Moran, candidate for governor in Massachusetts] and his crazy platform indicate the existence of great perils. . . ." Lodge was convinced that "behind all this movement is the desire to destroy all property and to break down law and order. Men like Hearst and Moran are not seeking a genuine cure for real ills, they are trying to bring on chaos by appealing to class prejudice and the worst passions." An apprehensive Lodge exhorted the President to bear down harder on labor. To such admonitions, Roosevelt replied testily that several recent speeches had been aimed "far more at agitators, at corrupt or sinister or foolish visionaries, at reckless slanders in the newspapers and magazines, and at preachers of social unrest and discontent than . . . at capitalists."

Yet the capitalists refused to be reassured. Roosevelt, the soul of conservatism, was perceived by conservative Americans as a wild radical. "The view of the [New York] clubs, of high finance, and the 'educated intelligence,' " he wrote, "is one of hatred, terror, but above all horror. They now think that I have become partially insane through excessive drinking."

By the fall of 1906 Roosevelt was in a funk once more, this time over lack of money for the Republican congressional campaigns. He had convinced himself that the Democrats were outspending the Republicans by a wide margin. "You would be dumbfounded," he wrote Lodge, "to know how universally the rich men have refused to contribute. . . ." Most of them were frank to say that they did not care whether Hearst won in New York State or not as long as their enemy, Roosevelt, was "at the head." "The more I see of very rich men acting singly or in corporations," he added, "the more firmly I feel that they are of no advantage to the country. . . ." But once more he put the screws on the Republican moneymen, and they coughed up.

Henry Adams was dismayed at the campaign expenditures of the Republicans. "As it seems likely that the President, Cabinet, all the Senators, Congressmen and Bank Presidents will have to go to the Penitentiary for election expenses," Adams wrote to Elizabeth Cameron, "I regard the country as safe. Roosevelt must go first . . . for starting the shindy." He wrote to his brother, Brooks: "Everyone seems to admit that both parties are wrecked, as long as Roosevelt is on their backs they will stay wrecked. Afterwards they will begin again, no doubt with a new socialist element, as in Europe. Fisher Ames, a hundred years ago, said that our system was a raft on the Connecticut River. One's feet were always under water, but the raft couldn't sink."

The Republicans won the midterm elections in 1906 but with considerably diminished margins. Hughes beat Hearst in New York, but Hearst showed "enormous strength," in Lodge's words. "We have got a terrible struggle before us to save the country from a movement which strikes at the very foundations of society and civilization," Lodge wrote to Roosevelt the day following the election.

While Roosevelt and Lodge shared their apprehensions about the coming socialist revolution of which William Randolph Hearst's political prominence seemed the harbinger, William James traveled to California to teach for a session at the new Leland Stanford Junior University. He wrote to a Harvard colleague: "You ought to see this extraordinary little University. It was founded only fourteen years ago in the absolute wilderness, by a pair of rich Californians. . . ." It had an endowment that yielded $750,000 yearly and 1,500 students, "*beautiful* architecture," and San Francisco only an hour away by train. "The landscape," James wrote, "is exquisite and classical. . . . The climate is one of the most perfect in the world, life is absolutely simple. . . . In fact, nothing but essentials, and *all* the essentials. Fine music, for example, every afternoon, in the Church of the University." James couldn't imagine "a better environment for an intellectual man to teach and work in for eight or nine months in the year, if he were then free to spend three or four months in the crowded centers of civilization—for the social insipidity is great here, and the historic vacuum and silence appalling. . . ."

The high point of James's West Coast venture was his lecture on "The Moral Equivalent of War." Since the Venezuela affair, when Grover Cleveland's bellicosity delighted Americans and brought the country to the brink of war with England, James had been troubled by the disposition of a people as allegedly peace-loving as the Americans to spring to arms. The threat of war with Great Britain had been followed by a war with Spain, accompanied by the wildest forms of jingoism and the disgraceful occupation of the Philippines and other indications that Americans were no different from any other people in their warlike and imperial propensities. As James reflected on the subject, it seemed evident to him that the "psychology" of human beings demanded an outlet for certain martial qualities, qualities such as hardihood, service to a higher cause, self-sacrifice, courage, loyalty. Peacetime life contained, for the great mass of men, little outlet for such attributes. Making money, holding a routine job, struggling to support a family and keep one's head above water, while doubtlessly requiring a commendable tenacity and often not a little courage, had about them little of the heroic. It thus followed, James speculated, that these basic but normally unexpressed qualities accumulated like water behind a natural dam until they burst out in some violent and destructive outpourings, at the heart of which lay frustration with the "ordinariness" of daily life. This, it seemed to James, was a root cause of all wars. And generally, terrible as they had been, wars had performed on one level the useful social function of giving an outlet to estimable, if not essential, qualities. Cultures that had gone for long periods without the bracing effects of war had, for the most part, become soft and decadent and been conquered and absorbed by people who manifested the martial virtues in greater degree. Stated thus, the observation seemed to give a kind of "scientific" or Darwinian legitimacy to war. Just as those individuals who were "fittest" survived, so those nations that were "fittest" defeated the less fit, thereby contributing to the upward progress of civilization. James, of course, did not subscribe to such a barbarous notion; he saw the problem as an intensely practical one: The inability of peacetime society to give expression to qualities *that human beings seemed to need to express* (and that, equally important, nations needed to have in their citizens in order to be vigorous and "healthy") clearly posed a dilemma. War, it seemed to James in 1906, had become too bloody and terrible to be any longer an acceptable agency of society for whatever purpose.

But if war satisfied a profound human need, then there must be found some nondestructive alternative, some "moral equivalent to war," some peacetime activity that would have substantial benefits for society generally but, more important, would provide an outlet for those martial virtues that James plainly admired and believed must find expression and thereby lower the psychological "pressure" or "temperature" that disposed peoples to rush into war so exuberantly.

The moral equivalent James proposed was service to the nation by young men of every class and condition who would be "drafted off" not to shoot their fellow human beings but to do the difficult, dangerous, and demanding tasks that had to be performed to keep a complex modern society functioning. Such work, requiring self-sacrifice, service, hardihood, and even courage, would have an especially exemplary effect, James felt, on the "gilded youth of the upper classes who would, thereby, learn at first hand of the permanently hard and sour foundations of our higher life" and be, in consequence, "better men and better citizens." At the other end of the social scale, warped and diminished lives would be given a new dignity. "All the qualities of a man acquire dignity," James declared, "when he knows that the service of the collectivity . . . needs them." For himself, James told his audience, "I devoutly believe in the reign of peace and in the gradual advent of some sort of a socialistic equilibrium. The fatalistic view of the war-function is to me nonsense, for I know that war-making is due to definite motives and subject to prudential checks and reasonable criticisms, just like any other form of enterprise." In his opinion, "a permanently successful peace-economy cannot be a simple pleasure-economy. In the more or less socialistic future towards which mankind seems to be drifting we must subject ourselves collectively to those severities which answer to our real position on this only partly hospitable globe. We must make new energies and hardihoods continue the manliness to which the military mind so faithfully clings. Martial virtues must be the enduring cement; intrepidity, contempt of softness, surrender of private interests, obedience to command, must still remain the rock upon which states are built."

There was nothing "to make one indignant in the mere fact that life is hard," James said, "that men should toil and suffer pain." That was life. "But that so many men, by mere accidents of birth and opportunity, should have a life of *nothing else* but toil and pain and hardness and inferiority imposed upon them . . . this is capable of arousing indignation in reflective minds." If "the whole youthful population" were to form "for a certain number of years part of an army" devoted to labors for the good of the whole, sent off to "coal and iron mines, to freight trains, to fishing fleets in December, to dish-washing, to clothes-washing, and window-washing, to road-building and tunnel-making, to foundries and stoke-holes, and to the frames of skyscrapers," they would be strengthened in body and in spirit. "Such a conscription, with . . . the many moral fruits it would bear, would preserve in the midst of a pacific civilization the manly virtues which the military party is so afraid of seeing disappear in peace. We should get toughness without callousness, authority with as little criminal cruelness as possible, and painful work done cheerily because the duty is temporary, and threatens not, as now, to degrade the whole remainder of one's life." To James, "it would be simply preposterous if the only force that could work ideals of honor and standards of efficiency into English or American natures should be the fear of being killed by the Germans or the Japanese. . . ." Mankind *must* find some more humane and socially useful way of organizing society and eliciting service to it.

"The Moral Equivalent of War" was not published in essay form until 1910 and then in *McClure's Magazine* and *Popular Science Monthly*.

That James, a kind of philosophical earthquake himself, should have been in nearby Palo Alto when the great San Francisco earthquake took place was almost too pat—another inspired notion of the Great Scriptwriter in the Sky. As James was leaving Cambridge for California, a colleague, Charles Bakewell, had said to him, "I hope they'll treat you to a little bit of earthquake while you're there. It's a pity you shouldn't have that local experience." At half past five on the morning of April 18, James sat up in his hotel room as the room began to sway. His first thought was "Here's Bakewell's earthquake after all." He wrote to his friend Fanny Morse: "It went crescendo and reached fortissimo in less than half a minute, and the room was shaken like a rat by a terrier . . . it was to my mind absolutely an *entity* that had been waiting all this time holding back its activity, but at last saying, 'Now, *go* it!' and it was impossible not to conceive of it as animated by a will, so vicious was the temper displayed—everything *down*, in a room that could go down, bureaus, etc., etc. . . . All the while no fear, only admiration for the way a wooden house could prove its elasticity, and glee over the vividness of the manner in which such an 'abstract' idea as 'earthquake' could verify itself into sensible reality."

When word arrived of the devastation in San Francisco, James took the train to the city. He reported the streets full of people with their possessions piled about them, "while the flames and the explosions were steadily advancing and making everyone move farther. The fires most beautiful in the effulgent sunshine. Every vacant space . . . occupied by trunks and furniture and people. . . . The order," James added, "has been wonderful, even the criminals struck solemn by the disaster. . . ." As evening came on, people began cooking their dinners at brick campfires in the middle of the streets.

The attention of the country was directed westward not only by the great earthquake but also by one of the era's most dramatic trials. The unlikely scene was the mining town of Caldwell, Idaho.

On a Saturday night in Denver, Colorado, February 17, 1906, after banks and courts had closed, police kidnapped Charles Moyer, president of the Western Federation of Miners (WFM), Big Bill Haywood, the union's secretary, and George Pettibone, a business agent of the union, hustled them on board a special train, and carried them to Boise, Idaho, where they were placed on trial for the murder of Governor Frank Steunenberg. Seven years earlier in the aftermath of a devastating miners' strike in Coeur d'Alene, Steunenberg, who had ordered the national guard into the town, had been killed by a bomb attached to his gate. Rewards totaling thousands of dollars had been offered for the apprehension of his killers. The Pinkerton detectives were called in, and seven years later Moyer, Haywood, and Pettibone were seized and charged with the murder.

A defense fund was established for the men, and money poured in. Newspaper reporters descended on Caldwell, along with a small army of union leaders and the families of the incarcerated men. Clarence Darrow was retained to direct their defense. To Haywood, who seems to have enjoyed his periods in jail, the time spent in the Ada County lockup was "the most quiet, peaceful period of my life." He read Buckle's *History of Civilization,* Carlyle on the French Revolution, a pile of English novels, including *Tristram Shandy* and *Sentimental Journey,* Marx and Engels, and Upton Sinclair's *The Jungle.* Haywood also designed a poster which depicted the kidnapping and quoted Debs: "Arouse, ye Slaves! Their only crime is loyalty to the working class!" It was smuggled out of the jail, printed up, and distributed around the country. More money rolled in. Socialists and nonsocialists, liberals and reformers, Christians and Jews joined in the chorus of protest at what appeared to many Americans to be a reprise of the Haymarket Affair, the difference being that in this instance the defendants had been some thousand miles from the scene of the crime. When the famous Russian writer Maxim Gorky arrived in New York on a visit, he sent a telegram to the prisoners conveying greetings from the Russian workers. Haywood replied that "our being in prison was an expression of the class struggle which was the same in America as in Russia and all other capitalist countries." Soon afterward the press disclosed that Gorky's "wife" was not legally married to him. Outraged moralists, Mark Twain among them, joined in a chorus of denunciation. Hotels refused to admit him lest he corrupt the morals of the other guests, and the astonished and indignant Gorky was forced to leave the country. Haywood attributed the hue and cry to Gorky's telegram. President Roosevelt got into the act by gratuitously characterizing Haywood and his fellow prisoners as "undesirable citizens."

All around the country demonstrations were held in support of the accused men. It was reported that 200,000 people had gathered on the Boston Common to protest their imprisonment. In Chicago 50,000 workers and other sympathizers marched through the city, and many more turned out in New York. The *Appeal to Reason,* founded by Mother Jones and Eugene Debs, put out an issue called the "Kidnapping Edition" and printed 4,000,000 copies, and Hearst's *New York American* devoted a special edition to the Moyer-Haywood-Pettibone case.

Months passed while the state labored to make a case against the defendants. The leading prosecutor was William E. Borah, attorney for the Barbour Lumber Company, the president of which was in the Ada County jail for fraudulently locating timber claims. While Haywood enjoyed his incarceration in the Ada County jail, the Socialist Party of Colorado nominated him for governor of the state in the elections of 1906, and he polled 16,000 votes, a very respectable showing for a man under indictment for murder.

In Caldwell the prosecution decided to separate the cases and try Haywood first on the ground that the evidence against him was the most damning. Haywood was described by a writer for *McClure's* as "a powerfully built man, built with the physical strength of an ox . . . a big head and a square jaw . . . a type of man not unfamiliar now in America, equipped with a good brain, and [who] has come up struggling and fighting, giving blows and taking them, who, knowing deeply the wrongs of his class, sees nothing beyond; whose mind, groping hopelessly for remedies, seizes eagerly upon a scheme like Socialism which so smoothly and perfectly solves all difficulties. Take a character like this, hard, tough, warped, immensely resistant, and give him a final touch of idealism, a Jesuitic zeal that carries the man beyond himself, and you have a leader who, like Haywood, will bend his people to his own beliefs."

As with most trials, the critical part of the trial came first: the choosing of jurors. Here Darrow was at his best. In the prospective jurors empaneled had been selected the most conservative members of the community, among them all the bankers. These, as Haywood put it, "Darrow disposed of . . . in short order. . . . He would show by his questions that there was little difference between a banker and a burglar. . . . It was like killing snakes." The final jury was composed largely of farmers. The principal witness for the prosecution was a miner named Harry Orchard, who claimed to have lit the fuse that blew up the Bunker Hill and Sullivan Mill mines at Coeur d'Alene. He implicated himself in the assassination of Steunenberg but declared that he had simply been acting on the instructions of the three defendants. In Haywood's view he had been well schooled by the head of the Pinkerton detective agency in Denver, James McParlan, who had earlier given the testimony that had resulted in the execution of the Molly Maguires in the Pennsylvania coalfields.

When Orchard's testimony was published, offers came to Darrow from individuals all over the West prepared to refute essential portions of his story. At the end of a parade of witnesses for the prosecution and the defense, Haywood himself took the stand, and Borah began to examine him. The sun was shining in Haywood's face, and he asked the judge to have the shutters closed: "I cannot see the senator's eyes." Later a friend told Haywood that the episode had disconcerted Borah. He had never heard of a man on trial for his life "who was so anxious to see the prosecutor's eyes. . . . [It] doubled me up like a knife," Borah is reputed to have said.

In Borah's final address to the jury he dwelt on Haywood's reputation for violent action and his statement at the time of the Coeur d'Alene strike that the governor should be "exterminated." Darrow concluded for the defense. "He stood big and broad-shouldered, dressed in a slouchy gray suit, a wisp of hair down across his forehead, his glasses in his hand," Haywood wrote. He began with the history of the Western labor movement, going over in detail the strikes that the Western Federation of Miners had conducted, many of them for an eight-hour day. Finally, he came to the particulars of the charge against Haywood. Could the jurors doubt that the mine operators and the public officials of Idaho and Colorado had conspired to undermine the power of the union by trying to hang its principal officer? "To kill him, gentlemen! I want to speak to you plainly. Mr. Haywood is not my greatest concern. Other men have died before him. Other men have been martyrs to a holy cause since the world began. Whenever men have looked upward and onward, forgotten their selfishness, struggled for humanity, worked for the poor and weak, they have been sacrificed. They have been sacrificed in the prison, on the scaffold, in the flame. They have met their death, and he can meet his, if you twelve men say he must. But, gentlemen, you short-sighted men of the prosecution, you men of the Mine Owners' Association, you people who would cure hatred with hate, you who think you can crush out the feelings and hopes and aspirations of men by tying a noose around his neck, not because he is Haywood, but because he represents a class, don't be so blind, so foolish as to believe you can strangle the Western Federation of Miners when you tie a rope around his neck. Don't be so blind in your madness as to believe that if you make three fresh, new graves you will kill the labor movement of the world. I want to say to you, gentlemen, Bill Haywood can't die unless you kill him. . . . If you kill him your act will be applauded by many; if you should decree Haywood's death, in the great railroad offices of our great cities men will sing your praises. If you decree his death, amongst the spiders and vultures of Wall Street will go up paeans of praise for those twelve good men and true who killed Bill Haywood. . . ." On the other hand, if the jury acquitted Haywood, the toiling masses would bless them; "men who labor, men who suffer, women and children weary with care . . . these men and these women and these little children, the poor and the weak and the suffering of the world, will stretch out their hands to this jury. . . ."

Darrow spoke for eleven hours, evoking every image that could arouse the hostility of Idaho farmers: railroad tycoons; Wall Street bankers; Eastern capitalists who owned the West. "While he spoke," Haywood wrote, "he was sometimes intense, his great voice rumbling, his left hand shoved deep in his coat pocket, his right arm uplifted. Again he would take a pleading attitude, his voice would become gentle and very quiet." When he finished, the jury retired. They were gone only a few hours. The courtroom filled with spectators to hear the verdict.

It was "Not guilty." The news was flashed quickly around the country, and everywhere workingmen and -women and their advocates hailed it with parties and celebrations. All over the West, miners danced on the mahogany tops of saloon bars and got gloriously smashed on the main streets of mining towns. Telegrams of congratulations poured into Caldwell from all over the world. Even the nuns at a nearby Catholic convent joined in the expressions of delight. Haywood's acquittal practically assured his companions, Moyer and Pettibone, of their freedom. One of the jurors asked Haywood to autograph a small American flag he drew from his pocket; another assured him, "William, they could have bleached my old bones before they could have convicted you. Now you be quiet for awhile."

Haywood, world famous, returned to Denver like a conquering hero. People collected at every stop from Pocatello, Idaho, to Leadville, Colorado, to cheer him and shake his hand. At Denver a huge and boisterous crowd awaited his arrival. The Socialist Congress at Stuttgart sent him a resolution which read: "The International Congress sends William Haywood the congratulations of the Socialist movement of the world in view of the magnificent fight he put up in the interests of the

organized workers of the United States. . . . The class conscious proletariat of Europe looks upon the enormous strength manifested by
this act of solidarity as a guarantee of unity in the future and hopes
that the American proletariat will show the same solidarity and determination in the fight for its complete emancipation."

One of the most revealing passages in the resolution denounced
the "bourgeoisie's total lack of tolerance and sense of honor." The fact
was, as we have noted, that there was widespread sympathy for Haywood among all "classes" in the United States, especially among the
reform-minded members of the Northeastern middle and upper classes.
It was also far from the case that the "entire capitalist press" was arrayed
against Haywood. Many newspapers, prominent among them those of
Scripps and Hearst, espoused his cause. Proof of the sympathy aroused
for the accused men was the fact that Haywood was besieged with
offers for speeches. The Tuileries Gardens of Denver offered him
$7,000 for a week's appearance, an enormous sum for the time. A
lecture bureau in California offered $15,000 for forty lectures, and
the Star Circuit, which booked lectures and vaudeville acts, proposed
$4,000 a week for eight weeks.

Haywood turned the offers down, but he did speak at a number
of rallies put on to raise money for the defense of Moyer and Pettibone.
In Chicago he spoke at Luna Park under the auspices of the Socialist
Party, with 45,000 paid admissions and other thousands who broke
down the fence and flooded the park. In Milwaukee there were 37,000.
In Chicago friends took Haywood to the cemetery where the Haymarket anarchists were buried, and there, at the foot of a monument
erected to the four men, he burst into tears. When he died in Russia
twenty years later, it was found that his will directed that half his ashes
be buried in Russia and half in the Waldheim Cemetery at Chicago
near the graves of the anarchists.

Pettibone was also found "not guilty," and the case against Moyer
was dismissed. But the WFM and the IWW proved more vulnerable
to factionalism than to persecution. Haywood and Moyer were constantly at odds. In Denver, Haywood found "that the spirit of intrigue
was more than I could overcome." Feeling the resistance of Moyer and
the federation to him and, perhaps more so, to his ideological disposition, he increasingly surrendered to the impulse to become a public
figure. He went on a highly successful lecture tour ostensibly under
the auspices of the WFM. On his first visit to New York City, a crowd
of 10,000 overflowed the Grand Central Palace to hear him speak and

constantly interrupted him with applause. Mobbed by his admirers after the meeting, Haywood found that "one little woman" who "kissed me repeatedly" was his sister, Mary, who lived on Staten Island. After New York it was Los Angeles, San Francisco, Seattle, Portland, and then back to Idaho. At that point the WFM officially withdrew its support, announcing the fact in the *Miners' Magazine*.

Haywood toured Europe, meeting with socialist and union leaders and addressing meetings of workers. When he returned to the United States, his position as a labor leader of international standing was well established, and he devoted his efforts to trying to organize the forest and lumber workers of the South. Elizabeth Gurley Flynn was the newly elected chairman of the IWW. Joseph Ettor had proved one of the union's most successful organizers, especially among the shoeworkers. The lumberjacks and millworkers of the South were both white and black, and Haywood set out to gather them in to defy the segregation laws of the South and unite them in a single union. In many of the Southern lumber camps the company paid its men in its own "money," or scrip, called batwings and cherryballs. Most companies were adamant against unions. Latent violence was in the warm Southern air, and any move to organize or strike brought on dangerous clashes between workers and company guards. At Grabow, Louisiana, at the Long-Bell Lumber Company, a strike for shorter hours and higher pay resulted in the deaths of several guards and company officials and three or four strikers. It was a common pattern. The turpentine and lumber companies of the Deep South encouraged the drug habit among their workers as a way of retaining them. "At every company store," Haywood wrote, "cocaine, morphine and heroin are sold. The workers, once addicted, cannot think of going away from their source of supply." At most camps the companies provided shacks for women who acted as the wives of the workers for the period they were employed by the company. When a "husband" left, he was replaced by another. From the South Haywood toured the Middle West as an agent for the *International Socialist Review*, giving speeches and selling subscriptions. On the West Coast the IWW was still glorying in its victory over the lumber companies and city officials of Spokane, Washington. A successful IWW tactic when local officials, acting at the instance of lumber companies, broke up meetings or refused to let the union leaders speak, was to have so many men defy the law that the town or city jail would soon be filled to overflowing with offenders and the police would simply give up, unable to arrest everyone. When a judge in Sioux City ordered an arrested Wobbly to show by the calluses on his hands that he was a real worker, the young man replied, "Take down your pants, judge, and let me see where your calluses are!" The story became a standard tale at Wobbly meetings.

Back in New York, Haywood engaged in a debate at the Cooper Union with Morris Hillquit, chairman of the Socialist Party. Haywood maintained that Hillquit and the party had deviated from the correct Socialist line by working to elect Socialists to political office.

Although it was not, of course, realized at the time, the trial and its attendant publicity represented the high-water mark of the radical labor movement in the United States. The brief story of the Industrial Workers of the World was not yet over, but it was from that point on a story of decline.

7

Conservation

The President continued to infuse routine political matters with elements of high drama. William James expressed the essence of Roosevelt's appeal to his countrymen. "Think of the mighty good-will of him," James wrote, "of his enjoyment of his post, of his power as a preacher, of the number of things to which he gives his attention, of the safety of his second thoughts, of the increased courage that he is showing, and above all of the fact that he is an open, instead of an underground leader . . . whose heart is in the right place, who is an enemy of red tape and quibbling and everything that in general the word 'politician' stands for."

"The President alone is still amusing and makes me laugh," Henry Adams wrote. "His views of himself particularly are humorous." The high point of the summer was the reunion of the Rough Riders at the Grand Canyon, an event the emotional dimensions of which were appropriate to those of the canyon. From Colorado Springs, Roosevelt wrote Kermit of a Rough Riders' reunion which was "delightful in every way." Five days of wolf hunting in Oklahoma delighted T.R. The party "got seventeen wolves, three coons, and any number of rattlesnakes. I was in at the death of eleven wolves. . . . It was tremendous galloping over cut banks, prairie dog flats, creek bottoms, everything. One run was nine miles long and I was the only man in at the finish except the professional wolf hunter. . . ." He also dispatched three bears. On his way home the President stopped in Chicago, where he found "a very ugly strike," and he warned the union leaders that "if the rioting . . . gets beyond the control of the State and City . . . the regulars [U.S. troops] will come." He wrote to Henry Cabot Lodge: "The labor people are utterly unreasonable."

A Pure Food and Drug Act was passed in 1906, and Roosevelt undertook to enforce it "with riot and clamor," as William Allen White put it. The act was accompanied by the Meat Inspection Act, a consequence (in part at least) of young Upton Sinclair's hair-raising description of the meat-packing industry in *The Jungle*. It provided for the Federal inspection of all companies selling meat in interstate commerce.

Rather typically, Roosevelt, after creating high hopes among his liberal supporters for realistic railroad rate regulation, ended up accepting legislation that failed to get at the most serious abuse: preferential freight rates. The Hepburn bill, which won his approval, provided for a commission to set *maximum* rates when *minimum* rates were really the issue. Ray Stannard Baker admonished the President but to little effect: "The taproot of Armour's power . . . is railroad favorites, and I have asked myself over and over . . . whether the power to fix a maximum rate, which you suggest, will touch this specific case of injustice. Armour's evil power arises in part from his ability to force the railroads to give him a lower rate on dressed beef than they give unorganized cattle-growers on their cattle." Roosevelt defended the bill in a four-page letter, but in the end he accepted some improving modifications in the Hepburn Act.

The most conspicuous (and characteristic) achievement of Roosevelt's second term was in the steps taken to protect the rivers and forests of the nation from exploitation by the "malefactors of great wealth."

That friendships were the breath of life to Roosevelt we have already had more than one occasion to observe. One of the most portentous of those friendships for the reputation of his administration (and the future of the country) was that with his fellow athlete Gifford Pinchot. Seven years Roosevelt's junior, Pinchot was a member of the President's inner circle, or tennis cabinet, as well as his boxing and wrestling partner.

His father, James Pinchot, was a connoisseur of the arts, a philanthropist, and a gentleman farmer and businessman with a strong interest in forestry. He admired the European management of forests, especially that of Germany. In the summer of 1885 the senior Pinchot asked his son a fateful question: "How would you like to be a forester?" There were at the time almost incomprehensibly vast American forests that were being systematically pillaged by lumber barons. Forest management had a history of more than 300 years in Europe, but there were no foresters and no forest management in the United States. Young Pinchot, who had inherited his father's love of the outdoors, was attracted by the notion. In the words of his autobiography, "the greatest, the swiftest, the most efficient, and the most appalling wave of forest destruction in human history was then swelling to a climax in the United States; and the American people were glad of it. Nobody knew how much timberland we had left and hardly anybody cared. . . . Public opinion held the forests . . . to be inexhaustible and in the way." Pinchot had been vacillating between medicine and the ministry; his father's question turned him to forestry. He intended, of course, to follow the family tradition and attend Yale, but Yale had no courses in forestry, and after four years of a typical carefree undergraduate life Pinchot went abroad to seek the advice of the man considered the dean of European foresters, Sir Dietrich Brandis, a tall, thin German, who had been knighted by Queen Victoria for introducing "systematic forest management in Burma and India" as early as 1856.

With the blessing of Brandis, Pinchot enrolled in the French Forest School at Nancy (it was a kind of homecoming—his grandfather had been a captain in Napoleon's army, and Pinchot spoke French almost as naturally as English). As part of the school's curriculum, Pinchot and his classmates visited all the great forests of Europe, and he got thereby his "first concrete understanding of the forest as a crop." He became "deeply interested not only in how the crop was grown, but also in how it was harvested in most forests every 150 years. Fires were forbidden in national forests with strict penalties for offenders. The Sihlwald, the famous Swiss national forest of Zurich, had been under forest management since before Columbus discovered America. "Its [the Sihlwald] production in wood and money," Pinchot noted, "was almost beyond belief."

When Pinchot returned from his apprenticeship abroad, he found Americans "obsessed . . . by a fury of development. . . ." It seemed to Pinchot as though everyone he encountered was "fiercely intent on appropriating and exploiting the riches of the richest of all continents—grasping with both hands, reaping where he had not sown, wasting what he thought would last forever." The notion was "Get timber by hook or crook, get it quick and cut it quick—that was the rule of the citizen. Get rid of it quick—that was the rule of the Government for the vast timberlands it still controlled." Public forests were disposed of in shady deals to lumber companies, which cut every stick of timber and left the land broken and eroded. Sheepmen and cattlemen grazed their flocks and herds in government-owned forests until no blade of grass or seedling was left to propagate new trees. Forest fires were started by careless hunters or cowhands or sheepherders and left to burn themselves out. In 1891, 12,000,000 acres of forest were lost to fires.

The Federal government owned some 2,000,000,000 acres, most of it in the West, "a domain richer in soil, water, forage, timber, and minerals," Pinchot wrote, "than any other similar area on earth." Into this world came young Pinchot with the ardent desire to teach his newly acquired knowledge to it. He was ideally equipped for his mission. Tall, handsome, rich, articulate, and charming, he was free from the need to make a living; he could devote all his remarkable energies to his mission of saving the forestland of America from continuing despoliation. Moreover, his family's wealth and social prominence gave him entrée everywhere. He did not wish to preserve American forests untouched; he wished rather to make them perpetually productive. In New York, for example, there were zealous tree lovers who opposed cutting down a single pine or fir. That was not Pinchot's pitch. To him the forests were a national heritage to be used profitably and enjoyed pleasurably by all Americans. "Forestry," he wrote, "is Tree Farming. Forestry is handling trees so that one crop follows another." He saw his mission as an educational one. Timber companies and ranchers, rather than being denounced as destroyers, must be made to see that in the long run, proper forest and range management meant greater profits. Among the influential sponsors Pinchot acquired was Carl Schurz. Accepting, in the Department of the Interior, the newly created position of forester, Pinchot began to create the essentials of the profession in the United States.

Hoke Smith, secretary of the interior in the Cleveland administration, "a big smooth-faced, powerful, confident man," became Gifford Pinchot's ally in his efforts to get legislation through Congress to protect the national forests. In February, 1896, Smith, prompted by

Pinchot, addressed to the National Academy of Sciences a series of questions having to do with the proper management of the forests under Federal domain. Perhaps the two most important questions were: "How shall the Government forests be administered so that the inhabitants of adjacent regions may draw their necessary forest supplies from them without affecting their permanency?" and "What provision is possible and necessary to secure for the Government a continuous, intelligent and honest management for the forests . . . including those reservations already made, or which may be made in the future." The result was the National Forest Commission, a permanent body which included the Yale chemist and physicist Wolcott Gibbs, as well as Charles Sargent, professor of arboriculture at Harvard, and, of course, Pinchot himself.

Pinchot and the members of the commission took a trip West in 1896, much of it on foot and horseback. At the Grand Canyon Pinchot met John Muir. The two men talked until midnight. "It was such an evening as I have never had before or since," Pinchot wrote.

Out of the trip came the Flathead Forest Reserve and later Glacier National Park, the Lewis and Clark Reserve, the Bitterroot Forest Reserve and the Mount Rainier and Grand Canyon National Parks, adding in all 14,000,000 acres to the nation's forest reserves.

The Forest Management Act of June, 1897, was called by Gifford Pinchot "the most important Federal forest legislation ever enacted." It opened the forest reserves to use under carefully controlled conditions. The secretary of the interior was authorized to sell "the dead, matured, or large growth trees after such trees" had been "marked and designated" by a forester.

In 1898 Pinchot became chief of the newly created Forestry Division of the Department of the Interior. It was an extremely modest enterprise with a staff of ten and an initial budget of $4,133,450, but, in Pinchot's words, "Every man in the Division was on his toes. We were all young together, all eager, all proud of the Division, and all fiercely determined that its attack on forest devastation must win. We were ready to fight it out on this line if it took the rest of our lives. With such a cause and such a spirit we couldn't lose." Soon the division was forced to enlarge its realm to take in such questions as "the relation of forests to stream flow, water supply, evaporation, erosion and irrigation." Yale proved a fertile recruiting ground for young men who felt a "calling" for forestry.

Armed with letters to many of the important politicians and ranchers and timbermen in the Western states, Pinchot went on a missionary tour throughout the Rocky Mountain region in 1899, preaching the new gospel. He was remarkably successful. Men who had been ready to dismiss him as an Eastern crackpot were converted to the new faith. His trip added to his passion for preserving the forests and to his alarm over the ravages of erosion evident wherever he went.

California was a different kind of revelation. "As I rode my hired horse through the California foothills," he wrote, "glorious in the lap of spring, I was enchanted. Every fence post seemed to hold a meadow lark, and great blankets of the richest colors kept the hillsides warm." The Mariposa Grove of redwoods was a revelation, and at Yosemite he spent hours with John Muir, hiking through "his" park.

Back in Washington, Pinchot introduced the practice of supplementing the staff of the division with student assistants, who were paid $25 a month and their expenses for summer work. In the summer of 1900, out of 232 applicants, 100 of them from Harvard and Yale, 61 assistants were chosen. The student assistants were in turn supplemented by "Collaborators," outstanding scientists such as Nathaniel Shaler of Harvard, men who had a knowledge of botany, geography, and related areas. In 1901 when the division became a bureau, it had grown to 179 persons, 81 of whom were student assistants and 25 of whom were collaborators. Soon they were supported by a private organization (to which, to be sure, most of them belonged) called the Society of American Foresters.

As the interest in forestry grew, the New York State College of Forestry was started at Cornell in 1898, and two years later Yale started a forestry school with the aid of an endowment of $300,000 from the Pinchots.

Gifford Pinchot's mainstay was W. J. McGee, "anthropologist, geologist, hydrologist—a fountain of almost universal knowledge," Pinchot called him. McGee had begun life as a blacksmith, educated himself, studied biology and geology, and made in Iowa "the most extensive geological and topographic survey ever executed in America without public aid," in Pinchot's words. A protégé of John Wesley Powell, McGee had been director of the Bureau of American Ethnology for ten years and had done pioneering work in what we today call ecology. He had done pioneering work as well in ecosystems—the relation of land, water, and indigenous plants in a particular area or watershed. "Every revolution," McGee declared, "whatever its material manifestations . . . is first and foremost a revolution in thought and spirit."

The revolution that was required in the United States in regard to its vast land areas was the recognition that they were there not for the exploitation and profit of individuals or great corporations but for the benefit of everyone, rich and poor alike. They were a great common treasure and resource, and it was the obligation of the Federal government, acting in the name of all the people, to prevent their despoliation and, so far as possible, to retrieve what had been lost or abused by rapacious individuals.

McGee related the destruction and monopolization of the land to the peculiar circumstances of America's birth. "When Independence was declared," he wrote, "and the Constitution was framed, no resources were reckoned except the Men who made the nation and the Land on which they lived." Trees and rivers were impediments. Nature was something to be subdued, overcome. The consequence was that the nation's apparently limitless resources "passed under monopolistic control with a rapidity never before seen in all the world's history; and it is hardly too much to say that the Nation has become one of Captains of Industry first, and one of the People and their chosen representatives only second." The issue that faced the country, McGee declared, was: Should this process be arrested and the benefits of the land go to the "people" or "into the hands of the self-chosen and self-anointed few, largely to forge new shackles for the wrists and ankles of the many?" The American people must "reclaim their own." The somewhat archaic language—"the few and the many"—recalled Jefferson and William Manning and their warnings that the few would always endeavor to take advantage of the many.

If McGee spoke in the stirring tones of a Henry George or an Edward Bellamy, the younger generation of men like Philip Wells, one of Pinchot's coadjutors, spoke a new language of "economic rent" and "unearned increment," of reforms "within the general limitations fixed by popular opinion as to fundamentals, and within specific limitations fixed by constitutional provisions." Writing years later to the journalist Mark Sullivan about those heady days, Wells observed, "Those who wished to protect the nation's natural resources (water power, forests, the mineral fuels and mineral fertilizers) inclined to the socializing pole; that is, they sought to enlarge the public control of these resources . . . both for the prevention of waste and, more essential, for the socializing of the raw resource value including unearned increment." Henry George was the most influential figure for them, although they rejected what appeared to them to be his excessive faith in private enterprise under the single tax system. For their enemies who raised the cry that they were infringing on the sacred rights of private property, Pinchot had a short answer: "I have very little interest in the abstract question whether the nation is encroaching upon the rights of the states or the states upon the nation. Power falls naturally to that person or agency which can and does use it, and the nation acts . . . [while] the states do not."

The opponents of the forestry movement were in large part Westerners whose lands were at issue. They argued with vehemence that the movement was dominated by effete Easterners with no interest in or sympathy for the economic needs of the West. They simply wished to seal up the nation's remaining resources and throw away the key. They wished "to keep everything petrified and stagnant," in the words of Colorado Senator Charles Thomas.

"Out in the Great Open Space where Men were Men the domination of concentrated wealth over mere human beings was something to make you shudder. I saw it and fought it, and I know," Pinchot wrote. But he continued to make converts even among that intractable tribe. He measured his success in converting lumber companies to sound forestry practices by the pronouncement of F. E. Weyerhaeuser, son of the head of the Weyerhaeuser Timber Company, that "Practical Forestry ought to be of more interest and importance to lumbermen than to any other class of men. . . ."

With Theodore Roosevelt in the White House, Gifford Pinchot anticipated new opportunities to promote his ideas about forestry. In his message of December 2, 1901, to Congress, Roosevelt had declared, "The fundamental idea of forestry is the perpetuation of forests by use. Forest protection is not an end in itself; it is a means to increase and sustain the resources of our country and the industries which depend upon them. The preservation of our forests is an imperative business necessity. . . . The forest and water problems are perhaps the most vital internal questions of the United States." The "water problems" had to do with protecting the major water resources of the nation from exploitation by individuals for profit. "Great storage works" were "necessary . . . to save flood waters." This was too vast an undertaking for private effort or even for the individual states. It should be undertaken by the national government, and the lands so reclaimed should be reserved by the government for actual settlers. "The reclamation and settlement of arid lands," Roosevelt continued, "will enrich every portion of our country. . . . Our people as a whole will profit, for successful homemaking is but another name for the up-building of the Nation." The message, in Pinchot's view, was "a landmark in the development of forestry in the United States." It gave to forestry "a new standing that was invaluable and it marked the beginning of government action in dam building, flood control and irrigation."

One of Roosevelt's first acts as President had been to place the Forest Service under the Department of Agriculture, a measure that Pinchot had urged. Despite his notable accomplishments, Pinchot believed that the movement to save the nation's natural resources from private exploitation suffered from want of a name that would be striking and comprehensive enough to take in the varied aspects of the protection of the environment. Forestry was, after all, only one aspect of the problem of protecting the nation's resources. There was a complex of issues relating to the land and its use. The forests were related to watersheds; "to streams and inland navigation, to water power and flood control; to soil and its erosion; to coal and oil and other minerals; to fish and game; and many other possible uses or waste of natural resources. . . . What had all these to do with Forestry?" As he rode in Rock Creek Park one day, it came to Pinchot that what was needed was a single word, one that could be used to dramatize the issue for the public and rally widespread popular support. "Seen in this light," he wrote later, "all these separate questions fitted into and made up the one great central problem of the use of the earth for the good of man." The idea was to him "a good deal like coming out of a dark tunnel. I had been seeing a spot of light ahead. Here, all of a sudden, was a whole landscape . . . [and] it was like lifting the curtain on a great new stage." The separate problems were, in essence, all "one gigantic single problem that must be solved if the generations, as they came and went, were to live civilized, happy, useful lives in the lands which the Lord their God had given them." The question was what single word could comprehend that "one single gigantic problem." The *E pluribus unum* of the natural world, as of the political life of the United States, was the word "conservation." With the exultation of Columbus discovering the New World, Pinchot wrote: "The Conservation of natural resources is the key to the future. It is the key to the safety and prosperity of the American people, and all the people of all the world, for all time to come. . . . Moreover, Conservation is a foundation of permanent peace among the nations, and the most important foundation of all." He immediately discussed his "brain child . . . with my Father and Mother," his untiring supporters in all his ventures. He tried it on his colleagues, who were captured by his enthusiasm. Then, during one of his rides with the President, he tried the name out on him, "and he approved it instantly." He not only approved it, but nailed its banner to the masthead of his administration. The whole notion suited him perfectly. It was exactly the theme and the tone he wished to strike. Even the fact that it was so close to "conservative" was a political asset. It evoked echoes of the ancient Protestant ethic of thrift, of saving and conserving, as Pinchot said, what the Lord had given. The greater part of the second term of Roosevelt's administration lay ahead. Conservation would become its major theme. A number of specific things had, of course, already been done. In 1903 Roosevelt had vetoed a bill to give Muscle Shoals to private power interests. Now all such measures had a name: conservation. Thus the creation of an Inland Waterways Commission, projected for several years, became a conservation measure. Senator Francis Newlands, sponsor of the reclamation bill, was elected vice-chairman of the commission. Pinchot, of course, was on it, and the President took a personal interest.

Recalling the success of the expedition taken in 1896 by the members of the National Forest Commission and the publicity that the trip had generated, Pinchot planned a similar journey by the commissioners and invited the President to join the party at Keokuk, Iowa, for the leg of the trip down the Mississippi. Twelve state governors also came aboard, and ten more joined at St. Louis. From Keokuk to Memphis people gathered at towns and villages along the riverbank to see the presidential party. At night they built huge bonfires and waited around them for the steamer to churn by. Wherever the boat was scheduled to stop, great crowds assembled, and the President delivered a speech on conservation, emphasizing the theme that Pinchot had proposed to him: "every river system is a unit from its source to its mouth and should be treated as such. . . ."

At Memphis Roosevelt declared "that the conservation of natural resources is the fundamental problem. Unless we solve that problem it will avail us little to solve all others." At the suggestion of the commission, he intended to call "a conference on the conservation of natural resources . . . to meet in Washington. . . . It ought to be among the most important gatherings in our history, for none have had a more vital question to consider."

Pinchot called the resulting conference "undoubtedly the most distinguished gathering on the most important issue ever to meet in the White House. . . ." All the governors, as well as some seventy national organizations concerned with some aspect of national resources, were invited.

Roosevelt addressed the assembled company, reminding them that "the conservation of our natural resources, though the gravest problem of today," was only part of the problem of "national efficiency. . . . We are coming to recognize as never before," the President continued, "the right of the Nation to guard its own future in the essential matter of national resources. In the past we have admitted the right of the individual to injure the future of the Republic for his own present profit. The time has come for a change. As a people we have the right and the duty of obeying the moral law, of requiring and doing justice, to protect ourselves and our children against the wasteful development of our natural resources. . . ."

The conference was not without its discordant notes. A number of Western governors declared their devotion to the doctrine of states' rights and insisted that Federal lands be turned over to the states. But "the general tone," Pinchot noted, "was one of overwhelming approval." Most of the governors signed a declaration stating "that the prosperity of our country rests upon the abundant resources of the land," that the land was "a heritage to be made use of in establishing and promoting the comfort, prosperity, and happiness of the American people, but not to be wasted, deteriorated, or needlessly destroyed . . . [and] that this conservation . . . is a subject of transcendent importance, which should engage . . . the People in earnest cooperation." Finally, the governors recommended "the enactment of laws looking to the prevention of waste in the mining and extraction of coal, oil, gas, and other minerals with a view to their wise conservation for the use of the People, and to the protection of human life in the mines."

The conference seemed to Pinchot, its principal architect, "a turning point in human history." The first gathering of its kind in the world, it soon had imitators in other nations.

The Immigrants

One of Roosevelt's happiest inspirations was his invention of presidential commissions. There had of course been presidential fact-finding commissions of various kinds throughout our history, but Roosevelt made them into a bold extension of executive authority. Bypassing an increasingly irritated Congress, the commissions, made up primarily of wealthy, public-spirited men of moderate, reformist tendencies, generally provided their own expenses and paid their own staffs. Sometimes grants from philanthropic foundations were solicited when costs were heavy. Starting with the commission on the anthracite coal strike in Pennsylvania in 1902, Roosevelt appointed eleven commissions to report on various aspects of American life. (Despite Oswald Garrison Villard's importunings, he refused to appoint a commission on the status of blacks.)

One of the most important was the Commission on Immigration. It was made up of three Senators, three Representatives, and three public members appointed by the President. As distinguished from the support of most of the commissions, the substantial sum of $600,000 was appropriated to pay its expenses, and three years were spent collecting and evaluating data. The results of the study were published in forty-two volumes, accompanied by "A Brief Statement of the Conclusions and Recommendations of the Immigrant Commission."

The commission gave special attention to the dramatic shift in the national and racial origins of immigrants from Northern and Western Europe—England, Ireland, Scotland, Wales, Germany, and the Scandinavian countries—to Eastern and Southern Europe—Italy first, then Russian-ruled Poland, Lithuania, Estonia, Turkey (the Ottoman Empire), and the various ill-assorted peoples who made up the creaky, ready-to-fly-apart Austro-Hungarian Empire of the Hapsburgs.

The new immigration included nationalities unfamiliar to most Americans. In addition to Armenians, there were numerous Magyars, Serbians, Montenegrins, Croatians and Slavs, Dalmatians, Bosnians, Herzegovinians, Finns, Greeks, Poles, Portuguese, Ruthenians, Slovaks, Syrians, and Turks.

Variety and volume told the story of the new immigration. In 1901, 487,918 immigrants entered the United States. The average yearly immigration over the preceding decade had run from 580,000 in 1892 to a low of 229,000 in 1898, but it climbed rapidly in the five years following the turn of the century, reaching more than 1,000,000 in 1905. Of that number, fewer than 85,000 came from Great Britain, 53,000 from Ireland, 25,000 from Scandinavia, and 40,000 from Germany, all traditional sources of immigration over the nineteenth century. But 275,000 came from "Central Europe," primarily the Austro-Hungarian Empire and 185,000 from Russia and Eastern Europe. These rates were maintained over the succeeding decade and interrupted only by the outbreak of the European War.

Beginning with some 2,000 immigrants in 1895, Asian Turkey sent an increasing number of immigrants, rising to 35,000 in 1913. Japanese immigration varied from 14,000 in 1902 to 30,000 in 1907 and then dropped off sharply as a consequence of the so-called gentlemen's agreement, whereby Japan consented to limit emigration.

By 1910 there were 22,686,204 Americans of foreign or mixed parentage out of a total population of some 76,000,000, of whom by far the largest number (5,264,004) were of German ancestry, followed by 3,122,013 Irish. Some 725,000 were of Polish antecedents, and 775,654 were Jews from Lithuania and Russia. By far the greater portion of the Italian immigrants came from the impoverished South. In 1912, for example, 26,000 Italians came to the United States from Northern Italy and 136,000 from the South, mainly from Campania,

Calabria, and Sicily. In a five-year period 250,000 Calabrians left their province; 150,000 of them came to the United States. Those left behind were largely the old and the unmarried women.

Immigration was a young man's game. Out of 8,000,000 immigrants who arrived in the United States between 1900 and 1910, only four out of 100 were over the age of forty-four. The vast majority were in their twenties or early thirties.

A notion of the geographical distribution of immigrants is indicated by the fact that in 1910 the census showed that west of the Mississippi and north of the Kansas-Nebraska line every state had at least 35 percent first- or second-generation immigrants in its population; Utah, Montana, the Dakotas, Minnesota, Wisconsin, Michigan, and Illinois had 50 percent or more foreign-born. Indeed, a line drawn from New Jersey southwest to St. Louis and thence northwest to the Minnesota-North Dakota border, comprising 18 percent of the continental United States and holding approximately half its population, contained at the same time 75 percent of all foreign-born whites and 82 percent of the new immigrants.

Fayette County in southwestern Pennsylvania produced 30,000,000 tons of coal a year. Out of a total population of 167,000, 48,000 were foreign-born, and many more the children of immigrant parents. The county had seventeen distilleries, which turned out 50,000 barrels of whiskey a year, and nine breweries, which produced 130,000 barrels of beer, most of which was consumed in the county.

In Chicago the Magyar section was adjacent to the Polish ghetto. Beyond spread blocks of Italian immigrants with some blacks intermingled. On the other side of the mills were successive blocks of Slovaks, Croatians, and Russians. Such communities were characteristic of the Mesabi and Vermilion iron ore ranges of Minnesota and the coal-mining regions of Pennsylvania.

As the tide of immigration swelled, an increasing number of the workers in all the "camps"—mining, lumber, and construction—throughout the Rocky Mountain states to the Pacific Coast were foreign-born. Employers were eager to replace native-born Americans, who, by general agreement, were volatile, aggressive, independent, and impermanent, with more passive foreigners.

One labor contractor, testifying before the Commission on Industrial Relations, rated construction workers in terms of nationality. At the bottom was the Hindu, "who ranks lowest in the scale of efficiency." Then came the Albanians, "who are just slightly more efficient." Italians were next, with Northern Italians outclassing their Southern cousins. At the top of the list of immigrant laborers were the Greeks, the Austrians, and the Swedes. The nationalities of the men employed by the Pueblo Steel works and the Rocky Mountain Timber Company were listed in testimony before the commission as 702 Americans (colloquially termed "white"), 615 Mexicans, 130 Slavs, 771 Italians, 192 Austrians, 28 Polish, 170 Greeks, and 25 Japanese. Russian, German, Swedish, Spanish, Irish, Slovakian, and Syrian, along with Bulgarian, Hungarian, and Rumanian, were also represented.

Montenegrins appeared as successors to the Swedes in Minnesota lumber camps near Deer River, and they were soon followed by Finns, Greeks, Poles, and Slovaks. Often the immigrants worked the iron mines in the summer and turned to lumbering in the winter.

The wage scale of immigrant workers was substantially below that of native-born workers. It varied also in relation to the particular industry in which the workers were employed. Immigrants working in the silver and copper mines of the Rocky Mountain states earned an average weekly wage of $13.60, which dropped to $7.86 in textile factories. At a time when a subsistence wage was calculated at $745 per year, the average annual wage of immigrants went from $722 for Swedes to $480 for Northern Italians and less than $400 for Southern Italians and Magyars.

Of the employees in the iron and steel industry in 1910, more than 50 percent were foreign-born, and their average salaries were $346, almost $400 below what was considered a subsistence wage. This meant, of course, that if families were not to starve, more than one member had to work. The common pattern was for the wife/mother to work as a domestic or at some cottage industry.

On the West Coast it is not surprising that hostility existed among native American workingmen toward the Chinese and Japanese. The two races were often used to drive down the already low wage level as well as to frustrate efforts at unionization. A union official in San Francisco, testifying before the Commission on Industrial Relations, expressed the views of most workingmen in the state. The greatest impediment to the labor movement, he declared, had been Collis Huntington's practice of bringing "the Chinese and Asiatics generally. . . . For white men would not go out to the ranches and be domiciled as were those Asiatics, and you could not blame them. They will not do it, and I hope to God they never will do it. I would rather see California without a solitary man within it, as a white man's State, than to see California Japanized or Chinaized. If this State is to belong to the Union let us have it for Americans, and not for the Japanese and Chinese as was brought here and whose sins we must suffer."

Of a sampling of 181,000 foreign-born industrial workers, 54 percent had been farmers in the old country and only 15 percent had had any experience in industries. In addition, farming life was predominantly village life, and the isolation of the American farm was unfamiliar to the vast majority of immigrants who became farmers in America. In many areas of New England and the Middle West immigrant farmers established themselves in self-contained communities; this was especially true of the Poles, many of whom settled on Long Island and became truck farmers supplying New York City with fresh vegetables. The Connecticut Valley was another stronghold of Polish farmers, who collected in Hatfield, Hadley, and South Deerfield.

The worst conditions of all existed in the labor camps where immigrant workers were assembled to work in mines, in quarries, brickyards, lumber mills, and canneries. New York State alone had 600 such camps, not counting lumbering operations. They were, for the most part, bleak and filthy beyond description. The New York State Department of Labor reserved its severest criticism for the railroad camps, which, it declared, "surpass anything investigated by this Bureau. Nowhere else has been found such an absolute disregard for comfort, health, morality, and justice." This situation bore most heavily on the Italians through the institution of the *padrone,* or labor boss, who assembled the work crews and took a substantial part of their salaries. The inspectors of the state Bureau of Industries and Immigration found some of the camps so filthy and vermin-ridden that the men had built themselves huts out of logs and tree limbs.

Some of the most surprising statistics concern those immigrants who returned to their homelands. Italians were especially disposed to return, in part because fares were cheap—about $35 from New York to Naples in steerage—and it was relatively easy to do so, and in part because of intense attachment to a particular town or cantonment. In the five years from 1907 to 1912 the roughly 900,000 Italians who emigrated to the United States were counterbalanced by some 500,000 Italians who sailed back the other way. We have no way of knowing, of course, how many of the 900,000 returned in that period, but there is evidence that more than any other nationality or "people" Italians became "commuters," traveling back and forth any number of times. A substantial number emigrated to the United States, worked hard, saved their money, and returned to their native villages to live in comparative opulence, admired by their fellow villagers for their cosmopolitanism.

Of the 430,627 Poles who came in the same period, 152,617 made their way back. By contrast less than 10 percent of the Jewish immigrants returned. Most of them had fled from more than poverty. Much the same was true of the Irish. Of 180,000 Irish immigrants, only 14,000 returned. On the other hand, more Magyars returned than stayed—i.e., 123,000 came and 87,000 returned. The same was true of Croatians, Serbs, Slavs, and Slovaks (of the last, 117,868 came and almost 70,000 returned). Of all immigrant groups of that period, 4,292,985 came and 1,452,239 returned to their homelands. Put another way, for every 100 immigrants that came from Northern and Western Europe—Ireland, Scotland, England, and Germany primarily—only 13 returned. For every 100 that came from Southern and Eastern Europe, 39 returned. Many undoubtedly returned bitter and defeated but radicalized and "nationalized"—that is, given fresh zeal to fight for independence, most particularly from the Austro-Hungarian Empire. Of those who returned, the great majority, it is reasonable to assume, were drafted into the respective armies of the Central Powers at the beginning of the European War. Many must have had friends and relatives in the United States, and the issue of the entry of the United States into the war on the side of the Allies was for them especially difficult.

We are inclined to think of immigration as a one-way street in which enormous numbers of foreigners came to the United States and found here, after some travail and hardship, happiness and success, so it comes as something of a surprise to discover how many rejected America after a trial and, for whatever reason or reasons, went home sadder but wiser. At the same time we can be confident, I think, that whatever the nature of their "American experience" they were not as they were before; certain fundamental ideas and attitudes had changed. Seen in this light, the United States was not only a refuge for millions of immigrants but also part of an important educational process for those who came and later went away.

In the remarkable reciprocity between old home and new, in the ceaseless movement of peoples from their homelands to America and back to their homelands and often back again, lies a whole largely hidden history as dramatic as any revealed history. Because they were able to come to the United States and here throw off their disguise, so to speak, and stand forth not merely as submerged portions of, say, the Austro-Hungarian Empire but as Croatians, Serbs, Slavs, Poles, and Slovaks, they demonstrated the reality of their national aspirations on the American stage. In addition, they raised money for the cause of nationalism and agitated strenuously. In the words of Emily Greene Balch, "To many an immigrant the idea of nationality first becomes real after he has left his native country; at home the contrast was between village and village, and between peasants as a class and land-lords as a class. In America he finds a vast world of people, all speaking unintelligible tongues, and for the first time he has a vivid sense of oneness with those who speak his own language, whether here or at home."

One of the most enthralling themes in American history is the means by which the wildly divergent immigrant groups or, as we call them today, ethnic groups adapted themselves to these new environments. Those stories were as varied as the groups themselves multiplied by the environments in which they settled. In other words, the experiences of Italians who settled the Southern states (not a large number, to be sure) were very different from those who landed in New York City, in the Colorado mines, or in San Francisco or Seattle. But all suffered from the sense of being aliens in a strange land.

"Poverty was only one half of our routine ordeal," the journalist Eugene Lyons wrote of his ghetto youth on New York's lower East Side. "The other half was an acute awareness of being aliens and intruders in a nation of Americans. Between the world of our text-books and the movies and newspapers and the other world of our homes and parents there was a deep gulf; different interests, preoccupations, ideals, languages. On the threshold of your home you removed your American self like an overcoat, and you put it on once more when you left home. We lived this double existence so continuously that the idea of an integrated life, in which home and out-of-home activities were part of the same pattern, was beyond our imagination." Lyons was convinced that no American "with roots deep in the American soil can understand the nostalgic homelessness of immigrant children, the pathos of second-generation aliens, *Land where our fathers died, land of the Pilgrim's pride* sung in the assembly hall by several thousand Jewish, Russian, Italian, and other foreign boys and girls whose fathers had never heard of the Pilgrims. We were 'Americanized' about as gently as horses are broken in. In the whole process we sensed a disrespect for the alien traditions in our homes and came unconsciously to resent and despise these traditions, good and bad alike, because they seemed insuperable barriers between ourselves and the adopted land."

It seemed to young Lyons (which was not, of course, the name with which he was born) that he and his friends and family were "caught and tangled in a mass of people, sodden with hopelessness, and in a stupor of physical exhaustion." It was easier to burrow into "the heap" than to "attempt the Gargantuan job of escaping," and "success" was extricating oneself from that swarming, teeming life, "a species of defiance and revenge against the clinging squalors and smugness of the lucky ones and, above all, against the social system that breeds such plague spots." One could claw one's way out by any means available, legal or illegal, or, as Lyons did, take up a "clamoring protest" that transcended the personal and embraced "all the disinherited and exploited." For him the socialism that he gave his allegiance to in his teens was "a conscious protest against ugliness and injustice as such." To him there was "a vast and unbridgeable difference between the radicalism that is accepted second-hand, from the outside, through the mind, and the revolt that is nurtured in one's very bones. Those of us who were—or thought ourselves—'socialists' instinctively, through spontaneous hatred for the reality as we savored it, could never quite get over a certain distrust of 'converts' to the cause from other social strata."

Before Lyons had ever read Marx, he "knew for a certainty that the whole world was one battleground, contested between the fat-bellied Capitalists and the down-trodden Workers, and that victory for the Workers, for my side, was inevitable. . . . The spectres of 'slack' seasons, of strikes for a living wage, of illness that cut off all earnings for a large family—the sight of my father's cadaverous face after a long day at the machine . . . these were less horrible when viewed as aspects of the perpetual class hostilities and as prelude to an ineffable triumph." From his Socialistic Sunday School Lyon graduated to the Yipsels, the Young People's Socialist League, "where we debated weighty questions and took courses in Marx and Spencer." The fondest hope was to escape by becoming "a Doctor."

Americans, made profoundly uneasy by the immigration of Eastern and Southern Europeans into the United States and by their disposition to collect in neighborhoods where they clung to their native ways, pointed to the extraordinary proliferation of foreign-language newspapers as an example of the resistance of immigrants to Americanization. But advocates of the immigrants were quick to point out that such newspapers were, in fact, an essential element in the process of Americanization. The great majority of the immigrants had had no newspapers in their homelands; to have a newspaper in America was to have already adapted a critically important American institution.

In 1913 there were 538 newspapers in the United States printed in twenty-nine foreign languages and published in thirty-five states. It was estimated that $27,000,000 was invested in such papers, and $10,000,000 taken in yearly in subscriptions. Of the number, 110 were Italian, 59 Swedish, 57 Polish, 42 Bohemian, 34 Yiddish, 10 Syrian, and 6 Chinese. *Atlantis*, a Greek daily paper in New York, had a circulation of 30,000. *Al-Hoda*, the only Syrian daily, had 10,000.

The content of such papers varied widely. The Yiddish and German newspapers devoted more than half their space to cultural news, while 38 percent of the stories in Italian papers dealt with crime: "trials . . . arrests . . . fights and brawls, bomb and black-hand [the secret Italian terrorist society], murder and suicide. . . ."

What all this meant, of course, was that immigrant journalism, was, if not exactly a rival to English-language journalism, very clearly a by-product of it. It might indeed be considered the most thoroughly American aspect of the experience of the immigrant. Equally important, the foreign-language newspapers provided jobs for thousands of young immigrant journalists, many of them of considerable, though generally unrecognized, brilliance, many of them persons who, like their "native American" counterparts, exerted a very strong influence on the political inclinations of their readers. As we have seen, the most prominent foreign-language editors were assiduously courted by ambitious politicians who wished to secure the votes of their fellow immigrants. Needless to say, their support was often contingent on favors for the nationality the editors/journalists represented or on less worthy considerations.

It was much the same with the theaters that put on plays in the languages of the immigrants. For most immigrants again they were an enthralling innovation. The benevolent associations performed an essential function by encouraging democratic participation in organizations of their own creation without analogues in the old country. The Czech colony in New York, which numbered some 30,000, outdid all other immigrant nationalities in the form of a five-story building— the National Hall—with a bar and restaurant and movie theater on the ground floor, the combined income of which maintained the building and amortized its cost. On the upper floors were meeting rooms for fraternal orders and for union meetings. There were, in addition, a dance hall and a theater with a school for the children of Bohemian freethinkers.

The Polish National Alliance had 800 branches with 50,000 members and maintained in New York City a home where Polish immigrants could seek lodging until they had decided where to establish themselves. In addition to providing aid (they were often burial societies as well), these associations strove "to keep alive a love of the old language, history, and tradition and to forward the cause of their people in Europe, where they suffer political oppression."

The public school was perhaps the greatest agency of acculturation. In 1910, of 18,000,000 children attending school, more than a fourth were the children of foreign-born parents.

While parochial schools clearly performed an extremely important function for the children of Catholic immigrants, middle-class reformers fretted over the fact that the instruction was primarily in the native tongue of the immigrant parents and thus impeded the adaptation of the children to American society.

An essential factor in the reconciliation of immigrants who remained in the United States to American life was the activities of those reformers who devoted their lives to easing the way for the new Americans. Jane Addams was the pioneer and the most famous—for all practical purposes, she *invented* the field of immigrant social work—but thousands of middle- and upper-class young women followed in her footsteps (and many middle-class young women ascended thereby to the lower rungs of the upper class), and hundreds of exposé journalists, taking their cue from the examples of Jacob Riis and Ida Tarbell, Lincoln Steffens and Hutchins Hapgood, made the lives of the immigrants vivid realities for millions of readers, thereby preventing them from simply disappearing from the consciousness of most Americans.

One of the leaders in the movement to give aid and comfort to the new class of immigrants was Emily Greene Balch, heiress of an old aristocratic Philadelphia family and professor of political economy at Swarthmore College. More of a scholar than an active social worker, she made the Slavs her "field," writing an informative book entitled *Our Slavic Fellow Citizens.*

An essential principle of the women and men engaged in "social service" was that the plans and programs for their immigrant clients must come not "out of our own heads," as the reformer Vida Scudder

put it, "or from superficial study [but out of] the great forces arising
from life. Identification of ourselves with the people must be the keynote of sound social advance. . . ." Indeed, it was the only way to avoid
misspent effort and eventual failure.

Helen Todd, who made child labor and the education of immigrant children her special concern, wrote in *McClure's* in 1913 that a
factory inspector had said, "What the working children need is what
all children need, but these especially—love from some one who has
the time and intelligence to love; work from some one who knows what
kind of work will be most possible and useful to them; but, above all,
play, music, stories, pictures, and the personality of a teacher who is
joyful, tender, intelligent. Discomfort, anxiety, and privation make
their faces old at ten years. They stand, little shabby creatures, between
the mockery of what our civilization has made of their homes and the
wreckage that machinery and speeded-up industry will make of their
lives. Meantime, there is our school. Would it not be possible to adapt
this child of foreign peasants less to education, and adapt more education to the child?"

When a survey of the Flatbush section of Brooklyn revealed that
2,500 Italian immigrants were living in the most deplorable conditions,
the Civic League called a meeting to attempt a remedy. The members
of the league decided to concentrate their efforts on organizing a
"garbage collecting system," grading and paving the streets, providing
a supply of clean water, and building a municipal playground adjacent
to the community.

Sarah Wood Moore, a member of the Philadelphia elite, started
the first labor camp school at Aspinwall, Pennsylvania, for Italian coal
miners. When she died six years later in her sixty-fifth year, she was
eulogized as someone who "had not only the imagination to conceive
a magnificent ideal, but the perseverance to achieve it in minutest
detail. Her birth and culture made her responsive to all refinements
of life, and gave her the insight of a truly democratic spirit which
discerns beauty of thought and action without regard to accidental
setting." Moore was not just an educational missionary to Italian immigrants but an ardent pioneer in adult education. "Whether in city
or camp, school quarters for the adult should be of the reading-room
type," she wrote, "and conversation should be a stated feature of the
course." At the labor camp at Ashokan Reservoir Dam, Moore created
her ideal classroom in a rustic high-ceilinged room forty feet long,
equipped with comfortable chairs, with tables improvised from saw-

horses and planks and long rows of bookshelves since "the workingman likes his school quarters in the heart of his living quarters and of the same homely pattern." He wanted his regular teacher, his own seat, and his own book, and he wished to learn the English words for the commonplace articles and tools of his daily life.

In the variety of the new immigration it was almost as though the United States were destined to prove in the new age, as Tom Paine had predicted, an "asylum for mankind." If America were to be a "gathered people," the gathering must be completed before the age was ended. Bible prophecy spoke of a final reconciliation of the nations of the world. A modern Englishman wrote of a new "cosmic man" shaped in America of all the desperate races and nations of the world.

It may be doubted if such thoughts occurred to most Americans, at least to the beleaguered "old" Americans. They felt rising anxiety at the "wretched refuse" that washed upon their shores in such vast numbers year after year. The roots of their anxiety were, as we have already had occasion to note, deep and tangled. In an age obsessed by genetics, by vaguely Darwinian notions of preserving or improving "the race" (the race, of course, being not the human race but the Teutonic, Anglo-Saxon race, which the Teutons and the Anglo-Saxons agreed was the culminating achievement of the evolutionary process), "racial mixing" was the ever-present nightmare. Upper-class dreams were filled with images of tall, handsome blond Anglo-Saxons mating with short, squat, dark, ugly Latins or Slavs or Ruthenians, not to mention Jews or, most alarming of all, blacks and Orientals.

In the war between capital and labor the newcomers appeared as reinforcements for the forces of labor, although in fact, with their widely divergent cultures, different languages, and common incomprehension of and inability to deal with the dominant American institutions, they were, at least initially, more of a handicap than an asset to embattled labor.

Then there was the religious issue. Most of the new immigrants were, like the Irish and many of the Germans, Roman Catholics. So added to the fear of genetic pollution was the ancient anxiety about the Pope's taking over the United States and making it, presumably, another papal state. The alarming new breed of immigrants might also be expected in normal circumstances to vote Democratic, thereby imposing a barrier to all efforts at municipal reform, for indeed, were not the deplorable condition of the cities, the corruption, the filth, the disease, the crime all the consequence of the masses of immigrants who crowded into them? A note of hysteria crept into scholarly as well as public discussions of the "problem." It might already be too late to arrest the progressive degeneration of the nation. The literature on the subject overflowed with the darkest predictions.

Finally, with the talk of revolution in the air, with the Socialists growing in strength each year and the anarchists increasingly visible and vocal, the conviction spread that political radicalism was directly related to the new-style immigrant who often, it was said, arrived in the United States the avowed enemy of capitalism (not avowed to the immigration officials, of course).

The Commission on Immigration discovered what presumably was already known: that immigration "is, with few exceptions, almost entirely to be attributed to economic causes." The commission also reported that immigration alone had made possible the extraordinary growth in industry and mining in the preceding thirty years. Of the wage earners in thirty-eight major industries three fifths were foreign-born in 1909 and only one-fifth were "native white Americans." In twenty-two industries foreigners were in the majority and in certain ones, such as sugar refineries, the number of foreign workers ran as high as 85 percent. In the clothing trades it rose to 94 out of every 100 workers.

Without welfare, without unemployment insurance, unable to speak the language, with no notion of the value of his labor, with little or no sense of solidarity with other workers, the immigrant was powerless, resented ("hated" does not seem too strong a term) by native working-class Americans and feared and despised by upper-class Americans. For the bolder and more enterprising like young Eugene Lyons, radical politics seemed the only hope. Everything that they experienced in their daily lives, in their contacts with the agencies of government, with their employers, and with the "oppressor class" seemed to confirm the most radical analysis of the causes of their misery and the remedies. If Marx and Engels and Alexander Berkman and Johann Most described an oversimplified world, they described one nonetheless familiar enough to most immigrants.

Further beclouding the picture, as we have seen, were the tenets of social Darwinism. "Race" was in the air, and decent, well-intentioned people rallied to its standard, suppressing their scruples since it came in the name of the most advanced scientific notions of the day. It was hoped the alchemy of being American would transform the "wretched refuse" into upstanding American citizens. But whether that would indeed happen and whether, if it did, the newcomers would make suitable breeding stock were clearly another matter.

Nativism, seldom far below the surface, became more assertive. By and large immigrants suffered from various forms of discrimination to the degree that they differed in manner, appearance, and culture from the predominant Anglo-Saxon norm. Certainly the Irish and the Germans, who, English and Scottish aside, most resembled the "native strain," had endured generations of prejudice and continued to experience it. But they had, after all, their own well-established "subcultures," even, in the case of the Germans, their own states.

The Japs, sheenies, Polacks, bohunks, spics, greasers, Chinks, wops (or dagoes) were assigned to dirty jobs, long hours, and low wages. At the same time they found themselves the objects of scholarly observation, if not exactly investigation. The academic world, infatuated with Darwinian-racist theories, declared them genetically inferior peoples, peoples without the freedom-loving blood and superior genes of Anglo-Saxons and Teutons (some scholars preferred "Nordic"). "Race" became the rage. Articles appeared in scholarly journals "proving" that certain races were irredeemably inferior. Important as environment was, it was now evident as a consequence of the remarkable advances in the study of genetics that heredity was where it was at, so to speak. The most famous of the new scholars of race was Madison Grant, chairman of the New York Zoological Society, trustee of the American Museum of Natural History, councilor, American Geographical Society, who wrote a runaway best seller—eight reprintings and four editions in seven years—entitled *The Passing of the Great Race* (guess which one!). Grant's work was introduced by another academic luminary, Henry Fairfield Osborn, research professor of zoology at Columbia University.

The most pressing task facing the country, Osborn insisted, was "the conservation and multiplication for our country of the best spiritual, moral, intellectual and physical forces of heredity; thus only will the integrity of our institutions be maintained in the future." Osborn, in his introduction, and Grant, in the body of his work, admitted that even the "lowest races" had some good genes, "but they are certainly more widely and uniformly distributed in some [races] than in others. Thus conservation of that race which has given us the true spirit of Americanism is not a matter either of racial pride or of racial prejudice; it is a matter of love of country, of a true sentiment which is based upon knowledge and the lessons of history rather than upon the sentimentalism which is fostered by ignorance." The future of the Republic was threatened by the erosion of American institutions and "their insidious replacement by traits of less noble character." All that, translated, said, "Keep those people with their inferior genes out of here!"

Grant's book is a long, tedious discussion of race, starting with Eolithic man, with charts, maps, and diagrams, appendices, a "documentary supplement" and a bibliography. In his introduction to the fourth edition, the author is more ominous than ever, declaring that "this generation must completely repudiate the proud boast of our fathers that they acknowledged no "distinction in 'race, creed, or color,' or else the native American must turn the page of history and write: 'FINIS AMERICAE.' "

Such ideas now seem, fortunately, hopelessly retrograde; that is not to say that some Americans do not cling stubbornly to them in the face of "new" scientific evidence which discredits them. But science is, of course, not the issue. It is a matter of morality. Racist notions, scientific or unscientific, are morally reprehensible, and that is all decent people have ever had to know about the subject.

But that is not, by any means, the last word on the subject of immigration. At the beginning of this work we made the ambitious claim that we would attempt to understand the United States as a vitally important part of a larger history—that of the human race—and that an American historian was under the most urgent and particular obligation to make such an attempt because we exist by virtue of the peoples of the world coming into the vast continent of America and making it a nation by their coming (and, as we have had occasion to note in this chapter, often going out again). In that perpetual and mysterious inflowing we were continually renewed. Not only did the newcomers bring their own aspirations and preconceptions with them, their expectations of a wider, fairer, more generous life (too often, as we have seen, cruelly disappointed), but they also brought with them their own particular *humanities*, their fullness and completeness as human beings formed by centuries of cultural interchange and cultural definition. We have, I suspect, never sufficiently appreciated or understood this simple and essential fact. In a certain sense it can never be understood; its potency exceeds our imagination. But it is there, nevertheless, and it is as much a part of our and the world's future as it is of our past.

Eugen Rosenstock-Huessy, the German historian-philosopher, himself an immigrant, accused the United States in 1918 of believing that its immigrants were "something 'natural.' " He wrote: "America does not consider that these English, Germans, Irish, Poles, Italians had already been stamped and educated by the law of the old fatherland before they filled the new world in the stormy drive for freedom. . . . Year in year out Europe delivered to America adult, full-grown freemen and colonists. Europeans were the bricks with which America could build its house."

That was Jane Addams's vision, too. "In the midst of the modern city which, at moments, seems to stand only for the triumph of the strongest, the successful exploitation of the weak, the ruthlessness and hidden crime which follow in the wake of the struggle for existence on its lowest terms," she wrote, "there come daily—at least to American cities—accretions of simple people [the immigrants] who carry in their hearts a desire for mere goodness." Indeed, it was among "this huge mass of the unsuccessful" that we had the best hope of finding a "medium" in which "the first growth of the new compassion" could take place. There people were "reduced to the fundamental equalities and universal necessities of human life itself, and they inevitably develop the power of association which comes from daily contact with those who are unlike each other in all save the universal characteristics of man." In that submerged mass of often desperate humanity were intimations "of a new peace and holiness," issuing forth "from broken human nature itself, out of the pathetic striving of ordinary men, who make up the common substance of life; from those who have been driven by economic pressure or governmental oppression out of a score of nations." Far more than the "successful," they "serve God for nought"; they offered reason to hope that we were "emerging from a period of industrialism into a period of humanitarianism. . . ." The larger cities were thus naturally the "centers of radicalism," as they had been traditionally the "cradles of liberty." The human possibilities of the city or, more accurately, of the immigrant in the city seemed to Jane Addams to extend even to the hope of peace. "It is possible," she wrote in 1907, "that we shall be saved from warfare by the 'fighting rabble' itself, by the 'quarrelsome mob' turned into kindly citizens of the world through the pressure of a cosmopolitan neighborhood. It is not that they are shouting for peace—on the contrary, if they shout at all, they will continue to shout for war—but that they are really attaining cosmopolitan relations through daily experience. They will probably believe for a long time that war is noble and necessary both to engender and cherish patriotism; and yet all of the time below their shouting, they are living in the kingdom of human kindness. They are laying the simple and inevitable foundations for an international order as the foundations of tribal and national morality have always been laid." So all those who cherished peace must eschew "unreal high-sounding phrases" and surrender themselves to "those ideals of the humble, which all religious teachers unite in declaring to be the foundations of a sincere moral life."

The Farmers

Among Roosevelt's numerous presidential commissions was one on country life, headed by Liberty Hyde Bailey, professor of agriculture at Cornell. Henry Wallace, publisher of *Wallace's Farmer* and perhaps the most famous farmer-editor of the Midwest, was another member, as was Walter Hines Page, editor of *The World's Work*. (One way to make sure the work of the commissions was well publicized was to appoint several prominent editors to each commission.) Inevitably Gifford Pinchot, perpetual, revolving commissioner, was a member. The Russell Sage Foundation paid the modest expenses.

The charge to the Country Life Commission was to consider how the "farmer should get the largest possible return in money, comfort, and social advantages from the crop he grows" as well as "the largest possible return in crops from the land he farms. . . . The great rural interests are human interests, and good crops are of little value to the farmer unless they open the door to a good kind of life on the farm."

The commission held thirty public hearings, to which farmers and, equally important, their wives came in substantial numbers to testify about their needs and aspirations. The commission, which also circulated thousands of questionnaires to farm families, eventually issued a report which deplored the pinched and narrow lives of many farm families and urged, above all, "a more creative social life" for farmers and their families. In Pinchot's words, "the great problem . . . was not a problem of crops, but of human lives."

The burgeoning of "presidential government, " especially in the form of commissions, caused first considerable uneasiness and then strong resentment in congressional bosoms. The Commission on Country Life was particularly offensive to representatives from the farm states, who viewed it as an unwelcome intrusion by the Federal government into matters reserved for the states. What Gifford Pinchot called their "venomous hostility" was expressed in the refusal of Congress to appropriate money to have the report printed and circulated. (The Spokane Chamber of Commerce put up the necessary $25,000 for publication of the report. In 1909 Congress passed the Tawney Amendment to the sundry civil appropriations bill, forbidding the President to appoint any "commission of inquiry" without the authorization of Congress.)

In 1900 the number of people engaged in agriculture was 10,433,219, and there were almost 6,000,000 farms. In the period between 1890 and 1900 a territory almost equal to the combined areas of France and Germany was added to the farm land of the United States. Amos Pinchot, Gifford's brother, testifying before the Commission on Industrial Relations, took note of the fact that the number of tenant farmers was increasing four times as fast as the number of owner farmers, who were often subject to heavy mortgages. Ranches in the 200,000- to 1,300,000-acre range were not uncommon.

Year after year small farmers were driven off their farms or forced into tenancy by the movement toward centralization and mass production, by the need for capital for increasingly expensive farm equipment, by the cost of money (high interest rates), and by the unpredictability of commodity prices. Professor Charles Alvord, manager of a 12,000-acre Texas farm that employed a largely Mexican work force, testifying before the Commission on Industrial Relations, described a labor system little different from that which prevails today on large ranches in the Southwest and Far West.

We should have by now no illusion that the story of American agriculture was one of verdant acres and smiling, prosperous farmers. Certainly there were many such, but there were millions of farms where desperate tenants (or small owners) lived in poverty and squalor. Had that not been the case, there would not have been, we may be sure, a Populist Party.

Moreover, even in the more prosperous farming regions, the lives of farmers and their families were often bleak and pinched, as the charge to the Country Life Commission suggested. Emma Goldman found the farmer of Montana very little different from "his New England brother . . . just as inhospitable, as close-fisted . . . unkind, greedy, and suspicious of strangers." Kate Austen explained the bizarre sexual practices of Missouri farmers to Emma Goldman as the result of the boredom and cultural aridity of their lives.

The trouble with the farmers was, in the words of the muckraking journalist Charles Edward Russell, "that for all their toil, skill, care, fortitude, and privations they had nothing to show except the bare fact of an existence kept by a hand-to-hand fight against adversity. Except in rare and favored circumstances, no one could win even a moderate fortune at farming. . . . To win even this barren fruitage he must not only work like a horse in a treadmill but endure a horrible isolation . . . industry, sobriety, integrity, frugality, all the virtues praised in song and story might work gloriously elsewhere but they broke down at the farm gate. Blight overhung the entire business. . . . The farmer fed all other men and lived himself upon scraps." Russell, in his years in Midwestern farm towns, "seldom saw a farmer . . . that did not look worsted in the battle of life."

In the opinion of Oscar Ameringer, a German-born reformer, much of the fault lay with the farmer himself. Without a tradition of husbandry to draw on, he looked on land as a commodity rather than as something held in trust, as it were, for the future generations. "What a tragedy," he wrote, "that so many American farmers have treated soil as dirt under their feet! What a disaster they did not look on farming as a great art, and freest, most soul-satisfying mode of human living! Instead they conceived it only as a means to make a profit, and so in the end made themselves the slaves of industry, capital, and speculators."

Ameringer believed that the Homestead Act should have forbidden the resale of land so acquired to large farm corporations. Many Homestead Act farms had been sold by farmers who remained on the land as tenants or were saddled with large mortgages. The farmers' indebtedness had reached $9,000,000,000, a sum so vast that if the interest had been paid in full, it would have been sufficient to buy the entire domestic wheat crop.

In all investigations of farm life, tenancy was the villain. It was to agriculture what low wages, long hours, and dangerous working conditions were to the industrial laborer. Tenancy in Texas had increased from 37.6 percent of all farms in 1880 to more than 53 percent in 1910. In Oklahoma the overall tenancy rate was 54 percent, and in the most heavily agricultural counties it was more than 68 percent. "Without the labor of the entire family," the commissioners noted, "the tenant farmer is helpless. As a result not only is his wife prematurely broken down, but the children remain uneducated and without the hope of any condition better than that of their parents . . . a very large proportion of the tenants' families are insufficiently clothed, badly housed, and underfed." Ninety-five percent were "hopelessly in debt."

T. A. Hickey, editor of the *Rebel* in Hallettsville, Texas, submitted a folder of letters written by desperate tenant farmers. The tone of a few suggests the whole: "Dear Hickey: The question now with us is, 'Can we stand the pressure?' The speculators are hovering over us like a gang of vultures. The trusts have raised the prices on almost all household commodities. The banks' high rate of interest and no price on cotton at all." Another tenant farmer, who had spent all his life working for a landlord, wrote: "[I] have worked and helped men pay for their land, school their children, build their fine houses and barns while me and mine lived in a shack and worked like Turks; our children grew up without education; and we are yet poor. . . . " He was broken in health. "Isn't it a shame to make a man slave for 60 years in order to spend the other few years of his life as an invalid?"

H. O. Sydow, an evangelical preacher and tenant farmer adept at conducting holiness tent meetings, began to preach on the text "Go now, you rich men, weep and howl for your miseries that shall come upon you. Your riches are corrupted and your garments are moth-eaten. . . . Behold the hire of the laborers who have reaped down your fields, which is of you kept back by fraud crieth, and the cries of them which have reaped are entered into the ears of the Lord of Sabaoth." Jesus, Sydow told his audiences, "preached an economic gospel as well as a spiritual. . . . We must change the system from private to public property of those industries that must be publicly used. Then everyone can sit down under their own vine and fig tree, where none can molest them or make them afraid. In a word Jesus denounced the system under which rent, interest, and profit is taken as robbery, and this is why the common people heard Him gladly." Sydow's landlord declared he was "tired of hearing socialism talked on his place," and Sydow was told he must move from the land he had farmed for ten years.

A. C. Walker of Baird, Texas, wrote to "Comrade Hickey" as "one of them, who are in the clutches of the capitalist's class. I could tell you of cases of renters and their conditions, sufferings, that you would not believe. . . . If I had money to invest in stocks or bonds, railroads or banks, my first investment would be in good Socialist literature for the workers. That is to my mind the only hope of deliverance from peonage. . . . Give us Socialism and the religion of our Lord and Savior Jesus Christ will move up on a higher plane of Christian living than ever before."

P. W. Reasoner of Blossom, Texas, wrote: "I have 50 acres of land myself, title clear, but I am unable to get shoes for my wife unless I have the cash. We are still here, and we are both getting old. I am nearly 70 years old and am a crippled old relief soldier. Our children are all married and gone; most of them are capital slaves. If we could get a good organizer in this country I believe that it would almost go socialistic. . . ."

Another letter writer blamed the unhappy state of the tenant farmers of Texas on the "big land hoarders" who forced "the renters to plant nothing but cotton, until cotton put us on starvation. They would not let us renters plant corn and raise stock."

Judge M. M. Brooks was a large landowner in Macon, Mississippi. His 5,000 acres of "black" cotton land were farmed by an uncounted number of tenants. In Brooks's opinion all the troubles of the tenant farmers were due to agitators (whom he called Jack Cades after the English highwayman) and their own shiftlessness. The agitators had been sent by the Lord "to try our patience. . . . They go running around the country talking about the tragedy of the tenant farmers when we were in absolute harmony before these Jack Cades began to sing their siren song. . . . The increase in tenancy is not because of the impoverishment of the tenants but it is their improvidence." The judge's principal wrath was reserved for those who kicked the Constitution around. "I have had enough of this," he declared, "and unless there is a return to decency in this country and to more patriotic desire to assert the sanctity of property rights and the permanency of the Constitution I fear they will be thrown away."

The Farmers' Educational and Cooperative Union of Texas was just such an organization of Jack Cades as Judge Brooks had railed against. In its "Declaration of Purposes," it declared, "This institution is based upon the principles of equity, justice, and the Golden Rule." It was dedicated to opposing "the mortgage and credit systems . . . to assist its members in buying and selling . . . to educate the agricultural classes in the science of agriculture . . . to strive constantly for harmony and good will among all mankind, and to especially cultivate fraternity—brotherly love—among members of the union," and to encourage "the rigid enforcement of law for the suppression of vice and immorality." Its members must be farmers and believe "in the existence of a Supreme Being."

At the end of the New Orleans dockworkers' strike, Ameringer found himself in the novel position of being offered a job by the Jeans Foundation to "uplift" the poor whites and blacks of the South. Andrew Carnegie was a member of the foundation's board of directors, as was the Ohio Republican Charles Taft.

Ameringer was born during the Franco-Prussian War in August, 1870, at Achstetten in the valley of the Danube. Apprenticed as a cabinetmaker, he was a wild and rebellious youth, scandalizing his pious neighbors. "There were only two courses for young hellions like me," he wrote in his autobiography, "gallows and hell—or America. So to America I went, partly pushed, but mostly drawn, some eight months before my sixteenth birthday . . . " and a few months ahead of the draft. In the United States the young immigrant made a precarious living playing the cornet in bands that enlivened the atmosphere of Cincinnati's numerous saloons. In addition, he devoured biographies of famous Americans from George Washington and Thomas Jefferson, a special hero, to Benjamin Franklin and Andrew Jackson, Tom Paine and Sam Adams, and in the process he taught himself to read English. Now he was ready to become a real American. He fell under the spell of Mark Twain and Bret Harte, Bill Nye and Artemus Ward. They completed the Americanization that Washington and Jefferson had begun; Ameringer learned American humor, "more spontaneous and bubbling than the beer-soaked, smoke-laden, mother-in-law belabored humor of Germany! And so, without homework, prescribed lessons, punishment, rewards or examinations, this best of all studies led me from book to book until, almost unaware, I had acquired the language, history, and some of the literature of my new homeland. . . . " Ameringer found that "by investing five cents in a schooner of beer and holding on to the evidence of purchase," he could eat his fill "of such delicacies as rye bread, cheese, hams, sausage, pickled and smoked herrings, sardines, onions, radishes, and pumpernickel." When work at a steady job was not to be found, he eked out a precarious living by following wagons loaded with coal to their destination and offering, for ten cents, to store the coal away. A bonanza came when he carried a ton of coal up a flight of stairs to a lawyer's office and received a quarter for his labors.

A young friend taught Ameringer to draw and paint, and soon he found work painting scenes on screens for the windows of saloons and private houses. Next it was landscapes and flowers on wooden bread bowls at $1 a bowl for "the aspiring wives of middle-class Germans." He made portraits from photographs and painted butterflies on ladies' kimonos. Pickaway County, stretching out from Cincinnati, was filled with the abundant farms of Germans, "farmers by the grace of God. To them the soil was not dirt under their feet to be ruined, raped, and robbed. They were not dirt farmers, but *Landbauern*, soil builders. Farming was a noble calling, far above that of merchant, lawyer, politician or money lender." They were "a proud, self-respecting lot all around." In the home of one of them, Dan Hitler, Ameringer was introduced to Milton and Dickens and to Plutarch's *Lives*, Gibbon's *Decline and Fall,* and books on European history.

He began to write humorous pieces and short stories, and bored with painting the bland faces of farmers and their wives and progeny, he organized a brass band. Gradually he found himself drawn into union activity and radical politics. He acknowledged a special debt to Steuben DeKalb Wham of Illinois, "one of the founders of the Populist and Socialist Parties" and Henry Heitholt, "in the long-ago a fellow cabinet maker, later frontier farmer, now retired oil man. . . ." Ameringer began to see his life as a "Utopian excursion in the realm of landless men and manless land."

Henry George's *Progress and Poverty* and Edward Bellamy's *Looking Backward* turned the cornet-playing young immigrant into a single taxer, a socialist, and an ardent reformer. He enlisted in Tom Johnson's brigade of idealistic young men, determined to rid Ohio politics of corruption. Newton D. Baker was an ally, and Frederic Howe, "as clean and sincere as they make them," was another. Ameringer ran for the Ohio legislature only to find that he had been used by both Democrats and Republicans, who were united in one thing: They both abhorred reformers. Ameringer's next venture was editing a Socialist newspaper, *The Labor World.* He found soon that the rewards were almost entirely psychological. "Running a labor paper," he decided, "is like feeding melting butter on the end of a hot awl to an infuriated wildcat." It became evident that from the point of view of a labor union official, the role of the editor of a labor journal was that of "court jester and press agent." Independent opinions and, more especially, radical views were deplored.

Ameringer then found himself working in Oklahoma, "the most promising field of uplift." The uplift was to be accomplished by education and organization, both with strong socialist bent. The year was 1907, a panic year when tens of thousands of Oklahoma farmers found themselves on the verge of bankruptcy and, in the more extreme cases, of starvation. Ameringer checked in with the state office of the Socialist Party in Oklahoma City. He, like Algie Martin Simons, who soon became a close friend, was convinced that farmers were poor material for Marxist propaganda. Call a farmer a proletarian, and you were as likely as not to feel the force of a large, weather-beaten fist. Farmers, Ameringer insisted to his more doctrinaire Socialist friends, were "capitalists exploiting wage labor. They owned the means of production. They had a good deal more to lose than their chains." Ameringer, who was thinking of those prosperous farmers he had seen in Pickaway County, Ohio, so informed the secretary of the Socialist Party, Otto Branstetter, who heard him out politely and then suggested that he might find a different kind of farmer in Oklahoma. So it proved. Ameringer's first speaking date was in the rural town of Harrah, twenty miles east of Oklahoma City. All roads to the town turned out to be under water; it took him the better part of a day and some wading to reach the town. The meeting was in a one-room schoolhouse, and the drenched audience included numerous babies and damp children. "All were wretchedly dressed: faded blue jeans for the men; faded Mother Hubbards and poke bonnets for the women. These people," Ameringer added, "had trudged in soaking rain, or come in open wagons or on horseback or muleback to hear a socialist speech—and they were farmers! This indescribable aggregation of moisture, steam, dirt, rags, unshaven men, slatternly women and fretting children were farmers! . . . I had come upon another America!"

The chairman had swum the rain-swollen North Canadian River in order to preside. After the meeting Ameringer was offered the hospitality of a "comrade's" home. He lived in a "typical tenant shack" of the kind Ameringer would soon "know so well, and hate so deeply." A soiled cotton comforter on a wooden pallet was the guest bed. Mosquitoes with stingers like augur bits were his nocturnal companions, and in the morning, after a sleepless night, breakfast consisted of corn bread, fat meat, molasses and "coffee" made of chicory. It was the beginning of a painful revelation for the young Socialist organizer. He found "toothless old women with sucking infants on their withered breasts . . . a hospitable old hostess, around thirty or less, her hands covered with rags and eczema, offering me a biscuit with those hands, apologizing that her biscuits were not as good as she used to make them because with her sore hand she no longer could knead the dough as it ought to be done." Ameringer saw young men and women not yet twenty years old, toothless, eaten by hookworms, malnutrition, and pellagra, and "tottering old male wrecks with the infants of their fourteen-year-old wives on their laps. . . . I saw humanity at its lowest possible level of degradation and decay." Their landlords, "well-fed hypocrites," marched off to church "while fattening like latter-day cannibals on the share croppers." Ameringer saw "wind-jamming, hot-air spouting politicians geysering Jeffersonian platitudes about equal rights to all and special privileges to none" while "addressing as wretched a set of abject slaves as ever walked the face of the earth, anywhere or at any time." It all seemed to him "a black betrayal of democracy, and an insult to Christianity."

There was an additional irony. Much of the land farmed by tenant farmers in the state was owned by Indians. The tenant farmers of Oklahoma were, in Ameringer's judgment, "worse fed, worse clothed, worse housed, more illiterate than the Chicago packing house wops and bohunks. . . . " Their living standard "was so far below that of the sweatshop workers of the New York east side . . . that comparison could not be thought of." They were not immigrants but "old American stock." They were "white, native, Protestant Americans working as the land slaves tenants and share croppers of the aboriginal Indians."

Determined to organize the tenant farmers, Ameringer "ate hog belly, corn pone, baking-powder biscuits, poke greens, and New Orleans molasses" until his stomach "cried for mercy." Mosquitoes and bedbugs made his nights hideous. Often the floors were simply packed dirt. More pretentious dugouts had floors composed of gypsum, salt, and wood ashes and a single glass window. The others depended for ventilation on an open door. Ameringer called Oklahoma "the tenant, bedbug and Indian country." Cowmen and cotton farmers had moved into the state from Texas. Sharecroppers and poor whites had arrived from the South, and from the North cow, hog, and wheat farmers had made their appearance. In addition, a number of the members of Debs's American Railway Union, defeated in the Pullman strike, had turned their hands to farming or mining.

Ameringer found that he could combine his talents as a musician with his spiel as a recruiter for the Socialist Party very effectively. He began his meetings (and interspersed them) with such rural favorites as "Turkey in the Straw," "Arkansas Traveler," and "Everybody Works but Father." At one point he joined up with a hypnotist named Jim Mooney, and the two of them spread the gospel of socialism wherever they could muster up an audience. "You are John D. Rockefeller," Mooney would announce to some disheveled bumpkin. "You own all the oil wells, refineries and tank wagons in the country." Indicating another hayseed, he would shout, "You are Pierpont Morgan. You own all the banks, railroads and insurance companies in the country. And you, over there"—to another—"are Andrew Carnegie, you own all the steel mills and libraries in the country. All of your pockets are bulging with money. . . . Now do business." The hypnotized subjects would immediately begin to buy and sell railroads and steel mills to each other to the uninhibited delight of their fellows. "The combination of hypnotism and socialism with clarinet obbligato was literally a howling success," Ameringer wrote. "The fame of our team spread all across the corner where Texas and Arkansas slobber over into Oklahoma, as the saying goes."

Oklahoma was divided by the tracks of the Santa Fe Railroad into the Indian Territory and "old Oklahoma," which had been opened to settlement by whites. Ameringer observed that many of the older settlers still lived in their sod huts. "Virtually all of them," he noted, "had cows, chickens, hogs, sheep, a vegetable garden, and had planted some fruit trees. All this meant a better balanced diet, explaining the greater energy and higher degree of health and education of the population as compared with that of the tenant population of Indian Territory." Ameringer's first meetings were modest in size, usually held in schoolhouses or churches, but as membership in the Socialist Party grew, summer encampments, the "lineal descendants of the religious and Populist camp meetings of former days, " were added. The audiences came in covered wagons and brought their own food. The organizers of the encampment provided toilet facilities, water, and firewood. Meetings were held in a large circus tent, and the atmosphere of a revival prevailed. Included in the ranks of the Socialists were bankers and merchants from the small towns that served as trading centers for the farms. Ameringer recalled a Socialist local in Kiowa County that included the town bankers, a druggist, and a lumberyard owner. An average of 5,000 people came to each encampment, which was generally welcomed by the townspeople because of the business it brought to nearby towns. In Elk City, Ameringer recalled, most of the local stores displayed the red flag and bunting of "international brotherhood." What Ameringer called the "local agitators" were nearly all ex-Populists and all of old American ancestry. In the fall of 1908 the Socialist Party held a week-long encampment near Hugo, the county seat of Choctaw and the Nation. Debs was the featured speaker.

The encampments started with the singing of Socialist songs, many of them derived from Populist tunes. After singing school there were lessons on history and economics. The textbook was Walter Thomas Mills's *The Struggle for Existence*. Frederick Jackson Turner's *The Frontier in American History* was another popular work, and Ameringer contributed a text written by him for children, entitled *The Life and Deeds of Uncle Sam: A Little History for Big Children*. By 1917 a half million copies had been sold to incipient young Socialists.

The noon dinner was the principal meal of the day, and once it was over, the campers gathered in the big tent for singing and instrumental music. Singers and musicians were recruited on the spot and coached by Ameringer, who prefaced his instruction with a brief lecture on classical music, which, borrowing from Bill Nye, he described as "a helluva lot better than it sounds." To make the point, selections were played from Mozart, Beethoven, Bach, and Wagner, plus "some gems from Stephen Foster." Kate Richards O'Hare, a militant young Socialist from western Kansas, was a popular speaker, as was Caroline Low, a former schoolteacher from Kansas City.

The labors of Ameringer, Low, Mills, O'Hare, and Debs himself bore fruit in Oklahoma. At the height of its influence, the Socialist Party counted in its ranks almost a third of the people of the state. It elected six members to the state legislature and a number more to county offices. Ameringer himself ran for mayor of Oklahoma City and was defeated by only a few hundred votes.

When Charles Edward Russell's Chautauqua tour took him to the Souris River region of North Dakota, he discovered that one farm in five had been foreclosed by the banks. Here he had his first encounter with sod houses, many of them eroded by rain and parched by the sun until they looked "like something with eczema." He could hardly imagine them to be the habitations of human beings. From one emerged a man carrying a baby. "Behind him was a glimpse of a dark and dismal cavern and of a work-weary woman. . . . The whole prospect seemed cursed and blighted with the extreme of poverty; hardly on the East

Side of New York had I seen anything so depressing. . . . They called this country North Dakota. It should have been called the Land of Broken Lives." The farmer seemed the victim of forces beyond his control. At every step middlemen preyed upon his crop. The banks charged exorbitant interest on the money he was forced to borrow to buy seed and fertilizer—in the aggregate as much as 18 percent. He was charged 8 percent "dockage" for presumed impurities in his wheat. Finally, the scales on which his crop was weighed were often fixed, and it is estimated that in one year more than 500,000 bushels of wheat were lost between the farm and the mill. The railroad rates were excessive, and year after year farmers slipped deeper into debt peonage until they were little better than slaves to the bankers and grain buyers.

One of the heroes of North Dakota was Edwin Ladd, president of the state Agricultural College, who undertook to press on the legislature some of the nation's earliest pure food laws. Ladd made no bones about his Socialist leanings, and when he wished to go abroad at the time of the Peace Conference, the attorney general of the United States denied him a passport on the ground that he was "a radical, a red, a dangerous person."

In an alliance with A. C. Townley, a short, sturdy reticent man, and a gifted organizer, Ladd formed the North Dakota Nonpartisan League, which directed its attention to protecting farmers from exploitation by inspecting scales, doing away with dockage charges, and building state-owned grain elevators and flour mills. In addition, freight rates within the state would be controlled. Recruited for the fight to wrest control of the state from the banks, grain speculators, and railroads, Charles Edward Russell started the *Nonpartisan Leader,* the official newspaper of the movement. Contemptuous at first, the ruling powers in the state took alarm at the growth of the Nonpartisan League. The state was soon flooded with leaflets and flyers denouncing the league made up of Socialists and anarchists as "a swindle, a fraud, a crime." Banks began to call loans and foreclose mortgages on farmers who were vocal in support of the league. By 1916 it was clear that the league was a serious threat. Russell and Townley recruited a popular young farmer from Hoople in the Red River Valley who had been a former football star at the University of North Dakota and was well known throughout the state to run for the Senate. He won, as did the whole state ticket except for the candidate for state treasurer, who was apparently defeated for no better reason than that he was a Catholic. The lieutenant governor, who chose the committees in the state legislature, although elected on the Nonpartisan ticket, turned against the league and stacked the important committees with conservative old-guard Republicans. Most efforts at reform were blocked by hold-overs from the prior election, but in the midterm elections of 1918 the Nonpartisan League completed its triumph and took the state firmly in hand. A series of spectacular reforms followed: a state-owned bank to lend money to farmers at reasonable rates; a state inspector of grades, weights, and measures; funds to build a state-owned mill and elevators; an inheritance and income tax; compensation for injured workers; an amendment to provide for the recall of public officers; state help in building private storage facilities. All in all, the session of the North Dakota legislature that followed the election of 1918 was undoubtedly the most productive (or "socialistic") session in the nation's history. A counterattack against the North Dakota "Bolsheviks" was promptly mounted. When the Nonpartisan League expressed opposition to World War I, it was branded treasonable. A number of its laws were delayed by litigation, tied up in the courts, and eventually declared unconstitutional by the United States Supreme Court. Efforts to build the elevators and establish the state bank were thwarted by the refusal of brokerage houses to float bond issues or banks to loan money.

The league soon extended to neighboring farm states. At the height of its influence it had more than 250,000 dues-paying members in thirteen states and certainly four or five times that number of sympathizers. "Not all of the Townley dream came true," Russell wrote a decade later. The "Stone Wall" of prejudice and reaction was too strong. But Russell was convinced that it made "North Dakota the most independently minded constituency in America. The spirit of the League survived long after its bones were buried."

In California the exploitation of farmers and farm workers by the big farm corporations was especially egregious. In the Durst fields, the hops pickers were forced to live in "a motley collection of tents, lumber stockades and gunny sacks stretched over fences." Tents were rented by the Dursts, who charged seventy-five cents a week. Here again was a congress of nations: Mexicans, Syrians, Spanish, Lithuanians, Italians, Greeks, Poles, Irish, Puerto Ricans, Swedes, Japanese, and Americans. For hundreds of workers the Dursts had provided eight malodorous toilets, crawling with flies. There was no water in the fields, and workers suffered from diarrhea, dysentery, malaria, and typhoid fever. "Lemonade" made from citric acid was sold for five cents a glass. When the workers struck under the banner of the IWW, violence flared. Armed county officials, trying to disperse a meeting of workers, fired or were fired upon. The district attorney and the sheriff were killed, a Puerto Rican black man was killed, and a young boy and a number of workers were injured. The sheriff's posse was driven off, and the governor then ordered militia to the hops ranch. Four IWW officials were arrested and charged with murder. Two—Richard Ford and Herman Suhr—were convicted of murder and sentenced to life imprisonment at Folsom penitentiary.

A state report on the California agricultural labor camps found that 96 percent were below the state board of health standards, while 40 percent had no bathing facilities and 70 percent had "filthy" toilets.

Under heavy pressure from the large agricultural corporations, the small farmers found an unusual ally in Aaron Sapiro. Sapiro was born in San Francisco in 1884 and, after the death of his father from alcoholism, was raised in an orphanage. A trustee of the orphanage, Rabbi Jacob Nieto, impressed with his unusual intelligence, arranged for him to attend the Hebrew Union College in Cincinnati. A history major and a rabbinical student, Sapiro earned a B.A. and a master's degree before deciding to become a lawyer rather than a rabbi and graduated from Hastings Law School near the top of his class. Launched as a lawyer, he became an apprentice in reform to Colonel Harris Weinstock and David Lubin, half brothers who had made their fortune as retail merchants and retired at an early age to devote their lives to good works. They had decided to concentrate their energies on the complex problem of farm prices. The fluctuations in commodity prices kept the farmers in a constant state of uncertainty that in bad times often brought with it financial ruin. Lubin had been one of the founders, in Rome, of the International Institute of Agriculture. Weinstock's career of service in the cause of reform culminated in his appointment by President Wilson to the Commission on Industrial Relations. Sapiro, following in the path of his mentors, was soon secretary of the National Liberal Immigration League, established to fight for more enlightened treatment of immigrants, especially those from the Far East. He was also secretary of the Western Assembly of the Jewish Chautauqua.

Weinstock's solution to the problem of marketing agricultural products was to form statewide marketing associations of farmers—in effect cooperatives—by means of which farmers could exercise some control over commodity prices. Weinstock enlisted Sapiro, who immediately set about to make himself an expert on the history of co-operatives in every modern nation. He traveled up and down the state addressing farmers' organizations, making "the marketing of a barrel of apples more exciting than a Tale from Boccaccio and the signing of a cooperative agreement seem as vital to social justice and progress as Magna Charta," in the words of a friend.

Perhaps the most important rural institution remained the Chau-tauqua. In the depressed farming regions of the Middle West, from the sun-baked Texas flatlands through the Oklahoma Panhandle, north to the bleak but beautiful Dakotas, Chautauqua lecturers like Oscar Ameringer and Charles Edward Russell and the most admired orator of them all, William Jennings Bryan, carried the message of socialism (or reform through the Democratic Party, of course, in Bryan's case) and of the hope of a better day.

The band of hardy Chautauquans who took to the lecture trail around the country, visiting Chautauquas in innumerable towns and cities, divided the circuit into the "Bed Bug Belt, the Cyclone Belt, the Broiling Belt, and the Hellish Hotel Belt." The Cyclone Belt, Russell decided, was the most dangerous, if not the most uncomfortable, since Chautauqua meetings were commonly held in large tents singularly susceptible to unanticipated tornadoes. One of the seasoned veterans of the circuit gave his secrets to the novice Charles Edward Russell. According to Russell, "he explained that the first thing to remember was that no audience really wanted to hear anybody, but only went because it had to go . . . [and] the man that could make all those people forget the miseries of the hard benches and the heat could have their support and money every time." The formula to follow was to keep the speech relatively short and fill it with homilies. Talk for ten minutes about the little red schoolhouse, then ten minutes on the value of early education and training in good habits, followed by reflections on the "dear old parson of the little old church on the hill. . . . Next get into the principles of success. This is what snatches them every time. Hon-esty, fidelity to duty, industry, specially industry (go heavy on indus-try—every farmer has his hired man), have been the touchstones of your own success. Tell about early struggles and privations and ring in a lot about the poor, poor farm boys that have become millionaires." The home was the final theme. "Show that it is the American home that has made America great." The talk must be larded with stories, and the stories must be old. "There is nothing an audience resents so much as a brand-new story." Another Chautauqua regular advised

Russell to stick to home and mother; the next best line was to be "optimistic and reassuring. The banks like that and the banks ran most of the Chautauquas."

One of Russell's most vivid memories was of the natural amphitheater at Ashland, Oregon, with a great crowd "waiting to hear Mr. Bryan for the nineteenth time." Many had traveled more than 100 miles to hear the orator. At Shelbyville, Illinois, some 30,000 turned out to hear him.

At the height of the fashion it was estimated that there were more than 22,000 Chautauquas in the United States and Canada.

As we have noted earlier, the Department of Agriculture performed important services for farmers, and with the increasing emphasis on the role of the Federal government in alleviating suffering and redressing inequities, the range of government services for the farmer was greatly expanded. It was the estimate of Wilson's secretary of agriculture, David Franklin Houston, that less than 60 percent of the arable land in the United States was under cultivation, and of that not more than 12 percent was "yielding reasonably full returns." Houston saw a great challenge to the Department of Agriculture to improve both the methods of farming and the quality of life in rural America. Not only must farming be profitable, but "it must also be comfortable, healthful, and attractive." It had been his experience as a young man in Illinois that the more prosperous farmers had "moved to town to enjoy educational and social advantages" and let their farms to tenants, who seldom farmed them as successfully as the original owners. "As a consequence," Houston wrote, "Illinois is one of the tenancy plague spots in the country. The remedy," he believed, "involved better methods of production through the use of good cultural practices, soil improvement, plant and animal breeding according to the best known principles, the control and eradication of plant and animal diseases, the standardization of products, the development of standard grain and cotton grades . . . , more economical methods and processes of marketing including the effective cooperation among producers, credit on reasonable terms, good roads, and modern schools." The last two were of special importance, Houston felt.

The means the secretary chose to effect such changes were through an Office of Information, directed to publish a growing stream of "farmers' bulletins," using "the simplest and clearest English and dealing with all the problems farmers encountered." County agricultural agents were given the best training in agricultural colleges and kept up-to-date on the latest improvements by refresher courses and seminars.

Houston's most successful innovation was that of calling on states to match Federal grants in order to facilitate the flow of information from the Federal and state departments and agencies to the farmer. In a number of states the department sponsored the starting of model farms where farmers could come see what was being done to make farming more productive. The Agricultural Educational Extension Act of May, 1914, provided that only when the secretary of agriculture and the state college of agriculture had agreed on plans for the best use of the money would Federal funds be released. Each rural county— some 2,850—was to have at least two agents, ideally a man and a woman, specialists who could "give advice in the more complex and difficult problems."

Roosevelt gave relatively little attention to farm issues; it remained for Wilson's administration to establish the Office of Markets and Rural Organization to develop new methods of rural finance and marketing. The Federal Reserve Board was authorized to make agricultural paper eligible and extend its period from ninety days to six months. The Farm Loan Act set up banking machinery designed to meet the special credit needs of farmers and keep interest rates down. Desirable as such measures were, their effect was often to aid the larger farms and the farm owners more than the small or the tenant farmers. In good times they subsisted; in bad times they suffered disproportionately.

10

Losing Ground: Black Americans

Theodore Roosevelt had a patrician's friendly disposition toward black Americans. He had admired and generously acknowledged the fighting qualities of the 25th Infantry at San Juan Hill and vowed that he would always remember their valor. As governor of New York he had backed legislation to desegregrate the schools. As President, as we have already noted, he had invited Booker T. Washington to the White House, thereby throwing the South into a vituperative rage, and had appointed a number of blacks to Federal offices.

In 1903, after an outbreak of lynching, Roosevelt issued a public letter denouncing mob law. "The spirit of lawlessness," the President declared, "grows with what it feeds on. . . . In the recent cases of lynching over three-fourths were not for rape at all, but for murder, attempted murder, and even less heinous offenses . . . the history of these recent cases shows the awful fact that when the minds of men are habituated to the use of torture by lawless bodies to avenge crimes of a peculiarly revolting description, other lawless bodies will use torture in order to punish crimes of an ordinary type. Surely no patriot can fail to see the fearful brutalization and debasement which the indulgence of such a spirit and such practices inevitably portends."

The letter was welcomed, of course, by blacks, but it caused deep resentment in the South.

These modest gestures had earned him the devotion of most blacks. But Roosevelt, whose mother had been a Southern belle, confessed to the newspaper editor, Henry Stoddard, that the principal attraction in considering whether to run for the presidency in 1908 was the assurance by Southern Democrats with strong Republican leanings that he could "break the 'Solid South.'" Roosevelt was told that he could carry Kentucky and Tennessee, and probably Georgia and Texas as well. It was a tempting prospect—to be the first Republican president to break into the phalanx of Southern states—and it may have made him wary of espousing measures on behalf of blacks that might have alienated large blocks of Southern voters. It should be noted, on the other hand, that Roosevelt was attracted to the notion of cutting Southern representation in Congress in proportion to the disenfranchisement of Southern blacks. But in general he thought it futile to try to alleviate the plight of blacks through political measures. He had no sympathy with the efforts of "little solemn creatures like Norman Hapgood." Nor was there much hope from "the heirs of the Wendell Phillips and Lloyd Garrison people, the Oswald Villards, Rollo Ogdens, Carl Schurzes and Charles Francis Adamses . . ." who had "frittered away their influence until . . . they literally have not the slightest weight with either Democrats or Republicans; and moreover they are as irrational on this as on other subjects, so that no help whatever can be obtained from them."

Black leaders had been sustained through the horrors of Reconstruction by the conviction that their lot would improve. With the slaves freed, Frederick Douglass had been uncertain how his energies might best be employed in other causes. Henry Turner, John Roy Lynch, Robert Brown Elliott, and hundreds of other leaders and millions of ex-slaves had found the courage to endure in their fight for their civil rights in their faith that in the United States, a progressive nation, blacks, like other Americans, must in time experience the beneficent consequences of "progress."

In his inaugural address in 1880 President Garfield had declared, "The elevation of the negro race from slavery to the full rights of citizenship is the most important political change we have known since the adoption of the Constitution of 1787. No thoughtful man can fail to appreciate the beneficent effect upon our institutions and people.

It has freed us from the perpetual danger of war and dissolution. It has added immensely to the moral and industrial forces of our people. It has liberated the master and the slave from a relation which wronged and enfeebled both. It has given new inspiration to the power of self help in both races by making labor more honorable to one and more necessary to the other. . . . No doubt this great change has caused serious disturbance to our Southern communities. This is to be deplored, though it was perhaps unavoidable. But those who resisted the change should remember that under our institutions there was no middle ground for the negro race between slavery and equal citizenship. There can be no permanent disfranchised peasantry in the United States. Freedom can never yield its fullness of blessings so long as the law or its administration places the smallest obstacle in the pathway of any virtuous citizen. . . . " Blacks deserved "the generous encouragement of all good men. So far as my authority can lawfully extend, they shall enjoy the full and equal protection of the Constitution and the laws. . . . It is alleged that in many communities Negro citizens are practically denied the freedom of the ballot. . . . Bad local government is certainly a great evil, which ought to be prevented; but to violate the freedom and the sanctities of the suffrage is more than an evil. It is a crime which, if persisted in, will destroy the Government itself. . . . If in other lands it be high treason to compass the death of the king, it shall be counted no less a crime here to strangle our sovereign power and stifle its voice."

Not surprisingly Southern blacks took hope at the President's words, but Garfield was assassinated, and no subsequent president cared or dared to espouse their cause. With each year that passed the terrible weight of prejudice pressed them down. Not only did they not make that all-American progress that was the nation's proudest boast, they lost ground. Decade by decade such rights of citizenship as they had enjoyed during Reconstruction were stripped from them as it became more and more evident that the intention of the South was to push them down into the most humiliating and degraded condition and keep them there under a banner bearing the slogan "This is a white man's country."

For no blacks was the dose more bitter than for those who had fought in the Union armies, many of whom bore the scars of their service to their country. Henry Turner had been a chaplain with the 2nd North Carolina Volunteers in some of the bitterest fighting of the war. As bishop of the African Methodist Episcopal Church he had come to urge emigration for American blacks, convinced that they could never have even the rudiments of justice in the land of the free.

That the situation of American blacks was not merely regional is clear from a statement issued in 1896 by a meeting of New England blacks which declared, "This movement is deemed necessary because the colored citizen is discriminated against in so many depressing and injurious manners not withstanding the letter of the law does not favor the same. It is exhibited by political parties, State and National; it exhibits itself in business, in the manufactories, in obtaining employment as salesmen and saleswomen, in benevolent associations, in seeking decent tenements. No distinction is made as to intelligence, character, deportment or means among the colored people. We believe that the moral influence of the colored men of New England should be felt outside of all partisanship, in favor of a national administration that places the welfare of all above the success of parties and leaders."

The fact that in some Northern cities black voters held the balance between Democrats and Republicans won them exemption from the grosser forms of persecution that they suffered south of the Mason-Dixon Line, but it was more a matter of degree than of real substance. Even their votes were debased; they were induced to sell them for the paltriest returns.

W. E. B. Du Bois acknowledged that "the better class of Negroes," disgusted with the venality and corruption of American politics and anxious not to attract unfavorable attention to themselves, took little interest in politics. "The black vote that still remained was not trained and educated, but further debased by open and unblushing bribery, or force and fraud; until the Negro voter was thoroughly inoculated with the idea that politics was a method of private gain by disreputable means."

While the Republicans continued to pay lip service to the principle of black rights, they were careful to do nothing for blacks that might alienate white voters. As for Democratic candidates, they were at pains to affirm that blacks were an inferior race and should be kept in their place. William Jennings Bryan dissociated himself from blacks. Speaking in New York in the presidential campaign of 1908, he expressed his support for the disenfranchisement of black voters in the South, arguing that Southern whites had treated blacks better than blacks would have treated whites had they had political domination. Bryan's running mate, John Kern, was said to have attributed his defeat for the governorship of Indiana in 1900 to the opposition of black voters.

At a postelection banquet he had declared, "I am proud of the fact that I did not receive a Negro vote. I was elected by the white vote but defeated by the ignorant nigger vote."

W. E. B. Du Bois had been a delegate at the first Pan-African Conference held in London in 1900. There were only thirty-two delegates, and Du Bois was one of the featured speakers. There he reiterated the theme that he had woven through *The Souls of Black Folk:* "The problem of the twentieth century is the problem of the color line, the question as to how far differences of race . . . will hereafter be made the basis of denying to over half the world the right of sharing to their utmost ability the opportunities and privileges of modern civilization." Du Bois evoked the teachings of the Prince of Peace and "that slow but sure progress which has successively refused to let the spirit of class, of caste, of privilege, or of birth, debar from life, liberty and the pursuit of happiness a striving human soul. . . . Let not the spirit of Garrison, Phillips, and Douglass wholly die out in America; may the conscience of a great nation rise and rebuke all dishonesty and unrighteous oppression toward the American Negro, and grant to him the right of franchise, security of person and property, and generous recognition of the great work he has accomplished in a generation. . . . Thus we appeal with boldness and confidence to the Great Powers of the civilized world, trusting in the wide spirit of humanity, and a deep sense of justice of our age, for a generous recognition of the righteousness of our cause."

Du Bois's "Credo" was published in the *Independent* of October 6, 1904: "I believe in God who made of one blood all races that dwell on earth. I believe that all men, black and brown, and white, are brothers, varying, through Time and Opportunity, in form and gift and feature, but differing in no essential particular, and alike in soul and in the possibility of infinite development. Especially do I believe in the Negro Race; in the beauty of its genius, the sweetness of its soul, and its strength in that meekness which shall inherit this turbulent earth . . . knowing that men may be brothers in Christ, even though they be not brothers-in-law. . . . I believe in Service—humble reverent service . . . of the Master who summoned all them that labor and are heavy laden, making no distinction between the black sweating cotton-hands of Georgia and the First Families of Virginia. . . . Finally, I believe in Patience,—patience with the weakness of the Weak and the strength of the Strong, the prejudice of the Ignorant and the ignorance of the

Blind; patience with the tardy triumph of Joy and the chastening of Sorrow—patience with God."

Du Bois, along with Frederick L. McGhee and William Monroe Trotter, was one of the principal founders of the Niagara Movement in July, 1905. He explained it as an association of "ministers, lawyers, editors, business men and teachers." The movement was devoted to the principles of freedom of speech, manhood suffrage, "the abolition of caste distinctions based simply on race and color," and a "belief in the dignity of labor." The members were pledged to "push the matter of civil rights," to try to improve relations between blacks and organized labor, "to study Negro history, to develop Negro businesses, circulate information of interest to blacks, encourage education and fight ill health and crime among black people."

At the second meeting of the Niagara Movement, at Harpers Ferry in August, 1906, the delegates made a barefoot pilgrimage to the site of John Brown's execution. Du Bois addressed them there in more militant terms than he had used the year before. "Our demands are clear and unequivocal," he declared. "First, we would vote; with the right to vote goes everything: freedom, manhood, the honor of your wives, the chastity of your daughters, the right to work, and the chance to rise. . . . We want full manhood suffrage, and we want it now, henceforth and forever. . . . Here on the scene of John Brown's martyrdom we reconsecrate ourselves, our honor, our property to the final emancipation of the race which John Brown died to make free."

Meanwhile, the tally of lynchings and race riots, by no means confined to the South, mounted. Scarcely a month passed without its dreadful harvest of broken and mutilated black bodies. In the spring of 1906 a white woman in Atlanta, Georgia, declared that she had been raped by a black man. In the riot that ensued three young blacks in no way implicated in the woman's charges were murdered by a lynch mob, dozens of others were injured, black property was wantonly destroyed, and black schoolteachers, lawyers, and doctors were forced to march "like criminals . . . at the behest of the mob."

A few months later in Brownsville, Texas, a far more lurid episode took place. There some soldiers of the 25th Infantry, a black regiment, frustrated and angry at their abuse by local whites, "shot up" the town on the night of August 13, 1906, killing one white man and wounding two others. All efforts to bring the culprits to justice were thwarted by the refusal of their fellows to cooperate in the investigation that followed the shooting. The inspector general of the army thereupon recommended that the three companies of the 25th Regiment, from which the offenders apparently came, be discharged without honor. The 25th was one of the finest units in the regular army with a long record of valor in the Indian wars and in the Spanish-American War. Black Americans considered it both a symbol of their aspirations for equality and a prospect of future hope. Some of the troopers had served for twenty-five years or more, and six had won Medals of Honor. The manner in which the announcement was made was additionally insulting. Secretary of War William Howard Taft released word to the press the day after the congressional elections of 1906, an election in which the Republicans had retained control of the House, with, in certain Northern cities, the traditional support of black voters.

The action was bitterly denounced by the black press, and pressure was immediately brought on Roosevelt to reverse Taft's action, which had had his approval. T. Thomas Fortune, the editor of the *Age,* the most influential black paper in the country, declared, "It is carrying into the Federal Government the demand of the Southern white devils that innocent and law abiding black men shall help the legal authorities spy out and deliver practically, to the mob black men alleged to have committed some sort of crime. The spirit invoked is not only vicious and contrary to the spirit of our Constitution, but it is an outrage upon the rights of the citizens who are entitled in civil life to trial by jury and in military life to court martial." W. Calvin Chase, editor of the *Washington Bee,* another prominent black newspaper, wrote: "If this is military discipline, then we say to h—— with military discipline." If the soldiers had turned in their comrades to the authorities, they would certainly have been lynched, Chase declared. The discharge had at an instant destroyed the President's standing with black Americans: "Jefferson Davis is more honored today than Theodore Roosevelt. Benedict Arnold would have a monument erected to his memory sooner than Theodore Roosevelt."

A black journalist named Richard Thompson wrote to Booker T. Washington's secretary: "Roosevelt has made the mistake of his life in that 25th regiment discharge. . . . He may correct this thing, if he takes it in hand and rescinds the order in time. If he stands pat, his name will be an anathema to Negroes from now on." S. Laing Williams, a black leader in Chicago, wrote to Washington: "Things in Chicago are at fever heat in the race matter. You cannot find a Negro who is not denouncing the President in frightful terms of abuse. I never saw or heard anything like it. Mass meetings are held. . . . " The rector of the Abyssinian Baptist Church called for punishment to Republicans at the polls, adding, "Thus shall we answer Theodore Roosevelt, once enshrined in our hearts as Moses, now enshrouded in our scorn as Judas." The Reverend Adam Clayton Powell, Sr., declared to a *New York Times* reporter: "It is hard to believe that the man with the big stick disarming and crushing colored soldiers is the same Theodore Roosevelt who three years ago declared that as long as he was president every man should have a 'square deal.' "

Black leaders found an ally in Senator Joseph Foraker of Ohio, who introduced a bill to the Senate in the fall of 1906 calling on the secretary of war to turn over to a Senate investigating committee the evidence on which the decision to discharge the soldiers had been made. An investigation by the Committee on Military Affairs was authorized by the Senate.

Typically Roosevelt reacted to the attacks on him with fury. He managed the neat trick of identifying his critics with the "capitalists", and "trusts" he was attacking, writing to the reformist minister, Lyman Abbott: "These creatures have no place in the Republican party and are entitled to the scorn and abhorrence of every patriotic citizen." At the same time Roosevelt affirmed his friendship for black Americans in general and tried to undo some of the political damage by appointing several prominent black leaders to governmental posts, but blacks in general were not appeased. The New England conference of black Methodists, meeting in Montpelier, Vermont, in July, 1907, declared that the discharge of the black companies had "done more to arouse our just resentment and unite all elements of our people than any act of any President since Emancipation."

Du Bois announced defiantly, "It is high noon, brethren—the clock has struck twelve. What are we going to do? I have made up my mind. You can do as you please—you are free, sane and twenty-one. If between two parties who stand on identically the same platform you can prefer the party who perpetrated Brownsville, well and good! But I shall vote for Bryan."

Booker T. Washington, meanwhile, did all in his power to dampen black criticism of the President. The fact was that black Americans had no political alternative to the Republican Party. As one black paper editorialized, "When one considers the record of the Democratic party he must admit that it is out of the question for the colored man to vote for Bryan. The 'Jim Crow' laws of every Democratic State, the exclusion from the jury of almost every southern court, the mockery of a fair trial before every southern tribunal, all stand as brazen reminders of the eternal enmity of the Democracy toward the Negro."

Southern newspapers were virtually unanimous in praising the President to the skies for his discharge of the black soldiers. The Tennessee legislature voted its approval, and in Texas, John Nance Garner, future Vice-President of the United States, introduced a similar measure in the legislature of that state. One of the few exceptions was Pitchfork Ben Tillman of South Carolina, who declared that the discharge was unconstitutional, no better than lynch law.

If blacks suffered from racial prejudice in the North only somewhat less than they did south of the Mason-Dixon Line, they were at least free to agitate for better conditions. In that generally thankless task black women were as active as their male counterparts. Fannie Barrier Williams, who had been enthusiastically applauded for her speech at the Chicago World's Congress of Representative Women entitled on "The Intellectual Progress of the Colored Women of the United States Since the Emancipation Proclamation," became a highly successful public speaker who espoused the cause of black women, "the least known and most ill-favored class of women in the country." Her particular crusade came to be against residential segregation.

Ida Wells Barnett, who had defied the mobbing spirit in New Orleans, continued her crusade against lynching. She also took a leading role in the formation of black women's clubs in Chicago where she made her home. Wells joined forces with Henry Turner and Du Bois to form "an anti-lynching bureau" of the Afro-American Council.

Increasingly, militant blacks, fighting for their people, found white allies. When Ida Wells found that her efforts to affiliate black women's clubs with the national association of women's clubs was rebuffed, she discovered a friend in Celia Parker Woolley, a Unitarian minister, who joined with her to form the Frederick Douglass Center, an interracial women's club where white and black women could meet on a basis of equality. Wells was disconcerted to discover that despite Woolley's good intentions, she, Wells, was expected to be grateful and deferential in her attitude toward her white coadjutor. Further disillusionment came with the discovery that the white members of the club were unwilling to sign a petition protesting the murder of the young blacks in the Atlanta riot.

Ida Wells found another ally in Mrs. Victor Lawson, the wife of the publisher of the *Chicago Daily News*. When Wells told her that young blacks were barred from the YMCA, Jessie Lawson and her husband contributed the money to open the Negro Fellowship League Reading Room and Social Center in the heart of the city's black ghetto, and when the *Chicago Tribune* began a campaign to segregate the city's schools, Ida Wells went to Jane Addams for help. Addams called a meeting of influential white liberals at Hull House, and Wells informed them of the drive to introduce segregation. A committee of seven was formed with Jane Addams as chairman to meet with the editor to inform him that the fairminded citizens of Chicago would not tolerate such action. That put a stop to the movement.

Whistled off what they felt was their legitimate prey—the derelictions of capital—by the president of the United States, some of the new journalists began to direct their attention to the subject of race relations in the United States. Among the leaders were Oswald Garrison Villard, acting, as he felt, in the spirit of his mother and his grandfather, and Charles Edward Russell, who was stirred to enlist by a meeting of the Republican Club in New York attended by Du Bois. Russell was fascinated by Du Bois's elegance, "by the logical and coherent arrangement of his matter . . . apt illustration . . . research and knowledge, . . . the polished and carefully chosen cameos of his language . . . the faultless fluency of his utterance . . . He astonished and charmed all that heard him," Russell added. He was the graduate of two great universities, "a man to mark and to be glad to know." Yet this remarkable man, one of the most gifted Americans of his generation, was daily subjected to "gratuitous insult and indignity. . . . In no part of the United States would his status among his fellow men be essentially above that of the criminal, the gangster, or the moral leper. In no part of the United States could he pass freely without unprovoked hostility. . . . He could belong to no clubs, except those made up of members of his own race. He could not enter a church or an elevator, a hotel, a restaurant, a theatre, or a railroad car, except a segregated one as though he were unclean or suffered from some communicable disease."

The terrible irony of the situation was borne home most vividly to Russell by a race riot in Springfield, Illinois, the hometown of the Great Emancipator. The riot lasted for three days. Three blacks were lynched. One was an elderly man who had been married to a white woman for twenty years; he was dragged from his home and hanged from a tree in his own yard. William English Walling, whose antecedents were Southern, wrote in the *Independent:* "Either the spirit of the Abolitionists, of Lincoln, and of Lovejoy must be revived and we must come to treat the Negro on a plane of absolute political and social equality, or Vardaman and Tillman [Southern Senators] will soon have transferred the race war to the North."

When Walling got back to New York, he called Russell and some other friends of radical disposition together to tell them of his plan to form "a great national organization of fair-minded whites and intelligent blacks that should throw some kind of shield between the Negro and his oppressor . . . a society or organization that might contend against the racial madness of the South." More kindred spirits were invited to future meetings: Villard; the well-known rabbi Stephen Wise; Mary White Ovington, a champion of racial reform. It was Walling's conviction that "the Southern treatment of the Negro was as blind and as stupid and as inimical to the interests of the white people as it was un-American, contrary to the spirit of our democratic institutions, and often wickedly cruel and immoral."

On April 27, 1908, a group that included Villard and a number of black leaders met for dinner in a restaurant on Fulton Street to discuss the "economic relationship of the races in New York City." Notice of the meeting had been sent to the newspapers. A Hearst reporter appeared and wrote a lurid account of the biracial gathering, suggesting that "coal-black colored men were leering at white women and forcing their attentions upon them, . . . and the whole meeting was portrayed," in Villard's words, "as a movement for social equality instead of for civic betterment." The result was a torrent of abuse from newspapers all over the country. Mary White Ovington's mail was filled for weeks with letters of obscene vilification. Adolph Ochs, the publisher of the *New York Times,* wrote: "This particular banquet, we think, provoking as it must the public disgust and indignation, will serve to call the attention of the community to certain forces of evil that have been rather actively at work of late. . . . " Ochs believed that "the odious exhibition" would produce a powerful reaction that would "check and destroy" such assaults on racial purity. "In the North," he wrote, "we may be said to have no Negro question, but there is a Negro question in the South, and it would be well-nigh impossible to do the Negroes of the South a greater injury than was done by these flabby-minded persons who assembled in New York City on Monday to talk about and to exemplify the social 'equality' of the races." Ochs attributed the meeting to the influence of the socialists, "the persons who are seeking by pen and speech and by all the arts of agitation and mob leadership, by revolution if necessary, to destroy society, and with it the home and religion."

The year 1909 was the hundredth anniversary of Lincoln's birth. A round-robin petition was circulated throughout the country calling for some concrete effort to improve the status of those Americans whom the Civil War had been fought to set free. Among the signers of the petition were Jane Addams and Ida Wells, representing Chicago. A conference was held in Chicago at the Orchestra Hall, and its highlights were an address by Du Bois and the singing of spirituals by a black chorus of a hundred voices under the direction of James Munday of the Negro Fellowship League, which Ida Wells had founded. Out of the Chicago meeting came the call for a three-day conference in New York City. The stated purpose was to "inquire how far the country had lived up to the obligations of the Emancipation Proclamation and how far it had gone in assuring to each citizen, irrespective of color, the equality of opportunity and equality before the law, which underlie our American institutions. . . ."

The call declared, "If Mr. Lincoln could revisit this country in the flesh, he would be disheartened and discouraged. He would learn that on January 1, 1909, Georgia had rounded out a new confederacy by disfranchising the Negro, after the manner of all the Southern states. . . . He would learn that the Supreme Court . . . has laid down the principle that if an individual state chooses," it may "make it a crime for white and colored persons to frequent the same market place at the same time, or appear in an assemblage of citizens convened to consider questions of a public or political nature in which all citizens, without regard to race, are equally interested. . . . 'A house divided against itself cannot stand'; this government cannot exist half slave and half free any better today than it could in 1861, hence we call upon all the believers in democracy to join in a national conference for the discussion of present evils, the voicing of protests and the renewal of the struggle for civil and political liberty." The call was signed by, among others, Jane Addams; Samuel Bowles of the *Springfield* (Massachusetts) *Republican* (whose father, Samuel Bowles, had been one of the leading abolitionists of his day and a founder of the Republican Party in Massachusetts); John Dewey; William Lloyd Garrison, Jr.; the venerable William Dean Howells, the dean of American letters; Lincoln Steffens; Lillian Wald; Mary Woolley, president of Mount Holyoke College; Du Bois; and the Reverend Francis Grimké, the black nephew of the famous abolitionist sisters Sarah and Angelina Grimké. Conspicuously absent was William Monroe Trotter, who had joined forces with Du Bois to start the Niagara Movement. Trotter told Du Bois, "I distrust white folk." His alternative was the exclusively black National Equal Rights League.

The black delegates to the conference, Du Bois most prominent among them, reviewed for their white friends the manifold offenses that were daily being committed against black citizens of the United States. For many sympathetic whites the meeting took on an air of revelation. They met "for the first time . . . the Negro who demands, not a pittance, but his full rights in the commonwealth. They received a stimulating shock. . . . They did not want to leave the meeting." At the insistence of the delegates it was prolonged two days beyond its scheduled time. The delegates decided to form an organization to be called the National Negro Committee. A committee of forty (including Charles Edward Russell, William English Walling, and Oswald Garrison Villard) was given the task of drawing up goals and bylaws for a permanent organization. A rift developed between Ida Wells and Du Bois, who omitted her name from the list of forty who had been nominated. The consequence was that Wells had subsequently little involvement with what came to be called the National Association for the Advancement of Colored People, an organization which she felt was dominated for the most part by white liberals.

The National Association for the Advancement of Colored People was rooted in the older traditions of Christian abolitionism. Its platform called for the removal of all distinctions based on race or color and for a general recognition of the principle of human brotherhood. It took as one of its primary objectives the collection and dissemination of information about the practical consequences of racial prejudice: the black children untaught or inadequately taught; the barriers to decent jobs; the discriminatory employment practices and the barriers to decent jobs for blacks; the crippling results of segregation. In Georgia, for example, 43 percent of the children of school age were black, yet less than 9 percent of the expenditures for education went to black schools. There were counties, the NAACP, as it was soon called, discovered, where blacks paid the greater part of the taxes, yet where from five to ten times as much money was spent on the education of white children as on blacks.

Soon the NAACP had an ally in the Constitution League, headed by a journalist named John Milholland, "an eager, sanguine man, all

Saxon in appearance, all Celt in sympathies and feelings; a blond man, with . . . active blue eyes, a swift and spontaneous manner," as Russell described him. Milholland's mission was to direct attention to the violations of the Constitution in the South's treatment of blacks and, by means of legal agencies and an aroused public opinion, to correct such abuses.

Two years after the Springfield race riot, the body of a white woman was found in an alley in Cairo, Illinois. An indigent black man called Frog James was suspected. He was arrested and locked up. A mob gathered and took James from the sheriff. A rope was placed around his neck; he was dragged to the center of town and hanged from a light arch above the street, and some 500 bullets were fired into his body. Some of the bullets cut the rope: The body was dragged up Washington Street, followed by a large crowd, and the head was cut off and stuck on a fence post. Finally, the body was burned. When Ida Wells heard of the incident in Chicago, she tried to organize a protest on the part of the black churches and social groups of the city and to ascertain the real facts. When she failed, she decided to go to Cairo herself. Her ten-year-old son had said to her, "Mother, if you don't go nobody else will." In Cairo she found the black population of the town thoroughly intimidated. No one wanted to talk to her about the lynching. The central issue was whether the sheriff of Cairo, a Republican who was popular with the black community, had done his best to protect his prisoner from the mob. Wells undertook to prove to a special commission formed by the governor that the sheriff had been derelict in his duty. She argued the case so persuasively that the governor refused to reinstate Frank Davis, the sheriff, and Ida Wells, proudly recounting the story in her autobiography, noted that no other black prisoner had been lynched in Illinois in the years that followed.

If lynchings were the most horrifying manifestation of white prejudice, the most debilitating was job discrimination. For a black man or woman confined to the most menial tasks the vote was, if not precisely a trivial matter, a decidedly secondary one. In 1910, 55 percent of all black males were farmers, and 21 percent domestic servants. Three-fourths of all employed blacks were confined to these two occupations. Most of the unions that made up the American Federation of Labor were as "lily-white" as New York City's exclusive Union Club. There were, of course, exceptions. The Brewery Workers' Union, "true to its international faith," in Oscar Ameringer's phrase, admitted blacks. But the only other AFL union to admit blacks was the United Mine

Workers. In New Orleans there were both black and white unions of stevedores or longshoremen affiliated with the AFL. The blacks had originally been introduced to the docks in order to break the power of the white unions. When they in turn organized, a great hue and cry was raised in the port of New Orleans. "White men, assert your supremacy, rescue your jobs from the niggers" was the cry that went up from pulpit and rostrum. The white longshoremen thereupon scabbed and broke the black strike. In Ameringer's words, this went on until in one such conflict "the white-supremacy strikers killed some ninety black strike breakers, whereupon the white-supremacy militia of white-supremacy Louisiana shot hell out of a similar number of white-supremacy strikers." The result was that the two unions—white and black—agreed to recognize each other and join forces to prevent their mutual exploitation. Ameringer was assigned by the AFL officers to coordinate the strike activities with the black longshoremen. It gave him his first insight into "the true nature of the thing called the race problem," he wrote. He found black workers had the same aspirations as white counterparts. "What they asked from life was living. Happiness within four walls, a loving mate, children, and the chance to rear them better than they had been reared. Health, laughter, beauty, peace, plenty, a modest degree of security in sickness and age. Some were good, some bad; some stupid, some crooked. They were wise and foolish; there were heroes and cowards. Most of them were a combination of all these faults and virtues." They were "more easily moved to song and laughter than their white fellow slaves. Beneath their monkeyshines was the wisdom born of suffering. . . . Mentally they were the equals of the white strikers. . . . In some respect the blacks even surpassed the whites on their own economic level." When Ameringer attended the meetings of black unions, he found them a combination of black church revival meetings and the rituals of secret societies. There were passwords, songs and hymns, vocal responses to the speakers: "Now he's talkin'. Tell 'em. Tell 'em." Month after month the strike dragged on while the shippers and the railroads tried to bring in trainloads of strikebreakers from Northern cities and the strikers fought to keep the port closed down and the ships idle at the docks.

The listing of 55 percent of blacks as "farmers" was highly misleading. Most of them were tenants. Like poor white farmers, many had slipped back from owning farms to tenancy. Debt peonage was another Southern labor practice that worked a particular hardship on blacks. Like a number of other Southern states, Florida had a debt peonage law that allowed an employer to whom an employee allegedly owed money to pursue such an employee if he decamped and to force him to return to work out his debt. It thus was only necessary for an employer to place an employee in his debt by the flimsiest of pretexts (such as the fact that he owed him for goods he was required to purchase from a company store and rent for a house he was required to rent from the company) to place him in an actual state of bondage, of slavery in all but name. This was the state of many black workers, especially tenant farmers and workers in the turpentine and lumber mills of Florida and Georgia. In the words of a sympathetic white lawyer, who, it may be said, did not dare voice his opinion publicly, once in debt a "negroe never gets out of debt I care not what may be his earnings." He was often held literally "at the muzzle of a gun . . . and when he happens to do anything that does not suit them they are tied up and beat most outrageously." If a worker fled such conditions and was pursued and captured, the costs of his pursuit and return to his employer were made an additional charge against him. When the United States attorney won a case against an employer accused of illegal actions in seizing a former employee, the lumber and turpentine industry in Florida raised an estimated $90,000 to carry the case to the Supreme Court, where the case was argued by a Georgia Senator and a Congressman from the same state.

While poor whites suffered from the debt peonage system, too, the system fell with crushing weight on blacks. The fact that the Supreme Court in 1904, hearing the so-called Clyatt Case on appeal, found for the defendant was a crushing setback for the reformers who were fighting debt peonage. In Alabama, where the system was especially pernicious, a laborer's accepting money and failing to work it out were "prima facie evidence of the intent to injure or defraud his employer" under state law. In such cases the employee, in addition to being forced to work off the alleged indebtedness, was subject to a fine of $300 (often more than his yearly wages) and was not permitted to testify in his own behalf. Booker T. Washington was generally disposed to conciliation, but he took up the case of a black man named Alonso Bailey, who had been seized under the state's debtor laws. "This simply means," Washington wrote, "that any white man, who cares to charge that a Colored man has promised to work for him and has not done so, or who has gotten money from him and not paid it back, can have the Colored man sent to the chain gang."

Washington was able to collect enough money—secretly, it might be said, from white friends sympathetic to the cause of blacks, among them Ray Stannard Baker—to carry the case to the Supreme Court, which returned it to the Alabama courts in 1908 on a technicality. When it returned to the Supreme Court two years later, Chief Justice Charles Evans Hughes delivered the opinion of the majority of the court that the Alabama law under which debt peonage was practiced was unconstitutional, while Justice Oliver Wendell Holmes submitted the opinion of the dissenting justices who upheld the Alabama law.

Baker, writing about the case for the *American Magazine*, spoke of Bailey as "a pawn . . . a sort of symbol of this new struggle for freedom." As long as "so many negroes are densely ignorant and poverty stricken, and while so many white men are shortsighted enough to take advantage of this ignorance and poverty, so long will forms of slavery prevail." The Bailey case made little difference in the treatment of Southern blacks trapped in peonage more dismal than that of Russian serfs. A black man who was victimized had first to have the courage to protest and then the good fortune to find a sympathetic white ear. Finally, money had to be raised to pay the costs of litigation. Under such circumstances it is not surprising that only a handful of blacks were able to secure justice.

Northern philanthropies to black causes, especially in support of segregated black schools and colleges in the South, increased substantially. The colleges, founded in most instances by Northern churches at the end of the Civil War, were desperately marginal enterprises, both intellectually and financially, but poor as they were, they were of critical importance to ambitious blacks struggling to obey Booker T. Washington's exhortations.

Oswald Garrison Villard was one of the directors of such an institution, the Manassas Industrial School, "a small, struggling imitation of Hampton." It had been founded by Jennie Dean, a black woman who had been born a slave. One of the school's principal benefactors was Andrew Carnegie. Carnegie was, in fact, Washington's bankroller, and much of Washington's influence among black Americans was due to the fact that he could put the bite on the Scottish philanthropist.

But aside from the continuing contributions of Northern churches and philanthropic organizations, the radical political groups took little interest in the plight of American blacks. This was conspicuously true of the Socialist Party. Du Bois joined the Socialist Party in 1911, but a year later he resigned to give his support to Woodrow Wilson, convinced that the Socialists were almost as indifferent to the problems of black Americans as the capitalists. He particularly resented the orthodox Socialist "position" on the race problem: that it was simply an aspect of the class struggle and would have to wait for a "solution" until after the revolution and the achievement of the workers' state, a development of which, it might be noted, Du Bois was highly skeptical. Speaking at an annual meeting of the Intercollegiate Socialist Society, he told the delegates, "I know and you know that the conspiracy of silence that surrounds the Negro problem in the United States arises because you do not dare, you are without the moral courage to discuss it frankly, and when I say *you* I refer not simply to the conservative reactionary elements of the nation but rather to the very elements represented in a conference like this, supposed to be forward-looking and radical. . . . You allow lynching and murder to become a national pastime. Nine out of ten of you have practically without protest sat by your parlor fires while 2,867 colored men have been lynched and burned and tortured in the last thirty years, and not a single one of the murderers brought to justice, not to mention the tens of thousands of Negroes who have been killed by mobs and murderers in that time. . . . The state socialism which you discuss is in America the socialism of a state where a tenth of the population is disenfranchised (not to mention the half who are women) . . . ; and you raise scarcely a single word of protest against it. . . . Under such circumstances you must remember that the integrity of your own souls and minds is at stake. You cannot thus play with a human problem and not spoil your own capacity for reason."

Du Bois was disturbed by the disposition of the enemies of black equality to base their arguments on Darwinism. This tendency had been evident early, but it had gained a new academic and scholarly status since the turn of the century. The reason was by no means exclusively hostility toward blacks. The continued stream of immigration, much of it from Central and Southern Europe, alarmed the "Anglo-Saxons," the old elite who felt its threat to their hegemony. In his address at the second National Negro Conference Du Bois launched an all-out assault on the Darwinists and their racial theories. "When a social policy based on a supposed scientific sanction leads to . . . a moral anomaly it is time to examine rather carefully the logical foundation of the argument," he declared. "What the age of Darwin has done is add to the eighteenth-century idea of individual worth the complementary idea of physical immortality of the human race." Darwinism,

Du Bois insisted, had been warped to give racism a respectable scientific gloss.

The residue of slavery, John Jay Chapman declared, was a land "still full of hard, hard hearts. . . . The depravity of the blacks and the lynchings by the whites have not yet ceased." Chapman wrote: "Burnings of Negroes at the stake still draw upon our nation the contempt and horror of mankind. But the spirit that is to put an end to these things has already been born. . . . The race question . . . puts each of us to the alternative of becoming a great deal holier, a great deal kinder, a great deal deeper in character, or else of being brutalized to some extent." Just as American blacks had "long wind and perfect faith: so must white Americans. The advocates of equality must be as patient, and school ourselves as thoroughly as they," Chapman declared.

11

The Election of 1908

As the months of his second term passed, Roosevelt found himself increasingly preoccupied with foreign affairs. When Kaiser Wilhelm made an inflammatory speech at Tangier, pledging German support for Moroccan independence, the French, who suspected the kaiser of being more interested in acquiring Morocco than in freeing it, warned him not to meddle. The kaiser's response was to call for an international conference on the issue. He asked Roosevelt to prevail on the French to attend. The President, well aware that Europe was a tinderbox ready to explode into war (there was already bitter fighting in the Balkans), got the British and French to agree to attend a conference at Algeciras, Spain, along with an American delegation. "I wish to Heaven," he wrote his secretary of war, William Howard Taft, "our excellent friend, the Kaiser, was not so jumpy and did not have so many pipe dreams." Roosevelt's friendship with Ambassador Jean Jules Jusserand seems to have been an important factor in France's acceptance of the Roosevelt plan for the conference at Algeciras. "With Speck I was on close terms; with Jusserand, who is one of the best men I have ever met, and whose country was in the right on this issue, I was on even closer terms," the President wrote. "He was one of the men who in every way deprecated and tried to prevent the growth in Germany of a feeling hostile to England."

The result of the Algeciras Conference was hardly what the kaiser had in mind: The settlement affirmed the independence of Morocco, while bringing some order into its financial affairs and placing the control of its police force in the hands of France and Spain . . . a very limited "independence," to be sure. The terms of the Act of Algeciras were ratified by a reluctant Senate under intense pressure from the President (the Senate added the proviso that the ratification should not be considered a precedent for the involvement of the United States in European affairs). "In this Algeciras business," Roosevelt wrote Whitelaw Reid, the American ambassador to England, "you will notice that while I was most suave and pleasant with the Emperor, yet when it became necessary at the end I stood him on his head with great decision." The effect of Algeciras was to strengthen the kaiser's paranoia. It seemed clear to him that, whatever he might do to curry favor with the American President on any issue involving a clash between the interests of Germany on the one hand, and Great Britain and now, apparently, France on the other, the United States would ultimately throw its weight onto the scales against Germany.

The British Foreign Office continued to resist Roosevelt's efforts to have Durand replaced, but did try to sweeten the pill by sending over as a military attaché the king's cousin Lieutenant Colonel Lord Edward Gleichen. "The best person to keep touch with the President," Spring-Rice had written to Edward Grey, the foreign secretary, "is the military attaché, and as Gleichen has been shot in the stomach and the neck, he is quite certain to meet with a favorable reception."

Roosevelt's importunings for the replacement of Durand finally bore fruit in the summer of 1906, when that unhappy diplomat was replaced by James Bryce, whose sympathetic volumes on the United States had already made him a favorite of the President despite the fact that he could not play tennis and was generally of a sedentary temperament. The Nation praised the appointment as a departure from the general disposition of foreign governments to send "rough riding and tennis playing diplomats to Washington lest they fall out of the category of most favored nation."

The always uneasy relationship between Japan and the United States was placed under a severe strain by the action of the San Francisco school board in October, 1906, in the aftermath of the earthquake, segregating Japanese, Chinese, and Korean children in separate schools for Orientals. The fiercely proud Japanese immediately protested, and the threat of a break in diplomatic relations and even the possibility of war hung in the air.

Roosevelt acted with firmness and tact. The school board was invited to Washington to confer with him and Secretary Root and their advisers. There they succumbed to the President's formidable charm; a compromise was reached. The segregation order was rescinded, and Roosevelt promised to support legislation to close the door to Oriental immigration through Hawaii and the Philippines. He had done his best "by politeness and consideration of the Japs to offset the worse than criminal stupidity of the San Francisco mob, the San Francisco press, and such papers as the New York *Herald*," he wrote to Lodge. "I do not believe we shall have war, but it is no fault of the yellow press if we do not have it."

In August, 1908, an American correspondent for the *New York Times*, William Bayard Hale, was granted an interview by the kaiser, who told the startled journalist that within a year or two the Americans would certainly have to fight the Japanese. To counter the Japanese, he intended to propose a treaty among Germany, China, and the United States. Germany would have to go to war against Britain because of that nation's betrayal of the white race through a treaty with Japan. Hale showed the interview to the German Foreign Ministry, which was horrified at the emperor's indiscretion, and the editors of the *Times* referred it to the President himself before publishing it. He in turn urged them not to do so in the interests of world peace. "I really like, and in a way, admire him," Roosevelt wrote of the kaiser, "but I wish he would not have brain storms." The trouble was, of course, that by any reasonable standard the kaiser was mad. He managed to air his scheme in the London *Daily Telegraph*, and the result was a diplomatic storm that caused him to flee to Pless, where he told his hostess, "Oh, I am most unhappy. I am always misunderstood."

Actually there was some fire beneath the kaiser's smoke. The Japanese, furious at the treatment of their nationals in California and intoxicated by their easy victory over Russia, were involved in overtures to Mexico; the Mexicans were blood brothers, they discovered, descendants of Japanese fishermen who had been blown across the Pacific centuries ago. Japanese training ships visited Mexico, and the grand admiral of the Japanese fleet was cheered as an ally when he spoke of the fraternal ties between Japan and Mexico at a state banquet. There were cries of "¡Viva Japón! ¡Baja los gringos!"

Roosevelt did not need the promptings of the kaiser to make him wary of Nippon. "My chief concern in foreign affairs," he wrote to Whitelaw Reid, "is over the Japanese situation. . . . " France, Britain, and Germany, awed by the Japanese defeat of Russia, were convinced that in a naval war the Japanese Navy would rout that of the United States and seize Hawaii and the Philippines. Roosevelt believed it essential that the Japanese not suffer that illusion. The United States Navy had a vastly improved gunsight that made its naval gunnery the most accurate in the world. Finally, there was the question of how best to deploy the fleet in the event of a war with Japan, which many military experts now considered inevitable. Admiral Mahan's principle, which Roosevelt made his own, was to be sure that portions of the fleet were not engaged by the Japanese piecemeal and destroyed. The obvious strategy was thus to withdraw the smaller U.S. Pacific fleet at the first sign of trouble, unite it with the Atlantic fleet, and *then* return to the Pacific waters and engage the Japanese with the full power of the American navy. Roosevelt was determined to find out if U.S. ships could shoot and if they were capable of long, sustained voyages with infrequent refuelings. The solution seemed to him to be a global voyage by the principal warships of the U.S. Navy. Senator Nelson Aldrich tried to stop the voyage by refusing to appropriate the necessary funds, but Roosevelt's response was to dispatch the fleet in defiance of Aldrich. "I made up my mind to send the ships that far [to China and Japan] and then let Aldrich take the responsibility for leaving them there at anchor or appropriate the funds to bring them back," Roosevelt wrote. "I felt sure that the country would not stand for ordering the ships back across the Pacific."

On December 16, 1907, the fleet sailed out of Hampton Roads, Virginia, down the coast of South America, through the Strait of Magellan, and north to Mexico. There, off Magdalena Bay, where, it was said, Japanese naval experts were stationed, the American warships held gunnery practice at sea, giving an awesome display of accuracy at long range. From Mexico the fleet proceeded up the West Coast to San Francisco. Australia and New Zealand invited the fleet for a visit, and Japan followed suit with an invitation to stop at Yokohama. The Suez Canal was finished just in time for the fleet to pass triumphantly through it on its return voyage, and it arrived at Hampton Roads in February, 1909, after thirteen months at sea and less than two weeks before the end of the President's tenure of office—a sensational finale! Henry Stoddard, the newspaper tycoon, noted of the President:

"He . . . thrilled over every incident as the cables brought the day to day news."

In November, 1908, Root and Japanese Ambassador Kogoro Takahira, under the stimulus provided by the voyage of the Great White Fleet, agreed that Japan and the United States were "animated by a common aim, policy, and intention" in the Pacific. They pledged they would "reciprocally . . . respect the territorial possessions belonging to each other" and concert their efforts to defend "the principle of equal opportunity for commerce and industry in China." That did not allay the fears of a former Stanford law student named Homer Lea. The frail Lea, after his graduation from Occidental College and Stanford Law School, had traveled to China, where he became a general in Sun Yat-sen's revolutionary army and a close adviser to Sun himself. He returned to the United States obsessed with the threat of Japan and the notion that the less militaristic nations—like Great Britain and the United States—must fall before the more warlike and aggressive, specifically Japan and Germany. His *bêtes noires* were the pacifists, the clergy, the feminists—all those who discouraged the growth of the United States as a great military power.

Lea's book *The Valor of Ignorance* took the line that war between Japan and the United States (and in all likelihood Germany) was inevitable. "This Republic and Japan," Lea wrote, "are approaching, careless on the one hand, predetermined on the other, that point of contact which is war. . . . We exaggerate, not Japan's capacity to make war, but our capacity to defend ourselves. . . . " Lea's scenario called for the Japanese to attack the Philippines in overwhelming force at Luzon, seize the main island (which Lea argued was indefensible) in some three weeks, and then capture Hawaii, Alaska, and California. Taken by surprise, the United States would become hopelessly mired in "confusion, ignorance, peculation, and a complete lack of every form of military preparation, armaments, supplies or means of securing them. . . . " Lea argued that "nations prefer to perish rather than to master the single lesson taught by the washing away of those that have gone before them. In their indifference, and in *the valor of ignorance,* they depart, together with their monuments and their constitutions. . . . "

Roosevelt gave his support to the Second Hague Peace Conference called by the czar for the summer and fall of 1907 and attended by forty-six nations. The most important consequence from the United States' point of view was the acceptance by the delegates of the so-called Drago Doctrine. Formulated in 1902 at the time of the Venezuela affair by Luis Drago, the Argentine foreign minister, the doctrine held that armed intervention must not be used by European powers to collect debts owed by American nations to foreign investors.

In the fall the Central American Peace Conference met in Washington. Proposed by Root, the conference included Costa Rica, Guatemala, Honduras, Nicaragua, El Salvador, and Mexico. Eight "conventions," including a treaty of peace and provisions for establishing a Central American Court of Justice, were agreed to by the attending nations.

As Roosevelt approached the end of his second term of office, he was not only far and away the most dominant figure in the United States, but the best known and, by all odds, the most admired individual *in the world*. Not since Abraham Lincoln had there been a public figure so universally acclaimed. Kings and emperors could not hold a candle to the cowboy President. A famous cartoon showed his head with its omnivorous grin, like the Cheshire cat, hovering over America. It might as well have been the globe. The British politician and biographer John Morley said of Roosevelt, "He is not an American you know, he *is America*."

By the end of 1907 Roosevelt had decided not to run for another term. According to Henry Stoddard, the President gave an odd, but oddly characteristic, explanation for his determination, or semidetermination, not to be a candidate. "I have been a crusader here. I have been a destructive force. The country needs a change. There was crusading to do when I took hold. There was something that had to be uprooted. I had to challenge and destroy certain influences or we would soon have had an intolerable condition imperilling everything." He had not been interested in the tariff problem or able to take it with the seriousness that it doubtlessly deserved, he told Stoddard. Nor was he interested in "the business problems of government," by which he presumably meant the day-to-day administration of the executive branch. "The conscience of business had to be aroused," Roosevelt continued; "the authority of the government over big as well as small had to be asserted. You can't half do that kind of job; it must be done thoroughly. I think I've done it. I didn't use a feather duster. I knew I had to hit hard—and be hit hard in return. We have had four years of uprooting and four years of crusading. The country has had enough of it and of me."

In addition, there was a severe depression in 1907, with millions of unemployed roaming the streets searching for jobs. "The tales of individual ruin are terribly pathetic," Henry Adams wrote to his English friend Charles M. Gaskell, "and strike very close on all sides, but at first one must try to save only society at large, which is having a severe strain, only just beginning." Roosevelt charged that the malefactors of great wealth had caused the depression to embarrass his administration. They in turn blamed his policies and programs.

Having made his decision not to run again, Roosevelt, typically, experienced misgivings over the wisdom of what he called, in a letter to Henry Cabot Lodge, "the great renunciation." He had, he confessed, "a definite philosophy about the Presidency. I think it should be a very powerful office, and I think the President should be a very strong man who uses without hesitation every power the position yields; but because of this very fact I believe he should be sharply watched by the people, held to a strict accountability by them, and that he should not keep the office too long." He was the kind of man, he assured Lodge (who knew very well of the President's tendency to suffer groundless fears and unnecessary apprehensions), that "when I am thru with anything I am thru with it, and under no temptation to snatch at the fringes of departing glory. When I stop being President I will stop completely. . . . " His plan was to go big-game hunting in Africa with his son Kermit under the auspices of the Smithsonian Institution. His best trophies would be sent to the Natural History Museum to be stuffed and displayed. The trip would get him off the national stage and give his successor an opportunity to establish his own administration free of the shadow of the Colonel. *Collier's Weekly* had offered him $100,000 for a running account of his travels, but *Collier's,* with Robert Collier as owner and Norman Hapgood as editor, was one of those muckraking journals the President had attacked so vigorously, and he decided to accept the much smaller offer of the much more respectable and "literary" *Scribner's,* a decision on which Lodge congratulated him somewhat excessively.

A cynic, and there were a number, might have thought it an odd way to remove himself from the public eye—an African safari complete with shot-by-shot accounts of the hero's exploits—(a moving picture crew was to accompany the party as well) but self-consciousness was not one of the Colonel's most evident qualities.

Roosevelt's first choice for a successor, according to Henry Stoddard, was Secretary of State Elihu Root, although William Loeb, Roosevelt's closest adviser, thought him unelectable. Root evidently agreed;

in any case, he begged off and Roosevelt settled on his friend William Howard Taft, then secretary of war, as his successor. After Loeb had informed Taft of the President's decision, Roosevelt himself told him, "Will, it's the thing to do. Our friends should control the convention; we don't want any uncertain note sounded there. We've all talked about candidates long enough; it's time for a decision. I'm for you, and I shall let it be known right away. That's as far as I can personally go. . . . My suggestion to you is to put yourself in Loeb's hands from now on. He knows the politics of this country as well as anyone I can think of."

The President was startled to find that many of his closest advisers were alarmed by his choice of Taft. Some still hoped that in the event of a deadlocked convention, Roosevelt might accept a nomination by acclamation for another term. Others simply considered Taft a weak candidate and felt that the convention should be an open one, thus avoiding the charge that Roosevelt had forced his own candidate on the party. Although the President made known to Taft his determination not to be a candidate in the upcoming election, he refused to make any public announcement or even to disavow his own candidacy, apparently on the not unreasonable ground that he would lose much of his power over Congress as soon as it was definitely known that he would not seek another term. He was familiar with the problems of lame-duck presidents and determined to avoid a similar fate if he could. He had, after all, declared in 1904 that if elected, he would not seek another term. Now he refused to do more than refer all those who importuned him to be a candidate to that earlier declaration.

Uncle Joe Cannon, the Speaker of the House, made clear that he was an anti-Roosevelt candidate. Philander Knox, attorney general under McKinley and Roosevelt, who had successfully prosecuted a number of antitrust cases and had resigned from that office to run for the Senate from Pennsylvania in the election of 1904, also had presidential ambitions. Finally, there was Wisconsin's Robert La Follette, with strong support in the Midwest. With the convention date approaching, Roosevelt announced his support for Taft. There was at once so much resistance from the Republican rank and file that the President, who had planned to remain aloof from the politics of delegate selection and preconvention maneuverings, decided that he would have to intervene actively to promote his candidate. "I don't understand this," Roosevelt was reported to have said to a rebellious Republican leader of a large Midwestern state. "They don't seem to know Taft as I know him. I've got to explain him to nearly all of our fellows."

Taft stood six feet two inches or so and weighed some 300 pounds. He was sleek as a seal and the soul of amiability. But his intellectual weight did not equal his physical. He meant well to all, William Allen White decided, "but he was deeply dubious . . . of any plan which would ameliorate the conditions surrounding the common man, or of schemes for using government property as an agency of human welfare. . . . " Ray Stannard Baker described Taft as "a large, dim, charming personality." The truth was that Roosevelt believed Taft to be what he wished to believe him to be. The picture he painted of his friend had little or nothing to do with reality. "To flaming hatred of injustice," he declared with characteristic enthusiasm and exaggeration, "to a scorn of all that is base and mean, to a hearty sympathy with the oppressed, he [Taft] unites entire disinterestedness, courage both moral and physical of the highest type, and kindly generosity of nature which makes him feel that all his countrymen are in very truth his friends and brothers." That Taft had a "kindly generosity of nature" was true enough. But it was also true that he had not the slightest perception of the real condition and needs of the Republic.

One of the principal criticisms of Taft was that he had obtained political eminence without ever having run for public office. The Taft family, wealthy and powerful, had settled on William to be the tribe's politician. As Ray Stannard Baker put it, "No money and no effort were too great to be given by the Taft brothers when Bill was to be benefitted and pushed forward." A friendly governor appointed him a judge. His friend President Benjamin Harrison made him solicitor general. Another friend, President McKinley, had appointed him governor of the Philippines, and Roosevelt had made him secretary of war. "Thus he was advanced," Baker wrote, "not by the rough impact of powerful convictions impressed upon an eager people, but easily and serenely by virtue of the charm of his personality and his loyal friendships with those high in public life." About many issues he was uninformed; about politics he was naïve. When, at the end of a speech he gave in February, 1908, at Cooper Union to launch his campaign for the Republican nomination, he had been asked, "What is a man to do who is out of work and starving?" Taft replied, "God knows, I don't."

When the convention met in June at Chicago, Henry Cabot Lodge was chairman. The President had arranged for a telegrapher to be stationed behind Lodge to flash the word to the White House if it seemed apparent that a Roosevelt stampede was developing. His intention, according to Henry Stoddard, was to demand "imperatively" that his name be withdrawn. The Taft forces, never entirely convinced that the President was prepared to step aside, were perplexed and alarmed that he had not already "imperatively" withdrawn.

Taft, his wife, his brother Charles, and close friends also received word by telegraph of developments in the convention hall. After all the nominating speeches had been made, the Taft circle breathed more easily. Then, according to Joseph Bishop, a member of Taft's staff, a telegram arrived with alarming news. It read: "A large portrait of Roosevelt has been displayed on the platform and the convention has exploded." It was the moment they had all feared. "Mrs. Taft," Bishop reported, "sat white as marble and motionless. Mr. Taft tapped with his fingers on the arm of his chair and whistled softly. No one said a word or looked at his neighbor." A few minutes later there was another bulletin: "The uproar continues with increased fury." It went on for forty-nine minutes by the clock before word came that Massachusetts had given twenty-five votes to Taft. Not long afterward the news that he had been nominated on the first ballot arrived at the temporary Taft headquarters.

The Republican Convention was a kind of last hurrah for the old-time Republican bosses. William Allen White sat beside Alice Roosevelt, who had just married the conservative Republican Congressman Nicholas Longworth. She tipped off White that Taft's running mate would be the "most reactionary of the Republican Congressmen," James Sherman of New York.

Taft hurried to the White House to express his gratitude to Roosevelt. A few weeks later, on his way to Cincinnati to deliver his acceptance speech, he stopped off at Sagamore Hill to consult Roosevelt on the text of his address. It was the last such gesture of beholdenness on the part of the Republican nominee.

Meanwhile, the Democrats met on July 7 at Denver, the farthest west a major national convention had yet ventured. In that salubrious mountain setting, far from Wall Street, the party reverted to its basic Bryanism. Once more there was a tent camp revival mood, the feeling of repentant sinners returned to the fold, chastened by their flirtation with big-city folk and big-city ways. Bryan had sounded the trumpet call for the faithful. "With malice toward none and charity for all," he had declared in the wake of the Parker debacle four years earlier, "let us begin the campaign of 1908; let us appeal to the moral sentiment of the country and arraign the policies of the Republican party before the bar of public conscience." Before he departed on a world tour in 1905, Bryan had written to Roosevelt, exhorting him to persist in his program of reform: "Stand by your guns! You have developed a reform element in the Republican party; you must lead it or suffer the humiliation of seeing the leadership pass to someone else." Now Roosevelt had, Bryan was convinced, attempted to pass the torch to someone without the zeal or conviction to carry it forward.

There had been an effort at a boomlet for the presidential candidacy of the president of Princeton University, Woodrow Wilson, an effort largely manufactured by Colonel George Harvey, the editor of *Harper's*. And William Randolph Hearst was a perennial candidate, whom no one took seriously. Bryan had dispatched George McClellan, Jr., to Grover Cleveland to find out how the former President felt about his candidacy in 1908, and Cleveland had announced, "I don't feel as bitterly about Bryan as I once did. You can tell him that if you like, in your own words." Bryan seemed delighted. "Thank God for that!" he exclaimed. He had returned from his tour in 1906 to vast outpourings of affection and loyalty. When the delegates gathered at Denver, Bryan was once more clearly in command of his party. The party platform dutifully expressed his political principles and condemned "the action of the present Chief Executive in using the patronage of his high office to secure the nomination for the Presidency of one of his Cabinet Officers." Such a "forced succession" was repugnant to republican principles. The House of Representatives was also chastised for its subservience to Roosevelt. The platform called, once more, for preventing trusts from becoming "private monopolies," "vigorous enforcement of the criminal law against guilty trust magnates," more effective control over the railroads, a national monetary system, an income tax on individual and corporate incomes, the popular election of Senators, the admission of Oklahoma, Arizona, and New Mexico into the Union, and "the preservation, protection and replacement of needed forests" and the nation's natural resources. Independence for the Philippines and territorial status for Alaska and Puerto Rico were advocated and the admission of "Asiatic immigrants who can not be amalgamated with our population" was opposed. (The Democratic platform was notably silent on the rights of black people while the Republicans congratulated themselves on having been "for more than fifty years the consistent friend of the American Negro. . . . We demand equal justice for all men, without regard to race or color. . . . ") The Democrats proceeded to nominate Bryan as the party's candidate for president. When Roosevelt heard the news, he wrote to Lodge that although Bryan was "a shallow demagogue," he had "many kindly and amiable traits." Certainly he was not "a bit worse than Thomas Jefferson, and I do not think that if elected President he would be a worse President. The country would survive, but it would suffer just as the country suffered for at least two generations because of its folly in following Jefferson's lead."

The Prohibitionists met at Columbus, Ohio, on July 15 and supported a series of liberal planks, including women's suffrage and a graduated income tax. They nominated Eugene Chafin for president and conducted a lively campaign aimed at the apparently hopeless goal of a national prohibiton law.

The Populists nominated Tom Watson again, but the glory days were an increasingly dim memory, and Watson himself was a tragic reminder of better days. The man who had fought so bravely for the rights of Southern blacks in the era of the Farmers' Alliance now indulged in racist harangues.

William Randolph Hearst, one of the most mercurial figures in American politics, rejected by the Democrats, founded his own Independence Party, which met in Chicago, listened to him denounce Bryan as "a trickster, a trimmer, and a traitor," and nominated Thomas Hisgen of Massachusetts for president.

The Socialist Labor Party, under the firm control of Daniel De Leon, gathered twenty-three delegates at a "convention" in New York City and demanded, not surprisingly, "the unconditional surrender of the capitalist class."

The Socialists, by contrast, turned out some 3,000 delegates (a substantial portion of their membership, it might be said), who gathered with an ebullient feeling that the future lay with them. But they fell almost at once to bitter ideological quarrels, most notably between those committed to class warfare and violent upheaval, if necessary, and the "Slowcialists," of the British Fabian variety, who eschewed violence and put their faith in educating the masses and freeing them via the ballot. The platform that emerged stated that "a bitter struggle over the division of the products of labor is waged between the exploiting propertied class on the one hand and the exploited, propertyless class on the other." That war was "the only vital issue before the

American people." Bill Haywood cast his lot with Debs's campaign for president and joined the "Red Special," a campaign train chartered by the Socialist Party.

It was soon evident that the Republican candidate was anxious to put as much distance as possible between himself and his patron. He not only noticeably abstained from seeking his predecessor's advice but also kept company with some of Roosevelt's bitterest enemies. It was the conviction of Stoddard and close Roosevelt friends that Charles Taft and other members of that proud and powerful Ohio clan had laid down the law to Will, never very resolute himself. He could not, they presumably said, appear to be tied to Roosevelt's coattails. He must be his own man and avoid any appearance of being under the political tutelage of his predecessor and benefactor. It was not bad advice, and Taft was wise to take it, but it might have been followed more tactfully and accompanied by private assurances that he was still unwaveringly committed to the President's policies.

At Cincinnati, on July 29, Taft reaffirmed his commitment "to the reform of known abuses, to the continuance of liberty and true prosperity." The man who had led the country on the path of "practical reform" was Theodore Roosevelt. "He laid down the doctrine that the rich violator of the law should be as amenable to restraint and punishment as the offender without wealth and without influences." The chief function of his administration, Taft assured his listeners and his party, would be "to clinch what has already been accomplished at the White House; to undertake to devise ways and means by which the high development of business integrity and obedience to law which he [Roosevelt] established can be maintained." The key phrase, several times repeated, was "practical reform"; it plainly meant very limited and cautious reform, nothing radical or extreme, nothing to alarm honest businessmen or law-abiding corporations.

As a campaigner Taft was not so much lackluster as absent. He devoted himself largely to golf. In the words of Henry Stoddard, "he played golf more persistently and with keener interest than he did anything else." Charles Evans Hughes and Roosevelt spoke with far more frequency and effect on behalf of Taft's election than the candidate himself.

As election day approached, Roosevelt was dismayed to hear that Taft's Unitarianism had become an issue with Protestant clergy of fundamentalist persuasion. Not only had there been "a real defection in the labor ranks . . . the country clergymen of the Methodist, Lutheran, Baptists," but even the Presbyterians were showing a tendency to "bolt." Lodge undertook to allay the President's anxieties. "The Congregationalists—very strong— are Republican to the core," he assured Roosevelt. "The Episcopalians are with us and their paper, *The Church Militant,* is urging Taft in strong editorials."

Taft polled 7,679,006 votes to Bryan's 6,409,106 and Debs's 420,820. Watson's vote fell from 117,183 four years earlier to 28,131, while the candidate of Hearst's new Independence Party polled 83,562, and Socialist Labor dropped sharply once more to only 13,825. In electoral votes Taft had 321 to 162 for Bryan.

With Taft the victor in the presidential race by a margin hardly less impressive than that of Roosevelt himself four years earlier, the colonel spent much of his remaining term of office concluding the diplomatic negotiations in progress and dramatizing the conservation issue. He also fired a parting shot at the American judicial system. In his message to Congress on December 8, 1908, he criticized the courts for their dogged conservatism, which threatened to defeat every effort at progressive legislation. William Allen White wrote congratulating him for "that fine electrical jolt to the reactionary courts. . . . I wish I had a million dollars. I would hire a ballet, and have those few brief sensible guarded remarks set to music and yipped and kiyoodled and yodeled into the pretty pink ear of Brewer and all his kitch and kind. Lord, Lord, how we do need to make the courts serve our democracy. . . . They make laws by interpretation, and execute them by injunctions, while the executive and legislative branches of the government are powerless to protest. . . ."

Even before the new President's inauguration a certain gloom had settled over Washington. Henry Adams was entertained by Mrs. John Garrett, the famous Baltimore hostess, "in full costume with all her jewels . . . listening to a Victor talking machine till bed-time." At dinner everyone had talked of the "good old times" a year ago, "when we were young and Theodore Roosevelt was President." Theodore was "wacking his last critics." "He is, beneath it all," Adams added, "a little saddened . . . although he bears it all bravely. In a few days Washington will groan with dullness without him. . . . " Meanwhile, Taft had "begun with a series of . . . stupidities which have thrown me into consternation." The root of Adams's dismay was Taft's appointment of Philander Knox as secretary of state. "He is not in the remotest degree fit for the post." The other Cabinet appointments were equally disheartening. "I have no candidate to offer, and no scheme to suggest," Adams wrote to Whitelaw Reid, "but if the new President is so bent on making a clean sweep of Roosevelt's men, why did we elect him expressly to carry on the Roosevelt regime?"

In the view of the Roosevelt loyalists, Taft added insult to injury by rather ostentatiously conferring with Uncle Joe Cannon at his Hot Springs headquarters. Charles Taft, emboldened by his role as his brother's Warwick, let it be known that he planned to run for the Senate from Ohio.

Inauguration day witnessed one of the worst storms in the city's history. There were several inches of snow on the ground and freezing winds. The ceremonies had to be moved unceremoniously indoors, but the descending President was characteristically euphoric. "Taft will give you four years of upbuilding," he told a dubious Henry Stoddard, "and I'm going off to Africa for a real fine time. I have done my Sorbonne and Oxford lectures. I've paid all my political debts. I'm footloose and fancy free, and when I'm back in Sagamore in a year or so as a private citizen, I'll be the happiest man you ever saw. It is time for me to go and for a man of Taft's type to . . . take my place," Roosevelt added; "he is a constructive fellow, I am not. The country should not be asked to stand four more years of crusading."

The trouble was that Taft was less a "constructive fellow" than a lazy fellow. And Roosevelt had to learn the hard way that you cannot pass on to a successor, however well intentioned he may, in fact, be, your own dreams and visions. The talk reported by Stoddard reminds us that an important part of Roosevelt's personality was an imperishable innocence.

Never had a president departed from office—the revered Washington included—to such an outpouring of affection and adulation. Gifford Pinchot spoke for his class, his generation, and the great company of middle-class reformers as well when he wrote of the change of administrations that "it was a dreadful day. Not because of the storm and the snow . . . but because the leader we loved was leaving us, because we should never know such days again." The Roosevelt administration, Pinchot wrote, had "found the public lands everywhere mishandled and misappropriated by corrupt politicians and their supporters for their own private profit, and it converted the Public Domain from private spoils into a great instrumentality for the public good. It convicted two United States Senators for public-land frauds, and stopped the looting of the property of the people." Finally, the President had "set and enforced standards of personal and civic honesty, capacity, and efficiency never before approached by any administration since the early days of the Republic . . . [and] his gallant contagious courage and marvelous executive effectiveness filtered down to the last messenger boy in the smallest Government division."

Walter Lippmann described Roosevelt as "the first President who shared a social vision." What Roosevelt brought to his office was not so much a new "social vision" as the determination to have honest and upright public officials. There was more truth in Lippmann's later and more considered judgment that he was the first president to realize the United States had become a "world power" with all "its responsibilities and its dangers and its implications, and the first to prepare the country spiritually and physically for this inescapable destiny. . . ."

Washington Gladden credited Roosevelt with rescuing the nation from the giant corporations. "Vast combinations of capital," he wrote, "were exerting a power of oppression such as no aristocracy of the Old World would dare to attempt; the railway managers were their thralls; some of the necessaries of life were largely under their control. . . . The extent to which this exploitation of the whole population had been carried by 'big business' was something fearful. The process went on noiselessly; silken toils were silently spun and woven about the limbs of the workers in their sleep. . . . That the burdens thus imposed would at length become intolerable, and that revolution would be the issue, was plain to all who could discern the signs of the times, but their voices fell on deaf ears. Fortunate it was for the country that the arrival of Theodore Roosevelt at the head of the nation was no longer deferred. Here was a man with eyes to see the extent and enormity of this veiled injustice, with words to describe it, and with an arm to smite it. The service which he has rendered to this nation in bringing into the light these furtive plunderings, in awakening the conscience of the land against them, and in setting the machinery of the law in motion for their prevention and punishment, is one of the greatest services it has ever fallen to any man to render." Roosevelt set himself to check the plunderers of the public, in Gladden's view, while disentangling "piratical business from honest business, to protect legitimate enterprise and prevent and punish predatory schemes. . . ."

The encomiums were endless. Roosevelt especially treasured that of William Allen White, who wrote: "How well you have kept the faith. How true you have been to all you hoped and believed in. . . . Of all the things you have done—and you have done so many—the best, it seems to me, is that you have lived so clean and so decently through it all that you have come out with the illusion of youth and strength and of a righteous faith. . . . I don't care much more than you do that your name and fame are secure. But it is a fine thing to have been nearly eight years in the most powerful place in the world and come out so clean that your faith in men and God is unshattered."

In Ray Stannard Baker's words, "Theodore Roosevelt was the first leader in whom I became deeply interested. He had become the hope of the young liberals, the 'insurgents' and progressives of that period. In the beginning we had great faith in him." What was of overriding importance was that Roosevelt aroused those hopes and, in doing so, suddenly made liberal politics an exciting prospect for young middle-class men and women who yearned for a better—or, in the older sense—a redeemed America.

The disappearance of Roosevelt from the political scene in 1908 took much of the savor out of life. He had banished boredom. "He has done it," Henry Adams wrote, "'by sheer force. I do not think I can name another considerable man in five hundred years past, who had his abnormal energy. It has never existed except in a lunatic asylum. . . . We are all timid and conventional, all of us, except T.R., and he has no mind."

Baker talked with the Colonel not long before he left office for his extended safari and suggested that the American people might turn to him again four years later, as they had to Cleveland. " 'No,' " Baker reported him as saying, "with a curious finality, a kind of sadness, a note which I never before heard him strike, 'revolutions don't go backwards. New issues are coming up. I see them. People are going to discuss economic questions more and more: the tariff, currency, banks. They are hard questions, and I am not deeply interested in them; my problems are moral problems, and my teaching has been plain morality.' " That was pretty much the fact of the matter.

Any great national hero has the capacity to invite what psychologists call projections. The public is able to project onto him all kinds of inchoate hopes and longings. Different segments of society as well as different individuals can discern in him different attributes, which, in fact, he may not possess, or ideas that he does not hold or holds only superficially. Roosevelt's protean nature allowed for just such projections in a remarkable degree. For those Americans who believed in "manliness," in the "strenuous" active life he was constantly proclaiming, he was a model figure. For the militant, he was the embodiment of militancy, always ready to leap to the defense of the honor of his country. Even for those of a pacific temper, like Jane Addams and Carl Schurz, he appeared, largely on the basis of his "interposition" in the Russo-Japanese War, the only world leader with the capacity for reconciling national conflict (Schurz had hailed him in the euphoria of the Russo-Japanese triumph as "a man in a position of almost unexampled moral power"). To the pious his constant evocation of the Almighty was reassuring, and to reformers, liberals, socialists, radicals, and intellectuals (largely overlapping categories), his serious literary and historical concerns as well as his loudly announced hostility to corporations was well nigh irresistible. Even workingmen and labor leaders were attracted to him by his pretense of even-handed justice, which in fact generally worked more to the advantage of the factory owner than of the factory worker. In short, he had the capacity to be all things to all men to a remarkable degree. Beyond all this, he simply held the fascinated attention of the country by virtue of his ability to create an air of drama by everything he did. After a succession of stodgy and virtually interchangeable presidents, Roosevelt's boyish enthusiasm for life was irresistible. He was a president made for the age of journalism. Although, like every occupant of the White House, he constantly inveighed against the bias and unfairness of the press, he played upon seasoned journalists and reporters like a master violinist on a Stradivarius, and they, in the main, adored him if only because he was such eternally good copy. Cartoonists, humorists, essayists, feature writers delighted to depict him in his latest scrap or adventure, his most recent tumble from a high-spirited horse, or the slaughter of the most recent bear.

Perhaps most important of all, Roosevelt made government service a highly attractive calling for hundreds of dedicated and idealistic young men. The Forestry Service was the prototype, but in the other departments and agencies of the government the same was true, and nowhere more so than in the Department of Justice, where brilliant young lawyers like Henry Stimson and George Wickersham prosecuted the malefactors of great wealth.

The circumstances surrounding the former President's departure for his hunting expedition cannot have been reassuring to his successor. To say that he went well equipped would seriously understate the case. Brooks Brothers and Abercrombie & Fitch vied in providing him with the most up-to-date hunting gear, and his wardrobe and armaments were reported in great detail to an enthralled public. Tens of thousands of cheering admirers gathered in New York in March, 1909, lining the shore to witness his departure. "I can see you now, as the ship moved slowly down the river," Lodge wrote, "waving your hand to us from the bridge and the picture will always be vivid in my mind." The papers have been filled for days "with minute accounts of your progress; of how you looked, what you wore and what you said or did not say from moment to moment. . . . The American people are reading these accounts . . . from day to day as if it was a serial story. They follow all with the interest of a boy who reads 'Robinson Crusoe' for the first time."

If Roosevelt had taken office with little more of a program than that of giving his fellow citizens a "square deal," he gradually developed the rudiments of a political philosophy which acquired the name of "nationalism." As we have noted, there was a large reform constituency before there was a national leader. Its principal exponents were the new journalists—Jacob Riis, Lincoln Steffens, Ida Tarbell, Ray Stannard Baker, Frederic Howe, Walter Hines Page, George Creel, Charles Edward Russell, and dozens of other, only slightly less well-known, members of the Fourth Estate. Its medium was, initially at least, *McClure's Magazine*, and its primary focus was municipal reform. Roosevelt, as police commissioner of New York City, had, of course, cut his political teeth on municipal reform, and Steffens and Riis had been his mentors. It was Riis who had alarmed and infuriated Roosevelt by asking him when he was police commissioner if he did not, in fact, intend to become president of the United States someday.

The reformers were constantly frustrated in their efforts by the doctrine of states' rights, which, by abjuring Federal action, left the citizens of the particular states at the mercy of the capitalists, who, routed in cities, commonly regrouped in state legislatures. What was desperately needed, in the view of many reformers, was a vastly enlarged theory of Federal or national powers as opposed to the ubiquitous and apparently irrepressible notion of states' rights.

This was the intent of Edward Bellamy's utopian novel *Looking Backward* and the Nationalist Clubs that sprang up everywhere to promote its principles. Roosevelt in his two terms as President had put flesh on the bare bones of nationalism. At the conclusion of his second term Rooseveltian nationalism was, as we might say, codified by one of the ablest of the new journalists. Herbert Croly was the son of David Goodman Croly, author of *Miscegenation,* and Jane Cunningham Croly, leader in a dozen women's causes, a follower of Stephen Pearl Andrews and a sometime member of his utopian communities. Croly was born in that vintage year for journalists, 1869. He served his literary apprenticeship on journals edited by his mother. Strongly influenced by Lloyd's *Wealth Against Commonwealth* and Bellamy's Nationalism, Croly set out to define what was most essentially American in our national life and what those elements suggested about the future of the Republic. His mission was that of providing a theoretical basis for the intervention of the Federal government on behalf of social and economic justice. The title of his book was *The Promise of American Life.* As we have argued earlier, the most decisive aspect of the collective consciousness of Americans was "promise," the dogged conviction, in the face of often overwhelming evidence to the contrary, in the midst, not infrequently, of unutterable misery, wretchedness, and want, that tomorrow would be better than today. We have seen how often this expectation was unfulfilled for large groups of Americans—for workingmen and immigrants, whose situation grew worse decade by decade in the period following the Civil War; especially for blacks, who sank deeper and deeper into the lower recesses of American society under the weight of prejudice—yet how, in the face of every discouragement, in the face of experience itself, the hope, the faith in the promise persisted irrationally and unquenchably. The dream of revolution was simply another manifestation, in political form, of that irrepressible expectation. "The faith of Americans in their own country," Croly wrote, "is religious . . . in its almost absolute and universal authority. It pervades the air we breathe. . . . Every new stage of our educational training provides some additional testimony. . . . We may distrust and dislike much that is done in the name of our country by our fellow-countrymen; but our country itself, its democratic system, and its prosperous future are above suspicion." Americans still believed, Croly wrote, "that somehow and sometime something better will happen to good Americans than has happened to people in any other country; and this belief, vague, innocent, and uninformed though it is, is the expression of an essential constituent in our national ideal. . . . An America which was not the Land of Promise, which was not informed by a prophetic outlook and a more or less constructive ideal, would not be the America bequeathed to us by our forefathers."

Assumptions about the future that rested on no more solid foundation than the faith that things must inevitably get better seemed to Croly a dangerous mixture of "optimism, fatalism, and conservatism." The idea that a better future would somehow "take care of itself," would somehow come about because we were the favored of the Lord, he believed to be no better than a belief in magic. The notion of a better future was nothing but "an idea, [and] that idea must be defined and human beings must undertake with patience and forethought to make it a reality." American history contained "much matter for pride and congratulation, and much matter for regret and humiliation." Nothing was to be gained, and much to be lost, by obscuring or glossing over the failures. What was at issue was no less than a new way of thinking about America's past *and* future. The future could no longer simply be evoked in fervent flights of patriotic oratory; it must be "planned and constructed rather than fulfilled of its own momentum." The conditions of American life had tended to "encourage an easy, generous, and irresponsible optimism," the result in large part of the abundant land and remarkable natural resources. Certainly the American experiment or whatever one wished to call it was "the first successful attempt in recorded history to get a healthy, natural equality which should reach down to the foundations of the state and to the great masses of men."

A constant theme throughout Croly's book was the danger of believing that the spectacular advances the nation had experienced in economic growth were somehow "automatic," that the nation had only "to slide down hill into the valley of fulfillment." Croly warned: "The discontented poor are beginning to charge their poverty to an unjust political and economic organization." The reformers, in abandoning "the older conception of an automatic fulfillment of our national destiny," of what he termed "optimistic fatalism," had already moved sharply, if sometimes unconsciously, in the direction of "purposive action" and "conscious national purpose." Stated in the simplest terms, the notion of a kind of inevitable and predestined fulfillment of the promise must be abandoned because it was every day more evident that the "traditional American confidence in individual freedom has resulted in a morally and socially undesirable distribution of wealth. . . . Efficient regulation there must be; and it must be regulation which will strike, not at the symptoms of the evil but at its roots. The existing concentration of wealth and financial power in the hands of a few irresponsible men is the inevitable outcome of the chaotic individualism of our political and economic organization. . . ." The economic problem was the problem, in essence, of "American national democracy, and its solution must be attempted chiefly by means of official national action." Croly, having stated his case, turned to the early history of the

Republic to substantiate it. The framers of the Constitution and Washington himself had been committed to the notion of a strong national government that used its powers boldly and aggressively to advance national policies. Alexander Hamilton's policy was, for example, the "energetic and intelligent assertion of the national good. He knew that the only method whereby the good could prevail either in individual or social life was by persistently willing that it should prevail and by the adoption of intelligent means to that end."

Thomas Jefferson had had a negative influence on American history because of his emphasis on states' rights, weak government, and a certain kind of anarchistic individualism. Croly called Hamilton "much the finer man and much the sounder thinker and statesman" and contrasted his nationalistic principles with "Jefferson's intellectual superficiality and insincerity."

It was Croly's thesis that even before the Civil War the "frontier mentality" had overshadowed the older Federalist view of the role of government and the nature of society. "For a long time American social and economic conditions were not merely fluid," he wrote, "but consistent and homogeneous, and the vision of the pioneer [that is to say, the notion that the aggressive and ingenious pursuit of individual gain must produce the maximum of general well-being] was fulfilled." But the success was transitory, and, in fact, in many frontier regions, notably in the territories administered by the Federal government, much of the success of the pioneer was the direct consequence of the authority exercised by the government. The irony was that the "captains of industry," the corporation lawyers, and the political and labor "bosses" utilized the ethic of the pioneer to justify the rise of the "business specialist" and the process of consolidation in the corporate world— the rationalization of the means of production in Marxian terms with considerable skill and sympathy. The capitalists, by Croly's reading, were not villains but simply enterprising individuals who took advantage of the opportunities offered them by the generally chaotic conditions of American life. Nor were the trusts the villains. They had succeeded in reducing the amount of waste, in effecting better working conditions and higher pay for their employees, and even in introducing a degree of stability into a volatile economy. At the same time they had proved "too wealthy and powerful for their official standing in American life" and for the good of the country. "They have not obeyed laws. . . . They have done much to excite . . . resentment and suspicion. In short, while their work has been constructive from an economic and industrial standpoint, it has made for political corruption and social disintegration. . . . Children, as they are, of the traditional American individualistic institutions, ideas, and practices, they have turned on their parents and dealt them an ugly wound." Moreover, they had formed an essentially antidemocratic alliance with political bosses for their mutual benefit.

Croly was critical of regulatory commissions appointed by state governments or by the Federal government. Their disposition was almost inevitably toward "incessant, vexatious, and finally harmful interference." The reformers, Croly wrote, "who expect to discipline the big corporations severely without injuring their efficiency are merely victims of an error as old as the human will. . . . They want to have their cake and eat it." The "problem" of the corporations—that is, their disposition toward criminal activity—was only a symptom. The real problem, and far more intractable, was an unjust distribution of wealth. "Reconstruction" must aim at placing the "industrial organization which has gradually been built up in this country" in "the service of a national democratic economic system." This could best be done "by some system of public ownership and private operation." It was Croly's belief that antitrust legislation should not discriminate in favor of the "small competitor" but should simply restrain the trusts from taking unfair advantage of him. It was a delicate problem, to be sure. Under the ground rules of fair play, established by the Federal government, the "small competitor" must, in the last analysis, be able to *compete;* otherwise, the government would be rewarding and thereby encouraging inefficiency.

By the same token, union activity should be encouraged, since unions seemed clearly to be the most effective means of raising the wages and improving the working conditions of the laborer. Indeed, Croly favored the closed shop, a requirement that all workers be enrolled in unions. Such a step would result in mitigation of the war between capital and labor and greater stability in all industrial operations.

Croly argued that the health of American democracy depended on its ability to fulfill for immigrants as well as for old-line Americans the promise of American life, which was, in the simplest terms, "the highest possible standard of living . . . economic freedom and prosperity." That promise had been made on the basis of apparently inexhaustible resources, he noted, "and it will have to be kept even when those natural resources are no longer to be had for the asking." The "democratic purpose" must rest on the principle of "human brother-hood," and "democratic organization" must be used "for the benefit of individual distinction and social improvement." In order to preserve democracy, "popular government" had "to make itself expressly and permanently responsible for the amelioration of the individual and society."

Some Americans clearly identified what Croly called "reconstructive policy"—i.e., government intervention in the economy in the name of social justice—as "flagrantly socialistic both in its methods and its objects." Croly was not inclined to dodge the word. A pragmatic rather than a doctrinaire socialism seemed to him perfectly compatible with the basic principles of democracy. Indeed, he was prepared to argue that such an approach was essential to the preservation of that democracy. If the necessary "reconstructive policy" were avoided because of the label "socialism," the United States would run the risk of failing in its most essential ideal: that of brotherhood. Private property should, Croly believed, be protected "in some form," but it should also be radically transformed in "its existing nature and influence. A democracy," he continued, "certainly cannot fulfill its mission without the eventual assumption by the state of many functions now performed by individuals, and without becoming expressly responsible for an improved distribution of wealth. . . . " It was Croly's conviction that the dominant form of socialism with its emphasis on revolutionary upheaval and internationalism was "headed absolutely in the wrong direction." The adoption by the United States, or by a majority of the citizens of the United States, of the "programme of international socialism" would, by setting class against class, accentuate the existing divisions in society, increase violence, and discourage brotherhood. "The only possible foundation for a better social structure," he wrote, "is the existing social order, of which the contemporary system of nationalized states form the foundation."

Americans, Croly pointed out, believed that every deficiency could be cured by money. What was in fact needed was not so much money as "collective purpose." In the reconstructed new order, individuality would replace individualism in a framework of collective action. Heretofore the word "individual" had been understood primarily in terms of individual striving for success and wealth, but the fact was that such a narrow goal inhibited the growth of true individuality, which rested on a much wider and more generous perspective. "As long as individuals are allowed to accumulate money from mines, urban real estate, municipal franchises, or semi-monopolies of any kind, just to that extent will the economic system of the country be poisoned, and its general efficiency impaired." Work must be made "disinterested," and the only way in which that could be done was to "adjust its compensation to the needs of a normal and wholesome human life."

Croly wrote: "The American people are not prepared for a higher form of democracy, because they are not prepared for a more coherent and intense national life." The opponents of "reconstruction" professed to see the ". . . extinction of American democracy in what they call the drift toward centralization. Such calamitous predictions are natural," he added, "but they are absurd." Croly insisted the days of "an individualist and provincial democracy" were clearly over. "There comes a time in the history of every nation, when its independence of spirit vanishes, unless it emancipates itself in some measure from its traditional illusions."

What was needed, above all else, in Croly's view, was a "process of national education" whereby the American people could draw the proper "inferences from the national experience, so that the national consciousness will gradually acquire an edifying state of mind towards its present and future problems." Croly put the issue in another way: The democratic ideal must be "nationalized." It must be raised from the provincial to the national; it must be retrieved from the hands of the powerful and predatory individuals who presently held it and placed in the hands of the people, and this could be done collectively only through the national government acting in the interests of all the people.

Croly had much to say in defense of a nonaggressive nationalism. It was, he argued, the principal obstacle to excessive centralization and the consequent danger of a harshly repressive world order. As for the decadent and repressive regimes that still held sway in Europe, those could probably be toppled only by war. "The ultimate object of a peaceable and stable European international situation cannot in all probability be reached without many additional wars," he concluded. The essential point was that such wars should be fought to accomplish such desirable purposes as extending democracy and improving social justice. Asian and African peoples, in Croly's view, lacked "the accumulated national tradition" that was the necessary basis of democracy. There must thus be destabilizing elements in the world scene, and European nations could and indeed should "undertake the responsibility of governing these disorganized societies," since "a few thousand resolute Europeans can hold in submission many million Asiatics," who, he was confident, would "be benefited by more orderly and progressive government." They needed such a "preliminary process of tutelage." The chaotic state of Latin American politics also distressed Croly. He feared that "no American international system will ever be established without the forcible pacification of one or more such centers of disorder. Coercion should, of course, be used only in the case of extreme necessity. . . . In short, any international American political system might have to undertake a task in states like Venezuela, similar to that which the United States is now performing in Cuba. . . . The construction of the Panama Canal," he added, "has given this country an exceptional interest in the prevalence of order and good government in the territory between Panama and Mexico."

In *The Promise of American Life* Herbert Croly wrote of Roosevelt: "No other American has had anything like so varied and intimate an acquaintance with the practical work of reform. . . . Mr. Roosevelt's reconstructive policy does not go very far in purpose or achievement, but limited as it is, it does tend to give the agitation for reform the benefit of a much more positive significance and a much more dignified task." More important to Croly, Roosevelt had treated "all public questions from a vigorous, even from an extreme, national standpoint. . . . The nationalization of reform endowed the movement," in Croly's opinion, "with new vitality and meaning. What Mr. Roosevelt really did was to revive the Hamiltonian ideal of constructive national legislation," which had languished during most of the nineteenth century.

One of the more interesting aspects of Croly's book was his attack on the notion of equal rights. By taking the line that all Americans had equal rights and equal opportunities, "mutual suspicion and disloyalty" were encouraged. Thus the failure of some individuals to prosper in the world or indeed to rise above the lowest level of want was attributed in large part to "individual wrong-doing," to personal weakness and ineptitude, to laziness or bad character, and the consequence was to arouse and intensify "personal and class hatred, which never in any society lies far below the surface."

The dream of the young intellectuals who had flocked to Johns Hopkins University had been of a new order of scholars, almost monastic in their devotion to the public good, who, through their researches and their painstakingly acquired credentials as experts, would transform American society from a cruelly exploitative and chaotic one to a just and orderly one. The dream was given a sharper focus by

Croly. The reeducation of "the American nation," as he preferred to call us, must be undertaken by "peculiarly competent, energetic, and responsible individuals," equipped to "perform the peculiarly difficult and exacting parts in a socially constructive drama. . . . " This meant in turn "a progressively higher standard of individual training and achievement. . . . American nationality will never be fulfilled except under the leadership of such men. . . ."

Finally, Croly evoked the time-honored American work ethic and attired it in modern garb. "Technical excellence" must characterize the labors of all Americans. Industry was not enough; skill was requisite; training was also of utmost importance. But underlying all else was the necessity for "intellectual and moral qualities essential to good work." So the true leaders would be the excellent workers, the enlightened thinkers, examples to their fellowmen "of heroism and saintliness."

The Promise of American Life soon took its place with Lloyd's and Bellamy's works as a basic text for nationalists and reformers.

12

Coming Down: The Taft Administration

In his inaugural address Taft paid his respects to his predecessor, declaring, "I have had the honor to be one of the advisors of my distinguished predecessor, and, as such, to hold up his hands in the reforms he has instituted. I should be untrue to myself, to my promises and to the declaration of the party platform upon which I was elected to office if I did not make the maintenance and enforcement of these reforms the most important feature of my administration. They were directed to the suppression of the lawlessness and abuse of power of great combinations of capital invested in railroads and in the industrial enterprises carrying on interstate commerce." The new President called for cooperation rather than conflict between the government and the giant corporations (many reformers would have said that there was too much cooperation already) and declared his intention of "saving and restoring our forests," a nod to the conservationists.

Despite the new President's reassuring words, the members of the newly formed National Progressive Republican League had reason to be apprehensive. They believed, in Ray Stannard Baker's words, "that only a start had been made during Roosevelt's administration; that the real battle was yet to come. . . ." It was soon apparent that their fears were justified, "that their efforts to understand and solve the important problems of railroads, water power, trusts, the tariff, and the like were to find small encouragement at Washington." The old guard was soon firmly in control of Congress, and Republicans "tainted with Teddyism," to use Joe Cannon's term, found themselves on the outside looking in when committee assignments were made. In the Senate, Nelson Aldrich, the rich New Yorker, was the conservative counterpart of Uncle Joe Cannon in the House. Petitioners for the President's support heard more and more frequently, "I am leaving that to Aldrich." Similarly, in the House Cannon ran things much as he pleased. "If I knew anything about the Government," Pinchot wrote, "I knew the fire had gone out of it. . . . Washington was a dead town. Its leader was gone, and in his place a man whose fundamental desire was to keep out of trouble."

After the appointment of Philander Knox as secretary of state (to succeed Elihu Root), Henry Adams wrote to a British friend: "With about fifty years experience, foreign service, social habitude and the help of half a dozen very intelligent and superior women, he will make a highly competent Foreign Secretary."

James Garfield, who as commissioner of the Bureau of Corporations had ridden herd on errant corporations and then as secretary of the interior had worked with Gifford Pinchot to consolidate the work of conservation, was replaced by Richard Achilles Ballinger, a Seattle lawyer with close ties to Western lumber and mining interests. "It is worse than I feared," Adams wrote to Elizabeth Cameron, of Taft's appointments. "Two owls and a hen, of whom one is Knox, another is [Franklin] MacVeagh [secretary of the treasury], a worse is Cannon, and the hen is fat and futile and fluffy. Never have I seen such a *débâcle* since Cleveland's second term. . . . Everybody cackles in consternation. . . . Nothing can be done. The whole concern is dropping to pieces." There were numerous other expressions of disenchantment. Taft took the stand that he was simply being judicial. Where Roosevelt had seen the role of the president as that of an aggressive opponent of the interests, his successor saw himself as a judge, balancing the scales between often extreme reformers and the legitimate interests of the business community. That attitude, Pinchot wrote, made him the unwitting "accomplice and the refuge of land grabbers, water-power grabbers, grabbers of timber and oil—all the swarm of big and little thieves and near-thieves, who, inside or outside of the law, were doing everything they knew to get possession of natural resources which belonged to the people. . . ."

William Allen White wrote to Taft to reproach him for the conservative trend of his administration and warn him that an "insurgent" movement was under way in the Republican Party in Kansas against his leadership. The people of his state, White declared, "will not stand for the Cannon-Aldrich leadership. . . . The people have begun to confuse you with the leadership. So they don't understand you, and perhaps you do not understand the people." Taft had snubbed Kansas Senator Joseph Bristow (White had managed Bristow's campaign), and White wrote: "When you discipline a man like Bristow who has the people behind him, you are merely disciplining the people."

Taft was soon faced with the first and most serious crisis of his presidency. In the last year of Roosevelt's administration, plans had been formulated to extend Federal control over "large numbers of immensely valuable water-power sites on navigable streams, on streams useful for irrigation, and in the National Forest," in Pinchot's words. There were also "rich coal lands, oil lands, iron-ore lands, and phosphate lands, millions of acres of them. . . ." All these, having been established by presidential fiat, could be as readily opened to private exploitation. Ballinger, Pinchot discovered, was in the process of turning over to private speculators valuable public lands in Alaska. The group was a Morgan-Guggenheim syndicate which owned the two principal railroads in Alaska and a steamship line. It also owned the copper mines of Kennecott and had its attention fixed on Alaska coalfields.

Pinchot began at once to use his very considerable influence and almost inexhaustible energy to frustrate Ballinger's scheme. When his appeals to Taft were turned aside and it became evident that Taft was determined to support his Cabinet officer, Pinchot went public in a series of magazine and newspaper articles as well as speeches, thereby defying both Ballinger and the President. Taft, aware of Pinchot's prominence as the symbol of the conservation movement and indeed of the entire Roosevelt program, did his tactful and ingratiating best to call off his unruly subordinate, but Pinchot refused to be muzzled. Newspapers took up the cause with enthusiasm. Reformers, liberal Republicans, and even Democrats rallied to Pinchot's side. The *Washington Post* of August 14 announced in a dark headline: "Pinchot-Ballinger War Likely to Reach Congress." It was not without significance that the name of the head of the Forestry Service preceded that of the secretary of the interior.

Taft confessed to his brother Horace: "I do regard Gifford as a good deal of a radical and a good deal of a crank, but I am glad to have him in the government." A few months later he wrote his daughter that Pinchot and Roosevelt had been much closer than he and Pinchot could ever be, "for they both have more of a Socialist tendency"; he described Pinchot to a friend as "a socialist and a spiritualist . . . capable of any extreme act."

Pinchot, for his part, had no intention of resigning. He was determined to dramatize the conservation issue in every way that he could. It was his plain intention to make the President fire him, and to this end he stepped up his campaign against the hapless Ballinger. The National Conservation Commission gave Pinchot its wholehearted support, but the *New York Times* and various conservative Republican newspapers congratulated Taft "for his thorough-going exposure of the methods of the muck-rakers [using Roosevelt's term to indict Roosevelt's protégé]. During the chief part of his predecessor's Administration they kept the Nation in a ferment by their indiscriminate, ill-judged, and baseless attacks upon public and private character."

In the *San Francisco Call* Fremont Older editorialized, "The West knows Ballinger too well. It knows his associations. The West knows Pinchot and his work. . . . It will wait to see who gets that Alaska coal, and whether Ballinger or his friends share in the profits."

Pinchot carried his case to the West Coast on a speaking tour. At San Diego he was greeted by a band of notables, among them John Spreckels, the sugar tycoon, S. S. McClure, and E. W. Scripps, head of the second largest newspaper chain in the country. When he gave a speech in Seattle on conservation, the *Washington Star* noted, "Mr. Pinchot met the members of the Pacific Coast Lumber Association for the first time, and was the subject of eulogy by every speaker. The change in public sentiment concerning the forest reserve system and the general conservation policy of the administration in this section is one of the most remarkable that ever occurred in the history of any country. Gifford Pinchot is today the most popular member of the administration in this part of the country. . . . 'He can have anything he wants.' "

Norman Hapgood and *Collier's Weekly* took up Pinchot's cause as its own, going so far as to hire Louis Brandeis to defend an official in the Department of the Interior who had been fired by Ballinger for protesting the proposed surrender of the Alaska lands. Congress decided to conduct an investigation of its own, and the *New York Journal of Commerce* observed, "Practically the whole attention in political circles is now centered upon the proposed Congressional investigation of the doings of Secretary Ballinger. With but few exceptions members of Congress still regard this investigation as of unusual significance because they think it is practically an investigation of the President." Indeed, it might have seemed to a casual observer that Gifford Pinchot was Roosevelt's true successor and Taft merely a pretender.

Finally, Pinchot forced Taft to request his resignation by writing the so-called Dolliver letter. Jonathan Prentiss Dolliver was a Senator from Iowa and chairman of the Committee on Agriculture and Forestry. Pinchot wrote to him to defend two officials of the Department of Agriculture who had publicly denounced Ballinger. In doing so, Pinchot defied a presidential order which forbade communications from officials of the administration to members of Congress except through channels. The letter had its desired effect. A furious Taft sacked Pinchot, and the chief forester admitted freely that the President "was perfectly justified in firing me. I had asked for it and I could not complain. . . ." Indeed, when he told his mother he had been fired, she flung her hand over her head and exclaimed, "Hurrah!"

The *Washington Evening Star* reported that "political Washington has stirring in its midst probably a greater tempest than it has had at any other period in recent history. It has all grown out of the summary dismissal by President Taft of Forester Gifford Pinchot." The *Washington Times* was even more agitated, noting that "the Ballinger-Pinchot conservation quarrel has in a single day precipitated the whole national political and legislative situation into chaos, and what some extreme people call anarchy." Reporters noted that the atmosphere at Pinchot's office was more that of a victory than of a defeat. It was indeed a victory. Gifford Pinchot had established himself as the hero of the embattled Republican Insurgents, the conscience of the Roosevelt wing of the party, and the defender of its most basic principles. As he himself wrote later, he had, in effect, founded the Progressive Republicans and ensured the candidacy of his hero in the presidential elections of 1912.

Attention now centered on the composition of the congressional investigating committee. In the House, after a sharp struggle in which the Insurgents were led by George Norris of Nebraska, Uncle Joe Cannon was defeated, and a joint Senate-House committee was appointed with a majority of opponents of the Taft administration. Congressman Charles A. Lindbergh of Minnesota, a friend of Pinchot and the Forest Service, was one of the Republicans who helped override the Republican regulars.

As the hearings proceeded, Brandeis proved brilliantly effective as attorney for the ousted officials. "Brandeis," Pinchot wrote, "was a wonder. He it was who won our case." It was his combination of "very remarkable dignity and gentleness of character and manner, combined with unyielding tenacity and inflexible resolution. . . . His poise was unbreakable, and his temper almost incredibly under control." Gifford Pinchot's brother, Amos, joined Brandeis as an attorney for the dismissed officials.

The congressional hearings on the Ballinger-Pinchot controversy lasted over a period of four months and received voluminous press coverage, thereby helping fix in the public mind, whether fairly or not, the image of President Taft as a friend of "the interests" and the enemy of conservation. Pinchot could hardly have asked for more. Or Brandeis. It helped materially to make him some years later the first Jewish member of the Supreme Court.

Reflecting on the significance of the Ballinger-Pinchot controversy, Oswald Garrison Villard noted that the President "was merely true to his training and ultraconservatism. His great vice was that he was extremely lazy and a great procrastinator." (Bryan called him the Great Postponer.) According to Villard, it was this disposition to put things off or half do them that led to Taft's decision in the Ballinger-Pinchot matter. "Taft put off reading the relevant papers in order to play golf with the Yale golf team. Then he ate a large meal, napped and rose too late to read the papers carefully, skimmed them and made the wrong decision—a decision in favor of Ballinger."

One of the planks in the Republican platform had called for tariff reform. The story was a familiar one. The "reform" took the shape of a bill that substantially increased tariff schedules instead of lowering them (perhaps this was the "cooperation" between business and government that the President had in mind). Henry Cabot Lodge, involved for the first time in "tariff making," was horrified at "the amount of ruthless selfishness that is exhibited on both sides. . . ." He acknowledged that there was much truth in Roosevelt's message from distant Africa, where he paused in his shooting of lions long enough to note that the difficulty was that there was "no real ground for dissatisfaction of a serious kind, with the present tariff; so that what we have to meet is not an actual need, but a mental condition among our people who believe there ought to be a change. . . ." Roosevelt was convinced that "the inevitable disappointment and irritation" which must accompany

any new tariff bill would die out in a few months if the country were prosperous. But it turned out that Lodge had somewhat misled the Colonel about the shortcomings of the Payne-Aldrich tariff. It was far more favorable to the trusts and big corporations than Lodge's comment had suggested. Rather than allay public outcry for tariff reform, the struggle in Congress had served, more than anything else, to dramatize the influence of business interests in that body and in Taft's administration generally.

There were soon numerous defections among Midwestern Republicans. Senators La Follette, Albert Cummins of Iowa, and Albert Beveridge of Indiana led the assault on the administration's policies. "Honestly I think the public is settling down on the conviction that President Taft is feeble-minded and his cabinet too . . ." Henry Adams wrote to his brother, Brooks. "We all like Taft, and avoid attacking him, but Knox and MacVeagh and [James] Wilson [secretary of agriculture] and Ballinger, are extreme cases of idiocy and age. . . . Wall Street . . . is cursing Taft quite as violently as they swore at Theodore. Indeed they profess to prefer Theodore. At least he did what he said, while Taft talks to everybody in their own sense." To Adams, it was the "top-heavy protective system which turns us into thieves and liars. We daren't touch it, for fear of the whole fabric falling. In that particular we are united in silence."

One shock after another befell Taft's ill-fated administration, culminating in the midterm election of 1910 that brought in a Democratic Congress. The setback seemed to lessen, if that was possible, the President's fitful interest in his duties. In the words of Senator Jonathan Dolliver of Iowa, "Taft is an amiable man, entirely surrounded by men who know exactly what they want."

While these events were taking place at home, the former President was making headlines with his dramatic doings in other lands. It is not hard to imagine the state of mind of President Taft as the papers were filled every day with accounts of the exploits of his predecessor while his own imposing person was comparatively ignored. He may have been excused for wondering at times who was indeed president and perhaps even more if a hunting trip to Africa was, after all, the best way to avoid the public eye. The safari was preceded (and followed) by a triumphal procession through Europe. In England Roosevelt went out of his way to snub egotistical young Winston Churchill. He had read Winston's biography of his father, Lord Randolph, and wrote to Lodge that he disliked the father and the son almost equally. "Both," he wrote, "possess . . . such levity, lack of sobriety, lack of permanent principle, and inordinate thirst for that cheap form of admiration which is given to notoriety, as to make them poor public servants." Winston Churchill was "undoubtedly clever but conceited to a degree which it is hard to express either in words or figures and . . . not at all sympathetic to me." Reveling in the adulation of Danes, Swedes, and Germans, Roosevelt was sincerely puzzled over the phenomenon. "I drive through dense throngs of people cheering and calling, exactly as if I were President and visiting cities at home where there is great enthusiasm for me," he wrote to Lodge. "As I say, I have been much puzzled by it." He concluded that his popularity was due to the fact that he was "a man who has appealed to their imagination, who is accepted by them as a leader, but as a leader whom they suppose to represent democracy, liberty, honesty and justice."

So it went during the whole year-long trip. Official honors and large enthusiastic crowds awaited him everywhere; public acclaim, such as had seldom been accorded a head of state or ruling monarch, continued in Britain, in Italy, in Germany; nations clamored for a visit from the former President. All this was, of course, reported, with what might have seemed but apparently didn't seem, excessive detail in the American press, and it swelled the hearts of the Colonel's critics as well as of his admirers to think that a former president of the United States should be so admired by the citizens of other nations. "The unceasing popular interest in what you are doing is a daily surprise to me . . ." Lodge wrote. The arrival of Roosevelt's party in Africa heightened the drama. The visits to European capitals, the cheering crowds had been simply the curtain raiser; now came the serious drama (although Finley Peter Dunne continued to make fun of the great American hunter; it might be noted that the former President, so far from resenting Dunne's parodies, delighted in them and in his friendship with Dunne).

In Africa, lion after lion fell before the Colonel's artillery. Rhinos, hippos, antelopes, wildebeests, and all manner of game were struck down, helpless as Democrats. When a skeptical George Creel asked one of Theodore Roosevelt's guides how the former President, "blind in one eye, and myopic in the other," could hit any of the animals that he accumulated on his safaris, the guide explained that when the Colonel leveled his gun, three other guns were also leveled. "Mr. Roosevelt had a fairly good idea of the general direction, but we couldn't take chances with the life of a former president."

Soon there was evidence that Roosevelt, even on safari, was beginning to have serious second thoughts about his "great renunciation." He wrote to Lodge from Nairobi: "The chances are infinitesimal that I shall ever go back into public life, but it would be the height of folly even to talk of the subject in any way. My destiny at present is to shoot rhino and lions, and I hope ultimately elephant." Nonetheless, it took no special perspicuity to discern, amid accounts of the slaughter of lions and hippos, a more than incipient yearning for the hunting fields of politics. People, he wrote to Lodge, must soon tire of "the advice of a man whose day is past. The last statement sounds melancholy," he added, "but it really isn't; I know no other man who has had as good a time as I have had in life; no other President ever enjoyed the Presidency as I did; no other ex-President ever enjoyed himself as I am now enjoying myself, and as I think it likely I shall enjoy myself in the future." Still, for anyone who knew the Colonel's restless energy and love of the public eye, there remained the feeling that when there were no more lions to be shot, there might be some awkward times.

In Kenya, in September, 1909, the Colonel killed his second bull elephant, and Kermit shot his first, making it an elephant, five lions, and three buffalo for the junior Roosevelt. The trip, Roosevelt assured Lodge, would have "permanent scientific value" because they would bring back with them "the most noteworthy collection of big animals that has ever come out of Africa." He was determined to try to capture for the readers of Scribner's the feeling "of the great game, the lions as they charged, the gray bulk of the elephants as we peered at them close at hand in the matted jungle, the hippos round the boat, the rhinos, truculent and stupid, standing in the bright sunlight on the open plains."

It became evident from Lodge's letters to Roosevelt that Lodge's true sympathies, personal feelings aside, tended much more to what was already defining itself as the Taft wing of the Republican Party than to "the radicalism of La Follette and Cummins," which seemed "rampant" in the Mississippi Valley, from Minnesota down to Kansas. As the dissatisfaction of the Insurgents, as the La Follette-Cummins faction was beginning to be called, increased, an obviously alarmed Lodge, well aware of his friend's disposition to speak out on matters that concerned him, fired off a series of letters to Africa, urging Roosevelt to say nothing to the press about the political situation at home until he, Lodge, had had a chance to explain things to him in their proper light. He should not even talk to Gifford Pinchot, recently sacked by Taft because of his attack on Ballinger. This seemed to

Roosevelt to be carrying circumspection too far. Pinchot was one of his closest friends and most ardent supporters. "There is a constantly growing thought of you and your return to the Presidency," Lodge wrote, "and I do not want your name made use of, on the one side to help men who are a little out of the administration and the party organization and are using your name for their own purpose." Despite his very evident misgivings, Roosevelt promised Lodge that on his return to the United States he would "speak as little as possible . . . and . . . when I do speak . . . exercise the most extreme care. . . . It is a very unpleasant situation."

The safari over, Roosevelt began his return—first by way of Cairo, and then on to Rome in early April. Everywhere he was greeted by crowds of eager reporters and crowds of enraptured citizens. In Rome he was forced to rebuke the Pope, who invited him to an audience conditional upon his not meeting with a troublesome group of Methodist missionaries. He would accept no such condition, he told the Pope. But when the Methodists crowed too loudly, he refused to see them, thereby rendering, he wrote Lodge, "what I regard as a small service to the cause of right-thinking in America." He was also forced to rebuke the kaiser, who invited him to visit at his Berlin schloss but neglected to include his wife, Edith, who had joined him in Rome. The Colonel let the kaiser know things were not done that way in the United States, and the kaiser immediately capitulated. Roosevelt found the German emperor and empress thoroughly *gemütlich*, "as nice a family as I have come across anywhere," he wrote to Lodge, "thoroughly good citizens in every way, very cultivated, very intelligent, very simple and upright and straight forward." He would be pleased to have them as neighbors at Sagamore Hill, and the kaiser, he felt, would make a first-class Senator or Cabinet officer and, "with a little change, a first-class President!"

Roosevelt was met by a reception committee on his return from Africa and given a tumultuous parade up Broadway. It was a spectacle hardly calculated to cheer President Taft and the Republican old guard. Still, he doggedly refused to discuss politics, the Taft administration, or his own political future. Nonetheless, his involvement, if reluctant, was inevitable. It began with his endorsement of Henry Stimson, Taft's secretary of war, for governor of New York.

Writing to welcome Roosevelt home from his famous safari, William Allen White deplored the Taft administration. "We need you, in our business," he wrote. "The American people are terribly sentimental. It seems to me they are the most sentimental people in the world; that is, they will do more for what seems the larger good, for the intelligently unselfish end, than any other people." But Taft was unable to make such an appeal. "No one dislikes President Taft," White added; "there is no anger at him. But no one feels any affection for him. . . . He has aroused no enthusiasm of high purpose." At the same time White made clear he was opposed to the movement to reelect Roosevelt as president.

To Roosevelt's credit, he did, it seems, "wish, in my own mind, and to you," as he wrote to Lodge, "to give Taft the benefit of every doubt, and to think and say the very utmost that can be said and thought in his favor. Probably the only course open to him was not to do as he originally told me before the nomination he intended to do, and as he even sometimes said he intended to do between the nomination and the election, but to do as he actually has done." The Colonel's phraseology, for anyone who knew him as well as Lodge knew him, was alarming, containing, as it did, hints of disloyalty and breach of faith. More ominous still, Roosevelt began to refer to the "Taft-Aldrich-Cannon regime." He reminded Lodge that "Taft was nominated solely on my assurance to the Western people especially, but almost as much to the East, that he would carry out my work unbroken; not (as he has done) merely working for somewhat the same objects in a totally different spirit, and with a totally different result, but exactly along my lines with all his heart and strength."

The problem was, of course, that no one except Roosevelt himself could have worked "exactly" along his "lines." The Roosevelt magic, as we have seen, lay far less in what he accomplished than in his unique style—the manner in which he accomplished what he did, which invariably gave maximum public effect to often modest achievements. Every action was accompanied, for one thing, by a blizzard of moralisms which gave the impression that America and humanity in general were nobler and better in consequence of what the President had prevailed upon a reluctant Congress to do. Another difficult element in the succession was Roosevelt's notion of loyalty. He thought Taft a fair and honest and, above all, loyal chap who would accept Roosevelt's advice and guidance without question. A touch more sophistication about human beings and their motives might have suggested that Taft, to the degree he was not a mere puppet, would try to be his own man and, in making that effort, would have to free himself from the tutelage not only of his predecessor but also of his predecessor's friends and supporters. There was also, of course, the simple fact that Taft was even more conservative in his instincts than Roosevelt himself. We have had ample opportunity to note how limited and tentative Roosevelt's own reforming impulses were. In the words of William Allen White, Taft "was convinced that we were mad." He "was a consistent, courageous, most intelligent conservative. He believed in the existing order. . . . It was his world."

Lodge tried to persuade Roosevelt to take an active role on behalf of Republican candidates in the midterm elections of 1910. From having feared his speaking out too critically of Taft, Lodge feared his silence even more. If Roosevelt remained on the sidelines, Lodge warned, his ill-wishers would say that he was doing so in the hope that a sweeping defeat in the fall "would make your nomination in 1912 inevitable." Lodge did not believe that Roosevelt single-handedly could prevent defeat, but he might "avert disaster and ruin" since "the great masses of the Republican party . . . believe in conservation, the control of corporations, the policy of reasonable protection, and, above all, believe in you." Lodge acknowledged that "the Republican party is on the eve of a defeat, but I do not want the Republican party destroyed or disintegrated. It is the best instrument, with all its defects, that we have to carry out what we both want done. The Democratic party is hopeless."

The Colonel's reply was not reassuring: "I went out of the country and gave him [Taft] the fullest possible chance to work out his own salvation." Many of Roosevelt's closest advisers had warned him against making Taft his heir apparent on the ground that Taft was, in many ways, an unknown quantity; if Roosevelt forced him on the party and he dropped the ball, instead of "hitting the line," Roosevelt would be blamed for Taft's failures. Taft had made his own bed.

It was in the midterm elections of 1910 that Oswald Garrison Villard first took serious notice of young Franklin Roosevelt, Theodore's distant cousin. He seemed to Villard to have great personal charm combined with shrewd political instincts. Elected to the New York State Senate in 1910, Roosevelt was introduced by Villard to a City Club audience as a young man "who . . . had the greatest political future before him of anyone of his generation. . . ."

Despite the disappointment of the former President's adherents at the course of the Taft administration, the year 1910 was an encouraging one for Progressives (or, as they preferred to be called in the Midwest, the Insurgents). The spirit of reform was sweeping the country as one state after another adopted the direct primary. "The initiative and referendum," White wrote, "was either established or on its way, going to the people as constitutional amendments in twenty states. . . ." In a dozen states people were voting directly for Senators, and a Federal income tax seemed well on the way to passage.

The feeling that the momentum was on the side of the Insurgents was strengthened in White by the fact that he was asked to write the Republican platform for the state of Kansas in 1910. He sent a copy to Roosevelt, who gave it "a green light." One plank in the platform pledged Republican congressional candidates to vote for a rule that would make membership on important House committees elective instead of appointive by the Speaker. Another plank supported jail sentences for willful violations of the antitrust laws, while still another urged strengthening of the Interstate Commerce Commission. The platform contained a ringing call for the direct election of Senators instead of their election by the state legislatures. Kansas Republicans in the state legislature were pledged to vote for a law "placing all public utilities, railways, telegraph, telephone, power companies, street railways, distributors of gas . . . under the control of a State Board." Finally, there was a provision for publicizing the sources and uses of campaign contributions.

In the words of William Allen White, "Reform was in the air. Political reform appeared first in the demand for the primary system, and, a few years later, for the recall, for the initiative and referendum, which spread to considerably more than half the states north of the Ohio, and for ballot reform. . . . So in Kansas, as in every state in the Missouri Valley and in many states in the Lake district, the Ohio Valley and Westward of Kansas to the coast, the young insurgents were coming out hammer and tongs. . . ."

The House and Senate were, in White's opinion, in the hands of "the most reactionary leaders along political and economic lines that were ever given command in Washington. They were not crooked or corrupt. They were deeply convinced that the rule of the dollar was by divine right."

In Kansas an Insurgent governor named Edward Wallis Hoch was followed by another reform-minded chief executive, red-headed Walter Roscoe Stubbs, who, as speaker of the state legislature, had led the fight to abolish the pass system—free railroad passes for journalists and politicians—in the state. After, as William Allen White put it, a "desperate struggle" the primary system was adopted. Efforts were made to regulate interstate commerce (overthrown by the Supreme Court), and cities were authorized to adopt the commission form of government. Kansas, and a number of other states, undertook to follow in the footsteps of La Follette's Wisconsin.

White threw his support to Joseph Bristow for Senate against the Republican machine's elegant Chester Long. Long rode about the state in a shiny limousine provided by a Wichita banker. Bristow, in dramatic contrast, toured in a battered Ford. Bristow was, in White's words, "a tall, lean, gaunt, Kentucky-bred creature, hungry-faced, fiery-eyed," looking somewhat like "an animated cadaver." He defeated Long, and the Insurgents controlled the Kansas legislature. "It was our day of triumph," White wrote. "I record this only because similar contests were going on in the latter part of the first decade of the 1900's in Iowa, in Illinois, in Indiana, in Michigan, in Pennsylvania, in Massachusetts, in New Hampshire, in Wisconsin, in the Dakotas, in Minnesota, in Colorado, in Wyoming, in Montana."

The growing conviction that Roosevelt would be the Republican candidate in 1912 was strengthened when the Colonel came to Kansas—to Osawatomie, the home of John Brown (not Roosevelt's type, needless to say)—and announced his support for the Republican platform in that state, "a position which shocked his friends in the East," a proud White noted. (Gifford Pinchot wrote the speech.) "We must drive special interests out of politics," Roosevelt declared, adding, "I stand for the square deal. . . . I mean not merely that I stand for fair play under the present rules of the game but that I stand for having those rules changed so as to work for a more substantial equality of opportunity and of reward for equally good service." White wrote in the 1940s: "It is hard to bring back today the sense of excitement, almost of tumult, that was in the air . . . in the summer and autumn of 1910. It was revolutionary."

After the elections, which saw four anti-Taft Republicans sent to Congress, William Allen White wrote triumphantly to Samuel Gompers, offering the help of the *Gazette* in labor's "struggle for collective bargaining, in its demand for a living wage, in its struggle for the right of a man to his job upon an equality of capital . . . or for any of the fundamental things that organized labor is struggling for in legislatures and out. . . ." White was convinced that the only thing that would "save democracy from ruin" was "an intelligent voting majority which will only be had as labor gets shorter hours, better wages and a higher social and economic status and a royal American privilege to look every man, class or profession squarely in the eye and tell it to go straight up."

The year 1910 witnessed the deaths of Julia Ward Howe, William James, and the artist John La Farge. The deaths of James and La Farge, Henry Adams wrote to Henry James, were "a limb of our own lives cut off."

Julia Ward Howe was one of the great figures of the time, "a daughter," John Jay Chapman called her, "of the great liberal epoch of the nineteenth century. . . ." An early abolitionist, a poet, a playwright, the wife of the romantic reformer Samuel Gridley Howe, she was the last surviving monument of a long-forgotten era (she had been born during James Monroe's Era of Good Feelings). She had written one of the nation's great hymns—"The Battle Hymn of the Republic"—after the Battle of Bull Run, and she had embraced every good cause in the years that followed, from temperance and justice to the Indians to peace and freedom for the Filipinos. "A doughty, gallant battler in the drawing room," she carried into her old age "an unfailing gayety," Chapman wrote. But Boston never quite accepted her. "Her house was full of Persians, Armenians, and the professors of strange new faiths. . . . She sat at the gate and entertained all men, including a lot of people who Boston thought ought not to be entertained. But there she sat, nevertheless,—all courage, all wit and all benignity. . . ." She was ninety-one when she died. Tiny, fragile, and beautiful as a piece of Sèvres china, she had lived through most of the history of the Republic.

William James almost single-handedly had created Harvard's golden age, but he had welcomed his retirement. "What an awful trade that of professor is," James wrote Grace Norton, "—paid to talk, talk, talk! I have seen artists grow pale and sick whilst I talked to them without being able to stop." He had become more and more wary of "all intellectualism, of the separation of thinking from life, of a world in which truth was thought to lie in sentences rather than in experiences." He wrote to his friend Theodore Flournoy, who had written to congratulate him on his retirement: "A professor has two functions: (1) to be learned and distribute bibliographical information; (2) to communicate truth. The 1st function is the essential one, officially considered. The 2nd is the only one I care for. Hitherto I have always felt like a humbug as a professor, for I am weak in the first requirement. Now I can live for the second with a free conscience."

James was well aware that his style was out of date and out of step with the new academic dispensation. He wrote to Flournoy: "I find that my free and easy and personal way of writing, especially in 'pragmatism,' has made me an object of loathing to many respectable academic minds. . . ." The scandal was increased by James's interest in psychic phenomena, less indicative of his belief in them than of his determined open-mindedness and zest for new realms of investigation. The increasingly critical attitude of young scholars toward his work troubled him. He remarked that he was determined to write at least one book in the new objective, impersonal mode to show that he could do it. At the same time he deplored the type of young scholar who was being stamped with the new Ph.D. like government-certified beef. They seemed to him a poor lot. What James saw himself as most resolutely opposing was less the illusions of the devout or the absolutist notions of metaphysical philosophers than " 'Science' in the form of abstraction, priggishness and sawdust, lording it over all."

Traveling in Europe after his retirement, James had met Sigmund Freud and Carl Jung and wrote to Flournoy that he hoped that Freud and his pupils would "push their ideas to their utmost limits, so that we may learn what they are. They can't fail to throw light on human nature; but I confess that he made on me personally the impression of a man obsessed with fixed ideas."

The key to James's character lay in his statement that he wished to defend "experience" against "philosophy" and do so *against all the prejudices of his "class."* So James did more than simply search for a way in which, consistent with his scientific skepticism, he could make a central place for religion in the life of the individual; he proclaimed a new form of *expressiveness* which broke down (or which at least began the process of breaking down) all purely formal relationships by a radical kind of "friendship," one characterized by "loving affection." John Jay Chapman wrote: "I cannot think that anyone ever met James without feeling that James was a better man than himself."

James was squarely in the "individualistic" tradition established by Emerson and reaching its ultimate expression in Whitman. "The mother-sea and fountain-head of all religions," he wrote to his friend Henry Rankin, "lie in the mystical experiences of the individual, taking the word mystical in a very wide sense. . . . We are . . . made convincingly aware of the presence of a sphere of life larger and more powerful than our usual consciousness." The "mystical experiences of the individual" carry "invincible assurance of a world beyond the sense, they melt our hearts and communicate significance and value to everything and make us happy. . . . Religion in this way is absolutely indestructible. . . . Something, not our immediate self, does act on our life! So I seem doubtless to my audience to be blowing hot and cold, explaining away Christianity, yet defending the more general basis from which I say it proceeds."

Pragmatism will build no cathedrals, erect no monuments to souls, real or mythic. It contains no communitarian or collective principle; it is individualism raised to its highest denominator, a translated Emerson, a denatured Whitman distilled for the upper middle class. It does not even incorporate friendship—the "loving affection" that James made the center of his own life. With James, the Poet as Prophet-Hero, so vividly delineated by Emerson, was replaced by the Philosopher-Hero, almost as irresistibly delineated by James. But character was still, after all, everything. And spirit.

"In general talk on life, literature, and politics," John Jay Chapman wrote, "James was always throwing off sparks. . . . It was easy to differ from him; it was easy to go home thinking that James had talked the most arrant rubbish. . . . Yet it was impossible not to be morally elevated by the smallest contact with William James. A refining, purgatorial influence came out of him. . . . My feeling is that James was enormously important to his own generation," Chapman added, "by breaking down the barriers that prevented them from giving rein to their instinctive feelings. Whether he will do this for a later time no one can tell."

If Protestantism had invented the individual and Emerson had secularized him or her with trappings of spirituality, William James defended the individual against the alarming skepticism of Science. Christian orthodoxy aside, Darwinism and its dutiful handmaiden Science had the unhappy effect of diminishing the significance of that relatively recently discovered creature the individual. James set himself the task of rescuing the individual from Darwinian Science. This meant, as in Emerson, the creation of a kind of quintessential religiousness, an indefinable but clearly evident "Will to believe," deeper than any particular religion, an impulse that fiercely resisted the reduction of man to a "scientific" element in a materialistic world. Josiah Royce, of course, shared in the task to a greater or lesser degree, as did the younger philosophers and psychologists whom James assembled at Harvard. The sacrifice of a beleaguered Christianity in such a cause seemed a modest price to pay for extricating the precious individual, who was, after all, such a tender vine, clearly desperately vulnerable to scientific skepticism, or, as it came increasingly to be called, objectivity. At the same time James's own nature was so passionately religious in its inner being that the effort was excruciating to him. He suffered Melvillean agonies over the conflicting need to view all the evidence dispassionately and his own ardent nature. To John Jay Chapman, the key to James lay in the fact that he "was the child of Christianity bridled by the languages of historical, metaphysical theory—a saint in chains. . . . You can find his jail at night through the light that streams out of his chinks. The light is the light of Christianity."

13

The Left

The continuing war between capital and labor and the severe depression of 1907, which caused widespread suffering, had given a notable boost to the socialists. To many Americans it seemed clearer with every passing month that whatever one called the American economy, it was clearly not working. Lillian Wald wrote to Graham Wallas, the English social philosopher, in 1908: "We are still 'at it' in these United States pushing along some very good Socialism mainly through the old parties and we have emerged from the recent elections with a good deal of cheer to everybody." The abortive revolutionary outbreak in Russia in 1905, although it was ruthlessly suppressed, seemed to many socialists a straw in the wind of radical social change.

In addition to those who called themselves Socialists with a capital S and joined the party, there were many more who, eschewing formal affiliation, flirted with socialism. Socialists, William Allen White noted, "appeared at respectable dinner parties." The dean of American socialists was John Swinton, a prosperous, cultivated man in his early seventies, who had been editing his radical prounion newsletter called simply *John Swinton's Paper* since the late 1870s. Emma Goldman described him as "tall and erect, with a silk cap on his white hair." The Swinton apartment in New York was, in her words, "simply and beautifully furnished and full of curios and gifts," the most striking of which, to her, was "a lovely *samovar* sent them by Russian exiles in behalf of Russian freedom." He had also "an exquisite set of Sèvres" given him by the French communards of the Paris uprising of 1871. Swinton, Goldman wrote, "made me see that Americans, once aroused, were as capable of idealism and sacrifice as my Russian heroes and heroines. I left the Swintons with a new faith in the possibilities of America." From now on, Goldman concluded, she would devote herself to "propaganda in English, among the American people."

Morris Hillquit and Eugene Debs were the acknowledged leaders of the Socialist Party, while Daniel De Leon dominated the Socialist Labor Party. Hillquit and Debs complemented each other. Hillquit was the practical organizer and tactician while Debs was the party's charismatic leader. Debs was born in Terre Haute, Indiana, in 1855, the son of immigrant Alsatian parents. He got his middle name from Victor Hugo and his first name from the popular novelist Eugène Sue. At the age of fourteen he left school to work as a painter on the Vandalia Railroad. After a stint as a railroad fireman, Debs became city clerk of Terre Haute and served a term as a state legislator before he turned full time to organizing railroad workers. Oscar Ameringer described him as "a great soul." Ameringer wrote: "People loved him because he loved people. Children used to flock to him as they must have flocked to the Carpenter." He recalled "greybearded farmers, who as American Railway Union strikers had followed him to defeat, rushing up to their Gene, crying, 'Gene, Gene, don't you remember me any more?' " Debs, always remembering, would throw his long arms around them, press "them to his heart until their eyes moistened in love and gratitude to the leader who had lost them their strike, their jobs and their home." He was, to Ameringer and to many others, "the dreamer, the poet, and the prophet of the weary and heavy-laden. He was the stuff of which the prophets of Israel, the fathers of the Christian Church, the Ethan Allens, Nathan Hales, Abe Lincolns, and John Browns were made. He was a riler-up of the people by the grace of God. . . . He won men by the force of his magnificent personality and the power of faith within him."

Outside New York City the strength of the Socialist Party was in the Middle West, especially in the state of Wisconsin and in the city of Milwaukee, but there were Socialists (most of them ex-Populists) through all the farming states of the region. Their leader was Victor Berger. Berger, the son of German immigrants, was thoroughly middle-class in his origins. He had received a university education and was a high school teacher when he became a convert to socialism, first with a small and then with a large S. Berger's friend Oscar Ameringer wrote of him that he was master of his library of thousands of volumes in English and German: "His knowledge of history was phenomenal. . . . [He] cared no more for money than Gene Debs." Ameringer and Berger were, in Ameringer's words, "far more than friends. We loved each other as did Damon and Pythias or David and Jonathan. . . . When we walked through the streets of Milwaukee, we walked arm in arm. When we occasionally visited a movie for a temporary respite from the madness around us, we often sat hand in hand."

Berger was quoted in the *Social Democratic Herald* of July 31, 1909, as declaring, "In view of the plutocratic lawmaking of the present day, it is easy to predict that the safety and hope of this country will finally lie in one direction only, that of a violent and bloody revolution." Each Socialist and worker, Berger declared, "besides doing much reading and still more thinking, [should] also have a good rifle and the necessary rounds of ammunition in his home and be prepared to back up his ballot with his bullets if necessary."

The Socialist journal *Appeal to Reason* was equally emphatic: "We would have no one under any mistaken impression so far as our position on confiscation is concerned. We want the capitalists themselves to know that we are organizing to take from them the right and power they have had since the beginning of capitalism to take from us the proceeds of our toil. . . . The *Appeal to Reason* unfurls the flag of confiscation and appeals to all the toilers of the Nation—in the mills and mines, on the railroads and the farms—to rally beneath its folds and hasten the day of their deliverance."

In Milwaukee in the spring of 1910 the Socialists elected their city ticket and a majority of the City Council. When Berger ran for Congress in the Third Congressional District, Ameringer, who knew the psychology of farmers as well as anyone, and spoke German, was recruited to work for him among the prosperous German farmers of Waukesha County. The county had a long tradition of abolitionism and, later, populism. The leaders of the Socialist Party in the state prevailed on Ameringer to accept the editorship of its paper *Voice of the People* and then persuaded him to run for governor of Wisconsin. The Socialists were in the process of making Milwaukee the best-run municipality in the United States. Not only was it widely acclaimed as a model city, but it was also a national showcase for socialism. Berger's wife, Meta, was a leading member of the Milwaukee Socialist Party and, in Ameringer's words, her husband's "equal in every respect." C. B. Whitnall was another leader of the Milwaukee Socialists and one of the founders of city planning in the United States. He started the city's first cooperative bank. Edward Melms was secretary of the party, and Emil Seidel, a patternmaker by trade, was the first Socialist mayor of Milwaukee, "a lover of men, and honest as the day is long," Ameringer wrote. Finally there was Daniel Hoan, Socialist mayor of the city for almost twenty-five years.

At the time the Socialists captured Milwaukee, Oscar Ameringer noted, it had been as corrupt as any large American city; "its press was as vile; its educators as cowed and kowtowing; its preachers, with rare exceptions, just as subservient to the almighty dollar. Its slum just as festering, its red-light district as foul, its justice as uneven-handed. Its banks and public-service corporations were as greedy, debauched and rapacious as that of the city's neighbor, Chicago. At best the municipal government was a milkcow; at worst a criminal conspiracy to rob honest men. Gold coast and red-light district, bankster and blackmailer, pickpocket and parson, during the campaign all of them were united in the holy crusade against the 'godless Socialists.'"

One of Ameringer's principal allies in the fight to oust the pillagers was a young poet, labor reporter on the *Milwaukee Leader,* and secretary to Mayor Seidel, named Carl Sandburg. Indeed, it seemed to Oscar Ameringer, when he looked back from the perspective of almost thirty years, that in all his wanderings he had never known a "cleaner, more idealistic and self-sacrificing aggregation of men than those Milwaukee Socialists . . . those forgotten men and women contributed hundreds of thousands of dollars to the cause of their hearts, and the overwhelming majority of them were wage workers, who had little time and money to spare. . . . They made their city a fine, safe, clean, and progressive place in which to live. At the end of their days they were as poor as when they went into Milwaukee politics and socialism, and often poorer . . . [T]hose were people who didn't talk endlessly about 'the American way,' but instead devoted their energies to making it a possibility for their city. . . . They lived and believed the great American ideals, enriching them with work, and labor, and sacrifice, and practical accomplishment. They aren't in the history books we give our children, but it is barely possible that they are a nobler monument to democracy as well as socialism than all the plutocrats we have found it so fatally easy to admire."

One of the most vigorous and influential Socialists in the Middle West was Algie Martin Simons. Simons, the son of a farmer, was born in a log cabin in 1870 in the town of North Freedom, Wisconsin. His father was an enthusiastic Populist, and young Simons imbibed rural radicalism with his mother's milk and his father's stump speeches on behalf of Populist candidates. At the University of Wisconsin he fell under the spell of Richard Ely's brand of Christian socialism and read Karl Marx. He was also an eager student of Frederick Jackson Turner. After his graduation from Wisconsin, Simons went to Chicago to become a social worker in the slum sections of the city. Within two years he had joined the Socialist Labor Party, convinced that capitalism was immune to piecemeal reform, and three years later he seceded from that organization to help form the Socialist Party. Editor at one time or another of five Marxist newspapers or journals, Simons was also a gifted public speaker and debater, translator, and political leader.

From 1900 to 1908 Simons worked to make his ideas the official doctrines of the Socialist Party, and, in the latter year he succeeded in inserting them into the party's platform, which asserted that "the small farmer . . . is to-day exploited by large capital more indirectly but not less effectively than is the wage laborer." In the party platform of 1912 he sponsored a statement to the effect that under a Socialist government the small farmer would keep his farm.

Simons adapted Turner's frontier thesis to his own political uses, arguing that the relatively late development of American rural radicalism was due to the fact that the frontier had only recently "filled up." He also borrowed from such diverse sources as William Morris and John Dewey. Morris's notion of the "instinct of workmanship" was united with Dewey's notions of practical and experimental learning. Capitalism, with its methods of mass production, frustrated the worker's instinct for workmanship. Dewey's pragmatic approach to education encouraged the student to be more critical of all the institutions of his society, especially of capitalism.

In 1911 Simons published a book entitled *Social Forces in American History,* in which he tried to develop a uniquely American form of Marxism. It was his argument that the majority of American Marxists were too rigid and slavish in their adherence to the German philosopher. American conditions required American solutions. Simons's severest criticisms were reserved for those of his fellow Socialists who equated American farmers with European peasants. Marx, for example, had referred to peasants as "the class that represents barbarism within civilization." That did not correspond to the Wisconsin farmers whom Simons knew. To him the small farmers of Wisconsin were ideal material for a revolutionary proletariat. "The American farmer," he wrote, "is a distinct and peculiar social factor. No other age has anything comparable to him. No other nation has his counterpart. His problems, his history and his future evolution present complications and relations unknown elsewhere. . . ." In Simons's view, the Western farmers were "the only hereditary rebels known to history." They were "the pick of the people of the eastern states of America and of Europe" and "even more susceptible to revolutionary propaganda than the city wage worker."

Simons was highly critical of the party's ideologists. "The Socialist Party," he wrote William English Walling in a letter published in the *Call*, "has become a hissing and a byword with the actual wage earners of America. It is becoming a party of two extremes: On the one side are a bunch of intellectuals like myself and [John] Spargo and Hunter and Hillquit; on the other side is a bunch of never works, demagogues, and would-be intellectuals, and veritable lumpen proletariats. The average wage earners, the men who are really doing the class struggle, are outside. Above all else we must have the union man. No one has denounced the efforts of the American Federation of Labor more than I, but I am forced to recognize that it comes much closer to representing the working class than the Socialist Party, and unless we are able to shape our policy and our organization as to meet the demands and incarnate the position of the workers, we will have failed of our mission."

John Spargo was equally outspoken: "In furtherance of the ambitions of a few men of small minds, and even smaller hearts, the whole movement is being dragged into the mire, and the heart of every sincere Socialist sickens with shame at the spectacle."

A leading Socialist theorist was Thorstein Veblen, the most acute observer of the new rich. An "American original," Veblen looked like a classic hayseed. His watch was pinned to his vest with a safety pin. He held up his socks by pinning them to his trousers. A wispy mustache and a short beard did nothing to enhance his appearance. Yet his brilliance and, perhaps even more, the force of his personality were evident to all who talked with him. He won his Ph.D. at Yale in 1884, and after seven years devoted largely to completing his education, he applied for a position in the Cornell economics department. When the University of Chicago opened a year later, Veblen moved there. But he was a restless spirit and a tireless womanizer, and he became a kind of itinerant scholar, wandering hither and yon and writing brilliant satires on American capitalism, thinly disguised as scholarly works.

Less well known was William James Ghent. Born in Frankfort, Indiana, a printer by trade, Ghent found himself increasingly involved in the socialist union movement. He wrote for labor journals and Christian periodicals of the left, like the *Independent,* and his principal weapon was satire. Although an avowed socialist, he remained aloof from the various political factions of socialism until 1904, when he joined the Socialist Party. In *Our Benevolent Feudalism,* published in 1902, he made fun of the capitalists by predicting a "new feudalism" in which capitalist barons would replace feudal lords. Already deferred to by preachers, teachers, and editors, the barons would soon complete their conquest of the law. The new feudalism would contain, in fact, twelve distinct social orders from the barons and "courtiers and court-agents" to "the editors of 'respectable' and 'safe' newspapers, the pastors of 'conservative' and 'wealthy' churches, the professors and teachers in endowed colleges and schools, lawyers generally, and most judges and politicians . . . workers in pure and applied science, artists and physicians." It would, Ghent wrote, "foster not only the arts, but also certain kinds of learning—particularly the kinds which are unlikely to disturb the minds of the multitude." The modern "villeins" would be divided into the villeins of the cities and towns, the skilled and unskilled, those of the rural areas, and "the villeins of the manorial estates . . . the mines and the forests"; then would come the "sub-tenants," the "cotters, . . . living in isolated places and on the margin of cultivation," and, finally, there would be "the tramps, the occasionally employed, the unemployed—the wastrels of city and country."

Frazier Hunt learned much of his radicalism from two Socialists in Alexis, Illinois, where he edited the *Weekly Argus.* Mons Johnson, a shoemaker, was a Swedish immigrant who subscribed to the *Appeal to Reason* and passed it on to those residents of Alexis who dared venture beyond the pieties of the Republican Party. Johnson's ally was Jim Pettit, the blacksmith, who, "broken by debt, uncollectible accounts and machine competition," joined Johnson and Ed Porter, a "silent old carpenter." The three men became Hunt's instructors in the afflictions of capitalism. To the *Appeal to Reason,* Hunt added the *Masses* and balanced this fare with William Allen White's *Emporia Gazette.* On a trip to Chicago, Hunt visited the radical Little Bookshop, run by a blind Socialist, and there, to his delight, he encountered "a slouching, ponderous figure of a man. . . . His left eye was gone, and there was about him the tired and discouraged air of one who had been touched by destiny but somehow or other had failed to take the cue; a beaten Spartacus who with a brave heart had led men to great but futile deeds." It was, of course, Big Bill Haywood. "He was easily my number one American hero at this moment," Hunt noted. With Haywood was Frank Little, a half-breed Indian with high cheekbones, black eyes, and straight black hair. Little and Hunt found an immediate rapport. The talk, stimulated by beer, went on until three in the morning, and Hunt remembered it as "the greatest evening I had spent in my life." He was stirred to the depths of his soul by "the warm and passionate side of the fighting faith of these militant Wobblies. . . . It was the emotional and not the hardheaded, practical side of Socialism that was so appealing to me. It was a human, moving religion for me. . . ." It was as though Haywood had planted in Hunt's heart a sympathy "with the little people and their right to decent lives and fair chances; and it had to do with a vague resentment against the brutality of power and wealth, the travesty of justice and the mockery of ignorant democratic government, and the failure of rich, lavish America to spread her abundance among all her people. It was all a bit hazy and emotional but I insist that it was the most vital part of my attempt at education."

Charles Edward Russell's decision to become a Socialist with a large *S* was based on the fact that the party "represented a protest and the biggest protest then in sight. . . . Big Business and Accumulated Wealth viewed it with shuddering horror, and having been thrown much in contact with its members I had found them to be the best people I had ever seen, and I thought I should be in luck to be allowed to go along with them." Russell found out that becoming a party member was nothing to be taken lightly. He had to fill out a membership form. "It is like joining a church," he wrote. "One must have had an experience of grace, one must show that one has come out from the tents of the wicked and capitalism."

To Russell, the penance required in the Church of Socialism was more severe than that laid on wayward Catholics. There was a chapter meeting every Saturday night "where we sat always until 2 A.M. and sometimes later, ardently discussing the points of pins and like vital matters. The party was managed on the broadest lines of democracy and, there was no limit to debate, but the meetings, though animated and prolix, were always orderly and although there were factions and often acrimonious squabbling over things of no moment . . . the great compensating fact about the whole business," to Russell, "was the unmistakable spirit of devotion to a cause in which all believed implicitly. About the Socialist creed clung a certain splendid significance of the universal man and the general fraternity that . . . obliterated the recollection of human weaknesses, whatever they might be . . . a tremendous impetus to endure and to struggle that came from a faith in an actual and reachable new day for everybody." Everyone was "comrade," including the presiding officer—"Comrade Chairman. . . . Whatever might be the personal frictions, we went home remembering that anyway this was a movement to establish a world without war, without poverty, without slums, without the spoliation of the worker, with an opportunity for all to live and know what life really means, and that was consolation enough." To Russell "the dream that led [the Socialists] on might have been impossible but at least it was a noble and beautiful dream."

The substance of the party's strength, he noted, not entirely accurately, was among Germans and Jews. "It left the great American Voter absolutely cold. . . . Despite all arguments and reasons, he continued to view Socialism as an uncouth plant of foreign growth unsuited to this soil and condition." The Socialist parades were especially popular. From the shouts and cheers of spectators the marchers were encouraged to believe they must carry the next election. But it was seldom so. "We had the cheering," Russell wrote, "and the old parties had the votes."

As a reward for Russell's faithful services to the cause, the Socialist Party of New York nominated him as its candidate for governor in 1910. Russell scrambled "madly from town to town and city to city, trying to tell people something that they did not wish to hear." On a typical evening in White Plains, eleven voters turned out, and nine stuck it out to the end.

George Creel submerged himself in *Das Kapital* but emerged with a deep antipathy to Marxism. He responded to the German's theory of surplus value, "but," he wrote, "everything else revolted me. Hate oozed from every line—hate of the competitive struggle, hate of achievement, hate of demonstrated superiorities. . . . At every point the Marxian class war had its base in monstrous envies." After communism, Creel explored non-Marxian socialism "and sweated over heavy doctrinal expositions until I had the luck to run across the clearer, simpler literature of the Fabians," as put forward by H. G. Wells, George Bernard Shaw, and the Webbs. They emphasized the achievement of socialism through "democratic processes" rather than through class war. What appealed especially to Creel about Fabian socialism was "the public ownership of natural resources and such utilities as were natural monopolies. Why should a man claim title to oil and coal deposits by the mere fact of discovery?" Creel asked himself. Still, the socialists were inherently doctrinaire, and Creel turned with relief to the "clarity and force" of Henry George as to "heaven." George offered Creel a plan for social reform that was free of class divisions and conflicts, that promised reform without violence or bloodshed, and that was clothed in the rhetoric of redemption that many Americans found irresistible. While finally rejecting organized socialism, Creel made up his mind "to stand for the highest degree of socialization short of a deadening level that did away with the incentive motive and denied proper rewards for initiative, industry, and ability." He would stand foursquare for the single tax to "end the monstrous injustice of having individuals appropriate the wealth created by the community."

A future leader of the American Socialist Party, Norman Thomas, was born in Marion, Ohio, in 1884. His maternal grandparents had been Presbyterian missionaries in Siam, and his grandfather, Stephen Mattoon, had translated the Bible into Siamese. After he had returned to the United States, Mattoon, a graduate of the Princeton Theological Seminary, became president of Biddle University, a Presbyterian-supported university for blacks in Charlotte, North Carolina. Norman's father, the Reverend Welling Evans Thomas, was a typical Presbyterian divine of his age, who, his son recalled, "lived for his family and profession" and "frowned on playing cards, marbles for keeps, dancing and theatre-going. He was sure that all drinking was immoral, and that smoking wasn't too much better."

Among the formative experiences of young Thomas's life was hearing William Jennings Bryan address a vast crowd on the steps of the Marion courthouse. Thomas also served as a newsboy for Warren Harding, editor of the *Marion Star*. He later recalled his boss as simply a "front" for Mrs. Harding. "He was very affable," Thomas wrote, ". . . very much of a joiner and personally popular. He was a fine small town or city booster. . . . He used to loaf around his office in shirt sleeves and, if memory serves me, very often with a chaw of tobacco in his mouth."

Starting at Bucknell University, Thomas switched to Princeton; he was a tall, thin young man disposed to slump a bit and enjoined by his mother to "stand up straight and look people in the face." At Princeton he came under the tutelage of Woodrow Wilson, and there he experienced Wilson's disposition "to take strong opposition or criticism as a sin against the Holy Ghost."

After graduation from Princeton, Thomas went to work at a mission slum center, the Spring Street Presbyterian Church and Neighborhood Center on the lower West Side of New York City. It was a rigorous education after Princeton. Thomas recalled such experiences as "sitting gingerly on a broken wooden chair while I talked to a sick woman on a filthy bed around which dirty toddlers played." He heard the Christian Socialist Albert Rhys Williams preach and found himself drifting toward socialism. He decided to become a Presbyterian minister with a vocation for working with the immigrant poor of New York City. After an idyllic interlude of world travel, which included a trip to Siam, where his grandparents were still remembered, Thomas returned to New York to study for his degree in theology at the Union Theological Seminary, the center of the Social Gospel movement, the most powerful voice of which was that of the Christian Socialist Walter Rauschenbusch. While at Union, Thomas courted Violet Stewart, daughter of a prominent banker and trustee of Princeton and heiress to a modest fortune. She had gone to the fashionable Brearley School and then studied nursing. After a trip to India to study the work of medical missionaries, she returned to New York and married Norman Thomas in the fall of 1910. The ceremony was performed by their friend Henry Sloane Coffin.

Thomas's social work was concentrated in Hell's Kitchen, and the gently nurtured Violet Thomas soon came to be known as "the angel of Hell's Kitchen." Thomas moved on to East Harlem, where his church was used not only by his own parishioners but by a Hungarian congregation as well. Increasingly he gravitated toward the peace movement and active involvement in the Socialist Party.

Colleges and universities were fertile grounds for recruiting ardent young Socialists. Upton Sinclair started the Intercollegiate Socialist Society, which had chapters in sixty colleges. A founder and leader of the Harvard chapter was Walter Lippmann. Lippmann was born in 1889, the son of wealthy and cultivated German Jewish parents. He traveled with his parents in Europe and attended private schools before attending Harvard. "I have come around to socialism as a creed," he wrote his girl, Lucile. "I do believe in it passionately and fearlessly— not that all men are equal, for that is a misapplication of democracy— I believe that people must express themselves in an organized society where religion is the dynamic." The Socialist Club was designed to advance "all schemes of social reform which aimed at the radical reconstruction of society." It was through the Socialist Club that Lippmann first met Lincoln Steffens and Jane Addams's ally, Florence Kelley, as well as Morris Hillquit and B. O. Flower. He decided it was "decidedly ridiculous for young men to be 'conservative,' for it means they will probably be 'stand-patters'—when they grow older."

Another major influence on Lippmann was the British Fabian socialist Graham Wallas, whose book *Human Nature in Politics* became a kind of text for Lippmann. It was Wallas who urged the proponents of socialism (of whom he counted himself one) to ask of "public enterprise . . . under democratic conditions" that it prove "a beneficent effect on the health, happiness and general culture of a community" or concede that "private enterprise is more beneficent. . . ." In that instance "the socialist case collapses. And good riddance to it."

Walter Lippmann married Faye Albertson, the daughter of a Congregational minister who had been a disciple of George Herron and was active in Christian Socialist circles. She provided a link with a classic Protestant America that plainly intrigued Lippmann. He wrote to Felix Frankfurter: "Faye and I are from such different beginnings. Think of it, Felix. She rode over the mountains as a baby in a prairie schooner and lived part of her childhood in a Georgia community devoted to the Brotherhood of Man" (the Herron-inspired commune).

In 1911 there were thirty-three American cities with Socialist mayors. One of them was Schenectady, New York, where the Reverend George Lunn, a Christian Socialist, had just been elected. Lippmann was persuaded to join his staff as an expert on at least the theory of socialism. It was not a successful experiment. Lippmann wrote to Wallas: "It wasn't long before I discovered that to raid saloons and brothels, to keep taxes below the usual rate, and to ignore the educational problems were the guiding principles of their 'socialist' administration. . . . On every vital question the socialists ignored their own point of view and fell in with what we have come to know as 'good government' or 'goo-goo' politics.

"I fought as hard as I could within the 'organization' without any result. When I saw that the policy and the program were settled . . . I resigned and attacked the administration in a socialist paper. This brought down on me the wrath of the leaders. . . ."

Graham Wallas's major work, *The Great Society*, had a strong influence in America. His dominant theme was the responsibility of the intellectual for the expansion of social justice. William James, two years before his death, praised Wallas's *Human Nature in Politics* for "being *real* philosophy. . . . The power of certain individuals to infect (for better or worse) others by their example is to me almost the all in all of social change."

Another young protégé of Wallas's was Learned Hand, recently appointed to a Federal judgeship. Hand wrote to Wallas that he believed "We Americans should go rather more slowly here till we have developed better machinery for collectivistic enterprises." He expressed himself puzzled at the dogmatism of Wallas's followers in the United States. They seemed disinclined, he wrote, to look upon politics "with the spirit of genial toleration or a sense that their message might not after all be the last word on the subject."

Roger Baldwin was another idealistic upper-class youth drawn to socialism. He was described, not very flatteringly, by Emma Goldman as "a very pleasant person, though not very vital, rather a social lion surrounded by society girls, whose interest in the attractive young man was apparently greater than in his uplift work."

The ties between the socialists and anarchists were, on the whole, friendly ones. Many people drifted back and forth across that loosely drawn line (Henry Adams, after all, called himself "a conservative Christian anarchist"). The arts provided an important connective tissue between the two parties of the left. They both were committed to the liberating function of the arts on the human personality. "To me," Emma Goldman wrote, "anarchism was not a mere theory for a distant future; it was a living influence to free us from inhibitions, internal no less than external, and from the destructive barriers that separate man from man."

While the anarchists were far fewer in number than the various socialist factions, it might be argued that they were the liveliest and most interesting of all radical groups. Much of this was due, of course, to the personalities of the movement's most conspicuous leaders: those two "old pals" Alexander "Sasha" Berkman and Emma Goldman. Of Berkman, Hutchins Hapgood wrote: "He felt at home in the world as few men do because his world was his own inner feeling, which never failed him." He conveyed the same feeling of assurance, of "at-home-ness" to others. "He was a great man, in the sense that there emanated from his personality some reality that had nothing to do with time— a certain feeling of permanence, of security against change, something living with and for itself. . . . I liked to be with him, not so much because of any nameable quality of mind, but because I felt surer of life."

In 1905 Emma Goldman realized her ambition to start a magazine that, as she put it, "would combine my social ideas with the young strivings in the various art forms in America." The first choice for a title was *The Open Road,* from the title of Whitman's poem, but copyright problems developed, and Goldman had to find another name for her publishing venture. Riding in the countryside with a friend, she saw the first green blades of spring thrusting up from the dark ground. " 'Mother Earth,' " I thought; " 'why that's the name of our child!' The nourisher of man, man free and unhindered in his access to the free earth! The title rang in my ears like an old forgotten strain." A few weeks later the first issue, sixty-four pages in length, appeared. It proved a potent amalgamation of radical social thought and avant-garde artistic expression.

Mother Earth prepared a special issue to honor the seventieth birthday of Prince Piotr A. Kropotkin, the father of modern anarchism. Emma Goldman called him "our common teacher and inspiration." Included in the issue were tributes by the English radical Edward Carpenter and by George Herron, the Christian Socialist and advocate of free love. Carnegie Hall was the scene of a mass meeting in which radical leaders praised the Russian philosopher. Kropotkin was not present, but he sent a letter which was read to the audience. In it he expressed his confidence in the eventual triumph of his ideas. "The more I live," he wrote, "the more I am convinced that no truthful social action is possible but in the science which bases its conclusions, and the action which bases its acts, upon the thoughts and inspirations of the masses. All sociological science and all social action which do not do that must remain sterile."

If the socialists had achieved a degree of respectability, the anarchists remained, for the most part, beyond the pale. In the aftermath of McKinley's assassination Congress passed a law which provided that no one "disbelieving" in organized government was to be permitted to enter the United States. Its main section read: "No person who disbelieves in or is opposed to all organized governments, or who is a member of or affiliated with an organization entertaining or teaching such disbelief in or opposition to all governments . . . shall be permitted to enter the United States." The Free Speech League rallied to challenge the constitutionality of the antianarchist bill, led by the elegant Bolton Hall, who attended meetings of the longshoremen's union, which he had helped organize, in high silk hat, frock coat, gloves, and cane.

Despite constant harassment by the authorities, anarchist circles were characterized by the same kind of exuberance and high spirits so often remarked on in the transcendentalists. In Emma Goldman's words, "Youth and freedom laughed at rules and structures, and our circle consisted of people young in years and spirit. . . . We had the joy of life in us, and the California wines were cheap and stimulating. The propagandist of an unpopular cause needs, even more than other people, occasional light-hearted irresponsibility."

Goldman and Berkman, in addition to their sponsorship of avant-garde art and ideas generally, had a genius for fastening on social issues and dramatizing them both through *Mother Earth* and through their highly publicized lecture tours.

Birth control was an issue ideally suited for Emma Goldman's talents. In 1909 she began a campaign that took her around the nation, spreading the word of birth control, anarchism, and peace. In her lecture tour Goldman was detained by the police in eleven different cities. Almost as notable as the constant police harassment was the variety of people and organizations that came forward to support her right of free speech. In New York even the conservative old Mayflower Society invited her to speak on birth control and applauded her remarks. The Free Speech League was equally bold; invitations to lecture poured in from groups eager to prove their devotion to the cause of free speech and doubtless anxious to hear the famous anarchist firebrand.

In San Francisco, the streets around the Presidio lecture hall where Goldman was to lecture (it grew increasingly difficult even to rent a hall) were lined with police "in autos, on horseback, and on foot." The presence of the police was equally evident inside the hall itself. The result was the reverse of what the police desired. Their presence helped attract a large and defiant crowd of some 5,000. Successive lectures turned out equally large crowds with people queuing up in long lines an hour before the lecture was to begin. In a lecture on patriotism, Goldman evoked bursts of applause by denouncing it as little better than jingo militarism, "the principle that justifies the training of wholesale murderers; a trade that requires better equipment for the exercise of man-killing than the making of such necessities as shoes, clothing, and houses; a trade that guarantees better returns and greater glory than that of the honest workingman." When a young soldier in the audience climbed onto the stage and shook Goldman's hand, pandemonium broke loose. "People threw their hats in the air, stamped their feet, and yelled in uncontrolled joy. . . ." The soldier, named William

Buwalda, was reported to his superiors. He was court-martialed, dismissed from the army, and sentenced to five years in Alcatraz for "attending Emma Goldman's meeting in uniform, applauding her speech, and shaking hands with that dangerous anarchist woman."

Buwalda's punishment aroused a storm of protest around the country, and the President was prevailed upon to pardon him after he had served ten months of his sentence. The next year, when Emma Goldman returned to San Francisco, she found the city officials openly hostile toward her. She was denied the right to speak in Victory Hall, and the crowd that had gathered to hear her was roughly dispersed by the police. William Buwalda, now a civilian, who had come to thank her for her efforts on his behalf and tell her at first hand the story of his arrest and prosecution, was arrested but discharged after a reprimand for associating with "dangerous criminals," and Goldman and her companion were charged with "conspiracy, making unlawful threats, using force and violence, and disturbing the public peace." Bail was set at $16,000, and they were placed in jail. In the dramatic aftermath money poured in from all over the country. Goldman and her friend Ben Reitman were acquitted, and Buwalda returned to the secretary of war the medal he had received for service in the Philippines, declaring that it reminded him "of raids and burnings, of many prisoners taken and, like vile beasts, thrown into the vilest of prisons. And for what? For fighting for their homes and loved ones; . . . of a country laid waste with fire and sword; of animals useful to man wantonly killed; of men, women, and children hunted like wild beasts, and all this in the name of Liberty, Humanity, and Civilization.

"In short, it speaks to me of War—legalized murder, if you will—upon a weak and defenceless people. We have not even the excuse of self-defence."

In San Francisco Abe and Mary Isaak were among the anarchist leaders. They had been Mennonite Russians, and in the United States they had lived in Portland, Oregon, where they helped publish an anarchist paper entitled *Firebrand*. When the Isaaks printed Whitman's poem "A Woman Waits for Me," the journal was suppressed, and the publisher arrested and imprisoned for obscenity. The Isaaks then moved to San Francisco and started a paper called *Free Society*, printed by them and their two sons.

One of the most conspicuous marks of the changing mood of the country was to be found in San Diego, a city known for its strong labor sentiment and tolerance of outspoken social and political views. In

1910 the City Council passed an ordinance severely limiting free speech.
When the ordinance was challenged by the anarchists and IWW, eighty-
four men and women were jailed. The result was that the city became
a kind of magnet for radicals of every denomination who were determined to speak their minds. The businessmen of the city, equally determined to drive out the invaders, organized the Vigilantes. They
raided the headquarters of the IWW, smashed the furniture, and kidnapped the men they found there. Carried off to nearby Sorrento,
they were forced to kneel and kiss the flag and sing "The Star-Spangled
Banner." After this ritual they were transported to San Onofre and
placed in a cattle pen guarded by armed men. After eighteen hours
without food or water they were forced to run the gauntlet between
lines of men armed with clubs and sticks. An IWW member named
Joseph Mikolasek was attacked by the police when he attempted to
address a union meeting. Badly beaten, he was followed to his home
by detectives and there shot to death when he tried to defend himself.
San Diego reportedly refused to allow Mikolasek to be buried in that
city. His body was sent by train to Los Angeles, where union men
turned out in numbers to honor him.

Emma Goldman was among those determined to test San Diego's
will. She and Ben Reitman set out for the city shortly after Mikolasek's
death. Through police complicity, Reitman was taken off the train
before it reached San Diego. When the train reached the city, the mayor
refused to let Goldman leave her car. He could not guarantee her
safety, he told her; the citizens were out for blood. Finally, Goldman
capitulated, but before she could get out of the station on a return trip
to Los Angeles, the train was attacked by the Vigilantes. She could
hear their "mad yelling and cursing—hideous and terrifying moments
till at last the train pulled out."

Back in Los Angeles, Emma was reunited with a terrified and
badly beaten Reitman. The Vigilantes had told him they would like
nothing better than to kill him, but they had promised the chief of
police they would preserve his life. They then proceeded to strip him,
to kick and beat him, and burn on his buttocks the letters *I.W.W.* They
poured a can of tar over his head and, in the absence of feathers,
smeared his body with sagebrush. One man tried to push a cane up
his rectum while another twisted his testicles.

In Denver Judge Ben Lindsey presided at Emma Goldman's lecture on birth control. Lindsey had recently been defeated for reelection, and he and his wife had received numerous threats against their

lives. In the copper-mining town of Butte, Montana, Goldman addressed an audience of miners and their wives on the social issues of the day. Her lecture on birth control was, she reported, especially well attended by miners' wives. Formerly they would not have dared inquire about such matters even privately; now they stood up in a public assembly and frankly avowed their hatred of their position as domestic drudges and childbearers. "It was an extraordinary manifestation. . . ."

All in all, Goldman visited thirty-seven cities and twenty-five states. She lectured 120 times to large audiences and had 25,000 paid admissions in addition to thousands of students and unemployed who were admitted without charge. Ten thousand pieces of anarchist literature, including many issues of *Mother Earth*, were sold.

Back in New York, Goldman was once more arrested for lecturing on birth control. At a protest meeting held in Carnegie Hall and chaired by her old Socialist friend, Lyman Abbott, doctors were mixed with political and literary figures, among the latter John Reed. On the eve of her trial a dinner was held at the fashionable Brevoort Hotel. The guests were a who's who of New York radicals and avant-garde artists. Rose Pastor Stokes, the radical poet, spoke for socialism. Robert Henri, the dean of American painters, was present, as were a number of his students from the Art Students League, among them George Bellows, Robert Minor, John Sloan, and Boardman Robinson. Goldman, free on bail, was the heroine of the occasion. Called on to speak, she dwelt on the issue of free speech.

The next day she argued her own case in court, making an eloquent defense of the right to disseminate birth control information and of birth control itself. If it was a crime to work for healthy motherhood and happy child life, then she was ready to admit to being criminal. When she finished her defense, the judge sentenced her to a fine of $100 or fifteen days in the workhouse. Goldman was carried off to the Queens County jail, where she occupied her time reading and writing while the cause of birth control received a great boost. In San Francisco forty women, many of them socially prominent, signed a petition demanding that birth control information be made available and affirming their willingness to go to prison for the cause. On Goldman's release from jail, another meeting was called for Carnegie Hall, and Rose Pastor Stokes announced that she would distribute birth control literature from the stage of the hall.

On November 11, 1912, socialists, anarchists, and radicals of various denominations met in Chicago to mark the twenty-fifth anniversary of the execution of the Haymarket anarchists. Red and black banners festooned the walls of the meeting hall, and portraits of Parsons, Spies, Lingg, and the others were hung with wreaths. The anarchist squad of the Chicago police force was conspicuous by its presence when the crowd gathered. Emma Goldman was one of the speakers. As she recalled in her autobiography, "all our hate and all our love were concentrated in my voice: 'They are not dead; they are not dead the men we have come to honour tonight! Out of their quivering bodies dangling from the noose, new lives have merged to take up the strains throttled on the scaffold. With a thousand voices they proclaim that our martyrs are not dead!' "

Despite all the particular instances of repression and, indeed, despite the untiring efforts of the Comstockians, whose efforts were, after all, directed most specifically at material considered "obscene," there was a remarkable degree of freedom of expression in the United States. Arthur Holitscher, a visiting German writer and dramatist, noted that in the schools of Chicago children twelve years of age discussed such matters as the recall of judges. "This simply amazed me," Holitscher told Hutchins Hapgood. "It would be impossible in Germany." In addition, although socialism was not taught in the schools, children were encouraged to read informative articles in socialist papers. "In Germany," Holitscher noted, "anything like that would be suppressed by the army."

The conviction of the socialists and anarchists that the future was theirs was strengthened by the outbreak of the Mexican Revolution. Porfirio Díaz had governed Mexico with an iron hand for almost thirty-five years. He had done much to modernize the country, but he had also fastened on it an increasingly repressive regime, which favored the upper class at the expense of the peasants and middle class. Frazier Hunt, on a newspaper assignment in Mexico in September, 1910, sensed trouble. He wrote: "There was something loose in the land—some inarticulate, half-thought-out demand that shortly was to express itself in words . . . land and liberty. Even ignorant peons could sense the strange portents in the air. They knew the meaning of injustice. They knew cruelty, neglect and abuse."

Reports filtered into Mexico City of uprisings around the country, but the newspapers dismissed them with the "comforting little phrase *no importante*." At the end of 1910 a small party of men, led by Francisco Madero, crossed the Rio Grande and began recruiting a revolutionary army. Madero was an idealistic member of the upper class who had cast his lot with Mexico's poor and exploited peasants. Accompanying him was an American soldier of fortune, Charles Sweeney, twice expelled from West Point. Attention focused on Mexico. Was it to be the harbinger of the anticipated revolutionary upheavals?

Journalists of all persuasions descended on Mexico to report on the revolution. George Creel had an inside track as a reporter: His cousin, Enrique Clay Creel, was the governor of Chihuahua. He had moved to Mexico after the Civil War and married the daughter of one of the most powerful men in the province.

Lincoln Steffens, convinced that the revolution was the beginning of a sequence of revolutions that would purify and redeem Western civilization, was in the vanguard. The cry of the "Reds"—"The Revolution! The Revolution will come out of this"—stirred an echo in Steffens's own heart. In Mexico he found "quiet, smiling hate, grasping caution, skeptical hope. . . . I entered into that Mexican revolution," he wrote, "in a state of mental doubt and confusion, which did not clear up till I was out of Mexico into the Russian Revolution." Ardent as he was, Steffens was too experienced and honest a journalist not to confess his confusion at the almost incomprehensible course of the revolution, if it could even be properly called that. The heroes and villains were disconcertingly difficult to identify.

Emma Goldman, Mother Jones, and Jack Reed were among the American radicals attracted to the Mexican Revolution. Reed became a correspondent with Pancho Villa, and members of the IWW in Southern California crossed the border to fight alongside the Mexican revolutionaries.

The American "left" acquired two unlikely recruits in the persons of Willard and Dorothy Whitney Straight. Willard Straight was a golden youth of the new century. Born in 1880, he had every gift of nature: He was tall, handsome, charming, a gifted artist with a notably patrician air (although his parents were schoolteachers from the Middle West). He grew up in Oswego, New York; attended Cornell, where he took a degree in architecture; and then traveled to China, where he found a job with the imperial customs service, made himself an expert on Chinese matters, reported on the Russo-Japanese War as a correspondent, and became a popular member of the international community in Peking. An English contemporary described him as "a sunny-faced American boy of the best type—good, kind, courteous, full of enthusiasm and the joy of living."

Straight was dismayed by "tale after tale of the roguery of American officials in the East, of the bribery of a consul and a group of missionaries, such things of Americans, of the great, the proud home of the Eagle, such rotten corruption by the representatives of one's own native land," he wrote in his diary, "was enough to make me wish for an absolute despotism that the stable might be cleaned."

To Straight the Far East became the new frontier of America. On the relations of the United States with China and Japan would rest the future peace and security of the nation. Soon he found a wider field for his restless energy, first as United States consul general in Japanese-occupied Mukden and then as representative of a consortium of American banking houses—Kuhn, Loeb, J. P. Morgan, the National City Bank, and other interests, which were contending with agents of other countries for the right to make enormous loans and undertake the building of a Manchurian railroad. Negotiating financial arrangements under such circumstances was like swimming in shark-infested waters. The Japanese had occupied Manchuria in the aftermath of the Russo-Japanese War, and Straight, who had lived in Japan for several years while his mother taught school there, saw at first hand their behavior as occupiers of a conquered land.

Straight's transition from consul general to representative of the most powerful financial interests in the country was aided by the fact that President Taft and Secretary Knox were interested in promoting American influence in China by means of American investment. The most important development in Straight's life had, however, nothing to do directly with high finance. Dorothy Whitney was the daughter of William Collins Whitney, who had made a fortune in New York City utilities and became a member of Cleveland's circle of inner advisers. Traveling in China, she met Straight and fell in love. Two years later they were married.

The revolutionary upheavals in China in 1911 brought an end to the prolonged negotiations over the Hukuang Railway and drove the Straights back to the United States, where Straight found life as an officer of the J. P. Morgan banking house a far cry from the drama and excitement of his China mission. His marriage became the center of his life, and his wife wrote: "Willard came and lifted me bodily out of the old life and it fell away. I never heard it fall. Almost imperceptibly things assumed new values and new proportions. I began to share his own vivid life of imagination and dreams as if no other realities had ever existed for me. . . . Life suddenly became an adventure, a quest on which I could risk everything. Safety did not matter any more." One of the adventures Willard Straight took her on was into the field of social and political reform. Bored to death with the world of finance, he reorganized and became president of the American Asiatic Association and realized a longtime dream by founding a magazine called *Asia* to disseminate knowledge of Eastern life and culture in the United States. *Asia* whetted his appetite for, in Herbert Croly's words, "a comprehensive medium of communication" which could be a vehicle for his own ideas of political and social reform. He had read Croly's *The Promise of American Life* with its almost messianic call for the Federal government to assume responsibility for the welfare of its citizens rather than leave such matter to the wavering and uncertain efforts of state and municipal reformers. Straight and his wife met Croly, and out of their conversations came the *New Republic*. It was to be the rallying ground for all those with a new vision of American life. Straight somewhat reluctantly agreed that the policies of the new journal must be determined by its editors—"the group as a whole," as Croly put it. "We'll throw a few firecrackers under the skirts of the old women on the bench and in other high places," Croly wrote. The magazine's comfortable offices, purchased by the Straights, were next door to a home for wayward girls. Its aim was "to infuse American emotions with American thought." Walter Lippmann, one of its editors, wrote: "We shall be socialistic in direction, but not in method, or phrase or allegiance. If there is any word to cover our ideal, I suppose it is humanistic, somewhat sharply distinguished from humanitarianism . . . between the noble dream and the actual limitations of life . . . vivid with the humor and insights and sounds of American life. . . ."

From *Mother Earth* to the *New Republic* was a substantial ideological distance, but many Americans of "the left" were equally at home in both camps.

It was just such vagueness and imprecision that drew the fire of British radicals. Alfred Zimmern wrote to Graham Wallas after a visit to the United States in 1911: "Meeting educated people here makes me appreciate the Oxford grounding; they are so incredibly casual and superficial in the way they attack concrete problems. . . . What I come back to again and again as a determining factor in American psychology is the size of the country. Americans live on too large a scale to live deep. . . . The result is that they seem to think only with the front of their head. What Meredith called 'fundamental brainwork' is so absent from most of their books and utterances that nobody even thinks of asking for it. Their speeches consist of not argument but of anecdote and generalization. . . . What is wanted is a new, more serious and steady habit of mind; otherwise, with this system of government, the good done in one whirlwind campaign will be swept away in the next."

14

The War Goes On

Two of the most publicized events of 1910 were the strikes of the garment workers of New York City and the employees of the *Los Angeles Times*—strikes with very different results. The garment industry was divided between the "giants"—the large companies, employing hundreds of workers—and the "moths"—small, fly-by-night ventures, employing sometimes no more than a dozen or so persons and subcontracting out much of the work. In New York in 1910 the women workers walked out of one of the more notorious sweatshops. Working as many as fourteen or fifteen hours a day for as little as fifty cents, they were among the most exploited workers in American industry. The garment industry had burgeoned in New York City in little more than a decade from a few thousand workers to some 70,000, most of them engaged in manufacturing shirtwaists. A state investigator who visited one of the garment "factories" noted that "the air was stifling," and the temperature "well up in the nineties and odoriferous with sewer gases. . . . The women were scantily clad, their hair unkempt, [and] their pale abject countenances, as they bent over their work, formed a picture of physical suffering that I certainly had never seen before." The International Ladies Garment Workers Union had been formed in 1900, but it had been racked from the beginning by bitter jurisdictional and ideological disputes between older and more conservative unionists and young radicals who inclined to the IWW, to Daniel De Leon's Socialist Labor Party, or to Eugene Debs's milder variety. The workers were, overwhelmingly, Jewish and Italian immigrants. Their complaints were based on the fact that the shop owners "simply refused to recognize the girls as human beings." The classic pattern that was by now so familiar in American strikes appeared: The employer hired thugs as "special police" to intimidate the women strikers. Clara Lemlich was beaten so severely that she had to spend several days in a hospital.

When a meeting was held at Madison Square Garden in June, 1910, to take a vote on an industrywide strike, one of the largest crowds in the history of the city turned up. Some 20,000 people crowded into the Garden while even more milled about outside. The band played the theme song of the French Revolution, the "Marseillaise," and the crowd inside and out sang revolutionary songs in three languages: Yiddish, English, and Italian. Clara Lemlich, still showing signs of the beating she had suffered, appealed for an industrywide strike. "I have listened to all the speakers," she declared; "I have no more patience for talk. I am one of those who feel and suffer from the things described. I move that we go on a general strike." There was a roar of agreement.

"Do you mean faith?" the chairman asked the hallful of workers. "Will you take the old Jewish oath?"

The crowd then swore in Yiddish, "If I turn traitor to the cause I now pledge, may this hand wither and drop off at the wrist from the arm I now raise."

The strike began in a spirit of euphoria. The women poured into the streets, singing in Yiddish, English, or Italian. As the strike spread to all establishments, violence against the strikers became commonplace. Pickets were assaulted and beaten; one woman was crippled for life by hired toughs. The courts backed the toughs, refusing to accept the testimony of witnesses concerning employer brutality and herding the strikers into jail. One judge, in passing sentence on a group of strikers, declared, "You are on strike against God." When George Bernard Shaw read the remark, he declared, "Delightful, medieval America, always in the most intimate personal confidence of the Almighty."

Within a few weeks 60,000 garment workers were on strike. Abraham Rosenberg, president of the International Ladies Garment Workers Union, remembered that many members of the union "cried for joy. . . . In my mind," he added, "I could only picture to myself such a scene taking place when the Jews were led out of Egypt."

The shop owners at once formed a manufacturers' protective association, hired "police" to protect their property, and declared they would never "surrender . . . control and management of factories to any set of men, whether calling themselves a 'union' or anything else."

A huge rally, attended by the city's radical elite, was held in Carnegie Hall. The Women's Trade Union League, headed by Margaret Dreier Robins, took an active role in the strike. Robins came from Chicago to participate. (Four years later the league, at her instance, established a training school for women union leaders.)

The Liberal Club, along with the National Civic Federation, was also much in evidence at the Carnegie Hall rally. Factory women who had been arrested were featured on the stage, and lawyer Samuel Untermyer and Socialist Morris Hillquit were among the speakers. "The office of Magistrate," one resolution passed by the meeting declared, "has been perverted into an instrument of persecution and oppression."

Efforts to persuade the shop owners to accept arbitration on an industrywide basis were rebuffed, but a number of employers reached separate agreements with their employees while the manufacturers' association stood firm against union recognition. The attention and publicity which attended the strike of the women garment workers encouraged the men in the industry, almost as badly exploited, to go out on strike as well.

Soon there were brigades of college women from Smith and Vassar joining their "sisters," young Jewish and Italian garment workers, on the picket line. Florence Harriman's Colony Club demonstrated its support for the strikers by inviting some of them to the exclusive club. Ida Tarbell, Lillian Wald, Samuel Untermyer, and domesticated capitalists like Anson Stokes, whose fortunes had already "aged," so to speak, lent their money and prestige to the struggle. Mrs. O. P. H. Belmont, mother of the duchess of Marlborough, hired the Hippodrome for a rally and raised $300. Rose Pastor Stokes addressed the strikers as "Friends and sisters." She brought them, she declared, "the message of 40,000,000 . . . working men and working women the world over. . . . 'Workers Unite! You have nothing to lose but your chains, and you have the world to gain!' "

A daughter of J. P. Morgan decided to build a model shirtwaist factory with unionized labor, and Wellesley students immediately ordered 1,000 shirtwaists from the still hypothetical factory. Vassar girls sold copies of the *Call* on the streets, and Barnard students kept a close eye on the treatment of the strikers by the police.

The President's daughter, Helen Taft, a student at Bryn Mawr and an ardent suffragist, visited the picket line and made one of the most naïve and revealing statements of the strike. "I never knew they were so down trodden!" she declared. "Really, I'll never put on a shirtwaist again without a shudder. . . . I shall certainly speak to papa about the terrible conditions. . . . Why, it's just like reading Nietzsche, isn't it?"

When one shop opened in defiance of the strike, strikers broke through the police lines and demolished the factory, throwing sewing machines out of the windows and smashing tables and chairs. Young John Purroy Mitchel, a friend and confidant of Florence Harriman, was the acting mayor of New York City. A graduate of Columbia and a lawyer, he had made his mark in city politics by his activities as an investigator of municipal corruption. Mitchel ordered an investigation which produced hardly surprising evidence that "both sides have been violent and disorderly, if not worse."

In the midst of the strike State Supreme Court Justice John W. Goff issued an injunction against the strikers on the ground that their fight for a closed shop constituted a "common law civil conspiracy." Goff denounced the union for a "systematic course of aggression by criminal acts." Following the judge's ruling, seventy-five strikers were arrested in a single day for picketing.

Many of the strikers were impoverished by the strike. There were numerous evictions, and strike funds were exhausted. At this stage Lincoln Filene, the reform-minded Boston department store tycoon, entered the picture with a plan for conciliation developed by Louis Brandeis.

Born in Louisville, Kentucky, and a graduate of the Harvard Law School, Brandeis had started his career as a highly successful corporation lawyer, but the Homestead strike and the writings of Henry Demarest Lloyd and Henry George had drawn him in the direction of social reform, and he had made himself an expert on public law. The fact that the majority of the underpaid and exploited garment workers were Jewish impelled Brandeis to take a leading position in both trying to mediate the strike and exploring his own Jewish roots. In the latter process, he became one of the founders and first chairman of the operating committee of the World Zionist Organization.

In place of the closed shop Brandeis proposed the preferential shop, a plan whereby nonunion workers would be gradually replaced by union workers but union membership would not be a requirement for employment. For a time the union resisted the Filene-Brandeis proposal as the "open shop with honey." *McClure's* noted, "These were men and women accustomed to enduring hardships for a principle. . . . Men and women who had fought in Russia, who were revolutionists, willing to make sacrifices, eager to make sacrifices. Their blind faith was the backbone of the strike." Finally, in September, the union leaders, over the objections of many of the more militant strikers, began negotiations with the employers. The agreement that emerged marked a vast improvement in working conditions and a substantial increase in wages for the workers. It was hailed in parades and rallies as a great labor victory and a harbinger of better things to come. The most widely publicized outcome of the strike was a mechanism invented by Brandeis, called the Protocol, a complicated plan designed to provide a method of settling disputes between employers and employees without the prolonged and bitter strikes that seemed to have become a fixture of the war between capital and labor. For a time the Protocol appeared to be the magic formula that would resolve conflicts that constantly threatened the peace and well-being of communities and, increasingly, of the nation itself, but, after two years of accumulating irritations, it threatened to break down in another disastrous strike. At this point an emergency plea went out to the newly appointed commissioners on industrial relations to exercise their good offices in an effort to preserve peace. After stormy hearings, under the chairmanship of Florence Harriman, that disclosed numerous points of disagreement among union leaders, the principal issues were reconciled. Sidney Hillman assumed the leadership of the union, and the commissioners proceeded with their hearings.

The fact that the strike initially involved women and that it happened in the nation's principal city, on center stage, so to speak, made the garment workers' strike of 1910 one of the turning points in American labor history. Perhaps it would be more accurate to say that it marked the beginnings of the transformation of the perception by upper- and middle-class Eastern Americans of working-class men and women or of the situation of the "masses," a word increasingly used to describe what had once been called the democracy or the dangerous classes. The world of the comfortable middle- and upper-class Americans in the large cities was as remote from the lives and the living and working conditions of the largely immigrant masses as if they had lived on separate planets. The strike of the shirtwaist makers with the consequent daily tales of police brutality and the general hostility of judges and city officials dramatized the plight of workingmen and -women as nothing else could have done. The way had been paved, to be sure, by a host of journalists, like Lincoln Steffens and Jacob Riis, who had painted vivid pictures of ghetto life, but words were one thing, and the sight of young women being harassed or beaten, abused, and mistreated had a far more powerful effect.

Another bitter strike in 1910 was that of the Bethlehem Steel workers in Pennsylvania. Charles Schwab, the president of Bethlehem Steel, was a self-proclaimed foe of unions. Half the employees of Bethlehem Steel worked twelve-hour days; one-third worked seven-day weeks. Working conditions were deplorable, dangerous, and unhealthy. "I have labored among my people in this community for nineteen years," a Catholic priest testified, "and I know that the Bethlehem Steel Company is a human slaughterhouse." When Schwab ordered that certain workers must work on Saturday and Sunday afternoons, men began walking out. Gompers moved in at once to sign the workers up in the Amalgamated Machinists' Union. Charges of violence and sabotage were made by Schwab, and the governor of Pennsylvania ordered the state police to Bethlehem. State police were a relatively new invention, but those in Pennsylvania were already notorious for their strikebreaking activities. There were immediate clashes between the strikers and the police. The union accused the police of "a campaign of slugging, arrests, murder, assaults, and riot without cause, the viciousness of which beggars description." Strikers who could do so armed themselves, and there were numerous gun battles, with casualties on both sides. "Under no circumstances," Schwab declared, "will we deal with men on strike or a body of men representing organized labor." In the face of such obduracy, the workers, their money exhausted and their families facing starvation, returned to work without winning any improvement in working conditions or increase of wages. The labor leaders were furious at the state's use of troopers to help break the strike, and the editor of the *Allentown Labor Herald* declared, "We want peace, but if it comes to fighting, we won't go against a machine-gun with a brick. . . . I want to tell you now, force to-day is the most respected thing there is in this world."

The most sensational event of 1910 took place in Southern California. Harrison Gray Otis, a Civil War officer and a descendant of

James Otis, the revolutionary leader in Massachusetts, and of Harrison Gray Otis, a leading figure in the Essex Junto which had plotted the secession of New England from the Union at the time of Jefferson's embargo, came to the small, sleepy town of Los Angeles in 1882. When Otis bought the *Los Angeles Times,* it was a union newspaper, but after a bitter strike in 1890 in which he broke the union, it became not only a nonunion but an aggressively antiunion, antilabor paper.

On October 1, 1910, the *Los Angeles Times* building was dynamited with a loss calculated by General Otis to be in excess of $500,000; twenty nonunion workmen were killed. It was the culmination of years of labor-capital warfare. "In all these years of dispute, contention, ignorance, delusion, and bad blood on the part of the antagonists, since the year 1890," Otis declared, "the Times has never editorially attacked organized labor as such. . . . It has steadily opposed and attacked the lawlessness and despotism of organized labor when it has shown itself to be guilty of these grave offenses. . . . It is the offenses, the crimes, the despotism, and the monstrous and inherent spirit of monopoly which possesses and obsesses unruly organized labor so largely that I have assailed day in and day out." To Otis "little or no real or permanent good comes out of present-day [union organization] in the long run. The conflicts, the strikes, the bad blood, the assaults, the violence and sure idleness and nonearning results . . . make the wisdom, the expediency and practical good flowing from the present-day organization of labor . . . extremely doubtful . . . free, independent, nonunion, unfettered labor is the true condition for the free-born, unenslaved American workman to live under." Otis, in his determination to undermine the union movement, paid his employees higher than union scale and then pointed to that fact as an argument against unions.

The *Times* bombing pointed up the disturbing fact that dynamite was a weapon increasingly employed by the more radical wing of the union movement. In a period of four years more than seventy dynamitings had occurred at steel and iron foundries that employed nonunion labor. It was suspected that the Bridge and Structural Iron Workers Union had been behind many of the bombings. Hutchins Hapgood's friend Olav Tveitmoe was known in West Coast labor circles as "the philosopher of the dynamite movement." He was a huge man, "his face," Hapgood wrote, "deeply lined, his eyes deepset and dreamy, his voice quiet and gentle. . . . One felt in him a sweet though Rabelaisian fullness of life. . . . He was like one of those great trees [the

California redwoods] he spoke of with so much love, or like the cliffs."
When Hapgood met him, Tveitmoe rhapsodized about the redwoods
and the beauty of the California coast. Tveitmoe and Haywood were,
to Hapgood, the poetic interpreters of the labor movement. They
preached a gospel which the new middle-class bohemians longed to
hear. Religion had failed, Darwinism and Science had failed, at least
in their eyes. The new vision was of an America, fair and free, open,
expressive, where men and women lived unfettered lives. All this was
to be achieved by the revolution in which radical intellectuals would
join hands with radical workers. And by dynamite.

From the point of view of labor, the bombing could hardly have
come at a worse time. In the eyes of many middle-class Americans the
IWW stood indicted for the systematic use of violence, though its leaders maintained with considerable truth that they were only responding
to violence practiced against them. The Socialist Party, under the leadership of Hillquit and Debs, was in the process of dissociating itself
from acts of violence by labor (and from the IWW). The Bridge and
Structural Iron Workers' Union had been suspected of at least one
bombing in Chicago. Gompers and the AFL, determined to keep the
skirts of the trade union movement clean, were untiring in their condemnation of violence. At the same time there was a growing sympathy
with the goals of "conservative" labor: shorter hours, better pay, and
an end of labor injunctions and industrial armies made up of Pinkerton
thugs. The socialists were definitely in the ascendancy, and there were
few informed Americans of liberal persuasion who did not accept the
proposition that socialism, in one form or another, was the inevitable
next step in social evolution. Even in Los Angeles, labor (and unions)
seemed on the verge of a substantial victory. Job Harriman, a middle-
of-the-road Socialist, was a candidate for mayor with wide support
from reform-minded civic groups. The city swarmed with labor organizers from the headquarters of one trade union or another, sensing
that the time had come to break the town's stubborn resistance to
unionization.

It was in this phase of the war between capital and labor that the
fatal dynamiting of the *Times* took place. Capital and labor squared off
immediately. Otis and his supporters, confident that the bombing was
the work of union men, hired the most famous detective in the country,
William Burns, to track down the culprit or culprits. The forces of
labor responded by charging that labor had been framed. The bombing, they declared, had been done by agents of the merchants' asso-

ciation to discredit the entire labor movement. Eugene Debs declared, "The *Times* and its crowd of Union-haters are themselves the instigators, if not the actual perpetrators of that crime and the murderers of the twenty human beings who perished as its victims." And Samuel Gompers weighed in cautiously with the comment, "The greatest enemies of our movement could not administer a blow so hurtful to our cause as would be such a stigma if the men of organized labor were responsible for it."

Such a position obviously contained serious risks to the labor movement as a whole. It may thus be taken as a measure of its desperation that its leaders, prominent among them Gompers, felt that they had no other course. It remained for the capitalists to prove that union men had done it. There was reason to hope that such a case would be impossible to prove, and even if union men were convicted of the crime, it must be on evidence so shaky that they would appear to be no more than the most recent martyrs to the cause, convicted and sentenced on trumped-up charges.

All this reckoned without William Burns, a formidable sleuth by the highest private-eye standards. Burns traced the bombers to Indiana and wove around them a web of evidence that even an unprejudiced jury must find convincing. Having identified them as the McNamara brothers, J. B. and J. J., Burns arranged to have them kidnapped and rushed secretly under heavy guard from Indiana to Los Angeles. The circumstances of the brothers' arrest added fuel to the fires of controversy that raged about the *Times* bombing. It brought to mind the earlier kidnapping of Haywood, Pettibone, and Moyer for complicity in the murder of Frank Steunenberg and strengthened the conviction of the prolabor groups that the McNamaras were victims of a plot hatched by Otis et al. The discovery by police of a bomb at Otis's home was ridiculed as simply another effort to discredit labor. With an astonishing recklessness, labor leaders, union men of all ranks, workingmen and -women without union affiliation and their by now considerable cohorts of middle-class sympathizers insisted that the McNamaras must be innocent and denounced the authorities who had brought them to trial. Thousands of dollars were raised for the brothers' defense, and Clarence Darrow, against his better judgment, was persuaded to take the case.

Taking advantage of the public reaction roused by the loss of life, the *Los Angeles Times* called upon "the plain citizens" of every county to form "a combine" for the "suppression of sedition and anarchy in the persons of the professional agitator." The paper proposed "an armed posse" to track down radicals. "There is no reputable citizen of Los Angeles who would decline membership of such a posse, and in an hour, if necessary, a brigade could be organized and armed with pick handles that would drive the lawless union laborites, closed-shop, murderous vermin into the sea." The police, the militia, and Federal troops must be relied on to protect "homes and . . . property," and, were these to fail, "a force of thousands of merchants and manufacturers and lawyers and bankers and nonunion workers and home owners" should be armed. Then "the carcasses of some of the labor leaders who instigated disorder and dynamiting and murder might be seen dangling from telephone poles."

It was clear to Darrow from the beginning of the trial that the evidence against the McNamaras was formidable. He confided his fears to Lincoln Steffens, who had arrived from England to cover the trial. Steffens wrote of Darrow's "long, lean, loose body, with a heavy face that is molded like an athlete's. . . . He is more of a poet than a fighting attorney. He does fight," Steffens added; "he is a great fighter as he is a good lawyer, learned and resourceful, but his power and his weakness is in the highly sensitive, emotional nature which sets his seeing mind in motion in that loafing body. His power is expressive. He can say anything he wants to say, but he cannot conceal much; his face is too expressive." He was a man of constantly changing moods. At one moment he might be "a hero for courage, nerve and calm judgment," and a few minutes later, "a coward of fear, collapse and panicky mentality." The evidence against the McNamaras disposed him to panic.

Steffens himself had started with the assumption that the McNamaras did the bombing and that "they did it as the appointed agents of labor, and they and their organization of ordinary working men must have suffered something worth our knowing about to get worked up to a state of mind where they deliberately, as a policy, could carry on for years dynamiting, arson, murder. What were those real or fancied wrongs, what are the conditions which produced this—act of war?" That would be Steffens's "story line." It seemed to him far better to concede the act and try to understand its causes so that peace might eventually be made in the war between capital and labor. He became obsessed with the notion. If the adversaries on the most bitterly contested battlefield could be brought to the negotiating table, peace might at least be made and the war concluded.

Steffens got permission to interview the McNamaras. They were appealing young Irishmen, bright, friendly, devoted to the cause of labor, nurtured in a tradition of violence. Steffens liked them both. He conceived of a plan whereby he might save their lives and begin the process of reconciliation. If the brothers confessed, Steffens told them, he would undertake to try to negotiate with Otis and the prosecutors a guarantee that their lives would be spared, that their sentences would be nominal, and that steps would be taken to create in Los Angeles an atmosphere more hospitable to unionization. The natural desire of the McNamaras to live was thus reinforced by the hope that their living would serve a worthy purpose.

Armed with the acquiescence of the McNamaras, Steffens sought out Darrow, who, believing his case hopeless, was ready to grasp at straws. Harry Otis, the general's somewhat more enlightened son, listened to Steffens sympathetically and undertook to bring his old man around. He succeeded, to Darrow's surprise. The McNamaras pleaded guilty to the bombing, and then the roof, in a manner of speaking, fell in. The news of the confession by the McNamaras was a devastating blow to the unions and their supporters. A newspaper correspondent in Los Angeles reported, "All over the city that sunny, warm afternoon, the eyes of men blinked and winked in vain efforts to repress the scalding tears that would well up. The shock was too great, the release of pent-up strain too sudden. So they wept, shaken by emotions beyond their control." When word of the confession reached Anton Johannsen, Hutchins Hapgood's prototypical workingman, he burst into tears and walked up and down the room, clutching the newspaper, sobbing, "That's the way they are, you fight for them and they turn on you— but I love them, the poor slaves!" To him it seemed that the McNamaras had betrayed the labor movement, and he bitterly resented Steffens's role in their confession.

"Jack Reed, 'my own boy,' " Steffens noted, "wrote a fierce poem, 'Sangar,' denouncing me. It was good poetry," Steffens added, in almost an excess of charity, "so that it was worth while." But to the labor "movement," the outcome of the McNamara trial was disastrous. The business interests everywhere and the conservative newspapers and journals made the best use of it to swing public opinion against unions and, indeed, against workingmen and -women generally. Many of the liberal fellow travelers of labor dropped off, disillusioned. Many others persisted in believing that the McNamaras had sold out the labor movement in return for their lives: that they were innocent but had pleaded guilty to escape the gas chamber.

Even Darrow, hero of dozens of court battles in behalf of labor, found himself under a cloud, denounced for accepting labor's money and betraying its cause. A hue and cry for severe punishment for the McNamaras arose around the country and, most conspicuously, by Steffens's account, from innumerable church pulpits. The judge, apparently unnerved by the clamor, sentenced the brothers to far more severe sentences than those agreed upon and berated them and the labor movement in terms that offered little ground for reconciliation.

Hapgood tried to explain the psychology of the dynamiters to his middle-class readers. "There are," he wrote, "ideas, if not men, behind the acts of the McNamaras. There is a whole system of ethics behind them—ideas to which the men holding them attach emotional and moral value." The attitude of loyal union men toward scabs had about it some of the fervor of any defender of the faith. "It is a moral law," Hapgood wrote, "believed in without question, as a Christian believes in the Gospel; and, as in the case of other religions, men are willing to commit crimes in the name of this religion, and die for it."

Emma Goldman found California "seething with discontent." The Mexican Revolution and the arrest of the McNamara brothers on the charge of dynamiting the *Los Angeles Times* building had labor, the liberals, and the radicals up in arms. They saw the case of the McNamaras as "another attempt of the plutocracy to crush organized labor."

In the aftermath of the McNamara case the *Survey* devoted an issue to the war between capital and labor. One contributor, Meyer London, wrote: "The American people must awake to the fact that a bitter, merciless war divides society. . . . It is a war with all war's fury, with all its injustice, with all its crime-breeding hatreds." Florence Kelley, secretary of the National Consumers' League, observed that workmen committed violent acts "as a cornered rat bites, not according to reasoned theories, but in the wrath and despair of baffled effort and vain struggles."

Robert Hoxie, a liberal economist, described the attack on the *Times* as "not merely the isolated act of an irresponsible pervert" but the consequence of labor's profound conviction that it could not receive justice in America.

In the opinion of a labor historian, "The McNamara case stopped the Los Angeles labor movement dead. . . . In addition, the shock of the McNamara crime sent tremors all through the American labor movement." Job Harriman, the Socialist candidate for mayor, who had been given a good chance to win that office, was overwhelmingly defeated. "Organized labor, and more particularly trade unionism," the editor of the magazine *Outlook* wrote, "is now thoroughly at sea. It is still staggering blindly under the sudden blow delivered full in its face by its own leaders. It is down, gasping for breath." General Otis, not surprisingly, took the outcome as a vindication of his antiunion stand. He declared, "It is proof of what we suspected from the outset—that this crime was either inspired by organized labor, or was done by desperate members of organized labor. . . . As to me and mine, we stand vindicated in our quarter of a century stand for industrial freedom."

The National Association of Manufacturers was stimulated to renewed efforts against organized labor by the outcome of the McNamara affair. Its journal, *American Industries*, denounced the closed shop as a socialist scheme for destroying American freedoms, and the association's president, John Kirby, Jr., referred to Gompers and the AFL as "these assassins." He added, "No country can exist half free and half throttled by criminal unionism."

When a congressional investigating committee pressed Clarence Darrow to repudiate the McNamaras' bombing, he refused. "There was no element that goes to make up what the world calls a criminal act, which is an act coupled with a selfish criminal motive," Darrow insisted. "J. B. McNamara, an obscure printer in a great labor fight in Los Angeles, took 16 sticks of dynamite . . . and went in the nighttime and deposited them in an archway of the Times Building, of course without any intention of killing anybody. . . ." The fire and the deaths that resulted from it were entirely accidental. McNamara did not do what he did for money; "he did not do it for malice. He was a union man in a great industrial struggle running over the years. He believed in it and believed it was necessary to the welfare of his class; he was thinking of the structural iron workers, of the men, women, and children living in poverty and want, and of the wonderful riches on the other hand, and in his mind he thought he was serving his class, and taking his life in his hands without reward. Now, if anyone can condemn him for it, they reason differently from myself . . . I can not."

Did Darrow then consider McNamara a martyr? "Well, he was risking his life for a cause he believed in; I would not have done it; I would not have advised it; but looking at it from his standpoint, he was a martyr."

The German journalist Arthur Holitscher, traveling in the United

States, expressed surprise at the way many Americans reacted to the McNamara bombing. "There were," he remarked to Hutchins Hapgood, "some newspapers and many individuals who, although of course they condemned the crimes committed, seemed, nevertheless, to feel that there were deep evils in the country which were in a sense responsible. This would have been impossible in Germany. There would have been nothing except ethical indignation expressed—nothing more. All this means to me that America has really great, popular and democratic possibilities."

Several years later the socialist editor of a prolabor Democratic newspaper secretly owned by Otis, a man named Frank Wolfe, reported to the Commission on Industrial Relations that Los Angeles was an armed camp. He charged that the Young Men's Christian Association had been recruited into the antilabor ranks and armed with guns. The president of the YMCA was a department store owner, and Wolfe declared that he had seen "great rows of lockers . . . filled with Springfield rifles and bayonets. . . . I do not suppose there is any community in the United States where there is as many armed camps as there is here. Everybody, every group that I know of has an arsenal, except union labor." The City Council had authorized the purchase of forty sawed-off repeating shotguns to distribute to "citizens' police" in times of riot.

Wolfe estimated that in the winter of 1913–14 some 40,000 men were out of work in Los Angeles alone. Under a municipal vagrancy law the police were permitted to arrest persons who had no job or habitation and put them on chain gangs to do roadwork. That was the way the well-to-do residents of Topanga Canyon had got a road built in that remote area. "Blanket stiffs, wanderers with their blanket rolled up and hung over shoulders were conscripted."

The continued friction between the railroads and their employees resulted in numerous strikes, which the IWW tried to use to reassert the notion of a single industrywide railroad union. The AFL responded to the challenge by establishing a special railway employees department to deal with union issues involving the railroads. The Harriman-controlled railroads, especially the Illinois Central, had long been the object of worker dissatisfaction. Headquartered in Chicago, the Illinois Central comprised 4,500 miles of track. Included in the Harriman interests were the Union Pacific, the Southern Pacific, and the Santa Fe. In June, 1911, unions in the Harriman system announced the formation of their own federation and demanded recognition and the beginning of collective bargaining over hours, wages, and working conditions. The railroad resisted on the ground that the roads would be at the mercy of the unions if they recognized such a federation. "It would have ten thousand times more power than the American Federation of Labor," the general manager of the Illinois Central declared.

The Harriman strike brought with it familiar tactics. The railroads hired "detectives" and "guards" and undertook to keep the trains running with nonunion workers. The strikers fought back by systematic sabotage of trains, destruction of company property, and the intimidation of strikebreakers. Violence began in New Orleans and spread rapidly along the Harriman lines. Four suburban trains were wrecked when rails were loosened on the Illinois Central lines near Chicago. Strikers and railroad agents were killed and wounded in considerable numbers as the strike ground on month after month. In McComb, Louisiana, a trainload of strikebreakers on the way to New Orleans was attacked, and a furious fire fight ensued. Three coaches were wrecked, and, when the train finally reached New Orleans, a reporter noted, "It looked as though it had been through the Boer War." The national guard was called out and shipped off to McComb with these orders: "If any man . . . lift a hand or makes a motion to hurl a missile, if any striker, strike sympathizer, or citizen makes a menacing demonstration . . . shoot, and shoot to kill."

Once more the employers made use of the weapon of injunction through the courts, and hundreds of strikers were hauled before magistrates and given heavy fines and prison sentences. A judge in St. Louis told a group of arrested strikers, "It is a mistake to suppose you have a right to get together and conspire to induce these men to leave the employ of the company. . . . I don't know what this strike is for. . . . I don't believe anybody else does. . . . Go back to work. There is no reason why you are out."

One of the most serious charges against the railroads was that, in their determination to break the strike, they had hired inexperienced, incompetent, or inadequately trained men, thereby endangering the lives of their passengers. A young newspaper editor, Carl Persons, who took this line in a union journal, supporting it with statistics, was indicted for "circulating through the U.S. mails, Matters Reflecting injuriously on the Conduct of the Illinois Central Railroad and its Officials." Persons was freed on bail, attacked and beaten by company thugs, and when, in self-defense, he shot one of his assailants, he was charged with murder and held without bail. When he was finally brought to trial, he was found not guilty.

The attitude of the officers of the Illinois Central toward unionization was well expressed by the testimony of one of them before the Commission on Industrial Relations. "Illinois Central Railroad Co.," he declared, "felt that it owed a duty to its stockholders, to its patrons, and to the country to resist in every legitimate and proper way the beginning of such a monstrous system."

In 1912, according to the records of the Interstate Commerce Commission, there had been 180,000 casualties and 10,000 fatalities on American railroads. A disproportionate number had occurred on the struck lines of the Illinois Central. "This enormous slaughter of human life," the Railway Employees Department of the AFL declared, "is not so much to be wondered at when taking into consideration the conditions under which the Illinois Central and Harriman lines operated during that period."

After the strike had dragged on for more than a year, representatives of the unions and of management met secretly to try to negotiate an agreement. The company had suffered heavy losses, seen its stock plunge to all-time lows, and been faced with bankruptcy. Of the strikers, 10 percent had been forced to seek charity and 68 percent to give up their homes. In December, 1914, the union abandoned the strike without having achieved any of its objectives. There had been little support for the strike among the newspapers of the country and, it must be presumed, among the general public. Strikes intended to win a closed shop, to establish an industrial union, or to force collective bargaining got far less public backing than strikes for higher wages or better working conditions. To many people the strikes in the former category smacked of radical politics, of communism-socialism-anarchism, of an effort by "labor" to impose its will on the country. As we have seen, this was particularly true with the railroads because Americans were so dependent on the railroads, and the more radical labor leaders, well aware of that fact, considered the industrywide organization of the railroads part of revolutionary tactics designed to replace capitalism with socialism. The *New York Tribune* warned that a federation—one big railroad union—"would be totally irresponsible," and the *Nation* declared that "the railways could not possibly concede to the workers' demands without producing socialism or anarchy."

Other less noticed battles took place continually. In Carteret, New

Jersey, the employees of the American Agricultural Chemical Company were told that they must accept a 20 percent reduction in their wages. This meant for those at the bottom of the pay scale $1.60 a day. The workers in the plant struck, and the company brought in 100 gunmen, who were sworn in as deputy sheriffs, ostensibly to protect its property. A few days later, in a clash with the strikers, the "deputies" fired for fifteen minutes, killing and wounding a number of strikers.

Child labor remained common. George Creel, who visited "the sweatshops of New York, the cranberry bogs of New Jersey, the cotton mills of the Carolinas, the coal mines of Pennsylvania, and the shrimp canneries of Louisiana," estimated that "at least two million children were being fed annually into the steel hoppers of the modern industrial machine . . . all mangled in mind, body, and soul, and aborted into a maturity robbed of power and promise." With the aid of Ben Lindsey and Edwin Markham, Creel published a book in 1913 called *Children in Bondage.*

15 ❧

The Paterson Strike

In Lawrence, Massachusetts, conditions in the textile mills were a public scandal. The state legislature had passed a law reducing the workweek in the textile industry from fifty-six to fifty-four hours. The industry replied by announcing that wages would be cut proportionately. The weekly wages of the lowest-paid workers (who made up the great majority of the industry's employees) was only $6 a week, with no vacations and all holidays deducted from the workers' pay. The spontaneous reaction of the Lawrence textile workers was to strike. By the end of January, 1912, 250,000 workers were out; among them twenty-eight nationalities were represented.

The governor of Massachusetts was a millowner, and both Charles Eliot, the ex-president of Harvard, and Harvard itself were investors in the mills. In the words of Emma Goldman, "The result of this unity between State, capitalism, and seats of learning in Massachusetts was a horde of police, detectives, soldiers, and collegiate ruffians let loose on the helpless strikers." The first two casualties among the strikers were a young woman named Anna Lapezzo, who was shot to death, and John Ramo, who was bayoneted. Two of the strike leaders, Arturo Giovanitti and Joseph Ettor, were arrested and charged with Lapezzo's death; Big Bill Haywood and young Elizabeth Gurley Flynn appeared on the scene to take their places. Emma Goldman had first heard Elizabeth Gurley Flynn address an open-air gathering at the age of fourteen; a girl with "a beautiful face and figure and a voice vibrant with earnestness," she had swept her audience away. Now a mature twenty-two, she was a veteran of dozens of union meetings and IWW rallies.

As the days wore on, the strike began to take on a special significance. To employers all over the country, alarmed by the growing radicalism of the labor movement (symbolized by the formation of the IWW), the strike was a confirmation of their anxieties; they perceived communism-socialism as eroding the foundations of the Republic. For radical labor leaders, the strike appeared a heaven-sent opportunity further to radicalize the labor movement, to give socialism a boost, and to unify the fragmented ranks of labor. The editor of the *Outlook* expressed a common apprehension when he wrote: "What [Haywood] desires is not a treaty of industrial peace between the two high contracting parties, but merely the creation of a proletarian impulse which will eventually revolutionize society. Haywood is a man who believes in men, not as you and I believe in them, but fervently, uncompromisingly, with an obstinate faith in the universal good will and constancy of the workers worthy of a great religious leader. That is what makes him supremely dangerous."

The business community tried to turn the strike into a patriotic issue—for America or against it. Much was made of the high proportion of "foreigners" among the strikers and of the militant socialism of the IWW. Many businessmen wore small American flags in their buttonholes. An alleged effort by an agent of the textile trust to hang a dynamite charge on the strikers by planting the explosive failed when the plot was exposed by the strikers, and the guilty party was fined $500. When a high official of the American Woolen Company committed suicide, rumor had it that he was afraid of being implicated in the plot.

Among those who appeared at Lawrence was vivid red-haired Margaret Sanger, a militant socialist. Margaret was twenty-nine; Haywood was forty-three. Sanger had a background not dissimilar to his. Her father was a stonecutter with radical inclinations, and Margaret had imbibed a distrust of capitalism from him. When an opportunity presented itself to reenact Mother Jones's children's crusade by sending a small party of child workers to Washington to testify before a congressional committee, Margaret Sanger was put in charge of them. By

Haywood's account, Samuel Gompers preceded the children on the stand and was denouncing the strike and its leaders when a child's voice called out, "You old son-of-a-bitch. You're telling a god-damned lie!"

"Young man," said the committee chairman, "that sort of language will not be tolerated here. Do not attempt it again!"

"It's the only kind of language I know and I'm not a-goin' to let that guy lie about us and get away with it!" the boy responded. The hearings had been arranged by Victor Berger, the Milwaukee Socialist, who had recently been elected to Congress.

Gertrude Marvin, a reporter for the *Boston American,* wrote a story for her paper sympathetic to Haywood and the strikers, but her editor threw it into the wastebasket with the comment "That big two-fisted thug has put it all over you!" She resigned from the *American* and went to work for the strike committee.

The strike was well organized and well supported. A fife and drum corps was organized, parades, entertainments, and interminable speeches kept the strikers diverted. The police of Lawrence were augmented first by police sent from adjacent towns and then by national guardsmen. A young Syrian boy who was in the strikers' fife and drum corps was bayoneted and killed by a guardsman.

Under the leadership of Mother Jones the wives of the strikers were active. Many children of the strikers were sent off to stay with sympathetic families in other towns. Their departures were recounted vividly as human interest stories by the press and aroused widespread sympathy for the strikers. When the police tried to prevent a contingent of children from leaving the Lawrence train station, their mothers attacked the police vigorously, and no further attempts were made. One cold morning after a group of strikers had been drenched by the hoses of mill guards, the women caught a police officer and stripped him to the buff.

While Haywood was addressing a strike meeting, two young pregnant Italian women appeared and expressed their determination to man the picket line in place of the men the next day: "I got big belly, she got big belly. Policemen no beat us." The next morning only women were on the picket lines. The women who had organized the female picket line and a friend, Bertha Crouse, were in fact so badly beaten by the police that they gave birth prematurely and, in Haywood's words, "nearly died themselves." Hired gunmen tried to assassinate Jim

Thompson, an IWW organizer, but he escaped naked from his bedroom with severe contusions on his head.

After six weeks the companies capitulated. All of the strikers' principal demands were met: higher pay, shorter hours, overtime, and no discrimination against those who had been on strike. Lawrence was the scene of an exuberant celebration. The members of the strike committee were of twenty-three nationalities. "We sang the *Internationale*," Haywood recalled, "in as many tongues as were represented on the strike committee."

Haywood and other IWW leaders hit the lecture trail to raise money for the defense of the men accused of murder, Arturo Giovanitti and Joseph Ettor. At Cooper Union in New York City Haywood told a large and responsive audience that "the vultures of capitalism intend to make horrible examples of Ettor and Giovanitti" in order to remind radical workers everywhere of the price of dissent. The two men had been miles away when the police shot Anna Lapezzo. "It was a wonderful strike," Haywood declared, "the most significant strike, the greatest strike that has ever been carried on in this country or any other country. Not because it was so large numerically, but because we were able to bring together so many different nationalities." Above all, the strike had been run "democratically." There had been no labor leaders bossing the strikers, but rather committees of strikers deciding on strategy and tactics. "The workers did their own bookkeeping. They handled their own stores, six in number. They ran eleven soup kitchens. . . . They had their own finance committee, their own relief committee. And their work was carried on in the open. . . ."

A strike by the textile workers of Little Falls, New York, followed, and this time the chairman of the strike committee was Matilda Rabinowitz, a fiery and determined, if diminutive, woman who steered the strike to a successful conclusion when a number of her male coworkers were arrested.

The next great strike scene after Lawrence was Paterson, New Jersey, described by Haywood as "a miserable place of factories, dyehouses, silk mills. . . . There is not a part of the workers' quarter for the childen to play in, no gardens or boulevards where mothers can give their babies a breath of fresh air." Included in the work force were Italians, Syrians, Armenians, French, Germans. Many workers were Russian, Polish, and Austrian Jews. Like the opponents of the strike in Lawrence, the Paterson millowners and executives and businessmen wore American flags in their buttonholes to suggest that the strike was somehow an unpatriotic act. Since the Paterson mills produced a large proportion of the flags sold each year in the United States, the strikers responded with a parade in which every worker and the members of his family wore a flag or carried a flag under which was printed:

> We weave the flag.
> We live under the flag.
> We die under the flag.
>   But damn'd if we'll starve under the flag.

A leader in the Paterson strike was Carlo Tresca, who came of a wealthy landowning Italian family. He had had to flee Italy because of his radical activity. Described by Max Eastman as having the manner of a "mildly liberal gentleman of the old school," he was Elizabeth Flynn's lover. "This was according to our code," she wrote later, ". . . to honestly and openly avow a real attachment." During a riot Tresca lost his vest. In it, when it was recovered, was found a copy of Elizabeth Barrett Browning's love poems with Flynn's marginalia affirming her love for Tresca. Big Bill Haywood called Elizabeth Gurley Flynn "the greatest woman agitator that the cause of those who toil with their hands has produced in a generation," and Theodore Dreiser described her as "a typical Irish beauty, with blue eyes, filmy black hair and delicate pink complexion. . . . She has the mature mentality, the habit of thought and finished expression of a woman of twenty-five." Hutchins Hapgood wrote that she had "the flame of a natural orator and the spirit and heart of a lover of the unfortunate and oppressed . . . the purity of her motives shone like a good deed in a naughty world." Hapgood and his wife took two of the children of the striking millworkers at Paterson into their home at the behest of Flynn, but it was not a successful experiment. The children were defiant and unmanageable and, above all, homesick.

Perhaps on the grounds that the IWW had declared war on capitalism and that all was fair in war, the public authorities in Paterson paid little or no attention to the law in harassing, beating, and jailing the strike leaders and the strikers. The mayor declared, in the immemorial accents of beleaguered officials, "I cannot stand for seeing Paterson flooded with persons who have no interest in Paterson, who can only give us a bad name. I propose to continue my policy of locking up these outside agitators on sight." Meetings of strikers were broken up, and socialist newspapers and journals were confiscated without legal pretense. Arrested leaders were given large fines and lengthy jail sentences; Patrick Quinlan, an eloquent young Irishman, was sentenced to seven years in prison for treasonable utterances. In the opinion of Haywood, "This action on the part of the police so thoroughly aroused the working class of Paterson . . . that it resulted in bringing about an amalgamation that would otherwise have required much hard work and a longer period to accomplish."

When the editor of the socialist *Passaic Weekly Issue,* Alexander Scott, denounced the Paterson police as "a bunch of drunken cossacks," he was charged under an obsolete, obscure statute, was convicted of inciting "hostility to government," fined $250, and sentenced to up to fifteen years in jail. More strikers, including such intermittent visitors as John Reed, were jailed.

Reed was put in a cell with Carlo Tresca, who at first suspected the young Harvard graduate of being a stool pigeon. Sprung after four days by an IWW attorney, Reed wrote an angry article for the *Masses:* "There's a war in Paterson, New Jersey. But it's a curious kind of war. All the violence is the work of one side—the mill owners. Their servants, the police, club unresisting men and women and ride down law-abiding crowds. Their paid mercenaries, the armed detectives, shoot and kill innocent people. Their newspapers, the Paterson Press and the Paterson Call, publish incendiary and crime-inciting appeals to mob violence against the strike leaders. . . . They absolutely control the police, the press, the courts. . . . When it came time for me to go out I said goodbye to all those gentle, alert, brave men, ennobled by something greater than themselves. *They* were the strike—not Bill Haywood, not Elizabeth Gurley Flynn, not any other individual. . . . Think of it! Twelve years they have been losing strikes—twelve solid years of disappointments and incalculable suffering. They must not lose again! They cannot lose!"

Violence increased on the part of both police and strikers. Houses were stoned and bombs exploded. At least five people were killed, and hundreds wounded, among them a number of policemen. The employers stubbornly refused to negotiate with the strikers. "These people," one of them declared, "will not be bound by any agreement and will continue to strike until they own the mills. It would be foolhardy to treat with an organization of that kind." The AFL now entered the picture belatedly in an attempt to sign up the strikers in a "conservative" union that would be more acceptable to the employers, but the federation's spokesmen were hooted off the stage when they tried to address the workers.

Upton Sinclair appeared on the scene and told the strikers a bit pompously, "I just simply could not stand it any longer, and I let my books go and came down here to congratulate you. Yours is the finest exhibition of solidarity ever seen in the Eastern states."

Walter Lippmann was a frequent visitor to Paterson, along with Max Eastman. Sundays took on a festive air. Denied the use of meeting places in Paterson itself, the strikers and their newfound bohemian friends met in an open field outside the jurisdiction of the authorities and there listened to fiery speeches, sang songs, drank wine, and ate bread and cheese. John Reed led the strikers in song as he had led the cheering section at Harvard football games.

In the midst of the strike Hutchins Hapgood brought Big Bill Haywood to the apartment of a wealthy young woman named Mabel Dodge. Hapgood had met Mabel Dodge through his friend the sculptor Jo Davidson, "the most entertaining man," Hapgood wrote, "I have ever known." Mabel Dodge lived in a luxurious apartment at 23 Fifth Avenue, "in the purely conservative world." When Hapgood met Dodge, it marked the beginning of a dramatic and in a sense "coalescing" event in the larger history of the new consciousness. It was as though a hundred disparate elements and individuals were searching for some moral or intellectual or, as Hapgood preferred to express it, "spiritual" center. Dodge, guided by Hapgood and propelled by "her enormous temperamental instinct," provided that center. Hapgood was, as he put it, "connected with all the isms and all the radical hopes and all the enthusiasms, however they expressed themselves of the wonderful new world we all felt was coming." It was a world that Mabel Dodge, young, rich, and with a kind of poignant beauty, was determined to get into.

Hapgood and Dodge, it turned out, shared a feeling for the "unseen cause of all things seen." Both had launched themselves on the search for the "Infinite." To Hapgood, Mabel Dodge's "sometimes graceless searchings, her terrific but formless needs, her occasional sharp unkindness, her extraordinary . . . jealousy, her inability to let go of anything even for a moment" was explainable only by virtue of the fact that she wanted, above all else, "to repose quietly and physically on the bosom of God. . . ." That feeling, Hapgood believed, bound them together. She was insatiable—for people, ideas, love, and intellectual dominance. Steffens described her as "an aristocratic rich, good-looking woman," who never "set foot on the earth earthy." (She wrote of Hapgood: "Everybody loved Hutch. He was the warmest, most sympathetic hound. God pursued him and he pursued God, looking into every dust bin for him. He never thought he would find him among the mighty, but always he was nuzzling among 'the lowly, lowliest, and the low.' ")

Big Bill Haywood held the company at Mabel Dodge's enthralled by his dramatic and touching account of the Paterson strike and the desperate straits of the strikers. He was at a loss as to how to arouse the public to the real nature of the struggle. "Why not bring the strike to New York? Make a big mass-play of the whole strike," Dodge suggested; "then the newspapers will have to notice it." Haywood was charmed by the notion. Where could such a play be held? "Why, of course, in Madison Square Garden," she replied.

John Reed, who had been a fascinated listener, announced, "And I will write the pageant! . . . We'll make a pageant of the Strike! The first in the World." The slogan of the pageant would be "Life without labor is robbery, labor without art is barbarity." It would both raise money for the strike and advertise it to the world.

Mabel Dodge's apartment became the command post for the projected pageant, and she the producer. John Sloan, one of Robert Henri's students at the Art Students League, was drawn in to paint the scenery for the pageant. Robert Edmond Jones, a Harvard graduate and sidekick of Reed, designed the poster to advertise the parade— "an heroic figure of a worker rising out of the background of factories, smokestacks and chimneys." A huge stage was built, and stage flats were painted to represent the mills of Paterson.

When the doors to the Garden opened two weeks later, a huge crowd was waiting. The line was estimated to have stretched twenty-eight blocks. The pageant began with a scene showing the mill in operation. Light shone through the windows of the Garden, giving it the effect of a giant factory, and workers walked wearily down the aisles "in groups, singly and by twos,—an occasional one glancing at a newspaper, another humming a song, some talking, all with small baskets, buckets or packages of lunch in their hands. . . ." The mill whistle blew, and then the sound of machinery was heard. All the workers rushed into the factory. The passage of two hours was simulated, and voices could be heard inside the mill, shouting, "Strike, strike!" The workers rushed out into the audience, "laughing, shouting, jostling each other," and then, with the audience joining in, began singing the *Internationale*.

Scene two showed the mills deserted. In Haywood's words, "They stood like monstrous spectres." Now the workers were on picket duty, singing strike songs they had composed. An Italian strummed a guitar. Policemen mixed with the strikers and then suddenly began to club and beat them. Shots rang out. A striker dropped dead; another limped off, wounded. The strikers followed the body of their dead companion to his home.

Scene three was the funeral of the dead striker. While the strikers formed a circle around the coffin, Elizabeth Gurley Flynn and Big Bill Haywood gave the speeches they had given at the graveside of the dead striker in Paterson. The next scene was that of the children of the strikers being sent from Paterson to other towns. They were on a "school strike" because the teachers had called the strikers "Anarchists and good-for-nothing foreigners." The children, wearing red sashes, departed singing "The Red Flag." The last scene depicted a strike meeting. A platform had been erected at the rear of the stage, and the worker actors gathered in front of it with their backs to the audience, "transforming the setting into a vast meeting." Haywood then addressed the audience as though it were all part of the strikers' meeting. The pageant over, a wildly cheering crowd rose to applaud the strikers.

Hutchins Hapgood wrote of the pageant in the *New York Globe* that the 1,000 strikers who had participated presented their story "without exaggeration, with gentleness, with a fine mass—not mob—feeling, and in doing it with such instinctive good faith they gave a performance of the utmost importance, not only socially but artistically. . . . They suggested a new art form, a form in which the workers would present their own story without artifice or theatricality, and therefore with a new kind of dramatic power. . . . The art of it was unconscious, and especially lay in the suggestions for the future. People interested in the possibilities of a vital and popular art, and in constructive pageantry, would learn much from it. . . . This kind of thing makes us hope for a real democracy, where self-expression in industry and art among the masses may become a rich reality, spreading a human glow over the whole of humanity. . . ."

The mood of elation produced by the pageant lasted for several weeks. The press was enthusiastic, calling it "a spectacular production," with "a poignant realism that no man will ever forget." An artistic success, the pageant was a financial disaster, ending up $2,000 in the hole.

The Paterson strike marked the melding of bohemia and the radical labor movement in the person of Big Bill Haywood. He and Margaret Sanger had formed an alliance at the Lawrence strike, and he had become a hero to Greenwich Village. Soon he was the center of the circle of intellectuals who met at Mabel Dodge's apartment or crowded into Margaret Sanger's smaller quarters. Haywood even tried his hand at writing "labor poetry," a very popular genre in the Village. "After meeting writers and artists among the groups who sometimes went to Mabel's salon, sometimes going to painters' studios or talking with an expressive woman, Bill would sit in Washington Square and write poetry," Hapgood wrote. One such meeting included Percy MacKaye, the poet, and Walter Lippmann. Haywood, as usual, was the center of attention, and "the talk was about labor, poetry, and justice. . . . Haywood glowed, and they reasoned." He "talked forcibly and feelingly against the poetry and literature of isolation. Still more feelingly he spoke for the poetry of work. . . . He sees so vividly how beauty and understanding and poetry might be found in the labor of the workers. . . . All things he touched on were suffused with his feelings toward the workers and their glorious destiny. He spoke of the solidarity of the working class. . . . He told how he got thirty-seven different nationalities to sing the same songs together. He commented on the wonder of that, of how this brought all these differing races in a feeling of unity, of solidarity of emotion and interest." To him there were, in the working class, no national barriers. There was "only an international humanity which wipes away prejudice and ignorance and brings man together in essential unity."

Haywood went with Hutchins Hapgood to the studio of Robert Henri. Henri was, in a manner of speaking, Haywood's artistic counterpart. He taught his devoted students to paint the commonplace: to see the beauty in ordinary scenes and ordinary people, to eschew the romantic and overblown, or, perhaps more accurately, since he was intensely romantic himself, to transfer the romantic vision from traditional landscapes and seascapes to cityscapes, to the swelling, intense life of cities. Henri and his students clustered about Haywood and bombarded him with questions about the strike. "Henri and his friends wanted new life, too," Hapgood wrote. Hapgood felt a kind of sad loneliness in Haywood. Far from his family and his Western roots, he seemed to be held prisoner by his intellectual and artistic admirers.

By May, 1913, the Paterson strike was plainly broken, and the desperate workers—those who had not been blacklisted for strike activity—returned to their jobs. They had lost more than $4,000,000 in wages during the strike, and the millowners had lost more than $5,000,000. The *Miners' Magazine,* exulting in the defeat of the IWW, wrote that "dead-beats and bilks shall be given to understand that no more money shall come from the sweat of labor to put on *Easy Street* the flim-flamming gang whose dirty vocabulary would pollute a garbage barrel and befoul a sewer," and Gompers declared that the IWW leaders "mislead the toilers into striking for impossible ideals and leave them betrayed and helpless and at the mercy of the vengeful employers." The Socialist Party showed little sympathy with the strike. When the strike leaders tried to place an advertisement in the Socialist Party paper, the *Call,* edited by Morris Hillquit, the ad never appeared, and Hillquit mentioned neither the Lawrence nor the Paterson strike in his *History of Socialism in the United States.*

During the strike more than 1,800 individuals, many of them women and a few children, had been arrested. A poem by Rose Pastor Stokes in the *Masses* pronounced its elegy:

> . . . Our fingers do not cease!
> We're starved—and lost, but we are weavers still;
> And Hunger's in the Mill!

The Paterson strike was broken, some said, because the energy needed to make it a success had been diverted into the pageant. The defeat at Paterson, along with the rejection of the IWW by the orthodox Socialists, marked an end to the prospects of the IWW in the East and, along with it, the notion of a great industrial union representing all the workers. Nonetheless, the strike had about it the purity of innocence; it was a moment as luminous and vivid as any in the century's history.

16

Greenwich Village

The seven months of the Paterson strike marked Greenwich Village's most exciting era. The Village, an area in lower Manhattan, coalesced into a symbol of new consciousness the center of which was, as we have noted, Mabel Dodge's apartment. Dodge, in Steffens's words, "read everything; she believed—for a while—everything; she backed everything with her person and her money, especially young geniuses." The young stage designer Robert Edmond Jones had a room to "play" with his models of stage sets, and John Reed had a room. "All sorts of guests came to Mabel Dodge's salons," Steffens recalled, "poor and rich, labor skates, scabs, strikers and unemployed, painters, musicians, reporters, editors, swells. . . ." Her "whim was her only master." There was something about Dodge, according to Max Eastman, that created "a magnetic field in which people became polarized and pulled in and made to behave very queerly. Their passions become exacerbated, they grow argumentative; they have quarrels, difficulties, entanglements, abrupt and violent detachments. And they like it—they come back for more."

Characters as diverse as the aristocratic young Pinchots, Amos and Gifford, and Marsden Hartley, the homosexual artist, sat on the floor with Big Bill Haywood and Margaret Sanger to listen to Emma

Goldman discuss birth control. Frances Perkins, another daughter of the privileged, rubbed shoulders with the Czech immigrant, Hippolyte Havel. Carl Van Vechten, enamored of the black jazz musicians he had discovered in Harlem, brought them to Mabel Dodge's evenings. Hutchins Hapgood proposed the notion of specific themes for the gatherings in her apartment. There was a Family Planning Evening with Alexander Berkman and Emma Goldman, and a Psychoanalytic Evening featuring Walter Lippmann. George Creel, with his flashy clothes and pushy manner, was somewhat of an outsider and a skeptic. "The works of Freud and Jung had just been discovered," Creel recalled, "and at every so-called *salon* the talk was of psychoanalysis and sex." To him it all seemed "pretty cheap and frowsy."

After the death of his wife Lincoln Steffens made his home in a room in Washington Square, "where youth lived and reds gathered, the young poets and painters, playwrights, actors, and Bohemians, and labor leaders of a radical trend . . . the thinking poor and the poor thinkers." John Reed lived upstairs. Steffens had known Reed's father, a U.S. marshal in Portland, Oregon. The elder Reed had asked Steffens to keep an eye on his impetuous son, who wanted to be a poet. "Get him a job, let him see everything, but don't let him be anything for a while," Reed's father told Steffens. Steffens gave Reed a job on the *American Magazine* to "use as a springboard from which to dive into life." Reed, "a big, growing happy being," would "slam" into Steffens's room at any hour of the night and wake him up to tell him about "the most wonderful thing in the world that he had seen, or done that night. Girls, plays, bums, I.W.W.'s, strikers . . . Bill Haywood, some prostitute down and out on a park bench, a vaudeville dancer, socialism; the I.W.W. program—all were on a live level with him. Everything was the most wonderful thing in the world. Jack and his crazy young friends were indeed the most wonderful thing in the world," Steffens wrote. "When that boy came down from Cambridge to New York, it seemed to me that I had never seen anything so near to pure joy. No ray of sunshine, no drop of foam, no young animal, bird, or fish, and no star, was as happy as that boy was. If only we could keep him so, we might have a poet at last who would see and sing nothing but joy. Convictions were what I was afraid of. I tried to steer him away from convictions, that he might play with life; and see it all, live it all, tell it all; that he might be it all; but all, not any one thing."

To Floyd Dell, a recent arrival from Chicago, Reed seemed "a hero out of a fairy tale background. We have as yet no sufficiently heroic tasks for such persons to perform," Dell added, "and we customarily put them in jail when they appear alarmingly upon our scene. . . ."

Mabel Dodge became hostess for the most famous hallucinogenic party in American history when a friend, Raymond Harrington, appeared. Harrington was an amateur student of the culture of New Mexican Indian tribes and had observed their use, for ceremonial purposes, of peyote buttons. He arrived in New York at Mabel Dodge's with a supply of buttons. It was decided that her apartment would be the ideal place to test their effects. Max Eastman and his wife, Ida Rauh, were present, along with Neith and Hutchins Hapgood, Robert Edmond Jones, and half a dozen others. Harrington brought a musical instrument to play Indian rhythms. The lights were arranged to resemble, so far as possible, Indian campfires, and, without the slightest notion of what made a sensible portion, the assembled group began munching away. Hapgood swallowed two buttons, and when he fled to the bathroom to vomit, it appeared to him that bright flames sprang out of his mouth. He subsequently became an Egyptian mummy. Neith Hapgood took a portion of a button, went peacefully to sleep, and had beautiful dreams of wandering in a forest. Harrington visited a tropical valley inhabited by enormous, brilliantly colored birds. Dodge, alarmed at the increasing signs of derangement among her guests, withdrew to her bedroom to pray. A doctor was summoned, and those still under the influence of the peyote were put in separate rooms to be treated for hallucinations.

Prominent among the curious collection of individuals who formed the initial stratum of the Village was the aforementioned Hippolyte Havel. Havel was, for college-educated intellectuals like Hutchins Hapgood, a kind of symbol of the exuberant culture of radical aesthetes that he and his friends were trying to create. Havel was the son of a Gypsy and, marvelously, a native of Bohemia. His favorite expletive was "God damn bourgeois." Always improvident, supported by a series of admiring, if often unfaithful, women as well as by his numerous friends, Havel was an expressive talker, a heavy drinker, a poet and writer, who gave a kind of legitimacy to the new bohemians.

Much of the social life of the radical intelligentsia centered on half a dozen bars and restaurants. There was Luke O'Connor's Working Girls' Home at the corner of Fourth Street and Sixth Avenue, called Hell-hole. The Hotel Brevoort was a particular rallying ground where the inner circle met. Trimordeurs, an Italian restaurant on

Mulberry Street, was the scene of a famous Village party. After an enormous Italian meal the chairs and tables were pushed back, and the guests, assembled largely by Hippolyte Havel, began to dance, "the first I ever saw," Hutchins Hapgood recalled, "that was wholly a matter of spontaneous rhythm. . . . There was no leader to give directions but, by natural right, Will Irwin [a leader in numerous radical causes] among the men and Fanny Lehman, a little anarchist girl, took the lead. Fanny danced with the fire of the coming Russian Revolution. . . . At this meeting all the elements were perfect, typical of the Village that was beginning. There were writers, artists, journalists, liberals, suffragettes, feminists . . . and there was especially another group who were merely women"—that was to say, women who were not attached to any man but who "belonged among the artists, the seriously socially-minded, the writers; but who were themselves none of these." They were some-how the cohesive element that held the group together. Louise Bryant was one.

Village women were not, in Hapgood's words, "victimized in any way. . . . The woman was in full possession of what the man used to regard as his 'rights,' and the men, even the most advanced of them, suffered from the woman's full assumption of his old privileges. To be sure, man retained the same 'freedom,' or what was called freedom, that he had always had, but his 'property' had been taken away from him, and no matter what his advanced ideas were, his deeply complex, instinctive and traditional nature often suffered, a suffering the woman was relatively spared. From the emotional point of view, the man, rather than the woman, was the victim." To Hapgood the woman, in the last analysis, held the real power. She had "the power and primitiveness of the earth. Woe to the more artificial male, dependent on the unconsciously remembered past and on willful desire to maintain the impossible structure of civilization—woe to his spiritual organization if he gets in her way! It is like opposing a force of nature. . . ." Although the women of the Village had a strong sense of "economic liberty," most of them were "still deeply held by the traditions of womanly restraint and by the unconscious belief that the ceremony [marriage] was a necessary condition to love-affairs. They provide a marked contrast to a generation of girls following them; their light and joyous spirit was changed, deepened, and made somber by elements of revolt, in the field of labor and in the suffrage fight, in marriage and relations of the sexes in general. When the world began to change, the restlessness of women was the main cause of the development called Greenwich Village, which existed not only in New York but all over the country. . . ." The Village in its earliest years was to Hapgood "a gay and happy, light atmosphere . . . harmless amusement in a Victorian world, holding firmly to the general tradition of sobriety in the home." Later things changed. A "deeper somber note" turned innocent pleasure into "violent debauchery and hopeless extravagance. . . ." Hapgood, still, as it seemed to him, in the thrall of Victorian morality, encountered "men and women caught in the throes of a passionate reaction, making statements . . . entirely contrary to the basis of social life and to the religious and esthetic values of human intercourse."

"On the sex side," Hapgood wrote: "there was of course all the normal weakness of human nature, but in addition to that the weakness of idealism, or an attempt to go beyond human nature. Marriage on principle was not tolerated, since it was an enslaving institution; but, whether married or living in what was called free union, the unnatural idealism of the group made it obligatory on the part of the male not only to tolerate but to encourage the occasional impulse of the wife or sweetheart toward some other man; or on the part of the woman, a more than tolerant willingness to have her man follow out a brief impulse with some other woman. This is called varietism, and was supposed to be hygienic and stimulating to the imagination. No doubt it was, but the time always came when human nature couldn't stand it and when one or the other broke down and separation, sorrow, and disappointment followed. And yet these libertarian ideas, associated with a principled reaction against what was felt to be a system of slavery, gave to this way of living a certain pathetic dignity."

Heterodoxy was a feminist club, composed, in Hutchins Hapgood's words, "of women, many of them of force, character, and intelligence, but all of them shunted on the path from the early suffrage movement into the passionate excesses of feminism, in which the 'vital lie' was developed that men had consciously oppressed women since the beginning of time, enslaved and exploited them. It is now hard for me," Hapgood wrote in 1938, "to put myself back into this almost insane atmosphere. Women of character and personal charm and beauty, although they felt the quality of men and had their husbands and lovers like other women, yet felt that in doing so they were merely gratifying some of their commonplace instincts."

A woman friend of Hapgood's, the dancer Elise Dufour, attended a meeting of Heterodoxy called to make plans for the production of a feminist play, Susan Glaspell's *The Verge*. "It seemed to me," she reported to Hapgood, "while these women were talking about *The Verge*, that I was in church, that they were worshipping at some holy shrine; their voices and their eyes were full of religious excitement. I was, I think, the only woman not under the spell. I tried at first to say a few things about the play that were in the line of ordinary dramatic criticism, which I thought had a reasonable basis; but when they all glared upon me, as if they thought I should be excommunicated, I spoke no further word."

Whatever the excesses of feminism might be, women were the ruling divinities of the Village. It revolved around them; they were its avatars, the priestesses of the new order.

Of course, Jack Reed and Mabel Dodge fell madly in love. Their romance was both inevitable and inevitably doomed. They shared the same unappeasable appetites, but Dodge was almost insanely possessive, and Reed was determined to remain free. "Mabel is wonderful, I love her," he told Hapgood, "but she suffocates me. I can't breathe." He ran away, and Mabel fled to the Hapgoods at Dobbs Ferry. Neith and Hutchins sat up with her all night. "She was weeping and smoking and burning holes in the blankets," Hapgood recalled, "repeating to all our suggestions of consolation, 'I want Reed back! I want him now!' "

Mabel Dodge's salon was not without imitators and rivals. Helen Phelps Stokes, a social-minded socialite, presided over an "alternative" salon to Dodge's, and Walter Lippmann soon found a central place in it. It included Upton Sinclair and Morris Hillquit as well as the socialistically inclined founder of a swank girls' school, Jessica Finch. (The school served as the somewhat incongruous setting for the 1911 convention of the Intercollegiate Socialist Society.)

Edith deLong Jarmuth, the daughter of a wealthy Seattle family, established one of New York's most famous salons in a handsome apartment on Riverside Drive. Exotic-looking, with long black hair and almond-shaped eyes, she was a magnet who drew radicals and intellectuals to her in droves. Inez Mulholland, a graduate of Vassar, became famous for her dedication to those who suffered from any form of discrimination. She was the ministering angel of the Village who went wherever there was a call for help.

The Villagers found a summer refuge in Provincetown, Massachusetts. There a restaurant run by Polly Holliday and Hippolyte Havel was the headquarters of the colony.

Hapgood felt that there was a definite regional basis for the desire to alter the stiff rectitude of the American character. Among his allies in the cause, a "very large proportion of the passionate individuals, not only in sex but in every other way, come from the undifferentiated physical contours—esthetically unsatisfying—of the Middle West." When Frederic Howe and Marie Jenney moved to New York and found an apartment on the edge of Greenwich Village, a new and exciting chapter opened in their lives. Jenney at last broke free of the home, got a job, and became active in women's suffrage activities. Howe was appointed head of the People's Institute, an offshoot of Cooper Union. "Brilliant young people, full of vitality, ardent about saving the world, floated in and out of our apartment," he wrote. ". . . Graduates of Harvard, Columbia, and Vassar, concerned for the well-being of society, but not for its conventions, formed an American youth movement. They protested against industrial conditions, suffered vicariously with the poor, hated injustice."

Art was as potent as politics; the two were to be mixed to produce the new consciousness. It was at Alfred Stieglitz's gallery-studio "291" that the most advanced artists found a friendly reception for their work. It was there, also, that the "wild" (fauve) art forms of Europe were first exhibited. "They were indeed the means," Hutchins Hapgood wrote, "by which life was lived, relived, and lived again in the little room. Representing then something relatively new in impulse and form, they made a wonderfully effective point of departure for the fresh stir of life, for recalling its meaning to the jaded and bored soul, and for again awakening hope of more abundance. . . . Through the new light that came from the free art forms, Stieglitz saw the possibility of enhancing our human relations, or at least a stirring way of pointing to this more vivid, more abundant existence. Incessantly he attempted to break up the dead areas, so that apropos of a picture by Marin, a drawing by Rodin, or a painting by O'Keeffe, Stieglitz would talk by the hour about 'life,' as it manifests, or should manifest, itself in all human relations. . . . He is full of love in the sense that he attributes great value to the object of his interest."

Another rising journalist who made his way to the Village was Frazier Hunt. Having made the leap from Chicago to New York (New York had replaced Chicago as the cultural and intellectual capital of the nation), he found lodgings in the Village with an artist friend, Jack Armstrong, who occupied a loft on East Fifteenth Street. Young Tom Craven from Kansas, uncertain whether to become an artist or a novelist, was working on a novel entitled *Paint*. A few blocks away Tom Benton from Neosho, Missouri, was "denned up in a miserable little studio painting away desperately at strangely distorted and discolored figures and scenes." The "old Art Institute gang," as Hunt called them, were much in evidence and leaders of the Midwestern art contingent.

The theater was another important channel for the new consciousness. The Yiddish theaters were a particular battleground. The issue was realism versus impressionism. It was debated in the cafés, on the stages of the theaters of the city, "the realist party," Lincoln Steffens recalled, "hissing a romantic play, the romanticists fighting for it with clapping hands and sometimes with fists or nails. A remarkable phenomenon . . . a community of thousands of people fighting over an art question as savagely as other people had fought over political or religious questions, dividing families, setting brother against brother, breaking up business firms, and finally, actually forcing the organization of a rival theatre with a company pledged to realism against the old theatre which would play any good piece."

The *Masses* was the semiofficial voice of the Village. The importance of the *Masses* in the view of Hutchins Hapgood was in the work of the young radical artists whose work adorned its pages: Art Young, Boardman Robinson, John Sloan, and Robert Minor. They were painters of the new realistic school whose scenes of streets, alleys, and vacant lots were referred to contemptuously by the artistic establishment as products of the Ashcan school of art. They took the name proudly as an indication of their concern with the masses. The masses, indeed, were on the tongue of every intellectual of liberal or radical inclination. They were, after all, the hope of the future.

The most prominent editors of the *Masses* were Max Eastman and Floyd Dell. Ida Rauh, Eastman's wife, was also active on the magazine. Needless to say, few coal miners or lumbermen read the *Masses,* and Morris Hillquit referred to it contemptuously as "the *Vanity Fair* of the labor movement." Oscar Ameringer wrote: "In the *Masses,* all the miners were six feet two inches tall, had the chests, arms, and legs of gorillas, and were forever breaking chains around their bulging biceps."

Eastman was, to Hapgood, a typical intellectual who dabbled in Marxism, a self-promoter, a "man seeking power." To Eastman, Hapgood was a dilettante, more interested in using radical movements as material for his newspaper columns than in advancing the cause of the revolution. Eastman was "handsome, eloquent, winning," in Frederic Howe's words. Associate professor of philosophy at Columbia, he symbolized the new alliance between the university and radical politics. His sister Crystal was a graduate of Vassar and a lawyer whose investigation of housing and industrial conditions in Pittsburgh had resulted in her being appointed secretary to the state's Workmen's Compensation Commission.

In this atmosphere of intellectual and cultural ferment, the People's Institute with Frederic Howe at its head became a center of radical thought. When Thomas Mott Osborne, the reform-minded warden of Sing Sing, was bitterly attacked for his efforts at prison reform, a meeting was held at the Cooper Union under the auspices of the institute. Osborne was a graduate of Harvard, class of 1884, who had worked in his father's farm machinery business until he decided on a career as a prison reformer. Appointed chairman of the New York State Commission for Prison Reform, he began his tenure of office by "serving" a week as a prisoner in Auburn prison. As a result of his experiences, he wrote *Within Prison Walls,* a scathing attack on conditions in prisons. The most dramatic moment of the meeting at Cooper Union came when Alexander Berkman appeared and demanded an opportunity to speak. He had spent ten years in prison and presumed that he knew considerably more about the subject than the members of the audience.

As we have had ample occasion to note, Americans of refined sensibility had never been able to stand America. Whenever the state of their finances permitted, they fled to Europe, most commonly to Britain with excursions to the Continent—to the baths in Germany, to Italy, and, in Washington Irving's wake, to Spain. Now cultivation and refined sensibility were far more widely spread about the country. New England and New York no longer exercised the hegemony that had earlier distinguished them. There was a potent and increasingly self-confident Middle West, an emergent Far West, and even a new South. There was a new sense of America. America had been acclaimed from the earliest days of the Republic as the hope of the world and the greatest nation on earth, and this spirit of rather touching brag and bluster had only been accentuated by the passage of time and the nation's spectacular growth. It had, at the same time, been deplored by upper-class Americans who, for the most part, considered Britain far superior to the United States. Emerson and Richard Henry Dana had been of that mind. And Henry Adams and James Fenimore Cooper. It was Emerson, after all, who wrote: "Great men and great nations are not braggards and buffoons but perceivers of the terror of life and arm themselves to face it."

Now, while the criticism of the United States did not diminish, indeed, if anything, grew louder and more vehement, it took on a new and more hopeful tone. If life could not be endured on Main Street or in Middletown or whatever arid and repressive small community one called home, there was Chicago or New York or San Francisco. What was going on was in part the democratization of the nation's cultural and intellectual class. The Eastern-New England-Harvard-Yale monopoly was being broken. Even as the Populists had tried (and failed) to break the hold of Wall Street on the nation's money supply, a new, essentially middle-class intelligentsia was setting out to break the Northeastern monopoly on culture, which required, in its initial stages at least, that all the culturally aspiring, all the renegades and runaways come to the East or to Chicago. It was not, of course, a new movement. It had been going on for several generations. John Hay had, after all, grown up in Salem, Indiana. William Dean Howells was a refugee from Martins Ferry, Ohio. But Hay and Howells took the the East on its terms. They became more Eastern than the Easterners without entirely shedding the feeling of small-town boys who had been lucky enough to acquire generous patrons.

The new migration, of which Greenwich Village was the center, had a far different quality. These invaders scorned the dominant culture; they intended to take over the city and then the country; they were fomenting revolution, not contemplating accommodation. So the Village marked not only the alliance of the intellectuals with labor, but the beginning of a genuinely "national" culture, the nationalizing, if you will, of American intellectual life. And for this a particular place and, above all, a particular group of friends, of people who knew and, at least to a degree, liked each other and danced to the same flutist, paid court to the same muses, was necessary. Yet Greenwich Village, as Hutchins Hapgood pointed out, was less a place than a state of mind or, as we would say today, life-style. "Wherever a group of individuals— men animated by a dislike of regular business or professional life, inclined toward the freedom of art and literature, the women of the same type, bored by some small place in the Middle West, the business office or domesticity, filled with a restless ambition to lead their own lives—came together, there was the Village."

In Walter Lippmann's exuberant words, "We live in a revolutionary period and nothing is so important as to be aware of it. The dynamics of a splendid human civilization are about us." There was an intoxicating sense of freedom, of new possibilities, new careers, new opportunities. Old forms, old oppressions fell away. The cake of custom was cracked, and everywhere the implications of the new freedom were explored. The new year of 1913 seemed full of promise to Emma Goldman and the friends and financial supporters of *Mother Earth* who met in her apartment in the Village: "poets, writers, rebels, and Bohemians of various attitude, behavior, and habit," as she put it. "They argued about philosophy, social theories, art, and sex. . . . Everybody danced and grew gay."

Six weeks later—February 13, 1913—the Armory Show opened in New York. It was the first exposure of the American public to the European avant-garde. To Mabel Dodge it was the most significant thing that had happened since the American Revolution. Hutchins Hapgood was no less ecstatic. He remembered the show "as I would a great fire, an earthquake, or a political revolution; as a series of shattering events—shattering for the purpose of re-creation." The show symbolized, for him and for thousands of others who saw it, or even read about it, an all-out assault on bourgeois values. "Whether," as Hapgood wrote, "in art, literature, labor expansion, or sexual experience, [it was] a moving, a shaking time. Postimpressionist art, experimental literature, sprang from the same impulse—the impulse of the day."

As Hapgood summed up the mood of the country, "There is a spirit of deep-seated unrest in the land, in the world. Political revolutions throughout the world have happened in the last few years, great strikes in the last few months, groups of people deemed radical a short time ago are now regarded as almost conservative. . . ." He could see no clear direction; no one group, faction, or party that displayed any clear capacity for leadership or knew in what direction the country was moving (the socialists, of course, insisted it was moving toward socialism). It seemed to Hapgood that the only encouraging sign was a kind of "spiritual" awakening in the country.

Of all the strange assortment of characters who gravitated to "the Village" in the first decade and a half of the century, none exuded a more powerful charisma than that wounded one-eyed giant, Big Bill Haywood. Into the night spots and hangouts of the intelligentsia, into the art salons, with some "slatternly girl" in tow he appeared as the dramatic and wildly romantic embodiment of the generation-long war between capital and labor. Into the theoretical discussions of revolutionary tactics he brought an acrid whiff of dynamite smoke, the impact of a mine guard's club. It was a strange turn for his tumultuous life.

He had always been, underneath the tough guy–brawler, an intellectual, and in the Village he was finally in his element, the archetypal hero of the labor movement, the prophet of the Red Revolution. John Reed and Margaret Sanger were only the best known of those who succumbed. It was certainly the case that middle- and upper-class reformers had played important roles in labor's struggle for justice. Terence Powderly was one such; the Swinton brothers were others. But by and large middle- and upper-class intellectuals, men like George Templeton Strong and Sidney George Fisher in an earlier generation, and the Jameses, the Adamses, and John Hay, had remained aloof from the war between capital and labor. Most of them continued to look on the "commonalty" with apprehension (and often fear) as well as with distaste. Even those who sympathized with the plight of workingmen and -women and tried to alleviate it did so out of humanitarian principles, not as the consequence of any strong affinity for the working class.

After the defeat of the Paterson strike, Haywood, who had lost eighty pounds from the effects of a stomach ulcer, went to France and then to England to meet with radical labor leaders in those countries, and when he returned to the United States he shifted his base of operations to the West Coast and took up the plight of the migratory farm workers. The IWW was too rough, too dangerous, too "Western," to succeed in the East.

Emma Goldman and Alexander Berkman were only slightly less potent figures in the life of the Village than Haywood. The same romantic aura surrounded them; they had been the precursors, the first venturers in the new realm of radical politics and advanced art. That they were immigrant Russian Jews gave them an ineffably exotic air. They mediated the world of European radical thought to the sons and daughters of the Midwest in the new dispensation. (Hutchins Hapgood and Emma Goldman contemplated a romance but decided to desist in the light of their respect for each other's lover.)

By the second decade of the twentieth century—what we might call the new romantic age—there were clear indications that canonization of labor by the intellectuals was under way. The new ethic saw Labor (with a capital *L*) and Unions (with a capital *U*) as the primary and essential vectors of the new age. If America was corrupt and materialistic almost beyond endurance, full of crass capitalists and greedy bourgeoisie, the working class at least was a great reservoir of as yet undefiled humanity. The Working Class, the Workers, and the Unions began to be more and more widely perceived as the redemptive element in American society. What the slaves, and later the freed blacks, had been to the abolitionists—the promise of a purified nation of black and white brothers—the Workers became to a new class in America: the radical (and liberal) intellectuals. America, it seemed, could not exist without the hope of a "saving remnant," without belief in "a company of redeemers." Only in the light of such expectations could the reality be borne. If the presence of Big Bill Haywood among the artist-intellectuals of Greenwich Village did not in itself produce that new consciousness—that new vision of the role of Labor in the redemption of America—it strengthened it and bore unmistakable witness to its existence. It was henceforth to be a major theme in the odd equation that constituted the American consciousness.

The period 1911 to 1914 was, all over the Western world, in Europe as well as America, an extraordinary moment when the visual and plastic arts reached the highest point of expressiveness in modern times. It was as though, anticipating the impending cataclysm of world war, the creative energies bloomed in astonishing brilliance and variety.

By statistical standards, Greenwich Village was a very modest enterprise, involving in its heyday a few hundred people. While much that was interesting and arresting came out of it, it produced very little, if any, great art. Its expectations in every line proved extravagant, but those extravagant expectations provided an extraordinary stimulus for a number of gifted people and changed in subtle but critically important ways the chemistry of American life. From Fresno, California, and Portland, Oregon, through Dubuque, Iowa, Peoria, Illinois, Nashville, Tennessee, from small towns and large cities all over the country, the name Greenwich Village evoked what Malcolm Cowley has called "a dream of the golden mountains."

In the 1950s Walter Lippmann looked back on the period between 1910 and the beginning of the war. "It was a happy time, those last few years before the First World War," he wrote. "The air was soft, and it was easy for a young man to believe in the inevitability of progress, in the perfectability of man and society, and in the sublimation of evil." Frederic Howe wrote in a similar vein: "The political renaissance was surely coming. It would not stop with economic reform; it would bring in a rebirth of literature, art, music, and spirit, not unlike that which came to Italy in the thirteenth century after the *popolo grasso* had made their pile and then turned to finer things. The colleges were to lead it; it was to have the support of the more enlightened business men; it would call forth the impoverished talents of the immigrant and the poor. The spirit of this young America was generous, hospitable, brilliant; it was care-free and full of variety. The young people in whom it leaped to expression hated injustice. They had no question about the soundness of American democracy. They had supreme confidence in the mind."

This was the spirit of what was called, for want of a better phrase, Greenwich Village.

17

It's Roosevelt Again!

By the midterm election of 1910 the principal question on the minds of those Americans preoccupied with politics (a substantial number, to be sure) was whether the Colonel would reclaim the presidency that he had so recently and lightheartedly abandoned.

The role that William Allen White envisioned for the Colonel was that of a wise and self-effacing leader and adviser rather than a presidential candidate in his own right. White wrote to Roosevelt in the summer of 1910: "The corporation in essence is selfish; it is the only entirely selfish organism in society. . . . It is society's centripetal force." The men who headed the great corporations were the men who surrounded Taft and dictated policy. Under such circumstances, Roosevelt was needed "as an unselfish leader working with the people as one of them, not as their ruler. We need a brother," White wrote, "and not a master nor a servant. . . . The alliance between politics and wealth that would merely aggrandize itself with no thought of its social obligation must be ever-lastingly smashed. There should be no compromise, no conciliation, no monkey business about that contest. It is fundamental. The people must control or be controlled. They can't go halvers with the Interests." It was Roosevelt's job to "go with them into this fight . . . as a friend and brother and equal of them all. They need you. They have a right to expect you to serve them, in this higher service, this more unselfish and more practical service without reward and without official honor."

While White had been unhappy at many of the things that Taft had done or undone, the country would be better off with another term for Taft, he felt, than to be involved in a bitter contest between the conservative and progressive wings of the party. The fact was that the American people no longer needed strong leadership. They were "beginning to walk alone." They had learned the lessons of the reformers better than anyone knew. "There is a distinctly growing, automatically organizing public opinion in America today," White declared, "that is the same in every section and corner of the Republic. It knows not class or occupation. It is national. It will triumph over every President, Congress or court that can be found. It is the outgrowth of necessity." With Roosevelt in the White House those Americans of conscience who had taken up the fight for social justice would feel secure and slacken their efforts, confident that the man in the White House would do what was necessary and thereby relieve them of the responsibility.

Roosevelt's principal rival for the leadership of the liberal wing of the party was Robert La Follette, the brilliant reform governor of Wisconsin. Born in the tiny town of Primrose, Wisconsin, in 1855, La Follette had grown up under the cruelly demanding conditions of the Northern frontier. Alternating school and work, he graduated from the University of Wisconsin at the age of twenty-four and soon afterward was admitted to the Wisconsin bar. One of his classmates was Belle Case, a brilliant student who earned a law degree in her own right. They were married in 1885. It was a classic "new marriage" in the Midwestern style. She worked in her husband's law office and became his political strategist. With her help he won two congressional terms, running as a Republican in a Democratic district.

The political boss of Wisconsin, Senator Philetus Sawyer, ruled the state party with an iron hand. He was the dutiful servant of the lumber, mining, and railroad interests, affable, accommodating, and corrupt. La Follette, dismayed by evidence of wholesale bribery on Sawyer's part, became increasingly the enemy of the party leaders and a champion of political reform: the direct primary, the regulation of the railroads, and the initiative and referendum.

Twice defeated for his party's nomination for governor, La Follette won the nomination and election in 1900 and took office committed to reform. Over the dogged opposition of the party stalwarts, "Fighting Bob," using the University of Wisconsin as his brain trust, welded the idealistic young men and women of the state, many of whom were ardent socialists, into an army of reform. He appeared as the most striking political phenomenon of the Midwest since Bryan's emergence in 1892. The Wisconsin Idea became a model for reformers all over the nation, and La Follette a hero to those men and women dedicated to the fight for social justice. Undoubtedly his most notable contribution was "putting mind to service in the cause of the public good." That had been the dream of the young idealists like Frederic Howe and Newton D. Baker at Johns Hopkins; La Follette had made it a reality at the University of Wisconsin, a number of the faculty members of which had been trained at Johns Hopkins.

The La Follette method was to define a particular problem—e.g., railroad rate legislation—appoint a commission of experts to research the issue, write an exhaustive report, and propose appropriate legislation. Armed with the facts, La Follette and his lieutenants would take the case to the people, mustering popular support and bringing intense pressure to bear on recalcitrant legislators. Frederic Howe wrote admiringly of "the close identification of the State university with the State government. . . . Through social legislation, education, and the expansion of State activities, Wisconsin was making itself an invaluable experiment in democracy." Felix Frankfurter was also an admirer of La Follette's "union between politics and the university, energizing organized knowledge in the interest of the state. . . ." It was, Frankfurter wrote, "one of the most vital contributions he has made. In fact all his concrete accomplishments are simply results of that viewpoint."

La Follette spread his gospel by means of a little magazine he edited. On the masthead he placed the motto "Ye shall know the truth and the truth shall make you free."

Lincoln Steffens sought out the new Midwestern knight of reform, convinced that he would find the typical rather priggish reformer. Before he met La Follette, Steffens inquired about him. A Milwaukee attorney was eloquent on the subject of La Follette's vices. "He's a fanatic," the man told Steffens.

"And an agitator?" Steffens asked, encouragingly.

"That's the worst of him. He's not only an orator, he's a born actor; and the way the man goes around spreading discontent is a menace to law, property, business, and all American institutions. If we don't stop him here he will go out and agitate all over the United States.

We're getting him now; you'll get him next. That man must be blocked."

A banker chimed in. "Yes, La Follette will spread socialism all over the world."

Milwaukee was full of socialists, Steffens interposed. Wouldn't they follow La Follette? No, the attorney declared, La Follette was not a socialist. "The socialists are reasonable men compared with this agitator, who is more of a Populist."

The more Steffens heard of La Follette, the better he sounded. "Bob La Follette's measures seemed fair to me," he wrote, "his methods democratic, his purposes right but moderate, and his fighting strength and spirit hopeful and heroic."

Steffens's personal impression of La Follette was positive. To the enthralled Steffens, La Follette poured out all his hopes, ambitions, and doubts—"the open book of an ambitious young man who, fitted in the schools and the University of Wisconsin with the common, patriotic conception of his country and his government, discovered bit by bit what the facts were, and, shocked, set out to fight for democracy, justice, honesty." In Steffens's words, "Bob La Follette was restoring representative government in Wisconsin, and by his oratory and his fierce dictatorship and his relentless conspicuous persistence he was making his people understand—all of them, apparently, not only the common people whom he preferred, but the best people too; they also knew. They might denounce him, they might lie to the stranger, but in their heart of hearts they knew. It was a great experiment, La Follette's: State reform that began in the capital of the State and spread out close to the soil."

Steffens described La Follette as "rather short in stature, but broad and strong" with "the gift of muscled, nervous power. . . . Every speech he made was an exercise in calisthenics. His hands and his face were expressive; they had to be to make his balled fighting fists appeal for peace and his proud, defiant countenance ask for the reasonableness he always looked for even in an audience he was attacking. His sincerity, his integrity, his complete devotion to his ideal, were indubitable; no one who heard him could suspect his singleness of purpose or his courage." In one speech he battered his hand so badly that it was in bandages for weeks.

When La Follette spoke at Michigan State College in East Lansing in 1908, the huge auditorium was packed with students, faculty, and townspeople, come to see and hear the Wisconsin giant killer. He completely captivated his audience. He talked for an hour and a half, and then his listeners urged him on for another hour. When he finished, an old farmer, sitting beside Ray Stannard Baker, turned to him and said, "I know now how the Apostle Paul must have preached."

Baker was another recruit to the La Follette camp. When he visited Milwaukee, he encountered "a short, thick, active man with a big head, red face and hair standing in a stiff pompadour." To Baker, La Follette was a master of the new politics. He had gone about overthrowing the entrenched politicians "as a scientist would have done." Baker visited the La Follettes home and described their family life. "There was the long table filled with the family, young and old," he wrote, "and often guests dropping in, and much good talk and laughter." Belle La Follette had gone to law school before the couple's first child was born, and Bob, already set on the path of politics, had helped out at home. Three more children followed. The boys, Robert, Jr., and Philip, seemed marked for politics. In the La Follette household, Shakespeare was the reigning literary deity (closely followed by Robert Burns), and the evenings were often spent reading aloud from his plays.

Baker and other young liberals—men like Amos and Gifford Pinchot; James Garfield; and Lincoln Steffens—believed that in Baker's words, "La Follette was the only truly progressive leader to whom the country could turn with any hope of success."

Roosevelt and La Follette, William Allen White observed, held the "allegiance of hundreds of thousands of men of both [Republican and Democratic] parties—chiefly, however, young Republicans north of the Mason and Dixon line. They were mostly college men," White added, "and they rejected Bryan," in large part because his appeal was primarily emotional.

Elected to the Senate from Wisconsin, La Follette found himself very much an outsider in Washington. "He is a wary Senator, carefully preserves his Wisconsin flavor, and seldom goes out socially," Florence Harriman wrote. It seemed to the infatuated Steffens that Roosevelt and La Follette were natural allies. He arranged a meeting between his new hero and a somewhat reluctant Roosevelt. "When they met at the White House, the president and the senator," Steffens recalled, "it was comic. They began to back off from each other before they met; their hands touched, but their eyes, their bodies, their feet walked away. I don't recall a word that either of them said. . . ." To Roosevelt, La Follette was all wrong—his flat Midwestern accent; his necktie; his shoes; the cut of his clothes; his unruly pompadour of black hair; his sturdy, somewhat truculent manner. Clearly he was not a gentleman.

Beside the elegant Steffens, the Wisconsin senator looked like a common laborer, dressed up for church. Roosevelt, who disliked Westerners, except cowboys, of course, suspected them of dangerously radical notions and a kind of collective insanity. "La Follette as a type," Roosevelt wrote somewhat later to Lodge, "is considerably inferior, in morality and capacity, to Robespierre."

La Follette intuited all that. To him Roosevelt's reform impulses were shallow and unsupported by any genuine commitments to change. For La Follette there was one overriding issue: "the struggle between labor and those who would control, through slavery in one form or another, the laborers." Everything else, even conservation, was secondary to that conflict. That certainly was very far from Roosevelt's view of things.

Eastern conservatives (and many Eastern progressives) shared Roosevelt's dislike of the flamboyant Wisconsonite. As Senator from Wisconsin, La Follette was treated with studied rudeness by the Senate's ruling elders. The Millionaires' Club, as that body was often called, "used against him the almost irresistible force of social ostracism," as Ray Stannard Baker put it. When he rose to speak, many Senators would walk out of the chamber ostentatiously. When he spoke on the Hepburn bill, the galleries were crowded with his admirers and with supporters of the bill, but the floor of the Senate chamber was half empty. La Follette, his voice thick with emotion, turned to the presiding Vice-President and declared, "I pause in my remarks to say this. I cannot be wholly indifferent to the fact that Senators by their absence at this time indicate their want of interest in what I may have to say about this subject. The public is interested. Unless this important question is rightly settled seats now temporarily vacant may be permanently vacated by those who have the right to occupy them at this time."

Two young Insurgents/Progressives with Midwestern roots were Albert Beveridge and George Perkins. Both had spent the mid-1880s in Kansas: Beveridge had practiced law in Dighton, Kansas, and Perkins had worked in Wichita as an insurance salesman. Beveridge, scholarly and well-read, moved to Indiana and began the political ascent that won him a senatorship from that state. Perkins went East, became the right-hand man of the House of Morgan, made a substantial fortune by the time he was forty, and retired to devote his life to reform, primarily, as it turned out, to the political fortunes of Theodore Roosevelt.

Beveridge was almost painfully earnest, and his friend William Allen White found his ambition "obvious and a bit ridiculous, but always innocent and shameless like a child's indecencies. He liked to talk sometimes sensuously," White noted, "and seemed to be stroking himself on the back with a pride in his oracular wisdom that was not offensive. . . ." Perkins was described by White as "a slim, silky-mustached, clear-eyed young man. . . ."

George Norris emerged in Nebraska as a Progressive bellwether. In Minnesota it was Moses Clapp, and in Illinois Joseph Medill McCormick and Harold Ickes. Chase Osborn was the Progressive leader in Michigan. Having won the Republican nomination for governor of Michigan with the aid of Frank Knox, Osborn had allied himself with the reform elements in the Republican Party. In the words of one of his supporters, he was "the Man of Iron who in 1911 and '12 shook and rocked Republican Michigan out of a . . . sleep, unsealed her eyes, and set her feet on the upward path." His achievements in Michigan made him a national figure in the Progressive ranks, and he had been recruited for the National Progressive Republican League by no less than Robert La Follette. With five other governors, nine Senators, and a number of Congressmen, the league had been formed at La Follette's home in January, 1911.

In Iowa, Albert Baird Cummins, a lawyer who had gained fame as the enemy of the barbed wire trust, led the Insurgents. Elected governor of Iowa in 1900, Cummins made that state a rival of Wisconsin in reform legislation. He broke the domination of the railroads and guided a primary law through the state legislature that became a model for many other states. But to Roosevelt, Cummins was the prototype of the wild-eyed Midwestern reformer who, in his zeal, gave encouragement to "idiotic reformers" everywhere.

Farther west, in Idaho, William Borah, prosecuting attorney in the trial of Big Bill Haywood at Caldwell, was another recruit to the Progressive cause. Edward Costigan of Colorado took on the mining interests in that state. Senator Jonathan Bourne of Oregon carried the Progressive banner, and in California Hiram Johnson, the prosecutor of Abraham Ruef and his cronies, became the leader of the Insurgent Republicans.

In the East, Gifford and Amos Pinchot were the mainstays of the movement in Pennsylvania, while in New England only Massachusetts showed a zeal for reform. There Charles Sumner Bird joined forces with Harvard historian Albert Bushnell Hart to lead the Progressive forces.

The admirers of La Follette, Gifford Pinchot among them, began to concert their efforts to bring La Follette forth as the successor to Roosevelt. If the Progressives could not recapture the Republican Party, their strategy was to form a third party and nominate La Follette as its standard-bearer. But that was not to be. Four years after he had solemnly and doubtlessly sincerely abjured presidential ambitions, Roosevelt now found the prospect of one more political safari irresistible. The Colonel soon moved to take firm control of the Progressive movement.

There was a brief, fierce struggle between the Eastern and Western factions of the Progressive Republicans—between La Follette and Roosevelt. "It was curious to watch the two men rise . . ." William Allen White wrote, "each struggling to take his country to the same goal, each bitterly scornful of the other's methods, and probably deeply suspicious of his inner aims." Roosevelt was the compromiser, content with half a political loaf rather than none. La Follette was the undeviating idealist who seemed to his critics as well as his enemies to have a martyr complex, ready to go down to defeat before he would compromise his principles. White loved and admired them both. He thought "adored" was not too strong a word. La Follette's hopes had rested primarily on winning the support of Eastern liberals and especially the liberal press. When he appeared at the Periodical Publishers' dinner in Philadelphia on February 2, 1912, it was with the hope of convincing that influential body that he had a fighting chance of winning the presidency. Woodrow Wilson, the Princeton professor and mildly reformist governor of New Jersey, had also been invited to speak.

For Wilson, the evening was a triumph; for La Follette, a disaster. Wilson spoke first. "Never was he in better form, more truly eloquent," Oswald Garrison Villard wrote. "He made one of his great speeches, and swept everything before him. The audience, largely composed of Republican reactionaries, was thrilled by him. . . ."

La Follette followed Wilson. He was exhausted from a wearying political campaign and distressed by the sickness of his daughter. He was, moreover, in a setting that was both unfamiliar and hostile. The greater part of his audience considered him a wild-eyed radical and a traitor to Republican principles. He had asked a waiter for some brandy and tossed it down. "It did not make him drunk," Villard wrote, "but . . . seemed to deprive him of a realization of what he was . . . saying." As he spoke, "he became confused and repetitious"; a kind of latent paranoia came to the surface in a bitter attack on his audience, men who, he charged, were "reactionary and eager to exploit the public," men "in a conspiracy against him." La Follette singled out Villard himself, who had always been a supporter. "He spoke for hours," Villard noted, "and completely spoiled the dinner." Guests began to slip away; others hissed; there were jeers and catcalls. When Villard left, it was after one o'clock in the morning and La Follette was still talking angrily and abusively. When it was over at last, La Follette's supporters were stricken. "To those of us who were there and were La Follette's friends," Ray Stannard Baker wrote, "it was a tragedy beyond tears. . . . [La Follette] sat in his chair white-faced and perfectly still while Mrs. La Follette and one or two other friends tried to keep up a cheerful conversation."

It seems safe to say that the Periodical Publishers' dinner was the most fateful meal in the annals of American politics. It was, in a real sense, La Follette's Last Supper, a meal that preceded his political crucifixion. It helped make, if it was not indeed decisive in making, one man president, and it may well have foreclosed for the other the possibility of achieving that office. Even today there clings to it something of the symbolic and bizarre. A weary and demoralized La Follette poured out all the accumulated bitterness of West toward East. Held in economic thrall by the self-assured and arrogant men of "Wall Street"— that is to say, patronized and condescended to as crude, uncultivated, and worst of all, politically radical, tainted with populism and socialism, with notions of free silver and free trade—the West spoke in the angry accents of its favorite son. The debacle served, as nothing else could have, to dramatize the width and depth of the chasm that separated the two great sections. A line running roughly down the Ohio River to the Mississippi and thence to the Gulf of Mexico separated the eastern third of the nation from the western two-thirds. Far more than a simple geographic boundary, it was a kind of fault line of the mind and consciousness. To the west of the line lay the better part of the continent, a land of enormous present and potential richness, the colonial possession of the East.

La Follette, it turned out, could not even count on his Midwestern allies. The fatal defection from his camp was that of Irvine Lenroot, a fellow Wisconsin reformer who had supported La Follette in the state and as a member of the Wisconsin congressional delegation. La Follette had been confident of Lenroot's support. Indeed, Lenroot, with close ties to the Progressive establishment through his labor in the cause of conservation as well as of municipal reform, was essential to the Wisconsin Senator's presidential ambitions. Now Lenroot cast his lot with the Roosevelt rebellion. Mrs. La Follette wrote to a friend: "Nothing that has happened has been so hard for me. We have managed to keep the personal relation but I realize that Bob and Irvine can never be the same to each other as before."

There were more disappointments to come. Although he had accepted the office of vice-president in the newly formed National Progressive Republican League, Chase Osborn was convinced that the primary purpose of the league was to advance the presidential aspirations of La Follette. At a rally of La Follette's supporters in Lansing, Michigan, Osborn put a damper on the proceedings by proposing that La Follette withdraw his name as a Republican standard-bearer in the coming election and throw his support to Albert Beveridge or Theodore Roosevelt as the Republican candidate. It was a blow to La Follette's hopes almost as severe as the defection of Irvine Lenroot.

By the fall of 1911 William Allen White, who, a year earlier, had cautioned Roosevelt not to allow himself to become a candidate for the Republican nomination, was singing a different tune. Taft was clearly beyond reclamation. "The courthouse bunch in every county in the nation had no enthusiasm for Taft," he wrote to Roosevelt, primarily because that by now thoroughly unpopular President must lose them votes locally if he were a candidate again and thereby weaken the party. White was convinced that the politicos intended to "tie up the [Republican] convention for a ballot or two between La Follette and Taft and an Eminently Respectful person [a yet unchosen middle-of-the-road candidate] and then let off the fireworks and stampede [the convention] to you." White was reconciled to that eventuality, he told Roosevelt. Taft was impossible, and "the country was not quite ready" for La Follette. "I think he is due in 1916," White added. To Senator Bristow of Kansas, White wrote that "there is absolutely no doubt at all but that Kansas would be for Roosevelt overwhelmingly against either La Follette or Taft or against both La Follette and Taft, and I think you will find that the sentiment of Kansas is the sentiment of the nation. . . . We can and will nominate Roosevelt."

But Roosevelt continued to vacillate. Henry Stoddard reported him as saying to the chairmen of three or four states where he was strongest, "I am not in this situation and I am not going to be dragged into it. Taft created it and let Taft take his spanking for it. There is no reason why I should. If I wanted four more years in the White House I would say so and go after it; but I don't want it. I've had enough. I couldn't go back without risking all I gained in the seven years I was there."

"You can hardly exaggerate the consternation into which the Roosevelt cohort has been thrown," Henry Adams wrote to Elizabeth Cameron, "by his actual cavortings now going on, and there is not one of your intimates but is squirming like a skinned eel at the hole into which he has thrown them. All are wondering what he wants them to do, or what he expects of them, while he assures them that he expects nothing. . . ." Even Elihu Root was convinced that Roosevelt did not in fact want to be president "but that he aims at a leadership far in the future as a sort of Moses and Messiah for a vast progressive rising tide of humanity." Henry Adams assumed that Champ Clark, the new Speaker of the House, or Bryan must become president. "The 'progressives,' " Adams wrote, "will vote for anybody rather than Taft; the conservatives will let anybody in sooner than Theodore. . . . The hatred of Theodore has become as insane as Theodore's own conduct; and the passion of the so-called progressives is red-hot." Adams reported that the psychiatrist, or "alienist," Morton Prince had undertaken to study Roosevelt as an example of a "double personality," one-half of which, a half that Prince called Sally, had "worked herself up to a personal and vindictive passion for beating Taft, and will stick at nothing to do it. This is *my* view," Adams added.

As the movement toward Roosevelt gathered momentum, White and others became disturbed at La Follette's intransigence. White wrote to various Progressive allies urging them to exert what influence they could to persuade him to support Roosevelt. "I feel that [La Follette] is exhibiting an animus against Colonel Roosevelt," White wrote to the president of the University of Wisconsin, Charles Van Hise, "which, even if based upon the facts . . . would be unmanly, undignified and politically suicidal to him, and absolutely disastrous to the cause for which we are all working." Roosevelt was, White admitted, "a very human person." He had done many things that White did not agree with and could not condone. "I feel very strongly about some of his faults," he added. "But, on the other hand, I believe that his faults are entirely secondary faults, temperamental rather than fundamental. I think he has done great service to the cause as a preacher. I have not regarded him as a great constructive statesman. . . ." Moreover, he had compromised on issues that he should never have compromised on. But his four years out of office, White believed, had made him "a

sounder, safer man and more progressive president than he ever was."
White was afraid that the La Follette forces would "tie up the organization of the convention to give the reactionary forces in that convention the immense advantages of organization, so that by force and
violence and cheating, they might force the progressive delegates into
a bolt and leave the reactionary forces in control of the party organization for the next ten years. . . ."

With La Follette's collapse his backers came in a delegation from
the Midwestern states (Governor Hiram Johnson of California was also
a member of the group) to urge Roosevelt to accept their platform
and become their candidate. Roosevelt's response was distinctly unfriendly. The platform, he implied, was much too radical. "I can stand
one-revolution men," he declared when he heard the names of the
delegation, "but two-revolution fellows are too much for me; they want
to be revolting all the time. I cannot be their candidate." The fact was,
he had already decided to contest Taft's renomination. When Frank
Knox, the Progressive Republican, visited Washington in December,
1911, he was "dumbfounded," he wrote to Chase Osborn, governor
of Michigan, at the widespread disenchantment with Taft in Republican circles. "Predictions of his defeat, if nominated, were on everybody's lips . . ." he wrote, "yet the White House assumes not to recognize
the situation." Knox, who included in his Eastern trip a visit with the
former President, reported that Roosevelt was concerned that the big
business interests, which "have no use for Roosevelt because of the
policy he has pursued toward corporations . . . will try to revenge themselves on both Taft and Roosevelt by using Roosevelt to defeat Taft
for the nomination, with the idea that Roosevelt would be defeated at
the election." According to Knox, Roosevelt, fearful of falling into the
trap of the party managers, wished to lie low until the election of 1916.
Then, if "the Republican party called upon him to again lead, he would
accept." By December Roosevelt, according to Knox, had so far overcome his misgivings as to hint that he would accept the Republican
nomination "if it came to him without solicitation or effort on his part."
Knox, determined to push Roosevelt's candidacy, enlisted his ally Chase
Osborn.

When Osborn, at Knox's behest, wrote to Roosevelt to sound him
out on the matter of being a candidate, Roosevelt replied noncom-
mittally but not discouragingly. Osborn thereupon urged the former
President to issue a statement to the effect that "if the people really
nominated me . . . I would be bound to accept." He concluded his letter

with the observation "It looks . . . as though you would have to make the greatest sacrifice and become President again." Roosevelt demurred. The time, he felt, was not ripe for such a declaration.

In January, 1912, Roosevelt decided to ask five governors to issue a public letter urging him to become a candidate for the Republican nomination. "It seems to me," he wrote to Herbert Hadley, the governor of Missouri, "that if such a group of four or five governors wrote me a joint letter, or wrote me individual letters which I could respond to at the same time and in the same way, that such a procedure would open the best way out of an uncomfortable situation." He was, he assured the governors, "honestly desirous of considering the matter solely from the standpoint of the public interest, and not in the least from my own standpoint. . . . I am not seeking and shall not seek the nomination. . . ." If it was clear beyond question that "the plain people . . . as a whole desire me, not for my sake, but for their sake, to undertake the job, I would feel honor bound to do so."

Knox drafted such a letter for the governors to sign, and Roosevelt revised it. Nine Republican governors, representing various regions from West Virginia to Wyoming, signed. The letter, dated February 19 and released to the press on that date, was replied to by Roosevelt four days later in a letter that doubtless had been drafted along with the governors' letter. In it, the former President indicated his willingness to be a candidate "in the interest of the people."

Henry Stoddard gave a dramatic account of the Colonel's decision to become a candidate. "I shall never forget the evening meeting in J. West Roosevelt's home in New York city early in February, 1912, when Roosevelt acquiesced," he wrote. "It was a gathering of many of the leading liberal Republicans and their money men. Everyone had his say. The weight was heavily on the side of Roosevelt's entering the race for his party's nomination. When they had given their testimony somewhat in the spirit of a revival meeting, there was a pause while," in Stoddard's words, "the Colonel . . . was evidently doing some hard thinking. Suddenly he raised his hands high, outstretching them as though in benediction. Quickly closing them he brought his fists down like a flash, each fist striking an arm of his chair with a bang and in a tone almost a shout, exclaimed: 'Gentlemen, they're off!' "

Roosevelt had decided to make the formal announcement of his candidacy in a speech at Columbus, Ohio, in which he would also state the platform on which he intended to run. On his way to Columbus, he stopped overnight in Cleveland. There he was besieged by reporters who wanted to know if he intended to run. "My hat's in the ring! The fight is on and I'm stripped to the buff," Roosevelt told them, and the famous words were immediately on telegraph lines to every corner of the nation. Numerous cartoons depicted his Rough Rider's hat in a ring. Taft responded with his own "fighting slogan," which was "Only death can take me out now!" In what appeared to be shaping up as a battle of slogans, La Follette added his: "I'm nobody's cloak. I'll fight to the finish!"

The touchiest point between the Midwestern (and Western) and the Eastern branches of the National Progressive Republican League was the issue of the recall of judges who were clearly the servants of corporate masters. In the Columbus address Roosevelt criticized the courts and suggested that the recall of judges might be undertaken "as a last resort."

Even this cautious endorsement of the principle of judicial recall raised a storm of indignant protest in the conservative press. Stoddard reported that Roosevelt was "staggered and depressed by the fierceness of the assaults upon him." Brooks Adams wrote later: "Theodore Roosevelt's enemies have been many and bitter. They have attacked his honesty, his sobriety, his intelligence, and his judgment, but very few of them have hitherto denied he has a keen instinct for political strife." Still, Adams believed he had made "a capital mistake" in his Columbus address.

Among those horrified by the speech was, predictably, Henry Cabot Lodge. He seldom differed from his hero, but in this instance he could not forbear to speak his mind. "The enemy," he wrote, "are just now holding you up as little short of a revolutionist. . . ." Lodge feared that Roosevelt had fallen far too much under the influence of the "Kansas crowd and the insurgents generally. . . ." In his defense Roosevelt replied that it was an associate justice of the Supreme Court who had encouraged him to make his criticisms of the courts. "Unless the Federal judiciary is willing to submit to temperate criticism where it goes completely wrong, and to amend its shortcomings by its own action, then sooner or later there is certain to be dangerous agitation against it." It was that agitation that Roosevelt wished to forestall. Even Taft had checked in on the side of judicial reform. "Make your judges responsible," he had declared in a speech in St. Louis. "Impeach them. Impeachment of a Judge would be a very healthful thing in these times."

In the aftermath of Roosevelt's announcement of his candidacy

Henry Cabot Lodge declared that he could not support him. The ostensible reason was the Columbus address, but the real reasons undoubtedly lay deeper. Lodge was by disposition and background considerably more conservative than his friend. In addition, he was above everything else a party man and a politician. His future lay in the United States Senate and nowhere else. Roosevelt had an enormous personal following; Lodge, a Senator in the days before direct election, depended on the goodwill (or on his political dominance) of the Massachusetts legislature, the General Court. If he offended that body, he had no recourse to the voters. The decision, he wrote Roosevelt, had made him "miserably unhappy," but his constitutional principles left him no alternative. Roosevelt replied graciously, urging him never to "think of this matter again." For him it was a closed issue. From this point on politics were seldom mentioned in the correspondence of the friends; matters personal and literary predominated.

To William Allen White the Columbus speech was both a mystery and a disaster. He called the phrase "most radical and indefensible," asserting that it "crippled him more than any one thing that he did in his life, [and] shocked millions of his countrymen whom he had gathered about him as followers. . . ." The whole speech, White felt, forced Roosevelt "to a position much further to the left than he would have taken naturally. . . ." Henry Stoddard described it as the minimum concession that Roosevelt was forced to make to win the support of La Follette's backers.

All over the country Roosevelt's friends and admirers rallied to the battle for the Republican nomination. "Sacrifice of time, of money, of comfort meant nothing," Stoddard wrote; "to win delegates was the one thought. Sacrifices were never made so freely as in the fight for Roosevelt's nomination." Many politicians who gave their all for the Colonel were subsequently punished by being barred from party offices and patronage for years to come. "If the experience was not the biggest thing in our lives," Stoddard wrote nostalgically, "it was the finest— the one we knew would be the best remembered by each of us in the years to come; there were no doubters, no timid ones; we believed we were engaged in a battle for the right, and we battled with the fervor of the righteous." When a group of the more prominent Progressives met in Washington to plan strategy, Jonathan Bourne, the Senator from Oregon, reminded them of the implications of their actions. ". . . the first thing we have got to decide is a matter of fundamental policy," he told them. "If we lose, will we bolt?" It was Bourne's conviction that such a commitment was necessary if the Roosevelt movement was to be taken seriously. It was a sobering note.

The Progressive strategy backfired. It had been the hope of the Roosevelt supporters that the threat of a bolt would force the Taft wing of the party to surrender. They found that it had the opposite effect. The right wing of the party saw an opportunity, even in losing, to divest the party of its troublesome liberal wing. If the Insurgents, or Progressives, as they were increasingly called, bolted, they would, in effect, abandon the party to its most reactionary elements.

Taft, meanwhile, displayed a disarming but politically damaging gift for saying the wrong thing at the wrong place. One example, cited by Henry Stoddard, was Taft's faux pas in respect to the Payne-Aldrich bill. When the President insisted, in 1912, on campaigning in the Midwest, where opposition to the Payne-Aldrich bill, which set a tariff schedule of some 38 percent, was an article of faith, he was warned to say as little about his administration's position on the tariff as possible, but in Winona, Minnesota, he devoted most of a speech delivered on behalf of an embattled Republican Congressman to a defense of the bill, which he praised as the best bill the Republicans had ever enacted. In Stoddard's words, "The whole West was immediately vocal with rage." Letters and telegrams flooded the White House; Taft, in the hope of appeasing his critics, declared that he had "dashed it off hurriedly between stations." It was at once pointed out by unfriendly newspapers that he had been playing golf in Bar Harbor, Maine, immediately prior to his departure for Winona. Might he not have better employed his time preparing the text of what was to be his major Midwestern appearance?

As the fight for delegates at the upcoming Republican Convention grew more bitter, charges were leveled from both sides. The Roosevelt camp joined with the hated Hearst in an attack on Boies Penrose, the boss of Pennsylvania Republicans, for accepting improper campaign contributions. In the midst of this intraparty imbroglio, word came of the wreck of the new "unsinkable" *Titanic*, crowded with the rich and famous, on its maiden voyage.

"Saturday evening," Henry Adams wrote to Elizabeth Cameron, "will be a date in history. In half an hour, just in a summer sea, were wrecked the *Titanic;* President Taft; the Republican Party, Boies Penrose, and I. . . . I know not whether Taft or the *Titanic* is likely to be the furtherest-reaching disaster. The foundering of the *Titanic* [which, incidentally, Adams had intended to sail on on its return voyage] is serious and strikes at confidence in our mechanical success; but the foundering of the Republican Party destroys confidence in our political system. We've nothing to fall back upon. . . . By my blessed Virgin, it is awful! This *Titanic* blow shatters one's nerves. We can't grapple it. Taft, *Titanic! Titanic*, Taft! . . . Where does this thing end!" The *Titanic* seemed to Adams a symbol of the situation of the Republic "drifting at sea, in the ice. . . . Our dear Theodore," Adams noted, "is not a bird of happy omen. He loves to destroy."

The Republican Convention was slated for June 18 in Chicago, and as soon as it was clear that Roosevelt intended to contest the nomination, a bitter fight for delegates began. The Republican effort was clouded by a growing conviction that Taft could not be reelected. The preconvention fight thus centered less on the notion that a president was to be chosen than on a desperate struggle for control of the Republican Party. Henry Stoddard was convinced that if Roosevelt had declared his determination to enter the race five weeks earlier, "his majority in the Chicago convention would have been too big to be tampered with." But he had procrastinated, and the Taft forces meanwhile strengthened their grip on the machinery by means of which the delegates were chosen. Stoddard recalled that Norman Mack, chairman of the Democratic National Committee, had said to him several weeks before the Republican Convention, "We can beat Taft hands down if you nominate him; I am not so sure about beating Roosevelt but I think we can. You fellows will split up if either man is named. If it is Taft we will nominate a liberal Democrat and get the liberal Republican vote; if Roosevelt is your candidate we will nominate a conservative and get the conservative Republican vote. That is why our folks think we have you beaten."

Stoddard gave the game away when he wrote: "Between defeat with Taft and possible success with La Follette, however, the bulk of Republicans, at least in the East, would have taken defeat." A La Follette victory would, of course, have meant a dramatic shift in the Republican Party's center of gravity from the East to the Middle West. That, above all, the Eastern Republicans, right or left, Taft or Roosevelt, were determined to avoid. When a newspaper reporter asked the President if he would become actively involved in the fight for renomination, Taft replied, "Even a rat will fight when cornered." The Roosevelt supporters made extensive use of the analogy.

It seemed to Henry Adams by the end of 1911 that "Theodore

is inevitable." When Adams encountered the President on the street, he looked "bigger and more tumbled-to-pieces than ever," and his manners had become "more slovenly than his figure. . . . He shows mental enfeeblement all over. . . . As yet it looks as if, for sheer lack of energy, we should have to choose between Taft and Bryan. One by one, Bryan has successively wiped out all his rivals, and Roosevelt has checked all his ardent admirers. Nothing remains but the two machines." Yet a week later Adams was convinced that the delegates to the Republican Convention would nominate Roosevelt "by a general yell." Adams added, "Whether Theodore can be elected I doubt, but no one doubts that Taft will be defeated."

18

The Rise of Woodrow Wilson

While the Republicans warred among themselves, the Insurgents against the old guard and the La Follette wing against the Eastern Progressives, a Democratic dark horse appeared on the presidential racecourse. The name of Woodrow Wilson was more and more on the tongues of those Democrats drawn to the cause of reform. Wilson's speech before the Periodical Publishers had given a substantial boost to his reputation. Some of the more liberal publishers of Democratic persuasion began to promote him assiduously as the party's likeliest candidate.

As an undergraduate at Princeton in 1876, Wilson had given indications of his obsession with politics and his own intense ambition. He and a classmate had determined to make oratory, which they believed to be the surest path to political eminence, their principal study.

Temperament and ideas in some ultimately inscrutable combination constitute the character of the individual. "My ancestors," Wilson wrote, "were troublesome Scotsmen, and among them, were some of the famous group that were known as Covenanters." (Was it mere chance that the League of Nations plan was called the Covenant?) Wilson's maternal grandfather was a Scottish Presbyterian missionary in Canada and then minister of a church in Chillicothe, Ohio. Wilson's father was a Presbyterian "of a severe, intellectual type," in the words of a Wilson Cabinet member, David Houston. A graduate of the Princeton Theological Seminary of New Jersey, the elder Wilson was a professor of rhetoric at Jefferson College in Pennsylvania (his undergraduate alma mater) and then, successively, professor at Hampden-Sydney in Virginia and the Presbyterian theological seminary in Columbia, South Carolina. Wilson adored his stern and demanding father.

Wilson's uncle James Woodrow was a scientist, a linguist, and a theologian, whose views of evolution resulted in a trial for heresy by his church. Wilson's first wife was the granddaughter and the daughter of Presbyterian ministers. Of Wilson's own religious faith, Houston, who knew the President perhaps better than any other Cabinet member, wrote: "With him God was an imminent presence. He was with him in the White House, and if he could discover what He wanted, he gave no heed to what anybody else or everybody else wanted or thought." In a sympathetic sketch of Robert E. Lee, Wilson wrote that there was a side to Lee "more dominant than even his love of wife, and children, and home, and that was his love for God. He believed in the living God, the Father, the Judge of the Earth. He had not the smallest doubt but that to God all things are possible, that by faith mountains might be moved. . . . Lee had one intimate friend—God." Much the same could be said of Wilson, who was undoubtedly well aware of that when he wrote his description of Lee. He told Ray Stannard Baker that he was secure in his Presbyterian faith; "the problems of religion were never again to disturb him. His was an immovable faith in God: he rested upon it and drew strength from it."

Wilson's favorite hymns were "The Son of God Goes Forth to War/ A Kingly Crown to Gain," and "How Firm a Foundation." He liked the old and familiar in clothes as well as morals, as, for example, a tattered old gray sweater. "All things work together for good," he had written to his fiancée, Ellen Axson. "Does it frighten you to know," he wrote in another letter to her, "that the city has temptations for me? It need not. I am quite sure that my religion is strong enough to make temptation harmless."

Despite his religious zeal, Wilson displayed an odd commitment to numerology. His lucky number, he believed, was thirteen. There were, he was pleased to point out, thirteen letters in his name. He sailed for Europe to the Paris Peace Conference on the *George Washington,* which would have arrived in Brest on December 12 if Wilson had not instructed the captain to time his arrival for the thirteenth.

He also referred frequently to the fact that the number of original states and stars in the flag was thirteen.

In 1879, while he was still a senior at Princeton, Wilson had written an article setting forth his views on congressional reform, which Henry Cabot Lodge, then editor of the *International Review,* published. In the *Overland Monthly,* five years later, Wilson recommended "making the leaders of the dominant party in Congress the executive officers of the legislative . . . by making them also members of the President's Cabinet." Although he called his plan Cabinet government, it was in fact very close to the British parliamentary system and revealed his addiction to British political traditions. "It must be a policy of wisdom and prudence," he wrote, "which puts the executive and legislative departments of government into intimate sympathy and binds them together in close cooperation. The system which embodies such a policy in its greatest perfection must be admired of all statesmen and coveted of all misgoverned peoples." As long as Congress remained "the supreme power of the state," it was "idle to talk of steadying or cleansing our politics . . ." he declared. Congress represented local interests and prejudices; the president, "on the other hand, is national; at any rate may be made so. . . ." He had no constituency "but the whole people," yet he had "no originative voice in domestic national policy."

Under "Congressional Government," Wilson wrote, "despotic power [is] wielded . . . by our national Congress . . . a despotism which uses its power with all the caprice, all the scorn for settled policy, all the wild unrestraint which marked the methods of other tyrants as hateful to freedom." He added: "Eight words contain the sum of the present degradation of our political parties: *No leaders, no principles; no principles, no parties.*" Wilson advocated a restoration of the presidency to that "first estate of dignity" from which it had fallen since the days of Washington, Adams, and Jefferson.

In 1900, sixteen years after the original publication of *Congressional Government,* Wilson wrote a new introduction in which he acknowledged that the office of president had gathered to itself powers not in evidence when the original edition was published. These were the result, in his view, of the war with Spain. "The greatly increased power and opportunity for constructive leadership given the President, by the plunge into international politics and into the administration of distant dependencies . . . has been the war's most striking and momentous consequence. . . . When foreign affairs play a prominent part in the politics and policy of a nation, its Executive must of necessity be its guide, must utter every initial judgment, take every first step of action, supply the information upon which it is to act, suggest and in large measure control its conduct. . . . There is no trouble now about getting the President's speeches printed and read, every word. Upon his choice, his character, his experience hang some of the most weighty issues of the future. The government of dependencies must be largely in his hands. Interesting things must come out of this singular change. For one thing, new prizes in public service may attract a new order of talent. . . . The President is at liberty," he wrote, "both in law and conscience, to be as big a man as he can . . . he cannot escape being the leader of his party . . . he is also the political leader of his nation . . . or has it in his choice to be . . . his is the only national voice in affairs. Let him win the admiration and confidence of the country, and no other single force can withstand him, no combination of forces will easily overpower him. . . . His office is anything he has the sagacity and force to make it."

In a biography of George Washington, Wilson wrote fulsomely that Washington "was bred a gentleman and a man of honor in the free school of Virginia society. . . . Virginia gave us this imperial man and with him a companion race of statesmen and masters in affairs. It was her natural gift . . . ; and Washington's life showed the whole process of breeding by which she conceived so great a generosity in manliness and public spirit." Although the milieu which produced Washington was very different from the Calvinistic setting in which Wilson was reared, it is clear that he yearned to emulate his state's great leader.

Wilson was a late convert to "democracy," as distinguished from "republican government," and it was Lincoln (supplementing, though not replacing Edmund Burke) who was the principal agent of his conversion. As with his rival Roosevelt, some of Wilson's most moving passages are his reflections on Lincoln and his significance for Americans. It was, he declared in an oration on Lincoln, one of democracy's most compelling mysteries that a frontier cabin "was the cradle of one of the great sons of men, a man of singular, delightful, vital genius, who presently emerged upon the great stage of the nation's history, gaunt, shy, ungainly, but dominant and majestic, a natural ruler of men, himself inevitably the central figure of the great plot. . . . Who shall guess this secret of nature and providence and a free polity?" Who could explain "where this man got his great heart that seemed to comprehend all mankind in its catholic and benignant sympathy, the mind that sat enthroned behind those brooding, melancholy eyes? . . . This is the sacred mystery of democracy, that its richest fruits spring up out of soils which no man has prepared and in circumstances amidst which they are least expected. This is a place alike of mystery and of reassurance." Wilson ended the Lincoln oration, to which he had clearly given much thought and considerable passion, with an affirmation of his own faith in democracy. "I believe in the ordinary man," he told his listeners. "If I did not believe in the ordinary man, I would move out of a democracy and, if I found an endurable monarchy, I would live in it. The very conception of America is based upon the validity of the judgments of the average man."

In Wilson's view, "the utility, the vitality, the fruitage of life does not come from the top to the bottom; it comes, like the natural growth of a great tree, from the soil, up through the trunk into the branches to the foliage and the fruit. The great struggling unknown masses of the men who are at the base of everything are the dynamite force that is lifting the levels of society. A nation is great, and only great, as her rank and file are great." Democracy was "a form of character. It follows upon the long discipline which gives people self-possession, self-mastery, the habit of order, and peace and common counsel and a reverence for the law."

Edmund Burke was the most decisive intellectual influence on Wilson. David Houston heard Wilson say on several occasions that he was so familiar with Burke's writings, "and they were so much a part of him, that he could not be sure whether he was using his own phraseology or Burke's." Wilson was also acutely aware, according to Houston, of the fact that he had what he himself called "a one-track mind."

We can perhaps best understand Wilson as a transitional figure in the emergence of the new consciousness. The unbending devotion to righteousness which was often touched with self-righteousness, the faith in Providence, and dogged individualism, his belief in the common man and in democracy—all were conspicuous features of the old consciousness. On the other hand, Wilson's faith in the ability of modern scholarship, especially in the area of the social sciences, to describe and impose order on society was a conspicuous element in the new view of the world.

It is hard not to suspect that Wilson's austere Presbyterianism made an unfortunate amalgam with his academic nurture. The least appealing qualities of each were reinforced and amplified by that conjunction (as, of course, were the positive qualities). Thus the often grim asceticism of his Calvinist forebears closed Wilson to much of the sensuous apprehension of life and made him stiff and unbending, awkward in his relations with people, and sometimes excessively severe in his judgments. Mind (as opposed to heart) is inclined to be rigid and unforgiving, and mind dominates the academy. Preacher and teacher alike are disposed to lecture or preach to the less enlightened and to assume an attitude of moral superiority. Such qualities complicated Wilson's role as a political leader and handicapped him in the achievement of his goals.

When Hutchins Hapgood met Wilson, he was put off by "his cold and concentrated personality," yet Wilson's "sense of assured and quiet power" struck Hapgood forcefully. "I didn't like him," he wrote, "but he seemed more of a vital inner force than his public career represented." William Allen White, who, like most Americans, put great store on a handshake, complained to his wife that the hand Wilson gave him "felt like a ten-cent pickled mackerel in brown paper—irresponsive and lifeless." To White, Wilson had "a highty-tighty way" about him that put him off. The fact was that Wilson's right, or "shaking," hand had been severely weakened by a stroke in 1896. White described him as "a spare, ascetic, repressed creature, a kind of frozen flame of righteous intelligence." Jo Davidson, the sculptor, a wise and observant man who made a bust of Wilson, told Ray Stannard Baker that he "admired the man, but found nothing to love, that the President seemed to be interested in no art, neither in painting, sculpture, nor music, nor to know much about any one of them. He was a moralist, a great leader, a powerful personality. . . . He invoked fear and respect, like God, but not affection." That Wilson was well aware of his shortcomings is suggested by his remark to Baker that "A high degree of education tends . . . to weaken a man's human sympathies."

David Houston, in his sympathetic assessment of his leader's character, remarked on Wilson's "deep suspicion of the ordinary run of professional politicians and an innate hostility to them." The story was told that when one of Wilson's aides suggested to him that he consult with his party's leaders in the House and Senate on administration policies, Wilson replied, "Utterly futile. A waste of time. I would never get anywhere if I should do that. Every fellow has his own views; I would be swamped." Even if there were no ideas worth adopting, Wilson's friend persisted, "you would get their cooperation in things you want to accomplish. They would feel that you had at least given their views consideration." Wilson repeated: "Futile! I tell you, futile!

I can make better headway be giving consideration to my own ideas, whipping them into shape, testing them out in my own way, and assuring their adoption by their own fairness and merit. I waste no time while I am engaged in such work. . . ." Henry Stoddard, who told the story, added, "Wilson was not distrustful or suspicious of people; he ignored his Cabinet and Senators because he did not regard them as his equal. . . ." He was especially short and scornful with politicians who came to plead for patronage for their districts or states.

Not only was Wilson suspicious of and generally hostile toward politicians, but he never had, in David Houston's words, "any large experience in the business world. . . . His lack of actual experience in business and of intimate contacts with its processes, details, and its managers, coupled with a suspicion of the plans and ideals of those in charge of big business . . . led Mr. Wilson at times to use extreme expressions and to take courses of action which the . . . present situation did not warrant, and it created in him a tendency unduly to distrust successful business men." The contrast between Wilson's attitude toward "the business community" and that of Roosevelt is instructive. Roosevelt was plainly attracted to successful businessmen, to capitalists. He numbered many among his close friends, and he admired their aggressive hunting instincts, their zest for profits, and their dedication to the strenuous life, even if the most strenuous part was making money. On the other hand, he was ready to engage in combat with particular capitalists or groups of capitalists who, in his opinion, put the law or the authority of the government at defiance. It was, after all, the *malefactors* of great wealth against whom his wrath was so publicly and dramatically directed. The relatively law-abiding knew they had nothing to fear from Teddy.

Whereas Roosevelt placed great store in friendships, Wilson had few close friends, indeed few advisers who were close to him in any personal sense. To those men and women who performed notable services for him, he seldom showed gratitude and rarely affection. He brought with him to Trenton none of his loyal allies from his Princeton battles. The same was true of his governorship of New Jersey. Only the shrewd and faithful Joseph Tumulty traveled with him to the White House. When Stoddard asked one of Wilson's associates to explain the President's cavalier attitude toward those who had aided him in his academic and political career, the man replied, "In pursuit of what he believed to be right Wilson was relentless as time. Public office was to his mind most emphatically a public trust and he acted as trustee. It might and would grieve him deeply to refuse to appoint a man whom he liked immensely but he would surely refuse unless he believed the man capable."

In private, Wilson displayed a special kind of charm of his own. Informed, extremely articulate, witty, fired by the play of ideas, he often dazzled friends and visitors. Ray Stannard Baker was attracted by Wilson's "singularly *living* face, alert, full of keen power," and Bernard Baruch found him "warm and human . . . in the circle of his friends he would dance a jolly jig or recite funny limericks, often at his own expense."

Oswald Garrison Villard first encountered Wilson in 1895, when he heard him speak in an extension course at the University of Pennsylvania. Wilson lectured on the abolitionists, accusing them of being dangerous fanatics who had helped bring on the Civil War. Villard took issue with him, defending the good name and good works of his grandfather. Later, when they met on shipboard, Wilson was considering running for governor of New Jersey, and Villard found him "approachable, mellow, altogether attractive, delightfully witty, with a story every five minutes."

John Jay Chapman took note of the loyalty Wilson inspired. A Princeton friend told him that there were "sixty men, professors and else . . . who were Wilson-mad, and would follow him to the death. Some of them didn't even *like* Wilson," the friend had added. Students were equally susceptible; he was voted the most popular member of the faculty four times. George Creel insisted that Wilson was "unfailingly generous, courteous, and considerate, possessing wit, humor, and winning geniality."

In his attitude toward women, Wilson was a product of his time and his region. The Southern journalist, Gerald Johnson, wrote that "he was Southern in his deification of women and his strong urge to protect them, and in his belief that women should govern in their own sphere and not soil themselves by participation in practical affairs." Of his first wife, Wilson wrote that she had grown up "in the best of all schools—for manners, purity, and cultivation—a country parsonage." If he had a conventional notion of women's role, he was strongly drawn to them, praising their "deeper sensibilities" and "finer understanding"; he became noticeably animated in the presence of a handsome and intelligent woman. One of his conquests was Mary Hulburt, whose first husband had died and who was separated from her second husband. Wilson wrote Hulburt more than 1,000 ardent letters, read her poetry when they were together, and delighted in their conversations. Indeed, his friendship with her seems to have been one of those classic male-female platonic friendships of which we have already observed a number of examples. Nonetheless, at Wilson's death, when his letters to Mary Hulburt were discovered, they threatened a scandal. Baruch, at the prompting of Ray Stannard Baker, bought them and deposited them in the Library of Congress.

Whatever his other qualities may have been, Wilson's real power lay in his remarkable gifts as an orator. George Creel heard Wilson talk to a group of high school students in Kansas City in 1904. "What thrilled me," Creel wrote years later, "was not merely the clarity of his thought, the beauty of his phrasing, but the shining faith of the man in the *practicality* of ideals. More than any other, it seemed to me that he voiced the true America—not the songs that people sing when they remember the words, but the dream of liberty, justice, and fraternity."

Ray Stannard Baker first heard Wilson speak at a dinner given in the ballroom of the Hotel Astor in New York. Wilson was then president of Princeton University. He had, a few weeks earlier, captured the attention of New York reformers by giving a bold speech to a group of bankers dining at the Waldorf-Astoria. Among his auditors had been such financial giants as J. Pierpont Morgan and George Baker. Wilson had told the assembled tycoons, "Banking is founded on a moral basis and not on a financial basis. The trouble today is that you bankers are too narrow-minded. You don't know the country or what is going on in it and the country doesn't trust you. You are not interested in the development of the country, but in what has been developed. You take no interest in the small borrower and the small enterprise which affect the future of the country, but you give every attention to the big borrower and the rich enterprise which has already arrived." A reporter observed Morgan "look glum and puff his cigar energetically."

Intrigued by Wilson's address to the bankers, Ray Stannard Baker sought him out in his book-lined study at Princeton and spent hours talking with him about the future of the nation. To Baker, Wilson seemed as "scientific" as La Follette, a man who approached political and economic issues with an open mind as far as that was possible, who sought out the facts systematically and then deduced from them some plan of action. Baker was an instant convert. "I left Princeton," he later recalled, "convinced that I had met the finest mind in the field of statesmanship to be found in American public life." In that conviction he seldom wavered, although at the moment it appeared to him that Wilson was "politically impossible. . . . He had not known until recently even the leaders of his own party in New Jersey" and could not name the head of the Democratic organization in Princeton. At fifty-five he was too old, Baker believed, "to begin an education in practical politics." It did not occur to Baker or, it must be said, to many others that there was even a "remote possibility" that the stiff Princeton scholar could capture the Democratic nomination.

Whatever Wilson's ambitions may have been, they required the proper conjunction of circumstances. The role of academics, especially La Follette's brand of reform-minded professors at Wisconsin, was one that had evoked a highly positive response among proponents of change. Wilson's widely publicized struggle against the reactionary alumni of Princeton had attracted favorable comment in the liberal press (Bernard Baruch, for one, took note).

New Jersey's Democratic machine, caught up unexpectedly in the mood of reform, needed a "progressive" candidate. Who better than the president of Princeton, New Jersey's most famous institution? The gentleman was approached. He was found receptive, if not eager. On July 10, 1910, he declared to a reporter for the *Newark Evening News*, "The mention of my name in connection with the governership, senatorship, or Presidency, is a matter [to] which I have never and do not now attach any importance whatever. Make it just as forcibly plain as you can, so that it may perhaps put an end to all these stories, most of them absurd, which have made me appear as being a candidate for office." Three days later he announced he was a candidate for office.

During the gubernatorial campaign he spoke often and eloquently, and somewhat to the surprise of party regulars, he was elected. According to Oswald Garrison Villard, who found him wandering around Trenton after his inauguration, the newly elected governor confessed, "I do not even know how to choose a secretary." Two men, who knew politics inside out, appeared most fortuitously to serve as his closest advisers: Joseph Tumulty, a shrewd and engaging Irishman, and James Kerney, also Irish, the owner and editor of the *Trenton Evening News*. While Wilson was receptive to their practical wisdom, he showed a dramatic flair of his own. He placed his desk in an open office and made himself "accessible to every citizen who walked in. . . ." In addition, he went to the seat of every county in the state to respond to questions about his administration and assure the citizens that he was determined to serve their wishes. At the time he was elected governor, Wilson was, in Villard's words, "a conservative if not a reactionary." He was strongly opposed to the closed shop and an opponent of the direct primary, defending the bosses as a political necessity. "It is unjust," he wrote, "to despise them." He opposed the regulation of public utilities by state or Federal government and declared that the whole notion of Federal regulation of corporations was "compounded of confused thinking and impossible principles of law." The Panic of 1907, he believed, had been caused by the "aggressive attitude of legislation towards railroads."

Even more important than the faithful Tumulty was the acquisition of Edward Mandell House (his title of Colonel was honorary), one of the most intriguing figures of the Wilson era. Born in Texas in 1858, House was unprepossessing in appearance. A short man with protuberant ears, a receding chin, and a sharp nose, he looked like an intelligent rat. (General James Harbord described him as "one of the few men with no chin, whom I have ever met, who were considered forceful. The upper part of his face and brow are good. His eyes are quite good and his expression very pleasant and affable.") House was conscious of a special destiny as a seventh son. He grew up a skilled rider and shot, but a serious accident left him physically frail. After several years at Cornell he returned home to plunge into Texas politics, becoming, in time, the *éminence grise* to four governors before he discovered Woodrow Wilson and attached himself to the New Jersey governor's rising political star. William Allen White wrote of him that he had an "almost Oriental modesty, a Chinese self-effacement. . . . He is never servile but always serving; gentle without being soft; exceedingly courteous. . . ." He accompanied another's remarks with "That's true, that's true."

Ray Stannard Baker noted that House had a revealing mannerism. When he was talking, he used "his small, delicate hands and fingers as though he were picking things apart, or pulling them out to look at." Another motion was complementary to the first: He "tapped and smoothed the imaginary object with his hands and fingers, his voice at the same time taking on an explanatory, reasonable, optimistic tone."

House, hearing that Wilson was a political comer, visited him at Princeton. He and Wilson, who valued loyalty above all other virtues, hit it off at once. Wilson was delighted to find a man who "wants . . . to serve the common cause and to help me and others." They were soon as chummy as schoolgirls, and Wilson wrote to House as "My dear friend," adding that it was as though "we have known one another always," while House wrote such lines as "My faith in you is as great as my love for you—, more than that I cannot say." John Jay Chapman, usually a shrewd judge of men, was much impressed by Colonel House. He wrote to his mother that he was "*extraordinarily intelligent,* very frank, very quiet—meets every point without evading it. . . ."

Wilson, on the other hand, in later years wrote to his second wife, Edith Galt, of House: "Intellectually he is not a great man. His mind is not of the first class. He is a counsellor not a statesman."

As governor Wilson pushed through the state legislature the strictest regulations for the control of the oil companies—the so-called Seven Sisters Law—ever passed in New Jersey. Never really warming to the gregarious ways of the Irish politicos who dominated the Democratic Party in the state, he nonetheless gathered them about him and learned what they had to teach him.

One thing we can say with confidence. Whatever else Wilson may or may not have been, he was no cloistered academic on whose shoulders the mantle of leadership unsuspectedly fell. He was intensely ambitious, and capable, when the occasion required, of a disconcerting ruthlessness. When he turned out one of his earliest and most devoted supporters, James Nugent, on the ground of his being involved in a shady political deal, the furious Nugent proposed a toast at a meeting of the state's militia officers: "To the Governor of New Jersey. . . . He is an ingrate and a liar. I mean Woodrow Wilson. I repeat, he is an ingrate and a liar. Do I drink alone?" Oswald Garrison Villard, who recounted the story, added, "He did not." In Villard's opinion, Wilson, despite his remarkable record of reform as governor of New Jersey, "was most concerned during his entire term in Trenton with his chances for the Presidency." That was also the view of one of his closest advisers, James Kerney. Wilson never really wished to be governor; his sights were set from the first instance on the presidency.

The man who aspired to become the twenty-eighth president of the United States was a physical wreck. He had been troubled since early manhood by headaches. He suffered so severely from nervous indigestion that he taught himself how to use a stomach pump in order to relieve his discomfort. His stomach troubles were so persistent that he referred to them as "turmoil in Central America." For almost a year after his stroke he was unable to write with his right hand. It may have been the difficulty of writing that made him so addicted to a battered portable typewriter. He was, in fact, the archetypal intellectual who treated his body as though it did not exist, and his body made him miserable in revenge. While his famous predecessor hunted wolves from horseback, Woodrow Wilson was prevailed upon only with considerable effort by his doctor to spend a reluctant few minutes a day exercising on a rowing machine.

Four years before he was elected President, Wilson had written of the office that it demanded "inexhaustible vitality. . . . Men of ordinary physique and discretion cannot be presidents and live, if the strain be not somehow relieved. We shall be obliged always to be picking our Chief Magistrates from among wise and prudent athletes." As President, Wilson, in consultation with his physician, worked out a program for the "careful, systematic, scientific conservation of every ounce of energy . . . an iron regimen, a fixed daily program that ordered every minute of his life with machine-like exactitude," wrote the admiring George Creel.

Florence Harriman and her more liberal Democratic friends had watched "with increasing interest and excitement" the growth of the Woodrow Wilson boom. The principal obstacles on Wilson's path to the presidency—his relative obscurity aside—were Grover Cleveland and William Jennings Bryan. Cleveland considered Wilson a fuzzy-minded intellectual. He had been especially indignant at Wilson's efforts to reform the Princeton undergraduate clubs. Although Cleveland had never been to college himself, the clubs appeared to him as bulwarks of tradition. In April, 1911, Wilson, hoping to win Bryan's support, had eulogized him for "having shown that stout heart which, in spite of long years of repeated disappointments, has always followed the star of hope . . . it is because he has cried 'America, awake!' that some other men have been able to translate into action the doctrines he has advocated so diligently." The effect of this encomium was largely nullified by the publication of a letter from Wilson to a friend eight months later in which he expressed the hope that Bryan might be knocked "once for all into a cocked hat." The fact was that Wilson viewed Bryan as a superannuated Populist whose day was long past. Credit for persuading Bryan to throw his support to Wilson in 1912 has been claimed by (or awarded to) several individuals. Florence Harriman claimed the honor, but Oswald Garrison Villard gave credit to the first Mrs. Wilson, who arranged a private dinner with Bryan and her husband in Princeton on March 12, 1911, and later told a friend, "That dinner put Mr. Wilson in the White House."

The first nominating convention was held by the Socialists in Indianapolis. There bitter controversy broke out between the "simon-pure Marxists"—or immediatists—and the revisionists—or gradualists. Ameringer, Berger, and Algie Simons were among those who belonged to the latter group. They insisted that ideological orthodoxy was the last thing to try to force on American Socialists. Berger warned the delegates, "Don't be like the ancient Hebrews who, when going on a journey, carried a bundle of hay to sleep on so as not to come in contact with a place on which a Gentile had previously slept."

That afternoon Tad Cumbie, the Gray Horse of the Prairie and the leader of the purists, appeared with a miniature bundle of hay pinned to his bright red shirt. "Well, Victor," said Tad, "here is my bundle of hay."

"Well, well," responded Berger, "I see you brought your lunch with you."

Berger, as a gradualist, argued, "Socialism is coming all the time. It may be another century or two before it is fully established." To him socialism with a small *S* was "anything that's right." It was Berger's conviction that "the mighty forces unchained by the industrial revolution were either driving mankind to destruction through war and bloody revolution or forcing it to adopt the co-operative system of production and distribution. . . . A socialist," he declared, "is anyone, irrespective of class, who places the common good above his own."

It was evident that the delegates at Indianapolis were discernibly different from those who had gathered four years earlier. Big Bill Haywood noted caustically that there were "seventeen or more preachers who could scarcely disguise their sky-piloting proclivities." There were many lawyers and some editors. Socialism was finally respectable, and the indignant Haywood and his IWW colleagues had to watch as Victor Berger, Morris Hillquit, and a strange company of Christian Socialists and middle-class reformers amended the constitution of the Socialist Party to make it less "revolutionary" and more evolutionary. They added Article 2, Section 6, proposed by a clergyman and seconded by Berger, which declared, "Any member of the party who opposes political action or advocates crime, sabotage or other methods of violence as a weapon of the working class to aid in its emancipation shall be expelled from membership in the party." In the words of the Reverend W. R. Gaylord, who introduced the motion, "We do not want any of it [violence]. We don't want the touch of it on us. We do not want the hint of it connected with us. We repudiate it in every fibre of us."

Particularly offensive to the respectable men and women who constituted the greater part of the new improved membership of the Socialist Party was the IWW's irreverent song "Hallelujah, I'm a bum." The "Marseillaise" and the "Internationale" were thoroughly acceptable by contrast. Victor Berger denounced it as being "as anarchistic as anything that Johann Most has ever written. . . . Every true Socialist will agree with me when I say that those who believe that we should substitute 'Hallelujah, I'm a bum' for the 'Marseillaise' and the 'Internationale' should start a 'bum organization' of their own."

The final act required to sanitize the Socialist Party was the expulsion from the National Executive Committee of Haywood himself, who responded by calling the delegates "a slippery desperate crew." To Haywood, the attack on the IWW was "base, libelous, . . . treasonous," and, worst of all, a stab in the back to Ettor, Giovanitti, and Caruso, awaiting trial on a framed-up charge of murder. It seemed to Haywood to give credence to every charge against the IWW and, indeed, retrospectively against the Western Federation of Miners that had been made by the hostile capitalist press since the days of the Haymarket Affair.

The day before the Republican Convention opened in Chicago, reporters, encountering Roosevelt, asked how he felt, and he "called out lustily, snapping his teeth, batting his eyes and grinning like an amiable orangutan," as William Allen White put it, "I feel as strong as a bull moose!" In addition to being a Roosevelt delegate from Kansas, White had been commissioned to cover the convention for the Adams Newspaper Service. On the same assignment were the cartoonist J. N. Darling, and the young journalist and novelist Edna Ferber, "a brunette," White wrote, "with a great mop of dark hair, blue-black, wavy, fine—the kind of lovely hair one is tempted to tousle. . . . We called her 'the angel child.' . . ."

To Florence Harriman, already committed to Woodrow Wilson, Chicago on the eve of the convention was "a strange phantasmagoric unbelievable chaos of sights, sounds and smells, slogans and emotions," a dizzy impression of "a flat, flat lake, sizzling asphalt pavements, bands circling and zig-zagging along Michigan Avenue, tooting and booming, 'Everybody's saying it, Roosevelt, Roosevelt.' " In the Coliseum thousands of excited, perspiring delegates, their shirts stuck to their backs, circulated, occasionally exploding into fistfights. "The sultry air was charged with dynamite. Delegates talked of drawing pistols and knives over disputed seats. Everybody jostled, pushed, whispered. Day and night the excitement grew, monotonous, continuous. Savages in the African forest, hearing the distant roll and boom of the tribal drums, could not better have been worked into a furious pitch of expectation than were the Americans who quivered and hoped and feared in the medley of trombones and telegraph tickers, hoarse oratory and shrill cries of the Coliseum medicine men."

One of the complications for the Roosevelt camp was that the Southern Republicans, who seldom, if ever, carried a Southern state for their party, appeared every four years and not uncommonly sold their votes to the highest bidder, "a corrupt alliance between the rich and the purchasable," in William Allen White's words. Thus almost a third of the delegates—those from the South—were, for all practical purposes, inaccessible to the Progressives. In those states without primaries the party machine controlled the selection of delegates, and here again the Progressives were shut out. Finally, in the organization of the convention itself the National Committee, made up largely of party loyalists, selected the temporary and permanent chairmen and the members of the credentials committee. The National Committee went further and nominated candidates in states where Roosevelt had won the delegate race. This made it possible for them to declare that those delegate seats were contested and refer the contested seats to the credentials committee, which, almost invariably, decided in favor of the Taft delegates. The throwing out of the Roosevelt delegates was done, White wrote, "with a sort of Gargantuan impudence, profligate and heroically indecent." Yet with all this, the support for Roosevelt among the mass of the Republicans and in the country at large was so strong that the insurgents were confident that public sentiment would, in the end, bring about the defeat of the Taft faction.

Fearful of an outbreak of physical violence on the part of the thwarted and angry Roosevelt delegates, the Republican National Committee had provided for 1,000 blue-coated policemen, who ringed the hall. Under bright bunting around the speakers' platform, hidden from the sight of the delegates, was barbed wire.

Elihu Root was chosen permanent chairman of the convention. To the Progressives, Root, a brilliant corporation lawyer and secretary of state under Roosevelt, was a turncoat. "Probably the most learned, even erudite, distinguished and impeccable conservative Republican in the United States," in White's words, "he was the idol of the American bar. . . . When he clicked the gavel on the marble block that topped the speaker's table, order ensued almost hypnotically. The gaunt, thin-lined features of this man so conspicuously the intellectual leader of a convention which had been melted by rage into a rabble, stood there calm, serene and sure in his domination of the scene. . . . I have never seen mass passion sway men before or since as that great multitude was moved those first hours after Root took command," White added.

When Root, as temporary chairman of the convention, made the opening speech, Roosevelt men groaned and began to drift out of the hall. "Work faster, kid, they're walking out on you," someone shouted from the audience. The next day a struggle to seat eighty disputed Roosevelt delegates was beaten back. The governor of Nebraska rose in the press section and began a cry, "We want Teddy." It did not matter what the enthusiasts wanted; the regulars wanted Taft. A fifty-two-minute-long demonstration followed for the Colonel while the Taft delegates sat grim-faced or shouted their own defiant slogans, sure of their eventual dominance. The Colonel, White wrote, "got . . . deeply, terribly angry at the injustice which he faced. . . . The mounting hatred on both sides . . . was a terrible reality," in White's words, worse by far than anything he had experienced in previous conventions. It hung in the air, palpable and ominous. It was heightened, if that was possible, by word that Roosevelt himself had decided to attend the convention, an unprecedented move that divided his followers. White was convinced that it was a mistake made under the sway of emotion. A Taft supporter had 10,000 handbills printed announcing that Colonel Roosevelt would walk on the waters of Lake Michigan at seven-thirty Monday evening. A favorite tune of the bands was "Everybody's Doin' It, Doin' it, Doin' It." Roosevelt arrived in a triumphal motorcade through miles of cheering citizens.

When it was clear that the battle for the nomination was lost, the Roosevelt loyalists gathered to plan their strategy. The critical question was whether or not to bolt the Republican Party and form a new political organization under the Progressive banner. "What a night . . ." Henry Stoddard wrote in his memoirs. "I never saw the Colonel so fagged; for hours his fighting blood had been at fever heat [that was the manner in which Roosevelt's admirers loved to write of their hero]. It was not the crowd that tired him, for he could always handle a crowd, but a score of important party leaders one after another had discussed with him all phases of the serious situation." One had even drawn Roosevelt into the bathroom for a private conference. As Stoddard recalled the night, after everyone had been heard out, George Perkins, Frank Munsey, and Stoddard gathered in the Colonel's bedroom with Roosevelt stretched out on the bed. Munsey declared, "My fortune, my magazines and my newspapers are with you." The next day, when Taft was nominated, the Roosevelt forces, led by Hiram Johnson, the Pinchots, Joseph Medill McCormick, and lawyer Bainbridge Colby, marched out of the convention hall to the jeers and catcalls of the victors. With hundreds of empty chairs the remaining delegates went through the required and perfunctory motions of adopting a party platform and renominating as Vice-President the aged and ailing James S. Sherman.

The Progressives adjourned to the Orchestra Hall and abandoned the Republican Party (rather than simply bolted), forming on the spot the Progressive Party and agreeing to hold a nominating convention in August. When White encountered Roosevelt later in the evening, he seemed "triumphant, full of jokes and quips," but for all his ebullience, White sensed a rage "bubbling inside him."

It was the opinion of Henry Stoddard that two diverse foes of Roosevelt had brought about his defeat in the Republican nominating convention of 1912: William Barnes, Jr., the reactionary boss of the Republican machine in New York State, and Robert La Follette. Barnes directed the ousting of Roosevelt delegates by the committee on credentials in order to organize the convention and elect Root as temporary chairman. La Follette, whom Stoddard disliked and charged with a rule-or-ruin philosophy, held the votes of the delegates from Wisconsin and North Dakota, and refused to release them to vote for Roosevelt, preferring, in Stoddard's view, to see the nomination go to Taft. It is unlikely that the switch of the delegates from those two states would have materially helped Roosevelt. Moreover, La Follette can hardly be blamed for trying to lay claim to the leadership of the Progressive wing of the Republican Party. He, far more than Roosevelt, represented the genuine radicalism of his Midwestern constituents; he and his supporters had been treated cavalierly by Roosevelt, who, as we have noted, dismissed them as "two-revolution men."

It seemed evident to Brooks Adams that at Chicago the capitalists who controlled the Republican Party declined to consider compromise. "Rather than permit the advent of a power beyond their immediate control, they preferred to shatter the instrument [the Republican Party] by which they sustained their ascendancy." Roosevelt's offense "in the eyes of the capitalistic class was not what he had actually done," Adams noted, "for he had done nothing seriously to injure them. The crime they resented was the assertion of the principle of equality before the law, for equality before the law signified the end of privilege to operate beyond the range of the law."

With the Republican Convention over, Chase Osborn wrote to Roosevelt that in his opinion, if the Democratic Convention meeting in Baltimore three days later nominated a reactionary, Roosevelt should run, "and, if possible, with someone like Wilson or Bryan; but if the Baltimore convention nominates a progressive," Osborn continued, "I am not so sure you should be a candidate. . . . Basically this is a fight between property rights and human rights; and between . . . honest men and thieves." Roosevelt, determined now to run as a third-party candidate, was alarmed at the hint of a possible defection from one of his strongest supporters. He urged Osborn not to make his views public. A liberal Democrat would not do, for the major concern of the "big reactionaries" was to beat Roosevelt "because . . . I happen to symbolize as no one else *at the moment* does the principles in which you and I so ardently believe."

The nation's attention now shifted to the Democrats in Baltimore. That city was, if possible, even hotter than Chicago. The 5th Regiment Armory was festooned in white and yellow cheesecloth, which improved the acoustics but did nothing for the circulation of air. The champions of Champ Clark chanted a Missouri folk song, "You got to quit kicking my houn' around," to which Wilson's rather unenterprising backers replied, "We want Wilson; we want Wilson."

James Beauchamp "Champ" Clark was the initial front-runner. Clark, a Kentuckian and ex-college president, had excellent liberal credentials. He had supported Bryan loyally for years and was considered a link with the party's Populist tradition, but he had recently allowed himself to be maneuvered into appearing as the candidate of those Eastern Democrats determined to wrest control of the party from the Bryanites, and that was to prove his undoing. Bryan's hold on the party was still too strong, and the memories of the "glory days" of Midwestern radicalism too vivid, for the party to be readily delivered into the hands of Clark's conservative backers. Bryan, leader of the Democracy, was no longer the Boy Orator of the Platte. His hair had thinned and grayed; he was paunchy from good living and slightly stooped. He wore his familiar wrinkled alpaca coat and a white vest and fanned himself with his palm-leaf fan. To White he was "a ridiculous man with tremendous power." The real manager of the convention, Bryan soon made that power felt in a characteristically quixotic way. He might face a revolt among the party regulars who had always disliked and distrusted him, but he still could touch those chords to which Democrats' hearts vibrated. He rose to make an eloquent and bitter attack on the capitalists in the party who had tried to dominate its councils for years by the sheer power of their purses and whom Bryan had continuously opposed.

Confident that they had the votes to elect their candidate, the Clark delegates listened first uneasily and then indignantly to Bryan's attack. While he was speaking, Bernard Baruch recalled, the Clark supporters "hooted, howled, moaned, threatened to lynch Bryan, fought in the aisles, and waved fists in his face."

Bryan's speech, reasserting his party's commitment, perhaps not so much to reform as to unrelenting hostility toward the predatory rich, seemed to William Allen White "a sinister exhibition," and the response to it "more emotional, more unrestrained, more savage" than the Republican regulars' response to Roosevelt in Chicago. It was the undertone of class and sectional hostility that alarmed White. The academic and intellectual element in the Democratic Party that had emerged in response to Wilson's candidacy was eclipsed by the traditional Democrats, the Irish and the South—"the rebel yell," White noted, "still ripped through the applause like a scythe down the swath."

At the end of the speech Bryan proposed a resolution that read: "In this crisis in our party's career and in our country's history this convention sends greeting to the people of the United States, and assures them that the party of Jefferson and Jackson is still the champion of popular government and equality before the law. As proof of our fidelity to the people we hereby declare ourselves opposed to the nomination of any candidate for President who is the representator or under obligation to J. Pierpont Morgan, Thomas F. Ryan, August Belmont, or any other of the privilege-hunting and favor-seeking class." A further paragraph declared, "We demand the withdrawal from this convention of any delegates constituting or representing the above interest." This was too much for the delegates. They rejected the second paragraph while adopting the first by a margin of four to one. When Bryan finished, he came to the back of the platform, took up the palm-leaf fan that was as much a part of him as his wide-brimmed hat, and said to a friend, "There, that'll fix 'em."

In Chicago Florence Harriman had been only a fascinated observer; in Baltimore she was an active partisan of Wilson and privy to the inner maneuverings intended to win the nomination for her man. When Clark was put in nomination, she noted, "Pandemonium broke loose—cheers and cheers and more nasal celebration of the houn' dog." Speech after speech "from incurably eloquent throats" followed, all to the effect that Champ Clark was one of the greatest leaders in the history of the Republic. Then came Wilson's turn. He was placed in nomination by a man who had opposed him for governor, Judge Westcott. "New Jersey believes," Westcott declared, "that there is an omniscience in national instinct. That instinct centers in her Governor. He is that instinct. We want Wilson." The delegates took up the chant; the old fires of reform blazed up. Baskets of white doves were released to whirl around the armory and let their droppings fall on the heads of the delegates.

When the balloting began, Clark led with 440 votes; for three days he maintained his lead, with Wilson holding steady in second place at 324. As a member of the Nebraska delegation Bryan was pledged to vote for Clark, but his lack of enthusiasm for the Kentuckian had already been demonstrated.

On the tenth ballot the New York delegation, controlled by Tammany and its wealthy allies, among them August Belmont and Thomas Fortune Ryan, shifted to Clark. Bryan, fearful that the Tammany break would start a general swing to Clark, giving him the nomination and Tammany control of the party, prevailed on the Nebraska delegation to switch to Wilson, and in announcing the fact he took the occasion once more to attack Clark as the tool of Wall Street. The speech checked the trend to Clark. Thirty-six more ballots followed while William McAdoo, Wilson's campaign manager, and his lieutenants bargained and pled for Wilson votes.

Florence Harriman hung over the gallery railing, "nibbling Peters chocolate and drinking sarsaparilla out of bottles." Talk spread of a Bryan move, and Bryan buttons reading "Longhorns from Texas, Jayhawks from Kansas" were much in evidence. Harriman met the Bryans: Mrs. Bryan, "a handsome woman with a motherly encompassing smile, serene as the prairie on a fine spring morning," and Bryan himself, wearing his familiar alpaca "deacon's coat" and Panama hat. Mrs. Bryan reminded Mrs. Harriman that "Eastern people" had been unfair to her husband, depicting him as a wild radical, and Florence Harriman found herself nodding agreement. "Most of the progressive measures in American politics that other people had adopted had originally been sponsored by the prophet from Nebraska."

Harriman boldly asked Bryan if there was any truth to the rumor that he was anxious to have the nomination for himself. The Great Commoner replied with "positive sincerity: 'I can never again be the candidate for the presidency for three reasons: first, my stand on prohibition, second my attitude toward the Roman Catholic church, and third because I am considered a hoodoo to the party.' " When the tide began to run decisively in favor of Wilson, White, rather to his surprise, found himself standing on a table and joining with the Wilson delegates in a wild dance of delight, cheering himself hoarse. Claude Swanson, a Virginia delegate, told Bernard Baruch, "I saw that my man Clark was dead. I wasn't going to lay down on that ice and get political pneumonia. No, Sir! I got up and cut some fancy didoes and came out for Wilson." At Wilson's nomination, Oswald Garrison Villard wrote: "My joy . . . was greater than that I have ever felt over any political happening. . . ." Thomas Marshall was nominated for vice-president.

The Democratic Convention was the longest that William Allen White had observed in his years of political reporting. "There at Baltimore," he wrote, "I saw the thing happen—the formation of a left-wing group led on the floor unofficially by Bryan, who even in victory looked like an adorable old rag baby but who had steel at the core." So, although the prize that he had sought so long continued to elude him, he, suppressing what must have been considerable misgivings, rescued his party virtually single-handedly from its long exile from power and from what was far more serious: the prospect of political irrelevance. If he had done nothing else, he would have earned its gratitude. At last a liberal spirit had asserted itself and the party crystallized in a new political image. It was a transformation far more significant than the delegates or the somewhat bemused party leaders realized. The Democrats had, in fact, entered a new era in their party's history. The crowning irony was that in order to do so, the party had had to draw on a thoroughly discredited and politically extinct tradition. In the person of William Jennings Bryan the spirit of the Populists secured the triumph of the genteel reformers. It had become respectable at last to be a Democrat.

White left Baltimore convinced that Wilson would carry his ill-assorted party with him. The Democratic Party, he observed, was a faith long tried and tested. It would prove true even to a professor.

Wilson's acceptance speech (he did not deliver it until more than a month after the convention) was vintage Wilson. It was not so much what he said as the way he said it. "We cannot intelligently talk politics unless we know to whom we are talking and in what circumstances. The present circumstances are clearly unusual. No previous campaign in our time has disclosed anything like them. The audience we address is in no ordinary temper. It is no audience of partisans. Citizens of every class and party and prepossession sit together, a single people, to learn whether we understand their life and how to afford them the counsel and guidance they are now keenly aware that they stand in need of. We must speak, not to catch votes, but to satisfy the thought and conscience of a people deeply stirred by the conviction that they have come to a critical turning point in their moral and political development. . . . The Nation has awakened to a sense of neglected ideals and neglected duties; to a consciousness that the rank and file of her people find life very hard to sustain, that her young men find opportunity embarrassed, and that her older men find business difficult to renew and maintain because of circumstances of privilege and private adventure. . . . Plainly, it is a new age. The tonic of such a time is very exhilarating." The great questions were the great questions of all times, questions of right and of justice. The problem was not that "wicked and designing men" had deliberately led the country astray "but that our common affairs have been determined upon too narrow a view, and by too private an initiative. Our task is to effect a great readjustment and get the forces of the whole people once more into play."

Wilson made it clear that he was not an enemy of the trusts per se but only of their unchecked power and their disposition to abuse it. He called for a reconciliation in the war between capital and labor. "No law that safeguards . . . [the lives of the working people], that makes their hours of labor rational and tolerable, that gives them freedom to act in their own interest, and that protects them where they cannot protect themselves, can properly be regarded as class legislation or as anything but a measure taken in the interest of all Americans."

There are fortunately only a few commonplace truths we live by. It is in the enunciating of them that the art lies. Since his undergraduate days at Princeton, Wilson had applied himself to the mastery of that art. All those who read or heard his speeches knew that the man who fashioned them was no ordinary man; this was not the language of politicians. It touched a higher chord.

19

The Swan Song of the Progressives

The day following Wilson's nomination, Chase Osborn called on all progressively inclined persons to line up behind the Democratic candidate. "The issue is clearly joined for the people," he wrote. "It is Wall Street vs. Wilson. It is even more than that. All of the evil forces of America will finally line up with Wall Street and Mr. Taft. Woodrow Wilson in character, temperament, preparation and fitness is above the average of American presidents. He is a Christian, a scholar and a fearless citizen. I hope Col. Roosevelt will not be a candidate. Republicans can vote for Wilson without leaving their party or bolting. The real Republican party has no candidate for president this year. . . . The action of the freebooters at Chicago is not binding upon the Republican party even if for the moment they are bearing aloft its stolen name sign." Wall Street was confident that it controlled both parties, but the fact was that "Wilson is not owned by anybody. He will lead the people against the financial overlords in orderly but earnest fashion."

Osborn persisted in his campaign to try to persuade Roosevelt not to run against Wilson, and he had numerous coadjutors. He wrote to Wilson himself: "I had very much hoped that Mr. Roosevelt would be nominated on the Republican ticket and you on the Democratic ticket . . . and then the public could not lose. I do not think they will lose because I anticipate your election and hope for it." But, he added, "I am a Republican and expect to remain one."

Roosevelt made no bones about his disappointment over the line Osborn had taken. He could not understand, he wrote Osborn, how any intelligent man could back Wilson, "excellent man though Wilson is individually," because it would mean strengthening the Democratic bosses in the large cities and giving power to the Democratic Party. But Osborn refused to retreat. "Woodrow Wilson," he wrote to Roosevelt, "represents what you represent. . . . It would be the greatest thing in the world for you to come out for him as I have done. . . . I have been your earnest, honest and unselfish friend and I still am."

Walter Lippmann wrote to Graham Wallas in July: "We are all elated that Wilson has got so far. . . . If [he is] elected we all expect him to outgrow his party in short order for once he begins to handle the situations he must face, his conglomerate supports will drop off."

The Roosevelt bolters had agreed to meet again in Chicago on August 5. Those Insurgent or Progressive Republicans like Chase Osborn and William Allen White who hoped that Roosevelt would throw his support to Wilson were doomed to disappointment. To the Colonel the Democrats were the embodiment of evil; he let his lieutenants know that he was in the battle to the end.

The Bull Moose Convention, as it came to be called after its leader's description of himself, resembled nothing so much as an old-time religious revival. It was clear from the first moment that it had only one passion: to nominate Theodore Roosevelt as the standard-bearer of the new National Progressive Party. The delegates, William Allen White noted, "were our own kind." Women were conspicuous among them: "women doctors, women lawyers, women teachers, college professors, middle-aged leaders of civic movements, or rich young girls who had gone in for settlement work," White wrote. Looking out over the convention, White judged complacently that there "was not a man or woman [delegate] who was making less than two thousand a year [the equivalent, when wages averaged $5 a week, of some $25,000 a year today]. . . . Proletarian and plutocrat were absent."

White, who was much in evidence, had created a Midwestern character for himself. Imitating his dead father, he wore "ice-cream" suits, white shoes, and a wide-brimmed Stetson. He found that the persona "worked" in the East. He discovered that he was "not out of key or focus with his New York environment." He had come out of

Kansas politics "a bleeding reformer," working with what was known as "the boss-buster crowd. . . . We were all fighting for a better world. . . ."

The best known of Roosevelt's women supporters was Jane Addams. Even Roosevelt's infatuation with the military life, so different from Addams's own pacifism, and his timidity on the issue of racial equality failed to shake her. Her friends urged her to extract from the former President a declaration of the principle of racial equality as the price for her public support. Wilson, she insisted, was no better than Roosevelt on the racial issue; worse, for he had the Southern Democrats around his neck. When she acquiesced in the Progressive platform, her friends "stood outside her door at the Congress Hotel and wept in the night hours." Her longtime ally Sophonisba Breckinridge excused her on the ground that "she could not do anything that was in the nature of compulsion or control." But Addams needed no excuse. Idealistic as she was, she had a deep vein of practicality (in William James's words, she "inhabited reality"). She had long known that the world was an imperfect place. "Aristotle," she wrote, "is reported to have said that politics is a school wherein questions are studied, not for the sake of knowledge, but for the sake of action." What overcame her misgivings on the military and racial issues was that the Progressives had pledged their party to work diligently for "effective labor legislation looking to the prevention of industrial accidents, occupational diseases, overwork, involuntary unemployment, and other injurious effects incident to modern industry."

The conditions in which people—especially women and children —worked was, in her mind, the most important single issue facing the country. The "economic conditions of our industrial cities" produced every year casualties greater than those suffered in the Civil War and Russo-Japanese War combined. "A new code of political action has been formulated," she wrote, "by men who are striving to express a sense of justice, socialized by long effort to secure fair play between contending classes. . . . Through the action of the Progressive party, remedial legislation is destined to be introduced into Congress and into every State legislature by men whose party is committed to the redress of social wrong. . . ." The question she asked herself "most searchingly," she wrote, was "whether my Abolitionist father would have remained in any political convention in which colored men had been treated slightly. . . ." She recalled that he had urged upon her only one standard of judgment: "I should be sorry to think that you were always going to complicate moral situations, already sufficiently difficult, by trying to work out another's point of view. You will do much better if you look the situation fairly in the face with the best light you have." She must face the fact that the "collective mind" of Americans was not yet sufficiently enlightened on the "negro question" to offer any hope for broad reforms. She decided to suppress her misgivings and to work for "a system of federal arbitration in interracial difficulties, somewhat analogous to the function of the Hague tribunal in international affairs."

Albert Beveridge, the intellectually inclined Senator from Indiana, had been chosen to make the opening address to the convention. When Roosevelt scheduled himself to follow Beveridge immediately, the Senator was furious. He wanted the stage of the convention's opening day for himself. He wired from his summer home in Maine: no exclusive, no speech. Roosevelt had prepared what he called a "Confession of Faith," 20,000 words long. Finally, Roosevelt agreed to appear on the second day of the convention.

Every state delegation entered the hall in marching order, singing and cheering. Hiram Johnson led the California delegates, carrying a banner which read:

> I want to be a Bull Moose,
> And with the Bull Moose stand
> With antlers on my forehead
> And a big stick in my hand.

The men from Michigan sang:

> Follow, follow,
> We will follow Roosevelt
> Anywhere, everywhere,
> We will follow on!

Oscar Solomon Straus, ex-secretary of commerce and labor and a power in New York politics and in Jewish circles, led the New York delegation, singing "Onward, Christian Soldiers," which became the convention's theme song. Hiram Johnson was, in Stoddard's words, "in the Seventh Heaven of delight, because he was in revolt. . . ." Charles Sumner Bird, whose name evoked memories of the great abolitionist leader, represented Massachusetts; Bainbridge Colby, the lawyer and reformer, New York; William Allen White, Kansas and the world. It was a strangely mixed bag. In addition to the governors of seven Western states, the Brooklyn boss Bill Prendergast was much in evidence. On the speakers' platform was an array of dignitaries of a class for the most part new to American politics: college presidents, heads of scientific foundations, and the like. "Our prize exhibit," White wrote, "was Jane Addams."

In his opening address, Beveridge struck exactly the right note: "Knowing the price we must pay, knowing the sacrifice we must make, the burdens we must carry and the assaults we must endure—knowing full well the cost, yet we enlist for the war. . . . We stand for a nobler America. We stand for an undivided nation. We stand for a broader liberty, a fuller justice. We stand for social brotherhood as against savage individualism. We stand for an intelligent co-operation instead of a reckless competition. . . . We stand for equal rights as a fact of life instead of a catchword of politics. We stand for the rule of the people as a practical truth instead of a meaningless pretense. We stand for a representative government that represents the people. We battle for the actual rights of man.

"For the party comes from the grass roots. It has grown from the soil of the people's hard necessities. It has the vitality of the people's convictions. The people have work to be done and our party is here to do that work. . . . And so the first purpose of the Progressive Party is to make sure the rule of the people. . . . The first work before us is the revival of honest business. . . . Present day business is as unlike old time business as the old time ox-cart is unlike the present day locomotive. Invention has made the world over. The railroad, telegraph and telephone have bound the people of modern nations into families." Business was an essential element in the modern world. "Warfare" against business was a fratricidal conflict. The purpose of the Federal Constitution was to "form a more perfect union and to promote the general welfare." That was "the heart of the Progressive cause."

The next day, while the delegates were still intoxicated by Beveridge's oratory, Roosevelt mounted the rostrum to deliver his own address. An hour-long demonstration intervened. If his "Confession of Faith" was excessively long, the delegates did not flag or waver, and the ending clearly redeemed the length: "To you men who have come together to spend and be spent in the endless crusade against wrong, to you who face the future resolute and confident, to you who strive in a spirit of brotherhood for the betterment of our nation, I say now as I said here six weeks ago, we stand at Armageddon and we battle for the Lord."

The concluding line seemed excessive to a skeptical Charles Edward Russell, who wrote: "It is rather painful to recall that at first a part of the enthusiasts that spoke confidently about Armageddon did not know what on earth it meant, some confusing it with a brand of breakfast food." The band, inspired by the reference to Armageddon, began to play "Onward, Christian Soldiers" again, and soon the delegates were bellowing out the hymn at the top of their lungs. Albert Bushnell Hart, distinguished professor of history and teacher of Theodore Roosevelt, caused a minor scandal by standing on a chair, "waving his arms and yelling like an undergraduate at a football game." An old-time newspaperman, sitting next to Russell, rose with the rest and sang "Onward, Christian Soldiers, battling hard for steel,/ For its booming profits save the Common weal."

The steel-mill owners were not the only capitalists with Progressive inclinations. The Harvester Company felt that it had been badly used by the Taft administration, which had proceeded to prosecute it under the antitrust laws. It threw its weight to Roosevelt. As Russell put it, "Other great Interests, including oil which might be described as the right wing of the Republican bird, Steel being its left, were entirely satisfied with Mr. Taft and content to have him reinstated. Dissension thus entered not so much into the ranks of the party as into the inner councils that were its life and being and sinews and success."

Whenever there was a lull in the proceedings, the band would strike up "Onward, Christian Soldiers." The veterans of less evangelically transported conventions realized that a less scripturally and more practically oriented campaign slogan was required, and they devised "Pass Prosperity Around," which became popular among Bull Moosers.

It remained to nominate the party's candidates for president and vice-president and approve the platform. The Brooklyn boss Bill Prendergast nominated Roosevelt. When Jane Addams came down the floor of the convention hall to second Roosevelt's nomination, the delegates rose as a man (and woman) to give her a heartfelt ovation, and White noted tears in TR's eyes while she spoke. Roosevelt's choice of a running mate was Hiram Johnson.

"It is time," the Progressive platform read, "to set public welfare in first place. Behind the ostensible government sits enthroned an invisible government, owing no allegiance and acknowledging no responsibility to the people. To destroy this invisible government, to dissolve the unholy alliance between corrupt business and corrupt politics is the first task of the statesmanship of the day."

Under the heading of "Social and Industrial Justice" was an impressive inventory of reforms ranging from the fixing of minimum health and safety standards in industry to a minimum wage scale, the prohibition of night work for women, and an eight-hour day "for women and young persons; one day's rest in seven for all wage-earners; compensation for death and injury in industrial accidents." One of the most significant planks was a paragraph calling for unemployment insurance and "the adoption of a system of social insurance." The platform also called for women's suffrage and virtually every other good thing.

After the party platform had been approved with cheers and shouts, the delegates sang "Praise God from Whom All Blessings Flow" and adjourned.

In the aftermath of the Bull Moose Convention, William Allen White wrote to his friend John Phillips, editor of the *American Magazine*, defending his adherence to Roosevelt: "If you had seen the crowd and understood the spirit of the session of the Progressive party, you would understand that Roosevelt is not the Progressive party, but that the fighting men in the progressive ranks of both parties are in this thing and mean business and no man on earth can divert them. The Progressive party is here to stay as the definitely radical party of this Nation, and if any man tries to divert it to his personal ends, so much the worse for that man. The Progressive party is here to stay, and I am satisfied it is going to have a place . . . in American politics for the next thirty years . . . a great stirring movement . . . , a movement to change the environment of poverty so that whatever of poverty is due to the environment may be removed. That is the meaning and the core of the whole Progressive movement. . . ." To White the Progressives were a heroic band engaged "in a wild charge against the impregnable wall of conservative inertia that all the world was trying to batter down." The most popular campaign slogan of the Progressive campaign was "Using government as an agency of human welfare." Like any good political slogan, this phrase was capable of a wide range of interpretations, from trust-busting to government ownership of railroads.

From his Socialist perspective Charles Edward Russell wrote: "I think I have never seen a great assembly that manifested a happier spirit. The fiery ardor of a crusade seemed to animate the mass of participants. They felt they were inaugurating a movement that would emancipate the nation from the grip of the terrible trust monster and the workingman from his state of virtual servitude. They were the heralds of a glad new day and let joy be unconfined. Even the old-timers in the press felt the reflex of an unusual zealotry. . . . Recourse was had to the scriptures as alone adequate to meet the spiritual requirements of the occasion." To the skeptical Russell it was simply a matter of "one variety of Big Business trying to defeat the other." He rejected the meliorist approach of the Progressive Party. "Some gentlemen in this campaign," he declared, "believe that two or three fragments of the Socialist program, with a few worn-out remedial laws, will spike the Socialist guns. They have jimmied the back door of the Socialist house, have stolen half a dozen silver-plated spoons, and think they have shut down the house, and they forget that the Socialist Party is not a party of reform, but of revolution." Russell insisted that "the Progressive Party is just as far from Socialism as from Democracy. Their planks are mere palliatives and nostrums, idle as the wind—not worth talking about."

For many Progressives the choice between Wilson and Roosevelt was an excruciating one. George Creel cast his lot with Wilson, while Judge Ben Lindsey and Josephine Roche, in Creel's words, "gave themselves to T.R. with an ardor that bordered on fanaticism, and were foremost among the Bull Moosers who shed their blood at Armageddon." Opponents called Lindsey, only a few inches more than five feet tall, the Bull Mouse, and Roche was called a Moosette.

Charles Zeublin, a Chicago socialist, wrote after the election: "Wilson was the best man in the field, but I had to support Roosevelt because the Progressive party is a generation ahead of the Democratic party. It has a definite, though moderate, Socialistic trend, while the Democrats are still harping on States Rights and competition. Our hope is that Wilson's independence will smash the Democratic as Roosevelt's did the Republican party, and we shall get a new alignment."

Among those who turned to Wilson as to a new prophet were Louis Brandeis and the Hapgood brothers, Hutchins and Norman, the latter the influential editor of *Collier's Weekly*. To Ray Stannard Baker the campaign that followed was "the most interesting and exciting" of his life. There was, he believed, less bunkum and sloganeering than ever before and more serious discussion of the issues.

Taft proved his own worst enemy. Arriving in New York during the campaign of 1912, he was met by reporters who asked him what he thought could be done to relieve the severe unemployment plaguing the country. Taft replied, "God knows." The answer, if candid, was generally considered unsatisfactory.

The President referred scornfully to the Progressive Party as "an army of colonels," meaning that it was made up of middle-class reformers and assorted intellectuals, officers without troops—that is to say, without an army of voters to support them. William Allen White deplored the "wolfish hostility" that Roosevelt's friends displayed toward Taft. Taft's backers insisted he must be equally bold. According to White, after Taft's speech writers had "made Mr. Taft say some harsh and cutting thing about Roosevelt in a public speech," the President went to his bedroom and wept with grief and remorse.

As the campaign moved to its conclusion, Taft grew increasingly bitter toward his erstwhile benefactor. Just before the election he was quoted as having said, "Whether I win or not is not the important thing; I am in this fight to perform a public duty—to keep Theodore Roosevelt out of the White House."

When one of Wilson's aides suggested that since the governor "had done a great deal to improve the laws protecting the women and children of New Jersey, there ought to be a women's organization to help elect him to national office," Florence Harriman came forward to help form the Women's National Wilson and Marshall Association. The efforts of the women's association were so successful that the campaign regulars soon began to grumble that they were eclipsing the candidate himself. The major theme of the campaign was to be the revival of Jeffersonian democracy in a new Democratic administration. Speaking in Union Square to a noisy crowd, Florence Harriman allowed herself a bit of conscious demagoguery. The election of Wilson, she told her listeners, would bring down prices. They were so high now that even her political enemies would hesitate to buy a bad egg to throw at her. The crowd laughed, and a voice called out, "What will make eggs cheap? Does Wilson lay them?"

During the campaign one of Wilson's supporters asked Harriman to use her influence with him to gain an audience for a Kansas City lawyer of liberal inclinations who had great influence in his state, a man named Frank Walsh. Harriman arranged for the interview and drove Walsh down to Sea Gate, New Jersey, to visit Wilson. The result was that a "bureau for social workers" was to be set up as part of the Democratic campaign, headed by Frank Walsh.

As candidate for president Wilson reiterated the theme that "the masters of the Government of the United States are the combined capitalists and manufacturers of the United States. . . . The Government of the United States at present is a foster child of the special interests. It is not allowed to have a will of its own. It is told every move: 'Don't do that, you will interfere with our prosperity.' And when we ask, 'Where is our prosperity lodged?' a certain group of gentlemen say, 'With us. . . .' "

Wilson declared, "The government, which was designed for the people, has got into the hands of bosses and their employers the special interests. An invisible empire has been set above the forms of democracy." It was his conviction that "Our government has been for the past few years under the control of great allied corporations and special interests. . . . As a result there have grown up vicious systems and schemes of governmental favoritism (the most obvious being the extravagant tariff), far-reaching in effect upon the whole fabric of life, touching to his injury every inhabitant of the land, laying unfair and impossible handicaps upon competitors . . . stifling everywhere the free spirit of American enterprise."

The most sensational event of the campaign was the attempted assassination of Roosevelt a few weeks before the election. Visiting Milwaukee, he was shot in the chest by John Schrauk, who had followed him from New York. The bullet, impeded by a thick manuscript of the speech Roosevelt was scheduled to deliver, penetrated the skin but failed to inflict a serious wound. The Colonel, true to form, protected his assailant against an infuriated crowd and, after the police had carried Schrauk off, insisted on delivering his address before accepting medical attention.

When the votes were counted, Wilson had compiled 6,286,214 to 4,216,020 for Roosevelt, 3,486,922 for Taft and 897,011 for Debs. Wilson and Roosevelt thus tallied more than 10,000,000 votes between them to Taft's 3,486,972 (all, presumably, hard-core conservative Republicans). Certainly it would be an error to assume that all the votes for Roosevelt were liberal or "Progressive." Many voters voted for him for purely personal reasons—because they liked him (or adored him). The electoral votes gave an overwhelming margin to Wilson, 435 to 88 for Roosevelt and 8 for Taft, who carried only Utah and Vermont. The combined vote of Taft and Roosevelt, essentially the conservative and liberal factions of the Republican Party, added up to something in excess of 7,600,000, almost 1,000,000 more than Wilson's vote, suggesting that the Republicans were still the majority party by a comfortable margin.

It should be noted that only 58 percent of the eligible voters cast votes in this hotly contested election. Almost 80 percent had voted in

1896. That percentage had declined to 73 percent in 1900 and to 65.2 percent in 1904. In 1912 the figure dropped another six percentage points. One conclusion may be that a substantial number of the non-voters were recent immigrants from Southern and Eastern Europe who had little understanding of or interest in American politics, but it was also undoubtedly the case that millions of Americans were simply disenchanted with the entire political system.

Taft was responsible for so many "contradictory and senseless men and measures" that his defeat was no surprise, Henry Adams wrote to Elizabeth Cameron. "So the wretched Woodrow Wilson has got the mess to brew, and our noble Theodore is licking his chops at the thought of 1916." In a subsequent letter Adams noted, "Mr. W. Wilson is loathed in advance by everyone within my circuit, Democrat or Republican. . . . I liked Taft and yet I now own up that I was totally wrong."

The Progressives were, on the whole, encouraged by their showing. They found consolation in the fact that half a dozen prominent former Bull Moosers won seats in the U.S. Senate, while as many gubernatorial candidates won in state elections. Confident that they could put together a coalition of liberal Democrats and Republicans in the presidential elections of 1916, they worked indefatigably to strengthen their party organization. In the words of White, "the Bull Moosers were holding meetings, particularly giving dinners, hearing speeches and singing songs. Everywhere substantial numbers of solid citizens turned out."

When the National Progressive Club met for a Lincoln Day banquet on February 12, 1913, the mood was euphoric. The membership was decidedly upper-class. The toastmaster was Bill Prendergast, "the Honorable," and there were speeches by Oscar Straus, Bainbridge Colby, Mary Antin (who had arrived in Boston from Polish Russia at the age of nine and had written *The Promised Land*), Senator Beveridge, and, of course, the Colonel. The program listed the committee members—names like the Pinchots, Frank Munsey, Hiram Johnson, Henry Moskowitz, and Mrs. George Plimpton, the cream of Gentile and Jewish upper-class liberalism. The menu was in French and ranged from *purée de gibier St. Hubert* to *petits fours* and *café noir*. The program contained the platform of the national Progressives and the New York branch.

After the election Ray Stannard Baker wrote euphorically: "Now we shall really get something done. . . . No president in the memory

of living men will enter the White House under more favorable conditions, or with greater opportunities for achievement than Wilson.
He has a clear field: he can be as great as he can be. . . . If he is truly
progressive, as he says he is, then he will have arrayed against him the
most powerful material forces in our life—the great financiers, the
great business interests with their engines of publicity and their power
of influencing the prosperity of the Nation."

It should be said that Taft's administration was not without a
modest quota of accomplishments, more than enough, one suspects,
for a chief executive of the pre-Roosevelt era. Perhaps most significant
was the addition of two new states. Arizona and New Mexico had been
pressing for statehood since the 1880s. The leading champion of statehood for Arizona was a Kentucky lawyer named Marcus Aurelius Smith,
who had arrived in Tombstone, Arizona, in 1881. Smith was the classic
type of Southern politician, a boon companion, a storyteller, an orator,
and a shrewd judge of men as well as of horseflesh. Within five years
he had become the dominant political figure in the territory, and in
1886 he was elected territorial delegate. A Democrat, he assiduously
cultivated all the "interests" in the state: mineowners, ranchers, railroad
tycoons, and even the growing contingent of Mormons. In 1880 the
so-called omnibus bill which provided for the admission of the Dakotas,
Washington, and Montana included, initially, Arizona and New Mexico. In 1891 some of Arizona's leading politicians met in Phoenix to
write a Constitution that looked toward statehood. The document that
was produced was decidedly favorable to the "development" of Arizona—that is to say, to the "interests." The same process was followed
in New Mexico, where a somewhat similar document, soon called contemptuously the Santa Fe rag baby, was drafted. As in Arizona, many
of the ordinary citizens of the New Mexico territory opposed both the
Constitution and statehood, feeling that their interests were better
protected by the Federal government than by those ambitious individuals who clearly intended to run the respective territories turned states.
There was also strong resistance to statehood for the territories in
Congress or, more particularly, from those Senators and Congressmen
who deplored the free silver or bimetallist convictions of the residents
of the Western territories. The election of Cleveland, a Democrat, in
1892, gave fresh impetus to the move for statehood in Arizona (New
Mexico was in the hands of the Republicans), but Cleveland shared
the Eastern suspicion of the West.

With the waning of populism, the territories resumed their fight for statehood, this time with wider public support. New constitutions were written. New Mexico and Oklahoma were enlisted, and optimism ran high, but almost ten years would pass before a reluctant Senate and president could be prevailed upon to approve statehood for the last three territories. The leaders of the opposition to statehood were Beveridge, Lodge, and Roosevelt himself. To these men and their like-minded colleagues, the Southwest was a backward region, populated by a disturbingly large number of "Spanish," many of whom did not even speak or write English. To Beveridge, Arizona was little more than "a mining camp." In addition, reformers like Beveridge saw the territories as the fiefs of big business—the giant mining corporations and the railroads—and there was, as we have had on more than one occasion to note, considerable truth in the charge. Certainly the Indians, workingmen, and the Spanish-speaking were far better off under the aegis of the Federal government. It was clear enough to men like Beveridge that the Rockefeller interests virtually owned Wyoming and the Guggenheims had a first mortgage on Utah. The support for statehood by such notorious spoilsmen as Boies Penrose and Matt Quay of Pennsylvania increased the apprehensions of the liberals. Oklahoma seemed to Beveridge much more "American," and he supported its admission. But Arizona and New Mexico had still to prove themselves worthy of statehood. The people of those territories must be "on an equality with the remainder of the people of the Nation in all that constitutes effective citizenship; they must have developed the resources susceptible of like development to bring their proposed new state up to the average of the remainder of the Nation," Beveridge wrote.

Senator Thomas Bard of California came vigorously to Beveridge's support, insisting that the citizens of Arizona and New Mexico were not intelligent enough to warrant statehood. Senator George Hearst, with substantial mining interests in the area, supported statehood. When it seemed to Beveridge that he did not have the votes to block the admission of the two territories as states, he employed an ingenious stratagem. Senatorial custom had it that as chairman of the Territorial Committee he must be present before a vote could be called for; since it was near the end of the session of the Fifty-seventh Congress, Beveridge hid out on the third floor of Gifford Pinchot's house until Congress adjourned. (Pinchot was an ally because as head of the Forestry Service he was convinced that the lumbering and mining interests were simply waiting for statehood to start to despoil the new states.)

In the next Congress a compromise proposal was put forward with the backing of Mark Hanna: Arizona and New Mexico would be admitted as a single vast state (thereby cutting senatorial representation from the area in half). When Arizonans in Phoenix heard that the proposal had the backing of the President, they changed the name of Roosevelt Street to Cleveland Street. The so-called Hamilton bill was defeated in large part through the efforts of Senator Bard, who was opposed to statehood for the territories in any form. The appointment of a former Rough Rider, George Curry, as governor of New Mexico seemed an encouraging sign, but the Progressives were alarmed by the reactionary character of the proposed Constitution. It was clear that it was securely in the hands of orthodox Republicans. When Taft succeeded Roosevelt, hopes for statehood rose. Taft, in fact, accepted the inevitability of statehood. The "Battle Hymn for Arizona" proclaimed:

> Don't let Federal Sucklings school you,
> Don't let Mercenaries fool you,
> Don't let Corporations fool you,
> Our Cause is marching on.

The radical Arizona Constitution, which called for initiative, referendum, and recall, included the recall of judges. Taft refused to accept the Constitution with this clause, and it was removed but immediately reinserted after statehood had been approved (February, 1912), at which the *Arizona Gazette* proclaimed: "Popular Government Succeeds Old Regime: Special Interests Dethroned."

In retrospect, it seems clear that Roosevelt's greatest mistake, one based on an often faulty judgment of people and a simple, almost simpleminded, notion of American politics, was not to yield to the importunings of his friends and run for (and presumably win) another term in office in 1908. He might then very well have passed on the office to a liberal or what was to be called a Progressive Republican, or that having failed, a liberal Democrat in the Wilson mold might have won the office. In any event, the Taft disaster would have been avoided, and with it the split in the Republican Party. The fact that he chose in effect to retire was due in large part to his notion of life as conflict, as a battle. He had taken on the malefactors of great wealth and defeated them, or at least so he and much of the country perceived it, and now, the battle won, there was nothing to do that particularly engaged him. He would rather hunt lions in Africa than contemplate some long-range program of social and economic reform. Implicit in Roosevelt's attitude was the view that there was not, after all, much wrong with the United States other than the intractability of a few rich and powerful men.

As time passed, William Allen White grew less sanguine about the prospects of the Progressive Party. In a letter to Roosevelt he analyzed the strengths and weaknesses of the new party. "As nearly as I can figure it out," White wrote, "we have attracted to ourselves thousands of men of the college professor, country lawyer, country doctor and country merchant type, men of considerable education and much more than the average intelligence of their fellows." These men, White guessed, amounted to 1,000,000 of Roosevelt's 4,000,000 votes. The rest were made up of the "sheep vote," the clerks and small farmers and the unskilled laborers whose minds were moved primarily by "tradition and noise." They were an unstable group not to be counted on to hold fast to Progressive principles once the "noise" of election times had faded away. The third group were the "Teddy votes," votes for Roosevelt by those who cared nothing for Progressive principles but were entranced by the "masculine sort of a person" the Colonel was (sublimated cowboys and big-game hunters?). It was White's conclusion that the new party could be held together only if Roosevelt would run again in 1916.

Yet even as they planned and organized and reassured each other that their party had a bright future, there were signs that their power was waning. It became increasingly evident that the fortunes of the party were tied directly to the actions of Roosevelt. Bull Moosers, seeking recruits for their party, frequently heard the line "I am for Roosevelt, but . . ." trailing away. These voters were so often encountered that they became known as Roosevelt butters.

Roosevelt's departure for Brazil in the fall of 1913 was doubtlessly motivated at least in part by the desire to escape from the consequences of the debacle of the election and the tremendous pressure exerted on him by the Progressives to assume firm leadership of the new party that he had almost inadvertently created. But he clearly had profound misgivings about the party and his relation to it. He was, above almost everything else, a party man, yet he had abandoned his party in the name of principle and/or personal ambition, and it was clear that in doing so, he had helped substantially to elect a Democratic president and inflicted a serious, if not fatal, blow to his own party. If his starry-eyed followers believed in the future glory of the Progressive Party, Roosevelt was too practical a politician to have any illusions about the life expectancy of his creation, and he had no disposition to hitch his wagon to a falling star. He knew in his heart that the Republican Party would be handing out patronage and enforcing party discipline long after the Progressive Party was no more than a romantic memory. The problem was how to find some reasonably respectable way back into the fold. That opportunity might not come until 1920; he could hardly expect to extricate himself from the Progressives sooner. They must experience at least one shattering defeat in a national election before they were ready to follow him back into the Grand Old Party. So once more he was off on a romantic flight guaranteed to keep him in the public eye and free him from the importunities of his supporters, now more of a political embarrassment than an asset.

Historians have racked their brains (and contended fiercely with each other) to "explain" the origins of progressivism. Was it a continuation of populism with a more urban slant? Was it based on the desire of "displaced urban elites" to retrieve the power that had passed into the hands of big-city bosses and their immigrant constituents? Was it a manifestation of a "socialized" Christianity; the result of the "new learning," a product of a Lester Ward style of social Darwinism? One of the above? All of the above? None of the above?

The answer seems relatively simple. A reader who has come this far on our strange journey will be conscious of the degree to which the Protestant Passion, the desire to redeem the world, was the most conspicuous part of our national psyche or consciousness since long before the beginning of the Republic. It was indeed this passion which brought on, in large part, the American Revolution itself. Prior to the Civil War it manifested itself most strikingly in the antislavery movement, but it had a dozen familiar forms: temperance, the women's rights movement, the peace movement, the reform of prisons and mental institutions, justice for the Indians, reform of clothes and diet, and dozens of others. The same families passed on their often battered ensigns of reform generation after generation. For these Americans, a faithful company, male and female, native or immigrant, the redemptive impulse was as natural as breathing. An already vigorous movement of reform on the state and municipal level found its focus and derived fresh impetus from Theodore Roosevelt, who, as its somewhat reluctant national leader, gave it a dramatic force and coherence it had lacked. The passion for reform made Roosevelt (and, subsequently, Wilson) far more than either of these leaders made it. The fact is the very word "Progressive" is misleading. It was the name adopted in the election of 1912 for dissenting Republicans who set out under the Bull Moose banner to "Battle for the Lord." As such it by no means encompassed the extraordinary range and variety of reforms and reformers. It was, moreover, remarkably transient. As a more or less organized political movement it lasted scarcely four years, yet it gave its name to an era. At the most it described a passion. One thinks again of Eugen Rosenstock-Huessy's comment "Our passions give life to the world; our collective passions constitute the history of mankind." Progressivism was just such a passion. Those who had experienced it felt for the rest of their lives that they had been to the mountain and looked from Pisgah into the Promised Land (their Moses might have had the features of either Theodore Roosevelt or Woodrow Wilson); they had been exalted and transformed; nothing would ever touch them so deeply again.

So progressivism was the brief crystallization of accumulations of reform sentiment, a nationwide political revival meeting of a kind not uncommon in our history when rational men and women pledged "their lives, their fortunes and their sacred honor" to make the world new once more.

It was, of course, limited in its vision of social justice and the uses of the state to achieve it. It left blacks and immigrants, workingmen and labor unions, and, to a lesser extent, women, outside its charmed circle. It was deeply rooted in an older morality—Puritanism plus lots of exercise with Roosevelt; Puritanism plus high thinking with Wilson—and it was in a sometimes uneasy alliance with the new scholarship, with science, and the handmaid of science, research. They—science and research—became the new divinities, the old morality and the new scholarship.

Finally, it is essential to keep in mind that the so-called Progressive movement, which would more properly be called what it was in fact called by contemporaries, "the struggle for social justice," was not merely an American impulse but a worldwide phenomenon. Such at least was the view of William Allen White. It seemed to White, from the perspective of the 1940s, that the Progressive movement had been part and parcel of the uprising of liberals and radicals in England and Europe. Even in ancient, primitive China, Sun Yat-sen was raising the banner of revolution. It was the culmination of a centuries-long process whereby humanity in general had developed "a sense of mercy." White wrote: "The natural aspiration for justice in the human heart took definite form. The struggle for liberty widened and became a more intelligent aspiration with a more certain and definite purpose. As people, the middle class, began to exercise functions in government, government changed," became more efficient and more humane. "The conscience of the world was moving," resisted everywhere by "economic and social privilege . . . with cunning and power. . . ." The Progressive movement was, in White's words, "the champion of the little businessman, the country lawyer, the doctor, the teacher, the preacher, the real estate dealer, the skilled worker—those whose labor organizations were rich and prosperous, the printers, the railroad men, the hard-coal miners." It was in no sense, White argued, "a class movement." The Progressives were thus, as he looked back on their fierce ardors, innocents with "no idea of the hidden forces beneath our feet, the volcanic social substance that was burning deep in the heart of humanity."

To White the Progressives, so confident of the originality and correctness of their ideas, had been simply the "product of the aspiration of the people." Into "the hearts of the dominant middle class . . . had come a sense that their civilization needed recasting, that their government had fallen into the hands of self-seekers, that a new relationship should be established between the haves and the have-nots. . . . We were joyous, eager, happily determined to make life more fair and lovely for ourselves by doing such approximate justice as we could to those who obviously were living in the swamps, morasses, deserts, and wildernesses of this world . . . this progressive movement . . . was profoundly spiritual." White did not quite do justice to the role of the Progressives when he wrote that "some way" the hearts of the middle-class Americans were turned to reform. It was, after all, the new clerisy, the expounders of the new Puritanism, the reforming journalists who had, in a very substantial degree, shaped that new consciousness and awakened the nation's conscience and hopes for deep-seated and essential reforms.

Perhaps we can best describe progressivism as the emergence in the arena of national politics of all the impulses to reform which had hitherto expressed themselves "socially" and "locally." They now found a focus which we call progressivism.

For one reform-minded Republican (who, needless to say, had no confidence in the capacity of the Democrats to achieve even a modest degree of social justice) his party's rejection of Roosevelt and progressivism was a prelude to revolution. Brooks Adams called his book, written in the aftermath of the Republican Convention, *The Theory of Social Revolutions*. His argument was that the holders of economic and political power would never relinquish or share it. He went back to the Greeks and the Romans to support his thesis. "Privileged classes seldom have the intelligence to protect themselves by adaptation when nature turns against them, and . . . the old privileged class in the United States," Adams added, "has shown little promise of being an exception to the rule. . . . If this class, like its predecessors, has in its turn mistaken its environment, a redistribution of property must occur, distressing, as previous redistributions have been, in proportion to the inflexibility of the sufferers." It was axiomatic, he declared, "that present social conditions are unsatisfactory." The cause of the "stress" in the social system was the intrusion of the courts as defenders of monopoly capitalism. The "capitalistic class" *must*, in Adams's view, acquiesce in the social and economic changes necessary to forestall violent revolution. "In fine," he wrote, "a government, to promise stability in the future, must apparently be so much more powerful than any private interest, that all men will stand equally before its tribunals. . . ." Whether, indeed, the government could muster so much energy and whether capital would bow its neck to the yoke of public control seemed to Adams extremely unlikely. "To resist [such efforts] perversely, as they were resisted at the Chicago Convention, . . . can only make the catastrophe, when it comes, as overwhelming as was the consequent defeat of the Republican party," he wrote. History had demonstrated time and again "that a declining favored class is incapable of appreciating an approaching change of environment which must alter its social status." The result must be revolution.

In addition to the high political drama of the political conventions, there took place a little-noticed event the symbolic implications of which were possibly larger than the conventions themselves. On August 14, 1911, in Coatesville, Pennsylvania, a black man named Zacharia Walker had been tied to an iron bedstead and burned alive by the citizens of the community. Apprehended in the midst of a robbery by a security officer of the Worth Brothers Steel Company, Walker had shot and killed the officer. Pursued and shot at, he tried unsuccessfully to kill himself. He was taken initially to a hospital for treatment of his wound but was then bound to his cot, placed on a pyre, and burned to death. The *New York Tribune* noted: "For hours today the scorched torso of the Negro Walker was kicked around by children on the highway a short distance from where he met his death." When John Jay Chapman read the story, it immediately awakened all his hereditary abolitionist instincts.

As we know, the lynching of blacks was a common occurrence in the South and by no means unknown elsewhere, as the Coatesville episode indicated, but the particular horror of the lynching and its relative proximity preyed on Chapman's mind. "I was greatly moved at the time the lynching occurred," he wrote, "and as the anniversary came round my inner idea forced me to do something. I felt as if the whole country would be different if one man did something in penance, and so I went to Coatesville, and declared my intention of holding a prayer meeting to the various business men I could buttonhole." The citizens of Coatesville, needless to say, treated Chapman as though he were the bearer of the plague. A young friend, Edith Martin, went with him, an act "which puts my mind at ease as if I had a big bull-dog to guard me," Chapman wrote to his anxious wife. She was, in his words, "a very remarkable woman, sort of healing priestess of the New Thought kind. . . ."

Chapman found it difficult to get a space in which to hold his "service of intercession." Because the meeting was to be held on Sunday morning, the churches were unavailable and, in any event, thoroughly unresponsive to the enterprise. Finally, he found a room in the Nagel Building and placed an ad in the reluctant *Coatesville Record,* announcing "A Prayer Meeting . . . Silent and Oral Prayer: Brief Reading of the Scriptures: Brief address by John Jay Chapman. In memory of the Tragedy, of August 13, 1911. O Lord receive my prayer." As word of Chapman's mission got about, hostility rose about him like a wall. "No one who has not been up against it," he wrote to his wife, "can imagine the tyranny of a small town in America. . . . There's a dumb, dead, unlistening decision to do what it *has been decided* must be done—what business demands—e.g., to not raise the lynching issue in Coates-ville. . . ."

"Who's back of this?" the editor of the *Record* asked fiercely.

"No one," Chapman replied; "at least I am."

Chapman was convinced that the townspeople would "rather like the idea of a prayer meeting" and would attend. He was profoundly mistaken. Besides Edith Martin there was an "anti-slavery old Negress," who lived in Boston and was visiting Coatesville, and a man who Chapman sensed was a spy sent to find out "what was up."

So the strange, quixotic event was played out. The prayers were prayed, the passages of Scripture read, and Chapman delivered his "address": "I will tell you why I am here; I will tell you what happened to me. When I read in the newspapers of August 14, a year ago, about the burning alive of a human being, and of how a few desperate, fiend-minded men had been permitted to torture a man chained to an iron bedstead, burning alive . . . while around about stood hundreds of well-dressed American citizens . . . coming on foot and in wagons, assembling on telephone call, as if by magic, silent whether from terror or indifference, fascinated and impotent, hundreds of persons watching this awful sight and making no attempt to stay the wickedness, and no one man among them all who was inspired to risk his life in an attempt to stop it, no one man to name the name of Christ, of humanity, of government! As I read the newspaper accounts of the scene enacted here in Coatesville a year ago, I seemed to get a glimpse into the unconscious soul of this country. . . . I seemed to be looking into the heart of the criminal—a cold thing, an awful thing.

"I said to myself, 'I shall forget this, we shall all forget it; but it will be there. What I have seen is not an illusion. It is the truth. I have seen death in the heart of this people.' For to look at the agony of a fellow-being and remain aloof means death in the heart of the on-looker." It seemed to Chapman a symbol of the paralysis of "the nerves about the heart in a people habitually and unconsciously given over to selfish aims, an ignorant people who knew not . . . what part they were playing in a judgment-play which history was exhibiting on that day. . . .

"Whatever life itself is, that thing must be replenished in us. The opposite of hate is love, the opposite of cold is heat; what we need is the love of God and reverence for human nature. For one moment I knew that I had seen our true need; and I was afraid that I should forget it and that I should go about framing arguments and agitations and starting schemes of education, when the need was deeper than education. And I became filled with one idea, that I must not forget what I had seen, and that I must do something to remember it. And I am here today chiefly that I may remember that vision. It seems fitting to come to this town where the crime occurred and hold a prayer-meeting, so that our hearts may be turned to God through whom mercy may flow into us."

The subject was not local; it was national. When Chapman had mentioned the lynching to a friend who lived not far from Coatesville, he had replied, "It wasn't in my county," and "that," Chapman said, "made me wonder whose county it was in. And it seemed to be in my county." Chapman lived on the Hudson River, but he knew that "this great wickedness that happened in Coatesville is not the wickedness of Coatesville. It is the wickedness of all America and of three hundred years—the wickedness of the slave trade. All of us are tinctured by it. No special place, no special persons are to blame. A nation cannot practice a course in human crime for three hundred years and then suddenly throw off the effects of it. . . . There is no country in Europe where the Coatesville tragedy or anything remotely like it could have been enacted, probably no country in the world. . . . Do you not see that the whole event is merely that last parable, the most vivid, the most terrible illustration that was ever given by man or imagined by a Jewish prophet, of the relation between good and evil in the world, and of the relation of men to one another?" So Coatesville was not only part of our national history but part of "the personal history of each of us. . . ." The first step, as in the process of redemption, was to recognize the evil, its full nature and historic life, to strip away all the excuses and evasions. "I say that our need is new life, and that books and resolutions will not save us, but only such disposition in our hearts and souls as will enable the new life, love, force, hope, virtue, which surround us always, to enter into us." To do so was to discover that what man really stands in need of "he cannot get for himself, but must wait until God gives it to him." Chapman had come to testify to that truth. "The occasion is not small," he said bravely to the three others who shared the small room with him; "the occasion looks back on three centuries and embraces a hemisphere. Yet the occasion is small compared with the truth it leads us to. For the truth touches all ages and affects every soul in the world."

It is hard not to compare Chapman's quixotic venture in Coatesville with the innumerable public gatherings in our history, addressed by prominent politicians and famous orators, which proved as ephemeral as mayflies. Chapman's words, on the other hand, will live as long as the Republic. The audience may remain modest, but the words, one dares to say, will continue to open hearts and change lives and the occasion thus truly prove "not small," for of such are the powers of history.

The Commission on
Industrial Relations

In light of the events we have described, it is hardly surprising that the war between capital and labor, a war the bloodiest campaign of which had come at its beginning—the Great Strikes of 1877—seemed to many Americans to be entering a period of accelerating violence and disorder. The bombing of the *Los Angeles Times* building and the sensational trial of the McNamaras had been followed by the garment workers' strike, the Lawrence strike, and, most recently, the Paterson strike. The Wobblies, effective and alarming out of all proportion to their members, were active in the lumber camps of the West and bore troubling witness to the increasing militancy of workingmen and women.

And these strikes were only the most dramatic. There were thousands more, little noticed outside the localities where they took place. "Through the length and breadth of the land there was armed warfare between the wage-earners and the profit-makers," Florence Harriman wrote.

Roosevelt had introduced a new executive instrument in the form of presidential commissions (if not new in form, new in the degree and effectiveness with which he utilized them). As the election of 1912 approached, a committee of citizens headed by Jane Addams persuaded President Taft to appoint a commission to study and report on steps that might be taken to make peace in the war between capital and labor. It seemed a safe enough undertaking to Taft. The President could render its investigations innocuous by appointing conservative members (Congress specified its general composition), but Congress rejected the individuals nominated by Taft as too favorable to capital. Moreover, Democratic Congressmen, anticipating a victory at the polls, wished to have the naming of the members of the commission in their party's giving. Positions on the commission would be appropriate rewards to individuals who had worked industriously in the Democratic campaign.

Under the terms establishing the nine-person commission, three were to represent "the public," three were to be employers, and "not less than three" representatives of labor. When Wilson won the election, he accepted the recommendations of Samuel Gompers for three AFL members. The real struggle revolved around the six members who were to represent business and the public.

The most prominent "public" member and chairman of the commission was the Kansas City lawyer-reformer Frank Walsh. Walsh was a man of formidable presence and enormous vitality (in George Creel's words: "broad shouldered, deep chested, wide of brow and granite chinned") and ineffable Irish charm. He was just the man to impart brilliant highlights to the drama he was about to direct. Creel described him as "A great lawyer, a persuasive speaker, and the most authentic liberal I have known." A newspaperman wrote: "If you asked a lawyer who was the greatest advocate in Missouri, it's dollars to jitney he will mention Mr. Walsh first."

Walsh had become a hero in Missouri by his brilliant defense of Jesse James, Jr., son of the bandit, who had been arrested without a warrant and charged with following in his father's footsteps. Walsh concentrated on denouncing the tactics of the police: "What a spectacle! Is it possible that this great commonwealth had to ally itself with hired detectives, with paid bloodhounds of the law, that the majesty of the law might be vindicated?" The emblems on the state flag should then be replaced "with the leering face of a detective and the drawling, snakelike shape of an informer!" James was so impressed by his defense attorney that he himself decided to become a lawyer, and he was later an attorney for reformers in Kansas City determined to oust the notorious Prendergast machine. A writer on *Harper's* characterized Walsh as "An idealistic and optimistic Irishman [who] combined . . . radical agitation and practical politics in a most uncommon fashion."

With his appointment as chairman of the commission, Walsh had found his calling. Under another chairman, it is safe to say, the hearings would have been far less enthralling. Walsh had the trial lawyer's instinct for a witness's most vulnerable point. Even more important, he won the respect and even affection of the diverse group of commissioners over whom he presided for almost two years.

Colonel House supported Florence Harriman's appointment to the commission on the ground that she was "the most logical, the most representative and the best woman appointee."

The most scholarly member of the commission was John Rogers Commons. Commons, born in 1862 in Hollandsburg, Ohio, had been graduated from Oberlin and then worked under Richard Ely at Johns Hopkins University. His Presbyterian background inclined him to radical economic theories, and his exposure, through Ely, to German "scientific" scholarship resulted, ultimately, in a pragmatic approach to resolving the conflict between capital and labor. His *The Distribution of Wealth,* published in 1893, had established his credentials as a critic of capitalism. In 1904 he joined the political science department at Wisconsin, despite the grumbling of some of the trustees, and soon was busy with his students drafting laws to improve the civil service, to regulate public utilities, and to establish a progam of workmen's compensation in the state under the aegis of La Follette. There, in his words, "I was born again." He also organized the state's industrial commission, which became a model for other states. "I was brought up," Commons declared, "on Hoosierism, Republicanism, Presbyterianism, and Spencerianism." He was small and frail, and his early career had been marked by numerous breakdowns, both physical and mental. Theodore Roosevelt described him as "a thoroughly good fellow, more of a radical than I am, but a sane radical," and Walsh called him "the most accomplished political economist of this time." Walsh and Commons, one large and expansive, the other small and precise, constituted the core of the commissioners. Walsh was responsible for the hearings; Commons, for the research. Commons was one of the few appointments that seemed to satisfy the progressively inclined. The professor, the *Survey* wrote, is "the one man in America who as an economist and investigator has thought out industrial reforms."

The labor representatives were James O'Connell, Austin Bruce Garretson, and John B. Lennon. O'Connell had been driven out of the presidency of the International Association of Machinists by the socialist faction in his union. Austin Bruce Garretson was an old-line railroad union man who supported the closed shop and the right to strike but disavowed violence. John B. Lennon of Illinois had been head of the Journeyman Tailors' Union, but he had also been ousted by the socialists in his union. The softhearted Lennon was a vice-president of the AFL. "Distressing testimony would make tears run down his cheeks . . ." Harriman noted.

To Gompers's indignation, the men he recommended and Wilson appointed were attacked in liberal circles as "wholly reactionary." John Haynes Holmes, the reformist minister, wrote: "Wake up, A.F. of L. you are today a hopeless drag upon the labor world." Gompers replied, "The workers are not bugs to be examined under the lenses of a microscope by the 'intellectuals' on sociological slumming tours. . . ." Such intellectuals "by their intolerance and arrogance . . . manifest their personal unfitness to consider Labor's problems. . . . Wisdom and understanding do not always accompany diplomas, degrees, or attach themselves to endowed chairs." What does seem clear is that Gompers, in order to get his candidates on the commission, joined forces with the most conservative wing of the National Civic Federation. That the federation was not unreservedly in support of the commission is suggested by the comment of its chairman, Ralph Easley, who described its original proposers as "radical preachers and charity workers," more interested in "a political Socialistic inquiry" than in discovering the truth.

The industry members were of a strong liberal disposition, all in all more liberal than the labor representatives. Harris Weinstock, a California department store owner with a reputation for enlightened labor policies, was active in the National Civic Federation. He was a believer in the efficacy of the referendum, initiative, and recall as a solution to the nation's ills; he had been the first president of the liberally inclined Commonwealth Club in San Francisco.

Thruston Ballard was a Kentucky industrialist whose flour mill in Louisville was a model of good employer-employee relations. A graduate of Cornell, Ballard had introduced profit sharing in 1899 with a third of the company's annual profits being distributed among the employees. He had also established the first eight-hour day in the flour mill industry and provided his workers with many amenities. Ballard was, in Harriman's words, "one of the most amusing and original men I have ever met and the most completely out-spoken." Florence Harriman we are already familiar with.

The *Outlook* was among the magazines that enthusiastically supported the appointment of the commission. "It is," an editorial declared, "somewhat as if, in the period prior to the Civil War, a President had appointed a Commission on Slavery. It may affect for untold good the future history of the United States, and the lives of innumerable men, women, and children."

Before it completed its task, the commmission held 154 days of hearings in Washington, New York, Paterson, Philadelphia, Boston, Chicago, Lead, South Dakota, Butte, Seattle, Portland, San Francisco, Los Angeles, Denver, and Dallas. More than 700 witnesses were heard in twenty-three categories, ranging from "Capitalists, bankers, directors, etc." to union officials, workingmen and workingwomen, educators, economists, sociologists, clergy, and "unclassified." In the words of Florence Harriman, "Each bore witness to what the economic struggle looked like from his angle, and many attempted to say how conditions might be bettered. There were immigrants and Yankee-born, there were meat-cutters and butchers, street car conductors, mayors and governors, miners and mine owners, Italian immigration officials, members of mill owners' associations, engineers and school teachers, railroad telegraphers and dispatchers, agents and signal men, truck builders and statisticians. There were doctors studying child hygiene, social workers from homes for Chinese working-girls, directors of schools of industrial arts, plumbers and pullman porters, superintendents of motive power on railroads, bankers and professors, manufacturers of ladies' cloaks, carpet layers and blacksmiths, owners of newspapers and reporters, secretaries of associated charities, boilermakers and shipbuilders, managers of placement bureaus and vocational advisers, merchants and cavalry men and state guards, councillors-at-law and plasterers, officers of child-welfare associations and structural iron workers, bricklayers and operating potters, men from bureaus of municipal research, painters, decorators and paperhangers, managers of docks and cargoes, bishops, the Minister of Labor from Canada, I.W.W.'s, and members of the Carnegie Peace Foundation, settlement workers, cigar-makers, civil servants, Chinese interpreters, seamen and detectives, farmers and wives."

What was perhaps most noteworthy about the commission—in addition to the volume of testimony it recorded—was its catholicity. It heard, with admirable disinterestedness, spokesmen for every conceivable political and economic point of view. It heard them all patiently and, on the whole, politely. Its broad-mindedness was demonstrated by the fact that two of its principal "stars" were Morris Hillquit, the leader of the Socialist Party, and John D. Rockefeller, Jr. Labor leaders under indictment for murder—such as John Lawson, an officer of the United Mine Workers—were followed to the stand by their ex-employers.

One of the most sensitive points at issue among the members of the commission itself was the role of "research." Some of the members, Florence Harriman and John Commons among them, were convinced that the greater part of the commission's budget should go to trained researchers. The commission's first director of research was Charles V. McCarthy, head of the Wisconsin Legislative Reference Bureau. McCarthy's greatest fame perhaps lay in the fact that as a student at Brown University he had scored touchdowns against both Yale and Harvard (the manager of the team was John D. Rockefeller, Jr.). A student of Frederick Jackson Turner, McCarthy was a La Follette liberal. He assembled a team of researchers that included Robert Hoxie, Selig Perlman, George Creel, and Sumner Slichter. To McCarthy there was "no greater problem any Amerian can work at than that of making a great statesmanlike program of social betterment." In his opinion, the commission was "of far greater significance than anything I know in this country today." Professors, scholars, researchers—they all were essentially the same—believed devoutly in the power of "social science," of patient research and scholarly investigation to search out the causes of unrest and propose remedies. Instead of legislation's being hit or miss, the result of behind-the-scenes struggles between competing interests, it must become "scientific," drafted by experts and passed by enlightened politicians who realized that a new and better era had dawned.

Walsh, as a product of the no-holds-barred political wars of Kansas City, was far more of a believer in what we today call guerrilla theater. He was hospitable to the efforts of the researchers, but he was convinced that in the last analysis only a coherent body of public opinion could provide the essential grounding for progressive legislation and that such opinion was created not by academic researches and scholarly monographs but through the channels of mass communication, primarily the newspapers and popular magazines of the country. Thus, when the commission's funds ran short and the question arose of whether the hearings or the "researches" were more important, Walsh had no hesitation in throwing his weight behind the hearings to the dismay of Harriman and Commons and, of course, the researchers themselves. To McCarthy the chairman's decision seemed hopelessly retrograde.

"Just at the time of the fruition of all our hopes and just at the time when opportunity comes knocking at his door, he is throwing it all away," he wrote.

Shortly after the names of the members of the commission had been made public, Mother Jones came to see Florence Harriman to ask what the commissioners on industrial relations meant to do for her "boys." Harriman described her as "a little old woman in a tidy bonnet . . . the sort of benign little body, if one lived somewhere on Main Street, one would like for a neighbor." She had come to Harriman to find out "if I was good for anything." The member of New York's Four Hundred and the founder of the exclusive Colony Club "wanted to laugh and cry at the little bonnet strings under that chin," for it was soon evident that the mild-looking little woman with the cool, direct eyes "had seen something more than Main Street. . . . Her boys were the two-hundred thousand members of the United Mine Workers of America. . . . For the next two years I was to find her name a legend wherever we went summoning the down-trodden to speak for themselves at our hearings." To Florence Harriman, she was "the most significant woman in America though her life has been alien to everything comfortable American womanhood is supposed to stand for. She has been a mother to men. She has kept alive their hunger for freedom. She has been a fire-brand, foul-mouthed and partisan, a camp-follower and a comforter in the industrial war. Humble men, rough men, men who speak the languages of every country in Europe and Asia are among her 'boys.'" Harriman wrote: "Other people seemed dead beside her, themselves not feeling, and unfelt."

Aware that the membership of the commission was not apt to be friendly to the interests of capitalism, the Rockefeller Foundation mounted its own "study." When the Rockefeller Institute for Medical Research had been decided upon, the responsibility for setting it up and staffing it had been turned over to Simon Flexner. Flexner, born in Louisville, Kentucky, of an old and aristocratic Jewish family, was a distinguished scientist who had discovered a dysentery bacillus, had been among the first to identify syphilis spirochete, and had produced a serum used successfully against meningitis. It was no exaggeration to say that the rapid rise of the Rockefeller Institute to eminence in the field of medical research was due primarily to Flexner's efforts.

Now Rockefeller wished to do the same thing in the field of the social sciences with particular regard to the conflict between capital and labor. As the counterpart to Simon Flexner, the Rockefeller Foundation chose Mackenzie King, former minister of labor in Canada, who had been widely applauded for his skillful handling of labor problems in that country.

Not only did the Commission on Industrial Relations cast its investigative net remarkably widely, but Walsh established an atmosphere of openness and informality that encouraged witnesses to speak their minds. In addition to investigating the horrendous conditions under which the great majority of Americans worked (that, of course, had been often done before), the commissioners probed the underlying social and political views of those who appeared before them. What resulted was an unique profile of Americans, a work without rival in both depth and comprehensiveness. If there is one "document" (the hearings were published in eleven formidable volumes) that tells what America did and thought in the era between 1901 and 1921, it is preeminently the commission's *Report*.

The commissioners began the hearings with testimony from leading large and small *S* socialists. As the principal critics of capitalism they could be counted on to provide a kind of ideological framework for subsequent testimony. In the absence of Haywood, who was ill, Vincent St. John, one of the officials of the IWW, led off. St. John was a classic rough diamond, direct, ungrammatical, and militant. He gave the membership of the IWW at 14,310 dues-paying members with perhaps twice that number who considered themselves members in spirit. Asked to begin by stating "the purposes, general scope and plan" of the IWW, he replied that its primary purpose was to organize the working class on a class basis. "That is, to organize and educate the workers with the understanding that the workers of this and every other country constitute a distinct and separate economic class, with interests that are distinct and separate from the employing class. . . ."

By St. John's account the IWW had a twofold mission: "to handle the everyday problem of the workers, which is one of shorter hours, better wages, and improved shop conditions, and ultimately the education of the workers so that they can assume control of industry." The union was a kind of school or training ground for that task. The commission was clearly most concerned with the role of violence in the philosophy of the IWW, and St. John was disarmingly forthright in responding to their questions. Yes, the IWW accepted the necessity for destroying property to "gain the point for the workers." Similarly, with violence against persons, the only question was whether or not it was necessary in order to gain the union's goals.

The commissioners pressed St. John further. Was he actually saying that violence was an accepted tactic of his union? "As far as the destruction of property is concerned," he replied, "the property is not ours. We haven't any interest in it at all; it is used simply—it is used to make the lot of the workers, as a class, harder. . . ." The employers "take us into the mills before we are able—before we have even the semblance of an education, and they grind up our vitality, brain and muscular energy into profits, and whenever we cannot keep pace with the machine speeded to its highest notch, they turn us out onto the road to eke out an existence as best we can, or wind up on the poor farm or in the potter's field." The employer showed no respect or concern for his workers, for their property, their muscles and bodies, and they felt no obligation to show concern for his. "We do not propose to do it," St. John declared, "and we do not propose to make any bones about that attitude clearly understood. . . . And the same holds true with regard to life and violence. Not that the Industrial Workers of the World are advocating the destruction of life to gain any particular point or the use of violence; because the destruction of life is not going to gain any point. . . . But we are not going to tell the membership to allow themselves to be shot down and beat up like cattle. Regardless of the fact that they are members of the working class, they still have a duty that they owe to themselves and their class of defending themselves whenever they are attacked and their life is threatened."

The commissioners persisted. "In other words," one of them asked, "your general policy is that whatever violence is necessary to carry the point, and if violence will carry the point, they must use it to gain the point?"

Mr. St. John: "Most assuredly; yes."

Yet that was not quite what St. John meant to say, as subsequent interrogation suggested. It was a subtle but extremely important issue. Was it self-defense against the violence perpetrated by the employer that he and the union condoned, or was it violence as a tactic?

The IWW considered "peaceful cooperation" between employer and employee—between capital and labor—impossible. "If a local of the I.W.W. took the line that the employers and the workers had a mutual interest . . . that would automatically expel them from the organization."

The commissioners doubtlessly turned from the rough and intractable Vincent St. John to the polished and articulate Morris Hillquit with some relief. There was nothing even vaguely threatening in the manner or the testimony of the urbane lawyer who took the witness stand.

Morris Hillquit, né Morris Hillkowitz, was a somewhat deracinated Russian Jew, born in Riga in Latvian Russia. He had come to the United States in 1886 at the age of seventeen, learned Yiddish from Abraham Cahan, the famous editor of the *Jewish Daily Forward,* and begun organizing Jewish unions on the Lower East Side of New York City. In the course of events he became active in the Socialist Labor Party.

When Hillquit appeared before the commissioners, the reorganized Socialist Party was at what was to turn out to be its apogee, the high point of its relatively brief history. Its predecessors and/or progenitors, according to Hillquit, were the Socialist Labor Party, formed in 1877, and the Social Democratic Party, organized in 1897. The Socialist Party in its latest manifestation dated from 1900. With Eugene V. Debs as its presidential candidate, it had recently (in the election of 1912) polled almost 900,000 votes, and it claimed a "dues-paying" membership of 115,000 in some 6,000 local organizations. It had recently purged itself of any association with the IWW, renounced the use of force, and expelled Big Bill Haywood from membership, primarily to make itself more respectable, thereby broadening its appeal to upper-class professionals and intellectuals. The election returns of 1912 seemed to have justified the strategy. While Debs's popular vote for president had been a small percentage of the total ballots cast, more than 300 Socialists had been elected to municipal offices; among them were 56 mayors of large and small cities.

Under questioning by the commissioners, Hillquit affirmed the goals of the party as "the nationalization of industries," said industries to be run "by responsible agencies of the people organized for that purpose." Hillquit declared, "Concretely stated, socialism demands the collective ownership of the principal tools, courses and resources of wealth production." He then went on, like any professor, to give the commissioners a lengthy lecture on the development of industrial capitalism. As a consequence of new methods of capital accumulation and new techniques of production, "1,000 individual workmen" had been deprived of "1,000 individual tools" and "substituted for those 1,000 individual tools, say, 10 great machines to be operated by the same 1,000 men. . . . The proper and equitable transformation," Hillquit argued, "would have been to have placed these 1,000 men properly organized in possession of this new complexity of machines. . . ." Instead, a new class had been created by the machines. The helper or apprentice of an earlier age saw his dependent position as transitory. He intended to become himself an individual independent producer in time. But under the new social and economic order, "the laborer . . . ,with very rare exceptions, is a laborer forever, and he breeds and produces a generation of laborers. . . . When the condition is such that for a majority of the workers his condition has become permanent and hereditary, we have for the first time in our history a perpetual hereditary working class."

The interests of the working class and the capitalist class were, by their very nature, opposed. But Hillquit, as distinguished from St. John, was careful to point out that this basic and unalterable hostility did not necessarily mean "personal hostility between the worker and the employer. Their relations may be very friendly, very cordial, but their interests are necessarily opposed to each other." Capitalism was "a system which works without general national plan, which works for individual profit and regardless entirely of social welfare, which is based upon the exploitation of labor and intense work. . . ." And it was, moreover, a system which created "the problem of unemployment. . . . Ordinarily, under normal conditions, there should be no unemployment in the United States," Hillquit declared. ". . . There are millions of citizens who stand in need of food, clothing, shelter, furniture, books, and so on, but we do not produce them, although we have the facilities for it." It was this kind of "inherent contradiction" in capitalism that socialism would cure. In addition, Hillquit was careful to point out, the Socialist Party sought to achieve its goals gradually: "We fully realize that social revolution is gradual; that social institutions are methods of historical growth and development; that no system of society can be changed in a day just because a certain number of individuals think it ought to be changed . . . and we also advocate every measure calculated to improve the condition of the workers—" such, for instance, "as better wages, shorter hours, abolition of child labor, State insurance, national insurance [protecting] the workers against old age, sickness, disability, and so on." A worker who was "badly underpaid, underfed, illy housed" could not readily "develop a social idealism."

When Hillquit finished his testimony, Samuel Gompers was invited to cross-examine him. Now began a battle of wits in which all the sore points between the Socialists and the American Federation of Labor were publicly ventilated. Gompers did his best to depict the Socialists as a party dominated by foreign theorists with little practical knowledge of the problems and needs of the ordinary worker, committed to undermining and eventually destroying the very things that had made the United States a great nation. Hillquit, for his part, attempted to depict Gompers as a kind of labor czar, more interested in retaining power through a labor aristocracy than in the welfare of the ordinary workingman. Hadn't Gompers, he asked, acquiesced in one of the workingman's oldest and most basic grievances: the ten- and twelve-hour day? Hadn't he dragged his feet on the issue of child labor? Wasn't he more interested in accommodating the employer than in fighting for better conditions? Had he not done his best to weed Socialists not only out of the leadership of his federation but out of the membership as well? The clear implication was that Gompers had betrayed and continued to betray the cause of the workingman by putting the selfish interests of the individual worker ahead of the interests of the working class.

Gompers, in turn, charged the Socialists with attempting to destroy the American Federation of Labor when it discovered that it could not take it over. That, Hillquit replied, was the Socialist Labor Party, the old, bad, radical Socialists. Gompers embarrassed Hillquit by quoting from various speeches and articles by Debs calling on the workingman "to sever his relation with the American Federation." Hillquit rebutted the charges as best he could, declaring himself "frank to add that the Socialist Party, at least a majority of its members, do believe that the present leadership of the American Federation of Labor is somewhat archaic, somewhat antiquated, too conservative, and not efficient enough for the object and purposes of the American Federation of Labor."

The Socialist Party was confident that in the future, presumably with new and more enlightened leadership, "the members of the A.F. of L. will be just as enlightened and progressive as members of any other organization. . . ."

One of the most interesting exchanges between Hillquit and Gompers came over the question of whether, in accordance with Marx's doctrine, the material condition of the workers was deteriorating. When Gompers put the question to him, Hillquit waffled. It was, and it wasn't. "The general consensus of Socialists' opinion [was] that the process of the making of a propertyless class of workers is on the increase . . . but that absolutely there is a noticeable improvement in the conditions of at least a large section of the working class." The issue was, of course, a crucial one. It had to do both with the "scientific" character of the Marxian analysis and, in the long run, with the chances of revolutionary upheaval in the United States. Gompers plainly asked the question in order to set up his own recital of the improvements in the condition of at least the members of the American Federation of Labor. That long and impressive inventory, credit for which Gompers attempted to appropriate to the AFL but which, in fact, was the consequence of a far wider reform movement, foretold the future of the American labor movement.

Gompers also showed considerable tenacity in grilling Hillquit about the degree to which Socialists were orthodox Marxists. "Do you," he asked, "regard the communists' manifesto of Marx and Engels as on the whole correct; as correct to-day as ever?"

Hillquit: "The general principles, on the whole, yes. The details, perhaps not. . . . What the author of the communist manifesto meant by the term 'communist' is what we mean to-day by the term 'Socialist.' "

"So you believe that the children of the working class are doomed to ignorance, drudgery, toil and darkened lives in the United States?" Gompers asked.

"Very largely," Hillquit replied.

The sparring between the two men continued. "Under socialism will there be liberty of individual action, and liberty of choice of occupation and liberty of refusal to work?" Gompers asked.

"Plenty of it" was Hillquit's firm response.

Would the attainment of socialism mark the end of man's social and political progress? By no means, Hillquit replied. "There will be something superior [to socialism] some time. In the meantime every stage of development is superior to the preceding stage; and by the same token capitalism is superior to feudalism. Socialism is superior to capitalism. That is all."

When it came Gompers's turn to testify, he offered the commissioners a classic American success story. There were 110 "national and international unions" affiliated with the AFL; 42 state federations of labor, 623 local city federations of trade unions, and 642 local unions federated with the federation until such time as there were sufficient locals to form a national union for a particular trade. The goal of the AFL was simply stated: "To make life the better for living in our day, and so that the workers may be in a better position to meet any problems with which the future generations may be confronted. In a word, to let no effort go untried by which the working people, as the masses of the people, may find betterment upon every field of human activity." The statement was a bit disingenuous since, as Hillquit had earlier pointed out, the federation had been conspicuously behindhand in supporting those reforms, such as the eight-hour day, which were of special concern to unskilled and unorganized workers.

When it came Hillquit's turn to cross-examine Gompers, the Socialist leader directed the majority of his questions at what he clearly believed to be Gompers's Achilles' heel: the disposition of the AFL to accommodate itself to employers' interests. Gompers's riposte was to submit twenty pages listing state and Federal legislation passed in the year 1912 that benefited the workingman. The year 1911 had seen sixteen major pieces of prolabor legislation; 1912 saw seventeen, the most important of which was the creation of a cabinet rank Department of Labor, the secretary of which was a former head of the United Mine Workers of America. Among the other important pieces of Federal legislation was one which specified that the employees of "all contractors and subcontractors doing work for the National Government . . . must hereafter observe the eight-hour day." In addition, eight hours would be maximum for all postal clerks, letter carriers, and postal employees. A children's bureau had been established in the Department of Labor to serve "the best interests of children by practicable and scientific methods." Steps had also been initiated to slow down the speedup increasingly common in industrial plants. The role of state prolabor legislation was far more extensive. Although confined to only eighteen states, it covered such matters as compensation for injuries, hours and conditions of labor, industrial safety regulations (in considerable profusion), and child labor prohibitions.

One of the most significant exchanges between Hillquit and Gompers involved their respective timetables for the achievement of "social justice for working men and women." Pressed by Hillquit, Gompers declared, "Working people, as all other people, . . . are prompted by the same desires and hopes of a better life, and they are not willing to wait until they have shuffled off this mortal coil for the better life, they want it here and now, and they want to make conditions better for their children. . . . The working people are pressing forward . . . making their claims and presenting those claims with whatever power they have . . . in a normal, rational manner, to secure a larger, and constantly larger share of the products. They are working to the highest and best ideals of social justice."

Hillquit clearly wished to depict Gompers and the AFL as concerned only with the bread-and-butter issues and indifferent to the larger visions of an enlightened and elevated humanity so prominent in the philosophy of socialism. But Gompers refused to take the bait, insisting that his union was committed "to the highest and best ideals of social justice." At the same time he wished to draw a line between visionary schemes and practical reform. "The intelligent, comprehensive, common-sense workmen," he declared, "prefer to deal with the problems of to-day . . . rather than with a picture and a dream which has never had, and I am sure never will have, any reality in the affairs of humanity. . . ." Such system as the Socialists advocated, Gompers insisted, would result in "the worst system of circumscriptional effort and activity that has ever been invented by the ken of the human kind." In his awkward formulation, Gompers was apparently predicting that socialism could attain its goals only at the cost of a system of repression and regimentation far worse than that of capitalism. He refused, he told Hillquit, "to permit my mind or my activities to be labeled by any particular ism."

Gompers came back repeatedly, in his testimony, to the fact that the United States was, in practical fact, a republic in which "the element and essentials to political freedom obtain. . . ." In consequence, despite the determined efforts of the business and industrial interests of the country to thwart the aspirations of the working people, the means of improving their condition were accessible to them and could be, and in fact had been and were being, used to improve their status in the larger society. That fact, Gompers declared, vindicated the policy of the AFL.

When Big Bill Haywood was available, he was called before the commission. Under the sympathetic questioning of Chairman Walsh and John Lennon, Haywood told the story of his early life in Salt Lake City and his experience as a miner, starting at the age of fifteen. Asked whether he thought a socialist system could be achieved by political action, Haywood declared, "Personally I don't think that this can be done by political action. First, for the very good reason that the wage-earner or producing classes are in the minority." Moreover, they were lacking in political sophistication and, above all, were chained to exhausting jobs, which allowed them little time for concerted political action. "I have had a dream," Haywood declared, "that I have had in the morning and at night and during the day, and that is that there will be a new society sometime in which there will be no battle between capitalist and wage earner but that every man will have free access to land and its resources. In that day there will be no political government, there will be no States, and Congress will not be composed of lawyers and preachers as it is now, but it will be composed of experts of the different branches of industry, who will come together for the purpose of discussing the welfare of all the people and discussing the means by which the machiney can be made the slave of the people instead of a part of the people being made the slave of machinery or the owners of machinery."

Weinstock, the follower of Hiram Johnson, pressed Haywood on the issue of the initiative, referendum, and recall. Would not that bring about the industrial democracy that Haywood desired? Haywood rejected the notion out of hand. He could not see how it had been of material assistance to the workers in any state that had adopted it. "Do you know the results we are hoping for? We hope to see the day when no child will labor. We hope to see the day when all men will be able to work, either with brain or with muscle; we want to see the day when women will take their place as industrial units; we want to see the day when every old man and every old woman will have the assurance of at least dying in peace. Now, you have not got anything like that to-day. You have not the assurance, rich man as you are," Haywood told Weinstock, "of not dying a pauper. I have an idea that we can have a much better society than we have got; and I have another idea that we cannot have a much worse one than it is at present. So you see that the program of the I.W.W. is not such a bad thing after all. . . ."

Another high spot of the commission's hearings was the appearance of Mother Jones as a witness. "Where do you reside?" Walsh asked her.

"Well," she answered, "I reside wherever there is a good fight against wrong—all over the country. . . . Wherever the workers are fighting the robbers I go there. . . . I belong to a class who have been robbed, exploited, and plundered down through many long centuries, and because I belong to that class I have an instinct to go and help break the chains."

At the end of her testimony Weinstock asked Mother Jones the now familiar question: What was her recommendation for wiping out industrial unrest? Her first recommendation was to do away with the detective agencies hired by the owners to intimidate strikers and break strikes. Then she would have the government take over the mines themselves. "They are mineral, and no operator, no coal company on the face of the earth made that coal. It is a mineral; it belongs to the Nation; it was down there through the ages, and it belongs to every generation that comes along, and no set of men should be permitted to use that which is nature's. It should be given to all nature's children in other nations."

From the leaders and theoreticians of the left, the commissioners went on to gather testimony from ordinary union members and workingmen and -women. One of the most articulate witnesses was Max Hayes. Hayes, forty-eight years old, had begun work as a printer's apprentice at the age of thirteen, worked as a typesetter for the *Cleveland Press,* been an active member of the International Typographical Union, and edited a socialist-labor paper called the *Cleveland Citizen.* As a socialist Hayes believed that the active involvement of socialists in the labor movement was the only practical course to pursue to achieve the classless society. He had no sympathy with the IWW or the Socialist Trade and Labor Alliance, which he saw as efforts to undermine the trade unions. He agreed with neither "Comrade Debs" or "Brother Sam Gompers . . . in his opposition to the Socialist movement. . . . My opinion is, after being in close touch, in daily contact, not with the officers of these organizations but with the rank and file . . . and I believe I am fully conversant with the views of the average worker—the man in the street so-called—that there is not the difference between the membership of the Socialist Party and the membership of the trade-union movement that people are frequently led to believe, because of the contentions, the rivalries, the jealousies, or the animosities that may exist between the so-called leaders of these movements." It was Hayes's conviction that "the very large bulk of the membership—a majority, I would say, of the membership of the Socialist Party—is composed of trade-unionists, and a very large proportion, that is, the largest proportion of the membership of the Socialist Party, is of the trade-union world." Especially in the Middle West, Hayes declared, he was constantly cooperating as a union organizer with local Socialist organizations. In Ohio, Indiana, and Illinois most conspicuously, the vast majority of the members of the United Mine Workers were, in Hayes's judgment, Socialists.

How, the commissioners asked Hayes, could he give his allegiance to the AFL when that body specifically rejected the goal of a workers' state and a classless society? "I am a member of the trade-union movement," Hayes replied, "because it is the bread-and-butter organization—the movement that meets the problems on the industrial field. . . . But I recognize the limitations of the trade-union movement, and hence I have come to the conclusion that it is absolutely necessary also to give a political expression to the wants and desires of the working class. . . ."

As an example of the practical achievements of his own union, the International Typographical Union, Hayes recounted the measures it had taken to improve the working conditions of its members: hours of work; sanitary conditions; wages. Each local union had a committee on sanitation. In the period from 1900 to 1914 the life expectancy of union members had increased from 41.25 years to 48.7. The Union Printers' Home in Colorado Springs with a hospital annex situated on 240 acres of land was a symbol of the achievements of unionism.

When Hayes was questioned on the nationalizing of major industries, he stated his emphatic support for nationalization, adding that "we would probably hire Brother Rockefeller as business agent of the oil division, or Judge Gary as manager of the steel department; but they would have to be workers."

21

Fat Cats and Experts

Some of the most interesting testimony before the Commission on Industrial Relations was that of the capitalists themselves and of the scholarly experts in the fields of political economy, economics, and sociology.

George Walbridge Perkins was a classic success story. He had risen dramatically from office boy to first vice-president of the New York Life Insurance Company and had then joined forces with J. Pierpont Morgan to form the United States Steel Corporation and International Harvester. In addition, he was a director of three railroads and the International Mercantile Marine, a company which he had been instrumental in forming. He was also a pillar of the liberal wing of the Republican Party. He told the commissioners that in his view, competition was no longer "the life of trade." Cooperation had taken its place. "I believe this," he declared, "because it is clear that competition, driven to its logical end, gave us the sweatshop, child labor, long hours of labor, insanitary conditions, and bred strife between employer and employee. I have long believed that cooperation between large industrial units, properly supervised and regulated by the Federal Government, is the only method of eliminating the abuses from which labor has suffered under the competitive method. I believe in cooperation and organization in industry. I believe in this for both labor and capital; but as in both cases the result places large power in the hands of a few men, I believe that such organizations should be under the strict regulation and control of the Federal Government in order that they may give the public the maximum amount of good and the minimum amount of evil." Perkins was convinced that profit sharing must be combined with wages if justice was to be done to workingmen. "One of the reasons why I believe in large corporations," he declared, "is that, the ownership being impersonal, you can have profit sharing, welfare work, pensions, accident, and benefit plans, which can not so well be had in small units of business where the ownership is personal. . . . I have long believed and often publicly said that the larger an enterprise becomes the more semi-public it becomes, and the more important are its responsibilities to the public generally." In Perkins's own United States Steel Corporation, 60,000 men were shareholders. Accident prevention had been a major concern of the companies of which Perkins was a director, and the accident rate in his plants had declined by 38 percent, he stated, over the previous decade.

Another enlightened and articulate tycoon was Daniel Guggenheim, whose father, Meyer, had captured control of the American Smelting and Refining Company after a classic struggle involving entrepreneurial skulduggery on a grand scale. The senior Guggenheim was, if possible, even more disliked in Colorado than the Rockefellers. Son Daniel and his brothers, Simon and Solomon, were active partners in the business, and Daniel, in particular, manifested the global thrust of American capitalism by developing company interests in Alaskan copper mines, Bolivian tin, Yukon gold, Chilean nitrate fields, and Belgian Congo diamond operations. Like so many second-generation capitalists, Daniel Guggenheim and his brothers were proud of what they believed to be their enlightened attitudes toward their workers. Asked whether he thought "labor unrest" was increasing or diminishing, Guggenheim declared that it had, in his view, been increasing for many years, and "it will continue to increase unless things are done to prevent it for the benefit of the laboring classes." What, Walsh asked, should be done? Guggenheim recommended steps to lower the high cost of living and moderate "the canker of envy." Beyond that the employer must accept the fact that he had obligations toward his employees. Even more important, the government must take more direct responsibility for improving the conditions of labor. Some critics thought the government had passed too much legislation already. Guggenheim disagreed. "I do not think we have begun to legislate to the extent that we shall in the future. I think we are many years behind the advanced countries in that direction, like England and Germany, in providing for the welfare of our workmen. I think the difference between the rich man and the poor man is very much too great. . . . I am a great believer in the legislation that is being discussed and thought of, where the Federal Government and the State—the employer and the laborer get together, and the laws being enacted where they all participate, covering the laborer's time of working life, and after his injury and after he dies. . . . [Workingmen and women] want more of the comforts and necessities of life and more of the luxuries, and they are entitled to them and ought to get them."

On the subject of charitable foundations Guggenheim was also explicit. While philanthropic foundations such as those the Guggenheims themselves had established performed a useful function, they were often in the position of "taking care of necessities," and that in fact was "the work of the State or the United States, to look after these people. The State must raise its money by taxation—by taxing the fortunes of the people when they die in a sufficient amount to enable it to do those things."

Of the capitalist witnesses, Henry Ford was the most arresting. He gave his testimony in "an absent-minded kind of way," Florence Harriman recalled. "I do not mean absent-minded. It was vague. He had gentle eyes like an animal." He was, nonetheless, an eloquent advocate of the eight-hour day. Ford's management style was a throwback to Andrew Carnegie—highly personal and paternalistic. He and a handful of stockholders, not thousands of large and small investors, owned the Ford Motor Company. He did not go to banks for loans; he did his own financing out of profits. He had recently established a wage policy that was a seven-day wonder. "The minimum daily income [for the worker] under the plan," Ford told the commissioners, "wages plus profits, is $5. The hourly profit-sharing rate, added to wages, is based on the wage rate, and so arranged or graduated as to give those receiving the lowest hourly rate the largest percentage of profits. . . . The working day is 8 hours instead of 9, as before; the week 48 hours."

Under the questioning of the incredulous commissioners—$5 a day!—Ford declared that three classes were eligible for the company's profit-sharing plan: (1) "Married men living with and taking good care of their families; (2) single men over 22 years of age who are of proven, thrifty habits; (3) young men under 22 years of age and women the sole support of next of kin." Close records of the habits and character of the employees were kept, "and every employee . . . able to use the money constructively for the good of self, dependents, and the community . . . is awarded a share." The company maintained a "corps of 40 men, good judges of human nature, who explain opportunity, teach American ways and customs, English language, duties of citizenship, who counsel and help the unsophisticated employees to obtain and maintain comfortable, congenial, and sanitary living conditions, and who also exercise the necessary vigilance to prevent, as far as possible, human frailty from falling into habits or practices detrimental to substantial progress in life." The Ford plan had not been adopted in order to increase profits; in fact, it decreased profits. It had been inaugurated "simply to better the financial and moral status of the men."

Ford took the line that virtually any worker who wished to improve himself or herself could find a job in the plant suitable to his or her capacities. If workers failed in one assignment, they were given another until one was found that they could perform satisfactorily. Under the plan absenteeism had fallen from 10 percent of the work force to three-tenths of 1 percent. "No man is discharged from the service of the company until he has proven utterly unfit from every standpoint. . . . A recent ruling of the company requires the approval of one of four men before a man can finally be dismissed." Of the four, two were Ford and his vice-president.

Was the system of rehabilitation successful?, one of the dazzled commissioners asked. A Catholic parish priest had written to Ford: "The work of the Ford Motor Co. has been of tremendous benefit to my people. Heavy drinking is characteristic of the Poles, I know. Your work, however, has resulted in sobriety now being the rule rather than the exception in my parish." In addition, the company provided space and facilities for an English-language school, taught on a voluntary basis by workers and staff, which enrolled some 1,100 workers. Why, a commissioner asked, had the Ford Motor Company devised such an elaborate and costly plan? It was based, Ford declared, on the assumption that the average worker could not support his family on the wages that prevailed throughout most industries and that the consequent anxiety and worry over this fact undermined his efficiency, or in his words, "made it utterly impossible for the human agency to deliver all the effort it was capable of in fulfilling the best and larger functions for which it was designed at work, at home, and in the community." The company thus had an opportunity "for breaking away from old-time habits and customs. . . . The institution of a new order, treating men like men in man fashion," he continued, "has brought out much of human salvage and proven that the barriers between employers and employees, thought to exist and [that] often do exist, can be largely removed." Then came the rather chilling observation that if "any employee . . . is not living a sober life, or is neglecting his duties as a father and a husband, and if he persists in such course he can not be an associate in our business."

How, a commissioner asked, could Ford call his system a profit-sharing system when he paid out the money weekly before he could possibly know what profits there might be to share? He simply guessed, Ford replied.

Finally, there was the fact that men were rehabilitated by the Ford system. "We have a great many [employees]," Ford declared, "who have been in prison and are outcasts from society. . . . We will guarantee to take every man out of Sing Sing and make a man of him." To the bursts of spontaneous applause that followed Ford's promise to reform criminals, Chairman Walsh replied sternly, "There must be no outward expression of feeling no matter how favorably the statement may impress you."

Ford informed the commissioners that he had more than forty-five plants "from Paris clear around the world."

Andrew Carnegie was the "star" capitalist. He spent the better part of his testimony boasting about his friendly relations with his workers, who called him Andy behind his back and considered his word as good as gold, except, of course, for the unhappy episode at Homestead. He captivated his interrogators by his informal manner and repertoire of stories, in all of which "Andy" was the hero. When Chairman Walsh asked, "What is your businesss?" Carnegie replied in a spirit that would have warmed Cotton Mather's grim heart, "My business is to do as much good in the world as I can. I have retired from other business."

In accordance with his philanthropic inclinations, Carnegie declared that "my first act upon retiring from business was to give $5,000,000 to the workmen of the Carnegie Steel Co. as a parting gift—$4,000,000 as pensions to the men and $1,000,000 to maintain the libraries and halls I had built for them. I say 'I.' My partners did not contribute to these gifts."

To Carnegie "sane publicity" was "the cure for most evils in American industrial life." He had read the testimony of his fellow capitalists, Daniel Guggenheim and August Belmont among them, and "last but not least, the testimony of that unaccountable being, Henry Ford, who declares he could make every convict in Sing Sing a competent, trust-worthy laborer in the vineyard. I am not disposed to question anything that prodigy asserts," Carnegie declared. "Success to him! By all means let us give him a trial. His success here would be no more of a seeming miracle than his success has been with the Ford car."

The most reactionary witnesses were not the great capitalists but the smaller businessmen who considered themselves the frontline fight-ers against unions and radical workingmen. When the commission took testimony in Portland, Oregon, M. C. Banfield, the leader in an em-ployers' association, attacked all unions as an infringement of the work-er's freedom. "Don't tie him down to eight hours . . . keep the men at work; idle hands find mischief. . . . This day and this hearing caused the greatest disturbance, the greatest dissatisfaction in the city among certain classes, of anything that has happened," he indignantly told the commissioners. Another employer witness declared, "You go to taking care of labor—put a man in the shade and fan him, and he will never develop, he will never create." J. V. Paterson, head of a ship construction company, was vehement in his attack on liberal Congress-men, on the clergy, and on Woodrow Wilson. If such persons interfere in the relations between employers and their workers, "We will fight you," Paterson declared. "We will rise with a counter revolution. . . . We have a right to do it. We have got the power. We certainly have the power. We will destroy you if it comes to that. . . . It is coming to a civil war, gentlemen, and we will fight." At the same time Paterson professed admiration for the IWW. The Wobbly organizer had ideals; "he has got something to offer above the sordid, rotten existence."

One of the commission's more ironic interludes came when its members examined the circumstances of the strike on the Harriman railroads, most notably the Illinois Central. That was the family of Florence Harriman's husband, Borden Harriman. The so-called Har-riman strike in 1911 had been an especially bitter one with the loss of many lives and much dynamited railroad property during its course. The railroad officials argued that the strike was intended simply to consolidate a general railroad union, in the spirit of the American Railway Union, and they cited in support of their charge a union circular which declared, "Let us make the federation of shop employees as nearly invincible as possible . . . , to compromise at this time would probably prevent the federation of the shopmen into a nation-wide organization."

In addition to spokesmen for business, the commissioners heard testimony from an array of experts: sociologists, economists, political scientists, and social workers. One of the most appealing witnesses was Frederick Taylor, the exponent of "industrial management." Taylor was one of that remarkable company of young engineers who, like George Westinghouse and Thomas Edison, were drawn irresistibly to the opportunities offered by the expansion of American industry. Born in Germantown, Pennsylvania, in 1856, the son of well-to-do parents, who sent him to Exeter and Harvard, Taylor, plagued by bad eyesight, dropped out of Harvard and went to work for the Midvale Steel Company, where he learned the skills of a patternmaker and machinist. Soon he was foreman of the machine shop, whereupon he attended the Stevens Institute of Technology and received his master's degree in engineering. Armed with both practical and theoretical training, Taylor set about designing large industrial machines. With a colleague he developed an improved process of tempering tool steel. But Taylor was not satisfied simply with the career of an inventor-engineer; he had a vision. It was of harmonious relations between capitalists and workers, or employers and employees. To Taylor the possibility of a mutually beneficial relationship rested on the nature of the employee's work habits as they related to his employer's machine. Every individual worker and every machine had some ideal reciprocal relationship, which could be discovered and described with scientific precision. In this relationship the worker's energy output was the minimum needed for the optimum performance of the machine, an interaction which had to result in the highest level of productivity. Looking about him, Taylor saw workers wasting time and energy simply by inefficient body movement or by an awkward and tiring position in relation to the machine. Even the shoveling of coal or slag could be made easier, more efficient, or scientific. In the Midvale plant Taylor's upper-class antecedents helped win him the right, despite the skepticism of his superiors, to try out his theories. The notion of higher productivity through so-called scientific management procedures was viewed as radical and eccentric by both capital and labor, which thought for the most part in terms of scarcity rather than productivity. That is to say, they were afraid that increased productivity would result in lower prices for the manufacturer and less work for the worker. It did not occur to them that higher productivity might mean higher wages for the worker and, in consequence, more money for him to spend for manufactured goods. To Taylor, talk of restricting productivity was the fundamental heresy of the capital class. To him there was "hardly any worse crime . . . than that of deliberately restricting output. . . . The world's history shows that just as fast as you bring the good things that are needed by man into the world, man takes and uses them. That one fact, the immense increase in the productivity of man, marks the difference between civilized and uncivilized countries [and]. . . it is due to that increase of productivity that the working people of today with all the talk about their misery and horrible treatment . . . have better food, better clothing, and on the whole more comforts than kings had 250 years ago." But the American mentality (for that matter, the world's) was one of scarcity, of reserve, of holding back, of putting by. Mental habits change far more slowly than the conditions that they confront. In the face of new conditions the movement is invariably reactionary except for the boldest spirits. The positive side of the mentality of scarcity is provision for the future—for old age, for children, for coming generations, for "the millions yet unborn" that figured so prominently in the rhetoric of the Founding Fathers. The negative side was a meager, small-spirited parsimony that saw the world as a kind of giant pie to be divided up among all its inhabitants. If some were to have large slices, it was inevitable that others must have very small ones. Taylor understood that the new world was quite different. It offered a breathtaking vision of a future in which the material things of life were not finite—limited items to be fought over sometimes to the death—but virtually infinite as the new technology created a constantly expanding realm of productivity. Whether that new world of heretofore undreamed-of material abundance could in the end satisfy humankind's ancient needs for beauty and meaning was a problem for the future. Feed and clothe men and women first, and then see what their other needs might be. That was certainly the sensible and, more important, the scientific way to proceed.

Taylor declared that every year "as many as a thousand or two thousand men . . . come under the principles of scientific management, who automatically receive an increase of 20 to 100 per cent in wages, and who become the best friends that their employers can have. That is to say, instead of being enemies of their employers, they become their warm, firm friends, and they enter upon careers of prosperity and development such as they have never had an opportunity to have before." In thirty years, Taylor declared, there had never been a strike of men working under scientific management.

Much of the commissioners' questioning had to do with Taylor's methods of overcoming the resistance and hostility of the workers to the introduction of his system, with its higher degree of specialization, into a particular factory. Taylor insisted that his system was not unfriendly to unions. He himself was neutral on the issue. To the charge that workers under his system, seeing that they were better provided for than those who had joined unions, failed to join a union or dropped out of a union they were already in, Taylor suggested that unions in their present form were a transitional stage in employer-employee relations. They were "fighting" organizations, which would in time be replaced by "educational institutions for mutual and helpful instruction."

Ida Tarbell, one of the original muckrakers and dean of women journalists, if not of the men as well, was an enthusiastic advocate of scientific management. It was her conviction that throughout American industry "there is a growing feeling that the man—the common man— is worth a great deal more than the employers and the managements of industry have ever dreamed; that there is a growing feeling among many people that the most important thing in the world on the side of business is the development of the common man. That to give him a full opportunity and full justice is the most important industrial problem that we have." The instrument by means of which this justice should and would be done was scientific management.

Taylor's scientific management techniques were highly controversial. The report of the Commission on Industrial Relations, referring to his testimony before it, noted that "it must not be overlooked that the whole scheme of scientific management, and especially the gathering up and systemizing of the knowledge formerly the possession of the workmen, tends enormously to add to the strength of capitalism. This fact, together with the greater ease of displacement . . . must make the security and continuity of employment inherently more uncertain."

Another expert witness was Ira B. Cross, assistant professor of economics at the University of California. "I do not know of any workman," Cross testified, "who is willing to go before a court feeling that he is going to receive a square deal. . . . It has taken centuries to educate the people to the belief that workmen are no longer slaves and that

they have rights before the courts, that they have equal rights with
their employers."

The same witness pointed to another basic cause of industrial
unrest: the fact that "the employers feel that they are endowed with
natural inalienable rights, and that they have the right to run their
business as they see fit. They feel that they have been given these rights
by the Constitution of the United States and the Declaration of Independence." However, the time had come, certainly in the opinion
of workmen with any degree of political consciousness as well as in the
minds of those concerned with reform, to realize "that there are no
such things as natural inalienable rights, that an employer can not run
his business just as he pleases; that there are other people in this world,
society, workmen, the public at large, that have rights, and that industry
should be run in accordance with the rights of society, and not in
accordance with what the employer thinks are his natural rights. The
employer should be taught that he does not have these natural rights.
Rights are given to the individual by the society in which he lives, and
it can and should protect itself at all times against the abuses of any
class of citizens."

Testimony before the commission brought out the extent of interlocking boards of directors in major corporations. Adolph Lewisohn, for example, was a director of eight banks, trust companies, and
mining and manufacturing corporations. The economist Roger Babson
told the commissioners that the only interest Wall Street had in the
industrial plants it controlled was in profits. "As long as dividends are
coming along Wall Street is satisfied with the management. . . . As a
rule it makes little difference whether they are being produced by fair
means or foul, by antiquated machinery or by modern machinery, by
good or poor management. They had no particular prejudice against
labor, as such, it was to them only an element in the production of
dividends." Babson supported certain forms of profit sharing, but he
wished to see it tied to greater productivity by individuals.

The Minnesota Congressman Charles A. Lindbergh was summoned as an expert on costs and prices. It was Lindbergh's conviction
that "No permanent reduction in the cost of living in favor of the
masses can be secured as long as there is no relative rule for fixing a
reasonable return for farm or other products and for labor, as compared with the so-called reasonable return for capital." There were,
in his view, "two remedies which can be applied. One is pure socialism,

which the people generally have refused to accept." The other was "to take from the banks the exclusive privilege of controlling the money and credit. . . ." The relationship between wages and profits must yield to some rational form of analysis and generally agreed-upon formula, "so that both the toilers and the capitalists, as long as the system is followed out, will receive a proportionately fair return for the services that are rendered in the one case by the employment of capital and in the other case by the laborer."

Amos Richards Eno Pinchot was another witness before the Commission on Industrial Relations. Amos, who had been graduated from Yale in 1897, fought in the Spanish-American War, and been graduated from the Columbia Law School, had joined his older brother, Gifford Pinchot, in helping start the Progressive Party. Young Pinchot aligned himself with the radical wing of the Progressives and declared himself for public ownership of forests, waterpower, and other energy sources, including coal and oil. He was also a strong advocate of unions and collective bargaining. He called the attention of the commission "to the fact that even college presidents and professors of economics, who are often the last to look at labor questions from a human or practical point of view," had come around to the support of unions.

Few men were better informed about the shenanigans of high finance than Samuel Untermyer, a former corporation lawyer turned reformer. He began by stating his position on socialism. "Notwithstanding its injustice and many other shortcomings, I believe in the capitalistic system as our only present solution. Socialism is a beautiful, iridescent dream," he declared. "It is useful mainly as a protest against the cruel inequities of existing social conditions. Civilization owes to socialism a great debt of gratitude for its idealism and self-sacrifice and for its restraint upon the grosser excesses of capitalism. . . . Socialism, communism, syndicalism, and like theories of government are thriving mainly on the abuses of capitalism—its stupid lack of imagination and of enlightened selfishness. Capitalism is more powerful, more rampant, more despotic, and less controlled by law or public sentiment with us than in any other country. It lacks the most elemental sense of justice and fights every inch of the way regardless of the merits of the controversy. Of all its blunders its blindness to and disregard of the welfare of the industrial workers who are its chief asset is the most flagrant, short-sighted, and unpardonable. . . . If capital were less obsessed with its own righteousness and sense of security the growth of socialism would soon come to an end." Untermyer then pointed out the shortcomings of the states' rights doctrine. "State lines mean little nowadays," he declared, "except the opportunity to obstruct reform and foster abuses. . . . Uniformity is impossible under separate State laws. . . . Without uniformity to take care of the elements of competition we can make no progress with industrial reform. The world has never known or dreamed of anything to compare with our stupendous corporate entities. They are fabulous in their size and concentration of money and power. They have grown up almost overnight and they are an ominous threat to our institutions, unless justly and rigidly controlled."

In Untermyer's view, there was "a lot of loose and irresponsible talk about our having too much law and too much . . . regulation of business. The fact is we are suffering from the absence of regulative law over these vast aggregations. . . ." Those laws that were passed were so watered down as a result of corporate pressures as to be almost useless.

At the hearings Terence Powderly appeared rather like a ghost of the past. After the collapse of the Knights of Labor, Powderly had become a highly successful lawyer and then an officer in the Bureau of Immigration. It was as an expert on Chinese immigration that he was invited to testify.

An important subject of scrutiny by the commissioners was the influence of the philanthropic foundations that were springing up in considerable numbers, following the lead of Andrew Carnegie. The Carnegie Institution of Washington held an endowment fund of $22,000,000, the income to be used in a wide variety of scientific and sociological researches. The Carnegie Foundation for the Advancement of Teaching was set up next, with an endowment of $15,000,000, its principal purpose being to provide pensions for retired college professors. Another Carnegie foundation with a $30,000,000 capital was established to reward deeds of courage. The Endowment for International Peace was founded to "promote peace and amity among nations," and the library fund, perhaps the most famous of all, was established to enable towns and cities to build libraries. The Carnegie Institute of Pittsburgh had, by 1914, provided scholarships for more than 3,000 students from forty-two states, many of them the sons of workmen in Carnegie enterprises. Women were admitted as well, but while some Carnegie Institute male graduates went on to jobs paying as much as $6,000 a year, the brightest women earned "splendid wages, fifteen, sixteen or seventeen hundred dollars a year." In 1914 the various benefactions of the various Carnegie institutions and foundations amounted to $324,657,399, approximately half the entire Federal budget for the year 1915.

The Rockefellers' first substantial benefaction was the Rockefeller Institute for Medical Research. The Rockefeller General Education Board made generous sums available for the appointment of professors of secondary education in prominent universities, provided only that such appointments be approved by the board. Ex-president Charles Eliot of Harvard testified before the Commission on Industrial Relations that the Rockefeller board, of which he was a director, had "brought into education . . . $200,000,000 . . . since 1905." Eliot, it is interesting to note, blamed "industrial unrest" primarily on the unions—"the closed shop, the boycott, union label, limited output."

When Carnegie was questioned by Commissioner Walsh about the danger of "great endowments" exerting undue influence upon educational institutions, Carnegie referred to President Eliot's testimony and then added that "he is one of my pensioners. He ought to know."

William H. Allen, an economist who had served as director of the Board of Municipal Research in Chicago, was highly critical of the role of foundations (many of which, it might be noted, contributed to the Board of Municipal Research). He urged that the government require a charter for all foundations "engaged in interstate philanthropy" and that a number of other steps be taken to prevent foundations from propagandizing for particular political and economic viewpoints. "No sooner does one of the great foundations turn toward or against a man or an institution than veritable hordes of people or institutions needing money or favor also turn. Newspapers turn. Subordinates turn. And the response is quicker, too, in the field of philanthropy and education than ever it was in the field of business, because dependence is more communicative than avarice." Allen went on to list seven books that contained extensive arguments against socialism. Of their six authors, one was dead and four of the remaining five were with Carnegie foundations, two as heads. The Rockefeller General Education Board distributed its largess to such groups as "The Boys' Corn Club movement," "The Girls' Canning Club movement," "Educating the Negro," and similar enterprises, with the accompanying news stories written by Ivy Lee, the Rockefellers' premier publicist.

Tom Watson expressed his opinion of philanthropic foundations succinctly: "Carnegie cuts his wages and robs his workmen of a million dollars. He gives ten per cent of it to Charity; and the Pharisees all cry out 'blessed by Carnegie.' Rockefeller plunders the people to the neat extent of Ten Millions per year on the oil monopoly. He puts little dabs of the booty here and there among Colleges and Schools and they flap their wings and crow; while the press says, 'blessed by Rockefeller.' The pity of it is that humbuggery is so victorious. . . . Where will it stop? How can human nature stand it always! Let no man dream that it can last. The sword of Damocles never hung by a slenderer thread than does the false system of to-day. When men suffer it is harder."

Amos Pinchot, who had testified in favor of unions, also had some reflections on foundations. He wondered aloud what the effect would be on the acceptance by "universities, schools and institutions" of generous grants of money from such sources. "Take, for example," he said, "the influence upon courses of economics in schools, colleges, and universities. Suppose a young instructor of economics were giving a course of lectures upon industrial production and the relations between capital and labor. . . . He might give his frank opinion of the results of absentee landlordism and of the whole structure of undemocracy and concentrated absolutism which companies like the Colorado Fuel & Iron and the United States Steel Corporation have inaugurated. Now, what I say is this: The gratitude which the faculty and trustees of a university ought to feel to an instructor who showed the students the utter unsoundness of production under a system of absolutism might seriously conflict with the gratitude which they could not but feel toward those whose gifts were making the university prosperous and useful." The result must be some "strain . . . a lack of sympathy between himself and the members of the faculty and the trustees, whose duty it was to care for the university's financial well-being." Sabbaticals might not be forthcoming, nor opportunities to attend scholarly meetings, perhaps not even promotions. The issue was not hypothetical. Pinchot informed the commissioners "that the smaller colleges of this country are full of instructors and professors who have not been deliberately driven from larger universities on account of economic opinions unfriendly to benevolent exploiters in industry, but who have nevertheless found their chairs in the large universities untenable, and have left them owing to influences which were irresistible but too subtle to complain about aloud."

John Haynes Holmes, the popular rector of the Church of the Messiah (later called the Community Church) in New York City, was another severe critic of philanthropic foundations on the ground that the money dispensed by such foundations properly belonged to the workers or, at the least, to the people in general. When asked his solution for "industrial unrest," Holmes declared that he looked for a "union between two great movements,"—that is, "socialism . . . state socialism, the public ownership of all those things which properly ethically belong to the public, by which I mean forest lands, mines, railroads, the telegraph, the telephone, public transportation, and public utilities; combined with cooperation . . . the coming together of the people to do their buying, manufacturing, distributing, and in that way solving the problems of their own economic life."

The most intriguing exchange between the commissioners and the multitude of witnesses who appeared before them was that involving Clarence Darrow. Darrow was another American original; he was, in addition, a man of the new age, skeptical, often cynical, a disbeliever in all the old pieties that his fellow Americans put so much store by. He was at the same time, not surprisingly, a driven and haunted man, poised between two worlds. Like Mark Twain, he viewed much of American life as a vast fraud or sham and the human being as a fragile and tragic creature. Yet he was as much a reformer and dreamer as William Lloyd Garrison or Wendell Phillips or his friend and client Big Bill Haywood. He too dreamed against his experience of a new and better human order. He had given his best talents to the exploited and the persecuted. "His clothes were a mess," William Allen White wrote of Darrow, "wrinkled, untidy—entirely clean but slomicky, if I may coin a word to fit his dishabille. He slouched when he walked, and he walked like a cat . . . he was essentially a lonesome soul, always seeking the unattainable . . . hobbled by his own cynicism, but always stumbling on . . . a complex man, a rebel like Eugene Debs." To White, Darrow and Bryan and Debs, so different in temperament, were "the outposts of that American revolution which rose in the last decade of the nineteenth century. . . ."

Hutchins Hapgood called Darrow "the great interpreter of the radical labor movement. . . . With great personal charm, unfailing eloquence, racy irony, and yet deep and genuine sympathy for the underprivileged, [he] was a towering figure." He was one of the few people, Hapgood wrote, who realized that a form of slavery still existed in the United States, "that along with our ideals of political freedom there was an industrial oligarchy or despotism; that this industrial situation is corrupting our political institutions, and that either we must straighten out our industrial condition or give up our political ideas. . . ."

Now Darrow, who had so often cross-examined witnesses, was himself cross-examined by the commissioners, who clearly found him a compelling and exotic figure. Walsh began with a leading question: Did Darrow believe that the laws were equally administered between the rich and the poor? By no means, replied Darrow, who proceeded to deliver a brilliant lecture on the relation of law to society. "Men do not act from logic and reason," he declared, "but from impulse. Any man with good intellect can give a good reason for anything he wants to say, and his opinion on either side of the case he is on is always logical if [he] is an able man. . . . The whole law has been made and administered by the controlling force of society, like everything else in the world, and it could not be any other way." The McNamara case still rankled with Darrow, and he brought it up as an illustration of the way that power abuses the law with impunity when it wishes to do so. Could Darrow give other examples? He was glad to oblige and started with the injunction against the strikers in the Pullman strike and the arrest of Debs, giving in the process a devastating critique of the use of the injunction in labor disputes. How might the law be changed to give a fairer hearing to workers? Walsh asked. Darrow could see no sure redress. Money bought the law. The law, in consequence, protected property.

What was the cause of the "general feeling of industrial unrest in the country"? Darrow replied, "Well, of course, life is unrest. It is idle to talk about curing unrest, because when you get it cured you are dead. It is that aspiration of people for power and to live; that is the cause. And you can not cure anything in this world. You can only help along to new adjustments and better adjustments." The great mass of people were not subtle reasoners, but they knew injustice when they saw it. "They know that all the oil there is in the earth [is] owned by one great corporation. . . . And they know that perhaps a dozen men in the United States are influential enough to shut down the wheels of industry when they want to; and they know that the coal mines are owned by a few people . . . and that the great mass of men are struggling along, in debt, hard up, can't get their teeth filled, and can't get anything the rest of us can get; that's about all they do know; and that's enough to know. And there will be unrest as long as that exists, and if you cure it why they will get restless about something else, of course." The only temporary remedy, in Darrow's opinion, was organization, union shops, and collective bargaining.

Harris Weinstock, who put his faith in the initiative, referendum, and recall, soon took the lead in questioning Darrow. Why, he asked, was he so skeptical about the ability of the mass of the people to make, through the ballot, such changes in the system as would make it more just and equitable? "Suppose the great body of the wage receivers of the Nation felt the time was ripe for the government to take over the coal mines, for example. . . . What could prevent it?"

"Congress, the Senate, the President, the Constitution and the Supreme Court."

Did not the people elect, or through their elected representatives appoint, all public officials to carry out their will?

Yes, but they came from very different segments of society, were elected at different times, and represented vastly different notions of a just order. To get them to act in concert on a particular measure at a particular time, "to get them all to say this thing together; never has been done in any very substantial way. You have to get them all, and have got to get them all at once. It is too clumsy."

What about the initiative, referendum, and recall—couldn't they bring about desired social order peacefully?

"All of them," Darrow replied, "are not worth a pinch of snuff. . . . Instead of trying to find out whether there are any fundamental causes that tend to the great inequality between men today we are tinkering at little fool symptoms and spending the time and life of a whole generation curing some little symptom and leaving the world no better off than before."

But were not the workers at fault in using violence to achieve their ends rather than depending on the law? Weinstock persisted.

"If you were a lawyer," Darrow replied, "you would not have such unlimited confidence in the law. The law cannot forbid any of the passions in the human heart. . . . The human heart does not take any account of statutes at all. It just acts. As the heart drives the blood around through the system, it does not take any kind of law."

"But must the law not protect life and property against the vicious and criminal?"

"Well, the vicious and the criminal have the property and should protect it themselves. . . . The idea of punishment is formed on the theory that a man knows right and knows wrong and fully and wickedly chooses the wrong. . . . A man is a creature of circumstances. He acts from motives. He goes where he must. Nobody is entitled to either credit or blame for what he does; they do it; that is all." The instinct to punish grew directly and simply out of the desire for vengeance.

As for the question of changing the condition of the workers, that was not a matter of law, of legislation or the Constitution; it was a matter of capturing the imagination of the public. "Nothing so changes and shifts as public opinion, and nothing is so powerful. We are . . . victims in its hands."

But what about the fact that "the American people . . . have the reputation of standing up for what is right and condemning what is wrong?" Weinstock asked.

"If they had that reputation, I never heard of it," Darrow replied. "I think they are about the poorest class on earth, as far as that goes."

"The American people as a unit?" Weinstock replied, obviously incredulous at this heresy.

"As to standing up for what is right, and going back on what is wrong. In the first place, we are not a Nation at all, we are a conglomeration of everything from everywhere. We have no nationality. You could depend pretty well on what an Englishman would do, because they are one people; or what the Germans would do; but you cannot tell what the Americans would do. It will take hundreds of years for them to get welded into a country. . . ."

Weinstock could hardly believe his ears. "Are we to understand . . . , Mr. Darrow, that the American people, you believe, stand up for the wrong and condemn the right?"

"Right or wrong cuts no figure. People like it because it is a spectacular thing; it is imagination that moves people. Something captures them. Right or wrong cuts no figure in the world anywhere as to moving people. . . . Napoleon is possibly the most popular idol of the world; maybe he had good qualities, but he was popular because of the great many people he killed, and his dash and brilliancy. Morals had nothing to do with it; just the spectacular part."

Weinstock returned to the question of punishment for wrongdoing.

Darrow: "I would not punish anybody for anything."

Weinstock: "You think it is a delusion and a snare?"

Darrow: "I think it is a barbarism. I don't think that anyone should be confined. I think that there are people that are antisocial in their nature and for many years to come there will be people that need confinement. It is not because of any wrong that they have done but because of a wrong that has been done to them, and they should be treated like hospital patients and kept until they recover or never turned loose."

Until such an ideal day, how would Darrow recommend dealing with criminals? "What we will do," he replied, "is to abuse them and misjudge them and practice all kinds of mistreatment." But he could already see a great change in public opinion toward a more humane treatment of confined persons. "The attitude is growing very fast. I don't believe it will be 25 years until there will be no more prisons, practically. We will be looked on as barbarians for doing those things. There will be people confined, but not in that attitude." To Darrow "everybody is innocent." Rockefeller, who represented to Darrow's mind "the most antisocial thing in the world of business to-day, is doubtless as innocent as anybody who looks at it in any other way and justifies himself to himself, the same as the rest of us. . . . You say a thing is wrong if it sort of shocks your sense of justice and fitness, and it is right if it does not. There is no way to base it. There is no foundation for right or wrong, so nobody can tell." No, there was a range of human emotions from fear and hate to love. Love, Darrow admitted, was "higher" than hate, and one might hope that the "higher" emotion would grow and expand, but he had little confidence that it would. "We are always being ruled by hatred and by fear, and the imagination of the world is always being captured by it," but perhaps "in the evolution of things" love would triumph.

As for the capacity of the law to ensure justice, Darrow quoted Anatole France: " 'Of course the law is perfectly equal; it provides that it is a crime for anybody to sleep under a bridge, whether he is a millionaire or a pauper.' But the millionaires," Darrow added, "don't sleep under bridges."

In other words, Weinstock declared, Darrow held that "while theoretically we are a free country, practically we are not; that while theoretically you and I and the rest of us have our civil and political rights, practically we have not."

"That applies to the weaker." In Darrow's view, the British workingman enjoyed more basic rights than his American counterpart.

"You mean," Weinstock persisted, "that all the progressive laws that have been passed in this country . . . and in the various Commonwealths in the last decade or two, including such laws as workmen's compensation acts, maximum and minimum wage acts, eight-hour day for women and safety acts, and the initiative, referendum and recall, are mere patches, are little makeshifts, that they don't touch the fundamentals, and therefore are of little value?"

"That is about the way I put that."

When John Lennon took over the questioning, he asked Darrow what he thought the outcome would be of "the struggle of the laboring class for better conditions."

"There is no doubt," Darrow replied, undoubtedly to the surprise of the commissioners, "but what the future is to have labor socialism. Whether you call it socialism, or labor, or any of the progressive ideas, the fact is that the imagination of men is working that way."

Were the commissioners then to understand that Darrow himself was an advocate of socialism? Not exactly. "Socialism says that you have got to abolish rent, capital, and interest, and have a cooperative Commonwealth where all production is done by the State—for the people collectively. Now it may be that they are right. The trouble is there is no way to determine exactly how anything will work out; there is no certainty that any one road is the only road. Of course, I am sympathetic with socialism, sympathetic with single tax and labor unions and pretty nearly any new thing that comes along; though I do discriminate a little I like to see the disturbance going on and giving them all a chance. If I was laying out a scheme I would say let's get the land monopolies first; let's take the mines and the forests and the railroads and see how they come out, and if that don't work let's get busy and do some more. We won't rest. I don't think anybody can tell in advance the absolutely necessary way or the easiest way. . . ."

Did the commission, in Darrow's view, serve any purpose? Yes. Since public opinion was "the greatest force there is in the country" and the commission had engaged the attention of the public, it was bound to do some good. "The recommendations that this commission will send out will have some effect on public opinion; whether you will get it into laws nobody knows. . . . But from my standpoint the more fundamental and radical your recommendations are the more good they will do; and the more you recognize the division of classes and the injustice of it, the more good it will do. . . ."

There was "no final remedy for unrest excepting the grave. We are all the time—society is all the time—in a state of unrest. . . . Society . . . is operating around certain orbits, and some great thing comes along and changes the orbits, and perhaps the resistance is less or perhaps it is greater. We can change only the immediate things. If we all get rich, we will have cancer or tuberculosis, or a tumor or corns, or something to bother us. . . .

"The righteous man suffers the same as the unrighteous. The good is crucified as often as is the evil, and evil triumphs as often as the good. There is no moral purpose in the universe that we can see." The commissioners might make of it what they wished; that was the way the world appeared to Clarence Darrow, a man of the new consciousness.

22

Ludlow

In the interminable war between capital and labor, the bloodiest battlefield may have been the mining towns of Colorado. During the hearings of the Commission on Industrial Relations, a coal miners' strike in Ludlow, Colorado, spread lurid headlines across the country. Since 1894 martial law had been declared ten times in Colorado as well as several times in Idaho. After the brutally suppressed coal mine strikes in 1903 the operators had replaced the American, Welsh, and Irish miners with presumably more tractable immigrants: Finns, Mexicans, Poles, Italians, and Japanese. A witness before the commission stated that the roughly 200 mines in Colorado had on their payrolls 7,786 laborers, representing thirty-two different nationalities, many of them illiterate in their native language (some of them thought Rockefeller was president of the United States). A miner of greater than average experience and sophistication described the camp superintendents as "a most uncouth, ignorant, immoral, and in many instances, the most brutal set of men that we have ever met . . . blasphemous bullies. . . ."

John Lawson, an official of the United Mine Workers and himself a miner, described the miner's sense of powerlessness in a community where everything, including the agencies of the law, was owned by the mine operators. "The miner," he declared, "is surrounded, not by his friends, not by people who have taken an interest in him, but he is in this land owned by the corporation that owns the homes, that owns the boarding houses, that owns every single thing there is there . . . not only the mines, but all the grounds, all the buildings, all the places of recreation, as well as the schools and church buildings." Company spies reported to their bosses any inclination on the part of particular miners to complain about conditions in the mines or in the camps, and such "troublemakers" were promptly given their walking papers.

The safety record of the Rockefeller mines was as deplorable as the wages and hours of work. Hardly a year passed without one or more serious explosions in which a number of miners were killed. When seventy-six miners were killed in the second Primero mine, the pastor of the First Presbyterian Church denounced the company from his pulpit, declaring that the miners' lives had been sacrificed on the "altar of corporate cupidity." He immediately received an indignant phone call from the mine's manager, L. M. Bowers, who denounced him as a bedfellow of the "muckraking magazines, socialistic preachers, trust-busting political shysters, and . . . the agitators and anarchists."

Under such conditions, it is not surprising that in the fall of 1913 the miners responded to the Western Federation of Miners' strike call. Violence soon flared. Military courts usurped the authority of the civil courts, the writ of habeas corpus was suspended, and strike leaders were arrested without warrants and held in prison without bail or formal charges. Bowers wrote to Rockefeller that the Black Hand was behind the strike. Members of the Black Hand had intimidated the loyal miners by "the hellish villainy that these creatures possess. . . . Hayes, vice-president of the United Mine Workers of America, together with representatives here in this State, are the principal mischief makers. They are able to load some newspapers with their lying statements and are permitted to gather gangs and crowds together on the streets, making speeches that would scarcely be permitted in any European country. Old 'Mother' Jones has been on the ground for two weeks," Bowers added, "but Saturday, we understand, the governor ordered her to be taken to the State line and ordered not to return."

The company erected eight large searchlights, each of which swept the countryside for miles. To Bowers it was all-out war. "I believe," he wrote to Rockefeller, "that if the business men do not awake from their indifference and take aggressive measures on a large scale to right the wrongs that are being inflicted upon the business of this country, we will see a revolution, we will be under military government and our Republic will end where so many others have ended."

It was clear that Bowers was determined to do all in his power to prevent such an eventuality. In November he wrote that he had secured "the cooperation of all the bankers of the city, who have had three or four interviews with our little cowboy governor. . . ." The bankers told the governor that they would lend the state all the money it needed to "maintain the militia and afford ample protection so that our miners can return to work, or give protection to men who are anxious to come here from Texas, New Mexico, and Kansas, together with some states further east. Besides the bankers, the chambers of commerce, the real estate exchange, together with a great many of the best business men, have been urging the Governor to take steps to drive these vicious agitators out of the State. Another mighty power has been rounded up in behalf of the operators by the gathering together of fourteen of the editors of the most important newspapers in Denver, Pueblo, Trinidad, Walsenburg, Colorado Springs, and others of the larger places in the State. They passed resolutions demanding that the governor bring this strike to an end, as they found . . . that the real issue was the demand for recognition of the union. . . ."

In another letter Bowers referred to "the uncalled-for and vicious demand of the union leaders in this State for recognition of the union and suppression of the open shop."

"You are fighting the good fight," Rockefeller replied, "which is not only in the interests of your own company but of the other companies of Colorado and of the business interests of the entire country and the laboring classes quite as much."

A few weeks later Bowers, suffering from indigestion and insomnia, reported that "there are several hundred sluggers camped within the strike zone, who have rifles and ammunition in large quantities secreted, and we are facing a guerrilla warfare that is likely to continue for months to come."

As the fighting spread, strikers attacked mines run by imported strikebreakers, and there were casualties on both sides. The Chandler mine, owned by the Victor Company, capitulated after being besieged for some thirty hours. Trinidad was reported in the hands of strikers, "including many fighting Greeks brought in from New Mexico," according to Bowers. "The President has not ordered out Federal troops," he complained in another telegram, "notwithstanding repeated appeals from the governor, chamber of commerce, bankers, coal operators and numerous other organizations. . . ."

Mediators, sent by President Wilson to try to negotiate a settlement, reported that the mine operators became "wild men" when the strike was discussed. "They fly into a rage, curse the federal government, and froth at the mouth." One of the mediators, dismayed at the intransigent spirit, wrote that "the state ought to be disenfranchised." The United Mine Workers considered calling out all the miners in the country.

On April 14, 1914, Bowers wired Rockefeller: "Following withdrawal of troops by order of the governor an unprovoked attack upon small force of militia by 200 strikers. Forced fighting resulting in probable loss of 10 or 15 strikers. Only one militiaman killed. Ludlow tent colony of strikers totally destroyed by burning; 200 tents; generally followed by explosions, showing ammunition and dynamite stored in them. Expect further fighting to-day."

Bowers's report was, to say the least, incomplete. In Ludlow two of the strike leaders, Louis Tikas and James Fyler, had been arrested and brought before a mine guard named K. C. Linderfelt, who had been commissioned a lieutenant in the state guard. After abusing the two men, Linderfelt broke his rifle over Tikas's head and then fired four bullets into his unconscious body. Fyler and four others—Bartoloti, Costa, Rubina, and a boy named Snyder—were killed. Under circumstances never entirely clear, the miners' tents were set afire. Twelve children and two women, hiding in an excavation under a large tent, died from smoke inhalation.

What was soon called the Ludlow Massacre brought Emma Goldman to Denver. She found that twenty-seven members of the IWW had been thrown in jail for trying to exercise their right of free speech and then put in the sweatbox for refusing to work. Goldman helped organize a protest march, and the Wobblies were freed. In New York Upton Sinclair organized a "Silent Parade" of protest in front of Rockefeller's office. Public excitement was heightened by the premature explosion of a bomb in a New York tenement house in which three anarchists and an unknown woman were killed. Rumor had it that the bomb was being constructed to blow up Rockefeller, and Berkman wrote Emma Goldman that the dead men had been badly beaten by the police at the Union Square demonstration of the unemployed some weeks earlier. "Though my sympathies were with the men who protested against social crimes by a resort to extreme measures," Goldman wrote, "I nevertheless felt now that I could never again participate in or approve of methods that jeopardized innocent lives."

Berkman was determined to make the funeral of the anarchists the occasion for a protest gathering. Although he was refused a permit to hold the rally by the police, he slipped through a police cordon around Union Square and managed to address the huge crowd gathered about the speakers' stand while the police stood by, not daring to try to intervene. The ashes of the anarchists were thereafter placed in an urn in the shape of a clenched fist and put on display in the office of *Mother Earth,* decorated with wreaths and red and black banners.

The *New York Times,* never conspicuous for prolabor sympathies, described the attack of the Colorado national guardsmen on the miners' camp at Ludlow as "Worse than the order that sent the Light Brigade into the jaws of death, worse in its effect than the Black Hole of Calcutta." George Creel was one of the first newspapermen to arrive on the scene. At a rally in front of the statehouse at Denver, Creel attacked those who were responsible, especially the governor and the Rockefellers, Sr. and Jr., who controlled a third of the mines of the state. "They were," he declared, "traitors to the people, accessories to the murder of babes." Lennon and Thruston Ballard were convinced that "there were several days when there was positive danger of a national revolution growing out of this Colorado strike."

As the fighting continued throughout the state, Rockefeller clearly began to lose his nerve, wiring Bowers to suggest that the operators agree to accept the mediation of "three disinterested men," but the manager wired back that it was too late for any halfway measures, that the mine operators of Colorado were determined to break the strike. "Daylight begins to break," Bowers wired. ". . . Throughout State thousands of subscribers stopping muckraking papers, who are largely responsible for this outbreak of passion among the working people." As public criticism of Rockefeller mounted, his telegrams urging mediation took on a tone of urgency. The Federal Council of Churches of Christ in America meanwhile entered the fray with a report highly "unfavorable" to the mine operators, pointing out, "The coal companies are determined that their men shall not be organized." Once again Bowers opposed any concession: "Our rugged stand has won us every foot we have gained, and we know that the organization is bankrupt in this field, while the big men in the union are at swords' points because of their failure here. So to move an inch from our stand at the time that defeat seems certain for the enemy would be decidedly unwise. . . . The political gang at Washington are at their wits' end to find some way to get out of the pit they help[ed] these leaders to dig, so we are encouraged to stick to the job till we win."

The strikes dragged on for four more months before the union, its treasury exhausted, its forces scattered and demoralized, called it quits. It had spent more than $6,000,000 in the course of the strike. It was a bitter defeat, and it was doubtlessly made more bitter by the flood of propaganda issued by the coal mine operators describing their beneficence to the miners, strikers and strikebreakers alike. Christmas candy was distributed "to all the children in our camps, numbering about 3,000 which inlude those of former strikers," the president of the Colorado Fuel & Iron Company announced piously.

Frank Walsh was well aware of the dramatic possibilities inherent in the Colorado strikes. The commissioners decided to hold hearings in Colorado. "If we have a good hearing there," Walsh assured his colleagues, "it will stamp our commission all over with success." After taking testimony from a parade of witnesses who gave hair-raising recitals of corporate villainy, of miserable conditions and ruthless exploitation by the operators, the commissioners returned to New York and summoned John D. Rockefeller, Jr., to the stand. Small, neat, prim, almost boyish, Rockefeller exuded the charm associated with uncounted millions. He made a striking contrast with his principal interrogator, Chairman Walsh. Seeing Mother Jones in the audience, Rockefeller went over to her, shook her hand, and said, quite audibly, "I wish that you would come down to my office at your convenience. There are so many things on which you can enlighten me."

That doughty old woman seemed disconcerted for one of the few times in her life. "I want you to come out to Colorado with me and see the things I have seen," she replied. "I am sure what you will see will make you do things which will make you one of the country's greatest men."

"I am afraid you are inclined to throw compliments," Rockefeller rejoined.

"Oh, no," she responded, "I am more inclined to throw brickbats."

Rockefeller's defense was the simplest possible one: ignorance, hence innocence. He had no idea of the terrible things that were being done in his name. He would never have condoned such actions. He didn't even know the wages or the hours of labor of the miners, had visited Colorado only briefly ten years before. He was not opposed to unions. As for better working conditions and higher wages, he "most heartily" favored them. "I have no desire to defend any conditions that are justly subject to criticism."

"You are like the church says," Garretson noted, "you are 'growing in grace.'"

At the end of Rockefeller's testimony the audience applauded. Clearly the capitalist had triumphed. Instead of being pilloried, as Walsh and some of the other commissioners had intended, the younger Rockefeller had appeared the very model of an enlightened capitalist (the *New York Times* noted that he had "never wavered from his entire self-possession and courteous humor"). Even Mother Jones was charmed. "I don't hold the boy responsible," she said. "When I have a good motherly talk with him I believe I can help him take another view of the situation among his miners out west," and Rockefeller announced, "I find we are in full accord upon most of the subjects in which we are mutually interested."

Walsh's aggressive and hostile interrogation of the polite and modest witness caused widespread criticism. The *New York Times* denounced his "illogical and absurd utterances," while the *Sun* observed that his "notions were at once . . . loose and violent." But Walsh had other cards to play. The commission's researchers had gathered a number of the letters between Rockefeller and the manager of the mines at Ludlow, L. M. Bowers, which indicated that he was far more familiar with the tactics and strategy employed by his manager than he had been willing to admit. Armed with the new evidence, Walsh called Rockefeller back to the stand several weeks later. The ambassador from Austria-Hungary noted that "Mr. Walsh showed considerable feeling and gave the impression that he was personally hostile to Mr. Rockefeller. . . . Mr. Rockefeller appeared to realize that Chairman Walsh intended to handle him roughly."

Walsh began by reading from the newly acquired letters, in one of which Bowers urged that the company refuse to bargain with the union "until our bones are bleached as white as chalk in these Rocky Mountains," to which Rockefeller had responded, "We feel that what you have done is right and fair and that the position you have taken in regard to the unionizing of the mines is in the interest of the employees of the company." Even George Creel, who had done so much to focus national attention on the situation in Colorado and on the Ludlow Massacre in particular, felt a twinge of pity for Rockefeller.

"In spite of my bitterness I could not help feeling sorry for the man who sweated under Frank's merciless questioning," he wrote. A reporter for the *Masses* noted, "Rockefeller's face grew whiter and whiter until it was ashy. His features seemed to sink back into the contours of his face. . . . Perspiration poured down his cheeks." The newspapers were filled with accounts of the session, and a triumphant Walsh, who had seen his prey almost escape earlier, declared, "I believe, after all, that the daily newspaper is the greatest avenue of information. The masses do not take time to read anything else." Walsh boasted, "I am sure you will not think it boastful when I say I turned the young man inside out and left him without a single justification for anything that took place in Colorado. Of course," he added, "to get at the truth I had to get a little rough at times, which I did not hesitate to do. . . ." To the charge that he failed to show "judicial poise," he told a reporter, "I consider that commodity as a great bar to human progress."

Walsh's tactics aroused indignation in many quarters where free enterprise was as sacred as the Holy Scriptures. The *Nation* denounced his tactics as "offensive and absurd." The *Washington Post* protested, "Mr. Walsh feeds solely upon rancor and hate." The *New York Herald* expressed the hope that "Mr. Wilson will undo the great mistake he made in letting this man loose upon the country." Given a free rein, "he would set afoot influences that would lay waste the industrial centers."

Liberal journals like the *Survey* and *Harper's Weekly* acclaimed him enthusiastically. *Harper's* spoke of Rockefeller's "sly hypocrisy" and deceitfulness, and the *Christian Socialist* devoted an entire issue to Walsh, praising his courage and his determination to unearth the truth.

Morris Hillquit (who seemed at times to act as a kind of prosecuting attorney with regard to Rockefeller) rubbed salt in the wounds: "He [Rockefeller] does not know whether the company owns the homes of the workers, whether it owns the saloons in the camps; he does not know whether it maintains a system of company stores; he does not know the first thing about the operations of a concern in which he has invested $24,000,000 and which employs 60,000 or 70,000 men, in which he is a controlling factor. . . . The most comical part of it, if it were not so serious, was the fact that the chairman of this commission had to inform Mr. Rockefeller about his investments, about the revenue on his investments, about the capitalization of his company . . . etc., and Mr. Rockefeller was only able to say, 'If you say so, I suppose it is so.' "

The "masses" (whoever they may be) adore to see the mighty brought down. An aura of invincibility had for so long clung to the great capitalists that they seemed somehow immune to the hazards and alarms of ordinary human existence. Now the greatest of them all, the epitome and superscripture of capitalism, was in the dock like a common criminal. Millions of Americans got a new and far sharper sense of the cruelties and inequities that masqueraded under the cloak of free enterprise. To those at the bottom of the social and economic scale, it came as a minor revelation that the capitalists might, after all, be called to account. Far more important than the commission's final and hotly disputed report, or any specific legislation that resulted from it, was the fact that the war between capital and labor had been dramatized on the nation's center stage before an enthralled audience of millions who would never again view such matters in quite the same way.

As Florence Harriman, who often disapproved of Walsh's prosecuting attorney manner, put it, "without the grilling from the chairman," Rockefeller "might never have gotten close to the terrible drama for which, because he was Capital, he was in the last analysis responsible." The Rockefeller grilling virtually concluded the hearings (there was some further testimony on labor conditions in Puerto Rico) and did so with public attention focused on the "crimes" of the greatest capitalist of them all, certainly the intention of the director of the drama, Frank Walsh.

A practical consequence of the Rockefeller barbecue was that the chastened tycoon, advised and guided by the ubiquitous Ivy Lee, journeyed to Colorado, ingratiated himself with the miners, joined in a square dance, and initiated the Colorado Industrial Plan to reform conditions in the mines and in the mining towns. From the union point of view, this new mood of benign paternalism was inimical to the long-run interests of the workers, and Mother Jones attacked Rockefeller and his plan. "You can't fool my boys," she said; "they know that this kind of scheme is a hypocritical and dishonest pretense."

In their final report the commissioners concurred in general observations, followed by supplemental reports by individual members. Frank Walsh, as chairman, led the supplemental list and also submitted the most liberal (or radical) statement. To the commissioners the crux of the question of industrial unrest was: "[H]ave the workers received a fair share of the enormous increase in wealth which has taken place

in this country during the period [1890 to 1912], as a result largely of
their labors? The answer is emphatically, No!" While the wealth of
the country had increased in that period from $65,000,000,000 to
$187,000,000,000 or 188 percent, the aggregate income of wage earn-
ers in mining, manufacturing, and transportation had increased only
95 percent, and their share of the "net product" had declined by more
than 4 percent. It seemed to the commissioners that "with the inexhaustible natural resources of the United States, her tremendous mechanical achievements, and the genius of her people for organization
and industry," there was "no natural reason to prevent every able-
bodied man of our present population from being well fed, well
housed, comfortably clothed, and from rearing a family of moderate
size in comfort, health, and security." Instead, most of the working
class existed in the most marginal fashion, and "about one-third were
living in a state which can only be described as abject poverty." The
greatest sufferers were children. In six large cities statistics revealed
that from 12 to 20 percent of the children were "noticeably underfed
and ill nourished."

In agriculture, tenancy was rapidly replacing ownership, and huge
farms and ranches, owned often by absentee landlords, were swallow-
ing up smaller ones. "It is industrial feudalism in an extreme form,"
the commissioners declared. In sum, "the unrest and dissatisfaction"
caused by "intolerable industrial conditions" would, if unrelieved, "in
the natural course of events rise into active revolt or, if forcibly suppressed, sink into sullen hatred." Evidence could be found in the
emergence of the IWW. Although that organization had relatively few
members, its "spirit and vocabulary" permeated "enormous masses of
workers, particularly among the unskilled and migratory laborers." In
addition to those who accepted "its philosophy and creed . . . numberless
thousands of workers, skilled and unskilled" felt "bitterly that they and
their fellows are being denied justice, economically, politically, and
legally." In the opinion of the commissioners, there were "four main
sources" of industrial unrest: "Unjust distribution of wealth and income. . . . Unemployment and denial of an opportunity to earn a living. . . . Denial of justice in the creation, in the adjudication, and in
the administration of law. . . . Denial of the right and opportunity to
form effective organizations. . . .

"The contest between capital and labor is more serious than any
of the other contests. Since the year 1877 it has frequently resulted
practically in civil war, with the army or militia called in to suppress

one side or the other, according to the will of the executive," declared the *Report.*

There was chronic unemployment and underemployment, the commissioners found, especially of the unskilled workers, "not simply because he is unskilled but also because he is poorly nourished and weakened by the effects of unfavorable conditions of living and, in many instances, by the unbearably severe conditions of work."

The *Report* compared such tycoons as J. Pierpont Morgan and John D. Rockefeller, Jr., to Louis XVI and quoted Morgan as saying that the directors of corporations were "not at all responsible" for the "conditions existing in the industries" which they directed. One persistent theme in the *Report* was the danger to democracy in the vast disparity of income between the rich and the poor. It pointed to the "growth of an hereditary aristocracy, which is foreign to every conception of the American government and menacing to the welfare of the people and the existence of the Nation as a democracy." This was coming about through alliances between the families of "these industrial princes . . . knit together not only by commercial alliances but by a network of intermarriages which assures harmonious action whenever their common interest is threatened."

One of the principal recommendations of the commission was the establishment of a permanent body with wide powers to enforce state and Federal labor legislation and adjudicate disputes between capital and labor.

A majority of the commissioners, led by Walsh, recommended "that the states and municipalities take over [the public utilities] under just terms and conditions," and a minority of four—Walsh, Lennon, O'Connell, and Garretson—argued for public ownership of coal mines and proposed that a six-day week and eight-hour day be established by law. The same four also recommended that Congress pass legislation "putting an end to the activities" of the Rockefeller Foundation since its funds had been accumulated out of "the wages of workers in American industries . . . by means of economic pressure, violation of law, cunning, and violence practiced over a series of years by the founder. . . ."

The minority report also called for women's suffrage on the ground that the denial of the vote had been "a most serious handicap to women in industry in their long and splendid struggle to secure compensation for their labor, humane working conditions, and protective laws."

Responses to the *Report* ranged from ecstatic to furious. The *New*

York Times called Walsh a "passionate Red," and its Los Angeles counterpart denounced the *Report* as the work of "mangy politicians" that would "live in political literature as rare specimens of envy, malice, and intellectual imbecility." The Ohio chapter of the Manufacturers' Association described the committee as made up of "notoriety seekers, dilettante reformers, anarchists, agitators, he-women and she-men," organized for "proclaiming, agitating, haranguing, and raising cain generally," and the *Iron Trade Review,* an organ of the iron industry, attacked the "Sociologists and Saloonists" who made up the committee, adding, "It is high time for the administration at Washington to suppress this mischief making coterie, which has no legal existence and ought to be driven from the national capital."

The *Labor Federationist,* on the other hand, declared that the *Report* would "go down in history as the greatest contribution to labor literature of our time." Eugene V. Debs wrote: "It peels the hide off capitalism." To the editor of the *Christian Socialist* it belonged with the Declaration of Independence. It was the workingman's Emancipation Proclamation.

Although the *Report* did not mark "the beginning of an indigenous American revolutionary movement," as the *Masses* had predicted, it is hard not to agree with that journal's statement that it was the "most remarkable official document ever published in this country."

It can be said with some assurance that the hearings of the commission marked the high-water mark of political toleration in the United States. The fact that unorthodox and "radical" viewpoints were given a fair and impartial hearing was a source of pride to those Americans who valued free speech. But the commission's hearings did far more. They broke the illusion of invulnerability that had enveloped the great capitalist overlords. When men like the elder and younger Rockefellers, Harrison Gray Otis, the "lord" of Los Angeles, and even Andrew Carnegie himself (though, it must be said, he was the most tenderly handled of all the tycoons) were summoned before a commission plainly composed of men (and a woman) sympathetic in the main to the cause of the American workingman and grilled about their words and actions, the myth was suddenly dissipated. Such men were, it turned out, reassuringly mortal. They fidgeted and perspired like common criminals before a merciless prosecutor. Like convicted thieves, they acknowledged their misdeeds, expressed contrition, and spoke plaintively of their philanthropic efforts as constituting extenuating circumstances.

One of the consequences of the *Report* was a private committee on industrial relations formed by various progressive politicians, among them Frederic Howe and Amos Pinchot, to apply pressure on Congress to draft legislation that would give effect to the *Report*'s recommendations.

Florence Harriman was distressed that the onset of the European War at the moment the commission's *Report* was published diverted public attention and aborted any hope of legislation to remedy the ills it had focused attention upon. When she expressed her chagrin to her husband, Borden, he consoled her by pointing out that "the eleven volumes of your published hearings are not dead. . . . Those eleven volumes may seem to be sharing the moldy fate of most government print, but they are the comédie humaine of America. They tell from a thousand angles the story of industrial unrest. The war is still on. Most of what the experts advised is still undone." The nation had to be made "conscious of the economic drama." He added, "It had to be staged and your unjudicial chairman was just the impresario that was needed. What could your experts do with a country that wasn't ready to admit that it needed them?" Florence Harriman took comfort in the thought that "during the two years that the Commission held its hearings,—its probe into the causes of the misery and unrest of the workers . . . held the public's attention, not only in the United States, but over the entire world. . . . We did succeed," she wrote, "in dramatizing the hidden facts of industrial warfare, and it is true that for the first time labor felt that a branch of the government was giving them a real say and a square deal."

In the slowly forming consciousness of the nation the *Report of the Commission on Industrial Relations* played a significant part. "The evidence is in," Walsh had exulted at the end of the hearings. "The case has gone to the great jury of the American people."

23

A Brilliant Start

Theodore Roosevelt had anticipated Woodrow Wilson in demonstrating the effective powers of the presidency. Wilson fell heir to a vastly enlarged presidency, and he was prompt to take advantage of that fact. At the same time Wilson undoubtedly had a tough act to follow. The "act" was Roosevelt's; Taft was simply an unhappy interlude. Beyond the circle of his supporters the new President encountered considerable skepticism. The dedicated adorers of Roosevelt, many of whom were in fact Wilson's natural constituency, viewed him with suspicion or active hostility; he had, after all, vanquished their hero. "This morning," Henry Adams wrote to Elizabeth Cameron, "Cabot dropped in and fulminated against Woodrow Wilson as usual, for Cabot raves against that great man, who seems, in truth, to be much of the Maryland schoolmaster type." A few weeks later Adams noted that Lodge's "hatred for the President is demented."

In the country at large Wilson had to deal with the commonality's inherent suspicion of professors and intellectuals and its feeling that a vast amount of drama and amusement had gone out of American life with the reluctant departure of the Colonel. Finally, he had to cope with Roosevelt's unrelenting hostility. This was not a quiet anger but a loudly and continually declared opposition to him and all his works. One might have thought that with Taft and the Republican old guard thrown down, if not humbled, Roosevelt would, after his initial disappointment, have welcomed Wilson's obvious intention to be as "progressive" as he and taken a justifiable pride in discovering that he had established a kind of tradition that his successor felt bound to carry on. In American politics no innovations instituted by one party can be considered to have entered the nation's political bloodstream until the opposition party has, in a sense, ratified them by that sincerest form of flattery, imitation. What Wilson's election proved was that at least until war put all calculations at odds, the Roosevelt Progressive program was the nation's. A more generous man or a man who did not, in Lincoln Steffens's phrase, "think with his hips" would have understood that more or less self-evident fact, but Roosevelt, in a manner of speaking, couldn't think at all. Where his impulses were sound, he soared to empyrean heights; where they were small and petty, he behaved in ways that embarrassed his friends and armed his enemies.

Wilson's prospects were further shadowed by the fact that the Mexican Revolution entered a new and more virulent phase on the eve of his inauguration. If Wilson (and all sensible and sober persons) were confused and perplexed by the often incomprehensible goings-on in Mexico, Theodore Roosevelt was not. He howled for intervention. Writing a weekly column in the *Outlook,* he denounced Wilson as a coward, a traitor, a Hamlet of indecision and timidity. He was convinced that "Wilson and Bryan are the very worst men we have ever had in their positions. It would not hurt . . . to say publicly what is nevertheless historically true, namely that they are worse than Jefferson and Madison." In another letter Roosevelt spoke of Wilson as "the worst President by all odds we have had since Buchanan. . . ."

Despite Roosevelt's vocal opposition, reformers everywhere took heart from Wilson's inaugural address, in which he went substantially further than any prior president in acknowledging the deplorable social conditions under which many Americans, especially immigrants, lived. "We have been proud of our industrial achievements," Wilson declared, "but we have not hitherto stopped thoughtfully enough to count the human cost, the costs of lives snuffed out, of energies overtaxed and broken, the fearful physical and spiritual cost to the men and women and children upon whom the dead weight and burden of it all has fallen pitilessly the years through. The groans and agony of it all had not reached our ears, the solemn, moving undertone of our lives, coming up out of the mines and factories and out of every home where the struggle had its intimate and familiar seat."

Other initial auguries were favorable. Wilson's Cabinet included some extremely able men. Josephus Daniels, the secretary of the navy, was, somewhat incongruously, a pacifist. The same was true of Bryan, the new secretary of state, who brought with him the quite unabashed air of an old-fashioned Midwestern politician. Henry Stoddard described him as sitting in his office, "shirt-sleeved (literally) with handkerchief tucked in his collar and a big palm-leaf fan in hand . . . like a Hottentot chief on his tropical throne," sniffing out government jobs for his followers. Certainly many of the Easterners in the administration viewed this flamboyantly Western intruder with scorn or amused condescension. When word reached the American ambassador to Great Britain, Walter Hines Page, that Bryan planned a visit to England, Page wrote Colonel House that he would rather return home than suffer the embarrassment of having the secretary appear as spokesman for his country. "It'll take years," he declared, "for American Ambassadors to recover what they'll lose if he carries out his plan [to visit England]. They now laugh at him over here. . . . Mr. Asquith [Herbert Asquith, the prime minister] . . . met Bryan once and he told me with a smile that he regarded him as a 'peculiar product of your country.' " John Jay Chapman met Bryan and reported to his mother, "He is a big, benevolent man with a musical voice who consoles and comforts everyone. . . . He is big, beaming, brilliant-eyed and handsome; and in all he said to me he was very ready and very intelligent."

Of all his Cabinet appointments, Wilson was most casual in his choice of secretary of war. When Wilson consulted Joseph Tumulty, the latter argued that this Cabinet post should go to a New Jersey man. When no suitable candidate came to mind, Tumulty got out a list of members of the state bar and judiciary and ran down the list alphabetically. Under *G* he turned up Lindley Garrison, a respected lawyer. Wilson had never heard of him, but the next day he was offered his post. Similarly Wilson had never met three other Cabinet members prior to his inaugural.

William McAdoo was appointed secretary of the treasury. McAdoo as an unknown and untried young engineer had made his name and fortune by building the tubes under the Hudson River, a project that had been abandoned by more experienced engineers. David Franklin Houston, secretary of agriculture, observed of his fellow Cabinet member that McAdoo had "dash, boldness, and courage" but was a "solitaire player" who had little patience with Cabinet discussions as they affected his bailiwick.

Houston, following the example of Gideon Welles, Lincoln's secretary of the navy, kept a diary of his years in Wilson's Cabinet. Not as complete or lively as that of Welles, it nonetheless gives revealing insights into the Cabinet and, even more, into Wilson's leadership. Born in Monroe, North Carolina, and educated at South Carolina College and Harvard, Houston had been president of the Agricultural and Mechanical College of Texas and subsequently of the University of Texas from 1905 to 1908. A friend of Colonel House's and a skillful maneuverer in the roiled waters of Texas politics, he had the interests of an intellectual and the instincts of a reformer. For eight years he was a loyal supporter of the President.

At his first Cabinet meeting Wilson announced his intention to press tariff and currency reform. The tariff was first on his agenda of essential legislation, but currency reform, he declared, would be the real test of the administration. It was possible that the administration "would work its ruin trying to serve the real interests of the people" by placing the currency on a sound basis. He also startled his Cabinet by announcing that he intended to address both houses of Congress in a joint session in person, something that had not been done since John Adams's presidency.

As Congress waited for the President's arrival, Houston noted that the members seemed "a trifle nervous, and something of a chill pervaded the air." Some Congressmen, he thought, "had a sullen look." When the President entered the chamber, everyone rose. When they were seated, Wilson, looking pale and tense, began: "I am very glad to have this opportunity to address the two Houses directly and to verify for myself the impression that the President of the United States is a person, not a mere department of the government, hailing Congress from some isolated island of jealous power, sending messages, not speaking naturally and with his own voice—that he is a human being trying to cooperate with other human beings in a common service. After this pleasant experience, I shall feel quite normal in all our dealings with one another."

On the issue of the tariff, the President told his audience that the practice of giving each group of manufacturers what it thought it needed to maintain a closed market had been established. The government in so doing had fostered privilege and monopoly "until at last nothing is normal, nothing is obliged to stand the test of efficiency and economy, in our world of big business, but everything thrives by concerted agreement.

"We must abolish everything that bears even the semblance of privilege or of any kind of artificial advantage, and put our business men and our producers under the stimulation of a constant necessity to be efficient, economical, and enterprising, masters of competitive supremacy, better merchants and better traders than any in the world. . . . We are to deal with the facts of our own day. We begin with the tariff. Nothing should obscure this undertaking. Later, currency reforms will press for attention."

The champions of high tariffs did not surrender without a struggle. David Houston noted that the lobbyists were everywhere. "It was impossible to move around without bumping into them—at hotels, clubs, and even private houses." The sugar lobbyists were particular "pests." Finally, an indignant Wilson denounced them. "I think that the public ought to know the extraordinary exertions being made by the lobby in Washington to gain recognition for certain alterations of the tariff bill. Washington has seldom seen so numerous, so industrious, or so insidious a lobby. The newspapers are being filled with paid advertisements calculated to mislead the judgment not only of public men, but also the public opinion of the country itself. There is every evidence that money without limit is being spent to sustain this lobby and to create an appearance of pressure of opinion antagonistic to some of the chief items of the tariff bill.

"It is of serious interest to the country that the people at large should have no lobby and be voiceless in these matters, while great bodies of astute men seek . . . to overcome the interests of the public for private profit."

The Underwood Tariff Act, signed by the President in October, 1913, was the first substantial reduction in the tariff rates since 1857. The reductions ran from 40 percent to less than 33 percent. Wool was put on the free list, and the tariffs on cotton were reduced between a third and a half. An impressed Oswald Garrison Villard called the bill "an astonishing success."

One of the new administration's most notable accomplishments was a direct tax on income. The first income tax had been imposed in 1862 as a wartime measure. It was repealed ten years later. An income tax had been included in the tariff bill of 1894, but the Supreme Court had declared it unconstitutional. The ratification of the Sixteenth

Amendment had opened the door to an income tax. Champions of protection opposed the tax for fear it would reduce the pressure to collect customs duties as the major source of government revenues.

It was also Wilson's desire to extend the hand of friendship to the "Latin-American nations." The United States should do everything in its power, he told the Southern Commercial Congress in Mobile, Alabama, to aid "the development of constitutional liberty in the world. Human rights, national integrity, and opportunity, as against national interests," were the issues that the United States had to face. "I want to take this occasion to say that the United States will never again seek one additional foot of territory by conquest," he declared.

The tariff victory and the passage of an income tax law were followed by an attack on one of the nation's most persistent deficiencies: the lack of any government supervision or control over the monetary system. A preoccupation of reformers and theorists of the new economics for a generation, such controls had been stubbornly resisted by the banking interests. On June 23, 1913, the President appeared before a joint session of Congress to deliver his message on currency reform. It was essential, he declared, to have a national banking system with control lodged in the government "so that the banks may be the instruments, not the masters, of business and of individual enterprise and initiative . . ." A basic Democratic concern was that of providing better credit facilities for American farmers. The currency bill, Wilson pointed out, "does the farmers a great service. It puts them on a footing with other business men and masters of enterprise, as it should; and upon its passage they will find themselves quit of many of the difficulties which now hamper them in the field of credit." Without the farmers, "every street would be silent, every office deserted, every factory fallen into disrepair. And yet, the farmer does not stand on the same footing with the forester and the miner in the market of credit."

The currency bill was sponsored by Carter Glass, the Virginia Senator. Glass, a man of characteristic Southern charm, had a curious way of speaking out of the side of his mouth, which led Wilson to remark that "Glass says more things out of the side of his mouth than a lot of people say with the whole thing." Known as the Owens-Glass Act, the bill to reform the monetary system became law in December, 1913; "the second great administrative victory" David Houston called it. In a real sense it was the fruit of almost half a century of popular agitation against a financial system that worked to the disadvantage of the poor (and indeed of the middle class as well) and that had caused incalculable hardship and suffering, especially among the farmers of the country. Wilson's administration produced what the Populists had called for twenty years earlier: an elastic currency that could respond to need for credit and that could not be manipulated by private banks. For their part, the banking interests had been busy promoting the notion of a centralized banking system when the election of Wilson brought the Democrats into office. The Democratic response was to appropriate the plans of the private bankers and substantially to extend them.

The Owens-Glass Act provided, among other things, for the organization of a Federal Reserve System with regional banks, the number and location to be determined. The Federal Reserve, by making money available to banks at rates of interest determined by its Board of Governors, could exercise control over the expansion of both currency and credit and thus play a stabilizing role in the economy, reducing, it was hoped, the wild fluctuations that had characterized it since the early years of the Republic.

Tariff reform and currency management having been accomplished, Wilson turned his attention in the new year to reform of the trust laws. The proposed trust legislation, he told Congress on January 20, 1914, "springs out of the experience of a whole generation. It has clarified itself by long content. . . . What we are proposing to do, therefore, is, happily, not to hamper or interfere with business as enlightened business men prefer to do it, or in any sense to put it under a ban. The antagonism between business and government is over. . . . The country is ready . . . to accept . . . with relief . . . a law which will confer upon the Interstate Commerce Commission the power to superintend and regulate the financial operations by which the railroads are henceforth to be supplied with the money they need for their proper development. . . ." The point was to free the railroads from the dominance of the financial institutions, which used the railroads' need for money to manipulate and exploit them. Businessmen, Wilson was confident, wanted something more than "the menace of legal process. . . . They desire the advice, the definite guidance, and information which can be supplied by an administrative body, an Interstate Trade Commission."

The Clayton antitrust bill instituted closer government control and supervision of corporations, extending, in effect, the number of business practices considered monopolistic. The Bureau of Corporations, designed primarily as a personal agency of Roosevelt, proved short-lived, but by 1914 the principle behind it had been incorporated into the Federal Trade Commission, to which, as one business advocate wrote, "we can submit business practices" for decisions "in advance as to the propriety, fairness and benefits of such proposed arrangements, each upon the merits of that particular case."

The Clayton antitrust bill also provided severe penalties for price discrimination, legalized strikes, picketing, and boycotts, and barred the use of injunctions in labor disputes, except when property damage was threatened (a substantial loophole, as it turned out). Samuel Gompers called the act, passed on October 15, 1914, "the Magna Charter of American labor." It was hardly that, but it was notable for the fact that it was passed in the face of the dogged resistance of big business.

Indeed, throughout his first term of office, Wilson, in Oswald Garrison Villard's words, "was rigid in keeping Big Business at arm's length. Never before in my memory," Villard wrote, "had the White House refused to receive the most powerful business men in the United States. They were literally outcasts." Among the proscribed were all members of the House of J. P. Morgan, one of whom, Thomas Lamont, complained to Villard, "That's all right if we are devils or improper persons to associate with but what puzzles us is why, if contact with us is so contaminating, we are being called upon by the State Department to help it advance its Central American policies by floating some loans."

The National Association of Manufacturers, which represented small business interests far more than those of the great corporations, alarmed by the success of the Wilson legislative program, began a drive to prevail on Congress to abjure all restrictive legislation. It was convinced that the Federal Trade Commission would become little more than a tool for the giant corporate interests. "The Country Is Suffering from *Too Much Law*," its stickers proclaimed. "Free Business from Political Persecution."

Wilson vetoed an immigration bill, to the indignation of many Californians. Legislation to restrict immigration had passed Congress three times and three times been rejected. "This last action ought to have been acquiesced in," Houston wrote. "We are getting entirely too many people who have no aptitude or qualifications for participating in our political activities and may never acquire any." He believed American institutions "will be menaced if the numbers of those of radically different experiences and habits continue to mount up, and particularly if they are permitted to congregate in race groups in our great cities or even in the rural districts. . . . These people furnish not only many of our worst agitators, but also very fruitful soil for the seed of revolution." America, Houston reflected, was "a nation where any cause can get a hearing; . . . all any advocates have to do is to convert the majority to their way of thinking; and . . . if they cannot do so, they must hold their peace." Houston did not indicate how long the advocates were to be allowed to try to convert the majority. Certainly it was an odd notion that once they had been judged to have failed, "they must hold their peace."

In the passage of all such legislation there was significant cooperation between the Wilson Democrats and the Progressive Republicans. Indeed, William Allen White, recounting Wilson's legislation program, constantly used the term "we"—for example, "In his first term . . . we had established a Federal Trade Commission. We had set up a Tariff Commission. . . . We had established the parcel post in opposition to the railroads. We had written a law providing for minimum wages for women and children in industry and had passed a law prohibiting child labor." (The last two laws were struck down by the Supreme Court.)

A euphoric Ray Stannard Baker wrote on January 14, 1914: "Washington is truly seeing a people's government. Progress is really being made. The great thing in the new currency law (a weak measure in many ways) is that it establishes finally the principle of governmental control of our national currency and banking system. The new trust bill provides for an industrial Commission which will establish the principle of governmental regulation of commerce and industry; a great step." It seemed to Baker that the hope of the future lay with the scientific *"thinkers,"* highly professional experts with "a real passion for public service." He added, "Neither Mr. Wilson nor his party alone originated these reforms. They were the outgrowth of years of agitation, muckraking, popular education, insurgency. Bryan, Roosevelt, La Follette and other radical and progressive leaders had a part in it. The Socialists had a part in it. Even the writers had a part in it. It was a great, slow-growing, public movement. . . ."

When Baker visited the President in September, 1914, he found Wilson "clear-eyed, confident, cheerful" in a "neat gray suit . . . affable and frank." He spoke of the success of his legislative program and of the importance of "conservation for *use,*" in the form of national parks.

Certainly Wilson, as both Baker and White suggest, did not carry through his legislative program without assistance from scores of able and dedicated Progressive Representatives and Senators from both parties, but what is most impressive about the achievement was the President's capacity to lead the liberal forces while neutralizing those conservative elements in Congress, many of them in his own party, that had so long impeded progress. Baker recorded a conversation with Wilson in which the President "made many references to this nation being intensely conservative—conservative-minded—and thought it due to our more or less rigid constitution, our diverse population elements, and our instinctive fear of interfering with the cement of our national institutions. But the only way for a party to live," Wilson insisted, "was to be going somewhere, moving—in short, being progressive."

There were, to be sure, danger signals. The economy was in a sharp decline, and Republicans were quick to place the blame on Wilson's legislation. Henry Cabot Lodge wrote to Theodore Roosevelt describing business as "very bad." He added, "I fear we are on the edge of a condition which will cause great suffering in all directions. It is not the fault of business or of the resources of the country. . . . The business crumbling which is going on is simply from fear." The Interstate Commerce Commission, in Lodge's view, had taken as its mission not the protection of the public but the destruction and prosecution of the railroads. The Pennsylvania and the New York Central had already laid off 30,000 men, and the New England railroads were "being torn to pieces. . . . Innocent stockholders have been deprived of their dividends," and these were "very largely women and children." In addition, the Department of Justice was "assaulting corporations without any distinction as to whether they are good or bad; whether they are violating the law or trying to live up to it." Even the Kodak Camera Company was under attack for restraint of trade.

As Woodrow Wilson and his supporters maneuvered one piece of progessive legislation after another through Congress, William Allen White wrote approving editorials in the *Emporia Gazette*. Why then, some of his Progressive friends began to ask him, did he not throw in his lot with Wilson and the Democrats. "I do not regard the Democratic party as progressive," he wrote in response to one such suggestion. "It can never be progressive. It must be historically and constitutionally the conservative party of this nation." The Wilson-Bryan phenomenon was a transitory one. The Democratic Party was "the inevitable residuary legatee of all conservatism in this country," White added. "I would sooner think of being a third-party Prohibitionist or a Socialist than of

being a Democrat . . . so long as [that party] is fettered by the ideas of
state rights and free trade. These two ideas make it inexorably conservative."

The letter is revealing. More than anything else it indicates the
depth of party feeling that had survived every vicissitude of party
politics in the stormy years since the Civil War. It was as though successive generations of Republicans had imprinted in their neural cir-
cuitries an inveterate hostility to Democrats. The ironic fact was that
decade after decade it was the Democrats, far more than the Republicans, who represented the feelings and aspirations of working-class
Americans. But all was nullified by the party's rigid commitment to
the principle of states' rights. That principle negated the party's inclinations toward social and economic justice and delivered every state
into the hands of the most ruthless and self-serving corporations. The
price of allowing the South to suppress all political activity on the part
of blacks was impotence in regard to those issues of greatest importance
to the majority of white Americans, especially those of the working
classes. By the same token nothing could be done to prevent the "progressive" degradation of the Southern blacks. Indeed, one of the principal concerns of many liberals was Wilson's views on the "Negro
problem." Many black leaders feared that his Southern background
would predispose him to antiblack attitudes or policies. Oswald Garrison Villard undertook to sound Wilson out on the subject. Five thousand black children were walking the streets of Atlanta alone with no
hope of bettering themselves because of lack of adequate education.
"That very week," Villard told him, "a seventeen-year-old Negro was
to be executed in Richmond for murder. They are killing that girl this
week," Villard added, "because being a child of a disadvantaged race
and compelled to live in horrible slums, more or less of an outcast, she
has had no chance to be anything else than what she is." Millions of
blacks, he told Wilson, were "living on the border line of destitution
in slums, which were breeding places of disease and vice. . . ." Moreover, there was no adequate cooperation between the races in trying
to alleviate such conditions.

Wilson seemed to Villard to be an attentive and sympathetic listener, and Villard appealed to the President to appoint a national race
commission modeled on Roosevelt's Country Life Commission and the
Commission on Industrial Relations. Its assignment would be "a nonpartisan, scientific study of the status of the Negro with particular

attention to his economic situation." The study would also investigate the physical health of black citizens, their homes, their "work and wages, education, religious and moral influences . . . legal status and . . . participation in government." The suggestion came formally from the National Association for the Advancement of Colored People, of which Villard was then chairman.

William McAdoo added fuel to the racial fire by ordering the segregation of black clerks in the Treasury Department. In addition, Secretary of State Bryan appointed white ministers to Haiti and the Dominican Republic, posts which, for years under Republican administrations, had been given to prominent blacks, the most famous being Frederick Douglass, minister resident and consul general to Haiti, appointed by Benjamin Harrison in 1889. Booker T. Washington wrote Villard that he had never seen his people so "discouraged and embittered" by the attitude of the administration. Villard continued his efforts to prevail on the President to appoint a commission. Finally, Wilson flatly refused. He was, he wrote, "absolutely blocked by the sentiment of Senators; not alone Senators from the South by any means, but Senators from various parts of the country." A week later he wrote that he "honestly thought segregation [in the various departments of government] to be in the interest of the colored people as exempting them from friction and criticism . . . and I want to add," Wilson concluded, "that a number of colored men with whom we have consulted have agreed with us in this judgment."

To this familiar argument Villard replied that blacks had lost ground in an administration committed to reform. Segregation had been given an official imprimatur by McAdoo's actions. Pressed by Villard, the President at last exclaimed, "I say it with shame and humiliation, with shame and humiliation, but I have thought about this thing for twenty years and I see no way out. It will take a very big man to solve this thing." Villard replied that the NAACP was "perfectly certain that there were solutions available for this problem but that they must be based on justice, fair play, and giving the Negro his rights."

An undaunted Villard continued to argue the case for what might be called black emancipation. In Washington he addressed a cheering audience of 3,000 blacks and whites with many more turned away. The President's "philosophy is wrong, his democracy gravely at fault," Villard told his audiences. "He has given us beautiful and worthy sentiments in his book called *The New Freedom*. But nowhere do we find any indication that his democracy is not strictly limited by the sex line and the color line." Years later when the memory of his efforts was still a bitter one, Villard wrote: "Not one thing was done by Woodrow Wilson or his administration to ameliorate the condition of the Negro."

24

Foreign Policy

By the end of Wilson's first year in office the most ominous cloud on the foreign front was the troublesome Mexican Revolution. Hailed by socialists and anarchists as the opening episode of world revolution, it aroused the enthusiasm of radicals everywhere. The only problem was that it was almost impossible to tell what was going on South of the Border. Francisco Madero's assassination on the eve of Wilson's inauguration had a strong influence on the new President. He had felt an affinity for the Mexican revolutionary, one of the most attractive of Mexico's leaders, and he was determined to do everything he could to assist in the overthrow of his successor, General Victoriano Huerta, whom Wilson viewed as an instrument of oppression in the hands of an aristocracy that had lived off the labor of the Mexican people for a century or more.

Wilson was determined not to respond to the cries of American investors in Mexico, who demanded that American troops be dispatched to protect their property. In Wilson's opinion, "the lying about Mexico was prodigious." He told Ray Stannard Baker that "his Mexican policy was based upon two of the most deeply seated convictions of his life: first, his shame as an American over the first Mexican war and his resolution that while he was President there should be no such predatory war. Second, upon the Virginia bill of rights: that a people had the right 'to do what they damned pleased with their own affairs.' . . . I have constantly to remind myself that I am not the servant of those who wish to enhance the value of their Mexican investments, but that I am the servant of the rank and file of the United States," Wilson declared. He urged patience. "Impatience on our part would be childish," he declared, "and would be fraught with every risk of wrong and folly. We can afford to exercise the self-restraint of a really great nation which realizes its own strength and scorns to use it." The proper role for the United States was as "Mexico's nearest friend and intimate adviser." As such the United States was "the more solemnly bound to go to the utmost length of patience and forbearance in this painful and anxious business."

When Wilson withheld recognition from Huerta's government, the move encouraged his rival, General Venustiano Carranza, who set up his own government under the banner of the Constitutionalists (a name that appealed to Wilson). Japan gave its support, in the form of guns and munitions, to Huerta, while Wilson spoke of his passion for "the submerged 85 per cent [of the Mexican population] who are struggling to be free." The President described Huerta as "a diverting brute . . . so false, so sly, so full of bravado, yet so courageous . . . seldom sober and always impossible yet what an indomitable fighter for his own country." Huerta referred to Wilson as the "Puritan of the North." Henry Lane Wilson, the American ambassador to Mexico, protested that Wilson's failure to recognize Huerta as the legitimate head of Mexico was simply encouraging anarchy and further bloodshed, but the President held the ambassador responsible in part for Madero's death (he had refused him asylum in the American Embassy) and considered him a creature of American financial interests in Mexico.

Meanwhile, pressures mounted on Wilson to intervene. American Catholics were vehement in denouncing the administration for its failure to take decisive action. As a Democrat, Wilson was especially susceptible to clamors from his Irish-American constituents. Cattlemen who owned large ranches in Mexico were indignant when the guerrilla leader Pancho Villa, a supporter of the slain Madero, began appropriating their steers and selling them across the border to finance his army. When such cattle drives were blocked, Villa set up a slaughterhouse on the U.S.-Mexican border and sold the beef to American packers over the vociferous protests of the owners. John Reed rode with Villa and reported on the war for the *Masses*. His articles were collected in a hastily edited book entitled *Insurgent Mexico,* which established Reed's credentials with the left. "I can't begin to tell you how good the articles are . . ." Walter Lippmann wrote to Reed. "I want to hug you, Jack."

Britain was especially upset at Wilson's anti-Huerta policy. "The best thing that can happen is to get as soon as possible a dictator who will keep order and give a chance for material and educational progress," Lord Bryce, the British ambassador, wrote. The kaiser touched on the heart of the matter when he declared, "Morality is all right, but what about dividends?" So far the British had also withheld recognition of Huerta out of respect for Wilson's convictions, but its navy needed Mexican oil, and on May 3, 1914, to Wilson's indignation, the British government accorded recognition to Huerta's regime. At practically the same time the Japanese minister delivered an angry note of protest at California's anti-Japanese legislation. The response of the Joint Army and Navy Board was to order five U.S. warships to Manila and recommend that the Pacific fleet be dispatched to Hawaii. (Josephus Daniels wrote that the admirals "sat up nights thinking how Japan was planning to make war on America and steal a march on us by taking the Philippine Islands and going on to Hawaii.") Wilson was so angry at what he considered the board's assumption of executive prerogative that he dissolved it.

American investors urged Wilson to offer recognition of Huerta with the understanding that he and Carranza would participate in free elections. For the moment it seemed as if Wilson might take their advice. William Bayard Hale, who had written a glowing campaign biography of Wilson for the election of 1912, thereby winning at least a portion of the President's heart, had been dispatched to Mexico by Wilson on a fact-finding expedition. The facts he found were, predictably, the facts that Wilson wished him to find: that Huerta's regime was shaky and must soon fall. The President thereupon notified Huerta that he must declare himself not a candidate in the election. Huerta's reply was to arrest 110 members of the Mexican Congress who were his political opponents, suppress all opposition, and declare himself the winner. This Wilson regarded as "an act of bad faith toward the United States." He announced that he would use "such means as may be necessary" to unseat Huerta. The result, of course, was just the reverse of what he intended. Huerta was greatly strengthened by Wilson's edict; the British, greatly alarmed. Sir Edward Grey, the British foreign secretary, smoothed the waters by, in effect, withdrawing British support for Huerta (as well as the British ambassador to Mexico, whom Wilson disliked), and Wilson in return prevailed on Congress to repeal the Panama Canal tolls, which were particularly offensive to the British. At this point the kaiser, a seasoned fisher in troubled waters, moved to support Huerta by large shipments of munitions.

Now another element was added. The USS *Dolphin* was anchored in Mexican waters off Tampico. Seven sailors went ashore on a gunboat to take on supplies and found themselves arrested by a minor government official who had orders to allow no boat to dock in the harbor. The men were promptly returned to the *Dolphin* with apologies for their arrest.

Admiral Henry Mayo, commander of the fleet of which the *Dolphin* was the flagship, decided that American honor had been besmirched and that the stain could be removed only by a twenty-one gun salute delivered by Mexican batteries in the town and the punishment of the officer who had made the arrest. Huerta refused, and the incident threatened to escalate into war. Wilson now issued a personal ultimatum to Huerta, demanding an apology before April 19. If Huerta remained adamant he would be punished by a naval blockade and the seizure of Veracruz.

On sober second thought Wilson was dismayed at the corner into which he had painted himself. A member of the Cabinet described him as "profoundly disturbed," and he ended a hastily called Cabinet meeting with an exhortation to prayer. Having created a situation in which war seemed inevitable, he told waiting reporters that "in no conceivable circumstances would we fight the people of Mexico." In the midst of around-the-clock conferences, word reached Wilson that a German ship, carrying arms for Huerta, was approaching the blockading ships. Was it to be permitted to pass through, thus making a mockery of the blockade, or stopped, thus raising the specter of war with Germany? While the President turned and twisted on the horns of his dilemma, affairs rushed to a denouement. Wilson was roused from his sleep for a conference call with Daniels, Bryan, and Tumulty. The German ship was due to arrive the next day. At that point a way out suggested itself. If the navy landed marines and seized the customhouse at Veracruz, the munitions could be intercepted without firing on the German freighter. The order went out: "Take Veracruz at once!"

The orders were carried out. The customhouse, the railroad yards, and the telegraph offices were seized by a landing party. Mexican cadets barricaded themselves in an abandoned fortification and opened fire on the sailors and marines. Soon they were reinforced by armed civilians. Before the guns of the USS *Prairie* began shelling the city, 4 Americans were killed, and 20 wounded. By the time the resistance had been quelled, 19 Americans and 126 Mexicans had been killed, and 71 and 96 Americans and Mexicans, respectively, wounded.

The next day at a press conference a reporter noted that the President looked "preternaturally pale, almost parchmenty—the death of American sailors and marines owing to an order of his seemed to affect him like an ailment." (Also, one trusts, the deaths of the Mexican nationals.) The Germans made a strong protest. The action of the Americans was in defiance of all the principles of international law, the German ambassador, Count J. H. von Bernstorff, insisted, and he was correct. Bryan went at once to the German Embassy to offer his government's official apology. In the midst of the general alarm and uncertainty about whether a state of war must now be presumed to exist between the United States and Mexico, the German freighter steamed down the coast, joined another German ship loaded with munitions, and both unloaded their cargoes at Puerta Mexico. The kaiser was delighted at the turn of events. He anticipated, correctly, a wave of Latin American hostility directed toward the United States and, he hoped, a protracted war between the United States and Mexico in which the Japanese might seize the opportunity to take the Philippines. "Mexico is a God-send to us," Bernstorff wrote to the German minister of foreign affairs.

At the funeral of the Americans killed at Veracruz, the President put the best possible face on an impossible situation. "We have gone down to Mexico to serve mankind," he declared, "if we can find out a way. We do not want to fight the Mexicans. We want to serve the Mexicans if we can." And in a letter to a friend he wrote: "I am looking for an exit."

Fortunately Argentina, Brazil, and Chile offered their services as mediators, but before the offer could be acted on, Carranza's forces finished off those of Huerta, who escaped to Spain on a German ship. The American forces in Veracruz were evacuated, and everyone breathed more easily.

Major General Frederick Funston, a boyhood friend of William Allen White, had been in command of the American soldiers at Veracruz. When White next saw his friend, Funston "broke out with dazzling, wrathful profanity . . . fire works of rage." White noted his comments. " 'God knows,' " he stormed, " 'it cut my heart out, but I had to withdraw American troops . . . under the sniping fire of those [multiple profanities] greasers from windows as we embarked. God, Billy, fancy that! Fancy the American flag, with me in charge of it, going meekly out of a dirty, stinking, greaser hole—withdrawing my command under fire!' "

A large part of the "Mexican problem" revolved around the complete incomprehension of the "gringos" for the "greasers." Their respective cultures and temperaments were diametrically opposed. "Business, which is business to us," Lincoln Steffens wrote, "is a game to the Mexicans, who don't distinguish between work and play as we do. All is fun to them, or a bore. They enjoyed the revolution. They must enjoy everything or hate it and neglect it. And so in Cuba and Puerto Rico, where the Americans were striving against despair to teach the natives the idea of private property. . . . Our State Department," Steffens added, "does, and it must, govern Mexico as it regulated the Mexican revolution, in the interest of the same kind of American investors who have corrupted the United States."

Steffens concluded that "the Mexicans, the Indians are an artistic people, like the Greeks, and that we Americans are so Roman, so moral, that any understanding between us is well-nigh impossible."

Mexico was not the sum of Wilson's foreign policy concerns. The problem of the Philippines remained, Haiti was a headache, and Cuba, under civil (supported by military) occupation, gave strong indications of a desire for independence. Criticism of American policy in the Philippines was persistent in liberal circles. Charles Edward Russell spoke for such opinion when he wrote: "After sixteen years of adroit evasion of this particular treaty, all the elements in America that favored side-stepping, that is, racial hypocrisy, the dementia praecox of imperialism, profit-mongering exploiters, . . . united to put through Congress an act that seemed the attainable summit of duplicity. While pretending to grant independence in ten years (totally ignoring the pledge 'as soon as a stable government can be erected therein') it was so cunningly worded and supplied with jokers that in reality it made independence virtually impossible."

As Russell noted, the Democratic Party platform in the election of 1912 called for "an immediate declaration of the nation's purpose to recognize the independence of the Islands as soon as a stable government can be established." It was a modest triumph for the supporters of independence, but they hailed it as at least a beginning. After his election Wilson asked a former Princeton colleague, Professor Henry Ford, to make a fact-finding trip to the islands. After more than two months in the Philippines Ford reported that desire for independence was widespread among the natives of the islands but bitterly opposed by American business interests there. While he reported favorably on U.S. administration of the islands, he believed that the time had come for independence or, at least, for greater participation by the Filipinos in the government. His recommendations were reinforced by a report from a young lawyer in the War Department, Felix Frankfurter. Since the islands were governed by a presidentially appointed commission, the easiest point of attack was in regard to the members of the commission. Wilson's first step was to appoint as governor general a man known to be a strong advocate of Philippine independence, Congressman Francis Burton Harrison. When Wilson talked with Harrison after his appointment, he found him "wonderfully well informed on Philippine conditions. . . ." Harrison's first official act was to read to a large crowd of Filipinos a message from the President which declared, "We regard ourselves as trustee acting not for the advantage of the United States, but for the benefit of the people of the Philippine Islands.

"Every step we take will be taken with a view to the ultimate independence of the Islands and as a preparation for their independence, and we hope to move towards that end as rapidly as the safety and permanent interests of the Islands will permit." To give practical effect to his words, the President, under the authority of the Jones Act of 1916, began to appoint Filipinos to civil service positions in the islands. At this point progress was slowed by the fears expressed by the most influential of the native Filipino commissioners, Manuel Quezon, that Japan had designs on the islands and might take advantage of the withdrawal of the United States to take possession of them. It thus turned out that while the governor general, ex-Congressman Harrison, was eager to advance the date of Philippine independence, one of the most influential natives wished to delay it. Quezon's strategy was to push a bill through the Philippine legislature calling for independence when there was 75 percent male literacy in the islands, an obviously remote eventuality in a largely illiterate population.

Finally, in January, 1916, under pressure from Democrats committed to independence, a bill presented to Congress authorized the

President to recognize the independence of the islands immediately and to withdraw within two years. The withdrawal was to be accompanied by a series of treaties ensuring the neutrality of the islands and their freedom from invasion by any warring powers. The so-called Clarke bill was defeated, and an indignant Charles Edward Russell wrote: "When we had beaten Spain in the Philippines, every consideration of fundamental good faith, American tradition, the principles of democracy we had professed, demanded that we should give the country over to the people who had struggled so long and so heroically to possess it. Instead of standing squarely upon our republican creed we went a-whoring after strange gods."

The Jones Act of 1917, also known as the Organic Act for Puerto Rico, made that island a U.S. territory and gave its inhabitants U.S. citizenship.

Haiti, which had won its independence from France in 1804, now fell on evil days. With the government in a state of economic collapse, a revolutionary mob seized the President of the Republic and the commander of the army and hacked them to death. The French, with extensive economic interests in the island, landed a naval lieutenant and nine marines to protect their legation. A few weeks later American marines landed, and, acting on the instructions of Secretary of State Bryan, went to the Haitian National Bank, a subsidiary of the National City Bank of New York, and carried off $500,000 in gold. The ostensible reason for this remarkable intrusion was that the presence of French naval personnel imperiled the Monroe Doctrine. The marines' arrival proved semipermanent—nineteen years, to be exact. Colonel Smedley Butler, commanding the marines, later described his mission as "doing the dirty work for the National City Bank." The Haitian legislature was disbanded by Butler, and a treaty which gave an air of legitimacy to the American occupation was extracted from the Haitians. Franklin Roosevelt, assistant secretary of the navy, found himself intimately involved. Six years later in Butte, Montana, he declared, "The fact is I wrote Haiti's constitution myself. . . . Until last week I had two votes in the League Assembly myself." It turned out to be necessary to kill some 3,250 Haitians who were unsympathetic to the presence of U.S. soldiers on their island's soil; 1 American officer and 12 men were lost. Many of the Haitian deaths, Major General George Barnett of the Marine Corps later testified, were "practically indiscriminate killings," intended to discourage resistance. On one occasion orders were given by an officer to shoot all prisoners. A marine lieutenant convicted of torturing Haitians was placed in an insane asylum.

A commission appointed by President Warren G. Harding in 1921 exonerated the marines on the ground that they were the victims of foreign policies that placed them in those islands, but it noted that "racial antipathies lie behind many of the difficulties which the United States military and civil forces have met in Haiti. . . . The failure of the occupation to understand the social problems of Haiti, its brusque attempt to plant democracy there by drill and harrow, its determination to set up a middle class however wise and necessary it seemed to Americans—all these explain why, in part, the high hopes of our good works have not been realized." The commissioners' report noted that the United States had spent some $23,000,000 in Haiti in a period of fifteen years and had "done nothing to fit the Haitians themselves for handling their affairs." In Oswald Garrison Villard's words, "If Russia was the 'acid test' of our fair play and democracy in Europe, Haiti . . . certainly should have been the 'acid test' of our fair play and democracy in the Caribbean. . . . The reasons given for this wanton attack upon a helpless little republic," Villard wrote, "were: (1) that there was lawlessness and disorder in Haiti which we could not permit in any country in the neighborhood of the Panama Canal; (2) that unless we rectified internal conditions, foreign intervention might result, especially as (3) both France and Germany claimed a special interest in Haiti because of their investments there; and (4) there was special danger after the outbreak of the World War that Germany might make Haiti a base for its submarines." The truth was that Haiti's problems were at least in part the work of the State Department and other interested parties anxious to create a pretext for U.S. intervention.

A few weeks after Haiti had signed a "treaty" under American guns, a treaty draft was presented to the president of the Dominican Republic, whose country was suffering similar problems, and was indignantly turned down. In November of 1916 with the island in a turmoil of revolutionary upheaval, the marines landed. The Dominicans were warned that their capital would be bombarded "without restriction" if they resisted. The American minister to Santo Domingo informed what passed for a government at the moment that the American receiver general of customs was hereafter to supervise the government finances. And for eight years the United States imposed martial law on the island, forbidding all meetings, censoring the press, and threatening court-martial for anyone who protested against the American occupation. In the United States Senators Joseph Medill McCormick, William Borah, and George Norris carried on a running battle against the American occupation, aided and abetted by the *Nation* and the *New Republic*.

In the instances of Haiti and the Dominican Republic, as to a degree in the cases of Cuba and the Philippines, altruism, however misplaced, was mixed in, in fairly generous amounts, with self-interest. The old redemptive zeal was as much in evidence as the desire to protect business interests. Cynics were convinced that piety was simply a cover for greed and self-interest, but such was surely not the case with men such as Bryan or with Wilson himself. They were victims of a deep conviction that it was America's business to set the world right. The conditions in the various islands were such as to invite the intervention of the well-meaning as well as the rapacious: terrible poverty, widespread illiteracy and disease, the ruthless exploitation of the mass of the populations by a handful of wealthy landowners for whom government officials were simply pliant tools—all these factors were present in abundance. They fairly cried out for rectification. American reforms, American education, American business practices and know-how, above all, American research and science must initiate a better era. The trouble was in part that particular forms of American exploitation accompanied American efforts at reform, making the respective native populations suspect that the powers in Washington were less interested in their welfare than in their pennies or their labor. The invaders-redeemers (human nature being what it is, those qualities were often contained in the same individuals) found, to their pained surprise, that Cubans, Haitians, or Filipinos had a startling different perspective on their generally unwelcome intrusions. The "natives" planted bombs or murdered and disemboweled unwary soldiers or sailors, shot at their benefactors from ambush, and in other ways expressed their resentment. The furious benefactors, offended as only a rejected benefactor can be, struck back with the vastly greater power at their command—often indiscriminately since one "native" looked disconcertingly like another.

What the benefactors had to learn slowly and painfully was that their benefactions were as much resented as their exploitations. It was a lesson that Americans had taught *their* great benefactor, Great Britain, 150 years earlier. Now we had to learn the lesson ourselves. We proved to be as slow and refractory pupils as the British. There is much evidence that we still have not learned it well enough to earn a passing grade.

In Nicaragua the situation was more ambiguous (or the impulse for reform less apparent). New York bankers had invested $15,638,700 there. In 1912 the marines took it over briefly for the ostensible purpose of protecting "our Nicaraguan canal rights." From that relatively modest beginning we went on to "protect" the Nicaraguans in 1922 by hunting down the "bandit" Augusto César Sandino who had, it turned out, some dangerous political ideas as well.

Europe was the great enigma, the tinderbox. Germany dominated the Continent. The French, still bitter over their humiliating defeat in 1871, hunkered down behind their presumably impregnable defenses and sought allies against Germany. Britain was characterized by that happy complacency that was often difficult to distinguish from arrogance. Yet there was also a sense of diminished power and, perhaps more important, diminished will in that quarter. "Everybody by common consent," Henry Adams wrote to Elizabeth Cameron, "seems tacitly to assume that England is done. It is curious how quietly they seem to accept it. They speak with just a little hushed voice, as though some one were dead. It sounds ghostly."

The decline of Great Britain was accompanied by the growing power of Germany and the truculence of the kaiser, who seemed determined to provide the most substantial arguments against autocracies. He meddled in his erratic way all over the globe—China, Japan, Africa, even (or especially) Latin America. His interest in Latin America went back to 1901, when he apparently made an effort to buy the Santa Margarita Islands off the coast of Venezuela. He also expressed an interest in acquiring Magdalena Bay in Baja California from Mexico in 1902, news which alarmed the American ambassador to Great Britain, Joseph Choate, who wrote to John Hay: "We have a decidedly exposed flank here and it seems pretty clear that property is for sale and the Germans are after it."

Wilhelm, who had a morning newspaper printed for him exclusively in an edition of one with gold letters, apparently invented the phrase "yellow peril," which became a catchword for anti-Oriental sentiments. He counted on war between Japan and the United States. Also born in the kaiser's somewhat disordered imagination was the notion of using Mexico (which he associated with the Panama Canal since they both were in the same part of the world) as a kind of long-range German ally to distract the United States.

It would be hard to overstate the negative influence of the kaiser on American opinion, especially in those circles most favorable to Great Britain. It had been the conviction of Hay and, to a lesser extent, of Roosevelt that Wilhelm II had undertaken a widespread campaign to capture the loyalty of German immigrants in various countries but especially in the United States. Germans abroad who had distinguished themselves in their adopted homes were showered with honors by the fatherland. "The Emperor condescended to receive them and permitted even German Jews to penetrate to the antechambers of the Court . . ." Ray Stannard Baker wrote. "Toward native Americans, also, he showed great affability. His paid pamphleteers discovered that, in essence, the Prussians and the Yankees were singularly alike. No form of seduction which occurred to the Prussic imagination was left untried. Gradually, the United States were permeated by the spies, advocates, and surreptitious promoters of the glory of the Hohenzollern dynasty." Journalists "trained" by Bismarck's "reptile press" came to the United States to spread his doctrines. Even the exchange of German and American professors, encouraged by the kaiser, was seen as primarily an effort to subvert German-Americans and serve "the Germanist cause here."

More and more travelers—tourists and journalists—returned from Germany with troubling accounts of that nation's increasing militarism and belligerency. After a visit Charles Edward Russell noted, "The Germans . . . are in many respects, an admirable people. I know them well, esteem their good traits, like to visit their country. The system and ideals of their government are utterly incompatible with any faith in democracy or principle thereof. The system and ideals are the system and ideals of a ruling class that is maddened with the lust of power, domination, glory—and profits. They have dangled before the German people the great gilt bauble of imperialism at the sight of which most populations are likely to go mad. Except for going thus mad," Russell added, "and for tolerating an autocracy in the twentieth century, the German people are not to be blamed for . . . the incessant rumblings of their gigantic military machine, forever threatening the world with war. . . . Almost hand in hand with the development to perfection of the German military machine on land and sea went the unexampled development of the German colonial empire and of German industrialism and commerce."

A German naval officer told Russell of his nation's ambitions. Rich and powerful as Germany was, it had no ports on the Atlantic. France, on the other hand, had five. The officer, "exceedingly well educated, wise, courteous, sophisticated, honest," spread out a map. "That tells the story," he said to the American journalist. "No one that looks at . . . the map can doubt what is to happen. With all these colonies, all this mounting trade, all this increase in manufactures, Germany must have a port on the Atlantic. We shall have Paris three weeks after we start. Then the war will be over." Would the Germans occupy Paris? Russell asked. "Not so foolish" was the reply. "We don't want that uneasy, restless conniving population to deal with. Let it alone. All we want is Northern France with the harbors. Then Paris won't matter, for France will be reduced to a fifth-rate power." The naval officer did not, of course, speak for the kaiser, but Russell encountered everywhere much the same tone. In Karlsbad, "a clearing house for the inside news of Europe," the air was electric with tension, and the conviction that war must come was expessed everywhere. The only questions were when and how. In France the mood was very different. The socialists to whom Russell talked scoffed at talk of war. Their comrades, the German socialists, were too strong to allow such an adventure. "Let the Germans come," they exclaimed with Gallic effusiveness. "We will welcome them with open arms as brothers." In the new revolutionary order national differences would become insignificant.

Russell traveled on to England, where, characteristically, the principal concern seemed to be the lack of grouse that year. He returned to the United States, deeply troubled, convinced that war was imminent, but when he offered a magazine a report on his findings, including an outline of the German plan for an attack through Belgium into France, it was rejected out of hand. It was mad to think that there would be war in Europe. The nations had too much to lose to be taken in by the kaiser's foolish posturings.

With rumors and rumblings of war in Europe, peace groups became more active than ever, lobbying Congressmen and elected officials of every persuasion. The hope for peace focused on arbitration treaties—that is, agreements between various countries to submit disputes to third-party arbitration. Roosevelt was indignant. "At this moment," he wrote Lodge, "there is a very grave crisis in Europe, and before the war clouds now gathering, all the peace and arbitration treaties and all the male and female shrieking sisterhood of Carnegies and the like, are utterly powerless." Roosevelt knew at first hand, he told Lodge (had the kaiser told *him?*), that German war plans "contemplate . . . as possible courses of action, flank marches through both Belgium and Switzerland. They are under solemn treaties to respect the territories of both countries, and have not the slightest thought of paying the least attention to these treaties unless they are threatened with war as the result of their violation."

25

The War Begins

Although, as we have noted, Europe seethed with rumors and alarms of war, Great Britain and the United States remained undisturbed. The years 1912 and 1913 had indeed been among the most remarkable years in modern history. In the tension between a dying world, an archaic consciousness, and a world struggling to be born, Western Europe blossomed in a fever of aesthetic creation. In Germany, in Russia, in the Austro-Hungarian Empire, in France, and in a lesser degree (or a more literary degree) in Britain, artists, poets, and even philosophers reached levels of achievement unparalleled since the Renaissance. In the visual arts, images quivered and dissolved and formed again. The material world melted into dreams and visions; figures floated in the air, metamorphosed, grew strangely angular; and disturbing music expressed astonishing dissonances, unsettling arabesques of sound. Bewildered critics and patrons were startled out of their conventional notions of art by "artists who took the name of 'Wild Beasts.'" Intimations had reached America in the Armory Show.

The year 1913 seemed in retrospect to Henry Adams to have marked "the dissolution of the old society in Europe in several very great empires." Italy had plunged into war to escape internal upheaval. France was on the verge. "Germany had raised its socialistic force to the highest power consistent with the old order" through such measures as old age and unemployment benefits. "Clearly," he wrote to his brother, Brooks, "all the world is scared and pessimistic and tending to suicide. . . . Another ten years—or even five,—at the rate of the last, will see moral *débâcle*."

While the triumph of the Republican old guard in the election of 1912 seemed to Brooks Adams a prelude to revolution, many others saw Wilson as the hope of the future and were thrilled by the tide of reform legislation that he steered through Congress so boldly in his first extraordinary months.

It was this world, full of doubts and hopes, pregnant with half-articulated promises, that received incredulously the news of a crisis in Europe. It all began innocuously enough.

As early as the First Balkan War in 1912, the German chief of staff, General Helmuth von Moltke, had declared that "a European war is bound to come sooner or later, and then it will, in the last resort, be a struggle between Teuton and Slav. It is the duty of all states who uphold the banner of German spiritual culture to prepare for this conflict. But the attack must come from the Slavs." Thus, when Serbian terrorists, recruited by Serbian officers, assassinated the archduke Franz Ferdinand (heir apparent to the Hapsburg throne), Austria, eager to humble the Serbs, was ready to undertake a general war, the major purpose of which would be the subjugation of the Slavic peoples of Central Europe to the Teutonic.

Austria mobilized for an attack on Serbia; Russia contemplated a partial mobilization as a warning to Austria that it could not pursue its designs on Serbia without the danger of Russian intervention. Meanwhile, the German ambassador to Russia informed Czar Nicholas II that Germany would regard even a partial mobilization as a threat and order mobilization of its own armies, "and in that case a European war could scarcely be prevented." The indecisive czar ordered full mobilization and then canceled the order and telephoned his cousin the kaiser, urging that the controversy between Serbia and Austria be submitted to the Court of International Arbitration at The Hague. The kaiser wrote on the telegram "Nonsense."

Wilhelm then sent word to the emperor Franz Joseph of Austria that he wished to state "most emphatically that Berlin expected the Monarchy to act against Serbia, and that Germany would not understand it if . . . the present opportunity were all to go by . . . without a blow struck." The Hungarian premier, Count Stephen Tisza, meanwhile warned of the possibility that an attack on Serbia might bring about the intervention of Russia "and consequently world war." An investigation, launched by Austria into the circumstances of Franz Ferdinand's assassination, in the meantime announced, "There is nothing to indicate, or even give rise to the suspicion, that the Serbian government knew about the plot. . . . On the contrary, there are indications that this is impossible." The Austrian ministry nonetheless went ahead with its "intentionally unacceptable ultimatum" to the Serbian government. The president of the French Republic, Raymond Poincaré, warned the Austrian ambassador to Russia, "With a little good will, this Serbian business is easy to settle. But it can just as easily become acute. Serbia has some very warm friends in the Russian people. And Russia has an ally, France."

In the midst of general anxiety about Russian intentions, a member of the Austrian Parliament asked the opinion of the prime minister, Count Karl von Stürgkh. It had been said that Russia dared not intervene because of the danger of revolution at home. A Russian émigré named Bronstein was a notorious advocate of revolution who held forth at the Café Central in Vienna. The Austrian secret police considered him a harmless windbag, and Count von Stürgkh replied scornfully to his questioner, "And who shall make this revolution in Russia? Perhaps Herr Bronstein from the Café Central?" Lev Davidovich Bronstein was the real name of Leon Trotsky; his fellow coffeehouse exponent of revolution was Vladimir Ilyich Ulyanov—Nikolai Lenin.

The Serbs, anxious to avoid war at all costs, offered to comply with most of the Austrian demands, insulting as they were, but they resisted the stipulation that Austrian police and judges be permitted to join in the search for and prosecution of the plotters. When the kaiser read the Serbian response, he declared it "a brilliant performance. . . . This is more than one could have expected! A great moral victory for Vienna; but with it every reason for war drops away. . . . On the strength of this *I* should never have ordered mobilization!" He sent word to Vienna urging an accommodating spirit. When Sir Edward Grey, the British foreign secretary, learned of the conciliatory Serbian reply, he warned the Austrians that persistence in attacking Serbia would make it clear beyond question that the only purpose was to crush that nation. Russia must react, and "the result would be the most frightful war that Europe had ever seen."

John Jay Chapman was in Kassel, Germany, in July, 1914, when Europe began to collapse into war. "The war scare is on," he wrote to

his mother. "People are surging in the streets. . . . If Russia gets involved Germany must go in." A week later he wrote to the *Times* of
London: "During the last month many persons of gentle breeding in
Germany, and high up in military circles, have seemed to be under an
obsession. . . . The religious zeal of the Emperor is not personal, but
tribal. We are in the presence of a military fanaticism which reminds
of Mahomet. I have been a little terrified for some years past in meeting
individual Germans. A gleam like hatred or like insanity would flit
across their personality, and give me a vague, queer chill."

In the midst of desperate diplomatic maneuverings, Secretary of
State Bryan submitted a proposal to all the major European powers,
asking them to wait a year between the occasion of war and actual
fighting to allow peaceful solutions to be explored. Apparently the
kaiser was the only head of state flatly to refuse Bryan's proposal as
submitted by House, saying, in effect, "With the German army and
navy trained to the moment, why should I give another nation a year
to prepare?"

The principal uncertainty was what course Great Britain would
pursue. That country gave every indication of an intention to remain
neutral. (In postwar postmortems it was agreed that a strong signal
from Britain that it would enter the war on the side of France would
have restrained Germany.) The fact seems to be that between the date
of the Austrian note on July 23 and August 4, when Britain declared
war on the Central Powers, the state of public opinion was such that
any effort to have "warned off" Germany with the threat that Britain
would enter the war on the side of France would have been vociferously
rejected by the great majority of the British. "Virtually nobody in
England," Charles Edward Russell wrote, "was ready for any such
adventure. . . . The opinion prevailed in the Cabinet and in the country
in general that Britain could remain aloof from the impending conflict." In large part this amiable complacency rested on a complete
misreading of the military potency of the respective armies—French
and German. It was simply taken as a dictum that the French Army
was, in every important respect, the equal, if not the superior, of the
German Army. The French border was heavily fortified with all the
most modern weapons, including the dreaded machine gun and battery
upon battery of artillery. It seems never to have occurred to the British
government, or to its military planners, that the Germans could penetrate those defenses. What must result, after some desultory fighting,
was a stalemate and a negotiated peace.

In the event of war the famous Schlieffen plan of the German general staff called for a massive and rapid German advance through Belgium in a great encirclement, intended to wheel about, with its hub at Verdun, sweep around in a semicircle, cross the Marne, capture Paris, and take the major elements of the French Army from the rear. Everything depended on the numbing speed and shock of the initial attack. At the outbreak of hostilities the German command thus requested that its armies be allowed to pass through Belgium. When King Albert refused indignantly to allow his country's neutrality to be violated, the German Army stormed into that country. Britain responded by declaring war. A cataclysm that would engulf the world had begun. Florence Harriman was in Paris when the German assault began. "People," she recalled, "ran every which way; tears were in the air."

The Schlieffen plan almost worked, but Count von Moltke, the German chief of staff, made just those modifications in the plan of attack and his subordinate officers committed just those errors that allowed the attack to bog down and the French to realign their forces to stop the German advance at the Marne. At that point, with the entry of the British into the war and the deployment of their units in support of the French, any hope of a swift and conclusive victory by the Germans was lost.

Militarily and psychologically Britain was even less prepared than France. "Never," Charles Edward Russell wrote, "went a great nation into a conflict so ill-prepared. On the land side nothing was ready, not even, so far as could be discerned, the vestige of a plan. . . . England in 1914 was without any equipment to carry on war in the modern way, without the machinery to create such an equipment, and but for the navy might in the first few months have been cut up like cheese. The war was not popular, the cause that had led the country into it was not well known, and the general ineptitude was painfully shown in the placard that appeared in all London shop windows. 'Business as Usual. . . .' "

In America, horror and incredulity were the most common reactions. "I had a feeling that the end of things had come," David Houston wrote. ". . . I stopped in my tracks, dazed and horror-stricken."

William Allen White was at his summer vacation home in Estes Park, Colorado, when the news came of the German invasion of Belgium. In the hills about there were half a dozen Kansas college professors and doctors and lawyers, who gathered at White's home to discuss the latest word from abroad. A University of Kansas history professor, Frank Heywood Hodder, refused to believe the newspaper reports. "It can't be so," he insisted. "They aren't telling the truth. Why, there's a treaty between Belgium and Germany that would prevent it!" White added, "When he had to accept the invasion of Belgium as a fact despite the treaty, the foundations of his faith in modern civilization completely caved in and he was a heart-broken man for nearly a week." It seemed incomprehensible to White and his academic friends as they sat on the porch, looking out toward the peaceful snow-crowned summit of Longs Peak, and tried to understand what it all meant. That the United States might become directly involved did not occur to any of them (though perhaps it might have to a similar group summering at an Eastern resort—Nahant or Saratoga). Nor did White at least have an inkling that it might signal the beginning of the vast worldwide revolutionary upheaval that so many intellectuals had come to anticipate and, indeed, looked forward to. While White "did not even dream how our whole economy would be bent toward making the materials and munitions of war," he did realize sadly that it meant at the very least a delay in the progressive program of reform proceeding so reassuringly under Wilson's guidance. The attention of the American people would inevitably be turned toward issues not congenial to the spirit of reform.

"From the moment the war began," Oswald Garrison Villard wrote, "the whole current of American life was changed and Mr. Wilson's great advances toward the New Freedom checked and finally stopped. The shadow of European events overhung everything—the markets, our sea-borne trade, the Treasury, the federal revenue." Walter Lippmann wrote to his friend Felix Frankfurter of the "awful disintegration" that threatened all liberal hopes; "ideas, books, seem too utterly trivial, and all the public opinion, democratic hope and what not, where is it today? Like a flower in the path of a plough."

Like a tropical storm that fills the atmosphere with dangerous and distressing charges of electricity, the war made itself felt in subtle ways. The world, it was apparent to at least some, had reached one of those dramatic and essentially incomprehensible turning points of which there have been perhaps scarcely half a dozen in recorded history, in which things do indeed seem to be out of control. All private hopes and expectations are rendered problematical, and the fate of nations hangs in the balance. Theoretically, of course, the socialists and, to a lesser extent, the anarchists were ready for it. They could fit it into the Marxist framework. It was the predictable conflict between decadent, imperialist capitalisms that was the necessary prelude to world revolution, the interim dictatorship of the proletariat, and, subsequently, the withering away of the state and true freedom for all humankind. Yet oddly enough it did not quite seem to fit. Presumably all the various socialisms had to do was to sit back and wait for the inevitable collapse, in mutual carnage, of the capitalists. The trouble was, of course, that the workers, not the capitalists, were fighting the war—millions of representatives of the middle class as well. "From the beginning," Hutchins Hapgood wrote, "we felt the War as a social upheaval rather than as a war. Even the Socialists forgot their stereotyped materialistic explanation and reacted with emotional imaginative complexity. It was personal and impersonal, a turmoil from within as well as from without. . . . Where were we? What were we? The War in our souls broke out. We were the Cause of the War; the violence and inconsistency of our emotions, the impotence of our ideas. What were our ideas worth? Had they ever contributed to make the War impossible?"

Hapgood wrote: "From month to month, my general state of feeling never varied from a deep-seated hostility. . . . From the beginning I knew that there was no guilty nation, that if the naïve idea of guilt was to be applied at all, it would have to be applied equally to all the great powers." In Europe there had been for years a conviction that war was coming. Only in Britain and in America had there been the illusion of peace.

Herbert Hoover, whose perspective on the world was very different from that of Hutchins Hapgood, perceived the prewar era as "the happiest period of all humanity in the Western World in ten centuries. . . ." It had been a time "of advancing human welfare and progress. The dignity of men and women and their personal liberty were everywhere receiving wider recognition. Human slavery had long since disappeared. Freedom of speech and worship, the right of men to choose their own callings, the security of justice were yearly spreading over wider and wider areas. . . . Fear had disappeared in the hearts of men. It was an era of released human spirit." There were, Hoover confessed, "squalor, privilege, slums, slum minds, greed, corruption and bad taste," but they had been recognized and were being "lessened year by year." The "middle class" constituted 80 percent of the population, and "hosts of individuals before our eyes were constantly rising from lowly surroundings to security and comfort. . . . In the material world there was a steady advance in the average standard of living and in the wealth of nations. . . . People were busy building railways and communications, roads and power plants, new ships discovering new mines, erecting magnificent buildings, beautifying their cities.

"Scientific research was daily unfolding new truth and breaking new frontiers of human progress." In the face of all this progress "the world stumbled into the Great War," and with that stumble "a period of Great Fear settled like a fog upon the human race—to last, perhaps, for generations."

Theodore Roosevelt's initial reaction was remarkably peaceful, especially when we consider his subsequent militancy. In September, 1914, he wrote in the *Outlook:* "Our country stands well-nigh alone among the great civilized powers in being unshaken by the present world-wide war. For this we should be humbly and profoundly grateful. . . . As regards the actions of most of the combatants in the hideous and world-wide war now raging, it is possible sincerely to take and defend either of the opposite views concerning their actions. . . . When Russia took part, it may well be argued that it was impossible for Germany not to come to the aid of Austria. . . . I think, at any rate, I hope, I have rendered it plain that I am not now criticizing, that I am not passing judgment one way or the other upon Germany's action. I admire and respect the German people. I am proud of the German blood in my veins. . . . Only the clearest and most urgent national duty would ever justify us in deviating from our rule of neutrality and non-interference. . . ."

From London Walter Hines Page, the American ambassador, wrote to his Johns Hopkins teacher and friend Woodrow Wilson: "Be ready, for you will be called upon to compose this huge quarrel. I thank Heaven for many things—first, the Atlantic Ocean; second, that you refrained from war in Mexico; third, that we kept our treaty—the Canal Tolls victory, I mean. Now, when all this half the world will suffer the unspeakable mutilation of war, we shall preserve our moral strength, our political powers, and our ideals."

More than 120,000 Americans, 30,000 of them teachers, were stranded in Europe by the outbreak of the war. An American committee, of which Herbert Hoover was a member, was hastily organized to help them get back to the United States. In Hoover's words, "the whole fabric of international finance had gone to smash." Business was at a standstill, and Hoover's own global enterprises were laying workers

off. The most colorful of the Americans caught by the beginning of
hostilities was a Wild West show in Poland, made up of twelve Indians
and ten American cowboys. The Polish authorities had seized their
ponies. They had a small zoo in conjunction with their show, and when
their money ran out, they fed the orangutan to the lion and tiger, and
then, unable to get transportation out of the country, they abandoned
the lion and tiger along with an elephant.

Britain, France, Holland, and Belgium (the part of it not already
overrun by German soldiers), as well as Germany, were filled with
alarmed Americans trying to get back to America. Those in Germany
experienced an arrogant contempt for Americans that seemed acti-
vated by the outbreak of the war. A couple from Ohio, trying to make
their way to Holland, were taken from their train at four different
stations, and each time the wife was stripped naked in the presence of
German officers. The episode stuck in Charles Edward Russell's mind
as a symbol of human behavior when the "mad dogs of war" were
turned loose. Some Americans were simply stripped of their money
and passports and left to make their way as best they could. Russell
volunteered his services to the American minister at The Hague, who
was trying to cope with the flood of refugees. "Every morning when
we went to work" at the legation, Russell noted, "we found a long
queue of them waiting at the front door, many penniless, some hysterical, all anxious and nervous." Suddenly reports of German insults
to Americans stopped. Every effort was made for their comfort and
safety. Each departing American received a bouquet of flowers. It was
the kaiser's order.

John Jay Chapman's son, Victor, an architectural student in Paris,
rushed off to enlist in the French Foreign Legion. Young Chapman
wrote to his mother that he was convinced that Germany would "go
down after a year or two. She is crazed," he added, "and will fight like
the Southern Confederacy, but she won't win out. The world is too
wise to make a truce with her." After the defeat of Germany there
would be, Chapman believed, "an opportunity for a Congress of Disarmament—compulsory disarmament—a thing to be carried out quietly, and enforced by gunboats." Anything that France, Britain, and
America were agreed upon could be made a political reality. "The
danger," Victor Chapman wrote, "is that between now and the end of
the war, these Powers may disagree among themselves." The worst
thing that could happen was that through a prolonged conflict the
Allies might begin "to think about national aggrandizement"; then "the

antagonisms will recommence, and the world will be booked for additional unpleasant experience. . . . The disturber of the peace must be restrained, not pillaged; and the hand of the constable must receive no part of the thief's property."

The outbreak of hostilities created an immediate crisis in international socialism. Delegates, among them Charles Edward Russell, were gathering for the International Socialist Congress at Rotterdam. American delegates included Oscar Ameringer; Emil Seidel, the Socialist mayor of Milwaukee; George Lunn, the Socialist mayor of Schenectady; Meyer London, Socialist Congressman from New York; and Morris Hillquit. Before they could sail on the *Vaterland,* word came of the outbreak of war. In Ameringer's words, "The thing we had predicted, feared, and that no one wanted, was upon us. The heap of artificially stimulated mistrust, hatred, lies, diplomatic chicanery, powder, oil, rags, and matches, exploded." The site of the congress was shifted to Brussels, but in a few weeks Belgium lay prostrated before the German armies. That was hardly the worst. Instead of opposing the war, the various European Socialist parties, many of them far more powerful than their American counterpart, fell in line with disconcerting speed. The German Social Democratic Party, the guide and model for the American Socialists, voted large sums to support the German war machine. Jean Jaurès, the leading Socialist and opponent of war in France, was assassinated. Emile Vandervelde, the famous Belgian socialist theorist, gave his support to the war government on the not unreasonable ground that his country had been invaded. And, finally, Georgi V. Plekhanov, the Russian Marxist, threw his support to the czar.

With the outbreak of the war Wilson issued a proclamation of neutrality and called on all Americans to be "impartial in thought, as well as in action." On September 26, 1914, Bryan requested the British to honor the Declaration of the London Maritime Conference of 1908–09. The British had announced that they would comply with the declaration "subject to certain modifications and additions . . . indispensable to the efficient conduct of naval operations."

When Bryan framed a strong protest over British restrictions on neutral trade, House urged Wilson to bring more subtle pressures to bear, emphasizing the effect of the edict on public opinion more than on the uncertain letter of international law. British Orders in Council (the phrase recalled to some the War of 1812) of October 29 and December 23, 1914, imposed further restrictions on neutral trade.

German ports were blockaded, and the North Sea was mined. The British went so far as to insist that neutral shipping proceed to British ports to be searched for contraband and take on their pilots to steer the ships through their minefields. Behind these edicts was the British disposition to fight a "cheap war." They had adopted the policy of recruiting an army through volunteers and clung to the illusion that what was an irredeemably land war could be won on the sea.

As it became increasingly clear that the war was resulting in a bloody stalemate on the battlefields, both Britain and Germany adopted a policy of trying to throttle each other economically—the British by mines and warships, the Germans with their U-boats. On February 2, 1915, Great Britain placed all goods, foods included, on its list of contraband. The Germans responded two days later by declaring "the waters around Great Britain and Ireland, including the English Channel . . . a war region." British ships in that zone would be destroyed "without its always being possible to warn the crews or the passengers of the dangers threatening." Neutral ships would also be in danger "in view of the misuse of neutral flags. . . ." On March 2, 1915, Prime Minister Asquith imposed a blockade of the German coast. No ships could enter or leave German ports.

Meanwhile, the United States reversed its initial policy of forbidding commercial loans to the belligerents. On November 4, the National City Bank made a $10,000,000 loan to the French government. A year later the dam broke when a consortium of banks negotiated an Allied loan of $500,000,000. By April, 1917, Americans had invested well over $2,000,000,000 in Allied war bonds, as contrasted with $20,000,000 in German bonds. If a nation's heart is to be found where its pocketbook is, there was no doubt of where the hearts of American bondholders were.

Within a month or so after the "guns of August" had opened fire, the polarization of the country had begun. It was along class, geographic, ethnic, and political lines. The geographic lines were perhaps the most basic. The Eastern upper class, especially, with its strong ties to Britain, grew increasingly pro-Ally with each passing month. "All the people who come to see me are simply and flatly anti-German and not pro-anything. Hatred of the German seems to be a ground on which all can stand," Henry Adams wrote. A few weeks later he wrote to Elizabeth Cameron: "The up-lifters and Progressives are quiet—almost—and one can hear an occasional whisper of sense. The social tide seems violently set, and we are allies. Even those who at first talked

German have now shut up." He added, "Apparently we are working day and night for the Allies, but also for money."

John Jay Chapman initially made a determined effort at neutrality. In his opinion, the proper course for the United States to pursue was do its best to prevent "cruel reprisals" at the war's end. "The antidote to war," he wrote, "is peace, to unreason, reason, to mania, sense. If America can remain neutral without violation to her self-respect, it is far better to do so. If America should enter the war, the world would lose the benevolence and common-sense which we now possess, and which is a strong factor in the whole situation. You and I," he declared, addressing his fellow Americans collectively, "would, in that case, become partisans, cruel, excited, and bent on immediate results." But when his son, Victor, enlisted in the Lafayette Escadrille, the famous French air unit, and was shot down over Verdun (the first American aviator to die in France), Chapman abandoned any pretense of impartiality. Young Chapman's death took on an enormous symbolic importance for Americans and Frenchmen alike and for Chapman, who was consoled by that fact. He wrote beside his son's name in the family prayer book: "For thou, O God, hast proved us; thou also hast tried us, like as silver is tried." Soon Chapman was writing impatiently: "I do hope the Americans will get into this war." He wrote to Lord Haldane: "President Wilson is rather wearing out our patience." Some months later he termed Wilson a "mendacious coward," a "putty-faced, untruthful person," who "rowed with one oar and backed water with the other." Like so many others of his class, Chapman had surrendered completely to his pro-British inclinations.

In Oswald Garrison Villard's opinion, "the first reaction of the public was against the whole military system in Europe, and a recognition—before the passions engendered by the war began to becloud people's judgments—that this was at the bottom of the conflict; that you could not build up huge military rivalries without insuring an inevitable explosion. . . ." On August 29, 1914, some 2,000 women joined in a peace parade down Fifth Avenue with Fanny Villard at their head. There were no flags, no speeches, but only a silent protest against the invasion of Belgium by the German armies.

The League to Limit Armaments was formed in December, 1914, to counteract the "outcry from . . . jingoes and militarists" that the United States "must follow in Germany's foot steps and militarize." Among the leaders in the league's activities were Nicholas Murray Butler, George Plimpton, Lillian Wald, Adolph Lewisohn, and Carrie Chapman Catt.

The league announced its policy to resist increased expenditures on armaments, declaring that "there has been presented to the United States an unexampled opportunity for constructive moral and political leadership in the work of the world. . . . This is assuredly the opportunity for which a people and a government like ours were raised up— the opportunity not only to speak but actually to embody and exemplify counsels of peace and sanity and the lasting concord which is based on justice and fair and generous dealing." When the President gave his support to the League to Enforce Peace, Lippmann and the *New Republic* hailed it "as a decisive turning point in the history of the modern world" and "one of the greatest utterances since the Monroe Doctrine."

Peace groups were active in every large city. Prominent among them were the Women's Peace Party, which Jane Addams helped found, the American Union Against Militarism, and the American Neutrality Conference Committee of New York City. The *Survey,* one of the best-known journals of reform, opposed supplying munitions to the belligerents. Henry Wadsworth Longfellow Dana, son of Richard Henry Dana and Longfellow's daughter, was another prominent recruit to the peace cause. The venerable Congregational minister Washington Gladden was dean of the pacifists. He had written five years earlier: "I believe that the day of disarmament is nigh, even at the doors, and that our nation is called of God to take the initiative in it. We are not in danger of aggression from any power under the sun; and it is perfectly safe for us to stop our shipbuilding and lift up the standards of peace before all nations . . . it is time that some great nation should pause in this mad race to ruin and call a halt to the rest. Our nation is the one that can speak with most commanding voice. It is her manifest destiny to lead the nations in paths of peace, and her opportunity is here, for peace has already become not merely a possibility, but a stern economic necessity."

At the same time there was in the East a "war" faction that grew more militant by the month. Its champion was the belligerent former President, who was soon blowing the trumpet call to arms. Those who wished to see the United States ranged alongside the Allies made "Preparedness" their slogan. The National Defense League, a highly conservative organization of businessmen and old guard politicians, was the principal propagandist for preparedness. In the words of David Houston, "In the field of military and financial preparedness, the President had pressed matters about as far as it was possible to carry them with any hope of having a majority in Congress and the public back of him." Part of the problem was that antipreparedness, or peace sentiment, was stronger in the President's own party than in the opposition ranks, if we except the very important group of Progressive Republican Senators on whom he depended for support of his domestic reforms.

Simultaneously, there was an ominous note in Wilson's frequent references to those Americans "born under other flags but welcomed under our generous naturalization laws . . . who have poured the poison of disloyalty into the very arteries of our national life; who have sought to bring the authority and good name of our government into contempt, to destroy our industries . . . for their vindictive purposes . . . and to debase our policies to the uses of foreign intrigue. . . . It is possible to deal with these things very effectually. I need not suggest the terms in which they may be dealt with." But the President did not stop with the foreign-born intriguers. He had "even greater contempt," Houston wrote, for the native-born "who had been guilty of disturbing the self-possession and misrepresenting the temper and principles of the country during these days of terrible war, when it would seem that every man who was truly American would instinctively make it his duty and his pride to keep the scales of judgment even and prove himself a partisan of no nation but his own." Such individuals with "their passionate sympathy with one or the other side . . . preach and practise disloyalty." No laws could "reach corruptions of the mind and heart," but every patriotic American must hold them in contempt for the "discredit they are daily bringing upon us." Although the President was careful to speak of the "passionate sympathy with *one or the other side,*" it was clear that he was not talking about his friends who wholeheartedly favored the British. His remarks were plainly understood to be addressed to those Americans who spoke out on behalf of the Central Powers—Germans, Austrians, and Hungarians for the most part.

Opinion in the West, where anti-British sentiment was strong, ranged from neutralist to pro-German. "Like almost all people in the big Eastern cities, I was passionately pro-Ally, but I know the West was not," Florence Harriman wrote. That was understating the case. The war brought prosperity, much of it to those very farmers of the Midwest who were most opposed to military involvement. It was what the Germans called *Blutsegen* or "blood blessing." Wheat rose to its highest level in years, almost $3 a bushel, while cotton went up to 40 cents a pound, and hogs proportionately. Many factories converted to war production; the price of farm goods rose markedly; steel production soared. "War," William Allen White wrote, "was producing in the United States its own intoxication, a kind of economic inflation that had spiritual reflexes. People felt happy because they were busy and seemed to be making money . . . naturally, as the Allies were our customers, they became our friends. . . ."

In Milwaukee, Oscar Ameringer wrote, the Poles, many of whom had been drawn into the Socialist Party, were "fighting the battles of Poland in the twelfth and fourteenth wards of Milwaukee." The Germans in the northern part of the city followed the lead of the German-language newspaper *Germania* in giving their support to the fatherland, while third- and fourth- generation Americans of German ancestry were torn between a policy of nonbelligerence and deep cultural attachments. The *Milwaukee Leader,* the voice of the Socialist Party in Wisconsin, took the line that it was a capitalist war that was "of no concern to the good people of Milwaukee and to the country at large."

The war put Oswald Garrison Villard, the *Nation,* and the *New York Evening Post* in a bind. Villard's affection for Germany and for things German—for German music (Beethoven, Brahms, and Wagner) and for German philosophy (Goethe, Schiller, Schopenhauer, and Hegel)—was profound. The staffs of both papers agreed that right favored the Allied cause, and Villard himself wrote the editorial affirming that conviction. *"The Nation,"* he wrote, "has always entertained and expressed the highest admiration for the German people, but never for the Germany of the Kaiser. . . . Never have we upheld the Germany of the mailed fist, of the autocracy of militarism; against its excesses, its encroachments upon civil rights, its assertion that it constitutes a sacrosanct caste, superior to any other, we have protested in season and out of season." While the world owed a great debt to "the spiritual leadership" of Germany, that debt could not excuse the crime of bringing on a terrible war. "For ourselves," Villard concluded, "we can only say that the one consolation in it all is that, if humanity is not to retrograde unspeakably, absolutism must pay for this denial of Christianity. Out of the ashes must come a new Germany, in which democracy shall rule, in which no one man, and no group of professional man-killers, shall have the power to plunge the whole world into mourning."

When Wilson addressed Congress in December, 1914, his efforts were directed toward forestalling any large-scale program of preparedness on the ground that such a step would seem to Americans as well as to the warring nations a prelude to American entry into the war and an incitement to pacifists and those opposed to American involvement. The nation, he told Congress, was not prepared for war and could not become so in any way compatible with our political institutions. "This is the time above all others," he declared, "when we should wish and resolve to keep our strength by self-possession, our influence by preserving our ancient principles of action . . . We are not asking our young men to spend the best years of their lives making soldiers of themselves." The national guard should be strengthened, and there should be a system "by which every citizen who will volunteer for training may be made familiar with the use of modern arms, the rudiments of drill and maneuver, and the maintenance and sanitation of camps. . . . More than this proposed at this time, permit me to say, would mean merely that we have been thrown off our balance by a war with which we have nothing to do, whose causes cannot touch us, whose very existence affords us opportunities of friendship and disinterested service which should make us ashamed of any thought of hostility or fearful preparations for trouble." The task of Americans was not preparation for war but rather "To develop our life and our resources; to supply our own people and the people of the world as their need arises from the abundant plenty of our fields and our marts of trade; to enrich the commerce of our own states and of the world with the products of our mines, our farms, and our factories, with the creations of our thought and the fruits of our character . . . as we strive to show in our life as a nation what liberty and the inspiration of an emancipated spirit may do for men and for societies, for individuals, for states, and for mankind."

The speech was a shrewd combination of idealism combined with a more material appeal. For those militant spirits eager for war he offered the prospect of civilian training as an outlet for their zeal. To the rest of the nation he hinted at the rewards to be gained by making available to the warring nations, "friends" of the United States, the products of American farms, mines, and industries. In other words, neutrality should be the profitable as well as the morally correct course.

By 1915 Jane Addams had perceived a disposition in the American press "to make pacifist activity or propaganda so absurd that it would be absolutely without influence and its authors so discredited that nothing they might say or do would be regarded as worthy of attention." Hull House itself came under attack as a nest of pacifist intrigue, and the City Health Department took revenge on it by "inefficient sanitary service" which lasted for many months. When Jane Addams returned from The Hague Peace Conference in 1915 and tried to report on the sentiment for peace among many of the ordinary people of Europe, she was astonished at the hostility she and her fellow pacifists encountered. "We had," she wrote, "been much impressed with the fact that it was an old man's war, that the various forms of doubt and opposition to the war had no method of public expression and that many of the soldiers themselves were far from enthusiastic in regard to actual fighting as a method of settling international difficulties." But when Addams and others made such statements, they were bitterly denounced as traitors, as weak and sentimental tools of the enemy.

Ameringer expressed the Socialist Party's view of the conflict in a poem called "Dumdum Bullets." Both the Allies and the Central Powers had accused each other of using bullets with the noses filed off to create the most devastating wounds. Ameringer's poem ran:

> A working-man, a little dumb,
> Made for his boss a little gun,
> A cartridge and a bullet
> With point sawed off to dull it.
>
> Another worker, just as dumb,
> Made for another boss a gun,
> A cartridge and a bullet
> With point sawed off to dull it.
>
> One day the poor, dumb workers met,
> Aimed at each other's wooden heads
> And each one sent a bullet
> With the point sawed off to dull it.
>
> Two bullets fled and said
> "Dumb dumb,"
> Two dummies tumbled over dead—
> Never knew what the bullets said.

But there were early signs of a serious schism in Socialist ranks. In addition to the prominent German and Austrian Socialists who immediately gave their support to the war, some prominent American Socialists began to waffle. Charles Edward Russell's statement that Germany's invasion of Belgium "imperiled every international convenant in the world and shook all foundations of international society" flew in the face of his own Socialist Party's analysis of the war as a contest between decadent capitalist nations for spoils. It cast Germany in the role of a rogue nation which, by a single lawless act, had placed the world in jeopardy. More and more American Socialists inclined toward Russell's position.

The greatest blow to the anarchists was Prince Kropotkin's support of the Allies. "It was a staggering blow to our movement," Emma Goldman wrote, "and especially to those of us who knew and loved Peter." The American anarchists stood firm, despite the defection of their hero. To them the war remained "a struggle of financial and economic interests foreign to the worker and . . . the most destructive factor of what is vital and worth while in the world." Goldman devoted herself to attacking in *Mother Earth* and from innumerable lecture platforms the notion of preparedness. "Readiness," she argued, far from preventing war, made it inevitable. As the campaign for preparedness gathered momentum, her lectures and writings took on a greater urgency. In San Francisco, Sasha Berkman edited the *Blast*. In New York it was the anarchist journal *Revolt* that carried on the battle against American involvement, and in Chicago *Alarm* was the spokesman for antiwar sentiment.

Both the British and the Germans did their tireless best to influence American opinion. At this game the British were clearly the more adept while the Germans compounded excruciating blunders.

The British realized from the first moment that they had to appeal to the idealistic vein in the American temper. When John Jay Chapman had lunch with Arthur Balfour, the first lord of the admiralty, Balfour professed complete sympathy with Chapman's notion of Allied war aims. Chapman's realistic wife believed it all would evaporate in talk "in the way of the moony educated English," but Chapman was encouraged. Lord Haldane told Chapman that the British Cabinet's goals were the independence of Belgium, the fulfillment of promises of limited hegemony to the Poles, Alsace-Lorraine returned to France, and, finally, disarmament. Chapman again was much encouraged. In order to enlist American sympathies, Chapman told Haldane, there must be some kind of British Emancipation Proclamation stating that nation's war aims and disavowing territorial aggrandizement.

Chapman reported the conversations to Wilson, and Florence Harriman carried similar encouraging words designed to play on Wilson's innate sympathy for the Allies. After a talk with Wilson, Chapman wrote to Lord Haldane: "I believe he understands the war better than any one in America. He has a kind of genius for understanding men and for using the symbols of government, and within him is a furnace. He has during the last few years controlled the American mind. . . . There must be some good in the American people or they never would have chosen such a man."

As a consequence in part of Chapman's good offices, Balfour was dispatched to the United States to play on Wilson's sympathies. In Steffens's words, "England sent man after man over here to get Wilson, till finally they found Arthur Balfour, a man, a liberal who could, as the President said, 'talk his language,' the liberal language, principles— bunk." A charming and adroit man, a philosopher, an author, an intellectual, and a man known for his "seraphic equanimity," Balfour appeared to be Wilson's British counterpart, an idealist, a scholar-intellectual, a believer in constitutional principles common to both English-speaking peoples. He played on all the Anglophilic impulses in the President that Frederic Howe had noted when he was a student of Wilson's at Johns Hopkins University.

One of the greatest mistakes of the Germans was to mount an aggressive campaign of espionage and sabotage in the United States (and Mexico). The ingenuity of the German agents was matched only by their ineptitude. The intelligence they collected could not possibly have compensated for the indignation aroused by their exposure. The able German ambassador, Count von Bernstorff, was the embarrassed witness of his countrymen's bungling. Bernstorff had been born in England and held honorary degrees from five American universities, including Princeton. He was a famous waltzer and tireless romancer, a good golfer and skilled poker player. He was always accessible to the press and wrote and spoke virtually flawless English.

The German intelligence activities were divided among three principal German agents. Captain Franz von Rintelen, who lived in New York before the war as the representative of a German bank and belonged to the swank New York Yacht Club, had elaborate plans to encourage strikes and sabotage in American war plants. In addition, he had been provided with a half million dollars to employ agents to build and place time bombs on ships carrying arms and munitions to the Allies. Under the name of Emil V. Gasche and a number of other aliases, Rintelen organized Labor's National Peace Council for the purpose of fomenting strikes among longshoremen and workers in munitions factories.

Major Franz von Papen, military attaché in the German Embassy, and his naval counterpart, Captain Carl von Boy-Ed, also had espionage duties. The better part of these activities went on under the watchful eyes of one or more American counterintelligence agencies. Among the targets for sabotage in the event that the United States entered the war were factories, bridges, canals, and wharves. A munitions explosion on Black Tom Island in New Jersey in July, 1916, which resulted in $22,000,000 worth of damage, was believed to have been the result of German sabotage. Six months later another explosion at Kingsland, New Jersey, caused enormous losses and indications again were of sabotage.

Each member of the German Embassy had his own office in New York and used the German-American Club on Central Park South as a kind of headquarters, meeting for highly secret sessions at the Manhattan Hotel on Madison Avenue at Forty-second Street, where the conference room was bugged by American agents. The fact was that all the German lines were tapped and conversations recorded by stenographers. The nemesis of all these busy spies of high and low estate was a Czechoslovakian who preferred to be known simply as Voska and whose "cover" was his leadership of the Bohemian Alliance in the United States. He had been expelled in his youth from Bohemia for socialist activities. In the United States he made a modest fortune, bought a marble quarry in Kansas, and became an ardent Czech nationalist. Working with a British counterintelligence agent, Captain Guy Gaunt, Voska set up a remarkable network of Czech agents in the center of the entire German intelligence operation. One Voska agent was the Countess von Bernstorff's personal maid; another was assistant chief clerk in the Austrian Embassy. One was a chauffeur for the German Embassy, and another operated a wireless station to which messages came in from Germany for the German Embassy. Before he was through, Voska had placed eighty men and women of Czech antecedents as clerks, scrubwomen, messengers, and waiters in German-American clubs, newspaper offices, consulates, and business firms. A photostat machine in his home copied stolen (or borrowed) documents. While the information so gathered was officially under the cloak of the British counterintelligence, it was passed along to the appropriate U.S. intelligence agencies, and much of it leaked through the *Providence Journal* to the *New York Times* and thence to the country at large.

A notable misadventure of German intelligence came with the so-called Albert Papers. An American secret service agent assigned to tail

George Sylvester Viereck, a prominent literary figure and a German-American with strong pro-German sympathies, noted that he was accompanied by a man—Dr. Albert, a German agent, as it would turn out—carrying a large briefcase. The agent decided to abandon the briefcaseless Viereck for his companion. They boarded a Sixth Avenue subway, and Albert fell asleep. He awoke as the El reached Fiftieth Street and ran to the egress before the train doors closed, leaving his briefcase behind. The agent seized it and escaped through a rear door with the doctor in pursuit. After a classic chase scene in which the agent changed from trolley to trolley one jump ahead of the frantic doctor, he escaped and turned the briefcase over to his chief, who took one look at its contents and rushed it off to Secretary McAdoo. It was a remarkable revelation of the extent of German espionage in the United States, and the government decided to leak the contents of the briefcase to the *New York World,* from the pages of which, published serially, it gave the Allied cause a substantial boost.

The Albert Papers were soon followed by one of Voska's richest coups, the Archibald Papers. Voska's agents discovered that an American in London named John Archibald was acting as a courier for the German Embassy, carrying papers considered dangerous to try to send by code. Tipped off by Voska, the British picked up Archibald and found a treasury of information, including plans for promoting strikes by Hungarian workers in war industries. There were canceled checks indicating payments for spies and saboteurs and a letter from Von Papen to his wife, speaking of "these idiotic Yankees." There was also mention of a visit by von Papen to Mexico to organize the Germans there for "self-defense."

The sensational acts of sabotage and the revelations, through Voska's agents, of German espionage activities doubtlessly did more damage to that nation's cause in America than all the Allied propaganda.

26

The European War

Historians, not surprisingly, are still contending over the causes of World War I. Most of the present-day theories of the causes of the war were put forward during the war by its contemporaries. The various brands of socialists had no hesitation in describing it as a war between rival capitalisms, a war caused by international capitalism in its frantic competition for colonies and markets and world domination. (A gloss on this theory was that it was caused by a cartel of international munitions makers as a way of increasing their profits—Krupp and Du Pont, for example). As far as it went, the theory of conflicting capitalisms was unanswerable, but it simply did not go far enough. There were too many other things like jealousy and national pride (and fear) mixed in, and simple human perversity and miscalculations on a global scale. Many people viewed the war as a consequence of autocratic governments. The kings and emperors were "bad"; the people were "good." This was a variation of Tom Paine's conviction that war was the by-product of monarchy. Do away with monarchy, and you would do away with war. This came to be, to a rather disconcerting degree, Wilson's view. The people were "good"; kings and tyrants were "bad." Replace monarchies with democratic republics, and you would have peace.

A wider and more comprehensive view was that the old European order was crumbling. That order was made up of basically incompatible elements in any event—a modern, ruthless industrial system imposed on an old, quasi-feudal system of castes and classes, hopelessly ill-suited to deal with modern realities. The World War simply accelerated the crumbling. (This explanation had a reassuringly scientific or even Darwinian tone to it.) International capitalists had discovered a virtually limitless field of activity in foreign nations and in "colonies." Railroads and hydroelectric power were in demand all over South America, Africa, and Asia. They required (and rewarded) limitless outlays of capital, much of it American, and corps of engineers, many of them American. Mining engineers, railroad engineers (designers and builders), and hydroelectric engineers were the critical links between foreign capital and its transformation into specific enterprises. The Guggenheims had mining interests all over South America, indeed all over the world. The efforts of the Morgan interests to lay predatory hands on public lands in Alaska had triggered the Ballinger-Pinchot controversy.

Lenin observed that "imperialism ran along the railroads." Certainly the competition among various industrial nations to build railroads in the preindustrial nations—Russia, China, Africa, the Near East—served to exacerbate national rivalries. Willard Straight went to China as representative of the Morgan interests to try to negotiate for American capitalists permission to build a major railroad line. Russia, Japan, and Germany were rival bidders. The decision of imperial Germany to build a Berlin to Baghdad railroad line, connecting Germany with Turkey, sent shock waves through the rest of Europe. Britain feared its passage to India would be outflanked by such a railway, and Russia was apprehensive that it would threaten its interests in the region of Constantinople and the Red Sea. Cecil Rhodes planned a Cape to Cairo railroad.

Behind everything else there was the fever of nationalism. Nationalism—the consuming desire of the peoples of the world to belong to separate, autonomous political and social units called nations—was hardly older than the nineteenth century, but it had become in that brief time the decisive fact of the modern world. The United States, by becoming "free and independent," had certainly helped set the style. Now everybody was doing it. Every little ragtag social unit that shared a common language, culture, history (often of oppression) wished to be its own boss, to bear the proud name of nation. Often the aspiring nation was hardly more than a tribe, and less viable economically. Certainly from the point of view of Americans, the impulse was understandable. It was a by-product, if not the direct consequence, of the growing feeling that dependence and subordination were incompatible with a people's full humanity. As we have argued from time to time throughout this work, "democracy" in its simplest and most basic sense is nothing more than the proposition that we, as particular individuals or as a collectivity called a people, know best what we need and want. We may be wrongheaded, obtuse, or unduly stubborn, but we wish to have, so far as it is humanly possible, our destiny in our own hands. The French Revolution was a revolution in the name of those principles against an oppressive internal order; the American Revolution, as the first successful revolution of a colonial people in modern times, was a revolution against what was perceived as an oppressive external order (a very mild one, relatively, but that is not the point; harsh or mild, it involved a state of subordination and dependence inconsistent with the notion of "freedom").

In a curious way the European War was also a consequence of the image of man projected by international socialism. Marxian socialism did a good deal to erode the earlier notion that there was an essentially religious or spiritual or transcendental dimension to life. Man and his world were matter, material, involved in a "dialectical" process destined in time to produce heaven on earth, the classless "workers'" society without coercive institutions in which the "state" had withered away and men and women enjoyed the fruits of their labor without the intrusion of capitalists. While the various socialisms, Marxian and non-Marxian, established standards of social and economic justice that helped, at least indirectly, to relieve some of the grosser inequities of the status quo, they also encouraged the notion that widespread violence might be a prelude to the new social order.

In every country there were socialists who planned and plotted feverishly in anticipation of the day that capitalism would collapse and they would take power. In some countries they constituted strong and reasonably respected political parties; they were particularly strong in Germany. In many other countries they were underground, ruthlessly hunted by the police, beaten and jailed and often shot, hanged, garroted, or simply assassinated by political adversaries. Everywhere there were factions and deviationists, groups committed to political violence rather than to achieving power by conventional political action. What we might call, in religious terms, the millennial expectation—the belief that a new and better age was dawning—had infected a good part of the world. War and violence on a global scale might be the price of the new age.

European wars were, of course, nothing new. There was, as we have noted, Pan-Slavism and Pan-Germanism as well as dozens of ancient rivalries, the origins of which were obscured by their antiquity. The German Empire dated only from the Franco-Prussian War in 1870–1871, when Bismarck assembled the various Germanic principalities into modern Germany with Prussia as its heart. Alsace-Lorraine was the principal prize that Bismarck had wrested from France as the fruit of victory. At the outbreak of the European War, Prussia contained three-fifths of the nation's population and area. It had been responsible for the partition of Poland and the seizure, in 1864, of Schleswig-Holstein from Denmark. In a period of some thirty years, Germany, with Prussia as its guiding force, had grown from a collection of principalities to the most powerful and progressive industrial nation in the world, but that growth had only whetted the appetite of the militarists who dominated Prussia and, through Prussia, Germany and, through Germany, the Austro-Hungarian Empire. That military caste was distinguished by arrogance of a peculiarly insidious kind.

In 1908 Austria had annexed Bosnia and Herzegovina, still nominally part of the Turkish (Ottoman) Empire and inhabited largely by Serbs. When Serbia protested, Austria mobilized, and Russia in turn announced its support of the Serbs. War was avoided when Russia prevailed on Serbia to acquiesce in the annexation. Meanwhile, there were rumblings of revolution in France. These events prompted Henry Adams to exclaim to Elizabeth Cameron, "Am I going off my head, or shall I lose the last vestige of mental balance soon? . . . The newspapers are quite crammed with cries of dissolving societies. Turkey is suddenly rotted out. Persia is worse. India is dreadfully uneasy. Russia is exhausted with convulsion. And now we have almost daily social disturbances in or about Paris. . . ."

In the same year the Young Turks had overthrown the fearful tyrant Abd-al Hamid. The Arabs and the Armenians hoped that their miseries were at an end, but the Young Turks proved as ruthless in their suppression of minority peoples within their domain as the old Turks had. They set out to Turkize all the disparate peoples within the empire. Those who resisted being made into Turks were jailed or killed.

In October, 1912, Bulgaria, Serbia, Greece, and Montenegro joined forces to attack Turkey. Ten days after the beginning of the war the Bulgarians won an impressive victory at Lule Burgas. What was known as the First Balkan War was ended by the Treaty of London in May, 1913. The Serbs were forced to disgorge the port of Durazzo (now Durrës, Albania), which they had captured.

A month later the Second Balkan War began; it ended shortly thereafter with the defeat of Bulgaria by Rumania and Turkey (small wonder Americans were anxious to avoid entanglement in European struggles).

A military mission was dispatched to Constantinople by the kaiser in 1913 under the leadership of General Otto Liman von Sanders, and thereafter the Turkish Army became a kind of adjunct of the German Army, trained and advised by German officers in all the weapons and tactics of modern warfare.

Such, briefly, was the background of what was called, at its onset, the European War. "Indescribable" is one of the words that comes most readily to the historian's mind, or pen. The horror of the war that began with the German invasion of Belgium is literally that: indescribable. One thinks of the words of the historian, Herbert Butterfield: "Sometimes when the human race has gone through one of its colossal chapters of experiences, men in the aftermath have been so appalled by the catastrophe, so obsessed by the memory of it, that they have gone back to the story again and again . . . as one generation succeeds another. . . ." No other event in history more fully deserves the name of tragic drama; in this the tragedy far overshadowed the drama, at least in the war itself. It was as though the mythical hounds of hell had been let loose; the demons that dwell in the darkest recesses of the subconscious were called forth.

With this nightmare, this orgy of death and destruction on a hitherto unimaginable scale, Americans had little to do directly, but they followed the course of events across the Atlantic with fascinated attention. They had, of course, only the most superficial notion of the grimmer realities of the war. Stories of German atrocities abounded, as did stories of Allied heroism and Allied successes (few, to be sure), but little or nothing of the reality of men in combat, in part because it was in fact incommunicable, but even more because the Allied propaganda agencies did not wish to have it communicated. It was their task ingenuously and persistently to misrepresent what was in fact going on. The war was terrible not alone in the virtually incomprehensible tally of casualties—the civilian loss of life, the permanently maimed—the employment on an unprecedented scale of massed artillery; the use of poisonous gas, barbed wire, and bombardment, and machine-gun strafing from the air (not, of course, to mention the machine gun itself) but in the particular and unique character of trench warfare, where men lived from day to day in the most wretched conditions imaginable; and in the manner of dying.

When Britain tried to recruit a volunteer army, it discovered the effect of generations of grinding poverty on the nation's young men. The same system which, in Charles Edward Russell's view, had brought about the war "had also undermined the physique of those toiling or starving millions until they were no longer able to respond to the demands the system itself imposed upon them. The supreme trial had come, the whole structure of modern society had been shown to be shaped toward colossal disaster. . . ." The French held 516 miles of the front, and the British 48. The difference measured the degree of military preparedness and capacity to respond to the crisis of the two nations.

Ideas would seem only secondarily involved in the terrible calculus of the battlefield, where the most primitive of human instincts predominate, but ideas, of course, determine the manner and form in which armies fight. This was indisputably the case in the battles of the World War. There the most rigid and arbitrary notions both of military maneuver and of human character prevailed. Factory workers existed to be used up in the merciless routines of the factory; transformed into soldiers, they existed to be expended for national honor, for glory, for the acquisition of empire. David Lloyd George, British secretary of state for war in the British ministry, who knew the vanity and pretensions of the British aristocracy from his earliest political days, wrote: "Whilst hundreds of thousands were being destroyed in the insane egotism of Passchendaele [one of the bloodiest battles of the war], every message or memorandum for [Douglas] Haig [the British commanding general] was full of those insistences on the importance of sending him more men to replace those he had sent to die in the mud. . . . As for the mud, it never incommoded the movement of his irresistible pencil" as he traced out the lines of the latest attack.

The Allied strategy, as the young British war correspondent Philip Gibbs (and many others) described it, "was to search the map for a place which was the strongest in the enemy's lines, the most difficult to attack, the most powerfully defended, and then after due advertisement, [so as] not to take an unfair advantage of the enemy, to launch the assault."

The Germans were brilliant in defensive tactics. They invented the concrete blockhouse, or pillbox, and the system of echeloned defenses in depth, the method of assault by infiltration, which broke the Italian lines at Caporetto, but they blundered "in all the larger calculations of war," nullifying their tactical genius.

A year after the war was over, Gibbs published a passionate work entitled *Now It Can Be Told*. His theme was that during the war it was impossible to write about the real horror of it for fear of demoralizing the folks at home and providing propaganda for the pacifists and those who wished to end the war by an immediate negotiated peace.

The initial German attack, as we have noted, was halted at the Marne in September, 1914. Meanwhile, a Russian army under General Aleksandr V. Samsonov, advancing toward Danzig, was checked and virtually destroyed at the Battle of Tannenberg in late August, 1914. A few weeks later another large Russian army, advancing toward Königsberg on the Baltic Sea, was also decisively defeated and driven out of East Prussia. A third and a fourth Russian army invaded Galicia and was checked at the Battle of Lemberg by an Austrian army under General Moritz Auffenberg von Kamarów. It was not a promising beginning for the Allied armies on the Eastern front.

Having checked the German advance at the Marne, the French launched an offensive directed at Ypres, just inside the Belgium border. The battle lasted into November, when a line was stabilized. It became the winter line, running from Ostend on the Strait of Dover south to the Chemin des Dames road, thence on to Verdun and St.-Mihiel and south and east to the Swiss border. The Russians meanwhile reestablished themselves in Galicia and west of Warsaw.

It now appeared to the Allies that the pearl of great price which might well bring victory to the Allied cause was Constantinople and the strait of the Dardanelles. With the Dardanelles in Allied hands, a line of transportation would be opened up between Russia and France and Britain, enabling the British to send arms and munitions to the Russians and the Russians in turn to ship footstuffs to the Western Allies. The project was Winston Churchill's, but it was plagued from the beginning with difficulties and delays. The attack was launched by British battleships on February 9, 1915, and for more than three weeks the heavy guns of the ships tried to silence the Turkish forts guarding the strait. Ultimately twenty-five ships joined in the bombardment while 100,000 British troops waited to make an assault. Instead of following the bombardment with an assault landing, the British commander, Sir Ian Hamilton, deciding that the transports were improperly loaded, returned to British bases in Egypt to reload, causing a delay of some six weeks while the Turkish forts were heavily reinforced. When the attack was renewed, three British ships were sunk, and two badly damaged by shore batteries. It was April before the first British soldiers were put ashore. When they landed, they were met by barbed-wire entanglements and murderous machine-gun fire from well-protected dugouts and gun emplacements. New Zealand and Australian troops bore the brunt of the fierce Turkish resistance and suffered staggering casualties. After establishing a toehold on the Gallipoli Peninsula, they found it impossible to advance. The campaign had been bungled from the beginning to end.

The first attack on Mons and Ypres saw the commitment of British regulars, virtually the entire British army at the beginning of the war. It suffered such severe losses that in effect a new army had to be created out of the survivors and more volunteers. The British refrained from instituting a draft on the ground that they and their French allies could finish the job by the summer of 1915. The Battle of Neuve-Chapelle started in March of that year. Almost half a million soldiers, backed by heavy concentrations of artillery, launched the attack. After the British had been stopped with heavy losses, the Germans launched a counterattack near Ypres (the second Battle of Ypres), preceded by poison gas. To the south the French made an unsuccessful attempt to drive the Germans out of St.-Mihiel, below Verdun. Again the attack was preceded by heavy artillery barrages, but the Germans easily repulsed the French infantry, and no more major campaigns were attempted through the summer months.

To Gibbs, 1915 was the worst year of the war. "There was a settled hopelessness in it which was heavy in the hearts of men—ours and the enemy's . . . there was no hope ahead. No mental dope by which our fighting-men could drug themselves into seeing a vision of the war's end." When sections of the trenches collapsed under the combined effects of rain and frost, leaving British and Germans alike exposed, the opposing troops sat on what was left of their parapets and called out, "Don't shoot! Don't shoot!" From time to time German soldiers crawled into the British lines to surrender. One of them said to Gibbs, "There is no sense in this war. It is misery on both sides. There is no use in it." The story was passed about of the sign raised over the German trenches that read: "The British are fools." It was quickly shot to pieces and replaced by one that read: "The French are fools," which suffered a similar fate. Then a sign appeared that read: "We're all fools. Let's all go home." A shout of laughter rose from the British lines.

"Death is nothing," a young British officer told Gibbs. "I don't give a damn for death; but it's the waiting for it, the devilishness of its uncertainty, the sight of one's pals blown to bits about one, and the animal fear under shell-fire that break one's pluck. . . . My nerves are like fiddle-strings."

Gibbs wrote of a section of the trenches not far from the terrible field of Ypres where the British soldiers huddled in filth and mud. "Lice crawled over them in legions. Human flesh, rotting and stinking, mere pulp, was pasted into the mudbanks. If they dug to get deeper cover their shovels went into the softness of dead bodies who had been their comrades. Scraps of flesh, booted legs, blackened hands, eyeless heads, came falling over them when the enemy trench-mortared their position or blew up a new mine-shaft."

The hardest sight for Gibbs to endure was the sight of the shell-shocked. He saw a shell-shocked sergeant after the battle at Auvelais, "he was convulsed with a dreadful rigor like a man in epilepsy, and clawed at his mouth, moaning horribly, with livid terror in his eyes. He had to be strapped to a stretcher before he could be carried away. He had been a tall and splendid man, this poor, terror-stricken lunatic." Another young soldier stood outside a dugout "shaking in every limb. . . . His steel hat was at the back of his head and his mouth slobbered, and two comrades could not hold him still." Gibbs could not bear to look at them; many tore at their mouths until they were scarred and bloody. Back in Britain, he could not endure the glib phrases about "our poor dear wounded" or read the "cheery" articles about how the brave soldiers were crushing the wicked enemy.

After the French retreat from Mons, Gibbs saw the bodies of dead German soldiers gathered into heaps, soaked with oil, and set on fire; "oily smoke" rose from the pyre.

Robert Graves, the British poet who fought at the Somme, wrote that "every night we went out to fetch the dead of the other battalions. . . . After the first day or two corpses swelled and stank. I vomited more than once while superintending the carrying. Those we could not get from the German wire continued to swell until the wall of the stomach collapses, either naturally or when punctured by a bullet; a disgusting smell would float across. The colour of the dead faces changed from white to yellow-grey, to red, to purple, to green, to black, to slimy."

The horror of the bitter but inclusive fighting did not inhibit the greed of leaders of the contending nations. In March, 1915, Russia pushed its claims to the shores of the Dardanelles, Constantinople, the shores of the Bosporus, and the islands in the Sea of Marmora. The Treaty of London, signed six weeks later, promised Italy, in return for entering the war on the Allied side, South Tyrol, Trieste, Trentino, Istria, Gorizia, Gradisca, Saseno, and the Dodecanese Islands as well as portions of Eritrea, Somaliland, and Libya (most of the latter territories belonged to Austria). The Sykes-Picot Treaty, signed on May 16, 1916, between Britain and France, divided up Turkey. The signatories agreed to recognize and protect an independent Arab state or confederation of Arab states while France would retrieve out of the Ottoman Empire Syria, Lebanon, Cilicia, and Mosul. Great Britain would get Mesopotamia and northern Palestine. Still another secret treaty was signed with Russia on March 12, 1917, eleven days before the beginning of the Russian Revolution and a month before the U.S. entry into the war. By its terms Russia recognized the right of France to Alsace-Lorraine and the Saar Valley. Russia also agreed to support the creation of a neutral state on the left bank of the Rhine to be occupied by French soldiers until Germany complied with the terms of whatever treaty might be written concluding the war.

If the Western front was more or less stabilized in the summer of 1915, the situation on the Eastern front deteriorated alarmingly as the Germans first turned back Russian attacks and then counterattacked with devastating effect. Constantly short of guns and munitions, the inadequately equipped Russians were no match for the Germans and Austrians, and the failure of the Allies to press against the Western front allowed the Germans with their interior lines to shift armies rapidly to the Russian front when they were needed. By the end of 1915 the Russian armies had been driven out of Poland and Galicia and eastward almost to Minsk, suffering in the process terrible casualties and paving the way for the Revolution.

Bulgaria meanwhile entered the war, and Serbia surrendered to the Central Powers. The British evacuated the Dardanelles. This combination of events, especially the crushing Russian defeats, was a serious setback to the Allied cause. The hope was to redress the balance by coordinated Allied attacks on the Western front, the French attacking in the Champagne while the British attacked what was known as the Noyon salient in a pincer movement designed to encircle the German defensive positions. The attacks, which began on September 25, had only limited success. The French lost more than 120,000 men in the first few days, and the attack had to be abandoned. The British had casualties of 110,000.

At the beginning of 1916 the German high command was convinced that the time had come to end the war with one final massed offensive directed at Verdun, the strongest fortress on the front and the key to the whole Allied defensive line. In what turned out to be their most serious strategic error of the war, the Germans staked everything on the assault. The German people had been assured that the war would be brief and glorious. For them the victories in Russia had not been sufficient to make up for the heavy casualties and the hardships that the war had brought with it, especially the food shortages caused by the Allied blockade.

The French motto at Verdun was *On ne passe pas* ("They shall not pass"). They did not, but more than 350,000 French were killed or wounded in the defense of the fort. For the first twenty-three months of the war the French had borne the brunt of the German attacks. Verdun was the symbol of that sacrifice.

On July 1, 1916, a newly constituted British army began an offensive that came to be known as the Battle of the Somme. It was essentially a rerun of the unsuccessful Allied offensives of the preceding year in the Champagne and at Loos. The rationale for the attack was that the Allies now had a clear superiority in men and in artillery and that it had only been their failure to persevere a year earlier that had cost them a decisive victory. The British casualties were 50,000 on the first day of the attack, but some ground was gained. The German tactic was to fall back slowly while exacting a heavy price in dead or wounded. Of the decisive battle of the Somme offensive that centered on Flanders, Gibbs wrote that "at last, after five months of superhuman effort, enormous sacrifice, mass-heroism, desperate will-power, and the tenacity of each individual human ant in this wild ant-heap, the German lines were smashed . . . and the enemy, stricken by the prolonged fury of our attack, fell back in a far and wide retreat across a country which he laid waste, to the shelter of his Hindenburg line. . . ." The dead numbered 400,000. Gibbs could not walk across the final battlefield, where "twelve hundred corpses littered . . . the earth . . . without treading on them there. When I fell in the slime I clutched arms and legs. The stench of death was strong and awful." The retreating crews had cut down fruit trees and blown up houses and churches until all was indescribable desolation. Terrible as was the agony of the British, the agony of the Germans was, in Gibb's view, worse. Often food could not be brought forward to the men under ceaseless shell fire. The British journalist found a soldier's letter which read: "We are quite shut off from the rest of the world. Nothing comes to us. No letters. The English keep such a barrage on our approaches it is terrible. To-morrow evening it will be seven days since this bombardment began. We cannot hold out much longer. Everything is shot to pieces." Gibbs wrote: "German soldiers were maddened by thirst." Another German soldier wrote: "I stood on the brink of the most terrible days of my life. They were those of the battle of the Somme." When it was over, "a handful of half-mad wretched creatures, worn out in body and mind, were all that was left of a whole battalion. We were that handful."

Gibbs saw thousands of German prisoners. They seemed to him "in the mass . . . decent, simple men, remarkably like our own lads from the Saxon counties of England. . . ." He found "among them all the same loathing of war, the same bewilderment as to its causes, the same sense of being driven by evil powers above them" that characterized the Allied soldiers. The officers were a different story. They refused to associate with their men. "They regarded them, for the most part, as inferior beings." The cavalry officers scorned the infantry officers and would not speak to them when both were prisoners of the British. Gibbs spoke to a captured German doctor who said, with an ironical laugh, "We go on killing one another—to no purpose. Europe is being bled to death and will be impoverished for long years. We Germans thought it was a war for *Kultur*—our civilization. Now we know it is a war against *Kultur*, against religion, against all civilization."

"How will it end?" Gibbs asked.

"I see no end to it. It is the suicide of nations. Germany is strong, and England is strong, and France is strong. It is impossible for one side to crush the other, so when is the end to come?"

A German communications sergeant in a trench not far from the British lines received one alarming message after another, "each more terrifying than the other, of enormous losses through the bombs and shells of the enemy, of huge masses of troops advancing upon us, of all possible possibilities, such as a train broken down, and we are tortured by all the terrors that the mind can invent. Our nerves quiver. We clench our teeth. None of us can forget the horrors of the night. . . . Our sleeping-places are full of water. We had to try and bail out the trenches with cooking-dishes. I lay down in the water. . . . Only a few sections got coffee. Mine got nothing at all. I was frozen in every limb, poured water out of my boots, and lay down again." Another soldier, writing to his wife, noted, "You can no longer call it war. It is mere murder. . . . All my previous experiences in this war—the slaughter at Ypres . . . are the purest child's play compared with this massacre, and that is too mild a description."

Behind the lines German deserters were shot in groups.

When he had finished recounting the horrors of the Somme offensive, Gibbs wrote: "But they are less than the actual truth, for no pen will ever in one book, or in hundreds, give the full record of the individual agony, the broken heart-strings, the soul-shock as well as the shell-shock, of that frightful struggle in which, on one side and the other, two million men were engulfed. Modern civilization was wrecked on those fire-blasted fields, though they led to what we called 'Victory.' More died there than the flower of our youth and German manhood. The Old Order of the world died there, because many men who came out of that conflict were changed, and vowed not to tolerate a system of thought which had led to such a monstrous massacre of human beings who had prayed to the same God, loved the same joys of life, and had no hatred for one another except as it had been lighted and inflamed by their governors, their philosophers, and their newspapers. The German soldier cursed the militarism which had plunged him into that horror." There were to be other battles after the Somme "as bloody and terrible, but they only confirmed greater numbers of men in the faith that the old world had been wrong in its 'make-up' and wrong in its religion of life. . . . Either the heart of the world must be changed by a real obedience to the Gospel of Christ or Christianity must be abandoned for a new creed which would give better results between men and nations."

General Erich Ludendorff, the German chief of staff, wrote: "The course of the Somme battle . . . supplied important lessons with respect to the construction and plan of our lines. The very deep underground forts had to be replaced by shallow constructions. . . . The conspicuous lines of trenches . . . supplied far too good a target for the enemy artillery. The whole system of defense had to be made broader and looser and better adapted to the ground. . . . Forward infantry positions with a wide field of fire were easily seen by the enemy. They could be destroyed by . . . artillery fire. . . . Positions farther back, with a narrower firing field and more under the protection of our own guns, were retained."

In the aftermath of the failure of the Somme offensive the strategy of active defense was adopted by the Allies: Carefully prepared limited attacks to achieve particular objectives were substituted for mass assaults. It became increasingly clear that the development of such tactics as massed machine-gun and artillery fire had swung the balance decisively to the defense. Movement and maneuver gave way to intricate defensive arrangements. The French, unnerved by the terrible casualties at Verdun and in the Somme offensive, began to stress tactics designed to minimize casualties. It was clear that they no longer had the heart for the kinds of attacks which had been so costly.

Despite the increasing demoralization of French and British forces, the only serious mutiny of empire soldiers was that of the 51st Highland Division at Calais in July, 1918. The case was far different with the French. Tens of thousands of French soldiers mutinied and in many instances killed officers bold enough to try to suppress them. In the words of Marshal Henri Pétain, "The French Army was exhausted. Hopelessness and pessimism spread to it from the interior, swamping as it did so the mood of artificial enthusiam, whipped up from above." Desertions were increasingly common. More than 21,000 soldiers deserted in 1917. In April the French 18th Infantry Regiment refused to leave its rest area for the front. A week later the 2d Colonial Infantry Division appeared on parade without packs or rifles. When ordered to get their arms, men shouted out, "Down with the war," and, "We're not marching." They would defend their lines against German assaults, but they would make no more attacks. The mutiny spread rapidly until it was estimated that out of twelve divisions in the Champagne section, only two could be relied on. Before it had run its course, the mutiny had affected seventy-five infantry regiments and twenty-three battalions of chasseurs in addition to twelve regiments of artillery. The task of suppressing the mutinies was given to Pétain, who combined severity of punishment with a notable improvement in the food and living conditions of the troops. Fresh vegetables and beds in rest areas helped bring the mutinous soldiers around. Some 24,000 were court-martialed, and many of those convicted were sent to French colonies; when colonial troops were involved, whole units were sent home.

By the early summer of 1917 it was clear that the Allies had been checkmated on every front. The flex defense of the Germans had yielded terrain but no substantial military gains. The Eastern front had collapsed. Gallipoli was still in the hands of the Turks, and the Italians had suffered a crushing setback at the hands of the Austrians.

27

Neutral America

Ten months after the outbreak of the war in Europe the sinking of the *Lusitania* gave fresh impetus to the campaign for preparedness. The *Lusitania* was sunk off the coast of Ireland in May, 1915, by German submarine *U-20*. More than 1,000 passengers and crewmen drowned; these included 139 Americans, many of them women and children. What was carefully kept from public knowledge was the fact that the *Lusitania* sank so quickly and with such high loss of life because the passenger ship was carrying gunpowder and munitions of war, which were ignited by the German torpedoes. The British and the U.S. officials who had conspired with them were at least as culpable as the German submarine crew. Hutchins Hapgood met Walter Lipmann on the street the day after the news of the sinking of the *Lusitania* and found him breathing fire and hot for America's entry into the war to avenge the sinking. "For the moment at any rate, he seemed to forget that the *Lusitania* was carrying war-materials to the enemies of Germany, and that there had been warnings in the press that such things might happen," Hapgood wrote.

Oswald Garrison Villard, arriving in Washington in the aftermath of the sinking of the ship, found that city in "a state of excitement" which recalled the blowing up of the *Maine* prior to the Spanish-American War. General Leonard Wood, former President Roosevelt, and several Cabinet members were calling for an immediate declaration of war against Germany. But Wilson and his closest advisers were determined not to panic. Word that the President was considering the appropriate course of action, "very earnestly but very calmly," was put out. What was most important was action that would "convey to Germany in unmistakable terms the righteous indignation of the American people for a violation not only of international law but of the fundamental decencies of civilization."

In the aftermath of the sinking Wilson warned Germany that its military actions could not "operate as in any degree an abbreviation of the rights of American shipmasters or of American citizens bound on lawful errands as passengers on merchant ships of belligerent nationality;. and that [our government] must hold the Imperial German Government to a strict accountability for any infringement of those rights, intention or accidental." The problem with submarine warfare was the "practical impossibility" of employing them "without disregarding those rules of fairness, reason, justice, and humanity, which all modern opinion regards as imperative. . . ." In other words, the United States was not disposed to tolerate Germany's most effective military weapon. The British controlled the surface of the world's oceans, and the Germans the waters beneath. The British were attempting to starve the Central Powers into submission by a blockade; the Germans were using the more radical method of sinking ships trying to supply their enemies. To tell the Germans that they must not use their submarines for fear of sinking a ship carrying American passengers was like telling a man fighting for his life that it was unethical to fire his revolver for fear of hitting a passerby.

That, in fact, was what Houston pointed out to the President. "Do you demand that Germany give up the use of the submarine in her efforts to destroy British trade? . . . England is violating the three-mile blockade. She is blockading at a distance. The long-range gun and the submarine make the three-mile rule obsolete. If I were England, I would do as England is doing, and, if I were Germany, I would use the submarine if I could justly and humanely do so to stop English trade. . . . War now is the war of whole nations."

Secretary of State Bryan, Villard, and many of those who wished at all costs to avoid American involvement in the war, felt strongly that Wilson should accompany a strong rebuke to Germany with a firm message to the British, who themselves every day violated international law by detaining American ships bound for neutral ports. British warships maintained a virtual blockade of the harbor of New York, stopping and boarding ships outside the three-mile limit. At the time the *Lusitania* was sunk, Britain was preventing American ships from entering the ports of Norway, Sweden, and Denmark. More than $415,000,000 worth of meat products were likewise under British detention. Soon the meat-packers were joined in their protests by cotton brokers and Western "copper men," complaining about arbitrary seizures. Villard carried his criticisms to the State Department counselor on international law, Robert Lansing, who listened sympathetically and assured Villard he would convey his views to the President. Lansing agreed "that the conduct of Great Britain was unbearable." He told Villard, "In fact, I have drafted just such a note in as strong language as I could write." Thus armed, Villard wrote an editorial for the *Post* which began, "Unless all signals fail, it is to be England's turn next. There is at this writing an excellent prospect that shortly . . . she will be haled before the Presidential bar of justice to receive from Mr. Wilson information as to how this government feels in regard to her violations of international law and practice."

Britain hastened, apparently on the basis of Villard's editorial, to "clarify" its position on American trade, and Wilson never issued the rebuke that Villard had predicted. "I felt then, and I feel now," Villard wrote in 1938, "that this was a turning point in our own attitude toward the war, this and the rescinding of the prohibition of loans to the Allies; . . . if that note had been sent and strongly backed up we might have kept out of [the war]. The failure to send the note undoubtedly gave the lie to our pretensions of being neutral in the conflict. . . ." Count von Bernstorff, a friend of Villard's, wrote to him in May, asking, "What would you think of the following proposal coupled with arbitration of some kind? We propose to give up submarine war if England will obey international law. We further propose to give up the submarine war temporarily to leave time for you to renew the above proposal to England." Villard, after consulting with Lansing, replied that he thought no such conditions could be attached to an agreement by Germany to suspend submarine warfare. "Have you thought of . . . suggesting," Villard concluded, "that Germany will agree not to attack any passenger steamers if England prohibits the sending of arms and ammunition by them? I have reason to believe that this would strike a favorable note with our government and our people."

When Wilson sent a draft of his message on the *Lusitania* incident to Bryan for his comment, the latter wrote: "My dear Mr. President, I join in this document with a heavy heart. I am as sure of your patriotic purpose as I am of my own, but after long consideration both careful and prayerful, I cannot bring myself to the belief that it is wise to relinquish the hope of playing the part of a friend to both sides in the role of peace maker, and I fear this note will result in such a relinquishment—for the hope requires for its realization the retaining the confidence of both sides. The protest will be popular in this country, for a time at least . . . because popular sentiment, already favorable to the allies, has been perceptibly increased by the *Lusitania* tragedy. . . ." The "jingo element," Bryan insisted, will "demand war." Germany would, in consequence, be more embittered "because we unsparingly denounce the retaliatory methods employed by her without condemning the announced purpose of the allies to starve the non-combatants of Germany and without complaining of the conduct of Great Britain in relying on passengers, including men, women and children of the United States, to give immunity to vessels carrying munitions of war. . . . The only way, as I see it, to prevent irreparable injury being done by the statement is to issue simultaneously a protest against the objectionable conduct of the allies. . . ."

Bryan told several of his fellow Cabinet members at a private luncheon, "The President has had one view. I have had a different one. . . . I have had to act as I have thought best. I cannot go along with him in this note. I think it makes for war. I believe that I can do more on the outside to prevent war than I can on the inside. . . ."

Wilson sent the note, and Bryan resigned on June 8, 1915. Four days later the *Louisville Courier-Journal* declared, "Men have been shot and beheaded, even hanged, drawn and quartered for treason less serious." Bryan, often ignored or patronized, put on the shelf as antediluvian in his ideas, an outdated relic of an earlier age—Villard, who professed admiration for him, wrote: "He is obviously lacking in taste, breeding, and knowledge of the world . . ."—acted with resolution and dignity in resigning from the Cabinet and with largeness of spirit in forgiving Villard's unkind thrust. "Tell Villard," Bryan said to the journalist David Lawrence, "that the Lord does not require us to win—He simply requests us to do our duty as we see it. We can never tell in advance what we can do—we can only tell by trying. If after trying we find we have failed we have nothing to regret."

Germany replied to the *Lusitania* note thus: "The Imperial Government . . . repeats the assurances that American ships will not be hindered in the prosecution of legitimate shipping, and the lives of American citizens on neutral vessels shall not be placed in jeopardy." American ships should carry special markings and notice of their dates of sailing and their routes should be given in advance to the German consulates. "The note was unsatisfactory," David Houston noted. "It was offensive." It denied the right of Americans to travel on merchant vessels of belligerent nationality. It was rejected, and further notes followed.

Pro-British Americans who wished for the entry of the United States into the war fastened on Wilson's moderate response to the sinking of the *Lusitania* as evidence of his weak policy and faltering leadership. In their own view, this was the moment, with public opinion thoroughly aroused against Germany, that the President should have declared war. But Houston, who knew both the President and the sentiment of the country, believed that Wilson "would have had strong partisan opposition to such a course, a large element in Congress against him and no such unity in the Nation as he did have when we did enter the war. . . . I have a suspicion that he would have had hard sledding."

William Allen White was among that large company of liberals who viewed the war in Europe with extreme disfavor. Kansas had been the home of a strong peace movement, among myriad other reforms. "War," White wrote, "brings men down to beasts quicker than whiskey, surer than women, and deadlier than the love of money." It was an interesting trinity of destruction: whiskey, women, and money. Even the sinking of the *Lusitania* did not seem to him to be sufficient cause for United States involvement. "Americans—South Americans and North Americans—hold the ark of the covenant of civilization," he wrote. "In a world war mad, we have the peace that passeth understanding. By God's grace we should keep it."

In an effort to dampen the war hysteria, Wilson declared, "There is such a thing as a man being too proud to fight. There is such a thing as a nation being so right that it does not need to convince others that it is right." The words were like a red flag to the proponents of war. They were quoted with scorn by innumerable Republican politicians. "The effect of our inaction in Mexico," Theodore Roosevelt wrote, "has been unspeakably dreadful. It has on the whole been surpassed in dishonor by the action of our government in reference to the great European War. . . ." A popular song was "I Didn't Raise My Boy to Be a Soldier." An indignant Roosevelt suggested it should be accompanied by the song "I Didn't Raise My Girl to Be a Mother." For those women who approved the song, their place was "in China—or by preference in a harem—and not in the United States."

When Bryan resigned, Wilson found himself in somewhat of a quandary seeking a successor. An obvious candidate was Robert Lansing, adviser to Bryan on international law and the son-in-law of John Watson Foster, Benjamin Harrison's secretary of state. Lansing had served on numerous international arbitration councils and as editor of the *American Journal of International Law*. Houston recalled that when his name was mentioned to Wilson as a strong possibility, the President "remarked that Lansing would not do, that he was not a big enough man, did not have enough imagination, and would not sufficiently combat or question his views, and that he was lacking in initiative." Houston was thus surprised when the President eventually settled on Lansing as Bryan's successor.

With pressures mounting for U.S. involvement in the war Ray Stannard Baker wrote in his journal: "It is a very ticklish situation; the country wants Mr. Wilson to be firm and yet almost no one wants war. How both these desires can be satisfied it is difficult to see. But the people have great confidence in Mr. Wilson; and are waiting for real leadership. He can do almost anything within reason and be supported." A few months later the President found himself at odds with his Cabinet, several members of which wanted war with Mexico and with Germany as well. Wilson, informed of developments in Mexico by Lincoln Steffens and persuaded that the revolutionary government was anxious to avoid a conflict, turned a deaf ear.

In the summer of 1915 Wilson yielded to the clamor for preparedness so far as to approve the establishment of the Citizens Military Training Corps at Plattsburgh, New York, designed to give rudimentary military training to 750,000 volunteers a year. The unabashedly Eastern upper-class character of the pro-British feeling was perhaps most dramatically illustrated by the fact that of the initial 1,400 volunteers for the corps, 43 were former members of the Porcellian Club at Harvard, one of the oldest and most prestigious of the undergraduate clubs. The citizen soldiers invited the old Porcellian member Theodore Roosevelt to address them. He welcomed the occasion to attack Wilson: "The man who believes in peace at any price or in substituting all-inclusive arbitration for an army and a navy should instantly move to China. If he stays here then more manly men will have to defend him, and he is not worth defending. To treat elocution as a substitute for action, to rely upon high-sounding words unbacked by deeds is proof of a mind that dwells only in the realm of shadow and sham."

In addition to authorizing the training corps, Wilson proposed a program of naval building described by the Speaker of the House as "the most stupendous and costly in the history of any country in peace time."

Secretary of War Lindley Garrison staked his political life on a plan for a "continental army" of some 400,000 "militiamen." The Senate accepted the Garrison plan, but the House defeated it by 13 votes, and Garrison resigned. However, more than a half billion dollars was voted for the army and the navy. Claude Kitchin, North Carolina Democrat and chairman of the powerful Ways and Means Committee, declared, "When this measure becomes a law thereby putting the arms of the munitions makers into the Treasury up to their elbows, with . . . heretofore undreamed of profits at stake, we can hardly conceive of a power in the nation strong enough to extract them." The munitions makers must thus constitute the nation's most powerful pro-war lobby, in Kitchin's view.

At Garrison's resignation, Wilson took the occasion to appoint the well-known reformer Newton D. Baker to replace him. An unfriendly Senator described Baker as "half pacifist and the other half Socialist." Ray Stannard Baker described the "other" Baker as a "light-footed, active man . . . all wires and energy, his eyes very black and his face full of wrinkles . . . a kindly, smiling, eager, affable man." When Baker, little more than five feet tall, mentioned that he loved flowers, his enemies nicknamed him Pansy, a word with homosexual implications. The appointment of Baker, who had earned one of the early Ph.D.'s at Johns Hopkins University and been the able coadjutor of Sam "Golden Rule" Jones in the reforming of Cincinnati, was reassuring to the proponents of American neutrality.

The stresses produced by the bitter divisions in the nation placed a heavy burden on the President's always precarious health. When Wilson left Washington for his summer retreat in Cornish, New Hampshire, in the summer of 1915, he was so tired and debilitated that his surgeon, Dr. Cary Grayson, was seriously alarmed. Grayson told Oswald Garrison Villard that Wilson had been seriously ill at the beginning of his administration and that his recovery had been something of a miracle. Now he seemed once more on the verge of a collapse. Grayson declared, "He sits by himself. He does not see enough young or old people, there is no gaiety around him and, in addition, he is carrying this frightful burden of his job. I feel that something must be done about it if there is not to be a serious breakdown. . . ." Grayson urged Villard to try to enlist Tumulty in an effort to prevail upon the President to live a more healthy life. All to no avail. The President was increasingly moody and often rude. Above all, he was inaccessible except to Tumulty and Colonel House. The death of Wilson's first wife, Ellen Axson, in 1914, had been a crushing blow; a year later he married a widow, Edith Galt. The first Mrs. Wilson had been popular with the public, and there was a general feeling that the President's prompt remarriage did insufficient honor to her memory.

Roosevelt had kept up a drumfire of criticism against his successor from almost the first moment of the war. Throughout 1914 and 1915 a series of articles and essays, all of them bitterly critical of Wilson, flowed from the Colonel's pen. At the end of 1915 they were collected under the title *Fear God and Take Your Part*. The volume was dedicated, ironically, to the memory of Julia Ward Howe, who had been an ardent pacifist in her latter years and opened with "The Battle Hymn of the Republic." Roosevelt praised Howe as the embodiment of "that stern and lofty courage . . . which shrinks neither from war nor from any other form of suffering and hardship and danger. . . . She embodied that trait more essential than any other . . . the valor of righteousness." Julia Ward's friends and descendants might have been excused if they felt that the Colonel had expropriated that splendid old lady.

Roosevelt argued that The Hague conventions—which forbade a nation to attack a nonbelligerent nation—were "part of the Supreme Law of our Land, under the Constitution. Therefore Germany violated the *Supreme Law of our Land* when she brutally wronged Belgium. . . ." The plain implication was that it had been our constitutional duty, at that point, to have entered the war to chasten Germany for a violation of the American Constitution. "Fear God . . . means love God," Roosevelt wrote, "respect God, honor God; and all of this can only be done by loving our neighbor, treating him justly and mercifully, and in all ways attempting to protect him from injustice and cruelty. . . ." In the case of a nation, loving God meant intervening wherever injustice or oppression manifested itself in the world. Such intervention was possible only if the mighty arm of righteousness was powerful. For the United States this meant a powerful army and navy, ready at any moment to speed to protect the weak or to right wrong. The best way for America to aid the cause of humanity was to develop "an intense spirit of Americanism. A flabby cosmopolitanism, especially if it expresses itself through a flabby patriotism, is not only silly, but degrading. It represents national emasculation. The professors of every form of hyphenated Americanism are as truly the foes of this country as if they dwelled outside its borders and make active war against it. . . . The leaders of the hyphenated-American movement in this country (who during the last eighteen months have been the professional German-American and Austro-Americans) are also leaders in the movement against preparedness. . . . They play the part of traitors, pure and simple. Once it was true that this country could not endure half free and half slave. Today it is true that it cannot endure half American and half foreign. The hyphen is incompatible with patriotism. . . . The pacificists who are seeking to Chinafy the United States are not only seeking to bring the United States to ruin, but are seeking to render it absolutely impotent to help upright and well-behaved nations which are oppressed by the military power of unscrupulous neighbors of greater strength."

As these comments suggest, the war in Europe worked a severe hardship on many American immigrants—Roosevelt's "hyphenated-Americans." In addition to the devastating psychological effects of having their mother countries involved in a war with enemies that were "friends" of their adopted land, many immigrants who had not become American citizens were summoned back to their homelands to enter in their armies. This was especially the case with Germans and Austro-Hungarians who had performed military service before immigrating to the United States. Those who had become citizens or who simply chose to remain ran the risk of having their loyalty impugned and indeed of being both persecuted and prosecuted. If Wilson and Roosevelt agreed on nothing else, they were of one mind and voice in denouncing "hyphenated-Americans." At the end of his rather limp *A History of the American People,* published in 1902, Wilson had expressed his view of the "new immigrants." He wrote: "Throughout the century men of the sturdy stocks of the North of Europe had made up the main stream of foreign blood which was every year added to the vital force of the country. . . . But now there came multitudes of men of the lowest class from the South of Italy and men of the meaner sort out of Hungary and Poland, men out of the ranks where there was neither skill nor energy nor any initiative of quick intelligence; and they came in numbers which increased from year to year, as if the countries of the south of Europe were disburdening themselves of the more sordid and hapless elements of their population. . . ." Even the Chinese "were more to be desired . . . than most of the coarse crew that came crowding in every year at the eastern ports."

The situation of immigrants from the belligerent nations was one of which Frederic Howe was acutely aware. At the outbreak of the war in Europe he had been offered the position of United States commissioner of immigration at the port of New York. The appointment of a well-known liberal rather than a party hack was evidence of Wilson's desire to recruit Progressives to his cause. Howe's small empire was, of course, Ellis Island, and he brought to that symbolic point of entry an impatience with bureaucracy and red tape and a warm sympathy for the immigrants who poured through it on their way to becoming Americans. Howe saw himself as a servant of the newcomers and his task as seeing that they were treated civilly, humanely, and, above all, justly. It proved to be a disheartening, uphill job. The physical setting was grim enough. "The buildings," Howe wrote, "were unsuited for permanent residence; the floors were of cement, the corridors were chill, the islands were storm-swept." The general atmosphere was that of a prison with small, bleak spaces enclosed by heavy wire mesh.

In his efforts at reform Howe immediately encountered the resistance of the professional bureaucrats, who were suspicious of outsiders and resentful of change. He soon came to the conviction that "in a generation's time, largely through the Civil Service reform movement, America [had] created an official bureaucracy moved largely by fear, hating initiative, and organized as a solid block to protect itself and its unimaginative, salary-hunting instincts." He found, "for the most part, only a petty struggle of groups and individuals to retain and exalt their own power." Howe wished Ellis Island to be "a kindly place" to the often fearful and apprehensive people who passed through its gates. He opened a school for children, equipped a playground, and removed the Stay Off the Grass signs, declaring that live babies seemed to him more important than live grass. On Sunday, concerts were given by immigrant groups playing music of their homelands. The Italians invited Enricó Caruso to sing on Italian day, and the famous tenor accepted. Soon congressional opponents of Wilson's administration, supplied with ammunition by hostile bureaucrats in the Department of the Interior, were attacking Howe for coddling the immigrants and destroying the morale of the agency. He was accused of being a socialist, and the newspapers joined in the clamor. He discovered that steamship lines, railroads, hotels, and food concessionaires all battened off the immigrants, and all resisted any efforts at reform that might reduce their profits. Howe's private investigation revealed more than $12,000,000 of government funds drained off through various forms of petty graft and misappropriation of funds.

On August, 19, 1915, the *Arabic,* a White Star liner, was sunk with the loss of American lives. Bernstorff reminded Lansing that the German response to the *Lusitania* notes had declared, "Liners will not be sunk by our submarines without warning and without safety of the lives of the non-combatants, provided the liners do not try to escape or offer resistance." Bernstorff asked Lansing to withhold any action until further word had been received from the German government. The advocates of peace in the United States took heart. It seemed as though the Germans were on the verge of renouncing unrestricted submarine warfare. Villard wrote exultantly that the President had, "by sheer force of moral indignation nobly expressed in the name of the greatest Republic in history," forced the Germans to yield on the issue of unrestricted submarine warfare, thereby avoiding America's entry into the war. The *Evening Post* printed a photograph of Wilson on its front page with the caption "This is the man who, without rattling a sword, without mobilizing a corporal's guard of soldiers, or lifting the anchor of a warship won for civilization the greatest diplomatic victory in generations."

On October 5 Bernstorff reported to the State Department that strict orders had been given to submarine commanders to see that no such episodes as the sinking of the *Arabic* took place. But on November 7 came word that an Austrian submarine had sunk the *Ancona.* After an exchange of notes the Austrians announced that the commander of the submarine had been disciplined for disobeying orders, and public clamor subsided. But the sentiment for preparedness continued to grow. Even some of the socialists and pacifists had gone along with the preparedness argument on the ground that being prepared was the best way to avoid having to go to war. "Sympathy for the Allies, unashamed, unquenched, glowed in the hearts of the American people," William Allen White declared somewhat extravagantly.

At the Manhattan Club in New York City at a dinner attended by a number of Democratic notables, Wilson decided to make his stand on preparedness clear. Bob Collier, of *Collier's Weekly*; Norman Hapgood; Mark Sullivan, the journalist; and William Allen White all were seated together in the gallery. To White the President looked sad, even glum. When he began his speech, his voice was strained, and his manner stiff. "Our mission is a mission of peace," he declared, "and we have it in mind to be prepared for defence, to protect our security." The President's plan called for an increase in the regular army to 141,836 officers and men and the creation of a "continental army" of 400,000 men, to be recruited in three increments for three years' service followed by three years in the reserve. At the end of three years the American armed forces would thus consist of 670,836 officers and men, made up of a regular army of some 140,000, a continental force of 400,000, and a national guard of 129,000. As he came to the end of the speech, Wilson's voice was firm and vibrant, but White knew it was "a bitter dose." It seemed clear to him that the President was a new man: "Neutrality had gone out of his heart. He was a partisan of the Allies against Germany."

A few days later Wilson led a Preparedness Day parade down Fifth Avenue, in a high silk hat and cutaway coat, his head "thrown back in exultation." For White, Wilson's presence in the parade symbolized the end of the "struggle for industrial economic justice and progressive political change." Fifteen years of "liberal advance" were over.

Roosevelt announced triumphantly that the President "had finally adopted my principle about preparedness . . . a year after I denounced peace-at-any-price, he followed suit . . . ; a year after I had attacked hyphenated Americanism Mr. Wilson followed suit—at least before the Colonial Dames. . . ."

For the President's plan (actually, ex-Secretary of War Garrison's plan), Congress substituted its own calling for a regular army of 186,000 and a federalized national guard of 425,000, plus a reserve corps and an officer training corps to be established at colleges and universities. The uniforms and equipment of the national guard and the standards of training were to be set by the War Department. The "continental army" disappeared.

Wilson's measures seemed wholly inadequate to the advocates of war. An increasingly militant Lippmann concluded, "Wilson is impossible. He has no sense of organization and no interest in the responsibilities of the socialized state. He has no grasp of international affairs and his pacificism is of precious little help to the peace of the world. . . . Roosevelt alone of men who are possible has any vision of an integrated community. . . ."

In the fall of 1916 the famous pacifist Madame Rosika Schwimmer won an audience with Henry Ford and persuaded him to underwrite the "peace ship," a vessel full of pacifists to be dispatched to Europe on the mission of negotiating a peace. The neutral countries of Europe, she assured Ford, would welcome such a move to end the war. He was the one man in the world who could dramatize the peace issue. Ford at first refused to be a party to the scheme, but Madame Schwimmer persisted, and the next day he gave in.

Oswald Garrison Villard was roused with the news that Henry Ford wished to see him at the Biltmore Hotel. When Villard arrived, Ford announced that he had chartered the ocean liner *Oscar II* to carry a party of distinguished Americans to Europe with the intention of stirring the neutral nations to an effort to mediate the war. Ford was ready to announce his project to a startled world. What, Villard asked, would he say to the press? "Oh, I always get on very well with the boys," Ford replied. "All you need is a slogan. . . . Something like— 'we'll get the boys in the trenches home by Christmas.' What do you think of that?" Villard pointed out that Ford did not plan to sail until December 4. "Well," Ford replied, "we'll make it, 'we'll get the boys out of the trenches by Easter.' "

Villard was convinced that Ford had no idea of the real difficulties of his famous and much to be ridiculed enterprise. In Frederic Howe's opinion, Ford was "lured into the enterprise against his will, his judgment and his desires by the plea that there was a possibility, a bare possibility, that he might be the means of saving lives." Newspapers in the United States and in the Allied countries gave Ford an unmerciful drubbing, accusing him of egotism, arrogance, and quixotic behavior. The last was undoubtedly true. It was a quixotic gesture, but it was, at the same time, both characteristic of Ford and a thoroughly "American" act. Rebuffed at every turn, Ford and his little company returned, discomforted, to the United States. The importance of the Ford peace mission, at least in Villard's opinion, was the fact that it finally discredited the whole idea of appealing to the neutral nations to act as serious peacemakers.

The stubborn resistance of many Senators and Congressmen to heavy "defense" spending continued. Henry Cabot Lodge, reporting the fact to Roosevelt in January, 1916, confessed himself "very depressed." Resistance centered in an incongruous alliance of Southern Democrats and Midwestern Insurgents. The country at large seemed no better; people were more interested in "the preservation of life, comfort and amusement" than in fighting for the honor of their country. Most disconcerting of all, there appeared to be "many good Republicans who are engaged in keeping as neutral as Wilson, and as silent about international duties. . . . The worst crowd we have to deal with are the so-called Progressive Senators." Almost all of them were for a general embargo on the shipment of arms and munitions to any of the belligerents. In February, 1916, Jeff McLemore, a Texas Democrat, introduced a resolution requesting the President to warn Americans not to travel on armed vessels. In presenting his bill, McLemore declared, "I believe this measure accurately embodies the wishes of an overwhelming majority of the American people, for in an hour like this the soul of a nation has ways of making itself manifest. . . . I am told the President regards my resolution as an attempt to interfere with his application of the Administration's foreign policy." To McLemore, it seemed clear that the President's policy favored the Allies and infringed American's neutrality. "Why," he asked, ". . . are we called upon to protect English ships, or French or Italian . . . ? As a member of Congress, I feel it a proud duty to uphold the hands of our President when he is in the right, but I must know that he is right. With my country it is different. I would prefer that my country be always right, but, right or wrong, my country forever. . . . I wish to submit this proposition, if we are to maintain an open sea for American travellers and tourists, let us maintain an open sea for the cotton, grain, and other products of our American farmers."

Wilson took the line that McLemore's resolution was a direct attack on presidential leadership, but it took all his prestige and all of House's political ingenuity to prevent the resolution from coming to an uncertain vote in the House. Among those Congressmen opposed to the administration's effort to have the resolution tabled were a number of Progressive Westerners, including Lenroot of Wisconsin.

One of the most significant consequences of the industrial boom produced by the war was the migration North of Southern blacks. As the war continued, the trickle swelled to a flood. Reports of high wages in defense plants and fewer racial barriers lured individual blacks and, more commonly, whole families North. Pioneers sent back encouraging reports. Not only tenant farmers, sunk in debt peonage, departed, but many relatively prosperous blacks who owned their own homes sold their houses and furnishings for what they could get—often no more than ten cents on the dollar—or, in numerous instances, simply abandoned them. Many belonged to "clubs" banding together for mutual support. In the words of one emigrant, "people almost gave away their houses and their furnishings." When the "club" departed, "the crowds at the train were so large that 'the policemen had to just force them back in order to allow the people to get on and off.' " One family departed one at a time "to secure better wages and more freedom. . . . This family sold their chickens and rented their cattle to some of the people in the community." Those left behind felt abandoned. One old black man told a reporter, "I sorta wanted to go myself. I didn't know just where I wanted to go. I just wanted to git away with the rest of them." A black woman in a small Georgia town declared at the height of the migration, "You could go out on the street and count on your fingers all the colored people you saw during the entire day. Now and then a disconsolate-looking Italian storekeeper would come out in the street, look up and down and walk back. It was a sad looking place, and so quiet it gave you the shivers."

Often a mass migration from a particular town or city would be triggered by white brutality toward a particular black. Abbeville, South Carolina, witnessed a general exodus after the lynching of Anthony Crawford. A black newspaper correspondent wrote that when Abbeville blacks departed, "the whites went almost into hysterics as some sections of Georgia and Alabama are doing because they are leaving for the North to better their industrial condition. Crawford is said to have been worth [the loss of] $100,000 in property. . . . The cry now is—'Go north, where there is some humanity, some justice and fairness." A thousand blacks had left Abbeville in a week.

In a Mississippi town that had lost half its black population, a black woman declared, "If I have to stay here any longer, I'll go wild. Every time I go home I have to pass house after house of all my friends who are in the North and prospering. . . . There ain't enough people here now I know to give me a decent burial."

Labor agents, commonly black, played a central role in recruiting Southern blacks for Northern industries. Some communities, to thwart the exodus, passed laws requiring agents to pay a huge fee—$25,000 in Macon, Georgia—for the right to recruit black workers. In other towns and cities upper-class black professionals—lawyers and doctors—whose own livelihoods were threatened by the exodus were enlisted to try to prevail on their fellows to remain at home. In Macon the police ostentatiously purchased rifles. Sometimes blacks who were known to be planning to leave were arrested and held in jail. A hundred blacks who turned up at the train station in Savannah to catch a train for the North were arrested and held at the police barracks. In Greenville, Mississippi, black passengers were forceably removed from trains, and at Brookhaven a chartered train carrying fifty blacks was held on a siding for three days. At Hattiesburg, Mississippi, the ticket agent refused to sell railroad tickets to blacks. The mayor of New Orleans telegraphed the president of the Illinois Central Railroad, urging that the line carry no more Louisiana blacks to the North. The migration caused considerable soul-searching among whites. The *Tifton* (Georgia) *Gazette* acknowledged that the citizens of the state had "allowed negroes to be lynched, five at a time, on nothing stronger than suspicion; they have allowed whole sections to be depopulated of them . . . ; they have allowed them to be whitecapped and whipped, and their homes burned. . . . Loss of much of the State's best labor is one of the prices Georgia is paying for unchecked mob activity against negroes often charged only with ordinary crimes. . . ."

With each passing month the nation grew more polarized. Vice-President Thomas Marshall, an unpretentious Hoosier, prided himself on remaining strictly neutral. "So far as I now know," he wrote, "I am the only living American, possessed of a voice, who followed that advice. I believed it to be my duty to obey not only the orders but the requests of my chief, and the only thing I got out of my loyalty was to be called by some people, an idiot, and by others, a fool."

28

The Election of 1916

For a beleaguered Wilson the Mexican situation seemed, for the time at least, more pressing than the European War.

The stories of atrocities against Catholic priests and nuns in Mexico made a long and terrible litany. Added to it were the names of a number of Americans. It was a litany that Theodore Roosevelt never tired of reciting as an example of the weak and vacillating policy of the Wilson administration. He believed it the mission of the United States to "put a stop to anarchy and murder and prevent further bloodshed" and "bring peace to the distracted land of Mexico." How this was to be done without killing large numbers of Mexicans and a good many Americans, he failed to make clear. "Insult to the American flag, nameless infamies on American women, caused [Wilson] not one single pulse of emotion," Roosevelt asserted. "Either we shall have to abandon the Monroe Doctrine and let other nations restore order in Mexico . . . or else we must in good faith ourselves undertake the task and bring peace and order and prosperity to Mexico as by our wise intervention it was brought to Cuba. . . . No man can support Mr. Wilson," Roosevelt concluded, "without being false to the ideals of national duty and international humanity. No one can support Mr. Wilson without opposing the larger, the true Americanism."

Lansing and Newton D. Baker became increasingly alarmed at the rumors of German activity in Mexico. William Allen White's old friend General Frederick Funston, in command of the Mexican border, heard reports that the German and Austrian consuls were providing funds for a band that was preparing to attack Texas. The "Plan of San Diego" was reputed to be the result of the combined efforts of Carranza and German agents to start a revolution among Mexican-Americans, Indians, and blacks in Texas, New Mexico, Arizona, Nevada, and California. The Japanese would, it was hoped, join in an assault through Texas up the Mississippi. A Berlin paper boasted of the effort to involve Mexico and the United States in war. "We consider it not worth denying that Germany is egging Mexico into war in order to prevent the export of arms to the Allies," it told its readers. "The fact that America's profitable arms traffic with France and England will suffer through a war with Mexico is, to be sure, a consequence that will cause us no tears."

Germans, many of them in the pay of the German government, others simply doing their patriotic duty, swarmed through Mexico. There were German-subsidized newspapers and German wireless operators as well as more than 50 German officers who held commissions in the Mexican Army. It was estimated that Germans in Mexico numbered more than 4,000.

The Union of German Citizens had twenty-two branches throughout the country, disseminating the propaganda of the *Vaterland* so effectively that "a great number of Mexicans have been convinced that we are right in our methods of conducting warfare and are now disposed to accept our communiqués," the head of the union reported. The Iron Cross Society was even more widespread, with seventy-five chapters in Mexico. Two of its members were fighting with Villa. So the effort went on with typical German thoroughness and equally typical obtuseness. Had Wilson had the slightest disposition to go to war with Germany, the activities of Germans in Mexico would have substantially increased it, in addition to helping justify the abandonment of neutrality in favor of direct support for the Allies.

The indefatigable Captain Franz von Rintelen had been busy with plans to restore General Huerta to power in Mexico. The scheme called for smuggling Huerta across the Mexican-U.S. border and supplying him with arms and munitions on the condition that he make trouble for the United States if that country were to enter the war on the side of the Allies. The time seemed ripe for a coup. Carranza was beset by

Obregón, Villa, Zapata, Díaz, and Orozco. In the continual bloody and inconclusive fighting (each Mexican "general" was backed by some faction in the United States, trying to preserve advantages for itself), Mexican nationals suffered most, but American residents in Mexico were also terrorized and murdered.

According to Rintelen's plan, Huerta was to travel in disguise on the train to El Paso but to leave the train at Newman, where he would be met by General Orozco and driven to Mexico. The State Department representative at El Paso, a man named Cobb, informed by telegraph of Huerta's impending arrival, met him with a contingent of U.S. soldiers at Newman and took him into custody. In the border town of El Paso sympathy was so plainly with Huerta that the mayor agreed to be his attorney. Cobb was apprehensive lest a compliant judge set Huerta free on bail and he slip over the border, sped on his way by sympathetic American hands. But while Huerta, uncooperative as ever, posed a severe dilemma for the President, nature took its course, and the general conveniently died, poisoned, his friends charged, by the Americans.

Many Americans who were cold to the involvement of the United States in a European war were eager for a showdown with Mexico. The *Chicago Tribune* editorialized, "Fate offers us a golden apple in Mexico and only bitter fruit in Flanders. If we win a war with Mexico we know what we get out of it—a secure continent. And it is practically impossible for us to lose."

Wilson found that Carranza was little better than Huerta. "I have never known a man more difficult to deal with," he wrote. Carranza had confiscated foreign property as freely as had his predecessor. Disappointed in Carranza and increasingly dismayed over the prolonged anarchy in Mexico, Wilson decided to place the U.S. bets on Pancho Villa. Villa, it was reported, when irritated by the bawlings of a drunken soldier who interrupted his conversation with an American journalist, had paused to shoot the disturber of his peace. Lansing urged support of Villa on the ground that such support might make Carranza more amenable. But after some months of anxiety about the latest U-boat attacks and revelations of German meddling in Mexican affairs, Wilson decided that it was too late in the day to trifle further with the volatile situation in that country and recognized Carranza as president. As Lansing put it, "Germany desires to keep up the turmoil in Mexico until the United States is forced to intervene; *therefore, we must not intervene.*"

The Americans were not, unfortunately, satisfied with withdrawing support from Villa. They betrayed him by allowing one of Carranza's generals, who was expecting an attack by Villa, to bring in reinforcements on American railroads. When Villa made his raid, his men were mowed down by Carranza's vastly superior force. He retreated over the Sierra with a handful of survivors and spent a winter of bitter hardship, planning revenge on all gringos.

Lincoln Steffens, an opponent of intervention, attached himself to Carranza, telling the suspicious Mexican leader, "I am here as a patriotic American to learn how to see my country through a revolution we need as much as you do." Carranza came gradually to trust Steffens and to include him in the meetings of his Cabinet. Steffens, for his part, alarmed that American business interests might force Wilson into war with Mexico, devoted his efforts to preventing such a move on the part of the United States. That task became far more difficult when on January 10, 1916, a band of Villa's men intercepted a train carrying seventeen American mining engineers, symbols to the Mexicans of the exploitation of Mexico's resources by Yankee capitalists. The Villistas stripped the Americans and then lined them up and shot them. One survived to tell the story.

In Mexico City at the American Club, Steffens found a number of his countrymen celebrating the fact that the Americans had been shot. "Why do you celebrate the killings of Americans?" the startled Steffens asked. "Don't you see?" they replied. "It means intervention. You don't suppose those blankety-blank pacifists in the Wilson administration can refuse now to send the army, do you?" Steffens, disturbed at the rumor that Wilson was contemplating war in the conviction that Carranza was determined to provoke it, hurried to Washington to try to convince the President that his information was false and that Carranza wished peace above all. At first Wilson refused to see Steffens, but when the journalist succeeded in getting information to him indicating that he was about to act on incorrect information, the President agreed to see him and, at least according to Steffens, accepted the evidence he submitted as valid, agreeing not to declare war on Mexico. While Steffens talked with Wilson, waiting outside to see the President were David Starr Jordan and Moorfield Storey, leading pacifists. When Steffens mentioned that they also wished to see him, Wilson replied, "Don't let them come near me. I won't see them. Those pacifists make me feel warlike."

Before he left the President's office, Steffens asked Wilson why he had at first refused to see him, and Wilson gave a revealing reply. "An executive," he told Steffens, "is a man of action. An intellectual—such as you and I—an intellectual is inexecutive. In an executive job we are dangerous, unless we are aware of our limitations and take measures to stop our everlasting disposition to think, to listen, to—not act. I made up my mind long ago, when I got into my first executive job, to open my mind for a while, hear everybody who came to me with advice, information—what you will—then, some day, the day when my mind felt like deciding, to shut it up and act. My decision might be right; it might be wrong. No matter. I would take a chance and do—something. . . . You have given me information, very valuable information, information which prevents a war. . . . I decided to re-open this, these" . . . tapping his forehead and touching his ears—"and—and it was right for once. You had some facts I lacked."

A month later came an episode that Wilson, with the elections of 1916 approaching, could not allow to go unpunished. Four hundred of Villa's horsemen attacked the town of Columbus, New Mexico, shooting anyone who appeared, burning houses, and looting stores. Wilson first obtained Carranza's permission (the Mexican president was as anxious as Wilson to rid himself of his murderous compatriot) for American troops to enter his country "for the sole purpose of capturing the bandit Villa." In March, 1916, General John J. Pershing was ordered to pursue and punish Villa and his men. In a few weeks the general with 6,600 men was 300 miles inside Mexico; the elusive Villa easily evaded the comparatively slow-moving expeditionary force. Report after report of Villa's capture or death proved erroneous. It seemed as though every dead Mexican was incorrectly identified as Villa, giving rise to the suspicion that all Mexicans looked alike to gringos. Secretary of the Interior Franklin Lane wrote: "My judgment is that to fail in getting Villa would ruin us in the eyes of all Latin America. I do not say they respect only force but, like children, they pile insult on insult if they are not stopped when the first insult is given."

Steffens, dismayed that Wilson had finally been prevailed on to intervene, wrote: "Woodrow Wilson was not only a well-grounded liberal of the old school of Jefferson; he was the strongest liberal who we could have had. . . . He was liberalism personified, and when he failed liberalism failed. And he did fail. He did not understand the economics of the situation." He invaded Mexico "a little," not enough to affect the outcome of the revolution seriously, but enough to enrage the Mexicans. In Steffens's judgment, Wilson blamed Carranza unjustly for not controlling his revolution, as though revolutions could be "controlled."

Roosevelt, who had been critical of Wilson for not invading Mexico to restore order, now denounced him for butting in. "He never did it . . . to secure justice and peace for Americans or other foreigners. He never did it to secure the triumph of justice and peace among the Mexicans themselves. He merely did it in the interest of some bandit chief." In the years of Wilson's presidency, Roosevelt wrote, "more of our citizens have been killed by Mexicans, Germans, Austrians and Haytians than were killed during the entire Spanish War." Despite the interventions in Haiti and Mexico, "thanks to the abject quality of Mr. Wilson's tameness, no benefit whatever, to us or to mankind, has come from this loss of life. . . ." Roosevelt insisted that American involvement in Mexico had made the United States "responsible for the frightful wrong-doing, for the terrible outrages committed by the victorious revolutionists on hundreds of religious people of both sexes."

With the threat of war against Germany in the air, two-thirds of the U.S. regular army were soon involved in chasing Pancho Villa. It was in this highly volatile atmosphere that the nation faced the presidential election of 1916. An interval of relative amity between the United States and Germany had been due less to any genuine accommodation of views about U-boat warfare than to the fact that the Germans had only a handful of U-boats of any considerable range. All the resources of the German shipyards had been meanwhile devoted to turning out a fleet of improved U-boats in a desperate race against the constricting effects of the British blockade.

On March 24, 1916, a British channel steamer, the *Sussex,* was sunk with the loss of a number of lives, Americans among them. In the weeks before the sinking of the *Sussex* three other British ships with Americans on board had been sunk without warning. The German reply to the American protest over the sinking of the *Sussex* was captious. The American note of protest in response was stern: "It now owes it to a just regard for its own rights to say to the Imperial Government that the time has come. It has become painfully evident . . . that the position that it took at the very outset is inevitable, namely, the use of submarines for the destruction of an enemy's commerce is, of necessity, because of the very character of the vessels employed and the methods of attack which their employment involves, utterly incompatible with the principles of humanity, the long established and uncontrovertible rights of neutrals, and the sacred immunities of non-combatants. . . . Unless the Imperial Government should not immediately declare and effect an abandonment of its present method of submarine warfare against passenger and freight-carrying vessels, the Government of the United States can have no other choice but to sever diplomatic relations with the German Empire altogether."

This time the Germans were more conciliatory. "In accordance with the general principles of visit and search and destruction of merchant vessels recognized by international law," the foreign minister replied, "such vessels, both within and without the area declared as naval war zone, shall not be sunk without warning and without saving human lives unless these ships attempt to escape or offer resistance." On the other hand, if the British did not show the same regard for the rules of international law, "the German Government would then be facing a new situation in which it must reserve to itself complete liberty of decision."

After the torpedoing of the *Sussex,* Walter Lippmann and the *New Republic* sounded a warning. "We no longer intend to be neutral between the violator and his victim," the magazine announced. The United States must be ready to use all its resources including, if necessary, "its military power against the aggressor." The editorial led to a break with Jack Reed, who accused Lippmann of playing the game of Wall Street, and Lippmann lashed back, noting that Reed had often "acted like a fool or a cad." Reed, Lippmann suggested, had simply been an ambitious social climber at Harvard. "I have never taken your radicalism the least bit seriously. You are no more dangerous to the capitalist class in this country than a romantic guerrilla fighter." He was simply "amusing and dramatic" in his revolutionary posturings.

The two most important presidential measures in the election year were the steps taken to increase the size and improve the armaments of the navy. Ten battleships were authorized, and six battle cruisers, plus fifty torpedo boats, a "fleet" of nine submarines and fifty-eight smaller "coast" submarines intended for patrolling local waters. Also created were a naval reserve, a naval war staff and a naval flying corps.

The election of 1916 could hardly have come at a more awkward time. The nation was deeply divided in its feelings about the war. The Progressives had been demoralized by Roosevelt's unwavering belligerence. Summoned to Oyster Bay by the Colonel, who was apparently interested in using the *New Republic* as a stepping-stone back into the

White House, Lippmann wrote to Mabel Dodge: "I spent last night . . . with Roosevelt and loved him more than ever," but when the *New Republic* criticized Roosevelt for what it thought was an unfair attack on Wilson, the Colonel denounced the editors as "three circumcised Jews and three anemic Christians," and a few weeks later Lippmann confessed that "TR gets on my nerves so much these days that I shall become a typical anti-Roosevelt maniac if I do not look out."

The peace faction was as active as the advocates of war. There seemed to be no clear consensus in the country about *anything*. The critical question for the Progressives was whether to hold their own nominating convention or return to the fold of the Republican Party, hoping to help nominate a candidate of liberal persuasion after the Taft debacle. Many Progressives opposed the notion of a separate convention. Would it not perpetuate the split in the Republican Party and assure Wilson of another term? Others argued that if the convention were held concurrently with the Republican Convention, it would serve as a kind of lever to force the Republicans to nominate a liberal candidate. The Progressives could then endorse him and help secure a Republican victory. It was soon evident that the original Progressive zeal had waned. Many Progressives were embarrassed by Roosevelt's suggestion that those opposing America's entry were somehow lacking in patriotism or, as he preferred to put it, Americanism. Responding to Roosevelt's attacks on Wilson, the Progressive Senator William Joel Stone of Missouri called the former President "the most seditious man of consequence in America," while William Allen White termed him "A Man of Wrath, raging at Wilson for his neutrality. And the more he raged," White added, "the more he forgot about the Bull Moosers—orphans in a storm." White himself was "more inclined to follow Wilson's foreign policy than Roosevelt's. . . ." One of the consequences of Roosevelt's all-out attack on Wilson's neutrality policy was that it revived his friendship with Henry Cabot Lodge. Once more the old friends were exchanging political speculations and congratulations on each other's public utterances. Their mutual hostility to Wilson and the advocates of peace, including the "college sissies" who had issued statements supporting peace, drew them closer than they had been since 1912.

Roosevelt admitted to Lodge that Republican prospects were poor for the coming election. He had no regrets, he wrote, at having forfeited the "Good will . . . of the David Starr Jordan and Jane Addams type of native American Progressive." He had found the California

Progressives a nest of antipreparedness sentiment, and it seemed highly likely that Wilson, "with his adroit, unscrupulous cunning, his readiness to about-face, his timidity about any manly assertion of our rights, and his pandering to the feelings of those who love ease and the chance of material profit, and . . . his willingness to follow every gust of popular opinion, will be supported by the mass of our fellow-countrymen. . . ."

As for the question of whether he himself should be a candidate for the presidency in the fall, Roosevelt wrote to Lodge that "it would be utterly idle to nominate me if the country is in a mood of timidity or of that base and complacent materialism which finds expression in the phrase 'Safety first.'"

In January, 1916, Roosevelt and his wife departed on a trip to the West Indies. Meanwhile, the regular Republicans, concerned with Roosevelt's potential for making trouble, circulated a prospective platform that, in Henry Stoddard's opinion, was "substantially a summary of Roosevelt politics." Stoddard joined Roosevelt in Trinidad, and the two men composed a statement which was wired to the leading newspapers. In it Roosevelt declared that he had no intention of entering into "any fight for the nomination. . . . Indeed I will go further and say that it would be a mistake to nominate me unless the country has in its mood something of the heroic; unless it feels not only like devoting itself to ideals, but to the purpose measurably to realize those ideals in action.

"This," the communiqué continued, "is one of those rare times in a nation's history when the action taken determines the life of the generations that are to follow. . . . Nothing is to be hoped from the present Administration. The struggles between the President and his party leaders in Congress are merely struggles as to whether the nation shall see its government representatives adopt an attitude of a little more or a little less hypocrisy and follow a policy of slightly greater or slightly less baseness."

It is hardly surprising that many of Roosevelt's countrymen took the statement as a declaration of the Colonel's intention to be a candidate for the nomination by the Republicans or, failing, that of the rejuvenated Progressive Party.

The Republicans, meeting in a lackluster convention in Chicago on June 7, adopted a weak and evasive platform and went through the required motions "as though through a mail order catalogue," in Henry Stoddard's words. Warren Harding, as chairman of the convention, gave the opening address; William Allen White described him as "a handsome dog, a little above medium height, with a swarthy skin, a scathing eye. . . ." On this occasion he was "meticulously clad in morning clothes with a red geranium as a boutonniere, and he had the harlot's voice of the old-time political orator." To White he was "the tip of the salient on the right."

If young reformers like Lippmann had any lingering attachment to the Republican Party of Theodore Roosevelt, the party's convention in Chicago in June severed it. Lippmann listened for nine stupefying hours to "bellow and rant punctuated by screeches and roars." It was, he wrote, "the quintessence of all that is commonplace, machine-made, complacent and arbitrary in American life." It was "the flag, red, white and blue, all its stripes, all its stars, and the flag again a thousand times over, and Americanism till your ears ached and the slaves and the tariff, and Abraham Lincoln, mauled and dragged about and his name taken in vain and his spirit degraded, prostituted to every insincerity. . . . The incredible sordidness of the convention passes all description."

The Republican strategy was to nominate Charles Evans Hughes in the hope that many Progressives, finding him a candidate to their taste, would return to the Republican Party. Hughes was an elegant man with a commanding presence. He had a quick, vigorous walk. "You could see in his stride," Stoddard noted, "that he was a purposeful man." He was famous for his integrity. He had been, successively, the mildly reformist governor of New York State (he had defeated William Randolph Hearst and Tammany for the office), associate justice of the Supreme Court (from which he had retired after six years), and now presidential nominee of the Republican Party. "The Republicans," in Stoddard's words, "adjourned in a deadened calm of over-confidence."

Having encouraged the calling of the Progressive Convention, Roosevelt, not surprisingly, found himself the choice of the delegates, who indeed had assumed that their chieftain was calling them forth to do battle for the Lord once again. The Progressive strategy was to have Bainbridge Colby nominate Roosevelt as soon as possible after the opening of the convention, but when Colby advanced to the platform, George Perkins, who had received a letter from Roosevelt rejecting the nomination, tried to intercept him, "crying out in a distraught and almost hysterical voice." He failed to check him, and Colby, in what must have been the briefest nominating speech in American history, put Roosevelt's name before the convention. The response was a burst of ecstatic cheering of relatively brief duration but of startling intensity, a cry of such passion as White had never heard before in a political arena and would never hear again, a tornado of sound that welled from the souls of the delegates and shook the rafters of the auditorium.

When the clamor subsided, Perkins read the Roosevelt letter. The last words, "But your candidate I cannot be," fell upon the delegates "like a curse," White wrote. "For a moment there was silence. Then there was a roar of rage. It was the cry of a broken heart such as no convention had ever uttered in this land before." With tears in his eyes White watched hundreds of delegates tear their Roosevelt buttons from their coats and throw them on the floor. Henry Stoddard wrote: "I shall never forget the scene of dismay, anger and defiance, with their old leader, in those closing hours. . . ." The convention was changed in an instant "from an intensely Roosevelt gathering to an intensely anti-Roosevelt gathering."

Oswald Garrison Villard wrote: "Only twice in my life have I seen men weep in a public assembly. Around me men of the frontier type could not keep back their tears at . . . the smashing of their illusions about their peerless leader." Villard telegraphed his paper that the Progressive Party had been destroyed at one fatal blow. "On its tombstone History will write: 'Created by Theodore Roosevelt for his own purposes and killed when it suited him.' In all the sizable graveyard of the third parties of our political history there lies none done to death so cruelly and so casually."

White was convinced that George Perkins was the agent of the liberal wing of the Republican Party, working in the Progressive ranks to confuse and demoralize the Roosevelt backers. He believed that Perkins had held back the letter from Roosevelt in order to aid the candidacy of Hughes.

Wherever Bull Moosers gathered that night, there was "a lodge of sorrow," in White's phrase. He called his wife long distance in Emporia and spent $9.45 "bawling like a calf into the receiver." Finally, Sallie cut him off, and he went to bed at peace. "It was the end of a great adventure, politically and emotionally probably the greatest adventure of my life," he wrote from the perspective of old age.

After the Progressive Convention had disbanded in anger and frustration, the National Committee (of which White was a member) met and voted by a narrow margin to support Hughes. White refused to vote. As he put it, "I was too freshly widowed to be in a mood for political romance." The dispirited White, after writing a friendly and reassuring letter to Roosevelt—"Don't worry. It will all come out in the wash. . . . Rest and wait"—confessed to a friend, "I am weak and weary, sick and sore. I am without star or compass politically and am up in the air and a mile west. . . . The whole trouble with our humanitarian platform, as I see it at the moment, is that it hit war. Kaiser Bill blew it up. . . . You cannot get people interested in minimum wages and laws for hours of service and equitable railroad rates in the face of the news from Verdun."

To White it seemed evident that the reason that the United States was "behind the civilized world in social and industrial legislation" was that "each of the old parties [was] half free and half controlled by reactionaries." Vast expenditures of energy were therefore necessary to achieve the most modest reforms, and nothing better could be hoped for until "a non-factional, non-sectional party" with progressive principles was founded out of two traditional parties. "The Progressives," White wrote to a friend, "should enlist those who are willing to take long marches with hard bivouacs, and in the end leave their unidentified political bones to mark the forward trail. . . . The problems which we have set forth will not be solved until either our party or some other party (and whatever comes it will not be the Democratic party, for Democracy is made irrevocably reactionary by the Negro question in the South)—until our party or some other party be entirely reconstructed, entirely free of the unthinking votes and the reactionary faction, rises . . . wholly consecrated to our ideals."

A few days after the collapse of the Progressives, Roosevelt dined with Hughes in New York City and pledged his full support, but Progressives by the thousands defected to Wilson and the Democrats.

The Socialist Labor Party had met in New York in the early spring, passed resolutions opposing American involvement in the war, and nominated candidates for president and vice-president, but the Socialist Party itself was too badly split to risk a convention. Two obscure candidates were nominated by mail referendum.

Meeting in St. Louis on June 14, the Democrats went through the motions much as the Republicans had, nominating Wilson again, with Thomas Marshall as his running mate. Placing Wilson's name in nomination, Senator Ollie James from Kentucky sounded what would be the major theme of the Democrats' campaign when he declared, "Without orphaning a single American child, without widowing a single American mother, without firing a single gun or shedding a drop of blood, he [Wilson] wrung from the most militant spirit that ever brooded above a battlefield the concession of American demands and American rights." Martin Littleton, a New York Congressman, coined the catchy phrase "He kept us out of war." What the delegates did not know was that the President, even as the convention met, had moved substantially closer to American intervention. He had approved a letter to Sir Edward Grey, the British foreign secretary, which read: "Confidential. Col. House told me that President Wilson was ready, on hearing from France and England, that the moment was opportune, to propose that a conference should be summoned to put an end to the war. Should the Allies accept this proposal and should Germany refuse it, the United States would probably enter the war against Germany. Col. House expressed the opinion that if such a conference met, it would secure peace on terms not unfavorable to the Allies, and if it failed to secure peace the United States would leave the conference as a belligerent on the side of the Allies if Germany was unreasonable. . . ." The memorandum, dated February 22, 1916, suggested a course of action as uncongenial to the Allies as to the Germans (to whom it was never communicated). Wilson's only change in the original memorandum was the insertion of the word "probably" before the clause "enter the war against Germany."

In his acceptance speech Wilson listed the accomplishments of his administration, a record "of extraordinary length and variety, rich in elements of many kinds, but consistent in principle." Above all else, it had overthrown the "Invisible Government" of capitalists and their lobbyist agents and established "a free and untrammeled government of the people."

David Houston, new to national politics, came away from the three party conventions—Republican, Progressive, and Democratic—"with a feeling of depression. They are not edifying spectacles," he added, "and they are an offence to the ear and to reason. . . . They are distinctly inartistic, not to say common or vulgar." The majority of the speeches were fountains of "bunk," and the demonstrations were "forced, childish, and trivial."

Perhaps the most notable fact about the Democratic Convention was that it was the first since 1892 that was not dominated by Bryan. His undeviating opposition to American involvement in the war had made him a liability. He had written to Postmaster General Albert Burleson on March 8, 1916: "My own supreme purpose at this time is to do what I can to prevent war. I believe that the interests of our party as well as the interests of the country and the world demand that *we shall not enter this war.* Any 'honor' that would require it is a sham honor and as for 'humanity' we have a higher mission than to go around the world looking for an opportunity to help one European monarch fight out his quarrels with another."

The Democratic platform, after congratulating the party, as all such documents must do, on its astonishing record of brilliant achievement (in this instance, with some justice), made a display of patriotism by denouncing groups that were intent on furthering "foreign interests" and went on to call for a child labor law, women's suffrage, self-government for the Philippines, and territorial government for Alaska, Hawaii, and Puerto Rico.

"I have come around completely to Wilson," Lippmann wrote Graham Wallas in August, "chiefly because I think he has the imagination and the will to make a radical move in the organization of peace. . . . Of course the campaign depends above all on what the former Progressives do. If Wilson can get 20 per cent of their votes he will be re-elected. . . . Wilson is by far the best party leader the Democrats have ever produced." While Felix Frankfurter considered the Republican Party the only hope for reform and urged Henry Stimson to do his best to "identify the Republican Party in the public mind as the liberal party," like many of his generation, he was determined not to be bound by party lines "in these transitional days." He added, "My groping of hope and loyalty to the Republican Party as the party that ought to be the liberal party, and largely tends that way, are perhaps valuable as reflecting the rather troubled viewpoint of not a few of the younger generation."

Frankfurter wrote to his friend Morris Cohen: "I have no illusion about Wilson. I still have a feeling of insecurity about him, but I do think that Hughes and the Republican campaign have systematically underestimated the impressive achievements of Wilson. . . ." Hughes, instead of educating the country about the crisis confronting it, had preferred to play safe. Furthermore, Hughes's notion of the president "as the administrative head of the government" compared unfavorably in Frankfurter's mind with "Wilson's notion of the presidency as a political leader and law maker."

The *New Republic* vacillated between Hughes and Wilson. It was, in fact, a contest between Croly and Lippmann. By September Lippmann had convinced Croly that Hughes was "pro-German" and that Wilson had become a wholehearted nationalist of the Croly persuasion. John

Dewey, Jane Addams, Amos Pinchot, and Frederic Howe came out for Wilson, breaking away from their Progressive allegiance.

Henry Adams saw little hope in either party. In the aftermath of the conventions he wrote to his English friend Charles Gaskell: "It is very curious—this living in the ruins of a dissolved world. No one seems to know it; no one has anything to say; no one does anything; no one speculates as to the past or the future; no one thinks. It is a great paralysis—all is waiting for something big to break. . . . Our old world is dead. The huge polypus waiting to pop over us is what we call the Middle West, which corresponds to your middle class. It has a stomach but no nervous centre,—no brains." Brains, of course, were exactly what the Middle West had, brains in abundance and brains for export, and a Puritan-derived moral sensibility not entirely dissimilar to Adams's own but much better suited to engage the world. Adams was not the only reviler of the West. When Roosevelt accused the West of being "yellow" because of its strong antiwar sentiment, William Allen White replied vehemently, "Man! you are clean, plumb crazy, wild as a bedbug about the West. . . . You must quit scolding the West. Here live the kind of people who support you and your ideals. Here live the men who are going to work out the economic and political problems that will confront this country after the war. And, if there is any fighting to do, here are the men who are going to do the fighting. The thing for you to do is to back off and get a little perspective on this election."

Thomas Edison, a lifelong Republican, got on the Wilson bandwagon. After listing his reasons for supporting the President, he added, "They say Wilson has blundered. Well, I reckon he has, but I notice he always blunders *forward.*" Two other notable additions to the Wilson ranks were the liberal young Wall Street financiers Bernard Baruch and Thomas Chadbourne. Baruch, "wiser than a treeful of owls," according to George Creel, proved to be a master of political strategy. Chadbourne, six feet seven inches tall, "with a Viking's look as well as build," was a source of funds and of good advice in dealing with the business community.

Baruch was one of that unique breed of Jewish families that had held assured social positions in the South since the days before the Civil War. Baruch's uncle Fischel Cohen had been on the staff of General P. G. T. Beauregard, the flamboyant hero of the First Battle of Bull Run. Beginning as a young man on Wall Street in 1890, Baruch had become a millionaire by the time he was thirty and was a partner in one of the leading brokerage houses in the city. His associates were men like Thomas Fortune Ryan, the Rockefellers, the Harrimans, and J. P. Morgan. He was a veteran of half a dozen of the Street's most spectacular financial transactions when a journalist friend, Garet Garrett of the *New York Evening Post,* undertook to prevail on him to dedicate part of his time and talents to public service. Already active in the Boys' Club movement, Baruch, a Democrat by birth, found himself attracted to Theodore Roosevelt's brand of reform politics, but in 1912, under the influence of "tall, explosive, voluble" Secretary of the Treasury McAdoo, Baruch began to take an active role in Democratic politics.

It was Wilson's "courage in fighting the snobbery and discrimination of the eating clubs" at Princeton University that first attracted Bernard Baruch to him. He recalled vividly that being a Jew had barred him from fraternities when he was an undergraduate student at the City College of New York. When Baruch met Wilson, he was at once impressed "by his sparkling clear eyes" and "keen mind," but he had no idea that he would soon regard Wilson "as one of the greatest [men] in the world." When panic threatened the cotton market and McAdoo was trying to raise a loan fund to support the price of cotton, Baruch subscribed $3,500,000 and encouraged several Jewish banking houses, among them Kuhn, Loeb and the Warburgs, also to subscribe, an action that not surprisingly brought him to the favorable attention of the President.

Baruch, obsessed with the notion that the U.S. government needed a plan to mobilize the industrial resources of the country in the event the nation was forced to enter the war, went to McAdoo with a plan for what he called a Defense Mobilization Committee, on which would be represented "the major industries supplying the armed forces." Wilson supported a bill to create such a body, and Congress passed it in August, 1916, as part of the army appropriations bill. The bill provided for a "Council of National Defense made up of the Secretaries of War, Navy, Interior, Agriculture, Commerce and Labor." An "Advisory Commission" of seven private citizens was also provided for. Among the men the President appointed were crusty Daniel Willard, president of the Baltimore & Ohio Railroad; Julius Rosenwald, head of Sears, Roebuck and Company; Samuel Gompers; and Baruch. By the time the United States entered the war the Advisory Commission "had mapped out a vast program to prepare the nation's economy to fight a war," as Baruch put it.

One of the things that upset Wilson about the skillful orchestration of his campaign by writers and publicists was that they insisted on pushing the slogan "He kept us out of war!" The President felt that it misrepresented his position and compromised his freedom of action to take the United States into war if, in his view, that became necessary. He complained to George Creel that the slogan gave the impression "that my policy is one of unchangeable neutrality, no matter what arises." Wilson then read from a speech in which he had declared, "The United States was once in the enjoyment of what we used to call splendid isolation. . . . And now, by circumstances which she did not choose, over which she had no control, she had been thrust out into the great game of mankind, on the stage of the world itself . . . and no nation must doubt that all her forces are gathered and organized in the interest of just, righteous and humane government."

Theodore Roosevelt had no interest other than defeating Wilson. He had declared to Henry Stoddard, "At best this war will be a stalemate for the Allies unless America gets into it. I don't say that Germany will win, but I do say that the Allies cannot. They may check Germany but no more." Roosevelt was convinced that the United States must sooner or later fight Germany. To him the only question was whether the nation should fight it with the Allies or, later, alone, after the European War had ended. The opponents of American involvement in the war were all "bleeding hearts" in Roosevelt's view, muddleheaded reformers with no notion of patriotic duty to "American destiny."

That the American people could "tolerate" Wilson seemed to Roosevelt incomprehensible, but then, he confessed to Lodge, "in retrospect" he was equally "unable to understand how they could have tolerated Jefferson and Madison in the beginning of the nineteenth century. Andrew Jackson had his faults, but at least he was a fighting man." Wilson was more of "the Jefferson and Buchanan type."

Hughes proved to be an uninspiring campaigner who had little taste for the rough-and-tumble of a presidential election and delivered himself into the hands of the old guard Republicans. In addition, he often appeared to have little grasp of the real issues. William Allen White was startled when Hughes asked him, "What are the Progressive issues? I have been out of politics now so long that I am not familiar with it. Just how should I express my sympathy with the Progressive movement?" White ran down a list of Progressive issues: an eight-hour day, old age pensions, workmen's compensation, minimum wages, and child labor laws. Hughes listened politely but, White felt, without enthusiasm or any notion of the importance of these issues to those who considered themselves independent Progressives.

Hughes's most disastrous error was in his treatment of the California Progressives whom Governor Hiram Johnson was eager to deliver to him. Hughes allowed himself to be taken possession of by Johnson's opponent, William H. Crocker. The California Progressive committeeman, Chester Rowell, concerned at the news that Hughes was to be placed in Crocker's hands, telegraphed the Hughes headquarters: "In any other State the Governor and Hughes' supporter would be obvious chairman and to refuse Johnson recognition will be taken by voters as indication of ostracism of Progressive participation." He added in a subsequent telegram, referring to Crocker's role, "These plans if unchanged will arouse such widespread resentment as to render California a doubtful State for Hughes."

Hughes compounded his error or that of his staff by greeting Crocker at a San Francisco meeting as California's "leading citizen," an accolade that many Californians thought properly belonged to Johnson and resented because of Crocker's identification with the railroad interests. Crocker's face and green-gray eyes, William Allen White wrote, "mirrored a low, incessant, gnawing greed—greed for power, for money, for destruction. . . . The word 'graft' was coined at the latter part of the old century to define that quenchless hunger for raw, quick, dirty money in American politics, which hardly sugar-coats its bribes, which glazes over its most iniquitous corruption."

On election night the early returns indicated a clear Republican victory. Gloomy Democrats predicted that the election of Hughes would mean a revolution. By midnight the *New York Times* had conceded Hughes's election. When the word was carried to Colonel House, he replied, vehemently, "Tell Mr. Ochs that his paper and the *World* by conceding the election this early are bringing about the defeat. I am not going to give in now." California was still unheard from, and House was convinced the state would end up in the Wilson column. "Don't stop counting until every last county's heard from," the Democratic headquarters in New York instructed its fellow Democrats in California. Returns from hamlets in the Sierra were being brought in by men on snowshoes. Word came that Kansas and Ohio had gone for Wilson, and at dawn Herbert Bayard Swope dashed in with the news that California appeared to be swinging Wilson's way.

When the votes were tabulated, it became clear that Wilson had won by the narrowest possible margin. The state of California, which was decisive, had gone for him by 3,773 votes, giving him 277 electoral votes to Hughes's 254. The popular vote was not as close: 9,129,606 for Wilson; Hughes 8,538,221. The Socialist candidate, despite the split in his party, had polled a respectable 585,113, while the Prohibition candidate got that party's stubbornly loyal 200,000-plus votes.

Henry Stoddard believed that Hughes's costliest mistake was his embrace of Crocker, symbol of the domination of the Southern Pacific Railroad. "The failure of the western Republican leaders to sense the opinion of the section is without parallel in political history. It cost a Presidency," Stoddard wrote.

In William Allen White's analysis, Wilson was reelected primarily by the votes of the Midwestern Progressives, many of whom strongly supported what they believed was his determination to keep the United States out of the war. He had, ironically, inherited the greater part of Roosevelt's following in those states.

The most sensational event of the summer of 1916 was not the party conventions but the explosion of a bomb in San Francisco. On July 22, 1916, Emma Goldman, Alexander Berkman, and Eleanor Fitzgerald, an editor of *Mother Earth* and Berkman's mistress, were having lunch in San Francisco on a "golden California day," all "in a bright mood," when the phone rang. A bomb had been thrown into a Preparedness Parade. A number of people had been killed and wounded. "I hope they aren't going to hold the anarchists responsible for it," Goldman exclaimed.

"How could they not?" Berkman replied, "they always have."

The effect of the bomb explosion on the antipreparedness movement and on the anarchists specifically was devastating. Four labor leaders—Thomas Mooney, Warren K. Billings, Edward Nolan, and Israel Weinberg—were arrested, along with Mooney's wife, Rena. Mooney, a member of the Molders' Union, had been a leader in California labor struggles. He had undertaken to organize streetcar motormen and conductors. The street railway association had posted flyers warning employees to avoid "dynamiter Mooney." Anyone associating with him would be immediately fired. Billings had formerly been president of the Boot and Shoe Workers' Union. His aggressive role as a labor leader had made him anathema to California business leaders. Nolan was another prominent labor leader, a machinist, and a sometime delegate to the machinists' national conventions. Weinberg was on the executive committee of the Jitney Bus Operators' Union. Rena Mooney was a music teacher.

The anarchists found themselves the victims of their own rhetoric when they tried to rally support for the labor leaders. They had proclaimed dynamite for so long as the principal weapon against the capitalist exploiters that when a bomb was thrown and people were killed, the not unnatural assumption on the part of the general public was that the anarchists were responsible. The consequence was a notable reluctance on the part of those groups and individuals most prominent in free speech controversies to come forward on behalf of the Californians. Although the evidence implicating the four men in the bombing was scanty, the issue this time involved national politics in a unique manner. The bulk of upper-class reform sentiment was Eastern. It was in these same upper-class Eastern circles that support for the Allies and for America's entry into war was strongest. Opposition to America's involvement in the war had its base in the Midwest and, to a somewhat lesser degree, on the West Coast. The event that had provoked the bomb attack was, most significantly, not a labor activity—a strike or a demonstration or an attack on an employer notoriously antilabor—but an assault on a body of patriotic citizens asserting *their* right to free speech and free assembly. It seemed, therefore, to the majority of Americans an especially horrendous act, cruel and "revolutionary." Amid the constant talk of impending revolution it aroused both fear and rage. In the words of Emma Goldman, "The McNamara confession was still haunting, ghostlike, the waking and sleeping hours of their erstwhile friends among the labour politicians. There was no single prominent man in the unions on the Coast who now dared to speak for his arrested brothers." With characteristic single-mindedness, Goldman took up the cause as her own. In her perplexity she turned to Frank Walsh, the Kansas City lawyer who had been the chairman of the Commission on Industrial Relations. Walsh was sympathetic, but he had pledged all his time and energy to trying to get Wilson reelected on the ground that he had kept the United States out of the European War. Walsh's attitude was, to Goldman, "additional proof . . . of the political blindness and social muddle-headedness of American liberals." Berkman soon joined forces with Goldman, and the two enlisted the Hebrew trade unions.

One of the most effective workers for Mooney and those arrested after the Preparedness Day bombing in San Francisco was Lucy Robbins. She and her husband, Bob, lived in Los Angeles. Lucy was a skilled carpenter, as well as an architect, a mechanic and a printer, who built what may well have been the first mobile home with cupboards and dressers and a small bathroom. It also contained a complete printshop, and the Robbinses earned their traveling expenses by doing job printing as they toured the country in behalf of radical causes. Arriving in New York, the Robbinses put their house-on-wheels in a garage and enlisted in Emma Goldman's campaign to secure justice for Mooney and the other labor leaders charged with murder. It proved a long and bitter battle. Although it turned out that the state's principal witness had perjured himself, the motion for a new trial was denied, and Mooney remained under sentence of death until 1918, when the governor of California commuted his sentence to life imprisonment. There was no direct connection between the Preparedness Day bombing in San Francisco and the conviction of Billings and Mooney on the one hand and the reelection of Wilson on the other, but the trial and conviction of the two labor leaders on the flimsiest of evidence foreshadowed the eclipse of the civil liberties of millions of Americans in the months that followed.

29

America Enters the War

With Wilson's reelection events rushed to a climax. A few days before the balloting, Baron Gottlieb von Jagow had been replaced as German foreign minister by Arthur Zimmermann, the undersecretary. Americans hailed the move as signaling a more moderate German policy, although the reverse was true. Jagow had been a stubborn opponent of unrestricted submarine warfare; Zimmermann proved himself ready to accept the judgment of the military and naval officers—the general staffs—that such warfare carried the only hope of a conclusive German victory, indeed, that it would make such a victory speedy and inevitable. Zimmermann was an excellent example of how deceptive physical appearance can be. In contrast with the quiet and withdrawn Jagow, a man whose reserve was often interpreted as Junker menace, Zimmermann had middle-class German origins and an expansive, jolly manner. He was a large man with red cheeks and bright blue eyes, the picture of friendliness and conviviality. General Ludendorff, the Chief of Staff, whom the kaiser referred to as "the top sergeant," and huge old Paul von Hindenburg, the commanding general of the German armies, had combined forces to push for an all-out submarine war. They argued that the United States could not possibly mobilize in time to affect the outcome if such a policy were adopted and the United States actually entered the war. The German civilian leadership under Chancellor Theobald von Bethmann-Hollweg had resisted the generals and admirals until Admiral Alfred von Tirpitz resigned his commission in disgust. Bethmann-Hollweg's manner reflected the desperate state of the German armed forces and of the people themselves. He smoked incessantly, his hair turned white, and he gave the appearance of an ill man.

The *Literary Digest* hailed the news of Zimmermann's elevation with the headline "Liberalization of Germany," and Colonel House on one of his tireless treks about Europe found Zimmermann "exceedingly cordial and delightful." He wrote to Wilson: "I have always liked him and I am glad we have resumed our friendly relations." James Gerard, U.S. Ambassador to Germany, described him as "a fine type of man. . . . my warm personal friend, just and friendly toward America. . . ." Zimmermann was, like so many other leaders in other times, a victim of his intelligence service, which supplied him only with information that confirmed his own prejudices. One of the most conspicuous of these was that, as he told Gerard, "there are half a million trained Germans in America who will join the Irish and start a revolution" if the United States entered the war. Gerard replied, "In that case there are half a million lamp-posts to hang them on."

American merchant ships continued to be sunk, and American lives lost. Wilson, increasingly uneasy, wrote to House: "The situation is developing very fast." If some formula were not found for peace, "we must inevitably drift into war with Germany on the submarine issue." That the President wished to avoid war can hardly be doubted. "Every reform we have won will be lost if we go into this war," he wrote. "We have been making a fight on special privilege. We have got new tariff and currency and trust legislation. We don't know yet how they will work. War means autocracy. The people we have unhorsed will inevitably come back into the control of the country, for we shall be dependent upon the steel, oil and financial magnates. They will run the nation." Secretary of the Interior Lane wrote to the editor of the *New York World*, who was clamoring for war: "The war will degrade us. That is the plain fact, make sheer brutes of us, because we will have to descend to the methods which the Germans employ." Nonetheless, it seemed to William Allen White in the winter of 1917 that the country was suffering "a period of national blind staggers." He contrasted

Wilson's style of leadership—"wise, scholarly and cautious"—with the kind of aggressive leadership that the country needed in his view: Roosevelt's leadership.

The closer Wilson moved toward war, the better Lippmann (and the *New Republic*) liked him. Wilson was, Lippmann wrote a friend, "a very considerable man." The nomination of Louis Brandeis to the Supreme Court helped complete the conversion. Abbott Lawrence Lowell, president of Harvard, and some fifty prominent Bostonians opposed the appointment on the grounds that Brandeis, as an advocate of liberal causes, lacked the judicial temper, and they were joined by Taft, now a member of the law school faculty at Yale. The *New York Times* dismissed Brandeis as "essentially a contender, a striver after changes and reforms."

In May, 1916, the President, speaking to the League to Enforce Peace, had declared that peace must be "made secure by the organized major force of mankind. It must not involve merely a new balance of power. It must not be a mere crushing of antagonists, a humiliating, hate-breeding peace. The rights of small nations must be recognized and peoples must not be handed about as so many cattle." A month after the election Wilson, with the support of his Cabinet, began to evolve his peace without victory strategy, urging the belligerents to make plain their purposes in fighting the war as the first step toward achieving a negotiated peace. As we have seen, there was widespread sentiment in Britain for such a course, although Allied censorship did its best to keep news of the British peace movements from reaching the American public.

It was the conviction of David Houston and most of the members of Wilson's Cabinet that the Allies were "in the right—that is, Great Britain, France, and Belgium are. I have been on their side since the first day the Germans moved," Houston wrote. "They ought to win, and I believe they will win, in the end; but I am not so blind as not to know that they are not fighting merely for the . . . things they proclaim. Their motives and purposes are very complex. The British for a long time have been very jealous of the growing naval power of the Germans." In addition, they were concerned about the Dardanelles, Asia Minor, Egypt, and India. In Houston's view, the war aims of the Allies were legitimate and should be stated openly. They would include, he assumed, the restitution of Belgium and France, the return of Alsace-Lorraine, a reconstituted Poland, an enlarged Serbia, a weakened Austria, and the eviction of the Turks from Europe and the Germans from Africa, as well as the safeguarding of backward nations.

Houston told the President that the people of the United States were, above all, determined not to become involved in "a mad race for military supremacy" or to aid one nation or another to dominate Europe. "It was sick of all that sort of mad business. It merely wanted a clean national house for itself, peace and law everywhere in the world, so that people everywhere might prosper and nations live together in neighborly fashion."

Wilson readily concurred, but he was convinced that a German victory must be avoided at all costs. It would "change the course of civilization and make the United States a military nation." The way to avoid such a disaster was for the United States to force the warring nations to come to the peace table. If the United States entered the war, that hope would be seriously compromised, if not lost entirely. The United States, instead of being a disinterested arbiter, would be simply another belligerent. Yet Wilson, believing as he did that only a negotiated peace could be enduring, moved, in the opinion of an apprehensive Count von Bernstorff, with maddening slowness. Part of the difficulty was that the President, misled by the elevation of Zimmermann to foreign minister, did not realize that the Germans were resolved to launch unrestricted submarine warfare. Furthermore, he did not trust Bernstorff, "neither his accuracy nor his sincerity," whereas Bernstorff was in fact his most essential ally. Again, a large part of the problem was personality. The Puritan President was put off by the libertine ambassador. Lansing also disliked Bernstorff; House was his only advocate.

The German generals, convinced that they could end the war in a few months by the use of submarines, were steadfastly opposed to negotiations of any kind. They believed that a negotiated peace would bring down the government. Only if the years of terrible suffering resulted in tangible gains would the Germans tolerate the leaders who had plunged them into war. "The German people wish no peace of renunciation," Ludendorff declared when the Austrians took the peace line, "and I do not intend to end being pelted by stones." With complete cynicism the German government made a "peace offer" based on the status quo, an offer which they knew would be totally unacceptable to the Allies but which they hoped would derail Wilson's own long-awaited proposal. The offer referred to Germany's "invincible power" and declared that if it were refused, Germany would be free of "all responsibility therefore before Humanity and History." The offer was being made, the kaiser informed his troops, "in the conviction that we are the absolute conquerors."

On December 12, 1916, the Germans sent Wilson their proposal "to enter forthwith into peace negotiations." In Houston's opinion, the note caught the President by surprise and proved somewhat of an embarrassment. Nonetheless, Wilson went ahead with his own exhortation, "as the friend of all nations engaged in the present struggle." In his understanding the belligerents on both sides had in mind much the same objects "as stated in general terms to their own people and to the world," a clause which much offended the British; indeed, it was said that the king wept when he read it.

Germany at once rejected Wilson's plea; the Allies delayed, believing that unrestricted submarine warfare would shortly be launched by the Germans and confident that it would, at last, bring the United States into the war on the Allied side. Still Bernstorff persevered. Both Lansing and House believed the President's efforts were futile; both men wished for American intervention on the Allied side. Bernstorff did win from the President, over Lansing's protests, permission to have coded messages from the German Foreign Ministry pass over the State Department cable in the interest of promoting negotiations.

On January 12, the Allies replied to Wilson's peace initiative, indicating a spirit as intractable as that of their enemy. They, too, were determined to win an unconditional victory. But Wilson was still unwilling to face facts. He told House, "This country does not intend to become involved in war. It would be a crime against civilization for us to go into it."

Three days earlier, at the German supreme headquarters, in the castle of Pless near the Polish border, the high command had met with the chancellor to make the case for unrestricted U-boat warfare. The secretary of the navy, Admiral Eduard von Capelle, assured those present that even if the United States entered the war in consequence, "from the military point of view, the assistance which will result . . . will amount to nothing." He was equally reassuring to the War Committee of the Reichstag: "We should not worry about American reinforcements to the Allied armies. We can assure you that not a single ship with troops will reach this side of the Atlantic. To stop them we have the U-boats; that, indeed, is why we have the U-boats."

The aides to the general staff had come armed with charts and statistics to prove their case beyond all reasonable doubt. The evidence was massive—tonnage tables, projected harvests, and grain shipments. Admiral von Holtzendorff, chief of the naval general staff, declared, "If we fail to make use of this opportunity, which, as far as can be foreseen, is our last, I can see no way to end the war so as to guarantee our future as a world power. On its part I guarantee that the U-boat will lead to victory." Bethmann-Hollweg spoke at length against the general staff's plan, predicting that it would inevitably bring the United States into the war and pointing out that those Germans most familiar with the United States, men like Bernstorff and von Papen, were convinced that the entry of the United States into the war must bring about Germany's defeat. His arguments fell on deaf ears. Sensing the hostility, the chancellor ended weakly, "But if the military authorities consider the U-boat war essential I am not in a position to contradict them. . . ." Holtzendorff declared, "I guarantee on my word as a naval officer that no American will set foot on the Continent!" The date set for the resumption of all-out U-boat warfare was February 1, 1917.

It remained only for the kaiser to sign his name to the fateful order. That done, the meeting adjourned, leaving Bethmann-Hollweg behind. When an officer of the royal court entered the room a few minutes later and saw the dejected figure of the chancellor, he asked, "What's the matter? Have we lost a battle?"

Bethmann-Hollweg replied despairingly, "No, but *finis Germaniae*. That's the decision."

When Ludendorff informed Walter von Rathenau, leader of the Socialists, of the council's decision, Rathenau expostulated with him. The nation could not be saved by arms. Arms had failed. Diplomacy must be tried. Ludendorff could not escape the logic, but he still would not abandon his conviction that the submarines would turn the tide. He kept muttering, "*Ich habe das Gefühl* ['I have the feeling']."

It now remained for Zimmermann to jolly the Americans along until the date set for the resumption of unrestricted submarine warfare. He entertained the American ambassador at a lavish dinner. "Our personal friendship encourages me in the assurance that we can continue to work in a frank, open manner, putting all our cards upon the table . . ." the German host declared. Gerard replied in a similar spirit. He was confident that with Zimmermann as foreign minister "relations between our two countries are running no risk."

Then Zimmermann, making use of the State Department's cable, authorized by Wilson at Bernstorff's request to conduct negotiations they hoped would lead to peace or at least to a resolution of the submarine question, sent a cable to the German ambassador, Heinrich von Eckhardt, in Mexico. The cable was, of course, sent in code, a code the Germans, proud of their mastery in such matters, were confident could not be broken. It had, in fact, been not broken in the formal sense but stolen, and it had enabled British intelligence—room 40, the cable intercept and decoding room—to monitor all of Germany's secret diplomatic communications. The telegram was sent on January 16 and routinely intercepted by the decoders in room 40. They realized at once that they had a momentous item in their hands. The text, when it was completely deciphered after almost five weeks, read:

"We intend to begin unrestricted submarine warfare on first of February. We shall endeavor in spite of this to keep the United States neutral. In the event of this not succeeding, we make Mexico a proposal of alliance on the following basis: Make war together, make peace together, generous financial support, and an understanding on our part that Mexico is to reconquer the lost territory in Texas, New Mexico, and Arizona. The settlement in detail is left to you.

"You will inform the President [then Carranza] of the above most secretly as soon as the outbreak of war with the United States is certain and add suggestion that he should, on his own initiative, invite Japan to immediate adherence and at the same time mediate between Japan and ourselves.

"Please call the President's attention to the fact that the unrestricted employment of our submarines now offers the prospect of compelling England to make peace within a few months. Acknowledge receipt. Zimmermann."

Undaunted by the Allied rejection of his peace proposal, Wilson on January 22, 1917, gave what was undoubtedly the most influential speech of his political career. He believed that a negotiated peace might still be achieved. The statements of the belligerents on their respective war aims suggested as much. They implied, "first of all, that it must be a peace without victory. It is not pleasant to say this. I beg that I may be permitted to put my own interpretation upon it and that it may be understood that no other interpretation was in my thoughts. I am seeking only to face realities and to face them without soft concealments. Victory would mean peace forced upon the loser, a victor's terms imposed upon the vanquished. It would be accepted in humiliation, under duress, at an intolerable sacrifice, and would leave a sting, a resentment, a bitter memory upon which terms of peace would not rest permanently, but only upon quicksand. Only a peace between equals can last. Only a peace the principle of which is equality and a common participation in a common benefit. The right state of mind, the right feeling between nations, is as necessary for a lasting peace as is the just settlement of vexed questions of territory or of racial and national allegiance."

The Allies were furious at Wilson's speech. The British, especially, felt betrayed. Wilson, for his part, was surprised by the intensity of their reaction to his peace proposals. The British reinforced their dismay by secret statistics which revealed that the nation had suffered far more severely from submarine sinkings than they had let the world know. Their treasury was virtually empty. The theme that Britain played upon skillfully was that far from the war's being, as it appeared, a stalemate, the Germans were on the verge of winning. Under such circumstances there was no hope for an equitable peace. A victorious Germany would impose its will on Europe and, through Europe, on the world. Could Wilson and the American people face the reality of a German victory?

Despite renewed pleas from Bernstorff, who warned repeatedly that "American war resources are very great," the wheel of fate rolled on inexorably. The submarines had already been dispatched, he was told, and there was no way to communicate with them. On January 31 Bernstorff, acting on instructions from his government, presented Lansing with the kaiser's order for unrestricted submarine warfare. "I know it is very serious, very," he told the startled secretary of state. "I deeply regret that it is necessary. Good afternoon." When the news was out and reporters swarmed about him, Bernstorff declared, "I am finished with politics for the rest of my life." He proved true to his word. After the Versailles Treaty and the establishment of the League of Nations, Bernstorff devoted himself to the cause of the League, and when Adolf Hitler came to power, he left Germany forever.

Under the terms of the German note, a new war zone was declared around Great Britain and along the coast of France and Italy. Any ship found in that zone would be sunk without concern for its nationality and without regard to loss of life.

Germany's hopes now centered on the United States' remaining out of the war if only for a few months to allow the U-boats to take their toll. Meanwhile, the United States existed in a strange limbo while Wilson debated the issue of war and peace with his closest advisers, House and Lansing, and, above all, with his own conscience. Everything that he had fought for and staked his political career on was in jeopardy. All his instincts leaned toward Great Britain. He was neutral in fact, not in spirit. Only his iron will and his profound conviction that the United States alone could act as peacemaker had kept him steady on the course that he had set for himself and his country. It had a kind of accidental constituency. Very few Americans shared their President's vision. Many opposed America's entry into the war because they hated Great Britain; others, overwhelmingly those of German birth or ancestry, because they loved Germany, not so much the kaiser but the whole warp and woof of German culture. Others opposed war because they were Christian pacifists who believed that war was never just and the taking of human life unacceptable to a Christ who had admonished the faithful to turn the other cheek. Still others opposed the war because they were socialists or anarchists (some of the socialists were Christian Socialists and thus doubly opposed) and believed that the war was a "capitalist war," the death struggle of capitalist nations, a prelude to international socialism. Certain capitalists opposed American entry into the war because it seemed more profitable to sell to the belligerents than to fight with or for them. The Westerners, in the main, opposed U.S. entry into the war because the East (and their nemesis, Wall Street) favored it. Relatively few Americans opposed entry into the war because they shared Wilson's vision of the United States as the great peacemaker and spreader of democracy in the world, the great restorer of order and harmony and justice among nations.

The Japanese, with an exquisite sense of timing, took advantage of the resumption of U-boat warfare to make their most forceful protest against the passage of two alien land bills, modeled after that of California, that were before the legislatures of Idaho and Oregon. Senators from the two states, appealed to by the State Department, managed to persuade the legislators to desist "at this critical hour." Wilson himself was not immune to apprehension about the "yellow menace." He startled David Houston and some of the other Cabinet members by declaring that (as Houston recalled his remarks) if, "in order to keep the white race or part of it strong to meet the yellow race—Japan, for instance, in alliance with Russia, dominating China— it was wise to do nothing [to aid the Allies] he would do nothing, and would submit to anything and any imputation of weakness or cowardice."

Houston, when his turn came to speak, declared that he had no apprehensions about Japan or China. They were "relatively weak intellectually, industrially, and morally. . . ." The real issue was the future of civilization. "Nothing worse can befall us than what Germany proposes, and no greater insult can be offered to any people. If we acquiesce, we ought not to pose as a nation of free people. . . . I am for asserting our rights, for standing with the Allies, for doing our part for our sake and for humanity."

But what, the President asked, should he say practically and specifically to Congress? All he could do on his own was to break off diplomatic relations with the Germans and arm American merchantmen for defense. For a week or more, in a succession of Cabinet meetings, the debate continued.

With the issue of war or peace clearly hanging in the balance, the pacifists redoubled their efforts. A National Pacifist Congress of some 500 men and women met in New York and exhorted the President to stand firm. The Association of German-American Pastors called for a day of prayer against "all evil counsel and base machinations which are at work to plunge our nation into war." The prowar forces, led by Roosevelt, who was beside himself with rage and disappointment, denounced the President as a coward and betrayer.

Meanwhile, in Berlin, a reassured Zimmermann told a friend, "You will see, everything will be all right. America will do nothing because Wilson is for peace and nothing else. Everything will go on as before." Zimmermann sent another cable to Eckhardt instructing him not to wait for America's entry into the war but to broach the alliance with Mexico at once. "If the President [of Mexico] declines from fear of subsequent revenge," Zimmermann added, "you are empowered to offer him a definitive alliance after the conclusion of peace, provided Mexico succeeds in drawing Japan into the alliance."

Meantime, bowing to the inevitable, Wilson had ordered Pershing to abandon his effort to chastise Villa and to withdraw his force from Mexico.

A few days after the announcement of the resumption of unrestricted submarine warfare, the head of British intelligence took the Zimmermann cable, still in the process of being decoded, to the British Foreign Office. Realizing at once that they had a trump card that might be just what was needed to carry the United States into the war, Lloyd George, after steps had been taken to prevent the Germans from realizing that their code had been broken, turned the text of the cable over to the American ambassador, Walter Hines Page, to forward to his government.

At the end of February Wilson, with the strong support of his Cabinet, decided to present to Congress a bill calling for the arming of all American merchant ships, a step tantamount to an unofficial declaration of war, and a few days later, on February 26, the President appeared before a joint session of Congress to urge the passage of the armed ships bill. Even as he was speaking, news came of the sinking of a Cunard liner, the *Laconia*, with the loss of two American lives. By this time Wilson had in his hand the text of the Zimmermann cable, and he placed it before Congress in hope of silencing the opponents of the bill.

When Henry Cooper of Wisconsin, the ranking Republican member of the House Committee on Foreign Affairs, proposed an amendment prohibiting the arming of munitions ships, there were 124 votes in its favor and 295 against, but in the Senate, La Follette and Cummins, along with ten other Senators, were determined to filibuster the armed ships bill to death. Wilson was furious at their delaying tactics. "The Senate of the United States," he declared, "is the only legislative body in the world which cannot act when the majority is ready for action. A little group of willful men, representing no opinion but their own, have rendered the great government of the United States helpless and contemptible."

Frustrated by La Follette's filibuster, Congress consoled itself by passing the so-called spy bill, which forbade criticism of the President in wartime or, indeed, by extension, of any policies designed to carry the war forward, such as enlistment of soldiers and sailors. The fact that the spy bill was passed in advance of any declaration of war was evidence of a deep uneasiness about the way in which at least some Americans would respond to the country's entry into the European conflict.

As the Wilson administration swung closer to war, the various peace organizations joined to form the Emergency Peace Federation, which held its first meeting in Chicago on February 28, 1917. Some 2,000 pacifists, many of them delegates of existing peace societies, attended the Chicago convention and endorsed an emergency program involving peace parades, rallies, and a media campaign to prevail on Wilson to stay out of the war. Its enemies—in effect the supporters of war with the Central Powers—denounced the federation as a pro-

German organization, a charge leveled at all peace groups. Its Washington headquarters were broken into by a mob of servicemen, and when Jane Addams finally had an audience with Wilson, the President was cold and unresponsive. She left convinced that he had made the decision to intervene. There was a final flurry of telegrams to the White House, urging continued neutrality, signed by Max Eastman; Addams; Lillian Wald; Paul Kellogg, the editor of the *Survey;* Norman Thomas, and hundreds of others. Secret polls purported to reveal a majority of Congressmen against American entry into the war; Midwestern Congressmen almost solidly so. But Wilson, who had been so eloquent on the subject of peace, now attacked the pacificists fiercely. "What I am opposed to is not the feeling of the pacificists," he told the convention of the American Federation of Labor on March 12, 1917, "but their stupidity. My heart is with them. I want peace, but I know how to get it and they do not."

The initial response to the publication of the Zimmermann telegram was predictable. To the enemies of Germany and the advocates of war it was verification of German perfidy, one in a series of incidents that demonstrated German determination to weaken and demoralize the United States. To those of a different persuasion it was a manifest fraud, manufactured by British intelligence to push the United States into war. One Senator declared it was "a forgery and a sham born in the brain of a scoundrel and a tool." Certainly, there had been many other such invented pieces of propaganda turned out by Allied "intelligence." Zimmermann, for inexplicable reasons, cut the ground from under those who, it was clear, were determined not to believe the cable authentic by acknowledging authorship. He had, he told astonished German reporters, sent it. Its verification was, in Lansing's words, a "profound sensation." Still, there were many Americans ready to defend Zimmermann and dismiss the telegram as irrelevant to the real issues. Oscar Underwood, Senator from Alabama, argued that Zimmermann was doing what a proper concern for German interests dictated, but the telegram undoubtedly weakened the forces opposed to war and strengthened its advocates. The *Chicago Daily Tribune* declared that the United States must now accept "active participation in the present conflict," while the *Cleveland Plain Dealer* asserted there was "neither virtue nor dignity" in refusing to declare war against the Central Powers.

The Hearst papers were especially insistent on the menace of a Mexican-Japanese alliance, their longtime *bête noir.* Japan, they warned, would seize the Far West and "Orientalize" it. Hearst, in fact, became the great expositor of the "yellow peril" through his network of papers and magazines. He warned constantly of an impending assault on the United States by Japan by way of Mexico. It would come, Hearst's journalistic soothsayers declared, through Texas and up the Mississippi, splitting the nation in half for piecemeal subjugation by the fierce warriors of Nippon. A Hearst film company made a serial starring Irene Castle based on such an invasion, led by a samurai complete with deadly sword. Japan was content to encourage the rumors, confident that they could only enhance its prestige as a formidable military power and enable it to up the ante at the peace table. Moreover, its protracted flirtation with Germany would serve it in good stead if Germany won the war, as the Japanese military leaders were convinced it must.

It was evident in Wilson's second inaugural address on March 4 that he was preparing the nation for the eventuality of war, although his remarks were directed particularly at the role that the United States might play at the end of the conflict. "We are making our spirits ready for those things," he declared. "They will follow in the immediate wake of the war itself and will set civilization up again. We are provincial no longer. The tragical events of the thirty months of vital turmoil through which we have just passed have made us citizens of the world. There can be no turning back. Our own fortunes as a nation are involved, whether we would have it so or not." The two events which had changed since the last time he had addressed Congress, the President noted, were the Russian Revolution and indications in Germany that the Socialists might take control of the government in that country. If the entry of the United States into the war "would hasten and fix the movements in Russia and Germany," Houston reported the President as saying, "it would be a marked gain to the world and would tend to give additional justification for the whole struggle." Of the various new developments, "the Russian Revolution was the most important, dramatic, and far reaching."

On March 9, after Congress had adjourned, Wilson gave the order to arm the ships. Nine days later he called the Cabinet together, and its members unanimously supported a declaration of war. Wilson left the meeting without stating his own views. The following day he issued a call for Congress to convene two weeks earlier than the date already set for the special session to hear his report concerning "grave matters of national policy."

The decision to propose a declaration of war to Congress was an agonizing one for Wilson. Since he has often been severely criticized for being an impractical idealist, it is important to stress the fact that his assessment of the military situation and of the consequences of America's involvement in the war was prophetic. He told Frank Cobb, editor of the *New York World*, that once the United States had entered the war, the country would succumb to prejudice and intolerance. Brother would be set against brother, and neighbor against neighbor. Moreover, Germany, with American manpower thrown into the scale against it, "would be . . . so badly beaten that there would be a dictated peace, a victorious peace," and at the end of the war there would be "no bystanders with sufficient power to influence the terms. There won't be any peace standards left to work with."

If the United States must enter the war, if it must abandon any hope for bringing about a peace without victory as a neutral determined to see justice done to both sides, the nation must then salvage what it could by making the entry itself the basis for a just peace. This Wilson concluded, in lonely hours of prayer and reflection, could be accomplished only if the United States, if he specifically, were to state at the moment of entry the conditions of a just peace and the determination of the United States to use to the fullest its influence and the power that must accrue to it for bringing the war to an end by intervention.

The recently adjourned Congress reconvened at eight-thirty on the evening of April 2 to hear the President deliver his war message. To David Houston it was "the most dramatic scene I ever witnessed and . . . the most historic episode in which I ever had any part." The members of the Supreme Court sat in a semicircle in front of the President. The floor of the House was packed, as were the galleries. A company of cavalry had escorted the President to the Capitol to protect him from pacifist demonstrators. Henry Stoddard was in the visitors' gallery when Wilson entered. Wilson, he wrote, "was the schoolmaster beyond all question—the perfect product of [that] conventional mold. His pale, immobile face, his protruding chin, his long thin nose firmly supporting eyeglasses, his carefully brushed hair, his slender figure seemingly elongated by a close-fitting frock coat, his dark gray trousers painstakingly creased, his ease, the manner of one conscious of his commanding place and of the importance of what others were to hear from his lips;—yes, he was the schoolmaster from head to foot." The Senators and Congressmen were tense and silent.

"With a profound sense of the solemn and even tragic character of the step I am taking," the President proposed that the Congress "declare the recent course of the Imperial German Government to be in fact nothing less than war against the government and people of the United States" and "formally accept the status of belligerent. . . . The present German submarine warfare against commerce is a warfare against mankind. . . . It is a war against all nations. . . . The challenge is to all mankind. . . . There is only one choice we cannot make, we are incapable of making: We will not choose the path of submission." At this point the great majority of those listening rose and applauded. Tears rolled down the cheeks of Edward White, the chief justice of the Supreme Court. For the rest of his speech Wilson was frequently interrupted by applause. Germany's autocratic government had become a menace to the nations of the world. Then, referring to the Zimmermann telegram, Wilson declared that it made unmistakably clear the malign intentions of the Germans "to stir up enemies against us at our very doors. . . . We accept this challenge of hostile purpose. . . . The world must be made safe for democracy." The country must fight "for the principles that gave her birth . . . God helping her, she can do no other." She must fight so a new and better order, a new age might, after all, rise from the wreckage of a Europe torn asunder by the evil spirits of imperial plunder and dynastic rivalries; so subject peoples, long suppressed and exploited, might recover the precious independence that Americans had enjoyed since the founding of their nation; so liberty, freedom, even, perhaps, equality—those magic evocations—might stir the hearts of men and women around the globe; so people everywhere might be free at last to speak their minds without the threat of imprisonment, torture, or death. "It is a fearful thing to lead this great peaceful people into war, into the most terrible and disastrous of all wars, civilization itself seeming to be in the balance. But the right is more precious than peace, and we shall fight for the things which we have always carried nearest our hearts, for democracy, for the right of those who submit to authority to have a voice in their own governments, for the rights and liberties of small nations, for a universal domination of right by such a concert of free peoples as shall bring peace and safety to all nations and make the world itself at last free. . . . The cause being just and holy, the settlement must be of like motive and quality. For this we can fight, but for nothing less noble or less worthy of our traditions. . . . A supreme moment of history has come. The eyes of the people have been opened and they see. The hand of God is laid upon the nations. He will show them favor, I devoutly believe, only if they rise to the clear heights of His own justice and mercy."

Tumulty reported that Wilson said to him after his war message that "from the very beginning I saw the end of this horrible thing; but I could not move faster than the great mass of our people would permit. Very few understood the difficult and trying position I have been placed in during the years through which we have just passed. In the policy of patience and forbearance I pursued, I tried to make every part of America and the varied elements of our population understand that we were willing to go to any length rather than resort to war with Germany . . . it would have been foolish for us to have been rushed off our feet and to have gone to war over an isolated affair like the *Lusitania*, but now we are certain there will be no regrets or looking back on the part of the people. . . . Our consciences are clear, and we must prepare for the inevitable—a fight to the end. . . . There were few who understood this policy of patience."

After Wilson had delivered his speech, fifty Democratic Congressmen, thirty-two Republicans, a Socialist, and an independent voted against declaring war. In the Senate Robert La Follette, Harry Lane, George Norris, Asle Gronna, and James Vardaman held out. In the acrimonious debate that preceded the vote in the House, William La Follette, a Congressman from Washington, declared, "When history records the truth about this awful act we are about to commit here, which means the maiming and dismembering of thousands of our noble boys and the deaths of thousands more, it will record that the Congress of the United States made this declaration of war under a misapprehension of the facts inexcusable in itself and that the people at large acquiesced in it on the theory that the Congress should have the facts." The war devastating Europe was not "a war of humanity," La Follette charged, "but 'a war of commercialism.' " His ancestors had fled France from the Edict of Nantes, and his first American progenitor had been burned at the stake by Indians; another had died on Sherman's march through Georgia, and now he, and those like him who opposed their country's entry into a ruinous war, had their patriotism questioned. "Is it a gauge of patriotism to vote calamity, debt, death, and destruction on our country? Have not those who view it the other way the same right to consideration and respect as those who see relief only through a sea of blood? God forbid that in free America such an unjust discrimination can ever be made. . . ."

In the midst of the Senate debate on the declaration of war Henry

Cabot Lodge left the chamber to meet a delegation of pacifists—a woman and half a dozen men. The pacifists were, by Lodge's account, "very violent and abusive." As they parted, "the German member" called out to Lodge, "You are a damned coward." Lodge responded by punching his accuser and declaring, "You are a damned liar." The pacifist struck back, and a series of blows were exchanged. "Then," Lodge reported, "all the pacifists rushed at me." But he was rescued by his secretaries and some bystanders. "I am glad [that I] hit him," Lodge wrote. "The Senators all appeared to be perfectly delighted with my having done so." The rumor spread that the elderly Lodge had killed his critic, "all of which," he noted, ". . . has made me extremely popular."

Florence Harriman recalled that in the aftermath of the declaration of war three leading Democratic Senators from the West (she did not give their names) appeared in the midst of a gathering of newspapermen at the Willard Hotel and cursed them for having "maliciously fanned public opinion to the war-point because Wall Street wanted a rupture." The furious Westerners "proclaimed over and over again what they knew to be true—that the West was still averse to 'going in.'" Two of the Senators were kept in line by the combined efforts of Wilson and House. "I could cite incident after incident," Harriman wrote, "to show how many of the Western states were in a dangerous condition of mind, from the Allies' point of view." Bryan resisted America's entry into the war to the last, urging a nationwide referendum on the issue a few days after Wilson's war message.

The reaction to Wilson's speech ranged, not surprisingly, from the ecstatic to the indignant. On the whole it was hailed with great enthusiasm. Hundreds of newspaper editorials acclaimed it; ministers praised it from their pulpits; state legislatures passed resolutions supporting it. William Allen White wrote in the *Gazette*: "Great times make great men. The great man who has come out of these times is Woodrow Wilson. If democracy—which is but another name for Christian brotherhood—makes a long forward stride in humanity out of this world crisis, more than any one individual in the world credit should fall to Woodrow Wilson." White was soon inveighing against "all the mollycoddles and sapheads" and "their weak and wobbly attitude toward the war." To White the war at once took on a "spiritual quality." Its "crux," he wrote, "is the struggle of the world away from the gross materialism of Germany to a certain higher spiritual standard of life contained in the world Democracy."

John Jay Chapman wrote to his friend Owen Wister: "What with the relief of getting into the war—which was so great that I didn't even care whether we lost it or not—I've come to look on Wilson as an interesting phenomenon operating in an environment which is essentially mystic and incomprehensible—weathercock to invisible currents—a super-politician—and *pro tanto* a great genius—the *genius of the moment*." Chapman rejected Wister's notion that Wilson was simply being flattered and jollied by Europe. "If he don't do anything to spoil it," Chapman wrote, "he will go down in European history as the greatest sage of the modern world—and one of the greatest ever."

A prominent Republican politician told Florence Harriman after Wilson's war message, "I want you to know now that I thank God every day that Wilson was elected and not Hughes. If Hughes had been elected and the same conditions had arisen we could never have gotten the country into the war without a revolution. The West would have said, 'Hughes was put there to make war,' and that it was Wall Street's war, whereas the fact that Wilson did everything to keep us out made the people know that when he said, 'Go in,' there was nothing else to do."

When word of the declaration of war reached Oswald Garrison Villard, he felt a wave of revulsion. "I knew," he wrote, "as I knew that I lived, that this ended the republic as we had known it; that henceforth we Americans were to be part and parcel of world politics, rivalries, jealousies, and militarism; that hate, prejudice, and passion were now enthroned in the United States." If Villard overstated the case, it was understandable. For three years he had been one of the leaders in the fight for peace and against intervention. His pacifist sympathies, which were part of the heritage of his family, of his maternal grandfather, William Lloyd Garrison, and his mother, had been reinforced by his pride in his German origins, the time he had spent there in his youth, and the many German friends he valued. The Republic, however, had survived shocks as severe. All had not been tranquility, justice, and harmony, as his words suggested. It had always been, in a great degree, an illusion that the United States could remain aloof from and uncontaminated by "world politics, rivalries, jealousies, and militarism." It had, to be sure, been Jefferson's dream, and Washington had warned against "entangling alliances," but the immigrants that filled up the vast, empty spaces of America brought the Old World with them. Moreover, America had had from the beginning a dream of redeeming the world that was as strong as, or stronger than, the dream of escaping from it.

The United States' entry into the war seemed to Big Bill Haywood a catastrophe almost beyond comprehension. He wrote that he was "struck dumb. For weeks I could hardly talk. I could not concentrate my mind on chess. . . . I could not read."

Henry Adams, on the other hand, wrote to Charles Gaskell that in his age and decrepitude he comforted himself with the fact that "we [the United States and Britain] are, for the first time in our lives, fighting side by side and to my bewilderment," he added, "I find the great object of my life thus accomplished in the building up of the great community of Atlantic Powers which I hope will at least make a precedent that can never be forgotten. We have done it once and perhaps we can keep it up. Strange it is that we should have done it by means of inducing those blockheads of Germans to kick us into it. I think that I can now contemplate the total ruin of our old world with more philosophy than I ever thought possible."

If the French and British governments were relieved and de-lighted by America's entry into the war, they were distressed by most of the principles the American President enumerated, especially his call for peace without victory. But ordinary people and intellectuals, idealists everywhere were enraptured. Wilson became, almost instantly, a hero of vast dimensions. When Florence Harriman met the French philosopher Henri Bergson in Paris in 1917, he said to her, "Tell the President that *he* is our Pope. Where we used to look to Rome for spiritual leading, now we look to Washington." When Harriman re-turned to Washington, she relayed Bergson's message and saw tears in the President's eyes. "All we can do is try our best, but we all make many mistakes," Wilson replied.

A combination of forces had propelled the United States toward war. There was the ardently pro-British sentiment of the Eastern upper classes, of the Eastern establishment, who desired to go to war so intensely that a number of them, like John Jay Chapman's son Victor, could not restrain themselves but volunteered for the British forces or France's Lafayette Escadrille. The pro-British sentiment was greatly enhanced by the virulent anti-German feeling, skillfully orchestrated by the Allied propaganda agencies. Here again, the British were the most accomplished and unprincipled. Atrocity stories, most of which were subsequently disproved (or never proved), were ground out like sausages.

Without question, the single most damaging fact for the German cause was the invasion of Belgium. Though the stories of skewered babies and crucified Belgium soldiers were in the main conscienceless fabrications (there are enough real atrocities in every war to obviate the need to manufacture them), there was no doubt of the destruction and suffering experienced by the Belgian people. Soon after the German invasion word came of their desperate state. Walter Hines Page pressed Herbert Hoover to undertake to get food to those threatened by starvation. Hoover began by calling a broker in Chicago and giving an order to buy 10,000,000 bushels of wheat futures. He then assembled a group of Americans in London, including a banker and several journalists, and the Commission for Relief in Belgium was born. Within six weeks some 60,000 tons of food had been delivered, and Hoover himself went to Belgium to supervise its distribution. In six months he was famous throughout the world. The Great Engineer had proved himself an organizational genius and become in the process the Great Humanitarian. Without question the greatest philanthropic enterprise in history, Hoover's commission prevented the death by malnutrition and disease, or outright starvation, of hundreds of thousands of Belgians.

The scale of the Belgium relief effort dramatized the perfidy and cruelty of the "Huns" as nothing else could have done. In all calls for preparedness or for American involvement in the war, the "rape of Belgium" was a constantly reiterated theme.

Equally important was the effort of the opposing powers to win the war not on the battlefield but by starving the enemy's civilian population. In this desperate tactic the British were as culpable as the Germans. The British had the greatest navy in the world and soon bottled up the surface navies of the Central Powers; the Germans had the greatest army, and with their technology and genius they developed as a neutralizer of the British naval superiority the most remarkable instrument of destruction yet devised, the dreaded submarine or U-boat. In the end the U-boat was Germany's undoing. It failed to starve the British into submission, and it made likely, if not inevitable, the entry of the United States into the conflict.

There was undoubtedly an important economic factor as well. The American economy, sliding toward what threatened to become a severe depression in the first half of 1914, shuddered at the initial impact of the war, as American ships were held in port and warehouses filled to overflowing, and then, with orders pouring in from the warring nations, rebounded to a giddy wartime boom. American neutrality required fair dealing with both "sides," but as German shipping was driven from the sea and Great Britain announced more and more restrictive measures, many of which the United States acquiesced in, the flow of American goods, money, and credit to the Allies far exceeded that to the Central Powers. The consequence was that the nation as a whole developed stronger and stronger economic ties to the Allies until it came to have a huge psychological and economic investment in an Allied victory. There was probably more than a little truth in Oscar Ameringer's observation that "America's declaration of war against the Central Powers was not written on a White House typewriter on April 6, 1917; it was written when the house of Morgan floated the first Anglo-French bond issue with the consent of the American government. It was sealed when the first boatload of war material left Hoboken for Liverpool. What followed was rationalization. . . ." In Ameringer's words, "it was in order to save the country, and with it its own administration, from the effects of a serious business slump that Woodrow Wilson sanctioned the huge loans and shipments of war materials to the Allies. The rest followed as the day follows the night."

As long as an Allied victory seemed inevitable or even possible, Wilson (or any other president) could not have pushed or carried the United States into the war, but the conviction that a clear-cut German victory would be unacceptable to the United States grew stronger with each passing month.

The obvious alternative was a stalemate and a negotiated peace in which the United States, as the neutral power, must play a decisive role. It was this course that most clearly appealed to Wilson, but it was soon evident that neither belligerent party wished him to play it. Both were determined to achieve a conclusive victory. It was evident to the Allies that they could do so only with the all-out economic aid of the United States. The Germans counted on their submarines.

There was a final and decisive factor without which all the others would have been nugatory, and this was the limitless arrogance (and consequent blindness) of the Germans. They committed blunder after blunder; ineptitude piled on ineptitude. It was indeed almost as though they had the deliberate intention of forcing the United States against all its predominant inclinations—even against its will—into the war. In the last analysis it was German underestimation of the American warmaking potential that made possible the fatal policy of the kaiser and his government, dominated in the last phase of the war by the generals,

With the nation officially at war, Wilson found himself besieged by the Colonel, who wished, above everything, to recruit and lead American soldiers into battle against the Germans. On April 23, 1917, Roosevelt dispatched a long letter asking Newton D. Baker to permit him to raise a division or more of volunteers. The letter was sprinkled with references to the administration's behind-handedness in preparing for war and was hardly calculated to win him his point or sweeten the disposition of the secretary or of the President, to whom Baker referred the letter and to whom it was in fact written. In addition to recruiting the divisions, Roosevelt wanted the right to sign up a passel of regular army officers he had fought with in the Spanish-American War. It was a highly inappropriate request. To have granted it would have been to have seriously compromised the administration's plan for a draft as the only fair and rational way of raising an expeditionary force. But Roosevelt was an authentic American hero, more popular or more deeply loved and admired by many Americans that the President himself. Rebuffed in his efforts to attain his objective "through channels," Roosevelt went, hat in hand, to the White House, to beg for his divisions. When Wilson coldly refused the request, he incurred the enmity of the Colonel's legions of admirers, among them William Allen White, who wrote in his autobiography: "I can still in my mind's eye recall the picture that I had from the day's press reports when Roosevelt, who more than any other thing on earth desired to fight for his country, walked up the curved path to the White House . . . and asked the President to be allowed to recruit a regiment for France. The frigid malevolence with which Wilson denied this strong man's plea . . . carved deeply in my heart a picture of Woodrow Wilson that I could not erase. . . ."

30

The Russian Revolution

When the Russian Revolution began in March, 1917, a few weeks before Wilson's speech to Congress requesting a declaration of war against Germany, it was far from clear what its course would be. The Czar hurried back from the front by train, followed by his generals and regiments of soldiers. The railroads were in the hands of a "revolutionary," Lomonosov, who ordered the men under him to allow the czar's train to pass but to impede the trains carrying his generals and auxiliary troops. Meanwhile, a council of the soviets under the liberal Pavel N. Miliukov left Petrograd to intercept the czar and force him to sign a document authorizing the formation of a provisional democratic government, a government that "would cut out and correct the worst abuses of old Russia and some of the defects of our western republics but would maintain otherwise intact the capitalist system," Lincoln Steffens wrote.

Meanwhile, shortages of food in Petrograd accentuated a growing crisis. The Russian Parliament, a body with only advisory powers, called for the abdication of the czar. Thoroughly demoralized by the increasing chaos in his country, he acquiesced on March 15, 1917, and a provisional government was organized under the leadership of Prince Georgi Y. Lvov. A rival for power was the Petrograd Soviet, which called upon the soldiers of the imperial army to lay down their arms and form their own councils under the direction of the Petrograd group.

The astonishment that word of the Revolution caused among Communists and revolutionaries of various denominations was scarcely less great than among the conservatives and liberals. In Steffens's words, "Radical theory looked for it in some highly developed capitalist system such as that of Germany, Austria, Italy, France or England. But no, it had come in a backward, half-developed capitalistic state, where, as in Mexico, the people were illiterate and labor unorganized." Steffens, like thousands of other radicals, met this doubt by assuring himself that "Russia was only the beginning and that 'the' revolution would soon spread all over Europe."

Will Irwin, a correspondent for the *Saturday Evening Post*, wrote prophetically of the outbreak: "This revolution will be difficult to stabilize. There have been centuries of oppression. There is no large middle class. There is almost total illiteracy in the people. There is no general experience in government. Russia cannot maintain a wholly liberal republic yet. Revolutions always go further than their creators expect. And in its swing, this one is more likely to go to the left than to the right."

When news of the beginning of the Russian Revolution reached the outside world, revolutionaries from every country began trying to get to Russia to observe the "future." Included were a number of surprised Russian revolutionaries, Lenin and Trotsky among them. Lincoln Steffens managed to get passage on a Swedish steamer and found in the "long and mysterious" passenger list the name of Trotsky as well as representatives of Wall Street with trunkloads of "bonds."

At Petrograd Steffens established himself in a "dark, cautious whispering" hotel, a spectator at the greatest upheaval of the century. The hotel where the American ambassador was quartered was surrounded by a vast crowd chanting what sounded like "Muni! Muni!" Finally, someone solved the riddle. It was "Mooney, Mooney," after Tom Mooney. To workers all over the world the conviction of Mooney had become a symbol of the repressiveness and corruption of capitalism. Witnessing the vast, strange stirring of a people into revolution, Steffens was more convinced than ever that "History is impossible. Putting together the stories I heard, the stories of the old government, of the new government, of old witnesses, of soldiers, sailors, workers, of the Soviets," he laid out "not the history, but my history. . . . It is not the truth; it is my compact version of some truth and some lies that counted like facts; for rumor is a revolutionist and a historian."

It was Steffens's conviction that the czarist government, not any body of "revolutionists," had brought on the Revolution. The government, confused, demoralized, corrupt, took exactly the steps best calculated to turn anger and unrest into revolution. It closed down the breadlines, hoping to drive off and disperse the crowds through hunger, then called the troops into the streets and ordered them to fire on the quietly waiting crowds of workers and ordinary citizens. The troops refused. An officer ordered them to fire again; again the soldiers refused; a nearby student mocked the officer, and the officer ran his sword through him. A Cossack from the most feared imperial troops rode out of the ranks and cut down the officer with his sword. The cry arose, astonished and exultant: "The soldiers *are* with us." And then: "The revolution! The revolution is on!" Steffens wrote, "That word, naturally, was the one that leaped to men's lips, and it means something big, hard, serious, slow." The word "revolution" had echoed throughout the industrial nations for more than 100 years. America had started it. France had taken it up. The Reverend Samuel Thacher at the Fourth of July celebration of 1796 had exclaimed: "All hail, coming revolutions!" They had come, burst forth, been suppressed, burst forth again, been again suppressed.

In the summer of 1917 Wilson, anxious to get some notion of what was going on, dispatched to Russia a mission headed by Elihu Root. Another member was Charles Edward Russell, whose support for the war had brought about his expulsion from the Socialist Party. Other prominent members were John R. Mott, head of the YMCA; James Duncan, vice-president of the American Federation of Labor; and Cyrus McCormick, head of the International Harvester Company. It was a remarkably mixed bag of capitalists, a representative of the American "worker," and a socialist. Steffens, who was in Russia as a working journalist, was careful to keep his distance. The mission was quartered in the Winter Palace of the czar with hundreds of other foreign observers. Wherever it traveled in Russia, it was shadowed by agents of the police and accompanied by speakers who announced to the people that the Americans had come to undo the Revolution and restore the czar. The imperial family—the czar, czarina and their children—were prisoners on their estate at Tsarskoye Selo, some twenty miles from Petrograd. Root's various public offices and his close association with Andrew Carnegie made him a special object of attention and criticism by the Russians. He was charged, among other things, with having returned to Russia political refugees from the czar's government. Root ignored the attacks on him, and in Russell's opinion, his speeches in Russia were "models of argument and eloquence and his personal kindness, unfailing wit, and genial acquiescence in whatever hardship or difficulty" won the hearts of the other members of the mission.

Both Russell and Steffens were able to witness the meetings of the "great council of the Revolution." It met in the hall of what had been the auditorium of the Cadet Corps of the imperial army. Now called the Council of Soldiers, Peasants, and Workman's Delegates, it numbered almost 1,000 men and women. Professors and intellectuals sat beside peasants who could barely write their names; fishermen pressed against middle-class revolutionaries. The back wall was decorated with crudely lettered posters, the most common sentiment of which was "Workers of the world, unite; you have nothing to lose but your chains." Outside the hall were tables at which the works of Marx and other socialist writers and theorists were sold. The dominant, indeed virtually the exclusive, color was red. The mood was rapt, euphoric. In Europe industrial capitalism in conjunction with decadent monarchies had fastened deathlike grips on the working classes of modern nations. In the United States there were, to be sure, many alleviating circumstances, but there, too, workingmen and farmers suffered acutely. Things were only comparatively better. Decade after decade revolution had been proclaimed. Indeed, it seemed to have actually started in the United States in those terrible days in the summer of 1877, when the whole country was virtually paralyzed by spontaneous outbursts of violence that broke out in every major industrial city. Good socialists held resolutely to the view that the World War, whatever else it might mean, heralded the collapse of the old order in Europe. The two events, one coming out of, made possible, by the other, had an irresistible theoretical congruence. The old order was dying in bloody horror; the new day was dawning. In the simple presence of workers and soldiers and peasants and intellectuals there was a fulfillment of dreams almost too compelling to enunciate.

The dawn of the World Revolution carried with it a heavy freight of social and political theories. It had, in fact, to do with the very nature of man, as an individual and as a member of society. The French Revolution had promised the perfectability of man and of society by the use of reason, of man's rational faculties, which had been locked up for centuries, so the argument went, by superstition, the most common form of which was the Christian religion, by tradition, and by the control of access to knowledge by ruling classes. In one form or another those ideas had remained in the air, so to speak. Karl Marx had given a particular gloss to them. For reason he substituted process or dialectic, forces working to bring about, inevitably, the triumph of the workers' state. Darwinism had been more ambivalent. Those who held power had cited the doctrine of survival of the fittest as the rationale for their holding power. They were the flower of the long evolutionary process. Their adversaries, typified by Lester Ward and Henry George, had replaced reason or process by science and the trained intelligence, thereby giving education a leading role in the redemption of society from ignorance and injustice. As we have seen, even Christianity had accommodated itself, to a degree, to the almost universal cry for radical social reform and, if not reform, for revolution. Now all these theories, all these hopes, all these "laws," the "dialectic" itself, "social" evolution—all seemed about to be vindicated. That was not, of course, the feeling of the defenders of the status quo; to them it appeared that the devil and his legions had been let loose in the world. Franklin Lane, Wilson's secretary of the interior, urged that it would be worth "a million lives" to destroy the Revolution and thereby "prove . . . the value of law and order." There had been no moment like it in modern history unless it was when the Bastille was stormed and the French Revolution appeared on the stage of history.

Russell was impressed with the unique spectacle of Russian legislators "snatched almost in a day from plow-tail and fish-net." They "carried it off . . . exceedingly well, no one can deny or doubt that fact; exceedingly well," he wrote. "Hour after hour they sit there, absorbed in the proceedings, listening to every word. . . . No conversation, no restlessness, no shifting about. It is amazing. They come early, they stay late, they seem incapable of weariness. And they are not dumb, driven cattle, either. They watch for points and applaud liberally. If a speaker says something they do not like they show dissent. They are insatiable of oratory, consume it, consider it critically, relish it, want more of it." One thinks, inevitably, of the "freeing of the word" when Calvin and the preachers of the Protestant Reformation began to speak the Word to their congregations—the immense power of the spoken word where before had only been silence. It had been the same in the United States when the abolitionists began to speak about the evils of slavery; when women began to speak about *their* rights. When they found a voice in public, the word was of enormous power, irresistible. The same phenomenon was now apparent in the Russian Revolution. The dumb could speak. The political word was released from the prison of censorship and repression. The Russian people had the intoxicating experience of speaking and listening. No wonder they were "insatiable of oratory."

Like Russell, Steffens was fascinated by the spectacle of the meeting of the workers' council; the soviets' delegates came from every corner of Russia "with their wives, women, friends, and swarming into the Soviet, they organized and went to work. They laid out their baggage, food, beds, and began debate which was constant, interminable." While the delegates debated, vast crowds stood outside the huge hall, waiting for word to be carried out to them about the course of the debates. Steffens's most vivid impression was of the "stink of the mob. . . . I could see the steam rising, as from a herd of cattle, over those sweating, debating delegates. They lived there. Once inside, they stayed inside. They cooked and ate there, and you saw men sleeping in corners and around the edges of the hall. No hours were kept. When delegates were tired, they lay down, leaving the majority to carry on; when they were rested, they awoke to keep the endless, uninterrupted debate going. But they did come to conclusions, that mob of Man, and their conclusions were a credit to the species. . . .The first law passed by that representative, stinking mass put them ahead of our clean, civilized, leading nations. It was against capital punishment. . . . And the second was against war and empire: the Russian people should never conquer and govern any other people." It seemed to an enthralled Steffens that the hope of humanity rested, in some curious and totally unexpected way, with that strange new entity, the soviet.

One thinks of Alexander Berkman's romantic idealization of the People. In the years since Berkman had attempted to assassinate Henry Frick, it had become an article of the faith of liberal and radical intellectuals that the People were a reservoir of simple goodness, decency, untutored and uncorrupted intelligence. Now the proceedings of the soviet, bizzare enough by conventional standards, gave substance to that faith. It was transporting. It confirmed what dreamers and idealists had proclaimed for generations to a skeptical world: The people, the ordinary men and women who labored in field and factory, the "masses," who were barely educated or not educated at all in any formal sense, were capable of governing themselves. They knew right from wrong, for instance, better than most politicians; above all, they understood their own needs and had an instinct for how they might be satisfied. They had, in addition and surprisingly, an inclination toward disinterestedness and a fraternal feeling for those people of other nations and races who shared their aspirations for a better social order. In short, their appearance on the stage of world history was one of that long history's most touching and dramatic moments, and everyone who observed the scene and was capable of any degree of sympathy knew it to be so.

Nikolai Tschaidze, the chairman, guided the whole assembly with a sure hand. "His strong, resolute, intelligent face" sported "a mattress of tawny beard," Russell wrote; his powerful voice reached the farthest corners of the hall. Sitting on the platform looking out over the assembly, Russell thought, "What a scene!" A Siberian fisherman who could neither read nor write spoke with astonishing fluency. "It is a good speech, it has ideas, the man knows what he wants to say, knows how to say it. He has wit, too. He cracks a joke." Russell was deeply impressed by the sea of faces before him. "The bodies," he wrote, "may be uncouthly clad or distorted with toil, but the minds shine out like strong flashing lamps. There, just below, near the front, sits a woman, big burning melancholy eyes fixed upon the speaker. What a face and what eyes! With those deep furrows torn into forehead and cheeks and an air as if she had been beaten down by the years, how old do you think she is? Sixty, at least. But they tell me she is about thirty-nine." She had been in Siberia for eighteen years for writing something that offended the government—a plea for universal education. And she had been a member of the Social Revolutionary Party.

The Bolsheviks sat together in the center of the hall. Lenin and Trotsky were conspicuous. Lenin's face was inscrutable; Trotsky was lively and animated. Trotsky had denounced Russell as an agent of J. P. Morgan who had come to Russia to betray the Revolution, but he was affable enough in conversation with the American, and he seemed to Russell "more human and wiser" than his comrade. Both Trotsky and Lenin were convinced that the time for talk had passed. Outside the Council hall, Russia was in chaos. Food supplies were dangerously short. Rival factions contended for power; nobody seemed in charge. Lenin and Trotsky believed in Marx's doctrine of the interim dictatorship of the proletariat. Discipline and authority were needed above all. The time had passed for endless talk and debate, intoxicating as that experience might be. There were, Russell estimated, no more than 160 Bolsheviks among the 1,000 or so delegates, but they had a program and a strategy to achieve it, and Russell sensed their fierce resolution.

The principal candidate for leadership was Aleksandr Kerensky, a typical Russian intellectual, "rather pallid, clean-shaven, gray-eyed, with large and regular features, . . . brown hair cut short and brushed straight back. . . . He went always carefully attired in a plain business suit of dark bluish gray," looking "more like a poet than a business man." His face, with "his large dreamy eyes," Russell noted, "was interesting but not strong; indeed it had a certain meditative cast that suggested trouble. . . ." Kerensky's power lay almost wholly in his remarkable oratorical gifts. To Russell he was the most powerful orator of the age. It was said that on a number of occasions tens of thousands of Russians had stood for hours under the spell of his eloquence. He was the perfect embodiment of the "speaking" phase of the Revolution. He presided over the release of the word from the dungeon of official suppression. When simple Russians heard him, their hearts flamed, and they discovered unsuspected powers of eloquence in themselves.

Russell, even if he had been denounced as a tool of the capitalists, had some standing with the Social Revolutionaries, and they invited him to meet with a group of them in the dining room of the old Cadet Corps to drink tea and hear their prospectus for the future of Russia (and, not entirely incidentally, the world). Several of them were members of the assembly; they all were young, and the majority were middle- and upper-class intellectuals. "In all good things," Russell wrote, "they seemed to have an invincible faith, a perfect democracy in which all men and women should share on equal terms, all power in the hands of the people, the socialization of the sources of supply, no privileges, no private monopolies, no imperialism." The land question, the most difficult of all, was to be solved not primarily by seizing the lands of the kulaks, or middle-class peasants, but by building roads and opening up vast, uncultivated areas to farming. The great estates, as well as the great holdings of crown land would, of course, be broken up and distributed to the peasants. Capital punishment would be abolished, prisons reformed, and a system of free education established. "A marvellous and unforgettable transfiguration has come over the visible face of Russia," Russell wrote. "Such an upsoaring of the general mind has hardly been known or knowable on earth as took place among the people between March and August, 1917. . . . All the first manifestations of the new day in Russia were idyllic. The released masses reacted not into excesses but into grandiose dreams. For the first six months of the Russian Revolution no nobleman's life was in peril, no mass movement of revenge was observable. The restraint of these freedmen was something to ponder; only from an unusual depth of character could such a manifestation come. No life in danger, no property rent violently from its owner's hands, no reprisals, but virtually a whole nation took itself to dreaming—and oratory." The principal dreamers, not surprisingly, were the Social Revolutionaries. "They saw an ideal state for Russia that should give the model to the world about to be remade after a new fashion, the universal brotherhood come at last, no more wars, no more hatreds, no more competitions, sufficiency and light for all, the grand utopia made real. The Terror had been banished from Russia; any good thing was possible anywhere!"

The Russian Revolution, like the Mexican Revolution before it, brought a spontaneous outburst of artistic activity. "What it means I don't know," Steffens wrote, "but that people, released, free, self-governing, flowered into theaters, and theaters of players, too. Some of them had no audiences. Only players, all players, but spectators or no, the Russians at that time and since have displayed a passion for the theater as a place to play in, to act in and make a show, a child's play of life."

To these bold dreams the Allies' immediate response was anxiety that Russian troops might now be withdrawn from the Eastern front and 2,000,000 German and Austrian troops set free to reinforce their companions in Europe. Delegations appeared promptly from France and Britain to urge the new revolutionary movement to remain in the war. The members of the British Labor Party who came to Russia were dismayed at what they saw of the Revolution. The British, right or left, liked things neat and tidy. What they saw in Russia was vast disorder, verging on chaos. "If this is democracy," one of the members of the delegations declared, "we don't want any democracy in our country." The British line was the totally uncomprehending one that Russia must stand by its treaty commitments whether the Social Revolutionaries or the czar were in power. Mrs. Emmeline Pankhurst, the champion of women suffrage in England, was fired off to Russia in the vain hope that as a British "radical" she might help prevail upon the Russian leaders to keep their country in the war. It must stand as one of the era's more preposterous diplomatic moves.

More and more people gravitated to the palace of the czar's former mistress, where the Bolsheviks had established their headquarters. There Lenin addressed them with quiet conviction. Steffens found his way to the headquarters with his interpreter. Lenin told a crowd gathered outside, "Comrades, the revolution is on. The workers' revolution is on, and you are not working. The workers' and peasants' revolution means work, comrades; it does not mean idleness and leisure. That is a bourgeois ideal. The workers' revolution, a workers' government, means work, that all shall work; and here you are not working. You are only talking.

"Oh, I can understand how you, the people of Russia, having been suppressed so long, should want, now that you have won power, to talk and to listen to orators. But some day soon, you—we all—must go to work and do things, act, produce results—food and socialism." Kerensky would not make socialism, Lenin warned. He did not have the conviction or the resolution. "But—" his voice strong and commanding—"when the hour strikes, when you are ready to go back yourselves to work and you want a government that will go to work and not only think socialism and talk socialism and mean socialism— when you want a government that will do socialism, then—come to the Bolsheviki."

Slowly the word spread—the Bolsheviki; it took on a mysterious power. The Bolsheviks knew what to do, it was said. The word " 'crackled' in everybody's mouth, ear and brain," Steffens wrote.

Steffens was closeted with the groping and uncertain Kerensky, who, not surprisingly, wished to conciliate the Western powers. One of the secret Allied treaties had recently been revealed; it gave Constantinople to Russia as its reward for participating in the war. The Russian people had been scandalized. That, it appeared, was what the war was about: spoils. Kerensky told Steffens that if President Wilson would denounce all secret treaties and agreements and reaffirm that the war was being fought to bring freedom and democracy to the peoples of the world, the Russians might be prevailed on to stay in the war. Kerensky, Lincoln Steffens observed, had not a plan of his own but was swept along by the events of the Revolution. "He was for a republic," Steffens noted, "a representative democracy, which in his mind was really a plutocratic aristocracy." The basic issue was that of carrying on the war. The people had no interest in doing so. Indeed, the war had become to them a struggle between competing capitalist systems, a struggle without meaning. In Steffens's words, Kerensky "was getting mad demands from all the allies and their representatives to go on with the war, to strike with a battle, if not for victory, then hard enough to keep the Germans engaged. . . . It was a comic and also a tragic show," Steffens added, that "provisional government's efforts, at our behest, to force a people who, newborn to freedom, as they thought, interested in a revolution full of possibilities—land, liberty, justice and the permanent peace with all the world—to carry on a war that they were through with against their very good friends, the German workers and peasants."

In May Kerensky became minister of war of the provisional government and launched an offensive against the German and Austrian armies. At that point, the Bolsheviks tried to seize power. They were vigorously suppressed. Lenin took refuge in Finland. Prince Lvov resigned, and Kerensky took over the reins of government on July 20, 1917. When he tried to fire General Lavr Kornilov in September, the Russian commander in chief turned on him in a coup d'état. The desperate Kerensky appealed to the Petrograd Soviet for help in suppressing Kornilov. The response of the Bolsheviks was to dispatch soldiers and, most important, sailors from the Kronstadt naval base, who shelled the Winter Palace and seized the ministers of the provisional government (Kerensky escaped in disguise). Lenin and Trotsky called the Second All-Russian Congress of the Soviets, which assembled on November 7, 1917. Some of the Social Revolutionaries, many of whom were pacifists, fled; a number of others were summarily shot as enemies of the state. "A few of the golden dreamers," Russell wrote, "made their way to Paris and ended their dreaming in melancholy exile and often in want." Tschaidze, whose chairmanship of the assembly Russell had admired, fled to Georgia, where he established the Georgian Republic with himself as president. The Bolsheviks invaded the Georgian Republic and defeated Tschaidze's hastily assembled and poorly equipped "army," and Tschaidze himself escaped to Paris to join an exile community that included Russians of both right and left. He committed suicide several years later, and his death put the seal on the hopes of the Social Revolutionary Party.

By the time these dramatic and momentous events had transpired, the Root mission was back in the United States, where its chairman received a cool hearing from the President, who suspected Root's politics and distrusted his advice. Steffens also returned, having written with considerable discernment and warm approval of the opening phase of the Revolution.

Perhaps the Bolshevik's most popular measure was their call for immediate negotiations with the Central Powers, looking to an end to the war and, if that proved impossible, an end to Russia's participation.

Trotsky gave a momentous radio broadcast, declaring on December 1, "We shall begin peace negotiations. If the Allied nations do not send their representatives we shall conduct negotiations alone with the Germans. We want a general peace, but if the bourgeois in the Allied countries force us to conclude a separate peace the entire responsibility will be theirs." Brest-Litovsk in eastern Poland was chosen as the site for the negotiations. The Russian peace delegation consisted of a brother-in-law of Trotsky; a Madame Byzenko, renowned for having killed a minister of the Kerensky government; a noncommissioned officer; a sailor; a workman; and a peasant distinguished by a long white beard and a susceptibility to wine. Also present were representatives of the other members of the Quadruple Alliance—the Austro-Hungarian Empire, Bulgaria, and Turkey—some 400 in all. After a week or so of negotiations the delegates were joined by Trotsky.

The Germans imposed a draconian peace on the Russians, and when they balked, the German Eastern army began an offensive which was virtually unopposed. In the Treaty of Brest-Litovsk, which was signed on March 3, 1918, Russia relinquished control over Estonia, Latvia, Lithuania, Russian Poland, Finland, and the Ukraine, representing some 40 percent of the steel and iron production and 75 percent of its coalfields—in all some 386,000 square miles. An argument often used in defending the Versailles Treaty was that severe as it was, it was mild in comparison with the treaty that the Germans had imposed on the Bolsheviks. Moreover, as apologists for the Versailles Treaty pointed out, the victory of the Allies' armies saved Russia from the worst consequences of the Treaty of Brest-Litovsk. On the other hand, it must be said that the Russians would never have acquiesced to the treaty's terms in the long run (just as the Germans could not be reconciled to the terms of the Versailles Treaty). They would certainly have resisted it by force of arms, and another conflict could have ensued.

When the Kerensky government broke up in November, 1917, the Finnish White Guards, supported by German troops, had attempted to seize Murmansk and make it into a German submarine base. The Russian commander of the Murmansk district, fearful of German intentions, asked for help from the Allies, and British marines were immediately disembarked in the city. On May 24, 1918, Admiral Dewey's old flagship, the *Olympia*, landed 100 American sailors. More British troops arrived and were rushed to protect the Murmansk—

Petrograd railroad at Kandalaksha. From Murmansk, Allied troops, including 50 American sailors, were shipped to Archangel, where they participated in a coup led by Nikolai V. Tchaikovsky, an old-time revolutionist, against the recently formed Bolshevik-dominated Russian provincial government.

In southern Russia the British supplied the White armies under Anton I. Denikin with munitions and money to fight the armies of Lenin and Trotsky. Forty thousand Czech soldiers were driving for the Volga in support of White Russians, while the British undertook to organize an expedition to drive down from the north, hoping to catch Moscow and Petrograd in a giant pincer.

By the summer of 1918 Wilson, acting, in the words of George Kennan, "reluctantly and against his better judgment, and only with a view to conciliating the European Allies," had yielded to Foch's urgent plea for American troops to be sent to Murmansk to guard military stores there. Wilson accompanied his acquiescence with a warning that the Americans would be withdrawn if there were any indication that they were being used against the Bolsheviks.

The journalist Frazier Hunt, learning of the expedition despite efforts to keep it a secret, jumped at a chance to join the Allied force. Called the North Russian Expedition, the troops were dispatched, primarily under the aegis of the British, to make contact with anti-Bolshevik Russians in the Murmansk area. Five thousand American soldiers were shipped off "to these Arctic regions," as Hunt put it. No reporter had found his way into "this dangerous, forbidden border for months." When Hunt arrived in Murmansk on Thanksgiving Day, 1918, he found the city swarming with a wild variety of peoples— "Italian troopers, English generals, Karelians in long parkas, Laplanders with their reindeer sleds, Canadian dog-team men, Russian laborers, Chinese workmen, French, Serbians, Poles." The city seethed with the "politics and intrigue of a Balkan capital."

Hunt discovered that the American soldiers had been scattered about in isolated detachments to block against attack by the Bolsheviks the various roads, rivers, and trails branching out from Archangel. The only way to reach most of them was by dog-sled. Hunt found a sympathetic YMCA official, a Major Williams from Baltimore, and arranged to travel with him by sleigh to deliver food to the soldiers. The Bolsheviks, or Bolos, as the soldiers called them, were all about, constantly probing the American positions. Moreover, the Russian enemies of the Bolsheviks were strongly opposed to the presence of foreign soldiers on Russian soil. "Some," Hunt wrote, "were Mensheviks, some Kerensky liberals, but all were against this foreign intervention. It was becoming more and more clear to me," he added, "that nothing short of a violent and brutal exposé would bring the intolerable conditions [of the American soldiers] to the attention of the highest authorities." But when Hunt tried to wire his dispatches to his American newspaper, they were intercepted by the British censors, who had no intention of allowing anything but the official version to reach the outside world. To Hunt the whole operation was "a dismal comic opera." Dissatisfaction of the Russian population at the high-handed actions of the expeditionary force had grown week by week. "Every phase of life within the district is controlled by the Allies and dominated by them," Hunt wrote. A Russian official told the American journalist, "As far as we can judge certain of the Allies are now working toward breaking the heart of the whole spirit of advancement in Russia and want a heavy-handed dictatorship established, so that life and business can go on under the old imperialistic conditions."

Under the cover of protecting the Allied supplies, the British commanding general, a General Knox, established a reactionary White Guard regime in Siberia. It was Knox who told the American commander, "You're fast getting the reputation of being a friend of the poor, and you must understand that the poor are nothing but swine."

When Hunt finally smuggled out an account of the Allied interference with Russian affairs, it was published in the United States and read in the Senate by Hiram Johnson. Wilson responded by promising to withdraw American troops as soon as the port of Archangel was free of ice.

An angry Oswald Garrison Villard wrote years after the event that "the full responsibility for this wanton invasion of a country with whom we were at peace will for all time rest squarely upon Mr. Wilson's shoulders and upon his head lies the blood of the Russian and our own soldiers." The Nation described the American policy as "combined burglary and starvation coupled with pious phrases."

If Villard's anger seems excessive, it is clear enough that the United States, by identifying itself with the Allied invasion, nullified what was in fact an initially friendly, if wary, disposition on Wilson's part toward the Russian revolutionaries. Paranoia is doubtlessly built into Marxist dogma, but American policies augmented rather than abated it.

31

Suppressing Dissent

With the entry of the United States into the war Wilson and his Cabinet determined on a policy of suppression toward those who opposed the war. All dissent, they believed, must be silenced in the name of national unity and patriotism. *McClure's Magazine* stressed the theme that "the coming 'ism' is not Socialism; the coming 'ism' is Patriotism." There was a "new righteousness which shall become a new passion—the *Love of Country*. We shall see that new passion develop in the American people until we have obedience to the law, *because it is the law,* and the will of the state will be sufficient." Socialists, anarchists, and pacifists must be gagged—frightened into submission or thrown into jail. "Force, Force to the utmost, Force without stint or limit" against the enemies of the United States, foreign or domestic, Wilson declared in a Flag Day ceremony. The disloyal and unpatriotic must be cast down "in the dust."

Behind such draconian measures lay an awareness of how deeply the nation was divided, East from West, hyphenated Americans from "natives," radicals from conservatives. Understandably anxiety blossomed into paranoia. Wilson had never been tolerant of opposition—not at Princeton; not as governor of New Jersey. He had the imperiousness of a man conscious of his own moral rectitude and confident to the point of arrogance in the correctness of his painfully arrived at decisions. He and a majority of his Cabinet were pacifists or at least pacifistically inclined. For two and a half years he had stood firm, if not always for a scrupulous neutrality, at least for peace *at almost any price*. He had been a rock of sanity, prudence, and restraint in a sea of angry and conflicting emotions. Now that he had to swallow the bitter pill, the psychic price was incalculable. The repressive policies of his administration may, additionally, have had something to do with his chronic ill health and the fact that he felt increasingly that it was his destiny to save humanity from its folly by the force of his implacable will.

Wilson had given a warning of what was to come in his second inaugural address. On that occasion he spoke of "the unity of America—an America united in feeling, in purpose, and in its vision of duty, of opportunity, and of service. We are to beware of all men who would turn the tasks and necessities of the Nation to their own private profit. . . ; beware that no faction of disloyal intrigue break the harmony or embarrass the spirit of our people." While Wilson was at pains to announce to newspaper editor Arthur Brisbane that he was opposed to any "system of censorship that would deny to the people of a free republic . . . their indisputable right to criticize their own public officials," including, presumably, himself, the implication was that criticism of governmental policies and, more important, of American involvement in the war itself would not be tolerated. It was soon evident that the limits of free speech would, with the President's approval, be sharply circumscribed. The Department of Justice brought in recommendations to expand the criminal code to include a wide variety of seditious activities. The President must be empowered to "prohibit the publishing or communicating of . . . any information relating to the national defense which, in his judgment, is of such character that it is or might be useful to the enemy." The Hearst newspapers collected a million and half signatures protesting the looseness of the bill's language. The House stubbornly refused to accept the more objectionable features of the bill, but the Senate was enthusiastic. Finally, in a joint Senate/House conference the Senate gave way on the issue of censorship itself, but under the heading "Title I, Espionage," espionage was broadly defined, and added to it were severe penalties for "crimes of obstruction or conspiracy that were likely to interfere with the execution by the administration of the acts of Congress." In this category were any statements made "with intent to interfere with the operation or success of the military or naval forces." Penalties of $10,000 and twenty years' imprisonment were provided for anyone who might "willfully cause or attempt to cause insubordination, mutiny, or refusal of duty . . . or shall willfully obstruct the recruiting or enlistment service." Title I was to prove the harshest and most oppressive of all the measures directed at suppressing opposition to the administration's policies. More American citizens were to be imprisoned under its provisions than any other section of the Espionage Act.

Title XII covered the use of the mails. "Unmailable matter," heretofore primarily obscene materials as measured by the standards established by Anthony Comstock and his vice crusaders, was broadened to include "letter, writing, circular, postal card . . . newspaper, pamphlet, book . . . in violation of any of the provisions of this act" or any material "advocating or urging treason, insurrection, or forcible resistance to any law of the United States." It was left to Postmaster General Burleson to determine what constituted actionable material. The first casualty was the *American Socialist*. The *Masses* was outlawed in August. In Max Eastman's words, "They give you ninety days for quoting the Declaration of Independence, six months for quoting the Bible, and pretty soon somebody is going to get a life sentence for quoting Woodrow Wilson in the wrong connection."

The King amendment (named for William King of Utah) was directed at the foreign-language press. It stipulated that an English translation of all material in a foreign-language newspaper or journal be submitted *in advance of publication* to the local postmaster. Those who failed to comply or whom the postmaster judged to have submitted seditious material simply had their publications barred from the mails.

The Espionage Act was fortified by the Trading with the Enemy Act in October, 1917, and the Sedition Act of May 16, 1918, which plugged every last hole through which free speech might escape. Burleson was tireless in pursuit of those he considered disloyal, especially "small-town editors . . . foreign language publications or little far-Western newspapers, . . . helpless small-fry who could not strike back," Eastman wrote. The solicitor general declared, in connection with the *New Republic,* " . . . I am not working in the dark on this censorship thing. I know exactly what I am after. I am after three things and only three things—pro-Germanism, pacifism, and 'high-browism.' "

No journal or magazine, especially those not in English, seemed too obscure or innocuous to escape the dragnet thrown out by Burleson. One of the publications barred from the mails was the organ of the Tenant Farmers' Union that Oscar Ameringer had helped start in Oklahoma; another victim was Tom Watson's *Jeffersonian*. Even the *Nation,* with the lead "Civil Liberty Dead," was held up in the New York Post Office as possibly seditious.

Different groups and individuals were drawn to specific issues in their opposition to the war. Many of the enemies of conscription did not directly oppose the war but believed that the American army and navy should be made up, like the British armed forces, of volunteers. Other enemies of conscription were opposed to the United States' entry into the war under any circumstances and fastened on conscription as the handiest means of expressing that opposition; the anarchists, under the leadership of Emma Goldman and Alexander Berkman, organized the No-Conscription League and planned a mass protest at the Harlem River Casino in New York City on May 18, 1917. Goldman estimated that 10,000 people turned out for the rally. Scattered through the crowd were soldiers in uniform who heckled the speakers. When they tried to prevent Goldman from speaking, she appealed to the audience to allow a soldier to speak in behalf of conscription. On the way home from the meeting, Goldman heard newsboys hawking papers that announced the passage of the conscription bill by Congress. It would go into effect on June 4, a few weeks away.

Goldman and Berkman, arrested for "conspiracy against the draft," were placed in the Tombs prison until $25,000 bail was raised. (The *New York World* announced that the kaiser had furnished the bail.) The trial of the two anarchists, Emma and her "dear old pal," as she called Berkman, was classic guerrilla theater, in a modern phrase, or, perhaps better, a modern morality play. They conducted their own defense with considerable skill and humor. An array of native radicals, among them Lincoln Steffens, John Reed, and Bolton Hall, testified in their behalf. The state's principal witnesses appeared bumbling and inept under cross-examination. But the defendants were frequently overruled by a hostile judge. "The atmosphere grew more antagonistic, the official attendants more insulting," Goldman wrote. "Our friends were either kept out or treated roughly when they succeeded in gaining admission." A recruiting station was set up in the street outside the courtroom, and the music of military bands could be heard distinctly throughout the proceedings.

At the end of the trial first Berkman and then Emma Goldman spoke in defense of the right of free speech and dissent. It was true that they had broken the law, but there had never been an ideal, "however humane and peaceful, which in its time had been considered 'within the law.' " Jesus, Socrates, Galileo all had been persecuted. "And the men who set America free from British rule, the Jeffersons and the Patrick Henrys? The William Lloyd Garrisons, the John Browns, the David Thoreaus and the Wendell Phillipses—were they within the law?" Goldman asked.

When she had finished speaking, the judge reminded the jury that their verdict had nothing to do with whether the defendants were "right or wrong," but only whether they were guilty as charged of disobeying the law. The jury deliberated for thirty-nine minutes and returned a verdict of guilty. The judge then inflicted the maximum penalty—two years in prison and a fine of $10,000. The records of the trial were to be sent to the immigration authorities in Washington with the recommendation that the defendants be deported at the expiration of their prison terms. The judge refused Emma Goldman's request for a two-day stay of execution so that she and Berkman could put their personal affairs in order. The prisoners were ordered to jail: Goldman to the Missouri state prison and her codefendant to the Federal penitentiary at Atlanta, Georgia. If a Supreme Court justice signed an application for appeal, the defendants could be admitted to bail. Louis Brandeis, recently appointed to the Court by President Wilson, agreed to do so, and Goldman and Berkman were returned to the Tombs to await the setting of bail. The matron there was, it turned out, an old friend, an ally in the birth control cause.

Scott Nearing, a former dean of Toledo University, was one of the organizers of the First American Conference for Democracy and Terms of Peace, held in Madison Square Garden on May 30, 1917. The delegates met in an atmosphere heavy with threats of violence. The police were out in force—400 of New York's Finest, a number equal to the delegates to the conference—and floodlights illuminated the area around the Garden. Some 20,000 pacifists attended the two-day meeting. Rabbi Judah Magnes called for Americans to "aid our government in bringing to ourselves and the world a speedy, righteous, and lasting peace." The convention then voted approval of the Russian peace demands: no annexations, no indemnities, and self-determination for all peoples. It went on to condemn the Selective Service Act and to denounce the efforts of the government to stifle dissent.

One of the principal speakers was Florence Kelley, daughter of the Republican Congressman and iron tycoon William "Pig Iron" Kelley, and a close associate of Jane Addams at Hull House. She warned of the dangers to the rights of the working class created by the war. Before the conference adjourned, plans were made for a national organization and a convention to be held some months hence. Bishop Paul Jones of the Episcopal diocese of Utah; Thomas Van Lear, the Socialist mayor of Minneapolis; Senator John Works of California; Paul Kellogg; and Crystal Eastman, Max's sister, were among those who endorsed the idea of a permanent body to pursue an early, negotiated peace.

The People's Council was the consequence of the American Conference for Democracy and Terms of Peace. It was a loose alliance of those Socialists who stuck with the party in its opposition to the war, various pacifist groups, and the Central Federated Union, the Socialist-sponsored union movement opposed to Gompers and to the war. Gompers in turn formed the American Alliance for Labor and Democracy, the guiding principle of which was all-out support for the war effort.

One of the more divisive issues in the leadership of the People's Council was what the pacifists felt was the disposition of the Socialists to try to use the peace issue to advance the Socialist cause per se and, furthermore, to be far too aggressive in their endorsement of the Bolsheviks, whose ruthless suppression of other revolutionists was beginning to cause disquiet in American radical circles.

Prominent among the well-known individuals who joined the fight against conscription was Helen Keller. When Keller heard of the arrest of Emma Goldman and Alexander Berkman for resisting the draft, she wrote to Goldman: "Believe me, my very heart-beat is in the revolution that is to inaugurate a freer, happier society. Can you imagine what it is to sit idling these days of fierce action, of revolution and daring possibilities? I am so full of longing to serve, to love and be loved, to help things along, and to give happiness. It seems as if the very intensity of desire must bring fulfillment, but, alas, nothing happens. . . . one thing is sure—you can always count upon my love and support." While others remained silent out of fear, Goldman spoke out; "nor," Keller wrote, "are the I.W.W. comrades holding their tongues—blessings upon you and them. . . . Never were courage and fortitude so terribly needed as now."

In Emma Goldman's words, "Noncombatants and conscientious objectors from every social stratum were filling the jails and prisons. The new Espionage Law turned the country into a lunatic asylum, with every State and Federal official, as well as a large part of the civilian population, running amuck. They spread terror and destruction. Disruption of public meetings and wholesale arrests, sentences of incredible severity, suppression of radical publications and indictments of their staffs, beating of workers—even murder—became the chief patriotic pastime." Rose Pastor Stokes was sentenced to ten years in prison for writing a letter to a Kansas City newspaper denouncing war profiteers.

The socialite Socialist Roger Baldwin was among dozens who went to prison rather than allow themselves to be drafted. During his trial Baldwin defiantly announced his commitment to anarchism and his resistance to the right of the state to coerce his conscience. Philip Grosser, a young Jew, refused to register for the draft on political grounds. He was turned over to the military authorities, court-martialed (an illegal procedure), and sentenced to thirty years in prison for refusing to obey orders. In prison he was subjected to every form of abuse and harassment; he was chained on several occasions, several times beaten, and finally confined to "the hole" at Alcatraz.

At Angel Island, a concentration camp for various categories of dissenters from the war, many men were systematically tortured. It was reported that at Leavenworth prisoners were forced to stand for the first week of their incarceration with "their hands crossed at their breasts, during the second week they hang by their wrists." Among those so tortured was Evan Thomas, brother of Socialist leader Norman Thomas.

In January, 1918, the Supreme Court handed down its decision upholding the constitutionality of the Selective Service Act (conscription had been going on for six months). With legal remedies exhausted, Berkman and Goldman prepared for their imprisonment. They wrote a farewell letter to their friends and fellow workers: "Be of good cheer, good friends and comrades. We are going to prison with light hearts. To us it is more satisfactory to be behind bars than to remain MUZZLED in freedom. Our spirit will not be daunted, nor our will broken. We will return to our work in due time. . . . The light of Liberty burns low just now. But do not despair, friends. Keep the spark alive. The night cannot last forever. Soon there will come a rift in the darkness, and the New Day break even in this country. Each of us feel we have contributed our mite toward the great Awakening." Their last act was the organization of the Political Prisoners' Amnesty League.

When Kate Richards O'Hare was sentenced to five years in prison for her opposition to the war, she told the judge that she welcomed a new form of service. "If it were necessary that Jesus should come down among men," she declared, "that he might save them, it may be necessary for me to become a convict among criminals to serve them. If this be true I will face prison; I will face the things that go with prison life, as serenely as I have court and judge and jury." O'Hare joined Emma Goldman at the Jefferson City prison for women.

A band of New York anarchists, among them Jacob Schwartz and Mollie Steimer, an editor of *Mother Earth,* were also sentenced to long prison terms, and Schwartz, who had been badly beaten by the police, died in his Tombs cell, leaving a note which read: "Farewell, comrades. When you speak before the Court I will be with you no longer. Struggle without fear, fight bravely. I am sorry to have to leave you. But this is life itself."

In a sense Emma Goldman welcomed the life of the prison. It enabled her to experience something "her old pal" Berkman had experienced much more intensely. In addition, it gave play to her bountiful humanity and her remarkable qualities of leadership. The prison was not immune to her ebullient spirit. The inmates, like the women of Blackwells Island, most of them coming from the depths of society, responded to her abundant energy. She was showered with gifts at Christmas from her admirers all over the world, and she shared them with the other prisoners until the prison was "filled with noisy hilarity." If she could not shape America or the world to her heart's desire, she could at least transform the prison into a community of society's outcasts. She was joined in the task by Kate O'Hare. Goldman was suspicious at first of the socially prominent O'Hare, with her upper-class accent and refined manners, but she soon found her an invaluable ally. The descendant of generations of "native" Americans, joining with the Jewish immigrant, symbolized the alliance between the reformers of the Protestant Passion and the radical immigrants. "We soon found common ground and human interest in our daily association," Goldman wrote, "which proved more vital than our theoretical differences. I . . . discovered a very warm heart beneath Kate's outer coldness. . . . We quickly became friends." With another political prisoner, a girl named Ella, still in her teens, Emma Goldman and Kate O'Hare were nicknamed the trinity. The three formed their own little world within the prison. O'Hare had been separated from her four children, a severe emotional burden on her. On the other hand, as Goldman put it, "the O'Hares had big political connections," and O'Hare's accounts of prison conditions published in the *St. Louis Post-Dispatch* brought reforms to the prison. In O'Hare's words, "The results gained by placing many hundreds of political prisoners in our penitentiaries have not been quite those sought by the political administration in power, or by the industrial forces controlling the administration . . . [and] as a by-effect, the searchlight of intelligent study and keen analysis has been turned into the darkest and most noisome depths of our social system—the prisons." That was certainly the case with Kate O'Hare's incarceration. It gave her a lifelong mission of reforming the nation's prison systems. "The political prisoners, in common with all sincere students," she wrote, "found that the prisons are the cesspools of our social system and that into them drain the most helpless, hopeless products of our body-, brain-, and soul-destroying struggle for existence. . . . There is no doubt," she added, "that it was a good thing for our country that a large group of well-educated, intelligent, socially-minded people should have gone to prison. . . . If I were ruler of the Universe I would see to it that many more respectable folk went to prison, for the good of their souls and the welfare of the country." In addition to devoting most of her life to prison reform, Kate O'Hare wrote one of the classics of prison life, entitled, simply, *In Prison.*

Matters did not go well for Berkman in the Atlanta penitentiary. He had been put in solitary confinement for circulating protests to the warden against the beating of inmates and the murder of a young black prisoner who was shot in the back for "impudence." Also in Atlanta was Eugene V. Debs, sentenced to five years for his opposition to the war.

Even after the entry of the United States into the war, Oscar Ameringer and Victor Berger had kept the *Milwaukee Leader* going, in large part by soliciting war bonds from the paper's supporters. But a copy of the *Leader* was confiscated by the postmaster general, and the second-class mailing privileges of the paper were revoked on the gound that it did not publish daily. Ameringer responded by calling a mass meeting, which was attended by 12,000 people. Four thousand dollars were collected to mail out issues to subscribers under the first-class permit, a far more expensive undertaking. The postmaster general responded by revoking the *Leader*'s right to *receive* mail. Letters addressed to the *Leader* were returned to the senders marked "Undeliverable under the Espionage Act." When the circulation of the *Leader* actually increased in the city itself, the Fuel Administration warned advertisers that if they didn't withdraw advertising, their fuel allocations would be reduced. A baker who had been one of the paper's original backers told Ameringer and Berger, with tears in his eyes, that he had been threatened by administrators at the Food Administration, which told him that if he did not drop his advertising in the paper, "they would refuse me the flour, sugar and coal necessary for operating my bakery. And that is all I've got in the world."

When all government efforts had failed and Berger and Ameringer stubbornly persisted in publishing the *Leader,* Berger, as editor in chief, was indicted on so many counts that, by Ameringer's calculations, if he had been convicted on all of them, he could have been sentenced to 1,500 years in the Federal penitentiary. Ex-Congressman Berger was released on a $1,000,000 bond with the injunction that he not write for the *Leader,* and to make doubly sure the injunction was obeyed, the files and papers of the *Leader* were confiscated. The judge who sentenced Berger was Kenesaw Mountain Landis, known as one of the nation's most liberal jurists (he had imposed a fine of $29,000,000 on Standard Oil).

At the conclusion of his trial Berger declared in court, "From my early youth, I have surrounded myself with the best and noblest minds of the ages. I am the sum total of the impressions they have left on me. I am what I am. I cannot be otherwise." He was reelected to Congress in 1918 while his case was on appeal, but that body refused to seat him because of his antiwar position.

The sentencing of Berger did not stop the harassment of the editors of the *Leader.* Dictaphones were planted in its barren offices and in the homes of Berger and Ameringer. When the two men wished to talk, they got into Ameringer's Ford and drove to the Milwaukee River, where they sat on a rock in the river and conversed.

Ameringer ran for Congress in the Second Congressional District of Wisconsin in 1918, but he was harassed by Federal agents, his posters were torn down, and his campaign literature was barred from the mails. Finally, he and five other Socialist congressional candidates were arrested and indicted for violations of the Espionage Act. Among them was Elizabeth Thomas, a Quaker and treasurer of the *Leader*. None of them came to trial since the purpose of the arrests was primarily to ensure their defeat in the elections.

The president of the League of Humanity was sentenced to a twenty-five-year jail term for an antiwar lecture he delivered in Davenport, Iowa. Louise Olivereau, a leader in a dozen reform movements, was arrested, tried, convicted, and sentenced to forty-five years in prison in Colorado for speaking against American involvement in the war.

John Purroy Mitchel, reform mayor of New York City, condoned the breaking up of Irish and socialist meetings by newly recruited soldiers. More than 100 instances of such attacks were recorded in the year following the entry of the United States into the war. In the same period, 3,465 individuals were convicted of "interfering with the operation of the draft," an extremely loose charge that could be stretched to cover any criticism of the U.S. entry into the war. Many people were tarred and feathered. Under the Espionage Act, 1,180 were prosecuted. The officials of the International Bible Students Association in Brooklyn, a fundamentalist Christian pacifist group, were sentenced to a combined 80 years in prison. In New York 3 men and a woman were sentenced to a total of 285 years in prison for passing out handbills objecting to U.S. intervention in Russia. A man in Lansing, Michigan, who had declared angrily that the government could go to hell, was given 20 years in jail and fined $10,000, and a member of the New York legislature, who had declared that the Russians "had more right to feel bitterly against the Americans [the soldiers] in Russia than we had against the Hessians in 1776," was indicted for "uttering disloyal, scurrilous, and abusive language about the military and naval forces."

In Los Angeles a liberal minister, who had announced that he preferred the ideals of the Communists to those of the Merchants and Manufacturers' Association, was given six months in jail and fined $1,200. When Oswald Garrison Villard spoke at Cincinnati, he was bitterly denounced by the American Legion and other patriotic groups. The hall he lectured in was besieged by Legionnaires, threatening to lynch him for his opposition to the war and to the treaty. He was forced to escape from the city by an indirect route, accompanied by three plainclothes policemen. A pacifist physician in Kentucky was badly beaten on the basis of a speech he was preparing to make. In Milwaukee a meeting of socialists and anarchists opposed to war was attacked by the police, and two young Italians were killed. Italian social clubs were raided, and eleven immigrants arrested for having provoked a riot. While they were in prison, a bomb was thrown in the police station. The prisoners were charged with responsibility for the bombing and sentenced to twenty-five years in jail.

The assault on free speech was not, of course, limited to the Federal government. States and even municipalities strove to outdo each other in patriotic zeal by persecuting their fellow citizens. In February, 1918, the Montana legislature passed the most repressive statute produced by the war. It purported to protect the Constitution (which, of course, it clearly violated), servicemen, the flag, and the United States against "disloyal, profane, violent, scurrilous, contemptuous, slurring, or abusive language . . . or any language calculated to bring [them] . . . into contempt, contumely, or disrepute."

Before six months had passed, Congress had produced a new sedition bill, almost as harsh as that of Montana and supported enthusiastically by the Senators from that state. One clause declared that "nothing in this act shall be construed as limiting the liberty or impairing the right of any individual to publish or speak what is true, with good motives, and for justifiable ends." Although Hiram Johnson was among its most vigorous supporters, the clause was rejected with little debate.

The academic world was not immune. The American Association of University Professors fell in line with a "guideline" for faculty members. "If," that document read, "a speaker should declare that all participation in war is immoral, or should praise the example of the Russian troops who deserted their posts and betrayed their allies, or should assert that the payment of war taxes is contrary to sound ethical principles—such a speaker may be presumed to know that the *natural tendency* of his words is to stir up hostility to the law and induce such of his hearers as are influenced by him to refuse to perform certain of the obligations of citizenship." Under that rather loose formula a number of faculty members were fired from their posts. In dismissing Professors Henry Wadsworth Longfellow Dana and James Cattell, a distinguished psychologist, the president of Columbia, Nicholas Murray Butler, announced, "What had been tolerated before becomes intolerable now. What had been wrongheadedness was now sedition. What had been folly was now treason. . . . There is and will be no place in Columbia University . . . for any person who opposes or counsels opposition to the effective enforcement of the laws of the United States, or who acts, speaks or writes treason. The separation of any such person from Columbia University will be as speedy as the discovery of his offense."

When Dana and Cattell were fired, John Dewey, who supported the war, issued a strong protest and Professor Charles Beard resigned. Scott Nearing escaped prosecution for an antiwar pamphlet, but the directors of the Rand School were fined $3,000 for publishing it.

Norman Thomas saddened his friends and enraged the proponents of the war by writing: "When universities refuse to permit or discuss free speech [referring to his alma mater, Princeton, which had refused to sponsor a debate on the subject], when mobs beat or kill agitators, when the government prosecutes critics of the war, it is liberty itself which is the chief victim. What shall it profit us to defeat Prussia if we prussianize our own selves?" For these subversive sentiments, Thomas was reported by the New York Post Office to military intelligence.

Emily Greene Balch, a member of the Wellesley College faculty and head of the department of economics and sociology, took a leave of absence in 1917 and 1918 to spare her colleagues' embarrassment over her pacifist views.

Most intractable and most vulnerable were the leaders and members of the IWW, who refused to be intimidated. They published editorials in their paper *Solidarity* calling for the expulsion from the union of any member who joined the army. On September 5, 1917, agents of the Department of Justice raided all the local offices of the IWW in the West. Haywood was among 160 Wobblies arrested and charged with violation of the Espionage Act. After seven months of accumulating evidence and a trial that lasted four months more, more than 100 were convicted and given sentences ranging up to 20 years—a total of more than 800 years. Among those sentenced to long jail terms were Haywood, Elizabeth Gurley Flynn, Carlo Tresca, and Arturo Giovanitti.

When the home of J. Edgar Pew, a wealthy oilman in Tulsa, Oklahoma, was damaged by a bomb, the *Tulsa World* accused the local IWW chapter of the act, although no evidence was produced to support the charge. "The first step in the whipping of Germany," the paper editorialized, "is to strangle the I.W.W.'s. Kill 'em just as you would any other kind of snake. Don't scotch 'em; kill 'em. And kill 'em dead. It is no time to waste money on trials and continuances like that. All that is necessary is the evidence and a firing squad." With that kind of encouragement, a mob formed and, with the complicity of the police, seized seventeen Wobblies who had been charged, in the want of any "crime," with vagrancy, whipped them until their backs were raw, and then tarred and feathered them.

In August, 1917, Frank Little, the half-Indian associate of Big Bill Haywood who had so enthralled Frazier Hunt, was taken from his boardinghouse in Butte, Montana, by a lynch mob and hanged from a nearby railroad trestle. One California newspaper proclaimed a general sentiment: "Hanging is none too good for the I.W.W.'s. They would be much better dead, for they are absolutely useless in the human economy; they are the waste material of creation and should be drained off in the sewer of oblivion, there to rot in cold obstruction like any other excrement." An investigator appointed by the governor of California to look into the causes of the strikes that were sweeping the state declared that "it was hard for him to believe that he was not sojourning in Russia conducting his investigations there instead of the alleged 'land of the free and the home of the brave.'"

As a result of the work by the American anarchists and their allies, the Mooney case, as we have noted, became an international *cause célèbre*. Workers' groups in Russia and other European countries organized demonstrations of protest, and Wilson finally responded by ordering a Federal investigation into the charges that the defendants were the victims of a judicial frame-up. He directed Felix Frankfurter, as a member of the Mediation Commission, appointed to mediate disputes between capital and labor, to look into the Mooney case, "which is greatly disturbing our Allies, Russia and Italy." Frankfurter's report was decidedly unfavorable to California justice, and it infuriated conservatives. Frankfurter also investigated the so-called Bisbee deportations; in Bisbee, Arizona, vigilantes led by one of Roosevelt's Rough Riders, Jack Greenway, had rounded up almost 1,000 Wobblies in the dead of night, shipped them off to a ghost town in New Mexico, and left them there, surrounded by desert, without adequate food or water.

When Frankfurter's report was critical of this high-handed abuse of the Wobblies' rights, Roosevelt publicly denounced him for "taking on behalf of the administration an attitude which seems to me to be fundamentally that of Trotsky and the other Bolshevik leaders in Russia; an attitude which may be fraught with mischief to this country."

Frankfurter rebuked his old leader: "Surely you must know what a great sadness it is for me to find disagreement between us on an important issue. . . . You are one of the few great sources of national leadership and inspiration for national endeavor. I do not want to see that asset made ill use of." But there was support from Learned Hand, who wrote: "I am glad that you stood up to him as well as you did, and you certainly had him backed against the ropes. . . . Your Bisbee report was absolutely right and courageous. . . ."

Frederic Howe's duties as director of immigration for the City of New York made him acutely aware of the prosecution of immigrants. American paranoia focused on Ellis Island. Politicians and newspapers took up the cry that all aliens who might be considered in any way to threaten the security of the United States or undermine the war effort must be deported. Ellis Island thus became a two-way transfer station—divided between those entering and those being deported. The net was cast wide and often indiscriminately for deportees. Those merely suspected of harboring dangerous sentiments were rounded up without due process of law and transported to Ellis Island to be shipped back to lands that were, in many instances, unwilling to receive them. Included were prostitutes and even women living with men in an unmarried state. Those accused seldom had interpreters. They were accused and convicted in a language they did not understand and often shipped off unaware of the charges against them. "Each day," Howe wrote, "brought a contingent of German, Hungarian, Austrian suspects, while incoming trains from the West added quotas of immoral men and women, prostitutes, procurers and alleged white-slavers arrested under the hue and cry started early in the war with the passage of the Mann White Slave Act."

Howe was indignant at the treatment of the aliens under his care. "That I should use my official power to get rid of people without evidence, and because some individual or group said they were undesirable, was abhorrent to my ideas of legal ethics and my sense of responsibility to my oath of office," he wrote. It seemed to him ironic in the extreme that the United States, avowedly fighting a war to make the world safe for democracy, should so trample on the rights of people within its own borders. He collected an archive of horror stories. One of the more bizarre involved a young immigrant woman in Knoxville, Tennessee, who had been seduced by her employer. The employer, wishing in time to be rid of her, reported her to immigration officials as an immoral woman. She was sent to Ellis Island for deportation to her homeland.

"Hysteria of the immoral alien," Howe wrote, "was followed by a two-year panic over the 'Hun.' . . . During these years thousands of Germans, Austrians and Hungarians were taken without trial from their homes and brought to Ellis Island. . . . From our entrance into the war until after the armistice my life was a nightmare. My telephone rang constantly with inquiries from persons seeking news of husbands and fathers who had been arrested. On my return home in the evening I would often find awaiting me women in a state of nervous collapse whose husbands had mysteriously disappeared, and who feared that they had been done away with." For his efforts to protect the rights of such men and women Howe found himself accused of that most heinous crime—of being "pro-German."

We are reminded by Jane Addams of the agony of conscience experienced by many pacifists. She was acutely troubled by the moral and philosophical problems raised by finding herself in opposition to the majority of her fellow Americans. "Our modern democratic teaching," she wrote, "has brought us to regard popular impulses as possessing in their general tendency a valuable capacity for evolutionary development." In hours of "doubt and self-distrust" the question haunted her: Has "the individual or a very small group the right to stand against millions of his fellow countrymen? Is there not a great value," she asked, "in mass judgment and in instinctive mass enthusiasm . . . ?" Was it not, above all, wrong to abstain "from this communion with his fellows"? Addams found solace in the thought that most great changes began in "a variation from the mass . . . with a differing group of individuals, sometimes with one who at best is designated as a crank and a freak and in sterner moments is imprisoned as an atheist or a traitor." The tormenting issue was when "the differing individual becomes the centro-egotist, the insane man, who must be thrown out by society for its own protection. . . . " When he was seen in this light, it was "perfectly natural for the mass to call such an individual a traitor and to insist that if he is not for the nation he is against it." Her friends pleaded with her to abandon her opposition to the war. She was, they argued, "committing intellectual suicide, and would never again be trusted" as a responsible person.

In the agonizing dialogue she carried on within herself and with the handful of like-minded friends, she recalled that "every student of our time had become more or less a disciple of pragmatism and its great teachers in the United States had come out for the war and defended their positions with skill and philosophic acumen." Was it not, after all, the *final war*, a war to end wars and spread the blessings of freedom or self-determination and democracy all over the world?

The attacks on Addams and her sense of isolation undoubtedly contributed to a severe case of pneumonia and a long and dismal period of bad health which followed. For three years, she wrote, "I experienced a bald sense of social opprobrium and wide-spread misunderstanding which brought me very near to self pity, perhaps the lowest pit into which human nature can sink."

Opposition to the war was not confined to pacifists and urban radicals. There stirred in the rural Midwest the old fires of populism. The Green Corn Rebellion, so called from the staple of the diet of the men and women who made up the ranks of the rebels, swept through the hill country of Arkansas, Tennessee, Kentucky, and Georgia, spilling over into Texas and Oklahoma. At its heart were the Pentecostal churches, the Holy Rollers, Nazarenes, the "hard-shell" and the "shouting" Baptists, and the fundamentalist Methodists. In the words of a historian of the movement, "Originally the Democratic Party claimed the allegiance of the great majority, but economic conditions exerted more pressure than precedent, and many turned to Socialism as a sort of gospel of despair." Far from being aliens, many of them had names that could be traced back to Washington's army at Valley Forge. The organizational form that the Green Corn Rebellion took was the Working Class Union and the Jones Family, both secret societies committed to violent action against the war.

Oscar Ameringer offered the following dialogue as an example of the mood of the rebellious tenant farmers. When he went to confer with their leaders, he was told, "We are going to stop this damn war the gang out East has foisted on us."

"But how?" Ameringer asked.

"On a given signal we'll slam the bankers, county officials, and newspaper owners in jail. . . . That will give us the money, government and press of our counties."

"And then?"

"We'll burn railroad trestles, bridges and blow up pipe lines."

When Ameringer expressed his skepticism that so small a group could accomplish such large objectives, the leaders of the Working Class Union told him that they had 70,000 members in Colorado, twice as many in Texas, and 19,000 Wobblies in Chicago, "waiting for the signal to break loose." They all were armed, and the coalfields contained enough dynamite to blow up the country. Ameringer tried to shatter their illusions. They could be sure, he told them, that their ranks were filled with informers and that the government knew of their intentions. Indeed, he would be surprised if a hidden Dictaphone were not at that moment recording their conversation and an informer were not among those present. For the record he would state his own views. "I am convinced," he declared, "beyond the slightest shadow of a doubt that the American people did not want this war, that it is not a war to make the world safe for democracy, nor a war to end war. I believe this war was foisted on the American people by their lying press, politicians, warmongers and munitions manufacturers, and by the bankers who are making billions out of the agony of mankind."

As for their rebellion, it was quixotic beyond words. It had not the slightest hope of success. Their numbers were fantasies of their imagination. There were not 19,000 Wobblies in the entire country, and most of those were in the Northwest. "All you will do," he warned them, "is destroy the splendid Socialist movement we have built in Oklahoma at such a high cost of labor and sacrifice. . . . Our movement will not recover from that blow for many years. Perhaps never. As for you and your following, you will all be hounded like wild beasts. Some of you will be killed. . . . You are marked men, so scatter, while the scattering is good."

Nothing Ameringer could say would deflect the rebels, and as he had predicted, when the rebellion fizzled out with a few bridges blown up and half a dozen of the rebels dead or wounded, the rest experienced the full weight of official wrath. They were rounded up by the hundreds. Jails were so overcrowded that 400 men were shipped to the state penitentiary, while thousands of men, women, and children took refuge in the Winding Stair mountain range, which ran into Texas and Arkansas. About 30 ended up in Leavenworth. There they sat until Kate Richards O'Hare, recently freed from the Jefferson City jail herself, led their wives and children to Washington to picket President Harding's White House in 1921. It was one of the most poignant and dramatic episodes in American history. The press gave it nationwide attention, and Harding, who, whatever his faults may have been, had a compassionate nature, ordered the pathetic residue of the Green Corn Rebellion set free.

The most relentless persecution was directed at Americans with German names. Dissenters had at least to draw attention to themselves by some statement or action judged by the organs of the law to be treasonable or by their neighbors to be in some degree offensive, but German-Americans had only to exist and have some identifiable German feature—most commonly, a name—to become victims of violence. When Frank Little, Bill Haywood's lieutenant in the IWW, was lynched by a mob, a man whose principal crime was that he had a German name was lynched at the same time. It was discovered later that he had invested in war bonds and supported the Allied cause.

A survey showed a German-born population of 1,337,000, with some 500,000 unnaturalized German citizens at the outbreak of the war and 10,000,000 Americans of German ancestry. In addition, there were between 3,000,000 and 4,000,000 "Austro-Hungarian enemy aliens." Some 6,000 "enemy aliens" were jailed under so-called presidential warrants which bypassed regular legal proceedings and left the accused individuals without the normal protection of the laws.

A Liberty loan speaker, urging his audience to buy bonds, called for the merciless killing of Germans, "the snakes of the human race," who must be "stamped out." He added, "No, I apologize to the snakes and to the animal kingdom. There is nothing in it so low and vile as a German." A friend said to Villard, "It must be terribly hard for you. I hear you have seventeen first cousins on the German front line." Villard was one of the founders (and the president) of the Philharmonic Society. A member of the board of directors visited him to ask him to resign from his office and from the board; another director led a fight to prevent the playing of Beethoven.

In those states with large populations of German descendants, like Nebraska and North Dakota, a special effort was made to prove loyalty to the United States by buying Liberty bonds. In North Dakota the first Liberty loan was oversubscribed by 140 percent.

George Creel found that anti-German propaganda had got out of hand. The Committee on Public Information was wary, he insisted, of "undocumented 'atrocity stories.' " But private organizations of patriots were less scrupulous. The promoters of the Liberty loan drives, for example, "flooded the country with posters showing 'bloody boots,' trampled children and mutilated women." The most bloody-minded were the National Security League and the American Defense Society; "at all times," Creel wrote, "their patriotism was a thing of screams, violence and extremes." Prominent among their demands was that no other language than English be taught or spoken. They conducted a campaign to change German street and place-names. The governor of Iowa, yielding to such pressures, issued an edict that "English . . . must be the only medium of instruction in public, private, denominational or other similar schools . . . [and] conversation on trains or over the telephone must be in the English language." Finally, those who could not understand English must conduct religious services in their homes. There were instances in which meetings of foreign-born citizens were stoned by patriotic Americans. There was tarring and feathering by self-appointed vigilantes. In some communities foreigners were forced to reveal their incomes to "committees" and then told what proportion they must contribute to Liberty bonds. A group of writers that included a number of former reformers and muckrakers formed an organization called the Vigilantes to travel through such states as Wisconsin,

Minnesota, and Missouri where opposition to the war was strong. Ray Stannard Baker was originally a member, but his determined effort at objectivity offended his fellow writers, and he was upbraided for refusing to distribute virulent anti-German pamphlets that seemed to him "inexcusably violent and unauthentic."

German as a language was eliminated from most school curricula. Professors of German extraction were subjected to investigations and forced to sign oaths attesting to their loyalty. German dishes were excluded from restaurant menus or their names were changed. People signed pledges not to buy articles of German manufacture, read German books, or sing German songs.

All these happenings, Oscar Ameringer wrote later, were the incidents that the history books, by and large, ignored—"the sweetless, wheatless, meatless, heatless and perfectly brainless days," when people "broke Beethoven's records, boycotted Wagner's music, burned German books, painted German Lutheran churches and Goethe's monument in Chicago the color of Shell Filling Stations today; strung up a Mennonite preacher in . . . Oklahoma, by his neck until he fainted, repeated the process until he fainted again, and then graciously relented; hanged another [Robert Praeger] to a tree in Collinsville, Illinois, until he was dead, and later, ransacking the room of the corpse for pro-Kaiser evidence, the executioners found that their victim had been refused service in the American army for physical defects." Pacifist Christians fared no better. Ameringer knew of other Mennonites and Seventh-Day Adventists arrested for refusal to serve in the army and tortured to death by their jailers. German-Americans or, more commonly, Americans with German names were called Huns, baby killers, kaiser lovers, and alien enemies. An old German friend of Ameringer's who had served in the Civil War and been wounded in the Battle of Lookout Mountain, was hunted down by a self-appointed committee that came to his house and demanded to see his naturalization papers. When the old man could produce none, he was carried off to the county seat, photographed and fingerprinted, and declared an "enemy alien." Many Germans were placed under a kind of house arrest. They could not leave their houses after nine o'clock at night (or whatever some committee of local vigilantes established as the curfew hour) or go more than a mile from their homes. One old German complained bitterly to Ameringer that the saloon where he got his daily mug of beer was a few hundred yards beyond the mile radius. Between them the Germans and the Socialists of Milwaukee managed to keep that city a kind of oasis of sanity "in the elsewhere universal madness," in Ameringer's words.

To Willard Straight, who was with the American Expeditionary Forces (AEF) in France, reports of the bloody-mindedness of the people at home were profoundly disturbing. It seemed to him, as he wrote his wife, that Americans were "like a team of draft horses that went along stolidly pulling their load and minding their own business." It took a lot of beating to urge them into a trot and then a run, but once running, "they look neither to the right nor left. You can't stop 'em or turn 'em—they're too stupid and too lacking in subtlety. They'll have to run till they're exhausted. . . . This is the state of mind of our public. They've come in late to the war . . . and they're trying to make up for their former indifference by their present intolerant chauvinism. . . . It's the people who have seen none of it, who sit in their studies and rant. They want to kill all the Germans, damn 'em. . . . What we want to do is to lick the Boche and get the peace we started into this war for. . . . I think many of us will have something to say to the loud-mouthed wild men who are now talking at home. . . . We are sowing seeds which will ripen into a harvest of jealousy and misunderstanding, once they have pushed their way through the soil of war."

The official measures of repression promptly adopted by the government were, in the last analysis, not so damaging to the legions of reform, radical or Progressive, as the divisions in their own ranks that followed Congress's declaration of war. Some Socialists and a few anarchists had already followed the example of Prince Kropotkin and announced their support for the Allies. Arturo Giovanitti, Italian immigrant, leader in the IWW organization, an antimilitarist, and an enemy of capitalism in all its forms, became passionately pro-Ally when Italy entered the war. There had, of course, been numerous defections even before the U.S. entry into the war, but that step created an immediate crisis for the Socialist Party. Its leaders called an emergency meeting for April 7 at St. Louis, and there Hillquit, Debs, and Berger called for a condemnation of the Wilson administration for breaking faith with the American people and urged all true socialists to work in every way to bring it to an end. Socialists should oppose conscription and miss no opportunity to advance the cause of peace. In a referendum on the so-called St. Louis Manifesto, it was approved 21,639 to 2,752. Among the defections were some leading Socialists; Charles Edward Russell, Upton Sinclair, Algie Simons, and John Spargo all pledged their support to Wilson and the war, some on the ground that the European allies were the lesser of two evils. The decision was obviously more difficult for the leaders than for the rank-and-file Socialists. Already in the public eye, they were far more vulnerable to arrest and imprisonment or, at the least, harassment and abuse. The case of John Spargo, a well-known writer on socialism, was representative, if not typical. A British miner, Spargo had immigrated to the United States in 1901 and become a leader in the Socialist Party. He was an adversary of Big Bill Haywood and his particular brand of revolutionary unionism as well as an outspoken opponent of United States entry into the war. Spargo had denounced preparedness as a sinister attempt "to commit this nation to militarism. . . . " After Congress had declared war, he took the line that the war might in fact advance the cause of socialism by hastening the downfall of reactionary regimes, a not wholly inaccurate conjecture. In addition, he believed that support of the war by the Socialists might help bring more workers into the Socialist Party. He thus joined with George Creel, head of the Committee on Public Information, the government's propaganda arm, and worked with Samuel Gompers as well to negate the People's Council.

Spargo and the Socialists who supported the war pushed for a commission to be sent to Russia to try to prevail on the revolutionary leadership to continue the war against the Central Powers. This effort culminated, as we have noted, in the so-called Root Commission.

Clarence Darrow explained his support for the war in an eloquent and loudly applauded speech in Madison Square Garden, and Charles Edward Russell, in his autobiography, noted bitterly that after the war "Parlor Pinkdom pardoned all his offenses but declined the least amnesty for mine, which only (and humbly) duplicated his." When he looked back on the war from the perspective of the early thirties, Russell was confident "that the United States brought peace to a war-shattered and despairing world and saved it from the illimitable disaster that threatened it." To him it was enough that "three old, medieval, autocratic monarchies that had ruled to military madness the destinies of 300,000,000 people" came tumbling down and were replaced by "a group of republics." The nations he had in mind were, presumably, Germany and its allies Austria and Hungary.

Russell's observation that "The greater part of the Socialist party membership was composed of Germans and Jews" was simply a fact. But it was used to justify or explain the opposition of many socialists to the war. The Jewish hostility toward Russia was eminently understandable. Russia had driven them from their homeland. Many other Jews held the memory of the Dreyfus case as a symbol of French anti-Semitism (as, of course, it was). The result, in any event, was to make them averse to a war in which France and Russia were the "good guys" and, it might be argued, less inclined to rationalizations that would allow them to support the war. "Essentially," Russell wrote, "Socialism is international. . . . Yet is is true that a majority of our members sympathized with Germany and hoped she would win." Germany's victory would be Russia's defeat.

To whatever side they gave their allegiance, it would be a mistake to impugn the motives or intelligence of the Socialist leaders. Honest men and good men differed. The tragedy was that out of their differences there often grew irreconcilable bitterness and enduring hostility. Men and women who had loved and trusted each other and worked valiantly and unselfishly in common causes for the benefit of those of their countrymen suffering most acutely from the gross inequities in American society came to denounce each other as traitors and turncoats and no longer spoke. If the "war damage" had been no more than that, it would have been bad enough. For lives lost and friendships shattered there were, indeed, no reparations. The schism was more than the sum of all the personal tragedies. It was a social disaster of considerable magnitude. It affected primarily, although not exclusively, the socialists and anarchists, in whose ranks were virtually all those Americans committed to political and economic reform. The ranks of reform were thereby much more than decimated. A general demoralization set in, a kind of debilitating spiritual lassitude that was more deadly than persecution.

In addition to the devastating effects of the United States' entry into the European conflict on American socialism and radicalism in general, it virtually destroyed the country's most promising liberal politician, Robert La Follette. La Follette, one of the six Senators who voted against American entry into the war, was burned in effigy on the campus of the University of Wisconsin, an institution that had benefited in innumerable ways from his warm support, a university the faculty and students of which had indeed achieved a degree of notoriety for their radical and progressive principles.

In North Dakota the Nonpartisan League, an offshoot of La Follette's Wisconsin Progressives, supported their onetime hero's plea for free speech but rejected his explanation of the "causes of the war and . . . his interpretation of the events leading up to it." When La

Follette, in a speech in St. Paul discussing the decision to enter the war, declared, "We had grievances," the Associated Press reported that he had said, "We have *no* grievances," bringing a storm of public denunciation. There was a movement in the Senate to expel him and a resolution dissociating the Senate from his views. A letter to the *New York Times* declared that only Aaron Burr was "more ready to betray democracy for his own selfish ends."

In Frederic Howe's opinion, La Follette was "the best-loved man in America." For a quarter of a century he had done "at least two men's work, fighting the special interests, assailing the trusts and the protective tariff in the Senate, and attempting to hold the railroads in leash." He represented in his person the resistance of the Middle West to the war. As a consequence, he was denounced by Wilson as a "willful man" and was mercilessly attacked by the press. Even old allies in manifold causes abandoned him. Again in Howe's words, "Threatened by disease and harassed financially, he bore his isolation without complaint; accepted no friendship which impaired his freedom, never compromised with conviction, and displayed unflinching courage. . . ."

Yet there was to be an antidote to all the frustration and the numerous setbacks and disappointments experienced by American radicals in and out of the labor movement. There came the electrifying word of the overthrow of the czar. In Emma Goldman's words, "the light of hope broke in the east. . . . The day so long yearned for had come! . . . The glorious tidings were the first sign of life in the vast European cemetery of war and destruction." Individuals as different in background and political views as Lincoln Steffens, Frank Walsh, and Big Bill Haywood were enraptured by the intimations of a new order, the form of which might be dimly discerned in Mexico and now, far more dramatically, in Russia. Forces of almost incomprehensible magnitude were manifesting themselves. Age-old wrongs, it appeared, were about to be made right. Only the dullest and most conventional spirit could fail to be moved by the spectacle. For Russian exiles around the world, perhaps especially for Russian Jews in the United States, the dream of a redeemed Mother Russia purged by the fires of revolution was irresistible. Thousands hastened back to Russia, "now the Land of Promise," as an ecstatic Goldman put it. "Like swallows at the first sign of spring they began to fly back, orthodox and revolutionists for once on common ground—their love and longing for their native soil." To Americans of all shades of political opinion, united only in their conviction that a new and more humane social order must unfold,

Russia assumed an enormous symbolic potency. The worldwide revolution that in time was to transform every society had begun in the unlikeliest of places: the backward and overwhelmingly agricultural empire of the czars. Marxist theoreticians were fertile with explanations of why this deviation from dogma had taken place. To the great majority of radicals and liberals that it had happened was enough. Big Bill Haywood from his prison cell at Leavenworth hailed it as the forerunner of the "Red Dawn," the beginning of a glorious worldwide revolution. He wrote to Margaret Sanger: "You remember what I said at the railroad station about 'it coming,' Margaret, all my dreams are coming true. My work is being fulfilled, millions of workers are seeing the light, Russia, Poland, Germany, France, Great Britain, Australia, South America, we have lived to see the breaking of the glorious Red Dawn. . . . The world revolution is born, the change is here. We will of course not live to see it in its perfection. But it is good to have been living at this period."

With the overthrow of the czar, Russia became a vast enigma for which, suddenly, both Germany and the Allies found themselves competing. George Creel suggested to Wilson that a representative of the Committee on Public Information be sent at once to Russia to initiate a propaganda effort there, and the editor of *Cosmopolitan* magazine, Edgar Sisson, was chosen for the job. Soon he was posting billboards and grinding out pamphlets in Russia, informing the people of the friendship and interest of the United States. He was disconcerted to find that Lenin and Trotsky made little distinction between "a democracy like the United States and an absolutism like Germany," as the indignant Sisson expressed it. "America is a financial empire and so is Germany," he was told. "Both exploit the working class, although the United States is slyer, covering up its capitalistic oppressions with a lot of smooth phrases. As far as we are concerned, they are one and the same, and it is our hope that each will destroy the other." It was soon evident to Sisson that Lenin and Trotsky were hand in glove with the Germans, receiving money from the German Imperial Bank and advice from the German general staff.

The Stockholm Conference, called by the Russians in September, 1917, was intended as the basis for a socialist program to take over the governments of the nations at war and make peace. The plan was not as bizarre as it might appear at first glance. In all the warring nations there were Socialist parties of varying degrees of political potency. Most of them had, to be sure, supported their respective governments at the outbreak of the war, but as the war dragged on with its dreadful toll of casualties, its profoundly reactionary character became more and more evident. In addition, the socialists in all countries were, at least initially, charmed and inspired by the Russian Revolution. England had a strong and vocal Socialist Party which, by 1916, had joined forces with those upper-class conservative Britons who feared that a more protracted struggle would mean the collapse of the British government and the end of traditional British life. There was thus in Britain a peace movement made up of the extreme left and fairly far right.

The fact was that in the crumbling ruins of the Austro-Hungarian Empire and the general dissolution of ancient autocracies, a number of brief Socialist regimes did rise to (or seize) power. Wilson made his own views evident in a letter to Lansing in May, 1917, writing: "I do not like the movement among the socialists to confer about international affairs. They are likely to make a great deal of mischief, especially in connection with affairs in Russia." The U.S. government announced that there would be no American representatives and that individuals from radical or pacifist organizations would not receive passports to go to Stockholm. The *Saturday Review* in London dismissed the conference as a gathering of "tricksters and traitors," and even Lincoln Steffens suspected it of being a cover for some scheme of the kaiser's.

The difficulty of securing passports was not, as it turned out, limited to the United States. The fear that peace might break out was shared by the warring nations. The conference had therefore to be postponed. The People's Council, determined to hold its own conference, tried to find a host town. It was said that Governor Lynn Frazier of North Dakota had offered the hospitality of his state. Fargo, South Dakota, a stronghold of radical farm protest, was also considered. Minneapolis was settled on, but the governor of Minnesota forbade the conference to convene in his state. Finally, William Hale Thompson, the reform mayor of Chicago, allowed it to meet in that city. There it was challenged by an avowed workingmen's organization—the American Alliance for Labor and Democracy—prompted by Creel and Gompers, whose mission it was to refute any implication that American labor did not support the war.

Wilson's encouragement of or acquiescence in the repression of dissent brought a strong reaction from liberals generally. John Jay

Chapman, who had welcomed the President's war message ecstatically, wrote to his mother early in 1918: "I hate Wilson, as everyone does. He's a mean man."

The question that must be addressed is how Wilson, a liberal intellectual, a man who in hundreds of speeches delivered over the years both before and after the beginning of his political career had praised the Constitution and the Bill of Rights as the foundation stones of the Republic and the essence of democratic government, could turn so quickly and unequivocally against those most basic tenets of democracy? The answer lies in his own temperament rather than in any intellectual rationalization, although certainly he made these as well. He was excessively sensitive to criticism or opposition, a trait that had been evident during his Princeton days. It is, to be sure, a trait not uncommon to us all, but I suspect it can be safely said that it is more evident the more a particular individual is fired by zeal for reform and the conviction that he is right and his opponents are willful enemies of the truth. What G. K. Chesterton in his life of Robert Browning called "the lust of idealism" often starts with love and ends with the slaughter of innocents simply because they could not understand what was best for them. If Woodrow Wilson stopped far short of the "terrible things" that the lust of idealism has prompted other leaders to do, he did, or condoned, things completely inconsistent with his avowed principles.

Frederic Howe, who was often a shrewd psychologist, believed that it was Wilson's loneliness that made him fearful, that inclined him to hate those who opposed him. "Conflict," Howe wrote, "disclosed the Wilson who had bewildered liberals while he was President; who had turned on old friends, who hated Cabot Lodge; who excoriated imperialism, and seized Haiti and Santo Domingo and sent battleships to Veracruz. It disclosed the Wilson who sanctioned the hate propaganda, the Wilson who imprisoned men who quoted him against himself. . . . Mr. Wilson could not bear criticism. Criticism brought his reveries of himself under inspection, and he cherished those reveries. He shielded them, nursed them, lived with them. His dreams had to be kept intact."

The Soda Fountain. Painting by William Glackens, 1935.
(Pennsylvania Academy of Fine Arts)

American Village. Painting by Edward Hopper, 1912. (Collection of Whitney Museum of American Art, New York. Bequest of Josephine N. Hopper. Photo by Geoffrey Clements)

The City from Greenwich Village. Painting by John Sloan, 1922. (*National Gallery of Art, Washington. Gift of Helen Farr Sloan, 1970*)

Mrs. Gamley. Painting by George Luks, 1930. (Collection of Whitney Museum of American Art, New York. Photo by Geoffrey Clements)

The Art Student (Miss Josephine
Nivison). Painting by Robert Henri,
1906. *(Milwaukee Art Museum Collection.
Photo by P. Richard Eells)*

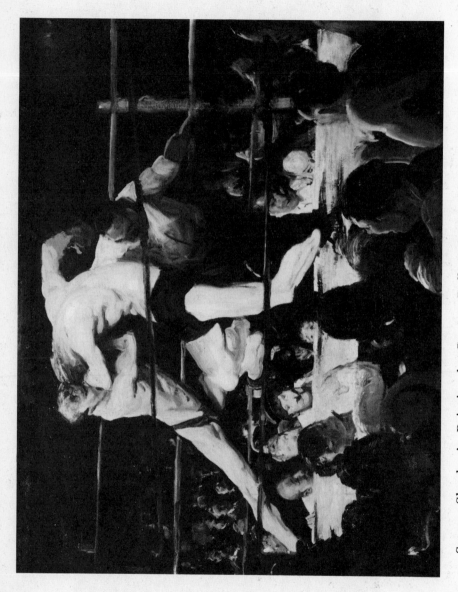

Stag at Sharkey's. Painting by George Bellows. (*The Cleveland Museum of Art, Hinman B. Hurlbut Collection*)

Gull Rock. Painting by Rockwell Kent. *(Courtesy Friends of the Earth)*

Trio. Painting by Walt Kuhn, 1937. (Colorado
Springs Fine Art Center Collection: Gift of the El Pomar
Foundation)

Storm Clouds, Maine. Painting by Marsden Hartley, 1906–07.
(Walker Art Center, Minneapolis. Gift of the T. B. Walker Foundation)

Marin's Island, Maine. Painting by John Marin, 1915. (*Philadelphia Museum of Art: The A. E. Gallatin Collection*)

32

Mobilizing the Nation

Reprehensible as were the suppression of dissent and the official and unofficial persecution of anyone who dared criticize the government, it is indisputably the case that the declaration of war triggered a mobilization of men and war matériel that astonished the world. Moreover, it was Wilson's qualities of leadership that, in the last analysis, brought all this about. Henry Adams, old and ill, confessed himself fascinated "by the singular cleverness and success of His Excellency the President of the United States, especially in upsetting his rivals and making the whole cohort of Republicans and Rooseveltians follow after him . . . [for] they obey him with as much docility as if they were not all the time cursing him with a vocabulary worthy of my extreme youth. . . . Never could I have conceived that in three short months we could have gone into a great war and adopted a conscription not unworthy of Germany, at the bidding of a President who was elected only a few months ago on the express ground that he had kept us at peace."

One of the first considerations was the means of financing the enormous cost of the war. The Progressive stalwarts, Midwest and West, under the leadership of La Follette, Hiram Johnson, George Norris, and James Reed of Missouri, were concerned that the financing of the war not result in increased benefits to those business interests that, in their view, had been most active in pushing the United States toward intervention. Deeply opposed to war on moral and philosophical grounds, they were also apprehensive lest it become the means by which all the reforms that they had fought so hard for were undone; they feared that the country would emerge from the war with capital substantially fatter and its grip on the political and economic system firmer than ever. Under La Follette's leadership they fought the excise taxes and so-called nuisance taxes which they believed imposed a disproportionate hardship on the poor. In this category were taxes on such items as chewing gum, soft drinks, letters, automobiles, theater tickets, gramophones, and moving pictures. La Follette's program called for the principal tax burdens to be borne by those who were the principal profiteers from the war; he espoused excess profits taxes, more steeply graduated income taxes, and, in good Midwestern fashion, high taxes on tobacco and alcohol. Congress passed a bill which provided for a sliding tax scale beginning at 2 percent on incomes of more than $5,000 and rising to 50 percent on those in excess of $2,000,000 a year, but the war effort was financed primarily by the sale of Liberty bonds. Some 9,400,000 purchasers subscribed to bonds in the sum of $3,808,766,150, and an additional $834,000,000 was raised by war stamps, which could be bought in small denominations, pasted in books, and turned in for certificates with maturity dates of January, 1923.

Wilson had two essential tasks: to direct the mobilization of America's vast resources and to fashion a philosophical rationale both for America's entry into the war and for a "peace without victory" at the conclusion of "a war to end all wars." He chose to create a kind of supergovernment run by him through a series of commissions to which he gave extraordinary powers and which he usually backed when their chairmen appealed for support. In line with his theory of the basically dilatory and obstructionist disposition of Congress, he bypassed that body as much as he dared, going to it primarily for greatly expanded powers for himself. His attitude toward Congress was reflected in his closest aides. When George Creel, head of the Committee on Public Information, was giving a talk to a socialist gathering which included many of his former associates, he was asked for his opinion of the "heart of Congress," and he professed ignorance, adding, "I haven't been slumming lately." The comment was reported in the newspapers. Congress was not amused and cut the funds for Creel's committee.

The Lever bill, passed on August 10, 1917, gave the President authority to establish controls over fuel, food, fertilizer, and the requisite machinery. It forbade the use of grains to manufacture "distilled spirits" and thus anticipated Prohibition, and it set the base price of grain at $2 a bushel. Wilson also had the power to fix the price of coal. Harry Garfield, son of the assassinated president and president of Williams College, was appointed director of the Fuel Administration.

However aloof and autocratic his disposition, Wilson unquestionably had a keen instinct for finding superior men to give effect to his plans and policies. Bernard Baruch was one such individual. As an early proponent of the Council of National Defense and a major financial contributor to Wilson's presidential campaign, Baruch was close to Wilson and was appointed by him to head the War Industries Board. There the "speculator," as he preferred to call himself (rather than "financier"), proved as able and autocratic as his boss.

At the beginning of the war the Council of National Defense had on its staff 408 persons, only 168 of whom were paid. The Women's Committee of the council listed among its volunteer members Anna Howard Shaw, Ida Tarbell, and Carrie Chapman Catt. Delegates from sixty women's organizations all over the country met with the Women's Committee on June 19, 1917, and plans were made to involve women in a wide range of organizations, but it was evident that many women were strongly opposed to American involvement in the war. The result was some distressing clashes between women who had worked together harmoniously for decades in various reform movements.

William McAdoo, the President's son-in-law, was another wartime "czar." McAdoo was made "director general" of the nation's railroads. Indeed, he wore half a dozen hats as secretary of the treasury and chairman of the Federal Reserve Board, the Farm Loan Board, and the War Finance Corporation, as well as administrator of the War Risk Insurance Bureau. As secretary of the treasury McAdoo had established a 2 percent interest on all government deposits and forced down interest rates. His railroad reforms were equally dramatic. In George Creel's words, "Worthless executives, drawing down hundreds of thousands of dollars in salaries and bonuses were kicked out; railroad workers were granted the right to organize and bargain collectively. . . ." In addition, McAdoo ended discrimination against women, establishing the principle of equal pay for equal work, and fought for child labor laws and workmen's compensation.

Samuel Gompers told Wilson that in his opinion, the only hope of holding labor behind the war was by specific promises for the improvement of working conditions and presidential support of the principle of unionization. The President's response was to appoint Gompers to the Industrial Relations Council of the War Industries Board. It was a feather in Gompers's cap and a gesture toward labor generally that helped minimize resistance to the war on the part of the unions.

Frank Walsh, the socialist chairman of the Commission on Industrial Relations, had been an active pacifist, but he, like Gompers, threw his support to the government. As a member of the War Labor Board and indeed co-chairman with former President Taft, Walsh had an opportunity to put into operation some modest reforms in labor practices that the Commission on Industrial Relations had recommended. Taft, the conservative, was strikingly liberalized by his own experience on the board. When Walsh accused Taft of being the board's "most radical member," the former president replied, "You're just a conservative."

A number of other committees operated under the aegis of the War Industries Board. Among them was the Committee on Supplies and Munitions, headed by Julius Rosenwald, the president of Sears, Roebuck. Under its direction aeronautical engineers, working around the clock, produced the blueprints for the Liberty engine, which was to power most of the airplanes manufactured in the United States and to be shipped to the Allies in substantial numbers before the end of the war.

The Aircraft Production Board was soon coordinating the design and manufacture of fighting planes. An Automotive Transport Committee pushed the production of military vehicles, while the Emergency Construction Committee directed the building of barracks and mess halls at designated enlistment and training sites.

The Committee on Raw Materials, chaired by Baruch, emerged as the most essential of the new agencies. To conserve steel, Baruch issued an order banning metal ribs in women's corsets, thereby not only bringing the New Freedom to the feminine torso but saving enough steel to make two warships. The board, in Baruch's words, "mobilized more than three hundred and fifty industries, from asbestos through caskets to lumber and zinc. No steel, copper, cement, rubber, or other basic materials could be used without our approval."

Baruch found that his two principal antagonists were the automobile industry, led by Henry Ford, and the steel industry, led by shrewd and stubborn Judge Elbert Gary. Meeting with Horace Dodge,

Ford, and other automakers, Baruch received a tongue-lashing from Dodge for daring to suggest that the government interfere with the decisions of industrial managers. That was little better than socialism, he declared. Ford was only slightly less testy. "Not even the fact of war," Baruch wrote, "was sufficient to win them from their laissez-faire convictions that government intervention was somehow un-American."

Seeing that appeals to reason or patriotism were unavailing, Baruch picked up a handy telephone and put through a call to McAdoo at the Railroad Administration. With the auto tycoons listening, Baruch said, "Mac, I want you to take down the names of the following factories, and I want you to stop every wheel going in and out." He thereupon read off the names of Dodge, Ford, General Motors, and the other automobile manufacturers that were refusing to cooperate. William Crapo Durant of General Motors was the first to capitulate. "I quit," he declared. The others followed. Later Dodge apologized to Baruch and invited him to come to his room for a drink of bootleg booze. Baruch refused; Dodge died of drinking the impure liquor.

The problem of bringing down steel prices was equally pressing. Baruch finally brought the steel manufacturers around by threatening to take over their factories. An unrepentant Gary charged after the war that "subversive influences in the government [by which it was clear he meant primarily Baruch] had sought to nationalize the steel industry as the first step toward undoing America's free enterprise system."

Another important member of the War Industries Board was Charles Schwab, at the height of his spectacular career as head of the Bethlehem Steel Company. Schwab was the classic (and comparatively rare) poor boy who made good. He had grown up in the shadow of the steel mills, driven stakes, worked as a laborer, and then, befriended by Carnegie, begun a dizzying ascent through the levels of management to become a top executive in the United States Steel Corporation and, subsequently, head of Bethlehem Steel.

The stenographer of the War Industries Board was a young man with an inordinate interest in the theater named Billy Rose.

The greatest contribution of the War Industries Board, in Baruch's view, was that it had "demonstrated the effectiveness of industrial cooperation and the advantage of government planning and direction. We had helped inter the extreme dogmas of laissez-faire, which had for so long molded American economic and political thought," he wrote. "Our experience taught that government direction of the economy need not be inefficient or undemocratic, and suggested that in time of danger it was imperative."

Edward Stettinius, head of the Diamond Match Company and later a partner in the House of Morgan, was appointed assistant secretary of war and put in charge of military procurement.

With Wilson as honorary head of the Red Cross and a Morgan partner, Henry Davison, as director, that organization took over a wide range of important duties having to do primarily with aid to the Allied ill and wounded and the needs and comforts of the soldiers in the field. By the end of the war it counted 20,000,000 members in 17,186 branches scattered about the country.

William Allen White, too old to serve in the trenches, put on the uniform of a Red Cross lieutenant colonel and set out for Europe as an "inspector" whose real assignment was to "write up" for various newspapers and journals the wartime activities of the Red Cross.

Among the friends White encountered in France were the Fishers, Dorothy Canfield, the writer, and her husband, John, who was driving an ambulance for the French. Ambulance driving was a well-established activity for many ardently pro-British Eastern upper-class Americans who longed to aid the Allied cause.

From his labors as head of the Commission for Relief in Belgium, Hoover was summoned by Wilson to become head of the United States Food Administration in May, 1917. It was at Hoover's initiative that Wilson formed his so-called War Cabinet, made up of the heads of the various committees and commissions that he had established to take charge of the different aspects of the war effort—munitions, food, fuel, shipping, railways, and trade—plus the secretaries of state, war, navy, and the treasury. If Herbert Hoover had not been born exactly in a cabin, the plain little four-room board and lath house in West Branch, Iowa, where he saw the light of day in 1874, was the next thing to it. After the deaths of his Quaker parents the ten-year-old Hoover was sent to live with an aunt and uncle in Newberg in the Willamette Valley of Oregon. There he had a classic American small-town boyhood, which included "baseball, jigsaws, building dams, swimming, fishing and exploring the woods with other village boys." The woods were, for him, a "never-ending journey of discovery . . . hunts for grouse and expeditions for trout." A visitor from the East planted in Hoover the dream of becoming an engineer. He heard that a new "free" university was being opened in California as a result of the philanthropy of Senator Leland Stanford. Public examinations were to be held in Portland. Hoover received a friendly reception from mathematics professor Joseph Swain, "a well-known Quaker," and was encouraged to enroll. When Hoover was graduated from Stanford with an engineering degree, he began a spectacular career as a mining engineer that, starting in Australia, carried him in time through a half dozen countries—including Russia, China, South Africa, and Canada—first as a representative of American mining interests and finally as a partner in his own company.

Hoover was a "new man," a representative of the new consciousness of the new age. Engineers were replacing inventors as culture heroes. They roamed the world, building railroads, bridges, and dams for hydroelectric projects, carrying American know-how and American capital to the remotest regions of the world. As men who unlocked the riches hidden under the earth, and harnessed the energies of coal and water, they were the new alchemists. Wherever they went, they turned dross into gold, primarily for the benefit of American (but also British, French, German, and Italian) investors since capitalism, as we have seen, was increasingly international. Hoover was not an eloquent writer, but he grew lyrical when he described his profession. Mining engineers, he wrote, were those fortunate individuals "who follow the gods of engineering to that success marked by an office of one's own in a large city." To reach that goal, they had to be prepared "to live for years on the outside borders of civilization; where beds are hard, where cold bites and heat burns, where dress-up clothes are a new pair of overalls, where there is little home life—not for weeks but for years. . . . The engineer learns through work with his own hands not only the mind of the worker but the multitude of true gentlemen among them. On the other hand, men who love a fight with nature, who like to build and see their building grow, men who do not hold themselves above manual labor, men who have the moral courage to do these things soundly, some day will be able to move to town, wear white collars every day, and send out their youngsters to the lower rungs and the frontiers of industry."

There was an unusual uniformity of opinion among those who met Hoover, still, at age forty-three, a comparatively young man. Walter Lippmann, working in George Creel's propaganda operation, described Hoover as a man "who incarnates all that is at once effective and idealistic in the picture of America." He found Hoover "an entrancing talker," adding he had "never met a more interesting man, anyone who knew so much of the world and could expound so clearly what to almost all Americans in 1917 were the inscrutable mysteries of European politics." Felix Frankfurter was equally impressed. He thought Hoover a "truly great man. Belgium has smelted him clean of any alloy of self concern. . . . Now he is an extraordinarily competent man completely devoted to keep life going in half the world—literally to keep life going." George Creel was one of the few dissenters. When Wilson asked how Creel got along with Hoover, he replied that Hoover always gave him the feeling of "a cockroach sliding around in a porcelain bathtub."

As the head of the Food Administration Hoover displayed the skill in organization that had made him famous as director of Belgium relief. Various incentives were offered farmers to improve their efficiency and increase production. The President in his war message had assured the farmers that the agencies of government "will do everything possible to assist farmers in securing an adequate supply of seed, an adequate force of laborers when they are most needed, at harvest time, and the means of expediting shipments of fertilizers and farm machinery, as well as of crops themselves when harvested. . . . This is our opportunity to demonstrate the efficiency of a great Democracy and we shall not fall short of it!" Among the measures taken by the Federal government to help the farmer become more productive were "the prevention, control, and eradication of the diseases and pests of live stock; the enlargement of live-stock production, and the conservation and utilization of meat, poultry, dairy, and other animal products; procuring, storing, and furnishing seeds for cash at cost to farmers in restricted areas where emergency conditions prevailed; the prevention, control and eradication of insects and plant diseases . . . and the conservation and utilization of plant products; the further development of the cooperative agricultural extension service . . . ; gathering and disseminating information concerning farm products . . . ; preventing the waste of food in storage, in transit, or held for sale; . . . enlarging the facilities for dealing with the farm-labor problem. . . ." In fifteen Southern states the number of community organizations established to help county agents increased from 1,654 to 2,508, and clubs organized among rural women multiplied from 250 to 1,042. The membership in rural boys' clubs in the region designed to train and entertain future farmers grew to 100,000, and those in the North and West to more than 400,000. Production of farm products increased substantially, and more than 1,000,000 head of cattle were grazed in national forests.

A few days after the formal declaration of war by the United States, David Lloyd George told the American Luncheon Club in London, "The road to victory, the guaranty of victory, the absolute assurance of victory, has to be found in one word, ships, in a second word, ships, and a third word, ships." In the second quarter of 1917 the Germans sank 1,360,000 tons of British shipping, making a total of 5,360,000 since the start of the war.

When Lloyd George spoke, it was estimated that one out of every four ships leaving British ports fell victim to a German submarine. Soon the phrase "bridge of ships" was on everyone's tongue. The problem was that America understood by its entry into the war that it was committed to rushing soldiers to France to fight alongside its allies. The British and French had a somewhat different view. In danger of running out of food and munitions, they wished, above all, for American supplies carried on American ships, armed or convoyed by destroyers. They doubted that American soldiers could be recruited, trained, and shipped overseas in time to play any significant role in the ground warfare. Indeed, they feared that shipping diverted to transporting American soldiers would be shipping desperately needed to supply the French and British armies. The French ambassador had said to David Houston a few days earlier, "I do not know whether you will enter the war or not, but if you do, we shall not expect you—and I am sure that I am speaking the sentiments of my government—to send any men to France except a detachment, for sentimental reasons, to return the visit of Rochambeau. We shall want you to aid us mainly on the sea and with credits and supplies."

Edward Filene, the department store tycoon, encouraged Allied fears by his calculation that it would take four tons of shipping for every American soldier sent overseas. The Emergency Fleet Corporation was given the assignment of building a large merchant marine fleet, and Major General George Goethals, builder of the Panama Canal, was put in charge. Henry Ford cooperated with a plan for a shipbuilding assembly line at his River Rouge plant. The government, meanwhile, took over 431 ships under construction in American shipyards, 97 interned German ships (among them the *Vaterland,* renamed the *Leviathan*), and 87 Dutch ships in American ports. Goethals set a production target of 1,700 steel ships and 1,000 smaller wooden freighters.

The proliferation of committees and subcommittees under the general jurisdiction of the War Industries Board seemed endless. Sergeant Irving Berlin was assigned by the Committee on Supplies to procure sheet music for the 390 bands that were to accompany the American Expeditionary Forces, the AEF for short. There was even a Brassiere War Service Committee.

The alien property custodian was A. Mitchell Palmer, a Quaker whose religious principles had induced him to refuse Wilson's offer of the office of secretary of war. It was Palmer's assignment to search out and seize in the name of the government all property owned by enemy aliens. Palmer discovered a surprising amount of war matériel manufactured or in the possession of enemy nationals hiding behind the façades of legitimate business enterprises.

However oppressive the rule of capitalism may have been, however harsh its treatment of its workers and arrogant its interventions in the political realm, it was difficult to fault its capacity to accomplish practical tasks demanding organizational skill and imagination of a high order.

One of Wilson's most important appointments was that of Creel himself to head the all-important Committee on Public Information, or CPI, as it was called, the brainchild of Newton D. Baker. In light of Creel's long history as a radical reformer, his brash manners and flashy clothes, it was a bold move by Wilson, and he was loudly criticized for it. If Creel was not quite as brilliant a success as he claimed in his autobiography, he did a remarkable job and raised the art of public relations, if we may call it that, to a new level of professional competence. Baker wrote, perhaps more ominously than he intended, that the victory of the Allies would rest, in the last analysis, on "the mental forces that were at work." To the CPI fell the power to control, in large measure, what Americans read and heard. In place of censorship Creel urged a policy of "voluntary agreement" under the terms of which newspapers and magazines would agree to print nothing that could damage the war effort or imperil the lives of American soldiers or sailors. *"Expression, not suppression,* was the real need," he insisted, adding, "During the three and a half years of our neutrality the United States had been torn by a thousand divisive prejudices, with public opinion stunned and muddled by the pull and haul of Allied and German propaganda. The sentiment of the West was still isolationist; the Northwest buzzed with talk of a 'rich man's war,' waged to salvage Wall Street loans; men and women of Irish stock were 'neutral,' not caring who whipped England, and in every state demagogues raved against 'warmongers.'. . ."

Soon there was a Division of News, and when Charles Dana Gibson walked in with a recruiting poster, a Division of Pictorial Publicity was promptly added. Someone had the inspiration to recruit thousands of speakers nationwide to give brief speeches in movie theaters to defenseless patrons. They were called the Four-Minute Men, and soon 150,000 "trained men were delivering the government's message to the people every week." Creel calculated that in the nineteen months of the war 75,000 men had addressed 7,555,190 audiences, exhorting them to support the war through a wide range of activities from the purchase of war bonds to reporting "slackers" and "draft dodgers" to the proper authorities. Creel labored valiantly to prevail upon government departments and agencies to make information about their activities available to the general public through the journalists and reporters who were members of his staff. His position was that the public wanted and had the right to know all news that would not endanger the war effort, and he was determined not to let the inefficient take refuge behind the plea that national security demanded secrecy. In terms of the collection and dissemination of the news that the government wished to have circulated, the Committee on Public Information did a remarkable job. In line with its policy of not publishing material which it did not know to be factually accurate, the committee, finding that it could not verify most of the atrocity stories turned out by the Allies, refrained from emphasizing them.

To the Four-Minute Men was added a corps of 300 "distinguished and effective speakers"—Americans, French, British, and Polish. The Chautauqua was enlisted as well. A Division of Advertising gave the government $2,000,000 worth of free advertising, and Guy Stanton Ford, chairman of the history department at the University of Minnesota, "called on every distinguished historian in the country" to write pamphlets setting forth the Allied position on every conceivable subject. Among the historians recruited to work for the CPI were Frederick Jackson Turner, Charles Beard, Guy Stanton Ford, J. Franklin Jameson, and Evarts Greene.

The most popular pamphlet was entitled *How the War Came to America,* and 7,000,000 copies of it were distributed, along with 70,000,000 other tracts, "used in schools, published as supplements by newspapers . . . an arsenal from which speakers, officials, and editors drew their ammunition." The motion picture makers cooperated in producing and distributing such films as *Pershing's Crusade, America's Answer,* and *Under Four Flags,* full-length films. Booth Tarkington, Gertrude Atherton, ancient William Dean Howells—now in his eightieth year— William Allen White, and dozens of other writers produced articles on American life and American ideals that were distributed free to newspapers and magazines. Wilson stated the country's war aims in placard paragraphs, which were plastered on billboards all over the country, as well as in Britain and, in translation, in France and Italy. Balloons carried leaflets with American propaganda over the German lines, and agents carried them into Russia. In George Creel's words, "an export licensing system that gave the Committee control over every foot of commercial film that left the country was what enabled us to force the acceptance of [the Committee of Public Information] programs in neutral countries." Gangster and underworld movies "that had done so much to give a false impression of American life" were denied export licenses.

There was, of course, censorship as well as the flood of organized propaganda. "Voluntary agreement" was simply a form of censorship, but papers, articles, journals, and radical newspapers that opposed the war were, as we have seen, rigorously suppressed.

Creel's task was certainly formidable. The image of the United States as a land of freedom, justice, equality, and opportunity that had been so prominent in the decades following the formation of the Union and that had dimmed under the incubus of slavery and the land-grabbing war with Mexico and been renewed with the preservation of the Union and the freeing of the slaves, had been severely tarnished by the bitter war between capital and labor, by the aggressive imperialism of the nation in the closing years of the century, and by the well-publicized stories of municipal corruption in the country's major cities. At the time of the entry of the United States into the war its international reputation was at an all-time low. If the war did nothing else, it replaced that negative image—both internally and externally— with a brilliant, glowing picture of democracy's last and best hope. With all the negative elements, with all the doubts, criticisms, and misgivings ruthlessly suppressed, the nation and the world were flooded with pro-American propaganda. Every familiar chord was struck not once but a thousand times. America the redeemer; America the pure in heart, the wise, the powerful, the benign, the particular vessel of the Almighty. Reams upon reams. We believed it with a great surge of hope and optimism, and so did much of the world, which needed desperately something to believe in. "Before the flood of our publicity," George Creel wrote, somewhat ingenuously, "German lies were swept away. . . . From being the most misunderstood nation, the United States became the most popular. A world that was either inimical or indifferent was changed into a world of well-wishers."

Creel flung his propaganda or "informational" network widely. Professor Charles Merriam, respected Harvard professor, was assigned to set up a propaganda mill in Padua, "for an attack on the morale of Austria." Other professional experts were given similar assignments.

One of the CPI's major propaganda efforts was directed at the much-abused hyphenated Americans. Josephine Roche, an ally of Creel's in the campaign to clean up Denver, was called to Washington to take charge of a Division of Work Among the Foreign Born. "She established close relations," Creel wrote, "with some twenty racial groups . . . and began a drive that carried down from cities to remote hamlets . . . ; through volunteer helpers Miss Roche went into homes and aided bewildered thousands to solve the problems presented by draft regulations . . . and other laws that confused them."

Another commission appointed by the President was the quasi-secret body known simply as the Inquiry, a group of scholarly experts on various nations and, as we would say today, "ethnic groups." The academic specialists—geographers, lawyers, historians, and political scientists—were instructed to examine the tangled state of international politics with special attention to national boundary lines and aspirations for self-determination. Walter Lippmann was its secretary, and Isaiah Bowman, director of the American Geographical Society, head of the section on territorial claims. "What we are on the lookout for," Lippmann wrote Newton D. Baker, "is genius—sheer, startling genius, and nothing else will do. . . ." The members of the Inquiry (the very unpretentiousness of its name and its semisecret or unheralded status were revealing) were a roster of some of the country's most eminent academics. Sidney Edward Mezes, one of the first of a series of distinguished California professors, who had taught philosophy at the University of Texas and been appointed president of the College of the City of New York, was the organizer of "the Inquiry." Bowman, the nation's most distinguished geographer, was a founding member; Charles Homer Haskins, the Harvard historian and graduate of Johns Hopkins University, was dean of medieval studies in the United States and the dean of graduate studies at the Cambridge institution. Haskins and the younger academics who worked under his direction were assigned the problem of the "northwest frontiers": Denmark and the Baltic countries. R. H. Lord, also of Harvard, was in charge of the question of Poland's boundaries and relations with Russia. Charles Seymour, of Yale, was responsible for the redistribution of the Austro-Hungarian Empire. George Beer, the Columbia historian of colonial America, was charged with collecting data and making recommendations for the disposition of the former colonies of the defeated powers. And so it went, through dozens of academic scholars, senior professors aided by graduate students or simply by former students who had caught the attention of their professors.

In the words of its chairman, S. E. Mezes, "The foreign and colonial services [of the European powers] were made up of permanent employees who had lived in these regions, come in contact with their officials and leading men, and in many cases made reports on those lands and the peoples inhabiting them." It was only recently that the American diplomatic and consular services had been put on any kind of professional basis, that men in the Foreign Service had been given secure tenure or treated as career diplomats. The Americans had thus to accomplish in a day, so to speak, what the foreign offices of the Allied powers had accumulated over generations: a body of practical information concerning the repeatedly changing boundaries of Europe and the often conflicting claims of various ethnic groups to their own "homelands." Included in the field of study of the Inquiry were Latin America and, since it was already boiling with revolution, Russia, which was made the object of especially intensive study—"of agriculture, industry, railroads, political habits and customs, racial affiliations, and the like." Perhaps the Inquiry's most important duty was the collection and updating of maps. "Basic maps," Mezes wrote, "were constructed for the whole of Europe and the Near East. . . . In volume this was one of the largest undertakings of The Inquiry . . . aiding, as it did, toward an understanding of the most contentious regions the Conference had to consider." One of these, which did not involve Americans directly, was the Near East, a tangle of ancient hates and modern rivalries. The Hamburg–Baghdad Railway, stretching from the North Sea to the Persian Gulf, symbolized Germany's imperial ambitions in the Near East.

33

Over There

If the Allies were, at least initially, more concerned with receiving American food and munitions, to the Americans the declaration of war meant, above all, soldiers. The essential question was how they were to be obtained. The Cabinet and the Council of National Defense were virtually unanimous in urging a draft rather than depending on volunteers. Either course involved risks. A call for volunteers might be answered in large part by Easterners. In the West, it had to be assumed, there would be little response.

On the other hand, as we have already seen, a draft was bound to be resisted by those opposed to the U.S. participation in the war. Considering the various hazards, the draft seemed the bolder and, in the long run, safer course.

In his appointment of John J. Pershing to head the American Expeditionary Forces, Wilson once more demonstrated his capacity for judging men. He had recalled Pershing from his futile pursuit of Pancho Villa in Mexico. A lesser man might have been tempted to make Pershing the goat of that ill-fated expedition, but Wilson had taken the measure of the man, and he laid on Pershing's broad shoulders the nation's heaviest responsibility aside from his own. Pershing, like

Wilson, was an excellent judge of men, and he assembled a brilliant staff devoted to him and effective instruments of his will.

Tall, handsome, broad-shouldered, with a kind of physical density and presence that impressed all those he met, Pershing had been born in the hamlet of Laclede, Missouri, in 1860, the son of a storekeeper. After his graduation from West Point at the rather advanced age of twenty-six, he had joined the 6th Cavalry in New Mexico soon after the capture of Geronimo. He subsequently commanded the 10th Cavalry (a black regiment in Montana). After a stint as professor of military science and tactics at the University of Nebraska, where he earned a law degree, Pershing was called to West Point as a tactical instructor (actually little more than an exalted drill sergeant). His strict discipline and his unfavorable comparisons of the West Point cadets with his black cavalrymen earned him the nickname of Black Jack Pershing.

Pershing fought in the Spanish-American War (he distinguished himself at San Juan Hill) and later against the Moros in the Philippines. As a military attaché in Japan he had been a witness of the Russo-Japanese War, and on his return to the United States, Roosevelt advanced him to brigadier general over 800 senior officers.

The general, Wilson and Newton D. Baker agreed, must have wide latitude for making his own decisions and running his own show. Baker recalled that his parting words to Pershing before the general left for Europe were, "I will give you only two orders, one to go to France and the other to come home. . . . If you make good, the people will forgive almost any mistake. If you do not make good, they will probably hang us both from the first lamppost they can find."

On May 28, 1917, Pershing sailed for Europe on the White Star liner *Baltic,* and a few weeks later—June 26—a token detachment of American regulars arrived at St.-Nazaire. It was then generally assumed by the Allied high command that the detachment, modestly augmented, would be the limit of American troop participation in the war. The soldiers nonetheless on July 4, 1917, made a brave appearance in Paris, where they were hailed with Gallic enthusiasm as the saviors of France. Pershing established his headquarters in the Rue Constantin and there discovered the true state of the Allied forces. There was open mutiny among many of the exhausted and demoralized French *poilus.* It was Pershing's settled conviction that the British and French forces were too depleted to win the war even with massive infusions of American arms and supplies. Fresh American soldiers would be required to ensure an Allied victory, he told Baker.

The British and French commanders wished to have such U.S. soldiers as could be rushed to France used primarily to replace their own undermanned regiments. They would thus be directly under the command of British and French generals. But Pershing was determined that the American soldiers must fight in their own divisions and corps under his command and that of his staff. In the short, bitter struggle that ensued Pershing won. Wilson gave Pershing his unqualified support because he was well aware that the ability of the United States to impose its will, or at least to exert a strong influence, on the peace negotiations ending the war would be greatly enhanced if distinguishable American units played a leading role in the conclusive battles.

Pershing boldly called for 1,000,000 American soldiers to be delivered in France within a year, adding that all training of recruits in the United States "must contemplate the assumption of a vigorous offensive." Newton Baker instructed his aide, Brigadier General Francis Kernan, to draft a memorandum making Pershing's determination to preserve the integrity of army units official U.S. policy. "In military operations against the Imperial German Government," the memorandum to Pershing read, "you are directed to co-operate with the forces of the other countries employed against the enemy; but in so doing the underlying idea must be kept in view that the forces of the United States are a distinct and separate component of the combined forces, the identity of which must be preserved."

Pershing set the size of an American division at 27,082 enlisted men and 979 officers, roughly twice the size of Allied and German divisions.

Floyd Gibbons was a successor to Richard Harding Davis as the-hero-as-war-correspondent. He had reported on half a dozen wars around the globe and entertained millions of readers with his accounts of hairbreadth adventures, in many of which he was the hero. Perhaps his most spectacular achievement had been to win the friendship of Pancho Villa, who hated gringos. He fitted out a boxcar, got it attached to Villa's train, and reported at first hand on three of Villa's most important engagements. When Pershing's expedition was dispatched to chastise Villa, Gibbons was the official reporter of the extended raid. With the threat on Germany's part of all-out submarine warfare and the prospect of America's entry into the war, Gibbons decided that his place was in Europe. He passed up an opportunity to cross on the same ship that carried Count von Bernstorff home after Wilson's request that the German ambassador be recalled and sailed on the Cunard liner *Laconia,* hoping to be torpedoed and thus have a "beat." The *Laconia* was indeed torpedoed off the coast of Ireland and sunk. Gibbons got off in a small boat and was rescued. He cabled a lurid account of the sinking to the *Chicago Tribune* the next day, and the story, reprinted all around the country, gave a substantial boost to the sentiment for intervention.

Gibbons was on hand to greet General Pershing when he landed in England on his way to France. He crossed the Channel with him, was one of two American correspondents with the first American troops to reach the front lines, and was with the artillery battalion that fired the first American shot into German territory; it was fired by Sergeant Alex Archer, Battery C, 6th Field Artillery, at 6:50:10 on October 23, 1917. Gibbons was responsible for reporting to the world Pershing's words at a ceremony welcoming him to France: "Lafayette, we are here."

On September 1 Pershing moved his headquarters to a town, Chaumont, in the section that had been assigned to the AEF whenever it should arrive. Georges Clemenceau, the French premier, well aware that the Allied cause hung by a thread, spoke bitterly of the "fanatical determination of the great chiefs of the American army to delay the arrival of the Star-Spangled Banner on the battlefield."

At Chaumont, Pershing's task was twofold: logistics and diplomacy. Of one of the supreme command sessions, General James Harbord, an aide to Pershing, wrote: "Our Allies hate each other and disagree on many subjects but they are a unit when it comes to casting lot for our raiment. They seem to look on America as a common resource, and while loudly proclaiming their wish to see America on the firing line as a National Unit, resort to all manner of subterfuge to defeat and delay that eventuality. . . ." Pershing had hardly left the meeting when the Allied ambassadors began besieging Wilson to send nothing to France but infantry and machine guns, a policy that would, of course, make it impossible for American troops to preserve their integrity as combat units.

The tasks to be accomplished by the initial detachments of engineers sent to France to prepare the way for American troops were enormous. In the words of one historian, "there were harbors to be dredged, docks to be built, piles to be cut to build the docks, unloading cranes, dredges, freight yards, storage sheds, refrigeration plants, and all the equipment to be provided without which a million Americans could not operate." The Americans constructed six ports of debarkation along the French coast from St.-Nazaire to Brest. Those two ports were greatly enlarged, and railroad lines were built to connect them with the forward training areas. The Services of Supply were under Charles G. Dawes. A graduate of the University of Nebraska, a successful banker, and a schoolmate of Pershing's, Dawes set himself up at the Ritz Hotel in Paris with a pet terrier and a piano. Arriving in France, Dawes was promptly advanced from major in an engineering unit to colonel and then, as director of the Services of Supply under Pershing, to general.

James Harbord, an army colonel with a record of distinguished service under Pershing, worked in the Services of Supply under Dawes and, like many other soldiers, kept an illuminating diary. "The Services of Supply," Harbord wrote, "is really the most stupendous industrial enterprise ever undertaken by the army; one of the most gigantic ever undertaken by any one. Certainly one which dwarfs the building of the Panama Canal, both in its difficulty, in the vast sums involved and in the tremendous potentialities of disaster if poorly done."

The tasks to be performed at home in conscripting and training almost 2,000,000 civilian soldiers were equally gargantuan. Dozens of training camps had to be constructed, most of them in the South, where the climate made year-round training exercises possible. The regular army, the national guard, and what was soon called the national army, made up primarily of draftees, constituted the three elements of the American Expeditionary Forces. The law establishing the draft provided that the actual decisions about who should be drafted and who exempted should be decided by local committees of citizens. The registration for the draft was to be done through 4,557 local draft registration boards. Senator Reed of Missouri, an opponent of the war, told Secretary of War Baker, "You will have the streets of America running with blood on Registration Day," which was set for June 5.

On the appointed day, or within a few days of it, 9,586,508 young men between the ages of twenty-one and thirty-one registered. Out of 2,810,296 initially drafted, 3,989 filed as conscientious objectors. They were allowed to seek some form of service "satisfactory to the government." Four hundred and fifty refused to accept alternative service and were sentenced to jail terms. Each draftee was assigned a number, and the numbers were then chosen by lottery. When draftees reported for induction into the army, they underwent a physical examination, and it came as a shock to the nation to discover how many young

Americans of working-class backgrounds were physically unqualified. It was a sobering testimony to the consequences of the nation's social inequities.

The most important innovation in the screening of draftees was the addition of a "neuro-psychiatrist" to the teams of doctors who examined prospective soldiers. In the 4th Division such a specialist recommended not only the acceptance or rejection of draftees but also the types of duty those accepted would be best suited for.

Soldiers were prevailed upon to take out life insurance, and by the end of the war 4,561,974 had done so. There were provisions, moreover, for allotments to the dependents of soldiers, taken from their pay. If a soldier died in the line of duty, his widow received a monthly income up to $75 until remarriage.

Two other steps that had important consequences were taken. First, the decision was made, as it had been made almost a century and a half earlier by George Washington at the time of the American Revolution, to avoid the recruitment and training of units by county and state and to train all units to be interchangeable. The other was to use existing regular army soldiers and national guardsmen as the nuclei of new units. The 26th, or Yankee, Division was the third division to be shipped overseas, and the first national guard division. The 42nd, or Rainbow, Division, made up of the best trained men in various guard units around the country, was assembled on Long Island, was given a brief period of accelerated training, had its first formal review in September, and was shipped overseas. When the Allies began to prepare for their spring offensive in 1918, Pershing had only four combat divisions under his command—the 1st, 2nd, 26th, and 42nd. But since each American division was almost twice the size of a French or British division, they were the equivalent of eight.

When Secretary of War Baker was summoned before a congressional committee to answer charges that the recruiting and training of an army had gone too slowly, he replied, "Has any army in history ever, since the beginning of time, been so raised and cared for as this army has been?" It was indeed true. "France," Baker reminded his congressional interrogators, "was a white sheet of paper, so far as we were concerned, and on that we had not only to write an army . . . we had to go back to the planting of corn in France in order that we might make a harvest." It was both a fact and a metaphor for the vastness of the energies and forces that had to be marshaled in a few short months.

It was September 6 before the first draftees arrived in the camps that had been prepared for them to begin their training in the art of war. Arthur Balfour said to David Houston that fall, "They tell me that you have already registered nine millions of men, that you have organized a number of officers' training camps, and that Congress has authorized or is about to authorize an expenditure of $21,000,000,000. Is it true or am I dreaming?" To Allies, desperate for credit, the sums were astronomical—almost $2,000,000,000 for the construction of ships, $640,000,000 for aviation, $350,000,000 for destroyers, $100,000,000 for medicine, $717,000,000 for heavy guns.

By the end of 1917 the British, in particular, were impatient to have American troops in combat. Having initially doubted that the United States would be able to recruit and train an army in time to participate in the fighting, the British, once it became clear that the United States intended to do just that, grew increasingly (though not publicly) critical of the delay in getting American soldiers to France. American spokesmen now promised twenty-four divisions by July, 1918.

Stateswide training was to be supplemented by training in France prior to combat duty. Combat-seasoned British and French officers were sent to newly formed divisions to make training as practical as possible. Rookies learned to build fire and communications trenches; to string barbed wire (and to cut it); to lay mines, saps, and trench accessories; to make dugouts and machine-gun emplacements, observation posts, and command posts. They learned to throw grenades and were given bayonet practice (an exercise which many soldiers found repugnant). Starting with three-mile hikes, draftees advanced to twelve-mile speed marches with full packs. In addition to close-order drill, they mastered open deployments for attack and road discipline for movement forward to the battle zone. Poison gas training was also stressed.

The AEF was organized into five army corps of six divisions—a total of thirty divisions plus two, the 81st and 93d, unassigned to corps. The First Army Corps was made up of the 1st and 2d divisions of the regular army, the 26th (drafted from New England), the 32d (Michigan and Wisconsin), the 41st (Washington and Oregon, North and South Dakota, Colorado, New Mexico, Montana, Idaho, Wyoming, and Minnesota), and the 42d (Rainbow) Division with troops from twenty-six states. (When the commander of the black New York 15th Regiment requested that his unit be included in the Rainbow Division, he was told that black was not a color of the rainbow.)

Divisions were made up in turn of three brigades. Two brigades included two infantry regiments and a machine-gun battalion. A third brigade was made up of three artillery regiments and a motor battery. A regiment of engineers, a battalion of Signal Corps troops, and an additional divisional machine-gun battalion completed a standard division. Six regular army divisions were scattered through the first three corps for training (and stiffening) purposes, and four marine brigades were attached to particular divisions where the military situation dictated.

The war raised once again in a highly visible form the issue of the status of black Americans. They must be drafted and must fight, to be sure, but how? They could not be integrated, it was assumed, into white units. Wilson, in any event, had no interest in pressing that issue. The most acute problem was that there were no black officers and no facilities for training them. Black soldiers therefore had to be commanded by white officers, an arrangement that black Americans, well aware of white prejudices, resented loudly. Plans were made for a black division to be composed of black national guard units, of which there were a scattering around the country. A training camp for black officers was established, and plans were made to organize two divisions of black soldiers. These, the 92d and 93d divisions, were shipped to France in May, 1918, but the great majority of blacks who were drafted were used in engineering units as laborers.

To Oswald Garrison Villard "the supreme wrong" done the black race "came . . . when the Negroes of the South, who were denied all participation in their government, multitudes of whom were deliberately kept illiterate and deprived of every civil right and personal liberty, were drafted to go to France 'to make the world safe for democracy'! What hypocrisy! What injustice! They were forced to die for the country which was still for them what Wendell Phillips had called it in Abolition days, 'a magnificent conspiracy against justice.' "

There were, of course, two famous black cavalry regiments in the regular army. The 25th Infantry had been disbanded by Roosevelt as punishment for the Brownsville raid. The 24th Infantry, stationed near Houston, Texas, smarted at the insults inflicted on them by Houston's whites. Assigned to guard a training camp under construction, the soldiers of the 24th had been subjected to innumerable indignities and harassments and had been beaten on several occasions by the city's police. Now they were out to exact vengeance. On the night of August 23, 1917, Sergeant Vida Henry of the 24th Infantry led some 100 black soldiers with Springfield rifles and fixed bayonets out of their camp for a raid on the law enforcement officials. Before the bloody night was over, 20 people, most of them white, were dead or fatally injured. Indicted for disobedience of orders, aggravated assault, mutiny, and murder were 63 soldiers. Of these, 19 were eventually convicted by army court-martial and sentenced to be hung. The rest were sentenced to life imprisonment. Wilson, on the advice of Newton D. Baker, commuted the death sentences imposed on 10. The significance of the Brownsville and Houston outbreaks was that they demonstrated an increasing militancy on the part of blacks. The offenders were, to be sure, black soldiers, but their actions, condignly punished as they were, made evident that forming in the black consciousness was a new kind of resolution that manifested itself in the actions of the soldiers, who felt most keenly the humiliations imposed on them despite their status as servants of their country whose comrades had suffered wounds and death in its defense.

The most publicized black unit was the New York 15th Infantry. In 1913 the New York legislature had passed a bill authorizing the formation of a black national guard unit, the 15th, to be organized in Harlem. Designated as the 369th U.S. Infantry at the time of U.S. entry into the war, the regiment was made a unit of the U.S. Army.

The 369th was the achievement of William Hayward, a forty-year-old transplant Nebraskan, whose father, Monroe Hayward, had been Senator from Nebraska. Arthur W. Little, an upper-class reform-minded New Yorker, was captain of a black rifle company and chronicler of the 369th. The officers of the 369th were, in the main, graduates of Harvard, Princeton, and Yale, many of them members of New York's most exclusive clubs—the Union, the University, the Racquet, and the Knickerbocker. Many, like Hayward, were the descendants of abolitionists. Hamilton Fish, captain of a famous Harvard football team for two years and scion of the famous Fish family (his grandfather had been secretary of state under Grant) commanded a company.

When the 369th finished eighteen days of training in a camp at Peekskill, it marched on Memorial Day, 1917, up Fifth Avenue with other national guard units to a wild reception. In the opinion of its officers, it was the smartest marching unit in the whole parade (with the best band in the AEF).

In the aftermath of the Houston affair there was considerable apprehension when the 369th was sent to Spartanburg, South Carolina, to complete its Stateside training. The mayor of Spartanburg warned of trouble. "With their northern ideas about race equality, they will probably expect to be treated like white men," he declared. "I can say right here that they will not be treated as anything except negroes. This thing is like waving a red flag in the face of a bull. . . ." A Chamber of Commerce spokesman told a newspaper reporter, "I can tell you for certain that if any of those colored soldiers go in any of our soda stores and the like and ask to be served they'll be knocked down. . . . We don't allow negroes to use the same glass that a white man may later have to drink out of. We have our customs down here, and we aren't going to alter them."

Hayward was determined to preserve peace between the soldiers and the townspeople. The band, conducted by James Reese Europe, immediately performed a public concert in the town square, and Noble Sissle, the drum major, sang a baritone solo. The concert was so successful that it became a weekly affair. But there were incidents. Captain Napoleon Bonaparte Marshall, a lawyer in civilian life, was ordered off a Spartanburg trolley. A black soldier was knocked into the gutter for walking on the sidewalk.

When a rumor reached the camp that two soldiers of the 369th had been hanged by the Spartanburg police, two platoons of black soldiers started off with loaded rifles, but word reached Hayward, and he caught up with the men just as they were entering the town. He drove to the police station with two of the soldiers to satisfy them that there was no basis to the rumor. Even the jail was inspected. The soldiers then obeyed the colonel's order to march back to camp. Hayward told Little later, "My, it was a narrow squeak! And the police showed those men through the jail, never realizing that they had been facing death at their hands a moment before, and until answers to questions had been made satisfactorily." By the time the search of the jail had been completed a crowd of whites had gathered without the slightest notion of what was afoot. As the soldiers formed and marched off, the crowd applauded. "It was the most incongruous demonstration I've ever seen," Hayward declared.

A most dangerous moment came when Noble Sissle, entering a hotel to buy a newspaper for Lieutenant Europe, was attacked and beaten by a white man. Immediately white soldiers in the hotel rushed to the defense of Sergeant Sissle, and for a moment a riot threatened. Then Lieutenant Europe called the soldiers to attention and ordered them to leave the hotel quietly.

It was evident that if another episode such as that which had occurred in Houston was to be avoided, the 369th had better be shipped elsewhere. It thus became one of the first American national guard units to be shipped to France, departing in November, 1917.

Training citizens to be soldiers was only half the job. Getting them to the front lines was as formidable an undertaking. The Germans were confident it could not be done. The Allies were skeptical. The problem was shipping—transports.

When the United States broke off diplomatic relations with Germany as an obvious prelude to war, the German ships then sequestered in American ports—103 of them—were promptly sabotaged, principally by means of smashing cast-iron parts, cylinders, pump casings, and so on. The repair of those ships by the new process of electric welding was accomplished so quickly that it was estimated by the admiral of the American fleet, Henry Thomas Mayo, that one year's time and $20,000,000 were saved, and a substantially larger number of American soldiers were transported to Europe in German ships sailing under the American flag than could otherwise have been carried across the Atlantic.

One of the most important contributions of the U.S. Navy was the extensive use of mines. A total of 56,611 American mines and 13,600 British mines were laid, the great majority of them in the North Sea. The navy, in addition, established twenty-eight aviation stations in Britain, France, Italy, and the Azores, as well as two training stations and six air bases.

Six German submarines operated off the coast of the United States between May and October, 1918, and destroyed seventy-nine U.S. vessels, most of them small coastal ships. Seven ships were sunk or damaged by German mines; they included the battleship *Minnesota*, which made port.

A great advance for the Allies in fighting the U-boats was the use of radio signals. British direction finders became so sensitive that they could take radio bearings on a German submarine from two points and fix its exact location.

The navy's most impressive achievement was the development of the convoy system for supply ships and troop transports. During the course of America's involvement in the war eighty-eight fleets with an average of a dozen ships sailed from the United States to France or Great Britain without the loss of a single transport. In order to crowd more men on each ship, the soldiers used their bunks in shifts, eight hours at a time. Month after month, starting early in the spring of

1918, more and more U.S. soldiers were crowded onto more and more transports to make the journey to the war zone.

Landing in England, American soldiers had their first experience with blackouts. English food was also a problem; tea, jam, oatmeal, and dark bread were unfamiliar, and men missed their coffee. The Germans, anticipating the arrival of American troops at Calais, made it a practice to greet them with bombs. "Here," wrote the historian of the 4th Division, "was a taste of real war—utter darkness, the dull drone of the motors, the roar of bombs as they crashed down on the city and camp shaking the stoutest buildings; the sound of falling masonry and breaking timbers; the rattle of anti-aircraft guns, like frantic pneumatic riveters, then a short silence followed by the tinkle of breaking glass. . . ." The soldiers also had their first experience with the "side door pull-mans," the French boxcars that carried "Hommes 40 Chevaux 8" with equal crowding and discomfort for horses or men. Bivouac areas were often dirty and uncomfortable. French barns were redolent of the filth of centuries. Even the French horses requisitioned to draw American guns proved a problem; they were used to being led, not driven. Many American units were armed with Chauchats, French automatic rifles called Hot Cats.

Customs, manners, habits—"life-styles"—were demoralizingly different. Friction between the French and Americans was conspicuous. The French had their way of doing military things; the Americans had theirs. The French, as the battle-seasoned veterans, expected the Americans to conform to the French mode. It seemed to the Yanks that their French allies were more preoccupied with defensive than offensive tactics. The Americans remarked to themselves that they had come to France to advance, not to bury themselves in muddy trenches.

It was not surprising that the British and French soldiers near the end of their resources after almost four years of horror were often contemptuous of the zeal for "action" displayed by American troops only a few weeks or months into the war and entirely unacquainted with the terrible, grinding character of trench warfare. On leave in Paris, American soldiers taught their British, Canadian, Australian, and New Zealand allies how to "shoot craps," usually very profitably. The Folies Bergères was translated by Yanks into "Foley's Place."

James Harbord, reassigned to command the 4th Marine Brigade on the eve of Château-Thierry, found the French "the most delightful, exasperating, unreliable, trustworthy, sensitive, unsanitary, cleanly, dirty, artistic, clever and stupid people that the writer has ever known. Intensely academic and theoretical yet splendidly practical at times, it will be a wonder if we do not feel as much like fighting them as we do the Germans before the war is over, for our alliance tries human patience,—American patience,—almost to the limit." The French would hold a position courageously in the face of heavy odds and then abandon it to "fall back on their soup-kitchen or for some equally important reason." But the next day "the colonel will come out and sob around over 'Mes enfants,' and they will kiss each other on both cheeks, and go out and die taking the position they gave up the day before." One French general, Duchesne, abandoned the Sixth Army without authority to spend several days in Paris "with a charmer." The highest ranks were constantly agitated by intrigues, some of which were aimed at overthrowing the French civilian government.

With the French, the shoulders, in Harbord's view, were as eloquent as words. "You were always told," he noted, "to proceed to some distant point where an officer will meet you with orders [but] . . . where you are going . . . is a secret from the person most interested, the American commander." When General Harbord was told that he would have to bring his entire and widely scattered division into line as a central element in the French attack plan and expressed his doubts about the possibility of completing such a movement over unfamiliar terrain with inadequate maps and severely damaged roads, he was "reassured by many shrugs of French shoulders." When he pointed out that there was no traffic control on the roads he was supposed to use to move his division forward, the answer was "more shrugs."

Frontline trench warfare was a shock to the Americans. Not all dugouts were like those described by Slater Washburn, a corporal in the 101st Artillery of the Yankee Division, near Soissons, where bunkers thirty feet deep were equipped with clean sheets and pillows, and the noncommissioned officers had a separate dugout to serve as a dining room and "clubroom."

There was time for sports and entertainment in the billets of units in reserve. Even in the front lines, men played baseball, soccer, and football. Washburn watched soldiers playing soccer. When German shelling began, they all dived for the nearest cover, leaving the ball in the middle of the field, and when the shelling stopped, they resumed their game.

Night movements of troops were common to avoid enemy observation. The historian of the 4th Division described such a march: "Staggering along the roads in inky darkness, their eyes filled with rain and perspiration, swinging in and out of the lines of transport, holding on to each other's packs so as to keep the chain intact, falling down shell holes, catching, in the murky darkness . . . a glimpse of a flash of red which told of the firing of a big gun . . . the men moved slowly until they were all in the trenches and settled down to snatch a fugitive bit of sleep." Often men fell asleep as they walked and were rudely awakened when they stumbled over some unevenness in the road.

Theodore Roosevelt, Jr., described the quarters of the 2d Division: "Tin cans and refuse of all kinds garnished the parapet. Gray dropsical rats ambled around the shelters. Men were soaked from one day's end to the other. Blankets were sodden with rain. Water slopped to and fro on the dugout floors, shining oilily in the flickering light of a candle-butt. The food, when it was brought up in marmite cans through slippery trenches crumbled by shell-fire, seemed tepid and diluted by the rain-water. Hands and feet were frost-bitten, or at least perpetually numb. At times a bursting German shell would throw to the surface fragments of a long-buried soldier. The earth could 'no more cover her slain.' "

The most romantic aspect of the war was, of course, the aerial combat in which British, German, French, and, eventually, American "aces" became "knights of the air," fighting famous aerial battles like the jousts of medieval knights. Almost without exception the aviators were young men of the aristocracy, many of them bearing famous names. Planes were used for a crude kind of bombing, to shoot down observation balloons, to strafe enemy troop concentrations, railheads, and roads, and to direct artillery fire, but most enthralling were the aerial dogfights between rival aces. Washburn found his battery at Soissons harassed by a German plane that flew over the town every morning as the doughboys were eating their breakfast, driving them to cover. It was said that the aviator was a countess who flew to avenge the death of her husband. "Man or woman," Washburn wrote, "[she] was one of the most daring flyers I saw at the front."

At the declaration of war the U.S. Army had two airfields and fifty-six more or less serviceable planes. By the armistice, nineteen months later, there were 11,000 fliers, 4,300 of whom were in France. The British had been using thirty-seven makes of engines, and the French forty-six. The superiority of the Liberty engine was established so quickly that by the end of the war 31,814 had been delivered to the

Allies. Plane production lagged behind, and most of the American fliers flew French or British planes until the end of the war.

Trench warfare, as we have noted, was dominated by artillery barrages on a hitherto unimaginable scale; by the machine gun, perhaps the deadliest defensive weapon ever invented; and by poison gas, another modern innovation.

Gas shells were fired almost daily when the wind direction was right. Their arrival was signaled by the cranking of a klaxon, and soldiers immediately put on their gas masks. Since there was a dispute over which gas masks, British or French, were the more efficient, Americans carried both. The gases most commonly used were chlorine and mustard gas. They had distinctive odors, and men could usually identify them quickly, but it was often difficult to don masks in time to avoid a breath or two of gas, which produced violent coughing and nausea—which in turn made it virtually impossible to wear a mask. The masks were, moreover, hard to breathe in. They induced excessive sweating and made any physical activity extremely arduous. If there was little movement of air along a section of the front, the gas was slow to dissipate, lying in low, damp areas for hours and sometimes days and seeping into dugouts and trenches. Dangerous as the gas was, the perpetual discomfort of the masks was, in the long run, more debilitating than the gas itself.

The most serious hazard of gas attacks was in its effect on the horses that drew wagons and artillery caissons. At Nantillois the movement of the 4th Division's artillery to new positions was impeded by dead horses. A "four-line" mule team loaded with bread stood in the street, the driver and one of the mules dead. Fifteen water carts, their horses dead in their harnesses, were scattered around the town.

In characteristic American style, training camps and rest and recreation areas swarmed with volunteers dedicated to cheering up the doughboys, the "Yanks." Besides the Red Cross and the YMCA there were innumerable private agencies catering to the needs of the doughboys. The Salvation Army was much in evidence, as were such organizations as the Knights of Columbus and the United Hebrew Charities.

Journalists and reporters were as numerous as do-gooders. They were insatiable in gathering stories for the "folks back home." A major theme was the ethnic diversity of the AEF. Floyd Gibbons quoted an Irish-born American soldier as praising a "Chink" machine gunner: "You oughter see that Chink talking Mongolian to a machine gun, and, believe me he sure made it understand him. I'm here to say that when a Chink fights, he's a fighting son-of-a-gun and don't let anybody kid you different." One company had "such a babble of dialects" that it called itself the Foreign Legion.

It was a "democratic army," too (so democratic that privates sometimes told officers where to go). Gibbons told of an American private serving as a general's orderly whose income tax for the preceding year had been in excess of $100,000. Such stories were legion and presumably reassuring to the folks back home.

The folks back home were fed a raw-meat diet of patriotism. The phonograph was at the height of its popularity, and there were dozens of war songs to be sung at bond rallies, parades, and benefits, dances, and parties for those training camp heroes who were departing and, in an astonishingly short time, for those wounded heroes returning. George M. Cohan, the Irish music hall star, wrote and sang the most popular of all, "Over There."

> Over there, over there,
> For the Yanks are coming
> The Yanks are coming
> Over there.

"Bring Back the Kaiser to Me," was a smash hit, as were "Goodbye, Broadway, Hello France!" and "Pack Up Your Troubles in Your Old Kitbag and Smile, Smile, Smile."

Meanwhile, the trickle of American soldiers to France turned into a flood. By the Fourth of July, 1918, Secretary of War Baker was able to inform the President that 1,019,000 American soldiers had embarked for France. By November there were 4,791,172 men in the military and naval services; on April 2, 1917, there had been 378,619.

But war was, finally, a serious business, and the real question was: Would the Yanks fight? If no one at home doubted, there were numerous skeptics on "the other side of the pond." First came the Germans, who did not believe that a mongrelized people without a military tradition could possibly stand up to sturdy Nordic soldiers led by officers schooled in the Continent's most fearsome military tradition, where fighting or preparing to fight was an artistocrat's principal reason for existence. The French and British were hardly less skeptical. Whatever the advantages of democracy might be (and they seemed precious few), fighting was a gentleman's calling. It was thus the case that a good deal rode on the initial performance of American soldiers in combat. The eyes of the world were upon them, and the honor of Old Glory was in their hands.

On March 13, 1918, the Germans, having withdrawn a number of divisions from the Eastern front in the aftermath of the Treaty of Brest-Litovsk, attacked the British front with sixty-four divisions; they were opposed by nineteen British divisions, with thirteen in reserve. In twenty-four hours the Germans had broken through first the British Fifth Army and then the Third on a fifty-mile front. The offensive reached within twelve miles of Amiens, and Paris itself was once more threatened and within the range of the German Big Bertha, which fired huge shells into the city at random. By March 26 the Germans had driven a wedge between the British and French forces, a gap plugged at the last minute by "engineers, auxiliary forces, camp followers, drivers, cooks," whoever could be rounded up. The Germans were checked at least for the moment more by the need to resupply their advance units and bring up supply and command echelons than by the ragtag forces opposing their advance. Lloyd George, elected prime minister on the slogan "Hang the Kaiser," sent a cable to President Wilson which began: "We are at the crisis of the war. Attacked by an immense superiority of German troops, our army has been forced to retire. . . . The dogged pluck of our troops . . . has checked the ceaseless onrush of the enemy, and the French have now joined in the struggle. But this battle, the greatest and most momentous in the history of the world, is only just beginning. . . . It is impossible to exaggerate the importance of getting American reinforcements across the Atlantic in the shortest possible space of time."

Having driven the British back all along the northern sector of the Allied lines, the Germans began what they believed to be a final assault upon the French, attacking in the Chemin des Dames-Soissons sector. The French lines began to collapse at once. General Ferdinand Foch replaced General Joseph Joffre. Pershing, calling upon the new commander in chief of the French Army, found him walking in his garden and offered him all the American troops and war matériel to use as he saw fit. Another response was the hastened departure of the 3rd and 4th divisions from their training camps in the States.

The 369th Infantry Regiment, which had been hurried out of Spartanburg, South Carolina, to avoid an outbreak of racial violence, was assigned to a French division. It soon became a battle-seasoned unit, the unlikely hero of which was Private Henry Johnson, a redcap porter formerly on the New York Central Railroad in Albany, New

York. Johnson was occupying a forward observation post opposite the German lines on the night of May 11, 1918, when a German patrol attacked the post. The Germans were on the outpost before its occupants had time to react. Their first warning was a grenade which seriously wounded one of the Americans. Johnson fired at the advancing figures, killed the leading German, knocked the next man down with his rifle, and then, drawing his bolo knife, killed another German with a blow to the head. With several bullet wounds in him, he then disemboweled another enemy soldier, upon which the patrol beat a hasty retreat, leaving behind them forty grenades, seven wire cutters, and three Luger pistols. In all, Johnson had dispatched five Germans, including one killed by a grenade as the patrol retreated. By Arthur W. Little's calculation there were no fewer than twenty-four men in the patrol. Johnson's exploit coincided with the arrival of the famous war correspondent Irvin Cobb, and a few days later the New York papers carried the story of "The Battle of Henry Johnson." Little noted proudly, "Our colored volunteers from Harlem had become, in a day, one of the famous fighting regiments of the World War."

The 1st Division, under the command of huge General Hunter Liggett, was rushed to the Mondidier area, northwest of the Oise River, at the end of May to halt the deepest German penetration. The Americans took the tiny village of Cantigny by assault and held it in the face of seven successive German counterattacks. Major George Marshall, one of Pershing's brilliant young staff officers, considered Cantigny the most crucial engagement of American troops, although its importance was obscured by the more spectacular events at Château-Thierry a few weeks later. "The price paid was a heavy one," Marshall wrote, "but it demonstrated conclusively the fighting qualities and fortitude of the American soldier." It was the fortitude of the troops under a "severe artillery bombardment" that was most significant to Marshall. "To be struck by these hideous impersonal agents without the power to strike back was the lot of the American soldier at Cantigny." The Germans had been especially anxious to discredit the fighting qualities of American soldiers; a captured order from Ludendorff instructed his troops to spare no pains to smash the Americans wherever they were encountered. Cantigny revealed the baselessness of the German hope. To the young American officer, Cantigny marked a "cycle in the history of America," the people of which had left the soil of Europe to escape oppression and now had returned as its liberators. In the words of General Liggett, at Cantigny the German got "the first cold foreboding . . . that this was not, as he hoped, a rabble of amateurs. . . ."

By June 1 the German advance had reached Château-Thierry on the Marne River. General Tasker Bliss called the German penetration "the very crisis of the war," and the French and British filled the air with accusations and counteraccusations. But now Pershing was ready. He had survived the combined efforts of the French and British to persuade him to commit his men where the supreme council felt they were more urgently needed. On June 3, 1918, the First Army Corps went into the line at the point where the Germans threatened the railhead at Château-Thierry.

The French lines had fallen back steadily, sometimes as much as ten miles a day. "No unit along the whole front," James Harbord wrote, "had stood against the foe." The roads leading from the front were crowded with refugees fleeing before the German advance. "Men, women, children, hurrying toward the rear," Harbord wrote, "tired, worn, with terror in their faces. Some riding on artillery caissons or trucks. Many walking, an occasional woman wheeling a baby carriage with her baby in it. . . . Some driving carts piled high with their little properties including all sorts of household effects, one old woman leading two poor little goats. . . . Little flocks of sheep, occasionally a led cow, sometimes a crate of chickens on a cart. . . . I have never seen a more pathetic sight."

Harbord's 4th Brigade, U.S. Marines, was given the mission of stopping the German advance on Château-Thierry. The Germans opened fire from the hills above the town on June 1. Initially they were checked on the north bank of the Marne by a machine-gun squad, led by Lieutenant John Bissell. At nine o'clock in the evening the Germans began their advance. As Floyd Gibbons described it, "Their dense masses charged down the streets leading toward the river. They sang as they advanced. . . . The American machine gun fire was withering. Time after time, in the frequent rushes throughout the night, the remnants of enemy masses would reach sometimes as far as the centre of the big bridge, but none of them succeeded in reaching the south bank. The bridge became carpeted with German dead and wounded. They lay thick in the open streets near the approaches." As soon as the German attack had been checked, Foch called for a counterattack by the marine brigade consisting of the 5th and 6th regiments in the Belleau Wood area.

When the marine brigade went "over the top" on June 6, 1918, Theodore Roosevelt, Jr., was in command of a battalion. Lloyd Gibbons was also there. Gibbons managed to get himself shot three times: once in the arm, once in the left shoulder, and once so close to his eye that he was permanently blinded. Finally, under cover of darkness, he was able to crawl back to the American lines. For his pains, he received a citation from Marshal Henri Pétain and the Croix de Guerre with the Palm. A month later he was back with the American units advancing on Amiens, and on July 18 he was with the marines once more as they launched their attack on Château-Thierry.

After Belleau Wood came the slopes of Hill 142 and the bitter fighting at the village of Bouresches. Having broken the German advance at its most forward salience and driven the attackers back, the marines withstood repeated and increasingly desperate counterattacks. "I cannot write of their splendid gallantry without tears coming to my eyes," Harbord wrote. "There has never been anything better in the world. What can one say of men who die for others, who freely give up life for country and comrades? What can be said that is adequate? Literally scores of these men have refused to leave the field when wounded. Officers have individually captured German machine guns and killed their crews. Privates have led platoons when their officers have fallen. Many companies have lost all their officers and been commanded by non-commissioned officers."

On July 7 an intelligence report was found on a captured German officer. It was based on the defense of Château-Thierry and the subsequent offensive by the 2d Division and read in part: "The Second American Division may be classed as a very good division, perhaps even as assault troops. The various attacks of both regiments on Belleau Wood were carried out with dash and recklessness. . . . The nerves of the Americans are still unshaken. . . . The individual soldiers are very good. They are healthy, vigorous, and physically well-developed men . . . who at present lack only necessary training to make them redoubtable opponents. The troops are fresh and full of straight-forward confidence. . . . They still regard the war from the point of view of the 'big brother' who comes to help his hard-pressed brethren and is therefore welcomed everywhere. . . . Only a few of the troops are of pure American origin; the majority of them is of German, Dutch and Italian parentage, but these semi-Americans . . . fully feel themselves to be true born sons of the country."

A common view was that the stand of the 4th Brigade "in its far-reaching effects marks one of the great crises in history." Even more important, it helped establish the right of the Americans to have their own sector of the front "and no longer be step-mothered by the French or English." An American staff officer, apparently Colonel Leonard Ayers, told Charles Seymour, "The Americans at Château-Thierry saved Europe and the world. And they did it contrary to orders. There was a gap of thirty miles. The French and British were all in. The Americans against orders filled the gap, advanced, and for the first time the tide definitely set against Germany."

Their reward was that when Foch mounted his counteroffensive on July 15, the divisions leading the assault were American. The Germans knew at once the game was over. The German chancellor at the time, Count Georg von Hertling, wrote not long before his death the following year: "At the beginning of July, 1918, I was convinced, I confess it, that before the first of September our adversaries would send us peace proposals. . . . We expected grave events in Paris for the end of July. That was on the 15th. On the 18th, even the most optimistic among us understood that all was lost. The history of the world was played out in three days."

Among the Americans wounded were two Roosevelt sons. Their father seemed to take a strange kind of comfort from the dangers to which they were exposed, as though they had been his surrogates. He wrote to Lodge: "Archie is badly crippled; whether permanently or not it is not yet possible definitely to say. . . . Ted was seriously wounded . . . [but] he will be back at the front in a few weeks. If the war lasts long enough he will either be killed or crippled. . . . Kermit also is now in the American uniform with Pershing . . . ; he is trying to get with the machine guns in the infantry; if he succeeds he will do admirably; but will at no very distant time share the fate of his brothers."

After Château-Thierry and Belleau Wood the ability of the American soldier to fight and of the general staff to coordinate the movements of divisions and corps could no longer be doubted. Pershing and his Americans were assigned the right wing of the Allied lines, roughly from Château-Thierry to Verdun and west and south of the Swiss border. Pershing commanded the First Army. General Harbord, who had commanded the 4th Marine Brigade at Château-Thierry and subsequently been given command of the 2d Division, was lent to the French Tenth Army. He brought his division from the Belleau Wood sector to the point of departure for the attack on Soissons in a brilliant maneuver. The night before the scheduled attack the 2d Division was still widely dispersed and some miles from the point of departure. "None of my units," Harbord wrote, "except the gunners were in place.

It rained hard; the forest was plutonian in its darkness; the road, beyond words to describe; trucks, artillery, infantry columns, cavalry, wagons, caissons, mud, MUD, utter confusion." All night the men of the 2d Division struggled forward. For the last few hundred yards the leading attack elements, exhausted from their nightlong trek, had to double-time to catch up to the rolling artillery barrage intended to cover their advance. The famous Moroccan Division of the French Army made up of North African Moslems—"the best shock and assault troops in France" Harbord called them—was in the center. The 1st Division, which had had a day in the line before the attack, was on the Moroccan left, while the 2d Division was on the right. Two other French colonial divisions were part of the attacking echelon. The task of the three divisions was to push forward toward the highway which ran from Soissons to Château-Thierry in an effort to reduce the salient which the Germans had carved out in their assault in May and early June. The main thrust was to be borne by the Moroccans and the 2d Division. The men of the 2d Division had had no sleep for two nights. Their only food was the cold rations they carried; their only water was that in their canteens. In thirty-six hours the division had been re-formed, "and under the most trying conditions, carrying such of its machine guns as it had been able to get to the front," with no more than one belt of ammunition to each gun. By ten o'clock on the morning of the eighteenth, the division had advanced some six miles into the German lines and captured more than fifty artillery pieces and 2,000 prisoners. By nightfall the 2d Division had taken another 1,000 prisoners and eleven batteries of German artillery and hundreds of machine guns and had outstripped the Moroccans, leaving them a mile behind. "Nothing in all history," Harbord wrote, "is finer than the spirit with which those men went forward, tired, hungry and thirsty. . . ." Food, communications, medical support—all were left behind, and it was hours before they caught up with the weary infantrymen. The American casualties had been extremely heavy; caissons bringing up ammunition and supplies passed ambulances, bumper to bumper, filled with the wounded.

One of the soldiers in James Harbord's 2d Division, which came into line just at the moment when the scheduled attack of the French Tenth Army started, was Sergeant Metej Kocak, a Hungarian immigrant who had worked as a coal miner before joining Company C of the 5th Marine Regiment (the 2d Division was composed of the 5th and 6th Marine regiments and the 9th and 23d Regular Infantry regiments). When the advance of the division was held up by German machine-gun nests, Kocak made his way forward to the emplacement guarded by a squad of German infantry. Single-handedly he routed the squad, charged another machine-gun nest, killed three of its defenders, and was about to be dispatched by half a dozen other defenders when members of his own platoon scrambled over the gun emplacement and the remaining Germans surrendered. As the attack continued, Kocak became separated from the men in his platoon. Encountering a group of Senegalese whose officers had been killed, he took charge of them and captured two more machine-gun positions before the day was over.

In General Harbord's words, "After forty days' bloody fighting at . . . Belleau, the division changed its zone of action from near Château-Thierry to near Soissons, and in two days of courage and devotion, drove an efficient and highly trained enemy over seven miles. . . . The United States Regular has again justified the proud boast that he has never yet failed to respond to every demand made upon him by his officers."

Relieved by a French division, the battered 2d withdrew to a rest area, and Harbord had a bath and a shave for the first time in five days.

After the destruction of the German salient, the most advanced point of which was Château-Thierry, Foch ordered an attack on another large salient in Picardy on August 8. Montdidier and Noyon both were captured, and by early September the Germans were in retreat all along the front.

The First Army was assigned to the sector east of the Moselle to Verdun and thence across the Meuse to the Argonne. The salient included St.-Mihiel, which had been held by the Germans since the early months of the war.

The fierce battle of the St.-Mihiel salient lasted only twenty-seven hours on September 12 and 13. In that time an estimated 100,000 Germans were routed from the strongest positions that could be devised, 15,000 prisoners were captured, and 150 square miles of territory, as well as the heights of the Meuse and the railroad network behind St.-Mihiel, were taken.

At the end of the St.-Mihiel fighting, which involved some 550,000 American soldiers, Pershing wrote: "An American army was an accomplished fact, and the enemy felt its power. No form of propaganda could overcome the depressing effect on the morale of the enemy of this demonstration of our ability to organize a large American force and drive it successfully through his defenses. . . . For the first time wire entanglements ceased to be regarded as impassable barriers and open-warfare training, which had been so urgently insisted upon, proved to be the correct doctrine."

An Allied war council on September 2, 1918, decided on a coordinated advance along the entire front from Ostend, Ypres, and Lille on the north to Verdun and the Moselle River on the south. The movement of the various armies—Belgian, British, French, and American—began on September 28. The American attack went slowly at first with heavy casualties. In the words of Major George Marshall, "As casualties and extreme fatigue wore down the organizations, and the strain of battle produced a form of nervous exhaustion, General Pershing increased his demands on subordinates and forced the fighting through every daylight hour. He directed the division commanders to move their personal headquarters forward, in closer contact with the fighting line, and exerted the strongest personal pressure upon all with whom he came in touch, to overcome the difficulties of weather and terrain, to cast aside depressions of fatigue and casualties, and to instill into the troops the determination to force the fight along every foot of the front."

Three American corps with a total of nine divisions were assigned objectives in the initial phase of the attack. A battalion of the 77th Division of the First Corps, fighting its way through the tangled forest in front of it, lost contact and found itself cut off from the American units on its flanks and surrounded by Germans. Called on to surrender, the division commander refused, and the "Lost Battalion" became a collective hero.

Pershing described the terrain through which the three American corps had to fight their way as a "vast network of uncut barbed wire, . . . deep ravines, dense woods, myriads of shell craters, and a heavy fog. . . ."

On the night of September 30 the 1st Division replaced the weary and depleted 35th in the Meuse-Argonne offensive. Casualties were heavy, especially in the combat patrols sent forward each night to keep contact with the enemy. The next day, when the 1st advanced, it encountered desperate resistance from two relatively fresh German divisions. The 16 Infantry, which began the day with 800 men and 20 officers, finished it with 240 men and 2 officers. Of 1,000 men in a battalion of the 26th, only 285 men and 6 officers (out of 30) were left when the battalion reached its objective. Much of the fighting was hand to hand. The next morning the 18th and 28th Infantry regiments of the 1st Division were ordered to continue the assault, this time on Montfancon Hill, a center of German resistance covered by a score of machine guns.

As the 1st Division advanced, the divisions on its right and left came under intense fire and held up, leaving the 1st dangerously exposed. On October 7 the 82d Division was rushed forward to relieve the pressure on the 1st. It, too, came under withering fire from well-fortified German positions on high ground. Its mission was to occupy the ground that the 1st had seized and then turn west against the German flank. In attempting to carry out the plan, the 2d Battalion of the 82d was checked by heavy machine-gun and artillery fire. It was clear that no progress could be made until the German machine guns had been silenced. Sergeant Harry Parsons, an ex-vaudevillian, was dispatched with sixteen men, among them Alvin Cullum York, a pious young man from Tennessee. Working its way cautiously around the German positions, the patrol got behind the German lines undiscovered. There they surprised a party of some 50 Germans gathered about a small hut to receive orders for a counterattack. The American patrol ordered the Germans to surrender, but at that moment a German machine gun opened up on the patrol, killing 6 and wounding 3. York was one of 7 who were unscathed. Taking up a position some forty yards from the German machine-gun nest, he picked off one member of the crew after another as though he were shooting squirrels in the hills of Tennessee. When a squad of Germans was sent to rush his position, York shot all 8 of them. Finally, the German officer in charge of the unit, unnerved by the accuracy of York's fire and the mounting toll of dead Germans, offered to surrender. Rounding up some 100 prisoners, including 60 from other machine-gun emplacements, York and those members of the patrol who had survived began the dangerous trip back to the American lines, picking up additional Germans on the way. When the count was finally tallied, York had killed some 25 Germans, and he and his comrades had brought back 132 prisoners, including 2 lieutenants and the major. It was the most remarkable individual achievement of the war, a feat that even eclipsed the famous exploit of Henry Johnson, the black railroad porter from Albany. It made Alvin York the most renowned American hero. A movie company offered him $75,000 to act in a film about the war, but the modest and diffident York, after a triumphal parade down Broadway, cheered by hundreds of ecstatic citizens, returned to the mountain town of Pall Mall, married his childhood sweetheart, and took up once more the life of a farmer.

In the final Allied offensive that smashed the German armies, the actions of the black 369th Infantry Regiment under Colonel Hayward in taking of the town of Sechault won the regiment the respect of the French units fighting alongside it. Arthur Little, now a major and battalion commander, recounted the achievements of the 369th: "recruited as fighting men, in ridicule; trained and mustered into Federal service, in more ridicule; sent to France as a safe political solution of a volcanic political problem; loaned to the French Army as another easy way out—these men had carried on.

"In patience and fortitude these men had served. Their triumphs in battle had been great; but their triumphs of orderliness, of cleanliness, of personal and civic decency, had been greater.

"France had wept over them—wept the tears of gratitude and love. France had sung and danced and cried to their music. . . . France had kissed their colored soldiers—kissed them with reverence and in honor, first upon the right cheek and then the left."

Little noted proudly that the regiment was under fire 191 days and lost in battle in killed and wounded 1,500 men, 1,100 of whom were lost in the Allied offensive from September 25 to October 6, 1918, the last major action of the war. The 369th never lost a prisoner or a foot of ground and took every objective assigned to it. "Our men sang while they marched," Little wrote; "they sang while they washed their clothes and while they dug their ditches; and, as for sentiment, their lives were just one, long continuous, and never-ending picture of love of home and country." The regiment won the coveted French Croix de Guerre, and 150 individuals won personal Croix de Guerre.

Without the excellent performance of American soldiers in combat all the other contributions of the United States to the Allied cause would have weighed far less in the scale of world opinion. The world being what it is, there were other intangible but important consequences. Americans and Europeans had not met in the ultimate test of battle since the War of 1812. In the meantime, the United States had become, in the opinion of those who, like Madison Grant, believed in the currently popular notion of racial superiority, "mongrelized" and thus, presumably, no match for the "purer" Nordic, Aryan, or Teutonic races. The performance of American soldiers in combat put a substantial crimp in such notions. Most important of all, American soldiers brought the war to a victorious conclusion.

34

The Fourteen Points

With the passing of each week Wilson found himself under increasing pressure, both at home and abroad, to make a clear and specific statement of U.S. war aims. The President had dispatched Ray Stannard Baker on a fact-finding mission to Britain, and Baker's reports of a growing movement there for a negotiated peace were alarming. In November, 1917, Lord Lansdowne, who had been a member of the Asquith government in 1916, published a letter in the *Daily Telegraph* (the *Times* refused to print it), calling for a negotiated peace. Among the British socialists who favored a negotiated peace was Graham Wallas, the philosopher-journalist, who was a friend of William James and Walter Lippmann. Wallas viewed the war as the last gasp of the old order. If it went on longer, he asked rhetorically, what forces would be left for reconstruction?

The British peace forces had been dismayed by the entry of the United States into the war. In their view, it threatened a break in the stalemate and encouraged the Allies to fight on in the hope of a conclusive victory. A prominent English socialist asked Oswald Garrison Villard, "Why, *why* did the Americans have to come in and spoil the whole business?" But Villard believed that the British "masses . . . as well as the middle class and all the Liberal and Labor elements, did not share this point of view."

A prominent British peace-by-negotiation group was made up of big-business men who believed that the war was doing irreparable damage to their economy and thereby paving the way for a Communist uprising. The members of the aristocracy who favored a negotiated peace believed, in Ray Stannard Baker's words, that "all law, all guarantees, were being swept overboard; the constitution was set at naught; the government was an autocracy." Lord Buckmaster quoted Benjamin Franklin's famous aphorism: "There was never a good war or a bad peace."

In addition to those Englishmen opposed to the war and/or in favor of a negotiated peace, there was a small but influential group of pacifists led by Bertrand Russell, who was under house arrest for seditious writings. Prominent among the socialist opponents of the war were Sidney and Beatrice Webb and George Bernard Shaw as well as the historians G. D. H. Cole and George Trevelyan.

Among the British intellectuals, those of the conservative, win-the-war-at-all-costs stripe made up what was called the Round Table. To them the critical issue was the reorganization and perpetuation of Britain's colonial empire. All other issues, such as the League of Nations, were secondary.

Support for a negotiated peace was by no means limited to Great Britain. It was the position of the Majority Socialists (as their party was called) in Germany and increasingly of Socialist parties in other countries. The doctrine that the workers of the world were bound together by common interests that transcended national boundaries seemed at last to be making an impression on working-class Britons, Frenchmen, Italians, and Germans. House sent Wilson a memo on May 31, 1917: "The pacifists in this country, in England and in Russia are demanding a statement of terms by the Allies which should declare against indemnities or territorial encroachment."

The publication of the text of the secret treaties by the Russians in the summer of 1917 increased the pressure on Wilson for an explicit statement of American goals. The government tried to prevent the text of the secret treaties from being published in the United States, but Oswald Garrison Villard published them in the Nation, while the New York Times contented itself by castigating the Russians for revealing them, calling it "beyond the pale . . . an act of dishonor." Like Lippmann, many liberals and socialists of strong pacifist persuasion salved their consciences by grasping at the President's assurances that the United States, by entering the war, would be in a position to ensure a just peace. "I would have dreaded the future of our cause," Lippmann wrote in the *New Republic,* "had we not found at this time such leadership as the President has given . . . consent was fading in the last four months for lack of a catholic idea."

The secret treaties gave the game away. They revealed the most shameless trading of peoples with no regard to their rights or wishes. Their patent cynicism revealed as nothing else could have the true nature of the conflict. The trouble was that the revelation of the secret treaties was six months too late. The United States had already entered the war; it no longer wished to know any such embarrassing facts. Our response was the classic "Please don't confuse us with the truth." Oswald Garrison Villard's *Nation* was the only magazine or newspaper to publish the full text of the treaties. Wilson professed ignorance of them. *He did not want to know.* At least he must not know officially.

Lincoln Colcord, a reforming journalist, recalled "dozens of conversations with Colonel House about the secret treaties going back as far as the summer of 1917. . . ." Time and again Colcord pressed on House the importance of repudiating the secret treaties. When, in defense of Wilson, it was claimed that House had never informed him of them, Colcord produced a letter stating that he was enclosing them "in the private mailbag for the White House . . . and you know the President alone has the key to the bag."

It was also the case that some Americans who had clamored for war began to have serious second thoughts. Felix Frankfurter, summoned to Washington by Newton Baker, with whom he had worked in the National Consumers' League, wrote to his wife: "When I see these boys . . . in Khaki, and talk with them, the sense of all the dislocating force of war rushes in on me, the vast tragic irrelevance of it to all that should be life, and I have no patience at all with those who see in war a great moral purgative. At best I can't regard it as better than as a purely temporary process forced on us in a world with other people. I hope we may utilize the unselfish impulses it arouses for I do believe that the President is right in saying that we went into it as a means of realizing a more decent opportunity for peaceful pursuits in an interdependent world. . . ."

Willard Straight, who had enlisted so exuberantly after the declaration of war, wrote to Herbert Croly that the war appealed to him less and less, and to his wife, Dorothy, he wrote that, "though I love soldiering I am more and more beginning to hate all it means. It's terribly unintelligent and unreasonable—the whole thing. I hate unfairness and greed and stupidity—and war is all that—and it is not redeemed by the fact that it brings out many heroic qualities in individuals and in peoples. It must in the end brutalize."

In August, 1917, Pope Benedict XV called for peace negotiations based on the renunciation of indemnities, on disarmament and the substitution of arbitration for war, on the resolution of territorial claims, and "the spirit of equity and justice." Belgium must also be evacuated, and its independence guaranteed.

Wilson and Lansing replied three weeks later, on August 27, expressing support for the Pope's peace initiative and reasserting American war aims, specifically resistance to "punitive damages, the dismemberment of empires, the establishment of selfish and exclusive economic leagues." The object of this war, Wilson declared through Lansing, "is to deliver the free peoples of the world from the menace and actual power of a vast military establishment controlled by an irresponsible government." The precondition for peace was that the German government be replaced by one the word of which could be trusted. Somewhere along the line Wilson's peace without victory had hardened into what was, in effect, the Allied position that Germany must surrender unconditionally and pay the penalty for its war guilt. The rationale was, equally clearly, that Germany had become an outlaw nation, with which it was impossible to negotiate in good faith. From this it followed that unless the German people freed themselves from this "ambitious and intriguing government," no negotiations and no peace were possible. Even as fair an observer as Louis Brandeis told Ray Stannard Baker that "Germany was an evil force to be utterly put down. There could be no compromise."

Despite the desperate condition of Germany, it was in a far better position strategically to profit from a negotiated settlement on the basis of the status quo than the Allies were. The Germans controlled the Continent from the Black Sea to the Baltic, including Poland, Rumania, Belgium, Alsace-Lorraine, and the eastern provinces of France. Turkey held sway over much of the Middle East. Germany was ready to accept a peace based on the partition of Russia, the acquisition of most of Belgium, and the incorporation into Germany of the French coast from Dunkirk to Boulogne. This was the proposal of the German Progressive People's Party.

Britain was equally obdurate. It declared that it would not accept mediation by neutrals and would fight on until it had delivered a "knockout blow" to Germany. Aristide Briand, the French prime minister, dismissed talk of negotiations as an "outrage." To the leader of the British press, Lord Northcliffe, even the suggestion of a negotiated peace could "only be regarded as hostile."

David Houston, troubled by signs of increasing obduracy on the part of the Allies, warned Wilson against "insisting that Germany be absolutely crushed." Indeed, he feared that the obstacles to a just peace might come more from the Allies, in their desire for revenge, than from Germany. "As the collapse of Germany becomes more certain, the demands of some of the Allies, particularly of France, will probably become unreasonable. This would be natural, but in the interest of world peace they will have to be held in check."

The Conference of the British Labor Party, the largest ever held in that country, met in June, 1918, to concert opposition to Lloyd George and to try to heal the breach in their own ranks over the war. It was at once evident that the concern of those Laborites who wished for a speedy end to the war centered on the notion that the entrance of the United States into the conflict had encouraged the "complete-defeat-of-Germany faction" to reject peace overtures from the Central Powers. "They feel," Ray Stannard Baker wrote from Britain, "that America, coming freshly and enthusiastically into the war, will become so intent on a 'knock-out blow' that it will fail to seize upon opportunities that may arise to secure a democratic peace by diplomatic means. It must not be forgotten," he added, "that a large proportion of the Labor party here is socialistic with a profound distrust of 'capitalistic' and 'imperialistic' governments. They have a deep-seated belief that even if the Allies crush Germany, these imperialistic and capitalistic forces in England and France would be so strong that there would be no assurance that they would seek a really democratic peace. . . . One could not attend the recent conference without being convinced of the strength of this feeling. . . ."

If sentiment for a negotiated peace was growing in Europe, the opposite was true in the United States. Here the support for unconditional surrender by Germany and a punitive peace grew stronger. When Lincoln Steffens returned from Russia, he visited Wilson and urged him to enunciate as official policy an idea he had once heard him express. "Let all the peacemaking nations agree," Steffens declared, "that any citizen of any country on earth shall be free to go to any other country on earth, himself and his money and his schemes, provided, however, that he go at his own risk and be subject in the foreign country to the laws and conditions of that country. In plain language: that all men shall have the run of the earth to risk their own lives and money, but that these adventurers shall not be backed up by their home governments and shall not, therefore, run their own countries into the risk of war." Wilson responded, "You got that idea in Mexico. It's an anti-imperialist principle, and it's sound. . . . That's one of the points of my foreign policy that I am criticized for: I don't back up our investors abroad. But I can't put that principle over on other governments."

Steffens was about to embark on a speaking tour around the country, and Wilson and House asked him to include in his talks a strong pitch for a nonpunitive peace, proposing in effect the President's as yet unannounced peace terms. Steffens agreed, but he was surprised and disconcerted at the degree of hostility that his audiences displayed when he broached the topic. Often people got up and walked out. He realized that most Americans were "psychologically fighting a war with the Germans" and "they could not—literally it was impossible for them— think of the president treating fairly with the Germans as human beings and with Germany as a civilized country." At Stanford University, in Santa Barbara, and in Los Angeles, Steffens's reception was hostile. In San Diego the authorities allowed him to speak on the Russian Revolution, but the next night, when he tried to speak on the terms for peace, "the army, the navy, the police, were all out, surrounding the church [where he had spoken the night before] and the waiting audience," and Steffens was forbidden to speak. He reported to Colonel House the nature of the public response. Wilson and House had already lined up an impressive list of "peace speakers" to travel around the country and spread the doctrine of peace. They were not dispatched. The anti-German propaganda had been too successful; the Germans could not be instantly transformed from Huns, murderous beast, rapists, and killers of children into foes deserving of fair treatment at the peace table. The consequence was, in Steffens's words, "President Wilson went to Paris to make an ideal peace with no intelligent peace opinion to back him in America." One of the causes of his failure was that the Allies knew "that he was alone, and that his people, the Americans, were not with him for a fair and permanent peace." Steffens himself found many doors closed to him. Magazines that had been eager for his articles refused them; people who had once turned out to hear him speak stayed home.

At this juncture House, with Wilson's approval, put the members of the Inquiry to work on drafting a comprehensive statement of American war aims. On January 8, 1918, the President appeared before a joint session of Congress to outline his Fourteen Points as the "only possible" basis for peace. They included "open covenants, openly arrived at"; freedom of navigation of the seas in war and peace, except as they might be closed by common action for the enforcement of international agreements; removal of economic barriers and the establishment of free trade wherever practicable; the reduction of all armaments to the level of self defense; the settlement of colonial claims in the interests of the native populations; the evacuation of all Russian territory and the freedom of Russia to determine its own political development without foreign interference; the evacuation of Belgium; the restoration of Alsace-Lorraine to France; the readjustment of the Italian frontiers; the right of the peoples of Austria-Hungry to self-determination; the evacuation of Serbia, Rumania, and Montenegro, with free access to the sea for Serbia. The disintegrating Ottoman Empire was also to have the right to self-determination, with the integrity of Turkey itself guaranteed. Poland must have its independence and access to the North Sea. Finally, there must be an international association of nations to enforce the terms of the treaty and prevent further outbreaks.

The last provision—for an international agency to police the treaty and "end all wars"—was the most dramatic and was at once referred to as a League of Nations. The idea was not new. In his acceptance speech on receiving the Nobel Peace Prize in Christiania (now Oslo), Norway, in May, 1906, Theodore Roosevelt had called for the strengthening of the Hague Tribunal and then added that "it would be a master stroke if those great powers honestly bent on peace would form a league of peace, not only to keep peace among themselves, but to prevent, by force if necessary, it being broken by others. . . . The combination might at first be only to secure peace within certain definite limits and certain definite conditions; but the ruler or statesman who should bring about such a combination would have earned his place in history for all time and his title to the gratitude of all mankind."

Henry Cabot Lodge, speaking at the dinner of the League to Enforce Peace, had expressed sentiments similar to those of Roosevelt.

He reminded his listeners that he had already made a recommendation for a league to promote international peace in an address at Union College a year earlier. Lodge called for some organization "in which the united forces of the nations could be put behind the cause of peace and law. I said then that my hearers might think I was picturing a Utopia, but it is in the search of Utopias that great discoveries are made. Not failure, but low aim, is the crime. This league certainly has the highest of all aims for the benefits of humanity, and because that pathway is sown with difficulties is no reason that we should turn from it."

In an address to the League to Enforce Peace in May, 1916, Wilson had called for the United States to "become a partner in any feasible association of nations" formed "to maintain the inviolate security of the highway of the seas . . . and to prevent any war begun either contrary to treaty covenants or without full warning and full submission of the causes to the opinion of the world—a virtual guarantee of territorial integrity and political independence." Now the League of Nations was put forward as the official policy of the United States and its principal "war aim."

That was realized at once by friend and enemy alike. Scott Nearing of the People's Council endorsed Wilson's programs, and the *San Francisco Chronicle,* a conservative Republican newspaper, referring to a British description of it as a "great charter," asked, "Why not the greater or greatest charter? Magna Charta was a small-town franchise compared with the proclamation of international liberty and democracy contained in the Presidential deliverance." George Sylvester Viereck, the tireless champion of Germany, called it, not unequivocally, "the most effective piece of propaganda ever designed by any human brain in the history of mankind."

The Fourteen Points speech changed the world's chemistry. Disaffected intellectuals returned to the fold; pacifists and socialists took heart. Hyphenated Americans were reconciled by the promise to free their homelands. The response, if overwhelmingly favorable, was far from unanimous. When William Allen White so far forgot his allegiance to Roosevelt as to praise Wilson for his statement of peace objectives, an angry Roosevelt wrote White that he had "bats in the belfry," illustrating his letter with bats. Wilson, he declared, was a threat to "the moral fibre of the American people." But the *Manchester Guardian,* a British journal, gave the most typical response: "Perhaps the greatest and commonest mistake which men make is to regard idealism as a sort of sentimental weakness, all very well for the cloister or the academy, but quite unsuited for the rough work of life and useless to the practical man. On the contrary, it is ideals which dominate the world, and nothing great is accomplished without them."

For better or worse the Fourteen Points was a document drawn up by professors and an intellectual or two (Lippmann and House). It was idealistic, visionary, and impractical. It showed little regard for or patience with the real world. It presumed the inherent goodness of individuals and the imminent triumph of reason. Perhaps that was all just as well. More worldly and realistic authors might not have had the heart to project such an impossible dream, in which case the world would have been the poorer.

Americans of all classes and sections responded to the President's suggestion that the nation's sacrifices (modest, to be sure, in comparison with its Allies) were justified by the faith that the war would put an end to wars and imperial conquests. To David Houston that spirit was exemplified by a rancher he met in Cut Bank, Montana, who had three sons in France. He was resigned to losing one or two of them. They were his contribution to "my country's cause and to the cause of civilization. What I ask is that they do not give themselves in vain." He was content to have them fight on for a day when "men may go about their business free from apprehension and disorder, till the nations can take steps to see that there shall never be another tragedy like this. See that they do not die for anything less worthwhile," he told Houston. "Fix the matter so that neither Germany nor any other nation can ruin the world."

From Rome, Ray Stannard Baker wrote Wilson that he found him a hero in Italy. Many walls bore the placard *"Parole Scultore di Wilson,"* with quotations from his latest speech. His pictures were in evidence everywhere, and Baker was told by an Italian friend that he had seen candles burning under the portrait of the American President in peasant homes.

However the peoples of the world might respond, their leaders were, in the main, less than enthusiastic. From France, Baker wrote to House: "Here as in England one often has the uncomfortable feeling that the Government leaders support Wilson more or less with their tongues in their cheeks, as a matter of policy. They want our powerful armies and our vast money resources, but they really think our war aims, as expressed by Mr. Wilson, a kind of moonshine . . . one cannot look to the French for the greater moral and political leadership. They are too close to the actual fighting; men cannot think with guns going off in their front yards. They are even less interested here than in England in the League of Nations, or in any constructive policy. All thought is here centered upon rooting the Germans out of France; getting them away from Paris so that Big Bertha will not be shooting into churches, and killing orphans. One sometimes actually feels like a kind of fool theorist to introduce here the subject of the League of Nations."

An increasingly uneasy Willard Straight wrote to his wife: "We should have made our bargain with the Allies when we first came in—or at least when we began to send troops in such large numbers. Now we will be apt to get nothing—not even the peace we fight for, but a peace which will, instead of being founded on a League of Nations, have the foundations for other wars." A weary and doubting Ray Stannard Baker wrote: "Between the forces of greed and revenge at one end of the scale, and the forces of doubt, weariness, and fear at the other, where now is the trumpet voice of great statesmanship? . . . I have moments of fear lest our sacrifices go for nothing. It came to me freshly, seeing . . . the familiar diplomatic and economic forces at work. . . ." The European leaders, he noted, "really want . . . a new world domination with themselves and ourselves dominating; what they decidedly do not want is a democratic peace. . . . As for Lloyd George, he is for anything that is uppermost at the moment. He rides exuberantly upon the crest of every wave. He has no yesterday and no tomorrow." The Allied leaders, Baker added, "allow the manufacturers and capitalists who own the plants to engage in the most ruthless profiteering."

It was clear to Baker that Britain and France were determined to punish Germany so severely that it could never recover its former status as a great European power. "It must pay for the war, pay for the rehabilitation of Italy, France and England, give up all its colonies and territories. Pay, pay, pay."

To one much-abused group—hyphenated Americans, especially those of German and Austrian-Hungarian antecedents—the President's Fourteen Points came as a benediction. They had suffered severely in their adopted country. Now they were encouraged to have hope by the promise of a wise and just peace. In a rare gesture of reconciliation Wilson invited representatives of thirty-three foreign organizations to join him in a Fourth of July celebration at Mount

Vernon. Shepherded by Josephine Roche, they were greeted cordially by the man who had so often attacked them.

As the Irish tenor John McCormack sang "The Battle Hymn of the Republic," each representative walked up to Washington's tomb, said a prayer, and placed a wreath upon it. This ceremony was followed by a speech delivered by the President. He recalled the beginnings of the nation 142 years earlier and concluded, "As the years went on, and one century blended with another, men and women came even from the uttermost ends of the earth. . . . We have called them alien, but they were never alien. Though they spoke not a word of the language of this country, though they groped dimly toward its institutions, they were already American in soul, or they never would have come. We are the latest manifestations of the American soul."

At the reception following his speech, reporters took note of the President's informal manner. It was a stifling summer day, and most of the delegates were dressed in hot black woolen clothes and "smothering under silk hats of every vintage." Wilson went from one group to another, shaking hands and urging the visitors to "peel off the funeral wrappings," removing his own to encourage the others.

The Mount Vernon gathering had a symbolic significance that extended far beyond the event itself. As we have noted, from the outbreak of the war many Americans, among them former President Roosevelt and Wilson himself, had been acutely concerned about the danger posed by the large, basically unassimilated immigrant population from the nations and ethnic groups that made up the Central Powers in the event that the United States were to enter the war on the side of the Allies. It was well known that the kaiser was confident that such anxieties would inhibit or preclude the direct involvement of the United States in the war. He made it abundantly evident that he expected every German-American to do his duty for the *Vaterland* long before the United States entered the conflict. Tensions in the various immigrant communities were intensified by the fact that hundreds of thousands of immigrants who wished to return to their homelands were prevented from doing so by the outbreak of the war. In addition, they suffered, as we have seen, harassment and persecution at the hands of public officials and violence and abuse from their neighbors. Their mail was intercepted; their magazines and journals were suppressed, their meetings broken up, their leaders arrested and, frequently, deported. In the face of such tribulations the token efforts of Josephine Roche and her staff availed little indeed. But the event at

Mount Vernon made it clear that the reconciliation of the hyphenated Americans was very much on the President's mind. That the desire to effect such a reconciliation was a critically important element in Wilson's formulation of the famous Fourteen Points cannot be doubted. It was as though he had said, "Trust me and the United States, and your friends and relatives in the homeland will realize their age-long hopes of freedom and independence. That is the price we will pay for your loyalty."

The President's July 4, 1918, address received worldwide attention. The *Manchester Guardian* declared it would "take rank with the best of Lincoln's speeches in the Civil War. It is a vindication of the highest democratic ideals of the United States in entering the war, which will live in history as long as the vindication of Athens in the speech of Pericles reported in the second book of Thucydides. . . . America is now convinced that the fortune of democracy, not in Europe alone but all over the world, depends on defeat of the German rulers in this war."

Lloyd George at a review of American troops the next day said, "President Wilson . . . made it clear what we are fighting for. If the Kaiser and his advisers will accept the conditions voiced by the President, they can have peace with America, peace with France, peace with Great Britain, tomorrow." The Allies were fighting not because they coveted "a single yard of German soil, not because we desire to deprive the German people of their legitimate rights. We are fighting for the principles laid down by President Wilson."

As the Allied fall offensive, spearheaded by fresh American divisions, began to drive the Germans back, it became clear that the collapse of the Central Powers was imminent. In October, Prince Maximilian became chancellor of Germany and at once asked Wilson "to take steps for the restoration of peace, to invite the Allied governments to send delegates to negotiate, and in order to avoid further bloodshed, to conclude an Armistice." Wilson replied that he would propose an armistice on the condition that the Germans immediately retire from Belgium and France. The Germans replied that they would evacuate all occupied territory and negotiate for peace on the basis of the Fourteen Points with the understanding that only details would still be subject to negotiation. Wilson's reply, dispatched on October 14, 1918, demanded the "destruction of every arbitrary power anywhere that can separately, secretly, and of its single choice disturb the peace of the world; or, if it cannot be presently destroyed, at least its reduction to virtual impotency." It was an odd and ambivalent sentence. It appeared to say that the German people must create a government that would accept full blame for the war and pledge itself to perpetual impotence in the European struggle for power. It was clearly an added imposition with the effect, if not the intention, of imposing conditions that no government could accept without falling. But the German response was accommodating. It assured Wilson that the "first act of the new government has been to lay before the Reichstag a bill to alter the constitution of the Empire so that the consent of the representative of the people is required for decisions on war and peace." It might be noted here, parenthetically, that Wilson's demand was based on the classic American assumption, a basic article of faith in the Secular Democratic Consciousness, that the "people" are in essence inherently wise and good and that the wickedness in the world was the consequence of autocratic governments that acted without regard to the feelings or interests of their constituents. The Classical-Christian Consciousness, on the other hand, had taken the view that mankind in general was disposed to vanity, arrogance, self-seeking, and other unattractive traits. By this reading, the people could not be counted on to act more wisely and humanely than their rulers, provided always that those who held power were most dangerous because they had the greatest opportunity to exercise that power destructively.

Impossible as Wilson's requirements were, they did not satisfy a number of the members of the Cabinet, among them Postmaster General Burleson, who declared that he would be satisfied with "nothing short of abject surrender with absolute military guarantees." In the words of Colonel House, "The outstanding problem was to have the terms [of the armistice] cover what must be practically unconditional surrender without imperiling peace itself. The military spirit in the United States was at its height during this period, and this feeling could not be ignored." The Allies, on the other hand, "were war-worn and war-weary. They had been bled white. Germany was retreating in orderly fashion and no one could say with certainty that she would not be able to shorten her line and hold it for months."

By October 23, 1918, the German government had been so forthcoming in responding to Wilson's demands that he felt it behooved him to take up with the Allies the question of an armistice. It was perhaps at this point that Wilson had his best opportunity to effect the outcome of the peace negotiations. He had resisted the impulse to deal unilaterally with Germany. The principal consequence of his exchange of diplomatic notes had been to force the Germans to face the real nature of their situation. In the process of extracting what seemed at least to the Germans like substantial concessions, Wilson had, in a sense, committed himself to ensuring that the Germans were treated justly in the peace negotiations. That, in fact, had been his declared intent from the beginning of the war. It had been the basis of his famous slogan "Peace without victory," which had enraged the Allies and many of his countrymen as well.

Before the armistice Clemenceau, Lloyd George, Balfour, and the Italian foreign minister, Baron Sidney Sonnino, sat down with House to discuss the Fourteen Points. The points were, as Stephen Bonsal, an American journalist who was present, noted, "read and reread. Now Lloyd George would read one with a wry face, and then Clemenceau would take a hand in the discussion." House would add a commentary, which had been prepared, in most instances, by Frank Cobb or Walter Lippmann. It seemed evident to House that the plenipotentiaries, rather than approaching agreement on the points, were, in fact, getting farther and farther apart. At this point he interjected, "If the Allies are unwilling to accept the Fourteen Points upon which Germany has based her request for an armistice, there can be, as far as I can see, only one course for the President to pursue. He will have to tell the Germans that the conditions they accepted are not acceptable to the powers with which America has been associated. . . . America would then have to take up direct negotiations with Germany and Austria." Lloyd George sprang to his feet. Would this mean a separate peace? It well might, House replied.

The next morning House had a communiqué to read from the White House: "I feel it my solemn duty to authorize you to say that I cannot consent to negotiations that do not include the Freedom of the Seas and the League of Nations. I hope I shall not be compelled to make this, our final decision, public."

There was reluctant agreement, with Lloyd George insisting on wording that would allow for future consideration of the issue of freedom of the seas, but it was not a happy start, and it is not too much to say that in the beginning might have been perceived the end. The Paris papers, used with great skill by Clemenceau, who was, after all, a former newspaper editor and thus able to deploy the various French journals like an adjunct to his own diplomacy, gave an indication of the way the wind was blowing by denouncing the Fourteen Points from the beginning. The *Echo de Paris* declared, "The Allies are bound by nothing that Mr. Wilson wrote or even typed on his typewriter."

Reparations was another point on which the Allied plenipotentiaries made a reservation. House made the best of the compromise, declaring, as he issued the agreed-to statement, that he welcomed them "because they emphasize complete acceptance of all the other Points. The Allied governments, reluctantly, I admit, but also undeniably, have committed themselves to the American Peace Program. This is indeed a turning point in history, and a triumph for our great President. There are, alas, so many key men in the Allied governments who, to put it mildly, are not sympathetic to this program. We shall hear from them later."

David Houston reported that the President came to the November 5 Cabinet meeting looking "less harried and less under a strain" than he had appeared for years. His manner was positively lighthearted. He told the Cabinet that the Allies had accepted the Fourteen Points as the basis of the peace negotiations with two minor exceptions: "Freedom of the seas" would have to be more carefully defined, and the restoration of Belgium must include financial compensation. The only cloud on the horizon, in Wilson's opinion, was "the possibility of revolutions in Europe under the stress of conditions and the influence of Bolshevik propaganda." Switzerland and Sweden, swarming with Russian agents and Russian money, were said to be trembling on the brink of revolution.

Ray Stannard Baker, who was in Rome, wrote on November 1: "Such a whirl of events, the very world on fire! Great battles in progress, dynasties crumbling, new nations being born. . . ." As Baker looked out over the beautiful roofs of Rome, over the ancient, cynical, wordly-wise city, over "the ruined baths of Diocletian" and the "weathered marbles" of the Colosseum that had seen so much of human ambition and tragedy, he felt a surge of hope. "There is," he wrote, "too little passion upon this earth, too little glorious and unrepentant living, too little faith in what is beautifully impossible." To be alive in a time when one even dared dream such dreams was a great joy. "I thank God," Baker added, "I am a part of it, that I, too, am taking a long breath and drinking out of the sea." In Wilson, he believed, the "new order has a leader of genius."

A week later Baker, recently arrived in Paris, noted in his diary: "Great news this morning. The German representatives are meeting

General Foch to ask for armistice terms. The war is practically certain to be over this week. At the last it has come swiftly. The Americans have taken Sedan and have cut the all-important railroad which the Germans might use in their retreat, and the British are close to the fortress of Maubeuge. Still more threatening for the Germans are the wide disturbances at home. Their fleet is in mutiny and there are strikes in Darmstadt and other places. Their situation is plainly hopeless."

The Allied terms for ending the war were severe. They called for the evacuation of the Western front in fourteen days, as well as the left bank of the Rhine and the occupation by Allied troops of bridge-heads at Mainz, Koblenz, and Cologne. Prisoners of war were to be returned at once, and perhaps harshest of all, all German naval vessels were to be surrendered and the Allied blockade was to remain in effect.

The provisional government of Germany, headed by the Majority Socialist Friedrich Ebert, received the terms, nominally accepted them, and three days later, on November 11, the armistice papers were signed in Foch's train. Word reached the United States in time for Wilson to read the terms of the armistice to a joint session of both Houses of Congress. "The war thus comes to an end," he concluded. ". . . it was the privilege of our own people to enter it at its most critical juncture in such a fashion and in such force as to contribute in a way of which we are deeply proud to the great result. . . . The arbitrary power of the military caste of Germany which once could secretly and of its own single choice disturb the peace of the world is discredited and de-stroyed. . . . The great nations which associated themselves to destroy it have now definitely united in the common purpose to set up such a peace as will satisfy the longing of the whole world for disinterested justice. . . . Their avowed and concerted purpose is to satisfy and pro-tect the weak as well as accord their just rights to the strong. . . . I, for one, do not doubt their purpose or their capacity."

Florence Harriman was working for the Red Cross in Paris when the armistice was declared. "I threw myself outdoors with the rest," she wrote, "and was carried with the stream of humanity flowing toward the Place de la Concorde. I came in time to see the crepe pulled down and the laurel wreath placed on the head of the beloved city. Six or seven people climbed on the railings. They started to sing 'Marseillaise,' but people could not sing. Their faces were bathed in tears, voices would not come, the old men sobbed aloud. I began to watch a poilu who stood quite still, apathetic. The look in his eyes said, 'We've suf-fered too much. We've touched depth. We cannot feel great emotion any more.' And all through that day of procession and dancing and singing and crying I saw other poilus standing quite unmoved, not more interested or alive than the millions of their comrades they had left forever at the front.... The sky was very blue in the afternoon.... All day without aim, I came and went with the crowds, with the tide that flowed from the Rue de Rivoli up around the Arc de Triomphe and back again to the Place de l'Opéra to Red Cross headquarters. If I had walked a hundred miles I would not have been tired. But I did not walk; something seemed to carry us along. In the evening we were still going and at café after café, we listened rapturously over and over again to the girls who stood on tables and sang the national anthems. The war was over, and it seemed as if everything in the world were possible, and everything was new, and that peace was going to be what we had dreamed about."

While Ray Stannard Baker was having dinner with an American friend, French girls came into the restaurant waving the tricolor and the Stars and Stripes, and all the diners began singing the "Marseillaise," followed by "Marching Through Georgia." After the euphoria had passed, Baker wrote soberly: "When one sees the ugly forces that exist in the various nations, the greedy, half-acknowledged territorial ambitions, the desire to reap commercial benefit from the war, the secret hostility among the victorious nations, one dreads the future, and wonders if peace can be had without the Allies flying at one another's throats." It seemed clear that everything rested on the shoulders of the unproved Wilson. "The fate of a drama lies in its last act," he wrote, "and Wilson is now coming to that. Can he dominate this seething mass of suspicion and disbelief? No European statesman, I am firmly convinced, believes in his inner soul that Wilson's program is anything but a wild dream, very pretty, but quite outside the realm of practical politics.... Occasionally in Wilson I see a likeness," Baker added, "to those rare moralists and idealists who from time to time have appeared upon the earth and for a moment, and in a burst of strange power, have temporarily lifted mankind to a higher pitch of comportment than it was quite equal to ... such leaders as Calvin, Savonarola, and Cromwell. ...." That Baker chose such classic Protestant types with whom to compare Wilson is significant. Certainly the austere scholar had in him that consuming zeal to redeem the world from sin and error that characterized in such a notable degree the three men Baker listed. Savonarola, to be sure, was a Catholic "protestant," but in spirit he was one with the others. Reflecting on the course of history, Baker wrote: "Nothing . . . is ever accomplished without an *excess* of faith, an *excess* of energy, an *excess* of passion." Wilson, he was convinced, would do much. America would do much. "We may even realize the League of Nations of the prophet's dream."

Back in England a few days later Baker experienced misgivings. "The real support for Mr. Wilson," he wrote, ". . . is found among the labor and liberal groups here. . . . It is plain also that in France, in the Government now in control, our American help is looked upon not as a means of reconstructing the world, but as a means of driving the Germans out of Alsace-Lorraine. Clemenceau rejects the idea of a real League of Nations and says nothing about future disarmament. The leaders are all 'realists' except Mr. Wilson, and it is doubtful if the allies were to win now with the present Governments in control, whether there would not be an old-fashioned trading peace, with scant effort to realize any of Mr. Wilson's ideals. Military victory is all they are after, but the labor and liberal groups here feel that Mr. Wilson is fighting for something beyond and above that—for a peace built upon new and sound guarantees."

Despite Frederic Howe's dismay (horror is not too strong a word) over the persecution of those who opposed the war and the ambivalence of his own feelings, he too surrendered to hope when the armistice came. "I felt," he wrote, "that the international millennium was at hand. The President's idealism had carried the world; his Fourteen Points had been accepted; armies were to be disbanded, armaments scrapped, imperialism ended. Self-determination was to be extended to all peoples, hates were to be assuaged, and peace to reign."

"This armistice," David Houston wrote, "marks the turning point in one of the world's great epochs. It may be thought of in comparison with the turning back of the Persians, the Fall of Rome, and the breaking up of the Feudal System, and the French Revolution. . . . It means or may mean the end of menace from medieval-minded, irresponsible despots; the return of Alsace to France; a number of new independent states, such as Poland and Czechoslovakia; the recovery by Italy of her natural boundaries; probably the Turks out of Europe; a measure of disarmament; and a scheme to settle disputes between nations without resort to war in so many instances. And so the world slowly and painfully progresses!"

At the news, an enthusiastic Walter Lippmann wrote to House: "Frankly I did not believe it was humanly possible under conditions as they seemed to be in Europe to win so glorious a victory. This is the climax of a course that has been as wise as it was brilliant, and as shrewd as it was prophetic."

Two weeks after the armistice Stephen Bonsal noted in his diary, "The hot fit is over and the satisfaction that we all felt on Armistice night is fading fast. I recall with amazement many of the foolish things we said and did; like millions of others we gave loose rein to our joy."

The closing weeks of the war coincided with the midterm congressional elections of 1918. It was in connection with these elections that Wilson made what was perhaps the most serious strategic error of his administration. His "open letter" to his "Fellow Countrymen," written on October 25, urged the American voters to send a substantial Democratic majority to Congress "if you have approved of my leadership and wish me to continue to be your unembarrassed spokesman in affairs here and abroad. . . . I am your servant," he continued, "and will accept your judgment without cavil. But my power to administer the great trust assigned me would be seriously impaired should your judgment be adverse. . . . I have no thought of suggesting that any political party is paramount in matters of patriotism. I feel too deeply the sacrifices which have been made in this war by all our citizens, irrespective of party affiliation, to harbor such an idea. I mean only that the differences and difficulties of our present task are of a sort that makes it imperatively necessary that the nation should give its undivided support to the government under a unified leadership and that a Republican Congress would divide that leadership. The return of a Republican majority to either House of Congress would, moreover, be interpreted on the other side of the water as a repudiation of my leadership. . . . I submit my difficulties and my hopes to you."

Will Hays, the chairman of the Republican National Committee, lost no time in calling it "an insult . . . to every loyal Republican. . . ." The majority of the nation's newspapers were Republican, and they excoriated the statement. Republican politicians at every level held it up to scorn and ridicule. Worst of all, the voters failed to respond, and the result was a Congress Republican in both branches, an outcome which Wilson himself had stated would be a repudiation of his leadership and which was taken to be so by many people on both sides of the water.

To George Creel the election was "the most inexplicable and disheartening" in our history. It indicated to the world "popular rejection of both the man [Wilson] and his policies." The principal target of the Republicans had been Point III of Wilson's Fourteen Points: "The removal, so far as possible, of all economic barriers and the establishment of an equality of trade conditions among all the nations consenting to the peace and associating themselves for its maintenance." Will Hays described Point III as an "absolute commitment to free trade with all the world, thus giving Germany out of hand the fruits of a victory greater than she could win by fighting a hundred years." Hays was reported by the *Times* of London to have declared that Wilson's " 'real purpose' is to reconstruct the world 'in unimpeded conformity with whatever Socialistic doctrines, whatever unlimited Government-ownership notions, whatever hazy whims may happen to possess him at the time. . . .' "

35

The Peace Conference

Statistics told the war's cost. They were terrible beyond comprehension. The deaths in battle came to 9,998,771. Men listed as prisoners and missing were counted up to 5,983,600. Since most of the missing were, in fact, dead, the total of battle-related deaths was calculated at almost 13,000,000. The number of wounded and maimed was 20,297,551. To these must be added the millions more who died of disease and starvation—the elderly, women, and children for the most part. Of the dead, 112,432 were Americans, half of whom had died of the influenza that swept U.S. military camps in Europe and America.

Months after the war had ended, its full horror dawned on Stephen Bonsal as he was traveling on a train carrying the "wreckage of war . . . the crippled and crushed survivors" of the Battle of Verdun, brought to that fortress "to celebrate the anniversary of some great feat of arms. . . . This train, crowded with those who survived, was a more horrible sight than any of the ghastly battlefields I have witnessed in so many lands," he wrote; "it was clear to me that those who had died in a moment of exaltation and inspiration were the lucky ones; to many of these death had been merciful . . . the overcrowded train . . . was filled with men and women who were dying slowly, the long-drawn-out death of conscious agony." With their grotesquely distorted faces and broken bodies they brought home to Bonsal the abysmal horror of war. He found himself wishing that "all who will be called upon to shape world policies in the next decade" might have been exposed to the sight of those maimed in body and spirit. Then perhaps at last swords might be beaten into plowshares and people might join in the forgotten prayer "Peace! Peace unto Jerusalem. They shall prosper who love Thee."

John Maynard Keynes was similarly appalled at the devastation of the French countryside. "The horror and desolation of war was made visible to the sight on an extraordinary scale of blasted grandeur. The completeness of the destruction was evident. For mile after mile nothing was left. No building was habitable and no field fit for the plow. . . . One devastated area was exactly like another—a heap of rubble, a morass of shell-holes, and tangle of wire. . . ."

With the armistice there began a new era in world history—a fierce and bitter struggle between the old discredited imperialist order that had brought on the terrible conflict and the new order that the American President had presented to the world in such dramatic and compelling fashion. There would be a "peace conference" that would not be a negotiation between the victors and the vanquished, but rather a contest among the victors over the disposition of the spoils.

Even as plans were laid for the conference, violence and revolution flamed across Europe. Turkey had collapsed under the pressure of a British offensive. Damascus and Beirut were captured, and the sultan of the moment sued for peace. An armistice had been concluded at Mudros on October 3, 1918. In Bulgaria an Allied army, made up of Serbs, Italians, Greek, French, and British troops, defeated the German-Bulgarian forces; soldiers threw down their arms, and the country was swept by political uprisings and Bolshevik intrigues. The Socialists contended with the Communists, and both with the royalists.

With the Hapsburg monarchy disintegrating, its component parts had met in Rome in April at the Congress of Oppressed Austrian Nationalities, where Czech, Yugoslav, Rumanian, and Polish representatives had declared the right of self-determination. By the end of June the Allies had officially recognized the independence of Czechoslovakia.

The Battle of the Piave, which cost the Austrians more than 100,000 casualties, had hastened the end of the war. The Italians then captured Trieste and Fiume.

The Yugoslav National Council met at Zagreb on October 29 and proclaimed the independence of Yugoslavia. Hungary followed suit, and a few weeks later the Yugoslavs proposed a union with Croatia, Slovenia, Serbia, and Montenegro.

The Rumanians and the Serbs were preparing to do battle with each other. The Rumanians threatened to seize Hungarian territory.

This much, but little else, was relatively clear. Where borders between the instant nations would be drawn; who could be left in and who out; the allocation of scarce resources; the demobilization of armies—all such matters were obscure, to say the least. Finally, there hung in the air the threat of revolution and the triumph of communism on the Russian model.

The first critical decision that faced Wilson was whether to go to the peace conference himself or to direct the American peace commissioners—General Tasker Bliss, Robert Lansing, and Henry White—from the White House.

The President's advisers urged him to remain in Washington, above the battles, and guide the negotiations from there. Colonel House, who was in England, took that line, as did Ambassador Page and most members of the Cabinet. House cabled: "Americans here whose opinions are of value are practically unanimous in the belief that it would be unwise for you to sit in the Peace Conference. They fear it would involve a loss of dignity and deprive you of your commanding position." Herbert Hoover and Bernard Baruch added their advice not to go, and General Bliss declared, "Jove should not come down from Olympus."

In the van of those who viewed President Wilson's venture into the murky waters of European intrigue with apprehension were the old-school, hard-line Socialists, who had opposed the war at every stage. Speaking for them, Oscar Ameringer wrote in an open letter to Wilson: "Stay home, Mr. President. If you go over there those hard-boiled highbinders will steal the very gold fillings from your teeth. Only you and the country back of you have the economic power to make them sign on the dotted line below the fourteen points you have borrowed from the Socialists' St. Louis platform. Tell them, from over here, not another American dollar, sack of wheat, pound of bacon, or ounce of copper, cotton, iron, zinc, or lead, until they sign on the dotted line, seal it, and give security for faithful performance."

Wilson's decision to go to Europe gave Ray Stannard Baker "a feeling of doom. . . . He occupies a pinnacle too high; the earth forces are too strong. He is now approaching the supreme test of his triumph and his popularity. They are dizzy heights he stands upon; no man has long breathed such a rarefied atmosphere and lived. All the old, ugly depths, hating change, hating light will suck him down. For all people are cruel with their heroes. They will pull them apart to see whether they have good, hard, heroic material all the way through. . . . Does he sit nobly on his cloud?"

David Houston was among those Cabinet members who were opposed to Wilson's participating in the peace conference. He "ought to go to Europe, talk with the leaders, visit Belgium, England, and Italy, make addresses in each country, canvass matters fully with his delegates, and then come home. The President would be stronger if he stayed at home and passed upon essential matters referred to him than he will be if he goes to Europe and engages in the daily wrangling." But the President was clearly determined to go. The American soldiers, he declared, expected him. So did the Germans. They "desired his presence to interpret and apply his conditions," which they had accepted as the basis for the armistice. "It is now my duty," he declared to Congress, "to play my full part in making good what [our soldiers] offered their lives to obtain. I can think of no call to service which could transcend this. . . . I realize the magnitude and difficulty of the duty I am undertaking; I am poignantly aware of its grave responsibilities. I am the servant of the nation. . . . I go to give the best that is in me to the common settlements. . . . I shall count upon your friendly countenance and encouragement."

"When the President ended this appeal," Houston noted, "many Republicans and some Democrats sat and looked sullen and as stolid as wooden men." Houston wondered how they could show "so little magnanimity and feeling."

Part of the problem was that by his ill-advised effort to influence the midterm elections of 1918, Wilson had crawled far out on a limb, and when the voters sawed it off, he appeared discredited and rejected. Demoralizing as that setback on the eve of the conference had been, it also strengthened Wilson's determination to attend.

Wilson had always "escaped" from difficult situations. He had escaped from angry alumni and a deeply divided faculty at Princeton and from the increasingly hostile politicians of New Jersey. So there may once more have been an impulse to escape an awkward, if not impossible, situation at home.

In the aftermath of the defeated hopes and disillusionment caused by the treaty, the debate revived. Frederic Howe was among those who came to believe that Wilson should have stayed at home. It was Wilson's "lone wolf" obsession that perhaps alarmed his supporters most. "England fed his isolated grandeur," Howe wrote. "England knew Wilson better than we did. She knew him as she knows so many things that no other country thinks it worth while to know. She had studied his written words; had penetrated into his hidden psychology." Lloyd George and his aides could play on his weaknesses like virtuosi.

"Who can tell," Florence Harriman wrote, "whether if he had remained the Absent Figure, the Great Myth, things would have moved otherwise than they have? None of us can live the winter of 1919 over. I should like to," she added, "I should like to feel the old hope of a new world again; and relive some of the gay hours of that crowded scene."

At the same time it seems clear (and it seemed so in retrospect to House and Baruch, among others) that Wilson's decision to go was correct. It is difficult, if not impossible, to imagine the conference without his presence or to believe that the Treaty of Versailles would not have been worse than it was without him (though it must be acknowledged that many of the treaty's critics thought it could not have been worse). In the words of Colonel House, "But for the presence of the President the Peace Conference never would have convened at all; certainly never would have gotten down to work. . . . Without his presence our peace ship never would have been launched. The pressure which he exercised upon his motley co-workers, never could have been exerted by cable. . . ."

Even as Wilson sailed for Europe, an angry and bitter Theodore Roosevelt issued a statement intended to cripple him in the peace negotiations. "Our allies and our enemies and Mr. Wilson himself," he declared, "should all understand that Mr. Wilson has no authority whatever to speak for the American people at this time. His leadership has just been emphatically repudiated by them. The newly elected Congress comes far nearer than Mr. Wilson to having a right to speak the purposes of the American people at this moment. Mr. Wilson and his Fourteen Points and his four supplementary points and his five complementary points and all his utterances every which way have ceased to have any shadow of right to be accepted as expressive of the will of the American people. . . . If he acts in good faith to the American people, he will not claim on the other side of the water any representative capacity in himself to speak for the American people. He will say frankly that his personal leadership has been repudiated, and that he now has merely the divided official leadership which he shared with the Senate."

It was an extraordinary statement to come from a former President directed against an incumbent President, and it revealed as clearly as words could the depths of Roosevelt's hostility toward Wilson. It is impossible to say with confidence the effect it had on Wilson's ability to achieve the goals that he had set forth so dramatically. Roosevelt was still a widely admired, if not revered, world figure of great prestige. On the other hand, both the British and the French were well aware of the fact that Wilson had placed his own credibility in jeopardy by his last-minute appeal to the voters to return Democrats in the fall elections of 1918.

Once he had decided to go (and the decision was reached promptly and apparently without serious misgivings), the next question Wilson had to consider was where the conference should be held. Geneva was proposed, but Wilson vetoed it on the rather odd ground that Switzerland was "saturated with every poisonous element, and open to every hostile influence." It must be Paris. Again Wilson's instinct may have been right, if his logic was elusive.

The French set January 18, the date of the signing of the humiliating peace with Germany in 1871 at Versailles, as the opening date of the peace conference. Wilson sailed for Europe on December 5, 1918, on the *George Washington*. Aboard the ship with Wilson were some 1,300 members of the peace delegation. Included were the President's White House staff, the peace commissioners with their staff, and the members of the Inquiry, augmented by junior aides and additional experts. There were almost as many journalists as instant diplomats, among them Frank Cobb for the *Saturday Evening Post* and Herbert Bayard Swope, whom Lippmann liked but was critical of as being a kind of public relations man for Bernard Baruch, who in return fed him market tips that enabled him to prosper beyond the dreams of most working journalists.

Wilson showed little disposition to take the peace commissioners into his confidence. The situation was especially galling to Lansing, who was also, of course, secretary of state. Ray Stannard Baker called him "a rather cold, precise, timid man, with a thorough and useful knowledge of foreign affairs." Josephus Daniels described him as "meticulous, metallic and mousy."

Prior to the armistice Lansing had made a list of the problems that must be dealt with by a peace conference. High on the agenda was the preventing of Germany from obtaining a route to the East north of the Black Sea. The Brest-Litovsk Treaty must also be abrogated, "and all treaties relating in any way to Russian territory or commerce."

The Baltic provinces of Lithuania, Latvia, and Estonia should become autonomous states of a "Russian Confederation," whatever that might mean. Finland should probably be an independent state as well. There should be an independent state or states composed of Bohemia, Slovakia, and Moravia, "possessing an international right of way by land or water to a free port." Lansing believed that Rumania, in addition to retrieving its former territory, should be given sovereignty over Bessarabia, Transylvania, "and the upper portion of the Dobrudja." Croatia, Slavonia, Dalmatia, Bosnia, and Herzegovina should be united with Serbia and Montenegro to form a single state. Italy must receive all the Italian provinces that had been taken over by Austria. Austria should be confined to the ancient boundaries of the archduchy of Austria. Primitive Albania should be under Italian or Serbian sovereignty or made part of Yugoslavia. The Ottoman Empire of the Turks should be reduced to Anatolia, and Constantinople should be made an international protectorate along with Armenia and Syria, which would be promised self-government as soon as possible.

Palestine was to be an autonomous state under a protectorate. Great Britain would get Egypt. All the land north of the Kiel Canal (which itself would be internationalized) should go to Denmark. Germany's colonial possessions should be allocated to the victors or used as indemnities for German "wrongs."

The underlying principles must be "the natural stability of race, language, and nationality, the necessity of every nation having an outlet to the sea . . . and the imperative need of rendering Germany impotent as a military power."

Lansing had, in full complement, the prejudices of his class and age. One of his principal objections to Wilson's Fourteen Points was their emphasis on self-determination. He thought it dangerous to put "such ideas into the minds of certain races," like "the Irish, the Indians, the Egyptians, and the nationalists among the Boers. Will it not breed discontent, disorder, and rebellion?" he asked. "Will not the Mohammedans of Syria and Palestine and possibly of Morocco and Tripoli rely on it? How can it be harmonized with Zionism, to which the President is practically committed? The phrase is simply loaded with dynamite. It will raise hopes which can never be realized. . . . In the end it is bound to be discredited, to be called the dream of an idealist who failed to realize the danger until too late to check those who attempt to put the principle in force. What a calamity that the phrase was ever uttered! What misery it will cause!"

Tasker Bliss was the U.S. chief of staff. Made permanent military representative on the supreme war council by Wilson, he proved to be one of the wisest and most effective men on that body and the information he provided the President was always fair and accurate. Called a "benevolent pachyderm" by one journalist, the corpulent and keen-witted Bliss was as popular with his subordinates and with the press as he was with his peers. He was described by one of the Americans as "the very personification of the gruff, silent, honest soldier . . . a strongly built man . . . a little stooping at the shoulders . . . thick gray eyebrows, bristly gray moustaches, thick hair on his neck and bald."

The third commissioner was Henry White, a Republican, "a tall, powerfully built, fine-looking man, with thick white hair, and full voice," as Baker described him. White, the most experienced diplomat of all the commissioners, had attended five international conferences beginning with the International Sugar Bounty Congress in 1888. He was "full of human kindliness," with a "wide familiarity with methods and forms which no longer move the world," in Baker's words. Charles Seymour called him an "old dear. . . . Just as nice as he can be but he is certainly doddering."

The members of the Inquiry, now charged with giving practical effect to their researches, were an arresting group. Charles Homer Haskins, at forty-eight one of the older members, was a graduate of Yale with a Ph.D. from Johns Hopkins University. After a stint at Hopkins as instructor in medieval studies, he had taught for ten years at Wisconsin and joined the Harvard faculty in 1902. Wilson had known Haskins since their days at Johns Hopkins, and he praised him as one of those "rare New England historians who did not regard the westward march of the American frontier as an aspect of the expansion of greater Boston."

George Lewis Beer was two years younger than Haskins. His fellow historian Charles Seymour described him as having had "a career in business with the Seligmans, then a traveler in Africa and Asia, then a gentleman of leisure who spends it working hard and writing good books on British colonial policy. . . . He is a snob—with perfect manners toward those he snubs. . . . " A model of sartorial elegance, Beer became Wilson's adviser on colonial mandates. In the opinion of Seymour, he "made one of the most vital contributions to the Covenant of the League and to the work of the Peace Conference" by translating General Jan Smuts's notions of mandates into terms "which fitted into Wilson's personal philosophy. . . ."

The Inquiry was, in many ways, an "in" group. Gordon Auchincloss, scion of the wealthy and socially prominent family, was a classmate of Charles Seymour at Yale and a law partner of David Hunter Miller. Auchincloss married House's daughter, and Miller was the colonel's closest adviser in Paris, particularly with regard to the League. Allen Dulles, a Princetonian and a nephew of Lansing, was one of the young "specialists" and Charles Seymour found his older brother, John Foster Dulles, a member of the reparations commission, "very charming." (Seymour noted that George Creel "looks common, flashy, with loud clothes," a man "of unlimited conceit.") The fact was that the American delegation was rather like an overseas campus of Yale. Yale (and Johns Hopkins) men were everywhere, and some, like Haskins, were products of both Yale *and* Hopkins. If Harvard supplied a corps of journalists, men like the Hapgoods and Lippmann, and a corps of brilliant lawyers like Stimson, Brandeis, and Frankfurter, Yale leaned toward diplomats and foresters, and Princeton toward tycoons. A rough division of academic labor thus seems to have occurred spontaneously. The American academics on the peace delegation were given $150 each so that they could replace their academic tweeds with the morning coats and striped pants more suitable for fledgling diplomats.

En route the American delegation watched movies: Charlie Chaplin and Douglas Fairbanks, favorites of the President and Mrs. Wilson. Wilson also met with the various members of the delegation to discuss the problems that lay ahead. Seymour noted of the President, "Moral factors appeal to him strongly, but he shows himself distinctly a practical politician—an idealist, but thoroughly aware of the foibles of human nature and willing to utilize them. . . . His whole attitude is the reverse of omniscience. . . . And always a strain of humor. . . . " Seymour left the meeting "enormously relieved," as he wrote his wife: "I think tremendous difficulties and dangers are ahead of us," he added, "and complete success impossible; but I do think [the President] has a policy and that in its broad lines it is the right policy."

Wilson himself was certainly conscious of the odds against him. George Creel recalled a conversation with the President on the deck of the *George Washington*. Wilson spoke apprehensively of the "quality of terrible urgency" that characterized the expectations of the American people. "There must be no delay," he told Creel. "It has been so always. People will endure their tyrants for years, but they tear their deliverers to pieces if a millennium is not created immediately. Yet you know, and I know, that these ancient wrongs, these present unhappinesses, are not to be remedied in a day or with a wave of the hand. What I seem to see—with all my heart I hope that I am wrong—is a tragedy of disappointment."

Thirty destroyers and fifty French and British warships greeted the President at Brest, with the bands on board each vessel playing "The Star-Spangled Banner." General Pershing came aboard the *George Washington* on December 13, 1918 (Wilson thought thirteen was his lucky number); Charles Seymour wrote his wife that Pershing was "the grandest man I ever saw. . . . "

Lincoln Steffens was in Paris when Wilson arrived. "The French government let the people have their way, and their way was singing and dancing, madly, gladly, sadly. There were regrets and doubts, but the rejoicing prevailed. And the next days—after joy—came hope, the hope for peace, a real peace. Was it possible? No more wars? The sophisticated sneered, the newspapers mocked, but there was a chance." The chance was Wilson. "The great American prophet of peace was sailing on a cloud through the air to save the Old World." Wilson was "a new kind of leader. . . . The Europeans believed in us, in our president, but they feared for him." And they prayed for him. Literally. "When Wilson traveled by train from Brest to Paris, at night peasant families knelt along the track to pray for him."

Florence Harriman stood in the windows of the peace commission's offices at the corner of the Rue Royale, looking out on the Place de la Concorde. "Presently we heard the guns at the station and knew that the President was in Paris. As the guns stopped a new sound rose like distant rumblings of thunder, *vox populi*, the roar of the populace, coming near and nearer—'Wil-son—Wil-son.' The crowd in the Place de la Concorde seemed to be one great single mass as it swayed back and forth. Emotion moved it as the wind moves water. Around the columns at the foot of the Champs Élysées coming directly toward our windows the procession appeared. Where the kings had sat in the state victoria beside the President Poincaré sat Woodrow Wilson. He held his hat in his hand and, as he looked at the cheering thousands, smiled the smile that took all Paris by storm." The Secret Service men were dismayed by the vast, uncontrolled sea of humanity that seemed hysterical, transported by emotion. People laughed and wept. The journalist William Bolitho wrote: "No one ever had such cheers. I, who saw them pass in the streets of Paris, can never forget them in my life. I saw Foch pass, Clemenceau pass, Lloyd George, generals, returning troops, banners, but Wilson heard from his carriage something different, inhuman—or superhuman. Oh, the immovably, shining, smiling man." The story was passed about that Clemenceau said to Wilson, "No one has ever had such a welcome in the world before." That evening Wilson, repeating the French premier's remark to a friend, added, "And in six months they may be dragging me in the dirt."

After his triumphant entry into Paris, Wilson crossed the Channel to visit England. The trip was tonic to him, the apotheosis of his career: an American cousin, student of Burke, returning to the mother country, the prophet of a new world. Some 200,000 Englishmen and women cheered Wilson in front of Buckingham Palace, where he went to meet the king. At 10 Downing Street he joined David Lloyd George to watch the election returns in the parliamentary elections, an election that Lloyd George won resoundingly. Wilson must have been acutely aware of the contrast with his own situation, where, as Theodore Roosevelt had just announced to the world, he had been repudiated by his countrymen.

Of his English appearances, the most dramatic was that at the Free Trade Hall in Manchester, the industrial city that was the heart of British radical politics. Clemenceau had just called, in the French Chamber of Deputies, for maintaining the old balance of power. Wilson accepted the challenge. The United States, he reiterated, "is not interested merely in the peace of Europe, but in the peace of the world. Therefore, it seems to me," he declared, "that, in the settlement that is just ahead of us, something more delicate and difficult than was ever attempted before is to be accomplished, a genuine concert of mind and purpose. . . . Never before in the history of the world, I believe, has there been such a keen international consciousness as there is now. . . . There is a great voice of humanity abroad in the world just now which he who cannot hear is deaf. . . . We are not obeying the mandates of parties or of politics. We are obeying the mandates of humanity." No man or body of men was qualified to say just how the new world order in all its complex details should be settled. Some agency must be established to provide "a machinery of readjustment in order that we have a machinery of good-will and of friendship. Friendship must have a machinery. . . . " Oswald Garrison Villard, who was present, wrote: "I am sure that if it had been Christ Himself returning to this earth, His reception could not have been more impressive or awe-inspiring." The atmosphere "defied description." Villard added, "Reverence, profound gratitude, the feeling that there stood the savior of the world, the creator of a new and better universe— all of those feelings were expressed on every countenance."

After traveling to Italy, Wilson made three speeches in one day: at the Quirinal, at the Capitol, and at the Italian Parliament. Two days later he was in Genoa and Milan and made five more addresses. Everywhere he was met by huge and deliriously enthusiastic crowds. No one had ever evoked such an outpouring of emotion before—no king, no pope, no general, no politician, not Roosevelt himself in his visit in 1909. Then it was back to Paris—ancient, cynical Paris, the world's most sophisticated city. With its grand boulevards and hectic night life it showed little sign of four years of war. Bernard Baruch described it as "a giant stage set on which was being played a complex, glittering drama, moving toward an historical denouement no one could foresee, but which everyone hoped would solve the problems of the world."

The President was quartered in the Palais Murat, an eighteenth-century mansion with frescoed walls and ceilings, overflowing with crystal and chandeliers. Numerous mirrors gave an illusion of unsubstantiality. The awed historian James Shotwell observed that "one can hardly tell how many rooms are real and how many only reflections." It was an appropriate metaphor for the conference.

At the Sorbonne on December 21 Wilson gave an address in which he declared, "There is a great wind of moral force moving through the world, and every man who opposes himself to that wind will go down in disgrace. The task of those who are gathered here to make settlements of this peace is greatly simplified by the fact that they are masters of no one; they are the servants of mankind, and if we do not heed the mandates of mankind we shall make ourselves the most conspicuous and deserved failures in the history of the world. . . ."

Two days later Wilson addressed the French Senate, then a delegation of the workingwomen of France and the League for the Rights of Man, and spoke twice more at the peace conference. It was, in all, an amazing performance. Arduous as his schedule was, the President seemed to draw strength from the adoring crowds that greeted him on every public occasion. In speech after speech the powerful and evocative phrases poured forth, weaving, almost hypnotically, the glowing vision of a just and peaceful world. All the terror and horror of war so evident everywhere seemed, at least for the moment, dispelled by the President's eloquence. What words could do, what eloquence could achieve, Wilson's certainly achieved.

Despite the strain of the endless round of official occasions, Wilson's closest associates found him more at ease, more friendly and relaxed in Paris than he had been in Washington. Bathed and sustained by an aura of adulation, he found the atmosphere far more congenial in France than in the United States.

He was under strong pressure to visit the battlefields, especially Château-Thierry and Belleau Wood, where Americans had fought so valiantly and with heavy casualties. Reluctantly he acquiesced, and an indignant William "Billy" Hughes, the Australian prime minister, who accompanied him, reported that the President had gone "right through the great areas affected in a closed limousine, stopping nowhere and seeing nothing." The inhabitants of ruined villages along the route had gathered to watch him pass, perhaps hoping for "some words of sympathy," Hughes wrote. ". . . But he passed them by without so much as a wave of the hand or a nod of the head." It was revealing of Wilson. He *was* disinclined to engage the physical world; he had a kind of myopia, not uncommon among intellectuals, which prevented him from seeing the physical objects that surrounded him. It was a dangerous and debilitating deficiency.

Besides the "star"—Woodrow Wilson—the cast of characters was astonishingly varied. There were, of course, the leading men, the Big Four, of whom one, Vittorio Orlando, the Italian premier, was hardly to be compared in importance with his colleagues—Wilson, Clemenceau, and Lloyd George.

Of the four leaders, Clemenceau was the most colorful. One American delegate compared him to "a Chinese mandarin of the old empire." Gray suede gloves worn to hide a skin condition were his trademark. Clemenceau, the reader may recall, had come to the United States as a political refugee at the end of the Civil War. He had had to flee France because of his radical republican activities, and after studying medicine in England, he emigrated to America, where he taught French and equitation at a girls' school and served as correspondent for the leftist newspaper *Le Temps*. Clemenceau married one of his pupils, returned to France with her (where his affairs of the heart soon became notorious), and plunged into politics. When his long-suffering wife, Mary Plummer, herself took a lover in 1894 (she must have been in her forties at the time), Clemenceau divorced her and had her deported to the United States.

The most decisive episode in Clemenceau's life was undoubtedly the German invasion in 1870–71, after which a defeated France was forced to surrender Alsace-Lorraine and pay the Germans a huge indemnity. Clemenceau stored the hope of revenge in his heart. A doggedly republican newspaper editor, he fought for a number of reforms: the eight-hour day, election of public officials (rather than their appointment by Paris bureaucrats), prison reform, and, as a devout free thinker, an end to religious training in French public schools. His greatest cause was that of the Jewish army officer Alfred Dreyfus. It was Clemenceau who published Émile Zola's brilliant defense of Dreyfus, *J'Accuse* (and suggested the title). Before the Dreyfus Affair was laid to rest, Clemenceau's editorials and essays on the issue had come to fill seven volumes. His closest friend was the Impressionist painter Claude Monet. Clemenceau's sardonic witticisms and brilliant epigrams circulated through Paris and, indeed, around the world. It was he who said, "War is too serious a business to be left to the generals." He had declared, "I wage war the way I make love. In domestic politics I wage war. In foreign politics, I wage war. Always, everywhere I wage war. . . ."

Clemenceau had come to power when French morale and capacity to continue the war were at an all-time low. In the words of Thomas Lamont, a member of the commission of reparations, "He lifted France from the slough and held her firm." The nation rallied around his stocky, indomitable figure and took courage from him. He went about in the front lines, risking his life repeatedly but putting new heart into the soldiers, most of whom had never seen a prime minister of France at close range. Indeed, he exposed himself so recklessly to machine-gun and mortar fire on trips of inspection to the front lines that a despairing aide denounced his *coquetterie* with death. Of all the national leaders gathered in Paris, Clemenceau was not only the most compelling but also the most malign. The story was told of how he got his nickname *le tigre*. It was said the Italians wired for help after Caporetto, saying, "The Germans are attacking with full force and they fight like lions." Clemenceau was reported to have replied, "Yesterday we captured 18,000 lions. Le tigre." His ardor in love and vehemence in politics had resulted in his fighting twelve duels, five with the epée and seven with the pistol. "I gave up dueling after seventy," he declared later. Ray Stannard Baker wrote of the French premier: "Clemenceau has a kind of feminine mind; it works well on specific problems, poorly on general policies. He is like an old dog trying to find a place to rest. He turns slowly around following his tail, before he gets down to it."

Herbert Hoover became a friend of the French premier. "His soul," Hoover wrote, "contained to his dying day all the bitterness of the sufferings of the French people. The widows, orphans, and ruined homes in France were the lenses he looked through . . . [he believed] the only way to deal with Germans was to make them impotent forever."

Certainly Clemenceau was not immune to the higher vision of the peace. "There must be," he declared, "no sacrifice which we are not willing and ready to make. . . . We must reconcile our interests which are only apparently conflicting. We must be inspired by our clear vision of the world that is to come, the vision of a greater and nobler civilization." But he could not free himself, in the last analysis, from his obsession with destroying Germany. Aside from anything else, obsessions make bad politics. It should be made clear that not all French parties agreed on a policy of humiliation and destruction of Germany. The French Socialists were strongly opposed to Clemenceau's program as well as to the observance of the secret treaties, especially that with Italy.

Bernard Baruch, a member of the drafting committee of the economic section, chairman of the raw materials division of the supreme economic council, and a representative of the economics and reparations commission, became a close friend of Clemenceau, who called him *le grand bandit américain* because of his opposition to heavy reparations. Baruch, visiting the French premier, would find him in gray gloves, gray skullcap, and gray slippers, looking like "a great, grey cat," and Clemenceau would greet him with the words "Well, *mon enfant*, what is the news?" When Baruch visited Clemenceau at his country home after the war, Clemenceau pointed to a stuffed crocodile behind his bed and said, "Poincaré," his political rival. Clemenceau nicknamed Baruch Prince d'Israël.

A story going around Paris had it that Clemenceau had said, "God Almighty gave mankind the Ten Commandments; and we rejected them. Now comes Wilson with his Fourteen Points—we shall see!"

David Lloyd George, the British prime minister, was exceedingly vain about his large head and disposed to judge others on the size of their noggins (he dismissed Neville Chamberlain, for example, as a "pinhead"). Born in Wales, the son of a schoolmaster who died when

Lloyd George was an infant, he had been reared by a shoemaker uncle who taught himself to read Latin so that he could tutor his young nephew. Lloyd George became a lawyer, married a farmer's daughter, and, at the age of twenty-seven, was elected to a seat in the House of Commons, which he occupied for fifty-four years. Winston Churchill, who was a member of his Cabinet and an admiring student of his political dexterity, described him as a lifelong enemy of the aristocracy and the possessor of the "seeing eye." Lloyd George, in Churchill's words, "had that deep original instinct which peers through the surface of things—the vision which sees dimly but surely the other side of the brick wall. . . . Against this, industry, learning, scholarship, eloquence, social influence, wealth, reputation, an ordered mind, plenty of pluck, counted for less than nothing." John Maynard Keynes called him "this syren, this goat-footed bard, this half-human visitor to our age from the hag-ridden magic and enchanted woods of Celtic antiquity." Keynes felt a "flavour of final purposelessness, inner irresponsibility. . . . Lloyd George is rooted in nothing . . . he lives and feeds on his immediate surroundings."

Perhaps not surprisingly he was almost as notorious for affairs of the heart as his French counterpart, although his wife was more patiently enduring than Mary Plummer. Lloyd George had a clear romantic edge by virtue of the fact that he had recently acquired a bright and handsome young mistress—Frances Stevenson, the teacher of one of his daughters—who acted also as his personal secretary and whose observations of her lover and of the peace conference dutifully recorded in her diary throw considerable light on the man and the events. He was fifty-six, she was twenty-three.

Lloyd George was referred to by William Allen White as "a horse-trading Welsh politician—expansive, emotional, but canny in the deep and bitter experiences of a lifetime in the peculiarly shady politics of the British parliament." Lloyd George shared many of Wilson's ideals, with, in White's phrase "a sort of academic enthusiasm." But when "the interests of the British Empire were at stake he deserted Wilson with the sweet and lovely complacency of the courtesan who has her child to support." The difference between the two men, White wrote, was that Lloyd George "knew he was harloting, and Wilson believed he was serving the will of God." Tasker Bliss called him "a greased marble spinning on a glass table top," while to Herbert Hoover, he was "a magnificent leader of the mob," a man whose "major principle was expediency."

Lloyd George professed to favor a nonpunitive peace that would not push the Germans into communism; there should be no excessive reparations and no amputations of German territory. After a meeting of the British delegation at Fontainebleau to hammer out its position, Frances Stevenson noted in her diary that "D . . . means business this week & will sweep all before him. He will stand no more nonsense either from French or Americans. He is taking the long view about the Peace & insists that it should be one that will not leave bitterness for years to come & probably lead to another war." But Lloyd George was no more to prevail than Wilson. So much has been made of Wilson's failure that insufficient attention has been given to the fact that it was as much Lloyd George's failure as Wilson's or perhaps indeed more, if we keep in mind that the prime minister had just won a smashing vote of confidence from the British electorate and was, therefore, in a much stronger position than Wilson to insist on a just peace. It could be argued that if Lloyd George had been more consistent, less mer- curial, less arrogant in his assumption that he could "sweep all before him," Clemenceau might have been overcome. On the other hand, it was an unequal contest. The most crucial issues were not, after all, resolved by a majority vote of the Big Four. Clemenceau held the trump cards. France had suffered far more than any other Allied power in the war, and nothing could, in the last analysis, be concluded without its concurrence or at least acquiescence.

The three—Wilson, Clemenceau, and Lloyd George—after a time got dreadfully on each other's nerves. Part of the difficulty lay in the degree to which each of them represented the essential characteristics of his respective people. It was positively eerie how strongly national traits came through in their own particular personalities. Wilson's per- petual moralisms, his preachiness, his self-righteousness were among the more conspicuous, if less attractive, qualities of his countrymen. Clemenceau's wit, his skepticism, and his paranoia clearly reflected attitudes of his countrymen. Lloyd George, the Celtic magician, with his lower-middle-class Welsh antecedents was the least typical, the most genuinely eccentric. "Moon-struck," Harold Nicolson called him. Cer- tainly in temperament he was the antithesis of Wilson. So, in addition to the practical problems of peace and, of course, bearing directly on the form the resolution of those problems was to take was the dramatic enactment of three extremely diverse peoples—British, French, and American.

A real power in all the negotiations was the supreme commander of the French armies, Marshal Foch, the architect of victory and beyond question the most popular man in France. Behind Clemenceau stood Foch, an unwavering advocate of the destruction of Germany. John Maynard Keynes described the French marshal "and his stout wife" as a "very bourgeois couple in their way of life," Foch a "peasant type, rather short, with decidedly bandy legs" and an ill-kept moustache, but a man without vanity or self-importance. He had no interest in or patience with civilians. His mind and character, in Keynes's words, were "of an extreme simplicity—of almost medieval simplicity . . . nine-tenths of the affairs of mankind are blotted out from his vision. . . . He is capable, therefore, in the appropriate circumstances of being . . . dangerous to the welfare of mankind. . . . Though a real figure he is small or—a peasant."

Finally, there was what we might call the X factor—Colonel House, his finger in every pie, conducting, it seemed at times, his own private treaty negotiations. Lippmann called him "the human Intercessor, the Comforter, the Virgin Mary," whose advice was widely sought because "it was believed to be a little nearer this world than the President's." When Ray Stannard Baker visited Colonel House in his apartment on the Left Bank, he found him resting on a sofa, with a dressing gown over his knees, "a little, light, deft, bright-eyed man, with a soft voice and winning manners."

One of the most perceptive and experienced Americans in Paris was Stephen Bonsal, the international correspondent. Bonsal had rescued Colonel House when House, roaming Europe as Wilson's emissary and alter ego, had been lost in Berlin. House was at once captivated by Bonsal's elegant assurance and wide knowledge of European politics and politicians. The two men became close friends, and at the beginning of the peace conference, House summoned Bonsal from Pershing's headquarters to be his aide and translator. As House was Wilson's alter ego, at least in the initial stage of the conference, so Bonsal became the alter ego of House, who (when Bonsal could be spared from his translating chores) dispatched him to visit the Central Powers and neutral nations and report back on conditions or to transmit the views of the supreme council to various political leaders, many of whom Bonsal had known before the war. Indeed, it seems safe to say that no American was more familiar with prewar Europe than Stephen Bonsal. In addition to acting as House's alter ego, he kept a journal of the daily progress of the conference, the inner details of which no one knew more and few as much.

The supporting cast ran into the hundreds, indeed, the thousands. Lloyd George's principal aide was Lord Robert Cecil, whom the American historian James Shotwell described as "a very tall man—six feet or more. When he sits down he slides into the chair and lets his body get under the table. . . . " David Hunter Miller, who had been actively involved in framing the original Covenant of the League of Nations, found him a man of "almost austere simplicity" with "a winning charm of manner" combined with "incredible frankness and . . . obvious sincerity," a remarkable combination of "the conservative, the practical, and the idealistic."

Bill Hughes, the Australian premier, was contemptuous of the idealism and, as he thought, the impracticality of the Americans. At one point he shook his finger at the American delegation and shouted, "Some people in this war have not been so near the fire as we British have, and, therefore being unburned, they have a cold, detached view of the situation." The combative old man was Clemenceau's only serious rival in exercising his wit at the expense of Wilson. He had an electric earphone and made it clear that he had come to secure New Guinea for Australia. When Wilson resisted, Hughes said, "Do you know, Mr. President, that these natives eat one another?"

To this anthropological information Wilson did not deign to reply. Lloyd George, hoping to strengthen Australia's case, asked Hughes, "And would you allow the natives to have access to the missionaries, Mr. Hughes?"

"Indeed I would, sir," was Hughes's response, "for there are many days when these poor devils do not get half enough missionaries to eat."

The representative of China was the brilliant and highly respected Dr. V. K. Wellington Koo, a graduate of Yale.

Ion Bratianu of Rumania, moody and taciturn, displayed an impressive black beard. The young foreign minister of Czechoslovakia, a hero of the revolution that had toppled the Hapsburgs, Eduard Benes, smiling and affable, won adherents with his charm and diplomatic skill.

The Polish delegate, Roman Dmowski, had a deeply lined face and striking "power of satire." Poland was in turmoil with seventeen different political parties contending (and often fighting) for power. It had declared its independence immediately after the armistice. After a sharp struggle a strong man emerged: General Joseph Pilsudski, a man Hoover described as "wholly without experience in civil government—with a strange mixture of social and economic ideas." In response to Allied pressure Ignace Jan Paderewski became prime minister in January, 1919. The great pianist turned diplomat was also a conspicuous figure in Paris.

A delegation of Carpathians from Orava appeared in Paris in the traditional peasant costumes of the region to make their case for union with Poland.

The Macedonians and the Armenians were there to argue the cases for their nationalities.

The Albanians, who had for centuries lived a strangely independent life in the mountains, had many of the characteristics of a primitive rural people. The representative of Albania was, in Sidney Mezes's words, "a broken-down old Turk who had no interest in Albania; but who was given a hearing because he was prepared to sacrifice the interests of Albania to those of Italy." He read from a manuscript which had evidently been written for him because he stumbled over unfamiliar words as he droned on and on. Meanwhile, the Albanians were fighting a desperate guerrilla warfare against the Serbs, who were determined to absorb them.

The most dramatic actor in the support cast was "Colonel Lawrence of Arabia," who moved mysteriously about in his desert costume, trying to rally support for his Arabs. Nicolson described Lawrence as gliding "along the corridors of the Majestic, the lines of resentment hardening around his boyish lips; an undergraduate with a chin," but Shotwell was clearly impressed, calling the romantic Englishman, "a Shelley-like person, and yet too virile to be a poet . . . bronzed by the desert, remarkable blue eyes and a smile around the mouth that responded swiftly to that on the face of his friend."

Bernard Berenson was much in evidence, drawing about him, in Florence Harriman's words, "the progressive liberal figures of the Conference"; he was classified as "interpreter first class."

The city swarmed with émigré Russian nobility; The Grand Duke Alexander lived at the Ritz, and Florence Harriman often dined with him. There were numerous Romanovs and scores of counts. Paris, Eleanor Roosevelt wrote her mother-in-law, "is full beyond belief and one sees many celebrities and all of one's friends."

Among the tide of humanity that swelled the city's population was a young Vietnamese radical named Ho Chi Minh, who had worked as a pastry cook under Escoffier and then as the maker of fake Asian antiquities. He and several of his friends had drafted a proposal for

Vietnamese independence, but without influential friends he was unable to get a hearing. The French socialists were more attentive.

"During the winter and spring of 1918–1919," Colonel House wrote, "Paris was the Mecca for the oppressed not only of Europe but of the earth. Pilgrims came in countless numbers to lay their hopes and grievances at the feet of those in the seats of the mighty. . . . There was much that was pathetic in it all. Delegates would appear overnight, and then, after many weary weeks of waiting, would disappear and would be replaced by others. . . . Nearly all had hearings but these were of necessity of a perfunctory nature, and were given less to obtain real information than to be courteous to some sponsor among the Powers."

"Ten thousand civilian visitors must have come here from every nation in Europe," William Allen White wrote. "For every nation on this globe had some vital interest at this conference. . . . Probably nowhere else on earth were ever assembled so many self-seeking visitors who knew, or thought they knew, exactly what they wanted. The air was filled with international horsetrading. . . . And from the Paris conference sprang the international agreements, patent pools, cartels, trusts, interlocking international directorates that . . . were organized compactly in one huge world-wide compact of plutocracy." That was perhaps the most ironic consequence of the war. All the hopes, all the bloodshed, all the revolutionary ardor, the terrible loss of lives, the maimed and the dislocated—all these had served to make the world not "safe for democracy" but safe, rather, in White's view, for the international "plutocracy."

The young American academics and intellectuals such as Walter Lippmann and Charles Seymour had their British counterparts in John Maynard Keynes, the brilliant economist, and Harold Nicolson, the son of Sir Arthur, a famous British political figure, and Arnold Toynbee, expert on the Near East. Of all those who wrote briefly or copiously on the conference, Nicolson and Keynes were arguably the most brilliant and mordant commentators.

The British delegates were quartered in the Astoria and the Majestic hotels. Keynes wrote of "the peculiar atmosphere and routine" of the hotel, where "the typists drank their tea in the lounge, the dining-room diners distinguished themselves from the restaurant diners . . . and the feverish, persistent and boring gossip of the hellish place had already developed in full measure the peculiar flavour of smallness, cynicism, self-importance and bored excitement that it was never to lose."

Harold Nicolson added his description: "The great hall of the Majestic was gay with the clatter of tea cups; the strains of dance music echoed from below the stairs . . . and the noise of motor cycles sounded from the streets." Like their American counterparts, the Englishmen believed in Wilson's "points" and "principles"—that "People and Provinces shall not be bartered about from sovereignty to sovereignty as if they were but chattels and pawns in the game." Nicholson wrote: "At the words 'pawns' and 'chattels' our lips curled in democratic scorn. . . . We were journeying to Paris . . . to found a new order in Europe. We were preparing not Peace only, but Eternal Peace. . . . We were bent on doing great, permanent and noble things."

The restaurants, theaters, and concert halls were crowded. "The City," William Allen White wrote, "was a place of parties, receptions, teas, conferences, caucuses, secret gatherings." The French outdid themselves, from not entirely disinterested motives, to entertain their legion of guests. The government rented the "gorgeous palace of a rather vulgarly rich man" so lavishly decorated with nudes that it came to be known by the hungry American journalists who frequented it as the House of a Thousand Tits. Henri Bergson was produced for the intellectuals to discuss his "creative evolution," and there was less high-brow entertainment as well. The Chinese rivaled the French in lavish dinners of innumerable and often unidentifiable courses presided over by V. K. Wellington Koo, who spoke perfect English and whose sister was married to a rising young army officer, Colonel Chiang Kai-shek.

There were, as astonishing as anything else, short skirts on women. It was, indeed, as though they had suddenly emerged, like butterflies from cocoons, from their Victorian swaddlings, and everywhere there was the intoxicating sight of female legs. Those stimulating, exciting legs were only the visible symbols of a more general sexual freedom. Paris was, after all, the city of love, licit and illicit. It was filled with young men, with officers on leave, with delegates from dozens of nations. Political intrigue sometimes seemed in danger of being obscured by sexual intrigue. An electric undercurrent of sexuality was evident and added to the atmosphere of unreality. Robert Gilbert Vansittart, an Englishman familiar with prewar Paris, found the city its old "hard self." He wrote: "There were a few modernizations, such as cocktail parties from which women barely tear themselves away in time to dress for dinner. Best-sellers are full of fornication. Sex, superseding slaughter, regained its place as topic of the hour, with a new laxity towards *ces messieurs* of perversion."

Then, of course, there were the journalists, a galaxy of them in the heyday of the Fourth Estate. A number had been reincarnated as diplomats. Norman Hapgood was the Danish consul; Brand Whitlock, ambassador to Belgium; Thomas Nelson Page, to Rome; and, of course, Walter Hines Page, to Britain. In Paris, White stayed at the Vouillemont headquarters with Ray Stannard Baker and half a dozen Americans attached to the peace conference. Oswald Garrison Villard was also quartered there, as was Ida Tarbell, who was writing articles on the conference for the *American Magazine*.

It was at the Vouillemont that William Allen White received word, early in January, of the death of his hero, Theodore Roosevelt. He read the headlines and cried out to Ray Stannard Baker, "Ray, Ray, the Colonel is dead—Roosevelt."

Although Baker was as devoted to Wilson as White to Roosevelt and had deeply resented Roosevelt's relentless attacks at Wilson, he replied sympathetically, "Yes, Will, it's a great blow. We are all sorry." Baker, White, and Tarbell "sat down to talk it over, and get used to a world without Roosevelt in it." White had not been affected so by grief since his father's death. The devotion survived the years. In old age White wrote: "I have never known another person so vital nor another man so dear."

It was Baker's assignment to provide "some one hundred and fifty correspondents representing various press organizations, individual newspapers, magazine and syndicates" with all the news the conferees cared to release. He added that "they were hungry and clamorous," utterly insatiable in their determination to have the news. To appease them, he set up a kind of professoriat made up of scholars in various fields of European and, indeed, world history, with the assignment of writing what we would call today background pieces, essaylike articles dealing with the culture and mores of the different nations involved in the peace treaty.

Occasionally, at Baker's behest, the secretary of state met with American newsmen in his tailcoat with silk binding, doublebreasted gray vest, striped trousers, and gray spats. "His game," William Allen White wrote, was "to convey absolutely nothing as pleasantly as possible." Newsmen plainly alarmed him. White, like the other journalists covering the conference, found it almost impossible to get at the truth. "The American people," he wrote, "only got the facts and not the truth." The truth was infinitely more elusive, and White came to believe that no one knew the full truth.

The principal agency of the conference emerged as the so-called Council of Ten with two representatives of each of the five Great Powers—Great Britain, France, Italy, the United States, and Japan. The halls of the palace on the Quai d'Orsay, where the council met, were, in the words of Mezes, decked out "with trappings that satisfied the senses; pictures were painted; the cinematograph was allowed to approach the fringe of the assemblies." The meeting room was some forty by sixty feet with a high ceiling and arched windows flanked by carved Doric columns and covered by green silk curtains; the gray carpet had faded red roses. The aides and advisers, the expert witnesses and the petitioners sat on small gilt chairs at individual tables. Clemenceau presided with, in Lord Robert Cecil's words, "drastic firmness." The length of the sessions corresponded to the length of the French premier's patience, and he did not hesitate to interrupt a speech he judged too long or repetitious. "These nationalistic quarrels," Charles Seymour wrote, "seemed to him entirely natural, even though inconvenient. His arid humor, his biting sarcasm displayed in an infrequent question, contrasted with the patient earnestness of President Wilson." Next to Wilson sat Lloyd George with Lord Balfour, "the British prime minister, consumed with an electric energy, always on the edge of his chair, questioning and interrupting; Balfour, with his long legs outstretched, his head on the back of his chair, eyes not infrequently closed, philosophic in his attitude." The Japanese were, of course, inscrutable, as they were supposed to be, "enigmatic as Mona Lisa," as Seymour put it. The Italians sat opposite Clemenceau, "Orlando, florid in manner, eloquent in speech"; his foreign minister, Baron Sonnino, a more arresting figure "with eagle features, powerful nose, and jaw set like a vise."

At the opening session, Wilson addressed the delegates, followed by Clemenceau, who declared defiantly the basis of the French position: "The greater the bloody catastrophe which devastated and ruined one of the richest regions of France, the more ample and splendid should be the reparation."

It was as though Wilson were engaged in mortal combat with Clemenceau and were determined to overcome the old "Tiger" with the weapon of words. In every speech he emphasized that he and the other Allied leaders were in Paris as representatives not of particular nationalistic interests but of the wounded humanity of the world. They must not "compromise upon any matter as the champion of this thing—this peace of the world, this attitude of justice, this principle that we are the masters of no people but are here to see that every people in the world shall choose its own masters and govern its own destinies, not as we wish, but as it wishes." Everywhere he went he saw American soldiers in uniform. "They came as crusaders, not merely to win a war, but to win a cause; and I am responsible to them, for it fell to me to formulate the purposes for which I asked them to fight, and I, like them, must be a crusader for these things, whatever it costs and whatever it may be necessary to do, in honor, to accomplish the object for which they fought." Not surprisingly a British delegate described Wilson's manner as "rather like a man preaching to others, or like a professor addressing a class of students. . . . If the President had something nasty to say, one could always tell long before hand by the very sweet and ingratiating tones he used. Always he would begin by saying, 'Well, my friend,' and everyone knew another sermon was about to be delivered.

"Clemenceau got very tired of this. On one occasion just as the President had said, 'Well, my friend,' Clemenceau shouted, 'Mon Dieu! Don't say that again! Every time you do, you send a cold shudder down my spine!' "

"Clemenceau," Lloyd George wrote in his *War Memoirs*, "followed [Wilson's] movement like an old watchdog keeping an eye on a strange and unwelcome dog who has visited the farmyard and of whose intentions he is more than doubtful." He added, "I really think that at first the idealistic President regarded himself as a missionary whose function it was to rescue the poor European heathen from their age-long worship of false and fiery gods. He was apt to address us in that vein beginning with a few simple and elementary truths about right being more important than might, and justice being more eternal than force. . . . They [the Allies] were therefore impatient at having little sermonettes delivered to them, full of rudimentary sentences about things which they had fought for years to vindicate when the President was proclaiming that he was too proud to fight for them." To Lloyd George, Wilson was "the most extraordinary compound . . . of the noble visionary, the implacable and unscrupulous partisan" that he had ever encountered.

Clemenceau, like any astute politician, was concerned to probe Wilson's point of vulnerability. It was, of course, not hard to find; it was the League. Wilson was surprised at the readiness with which Clemenceau accepted it early in the discussions, but the Frenchmen knew that the League was indeed the instrument by which he could lead the President where he wished. As he confided to his aide Jean Jules Mordacq, "When the moment comes to claim French rights, I will have leverage that I might not have at this moment."

Clemenceau said comparatively little; the burden of the French argument was carried by the indefatigable Léon Bourgeois, who first exhausted and then enraged the Americans and the British by his endlessly reiterated arguments against one after the other of the Fourteen Points or the articles of the Covenant of the League. Lord Robert Cecil implored him at one point, when he stopped for breath during a lengthy harangue, "Oh, M. Bourgeois! Do not begin that all over again. We have heard you so often and so patiently."

Lloyd George wrote that Wilson, at one point in the deliberations of the council, said, "Why has Jesus Christ so far not succeeded in inducing the world to follow His teachings . . . ? It is because he taught the ideal without devising any practical means of attaining it. That is the reason why I am proposing a practical scheme [The League of Nations] to carry out His aims." According to Lloyd George's account, Clemenceau "slowly opened his dark eyes to their widest dimensions and swept them around the assembly to see how the Christians gathered around the table enjoyed this exposure of the futility of their Master." Wilson was reported to have confided to House that only the sense that he was doing the Lord's work sustained him. But one may be forgiven some skepticism about Lloyd George's particular version. One of Clemenceau's widely reported wisecracks was "Wilson talks like Jesus Christ but acts like Lloyd George."

A story that circulated, whether apocryphal or not, seemed to Lincoln Steffens to sum up the "inner story" of the peace conference. Clemenceau was reported to have said to his fellow peacemakers, "We can make this a permanent peace; we can remove all the causes of war and set up no new causes of war. It is very, very important what you say, what you have been so long saying, Mr. President. We here now have the opportunity to make a peace that shall last forever, and the French people, diminishing, will be safe. And you are sure you propose to seize this opportunity?"

The others agreed, and Clemenceau, tapping his gray silk gloves gently on the table, then asked if they were ready to pay the price for a real peace.

The price?

"Yes, the price must be that you, Mr. Lloyd George, you English will have to come out of India, for example; we French shall have to come out of North Africa; and you Americans, Mr. President, you will have to get out of the Philippines and Puerto Rico and leave Cuba alone and—Mexico. . . . It is very expensive, peace. We French are willing, but are you willing to pay the price, all those costs of no more war in the world?"

No, they didn't mean exactly that.

"Then," said Clemenceau, "then you don't mean peace. You mean war. And the time for us French to make war is now, when we have got one of our neighbors down; we shall finish him and get ready for— the next war."

As much as Steffens relished the story, as clear a moral as it had for him, Clemenceau's proposition was less *true* than it seemed. "The next war," as it turned out, was one that France was no better prepared for than the one just concluded.

Besides the Council of Ten, the most important body in the initial phase of the conference was the Commission on the League of Nations, composed of fifteen members, ten representing the Five Great Powers and five representing the "lesser powers." Wilson presided, and prominent members were Lord Robert Cecil (who had drawn up his own plan for the League) and General Smuts of South Africa, who was credited with the idea of the mandates; Eleutherios Venizelos of Greece, one of the most commanding and dramatic figures in Paris; Dmowski, the Polish representative; and Bourgeois, Clemenceau's right-hand man. The commission met in an atmosphere of urgency. Wilson was due to return to the United States in a few weeks to address the opening of Congress, and he was determined to take with him the draft of the Covenant of the League of Nations. The commissioners had, in consequence, only two weeks to "organize, to deliberate, and to submit its report to the Conference," as Lansing noted. This meant a hectic rush to complete the document upon which, it was hoped, the future peace of the world would rest.

The original draft submitted by Wilson on January 10 provided for a Council of the League to consist of one representative from each of the Allied and "Associated" powers—the United States, Great Britain, France, Italy, and Japan—along with four representatives of the smaller nations chosen out of the general membership by the Assembly. No action could be adopted by the League without the unanimous vote of the Council. The Assembly did not vote except on four or five relatively unimportant matters. Even in those cases all the nations represented in the Council had to concur in the vote of the Assembly.

Thus the United States, of course, could always block or, in effect, veto any measure to which it was opposed (as could any other members of the Council). The charge that a "supergovernment" was set up over the United States was, Wilson pointed out time and time again, "sheer nonsense." Strictly speaking, the United States with its fellow Council members came much closer to constituting a supergovernment able to overawe and intimidate the rest of the world.

Article VI provided that a "covenant-breaking State" should be disciplined by "a complete economic and financial boycott, including the severance of all trade or financial relations." If such measures failed, the Executive Council of the League would recommend "what effective military or naval force to which members of the League shall severally contribute." Once the "covenant-breaking State" had been defeated, it would be "subject to perpetual disarmament."

For all those "Contracting Powers" that joined the League, existing treaties, inconsistent with the aims of the League, would become null and void.

One of the more interesting and idealistic sections of the Covenant was the second paragraph of Article IV, which required "the reduction of national armaments to the lowest point consistent with domestic safety and the enforcement by common action of international obligations." The signatories of the treaty were also to agree "to abolish conscription and all other forms of compulsory military service" and that "their future forces of defence and of international action shall consist of militia or volunteers. . . ."

An important addition to the draft that the members of the Inquiry had prepared was the section on the mandates, primarily George Beer's work, based on General Smuts's suggestions. The Smuts plan proposed a kind of trusteeship by the League over what were called the mandated territories, many of them formerly colonies of one or the other of the Central Powers. These entities, many of them islands, could not be simply turned adrift, the argument ran. They needed various kinds of assistance and, above all, protection from the rapacity of powers great and small. It was Smuts's inspiration to have the League take them under its wing as "the heir of the Empires" until they were ready for independent nationhood. They would be parceled out among the various members under the League's mandate, as tutors and protectors. The Smuts plan appeared in the draft of the Covenant in the following words: "As successor to the Empires, the League of Nations is empowered, directly and without right of delegation, to watch over the relations *inter se* of all new independent states arising or created out of the Empires, and shall assume and fulfill the duty of conciliating and composing differences between them with a view to the maintenance of settled order and peace." The League could, in turn, request various nations, free, presumably of the taint of colonialism, to act as tutors and protectors of such entities, under the "mandate" of the League.

Under Article XIII, which abrogated all treaties of member nations inconsistent with the terms of the Covenant, were six supplementary agreements dealing with the former colonies of the defeated powers as well as "all new States" arising from those empires: Turkey, Austria-Hungary, and Germany. The League of Nations was to be the "residual trustee" of the colonies "with sovereign right of ultimate disposal or of continued administration in accordance with certain fundamental principles. . . . These principles are, that there shall be in no case any annexation of any of these territories by any State either within the League or outside of it." Finally, the "rule of self-determination, or the consent of the governed to their form of government, shall be fairly and reasonably applied. . . ."

The League could delegate "its authority, control, or administration of any such people to some single State or organized agency which it may designate and appoint as its agent or mandatory."

Wilson read the hastily drafted Covenant to a plenary session of the peace conference on February 14. It was, he told the delegates, "a definite guarantee of peace." Many terrible things had come out of the war, "but some very beautiful things have come out of it. Wrong has been defeated, but the rest of the world has been more conscious than it was before of the majesty of right. People that were suspicious of one another can now live as friends and comrades in a single family. . . . The miasma of distrust, of intrigue, is cleared away. Men are looking eye to eye and saying, 'We are brothers and have a common purpose . . . and this is our covenant of fraternity and friendship.' "

When Wilson finished, House passed him a note: "Dear Governor, Your speech was as great as the occasion—I am very happy—EMH."

A few hours later Wilson was on his way back to the United States to meet a rebellious Congress. His departure left a curious hiatus in the conference. House met regularly with the council, and the commissions carried on their arduous labors, but the leader was gone, and there were still a number of unsettled issues, the most important being reparations, French security, and the left bank of the Rhine. Finally, there was the question of Italy's ambitions in the Adriatic and the determination of the Japanese to lay claim to the Chinese province of Shantung. House hoped that Wilson would stay in Washington and leave the day-to-day negotiations in his hands and those of the members of the peace delegation.

Before Wilson departed for the United States, House urged him to take a conciliatory line with Hoke Smith, the powerful Senator from Georgia. If he would only ask Smith to the White House and show him some attention, the Senator might become a valuable ally. But Wilson was adamant. "I shall do nothing of the sort!" he replied. "That man is an ambulance chaser. I scorn to have any relations with him whatsoever." The fact was that the President, after having earned his law degree and doing a stint of teaching, had hung out his shingle as a lawyer in Atlanta, believing that to be the surest road to political office, at the same time that Hoke Smith had begun his own practice. Smith, a young "good old boy" with an instinct for the law, had been an immediate success, and Wilson a humiliating failure, forced to return reluctantly to the academic world and to a future that seemed bereft of any political hope.

Ray Stannard Baker accompanied the President and Mrs. Wilson. Also along was the young assistant secretary of the navy, Franklin D. Roosevelt, who, in Baker's view, possessed "great charm of presence and of manner. He was enthusiastic and earnest, he was a mine of information regarding ships and the sea. . . ."

Wilson carried the initial draft of the League of Nations Covenant in the breast pocket of his coat as though he could not bear to be parted from that precious document. With Wilson on the high seas, Stephen Bonsal wrote in his journal that "the time has come to make what record I can of how what many regard as a miracle was wrought." The Peace Conference was hardly a month old.

Four days after Wilson's departure, as Clemenceau was on his way to a meeting with Colonel House, a young anarchist woodworker named Emile Cottin stepped out of a crowd and fired at Clemenceau's limousine, calling out, "I am a Frenchman and an anarchist!" As the car sped away, Cottin ran after it, firing seven or eight more shots, one of which hit Clemenceau and lodged near his heart. Clemenceau, the veteran of a dozen duels, said, "The animal shoots well."

Cottin's prosecutor wished to call for the death penalty, but Clemenceau intervened, declaring, to the delight of his countrymen, "We have just won the most terrible war in history, yet here is a Frenchman who misses his target six times out of seven. . . . Of course the fellow must be punished for the careless use of a dangerous weapon and for poor marksmanship." His recommendation was eight years in prison "with intensive training in a shooting gallery." The assassination attempt, the wound, and the old hero's lighthearted treatment of the whole affair greatly heightened Clemenceau's "public image."

Without waiting for the President to arrive in Washington to present and elucidate the Covenant of the League, his enemies in Congress began their attack upon it and upon him. Ironically, it was Miles Poindexter, Progressive Republican Senator from the state of Washington, who led the assault. Poindexter was an example of the disarray in the Progressive faction of the Republican Party. A strong advocate of Wilson's domestic program, he had parted company with La Follette on the issue of American entry into the war and joined forces with the "hawks." Now he came forth as a leader of the Senators opposed to the League of Nations. He was one of the Republican Senators reelected in 1918 despite Wilson's plea for a Democratic Congress, and he returned to that chamber in a defiant mood. He was followed on the floor of the Senate by James Alexander Reed, Senator from Missouri. Like Poindexter, Reed had begun his political career as a reformer. As mayor of Kansas City and a "gas and water socialist," Reed had led the battle against the street railways and the privately owned utilities and as a Democrat been elected in 1910 to the U.S. Senate, where he joined with Progressive Republicans, Poindexter among them, to help pass Wilson's legislation. Reed had been a supporter of Wilson's neutrality policy, and he had followed the President's lead on U.S. entry into the war, but he became disenchanted with what he felt was Wilson's excessive concentration of power in his own hands, and he turned, soon afterward, into one of the most intractable foes of the Treaty of Versailles and the League of Nations. Not surprisingly, Henry Cabot Lodge was the next important Senator to register dissent.

In an effort to blunt the criticism of Republicans in Congress, Wilson solicited the opinions of Elihu Root and former President Taft, assuring them that their objections would be presented to the peace conference when he returned to Paris. He then laid the Covenant before a conference of the House and Senate foreign relations committees and asked for their criticisms. Lodge refused to state his objections, but others pointed out various blemishes, among them the failure to exempt the Monroe Doctrine from the general provisions of the Covenant and to state that the League could not act on domestic issues, such as immigration. The right of a nation to withdraw from the League should also be spelled out, and recognition made of the fact that Congress, not the President, had the right to declare war or make peace.

Obviously three forces were at work against the President, the treaty, and the Covenant. First, Wilson had alienated many Congressmen and Senators by what seemed to them his high-handed and imperious way of conducting the war on the domestic front. Not only had he bypassed Congress in the creation and staffing of a multitude of wartime boards and commissions, but he had also been tactless and cavalier in his dealings with individual legislators. His manners repelled them as much as his policies. In the arena of foreign policy, his messianic proclamations alarmed some and infuriated others. Not only had he shown a lofty disregard for the views and feelings of Congress, but he seemed bent as well on personally directing the fortunes of the world. As we have had ample opportunity to note, the resistance to American involvement in the war was strong and widespread. Wilson's inspired rhetoric had carried the majority of Americans along with him by providing a rationale for U.S. participation, but especially in the West that accommodation was never more than skin-deep, and Wilson's sense that it was extremely unsubstantial made him particularly remorseless in suppressing all opposition to him and to his policies (to him they were indeed the same thing).

Perhaps equally crippling, Wilson inherited the bitter animosity of that considerable number of Americans who worshiped Theodore Roosevelt. With men like Lodge, the Roosevelt mania took the form of a personal animus so strong that it may be suspected that nothing Wilson might have done could have won their support. They hated him and all his works unreasoningly and *on principle*. If we add to this formidable array of enemies the loyal followers of La Follette and (not entirely synonymous) the pacifists and socialists, it is a wonder that Wilson was able to accomplish as much as he did. Under the circumstances it was wise for him to go abroad and to involve himself in the details of the peace conference. The fact was that his constituency was abroad rather than at home, and Wilson was by no means insensitive to that fact. Had he remained at home to "mind the store," as Lansing and many others believed he should, he might have found himself embroiled in daily wrangles with Congress while it was in session and with a host of lay critics when it was adjourned. If there was any hope for the League's acceptance in the United States, it depended, in large measure, on Wilson's ability to project the image of himself as a world leader.

The day before Wilson left to return to the peace conference in Paris, Senator Lodge offered his fellow Senators a resolution that in effect disavowed the President and the League. The most pertinent paragraph declared, "It is the sense of the Senate that while it is their sincere desire that the nations of the world should unite to promote peace and general disarmament, the Constitution of the League of Nations in the form now proposed to the Peace Conference should not be accepted by the United States." Invited a few days earlier to suggest changes in the Covenant, Lodge had declined. Now he proposed to forestall consideration of the League entirely. A Senator blocked a vote on the resolution, but thirty-nine Senators signed a statement declaring that they would have voted for the resolution if a vote had been possible under the rules of the Senate. Among them were such incongruous allies as Hiram Johnson, the leader of California Progressives, and Boies Penrose, the notorious Pennsylvania boss. Albert Cummins, another Insurgent or Progressive, added his name to those of William Borah; I. L. Lenroot, the La Follette lieutenant; and Reed Smoot, a seasoned member of the Republican old guard. The Republican strategy was to separate the treaty itself from the League of Nations Covenant. For some of the Senators the motive was more than mere party politics. They were convinced that a treaty was urgent and that attaching the League Covenant to it must cause delay. They genuinely believed that ample time was needed to review in detail every aspect of the League and resented the very evident determination of the President to wrest a favorable verdict from them, using the necessity of the treaty to do so. Others were undoubtedly, as David Houston charged, playing politics with "the election of 1920 particularly in view."

On the eve of his departure for France the first week of March, the President, in an address delivered at the New York Opera House, announced his intention to weave the League so thoroughly into the treaty that the Senate Republicans could not reject the League without rejecting the entire treaty and bringing upon themselves the opprobrium that must attach to a refusal to bring the war to an official end. It was a tactical error on Wilson's part. It was one thing to conceive of such a strategy; it was another to announce it to his enemies and, in effect, dare them to accept the challenge. The President's implication plainly was that the American people wished a definitive treaty *and* a

League. If the Senators by rejecting the League and the treaty with it defied the electorate, they would, it must be assumed, be punished at the polls. But the fact was that Republicans had received a substantial accession of power in the midterm elections of 1918, and only a relatively few would be vulnerable to the voters' anger if indeed such anger existed. Nonetheless, the assumption by the Senators that there was widespread popular support for the League made them initially cautious in attacking it directly.

36

Troubled Europe

While the Allied leaders sat in Paris "making the next war," in the view of the increasingly cynical Lincoln Steffens, Europe was racked by revolutionary upheavals and sporadic fighting. Germany, meanwhile, waited in a kind of limbo to hear its fate; Russia, for a moment at least, was under the control of the Bolsheviks. Bavaria was in revolt, and Austria had declared the Hapsburg Empire at an end.

Newspaper correspondents like Oswald Garrison Villard and Steffens found their way to Germany as best they could and sent back reports of starvation and revolution. Even before the Armistice the German government had planned to have the fleet slip out of the harbor at Kiel on October 29. On the thirty-first as the ships were getting up steam, the sailors had mutinied, joined forces with the soldiers in the port, elected a workers' council on the Russian model, and chosen a "commission" to visit Lenin. In Berlin there had been an immediate response from the Communists, and Karl Liebknecht, the Socialist leader, had flown the red flag from the kaiser's palace, where only a few hours earlier Wilhelm had held his last court before fleeing to Holland.

With the flight of the kaiser the chancellor turned over the government to the leader of the Majority Socialist Party, Friedrich Ebert.

A dozen Socialist and Communist factions contended for control in Berlin. The Spartacists, organized by Liebknecht and Rosa Luxemburg, represented the pro-Bolshevik wing of the radical movement. They were joined by elements of the Independent Socialist Party. There were parades, demonstrations, violent confrontations with the police, and, finally, a mass uprising of workers, 200,000 strong. The Communists were in control of Germany's greatest city. For a moment it looked as though the Socialists and Communists in some combination would assert their dominance, thereby marking a critically important advance in the world socialist revolution that radicals everywhere so eagerly anticipated.

In this atmosphere the Second Socialist International met at Berne, Switzerland, in February, 1919. It was a strange collection of revolutionaries. The most conspicuous delegate was Kurt Eisner, the intellectual Socialist Jew, premier of Bavaria. Eduard Bernstein, a German Marxist theoretician and scholar, was also much in evidence. Eisner was described by Oswald Garrison Villard, who slipped out of Paris to attend the gathering, as "a bald-headed, black-bearded man inclined to stoutness, who looked like nothing so much as an absent-minded professor. . . ." He was widely quoted as having declared, "The Wittelsbachs [the rulers of Bavaria] had ruled . . . for eight hundred years. With eight men I drove them out in eight hours." He had made an ex-sergeant minister of war, organized demobilized soldiers into a kind of state militia, and set up a republican government. The speech he gave to the delegates was, Villard thought, "one of the most remarkable and the bravest" he had ever heard. Eisner accepted the guilt of Germany in bringing on the war and appealed for an army of "German architects, builders, designers, and laborers . . . to build up where Germans had so wickedly destroyed. . . ."

Ramsay MacDonald and Arthur Henderson represented Britain. Rosika Schwimmer, who had persuaded Ford to undertake his ill-fated peace mission, was present as the Hungarian minister to Switzerland. The conference approved of the League of Nations, called for an international tribunal, the disbanding of all armies, free trade, and "free access to all countries." An enthusiastic Villard wrote to the *Nation:* "Though no Socialist myself, if I had the power to decide on which conference to rest the future of the world I would unhestitatingly, and with real joy, decide for this simple conference with its plain membership."

Two weeks after the Socialist International had adjourned, Kurt

Eisner was assassinated by Count Anton Acro-Valley. The count was a leader in an anti-Semitic society called the Thule, whose logo was a swastika. After Eisner's death a group called the Coffee House Anarchists held power for six days before they were ousted. A "Red Army" of some 30,000 men was formed, but it dissolved rapidly when food and munitions proved impossible to obtain.

The *Freikorps*, or militia, made up of men too old for military service, wounded veterans, German army officers, and boys in their midteens, was hastily mustered up. The *Freikorps* was dispatched to bring Munich and Bavaria into line. The "soldiers" of the corps were obsessed with the notion that the German Army had not been defeated by the Allies but had been betrayed by intellectuals, radicals, Jews (who were prominent in the left-wing parties of Germany), and politicians— the "November criminals" who had signed the armistice. When they reached Munich, the members of the *Freikorps* wreaked destruction, shooting down all who opposed them. Interrupting a meeting of Catholic workers, they shot or bayoneted a number of them. Armed with machine guns, mortars, and flamethrowers, they ruthlessly suppressed the uprising after ten days of bloody street fighting. Luxemburg and Liebknecht were arrested and murdered. In this atmosphere elections were held for a national assembly to meet at Weimar to draft a constitution and conclude peace with the Allies. The Majority Socialists polled 39 percent of the vote, and the Independent Socialists 7 percent, while the Communists refused to participate. Most ominously, in terms of the future, the National People's Party, the party of aristocrats, bankers, industrialists, and army officers, garnered 10 percent of the vote.

One of the grimmest aspects of the Allies' punitive attitude toward Germany was the naval blockade which prevented food from reaching that country and its allies during the period of the peace conference. To many people the Allied policy of withholding food from the German people as a means of destroying their will to resist and forcing on Germany conditions that only the most extreme desperation could have persuaded the nation to accept was both cruel and foolish. "The godly Presbyterian from the White House," Oswald Garrison Villard wrote bitterly, " . . . could not be induced to make a public stand against this indefensible cruelty to noncombatants; the screw of starvation was kept turned in order to compel the vanquished to sign whatever treaty might be drafted."

Villard was horrified at the conditions in Berlin. "As I went to lunch in the business center," he wrote, "I met long processions of workmen, horribly pale, gaunt and lean, and ragged, so overworked, starved and hungry-looking as to move my heart. . . . There is disorder in every direction," he added, "thieving, burglary, murder. . . ." Hundreds of thousands of unemployed workmen, their numbers swollen by demobilized soldiers, roamed the streets. Villard was convinced that Bavaria, and much of Germany with it, would turn "Bolshevik" within a few months if the Allies continued to block all imports of food. In Dresden the situation was, if possible, worse. The signs of famine were everywhere evident in the swollen bellies and stiffened limbs of children.

The Allied leaders, in Villard's words, believed that their military victory "gave them the right to deprive Germany of millions of her people, much of her soil, half of her coal supply, and three-fourths of her iron ore, all of her colonies, all her great steamships, the free use of her railroads, and free disposal of her industrial products. . . ." Pacifist Josephus Daniels, the secretary of the navy, exulted that "Germany had been rendered impotent for all time to come."

William Allen White noted in Cologne that the city was crowded with demobilized soldiers. Soup kitchens were running full blast. Jobs were scarce, and politics was everywhere. All factions seemed united only in fighting the "Reds." The Catholics were the most vocal anti-Red group, followed by the Socialists, the Social Democrats, and the Democratic People's Party. The sides of buildings were plastered with political posters and exhortations. The American soldiers and officers in the occupation forces showed a disconcerting tendency to make friends with the Germans in the towns and villages where they were quartered, and army headquarters was forced to issue a string of stern bulletins warning against "fraternization," warnings often ignored.

In Philip Gibbs's words, "the innocent were made to suffer for the guilty and we were not generous. We maintained the blockade, and German children starved, and German mothers weakened, and German girls swooned in the tram-cars, and German babies died. Ludendorff did not starve or die. Neither did Hindenburg, nor any German war lord, nor any profiteer. . . . But in the side-streets, among the working-women, there was, as I found, the wolf of hunger standing with open jaws by every doorway. It was not actual starvation, but what the Germans call *unternahrung* (under-nourishment), producing rickety children, consumptive girls, and men out of whom the vitality has gone."

It was not, of course, the Germans alone who suffered from the Allied blockade. The populations of all the nations that made up the Central Powers also suffered acutely, as Gibbs said, the innocent with the guilty.

With the armistice Herbert Hoover was once more summoned to feed the hungry French and Belgians. "We knew from the Belgian Relief experience," he wrote, "that there were legions of starving waifs and subnormal children throughout Europe who must have special care at once if they were not to become a generation of incompetents and criminals." What seemed most deplorable to Hoover was the Allied blockade "of food and other supplies" against "Twenty-three neutral, liberated, and enemy countries and Russia." He was convinced that both the "liberated" and "enemy" nations must have food at once "if we were to maintain the order and stability upon which peace and freedom of men could be built." Hoover's first experence of the temper of the allied ministers was profoundly disillusioning. He discovered that they were determined to maintain the blockade with the purpose of breaking the German spirit of resistance if any remained. The fact that such a policy must fall severely on the "neutral" or "liberated" nations and, in all nations, on those least able to tolerate acute hunger—the poor, the aged, women, and children—failed to budge them. "This morning session," Hoover wrote, "was at once an enlightenment in national intrigue, selfishness, nationalism, heartlessness, rivalry and suspicion, which seemed to ooze from every pore—but with polished politeness. . . . It was something of a shock to realize that the war and all its elevation of spirit had not changed the collective minds of the British, French or Italians. It was still Empire First—and against all comers. . . ." It was evident to Hoover that the Allies, dependent as they were on American food and loans, were deeply concerned that the President not use *their* needs to secure a treaty which they might consider prejudicial to their interests. Rather, they wanted to use American food and credits to coerce the conduct of neutral, defeated, and liberated nations. The so-called Clementel plan was to Hoover a shameless effort to establish Allied control of American resources by having those resources controlled by commissions dominated by the Allies. The normally reserved Hoover, Villard reported, cursed the French "with the ease and skill of a coal miner. . . . This humane and courageous fight of Hoover's for a sensible policy toward the defeated country and Russia stands out as his finest achievement," Villard added.

Even after Hoover thought that he had secured the agreement

of the Allies to lift the blockade, he found that the Allied blockade committee refused to issue the necessary orders, and the British navy refused to allow ships carrying food to pass through to German ports. Lest there be an uncertainty about British feeling, Winston Churchill declared in the House of Commons, "The evidence I have received . . . shows, first of all, the great privations which the German people are suffering, and, secondly, the great danger of the collapse of the entire structure of German social and national life under the pressure of hunger and malnutrition. Now is therefore the moment to settle."

Hoover concentrated on winning David Lloyd George as an ally. He explained the obstructionist tactics of Lloyd George's "minions" and prevailed on him to take the issue up at the next meeting of the council. "Never," John Maynard Keynes wrote of Lloyd George, "have I more admired his extraordinary powers . . . [as] he spoke . . . the creeping lethargy of the proceedings was thrown off, and he launched his words with rage. . . ." When he had finished speaking, a messenger arrived (by prearrangement, as it turned out) with word from the Allied commander in Berlin that "food must be sent into this area . . . without delay. The mortality amongst women, children, and sick is most grave, and sickness due to hunger is spreading. The attitude of the population is becoming one of despair. . . ." The dramatic impact was overpowering, and a reluctant Clemenceau at last gave way. Lloyd George laid the blame for the blockade on the French, a disingenuous act because the blame was largely that of the British. Winston Churchill had been one of the principal advocates of the blockade, and Lloyd George himself had campaigned for prime minister on a platform of merciless punishment of the defeated Germans.

When Hoover's part in the ending of the blockade became public knowledge, he found himself, for one of the few times in his life, the target of widespread denunciation. He replied in a statement headed "Why We Are Feeding Germany." First, he declared, there was the fact that his "Western upbringing" had taught him that "we do not kick a man in the stomach after we have licked him." Beyond that, he added, "I would say that it is because there are seventy millions of people who must either produce or die. . . . All we have done for Germany is to lift the blockade to a degree that allows her to import her food from any market she wishes . . . at full prices. Taking it by and large, our face is forward, not backward on history. We and our children must live with these seventy million Germans. No matter how deeply we may feel at the present moment, our vision must stretch over the next hundred years and we must write now into history such acts as will stand credulity in the minds of our grandchildren."

The total amount of food brought into Europe during the period when Hoover's mission was in operation exceeded 27,000,000 tons; in addition, 840,000,000 pounds of clothing and medical supplies were imported. More than $325,000,000 was distributed in the form of direct charity. The American relief organizations also moved 30,000,000 tons of coal and 1,000,000 tons of food within Europe. It was Hoover's settled view years later that "the blockade on food during those four months from the Armistice until March was a crime in statesmanship and against civilization as a whole."

Getting the blockade lifted was, of course, only half the battle. Food had to be bought, shipped to Europe, and distributed to the hungry in a dozen war-devastated countries. "Mission specialists" were dispatched to all the eighteen liberated and enemy countries and six to the neutrals. Their task was to establish "the machinery of economic rehabilitation." The Americans assured their hosts that they were not interested in "power politics" and would use food only to feed the people who needed it most urgently. A total of 2,500 men, recruited wherever they could be found, served as the agents of the mission. There was undoubtedly considerable truth in Hoover's proud observation that there was "never . . . such an exhibit of the power of the American way of life. . . ."

What preyed most on Hoover's mind and conscience was the fact that "there was a mass of waif, orphan, undernourished, diseased and stunted children in every town and city of the liberated and enemy areas. There were literally millions of them. They were not only pitiable little persons, but they were a menace to their nations. Unless remedied, their distorted minds were a menace to all mankind." The surveys conducted by the mission had indicated that as many as 12,000,000 children were seriously undernourished. When the American Red Cross confessed that it did not have the resources to tackle the problem, Hoover's mission took it on as "a free gift of the American people." He set up the children's feeding section under the American Relief Administration. Women of every country took the lead in the organization of chapters established to collect food and money. "Thus," Hoover wrote, "hundreds of thousands of men and women of these countries became partners with us." By his calculations the children's feeding section passed some 14,000,000 to 16,000,000 children through the process from undernourishment to health.

One of Hoover's most successful "missions" was that to Poland. Hoover had known Paderewski from his college days at Stanford, when as an undergraduate impresario he had scheduled the famous pianist for a performance. Paderewski and Roman Dmowski had used their talents so skillfully that in Hoover's words, they won an expanded Poland "beyond the powers of the nation to assimilate the minorities they took in. They secured entirely too many fringes of Germans, Czechs, Russians and Lithuanians for the good of Poland." At Paderewski's request, Hoover sent "a whole staff of expert advisers for his government departments of finance, railways and food. . . ." Indeed, it seemed at times that Americans, not Poles, were running the country.

Conditions in Europe were nowhere worse than in Finland. There, Hoover wrote after a visit to the war-devastated country, "it was a story of destroyed crops, of plundered and burned granaries, of stagnated imports and exports, a people eating bread made from a mixture of the bark of trees, a heart-breaking death roll amongst the weak and the children." Although the Finns, under General Carl Mannerheim, had thrown off German rule and declared themselves independent, the Allies refused to recognize the new nation, hoping that Communist Russia would collapse and that the status of Finland could then be negotiated with a new Russian government. Meanwhile, Finns starved to death, and Hoover turned his attention to trying to get the Big Four to take some action that would make Allied food available to the Finns. "By lack of recognition," Hoover wrote in a memorandum to Wilson, "they are absolutely isolated from . . . the rest of the world. They are unable to market their products. . . . They are totally unable to establish credit. . . . They are isolated by censorship. . . . If ever there was a case of helping a people who are making a sturdy fight to get on a basis of liberal democracy, and are asking no charity of the world whatever, this is the case." When the Big Four finally relented and recognized Finland, Hoover, with the assistance of thousands of Finnish women, set up another relief organization, which, in a few months, distributed 35,000,000 free meals to children.

The most alarming development of all was the seizure of power in Hungary by the Communists under the leadership of Béla Kun. The Big Four dispatched General Smuts to assess the situation in that country. There was an additional scandal over the fact that Italian

Army officers had sold millions of dollars worth of arms to Kun's Communists.

Kun clearly wanted to use the arrival of the mission to give legitimacy to his shaky regime, dependent as it was upon the army, but Smuts was determined to give no support. Instead, he presented an Allied demand for a neutral zone between Hungary and Rumania to be occupied by Allied troops. When Kun presented a counterproposal, Smuts, having decided that Kun was "just an incident and not worth treating seriously," in Harold Nicolson's words, withdrew, escorted his guests to the station platform, and steamed off, leaving the bewildered Communist and his aides staring after the train. Smuts predicted that Kun could not hold power for more than six weeks. Actually he proved surprisingly tenacious of power. It was August before he and a handful of his followers fled to Russia.

Pervading every issue, complicating the solution of every problem was the enigma of Russia or, more specifically, of the Bolsheviks. Winston Churchill was obsessed with them and called continually for an Allied invasion of Russia to oust them. In March and April, 1919, General Nikolai N. Yudenich gathered a motley army of White Russians, Finns, and Estonians, equipped with British and French arms and supplied by the Allies, and began an advance from Estonia toward Petrograd with the avowed purpose of capturing that city and making it the capital of White Russian resistance to the Soviets. A few miles from Petrograd, Yudenich's army revealed its true colors by disintegrating and plundering the army stores in the process.

At the same time the French demanded that the Americans provide food for the civilian population of Odessa, which was held by French troops supporting General Piotr N. Wrangel's White Russian army operating in southern Russia. The French troops, however, had no appetite for further fighting. Threats of mutiny forced the French government to recall them.

Lloyd George had perhaps the most realistic view of the hold of the Bolsheviks on the Russian peasants. "The peasants," he told Wilson, "accepted Bolshevism for the same reason as the peasants . . . accepted the French Revolution, namely, that it gave them land. The Bolsheviks were the de facto government. . . . To say that we ourselves should pick the representative of a great people was contrary to every principle for which we have fought." (This was in response to the suggestion by Baron Sonnino that the Big Four should simply designate, out of the thousands of refugee Russians in Paris, one as the "representative of Russia.")

A Latvian Soviet Republic was set up under Russian auspices in the winter of 1919, and all bourgeois enemies of the state were thrown in prison and/or shot, with particular attention to professionals—doctors, lawyers, teachers, and clergymen. When the Reds were overthrown by the Whites, led by German officers, a counterrevolutionary terror took place, with mass executions of Communists and leftists of various degrees. Wilson and the other members of the Big Four were denounced for their failure to recognize the right of the inhabitants of Estonia, Latvia, Lithuania, the Ukraine, and Georgia to determine the "sovereignty under which they shall live." The problem was, of course, that any effort to separate those peoples from "Greater Russia" would have meant war with Soviet Russia.

Wilson and Lloyd George prevailed upon a reluctant Clemenceau to approve of a conference to be held at Prinkipo, an island in the Sea of Marmora. The notion was that representatives of Estonia, Latvia, Lithuania, and the northern Russian "republic" with its capital at Archangel and under the leadership of Tchaikovsky (where Frazier Hunt had gone to report on the life of the American soldiers in the Allied expeditionary force) meet with emissaries of Lenin and Trotsky and Allied representatives to guarantee the "peace of the Baltic." The intention was clearly to try to extract from the Bolsheviks a promise not to extend their sway over the Baltic states, which had recently been part of Greater Russia. Somewhat to his surprise, William Allen White found himself appointed an American representative to the conference, apparently at the instance of Ray Stannard Baker, but more surprised to find that a fellow American delegate was George Herron, the Christian Socialist, the "young Isaiah" who had created such a stir on college campuses in the 1890s. Herron, who had started a Christian Socialist community in Georgia, had, the reader may recall, believed in "affinity" and free love. His wife had rebelled and divorced him, and Herron had married Carrie Rand, the daughter of his benefactress. White discovered that Herron owed his appointment to his friendship with Wilson, which dated back to the "glory days" when Herron had carried his doctrines of Christian socialism and sacrifice to the Princeton campus. Now in his fifties, he wore, in White's description, a square "French" beard and had a "soft but almost tragically insistent voice, an overwhelming (at least to me) self-assurance, cloaked by a quiet, repressed, and rather deadly manner ... utterly humorless." Dogged by scandal in the United States, Herron, as we noted earlier, established himself in Germany and became a prominent figure in radical German academic and intellectual circles. Wilson had used Herron's services in the early years of the war as a liaison officer between the Allies and the German radicals and Social Democrats, a handful of whom opposed the war. Bitterly disillusioned by the failure of German socialists to oppose the German invasion of Belgium and the war in general, Herron had written an angry book entitled *Germany Must Be Destroyed.* That he still enjoyed Wilson's confidence is indicated by his appointment to the projected Prinkipo Conference. White found him a treasury of information about the tangled politics of the Central Powers. When the Weimar Republic began its brief and troubled tenure of power, Herron, who knew many of the officials of the new government, was especially helpful to Wilson. White was impressed in spite of himself at the manners and knowledge of Herron, who, starting life as a poor boy from a Midwestern small town, had become "a solemn one-gallused intellectual."

Samuel Gompers was among the opponents of the Prinkipo Conference, and William Allen White recalled the meeting at the Vouillemont when he and Herron tried to persuade Gompers and his newfound ally William English Walling, whose defection to the Allied cause from socialist neutrality had cost him his wife's affection, to support the conference. Hearing Herron at his brilliant best, White felt he could understand the remarkable influence that the man exerted on Wilson and, it was said, on the leaders of the Weimar Republic.

White did not wonder that Wilson sought Herron's counsel; he was only sorry that he did not heed it more. He was convinced that Herron had the best grasp of European power politics and, more particularly, of the ambitions of the French to succeed to the role of dominant European power, of any of the numerous journalists, politicians, and diplomats to whom White talked interminably during his months in Paris. At last, after arousing considerable expectations, the Prinkipo Conference was canceled. According to White, the French persuaded the delegates from the Baltic countries that it would be a shameful thing to sit down at a table "with representatives of robbers, murderers, and arsonists who had overthrown the Russian government and brutally murdered the Czar."

The other, even odder "Russian gambit" was to dispatch William Bullitt, a twenty-eight-year-old "Yalie," a member of the Philadelphia upper class, to sound out Lenin on some accommodation with the

Bolsheviks. White, put off by Bullitt's upper-class Eastern manners, wrote that "he came from a different star, moving in a different social orbit, and we had to let mutual admiration rather than understanding grease the machinery of our relations." He described Bullitt as having "a quick brain, a precise, logical process," who "knew many things in many books" which the older and more practical White was inclined to doubt.

Bullitt picked an ex-social worker named Captain Petit and Lincoln Steffens as his companions. Traveling to Sweden to find a route that would get the party into Russia, the members of the highly informal "mission" acquired a Communist guide named Kil Baum. The oddly assorted group made, in Steffens's words, "a murderous peace commission."

Steffens wrote about the arrival of the mission that "Petrograd was a deserted city when we got there at night. Nobody was at the station, nobody in the dark cold, broken streets, and there was no fire in the vacant palace assigned to us. I . . . was called out by our Swedish and Russian guides to go looking through dead hotels for officials at midnight teas. . . . I was led from one tea to another till at last the guide found and presented me to [Grigori E.] Zinoviev, one of the three commissioners appointed to deal with us." Finally ensconced in a warm palace with servants, the group received "piles and piles of caviar . . . caviar and black bread and tea."

One of the first sights that greeted Steffens was Bill Shatoff, a Chicago Wobbly, who was chief of police in Petrograd. "He was a happy man," Steffens noted, "he had seen 'the' revolution; it had won; and he had seen a light. He was the first man," Steffens added, "to show me that after a revolution has happened you see everything in a new way." Shatoff had been an anarchist, and now he was chief of police.

As Steffens looked about him, the only thing he felt certain of was that "Soviet Russia was a revolutionary government with a revolutionary plan. Their plan was, not by direct action to resist such evils as poverty and riches, graft, privilege, tyranny, and war, but to seek out and remove the causes of them. . . . It was a new culture, an economic, scientific, not a moral, culture." It seemed to him that the determination of Americans to measure political matters by a moral yardstick hopelessly obscured the real, "scientific" nature of things. That appeared to be the only way out of the morass, the only way out of the endless and debilitating cycle of corruption, reform, corruption.

When Bullitt and Steffens gained an audience with Lenin, they found him a "quiet figure in old clothes," who greeted the Americans with "a nod and a handshake. An open inquiring face, with a slight droop in one eye that suggested irony or humor." When Steffens asked the Russian leader what assurance he could give that the executions that had so inflamed public opinion in the West could cease, Lenin flared out, "Do you mean to tell me that those men who have just generaled the slaughter of seventeen millions of men in a purposeless war are concerned over the few thousand who have been killed in a revolution with a conscious aim—to get out of the necessity of war . . . ?" Then, more quietly, he said, "But never mind, don't deny the terror. Don't minimize any of the evils of a revolution. They occur. They must be counted upon. If we have to have a revolution, we have to pay the price of revolution."

Lenin had initially been strongly opposed to terrorist tactics, he told his visitors, but, Steffens reported, "the plottings of the whites, the distracting debates and criticisms of the various shades of reds, the wild conspiracies and the violence of the anarchists against Bolshevik socialism, developed an extreme left in Lenin's party which proposed to proceed directly to the terror which the people were ready for." Even after an attempt on Lenin's life, he resisted the use of terror as a political instrument, but finally, he confessed to Steffens and Bullitt, "It is no use, there will be a terror. It hurts the revolution both inside and out, and we must find out how to avoid or control or direct it. But we have to know more about psychology than we do now to steer through that madness. And it serves a purpose that has to be served." The only solution that he could think of was to have the threat of terror so imminent that the enemies of the Revolution would flee before they had to be shot. "The absolute, instinctive opposition of the old conservatives and even of the fixed liberals has to be silenced," he declared, "if you are to carry through a revolution to its objective."

Bullitt and Steffens were told by Lenin that his conditions for an accommodation with the West were that all Allied armies, along with all support for White armies, be withdrawn from Russia and that the blockade of Russian ports be lifted. The Bolsheviks would, in return, stop fighting and allow the White Russians to retain whatever territory they held, announce a general amnesty for all political prisoners, and make good at least a portion of the debts owed to foreigners under the old regime. But the offer must come from the Allies themselves. Furthermore, it must come before April 10. Bullitt had the intoxicating illusion that he was about to alter the course of world history. He was convinced that the Allies would welcome such a bargain. He wrote to a friend: "In Russia today there are the rudiments of a government of the people, by the people, and for the people. The latest news indicates that the Bolsheviki are maintaining their power throughout Russia. . . ." Steffens was equally starry-eyed. "There," he wrote, "I got a true perspective on the Peace Making and the crumbling civilization of Europe. Lenin is a prophet so far as an understanding of physical, I mean economic forces, determine human conduct. He predicted and he understood better than the statesmen in Paris themselves did, what they did and did not do. . . . A great man, a delightful personality." Even Ray Stannard Baker, talking with a correspondent who had just returned from Russia, found himself wondering, "What if Lenin and those despised Bolsheviks had the creative secret of a new world, and we—we serious and important ones—were merely trying to patch the fragment of the old. . . . I have moments," Baker added, "when I wonder whether these ugly old shells of human organization are not too rotten to save, when I wonder if this Peace Conference is not, after all, fooling itself, and us." It was, in many ways, *the* inevitable and inescapable question. Certainly it was the question that every young man or women who had even flirted with the hope of a new and better social and economic order under the flag of some form of socialism asked himself or herself more than once. For some it was not even a question. The answer seemed self-evident: The Russian Revolution was, beyond any reasonable doubt, the dawn of the new socialist order.

When Steffens encountered Bernard Baruch and the latter said, somewhat challengingly, "So you've been over into Russia?" Steffens replied, "I have been over into the future, and it works." Then he asked himself a question that almost every American radical who visited "the future" was to ask himself: If Russia was heaven, and the Western capitalist world, hell, why were Steffens, Bullitt, and the other members of Bullitt's party so glad to be "home"? Steffens gave an answer that satisfied him and that was offered almost as often as the question was asked: "We were so accustomed to our own civilization that we preferred hell. We were ruined; we could recognize salvation, but could not be saved." Thousands of the faithful, who wished above all else to believe in the transcendent new order that had appeared, it seemed, in Russia, found what comfort they could in Steffens's answer, in *their* answer. It is significant that the question was cast in theological terms, in terms of repentant but unredeemed sinners. The sinners were those men and women who, knowing better, could not rid themselves of their "bourgeois" impulses and attitudes, who, for example, continued to feel queasy about political murders and mock trials. They could remain in the flock, tormented by guilt feelings over their unreconstructed middle-class attitudes; Americans had always been strongly attracted to doctrines and dogmas that allowed a full range to their feelings of guilt. Guilt, it might be said, is as important to Americans as "privilege" to the British or "reason" to the French.

Bullitt's mission was dismissed by Lloyd George as the work "of some unauthorized young man." Bullitt was furious but in all fairness to Lloyd George and Wilson, it should be said that the virtually unqualified enthusiasm of Bullitt and Steffens for Lenin and the Bolsheviks, word of which soon got around, seriously compromised the mission. To have returned with red stars in their eyes did not suggest scholarly (or even reasonable) objectivity. The question was inevitably miscast. It was *not* whether communism was better than or must supersede capitalism, whether it was heaven, and capitalism hell, but whether it was common sense and sound diplomacy to be so uncritically accepting of the Bolsheviks.

A prominent opponent of the Bolshevik regime was Herbert Hoover. How much of his hostility was the consequence of the fact that he and his partners had large holdings in Russia that the Bolsheviks appropriated without compensation is, of course, impossible to say, although he spoke of the failure of the Bolsheviks to honor the foreign investments made during the czar's regime as evidence of their depravity. Certainly in view of Hoover's background there were ample ideological grounds for his abhorrence; he noted, among other things, that the Bolsheviks had "embraced a large degree of emotionalism" which had given rise to a zeal among the Russian people "comparable only to the impulse of large spiritual movements. . . ." The Bolsheviks, he warned Wilson, would stop at nothing "to impose their doctrines on other defenseless people." At the same time, he warned Wilson against "military intervention," which would inevitably involve "years of police duty" and the possibility of the United States becoming the unwitting accomplice of an effort by France and Britain to reestablish "the reactionary classes." Americans "at home" would not stand for such an undertaking. Simultaneously Hoover insisted, "We cannot even remotely recognize this murderous tyranny without stimulating actionist radicalism in every country in Europe and without transgressing on every National ideal of our own." The wording of Hoover's letter is worth lingering over. How much influence it had on Wilson is impossible to say, but it displayed an attitude not uncommon among many Americans, especially those in public office, toward Soviet Russia, an attitude of unrelenting hostility that was to have profound consequences for the relations between those two nations. What was needed was a view of Russia somewhere between Hoover's hostility and the infatuation of Bullitt and Steffens.

The reaction of the Big Four to Russia was another instance of "folly and worse," in Villard's view. Villard was convinced that Lloyd George, who had concurred in the dispatching of William Bullitt to report at first hand on conditions in Russia, believed that he had to deny any knowledge of the mission in order to save his own neck. According to information that Villard received, Lord Northcliffe, the press baron, who perhaps wielded more power than any other Briton, told Lloyd George bluntly that he would lead a campaign to oust him from the leadership of his party if he recommended recognition of the Bolshevik regime. "Nothing more completely revealed Mr. Wilson's inadequacy for his Paris tasks, his mental tergiversations, his habitual refusal to face raw facts," Villard wrote, "than the treatment of Russia." One of the famous Fourteen Points had called for "such a settlement of all questions affecting Russia as will secure the best and freest co-operation of all nations in the world in obtaining from her an unhampered and unembarrassed determination of her own political development and national policy. . . ."

Villard was certainly unfair to Wilson. On the Russian issue, as on many others, the President went against his better judgment in order to gain half a loaf and, above all, to protect the idea of the League.

37

The Commissions

W hile the Council of Ten and the Big Four met continually, the
most important work of the peace conference was performed
by the various commissions of experts. There were more than fifty
commissions, which held among them 1,642 sessions. They had no
authority other than to make suggestions. American representatives
on each commission made up no more than a quarter of the membership, but they were often the best-informed members. Since many
American commissioners were graduates of the Inquiry and, in addition, the most disinterested members, they exercised a disproportionate influence. Charles Seymour told, with understandable pride,
the story of a dispute in his commission over where to draw a particular
boundary line. "A foreign delegate said at once: 'I suggest that we
accept the amendment without asking for evidence. Hitherto the facts
presented by the Americans have been irrefutable; it would be a waste
of time to consider them.' "

One of the major revelations of the peace conference for Frederic
Howe, a member of the commission on the Near East, was getting to
know some of the younger and, allegedly, more liberal British commissioners. He assumed that they must have the same view of the evils
of imperialism as their American counterparts, but he found that the

truth was different. " 'Imperialism' was not a dirty word to the British as it was to the Americans," Howe wrote. It did not have primarily economic connotations. It was rather "a white man's burden," a "sacred trust, undertaken for the well-being of peoples unfitted for self-government." The war had had nothing to do with financial interests; it had to do with responsibilities. It followed from this that all the Britons Howe met "seemed to feel, that America owed a debt to England, much as did Canada, Australia, and other colonies. . . . Conservatives or liberals, the empire was their passion. It was to be served, strengthened, carried on. Where the empire was in question," Howe wrote, "they were impervious to facts, blind to obvious evils, untouched by argument." No matter how "kindly and intelligent" they were, they thought talk of self-government absurd and conceded "nothing to the aspirations of other people for liberty. . . . To end imperialism was to end jobs, opportunities for preferment. It was like suggesting abolishing the church to the clergy, the army to the military caste, the navy to the marines."

Colonel George Marshall, whose duties as a member of Pershing's staff threw him into frequent contact with British officers, noted that their principal topic of conversation was what colonies Britain might expect to gain as spoils of war. One British officer suggested that the United States should take Syria, to which Marshall replied that the army was opposed to the acquisition of any colonies with excessively dry weather and "an abnormal number of insects." Bermuda was the only colony the United States would consider. At this the British officer, not realizing that Marshall was pulling his leg, became extremely agitated, describing Britain's ancient ties with Bermuda. Impossible! Quite impossible!

Even the Labor Party displayed a "confused veneration for the empire," in Howe's opinion. He came to suspect that Colonel Lawrence himself might be "a part of England's mysteriously efficient civil service." As though to underline his point, word came in April, 1919, of the British "butchery of the innocents" in the Jallanwala Bagh at Amritsar. Brigadier General Reginald Dyer with 50 Gurkhas and Sikhs had opened fire on 10,000 unarmed Indians. As a result, 400 were killed, and hundreds more wounded. "One thing is certain," Mohandas Gandhi told Frazier Hunt, "—India is not going to stop. We are trying now to win by nonviolence. If that fails the consequences will be too terrible to contemplate. . . . The whole movement may get out of my hands and beyond my power, and turn to awful violence, but even if we face anarchy it will be better than the present emasculated, half-beaten condition of India. The English have deprived us of all manliness, all self-respect, all self-reliance. They have impoverished us in body, mind, and soul. They have made us a slave nation. They have broken our hearts. . . . Only through universal education can we win back for India the things that have been taken from her. So it is that our revolution really means the cleansing of India of all its excrements and the coming of a new life. It will take a long time but we shall not falter."

As for the atmosphere of the commission meetings, posterity is fortunate that Harold Nicolson encountered Marcel Proust at dinner at the Ritz. He described Proust as "white, unshaven, grubby, slip-faced. . . . He puts his fur coat on . . . and sits hunched there in white kid gloves." Proust asked Nicolson how the commissions worked. When Nicolson started to reply in general terms, Proust protested. He wanted details. Begin over, he ordered. "You take a carriage to the Quai d'Orsay. You mount the elevator. You enter the chamber. And then? Be precise, my dear fellow, precise." So Nicolson was precise: the clothes, "heavy black suits, white cuffs and paper." Blue and khaki colors, pink blotting pads, and gilt chairs. "For smells you would have petrol, typewriting ribbons, French polish, central heating, and a touch of violet hair-wash. The tactile motifs would be tracing paper, silk, the leather handle of a weighted pouch of papers, the foot-feel of very thick carpets alternating with parquet flooring . . . the brittle feel of a cane chair-seat which has been occupied for hours."

Still Proust wanted more details. Nicolson was delighted to oblige. "The chandeliers blaze . . . " and the commissioners adjourn "for tea, brioches and macaroons. It is a large, slim room, and the tea-urn gutters in the draught. . . . On returning to the Majestic the sounds of dance music would reach us from the ballroom."

Proust could not have done better himself.

Two of the most important commissions were those on reparations and finances. Made up of bankers, economists (including John Maynard Keynes), and business leaders as well as politicians, these commissions were charged with calculating the absolute maximum that the defeated powers, particularly Germany, could pay without completely wrecking their economies.

In the words of Thomas Lamont, a member of the commission on reparations, "The subject of reparations caused more trouble, contention, hard feeling and delay at the Peace Conference than any other point of the Treaty of Versailles." The United States representatives on the commission were Norman Davis, Bernard Baruch, Vance McCormick, a prominent editor and member of the Democratic Executive Committee, and Lamont. The commission divided itself into three groups to consider the different aspects of reparations. The first question was what could be properly included in the category of reparations—damage inflicted by the Central Powers on the Allies for which they could be, under some color of justification, required to make restitution or "restoration." This ranged from such things as the destruction of railways, the flooding of mines, the chopping down of orchards and devastation of agricultural lands, and the bombarding of cities and towns to the actual expenditures of the Allies on their own military equipment and to the pensions paid to the veterans of the Allied armies. The second question was how much Germany could afford to pay without the complete destruction of its economy and the creation of anarchy and starvation in the nation. As one of the commissioners expressed it, "How much, at her utmost capacity, can Germany pay?" Everyone agreed whatever that sum was, that was what Germany must pay. The position of the American members of the commission was that the important thing was to fix a definite amount promptly so that the general air of uncertainty that hovered over the conference could be dispelled and Germany could be notified of the sum it was expected to pay.

Lloyd George, in his election campaign, had called for Germany to pay $120,000,000,000, a sum far beyond that nation's capacity. The debt was to be spread out over forty years, and the occupation of the Rhineland by the French Army was to be the guarantee for payment. The Americans countered by proposing an initial payment of $5,000,000,000 prior to May, 1921, and a subsequent sum of $25,000,000,000, provided Germany's ability to pay was not impaired by other exactions. With the British and French determined to exact the last farthing and the Americans resisting a figure they believed utterly unrealistic, John Foster Dulles, brother of Allen and a member of the reparations commission, suggested the establishment of a permanent commission on reparations to adjust the sum according to Germany's ability to pay in the future.

In addition, Germany, it had been agreed earlier, must pay Belgium an indemnity of $500,000,000 for invading and ravaging that country at the beginning of the war. The French pointed out that Germany had forced the French to pay an indemnity of $1,000,000,000 at the end of the Franco-Prussian War, in addition, of course, to seizing Alsace-Lorraine. "You wish to do justice to the Germans," Clemenceau said to Wilson. "Do not believe that they will ever forgive us. They will seek only the chance of revenge. Nothing will suppress the fury of those who hoped to dominate the world and believed success so near." Lansing reached a different conclusion. "The prevailing bitterness against France [by the Germans] because of the territorial cessions and the reparations demanded by the victor would," he wrote, "naturally cause the German people to seek future opportunity to be revenged."

In addition to demanding the German merchant fleet as a replacement for shipping lost to U-boats, the Allies called for the return of the cows, horses, pigs, and cattle appropriated by the Germans. To a Germany whose people were facing mass starvation, this seemed the cruelest exaction of all.

The notion that Germany could be made to pay the costs of the war was, in Colonel House's words, "a mad and wholly unwarrantable assumption. . . ." Much the same was true of the debts owed by the Allies to the United States. "These debts," he declared, "cannot be collected except by process of war. . . . Such conditions make for bad foreign relations, and we shall awaken to this when we begin to press for interest payments." The people of the United States "should have recognized that our foreign loans were not made as investments, but in order to defeat the Central Empires."

One question that came up repeatedly in all discussions among the commissioners on reparations was whether the industry and selfdenial required of the Germans to meet the Allied demands upon them would not, in time, mean "a greater, stronger Germany." The French delegates, already obsessed with Germany, "feared that they might push the thing so they would build up a gigantic machine . . . , a Frankenstein that would ultimately overwhelm them because of their increased efficiency, but they were willing to take the chance."

The crucial point in the reparations commission came with the defection of Smuts, who had originally taken a strong stand against heavy reparations. Wilson, who admired Smuts, perhaps excessively, for introducing the notion of mandates for ex-colonies, accepted Smuts's recommendations as opposed to the counsel of his own advisers, Baruch and Hoover among them. "We must . . . realize that we are dealing today with a much weaker Germany than the one we knew before the war, and we must recognize that any indemnities based on pre-war conditions would be impossible," Baruch had written to Wilson on March 29, 1919. "I knew," Baruch wrote in his autobiography, "that if Germany were left economically prostrate, all Europe would suffer."

John Foster Dulles made the point that the reparations had been set on the assumption that the prewar system of international credits backed by gold and silver through great international banking houses would be reestablished after the war and facilitate the payment of reparations. But this did not happen. The credit system broke down, and a desperate Germany inflated its currency as the means of avoiding payment.

The boundary question was, if possible, even touchier than reparations. Ancient hatreds complicated everything. Massacres broke out with disconcerting frequency as old scores were settled. In the words of Charles Seymour, "The Peace Conference was . . . placed in the position of executor of the Hapsburg estate." The heirs were Czechoslovakia, Poland, Rumania, Yugoslavia, Austria, Hungary, and Italy.

There was, of course, the matter of the secret treaties. When revolutionary Russia made the various treaties public, their revelations had caused considerable embarrassment in Allied ministries. The United States, on the other hand, took the line that the provisions of all such treaties were null and void to the degree that they were in conflict with the Fourteen Points, which the Allies had accepted, or appeared to have accepted, as the basis of the armistice and the peace negotiations.

Italy was a particular problem. Despite the fact that it might be argued that it had been more of a liability than an asset, it wanted the moon. Its goal was to push its frontier as far as the Brenner Pass to guard against future invasions from the north. That such a line would include a substantial number of Austrians, Slavs, and, ideally from the Italian point of view, Albanians did not disturb the Italians. In addition, Italy wished to extend its influence in the Adriatic by acquiring a number of islands (as well as coastline) and part of Syria in the Near East. Next to a "defensible" northern frontier, the Italians wished the port city of Fiume, which had been promised to Yugoslavia as its access to the sea. Italy's claims rested on the secret Treaty of London, negotiated as the price of its entry into the war on the side of the Allies. In addition to the Austrian Tyrol, it had been promised "certain important islands and ports of the Dalmation coast" and provinces at the head of the Adriatic, formerly part of the Austria-Hungary Empire. Orlando, in arguing his country's claims, was given to weeping. When

Balfour observed one such incident, he remarked, "I have heard of nations winning their way to empire by bribery, cajolery, by threats and by war, but this is the first attempt I have heard of by any statesman to sob his way to empire!"

To incorporate some 10,000 or 20,000 Italians living in Fiume into Italy would require taking over almost 500,000 Yugoslavs. This the Americans resisted since the readjustment of Italy's northern boundary had already resulted in the acquisition of some 300,000 Yugoslavs. The "American specialists" reported to the conference that handing over Fiume to the Italians "would be wholly unjustifiable and extremely dangerous." Wilson backed them up, and an angry Orlando withdrew to Rome, where he was met by thousands of furious Italians, who seemed disposed to blame him for the failure to prevail upon his fellow ministers to award Fiume to Italy. Italian papers called for the government simply to seize the disputed territories. The Fascists held a rally in Milan, and the Italian journalist Benito Mussolini in his paper *Popolo d'Italia* declared his defiance of Wilson and the Big Four.

The Czechs had established their claim to nationhood in part at least by deserting the Austro-Hungarian armies, and one of the first acts of the Allies was to recognize Czechoslovakia as an independent state. Of Czechoslovakia's 14,000,000 inhabitants, more than a third belonged to other nationalities, primarily German and Hungarian (or Magyar and Ruthenian). By the same token, Rumania, which had acquired Transylvania as well as large chunks of Hungary and Bukovina, had within its boundaries colonies of Székely Magyars as well as Germans. Rumania's principal concern was to receive the portion of southern Hungary known as the Banat of Temesvar, claimed by the Serbs; Serb, Magyar, German, and Rumanian villages were intermingled in the area. The territorial commissioners, after considerable cogitation, awarded the western third of the Banat to the Serbs and the remainder to the Rumanians; neither country was satisfied by the compromise, and both lobbied assiduously with the Council of Four to get the whole area.

Eleutherios Venizelos presented the claims of Greece. He wanted only southern Albania, most of Bulgaria, eastern Thrace, and a substantial portion of the Anatolian Peninsula, starting with the port of Smyrna (which, incidentally, the Treaty of London had set aside for Italy). One of the proposals for the dismemberment of Albania would have made the central portion of several hundred thousand people an autonomous Moslem state under an Italian protectorate. The northern part would have gone to Yugoslavia, and the southern part would have been divided between Greece and Italy. But the Albanians thwarted that plan by driving the Italians out of the city of Valona, and Albania's independence was subsequently recognized by the Council of the League of Nations.

East Galicia, with a large Ukrainian population—3,500,000—was made an autonomous province with guarantees for the rights of Ukrainians and provisions for a plebiscite in twenty-five years. Nothing could be done about the Polish-Russian boundary because the Allies were not at war with Russia and thus were unable to redraw that frontier.

The fate of the city of Teschen in Austrian Silesia is typical of the problems the commissioners and the council faced. An industrial center, it was claimed by the newly created Czechoslovakia as well as by Poland. In accord with the wishes of the Polish-speaking majority, the mining region adjacent to the city and the main railroad were awarded to the Czechs, and the eastern part of the city was turned over to the Poles. The electrical plant went to one state, and the gasworks to the other.

The problem of Poland was one of the thorniest of the questions faced by the peace conference. Poland had been divided among Germany, Austria-Hungary, and Russia. Point XIII of Wilson's Fourteen Points had promised that "an independent Polish state should be erected which should include the territories inhabited by indisputably Polish populations, which should be assured a free and secure access to the [North] sea. . . ." France was an enthusiastic supporter of the Polish claims on the ground that they would represent a major diminution of German strength.

The only available port was that of Danzig, lying between East and West Prussia. The city was thoroughly German. To reach Danzig, it was necessary to hack out between those two provinces a "corridor," one that contained a substantial German population. The issue was especially sensitive for the Germans. They were convinced that "with it stands or falls the position of Prussia as a great power, and therefore that of the Empire." The solution to the access-to-the-sea problem was to make Danzig a free city under the protection of the League of Nations, included in the Polish customs system but autonomous in regard to its own affairs. The Danzigers not only protested vigorously but mobbed Poles who showed up in Danzig. In the readjustment of the German-Polish frontiers, largely in Upper Silesia, Germany disgorged some 17,000 square miles and almost 3,000,000 people, including 1,000,000 Germans.

Common sense was generally the criterion in trying to reach decisions. Charles Seymour wrote: "If a chain of mountains or a river offered a natural frontier, it might seem advisable to depart slightly from the linguistic line. If an agricultural district of Jugo-Slavs were economically dependent upon a German-Austrian city, it might be wise to leave the district in Austria." In Seymour's words, the territorial boundaries resulted "from the labors and application of a body of technical experts who had taken pains to go into all phases of the situation." But he was not excessively sanguine about the long-term results of the commissions' labors. "Each state," he wrote a year later, "includes something of a nationalistic minority, which will look for support to its kinsmen, who form the majority in the neighboring state. Czecho-Slovakia and Rumania . . . include large minorities of aliens. . . .Germans and Jugo-Slavs are annexed in large numbers by Italy." In Yugoslavia itself ancient hatreds among Croats, Slovenes, and Serbs clouded the future of that nation. To protect minorities, especially Jews, who had been subjected to continuous persecution, the treaty contained provisions guaranteeing to minorities both freedom of religion and "linguistic" freedom—the right to retain their own languages and have their own schools as well as churches. Such injunctions were, obviously, easier to make than to enforce. Their existence in the treaty was, nonetheless, a great step forward.

The best testimony to the merit of the commissions' recommendations was that most were adopted without substantial modification or discussion by the council. The Americans were strongly in favor of permitting the union of Germany and what was called German-Austria since history, language, and shared cultural traditions as well as economic logic dictated such a union (more important, both Germans and Austrians wished it), but Clemenceau was adamant in opposition. Such a union must strengthen Germany, and his virtually exclusive concern was to weaken that country as much as possible if he could not destroy it. To the effort to charge Austria with a substantial portion of reparations, the Americans argued that whatever wickedness had been done had been done by the old Hapsburg Empire. The new Austrian republic should not be forced to pay for Hapsburg crimes. It should rather be strengthened in its democratic tendencies. But the conference, or the Big Four, or, more specifically, Clemenceau, Lloyd George, and Orlando, were unpersuaded. The treaty compelled Austria "to recognize her liability to pay full reparations. . . ."

The most mischievous commission was that on the causes of the war. Not surprisingly it assigned that responsibility to Germany and, more specifically, to the kaiser. "The war," its report declared, "was premeditated by the Central Powers together with their Allies, Turkey and Bulgaria, and was the result of acts deliberately committed to make it unavoidable. . . . Germany, in agreement with Austria-Hungary, deliberately worked to defeat all the many conciliatory proposals made by the Entente Powers and their repeated efforts to avoid war." Over the indignant protests of the Americans, Britain and France called for the trial of Wilhelm before an international tribunal as a war criminal. The opposition of the American delegates to the proposal to try the kaiser caused feelings to run "about as high as feelings can run," was the way James Brown Scott, the legal adviser to the American peace commission, put it. Wilson was also resolutely opposed to such a notion. Lloyd George, who had run for the office of prime minister with the slogan of "Hang the kaiser," found himself under heavy pressure from the more liberal elements in his own country as well as from Wilson to abandon the notion. The Japanese joined the Americans in opposition; the idea deeply offended their most basic notions of the power of the emperor. The Dutch finally settled the issue by defying all pressures to relinquish their unwelcome guest. Unable to get at the kaiser, the Allies demanded that the German government turn over to them for trial some 900 German politicians and military and naval officers to be tried for various crimes during the course of the war. Included in the list were all the members of the German general staff, which read like a roster of the German aristocracy and included Hindenburg, Ludendorff, and Bethmann-Hollweg. The Germans flatly refused to surrender the accused to an outside tribunal and offered, in their extremity, to try them in German courts. Although the effort to bring the kaiser to trial was unsuccessful, the Allies inserted in the final treaty the accusation that "William II of Hohenzollern" had committed "a supreme offence against international morality and the sanctity of treaties."

The commission on new states and the protection of minorities had, as one of its American members, David Hunter Miller. Allen Dulles, another American professor, joined the commission during its deliberations. Not surprisingly a number of the nations required to sign guarantees for the protection of minorities within their borders were indignant at what they felt were intrusions by the delegates to the peace conference into purely domestic matters. They argued that such a pledge was an insult, and some pointed out that the United States did not guarantee its own immigrant minorities education conducted in their native languages. In effect, the treaty provisions placed minorities under the protection of the League itself. The treaty with Rumania had a provision especially intended to protect Rumanian Jews, who had often been the victims of persecution of an especially egregious kind. Moslems and Greeks and Albanians were protected in Yugoslavia.

A clause on "religious equality," it was pointed out, would "unwarrantedly interfere with the internal policies of certain countries." Even in Great Britain a Catholic was excluded from succession to the crown.

The collapse of Germany and Austria-Hungary led to the collapse of Turkey with consequences as vast as, and more incomprehensible, than the consequences in Europe of the defeat of Germany. Every European power was determined to pick the bones of the Ottoman Empire. The various component parts of European Turkey were already bespoken. Under the terms of the Sazonov-Paleoloque Agreement of 1915, Russia was to get Constantinople and the straits of the Dardanelles and the Bosporus. Italy was to get "a just share" of the Mediterranean and the Dodecanese Islands. A year later Russia was promised four Armenian vilayets, or provinces, including Trebizond and Biltis. The Greeks pressed their right to Anatolian Turkey, a region of peasant farmers and sheepherders. The dramatic and eloquent Venizelos prevailed on a reluctant Council of Four to authorize the occupation by Greek forces of Smyrna. The resultant slaughter of Turkish men, women, and children by the Greek soldiers horrified world opinion, and Venizelos, blamed for the tragedy, fell from the world eminence he had achieved through force of his remarkable personality

The Armenians, seeking independence, had two delegations. One, representing Russian Armenia, was led by the poet and novelist Avetis Aharonian, and the other, representing Turkish Armenia, was headed by a mysterious Egyptian landowner, Nubar Pasha. The Kurds disputed the claims of the Turkish Armenians to large portions of territory. The Georgians and the Azerbaijan Tatars had conflicting claims to statehood and territory. The Georgians hinted at large quantities of manganese which might be available to nations that espoused their case, and the Tatars dropped hints about oil.

France was given "complete control" over the rich cotton-producing area of Cilicia and the prospectively rich copper mines of lower Armenia. In the words of the American representatives on the territorial commission charged with advising on the reshuffling of the Ottoman Empire, the area assigned to the French "defies every known law of geographic, ethnographic, and linguistic unity which one might cite. . . ."

The Arab portion of the Ottoman Empire was another prize to be distributed among the victorious Allies. Frederic Howe, who had traveled widely in the Middle East and become an amateur expert on Arab culture, had high hopes that the peace conference would do justice to the aspirations of Arabian nationalism. There might then be "a renaissance of this part of the world, a renaissance in industry, in culture, and in art that would make it again the centre of a civilization of its own," he wrote. He wanted to "be around when the hand of the Western world should be lifted from the people of the Near East, the glories of whose ancient civilization I dreamed of seeing restored." Through Howe's friend George Creel, head of the Committee on Public Information, Wilson had been prevailed upon to appoint Howe to the peace mission with a special assignment to advise on the Middle East.

Arab claims of independence had been strengthened by the performance of the Arab camel corps, commanded by Emir Feisal, son of the sherif of Mecca, and advised by T. E. Lawrence, who acted as liaison officer between General E. H. H. Allenby and Feisal and, in the process, became more Arab than the Arabs. "Neglectful of honors, indifferent to everything suggestive of personal aggrandizement," Howe wrote of Lawrence, "he seemed as detached from the Occidental world as was Feisal himself." Lawrence shared Howe's opinion of Allied treachery. "Turbaned, impassive" Feisal sat among the frock-coated diplomats, occasionally uttering some skeptical aphorism such as "When President Wilson spoke about self-determination for peoples, a smile went through all Arabia." He was accompanied by a black slave whom he had carried, wounded, from battle on the back of his camel. "Backward peoples," Feisal remarked, "are apparently peoples with oil, gold, natural resources, but no guns to protect them."

On Palestine the issue soon became that of a Jewish homeland or a separate state. The Jews themselves were divided. Auguste Gauvin, a French journalist, wrote: "Very few Jews want to go to their Holy Land and ours, and also unfortunately the sanctuary of the Arabs, except as tourists or to make a religious pilgrimage. Perhaps the whole question could be solved if it was placed in the hands of a competent tourist agency." As it turned out, the decisive influence was that of Chaim Weizmann.

Felix Frankfurter met Weizmann and fell at once under his spell. He was, he wrote years later, "quasimessianic . . . electric, . . . affectionate . . . radiated authority. . . ." With no concerns "except the realization of a Jewish Palestine . . . Weizmann seized the imagination and enlisted the will of people like Lloyd George, Balfour, Winston Churchill and Smuts," Frankfurter wrote. Frankfurter was in Paris at the instance of Brandeis and Julian Mack, a Federal judge. Both Mack and Brandeis were Zionists, and they instructed Frankfurter to observe and do what he could to further the cause. The Balfour Declaration had thrown the weight of the British government behind the proposal to establish Palestine "as a Jewish National Home." Frankfurter reported, "It was issued after detailed consultation, even changes in phrasing, between the Lloyd George Government and President Wilson in person."

Emir Feisal met with Frankfurter to discuss the issue of a Jewish homeland. The two men hit it off well—"exchanged mutual assurances," as Frankfurter put it. Feisal summed up his views in a letter to Frankfurter dated March 31, 1919, which read: "We Arabs, especially the educated among us, look with the deepest sympathy on the Zionist movement. Our deputation here in Paris is fully acquainted with the proposals submitted by the Zionist Organization to the Peace Conference, and we regard them as moderate and proper. We will do our best, insofar as we are concerned, to help them through; we will wish the Jews a most hearty welcome home."

At the same time Feisal, who was hospitable to the idea of a Jewish "homeland," made clear his objections to a Jewish state. "If the views of the radical Zionists . . . should prevail," he declared, "the result will be ferment, chronic unrest, and sooner or later civil war in Palestine. But I hope I will not be misunderstood. . . . I assert that with the Jews who have been settled for some generations in Palestine our relations are excellent. But the new arrivals exhibit very different qualities from those 'old settlers,' as we call them. . . . For want of a better word I must say that the new colonists almost without exception have come in an imperialistic spirit."

Balfour himself argued that his declaration had been misunderstood. ". . . neither my critics or my friends have really read my declaration . . . " he wrote. "I came out for a Jewish homeland in Palestine in so far as it could be established without infringing on the rights of the Arab communities, nomad as well as sedentary. Indeed I thought that in the terms of my declaration the rights of the Arab were safeguarded as never before. . . .I thought that our war aim was to give equal rights and even-handed justice to all the oppressed. . . . It was, I thought, merely a happy coincidence that this belated act of justice to the Jews would establish their national home at the Eurasian crossroads and would prove a protection to the wasp waist of our empire, Suez."

When William Linn Westermann, a member of the Inquiry and one of the territorial commissioners concerned with the Near East, was asked after the war if the prospective allocation of Palestine to the Zionists was not a violation of the principle of self-determination, he noted that there were six Arabs to every Jew in Palestine, "and the special privilege granted to the Jews there is contrary to the policy of self-determination. The justification for it" he added, "lies, in my mind, in the fact that the Jewish problem cannot be regarded as a local problem. It is a world problem and the problem of a very powerful people. . . . It must be treated as a world problem. It offers to the Jewish people an opportunity to carry out their idealistic aspirations, necessary for the Jews of the world, and bound to be helpful, rather than harmful, in the tangled situation in the Near East." It was also clear that the setting aside of Palestine as a Jewish homeland was in large part a consequence of the fact that the British desired "to have a buffer state on the eastern side of the Suez Canal." Moreover, the Balfour Declaration spoke of a "Jewish homeland" rather than of a "Zionist state."

"To the Jews of the diaspora," Westermann noted, "Palestine is to be the symbol of the political nationhood which they lost twenty centuries ago, and a pledge that the great tragedy of their humiliation may now be ended." There they would be free "to carry out their interesting plans for the social and economic betterment of the Jews who may come."

Frederic Howe's hopes for a just treatment of the Arabs proved as fruitless as so many other hopes. The terms of the secret Sykes-Picot Treaty were, in the main, observed. The considerable contributions of the Arabs to the British war effort, particularly their help in driving the Turks back from the Dardanelles, were ignored. In Howe's words, "agreements were thrown to the winds and betraying friends took possession of their ancient towns and country and when the Arabs rebelled against such treatment, the rebellion was crushed by their recent allies." Feisal was exiled to Switzerland.

38

Concluding the Treaty

When Wilson returned to Paris from his trip to the United States, he discovered, so at least his side of the story goes, that Colonel House, assuming the powers of the President, had bargained away what Wilson held to be the essence of the League. House was at the dock when the President's ship arrived and went at once to his stateroom.

After they had been closeted for a considerable time, Edith Wilson heard House leave and opened the doors of the connecting room. "Woodrow," she wrote later, "was standing. The change in his appearance shocked me. He seemed to have aged ten years. . . . Silently he held out his hand, which I grasped, crying: "What is the matter? What has happened?"

"He smiled bitterly. 'House has given away everything I had won before we left Paris.' "

Edith Wilson added, "I look back on that moment as a crisis in his life and feel that from it dated the long years of illness . . . the wreckage of his plans and his life." According to her account, her husband "threw back his head. The light of battle was in his eyes. 'Well,' he said, 'thank God I can still fight, and I'll win them back or never look those boys I sent over here in the face again.' "

That the judgment on House was too severe is perhaps less important than that the Wilsons believed it. In defense of House it must be said that Wilson's gains, as we have noted, were undoubtedly more illusory than real. Clemenceau had admitted to his aide Mordacq that he had acquiesced in Wilson's League plan in order to have more leverage subsequently. He had never intended to let Wilson have his prize without heavy payment.

Ray Stannard Baker, perhaps feeling House was his most serious rival for the President's affections, described him as "the dilettante— the lover of the game. . . . He stands in the midst of great events . . . and plays at getting important men together for the sheer joy of using his presumptive power." The colonel startled Baker by announcing that "if *he* had it to do he could make peace in an hour!" Did Baker relay that indiscretion to Wilson? Bernard Baruch had a similar reaction to House. He believed that House had become intoxicated by the power that he exercised in the President's name. Baruch recalled the colonel's saying to him "with his arms outstretched, 'Isn't it a thrilling thing to deal with the forces that affect the destiny of the world?' " Frank Cobb, the editor of the *New York World* and a member of the American peace delegation, was convinced, as he told Baruch, that House was "weakening and qualifying the basis of peace which Wilson had laid down." Henry Stoddard's explanation of the break between Wilson and House was that the President came to feel that during his absence House had cut the ground from under him by agreeing to so many Allied demands that there was nothing left for trading purposes on other features of the treaty. . . . The President needed a man who would take orders from him and not make compromises with others." Stoddard added that he had "never heard of a person to whom Wilson afterward ever mentioned the name of House."

Years later Lord Robert Cecil wrote, of the breach between the two Americans, that House was a high-minded and a "clear-sighted American . . . a delightful person to work with," open, candid and disinterested. "It was a bad day," in Cecil's view, when "the collaboration between Wilson and House ceased. But for that, the League might have been successfully steered through the American Senate and the course of history might have been very different."

It is difficult to convey adequately the atmosphere of tension that hung over the conference after Wilson's return. The armistice had been signed on November 11. It was now March 22. More than four months had passed since the armistice, and there was still no treaty to present to Germany. "Apart from the actual strain of continuous labor," Harold Nicolson wrote to his father, "there is the moral exhaustion of realizing one's own fallability and the impossibility of extracting from the lies with which we are surrounded any real impression of what the various countries and nationalities honestly desire." The conference was enveloped "in mists of exhaustion, disability, suspicion, and despair." Herbert Hoover wrote that "the whole air had suddenly become charged with currents of indescribable malignity."

It became a familiar sight to see the President of the United States tapping out a memorandum on his typewriter in a corner of the conference room during a break in the discussions. "The rest of us," Lloyd George wrote, "found time for golf and we took Sundays off, but Wilson, in his zeal, worked incessantly." Ike Hoover, his valet, reported, "He is so busy he never dresses for dinner anymore. He goes right to that meal in the clothes he has worn all day." It was also noted that he had developed a conspicuous tic in his left eye.

When Wilson replaced House at the negotiating table, it was soon evident that Clemenceau and, to a lesser degree, Lloyd George were thoroughly resistant to reopening the issues that they insisted had been settled with House in the President's absence. House or Wilson, it made little difference, one or the other must yield in the end to the combined pressure of Clemenceau and Lloyd George (with Orlando more or less tagging along). Lloyd George, it must be said, was, with certain striking exceptions, such as his dramatic effort in behalf of raising the blockade, an opportunist. He did not like Wilson; Clemenceau was far more his dish of tea. Thus, when Clemenceau turned up the heat, Lloyd George often lined up with the Tiger. Frances Stevenson, Lloyd George's combination secretary-mistress, noted in her diary: "He [Wilson] started to annoy D [David Lloyd George] . . . by talking of matters that have already been settled as though they were still open for discussion & as though he intended to reopen them. I am glad he has started to annoy D . . . as I think the latter was too prone to encourage & agree with him while he was here before. I do not think they will ever get a move on until President Wilson has been put in his place, & D. is the only person who can do it. Clemenceau cannot tolerate him at any price."

Lansing noted that the nations of Eastern Europe were arming speedily and the League itself was "being discussed with something like contempt by the cynical, hard-headed statesmen of those countries which are being put on a war-footing. . . . These men say," Lansing wrote in his journal, "that in theory the idea is all right, and it is an ideal to work toward, but that under present conditions it is not practical in preventing war. They ask, what nation is going to rely on the guaranty in the Covenant if a jealous or hostile neighbor maintains a large army."

Lansing's repeated efforts to elicit from Wilson some specific set of tasks for the American peace commissioners were unavailing. It seemed to him as though he and his fellow commissioners were "like a lot of skilled workmen who are ordered to build a house. We have the materials and the tools, but there are no plans and specifications and no master-workman in charge of the construction. We putter around in an aimless sort of way and get nowhere. With all his natural capacity the President seems to lack the facility of employing team-work and of adopting a system to utilize the brains of other men." As Lansing found himself less and less consulted by the President, he lapsed into a kind of abstracted manner. Baker often found him alone in his large office, doodling "grotesque figures or faces" on a pad of paper or writing with a "small neat hand" in his diary.

By the middle of March it was apparent that the meetings of the Council of Ten were too cumbersome and "stagy" to permit the accomplishment of any serious business, and the Council of Four—Clemenceau, Lloyd George, Wilson, and Orlando—began to meet in private, in "secret" it was said.

In contrast with the pageantry of the Council of Ten, the Council of Four met in the front room of Wilson's house. "There," Charles Seymour wrote, "one might have seen President Wilson himself on all fours, kneeling on a gigantic map spread upon the floor and tracing with his finger a proposed boundary, other plenipotentiaries grouped around him, also on all fours." Wilson showed a remarkable gift, in Seymour's view, for absorbing almost instantly the salient points of some complex issue. Maps, indeed, became the means by which claims were made or refuted and the making of spurious maps became a modest industry. In Isaiah Bowman's opinion, it would have taken a "huge monograph" (probably since written) to cover "all the types of map forgeries that the war and the peace conference called forth." Maps constituted a new "language"; they were flourished like posters, brightly colored and subtly argumentative. "A perverted map," Bowman wrote, "was a life-belt to many a floundering argument."

In addition to maps, true and false, Wilson relied on scale models of geographic areas. Douglas Johnson, one of the academic geographers who were members of the boundary commission, set up in Wilson's office "relief models of the eastern Adriatic coast . . . which showed . . . every river, mountain, valley, town, and railroad. . . . On the models were marked off the strategic, ethnological, and other frontiers." Similar models for other disputed boundaries were set up, and Wilson used them in conferences with his advisers and representatives of other governments.

American correspondents were indignant when the word reached them that the treaty negotiations were being conducted by the Big Four "meeting in secret to decide the fate of the world." "That settles it," William Allen White said to Oswald Garrison Villard as they left Baker's press conference. "That finishes the conference and Wilson. Lloyd George and Clemenceau will now take him upstairs into a private bedroom and fool him to death"; only the word used, Villard added, was much less elegant than "fool." In an atmosphere of "unhappiness, unrest, mutual dislike, intrigue, mad, selfish determination to get all the spoils possible at the expense of every body else," in Villard's words, the conference proceeded.

Robert Lansing was also offended by the secrecy with which the Big Four conducted their deliberations. "Confidential personal interviews were to a certain extent unavoidable and necessary," he wrote in his postmortem, "but to conduct the entire negotiations through a small group sitting behind closed doors and to shroud their proceedings with mystery and uncertainty made a very unfortunate impression on those who were not members of the secret councils." He noted in his journal, "The result of the present method has been to destroy their [the smaller nations'] faith and arouse their resentment. They look upon the President as in favor of a world ruled by Five Great Powers, and international despotism of the strong, in which the little nations are merely rubber-stamps. . . . Secret diplomacy, the bane of the past, is a menace from which man believed himself to be rid. . . . The whole world will rejoice when the day of the whisperer is over."

Baker came reluctantly to the conclusion (which he later apparently abandoned) that Wilson had been, in the later stages of the negotiations, "thinking too much politically. He took hold of the living soul of the world while he was its prophet," Baker wrote. "How much has he lost by becoming its statesman? Every time he has made a gesture of defiance—as in the Italian matter—the masses of the world have loved him; every time he has yielded to compromise—as in the Chinese settlement—the world has been cold. . . . He has wanted his League of Nations more than anything else; has he sacrificed too much for it?

No one else was willing to sacrifice anything. He will get his League, but can it rest upon such a basis of greed and injustice? . . . Great unrest, uncertainty, irritated impatience, has spread all over Europe," Baker wrote: ". . . above all, the soldiers of the various armies wished to be demobilized and sent home."

Wilson seemed to Baker near the end of his rope. "More and more," Baker wrote, "the President was coming to have a kind of mystic belief that the League, if he could get it accepted and organized, would save the world. He seemed ever more willing to compromise desperately to get it. . . . Wilson had for long been the prophet of the world; he had now to fight in the dust and heat of the arena in order to save from utter extinction even a small part of his grand plan."

The most widely criticized assignment of territory was directly counter to the recommendations of the territorial commission. This was the decision by the Big Four to award Shantung Province of China to Japan as its protectorate. Lloyd George had appealed to House to break down Wilson's resistance to giving Shantung to Japan. "The concession . . . is bad enough," he argued, "but it is no worse than the doubtful transactions that had gone on among the Allies," as was certainly true. Wilson continued to resist. He told House, "If I sign the Treaty—even under orders from Peking—I shall not have what you in New York call a Chinaman's chance." But the Japanese had witnessed all the other Allied powers grabbing off chunks of defeated Germany. They were determined to have something substantial for themselves. The sympathies of the delegates to the conference were with China. Polite and dignified Chinese delegates were conspicuously present to protest having part of their country given away for no other reason than to satisfy the imperial ambitions of Japan. The ubiquitous Japanese pushed their case relentlessly, threatening, like the Italians, to return home if their demands were not met. Rather than imperil the treaty, Wilson gave way reluctantly. "The Japanese, after all, were abominably crowded in their little islands," Baker wrote, in extenuation of the Wilson capitulation. "They also demanded *something*. . . . If we stood by China, broke up the conference and went home, who would then put Japan out of Shantung? . . . The only hope was in a world organization." When Wilson yielded, Lansing was, as Baker put it, "quite inconsolable. . . . Wilson had made a terrible mistake."

In Lansing's opinion, the cards that Japan played so skillfully in securing Shantung Province were, first, the agreement to withdraw its demand for an amendment to the Covenant denouncing racial inequality (an amendment especially awkward for the United States) and the threat to abstain from joining the League of Nations. The latter, Lansing believed, extracted Wilson's reluctant agreement to a measure that flew shamelessly in the face of his doctrine of self-determination. The Japanese were only bluffing, in Lansing's view. They had too much to gain in international prestige by being a member of the League. Japan did, to be sure, sweeten the pill by speaking of "the eventual restoration of [Shantung] to China."

As rumors of various compromises with the principles of the Fourteen Points spread, many of the Americans placed their hopes in at least salvaging the League itself. "The world is hungry for a League of Nations," Florence Harriman wrote in her diary in March, 1919. "It must have a League of Nations. It seems to me that God has given the world a new Pentecost to make a new Crusade. The old crusade was made to save an old tomb, the new is to bring the benison of God on every baby's cradle. A better chance for education, for housing; and for the female child an opportunity such as has never been dreamt of before—equal opportunity with the men. Surely a new spirit of God is moving in the trees. We must not be blinded by the little things, the small criticisms, but let us be grateful every day that we have been given the chance to take part in this great world movement towards brotherhood and peace."

Others were more pessimistic. Walter Lippmann, who had been instrumental in framing the original Fourteen Points, grew increasingly gloomy. When Bernard Berenson came to see him, he found him at his desk in the offices of the Committee on Public Information, still in uniform and wholly cast down about the direction the conference was taking. "I came to ask you," Berenson later wrote to Lippmann, "whether you were aware that we Americans were being betrayed, that no attention was being paid to our aims in the war, and that a most disastrous peace treaty was being forged." Lippmann had said nothing, but his eyes filled with tears. "I have loved you ever since," Berenson added, recalling the episode.

Ray Stannard Baker was convinced that the French had embarked on a concerted newspaper campaign to weaken and discredit Wilson both in the United States and in Europe. They emphasized the opposition to Wilson at home, depicting him as a visionary leader without real popular support. In addition, they placed great emphasis on the "disorder and anarchy" in Russia, thereby hoping to provoke Allied intervention, and finally, they printed a number of articles indicating that Germany was able to pay large indemnities. Lincoln Steffens made the same observation. The French were determined to "break his [Wilson's] plan, break his personal strength, which they called his obstinacy, break his power and popularity. . . . Clemenceau was the man who broke Wilson," Steffens wrote.

One of the most acrimonious disputes of the conference involved the left bank of the Rhine. It was, of course, inevitable and just that Alsace-Lorraine should be returned to France. The left bank of the Rhine was another matter. An area of some 10,000 square miles with 5,500,000 inhabitants, it contained rich coalfields and prosperous industries. Prussia acquired the region from France in 1814, and France had claimed sovereignty over it for only twenty years. Acquisition of the left bank as part of the spoils of war was a major objective of Clemenceau and the French government, but it was one that Wilson and his American advisers set themselves to oppose on the grounds that it would constitute a cynical abandonment of the principle of self-determination. A secret agreement with Russia required the severing of the left bank from Germany as a neutral state under French administration, a kind of buffer zone between France and Germany, and, not coincidentally, an enormous economic asset. Lloyd George said repeatedly, "We must not make another Alsace-Lorraine," but that in fact was exactly what Clemenceau was determined to do.

The southwest corner of the left bank of the Rhine constituted the Saar Valley. Before the war it had been responsible for 8 percent of Germany's vast coal production. It had been in French hands for some twenty years—from 1793 to the Treaty of Vienna in 1815. The 1,000,000 or more inhabitants all spoke German, but France wished to annex the region in return for the destruction of the French mines by the Germans, a destruction so thorough that it was estimated it would take at least five years to get them back into production. Britain and the United States set their faces against the annexation of the Saar by France, to Clemenceau's rage. Wilson was adamant. Clemenceau threatened, and Wilson replied, "Then if France does not get what she wishes, she will refuse to act with us. In that event do you wish me to return home?"

"I do not wish you to go home but I intend to do so myself," the Frenchman declared as he walked out.

Wilson was dismayed. "I do not know whether I shall see Monsieur Clemenceau again," he told several of his aides. ". . . I do not know whether the peace conference will continue."

"We are blocked in our plea for security," Clemenceau told Stephen Bonsal; "only our undoubted claim to Alsace goes uncontested. For the little else we may obtain we shall have to fight and fight hard." Wilson had no respect for the past, Clemenceau declared. He had told the American President, "I am the last, the only survivor of the Protest of Bordeaux—against the infamy of the Treaty that the Prussians imposed at the point of the bayonet. M. le Président, I speak for our glorious dead who fell in the two wars. For myself I can hold my tongue, but not for them." After the session, Wilson summoned Isaiah Bowman and announced, "I am in trouble. . . . I am in trouble. . . . I don't know whether I shall see M. Clemenceau again. . . . In fact, I do not know whether the Peace Conference will continue. M. Clemenceau called me pro-German and abruptly left the room. . . . I want to be fair to M. Clemenceau and to France, but I cannot consent to the outright transference to France of 300,000 Germans."

His strength and patience exhausted, the President let word get around that he planned to leave the conference. Instructions were sent to prepare the *George Washington* for a return trip. When Clemenceau got the news from Cary Grayson, Wilson's doctor, he showed his own alarm. "It's a bluff, isn't it?" he asked Grayson.

The doctor replied, "He hasn't a bluffing corpuscle in his body."

Clemenceau had warned Bonsal that Wilson's stubbornness might bring a reaction that would result in Clemenceau's replacement by a Foch-Briand-Poincaré coalition far more adamant in their demands. Bonsal considered such a development a definite possibility. On April 1, 1919, he wrote in his journal that the President must realize that while he had won the war, "he had lost the ideal peace he dreamed of. What should he do?" Bonsal asked himself. "Wash his hands of the whole matter and go home? In this case there would be no treaty and a state of anarchy not only in Europe but throughout the world would follow. The predatory powers would pitch in and take what they wanted, and the democracies we thought to help, and most certainly promised to help, would be despoiled. Or should the President consent to a treaty that will reveal some compromises in principle but at least one that will contain the Covenant, a bright star of hope and guidance in the dark heavens by night and a rainbow of promise in the troubled skies by day?" The answer was clear in Bonsal's mind. He should salvage what he could and, in House's phrase, "not run away." House read to Bonsal several times Gladstone's famous aphorism: "Men ought not to suffer from disenchantment; they ought to know that ideals in politics are never realized."

When House asked Steffens what he thought the consequence of the President's sailing home would be, Steffens replied that he felt confident that every Allied government involved in the treaty negotiations would fall. That prospect apparently unnerved Wilson. He abandoned the notion of leaving Paris.

On April 3 the President had a severe attack of grippe, marked by vomiting, coughing, and diarrhea; Clemenceau expressed his pleasure at the news. Frances Stevenson wrote that he had exclaimed to Lloyd George, " 'He is *worse* today,' and doubled up with laughter. 'Do you know his doctor? Couldn't you get around him & bribe him?' "

When Wilson returned to the conference table on April 8, he was, in Herbert Hoover's words, "drawn, exhausted and haggard." He sometimes seemed confused and groped for words. His valet, Ike Hoover, later told Herbert Hoover that the President had suffered a slight stroke. Certainly it would not have been surprising, in view of his history of minor strokes. Ray Stannard Baker noted that he had "never seen the President look so worn and tired. A terrible strain, with everyone against him. He was so beaten out that he could remember only with an effort what the council had done in the afternoon."

The discussions now centered on the issue of the Monroe Doctrine, which, the French argued, was counter to the principles of the League. Léon Bourgeois was untiring in his denunciations of the American reservations for the doctrine, and Wilson patiently at first and then impatiently reiterated the American position. The Monroe Doctrine, he insisted, was simply an early statement of the basic principle of the League itself: that strong nations should not impose by force of arms their will on weak ones. It is not clear whether the French opposition to the Monroe Doctrine reservations was tactical or emotional, but there was no question that Bourgeois and his coadjutor, Larnaude, orated with unstinting emotion on the subject. Another sticking point with the French was the provision that the native peoples of the mandated ex-colonies must not be recruited for military undertakings. This alarmed the French, who feared they would be barred from recruiting African and North African troops—Senegalese and Moroccans specifically—for the French Army.

Lloyd George, it turned out, had had a change of heart. He no longer talked of a just peace but boasted of what the British had gotten out of the treaty: the German Navy and merchant marine and a number of the German colonies. It was far more than he had dared to hope. It could be argued that these all were bribes offered by Clemenceau to Lloyd George as the price paid for a treaty that punished Germany excruciatingly if it did not go so far as to dismember the nation.

On April 10, Wilson attended a night meeting of those delegates working on the final form of the Covenant of the League in House's rooms at the Hôtel Crillon. The Monroe Doctrine was a point of contention. The French delegates were as usual making difficulties. Wilson answered them "in an extempore speech of witching eloquence," Charles Thompson, an American delegate, noted. "Now that a document was being drafted," the President concluded, "which was the logical extension of the Monroe Doctrine to the whole world, was the United States to be penalized for her early adoption of this policy? . . . Was the commission going to scruple on words at a time when the United States was willing to sign a covenant which made her forever part of the movement for liberty?" So vehement was Wilson, so pale and intense and, it seemed, so near the breaking point, that the French hastily abandoned the field.

There were more alarming signs. The President became obsessed with the notion that the French had surrounded him with spies. He sharply restricted the use of official automobiles and raised a row over a piece of missing furniture. His tic grew more noticeable.

The Big Four returned in the waning days of the conference to the Rhineland issue. Stephen Bonsal noted on April 14 that the French delegate, Larnaude, was furious: "His eyes grew very small and his nose swelled," Bonsal wrote; "he shook his finger across the Peace table and shouted: 'Unless you promise us an international force stationed on the Rhine, and unless steps are immediately taken to carry out your promise, there will be no League of Nations and perhaps no Peace.' And M. Bourgeois pounded on the table in complete approval of his colleague's ultimatum."

On April 15 Wilson capitulated on the demilitarized zone on the east side of the Rhine. A buffer zone was established running fifty kilometers east of the Rhine, an area in which Germany would not be permitted to erect any fortifications or military posts of any kind. In addition, an Allied commission would occupy the area for fifteen years to ensure that there were no violations of the treaty agreement. French troops would initially occupy the area and would withdraw in three echelons at five-year intervals if the German reparation payments were on schedule. House carried the news to Clemenceau, who embraced him. "At last," he said to Mordacq, "I've got almost everything I wanted." The Rhineland commission was to consist of four persons; the cost of the commission was to be paid by the Germans. By 1922 the commission included 1,300 persons, whose living expenses for eight months came to 178,000,000 gold marks. Castles were refurbished and lavish apartments provided for the principal officials. The whole enterprise became a gigantic boondoggle at the expense of the Germans.

The French newspapers had kept up a barrage of invective against Wilson and the Americans generally. The day after Wilson's capitulation the Paris papers, as though on command, overflowed with acclaim. One editorial writer exclaimed, "Honor to President Wilson, High Priest of the Ideal, Leaguer of the Nations, Benefactor of Humanity, Shepherd of Victory and Legislator of Peace." In the growing atmosphere of disappointment and anxiety, Baker wrote: "A treaty will be made, but it may never be signed, or if signed it will have little meaning. We are plunging inevitably into an unknown world full of danger."

As the time approached for submitting the treaty to the Germans, it became clear that no one was exactly sure what was in that large document of some 200 pages. Andrew Bonar Law, the Conservative leader in the House of Commons, and Jan Smuts described it as a "hopeless mess." In a final session Foch insisted that occupation of the Rhineland for a mere fifteen years was insufficient. Italy tried once more for Fiume. Lloyd George proposed giving it some of Syria in lieu of Fiume, but Clemenceau "had already decided to gobble down" that territory and opposed the suggestion.

"My last and most vivid impression," Keynes wrote, "is of . . . the President and the prime minister at the center of a surging mob and a babel of sounds, a welter of eager, impromptu compromise and counter-compromise . . . on what was an unreal question anyhow . . . and Clemenceau silent and aloof on the outskirts . . . dry in soul and empty of hope, very old and tired, but surveying the scene with a cynical and almost impish air; and when at last order was restored and the company had returned to their places, it was to discover that he had disappeared."

The Council of Ten had had 72 sessions; the Council of Foreign Ministers, known as the Five, 39 sessions, most of them relatively fruitless since the principals were making all the crucial decisions; and the Council of Four, 145 sessions.

The final draft of the League Covenant provided for the establishment of a "secretariat," consisting of a secretary-general "and such secretaries and staff that may be required." Its "seat" was to be at Geneva. The secretary-general was to be appointed by the Council with the approval of a majority of the Assembly.

The Council was to be made up of the Great Powers: Britain, France, Japan, and the United States. The lesser powers constituted the Assembly. All real power lay in the Council, which could veto any proposal of the Assembly.

The first meeting of the Assembly and the first meeting of the Council were to be summoned by the President of the United States. Article 7 provided that "All positions in connection with the League, including the Secretariat, shall be open equally to men and women."

Article 10 had stuck to the comparatively modest statement that "The Members of the League undertake to respect and preserve against external aggression the territorial integrity and existing political independence of all Members of the League. In case of any such aggression the Council shall advise upon the means by which this obligation shall be fulfilled." In cases of disputes between members of the League they agreed to submit the matter to "arbitration or to inquiry by the Council, and . . . in no case to resort to war until three months after the award by arbitration or the report by the Council."

For all former colonies the League would become "the residuary trustee with sovereign right of ultimate disposal. . . ." None of the former colonies was to be annexed "by any state within the League or outside of it," and in the future "the rule of self-determination, or the consent of the governed to their form of government," should be "fairly and reasonably applied. . . ." As "successor to the Empires" the League of Nations was "empowered . . . to watch over the relations . . . of all new independent States arising or created out of the Empires. . . ."

The mandatories, as they were now called, were to be taken under the "tutelage" of those members of the League that "by reason of their resources, their experience or their geographical position" were best qualified. Slavery or the slave trade and arms and liquor traffic as well as military bases and fortifications and armed forces were forbidden to the mandatories.

There were three classes of mandates, identified as A, B, and C. Class A mandates were perhaps the most shamelessly self-serving since they provided specifically for carving up the corpse of the Ottoman Empire and parceling out the pieces to the victorious Allies. But even here the mandates provided that when the respective peoples were able, in the opinion of the League, to stand alone (of course, that decision was reserved, under the League's Covenant, to the Great Powers, all of which had large economic interests in their mandated territories), they should be given their independence. B applied to Central African territories formerly belonging to the Central Powers; German East Africa went to Great Britain. The terms of these mandates also purported to protect the freedom of conscience and religion of the local inhabitants and banned trade in slaves, drugs, liquor, and arms. Class C mandates covered primarily the smaller islands of the Pacific. Samoa was assigned to New Zealand; New Guinea, to Australia. While there was a good deal of justified cynicism about the mandate system, the fact was that the recognition of the principle that the mandate was explicitly a temporary situation, looking toward independence for the mandates, made a subtle but important change in their status. It gave an unmistakable legitimacy to movements for independence and encouraged the most moderate elements to take the lead in such movements. It also created what proved, in the long run, irresistible pressures on the nations exercising the mandates to let their people go.

To the cynical the mandate system seemed to be intended primarily to avoid "the appearance of taking enemy territory as the spoils of war." As Lansing put it, "under the mandatory system Germany lost her territorial assets, which might have greatly reduced her financial debts to the Allies, while the latter obtained the German colonial possessions without the loss of any of their claims for indemnity." Whether this was the intention (and surely it was not), it was, in a measure, the effect.

Under the mandate system the British Empire grew by 1,607,053 square miles with 33,000,000 inhabitants; the French possessions of land and peoples by 420,000 square miles and 4,000,000 inhabitants; the Japanese, with Shantung, by 20,000,000 Chinese. Italy retrieved from Turkey, as mandates, 680,000 square miles of North Africa with a mere 880,000 inhabitants. But to state it in such fashion is in a sense to misstate it. The days of the mandates were numbered; the seeds of independence had been sown, and the ideal officially recognized. The new landlords would, in the main, find they had rebellious tenants and short leases.

Samuel Gompers used the occasion of reporting on the deliberations of the commission on international labor legislation, of which he was a member, to castigate the socialists. "It is due to the fact that proposals favored by the European Socialists were defeated . . . that American labor was able to endorse overwhelmingly the treaty and the labor provisions." At times, Gompers confessed, the socialists had been so aggressive that the "American labor mission . . . thought seriously of departing for home in despair. . . ." The attitude of the socialists was that they "shortly would be in control of most of the governments of the world, and therefore the workers would have a majority in all the international labor conferences" of the future. Gompers felt himself caught between "reaction and misunderstanding and willfullness" on the one hand "and utopian foolishness" on the other.

The efforts of the commission on labor resulted in Article 427, which declared in part that "labor should not be regarded merely [the word 'merely' was the result of a bitter debate in the commission; many delegates denounced the word as implying that labor was, in part at least, a commodity] as a commodity or article of commerce." The right to form unions was hinted at by the words "the right of lawful association for all lawful purposes." Moreover, "employees" (there were objections to the word "workers" as having too revolutionary a connotation) should have "a wage adequate to maintain a reasonable standard of life as this is understood in their time and country." The commissioners also called for an eight-hour day or a "forty-eight hour week as a standard to be aimed at." It was also stated that "men and women should receive equal remuneration for work of equal value."

To Gompers the existence of the commission was in itself a triumph for labor all over the world. "This," he wrote, "was truly an epoch-making step. The Covenant of the League of Nations is the written verdict and agreement of the civilized world that until justice is done to those who work, justice has been done only in part."

Toward the close of the sessions on the League a delegation of women from various countries asked for a hearing. They urged that the functions of the League not be limited to the prevention of war but be extended along "lines of international co-operation," that the League, in short, take under its wing all things having to do with the general welfare of the peoples of the world—such matters as fighting disease, racial and sex discrimination, and conservation of natural resources. The delegates were clearly impressed by the testimony of the women, and their ideas were represented in the final text of the treaty in a pledge to "endeavour to secure and maintain fair and humane conditions of labour for men, women, and children, both in their own countries and in all countries to which their commercial and industrial relations extend." They likewise agreed to take "international" steps "for the prevention and control of disease."

As the terms of the treaty itself got about, the initial reaction among the various peace delegates, at least among the Americans and many of the British, was one of anger and dismay. "I am much troubled over our peace terms," Smuts wrote to a friend. "I consider them very bad. And wrong. And they may not be accepted. The world may lapse into complete chaos. And what will emerge? I don't know what to do." To another friend he wrote: "Under this treaty the situation in Europe will become intolerable and a revolution must come, or again, in due course, an explosion into war. . . . I am bitterly disappointed in both Wilson and Lloyd George, who are smaller men than I should ever have thought. . . . The Germans behaved disgracefully . . . and deserve a hard peace. But that is no reason why the world must be thrust into ruin. . . . And so instead of making peace," he added, "we make war, and are going to reduce Europe to ruin. The smaller nations are all mad; they want credit, not for food for their starving population, but for military expenditure. It is enough to reduce one to despair." Smuts called it "the most reactionary [peace] since Scipio Africanus dealt with Carthage. . . . What a ghastly tragedy this is!"

Robert Lansing, reading his copy, wrote: "For the first time in these days of feverish rush of preparation there is time to consider the treaty as a complete document. . . . The impression made by it is one of disappointment, of regret, and of depression. The terms of peace appear immeasurably harsh and humiliating, while many of them seem to me impossible of performance." The notion that such an imperfect document could substantially reduce the chances of future wars seemed laughable to him. "The seeds of war . . . sown in so many articles" must "soon bear fruit. The League might as well attempt to prevent the growth of plant life in a tropical jungle. Wars will come sooner or later." The League was in essence "an instrument of the mighty to check the normal growth of natural power and national aspirations among those who have been rendered impotent by defeat. . . . Resentment and bitterness, if not desperation, are bound to be the consequences of such provisions. It may be years before these oppressed peoples are able to throw off the yoke, but as sure as day follows night the time will come when they will make the effort. . . . We have a treaty of peace, but it will not bring permanent peace because it is founded on the shifting sands of self-interest."

Norman Hapgood, Felix Frankfurter, Lincoln Steffens, and Henry

Morgenthau came to see Ray Stannard Baker to urge him to try to prevail on the President to make one last effort to improve the worst deficiencies of the treaty, but Wilson was too drained to respond. Even Lloyd George's nerve failed him at the last minute. "Liberal and labor" criticism in Britain had swelled to considerable proportions. He announced to Colonel House that he favored making "considerable changes" in the treaty to meet the storm of criticism. When Lloyd George went back to urge Wilson to reopen the most controversial aspects of the treaty, the President listened impatiently, twirling his thumbs while the prime minister declared that unless certain articles in the treaty were changed, the British army and fleet could not be counted upon to compel the Germans to sign. According to Baruch, who was present, Wilson heard the Briton out and then said angrily, "Mr. Prime Minister, you make me sick! For months we have been struggling to make the terms of the Treaty exactly along the line you now speak of, and never got the support of the English. Now, after we have finally come to an agreement, and when we have to face the Germans and need unanimity, you want to rewrite the Treaty." Still, if Lloyd George could persuade Clemenceau to accept the changes he now urged, Wilson would agree. The latter task, of course, was hopeless, as Wilson knew it to be. The treaty remained as it was with all its imperfections.

Harold Nicolson apportioned an equal share of the blame to Lloyd George. He wrote his wife that if he were a German, he "wouldn't sign for a moment." Balfour spoke to Nicolson of "Those three all-powerful, all ignorant men, sitting there and carving continents with only a child to lead them!" He talked of resigning.

Herbert Hoover was among those deeply disturbed by the final terms of the treaty. "Hate and revenge ran through the political and economic passages," he wrote. ". . . Conditions were set up upon which Europe could never be rebuilt or peace come to mankind. It seemed to me the economic consequences alone would pull down all Europe and thus injure the United States. I rose and went for a walk in the deserted streets at early daylight." A few blocks away he encountered General Smuts and John Maynard Keynes, equally sunk in gloom. Their diagnoses were much the same. The treaty spelled disaster instead of hope.

"It seemed to me a terrible document; a dispensation of retribution with scarcely a parallel in history," Ray Stannard Baker wrote. A few days later he added, "The President seems now to be losing the support he had among the liberal-minded people of the world, the idealists, the workers, the youth of all nations—without gaining the support of the conservatives. . . . Yet his principles remain. They are true; he has stated them once for all, but will he himself ever see the Promised Land? . . . How far," Baker asked himself, "must one work with the forces of his time, however passionate, ignorant, greedy? If he compromises, accepts the best he can get, he may not acquire the crown of prophecy, which is crucifixion, but he may win the laurels which posterity at length bestows upon the wise." Baker felt a deep division in his own mind about supporting the League founded, as it was, upon an "abominable" treaty. "How can I go home and support it, support the League of Nations, founded upon it, support Wilson? Yet I cannot commit the folly of mere empty criticism, harking back to what might have been done. I know too well the impossible atmosphere of greed, fear, and hatred he has had to work in. I have felt it myself, every day, every hour."

When the treaty was made public, "the world," in Lincoln Steffens's words, "was shocked. Nobody expected it to be as bad as it was." Several Americans in the peace delegation resigned in protest. In Steffens's view, Wilson might have still retrieved something from the debacle if he could have faced facts. "We and our president," he wrote, "might have had one of the most inspiring failures in this world of successes. If Wilson had said that he had failed and told why and pointed to a future of such glorious failures—to compromise, his story would have gone down in history as a classic, as one of the most magnificent and significant failures in the story of man. And we need some great failures," Steffens added, "especially we ever-successful Americans—conscious, intelligent, illuminating failures. But no, Woodrow Wilson chose success; so he goes down in history as just one more successful American, the founder of the League of Nations, the beginner of world government!"

Philip Snowden, one of the leaders of the British Labor Party, wrote on May 22, 1919: "Beyond all other statesmen who are responsible for the Peace Treaty, President Wilson is utterly discredited. He has not insisted upon the observance of a single one of the conditions of peace he had laid down. . . . His intervention in the European war has been disastrous from every point of view. If he had not brought America into the war a decent peace would probably have been secured. His intervention has intensely aggravated the European situation and has left Europe seething with jealousy, hatred, malice, and the certainty of a generation of war and bloodshed. The sooner he gets back to America and ceases to interfere in international politics, for which he has evidently neither the courage nor the knowledge, the better it will be for the peace of the world."

The editors of the *New Republic* rejected the treaty out of hand. "THIS IS NOT PEACE," they wrote. "Americans would be fools if they permitted themselves now to be embroiled in a system of European alliances. . . . The peace cannot last. America should withdraw from all commitments which would impair her freedom of action." The treaty was "morbidly sick with conflict and trouble." The *New Republic* did not hesitate to lay the blame on Wilson's doorstep for making Europe "a bureau of the French foreign office." The fact was that Lippmann and the young idealists of his generation had been as much betrayed as Wilson in their extravagant expectations, and it was ungenerous of them to pin the blame exclusively on the man they had shortly before praised so inordinately.

But the objections were drowned out in a chorus of praise from conservative newspapers. In an abounding irony, Villard's old paper, the *Evening Post,* which he had been obliged to sell, called the treaty "a voice from Heaven!" while the *New York Times* hailed it as "terribly severe but just."

Five young members of the American delegation, led by Adolf Berle, Jr., and Samuel Eliot Morison, met to discuss whether they should resign. They decided to hang on rather than to discredit the treaty. But Bullitt sent a letter of resignation to Lansing, and to Wilson he wrote: "I am one of the millions who trusted implicitly in your leadership and believed you would take nothing less than 'a permanent peace based on unselfish, unbiased justice.' But the government has consented now to deliver the suffering peoples of the world to new oppressions, subjections, and dismemberments—a new century of war. . . . Unjust decisions regarding Shantung, Tyrol, Thrace, Hungary, East Prussia, Danzig, and the Saar Valley and abandonment of the principle of freedom of the seas make new international conflicts certain. . . . I am sorry you did not fight to a finish and that you had so little faith in the millions of men like myself in every nation who had faith in you."

Bad as the treaty was, it had to be presented to the Germans for their acceptance. They were summoned to Paris to learn their fate. Francesco Nitti, the Italian prime minister at the time, wrote in 1922: "It will remain forever a terrible precedent in modern history that, against all pledges, all precedents, and all traditions, the representatives of Germany were never even heard; nothing was left to them but to sign a treaty at a moment when famine, exhaustion and threat of revolution made it impossible not to sign it."

The German delegation of 160 members, led by the foreign minister, Count Ulrich von Brockdorff-Rantzau, left Berlin on April 28, 1919, for Paris. Brockdorff-Rantzau, unfortunately for the success of his mission, was the personification of the Junker class, an imperious monocled aristocrat with the required dueling scars. The room chosen to receive the German delegates was the Trianon Palace Hotel at Versailles, the scene of France's humiliation in 1871. Several hundred of the higher echelons of the delegates to the conference were seated in chairs around the room, splendid with chandeliers and mirrors. Baker described the scene: "Clemenceau, short, powerful, impressive, stood at the head of the table; President Wilson at his right, Lloyd George at his left. Count Brockdorff-Rantzau, surrounded by his eight or ten German delegates, sat facing him." Clemenceau announced, "Gentlemen, plenipotentiaries of the German Empire, it is neither the time nor the place for superfluous words. . . . The time has come when we must settle our accounts. You have asked for peace. We are ready to give you peace."

In replying to Clemenceau, Brockdorff-Rantzau neglected to stand, an omission which, taken as a deliberate insult, infuriated the French. "We know," he declared, "the power of the hatred which we encounter here. . . . It is demanded of us that we shall confess ourselves to be the only ones guilty of the war. Such a confession in my mouth will be a lie. . . . We are far from declining any responsibility for this great world war having come to pass, and for its having been made in the way in which it was made . . . but energetically we deny that Germany and its people, who were convinced that they were making a war of defense, were alone guilty. . . ." Brockdorff-Rantzau went on to remind his hostile audience of the effects of the Allied blockade, which, he declared, had caused the deaths of "hundreds of thousands of noncombatants" who had perished since the armistice, "killed by cold deliberation after our adversaries had conquered. . . . Think of them when you speak of guilt and punishment." It was clearly not the right tone to take under the circumstances. Lloyd George snapped an ivory paper knife in two. Wilson said later, "The Germans are really a stupid people. They always do the wrong thing. . . . This is the most tactless speech I have ever heard." The usually cool Balfour said, "Beasts they were and beasts they are." (Count von Bernstorff told Stephen Bonsal that he believed humiliation at the way the German delegation had been treated plus cognac accounted for Brockdorff-Rantzau's behavior at the meeting with the Allies.)

"The session has lasted a brief moment of a spring day," Ray Stannard Baker wrote. "Through gardens of surpassing loveliness, past lilacs and chestnuts in the first burst of bloom, the Germans returned to their hotel. . . . The Allied leaders went back to Paris. It was over."

By his ill-considered remarks Brockdorff-Rantzau squandered whatever residual feeling many of those involved in shaping the treaty had in regard to the terms imposed on Germany. It was several days before such misgivings, strongly evident at the time that the text of the treaty became known, reasserted themselves. The reaction in Germany when the terms were known was one of bitter resentment. Crowds collected outside the headquarters of the military mission, chanting out the betrayal of the Fourteen Points as they applied to Germany. A speaker of the Majority Socialist Party called the treaty "a continuation of the war by other means." It was widely declared that if the Germans had had any notion of such severe terms, they would have fought to the end rather than lay down their arms. The president of the newly elected Assembly said, "The unbelievable has happened; the enemy presents us with a treaty surpassing the most pessimistic forecasts. It means the annihilation of the German people." After five hours of speeches the Assembly rose and sang "Deutschland über Alles." It was certainly an understandable, if ominous, response.

Among other provisions, Germany was not permitted to have a regular army or air force, military schools, or associations of veterans. A police force was allowed 204 field guns and 84 howitzers to preserve domestic order. The population of Germany was reduced by some 6,500,000. It lost a tenth of its factories, much of its coal production (in the Saar Valley), and a sixth of its farmland as well as its colonies and merchant marine.

There were another five weeks to wait while Germany agonized over the terms of the treaty. They were long, anxious weeks. On the first of May, when the working people and the socialists of Paris turned out to march and demonstrate, the police and the soldiers showed a savage disposition to suppress the annual event and punish the marchers. "We saw many bloody heads," Ray Stannard Baker wrote, adding, ". . . What folly! What unutterable folly!" The marchers chanted, *"À bas Clemenceau!"* and *"Vive Wilson."*

In Hungary there was a coup d'état engineered by the Hapsburg archduke Joseph, supported by Rumanian soldiers, who surrounded the halls of the ministry and set up machine guns commanding the building. Herbert Hoover, familiar with the situation at first hand, appeared before the Big Four and informed them that the restoration of the archduke "had done more to rehabilitate the Bolshevik cause than anything that had happened for a long time." If he were allowed to retain power, reactionary forces all over Europe would take new heart. Hoover was instructed to draft a telegram which contained the clause "the Allied and Associated Governments must insist that the present claimant to the headship of the Hungarian State should resign, and that a Government, in which all parties are represented, should be elected by the Hungarian people." Hoover's "man in Budapest" replied somewhat inelegantly the next day, "Archie [the archduke] on the carpet 7 P.M. Went through the hoop at 7:05 P.M." And so a new government, the fifth in a period of eight months, was established.

The news was not encouraging elsewhere. Yugoslavia and Italy were on the verge of war over Trieste. Baker wrote in his journal: "All the world seems to be going to smash. Paris is wretched with strikes of all kinds—accompanied by a nameless fear that these strikes . . . may result in revolution. We heard of bitter industrial struggles in China, widespread bomb outrages in the United States, deep-seated discontent in both England and Italy. . . ." In addition, rumors were circulating that Germany would refuse to sign the treaty, producing what—anarchy, revolution, more war?

Wilson took advantage of Memorial Day, May 30, to dedicate the American cemetery near Paris and identify the treaty with the sacrifice of American lives. He appeared rested and in strong, if somber, spirits. The event was inevitably reminiscent of Lincoln's dedication of the Gettysburg cemetery in the fall of 1863, and Wilson's speech was filled with echoes of Lincoln's famous address. The hillside, with rows of small crosses marching across it, and fringed by groves of acacia trees, was hot and dusty. Besides regiments of American soldiers, there were numerous diplomats and statesmen in attendance. "It would be no profit to us to eulogize these illustrious dead," Wilson declared, "if we did not take to heart the lesson which they have taught us. They are dead; they have done their utmost to show their devotion to a great cause, and they have left it to us to see that that cause shall not be betrayed whether in war or peace. It is our privilege and our high duty to consecrate ourselves afresh on a day like this to the objects for which they fought." They had come not merely to defeat Germany but to vanquish forever the repressive and authoritarian world that the Central Powers had stood for and "to see to it that there should never be a war like this again. . . . The peoples of the world are awake and the peoples of the world are in the saddle. . . . If we are not now the servants of the opinion of mankind, we are of all men the littlest, the most contemptible, the least gifted with vision." There must be a "new order of things in which the only question will be, 'Is it right?' 'Is it just?' 'Is it in the interest of mankind?' . . . I sent these lads over here to die. Shall I—can I ever speak a word of counsel which is inconsistent with the assurance I gave them when they came over?"

To Baker the speech was the greatest he had ever heard, "greatest in its emotional power over the people who were present, greatest in the conviction it gave of the speaker's utter devotion to his inner vision, and his determination to realize it." It was a speech "so perfectly turned, so sure, so musical, so appealing" that many who heard it wept.

A few days later, in Lansing's study at the Hôtel Crillon, Wilson was genial and friendly, praising the members of the various commissions for their contributions to the treaty, but there was a strong current of discontent among the three dozen or so delegates there. Most of those who expressed concerns about the treaty concentrated on the issue of reparations and the severity of the terms imposed on Germany. Wilson insisted that the terms were "just." If they were not, they should make them so. Yet his next words were disheartening to his auditors. The time to make substantial changes had passed. He was a "little tired" of people who came forth at the eleventh hour with cavils and objections.

In Germany the debate over accepting the treaty was carried by Matthias Erzberger, the leader of the Catholic Center Party, who defended the decision to sign by saying, "If someone had me handcuffed and was pointing a revolver at me, demanding that I sign a piece of paper on which I promise to fly to the moon in forty-eight hours, then any sane person, in order to save his life, would sign the paper."

On June 20, 1919, in the harbor of Scapa Flow of Great Britain, the crews of the German naval vessels detained there since the armistice scuttled their fleet: nine battleships, five heavy cruisers, and more than fifty destroyers. Three days later the Germans sent word they were prepared to sign, and on June 28 the representatives of the Weimar Republic returned to Versailles to the Great Hall of Mirrors for the ceremony.

Before the signing Wilson met for one of his rare press conferences with American correspondents. "All things considered," he told them, "the Treaty adheres more nearly to the Fourteen Points than I had a right to expect. Considering the incalculable difficulties we had to face, it comes remarkably near. Never forget that Germany did an irreparable wrong, and must suffer for it. . . . Think of the positive achievements of peace—the newly liberated peoples, who had not dared to dream of freedom, the Poles, the Czechoslovaks, the Slavs, the peoples of Turkey. The peace has given a new charter to labor, has provided for economic equality among the nations, and gone far toward the protection of racial and religious minorities, and finally and the greatest of all, it has banded the peoples of the world in a new League of Nations. It is a colossal business."

General Pershing and his staff were among the first dignitaries to arrive at the Hall of Mirrors. Lloyd George brought fifty disabled soldiers, and Clemenceau two old countrymen, friends of his for many years. There were, in addition to the potentates and plenipotentiaries, journalists, photographers, and a battery of secretaries, some 1,000 people, it was estimated. The German delegates were the secretary for foreign affairs under the Weimar Republic and the colonial secretary (though there were no colonies left), Hermann Müller and Dr. Johannes Bell, both men pale and nervous. While the treaty was still being signed, guns began to fire and shouts of exultation rose from the crowds waiting to hear the news. The fountains of Versailles, stilled since the outbreak of the war, were turned on, airplanes buzzed overhead, and the setting sun made the windows sparkle like "a jeweled palace in a fairy tale."

James Harbord, major general and head of the Services of Supply, described the "perfect delirium of joy!!" that possessed Paris at the news. "Windows opened everywhere at the first peal of the bells and guns, and people listened to the music a few seconds in ectasy [sic] before rushing down to mingle with the swelling throngs in the streets. The streets became avenues of color; flags waved from every apartment in the city, and Paris, sad for over four years, was transformed in an instant. Schools closed down and workers swarmed toward the center of the capital. Shops shut up and offices ceased work. Florists shops were taken by storm. Flowers were showered on every officer and soldier that passed. . . . It was a great manifestation of the Soul of Paris that words cannot reproduce." The "Marseillaise" was sung until voices grew hoarse. French and American and British soldiers linked arms and were joined by swarms of French girls, "soldiers of every color and colony, marching together. . . . Yank and Aussie, Italian, Portuguese, Pole, Czecho-Slovak, British, Hindoo, Anamite, poilu, black, white, red, yellow and brown, arm in arm they paraded up and down avenues and boulevards; tam o'shanters of the Chasseurs Alpins, Italian cocked hats, overseas caps, helmets, hats and bareheads, the four corners of the round earth; all glad that the war is ended. Nearly everybody in the city . . . was kissed by any one, man, woman, or child." To avoid kisses, one would have had to have hidden in a cellar. In the Café de la Paix 300 Americans, many of them roaring drunk, sang "Hail, hail, the gang's all here; what the hell do we care?"

General Dawes and General Harbord repaired to the Folies Bergères to see *Zig Zag*, the indiscreet sensation of the hour (Harbord called it "a fine clean show"). When the two generals emerged from the theater, the streets were still too crowded to pass through readily. At the grand opera an impromptu performance was devised. Chorus girls in teams of eight appeared, carrying flags bearing the names of the famous battles of the war. The American banners carried the names of St.-Mihiel and the Argonne and the Americans present cheered deliriously. When the pageantry, the singing, and the dancing were over, a French bugler in the balcony blew the notes of the "all clear" signal that had been sounded at the end of air raids. It seemed a fitting end to the day.

The armistice had been signed on November 11, 1918. The peace conference had *begun* ten weeks later on January 18. (It was January 22 before the delegates got down to business.) Three weeks later Wilson had departed for the United States, and he had been absent for almost four weeks. The first session of the conference after his return took place in the atmosphere we have described, on March 22. The treaty was presented to the Germans on May 8. The armistice, a state of political and economic limbo, had thus extended over six months, an unconscionable period of profoundly unsettling doubt, anxiety, and, above all, human suffering (it would be another five weeks before the Germans could bring themselves to sign the treaty). But of those six months, somewhat more than two (not counting Wilson's absence in the United States) had been devoted to *rearranging the world*. It is not surprising that there were major deficiencies in the treaty, though it might be argued that these were more the result of human intractability, greed, and vengefulness than want of time. And the villain was clearly that otherwise estimable and thoroughly charming old man

Georges Clemenceau. But Clemenceau, it turned out, was as critical as anyone of the treaty; Germany, grievously wounded as it was, had not been killed. When Hoover called on the prime minister before his departure from Paris, he found the old man in a pessimistic mood. "There will be another world war in your time," he told Hoover, "and you will be needed back in Europe." He recalled the telegraphic report on the downfall of the Archduke Joseph, last of the Hapsburgs. The telegram brought back his days in America and cheered him considerably.

One of the darkest consequences of the treaty was that it provided fuel for the myth of betrayal. As this account went, the German armies could have fought on to victory if they had not been betrayed at home by Socialists and Communists, many of whom were Jews, who were perceived as giving their allegiance to some amalgam of international socialism and international Jewry rather than to the fatherland. Of all the disastrous results, this, it turned out, was one that bore the most poisonous fruit.

Clemenceau, attacked on the one hand for accepting too soft a peace with Germany, was denounced by the Socialists for his ruthless suppression of opposition on the other hand and fell from power in the autumn elections of 1919, only a few months after his remarkable triumph. Lloyd George, faced with a series of bitter strikes and hard economic times, was voted out of office with the rest of his Liberal Party in 1922. He lived for another thirteen years, long enough to see the rise of Adolf Hitler, whom he visited and acclaimed as "the greatest living German." When war came in 1939, he refused Churchill's invitation to join the government, convinced that Great Britain would lose the war. His wife, Margaret, died in 1941, and Lloyd George married Frances Stevenson and retired to a cottage in Wales. Two years later he died of cancer at the age of eighty-two.

The corps of academics who had served as delegates returned, for the most part, to their academic posts, and several of them, Charles Seymour, most conspicuously, made their subsequent careers writing books about the peace conference and the causes and consequences of the war. Their role in the Inquiry and at the peace conference was pointed to as a brilliant example of the beneficent consequences of putting mind, as represented by "experts" and "specialists," in the service of society.

Paderewski had done his best to persuade Wilson to visit Poland before he returned to the United States. The President declined (he sailed the day of the signing of the treaty), but he. offered Hoover instead, and the latter made a triumphal tour of major Polish cities, leaving behind him a trail of streets and parks named after him and even, in Warsaw, a large statue in the central square. The most moving event was the parade of children who had been the beneficiaries of the soup kitchens established in Poland by the Children's Relief Association. Some 50,000 of them straggled past Hoover's reviewing stand, hour after hour, "laughing, chattering, squealing, trying vainly to look sober and to maintain some kind of marching order." The head of the French military mission, standing beside Hoover, was so overcome with emotion that he had to abandon his post, and he told Hoover afterward, "There has never been a review of honor in all history which I would prefer for myself to that which has been given you today."

To John Maynard Keynes, Hoover, "with his habitual air of a weary Titan (or, as others might put it, of an exhausted prize fighter)," was "the only man who emerged from the ordeal of Paris with an enhanced reputation."

39

The Treaty and the Senate

The mood on board the *George Washington* was one of uncertainty. There was every reason to anticipate resistance in the Senate to the Covenant of the League. More unsettling was the fact that those American delegates who should have been its warmest advocates were totally disillusioned, not just with the treaty but, above all, with the unexpected tenacity of the old order.

In the dark moments of the night Ray Stannard Baker found himself tormented by the thought that Wilson had raised expectations that were impossible of realization, the dream of "the people come to power; he has spoken the great true word, but has he the genius to work it out? Above all is the time ripe?" The last question may have been the most pertinent. Was the time ripe? Lenin and the Bolsheviks had forced the time; in a democracy the time must ripen.

Wilson returned to a tumultuous welcome. As the *George Washington*, escorted by battleships, airplanes, and dirigibles, entered New York Harbor, hundreds of smaller boats formed an enthusiastic convoy. Whistles blew; horns were sounded; guns fired. Wilson stood on the top deck in striped trousers and a Prince Albert coat with a golf cap on his head in place of his customary high silk hat.

Stephen Bonsal, arriving in Washington some weeks ahead of the

President, had been assigned by Colonel House the delicate task of explaining the treaty to Henry Cabot Lodge and trying to persuade him to support it. Bonsal and Lodge went over the Covenant article by article. "You good people who were over there in Paris seem to have been entranced by the President's eloquence," Lodge told Bonsal. "You thought that his was the voice that breathed over Eden, proclaiming a new era, that the old Adam was dead. . . ."

"Not at all," Bonsal replied. "We knew he was not dead, but we did believe he had a wicked clutch on the throat of civilization, and that unless it was broken the world which men of good will loved was doomed to end."

"As an English production it [the treaty] does not rank high," Lodge said teasingly. "It might get by at Princeton but certainly not at Harvard." But Lodge seemed on the whole encouraging, Bonsal reported to House.

Gilbert Hitchcock, the Nebraska Senator who was chairman of the Foreign Relations Committee, told Bonsal that he and his fellow Democrats were personally in favor of getting the treaty ratified "in almost any form." Hitchcock confessed that Lodge was an enigma to him. He had had at first "the impression that he [Lodge] merely wished to weave into the Covenant some of his great thoughts, so that this world charter would not, in the future, be regarded as a party document." But Lodge's hatred of Wilson impaired his judgment, in Hitchcock's view. Gerald Johnson repeated the familiar story that Lodge had met with Roosevelt shortly before his death, that the two men, without, of course, specific references to the treaty, the terms of which were then unknown, had agreed on a number of general principles which any acceptable treaty must contain, and that Lodge had pledged himself to fight for the inclusion of these in whatever treaty might be proposed to the Senate for ratification after his chief's death.

A few days after his return Wilson met with Hitchcock's committee. He read the members a little lecture that he had prepared, the gist of which was that Europe could not wait for a treaty without severe suffering. Unless the treaty were speedily ratified, the consequences might "prove disastrous to a large portion of the world, and . . . , at its worst, bring upon Europe conditions even more terrible than those wrought by the war itself." The implication was plain enough. If the Senate, in its partisan stubborn opposition, refused to ratify the treaty with the League as an essential part, it must take the responsibility for the terrible suffering that would in all likelihood result.

Patiently and, it is to be feared, patronizingly the President took up the principal objections that had been voiced to the Covenant and demonstrated either how each objection had been responded to by changes in the wording of the Covenant or that the objection itself was based on a misunderstanding of a particular article. To a modern reader the argument seems brilliantly sustained. But when the schoolmaster had finished, his pupils stared defiantly at him, quite unpersuaded. Among the more conspicuously and outspokenly unpersuaded was Senator Warren Harding of Ohio. He asked questions that the President had already answered. It seemed to Wilson that he had "a disturbingly dull mind," impervious to any explanation.

Two days later Wilson laid the treaty formally before the Senate, accompanied by a message that called the League of Nations the "only hope for mankind." His message declared, "We can go only forward, with lifted eyes and freshened spirit to follow the vision. . . . America in truth shall show the way. The light shines upon the path ahead, and nowhere else." The President stated that he was willing to accept what he called "interpretative reservations" designed to clarify the position of the United States on any issues in substantial doubt.

Henry Stoddard, sitting in the gallery, was shocked "by the pallor of his [Wilson's] face, the worn look that told a story no effort could wholly conceal." It was Stoddard's opinion "that Wilson could have insured the ratification of the Treaty within two weeks after his return to America had he chosen to do so on the basis of reservations suggested by Senators friendly to the League of Nations." Frank Kellogg of Minnesota went to the White House on July 15 as spokesman for some thirty-two Republican Senators (Lodge was not among them) with a plea that the President accept the reservations desired by those favorably disposed to the ratification of the treaty. Wilson's reply was that the points that Kellogg and his fellow Senators were concerned about were already covered by the Federal Constitution. "If that is so," Kellogg replied, "why not accept them? They can do no harm. We can furnish from 32 to 34 votes on this basis and with the Democratic votes you control you will have a safe margin for ratification."

"Thank you for your offer," Wilson reportedly replied, "I appreciate your purpose. I'll think it over and if I can agree with your view I will let you know." But Kellogg and his group never heard from Wilson, and most of them slipped quietly over into the opposition.

Wilson was especially vulnerable, or the treaty was vulnerable, on the Shantung issue. For one thing, China had many more friends in the United States than Japan had. What we might call the missionary establishment was powerful and articulate and tireless in its agitation against turning over a Chinese province to the Japanese as the spoils of war in contradiction of the principle of self-determination enunciated in the Fourteen Points and frequently reiterated. Senators, especially liberal Senators, lost no time in going to work on the Shantung issue. The Foreign Relations Committee voted to amend the treaty so as to give China to China, so to speak.

It is important to keep in mind that the Covenant of the League was in certain respects a seriously flawed document. There was some justice in the charges made by such an oddly diverse duo as William Bullitt and Robert Lansing. To critics of the treaty one of the most troubling concessions wrested from Wilson was the provision that the United States, Great Britain, and France enter into a formal alliance to resist any aggressive action by Germany and that they employ their military, financial, and economic resources for this purpose in addition to exerting their moral influence to prevent such aggression. The American peace commissioners had agreed that if the United States entered into the compact, one of the chief reasons for the League "disappeared." Lansing wrote in his journal: "What impressed me most was that to gain French support for the League the proposer of the alliance was willing to destroy the chief feature of the League." Another objection to the "affirmative guarantee" was that it would "permit European Powers to participate . . . in the forcible settlement of international quarrels in the Western Hemisphere, whenever there was an actual invasion of territory . . . while . . . the United States would be morally, if not legally, bound to take part in coercive measures in composing European differences. . . . But Wilson believed that the affirmative guarantee was essential to the success of the League."

When Bullitt was called before the Senate Committee on Foreign Relations to testify on the treaty, all his bitterness spilled out. He was, in a real sense, speaking for the idealistic young men of his generation who had invested so much hope in a settlement of the war that would bring peace and justice to the world. Denouncing what he considered the destructive compromises in the treaty, Bullitt added that Secretary of State Lansing had confided to him that he found "many parts of the Treaty thoroughly bad, particularly those dealing with Shantung and the League of Nations." Lansing, Bullitt declared, had told him, "I consider that the League of Nations at present is entirely useless. The Great Powers have simply gone ahead and arranged the world to suit themselves . . . and the League of Nations can do nothing to alter any of the unjust clauses of the Treaty except by unanimous consent of the members of the League, and the Great Powers will never give their consent to changes in the interests of weaker people. . . . I believe," Lansing had added, "that if the Senate could really understand what this Treaty means, and if the American people could really understand, it would unquestionably be defeated. . . ." At the same time Lansing was ready to admit that some of the arguments against the treaty "have been flagrantly unjustifiable and based on false premises and misstatements of fact and of law, which seem to show political motives and not infrequently personal animosity toward Mr. Wilson." The President's reaction, considering "the insolent tone assumed by some of his critics . . . was very human; not wise, but human."

Bullitt's testimony put Lansing on the spot, and he offered his resignation, which the President accepted, but many people agreed with Lansing that the principal deficiency of the League was that it created "an oligarchy of the Five Great Powers" and was thus reactionary.

Working against ratification of the treaty, with the League as an integral part of it, was America's profound suspicion of the ancient and depraved ways of the Old World. The tradition of noninvolvement by the United States in the conflicts that kept Europe embroiled in wars and struggles for dominance was as old as the Republic. The enemies of the treaty quoted ceaselessly the warning from George Washington's Farewell Address: "Why," Washington had asked, "forego the advantages of so peculiar a situation [separation from the rest of the world by two vast oceans]? . . . Why, by interweaving our destiny with that of any part of Europe, entangle our peace and prosperity in the toils of European ambition, rivalship, interest, humor, or caprice?" Washington was, of course, speaking primarily of the disposition of his countrymen, especially the Jeffersonians and radical Democrats, to embroil themselves in the conflict between Great Britain and France out of enthusiasm for the French Revolution. Like virtually all the Founding Fathers, Washington was a believer in what the British critic Wyndham Lewis has called "radical universalism"—specifically that it was the mission of the United States to redeem the world to republican government. But the French Revolution seemed to Washington and his fellow Federalists to be going too far and much too fast.

Senator William Borah of Idaho was as much an enemy of the treaty as Lodge was. He, more than anyone else, constrained American participation in the World Court. To Borah the European powers were still commmitted to war as an instrument of public policy. Any formal connection with them through treaties or international organizations had to entangle the United States in their intrigues. To Borah the Versailles Treaty, far from bearing any hope of peace, was a keg of dynamite waiting to be exploded by a new war, more dreadful than the one that had just ended. It was his conviction and that of his fellow isolationists, as they came to be called, that the world would "get along better without our intervention. . . ." He urged the recognition of the Soviet government of Russia and independence for the Philippines.

There were other and more rancorous attacks on the League. Lawrence Sherman of Illinois declared "history would forget the reign of Caligula in the excesses and follies of the American government operated under the League of Nations by President Wilson and Colonel House." James Reed of Missouri predicted that the League would permit the black races to rule the world. Another Senator insisted that it would turn over world domination to the Pope.

Anti-British feeling was never far from the surface in the West. Hiram Johnson argued that "greedy, conscienceless England" would, under the terms of the treaty, "control the habitable parts of the globe." Even the urbane William Allen White expressed his region's distrust of Britain, warning that if Americans came to believe that Britain was backing the League for selfish, imperialistic reasons, "the Republicans will whoop it up against England to justify the slaughter of the League and incidentally to bag the Irish vote and the pro-German vote; and, while the demagogues triumph, humanity will suffer." Once more valuable human and material resources would be expended preparing for and eventually waging war. To prove that it was not the "Cruel Stepmother, Britain must give Ireland dominion status. . . ." America would then ratify the treaty. The League thus became the focus of an odd assortment of classic American paranoias.

Numerous liberals, ex-Progressives, reformers of various denominations joined forces in the League of Nations Association to work for American acceptance of the League. (The radicals, the Socialists, Communists, and anarchists had been rendered political nullities when they were not, like Debs and dozens of others, safely locked up in Federal prisons.) But White, lecturing on behalf of the League, "found everywhere that the rigid belligerent attitude of the President toward the reservations was weakening his hold upon the people." To Senator Arthur Capper of Kansas he wrote that "sixty per cent of the Kansas people are against the League today, possibly more." But White was nonetheless convinced that Wilson "can pretty nearly be elected to a third term in this country, if the League is defeated and the Republicans make a record for universal service and a big navy and nominate for president any man who voted against the League."

Aside from the damage that the President was convinced further compromise would do to the League, there was the fact of his rigid and unyielding personality. A husband and wife team of "Freudian-oriented" historians has suggested that Wilson's stubbornness in regard to the League was a consequence of an Oedipus complex and an unresolved conflict with a dominating father figure or, more simply, a father whom Wilson adored and, according to the Freudian historians, feared and resented. We need no such theory to account for his determination to force the treaty through the Senate. He had shown the same resolution to work his will as president of Princeton. It was both a trait of his "character type"—Scotch-Irish Calvinist—and a quality commonly associated with inner-directed, highly ambitious individuals who conceive of themselves as governed by principle. There was an additional incentive in Wilson's case. He had initially, against his deeper instincts, committed himself and the country to a position of neutrality in the war. Events and the attitudes and opinions of those closest to him had combined to prevail on him to bring the United States into a conflict from which he had vowed to remain aloof. For a man of his sensibilities, the decision to enter the war had been excruciating. He had justified it primarily on the ground that the war was a war to end all wars and make the world safe for democracy. If it was simply a belated intervention to secure the fruits of victory for the Allied arms and perpetuate an archaic system of imperialistic aggression, it must then become apparent that the involvement of the United States had been a disastrous mistake or, almost as bad, the typical action of a great power concerned with its own interests. What was thus at issue was not merely the ratification of a treaty of highly dubious character but the vindication of everything that Wilson and, through him, the nation had professed to stand for, the vindication of all the repressive actions that his administration had condoned or encouraged, the voices of protest that had been ruthlessly silenced, the dissident aliens deported, the "traitors" imprisoned. If, indeed, the war, or at least America's entry into it, was to bring in its wake perpetual peace and harmony in the world, then any sacrifice, any severity, or any repression was justified. In his lust of idealism Wilson was not so far in spirit from the

Bolshevik leaders who thought the deaths of tens of thousands of "counterrevolutionaries" was a comparatively small price to pay for the attainment of a Marxist utopia. Wilson's repressions were, of course, on an infinitely more modest scale, but the *principle* was the same.

The President was further undercut when Lord Grey, the British foreign secretary, published a letter which hinted that the British were ready to accept ratification with the Lodge reservations. Even more damaging in liberal circles was the serial publication in the *New Republic* of John Maynard Keynes's assault on the treaty, *Economic Consequences of the Peace*, with its cruel portrait of Wilson. Senator Borah read long excerpts from Keynes's book in the Senate, declaring that it "must inevitably result that the economic system of Europe will be destroyed, which will result in the loss of millions of lives and in revolution after revolution." The treaty makers had "lightly wrecked the entire economic system of an entire continent and reduced to starvation millions of people and perhaps prevented the world peace from coming at all in this decade, there is no language too severe for such men. . . . The Treaty in its consequences is a crime born of blind revenge and insatiable greed."

One of the shrewdest assessments of Keynes's famous book was that of General Smuts: "America wanted a reason for denying Wilson. The world wanted a scapegoat. At that opportune moment Keynes brought out his *Economic Consequences of the Peace*. There were a few pages about Wilson in it which exactly suited the policies of America and the world's mood." Smuts had encouraged Keynes to write the book, but he was dismayed at the results. "I did not expect him to turn Wilson into a figure of fun," Smuts wrote. "These few pages about Wilson . . . made an Aunt Sally of the noblest figure—perhaps the only noble figure—in the history of the war, and they led a fashion against Wilson that was adopted by the Intelligentsia of the day . . . —the people who, admiring only their own cleverness, despise real goodness, real thought, real wisdom. . . ." Every review Smuts saw fastened on the brilliant, mordant lines about Wilson. "Wilson was already going down in America," Smuts added. "In their hearts the Americans wanted him to go down; they wanted to evade the duties he imposed on them. The book was absolutely to their purpose. It helped to finish Wilson, and it strengthened the Americans against the League."

By the end of August it was clear to Wilson that the treaty was in serious trouble, and he concluded that it was essential for him to appeal to Americans over the heads of their representatives in Congress. He decided to undertake a tour of the nation, speaking in a number of major cities and correcting errors and misapprehensions that he believed his Republican opponents had managed to disseminate. The news of the projected trip alarmed the Cabinet, already well aware that the President was in bad health and near exhaustion from his unremitting labors on behalf of the treaty and the League. Some even hinted that he might be endangering his life by such an undertaking. If that were to be the outcome, Wilson replied, he was ready to give his life for the cause.

Thus began his trip on September 4. In three weeks he traveled 10,000 miles, going as far to the northwest as Seattle and as far southwest as San Diego, making in all thirty-seven speeches. In St. Louis on September 5, Wilson told a large and responsive audience, "The real reason that the war we have just finished took place was that Germany was afraid her commercial rivals were going to get the better of her, and the reason that some nations went into the war against Germany was that they thought Germany would get the commercial advantage of them. The seed of jealousy, the seed of the deep-seated hatred was hot, successful commercial and industrial rivalry." Wilson's constantly reiterated theme was that without the League of Nations there could be no enduring peace. "I can predict with absolute certainty," he declared in Omaha, "that within another generation there will be another world war if the nations of the world do not concert the method by which to prevent it." At Denver, a few days later, he told his audience, "Stop for a moment to think about the next war, if there should be one. I do not hesitate to say that the war we have just been through, though it was shot through with terror of every kind, is not to be compared with the war we should have to face next time. . . . What the Germans used were toys compared with what would be used in the next war. . . . We went into this war to do a thing that was fundamental for the world, and what I have come out upon this journey for is to ascertain whether the country has forgotten it or not. I have found out already. The country has not forgotten. . . ." Wilson pledged that he would be true to his "clients." He added, "My clients are the children; my clients are the next generation. They do not know what promises and bonds I undertook when I ordered the armies of the United States to the soil of France, but I know, and I intend to redeem my pledges to the children; they shall not be sent upon a similar errand. . . . There seems to me to stand between us and the rejection or qualification of this treaty the serried ranks of those boys in khaki, not only those boys who came home, but those dear ghosts that still deploy upon the fields of France. . . . For nothing less depends upon this decision, nothing less than the liberation and salvation of the world."

Ray Stannard Baker followed the President's pilgrimage—for it was certainly that—with "painful eagerness" as though the future of mankind depended on its outcome. "To me," he wrote, "there was something sublime about that tragic venture, something indescribably great, beautiful, in what seemed to me its futility." But perhaps it was not, after all, futile. "Was he not trying to make the people understand? If he could not secure immediate support for his plan of world co-operation he was nevertheless laying the foundation for greater efforts in the future. *What he said was true: it could not die*."

Part of the problem was, as Baker suggested, that people did not wish to be preached to about their duty. The more insistent Wilson was that Americans do their collective duty by supporting the League of Nations, the more annoyed Americans in general became with him. A petition was circulated, calling for his impeachment for high crimes against the Republic in attempting to barter away its sovereign powers in the name of some visionary project of world peace.

While the President gave brilliant orations on the future of a peaceful, democratic world, economic conditions at home continued to deteriorate. "The domestic crisis appeared to many observers even more threatening than the problems of international relationships," Baker recalled. "Difficulties of reconstruction seemed overwhelming; business was struggling with all but uncontrollable inflationary trends, hordes of the unemployed were walking the streets; labor was disorganized and rebellious. There seemed nowhere any vital leadership."

"What do you make out about Wilson?" William Allen White wrote his fellow newpaper editor Victor Murdock, of the *Wichita Eagle*. "Is he stubborn, or sick, or stupid, or what? I had a great crush on him in Paris, but I haven't had much taste for what he has been doing the last two months. . . ."

Word that the President was on his way home reached Washington on September 26. The rumor was that he had had a collapse of some sort and had difficulty sleeping. Even the Cabinet had no direct word on the President's condition. When David Houston encountered his fellow Cabinet member Newton D. Baker at the Shoreham Hotel five days after the first word that all was not well with the President, Baker declared, "I am literally scared to death." The next day Houston saw Tumulty, who was obviously laboring under constraints about what he felt authorized to say. He did tell Houston that the President was paralyzed in one leg and one arm. That was alarming enough. Vice-President Marshall felt entitled to know the whole story of the President's condition, but a wall of secrecy surrounded the White House. Mrs. Wilson was inaccessible; Wilson's doctors had nothing to say. The city and the country were awash in rumors and wild stories, some of which declared the President dead. The impulse to secrecy, an apparent anomaly in a man who inveighed against all secret doings on the international scene, asserted itself once again.

The Cabinet was in a quandary. Vice-President Marshall called it into an emergency session. Dr. Grayson and Joe Tumulty came into the Cabinet room. The President's condition, Grayson asserted, had improved, but he was still in grave danger. It was too early to predict the outcome. Grayson was besieged with questions. Was the President conscious? Was he able to speak or write? Grayson replied that the President had heard of the Cabinet meeting and had asked "by what authority it was meeting while he was in Washington without a call from him."

After the first unhappy attempt to meet, the Cabinet did not try the experiment again. The White House remained shrouded in silence and mystery. Senator Lawrence Sherman of Illinois was quoted as saying that "the American people are living under the regency of Tumulty and Baruch." Other reports had it that Mrs. Wilson was running the country, a theory strengthened by her intensely protective attitude toward her ill husband. Meantime, debate on the League went on in Congress.

In order to get some notion of Wilson's condition, the Senate Foreign Relations Committee devised a stratagem. Senators Lodge, Hitchcock, and Albert Fall of New Mexico constituted themselves a committee to "lay before the President some papers relative to Mexican affairs and to confer with him regarding their disposition." A reluctant Edith Wilson conducted them into a darkened room where the President lay in bed. When Senator Fall, the prototype of the political hack that Wilson could not endure, said unctuously, "We have all been praying for you, Mr. President," Wilson answered, "Which way, Senator?" The delegation departed only mildly reassured.

Another group that gained access to the presidential chamber was made up of Senator Carter Glass of Virginia, Senator Claude Swanson of Pennsylvania, and Bernard Baruch. They urged him to accept some of the milder reservations of the treaty. "No," Wilson snapped at Baruch. "They are not reservations, they are nullifications. No, I shall not accept them."

Even Edith Wilson pleaded with her husband to compromise. "For my sake," she said, "won't you accept these reservations and get this awful thing settled?"

Wilson turned his head and reached out for his wife's hand, saying, "Little girl, don't you desert me; that I cannot stand. Can't you see that I have no moral right to accept any change in a paper I have signed without giving to every other signatory, even the Germans, the right to do the same thing?"

Ill as he was, the President managed to keep abreast of the developments in the Senate, where Lodge led the fight to amend the treaty to death. Lodge proposed fourteen amendments or reservations. They were rejected on November 18, 1919, by the Senate on a vote of 41 to 51, largely on party lines and at the urging of the President, who charged that the proposed changes in effect nullified the treaty. Wilson's response seemed to David Houston unfortunate. Indeed, he doubted that it was the President's own doing. The only course left, Wilson, or someone writing for him, declared, was for the nation to have a kind of referendum on the issue at the next presidential election. Houston noted in his diary, "This leaves the country and the world in confusion. Our action will impair our prestige and prevent us from assuming leadership at a time when it would be most gladly accepted and would count for most. It will retard the processes of recovery. It leaves us in a state of war with Germany. . . ."

Perhaps the most serious consequence of the U.S. Senate's failure to ratify the treaty was the weakening of American prestige in Paris. The American voice carried less weight in the territorial commissions especially. The Americans, for example, had strongly opposed the awarding of a substantial portion of western Bulgaria to Yugoslavia. It was an act that, in their opinion, was "unjustifiable according to any principle that governed the peace conference theretofore. . . . " Now, with the treaty unratified, the Americans were ignored.

"The Americans are charming," Clemenceau was reported to have said, "but they are far away." Far away and getting farther away all the time, someone might have added. The proponents of a diminished Bulgaria pointed out that the Bulgarians had treated the Serbians in a cruel and ruthless manner. Of the tens of thousands of Serbians in Bulgarian prisoner of war camps, more than half had died of disease and malnutrition. They had been equally merciless to the Greeks.

On April 26, 1920, at the San Remo Conference in southern France, the mandates for the Near East were divided between France (Syria) and Britain (Mesopotamia). Feisal meanwhile had proclaimed an independent Syria and given the French commander an ultimatum to withdraw his troops. Scattered fighting between the Syrian Arabs and French colonial troops went on for four months before the French established control and the French commander announced, "Emir Feisal has ceased to rule. Emir Feisal has been requested to leave the country with his family."

The Turks invaded Armenia and did their best to exterminate the Armenians. The Italians agreed to give up Fiume, but the Fascists toppled the government and occupied the city. Despite the Versailles Treaty, defense treaties were signed by half a dozen European countries—France with Poland, for example.

Then there was Russia. Professing sympathy with the aspirations of the Russian people, the Wilson administration took the line that the Bolsheviks represented only a "murderous minority." American policy makers saw their task as preserving some nominal relationship with Russia, preventing its dismemberment and waiting for the day when a new and more moderate government, representative of all the people, would come to power. Norman Davis, a spokesman for administration policy, declared that the United States had "little or no confidence in the wisdom of negotiating with the Bolshevists or the possibility of making any arrangements with them which can be depended upon," not, doubtlessly, an inaccurate reading of the situation. In the view of Davis, a specialist in Russian matters, it was "utterly impossible for two systems based on such diametrically opposed principles to work in peace and harmony." Yet Wilson in his Fourteen Points address in January, 1918, had praised the Russian revolutionaries for acting "very justly, very wisely, and in the true spirit of modern democracy." He had declared, "There is . . . a voice calling for these definitions of principle and purpose which is, it seems to me, more thrilling and more compelling than any of the many moving voices with which the troubled air of the world is filled. It is the voice of the Russian people. . . . Their power, apparently, is shattered. And yet their soul is not subservient. They will not yield either in principle or in action. Their conception of what is right, of what is humane and honorable for them to accept, has been stated with frankness, a largeness of view, a generosity of spirit, and a universal human sympathy which must challenge the admiration of every friend of mankind. . . . Whether their present leaders believe it or not, it is our heartfelt desire and hope that some way may be opened whereby we may be privileged to assist the people of Russia to attain their utmost hope of liberty and ordered peace."

If Wilson expressed such enlightened sentiments at the beginning of 1918, why, it might be asked, was he not disposed to recognize Russia, to welcome the initiative developed by Bullitt and back up his friendly words by acts? Instead, he had sent American forces under British authority to Murmansk to cooperate with the Allies in trying to suppress the Bolsheviks. To answer the question, it is necessary, first of all, to bear in mind that the Bolsheviks, in their merciless extermination of an older generation of revolutionary heroes and heroines, horrified Western opinion. If the friends of the Revolution turned away in horror from its excesses, it is hardly to be wondered that American liberals and radicals of less fierce dedication rejected the Bolsheviks. To students of revolutions there was every reason to believe that the most extreme phase would pass; in the French Revolution, for example, the Jacobins and the Mountain, the radical extremists of the left, had succumbed to a Thermidorean, or rightest, revolution. One did not have to be a champion of the czarist regime to believe that the Russian people deserved, and must in time get, a more moderate and humane government than that provided by the Bolsheviks. To Wilson it seemed a matter of common sense and simple humanity to do nothing to strengthen or perpetuate the Bolshevik tyranny. Indeed, the defense of their actions made by the Bolsheviks was that their dictatorship (of the proletariat) was simply a transitional stage on the way to the classless society in which all would be free. In delaying recognition of the Bolsheviks, Wilson was acting in a manner thoroughly consistent with his policy in Mexico—to throw his support to that Mexican leader who might reasonably be expected to do the most good for the Mexican people themselves.

The problem of Russia was compounded by Marxist dogma, or by Lenin's interpretation of it, which held the Western capitalist world to be the enemy to be distrusted under all circumstances and, as soon as possible, to be overthrown. It was thus impossible to be an orthodox Marxist and deal with capitalist democracies with any trust or candor. Capitalism was evil and could therefore not be compromised with; capitalism reciprocated.

Senator Robert Owen of Oklahoma joined with Borah and other Midwestern Senators to urge Wilson to recognize the Bolsheviks as the *de facto* government. But Wilson increasingly inclined toward a hard-line approach. The diplomats of Soviet Russia would be "agitators of dangerous revolt"; its leaders had plainly abjured "every principle of honor and good faith . . . upon which it is possible to base harmonious and trustful relations," he wrote.

Ironically one of the principal apostles of what might be called unremitting war on the Bolsheviks was the ex-Socialist John Spargo. It was, indeed, he who wrote the greater part of Undersecretary of State Bainbridge Colby's note that was to form the basis of the administration's Russian policy. (Spargo referred to it, somewhat immodestly, as "one of the most important diplomatic documents of the post-war period, belonging with the great documents announcing the Monroe Doctrine and the 'open-door policy.' ") When the note was sharply criticized by opposition papers and liberal journalists, Spargo undertook to defend it publicly, declaring that the destruction of bolshevism was "the supreme task of civilization." The United States was the hope of the world, Spargo argued, the most appropriate channel for the dissemination of ideas leading to social change. This meant a strong America, one that had access to the great markets of the world. The United States could not "be indifferent to such a demand as must come from Russia. Unless we find markets capable of absorbing the vast surplus of our manufactures," he wrote, "we must quickly pass into a period of prolonged industrial depression." Then, indeed, America might well come to fear homegrown Bolsheviks. "We are a capitalist nation living in a capitalist world in an era of capitalization," Spargo wrote. "Some of us believe that another form of society would be better. . . . In the meantime, however, only visionaries and addle-pated chatterers profess to be indifferent to the success or failure of our capitalist enterprises."

If Spargo's estimate of the importance of Bainbridge Colby's note was excessive, it was certainly the case that the Wilsonian policy vis-à-vis Russia had almost incomprehensibly significant consequences. It gave official sanction to the notion that Russian communism was a dreadful menace to the safety and well-being of the United States. Bolshevism was the mortal enemy, the paramount evil, the Antichrist, the antithesis of everything "American." That dictum, reinforced by the participation of American soldiers in the Allied effort to support the White Russians and overturn the Bolsheviks in their own country, produced a frame of mind in Russia equally paranoid.

It may certainly be doubted whether a more liberal and enlightened policy on the part of the United States would have allayed Russian fear and hostility, but it would have been far better for the general temper and the diplomatic strategies of the United States. The first President and the "Father" of the United States had warned his fellow citizens in his famous Farewell Address of the danger of inveterate hostility or excessive attachments to other nations. By making Russia the epitome of all evil, the Wilson administration (and, to be sure, its successors) did their countrymen a great disservice.

Toward the end of September, 1919, Colonel House once more sent Stephen Bonsal to Berlin. There he met and talked to Count von Bernstorff, a very different figure from the immaculate lady-killer Bonsal had known in Washington a few years earlier. "His shoes were cracked, his cuffs were frayed, and his trousers—how they needed pressing!" Bernstorff was touchingly grateful for a box of inferior army cigars that Bonsal gave him. He had been reduced to smoking brown paper.

The most arresting figure Bonsal encountered was the head of the Weimar Republic, Walther Rathenau. Bonsal came armed with a note from Colonel House: "Colonel Bonsal is my alter ego. Speak to him as frankly as you would to me." With this encouragement Rathenau talked long and brilliantly. "Now," he declared, "the fever of misunderstanding, the great madness under which we Germans and some others of the peoples of Europe have been suffering in hardly a less degree, mind you, has not run its course; it may be fatal still, or we may escape a fatal issue . . . " but the dangers were vast, and the Allies seemed determined to deprive Germany of anything that could be used to rebuild the devastated nation. "Today, economically," he told Bonsal, "Germany is dying, and the gangrened corpse that will result, I tell you again, speaking as an economist and not a politician, I tell you that gangrened corpse will infect the whole world. . . . The only vital, the only important thing to do today is to get together and see whether we can save ourselves and our children from the terrible consequences of the disaster in which, whatever may be our separate responsibility and individual guilt, we are all involved."

Germany, unable to pay reparations, inflated its currency until it stood at 62,000,000,000 marks to the dollar by the fall of 1923. When the Germans defaulted, French soldiers occupied the Ruhr. As we have seen, one of the commonest criticisms of the Treaty of Versailles was that its terms were so severe that Germany could not recover for decades and that its depressed economic condition would impose a severe burden on other European nations with interrelated economies. The economic consequences were, in fact, very different from those that Keynes had predicted. The Germany economy, after a devastating period of inflation, regained its equilibrium, and a decade after the end of the war it was producing 30 percent more coal and 33 percent more steel than before the war. Its highly efficient merchant marine had risen in tonnage from 650,000 tons at the end of the war to more than 4,000,000. After Hitler had taken power, Germany spent yearly more than seven times the amount on armaments than Keynes had calculated it could be expected to pay in reparations. The revival of Germany demonstrated, among other things, that psychological or emotional factors are far more important vectors of history than economic ones. But if the Treaty of Versailles did not have the economic consequences that Keynes (and many others) had predicted, it had consequences quite as destructive of any hope of prosperity and peace in the world.

The Senate continued to resist the treaty. Some Senators cited the Shantung giveaway; others focused on what they believed were sacrifices of American constitutional rights. On March 19, 1920, that body refused, by a margin of seven votes, to accept a substantially modified treaty, thereby ending more than a year of acrimonious debate.

40

The Consequences
of the War

The war altered every aspect of American life. American capitalism emerged a hero for its remarkable accomplishments in providing the sinews of war, not only for the the United States Army and Navy but for the Allies as well. Its prestige was enormously enhanced. Or perhaps, considering the bitter criticism to which it had been subjected since the Civil War, it might be more accurate to say that the reputation of capitalism was not so much enhanced as *created*. Moreover, capitalists, elated by their new popularity and their generally favorable press, took the offensive against those individuals and groups reckless enough to criticize them. Chambers of Commerce and the National Association of Manufacturers hired hundreds of highly paid publicists to proclaim the virtues of business, big and small, and to denounce their opponents as unpatriotic and, worst of all, as "Reds," unwitting dupes of Russia or wily agents of Bolsheviks. It was a novel notion—the idea that criticizing capitalism and capitalists constituted subversive activity. What had been, almost since the beginning of the Republic, a common exercise now fell under a ban. Criticizing capitalism could (and often did) result in the critics' being clapped in jail.

Capitalism, recently on the defensive in virtually every part of the globe, had seized the opportunity presented by the peace conference to create a new global financial order, in William Allen White's words, "of cartels and trusts and interlocking international directorates." It was, of course, not a wholly new development. European capital had helped settle America, opened mines, built railroads, created many of the great ranches of the West, bought state bonds, and speculated in American commodities. It had preyed on the vast, defenseless body of China and built railroads for the Russians. Now, in the aftermath of the war, while diplomats and heads of state did their best to patch together the old order as they paid lip service to the new and while revolution bubbled away beneath the surface, the quietly efficient men of finance and industry, who knew exactly what they wanted and how to get it, conducted their own, largely sub rosa "Versailles"; it was in time to have more far-reaching consequences than the deliberations of politicians, which, in any event, were largely subservient to the interests of the men of power. It must be said to their credit that the cartel makers were ready to conceive of the world as, if not one great human family, one great trading entity bound together by pounds and dollars and francs, by cartels and commodities. In some ways it was a not unpromising beginning. Joel Barlow, the Federalist poet whose *The Vision of Columbus* was widely acclaimed as the first American epic, anticipated the day when the United States, through a "Source" of "creative Power," the nature of which was never clearly defined, would become a great nation, combining with other nations of the earth in "one great empire," connected by common ideals and commercial ties and ruled by "a general council" of "the fathers of all empires."

> See, thro' the whole, the same progressive plan,
> That draws, for mutual succour, man to man,
> From friends to tribes, from tribes to realms ascend,
> Their powers, their interests and their passions blend.

Although it may be doubted that international cartels were exactly what Joel Barlow had in mind (he believed that love would guide the "general council"), it was nonetheless striking that the captains of commerce, finance, and industry most boldly anticipated the practical interrelatedness of the world; that a Japanese or Chinese peasant might become, in fact, a customer rather than simply a wretched Oriental, of unclean habits and inscrutable motivations.

"That organism," White wrote, "—somewhat financial, somewhat social, and of necessity more or less political—was growing conscious across national lines, even across ocean boundaries. Indeed it was passing the equator and spreading the sensitive pocket nerves of the well placed and overweening people of this globe . . . it sought unconsciously that world organization—that world sense of the power and the glory of the almighty dollar . . . which . . . makes a new kind of aim and purpose for the leaders of the world. . . ."

In a somewhat contradictory spirit the war demonstrated that the Federal government, faced by a severe crisis, could organize the human and material resources of the nation with remarkable speed and efficiency. The war thus helped shatter the states' rights myth and, with it, the notion that private initiative (or enterprise) was inherently superior to governmental action. The fact that the government could, in a time of national need, take over the productive facilities of the country and assume wide and even arbitrary powers was both a shock and a profoundly instructive lesson. Moreover, in exercising control over major segments of the economy, the government put into practice many of the labor practices that the unions and the reformers had been fighting for for years, and it did it virtually overnight. To a euphoric William Allen White the war seemed for a time to have ushered in "the most dynamic epoch in the world; the time when the greatest social, political, industrial, and spiritual changes of men were made," an era to be compared with the birth of Christ and the discovery of America.

It seemed to White that "the world, and particularly the American part of the world, is adopting a new scale of living and a brand-new scale of prices all at the same time. It has given us the worst case of social bellyache that it has been my misfortune ever to see or hear about. By a prodigal wave of the hand, somewhere along during the war, we have raised the laboring man into middle-class standards of living and he is not going back. . . . It is a mess," he added. "We have jumped about a hundred years in less that ten months in our economic growth. . . . " To the editor of the *Survey* magazine, Paul Kellogg, who asked how the wartime economy could be adjusted to peacetime, White wrote: "It seems to me that our practical objective should be to keep every man who wants work in a job three hundred days in a year, and that he should be kept at work at a living wage, that is to say a wage upon which he may maintain a family of six in the enjoyment of all the comforts of our civilization, electric lights, central heat and power, modern plumbing, convenient fuel for cooking, decent housing, good clothing, clean and exhilarating amusements, time for reading, and money to make profitable reading possible, some leisure for seeing his city, his state, and his country, and at least a high school education for such of his children as desire it." White was confident that such goals could be achieved "under our present institutions," but a constitutional amendment would be required, in his view, to give "Congress unlimited powers over commerce and industry," along with "a minimum wage commission with full powers. . . . This would soon wipe out the revolutionary ideals of labor. I should not fight Bolshevism with guns, but with steady employment." Radical as such a program might seem to many standpat Republicans, White believed that "some forward movement must be taken, and taken quickly, or the situation will become vastly more dangerous than it is now."

Aside from the radical curtailment of free speech (or the free curtailment of radical speech) and vastly increased pressures for social and political conformity, one of the more intangible consequences of the war was what we might call the democratization of American society. In the U.S. Army young men from different classes and different nationalities were drawn together in the "religion of combat," an experience, transcending all categories of civilian life, in which soldiers literally depended on each other, day after day, for their lives. The mystique of battle has been written of since the days of Homer. Distressing and terrible as war is, it engages the profoundest human emotions, and the trust, comradeship, and love that commonly characterize the relations of soldiers are, it seems safe to say, unique. Compared with all other armies, the American army was dramatically democratic. While most upper-class young Americans were given commissions, many on no better ground than the fact that they were college graduates, many middle-class young men were also commissioned, and some young men with working-class backgrounds earned commissions on the basis of their performances as noncommissioned officers. In addition, many upper- and middle-class youths enlisted or were drafted as privates (a substantial portion of these earned commissions). Beyond that, the fact of simply being thrown together gave young Americans of widely divergent social and regional origins a new respect for each other. Much the same thing had been true, of course, in the Civil War and, to a far more modest degree, in the Spanish-American War, but the World War involved a very different America, one of far more cultural and even racial diversity. It thus worked as a powerful counterforce to the disintegrative tendencies of American life. Nowhere was this more evident than in the emphasis placed on the remarkable ethnic mix of the American army. It was a theme that, as we have seen, war correspondents delighted to dwell on. Many newspaper and magazine stories were built on that astonishing heterogeneity. Reporters would seek out soldiers of Polish, Irish, Czech, Russian, Hungarian, Chinese, or American Indian ancestry and feature their qualities as fighting men and loyal Americans. It was the major theme of the book by Theodore Roosevelt, Jr., *Rank and File*. Much of this was, of course, for home consumption to negate the resistance of a substantial number of ethnic Americans—Irish, Germans, and Austro-Hungarians especially—to the war. But whatever the motive, the fact was that propaganda corresponded to reality. It seems safe to say that America emerged from the war far more democratic than when it entered.

One striking consequence of the war was the proliferation of organizations dedicated to the cause of peace. General Tasker Bliss, speaking at Edward Bok's Philadelphia forum—"What Really Happened at Paris"—reminded his audiences that the most imperative task facing the world was the limitation and, eventually, the abolition of all armaments. Modern wars, as distinguished from their predecessors, had become "total" wars, wars of extermination, "characterized by an intensity of national passions heretofore unknown . . . regarded by each side as wars for life or death, in which each, to save his life and destroy his adversary, will use every agent of destruction available to him; that, therefore, such agencies as the absolute blockade to starve people who heretofore were regarded as non-combatants, noxious gases, night and day bombing of cities from aeroplanes, the submarine, have come to stay until replaced by more destructive agencies."

William James had declared in 1906 in his lecture "The Moral Equivalent of War" that wars had become so terrible that they could no longer be used as instruments of national policy. World War I had proved the point beyond dispute. In consequence, peace organizations multiplied exceedingly until there were dozens of them, many with overlapping memberships. Fannie Fern Andrews, a Bostonian, belonged to nineteen different peace organizations, among them the International Commission for Permanent Peace, the Women's Peace Party, the Neutral Conference for Continuous Mediation (a wartime organization), the Women's International League for Peace and Freedom, the American Union Against Militarism, the Association to Abolish War, the Women's Committee for World Disarmament, the Committee on Militarism in Education, the World Peace Foundation, and the Central Organization for a Durable Peace. Not surprisingly the American Legion, a reliable voice for Americanism and reaction, was soon attacking the peace groups as treasonous and un-American organizations, in league with the Communists to undermine the United States. Henry Ford's *Dearborn Independent*, an equally dependable spokesman for reaction, carried the headline in March, 1924, "Do Bolsheviks 'Use' Our Women's Clubs?" The resolutions of the Annual Conference of the Women's International League for Peace and Freedom, the paper charged, had been dictated by the Communist, or Third, International. A resolution against chemical warfare adopted by the conference was another example of Red influence, "since gas may be used to quell riots, and they [the Reds] plan the beginning of the Revolution in the United States with riots." The Red International was in the process of infiltrating Chautauquas, churches, and peace societies. One *Independent* headline proclaimed that the "Socialist-Pacificist Movement in America" was "an Absolutely Fundamental and Integral Part of International Socialism."

A poem reinforced the argument:

Miss Bolshevik has come to town
With a Russian cap and a German gown,
In women's clubs she's sure to be found,
For she's come to disarm America.
She uses the movie and lyceum too
And alters text-books to suit her view;
She prates propaganda from pulpit and pew,
For she's bound to disarm America.

Many Americans who had been caught up in the world of radical reform, reform in all its manifold aspects—in the arts, in politics, and in social work—shared Hutchins Hapgood's mood of despair. "The years between 1914 and 1922," he wrote, "were for me years of the deepest discouragement and unhappiness. It seemed as if my personal fate was a part of the world's woe. . . . I was rudderless, like the rest of the world." The effects were evident all around him. Friends in Greenwich Village and Provincetown, Massachusetts, fell out among themselves. They quarreled over the war and over more personal matters. They had grim and wounding affairs, joyless encounters in which beds became battlegrounds. "Drink and sex," Hapgood wrote, "became a despairing ideal, instead of the constructive forms we had dreamed about. It affected even the coolest and most balanced of us all." Oswald Garrison Villard abandoned the hope of reform of government by concerted action of liberal spirits and placed what was left of hope in

"Labor," the workingman as the final vessel of redemption. That the leadership of labor would "always be wise and just," he added, "would be preposterous to assume; I am only sure that it can never be worse than the political and economic leadership of the capitalist countries which I have observed at close range." He had lost "any hope that the capitalist system would redeem or reform itself, without, however, adopting any hard or fast creed, just clinging to my old-fashioned liberal doctrines modified by . . . the economic revolution." Villard wrote to Hapgood that he had suffered acutely during the preceding four years because of "the sense of spiritual outrage at the injustice and wickedness that we are seeing." It was evident to him that "all the nations of the world were drifting as steadily as a glacier, and as irresistibly, in the direction of greater control of business and private enterprise which cannot end before they have taken over the public services and basic industries."

When Frederic Howe asked Lincoln Steffens in 1920, "What has become of the pre-war radicals?" Steffens answered "smilingly: 'I am learning to be an intelligent father.'" Brand Whitlock turned back to literature, his first love. Newton D. Baker occupied himself with his law practice. When Howe and Whitlock met, they talked nostalgically of the old battles against corruption in Cleveland and Toledo, of Tom Johnson and Golden Rule Jones. Those days seemed dim and distant. "I have gone through every political philosophy," Whitlock told Howe. "I can see nothing in Socialism. The philosophy of Henry George of a free state in which the resources of the earth will be opened up to use is the only political philosophy that has ever commanded my adherence. But the world is not interested in such a simple reform. It wants too much government, too much regulation, too much policing. And it may never change."

From the wreckage of his hopes and dreams Howe salvaged his faith in freedom, "the law of life," and the single tax, "the most nearly perfect expression of it that had been given to the world." He was ready to accept "a lot of evil to get free trade, to end private ownership of the railroads, to bring in the single tax." But these goals, he believed, could no longer be achieved by a demoralized and fragmented company of middle-class reformers; it must be achieved by "the workers— those who produced wealth by hand or brain. . . . By necessity labor would serve freedom, democracy, equal opportunity for all. . . . Much of my intellectual capital had flown," Howe added. "Drafts on my mind came back endorsed: 'No funds.' But I was still not bankrupt. . . . Did youth burn itself out? Has the movement become a class struggle, finding its leaders among the farmers and workers?"

There was a strong disposition on the part of liberals to plead *mea culpa*. In Lincoln Steffens's view, "It was liberals who, in the liberal sense, made the war in all the allied countries, and who made the peace, too. That was why liberalism was fading out . . . 'it had been tried and found wanting.' " It had become a creed, and "that creed had been exposed as false." Steffens, for one, "was still of the opinion that only a revolution could do the job."

To Howe, as to many of his class of liberal intellectuals (for they formed a class of a kind), the war had disclosed the "hysterias, hatreds, passions of which democracy was capable"; the government had revealed a willingness to sanction the making of money from the hardships and sufferings of the people. Wilson had failed dismally at Paris. Intelligence, idealism, "scientific" scholarship, the assiduous assembling of the pertinent "facts" by "experts"—all these, in which such high hopes had been invested, had failed. "Men did not believe in the truth," a disillusioned Howe wrote. The liberal reformers had "believed in discussion," he added, "in the writing of books and magazine articles, in making speeches. We liberals had the truth. If we talked enough and wrote it enough, it would undoubtedly prevail. . . . I believed in the mind and in facts. Facts were a Rock of Gibralter. . . . It was mind that would save the world, the mind of my class aroused from indifference, from money-making, from party loyalty and coming out into the clear light of reason. . . . I had built my life first around conventional morality, then about the mind. Conventional morals did not prevent men from making war, from corrupting the state, from destroying democracy. . . . And the mind had failed as completely as morals. Men did not think when social problems were involved. They did not use the mind. It refused to work against economic interest. . . . The new truth that a free world would come only through [the labor movement] was forced on me. I did not seek it; did not welcome it." Howe gave the next three years of his life to the labor movement. He founded a newspaper called *Labor* and wrote copiously for it. He became an advocate of labor-founded cooperatives and banks. He felt more confident "urging men to free themselves" than "appealing to men of my own class to stop exploiting somebody else." He helped organize the All-American Co-operative Commission, which published bulletins and disseminated information on the cooperative movement. At his urging the Brotherhood of Locomotive Engineers founded a bank, developed a coal mine, and bought two office buildings, and the Amalgamated Clothing and Textile Workers followed suit until there were nearly thirty "labor banks" in various towns and cities. Howe turned his attention also to the formation of a farm-labor party of "primary producers." The Conference for Progressive Political Action, which was formed in 1922, was funded by railroad unions. "In working with labor," Howe wrote, "I felt a satisfaction that I had never before experienced and a greater sense of personal integrity. I made friends with men who faced life without confusions. They were the kind of men I had known as a boy, kindly, generous, courageous." To him it seemed that the locomotive engineers were "the Vikings of modern industrial life. Association with them," he added, "is one of the outstanding experiences of my life."

Yet after three years Howe withdrew alternately to Nantucket and to Europe to cultivate his personal inner life. Indeed, encouraged by the growing popularity of Sigmund Freud's doctrines, many Americans retreated from the frustrating and disappointing world—the outer life—to the inner life—the id, the ego, the transcendent self. Hutchins Hapgood retreated to a highly private life in an enclave of friends in rural New England, but his children became union organizers, several of them working with John L. Lewis in the United Mine Workers.

Brooks Adams, revising *The Emancipation of Massachusetts*, wrote a new introduction that reflected the general postwar pessimism. He was dismayed by the apparent conflict between "the moral law and the law of competition which favors the strong, and from whence comes all the abominations of selfishness, of violence, of cruelty and crime." It had come to seem to Adams that the agent of chaos and disorder was competition, the very value that Americans most strenuously espoused. The "preface" for the new edition of *The Emancipation* became a tract, three chapters and 168 pages long, which began with, and placed primary emphasis on, the story of Moses. "Nature" now took the place of God or of "process," a willful, capricious Nature, reminiscent of the destructive playfulness of the Greek gods. The World War had been won by a fusion of "two economic systems which together" had held and administered "a preponderating mass of fluid capital, and which ... partially pooled their resources to prevail. ... Under our present form of capitalistic life," Adams wrote, "there would seem to be no reason why this fluid capital should not fuse and by its energy furnish the motor which should govern the world. ... America and England, like two enormous banking houses, might in effect fuse and yet go on as separate institutions with nominally separate boards of directors." But such an arrangement must be relatively short-lived. "It is not imaginable that such an enormous plutocratic society . . . could conduct its complex affairs upon the basis of average intelligence." A vast and expansive bureaucracy in turn would be challenged by those excluded from its benefits. "Here, the discontented say, you insist on a certain form of competition being carried to its limit. That is, you demand intellectual and peaceful competition for which I am unfit both by education, training, and mental ability. I am therefore excluded from those walks in life which make me a freeman. I become a slave to capital. I must work, or fight, or starve according to another man's convenience, caprice, or . . . will. . . . To such a system I will not submit." To buy off the discontented, the capitalist must, however reluctantly, share his largess. Or face a revolution. It seemed to Adams "to be far from improbable that the system of industrial, capitalistic civilization, which came in, in substance, with the 'free thought' of the Reformation, is nearing an end. . . . Democracy in America," he added, "has conspicuously failed in the collective administration of the common public property." Unless the "democratic man" could "supernaturally" raise himself to some higher level of perfection than he had yet manifested and change "himself from a competitive to a non-competitive animal," he must become "the victim of infinite conflicting forces."

Adams confessed himself startled by the assurance with which he had earlier stated the dogmas of Darwinism. "The last generation," he wrote, "was strongly Darwinian in the sense that it accepted, almost as a tenet of religious faith, the theory that human civilization is a progressive evolution, moving on the whole steadily toward perfection, from a lower to a higher intellectual plane, and, as a necessary part of its progress, developing a higher degree of mental vigor." It followed that "all belief in democracy as a final solution of social ills, all confidence in education as a means of attaining to universal justice, and all hope of the approximating to the rule of moral right in the administration of law, was held to hinge on this great fundamental dogma [Darwinism], which, it followed, it was almost impious to deny, or even to doubt." Neither Brooks Adams nor his contemporaries could any longer cherish such an illusion. "Each day I live," Adams wrote, "I am less able to withstand the suspicion that the universe, far from being an expression of law originating in a single primary cause, is a chaos which admits of reaching no equilibrium, and with which man is doomed eternally and hopelessly to contend."

Ray Stannard Baker believed the nation (and the world) were possessed by a fever of selfish ambition. "The world," he wrote in his journal in October, 1919, ". . . was never in such a state of disorganization and demoralization. All the passions of men seem to have been let loose; a far rebound from the discipline and sacrifice of war. At this moment in America we are facing a number of huge strikes; notably the steel strike. There have been fierce and brutal race-riots, only the other day one in Omaha in which the mob burned the courthouse and nearly killed the mayor." In Boston the police struck, an unheard-of event, and criminals rampaged through the city, unchecked. "Everyone is preaching rights rather than duties," Baker added; "each man is his own judge of what his rights are: if they are not instantly granted he tries to enforce them. No man thinks of sacrificing anything for any cause whatever. . . ."

From the perspective of the early 1940s Baker wrote: "Looking back along many years I can recall no period in which life in America looked bleaker than it did during the half dozen years following the close of the Peace Conference at Paris in 1918."

When Herbert Croly, who, Harold Laski wrote to Justice Holmes, "has the religious bug very badly," pressed William Allen White for an article for the *New Republic* on the election of 1920, White proposed as a topic "The Pharisees are running the temple and bossing the religion and handling the caucuses and the people are getting the worst of it." White's article was entitled "We Who Are About to Die."

The editors of the *New Republic* agreed that "a parvenue middle class, with a stake in the game, had appropriated the national inheritance and branded it with its own seal. . . . Americanization, which ought to mean a regeneration of mankind in this hemisphere with an open mind toward the future, [had] become a thing to frighten children with."

William Allen White wrote to his friend Victor Murdock, formerly editor of the *Wichita Eagle* and now a member of the Federal Trade Commission, that he was "very unhappy politically." It seemed to him that "any man is, who has any love of country or faith in its institutions, or hope for its future." He feared that if the "waters of progress" were damned, there would be in time "a tremendous breakover flood." He found comfort, nonetheless, in the "splurge" of progressive reform from 1903 to 1914. "We did get a lot of things done. Things that are well worth doing; things that are permanent. But I feel also that nobody much is paying attention to those things now." To Baker, White wrote: "What a God-damned world this is! I trust you will realize that I am not swearing; merely trying to express in the mildest terms what I think are the conditions that exist. What a God-damned world! Starvation on the one hand, and indifference on the other, pessimism rampant, faith quiescent, murder met with indifference . . . and the whole story so sad that nobody can tell it. If anyone had told me ten years ago that our country would be what it is today and the world would be what it is today, I should have questioned his reason. . . ."

Everywhere there were strange incongruities. The phonograph was the rage, and an updated version of ragtime called jazz swept the country. William Allen White wrote of "the Gargantuan cricket-song of the phonograph." Dancing was more important than politics, and making money most important of all. Life seemed somehow geared to record lengths, three or four minutes of frantic sound and then a new record. The coonskin coat and hip flask were fixtures of college life and football games. Tin lizzies and flapper skirts, stockings rolled daringly below the knees, rumble seats and furtive sexual encounters. Unbuckled galoshes and tailcoats and white ties or tuxedoes for formal wear. Many of those whose faith in redemption through Progressive political action was shattered beyond repair put their faith in sexual freedom. Of all the prewar movements, that alone survived. But it was changed, coarsened and vulgarized without the "spiritual" elements that, in Hutchins Hapgood's view, had distinguished it in its first "fine careless rapture." In Lincoln Steffens's words, there was "bitterness, cynicism, drink, sex-aplenty, but no science. There was a revolutionary spirit, but it shot off in the direction of art, morals, conduct. . . ." Steffens, recalling his "old theory that the war would cause revolution," felt only disappointment "to see and hear that sex was the thing. The revolutionary spirit of Germany, where conditions were the worst, turned to sex perversions and the establishment of a cult with newspapers to defend and promote the vices. In all Europe there was license. In America, where economic conditions were the best, we heard that all classes and ages had loosened up on drink and sex and that youth, which had found other outlets in Europe, were smashing through all the old moral inhibitions at home."

Strangest of all, this new, crudely materialistic America—at least it seemed so to the generation that had reached maturity before the war—began to have a surprising influence on the rest of the world. American cars, American clothes, music (jazz), popular songs, above all American movies began to spread around the world to the astonishment and despair of the upper-class guardians of the cultures of those nations that fell under the spell of things American. What was most astonishing of all was that this influence was not limited to Europe; one of the nations that fell most completely and helplessly under the spell was Japan. "We found the whole world dancing to American jazz," Steffens wrote from abroad, "—the Germans, too. And economically they all were dancing to our pipers. We went into the war a conceited, but secretly rather humble, second-rate country; we came out self-assured. Our soldiers, our engineers, our organizers and managers, our industrialists and financiers—we had measured ourselves with our European competitors and discovered our competence; we were beaten only in diplomacy. In actual fighting, in work, in resources, in riches, management, we were first-rate people, 'the' first world power!" It was a curious phenomenon. Even the "hardest-boiled, least sentimental of observers," the American correspondents in Paris, perceived it.

From the days of James Fenimore Cooper and Washington Irving, American intellectuals and literary figures had fled to Europe. Appalled by the Red-hunting, Prohibition-minded America, those who could flee did so at the end of the war. Europe, Paris especially, swarmed with émigré Americans, young writers and artists and intellectuals, many of whom still thought of themselves as socialists and awaited the completion of the Red revolution that had begun so encouragingly in Russia. On only one thing were they all agreed: America was impossible for anyone with refined sensibilities to live in. They thus became "expatriots," men and women who found refuge in Paris's Left Bank, in Berlin oddly enough, in Rome, in Provence. Suddenly it seemed as though the world was full of wandering Americans, searching for homes. Hutchins Hapgood encountered Lincoln Steffens and his young English wife and his friend William Bullitt, now married to Louise Bryant, Jack Reed's widow, in Paris. They had rented a house from Elinor Glyn in Auteuil, and Bullitt was writing a novel. George Cram Cook, the designer of so many of Eugene O'Neill's sets, dismayed his wife, Susan Glaspell, by deciding that his destiny was to become a monk in the Greek Orthodox Church, *in Greece*. He must, he announced, leave "his wife, home and children, and devote himself to his god, the Greek tradition . . . and live near the great symbol, the temple of Delphi."

At Nice, Hutchins and Neith Hapgood discovered another little colony of Americans, among them Marsden Hartley, recently in Berlin, his rooms filled with the strange canvases he had painted there. Ida Rauh, Max Eastman's ex-wife, was also in Nice, as was August Jaccaci, once art editor for *Scribner's*.

Grace and Sinclair Lewis visited the Steffenses on the Riviera. Frederic Howe and his wife appeared—Howe was studying the movement of history—and so did Max Eastman and his new Russian wife. In Italy parliamentary democracy was being pronounced a failure, and young Benito Mussolini was showing how government could be run far more efficiently. Steffens was intrigued. The Italian leader was trying not to stop corruption but merely to "regulate, control, govern" it.

While Steffens and a substantial company of émigrés lingered on in Europe, puzzled at the failure of the Revolution to spread across the map, the Versailles Treaty slowly unraveled. "There were wars, revolutions, distress everywhere," Steffens wrote. He challenged a group of correspondent friends to "name all the wars, big and little, that were going on in the world, and they could not do it. . . . Real wars . . . ; the economic conflicts were universal." Yet despite the desperate conditions of the poor, the revolutions did not come. Steffens blamed the "prevalence of liberal instincts and doctrines" as well as the failure of the radicals to "understand the plan for the peasants."

The prophetess of the new aesthetic was another expatriate, Gertrude Stein. From her Paris salon she extended her influence as far as Sauk City, Wisconsin; Sacramento, California; Nashville, Tennessee. Ezra Pound joined Stein in encouraging "the younger artists to despise old forms and the old stuff, to rebel, break away and dare." At the "exquisite apartment of the Billy Birds" writers, painters, and musicians gathered, and it was there Steffens met them all—Pound, Hemingway, Dos Passos, Lewis. But the most imposing figure was Stein herself. Jo Davidson, the sculptor, caught her massive poise, her rocklike solidity. She made her Ford car over to fit, "and her home befitted her, the furniture, the great paintings she bought, the perfect little dinners served there," Steffens wrote. The stream of visitors "felt there her self-contentment and shared her composure, but, best of all, the prophetess gave you glimpses of what a Buddha can see by sitting still and quietly looking."

41

Russia Again

The most dedicated seekers of the new world order headed for Russia—some, like Jack Reed, voluntarily; others like Big Bill Haywood, Emma Goldman, and Alexander Berkman, virtual exiles. How they reacted to the continuing and unsettling drama of the Revolution was to become the stuff of fierce ideological wars for the next two decades. A number of Russian-speaking American Communists were given important political offices by the Soviets. Reed became a kind of honorary Russian, and Lincoln Steffens urged House to use the good offices of Reed to try to reassure the Russians that American intentions toward them were honorable. Trotsky had appointed Reed Soviet consul general to the United States, but when Reed's ship docked in New York, Federal agents went through his luggage and seized his notes for *Ten Days That Shook the World*. "I am therefore unable to write a word of the greatest story of my life, and one of the greatest in the world," he wrote to Steffens, appealing to his older friend for help in retrieving his papers. "I was arrested the other day in Philadelphia," he added, "trying to speak on the street, and am held for court in September on the charges of 'inciting to riot, inciting to assault and battery, and inciting to seditious remarks.'" As soon as he could, he returned to Russia.

In September, 1919, Emma Goldman and Sasha Berkman, having served their sentences, were released from jail. Now they faced deportation proceedings. Both refused to testify. Berkman told the immigration authorities that "my social views and political opinions are my personal concern. I owe no one responsibility for them. . . . For the government to attempt to control thought, to proscribe certain opinions or prescribe others, is the height of despotism." Goldman added her own reflections on the government's actions, ending, "With all the power and intensity of my being I protest against the conspiracy of imperialist capitalism against the life and liberty of the American people." With the threat of deportation hanging over them, Goldman and Berkman set out on a "whirlwind lecture tour" to speak out in behalf of Russia. In Chicago and Detroit thousands of working-class and middle-class radicals and liberals turned out. "Monster demonstrations they were," Goldman wrote, "a tempest of vehement indignation against government absolutism and of homage to ourselves. It was the eloquent voice of the awakened collective soul, thrilled by new hope and aspiration. We merely articulated its yearnings and dreams."

After triumphant days in Chicago, lecturing to large and enthusiastic audiences, word came of the death of Henry Frick, whom Berkman had attempted to assassinate as an act of attentât at the time of the Homestead strike. Newspaper reporters descended on the country's most famous anarchists to record their reaction. "Mr. Frick has just died, what have you to say?" a reporter asked Berkman.

"Deported by God," Berkman answered, and Goldman added, "Henry Clay Frick was a man of the passing hour. Neither in life nor in death would he have been remembered long. It was Alexander Berkman who made him known, and Frick will live only in connection with Berkman's name. His entire fortune could not pay for such glory." Goldman forgot the Frick art gallery.

To Goldman the final irony of Berkman's deportation was the fact that the deportation order was signed by an old friend, Louis Post, assistant secretary of labor, who had been an ardent follower of Henry George, the former editor of the left-wing journal *Public*, and a defender of Goldman and other anarchists at the time of McKinley's assassination. It was to her a symbol of a general retreat into reaction by American liberals and radicals. One of the country's best-known champions of free speech had become its official squelcher. Like the former liberal reformers Newton D. Baker and Attorney General Mitchell Palmer, Post joined in the persecution of radical dissidents.

Convicted and shipped off to Ellis Island, Goldman and Berkman found scores of immigrants from a dozen European countries similarly confined for deportation. Ellis Island was a kind of tower of Babel with every language spoken by those awaiting shipment back to their native lands. It was December 21, 1919, when Berkman, Goldman, and a number of less well-known immigrants of Russian antecedents, some 500 "dangerous radicals," were shipped off. Goldman looked out her cabin's porthole. She could see the outline of the city's buildings. "It was my beloved city, the metropolis of the New World. It was America . . . repeating the terrible scenes of Tsarist Russia! I glanced up—the Statue of Liberty!"

After a difficult crossing Emma Goldman was once more in the land of her birth—Mother Russia, a land transformed by revolutionary zeal. "My heart trembled with anticipation and fervent hope," she wrote.

What awaited her was a bitterly disillusioning experience. Today it is almost as difficult to speak fairly and dispassionately about the Russian Revolution and the Bolshevik regime that was its most conspicuous consequence as it was in the moment Goldman and her fellow deportees stepped onto Russian soil. If American capitalism was the highest achievement of human history and its critics were a motley group of malcontents, atheists, ingrates, misfits, and, in the last analysis, traitors, the Russian Revolution might properly be seen, as it has been by many people, then and now, as some kind of terrible aberration, a hideous concatenation of everything alien to devout, God-fearing Americans, the ultimate consequence of infidelity and political radicalism. If that was the case, any measures designed to defeat and indeed to undo or reverse the Revolution might be considered legitimate. In the United States and indeed in many European countries, one's attitude toward the Russian Revolution became the test not only of one's patriotism but of one's morality.

On the other hand, if the individual saw capitalism as a ruthlessly exploitative economic system which degraded and abused those workingmen and women on whom its vast riches depended, the Russian Revolution and the other mini and quasi revolutions that appeared to be breaking out all over the globe held out the hope of a new and better human order. In the first volume of this work I undertook, following the lead of the German historian-philosopher Eugen Rosenstock-Huessy, to relate the American Revolution to what one historian has called "the age of democratic revolutions." According to this view of the development of the modern world, the age of revolution began with the English Civil War starting in 1642, the uprising of the parliamentary party against the autocratic power of the crown in the person of King Charles I. For almost twenty years England was without a king while a coalition of radical Protestant factions ruled the country, backed by Cromwell's Roundhead army. After the restoration of the Stuart rule under Charles II, the Puritan Revolution was "nationalized," so to speak, by the Glorious Revolution of 1688–89, which replaced King James II with William and Mary of Orange. The American Revolution was the lusty offspring of the English Civil War and the Glorious Revolution; it was conceived and carried on in the spirit of those earlier revolutions, and it established the principle of democratic participation in the processes of government. The Federal Constitution undertook to protect the legitimate interests of all segments of society and specifically rejected the ancient notion that social rank should confer special privileges, which had dominated every European society. All men were "born equal" and endowed with certain "inalienable rights." That was the story of the American Revolution in a nutshell.

The French Revolution extended the spirit of the American Revolution to embrace the notion that reason would in time achieve a perfected social order and that "the voice of the people was the voice of God," a notion alien to most of the Founding Fathers of the American Revolution. Karl Marx soon called attention to the fact that the toppling of kings and aristocrats meant little if economic power was unrestrained. Marx described in vivid terms the formidable array of images and stereotypes that the rich, the capitalists, could muster to justify their exploitation of the poor. The notion was not new by any means. In the American scene, individuals as diverse in their political inclinations as Gouverneur Morris and James Madison agreed that the rich and powerful would, if unchecked, exploit the weak and powerless. William Manning in his *Key to Liberty* was even more perceptive about the techniques used by "the few" to exploit "the many." As we have noted throughout these volumes, criticism of American capitalism has been a persistent element in political theory and discourse since the beginning of the Republic, reaching its peak in the last decades of the nineteenth and the first decade of the twentieth century.

In one sense the Russian Revolution was a crystallization or concretization of all the revolutionary aspirations of the preceding three centuries. It contained, or was perceived by most reformers and virtually all radicals to contain, the cumulative experience of earlier radical movements as well as the cumulative rage and hostility. Yet its paramount feature was hope for a new and more just universal world order. It was a hope as old as Plato's republic and in its ruthlessly authoritarian elements very much akin to the ideal state of the Greek philosopher.

Just as those Americans most sensitive to the moral horror of slavery had lived for decades in anticipation of the dismembering of the Union or a slave rebellion, Americans of the post-Civil War era had lived in fear or in anticipation of a social revolution. As an event in history the Russian Revolution was so vast, so titanic and protean that it was beyond comprehension—in its own initial agonies and from the "perspective of history."

When Emma Goldman and Alexander Berkman arrived, it was in its most volatile moment. Things changed from day to day. The Revolution had opened a Pandora's box of wildly conflicting political doctrines. In addition to Russian radicals of every description, revolutionaries from all over the world flocked to Russia to witness the beginnings of the world revolution and to take back with them tactics and strategies presumably guaranteed to produce similar results in their own countries. Since anarchy prevailed (not, it should be said, the kind of anarchy prescribed by the anarchists), people were free to make of the vast confusion and disorder what they wished. As the Revolution lurched along in its erratic and unpredictable course, it rolled over thousands of innocent devotees whose only crime was that they had the temerity to question one decision or another of the Supreme Soviet. With all the strange convulsions, with all the blind and frequently terrifying inconsistencies and mad excesses, there was also a wild euphoria. Workers from France, Britain, Bulgaria, Italy, Spain embraced Russian workers and each other, sang revolutionary songs, listened, enraptured, to revolutionary harangues, danced in the streets, and marched in endless parades that proclaimed the solidarity of the workers of the world, the new fraternal order of all peoples without regard to race or nationality. Middle-class revolutionaries clasped hands and stared into each other's eyes (when they could not otherwise communicate), seeing in them the irresistible gleam of the future, of trust and brotherhood, of a common dream of justice and equality that would make all the bad old ages past as remote and ephemeral as nightmares. (A young Irish writer—a literary, if not a political, revolutionary—spoke of history "as a nightmare from which I must awake.")

For the anarchists and those socialists who believed that revolution was compatible with the preservation of individual rights, most important among them the right of free speech, there were troubling indications that those in power were unwilling to tolerate dissent or even criticism. Opponents of the Bolsheviks were thrown into jail. Sometimes they simply disappeared. Emma Goldman met their old friend Bill Shatoff. He greeted Goldman and Berkman warmly and promised to unfold for them the marvels of the Revolution. But the Americans found that they were denied the opportunity to meet with fellow American anarchists who had preceded them. Every critic of the Lenin, Trotsky, Zinoviev triumvirate, which seemed to be running the country so far as it could be said to be running at all, was denounced as a counterrevolutionary. A counterrevolutionary was a person with a different opinion. Shatoff waved aside his friends' misgivings. "I just want to tell you," he assured them, "that the Communist State in action is exactly what we anarchists have always claimed it would be—a tightly centralized power, still more strengthened by the dangers to the Revolution. Under such conditions one cannot ride the bumpers, as I used to do in the United States. One needs permission. But don't get the idea that I miss my American 'blessings.' Me for Russia, the Revolution, and its glorious future!" Goldman was dismayed to learn that Communist party functionaries enjoyed all kinds of privileges denied the workers, not to mention the bourgeoisie. Soon she discovered that her friend Shatoff had functioned as virtual governor of Petrograd, ruling the city with an iron hand and turning over his enemies to the dreaded Cheka to be "liquidated."

Jack Reed was in Moscow. He tracked Goldman down and burst into her room "like a sudden ray of light," his familiar, ebullient self. He was on his way home to spread the word of the wonders of the Revolution, and to an already somewhat doubting Goldman he appeared quite unshaken in his faith in the revolution. "Wonderful, marvellous, isn't it, E.G.? Your dream of years now realized in Russia, your dream scorned and persecuted in your own country, but made real by the magic wand of Lenin and his band of despised Bolsheviks. Did you ever expect such a thing to happen in the country ruled by the tsars for centuries?" Goldman protested that the Bolsheviks had brutally cast aside the old revolutionaries who for decades had kept alive the dream of revolution and guided it in its first steps. Reed dismissed them contemptuously. Nothing was more to be reprobated than outdated revolutionaries. They were impediments to the Revolution, counterrevolutionaries. "I don't give a damn for their past," Reed exclaimed. "To the wall with them! . . . 'razstrellyat' (execute by shooting)."

Goldman protested, "Stop, Jack, stop, this word is terrible enough in the mouth of a Russian. In your hard American accent it freezes my blood. Since when do revolutionaries see in wholesale execution the only solution of their difficulties? In time of counter-revolution it is no doubt inevitable to give shot for shot. But cold-bloodedly and for opinion's sake do you justify standing people against the wall under such circumstances?" Under her questioning (she had heard, night after night, the sound of rifle fire), Reed admitted that some 500 dissidents had been summarily shot. What did the death of a few plotters matter "in the scales of the world revolution"?

"I must be crazy, Jack," she replied, "or else I never understood the meaning of revolution. I certainly never believed that it would signify callous indifference to human life and suffering, or that it would have no other method of solving its problems than by wholesale slaughter."

Reed tried to reassure her. She had heretofore dealt with revolution in theory. Soon she would come to understand the difficult imperatives of real revolution. "You'll get over that," he declared, "clear-sighted rebel that you are, and you'll come to see in its true light everything that seems so puzzling now."

Emma Goldman was famous in radical circles the world over, and the Russian leaders treated her warily. Her enthusiastic support for the Revolution would strengthen it in the minds of radical leaders in other countries, many of whom had grown uneasy over the arrest and often liquidation of well-known Russian revolutionaries. Conversely her criticism would be damaging, coming in the wake of the arrest and imprisonment of so many well-known socialists and anarchists.

In Goldman's words, the policy of the Bolsheviks seemed to be "the elimination from responsible positions [in the towns and villages to which she traveled] of everyone who dared think aloud, and the spiritual death of the most militant elements whose intelligence, faith, and courage had really enabled the Bolsheviks to achieve power. . . . People raided, imprisoned, and shot for their *ideas!* The old and young held as hostages, every protest gagged, iniquity and favouritism rampant, the best human values betrayed, the very spirit of the revolution daily crucified. . . . I felt chilled to the marrow of my bones."

The troubled Goldman sought an interview with Lenin. She and

Berkman were ushered through a series of heavily guarded rooms to the Russian leader's inner sanctum. Lenin sat behind a large oak desk, immaculately neat. A map of the world covered the wall behind him. The atmosphere was austere, but Lenin himself appeared positively jolly, laughing immoderately at whatever touched his risibility. He fired questions about America at his visitors: What were the chances of revolution there in the near future? Was the American Federation of Labor hopelessly under the influence of such reactionary leaders as Gompers? What about the IWW? How did they feel they could best serve the Revolution? Lenin asked. Berkman's answer was to inquire about the anarchists who were in Russian prisons. "Anarchists?" Lenin replied. "Nonsense! Who told you such yarns and how could you believe them?" The response of the Americans was to present him with a list of anarchists who had been imprisoned without any criminal charges made against them. Goldman told Lenin that she and Berkman could not cooperate with any regime "that persecuted anarchists or others for the sake of mere opinion." She went on to enumerate other brutal acts of the Bolsheviks. How, she asked, could these be reconciled with the high goals of the Revolution? Lenin's answer was that her feelings were simple "*bourgeois* sentimentality." "The proletarian dictatorship was engaged in a life-and-death struggle, and small considerations could not be allowed to weigh in the scale. Russia . . . was igniting the world revolution, and here I was lamenting over a little blood-letting." Lenin declared, "Do something, that will be the best way of regaining your revolutionary balance."

Goldman found that a number of her American friends from anarchist days, including some who had worked on *Mother Earth*, had no trouble rationalizing the arrest and execution of older revolutionaries, now denounced as counterrevolutionists. "They had," she noted, "no painful hesitations, no torturing doubts, no unanswerable questions. They were shocked to find me undecided. . . . My old values had been ship-wrecked and I myself thrown overboard to sink or swim. All I could do was to try to keep my head above water and trust to time to bring me to safe shores."

When a friend took Goldman to see Vladimir Korolenko, a well-known anarchist who spent much of his time trying to save the lives of friends accused of deviationist tendencies, the old man declared, "It has always been my conception that revolution means the highest expression of humanity and justice. The dictatorship has denuded it of both." To Korolenko it seemed apparent that the Russian Revolution "must retard social changes abroad for a long period. What better excuse needs European *bourgeoisie* for its reactionary methods than the ferocious dictatorship in Russia?"

Goldman and Berkman were sent on a mission to collect documents for a projected Museum of the Revolution. Christmas, 1920, was a dreary day for Goldman. She was on a Russian train with her "old pal Sasha," but she could not free herself from the depression that engulfed her. "Only a year had passed, and nothing was left but the ashes of my fervent dreams, my burning faith, my joyous song."

One of the most emotional reunions between Americans in Russia was that between Louise Bryant, the wife of Jack Reed, and Emma Goldman. Goldman had known Bryant through her friendship with Reed and considered her frivolous and self-centered. But Bryant had made her way to Russia disguised as a sailor to join Reed, enduring every kind of danger and hardship, only to find that Reed had been ordered to Baku to attend the Congress of Eastern Races. Reed had begged Zinoviev not to send him on the ground that he was in poor health, but Zinoviev insisted that Reed go as a representative of the American Communist Party. Reed had contracted typhus in Baku, and when he arrived back in Moscow, he had been more dead than alive. Louise had nursed him during his final illness. She begged Goldman and Berkman to remain for Reed's funeral. The sky was gray, and rain fell in a depressing drizzle during the ceremony. Reed was buried in Red Square as a tribute to his support for the Revolution. Emma Goldman found it ironic that there was "no beauty for the man who had loved it so, no colour for his artist-soul." At the conclusion of the short ceremony Louise Bryant fainted, and Berkman had to carry her to a waiting car.

When Goldman went to the offices of the Cheka to apply for a permit to allow imprisoned anarchists to attend the funeral of Piotr Kroptkin, the father of anarchism, who had become disillusioned with the Revolution, she discovered that the "presiding Chekist" was a young American named Brenner. He extended his hand warmly and addressed her as "dear comrade." Goldman spurned the outstretched hand. She did not shake hands with detectives, she told Brenner. Among the anarchists in the Moscow prison were Fanya and Aaron Baron, two American friends who only a few months earlier had rebuked Goldman for her lack of faith in the Bolsheviks.

If Emma Goldman had been prey to grave misgivings about the course of the Revolution almost from the moment she arrived in Russia, the brutal suppression of the strike of some 16,000 sailors, Red Army soldiers, and workers in the winter of 1921 at the naval base of Kronstadt completed her disillusionment. The strike of the Kronstadt sailors was based primarily on the issue of inadequate pay. The response of Lenin and Trotsky was to declare the strikers in a state of mutiny against the Soviet government, denouncing them as "tools of former tsarist generals who together with Socialist-Revolutionist traitors staged a counterrevolutionary conspiracy against the proletarian Republic." When the sailors and workers of the city refused Trotsky's demand to surrender immediately or suffer the consequences, he ordered the Red Army to attack. For ten days the besieged men held out against heavy artillery fire and aerial bombardment. On March 18, 1921, the "revolt" of the Kronstadt sailors and workers was broken with the loss of thousands of lives. Emma Goldman noted it was the anniversary of the Paris Commune of 1871, when 30,000 communards had been killed. In the wake of Kronstadt all intellectuals suspected of opposing the Bolsheviks were rounded up by the Cheka and either executed or sent to the penitentiary at Samara.

Goldman and Berkman decided that they could no longer appear even passively to support the Bolsheviks by remaining in Russia, but before they could leave, they witnessed the arrival of new contingents of American radicals, among them Ella Reeve "Mother" Bloor, Big Bill Haywood, and William Z. Foster. Emma Goldman was especially pleased to see Bloor, who had visited her when she was in the women's penitentiary at Jefferson City, and Haywood, an ally in many labor battles. She questioned him eagerly about Elizabeth Gurley Flynn, Kate Richards O'Hare, and other socialist and anarchist friends. Haywood had been sentenced to twenty years in jail for subversion. On bail while his sentence was appealed, he had made his way to Russia, where Lenin had assured him he was needed in the cause of the Revolution. Foster, who had returned to his earlier radical faith after the failure of the steel strike, came to see Berkman. With him was a young Kansan named Jim Browder, a member of the American Communist Party, whom Goldman had known as a militant Wobbly in America. Both Goldman and Berkman were soon aware that the Americans were avoiding them. It turned out that they had been warned that the two were less than wholehearted in their support of the Bolshevik regime. Thus began the estrangement of anarchist leaders from those American (and indeed European) radicals who gave their unquestioning loyalty to the Soviets.

The Red Trade Union Congress in 1920 provided Goldman and Berkman with their last chance to rally worldwide anarchist and socialist opinion on the side of the imprisoned anarchists. They drew up a petition calling for their release and presented it, with attendant publicity, to Lenin, who replied, in the words of Goldman, to the effect that "he did not care if all the politicals perished in prison. . . . He and his party would brook no opposition from any side, Left or Right." He would consent, however, to have the imprisoned anarchists deported from the country, "on pain of being shot if they should return to Soviet soil."

The most conspicuous non-Russian figure in the Red Trade Union Congress was Big Bill Haywood. Under heavy pressure from the Soviet manipulators of the congress he voted in support of the Communist strategy which demanded the liquidation of all militant labor organizations, most prominent among them the IWW itself. They must henceforth deploy their forces in the American Federation of Labor with the mission of subverting that organization to the use of the world revolution, to be directed from Moscow. "Soviet Russia," Goldman reflected, reviewing bitterly the consequences of the congress, "had become the modern socialist Lourdes, to which the blind and the lame, the deaf and the dumb were flocking for miraculous cures." She pitied the deluded, but for Americans like Foster and Browder, who should have, in her opinion, known better, she felt only contempt.

"I had reached the end," Goldman wrote in her autobiography. "I could bear it no longer. In the dark I groped my way to Sasha to beg him to leave Russia, by whatever means. 'I am ready, my dear, to go with you, in any way only far away from the woe, the blood, the tears, the stalking death.' " The Russian authorities were glad to be rid of their troublesome guests. They were given passports to depart through Lithuania, and by January they were on their way to freedom.

For a time it seemed as if they were to find refuge nowhere. Too conservative (or counterrevolutionary) for Russia, they were too dangerously radical for any other country. In the wreckage of American radicalism, they became nonpersons to those among their former comrades determined to remain true to what they believed was the opening act of the world revolution. Once one had accepted that rationale, of course, any horror was excusable. Monstrous evils required monstrous remedies. Once persuaded of this, all those who turned in revulsion from the terrible excesses of the Revolution were anathema, sentimental bourgeois, who in the last desperate hour faltered, whose nerves and faith failed them. It is unproductive to argue with revolutions. They come, and in their merciless course they crush those who oppose them and break the hearts of many who at one time considered themselves friends. But they represent such massive aggregations of our hopes and fears that they resist the moral yardsticks by which we measure the ordinary events of daily life. They demand to be judged by quite another standard. The Bloors, Flynns, Fosters, and Browders were, one feels, people of less character, less intelligence, or perhaps, simply less sensitivity to the pleasures and terrors of existence, armored by their radical catchwords and impenetrable Marxist clichés against the better impulses of the human heart. Yet of course, they were in a sense more "right" than Emma Goldman and Sasha Berkman. They were "right" in that the Revolution endured, silenced its enemies or even its mildest critics, and came in time to mitigate its worst excesses, achieve a new social order, and win at least the passive acceptance of the mass of the Russian people. And that in itself was a not inconsiderable triumph. In addition, as I think we must admit, it came, rightly or wrongly, to represent hope for millions of exploited people around the world. So it was, after all, a "world revolution," sustained, despite its very considerable errors and often grim tyrannies, by that common yearning for justice and equality that had fueled the American Revolution and its successors.

The long and bitter trip that Emma Goldman and Alexander Berkman took together from Homestead to St.-Tropez (their final resting place) was one of the most remarkable personal hegiras in modern history, a journey loaded or unloaded with symbolic implications of a very large order. With unfaltering courage and rare integrity they clung doggedly to their mission of proclaiming the truth and defending the rights of the individual whether it be in capitalist America or socialist Russia. For that courage and integrity, they were made exiles in the world, Ishmaels—"From going to and fro in the earth; and from walking up and down in it." Curiously enough, the reaction of Emma Goldman and her "old pal" to the Russian Revolution was both inevitable and ineffably American.

The question of whether Reed and/or Haywood became disillusioned with the Revolution before their deaths became a bitterly argued issue between the radical proponents of the Revolution and their adversaries. Reed seems to have suppressed whatever misgivings he felt. The case with Haywood is less clear. Hutchins Hapgood wrote of Haywood's last months in Russia: "There he was taken care of physically but his independent and free spirit wearied of the totalitarian discipline. . . ." Walter Duranty and Eugene Lyons, American journalists who saw Haywood in Moscow, reported that he longed for America. In a way it was the saddest exile of all. Compared with Haywood's long service to the cause of labor, John Reed was a romantic child playing with revolution. Haywood was as romantic in his own way as the younger man, and while he was lionized as a symbol of the international solidarity of the working class, he grew more and more aware of the profound alienness of Russia.

For Goldman and Berkman the issue was that of the integrity and inviolability of the individual, and this, indeed, was the real significance of American anarchism, making it the lineal descendant of transcendentalism. More than the capitalists, more than the various brands of socialists, the anarchists "kept the faith" in the classic American doctrine of the individual.

The sharpest split between Goldman and Berkman was over the question of the form and forum they should use to express their opposition to the Bolsheviks. Emma wanted to write for the American capitalist press on the ground that it was the only press read by any substantial number of workers to whom they wished to convey their message. Berkman objected strenuously that to do so was to play into the hands of the enemies of anarchism and socialism; it would simply provide the forces of reaction with ammunition to use against all radical movements. But Goldman persisted, and a storm of outrage broke around her head as the damning articles began to appear. Meetings were held to denounce her. Her former companions burned her in effigy. "I could see the similarity," she wrote of the attacks on her, "between the blood-lust [of the pro-Soviet Americans] and that of Southern whites at Negro lynchings." In Goldman's words, "In former days the liberal and radical groups used to take a common stand against every encroachment on political freedom and in opposition to economic injustice." Now they all were at each other's throats over the question of Russia.

42

Americans Against Americans

"The world I found on landing in New York," Oswald Garrison Villard wrote, "bore no resemblance whatever to that I had left behind me in Europe. It was then, and for years thereafter, like a different planet." What impressed Villard most strongly was that the "war hate," which had subsided in Europe, was still very evident in the United States.

The country's most striking pathology was the "fear of the Reds." The Red scare was, to be sure, some fifty years old. Americans had been crying out in alarm, "The Communists are coming! The Communists are coming!" or, "The Socialists are coming [or the anarchists]" since the 1870s. But while many labor leaders and ordinary workmen striking for higher wages had been beaten or killed by company guards, by Pinkerton agents, by national guardsmen, and even, on occasion, by soldiers of the United States Army, and while many more had been arrested, people had not, generally speaking, been prosecuted for their political opinions, which, it was presumed, were protected by the Constitution. During the war many men and women had, to be sure, been jailed for opposition to the draft, but now "Reds," a commodious category which could be expanded to cover anyone holding opinions objectionable to his or her neighbors, were clapped into jail on the grounds of treasonable utterances. In the words of the *Nation*, "Wilson and [Newton D.] Baker have lost their moral balance in this matter of militarism, the assertion of law and order and the suppression of civil rights and liberties. They are less honest than the Bourbons." Baker asked Congress for a standing army of 500,000, almost double the number Pershing himself recommended. A. Mitchell Palmer made himself the special scourge of the "Reds." A Federal judge in Boston named George W. Anderson revealed that *agents provocateurs* in the employ of the Justice Department had not only spied on Communist Party members but incited them to acts of lawlessness and helped draft the Communist platform, on the basis of which members of the min-uscule party were arrested for disloyalty. "I wish you would show me one case," Anderson said to the government prosecutor, "in which the Department of Justice has the authority to arrest persons and hold them two weeks without warrants. A more lawless proceeding is hard to conceive. Talk about Americanization; what we need is American-ization of those who carry on such proceedings. I can hardly sit on the bench as an American citizen and restrain my indignation. I view with horror such proceedings as this."

Undoubtedly the deteriorating economic situation gave added impetus to the so-called Red scare. Wheat fell in the months following the armistice from $2.20 to 60 cents; cotton, from 40 cents a pound to 5; hogs, from 25 cents a pound to 3. The accumulated resentments of workingmen broke out in a blizzard of strikes. Coal miners, railroad workers, steelworkers, and the construction trades all were on strike at one time or another. "All of Oklahoma seemed to be on strike," Oscar Ameringer wrote.

When Frederic Howe's phone rang, it was often a radical or liberal friend, harassed by the police or Secret Service, who turned to him as the only public official he knew with access to the White House. Could not the President be prevailed upon to stop the persecution of men and women whose only offense was exercising their constitutional right to speak out about issues that deeply concerned them?

Howe was convinced that the campaign against young men and women of liberal persuasion was part of a concerted effort by the business interests of the country to silence its critics. The war hysteria was the excuse. To Howe the "liberal movement," of which he had been a part, was "a renaissance of America rising from an orgy of commercialism." He could not reconcile himself to its destruction, "to its voice being stilled, its integrity assailed, its patriotism questioned, especially by a war that promised to give these democratic ideals to the world. . . . These young liberals felt that they had done no wrong, so far as America was concerned they could do no wrong. . . . They had stood for variety, for individuality, for freedom. They discovered a political state that seemed to hate these things; it wanted a servile society, a society that accepted authority without protest. The crushing of this movement and the men responsible for it," Howe wrote, "made me hate in a way that was new to me. I hated the Department of Justice . . . ; I hated the new state that had arisen, hated its brutalities, its ignorance, its unpatriotic patriotism, that made profit from our sacrifices and used its power to suppress criticism of its acts. I hated the suggestion of disloyalty of myself and my friends; suggestions that were directed against liberals, never against profiteers."

When Howe finally gained an audience with the President just before his speaking tour on behalf of the League of Nations, he found him "scrupulously attired, trim and erect, even debonair—every inch the gentlemanly President." Wilson's technique in dealing with suggestions that he did not wish to hear was to take the offensive, revealing a greater knowledge of the subject at hand than his petitioner. Howe felt that he had encountered a "stone wall." The President "understood the cases of arrested liberals, but he seemed determined that there should be no questioning his will. I felt," Howe wrote, "that he was eager for the punishment of the man who differed from him, that there was something vindictive in his eyes as he spoke. . . . I could not understand his apparent hatred of men who persisted in their belief in his own liberal opinions. . . ."

Howe's health suffered, and he feared himself near a nervous breakdown. He could not sleep. The ring of the telephone, so often disclosing a new horror, jangled his nerves, became "an evil thing." For months he lived in a state of fear of "something impending, something mysterious that hung over me." He carried his fears and anxieties to a well-known psychiatrist, who told him he was sick. "There are a lot of liberals like you. Some became war-mad and deserted their groups; some stuck by their convictions and were punished; others tried to adjust themselves as best they could to the war." There was only one cure, the doctor told Howe, for his "sickness." He must "blurt out" what he had on his mind; what was troubling him. Howe followed the psychiatrist's advice. A few days later, at the Cosmos Club, he declared to some friends, "Every one of us has done something he is ashamed of. All of us have been lying in some way or other. And many of us have been cowards." The other diners all denied any such feelings, but the "confession" relieved Howe's feelings, although, he wrote, "the fears that had possessed me would not wholly be exorcised. . . . I became distrustful of the state. It seemed to want to hurt people; it showed no concern for innocence; it aggrandized itself and protected its power by unscrupulous means. It was not my America, it was something else."

Lincoln Steffens got an audience with Wilson to try to prevail upon him to pardon Debs and others who had been sentenced to long prison terms for opposing the war, but again the President was grimly unyielding. No pardons for traitors.

The raids, the warrantless arrests, the prostitution of the legal system continued. The climax of irrational hysteria was reached in January, 1920, when some 6,000 persons were arrested—including girls of fourteen and sixteen years of age—and charged with being criminal anarchists. Avowed Communists were also arrested, along with any other persons found in their houses or apartments. Roscoe Pound, dean of the Harvard Law School, headed a list of well-known attorneys protesting the actions of Palmer and the Justice Department. A correspondent of the *Nation* charged that the Justice Department's "criminal acts" had been carried out "intentionally and purposely . . . to terrorize the foreign working population." The old middle- and upper-class hostility to workingmen and women and the fear of organized labor, which had ebbed (or been suppressed) in the decade prior to the outbreak of the war, resurfaced with surprising ferocity. The agents of the Justice Department seemed openly contemptuous of public opinion or confident that it would support them. Five newspaper reporters were present when an alleged Communist named Oscar J. Tywerewski was badly beaten by government agents. They were warned that they would be subject to prosecution if they reported the episode. Three radicals in the Hartford jail were tortured to the point of death. A fifty-year-old professor, whose only crime was teaching algebra in Russian, was badly beaten. Andrea Salsedo and Roberto Elia, accused of being anarchists, were held in secret confinement in offices of the Department of Justice and tortured until Salsedo jumped from the fourteenth floor of the building to his death.

Palmer tried to prevail upon Congress to pass a sedition law which read that anyone who "threatens to commit . . . any act of . . . hate . . . against the person or property of any officer . . . of the United States . . . shall be deemed guilty of sedition." Five Socialists were evicted from the New York legislature, and twenty persons in New York City were convicted of being members of the Communist Party. In Waterbury, Connecticut, a boy was sentenced to six months in jail for saying to a customer in a clothing store that Lenin was "the most brainiest man" who had emerged from the war era.

Ameringer and a number of other Socialist leaders had anticipated that the end of the war would bring a revival of Socialist activity. All the parties of the left, disillusioned by the war and its consequences, they reasoned, would rally to the Socialist standard. The reverse turned out to be true. Ameringer, reviving the *Leader* by heroic efforts, could muster up only 2,000 subscribers, rather than the 20,000 that he had hoped for. In his words, "the end of the war meant that the evil spirits it had aroused needed new objects for hatred. Trade unionists, Reds, radicals, pinks, foreigners, Negroes, Jews, and Catholics were at hand. . . ." In Oklahoma and a number of other Midwestern and Southern states, the Ku Klux Klan flourished. What the Socialists had looked forward to as an aggressive campaign to recruit new voters turned, instead, into a desperate defensive action against the Klan, which grew far faster than the Socialist Party. Walter Lippmann wrote caustically to Bernard Berenson: "The people are shivering in their boots over Bolshevism, they are far more afraid of Lenin than they ever were of the Kaiser. We seem to be the most frightened lot of victors that the world ever saw."

A small band of liberal lawyers fought the campaign of repression. Zechariah Chafee published *Freedom of Speech*, which focused on the unconstitutionality of the Espionage Act and on the Abrams case, in which three men had been sentenced to twenty years in prison for distributing treasonable pamphlets. Justice Holmes, dissenting, had observed that the hysteria of the times had "upset many fighting faiths" and that the "best test of truth is the power of the thought to get itself accepted in the competition of the market place," a modern paraphrase of Jefferson's famous admonition.

Chafee, Pound, and Frankfurter joined with nine other liberal lawyers in publishing a "Report upon the Illegal Practices of the United States Department of Justice." When Charles Evans Hughes read it, he was moved to reflect on "whether constitutional government as heretofore maintained in this republic could survive another great war even victoriously waged."

No one was immune. The Treaty of Versailles was supposed to "end all wars," yet pacifists found themselves under attack. In 1919 a list headed "A Who's Who in Pacificism and Radicalism" was made up;

it bore the names of men and women, like Jane Addams, Norman Thomas, Hillquit, Debs, Villard, Elizabeth Gurley Flynn, and many others, who had resisted the war and fought stubbornly for freedom of speech. It was an honor roll of Americans with the courage of their convictions.

Learned Hand wrote to Graham Wallas in January, 1920, trying to account for the mood of reaction and repression that had swept the country. "We never had the foundations in this country, in my time," Hand observed, "for a genuine spirit of toleration. It is a country where you are expected to conform and if you don't you are looked upon with suspicion. We all knew this, or at least knew it at times and in spots long before the war taught us. . . . The conception as a place of warm-hearted acceptance and toleration was always a mistaken one, I think, and the change is not so great as it seems. . . . Do not despair of us, by any means. We are not very temperate . . . but we will stop long short of the logical implications of what we have been doing."

Walter Lippman called it "the blackest reaction our generation has known. . . . My crowd is distinctly unpopular—parlor 'Bolsheviks' etc. . . . Popularity," he added, "would be a little bit discreditable when the world is so mad." Looking back from the relatively brief perspective of 1924, Howe wrote that "few people know of the state of terror that prevailed during those years, few would believe the extent to which private hates and prejudices were permitted to usurp government powers. It was quite apparent that the alleged offenses for which people were being persecuted were not the real offenses. The prosecution was directed against liberals, radicals, persons who had been identified with labor movements, with forums, with liberal papers which were under the ban. Many of them were young people, many were college men and women."

Hutchins Hapgood, who had found Oswald Garrison Villard rather stuffy and conservative when he worked for him on the *New York Post*, was impressed by his courage in opposing the wartime hysteria. Its effect had been to push Villard to a much more clearly defined liberal position on political and social issues, and Hapgood congratulated him on his inclination toward the left. Villard wrote a grateful response. He agreed that there had been a "great change," adding, "I do not see how anyone could have stood still during the last four years. One must have either moved to the left or to the right and I have gone to the left." He could not embrace either the Communist or Socialist creed, but he was convinced that one must "henceforth be either for or against the present political order. I do not wish my children to live in a world managed politically as the present world has been during the last five years." His own suffering had been due primarily, he told Hapgood, "to the sense of spiritual outrage at the injustice and wickedness that we are seeing. . . . I do know that nothing is going to save us humans except getting nearer and nearer to practicing the ethical teachings of Jesus and particularly a recognition of the fact that human life must be sacred and inviolable."

Not surprisingly, the actions of the government had, for many liberals, an effect quite different from that intended: They made the Bolsheviks "look good," or at least better than they had. It was clear that there was brutality, repression, and worse in Soviet Russia, but at least they were ostensibly directed at producing a more equitable social and economic order, while the less severe persecutions in the United States were wholly reactionary in character. Soon after young Eugene Lyons had been demobilized, he heard Norman Thomas speak. "I carried away the revelation," Lyons wrote, "that the Russian revolution had no boundaries, since it was the initial stage of the world revolution. The fight against capitalists in America, the battle to restore freedom to political prisoners and conscientious objectors, were just part of the world-wide defense of the Russian Revolution."

The drive to suppress all criticism, all opposition was accompanied by a renewed assault on labor and on labor unions. The closed shop was denounced by conservative spokesmen as an agent of revolution, as part of a Communist plot to subvert the nation. Private detective agencies combined forces with strikebreakers and officials of the Department of Justice to hunt down Reds in the labor movement. "For two years we were in a panic of fear over Red revolutionists, anarchists, and enemies of the Republic," Howe wrote, "who were said to be ready to overthrow the government. . . . Things that were done forced one almost to despair of the mind, or to distrust the political state. . . . The Department of Justice, the Department of Labor, and Congress not only failed to protest against hysteria, they encouraged these excesses; the state not only abandoned the liberty which it should have protected, it lent itself to the stamping out of individual freedom. . . . It became frankly an agency of employing and business interests at a time when humanity—the masses, the poor—were making the supreme sacrifice of their lives. . . . Civil liberties were under the ban. Their subversion . . . was an incident in the ascendancy of business privileges and profits acquired during the war. . . ."

The cases of Billings and Mooney, convicted after the San Francisco Preparedness Day parade, became a rallying point for the disaffected. Fremont Older, the reform-minded editor of the *San Francisco Call*, wrote: "That these two men are entirely innocent of the crime is now known all over the world. No one who has heard the facts doubts it, yet Mooney and Billings are both serving life sentences . . . and the state seems willing that they remain there until they die. . . . The little faith in human nature that I had left after the failure of the graft persecution has considerably lessened my experience in trying to bring about the release of these men." It was lessened more when Older found out that ten of twelve local labor leaders "were either actively conniving at keeping these men in prison or doing nothing to help them. This threw me into a despondent mood," Older added.

Before America's entry into the war the hearings of the Commission on Industrial Relations had dramatized labor's woes and delineated vividly the degree to which workingmen and -women (and children) had been left outside "the promise of American life," as Herbert Croly had titled his book: how unequal their lot; how profound the hardships and sufferings they endured. The war industries had, under pressure from the Federal government, established a standard of pay and, equally important, of hours and working conditions which, it was assumed, must become general throughout American industry after the war. But Wilson's prediction that the capitalists, once back in the saddle as suppliers of the nation's wartime needs, would be as difficult as ever to domesticate, proved accurate. It seemed that all that had been done had been undone. Ray Stannard Baker undertook an investigation of the latest phase of the war between capital and labor. He traveled extensively around the country and wrote twenty articles, which were soon collected in a book entitled, significantly, *The New Industrial Unrest: Reasons and Remedies*. In contrast with his articles before the war on the relations between capital and labor there was disconcertingly little public response. Baker concluded that "the people were emotionally and intellectually exhausted by the war. They wanted to be let alone; they wanted to get back to work."

Although there were no more than 75,000 Americans who gave their unflinching loyalty to the cause of Russian communism, every labor dispute, every strike, every shock to the body politic was ascribed to the machinations of domestic Bolsheviks. When workingmen in New York, Cleveland, Boston, and other large industrial cities marched in the traditional May Day parades, they were attacked by the police.

Eugene Lyons recalled the day as one of "blood and terror and ex-cruciating pain, of helpless anger. Workers' parades were smashed, radicals were brutally mauled, jails were crowded. The telephone rang continuously to apprise us of more raids, more brutality, more arrests." With all that, "the day was touched with rapture," Lyons added. "We felt ourselves in the thick of a great struggle for justice, only a few of us, but pitting our faith against something monstrous."

Palmer did his best to fan the flames by estimating that 5,000,000 fervent Communists were plotting to overthrow the government and establish a Communist reign of terror. In Centralia, Washington, four American Legionnaires were shot by Wobblies, and a Wobbly was in turn lynched by a mob. There was a rash of strikes, many revealing an alarming degree of bitterness among the workers. In August, 1918, a number of union officials met in Chicago and formed the National Committee for Organizing Iron and Steel Workers. Samuel Gompers was the honorary chairman of the committee, with John Fitzpatrick as acting chairman and William Z. Foster as secretary-treasurer. Workers were organized in seven steel-producing cities, including Johnstown, Youngstown, Chicago, and Cleveland. Foster's presence alarmed the steel owners, who were determined to do all in their power to defeat the union. Foster was a Bryan Democrat turned Socialist and Wobbly. He had been an ally of Big Bill Haywood and differed from many of his fellow Socialists in his belief that radicals should work within the trade union movement. He had abandoned Debs and the mainline of the Socialist Party during the war and given patriotic speeches in favor of Liberty bonds, thereby purging himself of his Wobbly connections. The steelworkers were certainly ripe for organization. Many had be-longed to unions that had been broken by the employers. Many others were immigrants with radical antecedents in their homelands and were eager to join the new union. Most steelworkers put in a sixty-nine-hour week. Their average income was $1,466 per year. In June, 1919, the national committee asked Judge Elbert Gary, chairman of United States Steel, to participate in calling a conference to arbitrate differences between millowners and the workers. Gary ignored the committee's request. The operators were determined to preserve the open shop. "The operators of the corporation respectfully decline to discuss with you, as representatives of a labor union, any matters relating to em-ployees" was the message.

When the owners refused to meet with the representatives of the union, the organizing committee called a strike for September 22, 1919.

"The workers in the iron and steel mills and blast furnaces . . . are requested not to go to work on September 22, and to refuse to resume their employment until such time as the demands of the organization have been conceded by the steel corporations." Their demands were "The right of collective bargaining; reinstatement of all men discharged for union activities with pay for time lost; the eight-hour day; one day's rest in seven; the abolition of the twenty-four-hour shift; an American living wage; double pay for overtime; the check-off and seniority; and the abolition of company unions."

Wilson urged Gompers to postpone the strike, and Gompers in turn appealed to Fitzpatrick and Foster, who declared "any vague, indefinite postponement would mean absolute demoralization and utter ruin for the steel union movement."

The *New York Times* expressed the views of the business community, declaring that the strike was not really for wages or improved working conditions but was "a strike for power, for the control of the industry." The same argument had been used to create public opposition to the Pullman strike twenty-five years earlier. The *Washington Post* chimed in that "The public is not in a long-suffering mood just at present." Public sentiment was certainly not in favor of the steel corporations. Gary's refusal to negotiate recalled George Pullman's recalcitrance to meeting with his workers. While liberal journals accused Gary of trying to destroy the union movement, the *Wall Street Journal* announced that he and the steel operators were "fighting the battle of the American Constitution."

The steelworkers responded enthusiastically to the call for a strike. Within a week more than 365,000 men had walked off their jobs. Soon there was violence. The bitterness and frustration on the part of the workers, which had been evident in every strike since the Great Strikes of 1877, were once more manifest, and once more they were met by brutal repression. Certainly the general atmosphere was not improved by the radical press, which hailed the strike as the beginning of the workers' revolution. The *Socialist News* declared, "Half Million Workers in Open Class War," and the *Call* announced that labor was entering the "last battle with the industrial overlords of America," while the editors of the *Communist* wrote glowingly of a war to "crush the capitalists." The steel trust, for its part, organized an extensive publicity campaign to make the point that the strike was the work of Reds and Bolsheviks. Many steelworkers, the trust declared (and the newspapers dutifully reported), made as much as $70 a day. A concerted effort was made to depict the strike as, in essence, a conflict between patriotic "native" American steelworkers and radical immigrants. Conservative newspapers announced, "Conditions Almost Back to Normal in All Steel Plants," "Workers Flock Back to Jobs," and similar headlines designed to demoralize the strikers. The millowners ran full-page ads in the newspapers of the cities where workers were on strike, exhorting them to go back to work and declaring that they were being misled by foreign agents. Returning to work was declared evidence of loyalty to the nation, an especially effective plea in the light of the wartime hysteria that had still not abated. "Stand by America," one such ad urged. "Show Up the Red Agitator for What He Is," "Beware the Agitator Who Makes Labor a Catspaw for Bolshevism," admonished others. In 1911, while still a member of the IWW, William Foster had written a book called *Syndicalism* in which he argued that unions must be the vanguard of the revolution. It was exhumed and widely quoted as evidence that the strike was political in intent.

Repeated incidents of violence, riots, and demonstrations increased public disenchantment with the strike and the strikers. Headlines that proclaimed, "Rioting Spreads . . . Guards Raid Pennsylvania Mill Pickets . . . Many Shot—2 Dead," further inflamed public feeling. At Farrell, Pennsylvania, in a battle between police and strikers, four strikers were killed, and eleven seriously wounded. Spies and strikebreakers employed by the trust added to the bitterness generated by its determination to break the strike. Black strikebreakers were brought in, and company agents were instructed "to stir up as much bad feeling as you possibly can." In Donora, Pennsylvania, a fight between black strikebreakers and white strikers resulted in two deaths. In Braddock, Pennsylvania, one striker was killed and twenty were injured in a battle between Italians and Poles.

In Indiana eleven companies of state militia, augmented by 500 special police and 300 deputies, were ordered into East Chicago and Gary to bully, harass, and arrest strikers. After a day of rioting the governor of the state called for Federal troops. Mother Jones appeared in Gary to encourage the strikers and declared to a cheering crowd, "We're going to take over the steel mills and run them for Uncle Sam," a declaration subject to various interpretations. The *Communist*, not surprisingly, continued to call for revolution: "Workers, act! out of your mass strikes will come . . . a state of the workers, [a] proletarian dictatorship which will crush the capitalists as the capitalist state now crushes the workers."

Gradually the propaganda of the steel companies eroded the resolution of the strikers. Amid scenes of increasing bitterness and violence they drifted back to work. By January, 1920, only some 100,000 remained on strike, and it was clear that the cause was lost. The National Committee for Organizing Iron and Steel Workers voted to call the strike off. Foster resigned from the AFL and turned his attention to the Communist Party. A number of unions which had supported the national organizing committee withdrew their backing. The steel trust had succeeded in breaking the union movement. Eighteen strikers had been killed, and hundreds wounded by Federal troops, national guardsmen, or local police and "deputies." None of the aims of the strike had been achieved. The consequences were devastating for labor and the union movement.

During the strike the Senate Committee on Education and Labor brought in a report which accepted without serious question the steel trust's version of events. The Senate report affirmed that a "considerable element of IWW's, anarchists, revolutionists, and Russian Soviets" had used the strike "as a means of elevating themselves to power."

The Interchurch World Movement, an ecumenical organization of liberal Protestants, made its own investigation. Its Commission of Inquiry had as its chairman Francis McConnell, presiding bishop of the Methodist Episcopal Church, and Daniel Poling, general secretary of the Interchurch World Movement. The "findings" of the commission were that the "fundamental grievances" of the strikers were: "Excessive hours; the 'boss system'; no right to organize or to representation." The steelworkers wished a shorter day and week with a living wage and the "substitution of industrial democracy for industrial autocracy."

The reason that the abuses had continued so long unredressed, according to the commission's report, was that "they were limited largely to foreigners of many races and languages without industrial tradition, education or leadership to organize." The hostility of American-born workers toward the immigrants had kept "the more skilled, more intelligent and better paid American workmen from taking up the cause of the foreign-speaking workmen." The crisis had come about, in the main, because of "the part these workingmen played in the war and the treatment afforded them for the sake of war production which gave them a new sense of worth and independence." Finally, there was a new spirit of democracy bred in the ranks of foreign-born workers because of the President's emphasis on democratic values. The commission cleared the strikers of the charge that they were the tools of radical agitators.

The strike was broken because the steel companies were able to mobilize public opinion against the strikers "through the charges of radicalism, bolshevism, and the closed shop, none of which were justified by the facts" and by the general hostility of the press, "giving biased and colored news and the silence of both press and pulpit on the actual question of justice involved; which attitude of press and public helped to break the strikers' morale." In addition, there was widespread fear of a "general labor war," as the prelude to a Red uprising. The strike was not, in consequence, given adequate support by the unions themselves.

Wilson's response to the outbreak of violent strikes was to call a National Industrial Conference, made up of representatives of labor, agriculture, and the general public. Among those appointed to the conference were John D. Rockefeller, Jr., Judge Gary, Charles Edward Russell, Lillian Wald, Ida Tarbell, Samuel Gompers, and the young head of the United Mine Workers, John L. Lewis. Also included was the ex-Socialist John Spargo, who promised not to push "any socialist aim or any socialist effort" and to "utter ne'er a word of regret against class consciousness."

Gary was, in William Allen White's words, "the dapperest man in the room," dressed in a brownish gray suit with a dove-colored vest and a flower in his buttonhole, "as if sitting for a portrait, with clothes creased, linen immaculate, and hands manicured. . . . He impressed one as a nerveless man." Short, stocky Gompers, with long arms and short legs, was in striking contrast with the elegant Gary and the slim, diminutive Rockefeller. He had, according to White, "leathery pink skin . . . moth-eaten hair, and a smooth-shaven face. . . . His face was mobile, his mouth was large and strong; his jaw . . . brutal and indomitable. He had the big nose of a ruler." There was, to White, something secretive about Gompers—"inscrutably oriental" was the term he used. He looked "curiously unwestern . . . like a Persian potentate." Yet his character was at the same time "western, fundamentally American."

The conference met in October, 1920, in the shadow of the coming presidential elections and, in Bernard Baruch's words, "achieved nothing." It seemed to Baruch that "labor's unrest, distrust and dissatisfaction have much justice," he wrote to William Jennings Bryan, "and the injustice involved must be found and eradicated. It is unthinkable that the right and . . . the generous thing should not be done toward . . . the working classes. . . ."

The fact was that the country was increasingly disinclined to question the virtues of American capitalism and its various tenets—competition, rugged individualism, laissez-faire—none of which pertained in practice but all of which served as an ideological covering for a revived and aggressive capitalism, exhilarated by its achievements in the war and determined to run the country according to its own predilections. We have had occasion, more than once in the course of this work, to note how fitful "progress" has been. American blacks, slave and free, for example, lost ground in the years between the founding of the Republic and the Civil War. After the war they enjoyed a brief period of ascent (though certainly not of ascendancy) before they were once more thrust down into a position of powerlessness and degradation by the dominant white society. Now labor had the same bitter experience. If the Great Strikes of 1877 had not resulted in a clear-cut "victory" for labor, they had nonetheless brought important gains, generated considerable public support (as well, of course, as fear and anger) for the cause of labor, and given workingmen and their leaders reason to believe that better days lay ahead. The Commission on Industrial Relations of 1913 represented the high point for labor in the war between capital and labor. Although the commission was split in its final report, the majority came out for a modest degree of socialism—public ownership of the railroads and utilities—and the predominant mood was clearly prolabor and anticapital. Although the report of the commission had discouragingly few practical consequences, it certainly appeared to have helped create a climate of opinion favorable to the aspirations of labor. Only four years after its report the mood of the country had changed dramatically. The reasons are not difficult to discover. The war had revived capitalism, but it had split the labor movement and the Socialist Party. It had exacerbated and polarized political feelings at every level of American society. Even to such conservative leaders as Samuel Gompers, the future of labor seemed bleak. Business was in the saddle and gave every indication that it intended to ride the country into submission. Earlier talk of compromise and accommodation was no longer heard, and even mild statements in support of labor were grounds for charges of Red sympathies.

One important result was that radical labor leaders like William Foster were driven out of the labor movement and into the Communist

Party, which made no bones of its loyalty to the Soviet Union and world revolution.

The other strike that attracted national attention was the strike of the police in Boston. Calvin Coolidge was the governor of Massachusetts, and his tough handling of the strikers charmed his countrymen. "There is no right to strike against the public safety by anybody, anywhere, any time," he had declared in an uncharacteristically ringing phrase. The time was September, 1919. The words, Henry Stoddard wrote, "rang through the country . . . like the clear, sharp peal of a Liberty bell." It might be said parenthetically that "Liberty" was not doing well that year in any event. These initial inspiring words were followed a few days later by another "ringing" declaration. "This is the people's cause," the governor of Massachusetts announced, adding that he was determined to support "all who are supporting their own government" and that "the authority of the Commonwealth cannot be intimidated, coerced or compromised."

This is the kind of talk Americans like, especially when it is directed at others. "Everywhere," Stoddard wrote, "people applauded; everywhere newspapers gave columns to the struggle to maintain the supremacy of government." There was very little effort to discover the facts: whether, for instance, the police had legitimate grievances that the authorities had failed to respond to. There was also, clearly, much antiunion sentiment involved in the widespread public opprobrium that poured over the heads of the unhappy policemen. The public, according to Stoddard, was "not slow to rally behind a governor with the courage to challenge Samuel Gompers' contention that public servants had a right to strike even though such action imperilled public safety." In the national mood of head cracking, of extirpating radicals and troublemakers of all kinds, the Boston police provided an ideal target for self-righteous editors and conservative politicians. The strike was promptly broken, and, as it would turn out, a President made (with a hand from fortune). "Never did any man in public life," Stoddard wrote, "win the interest and confidence of a nation so completely. . . ." News-hungry reporters began digging for equally inspiring utterances of this generally taciturn and heretofore notably obscure politician. A series of undistinguished speeches were hastily gathered up with the risible title Have Faith in Massachusetts and serialized by sympathetic newspapers. The new hero was widely acclaimed "for his modesty . . . his philosophy of life . . . for the courage with which he held to his beliefs."

Almost unnoticed was a newspaper article in the Boston papers on the arrest of two Italian anarchists, Nicola Sacco and Bartolomeo Vanzetti, on May 5, 1920, for armed robbery in the course of which a guard was shot and killed. The *New York Times* gave some seven inches to their conviction, fourteen months later, for armed robbery and murder with a sentence of execution.

Not surprisingly the situation of black Americans reflected the nation's mood of angry repression. Between June, 1919, and the end of the year there were twenty-eight race riots in various American cities. A riot broke out in Longview, Texas, over a letter written to the *Defender*, a black newspaper in Chicago, describing a lynching in that town. Whites, in retribution for what they perceived to be the slander of their community, burned down a number of the homes of blacks. A three-day riot took place in Washington, D.C., on the basis of a rumor of black assaults on white women. Evident in many of the outbreaks was the determination of blacks to defend themselves from white harassment and persecution, especially by the police.

The situation was highly volatile in Chicago, where hostile encounters between blacks and whites were almost daily occurrences. Ida Wells Barnett wrote to the *Chicago Tribune:* "Just such a situation as this . . . led up to the East St. Louis riot. . . . Will the legal, moral and civic forces of this town stand idly by and take no notice of these preliminary outbreaks? . . . I implore Chicago to set the wheels of justice in motion before it is too late and Chicago be disgraced by some of the bloody outrages that have disgraced East St. Louis."

A few weeks later a young black man, Eugene Williams, crossed the unmarked line that separated the black beach from the white on Lake Michigan. Whites stoned Williams until he drowned, and when nearby police refused to make any arrests, fighting began between black and white bathers. It soon spread all over the city. White gangs stabbed or shot blacks who strayed into white districts, and a day later mobs began pulling blacks from streetcars and beating them. On the worst night of the rioting, cars filled with whites drove through black districts, firing indiscriminately at homes and businesses; twenty people were killed, and hundreds wounded. Policemen, siding with white rioters, joined in firing at blacks. By the end of the week the arrival of national guard units and rain helped suppress the rioting. For six days the city had been in the grip of mobs, white and black. In that time 38 persons had been killed, 537 injured, and more than 1,000 homes destroyed. A grand jury, appointed to investigate the riots, reported that "the colored people suffered more at the hands of white hoodlums than white people suffered at the hands of black hoodlums." The *Chicago Tribune* called for stricter segregation of the races, including a separate system of transportation. In the prosecution of the rioters racial prejudice was again evident, as many more blacks were arrested and charged than whites, although blacks had suffered twice as heavily as whites.

On the evening of May 31, 1921, word that a white mob was planning to lynch a black man spread through Greenwood, the black section of Tulsa, Oklahoma. A young black shoeshine "boy" named Dick Rowland had been accused of attempting to rape a white elevator operator. Sarah Page claimed that Rowland had tried to tear off her clothes and been frightened away by her screams. A crowd of some 400 whites collected at the courthouse jail, and, as word of the prospective lynching ran through the Greenwood area, a man got up on the stage of the Dreamland Theater and told a group of angry blacks, "We're not going to let this happen. We're going to go downtown and stop this lynching." Those men who owned guns departed to arm themselves. Some fifty armed blacks then reported to the courthouse to offer their services in protecting the prisoner from the threats of the mob. The sheriff assured them that he was prepared to repel any efforts to storm the jail on the upper floor of the courthouse, but before the black party could be persuaded to withdraw, a white man tried to wrest a .45 caliber pistol from one of them. A shot was fired, followed by the crackle of gunfire, and a dozen individuals, black and white, fell wounded.

The mob now decided to invade the Greenwood area and put the torch to the homes and businesses of blacks. Hardware stores were broken into, and guns and pistols stolen, along with ammunition. A fire was set by the invaders sometime after midnight, and fire fighters who arrived at the scene were forced to retreat by the mob. In the next twenty-four hours more than 1,000 buildings in the Greenwood section were set ablaze: they included the recently completed Mount Zion Baptist Church, the handsomest structure in the area. The Tulsa police force meanwhile devoted its efforts to arresting blacks. Mary Jones Parrish described the scene near her house: "People were seen to flee from their burning homes, some with babes in their arms and leading crying and excited children by the hand; others, old and feeble, all fleeing to safety. Yet, seemingly, I could not leave. I walked as one in a horrible dream. By this time my little girl was up and dressed . . . [A] machine gun had been installed in the granary and was raining bullets down on our section." Before the night was over, some 6,000 blacks had been interned. One of them, the well-known black surgeon A. C. Jackson, was shot and killed as a group of blacks were being rounded up.

In addition to the buildings burned, more than 50 people (most of them black) were killed, and hundreds wounded. The *New York Times* reported that 9 whites and 68 blacks had been killed.

In the same week as the Tulsa riot, Moultrie, Georgia, was the scene of a lynching reported in the *Washington Eagle*. The mob was roused by a Confederate yell and the cry "*Whoo-whoo*—let's get the nigger." Some 500 whites rushed the sheriff, seized a black prisoner, cut off his genitals, and tried to make him eat them. In a Ku Klux Klan ceremony he was chained to a tree, wood was piled around him, and he was asked if he had a last wish. He asked for a cigarette and blew smoke in the faces of his tormentors. "The pyre was lit and a hundred men and women, old and young, grandmothers among them, joined hands and danced while the Negro burned. A big dance was held in a barn nearby that evening in celebration of the burning, many people coming by automobile from nearby cities to the gala event."

The desperate situation of black people—the discrimination, the poverty, and the hardships they endured—made them especially susceptible to a "Messiah," a prophet to lead them out of the wilderness of white prejudice. In 1917 a Jamaican immigrant (by way of England and Tuskegee) named Marcus Garvey arrived in New York City and started the Universal Negro Improvement Association. Like W. E. B. Du Bois in his youth (and Booker T. Washington, who had encouraged Garvey to come to the United States), Garvey was an eloquent advocate of black self-improvement. His larger plan was the rescue of Africa from white colonizers: "organize it, develop it, arm it and make it the defender of Negroes the world over." Garvey, who based his movement on the appeal to the "black masses," ordinary working-class black men and women, found himself at odds with Du Bois's more sophisticated approach to the emancipation of American blacks and with A. Philip Randolph, who was rising to power as a black leader through the union of Pullman porters. An enthralling popular orator (Du Bois's greatest appeal was to white audiences), Garvey visited thirty-eight states, preaching the doctrine of black pride. In two years his movement enrolled hundreds of thousands of black Americans, many of them living in the ghettos of Northern cities. Together they contributed some $2,000,000 to the movement. At the association's first national convention in New York in 1921, Garvey presided in a uniform of purple, green, and black with a helmet surmounted by white feathers. Fifty thousand of his followers marched from Harlem to Madison Square Garden, past the bemused stares of white New Yorkers. At the Garden those who could crowd in declared Garvey the provisional president-general of Africa. There were accompanying religious exercises by Garvey's African Orthodox Church, with a black Christ and black Madonna. Also much in evidence were Black Cross nurses, the African Motor Corps, and, most splendid of all, the Black Eagle Flying Corps.

Garvey was tireless in expounding his theme that all things black were beautiful and indeed superior to things white. He enthusiastically supported the manufacture and sale of black dolls for black girls and told his audiences, "Every student of history . . . knows that the Negro race once ruled the world, when white men were savages and barbarians living in caves; that thousands of Negro professors . . . taught in the universities in Alexandria. . . . When Europe was inhabited by a race of cannibals, a race of savages, naked men, heathens and pagans, Africa was peopled with a race of cultured black men, who were masters in art, science and literature; men . . . who, it was said, were like the gods. . . . Why, then, should we lose hope? Black men, you were once great; you shall be great again. Lose not courage, lose not faith, go forward."

Garvey presented himself as the champion of 400,000,000 blacks. Blacks, he told his listeners, could live in the United States another 5,000 years and "never get political justice . . . or political equality. . . . We are not preaching a propaganda of hate against anybody. We love the white man; we love all humanity. . . . The white man is as necessary to the existence of the Negro as the Negro is necessary to his existence. . . . We shall march out, yes, as black American citizens, as black British subjects, as black French citizens, as black Italians or as black Spaniards, but we shall march out in answer to the cry of our fathers, who cry out to us for the redemption of our own country, our motherland, Africa. . . ."

43

The Republicans Recapture the White House

Two of the most significant events of the postwar period were the Eighteenth and Nineteenth Amendments to the Constitution, the first forbidding the manufacture and sale of intoxicating liquors and the second giving the vote to women.

From the early days of the Republic the control or prohibition of liquor had been high on the agenda of reform. Most abolitionists, notably William Lloyd Garrison himself, had been teetotalers. At the height of the pre-Civil War movement for reform a number of states had passed prohibitory laws. There had been a strong temperance element in the Republican Party from its inception (Lincoln, the reader may recall, had been a temperance lecturer), and when it proved indifferent to the cause in the years following the war, the Prohibition Party had reasserted itself with marked effect on a number of Midwestern elections. Most Populists were prohibitionists or, at the least, temperance men and women; William Jennings Bryan was a prohibitionist and a teetotal abstinence man. Temperance and/or some form of prohibition had been a central issue in the women's rights movement from the first. Susan B. Anthony had started her public career as a temperance lecturer. Frances Willard had made prohibition the dominant issue for millions of reform-minded women. Most Spiritualists and all Methodists were advocates of some program or another to do away with alcohol. So it is not surprising that the Midwestern variety of Insurgency or Progressivism contained a strong element of prohibitionism. In a considerable degree it was an East-West issue.

A revival campaign for a national Prohibition law was clearly a by-product of the era of reform. To the persistent Protestant evangel against the demon alcohol as an offense to God, as a social evil and a major impediment to the realization of a redeemed Christian republic, was added the new concern for the human body as "the Temple of God," to use the title of Victoria Woodhull's essay. The same refrain was carried by reformers of all orders and denominations, from Unitarians and Baptists to Presbyterians and Methodists, from Spiritualists to Christian Scientists and Christian Socialists (although the Socialist Party steered clear of the issue because of its desire to cater to the radical elements among the German and Irish workers). To drink, even in moderation, was to poison the body and compromise the fight for social justice. "Research" and "science" were recruited to strengthen the case for prohibition. Studies showed that insanity, criminal behavior, a variety of diseases, and early death awaited not only the alcoholic but anyone who indulged. Colleges began to insist that their athletes not drink.

A drive was also instituted in professional baseball to squelch drinking (an uphill battle), and Connie Mack, the famous manager of the Philadelphia Athletics, announced, "Alcohol slows a man down. I don't bother with youngsters that drink." Henry Ford and other industrialists instituted in their plants programs directed at informing their workers of the dangers of strong drink (the most serious danger for Ford workers was that they would be fired if they were even suspected of drinking to excess).

The Woman's Christian Temperance Union, the leader in so many social reforms, prevailed on (or bullied) publishers to include lurid accounts of the dangers of intemperance in school textbooks. The ancient link among alcohol, prostitution, and venereal disease was given fresh potency by "studies" that offered alarming statistics. A physician declared that 70 percent of venereal infections in men under the age of twenty-five were contracted while the men were inebriated. A group of prisoners in the Western Penitentiary at Philadelphia exhorted the state legislature to pass a prohibition law, declaring that 70 percent of the crime in the state was the consequence of drinking hard liquor. Of all divorces, 20 percent were attributed to alcoholism, and 45 percent of children in orphanages and children's homes were said to be the offspring of alcoholics. In addition, uncounted thousands of children were beaten and abused by drunken parents. The Committee of Fifty, composed of doctors and scientists devoted to the study of the effects of intemperance, reported that it was the sole cause of crime in 16 percent of all arrests, the primary cause in 31 percent, and a contributory cause in almost 50 percent.

Sociologists and psychologists, who were placing increasing emphasis on the environment as a determining factor in human behavior, argued that poverty was less the result of bad genes than of bad surroundings; saloons and drunken parents produced delinquent children. Virtually all the reform journals from *McClure's* (a leader in the fight for prohibitory laws) to *Harper's Weekly*, the *Atlantic Monthly*, the *Survey*, and *Collier's* carried frequent articles on the disastrous consequences of excessive, or even moderate, imbibing. Dr. Henry Smith Williams, an authority on the effects of alcohol, declared it the "most subtle, the most far-reaching, and judged by its ultimate effects, incomparably the most virulent of all poisons." If you were a drinker, you were "tangibly threatening the physical structure of your stomach, your heart, your blood-vessels, your nerves, your brain; . . . you are unequivocally decreasing your capacity for work in any field, be it physical, intellectual, or artistic; . . . you are, in some measure, lowering the grade of your mind, dulling your higher aesthetic sense, taking the finer edge off your morals . . . and . . . you may be entailing upon your descendants yet unborn a bond of uncalculable misery. . . . As a mere business proposition: Is your glass of beer, your bottle of wine, your high-ball, or your cock-tail worth such a price?"

The editor of the journal in which Williams's article appeared added that scientific investigation had shown that "every function of the normal human body is injured by the use of alcohol—even the moderate use, and that the injury is both serious and permanent."

In the face of such evidence it was a bold spirit who dared say a good word for "spirits." The consensus among the informed and the reform-minded on alcohol was virtually unanimous; the real question was what to do about it. Most socialists of various denominations took the line that alcoholism, like poverty, was a side effect of an exploitative capitalism that produced the conditions that drove workingmen to drink as the only escape from their misery (and others to drink because of the grindingly competitive character of American life) and that robbing the workingman of the consolation of his glass of beer was hardly the way to remedy the situation. In 1912 at the Socialist Convention the delegates adopted a resolution which read in part: "Poverty, overwork and overworry necessarily result in intemperance. . . . To abolish the wage system with all its evils is the surest way to eliminate the evils of alcoholism. . . . " Taking a contrary tack were such prominent Socialists as John Spargo, who pointed out that European Socialists had taken a position in favor of Prohibition. Strong drink, according to Spargo, was one of the means by which capitalism diminished revolutionary ardor and kept the masses in a passive state.

Between 1900 and 1906 many states and counties passed antisaloon or prohibitory laws until, by some estimates, approximately 40 percent of the country's population was living in dry territory. In New Hampshire 183 out of 224 towns were dry and in Vermont, 221 out of 246. In Ohio 1,150 towns were dry; there were 708 dry towns in Wisconsin, and 26 counties in Illinois. The South followed suit; by 1907 two-thirds of the Southern counties were dry. Often conflicts developed where the rural populations of counties forced cities within their boundaries to go dry. Most of the Rocky Mountain states went dry in the years following, and the Prohibition movement seemed to have acquired an irresistible momentum. But soon there were defections. As had happened many times in the past, towns, counties, cities, even wards, backslid. Just when it appeared the tide had turned strongly against it, the cause of Prohibition was saved by the outbreak of the European War. Even before the entry of the United States into the conflict, the forces urging preparedness had called for "an entire or partial ban upon the liquor traffic," in the words of the *Bankers Magazine*. The argument for moral austerity was reinforced by the argument that the grain used to make alcohol was needed to feed the starving Belgians or the hungry British or French. The preparedness prohibitionists did all they could to identify opposition to Prohibition with the German-American population and thus, somehow, with Germany and, by extension, with treason. Undoubtedly the growing suspicion of and hostility toward those immigrants who had come from the nations that constituted the Central Powers gave added impetus to the Prohibition movement. It was almost like a rebuke by the old-time American-born reformers to the dangerous class of hyphenated Americans, many of whom strongly opposed the entry of the United States into the war.

With Prohibition increasingly identified with "loyalty" as well as austerity and morality, its opponents found themselves outmaneuvered. On December 18, 1917, Congress adopted and submitted to the states the Eighteenth Amendment, prohibiting the manufacture, transportation, or sale of liquors with an alcohol content of more than one-half of 1 percent.

Almost two years later, with the amendment ratified by a two-thirds vote of the states, Congress, in October, 1919, passed, over Wilson's veto, the Volstead Act, providing the enforcement apparatus. It was a strange moment in the history of the Republic. Vineyards and breweries and distilleries closed down all over the country. Tens of thousands of workers found themselves without jobs, and millions of Americans without the consolation of a sip or a nip.

The triumph of Prohibition in the United States was, in the mind of dedicated prohibitionists, simply the first step in the redemption of the world from alcohol. The Reverend A. C. Bane declared at a convention of the World League Against Alcoholism in 1917, "America will 'go over the top' in humanity's greatest battle, and plant the victorious white standard of Prohibition upon the nation's loftiest eminence. Then . . . we will go forth with the spirit of the missionary and the crusader to help drive the demon of drink from all civilization. With America leading the way, with faith in Omnipotent God . . . we will soon . . . bestow upon mankind the priceless gift of World Prohibition."

The redemptive zeal could not be suppressed. It manifested itself in Prohibition as surely as in the somewhat more sophisticated notion of the redemption of the world by the League of Nations. For better or worse, the relationship of Americans to strong drink is one of the most persistent and perplexing issues in our history. Outside of the issue of slavery and, subsequently, of the status of black Americans, no issue has more persistently troubled the mind and the consciousness of Americans than that of temperance, of the drinking or nondrinking of alcoholic beverages. As we have noted time and again, the forces of temperance endured from generation to generation, preserving in families unbroken lines of teetotalers from father to son to grandson. Few families failed to number among their members chronic alcoholics carried to early graves. The problem of alcoholism was not a figment of the imaginations of repressive-minded Puritans; it was one of the most enduring symptoms of the psychic cost of being an American. Decade after decade it seemed to give the lie to the proposition that Americans were a "happy" people.

In an era that witnessed the accomplishments of women like Jane Addams, Ida Tarbell, Emma Goldman, Mother Jones, Kate Richards O'Hare, Florence Harriman, Elizabeth Gurley Flynn, Mabel Dodge, Edith Wharton, Willa Cather, Florence Kelley, and literally thousands of other remarkable women, one could hardly speak of the "emergence" of women (it could be argued they had "emerged" in the 1840s), but it is certainly true that they achieved a new kind of potency in American life; it is impossible to imagine the age without them. Still, they could not exercise what was considered by many Americans the most basic right of a citizen: the right to vote. Oswald Garrison Villard, proud in the spirit of his mother and his wife, had been one of eighty-four men who marched in the first "joint suffrage parade" in 1911. As the parade formed under the windows of the University Club, Villard could see the faces of his fellow club members, peering indignantly out of the windows. From the club to Union Square the marchers were booed and hissed. The men were the special objects of the spectators' jeers. "Did she make you come?" and "Who's doing the cooking while you're out?" At Union Square, the terminus of the parade, Fanny Garrison Villard spoke, as did Anna Shaw, who declared the parade a great success. She hoped that there would be 500 men at the next one and 20,000 women, concluding, "I do not know when I have enjoyed a day more and wish I could do it over again tomorrow."

Among the most vocal opponents of women's suffrage were, not surprisingly, a number of Southern Senators, prominent among them Pitchfork Ben Tillman of South Carolina, who declared that the vote would "mar the beauty and dim the luster of the glorious womanhood with which we have been familiar." George Creel replied that a substantial portion of that "glorious womanhood" was working sixty hours a week in Southern cotton mills at starvation wages. Henry Cabot Lodge was another conspicuous enemy of women's suffrage.

When a heckler called out to Anna Howard Shaw, "What about women sitting on juries?" Shaw replied, "My dear man, there are thousands of poor creatures—scrubwomen in the great office buildings, washerwomen, clerks in department stores on their feet from dawn to dark who would thank God for the chance to sit *anywhere*."

On June 4, 1919, Congress passed and sent to the states for ratification the Nineteenth Amendment, giving women the right to vote. Fourteen months later, August 26, some eight weeks before the presidential election of 1920, the requisite number of states had ratified, and the amendment became the law of the land. Seventy-two years had passed since Elizabeth Cady Stanton had startled the delegates to the Seneca Falls conference on the rights of women and distressed her father, Judge Daniel Cady, by proposing that women should have the vote.

After Wilson's stroke only his iron will sustained him. He clung tenaciously to his office and even exercised a degree of control remarkable for one so physically shattered. Yet there was an inevitable feeling of drift and uncertainty in the country and numerous problems that demanded the attention of a healthy and vigorous chief executive. "He has been ill since last October," Ray Stannard Baker wrote, "and he cannot know what is going on. He sees almost nobody; and hears no direct news. This sick man, with such enormous power, closed from the world, and yet acting so influentially upon events!"

Although Edith Wilson did not block access to her ill husband or "run the country," she did, it seems, prevent a reconciliation between the President and Colonel House. She could not forget Wilson's reaction to what he believed was House's betrayal of his most cherished principles while he was in the United States presenting the Covenant to Congress and the American people.

In January, 1920, at a Jackson Day banquet in Washington, a message from Wilson was read: "Personally I do not accept the action of the Senate of the United States as the decision of the nation. . . . If there is any doubt as to what the people of the country think on this vital matter the clear and simple way is to submit it for determination at the next election to the voters of the nation, to give the next election the form of *a great and solemn referendum*—a referendum as to the part the United States is to play in completing the settlements of the war and the prevention in the future of such outrages as Germany attempted to perpetrate."

On March 19 the treaty once more was placed before the Senate. This time it was rejected by 49 ayes to 39 noes, 9 votes shy of the necessary two-thirds. On May 15, a resolution by Philander Knox calling for a separate treaty with Germany passed by a vote of 43 to 38. A week later it passed the House, 228 to 149, and Wilson vetoed it. An effort to pass it over the President's veto failed. Henry Stoddard suspected that Wilson was content to witness the demise of the Versailles Treaty (7 or 8 Democratic votes would have given it the required two-thirds) on the ground that the party must now make him its nominee. He would then run on the issue of ratification of the treaty and be triumphantly vindicated. He believed, in Stoddard's words, "that the people would rise en masse behind his banner. . . . "

The *Nation* observed that Congress had saved the country from "acquiescing in a treaty which embodies so gross a breach of faith with the American dead in France and the Americans living everywhere who took at full value and held in honor the assertions of the President that we were in the War to safeguard democracy and advance the cause of human liberty."

A popular bit of doggerel read:

Who killed the Treaty?

"I," said Hank Lodge;
"With my little dodge
I killed the Treaty."

Who saw it die?

"I," said Bill Borah;
"It got my angora.
I saw it die."

Who'll dig the grave?

"I will," said Sherman;
"They say I'm pro-German,
I'll dig the grave."

Who'll toll the bell?

"I will," said Smoot;
"At knells I'm a beaut
I'll toll the bell."

Mrs. Wilson summoned David Houston to the White House at the end of January, 1920. "Of course, you know I did not ask you to take the trouble to come here merely to drink tea," she said to her guest. "The President asked me to tell you that he is very anxious for you to accept the Secretaryship of the Treasury." Houston assented; he was willing to do anything Wilson requested.

Houston proved a hard-nosed secretary of the treasury, believing, as he did, that there was no shortcut to economic recovery. He was also convinced that the Allies, as he noted in his journal, "must be reasonable in their exactions against the Central Powers. They must give them a chance. They, too, have been hard hit. . . . The world cannot recover as long as the central part of Europe is in chaos; and unless assistance is rendered, Germany and Austria will sink deeper into the mire and draw others in with them." But his advice did not prevail. Huge reparations continued to be exacted from Germany and Austria.

On the domestic front Houston anticipated a difficult period of adjustment for farmers as war-inflated prices fell. One consequence would be what he called "an agrarian movement" of angry farmers faced with retrenchment and foreclosures. Ignorant of the underlying causes of their difficulties, they would, he predicted, blame the bankers as they invariably did for their economic woes.

As secretary of the treasury Houston had the task of paying off the debts incurred by the war. The year 1920 was, he reported proudly, that in which "the largest collections were made from the people through taxation," something in excess of $6,700,000,000.

The problem of war debts was a serious one. Prior to our entry into the war the United States had "lent" the Allies billions of dollars. These were considered debts of the traditional kind, drawing interest and subject to repayment at some specified date after the end of the war. After our entry we continued to lend large sums of money, primarily to Great Britain and France. These also were considered debts subject to repayment, but they were obviously of a different character from loans made during the period of American neutrality. In any event the United States government made clear that it expected the prompt payment of all debts. To discreet British inquiries about whether some loans might be extended or forgiven, the unequivocal answer was no. "The views of the United States Government have not changed," the chancellor of the exchequer was crisply informed, "and it is not prepared to consent to the remission of any part of the debt of Great Britain to the United States." The British, in turn, had no notion of not extracting the last penny of reparations from Germany. In fact, they took the line that they would pay the United States what it was owed when Germany paid Great Britain. This did not suit David Houston. The United States, he noted, "had vigorously protested against the excessive amount of reparations which was fixed [for Germany]." It was "an impossible amount," and for the British to attach their payments to a schedule of reparations was simply unacceptable.

Shortly after he had assumed the duties of secretary of the treasury, Houston and his wife were invited to dine at the White House. It was their first visit since the President's stroke, four months earlier. It was, Houston wrote, "a somewhat pathetic experience." Wilson "made a brave show of good spirits." He told his favorite stories "and was exceptionally kindly and friendly." Houston was deeply touched when, as he and his wife parted from the Wilsons, the President laid his hand on Houston's arm and "with some emotion" said, "Houston, old man, God bless you." It was, Houston added, "the first evidence of personal affection or emotion I ever saw him exhibit."

The first Cabinet meeting attended by the President since his stroke was held in April, 1920. Almost seven months had passed. The change in his appearance was startling. Since he could walk only with great difficulty, he had seated himself at the head of the table around which the Cabinet commonly met before any of the members arrived so that his disability would not be evident. The President, Houston noted, "looked old, worn, and haggard. It was enough to make one weep to look at him. One of his arms was useless. In repose, his face looked very much as usual, but, when he tried to speak, there were marked evidences of his trouble. His jaw tended to drop on one side. . . . His voice was very weak and strained. . . . He put up a brave front and spent several minutes cracking jokes."

There was a long silence. The President seemed to be waiting for someone to take the initiative. After some desultory conversation Dr. Grayson appeared at the door, and a few minutes later Mrs. Wilson came in to suggest that the meeting had best be ended.

With the League defeated in the Senate, the President's attention now shifted to the upcoming presidential elections. Despite his illness and virtual incapacity (it was still by no means clear what his condition was, so carefully was he guarded by his wife and Dr. Grayson), Wilson apparently clung to the hope that the delegates at the Democratic Convention meeting in San Francisco would nominate him as their presidential candidate or, failing that, choose an eloquent champion of the League who would make that the central issue of the campaign.

As the elections of 1920 approached, it proved hard on political prognosticators. The mood of the country, hysteria over Reds aside, remained highly uncertain. In the months prior to the Republican Convention the front-runner was General Leonard Wood, formerly governor, first of Cuba and then of the Philippines, and chief of staff of the United States Army. Wood was a huge man who emanated energy and ambition. Oswald Garrison Villard wrote, somewhat unflatteringly, of him: "Of all the men whom I have known and studied

Leonard Wood seems to me to have been the most blindly ambitious. . . . The moneyed interests supported him enthusiastically when
he sought the Presidential nomination and they poured out money in
such quantities that . . . the General was the center of a scandal. . . .
He lacked vision and background, read little, knew nothing about
economics and modern trends, and would have taken the Big Business
viewpoint as to labor and strikes."

His principal rival was Frank Lowden, governor of Illinois. There
was also a bit of a boom among Progressives for Herbert Hoover. There
had been talk as early as 1918 of drawing Hoover into political activity
on behalf of the Democrats. Florence Harriman felt the "great engineer" lacked the "flare" for politics. "He's like a cat with water: gingerly
impatient with our political talk," she wrote in her diary. "He doesn't
like the amusing indirectness of getting things done in a political way,
and that means he won't like Congress!" Ray Stannard Baker noted
that Hoover was "an able and skilled administrator, with years of training in large affairs. . . . There is no other public man in America who
knows every phase of the foreign situation as comprehensively as Herbert Hoover, and none who has been able to deal more skillfully with
complicated international problems." But when Baker had an opportunity to talk further with Hoover, he was disconcerted by the man's
limitations, his stubborn conventionality and lack of vision. The Hoover
boom died aborning, and the remnants of the Progressives in the
Midwest went to the Republican Convention of 1920 committed to
Wood as the closest candidate they could find to their adored Roosevelt,
although William Allen White was frank to confess that he disliked
Wood's "military showmanship."

Henry Stoddard tried to start a boom for Coolidge. He recruited
some fellow publishers who had been equally entranced by the Massachusetts governor's handling of the Boston police strike, but they
found their path blocked by Senator Lodge, who controlled the Massachusetts delegates and rejected out of hand the notion of nominating
for president on the Republican ticket "a man who lives in a two-family
house."

Once again White was both a delegate and a journalist covering
the convention for a syndicate of newspapers stretching across the
country. White's Kansas friend (and governor of the state) Henry Justin
Allen was given the task by Wood's managers of writing a speech for
their candidate, but they objected so strongly to any statement that
might be considered in the slightest degree controversial that the result

was a tepid talk that aroused no enthusiasm. Wood's supporters thereupon accused Allen of deliberately sabotaging their candidate.

White sat with the Kansas delegation in a blue and white striped shirt, fanning himself with a new $25 Panama hat. Watching the convention go about its business, he decided he had never seen one "so completely dominated by sinister predatory economic forces as was this." It gave off emanations of "plutocracy" and "amalgamated wealth." Indeed, it symbolized and ratified the "return of the capitalists," the remarkable revival of the forces represented by the National Association of Manufacturers in league with Wall Street. "Every delegation that I knew much about," White wrote, "was loaded with one, two, or half a dozen representatives of national commodity interests—oil, railroads, telephones, steel, coal, and textiles." Harry Daugherty, a lobbyist for Ohio industry, had warned White and other Progressives that Warren Harding, Senator from that state and a small-town newspaper editor—a handsome, affable man without a mind of his own—would be chosen in the proverbial "smoke-filled room" by the leaders of the Republican right wing and nominated after other candidates had been given "a play."

For two days the deadlock between Wood and Lowden continued in temperatures which soared above 100 degrees in the convention hall. "The multitude sweated, stank, and lifted from the floor sheeplike faces which fell under the hypnosis of the American madness of the hour," White wrote. When he saw Harding on a hotel elevator, the Ohioan had a two days' growth of beard, his eyes were bloodshot, his clothing was disheveled and it was clear to White that he had been drinking. He looked little like the "oiled and curled Assyrian bull" that, four years earlier, had turned back Roosevelt's bid for fusion between the Republican regulars and the Progressives to the "yipping delight" of the delegates.

Finally, word came to White of the move to nominate Harding. His response was, "If you nominate Harding, you will disgrace the Republican party. You will bring shame to your country." But the Kansas delegation led the move to Harding, and White marched with his delegation around the humid hall. In the years that followed, White tried to understand the impulse that led him to rise and join his fellow Kansans. It seemed to him, finally, that it was "the death of Theodore Roosevelt and the rout of his phalanx of reform, together with the collapse of Wilsonian liberalism. . . ." Those developments, coupled with "the eclipse of the elder La Follette's leadership," had created in

White's heart "a climax of defeat." He concluded, "I was too heartsick to rise and fight." He salvaged something of his conscience by casting one of nine votes for Hoover in the closing minutes of the convention.

From Roosevelt to Harding traced a path that seemed to White to measure the decline of the Republic. Harding had been sponsored by Cincinnati's "iron boss," George Cox, as a pliant tool of Cox's machine. Elected to the Senate, he became, in George Creel's words, "the unasking, unquestioning rubber stamp for Lodge, Penrose and other Republican leaders." To Baker, Harding appeared "a large, benevolent-looking, vague, tired human being," with nothing "sure, strong, clear, about him or his speech. . . . Not a word of vitalizing leadership, not a suggestion of courage, vision, power. It was pathetic. . . ." During the opening days of the convention Harding had been the essence of geniality. With little notion that the nomination could come to him, he spent most of his time greeting old friends. His principal concern was not to miss the opportunity to file for Senator from Ohio. His friends insisted that in the event of a deadlock in the convention he stood an excellent chance of becoming a compromise candidate: a man without strong convictions—or powerful enemies.

Once nominated, Harding tried to persuade Hiram Johnson to run on the Republican ticket for vice-president, but Johnson refused, and a delegate from Oregon began chanting the name of Coolidge. The Oregon delegates had come to the convention to vote for Coolidge for president. Since they had failed in that effort, they were determined to press for his nomination as vice-president. They succeeded. The "floor," indifferent to the wishes of the party leaders, rose up spontaneously for Coolidge.

Oswald Garrison Villard was sitting with newspapermen from Massachusetts when Coolidge was nominated for vice-president. The newsmen "laughed heartily, thinking it was a great joke." Robert O'Brien of the *Boston Herald* took a more serious view. "You know . . ." he told Villard, "I have known all our public men since Grover Cleveland's time. This is the worst man I ever knew in politics." O'Brien then turned to a Quaker friend and said, "I will bet thee a dinner that Harding will die and Coolidge become President." Creel thought Coolidge only a shade better than Harding, referring to the governor "as distinguishable from the furniture only when he moved."

In addition to nominating Harding and Coolidge, the delegates did manage to get a few Progressive planks drafted by the League of Women Voters into the platform presented to the convention: support of the principle of "collective bargaining" (at Gompers's instance), a promise to recognize Soviet Russia, and an endorsement of a World Court to decide disputes between nations.

All efforts to get a plank endorsing a League of Nations with the "reservations" earlier insisted upon by the Republicans were turned back by William Borah and Joseph Medill McCormick. Elihu Root was appealed to to draft a compromise. His plank was, in White's words, "fearfully and wonderfully made. It meant nothing except that it frankly did mean nothing. . . .

"The Republican party of 1920," White added, "had [a] bitter hatred of Wilson and anything Wilson stood for. . . . It was 'isolationist' for spite and hatred, governed by its emotions, and not amenable to reason. Out of that witch's pot of mad malice rose the stench which produced Harding's election and became the Harding administration." Yet Wilson, as White reminded his readers, was in large part responsible for that witch's pot. His "suspicious jealousies, bitterness, and cold malevolence toward his opponents" spawned a countervailing hostility that helped overturn the dearest hope of his heart.

Henry Stoddard, self-styled Progressive and devoted disciple of Theodore Roosevelt, saw nothing inconsistent in throwing his support to Warren Harding once Roosevelt's death had removed him from the scene. He was proud to be a member of the delegation that traveled to Marion, Ohio, to inform Harding officially of what he already knew: that he was his party's candidate for the presidency. Stoddard, Harry Daugherty, Senator T. Coleman Du Pont of Delaware, and several other politicians walked to Harding's "modest village home" to greet the candidate, "physically a splendid type of manhood" (of his intellectual qualifications Stoddard, perhaps wisely, said nothing). The candidate, apparently on his own, found his campaign slogan. Whatever the question was, Harding had an infallible answer: "Don't let's cheat 'em!"

There was a substantial measure of heartbreak for the Progressives in the outcome of the Republican Convention. All their hopes and aspirations lay in the dust. The capitalist counterrevolution was triumphant, and the Progressive dream of "distributive justice," of a more just and humane society, seemed as ephemeral as the evening mists.

When James Bryce wrote to William Allen White early in 1917 to ask what "the radicals or progressives of the West" wanted, White had replied that "they wanted government ownership of the rail-

roads. . . . They want drastic inheritance taxes, and they want the proceeds of the inheritance taxes spent in internal improvements under
expert direction. They want to break the alliance between politics and
big business. They want to equalize opportunity much more than it is
equalized, for instance, on the Atlantic seaboard." They wanted old
age pensions "and that the national resources should be operated along
socialistic lines—the coal, the oil, the water power, the forests and the
minerals"—all these and a "rural credit law which will take care of the
tenant farmers. . . . They desire a genuine redistribution of the wealth
of the country," and they desired it now "and at any commercial cost. . . ."
None of those Progressive goals had been achieved; indeed, they seemed
further off than ever. White puzzled over the deeper meanings of the
reaction. Certainly the war must carry a heavy responsibility for the
collapse of the liberal and/or radical cause. But to say that was to
obscure the real issue. What had happened to the American people?
Why had the populace at large, the millions of voters who went to the
polls (as well as the millions who stayed away), withdrawn their support
from the bright visions of the Progressive heyday? "Perhaps," White
reflected, "our own pride and fear and newly acquired and not quite
understood leadership of the world gave us a vulgar, rapacious arrogance which dramatized itself in the idolatry of the power of money.
If it had not produced a Harding it might, indeed probably would,
have expressed itself in some other way as evil, as tragic, and as shameful." While "evil," "tragic," and "shameful" may seem a bit excessive
to describe poor Harding's regime, the words bear eloquent testimony
to the feelings of a devoted Progressive who was also an experienced
politician with a journalist's eye for the unvarnished fact. So we come
back again to the trauma of the war, which had so divided the nation,
and, more than the war, those things ancillary to it or the consequences
of it: in the United States the ruthless hunting down and systematic
denigration of all who opposed it. And, finally, to the paranoia produced in the United States by the Russian Revolution. Here Americans
may well have been victims of their own rather simpleminded notion
of how history "happened," of its vectors and its underlying structure.
Americans, for example, had always believed, as we have often had
occasion to note, in progress, progress "on and up." They had believed
in a benign God who had singled out the people of the United States
as, somehow, his Chosen People, the Chosen of Second Dispensation,
a Christian people. As the religious view of a providential God favoring
His own lost some of its potency, it was shored up by the conviction

of the Enlightenment that the people could perfect themselves and ultimately their society by the use of Reason. Their vision of the future was, in any event, a highly optimistic one, in which tomorrow would be better than today *ad infinitum.*

The Russian Revolution was the first serious challenge to the complex of ideas that constituted the American consciousness. There appeared with startling suddenness on the stage of world history a wholly "new" nation, one that arrogated to itself what had previously been America's virtually unchallenged mission: to adumbrate the future; to establish the terms on which the future must take place. Soviet Russia not only challenged the United States' claim to be the custodian of the future, but cast the United States in the role of a reactionary villain, the enemy of equality and social justice in the world. As the principal capitalist nation it was the principal obstacle to a worldwide utopian order (or at least the Marxist version of utopia) in which equality and justice would reign supreme. To a people who viewed history as the unfolding of God's plan for mankind, the hostility of the Russians toward all forms of religion (except, of course, the religion of Marxism, which they insisted was not Religion but Science) was an outrageous blasphemy. To the Darwinian, who believed in history as ruthless competition for the survival of the fittest, the rise of Russia appeared as the ultimate test of American power and American will, a final struggle for supremacy: the American way or the path of the godless Bolsheviks. For the dedicated non-Communist socialist, anarchist, or liberal reformer it raised a whole different set of questions and anxieties, the most troubling of which was that the Russian Revolution might be "right," might indeed be the wave of the future that, after it had purged itself of its excesses, would point the way to the universal order that every reformer yearned for. The power of the Revolution was that it rode on the crest of that passion for social justice which, as we have seen, had swelled to a great tide in the late nineteenth and early twentieth centuries. So there was this tormenting question: Was the Revolution, with all its horror and brutality, its indifference to life and relentless extirpation of counterrevolutionaries and, what was even more troubling, of dissident revolutionaries, after all, the hope of mankind? Were the doubts and misgivings that it raised in the minds of all but the most fanatical merely bourgeois sentimentalities, fatal weaknesses in soldiers of the class war? Perhaps the shrewdest ideological ploy of the Marxists was to plant just this anxiety: that any hesitation about injustice or brutality carried out in the name of the Revolution was the consequence of one's inability to transcend an irrelevant or counterrevolutionary middle-class morality. If the "end" was justice for all, to cavil at the "means" was at the best sentimentality and at the worst the betrayal of the workers.

It is small wonder that Americans were confused, demoralized, and alarmed by world events clearly beyond their control. The isolationism represented by Borah was one perfectly understandable, if not entirely rational, response. Another was to identify any native dissent or dissenters as furthering the cause of the Reds, the bloody-minded atheistic Communists bent on the destruction of America and, equally important, of American influence in the world. Still another response—that initially of a small portion of the surviving radical-liberal alliance which had so recently dominated, if not the actual political life of the country, then the major channels of public discourse—was to abandon all pretense of critical judgment and simply to accept whatever the rulers of Soviet Russia did and whatever their theoreticians declared as the right and true. Once an intelligent man or woman had crossed that line, he or she could no longer be reached by rational argument or even by simple facts. If the Supreme Soviet had declared, on the basis of the Marxist doctrine, that the earth was flat, one suspects that the faithful would have swallowed the new dogma without a hiccup.

Such views, of course, helped explain the resurgence of capitalism. Capitalism, once widely denounced from pulpit and platform as godless greed and self-seeking, had, it now appeared, formed a *concordat cordial* with God in the form of Protestant Christianity and, most surprising of all, with the evangelical and fundamentalist wings of Christianity that not long ago had been among its severest critics. Faced by a choice between capitalism, newly affiliated with the Almighty, and "godless communism," the choice was plainly capitalism.

So it might perhaps be said that the most serious charge that could be leveled against bolshevism was that it made capitalism respectable by comparison. Prior to the Russian Revolution, as we have seen, it was almost impossible to find an intelligent and liberal spirit who had a good word to say about it. Not only was no one of any intellectual pretensions prepared to defend capitalism, but it was not regarded by its friendlier critics as so much a final system as an evolving process, moving toward greater and greater social justice. Now, since communism was proclaimed as the final form of social and economic organization, as that utopia for which humanity had so long yearned, capitalism was increasingly put forward as "a final form" in its own right. It was declared a superior utopia to communism rather than an evolving political and economic process. The finality of communism produced the counterfinality of capitalism. Moreover, social reforms long advocated were increasingly attacked as "communistic" or "socialistic." Such charges were not, of course, new, but now they were identified with lack of patriotism, if not outright "godless" treason. If communism was the ultimate enemy, and Russia its home, then it followed that Russia was the ultimate enemy and that anything that smacked of communism (and the range was wide) was suspect or, far worse, un-American.

Three weeks after the Republican Convention the Democrats opened in San Francisco. The geography was eloquent. San Francisco was a Pacific coast city boasting a unique urbanity, the best restaurants in the country, the most exhilarating panoramas, the most hospitable inhabitants. The site was a belated recognition of the importance of the Western Democrats. Wilson, hopeful to the end, apparently relied on Postmaster General Albert Burleson and the secretary of the navy, Josephus Daniels, to lead the fight to secure his renomination. Secretary of State Bainbridge Colby was dispatched to reinforce Daniels and Burleson. If that was the plan, it failed to materialize. Colby and Wilson's other emissaries found a mood of stubborn resistance to Wilson among the delegates. His bad health, his obsessive concern with the treaty and the League had left most Democrats disenchanted. If Colby was, in fact, waiting for an opportunity to put Wilson's name in nomination and stampede the convention, it never came. Wilson's party and his country had rejected him. He had fallen in a few months from heights no American president had ever ascended to—a world leader, a symbol for millions of the hope for a world freed at last from the threat of war and tyranny.

When Al Smith, the reform governor of New York, was placed in nomination, the delegates burst into the old songs—"Tammany," "The Sidewalks of New York," "Daisy Belle"—while an organ played. "Al Smith is the greatest governor New York has ever seen," Florence Harriman, a delegate, wrote, "and he was a fish peddler in his youth! Of course," she added, "his religion (R.C.) bars him from the Presidency, at least for the present." Mrs. Harriman gave her support to William McAdoo, the "Crown Prince," as his enemies called him. "Now," Harriman noted at 11:30 P.M. of the convention's opening day, "to soft organ-music a man is reciting verses of the 'Battle Hymn of the Republic.' A beautiful soprano voice floats from the far-distant corner of the top gallery singing the air of the chorus. Then the whole twelve thousand people . . . join in singing the chorus. It is grand and impressive and gives one chills up and down one's spine." Bryan appeared on the speaker's platform, in his old familiar alpaca coat, arm in arm with Carter Glass, the courtly Virginian, the latter to speak for the platform committee. "We favor the League of Nations." Enormous applause. "All the planks of the League of Women Voters are included in the platform," Florence Harriman noted proudly.

Slowly but surely the nomination slipped away from McAdoo as James Cox, the lackluster governor of Ohio, gained strength. To Florence Harriman the principal objection to McAdoo seemed distressingly personal: He was Wilson's son-in-law. In the end it was another Ohio newspaper editor-cum-politician who won the nomination. Cox was an able and intelligent man, but he lacked "color." There was no passion or vibrancy in his temperament or in his speeches. He was everything that Wilson was not—agreeable, personable, accommodating, and unexciting. With his nomination the Democrats, like the Republicans, declared officially that the days of reform were over, that politics-as-usual was back in command of the party.

Cox chose as his running mate the handsome young political "comer," Franklin Delano Roosevelt, whose ready smile and ebullient manner reminded many people of his famous cousin. Walter Lippmann wrote to Roosevelt that "your nomination is the best news in many a long day. . . . When parties can pick a man like Frank Roosevelt there is a decent future in politics." An enthusiastic reporter for the *New York Post* described the vice-presidential nominee as having "the figure of an idealized college football player, almost the poster type in public life . . . making clean, direct and few gestures; always with a smile ready to share. . . . He speaks with a strong clear voice, with a tenor note in it which rings—sings, one is tempted to say—in key with . . . [an] intangible, utterly charming and surely vote-winning quality."

In a more pessimistic mood Lippmann wrote to Graham Wallas: "There is no pretending that the atmosphere is cheerful here. It is not. The hysteria has turned to apathy and disillusionment in the general public, and cynicism in most of my friends. I feel that we shall not have immediate influence in America for perhaps a decade, but I am not discouraged because we can use the time well to re-examine our ideas." Lippmann described the presidential candidates as "provincial, ignorant politicians entirely surrounded by special interests, operating in a political vacuum. Nobody believes in anything. Nobody wants anything very badly that he thinks he can get out of politics . . . nobody will be enthusiastic about anything until a generation grows up that has forgotten how violent we were and how unreasonable."

The Socialist Party Convention meeting in New York early in May had unanimously nominated their imprisoned leader, Eugene V. Debs. The Socialist Labor Party nominated W. W. Cox, while a political new-comer, the Farmer-Labor Party, entered a candidate, P. P. Christensen of Utah. The Single Tax Party made an unexpected appearance as well, and of course the Prohibitionists checked in with a quadrennial candidate.

After its brief April session the Cabinet did not meet again until October, 1920. Now it was evident that the President's eyesight was badly impaired. Each Cabinet member was announced to Wilson, who said some perfunctory word of greeting. The outcome of the presidential election was discussed, and the President expressed confidence that Cox would defeat Harding. Houston, anxious to prepare the President for what seemed to him inevitable defeat, pointed out "that the issues were very complex, that people had been hit in many directions by the war and its aftermath, that there was much soreness and some hysteria, that there had been no effective presentation of the Democratic views," that Cox had waged an inept campaign in which he had attempted to put as much distance as possible between himself and the President *and* the League of Nations.

"You need not worry," Wilson replied. "The American people will not turn Cox down and elect Harding. A great moral issue is involved. The people can and will see it. In the long run, they do the right thing."

Later Houston noted in his journal, "What a drop there will be to either Cox or Harding. If Mr. Harding is elected, the contrast will be painful. It will be somewhat tragic to have a man of Mr. Wilson's intellect and high standards succeeded by a man of Mr. Harding's mediocre mind and ordinary standards of thinking and action. . . . Mr. Harding will not be a leader. He cannot be. He has never stood for any great cause. He knows very little, has no vision, very little sense of direction, and no independence. He was not nominated to lead. He was selected because he was colourless and pliable. If he is elected he will be the tool of such tried leaders as Lodge, Penrose and others."

Warren Harding looked presidential, but his statements on the

League were confusing and suggested that the candidate himself was befuddled. He declared the League impotent, a strange charge since it was the refusal of the United States to enter it, it might be argued, that made it impotent. Then he stated boldly that the proper substitute for it was "a society of free nations, or an association of free nations, or a league of free nations, animated by considerations of right and justice, instead of might and self-interest, and not merely proclaimed an agency in pursuit of peace, but so organized and so participated in as to make the actual attainment of peace a reasonable possibility. Such an association I favor with all my heart. . . . One need not care what it is called."

Some of Harding's classic sentences defied parsing (or understanding): "No one may justly deny the equality of opportunity which made us what we are. We have mistaken preparedness to embrace it to be a challenge of the realities, and due concern for making all citizens fit for participation will give added strength of citizenship and magnify our achievement." And again: "Our revisions, reformations, and evolutions reflect a deliberate judgment."

When the election returns were counted, Harding was the victor by a margin of more than 7,000,000 votes—many of them the votes of the newly enfranchised women voters—16,152,200 to 9,147,353—and 404 electoral votes to 127. In 1912 Wilson had won with 6,286,214, while Roosevelt and Taft had tallied some 7,500,000 between them. One of the least qualified presidential candidates ever to run for the office had been elected by the largest percentage of the popular vote in the nation's history.

When one recalls the impassioned and apocalyptic rhetoric of the champions of women's suffrage, predicting that it would bring with it a nobler and purer America, it is ironic to reflect that the first national election in which women participated resulted in the victory of Warren Harding.

Debs polled more than 900,000 votes; the Prohibition candidate (a candidate, it might be said, without an issue since the passage of the Volstead Act) received 189,408 reflex votes. The vote was a crushing repudiation of Wilson and the Democrats, a vote for business as usual.

One of the most poignant moments of Wilson's last months in the White House came when Mrs. Wilson invited Ray Stannard Baker and a few of the President's closest associates to the White House to view the films of his triumphant entry into Paris on the eve of the peace conference. It was the first time Baker had seen the President since his stroke. He was shocked at his appearance. He came "shuffling slowly with a cane . . . his left arm inert, his left side drooping . . . a stooped, gray-faced, white-haired old man," yet he gave Baker such a "sense of unconquerable will, of untamable life, as cannot well be described." The White House itself gave off a mortuary air. The furniture had been packed away except for a few shrouded chairs; the rooms echoed emptily to the steps of the little party of guests. They were seated on the chairs; the movie projector whirred and the film began. "With the first brilliantly lighted episode," Baker wrote, "we were in another world; a resplendent world, full of wonderful and glorious events. . . . There was the President himself . . . very erect, very tall—lifting his hat to shouting crowds." There was the president of France, the Arc de Triomphe, marching men, statesmen and dignitaries, and always the wildly cheering crowds. Then the film was over. Darkness fell on the little party. As the lights were turned on, eyes turned to the President. He rose laboriously, assisted by an aide, turned, and shuffled out of the room alone, "without looking aside and without speaking."

Wilson's last message to Congress, a substantial portion of it written by David Houston, was a wise and moderate document. The war had made the United States "a great creditor nation." We had lent more than $9,000,000,000 to the Allies. Moreover, we had an excess of exports over imports running at some $4,000,000,000 a year. In the face of this enormous imbalance, we insisted on prompt payment of all debts by a war-devastated Europe and then seemed determined to erect *tariff barriers to redress the balance*. It was a wildly inconsistent and illogical policy that could result only in global financial disaster. "If we wish to have Europe settle her debts, governmental or commercial, we must be prepared to buy from her, and if we wish to assist Europe and ourselves by the export either of food, of raw material, or of finished products, we must be prepared to welcome commodities which we need and which Europe will be prepared, with no little pain, to send us. Clearly," Wilson added, "this is no time for the erection of high trade barriers." But a Republican Congress was determined to revert to its atavistic ways. Protection was less a rational policy than an ancient article of faith.

The last Cabinet meeting of the Wilson administration took place on March 1, 1921. When the President was asked if he would take advantage of his new status as a private citizen to write his own account of the events of his administration, he replied in the negative. What, then, would he do? He replied, sardonically, "I am going to try to teach ex-presidents how to behave." He paused a moment and added, "There will be one very difficult thing for me, however, to stand, and that is Mr. Harding's English." So he was a schoolteacher to the end.

The secretary of state made a brief speech on behalf of himself and his colleagues. It had been "a great distinction to serve you and with you in the most interesting and fateful times of modern history. It has been a most satisfactory and inspiring service. We shall keep watch of your progress toward better health with affectionate interest and pray that your recovery may be rapid."

Houston started to speak, but he noticed that Wilson, his lips trembling and tears in his eyes, was trying to say something. He paused, and with obvious effort the President said, "Gentlemen, it is one of the handicaps of my physical condition that I cannot control myself as I have been accustomed to do. God bless you all." The members of the Cabinet rose and passed out of the room, shaking the thin, blue-veined, palsied hand as they left.

On inauguration day, Joseph Tumulty described the ride from the White House to the Capitol. "From the physical appearance of the two men seated beside each other in the automobile, it was plain to the casual observer who was the outgoing and who the incoming President. On the right sat President Wilson, gray, haggard, broken. He interpreted the cheering from the crowds that lined the Avenue as belonging to the President-elect and looked straight ahead." When Baker visited the Wilsons a few days after the inauguration, he received their blessing as the editor of Wilson's papers and as his official biographer. Wilson looked more gaunt and weary than ever; only the eyes burned undimmed in the drawn face. A book of detective stories and a worn Bible and some chocolates were on a stand by his bed. Behind the burning eyes Baker sensed an unfathomable bitterness and even more an oceanic sadness. Already the country was trying to forget him. His successor promised "normalcy," whatever that was.

In defeat Wilson's religious faith gave him strength to endure disappointment and humiliation. "It is all right," he told an interviewer. "Perhaps we shall be the better for the delay; the world was led to it [the League] by its sufferings; it might not have worked just yet; to be a sure success a League of Nations must come not from suffering but from the hearts and spirits of men. We are still in darkness but I am sure it is the darkness that eventually lightens. I realize now that I am only an empty tenement, a tool that has served its purpose in God's hand. I was stricken because it was His way of doing things. It was His will to set me aside; He knows what is best. I am content with the record as it stands."

The new President made an encouraging start. He assembled, on what principle it is not entirely clear, one of the ablest Cabinets of any president since Lincoln. Charles Evans Hughes made a highly distinguished and competent secretary of state. If Andrew Mellon was not only a representative of big business but himself a millionaire many times over, he was an able man, a great connoisseur, and a capable secretary of the treasury. Hoover had already demonstrated his remarkable organizational ability and was an excellent appointment as secretary of commerce and labor. Will Hays made a good postmaster general in that not very demanding office, and Charles Dawes, as director of the budget, instituted a number of important reforms.

Harding's worst Cabinet appointment, Senator Albert B. Fall as secretary of the interior, obscured his better ones. Hearing of Fall's appointment, David Houston noted that "he was one of a crowd that we had been fighting for a number of years . . . he had about the same interest in the conservation of the natural resources of the nation that a tiger has in a lamb . . . " and William Allen White described him as "a tall, gaunt, unkempt, ill visaged" man with "a disheveled spirit behind restless eyes," looking like a "patent medicine vender . . . a cheap, obvious faker. . . ."

Harding improved the good impression his Cabinet appointments had made by pardoning a number of individuals imprisoned under the wartime Espionage Act, the most famous being Eugene Debs. William Allen White encountered a group of his friends outside the White House shortly after the inauguration. It included Oswald Garrison Villard. The party had an appointment with Harding to plead for the pardon of Debs. Villard asked White to join them, and he readily agreed. When White and Villard had finished making the case for a pardon and the President had responded politely, one of the women in the party called out, "Mr. President . . . we demand a yes-or-no answer right now!" Harding replied that his office forbade him from replying "as I should like to if I were elsewhere!" When the others had left, Harding told White, "Of course, I want to do something for old Debs. I think I can."

When Lincoln Steffens visited Debs in the Federal penitentiary at Atlanta to inform him that Harding intended to pardon him, Debs expressed no elation. "He was a happy man in prison," Steffens wrote, "he loved everybody there, and everybody loved him—warden, guards, and convicts." Debs pressed Steffens for details about the Russian Revolution. He had protested its "outrages." "It was not socialist," he insisted. ". . . Like so many reds who rejected Bolshevism, Debs the socialist could not abide the violence, bloodshed, tyranny," Steffens added. "They all had their mental pictures of the heaven on earth that was coming, and this was not what they expected." Steffens urged Debs to "wait and hear more about it, even go to Russia and see for himself, before judging of the Soviet Republic."

Prior to his release from prison Debs was brought to Washington for a meeting with Attorney General Harry Daugherty. Daugherty wrote: "We talked freely for several hours. He unfolded frankly his ideas on government, his ideas on religion, his own case, the cause of Socialism, his beliefs and disbeliefs. A more eloquent and fascinating recital I never heard. . . . I found him a charming personality with a deep love for his fellow man."

Debs was released from Atlanta on December 24, 1921. Soon afterward he made a speech "denouncing . . . the revolution and all its works . . ." as Steffens put it.

The idea of the League of Nations proved remarkably tenacious. Many of the old Progressives found a new cause and took a new lease on life as advocates of the League. Most peace groups endorsed it. William Allen White was one of a number of prominent Republicans, a group that included Herbert Hoover and Elihu Root as well as Charles Evans Hughes and William Taft, who addressed an open letter to Harding asking him to support the League of Nations.

For the very considerable body of liberals/Progressives who had staked so much on American participation in the League of Nations, the World Court became an issue of almost as much emotional intensity. American participation would be a face-saving act that would demonstrate that the United States was not entirely sunk in the selfish pursuit of material gain. Harding found himself, in White's words, "sadly beset" by a formidable array of prominent Republicans including once again Hughes, his secretary of state, and Hoover, his secretary of commerce in his own Cabinet, and Root and Taft outside. In the Senate a faction led by Borah pressed him relentlessly to keep out. Harding's "solution" was to call a disarmament conference in Washington to demonstrate his commitment to peace. William Allen

White wrote that "the response of the people to that call, a glorious flare-up of faith which Wilson had fanned to flame in 1917 and 1918, was lovely to behold. . . . The nation rejoiced in pride at America's part in summoning the conference." White went to cover the conference "with something like the exultation of spirit that had taken me to the peace conference in Paris." It was a moment of pure euphoria when it seemed that something might indeed by salvaged from the debacle of the war. The extremity of feeling which it aroused and the excessive hopes which it engendered were perhaps the most vivid demonstration of the trauma of the Versailles Treaty itself and its subsequent rejection by the Senate.

The U.S. Senate and House of Representatives, the Supreme Court, the diplomatic corps, and journalists by the dozens surrounded the actual delegates seated about a U-shaped table for the opening ceremonies. A Baptist minister gave the invocation (something notably missing from the Paris Peace Conference, the pious noted), issuing thereby, as White noted, "official credentials to God in the Disarmament Conference." Harding followed with a greeting to the delegates, declaring, "Inherent rights are of God and the tragedies of the world originated in their attempted denial." He asked, "How can humanity justify or God forgive the World War unless its fruits shall be fruits of permanent peace? . . . We have no fears; we have no sordid ends to serve; we suspect no enemy; we contemplate or apprehend no conquest. . . . We only wish to do with you that finer nobler thing which no nation can do alone."

The climactic moment of the opening ceremony came with the speech by Secretary of State Hughes. Strikingly handsome, erect, and commanding in manner, he spoke with obvious feeling and moving eloquence. "His words," White wrote, "rang out with a trumpet clearness. . . ." America was, belatedly, asserting its role of leadership in the world; "a genuine hush of awe" fell over the large audience. Hughes's dramatic proposal was that the assembled nations agree to the destruction of a total of 2,000,000 tons of naval vessels as proof of their dedication to the cause of world peace. The effect was like a bombshell in White's opinion. At the end of Hughes's address many of the Senators in the gallery rose to their feet to lead the cheering "in a mad chorus of approval; that lasted for ten minutes and sounded more like an American political convention than an international gathering. . . . Hats waved, handkerchiefs fluttered, men shook one another's hands, hugged one another, slapped one another, exhibited every kind of animal delight of which human beings are capable in their high moments." Rules of order and laws of decorum were forgotten in the exuberance of the transcendent instant. The crowd began a chant for the French prime minister, Aristide Briand. William Jennings Bryan thought the cry—"Bree-an, Bree-an"—was for him and started to rise, but friends sitting beside him yanked on his coattail, and he "fell back into his chair smiling kindly, but dazed and confused." It fell to Arthur Balfour, with his "exact but hesitant British manner" and splendid English, to quiet the crowd.

White, who had been witness to most important national gatherings and conventions since the McKinley nomination in 1896 (including the ecstatic days of the Bull Moose Convention), reflected in old age that "of all human conclaves I have ever witnessed, the gathering of the Disarmament Conference in Washington furnished the most intense dramatic moment I have ever witnessed."

William Allen White made the new President his special study. Judson Welliver, Harding's personal secretary, told White that the President was constantly asking him his opinion of difficult issues and confessing, with disarming frankness, his own ignorance. On a controversial tax bill Harding broke out: "Jud, you have a college education, haven't you? I don't know what to do or where to turn in this taxation matter. Somewhere there must be a book that tells all about it, where I could go to straighten it out in my mind. But I don't know where the book is, and maybe I couldn't read it if I found it! . . . My God, but this is a hell of a place for a man like me to be!"

When White interviewed Harding, he found that the President wanted to chat about the problems and pleasures of being a small-town newspaper editor. He began by asking the current price of paper and the possibility of broadening the readership of his paper, the *Marion* (Ohio) *Star,* by carrying more syndicated national and foreign news. "There was never a day in all the years that I ran the paper," Harding told his fellow editor, "that I didn't get a thrill out of it." Then the troubled President confided to White that some of his confidants and political allies were under indictment for violation of the antitrust laws and wanted him to dismiss the indictments. "I can take care of my enemies all right," Harding broke out. "But my God-damn friends, White, they're the ones keep me walking the floor nights."

It seemed clear to White at the end of Harding's first year in office that he "tremendously desired to do what he regarded as the right thing, that he saw—as clearly as he could see anything—the opportunity to make a name in history." But he was caught between his desire to do good and his loyalty to his old friends, who were determined to use him to fatten their already swollen purses.

Shortly before Harding departed on a trip to Alaska, it was brought to his attention that more than 200,000 steelworkers were still working twelve-hour days. The President spoke to the two giants of the steel industry, Judge Elbert Gary and Charles M. Schwab, and extracted from them a pledge to go to an eight-hour day for all their employees, thereby setting a standard for the industry.

White wrote of the President's inclination to stand by the "cheap and sometimes corrupt little men" who were "using the powerful leverage of [Attorney General] Daugherty's name for unbelievably corrupt semipublic transactions." Those who had begun to denounce such behavior were harassed by what White called "the spy service of the Department of Justice." Washington was "a buzz with a thousand little stories, rumors and suspicions of irregularity, sometimes amounting to crookedness. . . . But there were counter stories, little hero talks of the President's kindness, of his dawning consciousness of the truth and his growing resolve to serve it." Harding looked ill, and White diagnosed his trouble as "part terror, part shame, and part utter confusion." On the way back from Alaska Harding fell ill in San Francisco and died a few days later on August 2, 1923. What he proved in his brief tenure of office was that he was a man of extremely modest talents whose heart was in the right place; an old-fashioned small-town newspaper editor and politician entirely out of his element. His administration was most distinguished by the pardons that he gave Americans whose only crime had been the exercise of their right of freedom of speech presumably guaranteed to them under the Constitution of the United States. In addition to Debs, he pardoned Kate Richards O'Hare and dozens of other lesser-known radicals who had been rounded up and clapped into Federal penitentiaries in the process of making the world safe for democracy.

Harding's successor, another political accident, it might be said, was not an improvement. A gloomy Oswald Garrison Villard wrote: "And now the Presidency sinks low indeed. I doubt if it has ever fallen into the hands of a man so cold, so narrow, so reactionary, so uninspiring, so unenlightened, or who has done less to earn it than Calvin Coolidge." The country was now led by a man "whose writings and public utterances reveal no spark of originality, no vision, no tolerance, no sympathy with progress and advance. Every reactionary may today rejoice; in Calvin Coolidge he realizes his ideal, and every liberal must be correspondingly downcast."

The Genius of
Woodrow Wilson

Harding's death was the prelude to a succession of scandals involving members of his Cabinet and leading Republicans in his administration. Corruption was exposed in the Veterans Bureau and the Justice Department. More malodorous were the actions of the secretary of the interior, Albert Fall. Fall had prevailed on Harding to give him jurisdiction over naval oil reserves at Teapot Dome in Wyoming and Elk Hills in California. He had then leased the Teapot Dome lands to oil entrepreneur Harry Sinclair. The Elk Hills went to Edward Doheny, a rival to Franklin Roosevelt for the vice-presidential nomination at the Democratic Convention in 1920. Fall was richly rewarded by Sinclair and Doheny. When his defalcations were exposed by Thomas Walsh, a Democratic Senator from Montana, Fall went to jail.

Six months after the death of his successor, Woodrow Wilson died, on February 3, 1924. It would be hard to imagine two individuals more diametrically opposed. Poor Harding soon became a byword for presidential ineptness, taking his place with such hapless figures as James Buchanan, Millard Fillmore, and Benjamin Harrison. Wilson joined the ranks of the "great" presidents and became in consequence the subject of endless evaluations and interpretations by industrious historians.

A central issue in any assessment of Wilson's presidency has to do with what is often called his failure at the Paris Peace Conference. Indeed, some critics have emphasized three failures: his failure to keep the United States out of the war; his failure to achieve his Fourteen Points (plus six corollaries), a total of twenty, of which it was alleged he attained only four; and, finally, his failure to prevail on the Senate to ratify the Versailles Treaty.

The first and most grievous of Wilson's failures in the minds at least of millions of German and other hyphenated Americans, of individuals as diverse as Oswald Garrison Villard and Oscar Ameringer, of pacifists like Jane Addams and Socialists like Kate Richards O'Hare, was the failure to keep the United States out of the war. To the end of his life Villard could not forgive Wilson. The bitterest comments in the closing pages of his autobiography are reserved for the man he felt had betrayed him and all those committed to the cause of peace and progress.

Faced early in his administration with the crisis in Mexico and the threat of war with Japan, Wilson said to David Houston, "It would be the irony of fate if my administration had to deal chiefly with foreign affairs. . . ." War was, of course, the central issue of his administration. For six of his eight years in office, the European War and its aftermath were the most critical political facts that he had to confront. Of his attraction to Britain and his sympathy for the Allied cause there can be no doubt, nor of his devotion to peace and his desire to keep the United States out of the war. Two things combined to force him, against his deepest instincts, to lead the United States into the war: the desperation tactics of Germany in relying on an all-out unrestricted U-boat campaign to starve the Allies into submission, confident that the United States could neither mobilize an army nor transport it to Europe in time to affect the outcome of the war, and, beyond that, the real danger that Germany might win a decisive military victory and hence dominate the world for the foreseeable future. As long as the prospects of an Allied victory or even a negotiated peace without victory seemed reasonably good, there was no necessity for the United States to intervene and many reasons why it should not. But it may well have been the case that a substantial majority of the American people could not view with equanimity a conclusive German victory. What Wilson and the Allies could not, of course, foresee was the rise to power of the Bolsheviks and the withdrawal from the war of Russia, which released almost 1,000,000 German and Austrian soldiers to fight on the Western front. *If* the United States had not entered the war when it had, the transferral of the armies of the Central Powers from the Eastern to the Western front, combined with a modest degree of success in the U-boat campaign, might have given victory to German arms—though it may well be doubted if "victory" could have meant much to the exhausted adversaries. It is interesting to ponder whether, if the Germans had refrained from launching their unrestricted U-boat warfare in February, 1917, thereby depriving Wilson of a perhaps essential casus belli, he could have overcome the widespread resistance in the nation to American involvement. It is certainly not beyond the realm of possibility that there would have been a revolt of some kind in the West, sporadic outbreaks of violence, organized and large-scale opposition to the draft, sabotage, and a Green Corn Rebellion on a much more significant scale.

We can say with some confidence that the course the Germans chose to pursue was fatally wrong. It brought a reluctant and deeply divided United States into the war and thereby upset all German calculations and sealed that nation's fate.

The question still remains, however: Should the United States have entered the war? What would the consequences have been if it had stayed out and (1) the Allies had won a conclusive victory, or (2) the Germans had won a conclusive victory, or (3) there had been a negotiated peace based on the relative strength (or exhaustion) of the belligerents?

(1) seems least likely from all we know about the course of the war up to and after the entry of the United States, but in the event of (1) it seems clear the Allies would have had a relatively free hand to divide up the world on the basis of the secret treaties. The old imperialistic system would have been in large part preserved, with such compromises and accommodations as were required to produce a peace; it would have been a most egregious display of horse trading on an international scale. The United States would certainly have been in no position to have influenced substantially the terms of peace. There would almost certainly have been no League of Nations or any serious discussion of such an international organization. It might well have been the case that instead of the sporadic outbreaks of socialist revolution, the outraged populations of Europe might have followed the example of the Bolsheviks. Europe might well have been swept by that wave of socialism/communism that had so long been anticipated or, equally likely, by right-wing dictatorships. It is hard to imagine that *nothing* would have happened.

(2) was not beyond the range of possibility. Indeed, it was more likely than (1) in view of the withdrawal of Russia from the war. Of the three possible outcomes (2) would have been the worst. It is reasonable to assume that German peace terms would have been even more severe than those imposed by the Allies on Germany. German arrogance and the German appetite for conquest held no promise of a peaceful and orderly world (except the order of military domination). Russia and Germany almost certainly would have fought if Germany had tried to enforce, and Russia to evade, the draconian terms of the Treaty of Brest-Litovsk. Russia was in no condition to repel the armies of a victorious Germany. It must have succumbed. The United States could hardly stand by and see Germany take over most of the world without offering some opposition. It is not unlikely that Germany and the United States would eventually have become involved in a war as devastating as the one recently concluded.

(3) seems the most likely outcome if the United States had remained out of the war. What (3) would have certainly avoided was the brutally punitive peace imposed by the victorious Allies, the magnitude of whose victory was indisputably the consequence of the United States' entry into the conflict. But there are no grounds for believing that (3) would have contained any major portion of the principles enunciated in Wilson's Fourteen Points, most prominent among them the League of Nations itself. The best that could have been hoped for under (3) was a kind of *modus vivendi* or *status quo ante bellum*, with little to show for the terrible suffering and bloodshed. Again there is a real question whether the abused peoples of the world would or could have tolerated such an outcome.

Finally, there is the fact that not only would the Wilsonian ideals not been projected into the world's consciousness and the United States have failed to play an essential role in resolving the greatest crisis in modern history, but the ideal of a redeemed and reconciled humanity—the emancipation of a world—which we had professed since our birth as a nation would have been discredited. We would have suffered a severe loss of prestige in the world and a diminution of our own vital spirit.

Which bring us to Wilson's second failure—his failure to achieve the high-minded principles put forth in the Fourteen Points. British and French critics were harshest in indicting this particular failure. We have already mentioned John Maynard Keynes's malicious characterization of Wilson. Keynes called him "This blind and deaf Don Quixote," who was "entering a cavern where the swift and glittering blade was in the hands of the adversary." He added that "there can seldom have been a statesman of the first rank more incompetent than the President in the agilities of the council chamber."

Winston Churchill wrote: "Before him lay the naughty entanglements of Paris; and behind him, the sullen veto of the Senate. . . ." By Churchill's account, Wilson "did not wish to come to speedy terms with the European Allies; he did not wish to meet their leading men around a table; he saw himself for a prolonged period at the summit of the world, chastening the Allies, chastising the Germans and generally giving laws to mankind. He believed himself capable of appealing to peoples and parliaments over the heads of their own governments." What Churchill does not mention is that he himself was one of those reactionary European statesmen who did their best to defeat Wilson's plan for a just peace. As one of the leaders in the House of Commons, Churchill supported the blockade of Germany and the neutral states; he also was a strong advocate of mustering an Allied army to oust the Bolsheviks from power in Russia. In the words of David Lloyd George, Churchill had "Bolshevism on the brain."

Clemenceau was even more biting than Churchill in his criticism of Wilson's role. "Later there comes on the scene," he wrote in his sardonic style in the *Grandeur and Misery of Victory*, "President Woodrow Wilson, armoured in his Fourteen Points, symbolized by many pointed wisdom teeth that never let themselves be turned aside from their duty. . . . Doubtless he had too much confidence in all the talky-talk and super talky-talk of his 'League of Nations' . . . which was nothing more than an epitome of the Parliaments of all nations, to which all historic disagreements, all diplomatic intrigues, all coalitions of national, or even private egoisms were to come and concentrate, multiply, intensify, and perhaps sometimes even find some temporary mitigation. . . . There are probably few examples of such a misreading and disregarding of political experience in the maelstrom of abstract thought." Of course, the idea that "all men should be free and equal" was a classic example of "abstract thought"; the United States had been born out of the womb of abstract thought.

One of the most perceptive analyses of Wilson's plan for reordering the world was that of Harold Nicolson. He wrote: "It was not that the ideas of Woodrow Wilson were so apocalyptic: it was that for the first time in history you had a man who possessed, not the desire merely, not the power alone, but the unquestioned opportunity to enforce those ideas upon the whole world. We would have been insensitive indeed had we not been inspired by the magnitude of such an occasion." But Nicolson went on to argue that Britain and France could not stake their future upon the unsteady will of the American people who had shown, since the days of the Mexican War and the Louisiana Purchase, a disconcerting tendency to act in opposition to their professed principles. "The Anglo-Saxon," Nicolson added, "is gifted with a limitless capacity for excluding his own practical requirements from the application of the idealistic theories which he seeks to impose on others." To the British this appeared to be most strikingly the case in the treatment by the Americans of blacks, Indians, and Orientals. To the Americans it seemed clear in the disposition of the British to denounce colonialism while doggedly holding on to their own colonies (and indeed trying to add substantially to them at the cost of the defeated powers). The non-American members of the peace delegation, according to Nicolson, had the uneasy feeling "that America was asking Europe to make sacrifices to righteousness which America would never make, and had never made herself. . . ." This produced "a mood of diffidence, uncertainty, and increasing despair. . . . The whole Treaty," Nicolson argued, "had been deliberately and ingeniously framed by Mr. Wilson himself to render American cooperation essential." Without American cooperation the whole structure might well collapse, and there were, from the first, serious doubts about whether Wilson could carry his fellow Americans with him.

Much of the discussion about the peace conference has revolved around the proposition that Wilson bargained away the Fourteen Points by ineptness or as a consequence of allowing himself to be manipulated by his shrewder and more experienced confreres. The criticism, often leveled at Wilson by those favorable to his ideals, is that he somehow sold out. If, the argument often goes, he had been more flexible, less secretive, more candid with the American peace commissioners, sought and followed their advice more frequently, more this, less that, then the treaty that finally emerged might have been closer to his original vision. The fact was that Wilson was caught in the classic no-win situation, the double bind. Every step he took, every compromise forced upon him made the hope of a just peace more remote. The most basic fact of the peace conference was that a majority—three out of four of those who undertook to fashion the treaty—had little or no sympathy with Wilson's aims and gave no more than reluctant lip service to them.

That was, as we say, the bottom line. All the charges that Wilson "failed" are based on the assumption that he could, by greater force of character or greater guile or greater resolution, have "won."

The issue of the League has to be, to a degree at least, separated from that of the treaty, although it seems clear enough that Lloyd George and Clemenceau callously used Wilson's devotion to the idea of the League to extract numerous concessions from him. The point to be emphasized here is that Wilson's vision of the League was only a heightened and intensified and more sharply focused form of the visions that had been bred out of the world's agony, the agony of the industrial age which was in the process of tearing up the complex network of social usages and customs formed in the various branches of the human family over centuries, in some instances, over millennia.

Certainly there was no indication that the Allies had the slightest disposition toward either an equitable and enlightened peace or anything like a League of Nations. William Allen White was convinced that the French supported the notion of a League of Nations primarily as a means of preserving the old balance of power arrangements. They wished for a League which they had every intention of dominating. They wished, in White's words, "to control Central Europe and the Near East. They were willing to give, and England was willing to take, colonies in Africa for exploitation under the fairly decent but always imperial habits of the British. . . ." In addition, the French were willing to give the British a free hand in the Far East. "Japan was a stepchild, and China a poor orphan." In White's view, Wilson "often took things that were bad, not knowing how bad they were. . . . He was sitting in a game with two sharpers [Lloyd George and Clemenceau] who knew the cards, who had marked the decks and knew the value of the chips. Yet [Wilson] was for all that, by reason of the nobility of his ideals, the brave, fine way he stuck to them, and even for what he achieved, a truly great and noble figure in Europe that year."

One of Wilson's severest American critics was Felix Frankfurter. He wrote to Walter Lippmann: "At least at bottom, if not *the* bottom fact, is that neither the President nor the Colonel had any adequate conception of what the problem of peace making was. I do not mean the actual detailed question, but the technique of peace making, the processes which would come into play, the forces they would encounter and the forces they could rely upon. Without exception, the saddest day of the war for me was Labour Day of last year when the Colonel outlined to me the plan for the Peace Conference. I knew then . . . that they were the naïvest children in the world and the President's efforts to achieve his principles were doomed to failure." Frankfurter believed that the outcome of the British elections had made Lloyd George "utterly dishonest in regard especially to the reparation clause." In the American headquarters at the Majestic and the Crillon hotels there were, in Frankfurter's view, "all the necessary knowledge and vision to approximate the world order that was attainable," but that knowledge and that vision were frustrated. If there had been "public courage on the part of two or three of our own people," he concluded, "this Treaty would never have been." Brandeis, for example, could have saved the day, Frankfurter believed.

Frederic Howe, whose experience of practical politics was far more extensive than Frankfurter's, was convinced that Wilson's only hope had been to remain "a Messiah," a prophet of the new humanity who refused to compromise his principles under any circumstances. Then he might have rallied such a body of public sentiment in the United States and around the world as to have proved irresistible. "But," in Howe's words, "he chose to barter. When he began to barter, he lost all; he lost his own vision of himself, and he had to keep that vision intact."

Those Americans closest to the treaty negotiations proper—the League itself aside—were disposed to justify the decisions of the President. Bernard Baruch and Herbert Hoover never abandoned their conviction that Wilson had fought a noble and, in large measure, successful fight in Paris. Hoover wrote years later: "Destructive forces sat at the Peace Table. The future of twenty-six jealous European races was there. The genes of a thousand years of inbred hate and fear of every generation were there in their blood. . . . Clemenceau had secured a vote of confidence to render Germany innocuous for all time, and collect every centime of French losses. The oppressed races were there, with their recollection of infinite wrong." In Hoover's view the Europeans thought "Americans were a foolish people, pliable to ingenuous Allied propaganda; that President Wilson was a visionary idealist wholly out of tune with European realities; that having won the war they were going to have the spoils of victory; that they were going to establish their power over Europe against the Germans or any other combinations once for all." In this atmosphere the President's "expression of American ideals was the only spiritual expression in the

Conference. At every step he fought the forces of hate." He "made the major contribution to lifting oppression from millions of people and settling them upon the road to hope."

Sidney Edward Mezes, the chairman of the Inquiry, wrote: "The war released blind forces in all fields of human interest, and the Powers of the world were as helpless in 1919 to compose those forces as they had been in 1914 and are now. . . . No human conference could have relieved us of all these present evils." In contrast with such earlier alterations of the map of Europe, the Paris conference "faced vastly greater problems, studied its problems in a more scientific way, and sought more earnestly to harmonize its settlement with the principles of justice."

Florence Harriman wrote: "There were the secret treaties, old bargains, often shameful, made in the days before the Fourteen Points shone like stars promising Peace on Earth. It is the custom to vilify the peacemakers who gathered around the table and drew the Treaty of Versailles. But their problem was one of the most difficult in history. Every nation in Europe wanted to recoup for the outrageous sacrifices made in the years of madness."

The League with all its shortcomings and deficiencies was in itself a remarkable fact. The notion of the mandates, however abused in practice, was the right notion. It stated a new anticolonial principle. Many of the smaller nations were given a kind of provisional protection against larger and more powerful neighbors. The failures of the League were more sharply delineated because of the extravagant expectations its creation had aroused.

General Jan Smuts, who knew Wilson well, wrote of him: "At a time of the deepest darkness and despair he had . . . raised aloft a light to which all eyes . . . had turned. He had spoken divine words of healing and consolation to a broken humanity. His lofty moral idealism seemed for a moment to dominate the brutal passions which had torn the Old World asunder. . . . It was not Wilson who failed. . . . It was the human spirit that failed at Paris. . . . What was really saved at Paris was . . . the Covenant of the League of Nations. . . . The Covenant is Wilson's souvenir to the future of the world. No one will ever deny him that honor. The honor is very great, indeed, for the Covenant is one of the great creative documents of human history."

The Greek prime minister, Eleutherios Venizelos, expressed the feeling of many of the smaller nations of Europe when he declared,

"Without a League of Nations southeastern Europe would face the future with despair in its heart."

Lincoln Steffens, whose life was an unending examination of the relationship between moral imperatives and political realities, offered a shrewd insight into Wilson's character. "Did not Mr. Wilson and did not we realize that such a League would become an instrument in the hands of England and France and—perhaps—less so—the United States for the extension of power over both backward and forward nations," Steffens asked, "and that otherwise we would not join it? We did not. And Mr. Wilson did not. He was sincere. He meant well. . . . But he agreed to a warlike division of the defeated countries; he made a treaty of peace that was full of war. How could he do that, he an historian, a highly intellectual man, a very enlightened democrat?" Steffens's answer was that "Wilson was a righteous man and, as such, personified us, his people. He had ideals; they were high and they were sincere. But they were so high that he did not expect to realize them." Americans, Steffens reflected, must "learn to do wrong knowingly. Wilson could not. He had to be, so he was, right. It was as if every night he thought, talked, prayed over what he had done that day till he could go to sleep feeling that he had not sinned or erred, that there was a good reason for his acts." The same had been true of his predecessor and enemy, Theodore Roosevelt. He, too, had had to be morally justified in every action.

In the last analysis the League was the consequence of a utopian mode of thinking which had always been characteristic of America and had more recently captivated the world. The most striking manifestation of that form of thinking was, of course, socialism, with a small *s* and Socialism with a large *S*. All the socialisms and communisms and anarchisms and syndicalisms had in common the profound conviction that their triumph by "ballots or bullets" would bring a new day—*the* new day, in fact: the end of tyranny, injustice, and (when all nations were socialist) peace and prosperity. They all were, politically speaking, "quick fixes." Wilson was not a socialist in any formal political sense, but he clearly had been affected by socialist doctrines and shared, to a substantial degree, its utopianism. Moreover, his young aides and advisers, including most conspicuously Walter Lippmann, were or had recently been avowed and active Socialists with a large *S*. The notion of the League thus had in it some of the arrogance and coerciveness that were inherent in all Socialist/Communist thought—"we intellectuals, men and women of superior intelligence, moral perception and understanding know what is best for you, 'the people,' whom we love. That love makes it necessary for us to do things that you may not understand or may even, unfortunately, stubbornly resist. We must, therefore, out of our love for you and for your own good, coerce you in some small and some not so small ways." G. K. Chesterson spoke, in his essay on Robert Browning, of such a mood as "a kind of disease of public spirit" common to despots. But it is common as well to large-scale reformers of society, whatever they call themselves. "They represent," Chesterton wrote, "the drunkenness of responsibility. It is when men grow desperate in their love for the people, when they are overwhelmed with the difficulties and blunders of humanity, that they fall back on a wild desire to manage everything themselves. . . . This belief that all would go right if we could only get the strings into our own hands is a fallacy almost without exception, but nobody can justly say that it is not public-spirited." Chesterton spoke of the appearance in history of "these great despotic dreamers . . . who have at root this idea, that the world would enter into rest if it went their way and forswore altogether the right of going its own way. When a man begins to think that the grass will not grow at night unless he lies awake to watch it, he generally ends either in an asylum or on the throne of an Emperor." Wilson was far, of course, from being a great despotic dreamer, but he came dangerously close to succumbing to "a wild desire to manage everything," and he did drive himself to a disastrous physical breakdown. In a curious way the White House became his asylum, a national sanatorium occupied by a tragic remnant of his real self.

We come finally to the third of Wilson's failures: the question of whether Wilson's obduracy "lost" the treaty and America's participation in the League. Here the answer seems clear. More tact, more compromise, more skill, and better management could have secured the ratification of the treaty by the Senate. Wilson's unreasonable stubbornness cost the ratification. But it must be said he had endured a great deal. He was half-dead; only his iron will kept him alive. In those terrible last months he clung to the League as to life itself. It came to seem to him that some essential element of the truth, of faith and honor was involved. As he did so regrettably often, he saw his opponents as his mortal enemies, in this case determined to kill him and his League as well. So he persevered. It may be doubted if it mattered much.

The League was badly flawed, and there is no reason to believe that the refusal of the United States to join seriously impaired its ability to prevent the numerous wars and contests for empire that marked its existence. Its successor is situated in the United States and is remarkably like the original in its deficiencies, but it is still a hope, a prospect, and a force, in the main, for good. It points a direction: it helps moderate our most unruly passions or at least provides a forum for them. So we must be grateful to it and to the man who dared imagine it and so salvage something from an otherwise unmitigated disaster.

But larger and more complex problems remain. After the first attack of the Americans on the Marne, a young German officer, Eugen Rosenstock-Huessy, who had been a tutor at Heidelberg and had earned a doctorate in law, wrote an essay which he entitled "The Crusade of the Star-Spangled Banner." He wrote: "The pre-war era in Europe was a period during which all forms gradually decayed." The war had demonstrated the emptiness of forms, from the coats of arms of nobility to the doctor's hood. The European War had become, with the entry of the United States, a "World War." At that time the American President "appears before us in the double role of the true neutral and of the first 'disinterested belligerent'. . . . A completely new war is in process, an American-European war, with other aims, about other issues than the three-year war of the European powers. In this new conflict it is no longer a question of trade and empire; for welfare and riches are everywhere gone. Here it is a question of the forms of life and of faith. . . . From 1914–1917 the issue was the great disruption over the goods of this world; the war, as hereditary divider, was supposed to decide about trade, colonies and wealth." In this sense it was a civil war with all the fury and destructiveness of such a conflict. But for the United States it was a crusade. "A Crusade, a disinterested, selfless war is now the battle against the sultans and emperors of the old war. . . . The people of good will, no, quite simply, the good people are fighting against the evil, the German militarism which enslaves human beings, which considers them evil and therefore rules them with distrust and policemen." The American with his faith in "psychology" believed that he could "practice the inexplicable magic of the management of souls. The art of psychology takes the place for him of the brutal power which he incontestably believes is dominant in the empires." America thus came to the aid of France, the "only sister republic in old Europe which is also built upon 'psychology,' on leading the masses or deceiving the masses, on the sovereignty of the people. . . ." The crusade was "directed from across the sea with a fantastic exaggeration of all power and resources and with swaggering and boasting. But because the melting pot of the new world is boiling over here, because the power of imagination is inflamed, because the future of mankind must be saved from the Huns, therefore the measures of this world of ideas will have to be somehow satisfied by the events before the ardor can cool off." America's dogma was "Man is good! Tyrants falsify and commit violence with his true nature. Human nature creates out of itself peace and freedom, the brotherhood of man and justice. Only princes prevent this natural harmony." It was indeed a throwback to or an evocation of Tom Paine's *Common Sense*, so confident in its conviction that wars and other forms of wickedness were the doing of kings and emperors, lords and barons. Wilson was, in mind and spirit, far closer to Tom Paine and Thomas Jefferson than to Edmund Burke or Walter Bagehot. "The President," Rosenstock-Huessy wrote, "today calls the faithful new world to a united world order against the dying old world. Not unintentionally did he declare war on Good Friday. His address at the grave of Washington on July 4, 1918 displayed every known magical power that can today sweep human hearts to faith." Wilson's failure (and America's), Rosenstock-Huessy insisted, was that he (they) ignored the darker passions of the human heart that Christian dogma acknowledged under the rubric of original sin. The wickedness of kings and emperors was simply an epitome of the general human disposition to "self-aggrandizement" (unlawful power), vanity, and insatiable greed.

What Rosenstock-Huessy called the Crusade of the Star-Spangled Banner (contrasting it, unfavorably it should be said, with the Crusades of the Cross) can be seen in this light as the culminating act of the Secular Democratic Consciousness. In its division of the world into the "good" democracy and the "evil" autocracy (Wilson, of course, fastened on the kaiser as the symbol of that transcendent evil), the United States and Wilson played into the hands of Clemenceau. If Germany was "evil," then clearly the task of the victors was to destroy Germany— i.e., evil—so that the world could be harmonious and peaceful. Seen in this light, Wilson's failure was not in a compromised and crippling peace, not in concessions to the French and British or indeed to the Japanese and Italians, but in his failure to be true to his own Christian doctrine of original sin and to keep steadily in mind that victor and vanquished stood under the judgment of the same stern Calvinist God. That was why Wilson could encourage the persecution of all those who refused to support the crusade wholeheartedly. They, too, were evil and must be extirpated. So perhaps the final irony was that one of our most personally pious and devout presidents was also the most heretical in the vision that he tried to impose on the world. When all that is said and done, however, the fact remains that in reviving the dream of the Reverend Samuel Thacher, the dream of the "emancipation of a world," Wilson did vastly enlarge the notion of human brotherhood and play a crucial role in dismantling an archaic and decadent order.

That he did so at a terrible personal cost is hardly surprising. He was undoubtedly thinking of himself when he wrote of Lincoln: "There is a very holy and very terrible isolation for the conscience of every man who seeks to read the destiny of affairs for others as well as for himself, for a nation as well as for individuals. That privacy no man can intrude upon. That lonely search of the spirit for the right perhaps no man can assist."

The two words most often used in relation to Wilson by those whose hearts he had touched were "messianic" and "prophetic." In the words of Bernard Baruch, "His prophetic vision gave the bloody business of war a meaning to those who did the fighting and dying. His messages, couched in some of the most moving and noble language to be found in state papers, communicated his own high purpose and inflexible will to the world." Baruch wrote: "Next to my father, Wilson had the greatest influence on my life. He took me out of Wall Street and gave me my first opportunity for public service. His political philosophy helped shape my own. His practical idealism, ability, and conduct still provide the standard by which I measure public men." The peace conference remained for Baruch "a great crusade, and I count it the finest privilege of my life to have been part of it."

Frederic Howe, who had such ambivalent feelings about Wilson, was convinced that victory came out of Wilson's defeat—but not the kind of victory he intended or one that he would have welcomed. "As an evangelist," Howe wrote, "he . . . helped to free Ireland. He heartened the Egyptians, the Arabs, and the Indians. He set aflame fires that are slowly driving the white man from other people's countries. . . . As an evangelist he takes his place among the great men of history. . . . His phrases won permanent victories, they inspired peoples; possibly they won the war. They left humanity better for what he said; he enriched it by the unsullied idealism of his messages. . . . The pinnacle from which he fell," Howe wrote, "was within himself. That was the tragedy of the Peace Messiah."

Franklin Roosevelt, who served for over seven years as Wilson's assistant Secretary of the Navy, told Frances Perkins years later: "He [Wilson] was a Presbyterian, you know, and a tough one, and he was perfectly sure that all men are sinful by nature. He figured it out that Western civilization would attempt to destroy itself through the natural sinful activities of modern man unless . . . by the grace of God the decent people of Western civilization resolved to support the doctrine of the Golden Rule."

What Wilson was in effect calling for was nothing more or less than the salvation of the world. It was the millennial expectation stated in the language of international politics. The world was ill with war, poverty, exploitation. It must be made well, healed, restored, saved. Wilson was the physician, the healer, the redeemer, the Messiah. The message was irresistible and will always be so when a truly prophetic voice declares it.

In the end Wilson's principal failure was thus an intellectual one, indeed a theological one, rather than a tactical or political one. He failed his own religious convictions. The Christian faith that he professed so ardently taught that people were not "naturally" good but tainted by original sin—that is to say, had base impulses that constantly compromised their better instincts, that greed and selfishness were ineradicable elements in their nature. All triumphs over evil were thus limited and contingent; the battle of the "higher" over the "lower" was unending.

In yielding to the Enlightenment view of human nature, brought up to date by Darwinians and Freudians, Wilson was, of course, doing no more than yielding to the spirit of the age, represented at its most insistent and beguiling by such young men as Walter Lippmann and Frederic Howe. In any event, he could hardly have accompanied the Fourteen Points with a reminder of the inevitable limits to human pretensions and a sermonette on original sin. The potency of the points rested on the shared and unquestioning faith of those who heard them in the possibility of an immediate and universal panacea.

Rosenstock-Huessy has declared it as a kind of law of history that everything of a powerfully reforming nature must happen *too early*, before the generality of the people are ready for it, so that it may happen *in time*; at the right or appointed time. So Wilson's final reconciliation to being too early was a saving insight. If he had been too bold, too arrogant, too swept away by the adulation that fell so intoxicatingly upon him, he had paid a terrible price, and having paid the price, he was given the grace to perceive a larger truth and find consolation in it. So it turns out, he had not so much been defeated as chastened. He had, indeed, prepared the way.

Despite all the vicissitudes of American and world politics, the dream endured. What had been done could not be entirely undone. The same could be said for the critically important social legislation passed during Wilson's first administration. Much was lost in the confusion and disorder of the war and the boom times that followed it, but a residual memory remained. Many of the young men and women who had cast their lot with Wilson and the Democratic Party and who had suffered acutely over the failure of much that they had aspired and worked for retained the ideals and the hope that first Roosevelt and then, more dramatically, Wilson had inspired. Dismal as the prospects seemed to them, their time would come.

If, as Alfred North Whitehead wrote, "style is the ultimate morality of mind," Woodrow Wilson rates high marks; he was one of our great stylists. The Roman historian Livy declared centuries ago, "History at its most profound is oratory." Livy had a devoted disciple in young Wilson, who, while still an undergraduate at Princeton, had formed a pact with a classmate "to school all our powers and passions for the work of establishing the principles we held in common; that we would acquire knowledge that we might have power; and that we would drill ourselves in all the arts of persuasion, but especially in oratory . . . that we might have facility in leading others into our way of thinking and enlisting them in our purposes." If ever a purpose was pursued with single-minded devotion, it was Woodrow Wilson's youthful determination to "have power" and to achieve it by developing "all the arts of persuasion . . . especially that of oratory. . . ." That he did so is indisputable.

Years after the peace conference, Colonel House and Stephen Bonsal reviewed its history. "I have no patience," House said, "with those who speak of the President's venture in altruism, although many say it with kindness in their hearts, as 'a magnificent failure.' Much was accomplished, and though, as we all know now, Wilson left the world far from safe for Democracy, he liberated in Europe many millions of people and gave hope and courage to many millions more, who, as yet, are not 'redeemed.' Wilson died a martyr to the noble cause that will ever be associated with his name. It may be a trite saying, but it is a true one, 'The blood of the martyrs refreshes the tree of liberty as it also invigorates the Church.' " House then quoted Carlyle: "Nothing that is worthy in the past departs; no truth or goodness realized by man ever dies, or can die; but it is still here, and, recognized or not, lives and works through endless changes." Wilson was a modern Christian from John Bunyan's *Pilgrim's Progress* leading his fellows—Everyman—"through many dark glens, along many a precipice . . ." to the "Shining Gate and . . . the City of Peace."

If we were to grant the charges of his critics (and, as we have seen, these were legion)—that Wilson was rigid and unyielding (many said he yielded far too much); that he was often politically inept; that as he himself said, he had a one-track mind; that he was not above "petty rancors" (Lloyd George's phrase); that he was deficient in compassion and overly disposed to abstract thought (Clemenceau's charge); that he was excessively preachy and moralistic (virtually everybody's charge); that he was what we would call today a racist, which is to say, he shared the prejudices of his section and his party; that he was often vindictive toward those he believed to be his enemies (i.e., those who differed from him); a monomaniac who believed that he could control the destinies of the world—certain facts remain indisputable: He was a "great man" in any proper meaning of those sometimes loosely used words; he changed the course of history; he expressed the highest ideals of America, ideals that have often been more honored in the breach than the observance, and did so with an eloquence that thrilled the souls of uncounted millions, not simply in the United States but all over the world. Almost single-handedly he created a new global consciousness that looked beyond national divisions and ancient rivalries to a better human order and, finally, to peace. In the light of these very considerable facts, his undoubted and generally regrettable deficiencies (some were simply the reverse side of his attributes) assume their proper proportion. In aiming so high (and falling so far), he nonetheless opened a new chapter in the long history of the race, and those who walked in the light of his vision were not as before.

We think again of the words on the Great Seal of the United States: *Novus ordo seclorum* ("A new age or new order of ages now begins"). It was that chord that Wilson touched.

45

Religion

In the realm of religion during this period in the United States, there were five main currents: denominational Protestantism, Christian socialism or, as it was more commonly called, the Social Gospel (not all adherents of the Social Gospel were Socialists), evangelical fundamentalism (not all evangelicals were fundamentalists), domestic and foreign mission work, and, finally, a theological movement that came to be known as neo-orthodoxy.

The rigid and repressive attitudes associated primarily with small-town Puritanism continued to alienate young men and women who were moved by the impulses of reform. The Protestant Passion of the "Thou shalt" had dwindled to the negative injunction "Thou shalt not." George Creel was typical of many boys and young men of an inquiring disposition. Before he had ever heard of Darwin, he had begun to rebel against his mother's Episcopalian faith. "It was the cruelty, even savagery, of the Old Testament tales heard in Sunday school that first turned me against so-called Christian teaching," he wrote late in life. "I liked the poetry of the Psalms, but I thought King David a lecherous, treacherous old man," guilty of adultery and murder. "If that was Christianity, I wanted no part of it. Later on," he added, "I came to believe in God the Creator, and bowed before Christ as a great teacher, but I could not swallow denominationalism, or get over my distaste for those who made their own particular brand of devotion to the Galilean an excuse for hateful intolerance." Reading Thomas Paine, Creel decided that, like Paine, he was a deist.

Ray Stannard Baker also felt the pulls and tugs of conventional religion versus the new religion of scientific reform. He read Henry Drummond's deistic *Natural Law in the Spiritual World*, Emerson on "Compensation," and Andrew White's tome on the war between science and religion. Benjamin Kidd's *Social Evolution*, with its mild ethical Darwinism, appealed most to him. Kidd, whose book went through a number of editions, had written: "The fact of our time which overshadows all others is the arrival of Democracy. But the perception of the fact is of relatively little importance if we do not also realize that it is a new Democracy. There are many who speak of the new ruler of nations as if he were the same idle Demos whose ears dishonest courtiers have tickled from time immemorial. It is not so. Even those who attempt to lead him do not yet quite understand him. . . . They do not perceive that his arrival is the crowning result of an ethical movement in which qualities and attributes which we have been all taught to regard as the very highest of which human nature is capable find the completest expression they have ever reached in the history of the race."

Like Baker, Hutchins Hapgood and Lincoln Steffens searched for a "spiritual" dimension to life that would be essentially Christian but that rejected the "coldness" of the major denominations. Steffens's indictment of the churches was that they did not preach Christ's concern with the poor and downtrodden but offered instead a religion of pious middle-class assurance. "Wherever I was on a Sunday—and I was in many, many places—" he wrote, "I went to church—to many, many churches of many denominations; and I never heard . . . Christianity, as Jesus taught it in the New Testament, preached to the Christians." It was in politics, among the reformers, that Steffens saw the true teachings of Christ exemplified. "I began to try it myself," he wrote, "and it worked. Christianity, unpreached and untaught and unlearned among the righteous, works wonders still among the sinners."

Washington Gladden in 1908 stated the essentials of the Social Gospel-cum-Christian socialism. "Organizations of employers," he wrote, "have arisen in late years, whose attitude toward organized labor is more hostile than anything which has been known in our history. And

I fear that it will be found," Gladden added, "that there are thousands of employers in all parts of the country who, a few years ago, were disposed to be reasonable in their treatment of the labor unions, but who, today, are maintaining toward them an attitude of almost vindictive opposition." It seemed clear to Gladden that "if the wage-system means perennial war, the wage-system must pass, and some less expensive method of organizing industry must take its place. The alternative now constantly in sight is Socialism. Socialism proposes that the functions of the capitalist and *entrepreneur* shall be merged in the commonwealth." Gladden was free to admit that he had never regarded "this possibility with enthusiasm." The American populace, in his view, was not, "in its prevailing ideas and tempers, sufficiently socialized to work the machinery of Socialism." There remained too much to be done to raise the general level of literacy and intelligence in the country; "a stupid, illiterate population can but mock Socialism with a sort of bureaucratic tyranny. . . . " Gladden's proposals, like those of so many other critics of the "wage-system," would add to the post office— "a socialistic institution"—the telegraph and the railways. "All these," Gladden wrote, "are steps in the direction of Socialism which we are likely to take at no distant day. All the industries which I have named are virtual monopolies, and the people must own all monopolies. That is the essence of democracy, on the economic side. There must be no monopolies of goods or services necessary to the life of the people which the people do not themselves control. If democracy is to endure, it must assert and maintain this prerogative." Above all, the economy must be "Christianized," made humane and responsive to the needs of people. "Any organization of society which is founded on selfishness will come to grief. That is the bottom trouble with the world to-day; and the only radical cure for it is a change in the ruling principle of life." It seemed to Gladden that "collective ownership and control will be and should be greatly extended; that many of the industries which are now in private hands will become departments of public service. I believe that such cooperation of all the peoples through the state will result in great economies, and will put an end to some of the worst oppressions."

Baker was deeply impressed by Professor Walter Rauschenbusch at the Rochester Theological Seminary in New York. Rochester, in part as a result of Rauschenbusch's reformist zeal, was busy cleaning out its political stables. The professor had written "some prayers for the new age" that charmed Baker. He got Rauschenbusch's permission to put one of his prayers on the back of the February, 1910, issue of the *American Magazine*. It read in part: "O God! thou great governor of all the world, we pray thee for all who hold public office and power, for the life, the welfare, the virtue of the people, are in their hands to make or mar. We remember with shame that in the past the mighty have preyed on the labors of the poor; that they have laid nations in the dust by their oppressions and have thwarted the love and prayers of thy servants. . . . We rejoice that by the free institutions of our country the tyrannous instincts of the strong may be curbed. . . . Purge our cities and states and nation of the deep causes of corruption. . . . Raise up a new generation of public men, who will have the faith and daring of the Kingdom of God in their hearts. . . . Bring to an end the stale days of party cunning. . . . Breathe a new spirit into all our nation. . . ."

The publication of Walter Rauschenbusch's prayer in the *American Magazine* may be taken as marking the popularization of the Social Gospel, the doctrine that organized religion, through the churches, had a direct responsibility for reforming as well as alleviating social ills.

Christian fundamentalism, which had provided the inspiration for populism and rural radicalism in general, identified itself more and more closely with capitalism, in order the better to oppose communism. It still clung to "enthusiasm," to revivals and shoutings, to tent meetings and "awakenings." Here hell still burned and sinners suffered an eternity of torment. The words of the Bible were to be understood literally; the millennial expectation depicted so vividly in Revelations was an imminent possibility. The revivalistic spirit of Jonathan Edwards, Lyman Beecher, and Dwight Moody was carried on by the evangelist, Billy Sunday, who reached the height of his popularity in the first two decades of the new century. To Emma Goldman, Sunday's "vulgar manner, his coarse suggestiveness, erotic flagellations, and disgusting lasciviousness . . . stripped religion of the least spiritual significance." She deplored the "atmosphere of lewd mouthings and sexual contortions with which he goaded his audience to salacious hysteria." But if Sunday's antics offended Goldman, they drew tens of thousands of the devout and merely curious to his meetings, and he, far more than Walter Rauschenbusch or Washington Gladden, spoke to the mass of Protestant Americans, though it should be added, Sunday inclined to the liberal side on theological issues.

Derived directly from the Social Gospel movement was the work of domestic missionaries to the immigrant groups of the large industrial cities. Young men and women were sent abroad as immigration fellows to study the languages and cultures from which the immigrants came. Religious journals, devoted to studying and improving the conditions of immigrant life, were also started. William Shriver, a young minister, published in 1913 a study of immigrants entitled *Immigrant Forces*. Shriver gave his definition of "social service" as a group endeavor, getting people together, "to make a careful study of the working people in a community and by collective effort to improve those conditions, by bringing influence to bear upon the employers, and by helping organization among the workers themselves. . . . It is service in behalf of a group of people who have common interests, whose life is gladdened by the common welfare. . . . In its ideal sense, social service is wholly unselfish, it aims solely at the common welfare as distinct from that of a party, a sect, a business interest, or a particular institution."

The Congregationalists alone maintained 724 churches and missions among the foreign-speaking immigrants in the United States and expended $420,000 yearly to maintain them. The congregations ranged from Armenian (29) to "Dano-Norwegian" (80), German (226), Japanese (21), and Italian (21) to Hindu, Turkish, and Mexican, with 117 churches and missions ministering to Swedish immigrants.

The Baptists had 369 churches and missions with combined congregations of 30,746 among German-speaking immigrants, and 14 serving the hardy Protestant Poles.

The Presbyterians were especially active among the Bohemians, a number of whom were Protestants and perhaps a majority of whom were freethinkers and thus presumably susceptible to evangelizing by Protestant missionaries. The Presbyterians were also active among the Magyars and the Italians. Mexicans were virtually a monopoly of the Presbyterians, with 44 churches and missions.

The Northern Baptists and Methodists had more than 700 churches among Swedish-Americans, while the Presbyterians had some 1,500 churches with more than 120,000 members among German immigrant groups.

Among them, these Protestant denominations employed 2,201 salaried men and 454 women, most of whom ministered to the immigrants in their native tongues. They maintained 3,376 churches and missions and spent, in the year 1912, $2,256,963 in the work. Omitted from these figures are the Episcopalians, not to mention dozens of other evangelical and fundamentalist churches, some of which were not, to be sure, oriented toward missionary activity among the foreign-born.

William Shriver, who printed these statistics, estimated that they should be multiplied by at least seven to get an accurate picture of Protestant missionary activity among immigrant groups. Even if we took a more modest figure, it would still represent an impressive commitment by the churches. Nonetheless, the number of immigrants directly affected was only a fraction of the immigrant population. Those immigrants who were drawn into the network of Protestant missions made the transition to American society more rapidly and effectively than their compatriots who retained their traditional faiths. As a consequence, they came to constitute a disproportionate number of the political and business leaders of the immigrant communities to which they belonged. Plainly numbers alone do not tell the story. It is also the case that American missionaries went to the countries from which the immigrants came for the purpose of evangelizing and, in the process, brought with them such institutions as the Young Men's Christian Association and the Boy Scouts (there were Boy Scouts in the Czech center of Gary, Indiana, and in Bohemia as well).

A by-product of Christian socialism and the Social Gospel movement generally was the so-called Labor Temple, a building provided, usually by a Protestant denomination, for the use of workingmen and union members who might or might not, as they wished, have religious services in conjunction with their meetings. A typical week of activities in a temple on the Lower East Side of New York City in 1913 presided over by the Reverend Charles Stelzle, an ex-machinist, included a talk by the secretary of the American Federation of Labor, a "People's Service" on Sunday evening, an illustrated lecture on Monday "with Motion Pictures," a religious forum, and, on Saturday night, a "People's Popular Program. Vocal and Instrumental Music, Motion Pictures, etc."

At the very moment when the nation's cities seemed hopelessly sunk in misery and corruption, a new spirit manifested itself. In John Jay Chapman's words, "compassionate persons" appeared; men and women "filled with love and pity" took on themselves responsibility for the poor and dispossessed. "This new gospel of love," Chapman wrote, "now absorbs whole classes of people in American life, and swallows the young as the Crusades once swallowed them. I hear schoolmasters and learned men complain that their most brilliant classical scholars insist upon doing settlement work the moment they graduate." They could not explain why they abandoned learning for work among the poor, but they nonetheless expressed, "by their conduct, a more potent indictment of the cultivation and science of the older, dying epoch than could be written with the pen of Ezekiel. The age has nothing in it that satisfies them: they therefore turn away from it . . . In doing so they create a new age. . . . All these new saints of ours—new Christians and loving persons who crowd the slums, and rediscover Christ in themselves and in others—lack power to explain; they merely exist."

In addition to the intense activity of the domestic missions, foreign missionary ventures flourished in China and Japan, in the Near East— notably in Syria and Lebanon—in Africa, and in the countries of Latin America.

Between 1860 and 1910, 119 American women served as missionaries in Shantung province; of these, 71 came as single women. Lottie Moon's thirty-five years of missionary endeavor made her the most famous of the woman missionary band. On the male side, Calvin Mateer, who baptized an infant son of missionaries named Henry Luce, was the most commanding figure. Mateer headed Tengchow College, which turned out a number of distinguished Chinese Presbyterians, teachers and scholars and followers of Sun Yat-sen. By 1912 the graduates of Tengchow College held 380 teaching positions in eleven Chinese provinces. Others were scattered around in government service and in various fields of reform. The remainder were concentrated in the fields of medicine, business, and journalism. At the end of his career Mateer was struck by the accelerating rate of change in China. "Old customs and prejudices are giving way," he wrote exultantly. "The bright dawn of better things is upon us. The most conservative and immovable people in the world, persistently wedded to the old ways, are getting used to new things. . . . I often wish I were young again."

The power and importance of what we might call the Near East missionary establishment were revealed at the Paris Peace Conference. During the conference and after it had adjourned, American missionary leaders like Cleveland Dodge and Howard Bliss exerted a strong, though in the end futile, pressure for settlements favorable to the national interests of the Armenians and Syrians in particular. General James Harbord, whom we have already encountered as an aide to Pershing and subsequently as commanding general of the 1st Division at St.-Mihiel and head of the AEF Services of Supply, was the head of a Near East mission, formed in large part as a consequence of missionary agitation to make recommendations for United States policy in the region. Assiduous lobbying was done by the American Committee for Armenian and Syrian Relief, the American Committee for Relief in the Near East, and the American Friends of Armenia. Behind all these groups was the American Home Mission Board. In addition, the native leaders of the Near Eastern peoples were in large part trained in mission-run schools and colleges—the Syrian Protestant College, Robert College, and Constantinople Woman's College.

Seven other missionary-founded colleges in the Near East included the American College at Van in eastern Anatolia, Central Turkey College, with separate campuses for men and women, and at Smyrna, the International College. In Bulgaria, no longer within the Ottoman Empire, the American board founded the Collegiate and Theological Institute at Samokov, and, in Greece, the Thessalonica Agricultural and Industrial Institute.

The accomplishments of the Near East missionaries and their Protestant allies at home were substantial. In the words of the historian of their activities, Joseph Grabill, they "developed Near East Relief, an aid and recovery program not unlike the Marshall Plan and Point Four, . . . [and] they helped promote the League. They advocated a strategic presence for the United States in the Near East [mandates over Armenia or all of Asia Minor] and . . . support for Iran, Greece, and Turkey."

The case was much the same in China. The principal opposition to placing Shantung Province under control of the Japanese came from American missionaries. But that was, of course, only a small part of the story. The "Westernization" of the Far East was carried on primarily by missionaries. By 1910 there were 10,000 women, divided almost equally between married and unmarried, in seventeen Far Eastern missionary fields; 332 were physicians. There were almost twice as many men active in the various mission fields and many more male physicians. Bengali children were taught by the most up-to-date pedagogy in schools run by teachers who had been students of John Dewey or were graduates of teacher-training schools run on Deweyan principles.

Andrew Carnegie had testified before the Commission on Industrial Relations that one of the "greatest triumphs in this age . . . is the elevation of women. [Laughter]." "I want to tell you something I can never forget. I was traveling in China. . . . Sitting with the mandarins . . . we began to talk, and the question of course came upon the different views of the future and religion, and so forth, and one of the mandarins said to me, 'Mr. Carnegie, the greatest work of your Christ is the elevation of women. . . . They are not elevated in China, but that is Christ's great work. He has elevated women beyond any human being that ever lived.' " Vast and virtually invisible, the missionary enterprise played a crucial role in the spreading of the new consciousness around the globe.

Following the lead of Continental theologians, American clergy began to question whether the church and the Christian community generally had not, in their enthusiasm for secular social reform, deemphasized dogma and doctrine until nothing was left of orthodoxy except some platitudes about loving one's neighbor. Shailer Mathews, dean of the University of Chicago Divinity School and a leader in the Social Gospel movement, had misgivings about the tendency of the Protestant churches or, more notably, the liberal ministers involved in social work to emphasize the "Social" at the expense of the "Gospel." He wrote: "A danger to which Protestantism—particularly progressive Protestantism—in America is exposed is that its churches shall become mere agents of social service. There are many people who, in reaction from extreme orthodoxy, have come to feel that the sole business of the church is to push social reform. This danger is particularly strong in America just now because social workers have come to see that the Church, instead of being hostile to their ideals, is the greatest force by which their ideals can be put into operation. Such a valuing of the Church brings no small satisfaction to those of us who have endeavored to set forth the social significance of the spiritual life. But we cannot let social service take the place of God."

The movement of the new, or neo, orthodoxy stressed the biblical emphasis on man as a "fallen" creature, tainted by original sin and thus by no means "naturally good" or even, prospectively, "perfectible." This was a view of human nature that characterized the Classical-Christian Consciousness of the majority of the Founding Fathers. As such it was the most serious challenge yet launched against the optimistic Enlightenment view of human society that had dominated the mental world of most Americans for more than 100 years. Curiously enough, it was reinforced by the widely discussed Freudian view of human nature, in which the "libido," with its ravenous sexual appetites, and the "id," or subconscious, with its own irrational needs and hungers, were constantly warring with the "ego," the conscious, socially responsible element in the individual. The Freudian terms could be translated, to a disconcerting degree, into the terms of the Manichean heresy of the struggle of good and evil or, indeed, of original sin. But this connection was not commonly made, and Freud, by depicting God simply as an enormous projection of his famous father figure, did his bit to undermine conventional Christianity. It might be said that he adapted the rather gloomy view of human nature that was a major element of the Judeo-Christian world view and stripped it of its redemptive elements, such as the promise of eternal life. Between the Marxist's merciless analysis of most thoughts and actions as merely rationalizations—social stereotypes and institutions—of man's disposition to exploit his weaker neighbors and nations, and Freud's account of the id playing its bag of tricks on the ego, the composite picture of man that emerged was not a cheering one; it must be said, however, that it seemed to have an irresistible attraction for American intellectuals (Marxism at least dragged in the hope of salvation via the triumph of the workers and the withering away of the state).

New Thought—Christian Science, Science of Mind, and similar sects—remained much in evidence. The New Thought sects were apt, as John Jay Chapman put it, "to take names that appealed to the prejudices of the age and suggested that their truth was new and yet old; scientific and yet Christian; hygienic and spiritual, combining the utmost obscurity of statement with the most positive practical results." These new religions "arose out of some first-hand private tragedy, grief, disease, or nervous disorder, self-cured, without a doctor, without a church—but not without God. The new forms of religion had this in common with the old," Chapman added, ". . . they focalized the attention of the worshipper upon some super-sensuous abstraction and thereby filled him with power." They made it possible once more to invoke the name of God. "It was, through such rifts, cracks and jagged holes in the roof of the prison that a hurricane of the spirit tore and blasted its way back to humanity. . . . The new American mysticism, for all its eccentricities, dropped an anchor for a generation that had been living in continuous flotation . . . a religion of good works sprang up, which had the spontaneity of a natural force; it was insuperable." To Chapman, both "Uplift" and "New Thought" were parts of the same great spiritual revulsion . . . and acceptance of life as something that we subserve." It was also true that New Thought was far more "personal" and inward-turning than conventional Christianity, more individualistic, less oriented toward reform; ". . . the goal toward which the age has been groping its way during the last thirty years could better be described as the Right to Feel than as the Will to Believe." Chapman regretted "the loss of the old cultivation," yet he knew it was never "quite right," and he believed that he was living "in the age of a great regeneration. There is hardly a man in whose face I do not see some form of it. A new hope is with us." The new mission was very different from that of the abolitionist movement, but both were "forms of the same power." The spirit was felt in all men. "In some, it moves the heart, crying, Abba, Father. Others it leaves speechless, but makes their lives beautiful through unselfish labor." The warfare between religion and science was in a truce, if not at an end. The churches had grown liberal, and thoughtful people were increasingly aware "of the realities which lie . . . behind the noisy dogmas . . . of human thought. . . . Great and small, learned and unlearned meet upon that plane of common humility which is their only meeting ground. It is a period when the power and first-hand mystery of life is recognized on every side. . . . "

In the decline of the power of orthodox Christianity, if not necessarily of church members, cults and sects came to the fore. Rabindranath Tagore, a Bengali whose family had tried to combine Western practicality and Eastern mysticism, became the rage in upper-class circles. Tagore was an Indian nationalist, a poet and philosopher. He was a striking figure, more than six feet tall, with a flowing white beard and voluminous white robes. More important, he was one of the first of a long line of Indian wise men, gurus, who found responsive audiences and infatuated disciples in the United States.

Civil religion—the faith that the United States was the finest, the noblest, the freest, most powerful, wise, prosperous, and benign nation on earth or in history's annals—persisted, grew, if anything, larger and more offensive. It was not confined to the conviction that the United States was the greatest nation in the world. Arnold Bennett, on his tour of the United States in 1911, was assured in every city or hamlet he visited that *it* was the greatest and truest and most authentic and representative city (or the "greatest little town") in the United States. Chicagoans commiserated with him for having had to linger in New York City and assured him that it could in no way be taken as representative of the real America. Bostonians told him with sublime confidence that Boston was not only the most historic (and best preserved) of any American city but also the most genuinely American (as well as the most British) of cities. "And when I entered Indianapolis,"

Bennett wrote, "I discovered that Chicago was a mushroom and a suburb of Warsaw, and that its pretension to represent the United States was grotesque, the authentic center of the United States being obviously Indianapolis." Everywhere he was pressed to affirm this or that city as comprehensively and preeminently American. There was often a kind of plea for reassurance in the query. "You are aware of the self-consciousness of Chicago as soon as you are aware of its bitumen," Bennett wrote. "The quality demands sympathy and wins it by its wistfulness. Chicago is openly anxious about its soul." He liked that quality in Chicago; he wished more cities were concerned about their souls.

The German author Emil Reich in his book *Success Among the Nations* described the nature of America's civilization: "The Americans are filled with such an implicit and absolute confidence in their Union and in their future success that any remark other than laudatory is unacceptable to the majority of them. We have had many opportunities of hearing public speakers in America cast doubts upon the very existence of God and of Providence, question the historic nature or veracity of the whole fabric of Christianity; but never has it been our fortune to catch the slightest whisper of doubt, the slightest want of faith, in the chief God of America—unlimited belief in the future of America."

46

Education

"Americans," Herbert Croly wrote, "are superstitious in respect to education, rather because of the social 'uplift' which they expect to achieve by so-called educational means. The credulity of the socialist in expecting to alter human nature by merely institutional and legal changes is at least equalled by the credulity of good Americans in proposing to evangelize the individual by the reading of books and by the expenditure of money and words. . . . Do we lack culture? We will 'make it hum' by founding a new university in Chicago. Is American art neglected and impoverished? We will enrich it by organizing art departments in our colleges, and popularize it by lectures with lantern slides and associations for the study of its history."

John Jay Chapman wrote: "The savage, terrible hordes of America waked up in 1870 to the importance of salvation by education. Perhaps they valued education too highly, and in their ignorance demanded more than even education can give. . . . The Pope during this epoch was Charles William Eliot." Buildings in the neo-Gothic styles favored by donors and alumni sprouted like mushrooms across the American landscape, but what went on behind these handsome façades was more social than intellectual: Clubs, secret societies, such as Woodrow Wilson had broken his teeth upon at Princeton, fraternities, and sports flourished. "Our colleges," Chapman wrote, "perform a wonderful social service: they are boys' clubs and men's clubs. Educationally they are nearly extinct so far as the old humanities go." To Chapman, Eliot symbolized Harvard's shortcomings. "There is about as much love of learning in Charles Eliot as there was in Jay Gould," he wrote.

"I cannot bear to be called 'a loyal son of Harvard,' " Chapman wrote to William James. "This chest-thumping, back-slapping, vociferous and cheap emotionalism, done to get money . . . is too much like everything else." The "decay of scholarship and decent feeling" was evident in the collection of eulogies gathered to celebrate Eliot's retirement in 1909. "Everything seems to be a base-ball team—jollying, rough good-feeling, and a thorough-going belief in money and *us*. . . . Harvard is a base-ball team, and they'll bid high to get the best man they can, even if they have to outbid the Sioux City Nine." Eliot's philosophy was "boom, boom, boom. . . . Is there something that operates without money—not anywhere? . . . Eliot and the crew of howlers . . . are submerged in their improvements. . . . It is no one's fault. They done the best they knew; and the next generation can pick up the pieces and painfully recover and reconstruct the idea that a university is a place of thought, truth, religion." Chapman added: "Eliot in his financial rhapsodies drew golden tears down Pluto's cheek, and he built his college. The music was crude; it was not Apollo's lute; it was the hurdy-gurdy of pig-iron and the stock-yards. To this music rose the walls of Harvard, and of all our colleges—our solemn temples, theaters, clinics, dormitories, museums . . . clubs, parades, intelligence offices and boat rides, the Harvard Brigade that beats up trade for the College—foolish would be the man who should blame any individual for these things. . . . They are the symbols of contemporary America— inevitable, necessary. . . ."

By Chapman's era at Harvard the neglect of the undergraduates that had so embittered Charles Francis Adams (and others) had produced a kind of crisis marked by nervous breakdowns and suicides. When the "authorities," Chapman wrote, discovered "something was wrong at Harvard," it was concluded that "nobody loved anybody there, and that the thing to do was to give weekly teas at Brooks Hall, to ask everyone, to get ladies from Boston, Bishops from anywhere, social people at any cost, social talent to bridge the gulf between instructors and instructed. . . . It was shoulder-to-shoulder, never say die, love one love all, more tea, more ladies . . . , it was a real dawn, somewhat grotesque and naïve . . . but Harvard," Chapman wrote, "has been a more human place ever since. Indeed, what Harvard truly needed was the outside world—ladies, Bishops and tea."

More than by bishops or teas or philanthropic tycoons, Harvard was rescued from the intellectual doldrums by William James and the colleagues he attracted to Harvard, notably Josiah Royce and George Santayana. Oswald Garrison Villard recalled the Colonial Club, a group of Harvard faculty members, led by James and Royce. "When they spoke," Villard wrote, "everyone listened; I recall particularly James's seriousness and earnestness and the impression he gave of a controlling desire within him to get to the bottom of things, really to arrive at the facts."

To Hutchins Hapgood the Harvard of William James was like being released from a prison of the soul. He found in it "something constantly soothing, hygienic, and elevated. . . . I found freedom of the spirit all about me. It was an indescribable cool pleasure to come in contact with emancipated intelligences, with men of real culture and power who were not burdened by themselves but moved about freely in the world of intuition and thought; men like James, Royce and Santayana. . . . I found free instead of imprisoned souls. I had come from a town where most people seemed to me painful or benumbed slaves, where the intensity of life revealed itself only in ugly passions, inarticulate. I came into serene elevation. . . . I found myself where I needed to be. I found myself morally at home."

Between John Jay Chapman's and Oswald Garrison Villard's undergraduate days and those of Walter Lippmann and John Reed, some fifteen years later, Harvard (and American universities in general) benefited from the intellectual ferment of the Progressive era. "It has been such a wild time," Lippmann wrote his "girl," Lucile Elsa, in 1908. "Metaphysics, Socialism, are theories, Schopenhauer, a vitality in religion—every night till late in the morning and then dissatisfaction and bed." He added, "Dissatisfaction is the price we pay when we're young for vision . . . it is better never to see and to realize, than to see and realize and not transcend the vision." The ideal of Lippmann and his friends was "to build a citadel of human joy upon the slum of misery . . . to give the words 'the brotherhood of man' a meaning." Every Thursday morning at eleven he had tea with James and his wife, and these were the high spots of his week. The talks were, he wrote his parents, "the greatest thing that has happened to me in my college life."

George Santayana, with his modern Epicureanism, appealed to

Lippmann, and he wrote to Lucile: "Our lives must be given over to the most beautiful ones, for beauty alone, physical or intellectual or spiritual, has the power of completeness. . . . Beauty alone is immortal, not skin-deep as cynics say, because fullness is the essence of immortality." In addition to reveling in beauty, he longed "to reach some small portion of the 'masses' so that in the position not of a teacher but of a friend, I may lay open real happiness to them."

Harvard's other saving grace, at least among its sister institutions in the so-called Ivy League, was its admissions policy. "At Harvard, class distinction counts for nothing," Lippmann wrote to a friend. "Men of all types and purposes are thrown together in dormitory, dining hall and on the athletic field . . . the scientific student is expected to know poetry, and the aesthete is generally interested in physics."

Graduate education, fired by the Johns Hopkins-Clark University ideal of putting mind to work in the service of society, in Frederic Howe's words, reached its apotheosis at Robert La Follette's University of Wisconsin and approached the ideal at other reform-minded public institutions, primarily in the Middle West. Science ruled, and the scholar was its handmaid. James Bryce, lecturing at Johns Hopkins on the failure of democracy, told his students that "America, with no leisure class devoted to statecraft as in Great Britain, was to be saved by the scholar."

Generally, the nation's colleges and universities were bastions of conservatism. Emma Goldman found the University of Wisconsin refreshingly radical after the Eastern institutions of higher education. "Professors and students were vitally interested in social ideas. . . ." The professors "proved to be exceptions to the average American educator. They were progressive, alive to the problems of the world, and modern in interpretation of their subjects." From Goldman's observation of other American colleges, the professors and students knew and cared little about "the social struggle." Although Michigan State University was "only ten hours removed from the University of Wisconsin," she noted, ". . . in spirit it was fifty years behind. Instead of broad-minded professors and keen students, I was confronted by five hundred university rowdies . . . whistling, howling, and acting like lunatics."

When Goldman returned to Wisconsin a year later, she found the professors considerably less "reckless" than they had been on her earlier visit. The apparent reason was that the state legislature was considering the university's appropriations bill. The changed atmosphere reminded her that professors were "also proletarians; intellectual proletarians, to be sure, but even more dependent upon their employer than ordinary mechanics." The University of Kansas, once the bellwether of radical reform, seemed subdued, content to live on past glories. "Had it not been the stronghold of free thought?" Emma Goldman reflected. There was no sign of unorthodoxy now. "The Church and Prohibition had . . . performed the last rites at the internment of liberalism . . . smugness, and self-complacency characterized most cities in the State of Kansas," she noted.

In the state universities of the Midwest the majority of the students—56 percent at the University of Michigan—came from "the homes of farmers and mechanics." The historian of the University of Kansas wrote: "The great mass of them . . . are poor. In order to obtain an education many of them have for years practiced self-denial and suffered privations, the description of which would stir your hearts with admiration and fill your eyes with tears of sympathy."

In addition to the denominational colleges and the land-grant universities, there were numerous more or less ephemeral colleges established, as we would say today, as alternative institutions by persons dissatisfied with the more conventional forms of higher education. Such was the One Study University near Mastersville, Ohio, where the students took one subject intensively at a time before going on to another. Arthur Le Sueur, a lumberman, millworker, railroad hand, farmer, and, finally, lawyer, established the Peoples College at Fort Scott, Kansas, on the principle that "the psychology of education in the practical line of the schools is to educate the ambitious to acquire; the prime thing in life that is inculcated in the children is to follow the example of those who have been able to amass fortunes. . . ." The Peoples College, on the other hand, tried to "inculcate the idea that the most dishonorable thing in life is parasitism—the will to live on the labor of another. . . . We aim to prevent that by making a practical demonstration of cultural and vocational training and bringing the student in touch with the workers' viewpoint, showing the desirability . . . of service and the dishonorableness of living upon the labor of others without contributing to the welfare of society."

But there was already, as we have noted, a strong countermovement toward "scholarly" objectivity, detachment, and political and social neutrality, a movement encouraged by trustees who made clear that they frowned on professors who involved themselves in liberal or radical causes. The memory of William Rainey Harper's sacking of Edward Bemis for his municipal ownership of utilities' heresies remained fresh in academic minds.

It seemed to critics as diverse as Brooks and Henry Adams, on the one hand, and John Jay Chapman, on the other, that if the disposition of scholars to devote themselves to increasingly esoteric studies—aimed, it was said, at "pushing back the frontiers of knowledge"— made them relatively immune to the ire of trustees, it also made them distressingly irrelevant. That irrelevance, Brooks Adams argued, was just the point. Convinced after the Republican Party's rejection of Roosevelt in 1912 that a social revolution of devastating proportions was inevitable, Adams saw American universities as the docile creations of capital. "In the United States," he wrote, "capital has long owned the leading universities by right of purchase, as it has owned the highways, the currency, and the press, and capital has used the universities, in a general way, to develop capitalistic ideas . . . [C]apital has commercialized education. . . . Capital has preferred the specialized mind and that not of the highest quality, since it has found it profitable to set quantity before quality. . . ." After 1870 the emphasis in higher education had switched rapidly from ethical and literary studies to "the intrinsic value of the fact. . . ." According to Henry Adams the aim of the New University came to be "to teach everything, little attention being given to the coordination of the parts. The result could not be otherwise than wasteful and disjointed. . . . The theory on which the modern University system rests is fallacious. The worth of the University lies not in the multitude of units taught, but in the coordination of parts and the intensity of effort." There was a wasteful duplication of courses and topics; colleges made no effort "to add to their efficiency and stop their waste by intelligent cooperation among themselves. . . . The student at college is launched upon an unknown sea, like a mariner without chart or compass. He has little to guide him in ascertaining what departments are really kindred. Even the courses of history are often arranged according to the taste of professors, and with no relation to historical sequence." The result was that the university served to neutralize the intellectuals and scholars who might otherwise have been capital's most vigorous critics.

To William James, as to John Jay Chapman, the direction of higher learning was more of a threat to the moral and spiritual values of the society than to the intellectual. James was especially dismayed at what he called "the Mandarin disease," the increasing emphasis on the Ph.D. as a "Teutonic" invention—entirely alien, in his view, to the essential character of American life. "To interfere with the free development of talent, to obstruct the natural play of supply and demand in the teaching profession, to foster academic snobbery by the prestige of certain privileged institutions, to transfer accredited value from essential manhood to an outward badge, to blight hopes and promote invidious sentiments, to divert the attention of aspiring youth from direct dealings with truth to the passing of examinations . . . ought surely to be regarded as a drawback. . . ." James called on the colleges and universities to "give up their unspeakably silly ambition to bespangle their lists of offices with these doctoral titles" and to "look more to substance than to vanity and sham. . . . Are we Americans . . . destined after all to hunger after similar [Germanic] vanities on an infinitely more contemptible scale? And is individuality with us also to count for nothing unless stamped and licensed and authenticated by some title-giving machine? Let us pray that our ancient national genius may long preserve vitality enough to guard us from a future so unmanly and so unbeautiful!"

James himself was criticized by younger scholars for writing "too personally." One apparent sign of scholarly detachment, he noted, was writing badly. "Of all the *bad writing* that the world has seen," he wrote to his friend, Theodore Flournoy, a professor at the University of Geneva, "I think that our American writing is getting to be the worst." The academic world had "unchained a formlessness of expression that beats the bad writing of the Hegelian epoch in Germany." Academic philosophy was becoming an "awful abstract rigmarole" which was used to obscure the truth, not to illumine it. "It means," he wrote to a friend, "utter relaxation of intellectual duty, and God will smite it. If there's anything he hates, it is that kind of oozy writing."

When James traveled to Italy in 1905 to give a paper at a philosophical congress in Rome, he was charmed by the "enthusiasm, and also a literary swing and activity," among the young Italian students he met that had no counterpart "in our own land" and that "probably our damned academic technics and Ph.D.-machinery and university organization" would prevent "from ever coming to birth." The Italian enthusiasm, he wrote to Santayana, "has given me a queer sense of the gray-plaster temperament of our bald-headed young Ph.D.'s, boring each other at seminaries, writing those direful reports of literature in the 'Philosophical Review' and elsewhere, fed on 'books of reference,' and never confounding 'Aesthetik' with 'Erkenntistheorie.' Faugh! I shall never deal with them again. . . . Can't you and I, who in spite of such divergence have yet so much in common in our *Weltanschauung*, start a systematic movement at Harvard against the desiccating and pedantifying process?"

John Dewey was accomplishing at Chicago much the same mission as James—to give life to an institution otherwise intellectually timid and innately conventional. "Chicago University has during the past six months," William James wrote to Sarah Whitman, "given birth to the fruit of its ten years of gestation under John Dewey. The result is wonderful—a *real school*, and *real Thought*. Important thought, too! Did you ever hear of such a city or such a University? Here we have thought, but no school. At Yale, a school but no thought. Chicago has both. . . ." James wrote to F. C. S. Schiller: "Dewey's powerful stuff seems also to ring the death-knell of a sentenced world. Yet none of *them* [his colleagues] will see it." Soon "the living world will all be drifting after *us*."

Dewey had set himself the task of translating the new consciousness into a set of educational principles and practices applicable especially to the curricula of elementary and secondary schools. A disciple of James, a self-styled pragmatist, Dewey embraced Darwinism as a liberating doctrine with its own morality. "To idealize and rationalize the universe at large is after all a confession of inability to master the course of things that specifically concern us." But the new Darwinian social science offered "a method of locating and interpreting the more serious of the conflicts that occur in life, and a method of projecting ways for dealing with them; a method of moral and political diagnosis and prognosis."

In John Dewey's words, "The human mind, deliberately as it were, exhausted the logic of the changeless, the final, and the transcendent, before it essayed adventure on the pathless wastes of generation and transformation. . . . The influence of Darwin upon philosophy resides in his having conquered the phenomena of life for the principle of transition, and thereby freed the new logic for application to mind and morals and life. . . ." Theologians and the religious in general had found comfort in evidences of design in the universe—"the marvelous adaptations of organisms to their environment, of organs to the organism . . . the foreshadowing by lower forms of the higher; the preparation in earlier stages of growth for organs that only later had their functioning. . . ." These facts "added such prestige to the design argument," Dewey wrote, "that by the late eighteenth century it was . . . the central point of the theistic and idealistic philosophy. The Darwinian principle of natural selection cut straight under this philosophy. If all organic adaptions are due simply to constant variation and the elimination of those variations which are harmful in the struggle for existence . . . there is no call for a prior intelligent causal force to plan and ordain them." What resulted, in Dewey's view, were shifts from the notion of "an intelligence that shaped things once for all to the particular intelligences which things are even now shaping; shifts from the ultimate goal of good to the direct increments of justice and happiness that intelligent administration of existent conditions may beget. . . ." The overtones of Emersonian individualism are unmistakable. It was evident to Dewey that man, not God, was master of the processes that would produce, scientifically, the new and better social order.

The implications for the reform of education were apparent. It must concern itself primarily with educating students to think for themselves, to explore all issues with an open mind, to eschew all rote learning, to question all received authority, and to realize, above all, that they could understand, control, and direct the evolution of human society. In an influential essay entitled "Morality Is Social," Dewey wrote: "Intelligence becomes ours in the degree to which we use it and accept responsibility for the consequences. . . . Thoughtless, self-centered action" was, above all, antisocial action. The critical question was not whether such action was "good" or "bad" according to tradition or edict, but whether its results were socially harmful. "Scientific social psychology," manifested in the new "progressive education," must produce a new type of socially responsible citizen.

That Dewey's philosophical views were in the main shallow was far less important than the fact that their practical consequences were on the whole exemplary. Jane Addams described him as a pioneer in insisting upon "an atmosphere of freedom and confidence between the teacher and pupil, of a common interest in the life they led together." She wrote: "John Dewey calmly stated that the proper home of intelligence was the world itself and that the true function of intelligence was to act as critic and regulator of the forces which move the world."

Dewey's influence spread far beyond the boundaries of the United States, as Addams discovered when she visited Peking and was told by the members of the Philosophy Club in that city that "the philosophy of Dewey and his concepts of conduct could be compared to no one but to Confucius himself."

The Mexican minister of education proclaimed himself a disciple of Dewey's. The murals of José Clemente Orozco that decorated the walls of education buildings in Mexico were, it was said, conceived in the spirit of Dewey's theories of education, with their vivid depiction of the life of the Mexican people. The murals were the visual representations of Dewey's conviction that all true education must relate directly to the life of the people themselves. In Dewey's words, "Better it is for philosophy to err in active participation in the living struggles and issues of its own age and times, than to maintain an immune monastic impeccability. To try to escape from the snares and pitfalls of time by recourse to traditional problems and interests—rather than that, let the dead bury their own dead."

Ironically, the principles that Dewey enunciated eloquently and voluminously (his collected works are in many volumes), which traveled around the world at only slightly less than the speed of sound to penetrate virtually every institution devoted to the training of teachers, were rudely rebuffed by the high priests of higher education in the United States. The colleges and universities rejected his doctrines as tending to compromise the purity of their highly specialized and increasingly esoteric studies.

It was also the case that higher education, once overwhelmingly Protestant-Christian in its atmosphere and inner rationale, became entirely secular. "Science after Darwin's time was seized with a fever of world conquest; its language must dominate. In correct circles it became bad form to use any word that was tinged with theology," John Jay Chapman wrote. "New words were invented; modern psychology was developed. . . . The word 'God' was, of course taboo, unfair, incorrect, a boorish survival." Religion was an illusion; "methods of accurate research had recorded a zero." Dewey wrote: "Intellectually, religious emotions are not creative but conservative. They attach themselves readily to the current view of the world and consecrate it. They steep and dye intellectual fabrics in the seething vat of emotions; they do not form their warp and woof." Dewey could not think of "any large idea about the world being independently generated by religion."

Lester Ward remained doggedly optimistic. He was pleased to report in 1906 that the high school system in the United States had grown impressively and was "almost turning out scholars." The "certificates from many of them place their holders on the threshold of the higher institutions. . . . The several American States are rapidly establishing what they call State Universities," he added, "some of which already take rank with the older endowed universities."

From his professorship at Brown, Ward was less disposed to write off private colleges and universities as a negative influence on education, but he still took the line that they might ultimately be replaced by public universities. "It is certain," he wrote, "that they are freer and more democratic than endowed institutions. . . ." But the "action of society in inaugurating and carrying on a great educational system, however defective we may consider that system to be, is undoubtedly the most promising form thus far taken by collective achievement. It means much even now, but for the future it means nothing less than the complete social appropriation of individual achievement which has civilized the world. It is the crowning act in the long list of facts that we have only partially and imperfectly considered, constituting the socialization of achievement." Yet Ward was highly critical of what passed for academic scholarship. Much of it seemed to him "intellectual gymnastics . . . exercising the intellect on sham problems in the same manner that acrobats cultivate their bodily agility."

Despite (or perhaps because of) her affection for Dewey, Jane Addams became increasingly uneasy about the relation of Hull House to the University of Chicago. She warned against allowing the university to "swallow the settlement, and turn it into one more laboratory; another place in which to analyze and depict, to observe and record." A settlement house which allowed itself to be thus preempted was "merely an imitative and unendowed university, as a settlement which gives all its energies to classes and lectures and athletics is merely an imitative college." To Addams the failure of the university lay in the fact that after it had passed from "teaching theology to teaching secular knowledge," it should have shifted from trying to save men's souls to trying to give its students the power to adjust "in healthful relations to nature and their fellow men." But the college failed to do this and made the test of its success the mere collecting and disseminating of knowledge, elevating the means into an end and falling in love with its own achievement.

One of the principal shortcomings of the educational system, Addams argued, was that "We distrust the human impulse as well as the teachings of our own experience, and in their stead we substitute dogmatic rules of conduct." At the end of *Democracy and Social Ethics* she quoted the prophet Micah: "to do justly and to love mercy and to walk humbly with thy God." It was the latter injunction that seemed to her of special importance, "to walk for many dreary miles beside the lowliest of His creatures, not even in the peace of mind which the company of the humble is popularly supposed to afford, but rather with the pangs and throes to which the poor human understanding is subjected whenever it attempts to comprehend the meaning of life."

Addams was alarmed at the growth of largely autonomous departments in the major universities. They were characterized by "invisible walls which . . . stubbornly separate one academic department from another. There is nothing in creation like it," she added, "excepting the unbreakable division walls between the different departments of the United States government."

Some attention to the word "popular" will give us a useful clue to the nature of the alienation between the world of the academy and the world outside. For the first generation of post–Civil War academics the distinction had little meaning. They considered it an essential part of their responsibilities as scholars and intellectuals to communicate the results of their experiments or cogitations to as wide a circle of the informed public as possible. To this end they lectured frequently to "lay" audiences—the Chautauqua circuit was a favorite—and to various clubs and societies of amateurs in the fields in which they were experts. Asa Gray, Louis Agassiz, Benjamin Peirce, and dozens of others considered it no condescension to carry their knowledge wherever there were those ready to hear. As the last decades of the century wore on, general-circulation magazines, such as the *Nation, McClure's, American Magazine,* and *Everybody's Magazine,* and the older journals, such as the *Atlantic Monthly* and *Harper's Weekly,* carried a substantial number of scientific articles written by professors (or, when their prose tended to be impenetrable, articles by them in conjunction with the editors of the magazine). *Popular Science* was one of the most successful journals of the day and counted among its contributors such figures as Charles Sanders Peirce and William James, not to mention an array of stars from the natural sciences. Gradually, however, "popular" took on distinctly negative connotations. "Popular" became synonymous with "simplified," and "simplified" with "degraded" or "meretricious." Serious scholars eschewed anything that suggested a wider public than their fellow academics. To be accused of being "a popularizer" was to invite ridicule and contempt. As the academic world drew into itself and erected a complex set of specialties, each with a language as arcane as medieval Bulgarian, it became its pride that it would make no compromise between the academy and the public, between "inside" and "outside." That fact alone gives to the stormy academic controversies of the late-nineteenth and early-twentieth centuries an archaic air. They were argued out in public. The disputants vied for public attention and approval. One reason may have been that the academic world (or the more seriously scholarly portion of it) was so small that it had yet to constitute a critical intellectual mass; the informed public must perforce be included. But there was certainly a deeper reason: the conviction that the informed mind must act responsibly on the most challenging social and political issues of the day. Frederic Howe revealed the rationale for the intertwined nature of the academic world and the public world when he wrote so glowingly of his days at Johns Hopkins.

So there were two discernible and closely related tendencies. One was the increasing ubiquitousness of graduate study, accompanied by an increasing disposition to conceive of scholarly activity as objective and detached from the political and social struggles going on outside universities' cloistered walls; the other was the growing disposition in the large universities to make undergraduate education merely a by-product of graduate studies.

"I am at a loss to learn what function a University now performs," Henry Adams wrote to his brother. "They are ornamental but expensive; and as you say, not one graduate in ten retains a shadow of liberal education. . . . The average man of highest education is a greater imbecile than the old-fashioned boor, who at least recognized an inexplicable phenomenon when he saw it. Our educated class will not recognize the day of judgment, until they are resting in hot oil." Brooks Adams responded, "Save as an amusement for the antiquary, history and economics which deal with the past without reference to the present have no significance. Research for its own sake is futile."

Whether the growth of "research for its own sake" was the result, as Brooks Adams argued, of "capital's" desire to discourage critical generalizations or simply the consequence of a kind of inner dynamic that worked its way heedless of any rational argument, the outcome was disheartening. "What is the most important thing in education?" John Jay Chapman asked rhetorically, and answered, "It is the relation between teacher and pupil. Here is the focus of the whole matter; this tiny crucible must boil or your whole college will be cold. The Business Era chilled this heart-center of University life in America; because during this Era, natural law operated to bring the youngest scholars under the control of unenthusiastic instructors. Persons of individual power were the very ones who were discharged. Thus the instructors—without anyone's being aware of it—were picked out *because* of their unenthusiasm. So terrible is natural law."

Much of the unhappy moral and spiritual condition of the United States, in Chapman's view, was due to the decline of true learning. Professional scholarship had taken its place. With the proliferation of institutions of higher education, the great tradition had fallen on barren soil. The emotions of the youth in every vigorous society should be fed upon the great works of the past, he insisted: "songs, aspirations, stories, prayers, reverence for humanity, knowledge of God—or else some dreadful barrenness will set in and paralyze the intellect of a race. . . . To cut loose, to cast away, to destroy, seems to be our impulse. We do not want the past. This awful loss of all the terms of thought, this beggary of intellect, is shown in the unwillingness of the average man in America to go to the bottom of any subject, his mental inertia, his hatred of impersonal thought, his belief in labor-saving, his indifference to truth. . . . The commercial mind seems, in its essence, to be the natural enemy of love, religion, and truth; and when, as at the present moment in America [1913], we have commerce dominant in an era whose characteristic note is contempt for the past, we can hardly expect a picturesque, pleasing, or harmonious social life."

47

The New Technologies

The new consciousness had a technology to go with it. The first decade of the new century saw a kind of explosion of technology, one that had two principal elements: the technology itself—telephone, automobile, airplane, "moving picture"—and the utilization of that technology. Europeans, as we have had occasion to note before, often preceded Americans in inventions (the Italian Guglielmo Marconi developed the wireless) and almost invariably in what was coming to be called pure science, but the particular genius of Americans was expressed in making new inventions available to a broad market and, above all, in *organizing* mass production.

The most important, if not the most dramatic, development was in the field of electrical energy. Electricity became so inexpensive that its use multiplied a thousandfold in a few years. From being a luxury it soon became a necessity. It found a wide variety of uses. By 1920 there were hundreds of electric steelmaking furnaces in the United States. Forty thousand electric stoves were manufactured in the same year. There were, as we have noted in an earlier volume, electric streetcars and electric elevated railroads. The waterpower of Niagara Falls was harnessed, and dams began to appear on major rivers to meet the insatiable demand for electric power. The dynamo became for Henry

Adams the symbol of the industrial age, and he contrasted the frame of mind that had produced it and worshiped it with the medieval temperament that had worshiped the Virgin. In his almost perversely private way he wrote a letter/book to his nieces reflecting on the relation of the Virgin to the dynamo after visits to Mont St.-Michel and Chartres, and he and Brooks Adams decided that the nation controlling the largest force of energy must dominate the world.

Like Adams, Arnold Bennett, the English writer, found the "most powerful ecclesiastical symbol" for America in the electric dynamo that supplied power for the city of New York. There were only the huge bulks of machines with an occasional dwarfed human figure in "a hall enchanted and inexplicable." By the great turbines, "I was," he added, "more profoundly attracted, impressed and inspired than by any other non-spiritual phenomena whatever in the United States. For me they were the proudest material achievements, and essentially the most poetical achievements, of the United States."

By 1917 Americans were paying $175,000,000 a year for more than fifty electrical appliances for use in the home. Comfort and convenience, foreign travelers had noted from the beginning of the nineteenth century, were American obsessions. Those middle-class families least able to afford servants were the first to make use of the new laborsaving domestic appliances: vacuum cleaners; washing machines; refrigerators; electrical stoves and heaters. In 1904 the Franklin Institute awarded a gold medal to Schuyler Wheeler, an associate of Edison's, for inventing the electric fan (which had, in fact, been agitating the air since 1886).

The presiding genius of the age of electricity was, of course, Thomas Alva Edison. Edison, whom we have already encountered, was born in 1847 in a classic Midwestern small town, Milan, Ohio, and reared in Michigan. He was an indifferent student and a fledgling entrepreneur, selling newspapers and operating a candy concession on railroad trains. He became a telegraph operator while still in his teens and moved to Boston in 1868 to work for Western Union. There, a year later, he patented his first inventions—an electographic vote recorder and a stock ticker tape. They were suggestive of young Edison's preoccupation with the practical world of politics and business. At the age of twenty-three he joined with two other young engineers to form a consulting business. When it was dissolved two years later, Edison's share of the profits enabled him to set up a modest laboratory with several other young engineers to concentrate on improvements of telegraphy. These came so rapidly that in 1872 he applied for 38 patents. Three years later he invented a resonator for analyzing sound waves, and the next year he made a carbon telephone transmitter which greatly improved the quality of sound. He moved his much expanded laboratory to Menlo Park in New Jersey the same year. Five years later he registered 86 patents; he had clearly developed a technique for the mass production of inventions. Before he was through, he had registered thousands of patents in the United States and some 1,200 abroad for inventions of his and his associates. As significant as Edison's extraordinary fecundity of invention was his business acumen. Some of his patents he sold, and others, which promised quick profits, he undertook to manufacture himself in his Edison company. Although his contributions to the motion picture projector were relatively modest, he saw its commercial possibilities and was one of the earliest and most enterprising filmmakers and distributors.

In the more directly industrial line Edison turned to the invention of ore-mining machinery and metallurgy and the development of a storage battery. He also devised an efficient dictating machine and the mimeograph. In his lack of formal scientific training and his dependence on simple perseverance—the familiar trial-and-error approach of most nineteenth-century American inventors—Edison was a representative of an earlier era. He dismissed the notion that he was a genius by declaring that genius was, in fact, "one percent inspiration and ninety-nine percent perspiration," the kind of sentiment adored by his fellow Americans.

Edison's air of a homespun philosopher charmed Americans. For a nation infatuated with technology and with "getting ahead," Edison was the perfect exemplar. The practical nature of his inventions seemed to fulfill the promise of ever more bountiful comfort and convenience. In his shrewd perception of the "multiplier effect" of associating inventors in a common laboratory, where cooperation and organization counted for everything, he was a precursor of the new age. The ability to organize human talents and energies (which had its analogies in the factory and office) and direct them to the solution of particular practical problems was as important as his genius for invention.

Perhaps in reaction to the public adulation which was accorded Edison so unstintingly in his lifetime, historians, especially historians of science, have been disposed to downgrade his accomplishments as an original inventor. But that, after all, is beside the point. Edison embodied any number of qualities admired by his contemporaries and was, by any reasonable measure, one of the most remarkable of American heroes. He had a self-made man's scorn for academics and for universities and scholarship generally. "What we need," he declared in a characteristic statement, "are men capable of doing work. I wouldn't give a penny for the ordinary college graduate, except those from institutes of technology. Those coming up from the ranks are a darned sight better than the others. They aren't filled up with Latin, philosophy, and the rest of that ninny stuff. . . . What the country needs now is the practical skilled engineer, who is capable of doing everything. In three or four centuries when the country is settled, and commercialism is diminished, there will be time for the literary men. At present we want engineers, industrial men, good business-like managers and railroad men," men, in short, like Thomas Alva Edison. While Edison was proud of his village-atheist approach to conventional religion (one of many qualities he shared with his friend Henry Ford), he declared that he believed "beyond the possibility of a doubt that some vast Intelligence is governing this and other planets."

It was notorious that Edison was testy and irascible, but his biographers stressed that while it was true that their hero had a strong temper and was subject to spells of moodiness and depression, he was "a normal, fun-loving typical American. His sense of humor is intense, but not of the hot-house, overdeveloped variety." Citified humor? "His laugh is sometimes almost aboriginal; slapping his hands delightedly on his knees, he rocks back and forth and fairly shouts his pleasure." He was a lively mimic of "the sanctimonious hypocrite, the sleek speculator. . . ."

But work was the key to everything, the magic alembic. It could batter down any walls, solve any problem. The country resounded for years with stories of the hero's prodigious capacity for work: five days and nights without sleep on the trail of some knotty problem; nineteen hours of work per day seven days a week. At the age of sixty-four, determined to solve the problem of an indestructible diamond disc for his phonograph, he, along with his "faithful experimenters"—facetiously called "The Insomnia Squad"—"stayed steadily at work for a period of over five weeks—working, eating, drinking and sleeping (occasionally) there [the laboratory]." Edison went home only five times to change his clothing but neglected to shave.

The phonograph was his principal passion. In the words of his biographers, "He decided to make a thorough study of [music], not only of composition, but also of the human voice, its powers and limitations. He . . . designed and constructed a special kind of studio for the purpose of studying the different effects of various styles of orchestration." In a ten-year period he listened to some 25,000 compositions, keeping careful notes on those best suited for reproduction on his phonograph cylinders, grading them from "beautiful" to "punk."

When the studios and laboratory at West Orange burned in a disastrous fire in December, 1914, Edison, "while the fire was still raging, . . . gathered together his top executive officers and heads of departments" in the one building not affected by the fire and announced that he would begin rebuilding the next day. His staff members were given their assignments on the spot.

Perhaps conscious that he had become a national institution (indeed, he could hardly have avoided the thought, which was endlessly proclaimed), Edison in 1918 formed the Edison Pioneers, with three classes of membership. The first class of membership was reserved for Edison, "The Pioneer, his wife and descendants" and for such other individuals who had "rendered pre-eminent service in connection with Mr. Edison's work." The second category was reserved for those persons "who were associated with Thomas A. Edison . . . up to and including the year 1885." The last class was made up of those associated with him between 1886 and 1900. By 1925 the past presidents of the Edison Pioneers included two notorious swindlers, Samuel Insull and Charles Clarke.

Edison's admiring biographers (three of them collaborated on the same volume) listed the total assets of the "Industries in the United States directly founded upon or affected by the inventions of Thomas A. Edison." They included thirteen separate categories, starting with "central station lighting and power" with an investment of $10,300,-000,000, and incandescent lamps, telegraph systems, motion picture theaters and production, and radio sets and broadcasting. The total they calculated in terms of investment came to $21,585,000,000, producing sales of $6,311,500,000 and annual payrolls of $2,057,000. Allowance having been made for a degree of exaggeration, the figure is impressive. Added to his friend Ford's vast resources, it accounted for a substantial portion of the nation's industrial production.

In the years since Alexander Graham Bell had demonstrated his wonderful telephone at the Centennial Exhibition at Philadelphia, rapid strides had been made in perfection of the instrument. At the same time Bell and his associates set out to inform the public of their invention by a series of widely publicized lectures and demonstrations.

The first was at the Essex Institute in Salem, Massachusetts. Bell's assistant, Thomas Watson, to whom Bell had spoken the immortal line "Mr. Watson, come here, I want you," was in Boston. Bell interspersed his lecture with contributions by telephone from Watson, who played various musical instruments and sang "Auld Lang Syne" and "Do Not Trust Him, Gentle Lady."

In a few months 778 telephones were in use, 6 of them as part of a burglar alarm system in Boston. Bell offered his invention to Western Union for $100,000, but the company turned it down as having no practical value. Western Union soon repented and produced a rival "phone," but Bell and his associates sued and won their case, and Bell stock soared to $1,000 a share.

A crucial step in the broader utilization of the phone was the switchboard. Cables were improved and placed underground. Means to put several telephones on a single line were devised. What was especially intriguing about the refinement of the technology of the telephone was the remarkable variety of individuals who contributed to it. Bell himself was a Scottish immigrant who had come to Boston by way of Canada, "a tall, slender, quick-motioned man with a pale face, black side whiskers and a drooping mustache, big nose, and high sloping forehead crowned with bushy, jet-black hair." He had been fascinated since childhood with the artificial creation of sound, and he and his brother had invented a talking device that could say "Mamma." Like his parents, Bell made his calling the teaching of deaf-mutes. In Boston he was employed by the school board to produce "visible speech" for deaf-mutes. His success in that project led to his appointment as professor at Boston University. Two private pupils, both mutes, became intimately involved with Bell in his experiments with the telephone: Georgie Sanders and Mabel Hubbard, a girl fifteen years old who had been deaf since infancy. Four years later Hubbard became Bell's wife, and her father, Gardiner Hubbard, a wealthy lawyer, financed Bell's experiments. "If I can make a deaf-mute talk," Bell declared, "I can make iron talk." Using an ear from a human corpse, Bell demonstrated a tracing of the vibrations of the human voice on smoked glass.

The venerable Joseph Henry, first director of the Smithsonian Institution, gave Bell encouragement at a critical stage in his experiments, and Georgie Sanders and Mabel Bell assisted him, along with young Thomas Watson. One of the problems that soon developed was the tendency of switchboards to overload, thus keeping lines busy and delaying calls. In Kansas City, Missouri, an undertaker named Almon B. Strowger believed that a telephone switchboard operator was conspiring with a rival to prevent him from sending or receiving calls. He decided that the most effective antidote would be an automatic switchboard on which numbers could be dialed. He found some partners and moved to Chicago in 1891 to develop an automatic switchboard. Before he was through, he had established a factory with 3,000 employees.

John Carty, who began his career as an errand boy in an electrical shop in Boston, discovered a technique for reducing static and interruptions on telephone lines, was put in charge of undergrounding telephone lines in New York City, and became president of the Western Electric Company while still in his thirties.

Michael Pupin was a Serbian immigrant who arrived in New York at the age of fifteen with five cents in his pocket, unable to speak a word of English. After a period as a farm boy he was admitted to Cooper Union and subsequently to Columbia University, where he helped pay his tuition by coaching wrestling and boxing. He continued his studies abroad but returned to the United States and to a professorship at his alma mater. His contribution to telephone technology was the loading coil, which made long-distance calls possible. His device, for which the telephone company paid him $500,000, saved the company more than $3,500,000 in the first year of its use.

Willis Whitney, born in Jamestown, New York, was another of the electrical wizards of the new era. He was graduated from the Massachusetts Institute of Technology in 1890 and received his Ph.D. from Leipzig six years later. He returned to MIT as assistant professor of physical chemistry. Edwin Rice, Jr., who was setting up the General Electric experimental laboratory in Schenectady, New York, prevailed on Whitney to leave MIT for the new laboratory. Whitney and his young associates—he was thirty-two, apparently the classic age for young physical chemists to begin their important experimental work— decided "that the best contribution that could be made to God's will was to study and understand nature and use it correctly."

Whitney prevailed on William Coolidge, a young chemist with a background strikingly like his own, to join him at Schenectady. Coolidge was a small-town boy from Hudson, Massachusetts. He had also gone through MIT, earned his Ph.D. at Leipzig, and taught at MIT. After four years of work in the GE laboratory with twenty research chemists and a number of technical assistants, Coolidge produced the tungsten filament incandescent lamp, which burned at least twenty times longer and gave more light than the existing lamp. At this point another young scientist was recruited, this time from the Stevens Institute. Irving Langmuir was a variation on a theme, inasmuch as he had grown up in Brooklyn, New York, in a family already highly oriented toward science and had received his degrees, respectively, from Columbia and Göttingen. Whitney set him to work on the problem of the gases created within the light bulb by the high temperatures of the lamp's filaments. In brief, Langmuir discovered that if he increased the diameter of the filament, coiled it, and put an inert gas in the lamp bulb—nitrogen or argon—he could produce a lamp that used one-half watt per candlepower of illumination and lasted 300 hours.

Whitney urged his colleagues to have "fun" with their work. Only if it was fun could it be genuinely productive and original, he reminded them. His constant query was "Are you still working on that problem no one else had found an answer to?"; this meant "Are you still engaged in the most exciting exercise there is in life?"

The importance of Willis Whitney in the development of the modern research laboratory was that he had passion and a vision of "working into new levels of nature's infinite mines." To him the universities, even his beloved MIT, were woefully lacking in that passion. The frontier of scientific investigation thus shifted to the corporate research laboratory. General Electric, with its company of brilliant young men, was imitated by DuPont and American Telephone & Telegraph. The gathering of inventors and researchers into a single laboratory to work together on complex problems was not entirely new, of course. Edison was its initiator. But earlier efforts, like those of Alexander Graham Bell, had been by individuals backed by sympathetic friends, family, and prospective investors. The idea of a large corporation's putting its vast resources to work refining existing products and developing new ones in hopes of future profit was new. The consequences were significant. A kind of multiplier effect was created, and technological innovation was astonishingly accelerated. By 1920 there were hundreds of industrial research laboratories. Langmuir went on to make important modifications in the vacuum tube, invented by Lee De Forest, which had the effect of powerfully amplifying sound. Now phone calls could be made across the continent. In January, 1915, Alexander Graham Bell, using a replica of his original telephone, called Watson once more, this time in San Francisco, and spoke the same message: "Mr. Watson, please come here, I want you." Watson replied, "It would take me a week now."

To Arnold Bennett it seemed that the telephone was a classic American device. "Many otherwise civilized Europeans," he noted, "are as timid in addressing a telephone as they would be addressing a royal sovereign." To the European the telephone was still "a toy, and a clumsy one, compared with the inexorable seriousness of the American telephone." Bennett thought of the telephone lines "as being threaded, under pavements and over roofs and between floors and ceilings and between walls, by millions upon millions of live filaments that unite all the privacies of the organism—and destroy them to make one immense publicity!"

Above all, the phone served the American woman; it was a kind of extension of her personality and a new form of articulation. In part this was due to the superior technical quality of the American telephone, which conveyed the voice with such speed and clarity that it invited the most intimate reflections. Its triumphant field was in suburban communities. There "a woman takes to the telephone as women in more decadent lands take to morphia. You can see her at morn at her bedroom window, pouring confidences into her telephone. . . ." Fascinated by the ubiquity of the telephone "more wonderful and terrible" in the United States than anywhere else, Arnold Bennett sought out its "intricate and marvelous secret organization," the telephone exchange, a vast hall filled with "operatives," young women, attractively attired, surrounded by comforts and conveniences. "We were silent for a time," he wrote, "as though we had entered a church. We were, perhaps unconsciously, abashed by the intensity of the absorption of these neat young women."

The automobile was the fruit of a generation or more of experimentation. A trackless steam engine had been built in England in the early decades of the nineteenth century. In 1799 a French mechanic named Philippe Lebon built a cylinder with a piston driven by the explosion of streetlighting gas ignited by an electric spark; with the explosion of the gas, the piston returned to its original position. In 1862 another Frenchman, Jean Joseph Lenoir, applied Lebon's principle of an internal-combustion engine to build a one-and-one-half-horsepower engine, which he placed in a road vehicle.

In 1876 a German named N. A. Otto invented an engine in which vaporized gasoline was compressed before being fired; compression added greatly to the weight-to-power ratio of his engine. He next developed a four-cycle engine, which is essentially the engine used in cars today. As the piston moves from the head of the cylinder, a mixture of gasoline and air is drawn in through valves, which close, and the return movement of the piston compresses the gasoline-air mixture; a spark ignites the compressed mixture, and the piston is driven to the end of the chamber. The cycle occurred more than 1,000 times a minute. The Otto Engine Works turned out many gas engines to do the work of steam engines, but Otto was less concerned with developing a motorized vehicle than with perfecting his engine. He gave the former task to Gottlieb Daimler. Daimler was the original genius of the automobile, and his inventions and improvements resulted in the first practical motorcar, built in 1884. He named the car Mercedes after his daughter. Among his numerous achievements were the water-cooled engine, the clutch, the transmission, the carburetor, and the V type of engine. Another German, Karl Benz, was almost as active and inventive as Daimler. The first foreign automobile imported into the United States for the Chicago World's Fair in 1893 was a product of Benz's factory.

The work of Benz and Daimler was complemented by two French inventors, Émile Levassor and René Panhard. Many of their innovations had to do with improved chassis and suspension. The first automobile race from Paris to Rouen in July, 1894, a distance of some eighty miles, was won by Panhard-Levassor and Peugeot cars driven by Daimler engines.

In the United States the earliest successful automobile was built by George Selden, a Rochester, New York, patent attorney and a graduate of the Sheffield Scientific School of Yale University. By 1877 Selden had built a practical three-cylinder engine in his own home, but he was unsuccessful in his efforts to get financial backing. For fifteen years he struggled to finance the manufacture of his automobile. Meanwhile, he was overtaken by numerous other inventors and automobile manufacturers, among them the Duryea brothers, Charles and J. Frank, who made an improved vehicle with a fixed front axle and steering knuckles as well as pneumatic tires. Their car won the first American road race in 1895 from Chicago to Waukegan; the speed was ten miles an hour. The next year the Duryeas built thirteen cars.

Dozens of ambitious young inventors were working away at various motorized vehicles, some electric, some steam-driven. In Kokomo, Indiana, Elwood Haynes built the car he drove on the streets of Chicago in 1895. Alexander Winton, a bicycle repairman in Cleveland, Ohio, was at work on an improved automobile, as were Ransom E. Olds in Lansing, Michigan, and Henry Ford, a Detroit mechanic. Interestingly enough, while the developments in electricity were virtually an Eastern monopoly, the automobile and airplane had their genesis in the Middle West. This division of labor was doubtless due to the fact that the development of electricity was a far more sophisticated and scientific enterprise than making horseless carriages. It required a high degree of professional training as well as expensive facilities. In the Midwest, on the other hand, there was a long "mechanic" tradition involving farm machinery and its repair.

The early automobiles were expensive to build and initially little more than popular curiosities; they were indeed dismissed by most people as the toys of the rich, but Ransom Olds in 1900 produced a one-cylinder two-passenger car with a curved dashboard which sold for a modest $650. Olds sold his patents and his plant and started another company to manufacture Reo trucks.

The Duryea brothers were the first American automobile makers to make more than one car from the same pattern, but in 1899 some thirty companies manufactured more than 2,500 cars. Most of this output was centered in New England and constituted electric and steam vehicles. The Middle West was the home of the gasoline engine car companies. The *Motor Age,* which immediately appeared to cater to this new type called the motorist, estimated that there were 1,000 shops devoted to making automobiles, no more than 100 of which had actually produced cars. Ray Stannard Baker wrote an article for *McClure's* entitled "The Automobile in Common Use." "Five years ago there were not thirty self-propelled carriages in practical use in all the world. A year ago there were not thirty in America. And yet between the first of January and the first of May, 1899, companies with the enormous aggregate capitalization of more than $388,000,000 have been organized in New York, Boston, Chicago, and Philadelphia for the sole purpose of manufacturing and operating these new vehicles." Among the advantages of the new vehicle, Baker pointed out, was the fact that it was lighter than a horse-drawn carriage when the weight of the horse was taken into account; "it could not possibly explode (as the old steam vehicles frequently did); it would climb hills and on the level ground go at variable speeds from two miles an hour to twenty or more."

There was a strong movement by horse lovers against the automobile, to which J. Frank Duryea replied that "the horse is a willful, unreliable brute." The long tally of "accidents due to horses . . . prove that the horse is a dangerous motor and not the docile pet of the poet. The mechanical motor is his superior in many respects. . . ." This sentiment found wide acceptance by champions of the new machine. It was also pointed out that the automobile did not defecate on the city streets.

Alexander Winton promoted his car by driving the 720 miles between Cleveland and New York City with a newspaper reporter named Charles Shanks, which gave rise to numerous jokes about "shank's mare," but provided excellent publicity for the motorcar, which, it was estimated, was seen by more than 1,000,000 people in the course of its run. When Ransom E. Olds drove from Detroit to New York in ten days at an average speed of 14 miles an hour, the attendant publicity enabled him to sell 750 cars in New York City the following year, by far the largest number sold in any preceding year. Two years later he sold 4,000 cars.

The improvements in the performance of motorcars were spectacular. A Ricker, the fastest car of its day, made 26 miles an hour in 1896. Ten years later a Stanley Steamer averaged 127 miles per hour. Barney Oldfield, driving a specially built Ford "999," won numerous races and became a national hero. At the Vanderbilt Challenge Cup in 1904 the winner averaged 52.2 miles per hour.

In addition to the widely publicized automobile races starting in 1900 at Madison Square Garden, automobile shows became a popular form of entertainment. Colonel Albert Pope, a promoter of the new vehicles, described the shows as "a sort of festival for society and the automobiling class."

As early as 1910 Charles Duryea was able to say, "The novelty of owning an automobile has largely worn off. The neighbors have one of their own. The whole family has become so accustomed to auto riding that some members prefer to ride alone or remain behind while others go." By 1912 the number of motor vehicles registered in the United States stood at 944,000, and there were undoubtedly more cars on the road since some states did not require registration. New York led with 62,000 registered vehicles, and California with 44,000 was next. Wyoming was lowest with only 360. California had the highest ratio of cars to population—one car for every 40.3 people, far ahead of second-place Rhode Island (62.9). More than 700 factories and suppliers employed 85,359 people and paid wages in excess of $58,000,000.

As a mechanic and inventor Henry Ford was hardly to be distinguished from other young men. Where he differed was in his vision of a nation of automobile owners driving a single standardized, inexpensive, and durable "universal car." Cars were initially so expensive that in order to sell them to the only people who could afford them, the disposition of most car makers, Olds being perhaps the principal exception, was to make beautiful creations, marvelous machines that gleamed with brass and nickel, machines of breathtaking elegance, suggesting opulence and, above all, speed, for everyone wished to go faster than anyone else. It was Ford's brilliant insight that cars might be produced not lovingly, one by one, as objects of great aesthetic power but rather as one made galoshes or any other mass-produced item.

Ford's father wanted him to be, as the father was, a farmer, but Ford was fascinated by machines. He went to Detroit while he was still in his teens, to work as a machinist, as a shipyard mechanic, and then as an employee of the Westinghouse Air Brake Company. His father lured him back to the farm by giving him forty acres of woodland. Ford built a sawmill, lumbered off the land, and set up a little machine shop, in which he began the manufacture of an inexpensive steam automobile. The enterprise failed for lack of capital, and Ford went back to Detroit to work as an engineer for the Detroit Edison Illuminating Company. After work he spent hours in his shop, building a gasoline-powered automobile, which, when he tested it in 1893, ran at the unusual speed of twenty-five to thirty miles per hour. In 1898, with a better prototype, Ford collected $50,000 from optimistic investors and started the Detroit Automobile Company; he was chief engineer at a salary of $100 per month. The company failed to prosper and Ford sold it to a firm that began making Cadillacs. After a brief time in a machine shop he started the Ford Motor Company with a capital of $100,000. The company turned out its first car in 1903.

From the beginning of his endless experiments with automobile engines Ford was looking, as he put it, for the "universal car," the car with the best output of power to weight, the most durable parts (he experimented extensively to find the best combination of steel and vanadium for each part of the engine), the greatest economy and simplicity of construction, and the greatest safety. It was, after all, a marvelous conception—the universal car—a notion as luminous and brilliant in its own way as Michelangelo's vision of Creation on the

Sistine ceiling. Ford wanted replacement parts so inexpensive that "they could be carried in hardware shops just as nails or bolts are carried." Soon Ford parts could be bought from dealers around the country instead of having to be ordered from Dearborn.

Eight different models preceded the universal car. In 1908 Ford built 6,181 cars with a work force of 1,908, and the following year 10,607 Model Ts were sold, the largest number sold by a single automobile manufacturer in any prior year. The company also sold two other popular models, R and S, four-cylinder runabouts. In 1909 Ford decided that he would concentrate exclusively on the Model T. He told his principal executives, "I will build a motor car for the great multitude. It will be large enough for the family but small enough for the individual to run and care for. It will be constructed of the best materials, by the best men to be hired, after the simplest design that modern engineering can devise. But it will be so low in price that no man making a good salary will be unable to buy one—and enjoy with his family the blessings of hours of pleasure in God's great open spaces."

If Ford's sales staff was dismayed, his rival automakers were jubilant. "If Ford does that," one of them was quoted as saying, "he will be out of business in six months." The fact was, of course, that the sales of Model Ts rose spectacularly. Ford made constant improvements in his assembly lines. In 1910 it took fourteen hours to assemble one Ford car at a cost of $8.75. Two years later the average time for assembling a car had been reduced to two man-hours and the cost to $1.25. In the development of the moving assembly line, Ford borrowed from the overhead trolley used by Chicago meat-packers in dressing beef. One detail of production after another came under Ford's scrutiny—the making of magnetos, castings, the piston-rod assembly—and each was improved with the intention of making the operation possible by unskilled labor and by Frederick Taylor's principles of efficiency of movement. There were no titles and as few "experts" as possible among the work force. "When a man is really at work," Ford wrote, "he needs no title. His work honours him." Ford encouraged direct contact between every worker and every supervisor; there were no "channels" or chains of command. Workers were encouraged to make suggestions about ways of improving productivity, and their ideas, when practical, were immediately incorporated (Polish workers were most fertile in practical suggestions). "There is," Ford wrote, "no question of red tape or going over a man's head. . . . One thing we will not tolerate is injustice of any kind." Ford's engineers made studies of which operations could be performed by handicapped individuals; blind workers were set to sorting parts which, it turned out, they could usually do more efficiently than sighted workers.

We are already generally familiar with Ford's labor practices from his testimony before the Commission on Industrial Relations, and if practice often fell short of theory, he still had a strong claim to being the nation's most enlightened employer of a large labor force. Ford was especially proud of employing 9,563 "substandard" or handicapped men, 234 of whom had only one foot or leg and 123 with amputated arms or hands.

Beginning with the production of 18,664 cars in 1909–10—they sold for the price of $950—Ford virtually doubled his production each successive year while lowering the price of his Model Ts until the war slowed production. In 1918–19 he manufactured 533,706 cars, which sold for $525, a little more than half the cost of the same car nine years earlier. In the year 1920–21 he sold 1,250,000 Fords at prices ranging from $440 to $355 (with no "extras"). In addition he built assembly plants in Britain and a number of other countries.

Henry Ford's autobiography, *My Life and Work*, full as it is of pieties and platitudes, is nonetheless a compelling document, especially in his lucid and eloquent description of his development of the production processes that made his automobile the most famous conveyance in the world and, perhaps above all, in his account of the relationship between the men and the machines in his factories. Like Edison, Ford apotheosized work; like the great inventor, he saw American society in explicitly moral terms, although Ford was more critical of the status quo than Edison was. Ford's theory of business was one that "looks toward making the world a better place in which to live." The lesson of the success of the Ford Motor Company was that it had done just that, in Ford's opinion, and made a profit doing it. The present organization of society, he wrote, was entirely satisfactory if making money was the end of life. "But I am thinking of service. The present system does not permit of the best service because it encourages every kind of waste—it keeps many men from getting full return for service"— that is to say, the worker was not adequately rewarded for his or her work. It was all "a matter of better planning and adjustment, and a more humane attitude toward the needs of the working man himself. . . . The natural thing to do is to work—to recognize that prosperity and happiness can be obtained only though an honest effort."

Since people must work, "it is better to work intelligently and fore-handedly." Ford made it clear he was no reformer. In his view, re-formers wanted to smash things. He, on the other hand, wanted to make things simple and rational. His exhortation was "Simplify!" Habit was the enemy of change. Life was "not a location but a journey. . . . Everything is in flux, and was meant to be. Life flows." Nothing failed like success when it encouraged routine and discouraged in-novation.

Those who observed Ford at close range were impressed by his capacity for complete absorption. He would break off in the middle of a conversation or rise from the dining table, leaving his lunch un-touched, to go off to work out a problem of mechanics. "He saw the labor problem in personal terms," Frederic Howe wrote. "He had no faith in labor-unions, apparently little faith in the experts he employed. He had few intimates among men of his class, but loved to visit with the farmers and men with whom he had grown up in the town of Dearborn. Life to him seemed bounded by the moralities of a small town, moralities of kindness, of doing your job as well as it can be done, of hating waste in any form, especially hating personal vices like smoking, drinking, or gambling. To him the banker was an exploiter, the railroads were the last word in inefficiency, and should be owned by the government and operated for service. . . . War was the most immoral thing of all. It was caused by international bankers, by mu-nition-makers, and by a parasitical, exploiting class." This view he shared with the socialists and with many of the profoundly conservative men and women of the Midwest.

It seemed to Lincoln Steffens that Henry Ford, "the industrial leader in a land of industrial pioneering, was a prophet without words, a reformer without politics, a legislator, statesman-radical." Steffens wrote: "I understood why the Bolshevik leaders of Russia admired, coveted, studied him. He was a labor leader, for example. With no sentiment at all about the workers, handling labor as he did raw ma-terial, he learned by experience to stand for high wages. . . . He outbid his rivals and so discovered that high wages improved the market for cars." Ida Tarbell was another reformer who fell under Ford's spell. It seemed to her that at last the long and bloody war between capital and labor was at an end. Ford had discovered or stumbled upon the fact that "a worker" was also "a consumer."

To Tarbell and Steffens the conclusive evidence of Ford's genius was that he dispelled "the myth of the stockholder." Ford discovered that the stockholder was a reactionary element in business, especially in an innovative, rapidly changing industry. "They were for dividends, stock melons. Ford," Steffens wrote, "saw that dividends were a leak, a waste. . . . His stockholders, being naturally for the division of profits among themselves, not among the workers and consumers, resisted Ford." So Ford bought them out, saved his money, and financed his own expansion (he kept a reserve of $50,000,000). "This was Russian and revolutionary." The stockholders were too narrow and selfish in their outlook to realize that "good wages to labor, good earnings to farmers, prosperity in the masses, made a good market for cars." When Steffens reminded Ford that there were no stockholders in Soviet Russia, that there he would "be free of the private bankers and land-lords," Ford's face took on "the expression of released joy." Steffens reported him as saying, "My God, is that it? Why, that would free business!"

Ford summed up his philosophy as follows: "Don't cheapen the product; don't cheapen the wage; don't overcharge the public. Put brains into the method, and more brains, and still more brains—do things better than ever before; and by this means all parties to business are served and benefited."

Among his other classic American precepts: "Money is only a tool in business. It is just part of the machinery. . . . The highest use of capital is not to make more money, but to make more money do more service for the betterment of life. Unless we in our industries are helping to solve the social problem, we are not doing our principal work. We are not fully serving."

It was a message as simple as the Model T, and Ford, it may be suspected, repeated it almost as often as he made the famous car. It confirmed the feeling of many of his countrymen that he was the ideal American, the greatest man of his age.

There was another less attractive side to Ford. Like many geniuses, he was, or became, a little mad. In that, too, and in a growing paranoia about Jews and Bolsheviks, he was thoroughly American, a farm boy with enormous power, loose in a bewildering world. When Frazier Hunt tried to interview him, the motor king asked him if he had read the *Protocols of the Elders of Zion*. Hunt replied that he had not, and Ford stalked from the room. He would not talk to the journalist until he had absorbed the bizarre forgeries on which Ford based his anti-Semitism. When Hunt returned, Ford told him that he believed in reincarnation. "What we think of now as the mysteries of life and death were [once] known," he declared. "There was no riddle of life then. All the complete whole—everything—was known then."

It was highly appropriate that Ford and Edison should have become close friends, going off each fall for extended camping trips. They camped, to be sure, with some elegance in a caravan that included, appropriately enough, a truck with an electric generator so that they could enjoy the advantages of Edison's most famous accomplishment, the electric light. One of the bonds between them was Ford's determination to re-create at Dearborn, Michigan, Edison's laboratory at Menlo Park. They also shared the same devotion to hard work and simple living and the same contempt for Wall Street and the stock market.

By 1920 there were more than 8,000,000 passenger cars registered in the United States, far more than the rest of the world combined. But statistics are, of course, only a small part of the story. In addition to the hundreds of thousands of people employed in manufacturing cars and the millions more whose livelihoods were directly or indirectly involved in the use of the automobile—from filling station operators and attendants to motel and resort owners and employees—there were the more elusive psychological aspects of the automobile. First of all, it gave practical effect to the notion of freedom, in its more obvious physical manifestations. The owner of an automobile could range through space in an unprecedented manner. Henry Adams's suspicion of the modern world did not extend to the automobile. He was one of the first to own one. He wrote to his English friend Charles M. Gaskell that he had "bought an automobile, a pretty Mercedes, 18 h.p., and hope to live in it. . . ." He found "that a gait of about 25 miles an hour on a straight country road hypnotises me as a chalk line does a hen. . . . Every few days I rush out into the country fifty miles to breakfast. . . . The auto is a great tyrant. I have to invent space for it." Inventing space for it was a task Americans proved thoroughly up to. They were soon touring in the marvelous contraptions, "gypsying" it was called. There were campgrounds, or simply wayside fields to cook and sleep in, and soon motor hotels, or motels, where the more affluent could drive up to their own cabins to spend the night. There were magazines and newspaper columns devoted to the new pastime. Journalists wrote it up; automobile clubs provided road maps for the touring family. "You are your master," *Motor Car* rhapsodized; "the road is ahead; you eat as you please, cooking your own meals over an open fire; sleeping when you will under the stars, waking with the dawn;

swim in a mountain lake when you will, and always the road ahead. Thoreau at 29 cents a gallon. . . . Time and space at your beck and call; your freedom is complete."

The car brought out the latent poetry in every American's soul:

Breezes tugging at the topbows,
Motor singing glad refrain,
Far from the clamor of the city
In the open—born again!

Americans could escape from the stultifying details of daily life to a realm of speed and fantasy: the power of innumerable horses, the exhilarating sense of movement, of flight only slightly less free than that of birds or airplanes. The automobile changed radically the relationship of human beings to the physical world, to nature, to one another. It became a courtship machine, a mobile love nest (with the invention of that splendid space the rumble seat), a symbol of success, of America. All our boasts, all our vainglory seemed at last ratified and confirmed by the automobile. How was revolution possible in a nation with 10,000,000, 20,000,000, 50,000,000 motorcars! In a society in which many people suffered from an acute sense of powerlessness, in a jungle of machines and increasingly impersonal agencies, one had one's own "power source" immediately at hand. To be "empowered," one needed only to turn on the ignition (or twirl the crank), and an obedient engine of the power of an infinite number of horses would be at one's command. The engine itself became the god of youth. Mysterious to their elders, it yielded up all its mysteries to its young devotees. It represented, perhaps above all, the conquest of the vast space that constituted America.

The fact was the country was still in the process of formation; it was still "gelling," "setting up," so to speak. It had masses of poorly assimilated recent immigrants. East was divided from West. Class lines were still conspicuous and bruising. The automobile had a profound, if subtle, impact on all these unresolved issues. Indeed, in a curious way, one has the feeling that it was perhaps less the mission of the United States to spread freedom in the world than to *produce* the automobile; we clearly did not invent it, but we incorporated it almost instantaneously into our economy and our culture.

That man would fly was inevitable. The only question was when and where. Icarus tried too soon. Leonardo da Vinci worked on the mechanics. An Australian, Lawrence Hargrave, built a kind of flying wing in 1891 that was driven by a compressed air engine and flew 128 feet. Samuel Pierpont Langley, secretary of the Smithsonian Institution, tried compressed air, steam, and giant rubber bands to propel an airplane. Langley was one of the foremost astronomers of the day, and he proceeded scientifically, studying the lifting qualities of certain surfaces and working out mathematically the formulas for the relationship between wing surface and weight. On May 6, 1896, he flew the first machine-powered (steam engine) heavier-than-air machine some 3,000 feet at Quantico, Virginia.

Langley was a coeval of that remarkable first generation of American inventor-scientists, almost all of them small-town boys. He had been born in Roxbury, Massachusetts in 1834. He attended the famous Boston Latin School and then toured Europe with his chemist-brother, John, visiting the great centers of science there. A professor of astronomy at the University of Western Pennsylvania, he began pioneering studies of solar radiation. Appointed the third head of the Smithsonian in 1887, Langley continued his experiments in radiation and established the National Zoological Park and the Astrophysical Observatory. The fact that a scientist who had made such important discoveries in the realm of "pure" science also took such an intense interest in as practical a problem as heavier-than-air flying machines was characteristically American.

Somewhat reluctantly Langley was persuaded to extend his experiments to the development of a machine that could carry a person, a pilot. With the backing of the army, which was interested in the military possibilities of manned flight, Congress appropriated $50,000 for his experiments. The problem was to find an engine powerful enough and light enough to propel a craft large enough to carry a man. Langley worked slowly and carefully, concentrating on such problems as the size and pitch of a propeller to pull such a machine through the air. By September, 1903, he was ready to launch his man-carrying airplane. He decided to fly it from the roof of a houseboat. In two attempts, a few months apart, the machine failed to take to the air because of accidents in the launching process itself. A disheartened Langley, then sixty-nine and in poor health, abandoned the project. Although his machine was later flown and thus proved airworthy, his efforts were widely ridiculed.

Gliding experiments were meanwhile going on in various places—in Algeria, France, Germany, and Britain and on the shores of Lake

Michigan. Hiram Maxim, who had invented the machine gun and who thought big, built a steam-driven flying machine in 1893 at a cost of some $100,000; it was designed to carry a crew of three and a ton of cargo. He constructed a track a half mile long to test his plane on and proved, in a series of tests on the track, that it would fly, but in a trial run the huge machine crashed.

Conscious of the various efforts that were being made to build a machine that could carry a man, Wilbur and Orville Wright, two brothers who ran a bicycle shop in Dayton, Ohio, built a glider. "With this machine," they later wrote, "in the autumn of 1903, we made a number of flights in which we remained in the air for over a minute, often soaring for a considerable time in one spot without any descent at all." (One of the Wright assistants proposed covering it with feathers to increase its hovering ability.) What the Wrights concentrated on in their experiments with their glider was an improved means of stabilizing and guiding their craft (most previous efforts had been limited to the pilot's shifting of his weight). They developed a system whereby the surfaces of the wings could be warped by hand-operated levers attached to wires to permit the plane to maneuver. For three years they concentrated on improving the flying qualities and maneuverability of gliders. In 1903 they began a series of tests near Kitty Hawk, North Carolina, with a gliderlike machine that had an engine mounted on it. A track was built, and the machine was towed along it by an automobile. On December 17, 1903, the machine flew for the first time. The duration of the flight was twelve seconds. The effort was repeated; each time the machine stayed aloft a little longer. The fourth time it covered a distance of 852 feet in slightly less than a minute. The Wright brothers returned to Dayton, where they kept their achievement more or less a secret while they tried to sell their machine first to the United States and then to Great Britain. Meanwhile, a Brazilian who lived in France, Alberto Santos-Dumont, flew in a public demonstration in October, 1906. Soon it seemed that half of France was airborne—Henri Farman, a bicycle racer, the Voisin brothers, Delagrange, Louis Blériot, Levassor. Meanwhile, Alexander Graham Bell, not content to rest on his laurels as the inventor of the telephone, had been tirelessly engaged in studying aeronautics and had built a series of spectacular kites to fly at his summer home in Nova Scotia. Now he hired a mechanical genius, Glenn Curtiss, a motorcycle racer, to help him build an engine that would drive one of his giant kites.

Afraid that their own private invention of warping the wings for control would be discovered and their principal contribution to manned flight obscured, the Wrights decided that Wilbur should take one of the Wright-built planes to France to demonstrate its superior flying qualities at the center of the new flying mania while Orville conducted a similar demonstration for a party of American army officers. The army had established certain standards for the Wrights to meet: a speed of 40 miles an hour with a bonus of $2,500 for every mile an hour above that. The demonstration flights were an impressive success; the Wrights won a contract to build planes for the army. Glenn Curtiss meanwhile improved on their technique for stabilizing and maneuvering a plane by inventing ailerons (French for "small wings"), which could be more readily controlled and which, in a sense, completed the necessary technology for successful flight. What followed was the fastest and most spectacular development of a new mode of transportation in history. Wind tunnels were built, and model planes tested, to determine the most efficient design of body and wing. Soon speeds of more than 100 miles an hour were reached, an unheard-of velocity. Prizes were offered for every important extension of range, speed, and maneuverability.

The outbreak of the European War in 1914 provided an additional stimulus. Six or seven years after the first demonstrated, sustainable manned flight, airplanes were engaged in spectacular aerial "dogfights" above the battlefields of Europe. By 1914 Curtiss had built a machine with a wingspan of 133 feet as well as a hydroplane, a plane which the British bought. The Sikorsky, built in Europe, could carry eighteen passengers, and at the war's end a British Vickers plane flew across the Atlantic from Newfoundland to the British Isles, averaging 118 miles an hour. The air age was well launched.

"Moving" pictures were at least as old as the eccentric photographer Eadweard Muybridge's zoopraxiscope. Much of the technology, including the celluloid film, was developed in Europe by an Englishman named William Friese-Greene, who wrote of exposing "a negative on travelling bands, 3,000 times in five minutes." By 1893 the Edison laboratories had developed a film which carried a series of minute photographs, each lit by a light at one seven-thousandths of a second. A half dozen inventors contributed to the efforts to produce a continuous "picture" of motion. C. Francis Jenkins, a native of Richmond, Indiana, a stenographer in the Treasury Department, was obsessed with developing a practical machine for projecting moving pictures.

By 1891 he had built what he called a phantascope, which he demonstrated to some friends. Three years later he was ready for a public demonstration in his hometown. The scene that he projected was that of a vaudeville dancer in Washington, D.C. Although his mother objected to the subject as indecent, the *Richmond Telegraph* of June 8, 1894, gave an enthusiastic account of the demonstration. An electric motor turned a wheel with pegs that fitted into holes along the edge of the film, which passed before a beam of light, essentially the motion picture projector as we know it today. A thousand images a minute passed the light beam. Soon Jenkins's invention was being turned to commercial use by ingenious itinerants, who went from town to town, photographing local scenes—firemen in a drill, a train coming into the station—developing the film and then showing it to the townspeople at the grange hall or opera house. An enterprising young man named Alexander Black had hit on the idea of offering a series of projected single photographs to constitute a "play." In 1900 Ferdinand Zecca, a French director, produced a photoplay entitled *L'Histoire d'un Crime*, which laid claim to being the first "motion picture" in dramatic form.

Although the Edison laboratories had made comparatively modest contributions to the development of the motion picture, Edison was quick to form a company to make films. It employed Edwin Porter, a stage director, to write and direct "films" to be shown to the public. One of his first efforts was the sensationally successful drama *The Great Train Robbery*.

A young playwright-actor, David Wark Griffith, discouraged by the flop of his most recent effort, a "problem play" about California hop pickers, was encouraged to write plays for the new medium. Griffith shared the famous director David Belasco's view that "always when you look at a picture on the screen you will be conscious of its lack of living quality. And this the celluloid drama will never to able to surmount. You will always have the subconscious knowledge that it is mere photography after all." But Griffith needed money desperately, and he was told that the mere outline of a story (since little dialogue was needed) would bring $5. In addition to Edison, there were a number of other film companies that had appeared to exploit the new technology, among them Vitagraph, Pathé, Selig, and the Essanay Company. They were busy turning out such films as *The Curse of Drink, The Gambler's Fate, The Face on the Barroom Floor,* and *A Kind-Hearted Bootblack*. No one, of course, considered them art; they were a curiosity more than anything else. Established actors and directors scorned them, although Cecil B. and William De Mille, whose most recent play had failed dismally, were interested in the medium for essentially the same reason as Griffith—to recoup their fortunes. That there was an audience for such jejune efforts could not be denied. By 1908 there were 600 "storefront" theaters in New York City alone.

Young Griffith tried to palm off the story of Puccini's *Tosca* on Edison's director, Edwin Porter, but Porter recognized the plot and refused it. He did, however, offer to give Griffith a part in his movie *Rescued from an Eagle's Nest* at the substantial salary of $5 a day. After the Edison experience Griffith took a play that he had written to the American Mutoscope and Biograph Company located on three upper floors of a house, the ground floor of which was a salesroom for the Chickering Piano Company. Every week Biograph, when David Griffith appeared at its doors, was making two or three one-reeler films that ran from five to twelve minutes each. The company was without an experienced director and in serious financial difficulty. After selling plots for several films, Griffith and his wife were hired to act in them, and soon Griffith was directing films as well. He completed ten films in his first month of directing, the first in two days. It was soon evident that he had a gift for handling actors; he was especially attracted to the idea of using groups of people in action scenes. Since virtually all films were made with a fixed camera as though seen by an audience through a stage proscenium, Griffith's innovation of moving the camera closer to the actors—a close-up—was striking.

By the time the year was over Griffith had shot more than fifty pictures. Soon such young actresses as Lillian and Dorothy Gish, Mae Marsh, Mabel Normand, and Mary Pickford were playing roles in Griffith's films, and he was extending his innovations in lighting, characterization, and the use of groups of actors. In 1910 he followed several other motion picture companies, the Selig Company and the New York Motion Picture Company, to California, where the year-round mild climate, the natural light, and wide-open spaces made an ideal site for filmmaking. There Mary Pickford starred as an Indian maiden in Helen Hunt Jackson's *Ramona*.

One of the severest limitations of the new medium was the fifteen-minute running time of a single reel. It was 1909–10 before a director named J. Stuart Blackton made history by producing *The Life of Moses* in five reels, in addition to a three-reel version of *Uncle Tom's Cabin*.

In 1911 Griffith, now acting as producer of some films and director of others, made seventy films, introducing such innovations as crosscutting. In addition, he incorporated a number of techniques developed by other directors. He had also pioneered in the use of a moving camera and became a master of the close-up as well as of the use of multiple cameras, which allowed far greater flexibility both in cutting and editing and in tracking shots.

The year 1913 saw a major breakthrough for Griffith in the filming of *Judith of Bethulia*, a biblical drama that enabled him to achieve new effects of scenic opulence and the use of masses of people against exotic backgrounds. *Judith* was Griffith's longest picture to date—a four-reeler—and it anticipated his two greatest pictures: *The Birth of a Nation* and *Intolerance*.

The Birth of a Nation, perhaps more than any other single film, marked the coming of age of the American film industry. It made reputations and careers and fortunes. An ambitious nickelodeon owner, Louis B. Mayer, secured the New England rights to the film, and it launched him on a meteoric film career of his own. Unhappily the film also projected what was perhaps the most degrading image of Southern blacks ever created in any medium. The protests of the newly formed National Association for the Advancement of Colored People, of Jane Addams, Oswald Garrison Villard, and Charles Eliot, as well as of hundreds of black leaders, were ignored, but the denunciation of the film's depiction of Southern blacks persuaded Griffith to make a vindicating film under the title of *The Rise and Fall of Free Speech in America*. It was this film which appeared as *Intolerance*, another spectacular epic.

If D. W. Griffith and Edwin S. Porter were the most imaginative innovators in developing new film techniques and incipient "stories," a remarkable group of Jewish immigrants emerged as the entrepreneurs of the new medium. Their role in expanding the creative potential of the flicks, as they were initially called, went far beyond mere merchandising, although they did that exceedingly well. They were committed to constant innovation, to longer and longer films and more complex stories, to attracting well-known actors and actresses from the legitimate theater and drawing more sophisticated (as well as larger) audiences to their increasingly lavish movie palaces.

Adolph Zukor had come to the United States at the age of fifteen, an orphan, without family or friends, small in size, almost stunted. He joined forces with a Hungarian refugee a few years older named Maxie Schosberg. Together they formed the Novelty Fur Company. Having lent three thousand dollars to a penny arcade which fell on evil fortunes, Zukor undertook to rescue the enterprise, became fascinated with the nickelodeon that was one of its attractions and joined forces with another furrier, Marcus Loew, to open a chain of theatres in the form of simulated railroad cars where the audiences could view travel scenes such as the Grand Canyon and the Rockies. From there it was just a step to showing films like *The Great Train Robbery.* They were such a success that Zukor abandoned his railway cars and opened his own movie theatre. When he introduced the Italian movie, *Quo Vadis,* a four-reeler, he charged the unheard-of price of one dollar for admission and filled his theatre. Running out of foreign films, Zukor formed his own filmmaking company and began adding theatres to what was soon a chain.

Samuel Goldfish had arrived in the United States at the age of twelve, a refugee from Poland who had worked his way across the Atlantic in steerage. His first job was in a glove factory at Gloversville, New York. After a stint as a glove salesman, Goldfish came to New York City to start his own glove agency. Jesse Lasky was a second-generation Jewish immigrant who had tried his hand at gold mining in Alaska and worked subsequently as the only Caucasian in the Royal Hawaiian Band. Meanwhile Jesse Lasky's sister, Blanche, also a cornetist, who had toured with him as one of the Musical Laskys, had married Goldfish. When Jesse Lasky's effort to start a cabaret ended in failure, he joined forces with his brother-in-law, Sam, and an only moderately successful actor turned playwright, named Cecil B. De Mille, whose ambitious mother, Anna, was the daughter of Henry George, prophet of the single tax. Together they formed the Lasky Feature Players Company and signed the popular stage actor Dustin Farnum to make a movie of his Broadway success, *The Squaw Man.* Cecil B. De Mille directed the film which was shot in three weeks in an old barn in Hollywood near the corner of Sunset Boulevard and Vine Street, country roads that passed through orange orchards. Zukor, impressed with the initial efforts of the new company and hungry for films to show in his expanding chain of theatres, persuaded the Lasky-Goldfish-De Mille trio to merge, forming Famous Players–Lasky.

The principal rival to Famous Players–Lasky was Lewis J. Zeleznick. Zeleznick, who changed his name to Selznick, had, like Sam Goldfish, fled Russia and its pogroms at the age of twelve. After serving an apprenticeship as a jeweler, he opened a jewelry store in New York City. When it failed he sought out a friend named Mark Dintenfass, an ex-herring salesman who had launched himself as a movie maker. Selznick discovered that Dintenfass held a substantial block of stock in the Universal Film Company. Armed with Dintenfass's stock, Selznick joined forces with Carl Laemmle to take over control of Universal. Too headstrong and reckless to work for or with anyone else, Selznick was soon turning out hits with stars lured from other studios. Hearing of the czar's fall in the opening act of the Russian Revolution, he sent a cable to the ex-emperor: "When I was a boy in Russia your police treated my people very bad. However no hard feelings. Hear you are now out of work. If you will come to New York can find you a fine position acting in pictures. Salary no object. Reply my expense. Regards you and family." The cable received wide publicity and helped to promote Selznick's film, *The Fall of the Romanoffs*. Selznick's major contribution to the nascent film industry may well have been the standard he established as the archetypal film mogul. He collected Ming vases and starlets in his twenty-two-room New York apartment, had four Rolls Royces and gave his teen-age sons thousand-dollar-a-week allowances. In the words of Budd Schulberg "hopeful young actresses nicknamed him C.O.D. because the passions of his leading ladies were invariably tested on his red-velvet casting couch."

Another important addition to the ranks of early filmmakers was young Benjamin P. Schulberg, whose parents had fled for their lives from Minsk in Polish Russia carrying him with them as an infant. From an early age young Schulberg had shown a precocious literary gift and, with the advent of films, begun to dream of becoming a writer of films. As an aide to Franklin Pierce Adams, whose "Conning Tower" was one of the most popular columns in the *New York Mail*, Schulberg was assigned to write reviews of the one-reel movies that passed through the nickel-a-show store-front theatres in rapid succession. Vachel Lindsay's *Art of the Moving Pictures* was a further inspiration and soon Schulberg was writing scripts for Edwin Porter, who was shooting movies for Adolph Zukor.

In 1913 at the First Annual Ball of the Screen Club, an association of filmmakers and fans of the new medium, Schulberg, then only twenty-one, composed "An Appreciation," which read in part: "Marvel of science, mirror of art, product of the ingenuity of man and the inventive power of his mind—we speak to you, the Motion Picture!

"Not with the sword, not with the oppression and persecution of cruel might, but with more human sobs and smiles, you have conquered the world!

"You are the struggle and the victory! You are Aspiration and Achievement—Hope and Realization!

"You are King in the Land of Mechanical Wonders, supreme in the domain of daring dreams! . . .

"You are the soul of skill and the spirit of Service, the essence of energy, and the germ of enterprise. You thrill with the common sympathy of the universe, and throb with the throes and thralls of united humanity.

"You translate the world's sorrows, and delineate life's joys. You bear the burden of the earth, the load of care and misery and evil, the pathetic definition of futility and fatality; yet we catch the gleam of a sunbeam, the lilt of a song—and we laugh! . . .

"Motion Picture, you are great. You are the agent of the age, the messenger of futurity!"

Furriers, jewelers, junk men (L. B. Mayer), glove salesmen, cornet players, penny arcade proprietors, what the early movie makers had in common was an uncommon instinct for engaging the fantasy life of their countrymen, an unaccountable extravagance of the imagination combined with more or less equal parts of commercial shrewdness and marketing skill. Derided and despised, they emerged from the obscurity of the ghetto to assume command of the most potent popular art form devised by the species. The long and dramatic history of the race burst forth, as it were, in images, compelling, irresistible images, flickering across the mind, across the world—bathing beauties, Keystone Kops, Little Rascals, engaging bums, sirens of the silver screen, sweethearts and heroes, larger than life and infinitely rich in promise.

Of all the odd and exotic moments in the nation's history there was none stranger than the conjunction of Thomas Edison's moving picture machine and the exotic company of Jewish immigrants from Russia, Poland and Latvia waiting in the wings, as it were, to develop the dazzling potentials of the new medium, eager to be the purveyors of America's dreams and, as it would turn out, the world's dreams as well.

Hugo Münsterberg, the Harvard philosopher and pop psychologist, was one of the few intellectuals to take the "movies" seriously. In 1916 he published *The Photoplay: A Psychological Study*. Serious critics scorned the movies as debased spin-offs from the "legitimate" theater, but Münsterberg saw them as a wholly new art form with profound philosophical and psychological implications. The perspective and movement in the film were curious combinations of fact and symbol. The viewer was free to fill them with his or her own fantasies. The close-up was a form of attention. As contrasted with the stage, the "movie" encouraged the "subjective play of attention." The flashback was memory. The cutting from scene to scene produced an effect of simultaneity, and its general effect was to eliminate or transform time and space. The film was successful in "overcoming the forms of the outer world, namely space, time, and causality," thereby demonstrating the "freedom of the mind . . . over the unalterable law of the outer world." In the "turmoil of a technical age" a new form of beauty had been created which "by its very technique . . . more than any other art [was] destined to overcome outer nature by the free and joyful play of the mind."

Vachel Lindsay, poet of democracy, captured the magical quality of the movies in his verses to America's new "stars":

> Mary Pickford, doll divine,
> Year by year, and every day
> At the moving-picture play,
> You have been my valentine. . . .

And to Blanche Sweet:

> . . . we walk serenely
> Down the odorous isle.
> We forgive the squalor
> And the boom and squeal
> For the Great Queen flashes
> From the moving reel . . .
> She will stand like marble,
> She will pause and glow,
> . . . Keep a peaceful reign,
> Ruler of her passion,
> Ruler of our pain!

The beginning of the new century saw technological refinements and innovations of incomprehensible consequence. All that we can say with certainty is that *everything was different* from what it had been before; the world had never experienced such astonishing and dramatic transformations in so brief a time.

48

Art and Architecture

America, as we have noted before, inherited, as part of the re-formed consciousness of Protestant Christianity, a strongly icon-oclastic disposition—that is to say, a prejudice—against symbolic representations of life, against the icons that constitute so rich a portion of Catholic Christianity. Reacting from the remarkable proliferation of images that characterized the late Renaissance, American Puritans banished all images from ecclesiastical architecture and even music from the austere meetinghouses where the Word flourished, the Will prevailed, and the sensuous was rigorously excluded.

It thus followed that Americans who wished to express their perceptions of reality in visual form labored under a considerable handicap. They were working against the grain of the society as a whole. The Word had far more status than the Image. The Centennial Exposition in Philadelphia in 1876, when the outraged descendants of Puritans physically attacked "foreign" painting and sculptures they considered wickedly sexual, was a psychological watershed for the visual arts in the United States. Americans in large numbers were, for the first time, "exposed" to art that "exposed" the human body. While many reacted with shock and outrage, many others, of at least comparatively more sophisticated instincts, were astonished and exhilarated. Thomas Eakins and Eadweard Muybridge were leaders in the move to reveal the human body as an object of beauty and power. Their photographs of nude men and women and Eakins's paintings of wrestlers, rowers, boxers, and swimmers moved American art from the landscape to the body (although the landscape certainly continued to be the dominant theme in American painting). Eakins exerted his principal influence as a teacher at the Pennsylvania Academy of Fine Arts. There a succession of gifted young men and women received inspiration from Eakins, who was a compelling teacher as well as a painter seriously rivaled only by Winslow Homer. That Eakins was deeply rooted in what we might call the nature tradition in American painting, a tradition going back to Thomas Cole and Asher Durand, is indicated by a letter he wrote as a young man when he was studying the Spanish painters in Madrid. "The big artist," he wrote ". . . keeps a sharp eye on Nature and steals her tools. He learns what she does with light, the big tool, and then color, then form. . . . The big artists . . . had the greatest confidence in nature, and when they made an unnatural thing they made it as nature would have made it, and thus they are really closer to nature than the coal-scuttle painters ever suspect. In a big picture you can see what o'clock it is, whether morning or afternoon, if it is hot or cold, winter or summer and what kind of people are there and what they are doing and why. . . . The sentiments run beyond words."

As a man of the new age and the new consciousness, Eakins saw no conflict between science and art. One complemented the other. The camera was the artist's best resource to assist him in capturing reality. Hence his encouragement of and involvement with Muybridge's photography. He made himself an excellent photographer as well. Homer, whom Eakins admired as the finest painter of his generation, continued, of course, to paint with no evidence of diminished power until shortly before his death in 1910. For ten years Eakins, supported by his father, taught anatomy at the Pennsylvania Academy without pay. "If America is to produce great painters," he told his students, "and if young art students wish to assume a place in the history of the art of their country, their first desire should be to remain in America, to peer deeper into the heart of American life." When Eakins insisted that his women students work from a nude male model, just as his male students worked from female models, it was too much for the Victorian sensibilities of the trustees, and he was forced to stop teaching. Eakins and a number of his students formed the Philadelphia Art

Students League, modeled after the league in New York. Later he taught for six years at the National Academy in New York, where he completed one of his most ambitious paintings, "The Clinic of Professor Agnew."

The years covered by Eakins's teaching career—from the mid-seventies to his death in 1916—also marked a substantial advance in what we might call the professionalizing of art in America. While most artists still had to make their livings as illustrators and cartoonists, the growth in the number of art schools and, more important, the improvement in the quality of instruction made study abroad less essential. Indeed, as we have noted, Eakins warned his students against foreign influence (ironically, the warning came at the very moment the French Postimpressionists were changing the European art scene beyond recognition). One of Eakins's most gifted students was Thomas Anschutz, who, like his master, concentrated his attention on people doing everyday tasks. Born in Newport, Kentucky, and reared in Moundsville, Ohio, and Wheeling, West Virginia, Anschutz gave special attention to blacks, revealing a deep sympathy for the toil and sorrow of their lives. At the age of twenty-one he came to New York to enroll in the National Academy of Design, but he decided it was "a rotten old institution" and headed for Philadelphia to take Eakins's life class. He became an assistant in anatomy and then a lecturer and joined Eakins and Muybridge in their experiments photographing movement. Anschutz's most brilliant painting was a scene of workers taking their luncheon break outside a factory, but the body of his surviving work is small, and it was as a teacher of such artists as Robert Henri that he made his impact felt most sharply. He was the "teaching link" between Eakins and Henri (although Eakins, in fact, outlived his pupil).

Another important member of Eakins's generation of teacher-painters was William Merritt Chase, who was born in Indiana in 1849. After studying in Munich toward the end of the period of German domination of the art world, he returned to the United States in 1878 to establish his studio in the famous Tenth Street Studio building. He soon became a kind of artistic impresario, helping break the grip of the National Academy of Design on the art world by founding the Society of American Artists in 1878, but it was as a teacher at the recently founded Art Students League that Chase, an urbane man who carried a cane and wore a pince-nez on a ribbon, had his greatest influence. His own school, the Chase School, later became the Parsons School of Design. Rockwell Kent and Joseph Stella were among his better-known students. Chase urged his students to look for "any un-paintable material considered suitable to break through the academic jam." He was one of a group of mildly Impressionist painters who in 1895 banded together to support one another's work, calling themselves the Ten. One of the most prominent of the Ten was Childe Hassam, whose impressionistic scenes of Central Park and Fifth Avenue caught the tone of New York society.

The war between capital and labor and the general movement for social reform affected artists as well as writers. Anschutz considered himself a socialist, and he exhorted his students to search out and portray workingmen and women in scenes of urban life. Another influential figure at the Art Students League was an older teacher, George de Forest Brush, born in Shelbyville, Tennessee, in 1855 and reared in Danbury, Connecticut. Like many other American artists, Brush studied under Jean Léon Gérôme at the École des Beaux-Arts. After six years in Paris he returned home and worked as an illustrator for *Harper's* and *Century* magazines before he began teaching at the league. Conventional in style and theme, Brush was an enthusiastic follower of Henry George, of whom he did several portraits. In the words of a painter friend, Barry Faulkner, Brush believed "the capitalistic system to be brutally evil. . . . He bought no stocks or bonds and the only investment his theories allowed him was the farm in Dublin [New Hampshire]."

Robert Henri, also a specialist, became the most influential of the teachers at the league. Like all great teachers, Henri taught art as a subdivision of life. Art to him was not simply something done by people who called themselves artists but something that pervaded every aspect of life, and it was as essential to human beings as breath. The task of the artist was to reveal to his or her compatriots those aspects of life which presented themselves to the eye. To perform his mission, the artist had to be open to experience, spontaneous, responsive, socially responsible. First, he himself must see the world freshly, and then he must reveal it to others. Forbes Watson, a painter, critic, and student of Henri's, in his introduction to a collection of his teacher's musings and aphorisms, many of them taken down by students, recalled a group of Henri's students on a bench in Union Square arguing heatedly about what Henri had said to his class that evening. "The discussion," Watson wrote, "was so ardent that no one hearing it could have believed that these young men who had worked all day at manual labor, and painted for hours at the Henri School, were about to sleep on a bench in a park because they could not afford to hire a room for the night." But the students "followed Henri without complaint even when they suffered thereby great material hardships. They did not make the slightest compromise with the ideals Henri held before them." In his war with the existing art establishment Henri, Watson wrote, was "not fighting . . . for a theory of painting. . . . He merely demanded from the reactionaries in power a fair and free opportunity for the young independent American artist."

Paintings, Henri told his students, were "sign-posts on the way to what may be. Sign-posts toward greater knowledge. . . . Art when really understood is the province of every human being. . . . When the artist is alive in any person, whatever his kind of work may be, he becomes an inventive, searching, daring, self-expressing creature. . . . He disturbs, upsets, enlightens, and he opens the way for a better understanding. . . . The world would stagnate without him. . . . The work of the art student is no light matter. Few have the courage and stamina to see it through. You have to make up your mind to be alone in many ways. Cherish your own emotions and never under-value them. . . . I have little interest in teaching you what I know. I wish to stimulate you to tell me what *you* know. . . . For an artist to be interesting to us he must have been interesting to himself. He must have been capable of intense feeling, and capable of profound contemplation. . . . Through art mysterious bonds of understanding and of knowledge are established among men. They are the bonds of a great Brotherhood. Those who are of the Brotherhood know each other, and time and space cannot separate them." That could be said for Henri's students; they constituted a part of that "great Brotherhood." As William James charged students with his own vitality and "loving affection," so Henri filled them with his own "Art spirit," as he called the collection of his reflections.

Another young artist-socialist was Rockwell Kent. Kent, born in 1882, was the prototype of the illustrator-artist-political radical. He was an inebriate of nature with a capital *N*. Monhegan Island in Maine was his equivalent to John Marin's Deer Island. "Monhegan!" Kent wrote exultantly on his first visit. "We've reached the harbor's mouth; we've entered it; we've reached the wharf; we're moored; I've jumped ashore. My bag in hand I race up the hill, and . . . like a puppy let out of his pen I'm off at a run to see, to climb, to touch, and to feel this wonder island that I've come to." Kent was a kind of artist equivalent to Jack London. He had the same ardent and romantic nature, the same Emersonian-Whitmanesque fascination with the rough, material aspects of American life, the same romantic zeal for the revolution and the workers. Unlike many of his contemporaries, Kent was content to remain essentially an illustrator, in some instances of his own books, convinced that was the proper role for the revolutionary artist.

Edward Hopper was born in Nyack, New York, the same year as Rockwell Kent (1882), and he, too, was a student of Henri's. After completing a course at the Correspondence School of Illustrating in New York City, Hopper spent five years studying with Henri. When he went to Paris in 1906, he was already an accomplished artist. Back in New York Hopper determined to make himself master of the city's moods, above all, the haunting loneliness of urban spaces, but aside from a painting sold out of the Armory Show, he could not find a market for his paintings and was forced to support himself and his family as a commercial illustrator. During the years between 1907 and 1920 he turned to etching. In addition to his city scenes, Hopper, like Marin and Kent, was strongly attracted to the Maine Coast.

In 1906 Alfred Stieglitz opened a small gallery at 291 Fifth Avenue, which soon came to be known simply as "291" and later as An American Place. There he encouraged young artists who, influenced by the currents of radical experiment in European painting, were taking a markedly different course from the Eakins-Anschutz-Henri style of realism in their concern with form rather than subject matter.

Three years later Gertrude Vanderbilt Whitney, whose fortune obscured her real talents as a sculptor, also opened a small gallery to exhibit the work of painters excluded from more conservative galleries and exhibitions. The work of the German Expressionists and the Italian Futurists began to influence the work of young American painters working abroad. The Italians were proclaiming the beauty and power of the machine; the Duesenberg, they declared, was more beautiful than the "Winged Victory." All academic art must be rejected in the wake of the machine age. The doctrines of Sigmund Freud also began to make themselves evident in paintings. The most radical artists insisted that their proper task was to explore the world of symbols and dreamlike states that slumbered in the unconscious.

All these impulses—the determination of the young artists working in the Eakins tradition to explore the commonplace and identify themselves with radical politics and the increasing interest in the disintegrative elements of what the socialists and anarchists referred to contemptuously as bourgeois society—came to a climax in 1907, when the jury of the National Academy of Design rejected the paintings of a group of Henri's students, most prominent among them John Sloan, George Luks, and William Glackens. Robert Henri, furious with the academy, refused to allow his own paintings to be exhibited, and the next year the Macbeth Gallery in New York exhibited the paintings of a group selected, in large part, by Arthur Davies. Davies, a courtly and elegant man, whose own paintings featured dreamy classical landscapes with processions of tunic-clad females and unicorns scattered about, was an incongruous ally in the battle against the National Academy. The show, a manifesto for the "new" realism, was billed modestly as "Eight American Painters." They included Henri himself, Glackens, Sloan, Luks, Everett Shinn, Ernest Lawson, and Maurice Prendergast, an older painter who had spent much time in Paris and who was strongly influenced by the Impressionists. Glackens, Luks, Sloan, and Shinn all were newspaper artists working for the *Philadelphia Press*. Far from thinking this an impediment to their development as serious artists, Henri encouraged such work by his students on the ground that it kept them in touch with the everyday world.

Glackens, Luks, and Sloan all were born within four years of each other (1867, Luks; 1870, Glackens; 1871, Sloan). Luks and Sloan were small-town boys (Glackens was a Philadelphian); all considered themselves socialists with a large or small *s*. Following the lead of Eakins, all were interested in sports. Luks, fascinated by professional boxing, invented a past in which he had been a feared middleweight named Chicago Whitey, the Terror of the Windy City. He had also done a comic strip for several years for the *New York World*. Lawson, born in 1873, had played professional baseball for several years. Sloan staked out bars as his particular province; one of his most famous paintings was "McSorley's Bar." Sloan also had a fondness for alley cats and ash cans which helped give the contemptuous name the Ashcan School to him and his friends. They were also known as the Eight from the Macbeth Gallery show, although they were, in fact, a disparate group whose principal common denominator was the rejection of their work by the National Academy.

Prominent among the younger artists was John Marin, whose grandfather Jean-Baptiste Marin had migrated from France in the 1840s. Marin was born in December, 1870 (notice again this year); his mother died a few years later, and Marin was reared by his pious, Bible-reading Yankee maternal grandparents in Weehawken, New Jersey. Marin's passion for nature, for the outdoors, hunting, fishing, exploring, calls to mind Winslow Homer (and, of course, legions of other American landscape painters). For a decade or more Marin drifted from one job to another, often working as an architectural draftsman and painting on his Sundays off, developing his own unique calligraphy. When he was twenty-nine, the austere aunts who had supervised his education after the deaths of his grandparents, deciding that he had no future in the business or professional world, agreed to his attending the Pennsylvania Academy of the Fine Arts. Marin was not a responsive student. He noted that one of his classmates could render a classical plaster cast with remarkable fidelity. "But I thought to myself, 'What is it for? A man paints a boat to look like a boat. But what has he got? The boat doesn't do anything. It doesn't move in the water, it is blown by no tempest. . . . Art must show what goes on in the world.' " The art of the new consciousness could hardly have a more apt slogan: "Art must show what goes on in the world." By this time Marin's father, prosperous and reconciled to his son's odd inclination for painting, "forked up," as Marin put it, money for the obligatory Paris art training, and his son departed for France at the age of thirty-five. The critic Paul Rosenfeld recalled his appearance: "His lean, dry, somewhat swarthy face with its sharpened nose already was reminding people of a wizened apple or the visage of a wren. A slight, medium-tall, somewhat slouchy figure, he had, together with the look of a Yankee farmer, the curious personal dignity and simplicity of the type."

Marin met Stieglitz in Paris in 1910, and Stieglitz returned to New York with a batch of Marin paintings for a show at "291." It had a surprising success. The paintings were not only "advanced," reassuringly "abstract," but beautiful. "To create lovely things one must see lovely things," an enthusiastic reviewer wrote, "hope lovely things, and desire lovely things, and that is what John Marin, in his intense and simple fashion, is greatly doing." By 1915 Marin had found and virtually appropriated the Maine coastline.

A friend of John Marin's who was also to be strongly associated with the Maine coast was Marsden Hartley. Seven years younger than Marin, Hartley came natively by the state. Born into a working-class home in Lewiston, Maine, he was one of nine children, only five of whom survived. Hartley had a difficult childhood (his father, an English immigrant, worked in a cotton mill). Like Frank Lloyd Wright, he felt that his father was a weak and inadequate man, incapable of providing for his family and of showing affection. Hartley's mother died when he was eight. "From the moment of my mother's death," he wrote, "I became in psychology an orphan, in consciousness a lone thing left to make its way out for all time after then by itself. . . . I had a childhood vast with terror and surprise. If it is true that one forgets what one wishes to forget, then I have reason for not remembering the major part of those days. . . ."

Hartley's father married again and moved to Cleveland, where young Hartley found a friend and sponsor in a painter named John Semon. His work showed such promise that he was given a scholarship at the Cleveland Art School. There a drawing teacher gave him Emerson's *Essays,* which became his Bible—the "greatest book" of his life. Hartley responded most strongly to Emerson's praise of intuition and his notion of the spiritual. At the end of his first year of study one of the trustees of the Cleveland Art School, impressed by his progress, offered to underwrite five years of study in New York. In addition to his undoubted talent, Hartley was a compelling figure; a tall, thin, ascetic-looking youth, with an aquiline nose and brilliant, burning eyes, he was the prototype of the young artistic genius. His working-class background coupled with his aristocratic features encouraged the notion that he was a changeling, a young prince abandoned in a workman's hovel, and gave him, for his wealthy sponsor, an irresistibly romantic aura.

In New York Hartley attended William Merritt Chase's New York School of Art. Hartley began spending his summers in Maine, enraptured with his reading of Emerson and Thoreau. "There is nothing," he wrote to a friend, "that sets all things at peace with me as a communion with Nature. She seems to have a balm for every pain and a cheerful song for every sorrowing heart. . . . One learns to look for art in everything and one aspires or should aspire to see art in everything. Beauty is my own aim in life, beauty in character, in thought, in work, in deed, and in expression on canvas of Nature divine, and the glorification of the God of all, who provided us with these beauties." Inspired by such reflections, Hartley became devoutly religious and after a year at the National Academy of Design (its tuition was $10 a month, as opposed to the New York School's $15) Hartley joined a utopian socialist commune in North Bridgton, Maine. The members of the commune were guided by Christianity-cum-Spiritualism-cum-Nature, a thoroughly American amalgam. Whitman, through Horace Traubel, his biographer, was the next strong influence on Hartley. As a consequence of his friendship with Traubel, Hartley found himself drawn into a group of homosexual artists and intellectuals.

Unable to sustain himself by his painting, Hartley next stopped at another commune of radical artists and mystics, Green Acres, in Iliot, Maine. Founded by Sarah Farmer, the daughter of abolitionist followers of Emerson, Green Acres had become a school for the Bahai faith, and it had a full complement of Indian mystics and swamis. Hartley's paintings, especially those of the Maine coast, now began to sell; he acquired several wealthy patrons, and his mature style of vivid colors laid on in strong brush strokes emerged with great power and vitality. Desperately anxious to have a major show and encouraged by Arthur Davies (John Sloan found his paintings too charged with "mystical" implications for his taste), Hartley took his work to Stieglitz, who agreed to have a show for him at "291." Hartley's exhibition established him as one of the brilliant young practitioners of the new art. He discovered Albert Pinkham Ryder with exaltation and declared himself "a convert to the field of imagination into which I was born. . . . I had been thrown back into the body and being of my country." Hartley found the old and largely neglected artist in his little studio on Fifteenth Street and felt that he had made contact with a buried tradition in American painting. Ryder, Hartley wrote, "saw with an all too pitiless and pitiful eye the element of hopelessness in things, the complete succumbing of things in nature to those elements greater than they that wield a fatal power." The comment is worth noting; it marked a strong movement of Hartley's imagination away from the sunny Emersonian view of nature to the darker and more Melvillean end of the scale, where nature was profoundly ambivalent.

In his involvement with Stieglitz and "291" Hartley found a kind of foster father. Most important of all, he became part of the Stieglitz circle, which included Marin and Arthur Dove. When Hartley was sent to Europe for a year through the efforts of Stieglitz and several wealthy art patrons, he found himself much more strongly attracted to German expressionism than to the French Neoimpressionists. He was also introduced by the painter Max Weber to American Indian art and cubism. The result was a body of work in which German militarist images were juxtaposed with symbols derived from Indian pottery. They suggest, in an almost eerie manner, the startling potency of the German military spirit that led to the outbreak of the European War, the coming of which forced Hartley to leave Berlin and return to the United States.

In 1910 Stieglitz put on a show at "291" made up exclusively of "modern" works. One of the most important new artists to exhibit (a

student of Robert Henri's) was Walt Kuhn, at thirty-one one of the
more powerful of the younger painters. Out of the Stieglitz show and
another show a year later at the Madison Gallery came the Association
of American Painters and Sculptors. Other members of the association
were George Bellows, who, like Eakins and Glackens, was fascinated
by prizefights and whose painting "Stag at Sharkey's" established him
at once as a leader of the Neorealists, and Guy Pène du Bois. Another
charter member was the moody Gutzon Borglum, a student of Rodin's
with big ideas. The sculptor Jo Davidson, a close friend of Hutchins
Hapgood's, was also a member. The unlikely leader of this band was
Arthur Davies. It was Davies and Kuhn who decided that it was time
for America to be exposed to the most advanced work of European
painters and sculptors as well as to the work of American modernists.
Reserving the cavernous 69th Regiment Armory on lower Lexington
Avenue in New York, they set out for Germany to select from a vast
show at Cologne works to be exhibited in the United States. Repre-
sentative work of the French "wild beasts" (Fauves), as well as of the
Expressionists and the Cubists, were chosen, along with the sculpture
of Wilhelm Lehmbruck, Aristide Maillol, Alexander Archipenko, and
Constantin Brancusi. Among the painters whose works were included
were the Cubists Fernand Léger, Marcel Duchamp, and Georges
Braque. There were several Picassos, and paintings by Odilon Redon,
André Derain, Maurice Vlaminck, and, of course, Henri Matisse, Georges
Seurat, Vincent van Gogh, Paul Gauguin, and Henri de Toulouse-
Lautrec. It was an astonishing collection, and Kuhn, when he returned
from Europe with his treasures, wrote to Walter Pach, who had helped
assemble the show: "It will be like a bombshell. . . . Everybody is elec-
trified. . . . I feel as though I had crowded an entire art education into
these few weeks. . . . We have a great opportunity in this show, and
must try to make it truly wonderful. . . . We want this old show of ours
to mark the starting point of a new spirit in art, at least as far as America
is concerned. I feel that it will show its effect even further and make
the big wheel turn over both hemispheres."

The organizers of the show and their friends proved to be masters
of publicity, not surprisingly since most of them had strong ties with
newspapers, for which they had worked as illustrators and cartoonists.
Guy Pène du Bois filled a whole issue of *Arts and Decoration* with an-
ticipations of the show. The members of the Association of Painters
and Sculptors festooned the hall with streamers and garlands of pine
to make a connection with the pine tree symbol of the first American

Revolution. As that had been a revolution in political consciousness, this would be a revolution in aesthetic consciousness.

In the democratic mode, the show, which opened Febuary 17, 1913, included works of American artists considered to be in the spirit of the new artistic consciousness, often with little attention to the quality of the works themselves. The result was a wildly heterogeneous collection of 1,600 works of art hung on about 2,400 feet of wall space. The lawyer-collector John Quinn, formally opening the show, declared, "The members of this association have shown you that American artists—young American artists, that is—do not dread, and have no need to dread, the ideas or the culture of Europe. They believe that in the domain of art only the best should rule. This exhibition will be epoch-making. . . ."

Some 70,000 people paid to see the show. It is small wonder that many of them came away bewildered and confused. There had, of course, been numerous instances in the long history of art when work accepted as constituting the proper canon of art had been challenged by an upcoming generation of artists with a different vision of the world (Eakins's painting of an operation at the Gross Clinic in Philadelphia had been barred from the Art and Sculpture Hall of the Centennial Exhibition in 1876 on the ground that its subject was unsuitable for art; it was exhibited in the Medical Building as a compromise), but never before had the artistic establishment been challenged by such a wild variety of new theories and modes of artistic expression.

It was all the more disquieting for a generation acutely aware that chaotic and inexplicable forces were calling into question every bit of traditional wisdom. It was as though all the strange and unsettling intellectual currents in the air had been crystallized in the form of particular objects—paintings and sculptures. The show was at once exhilarating and alarming. It made, as we say today, a statement, and if it was not at all clear exactly what that statement was on the affirmative side (except that anything might claim to be art), it was plain enough that it emphatically declared the old order defunct.

The most controversial painting in the show was Marcel Duchamp's "Nude Descending a Staircase." It provided a field day for scoffers. In the spirit of finding the concealed ponies in a landscape, a newspaper offered a reward for any schoolchild who could find the nude. The most popular description of the painting was "An Explosion in a Shingle Factory."

Theodore Roosevelt, recently defeated in his bid to win another presidential term as the candidate of the Bull Moose or Progressive Party, proved himself as mildly progressive in art as in politics, undertaking to review the show for the *Outlook* under the newspaper lead of "A Layman's Views of an Art Exhibition." It was appropriate that Americans should see the "art forces . . . in Europe, forces which cannot be ignored." He was pleased to see "not a touch of simpering, self-satisfied conventionality . . . no requirement that a man whose gift lay in new directions should measure up or down to stereotyped and fossilized standards." But he had only criticism for "the lunatic fringe"— the Cubists and Futurists.

A number of paintings were sold out of the show. Duchamp's nude was purchased by West Coast art dealers for $324, while a painting of Paul Cézanne's brought $6,500.

Not all American painters were captivated by the Armory Show. Thomas Hart Benton and his fellow artists from the Chicago Art Institute deplored the disposition of the younger American painters to show excessive deference for European trends. The mission of American artists, in Benton's view, was to explore characteristically American themes, specifically the small-town and rural Midwest.

The decorative aspect of the era, the strong emphasis on design and on craftsmanship, had its roots in the Beaux-Arts tradition, in the teachings of William Morris and the work of the Pre-Raphaelites in England. It was also directly related to the new consciousness, which undertook very self-consciously to rebel against the machine-made artifacts that threatened to inundate the nation. The movement, which is associated most conspicuously with the names of Louis Comfort Tiffany, Frank Furness, and John La Farge, stressed in its initial manifestation extreme sinuosity of line and elaborate ornamentation, which reached its high (or low) point in the so-called Moorish Room of Cornelius Vanderbilt's New York residence. Designed by George Browne Post, it carried decoration about as far as it could go. The Morris strain, on the other hand, emphasized the linear and angular, the tones of wood rendered in direct and somewhat rustic manner, hand-woven fabrics, Oriental rugs, natural wood finishes, simplicity, glass bowls and vases, and an extravagance of pottery forms. At times the sinuosity turned into the bizarre. It was almost as though the *line* had escaped all constraint. It wound around the margins of books, across wooden surfaces; it appeared in ornamental iron grillwork. A Freudian might have suspected it was the libido emerging from its subterranean hiding place in the sternly rectilinear Puritan psyche.

Women designers and craftsmen were conspicuous in the movement. The pottery of Hanna Tutt and Sadie Irving was widely acclaimed. Sarah Whitman, the wealthy Bostonian to whose salon John Jay Chapman, William James, and most of the literary lights of the day repaired, designed books, as did Margaret Armstrong. Armstrong, with strong liberal inclinations, made a specialty of working on books by and about blacks. She designed a book of poetry by Paul Laurence Dunbar that was illustrated with photographs by students at the Hampton Institute.

The most effective propagandist of the craftsman movement was Gustav Strickley, whose magazine the *Craftsman* probably did more to develop a conspicuous style of interior design and decoration than any similar journal in our history. But it did not stop with a simple crafts approach; Strickley and the *Craftsman* expounded a philosophy in which the words "indigenous," "honesty," and "integrity" appeared like a litany. Be true to your materials. Do not make plaster look like wood or wood like plaster. Respect and learn from nature. Make every part and furnishing harmonious.

An ancillary development was the poster and magazine cover. Here the undisputed master was Will Bradley, who was influenced by the British graphic artist Aubrey Beardsley and by Japanese prints. Bradley's feeling for design was unrivaled. His posters set the standard to which all others were compared. Boldly and brilliantly conceived, they proclaimed an exciting new freedom of form and movement. From the crowded, busy surfaces of the existing illustrator's style there emerged a compellingly fresh treatment of space. And everywhere there was that newly liberated line, coiling about. But Bradley and his followers came under attack in the Progressive era as mirroring a European decadence, and the coiling line, identified with the feminine anima, was superseded by the more severely "masculine" rectilinear line. In part what came to be called the Arts and Crafts movement was overtaken by the new spirit of reform, which suggested an alternative tactic to establishing a bastion of art against the barbarian force of the machine; the machine might be tamed and the capitalist chastened. The machine might indeed, as the Italian Futurists suggested, become art, as it had been, of course, at its inception. Nonetheless, the Arts and Crafts movement, which survived at least to the end of the first decade of the new century and left its impact on American art and, perhaps more notably, through Frank Lloyd Wright, on our architecture, remains an interesting and important anomaly in the nation's cultural history. Looking at the objects it produced, one is struck by the sense that for a time some of the nation's most creative energies found expression in a collection of extravagantly beautiful objects and images, many of which give powerful sexual emanations; their effect cannot have been other than therapeutic.

On the Pacific coast a school of landscape painters matched the journalists and writers of the area in creating their own independent movement, which centered in the California School of Design, established in San Francisco in 1878. Less influenced by the French Impressionists and Postimpressionists than the Eastern painters were, the West Coast painters inclined to a modified impressionism imported by Emil Carlsen, director of the Califonia School of Design, and by his successor, Arthur Mathews.

Born in Wisconsin in 1860, Mathews grew up in Oakland, California, where his family moved when he was seven. He worked as a draftsman and illustrator before going to France to study under Jules Lefebvre. Among the principal influences on Mathews were John La Farge and the French painter, Pierre Puvis de Chavannes. In his role as director of the California School of Design from 1890 to 1906, Mathews transmitted his so-called decorative style to many of his students. He and his wife, Lucia Kleinhans, who was an equally gifted artist, took as their mission the integration of such practical domestic objects as furniture, stained glass, boxes, and lamps with easel painting. They designed and carved their picture frames in accord with the subject and the tones of the paintings. The masters of a subtle but powerful palette, Mathews and his wife went further than any artists of their generation in combining fine art with the crafts. The harmonious surfaces of their paintings remain entirely captivating. While the themes—Naiads, the three Graces, Sacred and Profane Love—are those of high Beaux-Arts, the spirit and technique transcend the limits of the subject matter. While it may well be true that the powerful personalities of the Mathewses helped immunize the West Coast painting from the currents of modernism that swept the East, the consequences were by no means negative. California developed a style of its own and a confident independence of the East.

The fact that the Mathewses went very much their own way has led to their neglect by art historians, but since we do not have to concern ourselves with who is "in" and who is "out," who is (or was) advanced, and who retrograde, we can simply say that "if beauty is its own excuse for being," the Mathewses need no apologies.

In architecture the influence of Louis Sullivan continued to emanate from Chicago, most strikingly in the person of one of his students, Frank Lloyd Wright. Wright was born in 1867 at Richland Center, Wisconsin, on the farm of his maternal grandfather, Richard Lloyd Jones, a Unitarian minister. Wright's father, a Baptist minister, lived in Weymouth, Massachusetts, and Wright grew up there, but it was his lifelong conviction that his roots were in the Middle West. Wright's father was a classic American "failure" who tried successive careers as a preacher, doctor, lawyer, and music teacher without ever being able to support his family adequately. His mother was Wright's inspiration and guiding star. Determined that he should be an architect, she filled his room with engravings of famous buildings. His mother and father were divorced, and Wright and his mother found refuge on his grandfather's farm, a "hive of work, prayer and song." From Madison, Wisconsin, Wright went to Chicago, then in what Theodore Dreiser called its "furnace stage," the most vital and exciting city in the country. At the home of an uncle he met Jane Addams and, through her, the radical intellectual elite of the city. Louis Sullivan hired the ambitious young Wright as a draftsman, to be his "pencil," as he put it. Sullivan, as we have noted earlier, was a kind of Whitmanesque apostle of democracy. He identified all traditional architecture as "feudal" and called for a democratic architecture that would embody the ideal of "the individual man . . . self-centered, self-governing—an individual sovereign, an individual god."

When Jane Addams invited Wright to lecture at Hull House, he chose as his topic "The Art and Craft of the Machine." Addams's own efforts to place traditional crafts in a practical relationship to the machine were opposed to the William Morris dream of revived feudal order, and Wright took his cue from her. He admitted that the machine had rendered nugatory "every type or form sacred to the art of old" and left a "pandemonium of tin masks, huddled deformities and decayed methods." But Wright looked to the machine to demonstrate "intellect mastering the drudgery on earth." The machine, used properly, might free man from his ancient sentence to earn his bread by the everlasting sweat of his brow, thereby creating for the first time in history the conditions for a true democracy. "Every age has done its work," Wright declared, "with the best tools or contrivances it knew, the tools most successful in saving the most precious thing in the world—human effort." And he wrote to a friend the same year (1901): "The art of the future will be an expression of the individual artist through the thousand powers of the machine, the machine doing all the things that the individual worker cannot do, and the creative artist is the man that controls all this and understands it."

The city, with its "muffled persistent roar" and "ceaseless activity," was the center and testing ground of the new human order, a "monster leviathan . . . whose heavy breathing, murmuring, clangor . . . rose to proclaim the marvels of the units of its structure." The artist must transmute this "greatest of machines, the city" and give it "A SOUL."

Happily married and with a growing family, Wright now entered the most productive period of his career, designing a series of houses and several public buildings, most of them in Oak Park, the suburban area of Chicago where he himself lived, which gave dramatic form to his ideas. By the time he came in 1908 to write an essay for the *Architectural Record*, "In the Cause of Architecture," he had turned sharply toward Nature, and he said little about the machine. What Wright proclaimed was "Indigenous Architecture." Nature, in his words, "furnished the materials for architectural motifs out of which the architectural forms as we know them to-day have been developed. . . ." Instead of adhering slavishly to dead formulas, the modern architect should turn back to Nature; "her wealth of suggestion is inexhaustible; her riches greater than any man's desire. . . . A sense of the organic is indispensable for an architect," and this he learns best from Nature. Wright identified himself with the "New School of the Middle West." Its principles, he wrote, were, first, "Simplicity and Repose." From this it followed that a house should contain "as few rooms as will meet the conditions which give it rise and under which we live, and which the architect should strive continually to simplify; then the ensemble of rooms should be carefully considered that comfort and utility may go hand in hand with beauty." The ground floor need contain no more than living room, dining room, and kitchen. Indeed, there need be only a living room "with requirements otherwise sequestered from it, or screened within it by means of architectural contrivances." He added, "Openings should occur as integral features of the structure and form, if possible, its natural ornamentation." Then came one of his severest and most radical stipulations: "An excessive love of detail has ruined more fine things from the standpoint of fine art or fine living than any one human shortcoming—it is hopelessly vulgar. Too many houses, when they are not like little stage-settings or scene paintings, are mere junk-shops. Decoration is dangerous unless you understand it thoroughly and are satisfied that it means something good in the scheme as a whole." Appliances and fixtures were to be in the main avoided or designed in harmony with the total structure; pictures should be thought of as decoration and used accordingly; they should not clutter walls. The furniture, like the fixtures, should be integral with the house, designed for it. There should be as many kinds of houses, built along these general principles, as there were people to live in them. Most important of all, "a building should appear to grow easily from its site and be shaped to harmonize with its surroundings if Nature is manifest there. . . ." Midwesterners who lived on the prairieland should live in houses that accentuate "this natural beauty, its quiet level. Hence gently sloping roofs, low proportions, quiet sky-lines . . . and sheltering overhangs, low terraces and out-reaching walls, sequestering private gardens." Colors must harmonize with the mood of the house and its setting—"soft warm, optimistic tones of earth and autumn leaves in preference to the pessimistic blues, purples or cold greens and grays of the ribbon counter. . . . Develop the natural texture of the plastering. . . . Reveal the nature of the wood, plaster, brick or stone in your designs; they are all by nature friendly and beautiful. . . . Buildings like people must first be sincere, must be true and then withal as gracious and lovable as may be. Above all, integrity."

Wright's doctrines were often repeated and amplified, but their essence was "In the Cause of Architecture," as revolutionary a creed (and doubtless as Midwestern a one) as the history of American domestic architecture vouchsafes us. It belongs with Andrew Jackson Downing's treatise on the cottage and breathes the same spirit of democratic idealism. The two men were, indeed, surprisingly alike in their views. Both were preoccupied by the relationship of the architecture to the kind of human existence that takes place within it. Both men wished to make that life simpler, more honest, more generous, more humane. Both were in the tradition of the great dreamers and reformers. To Wright, as to Downing and, it might be said, to Harriet Beecher Stowe as well, Americans were cramped and smothered by the awkward and arbitrary structures in which they lived, buildings dictated more by fashion than by the psychological needs and physical well-being of those who lived within them.

Wright's houses are, for all practical purposes, servantless houses, houses with an air of informality, of easy movement from one area and activity to another, houses that encourage, if they do not dictate, new kinds of intrafamily relationships. Wright was a socialist whose political ideas were as radical as his architectural ones. He wanted factories and office buildings to be as beautiful and inhabitable as his homes. He did not stop with homes and factories; his utopian vision took in whole cities, and he designed one: Broadacres, never built. "We see I am cast by nature for the part of an iconoclast," he wrote to a friend. "I must strike—tear down, before I can build—my very act of building destroys an order."

Like many radicals of his generation, including the Greenwich Village circle, Wright rebelled against the standard bourgeois marriage. In 1907 he declared himself in love with Mamah Borthwick Cheney, the wife of a former client. "Love should be its own protection or its own defeat," he declared. "I loved my children. I loved my home. A true home is the finest ideal of man, and yet—well, to gain freedom I asked for a divorce." Those ideal domestic spaces that Wright had created for himself and his wife could not, after all, prevail against normal human perversity. His wife, perhaps concerned with the welfare of their six children, refused to divorce him. The result was that Wright turned against the upper-middle-class respectability and prosperity of Oak Park and departed for Europe with Mrs. Cheney. When he returned, he returned with a new concept of the architect's role and of his own future. In the Valley of the Jones, as Wright called the setting of his ancestral home, where his grandfather had presided like a feudal lord, Wright built Taliesin as his home and studio. It was to be a place where "life and work were one," a structure that belonged to the land it rested upon so naturally, but in 1914 a servant, who had gone insane, set the house on fire, killing Mrs. Cheney and three of her daughters. A shattered Wright spent most of the next six years in Japan, leaving behind as his memorial the Imperial Hotel, built to conform to his theories and to withstand the earthquakes that shook Tokyo intermittently.

The high Victorian interiors that Frank Lloyd Wright (and others as well) protested against were filled with a jumble of knickknacks, whatnots, furbelows, and any number of *things*. Heavy curtains barred any stray beam of sunlight and gave an exaggerated and much admired effect of light and shadow—chiaroscuro. Such interiors were related to the general air of repression that characterized the age, of things hidden or obscured. Wright wished to sweep away the clutter of objects and open the dark interiors to sunlight and air.

In California Wright's counterparts and, to a degree, disciples were the Greene brothers, Henry M. and Charles S. Henry was a year younger than Wright, and Charles two years Henry's junior. They established themselves in Pasadena, where they developed a striking "indigenous style" that was plainly influenced by Japanese architecture as well as by the Arts and Crafts movement and Art Nouveau. The Greenes set out to design not Tudor mansions or Gothic cottages but houses expressive of the climate and landscape of Southern California, where pellucid skies and perpetual sunlight suggested a new way of living and a new relationship between indoors and outdoors. Porches and loggias coming into favor even in far less temperate climes were important features of Greene houses, as were long, overhanging eaves to protect interiors from excessive glare and heat. This meant houses carefully oriented to the sun's seasonal journey. Naturally finished and carefully treated surfaces with respect for the qualities of various materials were as characteristic of Greene houses as of Wright's. Like Wright, the Greenes gave loving attention to interiors and, above all, to the furnishings.

The California cottage style, an adaptation of the Greene and Greene principles to far more modest structures, also flourished, and Irving Gill, who had worked in Sullivan's office with Wright and helped design the Transportation Building at the Chicago World's Fair moved to the San Diego area and introduced what we might call modified adobe, Southwest, not on the whole a very rewarding style but an interesting example of the enthusiasm for the indigenous. Finally, there was the Spanish colonial, which appeared unaccompanied by any elaborate architectural rationale but proved irresistible. With, in the case of more pretentious houses, interior courtyards or patios, fountains, gardens, and palm trees, it was preferred by the movie moguls who, by the end of this period, were migrating in considerable numbers to Southern California.

In the northern part of the state Bernard Maybeck and Julia Morgan were developing their own particular style. Morgan's work was done in a kind of modified Beaux-Arts style, with classical proportions and a captivating spirit of light and air. She was William Randolph Hearst's architect and the designer of his "castle" on the California coast near Morro Bay. Maybeck staked out his claim to national attention by his elegant Palace of Fine Arts at the Panama-Pacific Exposition in San Francisco in 1915. The graceful colonnade and classical façade of the palace survive and, somewhat ironically, house Frank Oppenheimer's brilliantly conceived Exploratorium, a chamber of scientific wonders designed primarily for young people.

While Wright's influence was widely felt, most American buildings, domestic and public, remained highly eclectic and overwhelmingly traditional. The recoil toward reaction that followed the outbreak of the European War in 1914 was felt at every level of American life. The tragedy of Wright's personal life coincided to an almost eerie degree with the world upheaval that called every innovative notion into question. To Arnold Bennett, the British novelist, the great architectural monuments—the American equivalents of palazzi and cathedrals—were the towering office buildings and the railroad stations that continued to be built in the formidable Beaux-Arts style. A New York insurance company united "all the splendors of all the sky-scrapers," Bennett wrote. "Its foyer and grand staircases will sustain comparison with those of the Paris Opera. . . . Within the foyer and beyond the staircase, notice the outer rooms, partitioned off by bronze grilles, looming darkly gorgeous in an eternal windowless twilight studded with beautiful glowing green disks of electric-lamp shades. . . . The desired effect is at once obtained, and it is wonderful." So it was in one establishment after the other, with the greatest magnificence retained for the chambers of the rulers of these imperial headquarters of commerce. In the inner sanctums "ceilings rose in height, marble was softened by the thick pile of carpets. Mahogany and gold shone more luxuriously . . . a noble apartment, an apartment surpassing dreams and expectations, conceived and executed in a spirit of marvelous prodigality." One such business baron, luxuriating "in the brilliant symbolism" of his office's "grandiosity," his gilt-framed portrait "repeating him above his head," confessed proudly to Bennett that "My wife used to say that for ten years she never saw me."

To those Europeans who declared that America had no great art, Bennett offered in refutation the Pennsylvania Station in New York City. It was "full of the noble qualities that fine and heroic imagination alone can give." It required a railroad man "poetic and audacious enough to want it, architects with genius powerful enough to create it, and a public with heart enough to love it. . . ." These things seemed to Bennett "a surer proof that America is a great race than the existence of any number of wealthy universities, museums of classic art, associations for prison reform. . . . Such a monument does not spring up by chance; it is part of the slow flowering of a nation's secret spirit!" It was true, though, that it took a foreigner to see. The issue was, after all, imagination, imagination on quite a spectacular scale, an imagination appropriate to the landscape, breathtaking in its presumption and dazzling in its achievement. It stood somehow, in its arrogance and audacity, beyond judgment like a force in nature, creating a category of its own, putting its critics on their mettle.

Art historians have been busy for some time now describing, analyzing, and categorizing what we would call the art of the new consciousness. The currents, schools, and styles are certainly diverse, but it is clear enough that there were two distinguishable trends: Stieglitz and the artists who clustered about "291" and the students of Robert Henri, more politically oriented as a group. There were certainly conspicuous overlaps and crosscurrents, and it is evident that despite a determined effort to utilize the city, city buildings, and city themes, the older Emersonian infatuation with nature and, equally, the zeal for social reform, taken together, reasserted itself with irrepressible vigor. To say American art came of age in this period would be to scant what had already been accomplished and perhaps anticipate a swelling future, but we can say with certainty that American art and artists were both conspicuous beneficiaries of the new consciousness and, at the same time, contributors to it. The most striking thing about the movement was the revelation of a dazzling new realm of images, of line and form and color, vivid iconographies of the individual psyche. At the moment that the buried images and fantasies of a culture are set free they emerge with a startling power. Emerson had, in a sense, called Whitman to life to enact that which Emerson was too conventional to do more than advocate.

Louis Sullivan in architecture and Robert Henri and, to a lesser extent, William Merritt Chase had, in similar fashion, summoned up the Faustian (or Freudian) intuitions of their students to create in the realm of the visual arts what Whitman had achieved in verse. Many of the artists went back to reclaim a Whitman who had been largely buried under Victorian pruderies and inhibitions. The final point to be made is that in the strange ferment of our period, the intellectual and aesthetic foundations of the unfolding century were laid in the arts as in politics, economics, and technology.

49

The Popular Novel

Describing the birth of a new consciousness is not only, as Jane Addams noted, one of the most demanding tasks for the historian but also a protracted undertaking since a new consciousness usually takes decades and, in most instances, generations to come to term. On occasion a widespread change of outlook can happen almost overnight. The most dramatic example of the latter would be the change in national psychology brought about by a sudden warlike event, such as, for example, the bombing by the Charleston militia of Fort Sumter. In an instant most of the Northern doubts and misgivings about the proper course to be followed by the Federal government vanished or were suppressed.

The birth of a new consciousness is, however, a transformation of a different order of magnitude or even of a different character. It goes deeper into the collective psyche, and it is far more enduring; its timetable is different for different classes, sections, generations. It is most rapid in the younger generation, most stubbornly resisted by the older generation. It is more urban than rural, and it is usually carried along by the intellectual leaders of the middle class. Even grass-roots movements like populism (which was in many respects highly conservative) draw their leaders most frequently, although not exclusively, from better educated, more articulate, more self-conscious individuals.

All this is too evident to require exposition, but it is nonetheless important to keep in mind. Especially in the early stages of the emergence of a new consciousness, progress is generally slow, and there are numerous setbacks and interruptions. The free love movement is a case in point. Beginning in the post–Civil War period, in a time of radical social experiments, it grew rapidly in the decade of the seventies and certainly appeared to those involved to be the famous "wave of the future," but a reaction set in. The reaction was symbolized by but clearly not limited to Anthony Comstock, and by the end of the century it was as though the free love movement had never happened; it was erased from the collective memory of the American people. Its high priestess, Victoria Woodhull, even tried to have the newspaper accounts of her involvement removed from the papers' files. When free love reappeared, most dramatically in Greenwich Village, roughly in the years from 1910 to 1917, its new advocates were a very different type from its original champions and, moreover, unaware of the antecedents of the movement they believed that they had initiated.

A new consciousness registers first and most dramatically in the arts. The Armory Show was, by that token, as powerful a representation of the new consciousness as one could conceive. As contrasted with that of literature of the period, with novels or poems, or criticism, its impact was immediate and inescapable. Whether one accepted it or not, was thrilled or horrified, there could be no shadow of a doubt that it registered a new way of perceiving the material world. Broadly put, it appealed to the young intelligentsia and horrified their elders.

In literature the problem of registering the new consciousness proved far more complex and laborious than in art. In art one had only to paint in the new style, find a wall on which to hang the paintings, and invite the public to view them. In literature there was an establishment, a powerful autocracy made up of the official arbiters of literary taste, who decided what should be published and what should not. They were writers/critics/editors, men like William Dean Howells and Thomas Wentworth Higginson, Walter Hines Page and Henry Holt. They edited the literary magazines, like the *Atlantic Monthly*, *Century*, and *Independent*. Ellen Glasgow described them: "Life had been easy for them, and literature had been easier. They had created both the literature of America and the literary renown that embalmed it. . . . When they were not . . . 'encouraging one another in mediocrity,' they were gravely preparing work for one another to praise." It seemed to Glasgow that she was surrounded "not by a vigorous immaturity, but by an immaturity that was old and tired and prudent, and loved ritual and rubric, and was utterly wanting in curiosity and the new and the strange." They had gobbled up such diverse figures as Mark Twain and Hamlin Garland. Of Garland, Glasgow wrote: "His first volume of stories, *Main-Traveled Roads*, showed an almost savage fidelity to life; but, when he left the West and came to New York, he was tamed of his wildness as well as his originality, by the civilizing influence of Mr. Howells."

What was most significant was the fact that the establishment controlled a multimillion-dollar publishing industry, one that consumed an enormous amount of good, bad, and indifferent literature every year. The popular novel was the kingpin of the industry, and the writers of novels the lords (and, almost equally, the ladies) of the literary world. We have earlier discussed the general form of this flood of second- and third-rate literature: romantic tearjerkers with stock characters, situations, and themes.

The most common "plot" was that of a young man, the hero, usually described in almost the same phrases by a wide variety of writers. He is strikingly handsome and well set up, with broad shoulders and, invariably, blue eyes, and dark hair with a slight wave. He is immaculately dressed. Whether a workingman-prizefighter (as in Jack London's *The Game*), a Nebraska farm boy, a Southern poor white, or an ornament of Fifth Avenue, he was, in fact, Howard Chandler Christy's archetypal young man. It was as though the visual stereotype were too powerful for the most determinedly "individual" or "original" writer to break. The women, at least in novels written by women, were somewhat less stereotyped. Virtually all of them are "new women," the exception being the female heavies, who are apt to be older women, vain, spoiled, self-indulgent, shallow, and unscrupulous in the techniques they use to snare males.

The hero, incidentally, is most commonly a journalist, sometimes an art critic, occasionally a writer. The hero meets the heroine; they fall madly in love, but one or both are already married to spouses they have grown indifferent to. Usually the woman is in this fix since it is a basic assumption of these novels that virtually all marriages are cold and loveless. Often their marriages have been born in romantic love, but the husband has grown increasingly preoccupied with his business, with getting ahead and making vast sums of money. It is delicately indicated that the physical side of the marriage is inoperative and that the husband finds his sexual satisfactions elsewhere. Convention and other complications make it unthinkable for the hero and heroine to run off together, although they usually contemplate it for a number of chapters, carefully canvassing all the arguments pro and con. They part. Various adventures or again, more commonly, misadventures befall them, making them older and wiser (and less romantic). The mates that have kept them apart die from a wide range of causes, running from suicide (Gertrude Atherton's *Patience Sparhawk and Her Times*) to falling off a cliff. The hero and heroine get married. Not infrequently virtually everybody dies.

A major category of popular literature dealt with the apparently endlessly absorbing details of high society (a subdivision was Anglo-American high society, as in Atherton's popular *American Wives and English Husbands*). As we have had occasion to note before, virtually all these novels depicted high society as selfish and frivolous. The merciless struggle for success was central. Typically an ambitious young man rises to the pinnacle of riches by unscrupulous means only to discover that all his wealth means nothing without (1) the love of a good woman, (2) God's grace, or (3) both. Often the repentant sinner resolves to devote his remaining days to improving the lot of his less fortunate fellows. Alternately he runs away, goes off on some anonymous journey around the country or around the world, and comes back, at last at peace with himself, to a faithful wife, whom he has ignored or mistreated in his days of wealth and power. This was the theme of William Allen White's best-selling novel *A Certain Rich Man*, which was published in 1909.

John Barclay of Sycamore Ridge, a small Midwestern town, is the hero of White's novel. Barclay makes a fortune in grain mills and elevators and railroads—by tireless work and ruthless methods. The slogan "Barclay's Best" was on the side of freight trains rumbling across the country; it was emblazoned on mountainsides and even painted on the base of the Statue of Liberty. The futility, indeed wickedness of Barclay's course is pointed out to him by his mother. She upbraids him for "all this money-getting. I am foolish, John, but some way, I want my little boy back—the one who used to sit with me so long ago and play on his guitar and sing 'Sleeping, I Dream, Love.'" But this is a new world, her son protests. "I know, dear—it is a new world; but the same old God moves it. . . ."

Barclay dismisses his mother's warnings. He is astonished and indignant when Congress passes laws to limit his despoiling of the people—the consumers of his wheat and the passengers on his railroad trains. "The men who make the wealth and maintain the prosperity have got to run [the country] in spite of the long-nosed reformers and socialists," he rages. When Barclay finds himself the object of a suit for fraud and illegal combination, his mother is almost relieved. "If you could come out of jail with that horrible greed for money purged from you!" she exclaims. The voice of the people, which is no more than the voice of God, has humbled him to the dust. "The last century gave us Schopenhauers and Kants, all denying God, and this one gives us Railroad Kings and Iron Kings and Wheat Kings, all by their works proclaiming that Mammon has the power and the glory and Kingdom. O ye workers of iniquity!" Barclay yields to his mother's exhortations. He is contrite. He feels uplifted, born again. "Oh, mother, mother, I feel like a child!" "Then Mary Barclay knew that her son had let Him in. . . ."

A Certain Rich Man may well be taken as the prototype of the novel of success and repentance. It was extravagantly praised by the critics and enthusiastically read by the public.

David Graham Phillips was the beau ideal of the popular male novelist. Born in Madison, Indiana, in 1867 and educated at Yale, he had a career as a journalist before trying his hand at fiction. His first successful novel—he wrote more than twenty—*The Great God Success,* created a scandal which ensured its sales. The hero, Howard, a recent graduate of Yale, applies for a job on a New York daily paper. The editor regards him with skepticism: "I thought Yale men went into something commercial; law or banking or railroads." Howard replies virtuously that he hasn't "the money-making instinct." The editor warns him that in journalism the "room is at the bottom" rather than at the top. It was a "dragon that demands the annual sacrifice of youth. It will have only youth." Howard realizes that he must practice a severe discipline to learn to "write for the people." At the same time he finds it "the most fascinating work imaginable for an intelligent, thirsty mind— the study of human nature under stress of the great emotion . . . he was always observing love, hate, jealousy, revenge, greed . . . in all his better stories . . . there was the atmosphere of sincerity, of realism, the marks of an acute observer, without prejudice and with a justifiable leaning toward a belief in the fundamental worth of humanity."

Reveling in his freedom and in the romance of being a newspaper reporter, Howard falls in love with Alice, a pretty young woman who has been unable to find a job and is on the verge of accepting money from young men in return for sexual favors. For four years she and Howard live together "in a Bohemian quicksand." At the age of thirty Howard realizes that he has come to depend on "a dangerous facility, a perilous inertia." He is making a good salary at work he enjoys, but he has lost his drive and his ambition to get ahead. He blames this state of affairs on Alice. He does not love her and cannot consider marrying her; she is too far beneath him in caste. Above all, she does not "inspire ambition in him." By satisfying his "amatory needs," she has prevented him from pressing "that search which men and women keep up incessantly until they find what they seek"—a suitable mate.

The dilemma is resolved by that familiar deus ex machina, Alice's illness and death. Too late Howard realizes how much he has loved this artless and unselfish young woman who gave herself to him so generously. Her death provides the spur to his ambition that her life did not. To forget his sorrow, he sets out to perfect his literary style and to find a cause in which he can enlist his journalistic talents to the full. His life is simplified into "work and sleep . . . the two periods of happiness" in his otherwise drab existence. This regimen is interrupted when Howard meets a handsome but jaded young society woman, Marian Trevor. She is engaged to marry Teddy Danvers, depressingly like all prospective husbands in such novels: " 'a good deal of a chump' " but "a decent fellow, good-looking, good-natured, domestic in his tastes, and nothing but money." Miss Trevor, a friend assures Howard, is quite "capable of leading him a dance if he bores her. And bore her he will. But that is nothing new. This town is full of it."

"Full of what?" Howard asks.

"Of weary women—weary wives. The men . . . have just one interest and that is usually small and dull—stocks or iron or real estate or hunting or automobiles. Our women are not like the English women—stupid, sodden. They are alive, acute. They wish to be interested. Their husbands bore them. . . . It's the American blood coming out—the passion for achievement. They want a man of whom they can be proud, a man who is doing something interesting and doing it well."

Marian and Howard fall in love. She decides to go through with her marriage to Teddy Danvers, but the marriage, in fact, does not take place. Marian and Teddy have a bitter quarrel over her friendship with Howard, and Teddy looks "at her neck, bare arms, with the baffled desire of brute passion." After he has stormed out, she begins to cry hysterically. When her cousin finds her, she sobs out her story. She has thought of Teddy as "a brother" and a "friend," but he has treated her "like a—like a *thing*." The cousin declares, "Of course Teddy's a brute. . . . I thought you knew. He's a domesticated brute, like most of the men and some of the women. You'll have to get used to that." In this context "brute" means abnormal (or perhaps normal) sexual appetites.

In the end it is Danvers who runs away, leaving behind a note accusing Marian of having "fallen under an evil influence." Now driven more than ever by the demon Success, Howard embraces "yellow journalism" to increase the circulation of his newspaper. His spectacular success emboldens him to renew his courtship of Marian. They marry, but Howard soon finds himself distracted by his ambition to succeed on a grand scale. Having achieved wealth, he turns to the pursuit of power; he becomes a restless and inattentive husband, but at least he is an achiever, far better than the selfish parasite Teddy Danvers. Marian turns increasingly to a hectic social life to fill her otherwise empty days. "In her own way she has become as self-absorbed, as ambitious as he." He takes on the mantle of a reformer and throws his paper's weight behind a Progressive candidate, but when he finds that his large investments in a corrupt and mismanaged coal company are in jeopardy, he decides to cover up its defalcations. At the end of the novel there is no repentance and reform. Howard is disgraced and loses much of his wealth, and Marian must face the fact that their hearts have grown cold toward each other and that they have sacrificed both love and humanity to the Great God Success.

The Great God Success was published in 1901 under an assumed name because the subject matter—specifically the unmarried relationship between the hero and Alice—was thought to be scandalous.

In 1910 Phillips chose an even more daring subject, the fall and *rise* of a woman of easy virtue. In *Susan Lenox: Her Fall and Rise* Susan, desperately poor and unable to find work, begins to accept favors from men and becomes what would later be termed a call girl. The novel was considered too bold by far to be published when it was written, and it was not until 1917, six years after Phillips had been murdered by a paranoid violinist, that the novel was published.

At the end of Phillips's novel Susan Lenox finally frees herself from her dependence on men. She reflects that the man who launched her career as a successful actress told her that she was "born lucky because she had the talent that enables one to rise above the sordidness of that capitalism he so often denounced—the sordidness of the lot of its slaves, the sordidness of the lot of its masters." The price was that she must be "Alone—always alone. . . . And always to be alone. . . . A billow of heartsick desolation" surges over her, but she consoles herself with the thought that at last she is truly free. "She was free—forever free! Free . . . from the wolves of poverty and shame, or want and rags and filth, the wolves that had been pursuing her. . . . Free to live as *she* pleased instead of for the pleasure of a master or masters."

Newton Booth Tarkington was another Hoosier author, two years younger than David Graham Phillips. His parents were New Englanders who had moved to Indianapolis while preserving close ties with the East. Tarkington's uncle Newton Booth was a famous lawyer and jurist and one of the early governors of California. Tarkington was sent East to Phillips Exeter for his secondary schooling and then, after two years at Purdue University, transferred to Princeton. His consuming ambition was to be a writer and illustrator. After five discouraging years he hit the jackpot with his first published novel, *The Gentleman from Indiana.*

The book is a skillful evocation of the town of Plattville, Indiana (Tarkington was one of the first and most successful exploiters of the Midwestern small-town locale). The novel begins with a vivid picture of the Great Plains: "There is a fertile stretch of flat lands in Indiana where unagrarian Eastern travelers, glancing from car-windows, shudder and return their eyes to interior upholstery, preferring even the swaying caparisons of a Pullman to the monotony without. The landscape lies interminably level; bleak in winter, a desolate plain of mud and snow; hot and dusty in summer, in its flat lonesomeness, miles on miles with not one cool hillslope away from the sun," interminable fences interspersed with large barns and stiff defiant farmhouses, small towns with a few brick buildings clustered near "small frame railroad stations." It is to such a town, slightly larger and more sophisticated than its sisters, that John Harkless comes to run the town newspaper, a failing venture that he has bought unseen. Harkless is a college graduate, an educated man of cultivated tastes who, born in Indiana, has cherished a romantic dream of becoming a newspaper editor. In Plattville his dream is realized. He courageously opposes the local vigilantes, the White Caps—a kind of local of Ku Klux Klan that terrorizes the town—and for his pains is beaten and almost killed. During his long recuperation Helen Frisbee, the daughter of a derelict whom Harkless has befriended, secretly takes up the editorship of Harkless's paper, which must otherwise collapse and leave the field to the most brutal and reactionary elements in the county. She proves to be a brilliant editor; among her successful innovations is a "women's page."

When Harkless, well again, returns to his paper and it is more successful than ever, he realizes that Helen has saved it from failure. They avow their love. They agree their place is with the people of Plattville, their friends and neighbors. They see them celebrating Harkless's return. "Look," said Helen, "aren't they dear, good people?"

"The beautiful people!" Harkless replied.

The Gentleman from Indiana was an old-fashioned romance with a new-fashioned woman, capable of taking over and running a faltering newspaper but eager to succumb to love and make her own life subordinate to her husband's. Tarkington utilized the myth of the "escape and return" (as old as Odysseus). Harkless, born in Indiana and educated in the East (as was Tarkington), returns to his true home in the Midwest.

By 1918 Tarkington had joined the ranks of those who viewed the small town as a cultural desert. "The magnificence of the Ambersons" begins in the panic of 1873. When others are losing their money, Major Amberson makes his fortune, a fortune that enables his family to dominate the town of Midland as it grows into a city. The novel opens with what is perhaps the most perceptive sartorial inventory of small-town life in our literature. From clothes it proceeds through architecture—Tarkington is especially eloquent and detailed on porches and parlors, indeed domestic spaces in general (the lawns of the prosperous display cast-iron stags, wounded lions, and other ornamental figures)—and then to the geography of the town, its transportation, and its social life, its sports and politics and funerals. Looming over everything is the extravagant mansion of the Ambersons, the woodwork of which alone is said to have cost $60,000! Visitors to Midland are told by the awed locals that the Major's wife and daughter have been to Europe and since their return have tea every afternoon at five o'clock. Instead of making salad with vinegar and sugar, they pour olive oil on lettuce with the vinegar and add olives, green things, "something like a hard plum."

The novel which follows the fortunes of the Ambersons, especially the Major's spoiled grandson, George Amberson Minafer, is also the story of a small town's transformation into a booming industrial center. Played as a counterpoint to the triumphs and tragedies of the Ambersons and, above all, the priggishness and snobbery of George is the destruction of Midland by the spirit of boosterism. The town grows apace, but it grows "dirty" and soulless as the spirit of boosterism comes to dominate everything—its motto becomes "The more dirt, the more prosperity." Most of the Ambersons live elsewhere and only draw their income from what is now a small city. But things go badly for the family fortunes, so ill attended, and when the old Major dies at last, it turns out that his estate is bankrupt. George, finally humbled, reflects that "the city had rolled over his heart, burying it under. . . . The city had rolled over the Ambersons and buried them under to the last vestige. . . . George Minafer had got his comeuppance, but the people who had so longed for it were not there to see it, and they never knew it." For all its determined "realism," *The Magnificent Ambersons* ends on the old, familiar romantic note of reconciled lovers.

Tarkington went on to become one of the most prolific novelists of the era. Before he was through, he wrote more than forty novels, most of them set in small Midwestern towns, and wrote some of the most delightful and enduring accounts of boyhood in our literature. If many of Tarkington's novels are unreadable today, the same may be said for most of the novels of most of his contemporaries, but one suspects that his youthful heroes Penrod and Sam are immortal and have ensured their creator of a secure, if modest, place in posterity.

Upton Sinclair was born in 1878 in Baltimore, Maryland, and educated at the City College of New York. Between his graduation at the age of nineteen and his first best-selling novel, Sinclair published four historical romances. An enthusiastic recruit to socialism, he decided to write an exposé novel, of the type so much in vogue, about a family of Polish immigrants whose men worked in Chicago slaughter and packinghouses. The defalcations of the beef trust had already been exposed by Charles Edward Russell. Sinclair, whose primary purpose was to arouse public sympathy for the plight of the Berczynskas family and his hero, Jurgis Rudkus, and to encourage immigrant workers to unionize, was swept away by his researches into the conditions in the packing plants. The most vivid (and nauseating) part of the novel depicts the filthy and dangerous conditions in the plants. The novel, dedicated "To the Workingmen of America," ends with a stirring call for socialist revolution. The tide of socialism would be "irresistible, overwhelming—the rallying of the outraged working-men of Chicago to our standard!" a Socialist orator proclaims in the closing paragraph of the book. "And we shall organize them, we shall drill them, we shall marshal them for the victory! We shall bear down the opposition, we shall sweep it before us—and Chicago will be ours! *Chicago will be ours!* CHICAGO WILL BE OURS!"

The Jungle was an instant sensation and a runaway best seller. The reaction, as it turned out, was not so much sympathy with the plight of the immigrant workers as horror over the conditions under which America's meat was prepared for consumption. The book made Sinclair a rich man at the age of twenty-eight and helped secure passage of the Pure Food and Drug Act (he complained that he had aimed at America's heart and hit its stomach). Sinclair, in line with his Socialist principles, used much of the profits from *The Jungle* to start a utopian colony, Helicon Hall, at Englewood, New Jersey. He was active as a reporter and participant in the Paterson strike in 1912 and wrote another exposé novel, *King Coal,* based on the Colorado coal strikes of 1913 that attracted the attention of the Commission on Industrial Relations.

The most flamboyant literary figure of the age was Jack London, born in Oakland, California, in 1876 (two years before Upton Sinclair, whom, in many ways, he resembled). Although London's antecedents were definitely middle-class, his family fell on evil days, and London experienced real hardship in his youth. He educated himself in the public library, reading everything he could get his hands on, and worked, when he was old enough, as a seaman, a longshoreman, a janitor, a jute mill hand. After a year or more on the road, hoboing it around the United States, London returned to Oakland, where he resumed his high school education, discovered socialism, attended the University of California briefly, and then departed for the Klondike in the gold rush of 1897. He was twenty-one when he embarked on the adventure that was to supply him with a lifetime of story material. Back in Oakland, he turned to writing stories of the "wild." He struck gold much more readily with his pen than he had with his miner's pick. At the age of twenty-two he sold a story of life on the Yukon to the *Overland Monthly.* Eight more stories followed within the next year in the *Overland,* with additional stories in the *Atlantic Monthly.* It was a spectacular beginning for the young author. A collection of London's short stories, entitled *The Son of the Wolf,* was published in 1900, two years after the publication of Ernest Thompson Seton's *Wild Animals I Have Known,* which featured Lobo, the wolf (the taste of Americans for wolves was apparently substantial).

The stories poured out, as many as 200 a year, an astonishing torrent of words. And the money rolled in. London provided handsomely for his mother and spent his easy money like a young prince.

His ranch, Glen Ellen, near Sonoma, California, became a fabled retreat to which starry-eyed journalists, many of them young women,
made their way to compose breathless reports of the famous writer
working at a rough desk of oak boards beneath a tree or riding his
spirited horse, accompanied by his half-wolf dog, through the streets
of Sonoma.

The Socialists adored him (they still do) because of his more or
less working-class background and his generosity to the party. By 1906
he had published ten volumes, five of them about the Klondike, most
of them celebrating the disposition of man in the wilds to revert to
primitive savagery. *The Call of the Wild, The Sea Wolf,* and *White Fang*
are the best known. To an age entranced with Darwinism the theme
had a strong appeal. In addition, London was a marvelous storyteller.
His best tales of the Klondike entered at once into the rather limited
canon of enduring works that, whatever their literary merit, compel
our attention.

If ever a writer was corrupted by success, it was London. When
he wandered, be it ever so slightly, from the sea or the Alaskan gold-
fields, his stories and novels were distressingly banal. When he tried
to write sympathically about "working-class" characters, his efforts were
laughable. *The Game,* subtitled *A Transcript from Real Life,* appeared first
as a two-part serial in the *Metropolitan Magazine* in 1905. Joe Fleming,
a sailmaker and prizefighter who looks and dresses like a Howard
Chandler Christy figure, is the support of his mother and sisters. He
is also engaged to Genevieve, a working-class girl who looks like a
Gibson girl and works in a candy store. Genevieve is opposed to prize-
fighting, and Joe promises to give it up after one more fight. "Joe's
masculinity, the masculinity of the fighting male, made its inevitable
appeal to her, a female, moulded by all her heredity to seek out the
strong man for a mate and to lean against the wall of his strength
[natural selection]. She did not understand this force of his being
[sexual attraction] and laid its compulsion upon him. . . ." Joe, trying
to explain to her his feeling about fighting, urges Genevieve to press
his biceps. "Hard all over, just like that," he tells her. "Now that's what
I call clean. Every bit of flesh an' blood an' muscle is clean right down
to the bones—an' they're clean, too . . . clean all the way in. I tell you,
it feels clean. It knows it's itself." Joe and Genevieve, it turns out, are
"working-class aristocrats. In an environment made up largely of sordidness and wretchedness, they had kept themselves unsullied and

wholesome." They had a common regard for "the niceties and clean things of life, which had held them aloof from their kind." Genevieve had as sheltered a life as any young society belle, shunning "all that was rough and brutal. . . . Springing from a long line of American descent, she was one of those wonderful working class blooms which occasionally appear, defying all precedent of forebears and environment. . . . Quiet, low-voiced, stately and dignified, she somehow had the knack of dress. . . ." No wonder she looked, in the illustrations, like a Gibson girl. Joe Fleming had, of course, bright blue eyes and dark hair that "drew and held the gaze of more than one woman" far above him in the social scale. Genevieve agrees to go see his last fight. When she sees him "naked" (he has on only his boxing shorts), she almost faints. Her face "was burning with shame at the beautiful nakedness of her lover. But she looked again, guiltily, for the joy that was hers in beholding what she knew must be sinful to behold. . . . The mothers of the past were whispering through her, and there was the clamor of the children unborn." Looking at him made her feel that she was engaging in "sacrilege or blasphemy."

The sappy illustration of Joe, accompanying the text, shows him "naked" in his boxing trunks but sans nipples and navel. There were obviously limits to what the public would tolerate. John Ponta, Joe's opponent, is squat, ugly, and brutal-looking, obviously a member of some lesser breed. When the fight begins, it is clear that clean Joe Fleming is the master of his lowering enemy, but Ponta, fighting like an animal, lands a lucky punch that stuns Joe and then follows with a flurry of blows that kills him (that, presumably is the "real" part of the story. Prizefighters are killed in the ring; one has to suppress the uneasy thought that Joe may have been fatally weakened by the absence of nipples and navel).

It is not surprising that with such a voluminous output London wrote an uncommon amount of poor stuff or, indeed, that he became an alcoholic (he even wrote a book about his alcoholism), or, finally, that he burned himself out and died at the age of forty. He managed in his relatively short life to create a persona for himself as wildly romantic as any of his Klondike tales. In doing so, he demonstrated the capacity of the publishing world to devour a young and still unformed talent. Despite such pieces as *The Game*, full of middle-class snobberies, socialists have continued to argue that London in his best stories, the stories of the "wild," was really writing symbolic tales about the wildness and savagery of the capitalist class that was a wolf to the working class. Kindness suggests that we draw a veil over this thesis.

If the critic Waldo Frank was too severe in his judgment of London, there was nonetheless much truth in his indictment. London, Frank wrote, "no longer believed in the Puritan God. He no longer believed in the Constitution. He signed his . . . letters 'yours for the Revolution . . .' " but he fell victim to "an infantile romanticism under which he deliberately hid his own despair." He became a literary corporation. London's confessional novel, *John Barleycorn*, "reveals no trace of self-consciousness, no suggestion of the sanctity of art, no hint of the values of life."

Upton Sinclair and Jack London, the most famous Socialist writers, collaborated on "An Anthology of Social Protest" entitled *The Cry for Justice*. Subtitled *The Writings of Philosophers, Poets, Novelists, Social Reformers, and Others Who Have Voiced the Struggle Against Social Injustice*, the anthology covered 5,000 years and was drawn from twenty-five languages. London, in his introduction to "this Holy Bible," wrote that a reader of the work would discover "that this fair world so brutally unfair, is not decreed by the will of God nor by any iron law of Nature. He will learn that the world can be fashioned a fair world indeed by the humans who inhabit it, by the very simple, and yet most difficult process of coming to an understanding of the world." London praised "the gospel of service" as the key to reforming the manifold social injustices of American life and indeed of the world. From Plato to Charlotte Perkins Gilman and Henry George and, of course, to George Herron, Sinclair, and London themselves, the pieces in the anthology dealt with the ancient fight for social justice.

One of the most popular of the popular novelists with Midwestern origins (and one who grew increasingly radical) was Winston Churchill, born in St. Louis, Missouri, in 1871 (the period from 1869 to 1874 was especially prolix in popular novelists). A descendant of Jonathan Edwards and of John Dwight, the founder of Dedham, Massachusetts, Churchill felt strong ties to New England. He won an appointment to the Naval Academy at Annapolis, and after serving the required time in the navy after his graduation, he turned to journalism. A stint as editor of *Cosmopolitan* magazine (an important post for such a comparatively young man) followed. Churchill then married an heiress and moved to New Hampshire to take up his career as a full-time writer. His first efforts were historical novels, costume dramas of the American revolutionary era and antebellum St. Louis. Meantime, he took up the banner of Progressive politics. Elected to the state legislature, he took on the lumber and railroad interests, but when he ran for governor, the same interests brought about his defeat.

He took his revenge by writing *Coniston,* published in 1906. It is the story of a corrupt political boss, Jethro Bass, closely modeled after a real-life ruler of the state, a "new man," venal and ruthless, who had risen in the period following the Civil War. In an afterword Churchill explained his purpose in writing the novel. America and traditional American values were threatened by ignorance and inattention, by, above all, a lack of knowledge on the part of the public itself. "Thus," Churchill wrote, "the duty rests to-day, more heavily than ever, upon each American citizen to make good to the world those principles upon which his government was built. . . . In America to-day we are trying—whatever the cost—to regain the true axis established for us by the founders of our Republic."

A Modern Chronicle is a satire on social climbing and the increasingly common dissolution of an upper-class marriage by divorce. With *The Inside of the Cup* Churchill returned to social criticism, tracing the connection between capitalism and the churches. *A Far Country* concentrated its fire on Spencerian economics and the mindset which opposed reform on "scientific"—i.e., Darwinian—grounds. *The Dwelling Place of Light* is Churchill's most radical attack on the existing social order. The heroine is a young woman of upper-class antecedents who, appalled by the tactics of the millowners, joins the Wobblies under the leadership of Big Bill Haywood. The novel was clearly based on the Paterson strike of 1912.

Novels of both exotic places and ancient times—Renaissance Italy or classical Greece—were popular, and the appetite for stories with British lords and ladies in them seemed insatiable. Finally, there was the genre of the "wild." If Jack London did not invent it, he was by far the most famous practitioner. Ernest Thompson Seton and Stewart Edward White were not far behind. Wildlife, wild human passions in wild nature had a strong appeal to Americans whose lives seemed increasingly tame. Dog stories were extremely popular—*Lassie* and *Bob, Son of Battle.* Ernest Thompson Seton's marvelously evocative stories of animals that behaved not only like people but better than people were morality tales of love and loyalty in the wild. Most of the "wild" or "nature" writers were, like London and Seton, political reformers or socialists who meant to contrast the falsity and inequity of "civilized" American life with the stern and unrelenting "truth" of the natural world and the men and women who inhabited it on a kind of sufferance that might be withdrawn at any moment if they did not "obey the rules" that the wilderness imposed.

Stewart Edward White covered the "wild" in increments or by terrain features—mountains and mountain ranges, the Black Hills, rivers, forests and forest fires, the desert, Arizona. In a whole series of novels he wrote a kind of fictionalized geography of the United States.

Ernest Thompson Seton's second wife described him fairly enough as a writer about animals whose work "has never been excelled, if equalled; an artist acclaimed as at least among the best in the line of his own work; an architect and builder . . . ; a deep student of American Indian life; a lecturer and story-teller *par excellence;* the founder and projector of the first of all outdoor youth movements" (the Boy Scouts of America). Seton was born in England in 1860, the tenth son of an ancient Scottish family. His family suffered financial reverses, as the saying goes, and emigrated to Canada. There they became pioneer farmers in the province of Ontario. The family prospered sufficiently so that Seton was able to go to London on a meager allowance to study art. Back in Canada, he camped and hunted and began to write and illustrate stories about animals and nature. His first book, *Wild Animals I Have Known,* published in 1898, made his fame and fortune. Included was his most famous story, "Lobo, the Wolf." His purpose, he wrote, was to quicken the sympathies of his readers "toward the noble creature who, superior to every trial, died as he had lived, dignified, fearless, and steadfast. I have tried," he continued, "to stop the stupid and brutal work of destruction by an appeal—not to reason, that has failed hitherto—but to the sympathies of the coming generation." The logic of preserving great paintings was similar to the logic of preserving animals. "There will always be wild land not required for settlement; and how can we better use it than by making it a sanctuary for living wild things that afford pleasure to all who see them?"

At one of Seton's lectures a handsome young woman who had been thrilled by his vibrant voice and compelling figure spoke to him after his talk. She became his mistress and, after his divorce, his wife and collaborator.

One of Seton's most significant accomplishments was to picture the American Indians in a highly sympathetic, if somewhat romanti-

cized, fashion. If he did not initiate the modern interest in the abo-
rigines, he certainly anticipated it. In some 3,000 lectures and in his
work first with the Boy Scouts and then, when he split with the Scouts
over what he considered their excessive emphasis on military forms,
with the Woodcraft Guild, he helped lay the foundations of our modern cult of nature.

Among the various "wilds" the Wild West emerged as a particular
and distinctive "wild" largely through the efforts of one man, Owen
Wister, who was, like so many other glorifiers of the West, an effete
Easterner. Albert Bierstadt and Frederic Remington, archetypal Easterners in their own particular and respective manners—Bierstadt the
German immigrant, Remington the Yale dandy—had given a powerful
visual form to the Wild West. Buffalo Bill and dozens of Ned Buntline
sagas of the West had fleshed it out, but it was Wister, an upper-class
Philadelphian, a grandson of Fanny Kemble, and a graduate of Harvard, who gave the myth its archetypal form. Like his friend Theodore
Roosevelt, he had spent summer vacations in the West while a student,
and he decided to become its chronicler. The Virginian is an otherwise
nameless hero who goes West for reasons never quite clear and becomes the prototypical cowboy. "What," Wister asked, "is become of
the cow-puncher, the last romantic figure upon our soil? For he was
romantic. Whatever he did he did with all his might. The bread that
he earned was hard earned, the wages he squandered were squandered
hard. . . . He will be here among us, invisible, waiting his chance to live
and play as he would like. His wild kind has been among us always,
since the beginning: a young man with his temptations, a hero without
wings." Wister was an archconservative who feared and hated the immigrants flooding into American cities. "No rood of modern ground
is more debased and mongrel with its hordes of encroaching aliens,
that turn our cities into Babels and our citizenship into a hybrid farce,"
one of Wister's characters declares, "who degrade our commonwealth
from a nation into something half pawn-shop, half broker's office. But
to survive in clean cattle country requires the spirit of adventure, courage, and self-sufficiency; you will not find many Poles or Huns or
Russian Jews in that district." The polyglot peoples of Europe are
hothouse types. "The Frenchman today is seen at his best inside a
house; he can paint and play comedy. . . . The Italian has forgotten
Columbus and sells fruit. . . . But the Anglo-Saxon is still forever
homesick for the out-of-doors."

Not only does the Virginian face down all the bullies among the cowhands, but he also proves that he is no effeminate tenderfoot but as "Western" as the best of them. Indeed, it turns out that the aristocratic Easterner is the true "cowboy," the noble son of nature, the knight of the plains, far superior to the rough, if amusing, native sons, who, although good sorts, are inescapably lower-class and thus made to be dominated by their betters.

In the simplest terms *The Virginian* was Darwinism applied to the Rocky Mountain states, Darwinism teaching by example. "Equality is a great big bluff," the Virginian announces to a liberally inclined schoolteacher. "I look around and I see folks movin' up or movin' down, winners or losers everywhere. . . . All America is divided into two classes— the quality and the equality. The latter will always recognize the former. . . . Both will be with us until our women bear nothing but kings." The law is the law of the survival of the fittest, and the Virginian accepts the lynching of a friend because the friend has willfully violated not so much the law as "the customs of the country."

The Virginian became one of America's all-time best sellers. It went through thirty-five printings and sold more than 3,000,000 copies. It was made into a play that ran for ten years on Broadway. It cemented the alliance between big business and the cowboy West. The fact was that as we have noted earlier, the Eastern tycoon was, and remains, infatuated with playing cowboy-rancher and identifies most strongly with what he conceives to be the cowboy ethic.

Perhaps in the last analysis the point to be most firmly made about these novels (if you read enough of them, they all merge into one vast indistinguishable novel and your brain turns to mush) is simply the number of them. As much as the era from the 1890s to 1915 or 1920 was the age of anything, it was the age of the novel. In 1910 more than 600 titles of novels were *in print*, 370 from one publisher alone, A. L. Burt. Burt listed 22 novels by the English writer, E. Phillips Oppenheim, who specialized in mystery and detective stories. Among the more prolific, enormously popular in their day and now largely forgotten, were Harold Bell Wright, Joseph Lincoln, F. Hopkinson Smith, Eleanor Atkinson, Beta Ruck, Carolyn Wells, Mary Waller, Elinor Glyn, Rex Beach, Anna Katherine Green, Ethel Dell, Eliza Calvert Hall, Mary Johnson, Natalie Sumner Lincoln, and Margaret Deland. Each of these novelists had dozens of novels to his or her credit. Margaret Deland wrote one of the most daring novels of the romantic genre. In *The Awakening of Helena Richie*, Helena Richie is a mysterious figure with "a past" who settles in a small town but refuses to become a part of it. She is "awakened" to a richer emotional life by accepting the guardianship of a young orphan, David. Just when she becomes devoted to David, it comes to light that she has for some years been the mistress of a successful and highly respected lawyer. She is told that under the circumstances she must, of course, surrender her guardianship of David. He cannot grow up in the care of a tainted woman. Helena Richie becomes a convert to Christianity, renounces her life of sin, and is allowed to keep David.

No matter how indifferent a particular novel or novelist might be, there were always in the army of ubiquitous critics some who were ready to proclaim it, or its author, worthy to stand with the immortals. An uncommon fuss was made over *The Awakening of Helena Richie,* and Margaret Deland was elevated to the ranks of the immortals by certain critics who compared her favorably to Hawthorne, the Brontës, and Henry James.

The inevitable question is what, if any, reality these novels described. Certainly they satisfied a deep psychological need, or they would not have been published and read in such vast numbers. Since the greater portion of their readers were, as we have noted from time to time, women, they spoke to their needs most directly. Perhaps their truest common perception, those written by men as well as women, was that American wives were bored—i.e., they read novels to relieve their boredom, and in that boredom-relieved-by-reading-novels, they took comfort in the thought that other wives, even fictional wives, were inexpressibly bored by their successful, achieving, one-dimensional husbands. Seen in this perspective, the vast tide of romantic novels was both an underground system of communication and a form of therapy for middle-class American women suffering from a kind of group neurosis that resulted from their unhappiness with and, on occasion, outright rejection of their traditional roles. "Your amusements," Gerty Bridewell tells her philandering husband in Ellen Glasgow's *The Wheel of Life,* "are built on our long boredom."

There are two facts worth noting about the literature of the period. Virtually all the authors of either sex served apprenticeships as journalists, newspaper people, or contributors to and editors of popular magazines. The magazine medium stimulated the writing of short stories and novels that could initially be serialized. The short story was better suited to the magazine format than the serialized novel. Much of the tedious and excessive plotting in the novels, as well as the arrangement of chapters, was dictated by the requirements of the magazines. One has only to compare the short stories of Sarah Orne Jewett, Mary Wilkins Freeman, Alice Brown, Kate Chopin, Charlotte Perkins Gilman, and others with contemporary novels to realize how far short the latter fell. Even the short stories of the best novelists—Willa Cather and Edith Wharton specifically—are substantially better as literary works than most of their novels.

50

The Literary Scene

The most crucial individual in the literary expression of the new consciousness was Theodore Dreiser. He was born in the town of Terre Haute, Indiana, in 1871, but most of his youth was spent in the town of Warsaw. There he grew up in an atmosphere that was almost a parody of the contradictory American attitudes toward sex. The family was notably close, with that flow of affection perhaps most commonly felt in lower-middle-class immigrant families like the Dreisers. Three of Dreiser's sisters—Emma, the original for the title character in *Sister Carrie;* Mary or Mame, the inspiration for *Jennie Gerhardt;* and Sylvia—were, by the definition of the times, "loose." Mary had been seduced and become pregnant at sixteen. Her lover, a successful middle-aged lawyer, tried to get her to have an abortion, but she refused and returned home to have her child (who was stillborn but who survived as Vesta in *Jennie Gerhardt*). Sylvia had a child by the scion of a wealthy Warsaw, Indiana, family. She went to New York to have the child at the home of her sister Emma. The mistress of Dreiser's adored older brother Paul was the madam of a brothel who befriended the Dreisers when they were in straitened circumstances. On the other hand, Dreiser's father, John Paul, was a devout Catholic and preached to his children the most severe code of sexual morality, with warnings of hellfire and eternal damnation for the unrepentant sinner. Much of Dreiser's most painful soul-searching was directed at resolving the issue of his own sexual drives and, equally important, of giving himself a good conscience about the sexual "generosity," as he came to see it, of the sisters he loved.

Dreiser's father, a German immigrant, had suffered the kind of disaster familiar in our history. His flour mill had burned down, and he had been badly injured. He thus had difficulty supporting his family, working at a series of menial jobs while his wife took in boarders. To young Dreiser and his brothers and sisters, he was a harsh and demanding figure, made sullen and bitter by his sense of failure. Theo's older brother Paul changed his name to Dresser and became one of the most popular songwriters, singers, and entertainers in the country. Dreiser himself longed to escape from Warsaw and to have a life as colorful and opulent as his adored brother. He did, in fact, "succeed" to a modest degree as a newspaperman and editor. It was while he was an editor that his friend Arthur Henry, who aspired to be a novelist, persuaded Dreiser to undertake the project of writing a novel. Dreiser hit on the idea of writing a story of a small-town girl who comes to Chicago to try to find work, hoping thereby to alleviate the desperate financial straits of her family. Sister Carrie finds jobs scarce and exhausting. She is rushed by a flashy traveling man, Charles Drouet, and slips into the role of his mistress. A prosperous saloonkeeper named George Hurstwood becomes infatuated with her, sacrificing family and respectability and finally stealing money to carry her off to New York. Carrie, finding she has a natural talent as an actress and singer, becomes a popular music hall figure. Hurstwood's subsequent psychological disintegration is the most powerful portion of the book. The ending of Sister Carrie is conventionally "liberal" and indeed moralistic. Carrie's mentor in her new life tells her, "You can't remain tender and sympathetic and desire to serve the world without having it show in your face and your art. If you want to do most, be good. Serve the many. Be kind and humanitarian. Then you can't help but be great."

Dreiser had a contract with Doubleday & Page for the publication of the book, but the publishers, Walter Hines Page in particular, were so appalled at the theme of the novel and its sympathetic treatment of Carrie that they did their best to back out of their agreement. When they finally consented to publish it, they did so in an edition of only 1,500 copies and discouraged sales and reviews. The efforts of Doubleday & Page to consign Sister Carrie to oblivion enraged Dreiser and helped bring on a severe nervous breakdown. For almost a year he suffered acutely from psychosomatic ailments. Unable to write or work, he went through a process of deterioration startlingly similar to that of Hurstwood in *Sister Carrie*. He was rescued by the intervention of his brother Paul, who persuaded him to go to a sanatorium. After his recovery from his nervous breakdown Dreiser worked as an unskilled day laborer until he returned reluctantly to editorial work with the publishing house of Butterick. Ten years, which he considered wasted years, intervened between the initial appearance of *Sister Carrie* (which was reprinted, to considerable acclaim, in 1907) and the publication of his next novel, *Jennie Gerhardt.*

As Carrie Meeber was derived from Dreiser's sister Emma, so Jennie Gerhardt was based on the life of his sister Mary. Jennie becomes the mistress of wealthy Lester Kane, who seduces her, if "seduces" is indeed the proper word, for Jennie, herself deeply sexual, is responsive to Kane's advances, if not provocative. Of Kane, Dreiser wrote: "He wanted the comfort of feminine companionship, but he was more and more disinclined to give up his personal liberty in order to obtain it." Kane's philosophy was "not to fuss and fume, not to cry out about anything, not to be mawkishly sentimental, to be vigorous and sustain your personality intact. . . ."

When Kane's scandalized family learns of his illicit relationship with Jennie, they force him to leave her and make a conventional marriage to a wealthy widow. Kane cannot, however, get over his love for Jennie; life becomes empty and bitter to him, and he dies in part of ennui and self-indulgence. There is a classic deathbed reconciliation which serves to remind us that Dreiser took conventional romantic plots and imbued them with a quite new element.

Having, in *Sister Carrie* and *Jennie Gerhardt*, smashed beyond repair the existing literary taboos on the discussion of sex and, even more important, created two unforgettable heroines, Dreiser turned to that other great American theme, the predatory tycoon, in two novels, *The Financier* and *The Titan*. The tycoon, or the ruthlessly ambitious businessman, was, as we have seen, already a stock figure in the novels of the era. From Howells's *The Rise of Silas Lapham* through William Allen White's *A Certain Rich Man,* we had dozens of novels which centered on the wicked manipulations of "merchant princes," "railroad barons," and "bonanza kings."

Dreiser fastened on the most striking of them all, Charles Yerkes. Yerkes's life had all the drama that any writer could ask for: divorces, seductions, spectacular successes, and equally spectacular failures. In *The Financier,* Yerkes's literary counterpart, Frank Cowperwood, is a man of strong intellectual and aesthetic interests; Yerkes was a collector and, more rare among tycoons, a connoisseur of art and, like Dreiser, a man of immoderate sexual drives. "There was . . . in him," Dreiser wrote, "in some nebulous, unrecognizable form, a great artistic reality." Yerkes combined sex and power in a classic American amalgam. In *The Financier,* as in its successor, *The Titan,* Dreiser does what he did brilliantly in *Sister Carrie* and *Jennie Gerhardt:* He takes an apparently unsympathetic figure and brings him to life by applying one patient, realistic detail after another. He does this without the intrusion of moral judgment, without a contrived repentance (like that which concludes White's *A Certain Rich Man*), and without sentimentality. In the process he gives us keen insight into the quality of imagination and the interior life of a great capitalist. Dreiser had done painstaking research into Yerkes's own life, and his descriptions of Yerkes's-Cowperwood's manipulations are textbook accounts of high finance.

The *Financier* and *The Titan* were massive chronicles of capitalism, but Dreiser's real significance is in his skill as a portrayer of women. In the process, as the critic, Randolph Bourne, put it, he "made sex human," not an inconsiderable achievement. Women were the unmapped territory that Dreiser set out to explore. When his own marriage broke up (his wife refused to divorce him), he began a career of insatiable, obsessive sexual adventuring. He had few close masculine friendships—Arthur Henry and Henry Mencken were perhaps the most notable—but his most intimate relations, intellectually and psychologically, were with a series of women, indeed with a number of women simultaneously (much of his later diary is taken up with accounts of his efforts to keep three of them from discovering the extent of his involvement with the others). As the editor of Dreiser's graphic diaries points out, "To every bedroom he carried along a manuscript." One diary entry reads: "No sooner get in than we begin undressing. Fire in the grate. We play in the rear room before mirror, then go into the bedroom. Stay in bed from 2 to 6, playing. Between rounds she reads *A Story of Stories* and likes it."

Dreiser's days and nights were taken up "copulating" with his women friends. But that was obviously not the whole story. Most of the women in his life were indubitably "new women." They had their own intellectual and artistic interests (some were married; others were single or divorced). They read and criticized his manuscripts; they typed; they helped with his research. His dependence on them reached well beyond the merely physical. It also seems clear that Dreiser very consciously saw himself as a pioneer or crusader in destroying the repressive sexual attitudes of men and women alike. His fornicating was, in a manner, doctrinaire. In another sense it was as though the tides of repressed American sexuality were flowing through him. Every act of intercourse was, as we would say today, a statement. It partook of dogmatism; it was the practical expression of an ideology. It must also be noted that many of the women sought Dreiser out, drawn irresistibly to him through his novels as a man who had a particular sympathy for and delicacy of feeling about their sex. They were literary "groupies" who wished nothing more than to draw sexual and intellectual energy from his apparently inexhaustible reservoir. Like his hero Cowperwood, Dreiser wanted from women "personal reaction of thought and feelings, a certain kinship of soul or understanding . . . and if he could not have that he was not interested." (Dreiser echoed the free love reformers with his view that men and women must have "affinities" and "variety.")

Dreiser noted in *Jennie Gerhardt* that physical attractiveness aside, men are drawn to "the non-defensive [female] disposition" like flies to a "honey-jar," that "Nothing is brought to it and much is taken away. Around a soft, yielding, unselfish disposition men swarm naturally."

Dreiser came to believe that lower-class women, working girls, and, closer to home, his own sisters had their sexuality intact. Unlike middle- and upper-class women, they were "non-defensive"; they did not restrain their sexuality or repress their natural instincts, dangling their sexual favors as the price of marriage, favors which then proved all too often illusory. The women of the higher classes not only denied themselves the uninhibited pleasures of sexual intercourse but forced men into the role of licentious beasts, always clamoring for what was yielded up coldly and reluctantly.

Increasingly Dreiser was inclined to blame the unhappy social conditions in America on capitalism. His remedy, it might be said, was "Sex and Socialism," a duality which, as we have seen, a great many of his fellow literary and artistic contemporaries also endorsed. His "philosophy" was shallow, even juvenile, a muddle of half-digested Marxist, Darwinian, and Nietzschean notions, the effect of which was that human beings were the victims of forces beyond their control and that the law of life was survival. For literary purposes this was not a bad base, not indeed too far removed from the Greek idea of the capriciousness of the gods or Thomas Hardy's belief in tragic destiny.

Sherwood Anderson is one of the most appealing figures in American literature. As tousle-headed as a small-town boy from one of his novels, and as unselfconsciously friendly, he valued loyalty exceedingly and was all his life irredeemably Midwestern. More than any other writer except Thomas Wolfe, whom he much resembled in temperament, his books were so autobiographical and his autobiography so fictional that he exists for us in a mysterious realm of his own creating. A reader can go from his exuberant, searching letters to his friends to his novels and short stories hardly conscious of a dividing line between fiction and reality. Subject to swings of joy and depression of an almost manic-depressive character, Anderson wished, like Whitman and the Twain of *Huckleberry Finn*, to bespeak America. The historical figure he identified with most closely was Lincoln; he wished to be, in some way, the Lincoln of our literature. And if we are looking for a representative American figure, not simply a literary luminary, we can hardly find a better example than the small-town boy who was born in Camden, Ohio, in 1876, the third of seven children, son of an improvident harnessmaker and his patiently enduring wife.

As a boy in a series of small Ohio towns Anderson was known as Jobby because of his bustling pursuit of odd jobs. He was, among other things, a farm hand, a newsboy, an exercise boy at racetracks, and a factory worker. In the spirit of the ambitious young man, determined to be a success, Anderson was the prototype of the Protestant ethic: industrious, thrifty, and even, in his own fashion, pious—which is to say, obsessed with the meaning of life and the nature of truth. We may know the boy Anderson better than any other American juvenile because he is vividly and tenderly portrayed in the first half of *Windy McPherson's Son*.

At the age of twenty Anderson left Clyde, Ohio, to make his fortune in Chicago, where he worked as a common laborer. During the Spanish-American War he enlisted in the army and served a brief stint in the Cuban occupation force before he was discharged. He already had a way with words, and he became a copy writer for a Chicago advertising firm. His energy, talent, and ambition led to his rapid advancement. In 1904, at the age of twenty-eight, having achieved a modest measure of success, he married Cornelia Lane and two years later started his own business, a mail-order house which he named United Factories. For the next six years he pursued a business career with growing doubts about whether commercial success was indeed his destiny. By the fall of 1912, on the verge of a nervous breakdown, he "walked away" from his mail-order paint firm in Elyria, Ohio. By his own account, he simply stopped in the middle of dictating to his secretary and walked out of town to take up the life of an artist and a writer. The truth was somewhat more complicated but equally dramatic. He soon found he could not support himself by writing fiction. Seeking a job that would give him time to write, he sold his business and went back to work as an advertising executive. For the next nine years he labored with increasing resentment in the salt mines of the advertising world in order to support himself and his family.

From the first words he wrote in his new role as author, Anderson was determined (like so many of the other writers we have taken note of) to break through the false and constricting conventions of the contemporary novel. From the first he was more successful than any of his contemporaries, with the exception of Theodore Dreiser and Willa Cather. The stories he wrote fitted into the already well-established small-town genre, but they had about them a directness and intensity of feeling, a passion that was novel, and they made their way quite readily into magazines and newspapers. In 1916 Anderson published his first novel, *Windy McPherson's Son*, divorced his wife after a long and harrowing effort at reconciliation, and married Tennessee Mitchel, a music teacher.

Windy McPherson's Son is in reality two novels, loosely joined together. The first is the story of Sam McPherson—Sherwood Anderson growing up in Caxton, Iowa. The real hero of the "first novel" is the small-town dreamer and litterateur John Telfer, who gave the town and, above all, Sam what glimpse it and he had of a larger world where the imagination roamed over the whole dramatic and compelling surface of reality. When someone refers to a local woman who paints china as an artist, Telfer breaks out indignantly: "An artist is one who hungers and thirsts after perfection, not one who dabs flowers on plates to choke the gullets of diners. . . . An artist tests his brains against the greatest brains of all times; he stands upon the peak of life and hurls himself against the world."

Sam McPherson comes to realize that his father is a "blustering, pretending, inefficient old man," forever talking of his grand experiences as a soldier in the Civil War. "The realization of the fact that his father was a confirmed liar and braggart . . . for years cast a shadow over his days and the shadow had been made blacker by the fact that in a land where the least fortunate can laugh in the face of want he had more than once stood face to face with poverty." John Telfer bespeaks Anderson's artistic creed, and Mike McCarthy, the free Irish spirit of the town who has murdered a man in a drunken rage, speaks Anderson's philosophy of life. Jailed and beleaguered by a mob of his townspeople who wish to lynch him, McCarthy calls out, "Oh Father! help us men of Caxton to understand that we have only this, our lives so warm and hopeful and laughing in the sun, this life with its awkward boys full of strange possibilities, and its girls with long legs and freckles on their noses, that are meant to carry life within themselves. . . ." Not a very likely outburst for an Irish drifter, but very much Sherwood Anderson.

When Sam leaves Caxton to make his fortune in Chicago, the novel slumps into a by now familiar pattern: success, bought at the price of compromising ideals, a "good marriage," growing restlessness, and dissatisfaction on the part of Sam with his life and with his wife. Finally, he breaks away entirely as Anderson himself, of course, had done. But his breakaway and his description of his vagabond life, as he searches for truth, are flat and conventional after the vividness of his Caxton childhood. The woman he marries, his boss's daughter, Sue Rainey, is clearly a "new woman," and she warns Sam, "You will have to make a mother of me and keep making a mother of me. You will have to be a new kind of father with something maternal in you. You will have to be patient and studious and kind. You will have to think of these things at night instead of thinking of your own advancement." At the end of the novel, after various adventures, the most notable of which is his effort to assist young women strikers to form a union and win their strike, Sam McPherson returns to Sue. It is a tentative return with no guarantee that things will work out any better between them. His wife is too absorbed in their children; he, too preoccupied with the meaning of life. "I cannot run away from life," Sam McPherson reflects, "I must try to face it. I must begin to try to understand these other lives, to love."

Despite Anderson's determination to write freshly and "truly," the novel as a whole hardly rises above the common run of similar works. Certainly the theme of flight in search of one's self and return is by now a well-established convention. Two things distinguish *Windy McPherson's Son* from the common run of popular novels. Perhaps the most important is Anderson's bold and explicit treatment of sexuality. In the city Sam "began to understand how distorted, how strangely perverted, his whole attitude toward women and sex had been. 'Sex is a solution, not a menace—it is wonderful,' he told himself." The other element is found in the lyrical cadences of Anderson's prose, a quality that recalls Whitman's passion to articulate America and that is found also in Willa Cather's writing.

Life had opened up for Anderson in Chicago. Margy Currie, a young painter who had been married to Floyd Dell, a Chicago newspaperman, took an interest in Anderson and his stories. She introduced him to Dell; he also met Ben Hecht and Burton Rascoe, who was reviewing books for the *Chicago Tribune*. "We were all from the Middle West," Anderson wrote. "We were all full of hope. It was the time in which something blossomed in Chicago and the Middle West." Frank Norris and Francis Hackett were fighting for recognition for Theodore Dreiser. Anderson described Dell descanting on literature: "I had never before heard such talk. How it flowed from him. What vast fields of literature he covered. He became excited. He shouted. The intense little figure became more and more erect." There is obviously a good deal of Floyd Dell in John Telfer, the small-town litterateur in *Windy McPherson's Son*.

Anderson met Carl Sandburg in the spring of 1917. Sandburg liked Anderson's "chants," Whitmanesque "songs" in praise of the great essences of America. They hit it off at once, although Anderson commented to Waldo Frank about Sandburg's "closed-in icy places" and reported Ben Hecht's observation that Sandburg was "a true poet who could not write poetry."

As Anderson put it in his *Memoirs*, "Edgar Lee Masters had written his *Spoon River Anthology;* down the state Vachel Lindsay was shouting forth his stirring verses; Sandburg was writing his magical *Chicago Poems;* and Margaret Anderson, still working as editor on some church paper, was soon to break loose and start her *Little Review*. All over the country . . . there was an outbreak of new poets. Something which had been very hard in American life was beginning to crack, and in our group we often spoke of it hopefully. And how exciting it was. Something new and fresh was in the very air we breathed. . . . What ho! for the new world. . . . What nights we did have, what excursions at the week ends. . . . We were, in our own minds, a little band of soldiers who were going to free life (first of all, to be sure, our own lives) from certain bonds."

One of the consequences of the publication of *Windy McPherson's Son* was a profoundly important friendship with two young critics who had just started a literary magazine called the *Seven Lively Arts*. Waldo Frank was a small, pale urban Jew, a classic intellectual—well educated, widely read, sophisticated in his tastes, and completely committed to the discovery and nurturing of literary expressions of the new consciousness. Van Wyck Brooks, no less intellectual, was an archetypal WASP: scion of a long line of New England teachers and preachers, a graduate of Harvard, and, most recently, a professor of literature at Stanford University. As editors of the *Seven Lively Arts,* Frank and Brooks had formed one of those fruitful Jew-WASP alliances that we have noted in the marriages of Felix Frankfurter and Walter Lippmann, in the alliance of Herbert Croly and Lippmann in the *New Republic* and, in the legal realm, of Frankfurter and Henry Stimson. Anderson began to send his stories and articles, specifically many of the stories that were to make up *Winesburg, Ohio,* to Frank and Brooks's magazine. Thirsting for literary contacts and for encouragement, he wrote incessantly to the two younger men (Frank was thirteen years younger and Brooks ten years younger), who, by virtue of their magazine, yielded a power disproportionate to their ages and their experience. Soon the three became friends (Frank and Anderson were especially close), forming a remarkable triumvirate: second-generation immigrant New York Jew, upper-class New England literary WASP, and Midwestern small-town "graduate." To Anderson, Brooks and Frank represented the literary avant-garde and the most enlightened element in the new or post-Howells Eastern literary establishment. He regarded them with some awe, importuned their approval of everything he wrote, and chided them for not paying more for the material he sent them. At the same time he reminded them frequently of his far wider experience in the world, experience that ran the gamut from fieldhand and factory worker to successful businessman, and he cautioned Frank especially against succumbing to excessive intellectualism. He felt, in their friendship, as "a crude woodsman that has been received into the affection of princes!"

Anderson was acutely aware of his intellectual shortcomings. He had, he admitted, a limited vocabulary. There were many words he knew that he dared not try to pronounce. He must, he decided, stick to the language he knew, "the language of the streets, of American towns and cities, the language of the factories and warehouses where I had worked, of laborers' rooming houses, the saloons and farms."

He wrote to Waldo Frank in the fall of 1917: "As for myself, you know something of what I have dreamed. At my best I am like a great mother bird flying over this broad Mississippi Valley, seeing its towns and broad fields and peoples and brooding over some vague dream of a song arising, of gods coming here to dwell with my people. At my worst I am a petty writer not big enough for the task I have set myself." He added, "I have been to Nebraska, where the big engines are tearing the fields to pieces; over the low hills runs the promise of the corn. You wait, dear Brother, I shall bring God home to the sweaty men in the corn rows. My songs shall creep into their hearts and teach them the sacredness of the long isles of growing things that lead to the throne of the God of men."

American dreams and dreamers became a major theme of Anderson, and, of course, success and failure. Having succeeded in business, he had to cast himself adrift in the far more uncertain waters of artistic achievement, and he was constantly tormented by a feeling of possible failure. "I found it necessary to my continued existence," he wrote Frank in 1917, "to utterly and finally embrace failure, the one terrible, hard thing for an American to do." The American obsession with success was an inescapable element in the American character. "The desire for gain that does not belong to us, gain in money or fame, goes far. We are success-worshipers. . . . The Jews, you know so well, have it, but in their case it is offset by a passionate something that is racial. When it gets into our cold Anglo-Saxon veins, it is terrible."

In 1919 Sherwood Anderson collected the sketches and short pieces, many of which had been published in the *Seven Lively Arts* and Margaret Anderson's the *Little Review,* under the title *Winesburg, Ohio.* They were given a modest degree of unity by the appearance in many of the sketches or chapters of young George Willard and his mother, Elizabeth, and, of course, by the fact that they all happened in Winesburg. A deeper unity was in the direct and unblinking observation of a gallery of small-town figures and the events which revealed their innermost thoughts and feelings. Anderson called his characters grotesques, individuals whom life had scarred and bruised. The tone of *Winesburg* is certainly somber. There is little of the joy and beauty that Anderson assured himself he was committed to conveying in his writing, and even the love was warped and distorted; but the air of truth was there, and those who were open to the new consciousness read it with a thrill of recognition. In a time far different, when Anderson's crusade not only has been won but has in some substantial measure run out and turned back on itself, it is difficult to capture the sense of liberation that the book brought with it. Not since *The Adventures of Huckleberry Finn* had an American author struck so deep and authentically American a note. To those who struggled to understand or articulate the new consciousness in literary form, it came like a revelation. The pain and anguish of its creation were unmistakable. The more perceptive critics understood that the American literary scene would never be quite the same again.

A year later, 1920, *Poor White* appeared, and the following year a collection of short stories, *The Triumph of the Egg*, which took its title from the most powerful and racking story in the collection. With the publication of *The Triumph* the canon of Anderson's work was in a sense complete. Anderson wrote a best seller, *Dark Laughter,* which contrasted the open, free, spontaneous life of American blacks with the uptight repressive life of white society, and half a dozen other books before his death in 1941 of peritonitis. He encouraged younger writers, Ernest Hemingway and F. Scott Fitzgerald among others; he lived for almost a year in New Orleans with William Faulkner and corresponded with Gertrude Stein; in fact, he introduced Hemingway to Stein, thus serving as literary midwife in one of our history's more significant literary friendships. It might be said he even specialized in friendships, maintaining his friendship with his "dear Brother" Waldo Frank and with Van Wyck Brooks. He was less successful in marriage—three divorces—in part, one suspects, because the women he married were not yet ready for the degree of sexual emancipation that Anderson demanded.

Anderson called himself a literary Billy Sunday, referring to the popular evangelist. He was in the great American tradition of preachers and moralists, the tradition of Emerson and Thoreau, of Melville and Whitman and Hawthorne and the "people's poets"—Bryant, Longfellow, Whittier, and Lowell. America to him was "a land of children, broken off from the culture of the world. . . . For the Americans of the future," he wrote to Van Wyck Brooks, "there can be no escape. They have got to, in some way, face themselves." Anderson himself could see no very bright future for America until "a few people," a new "leisure class," could "shake off the success disease" and "really get over our American mania for 'getting on.' "

When Paul Kellogg, the editor of the reform journal the *Survey*, asked Anderson to contribute to a symposium on how to create a "liveable world," Anderson replied with his plug for his new leisure class. "I want men and women," he wrote, "who, at any physical cost to themselves and others, will refuse to continue to work as we understand the word work." With "such surplus energy loose among us, we may begin to do some of the things that now seem entirely out of our reach. We may begin to make towns, houses, books, pictures, gardens, even cities that have beauty and meaning. . . . So you see I want a body of healthy young men and women to agree to quit working, to loaf, to refuse to be hurried or try to get on in the world—in short, to become intense individualists. Something of the sort must happen if we are ever to bring color and flair into our modern life."

What Dreiser and Anderson shared most notably with the important women writers of the period—Wharton, Cather, Glasgow, and Atherton—was a gloomy view of the relations between men and women, especially in the institution of marriage. Even H. L. Mencken, whose view of that holy state was anything but rosy, was led to protest. After all, Mencken pointed out, in nineteen marriages out of twenty the couples "muddled through." If writers like Dreiser and Anderson professed to be dealing with real life, shouldn't they give their attention to at least an occasional successful marriage? A fortune, Mencken predicted, awaited the novelist, "male or female, who writes a genuinely realistic novel about a happy marriage." Dreiser's heroes "imitate the colossal adulteries of a guinea pig, a movie actor or a Wall Street broker . . . and even Miss Cather deals with husbands who flee to the wars to escape their wives. . . ." They all were apparently afraid that if they wrote of a happy marriage, they would be charged with "sentimentality" and classified with hack writers like Harold Bell Wright. In consequence they described marriages which resembled "nothing so much as a series of raids by Prohibition enforcement officers, with a leap off the Brooklyn Bridge as climax." Of course, Mencken failed to note that all the authors in question had had either disastrous marriages or none at all. He assigned the newest literary luminary, Sinclair Lewis, whose recently published *Main Street* had become a best seller, to the task. Lewis, whose marriages, real and literary, were no more successful than those of his fellow authors, declined.

For the male authors of this period, America was, above all, dreams: of success; of erotic love; of beauty and dignity in a disorderly world. The dreams of young men were clearly different from those of young women. They both dreamed of escape from narrow and repressive environments, from small towns, from rigid conventions of class, as in Edith Wharton and Ellen Glasgow; they both dreamed, as we have seen, of a new and finer, more generous, and more "equal" relationship between men and women. But the best of the men writers were tormented by the need to define or explain or articulate America. They responded to Sherwood Anderson's image of himself as a "great mother bird" hovering over the Mississippi Valley. Such grandiose and extravagant images came naturally to them. America, they perceived, had been a dreamworld from the beginning; its simplest realities had begun in dreams. All the writers and critics partook of Thoreau's individualistic anarchism. Waldo Frank, a second-generation Jewish immigrant, was as susceptible to the disease as the Midwestern Anderson, and as ready to identify with Lincoln and Whitman.

Frank, in a little book entitled *Our America,* set out to restore a moral and spiritual dimension to American life. "Cultural America in 1900," he wrote, "was an untracked wilderness but dimly blazed by the heroic ax of Whitman. . . . In this infancy of our adventure, America is a mystic Word. We go forth all to seek America. And in the seeking we create her." America must have a new definition of "Success." Heretofore Success has meant "suppression of life. . . . The man who dreamed, loved, created rather than possessed, was a byword and a pariah." But the "new singers" have taught the "sanctity of Failure." Now "the whole structure of pat words, pat panaceas, pat utopias is crumpling. . . . Society is rotten: the State is a pious criminal: the old truths are tawdry lies. . . ." But men like Alfred Stieglitz, Frank believed, were prophets and rallying points for the new age. Young Americans must generate an energy springing from the love of life; that energy, "to whatever form the mind consign it, is religious. Its act is creation. And in a dying world, creation is revolution." Anderson wrote to Frank: "In the midst of all our terrible American trick of specializing, you have remained alive to a thousand things and to open your mind and your soul to all of us."

Before there could be a renaissance of American poetry, there had to be journals to publish the new poetry. Most of the older journals, like the *Atlantic Monthly* and the *Independent* (which, to be sure, did publish a handful of Robert Frost's relatively "easy" poetry), were presided over by members of the literary establishment to whom the new poetry seemed more like the babbling of lunatics than genuine verse. For poetry, as for literature, a "support system" of sympathetic critics and editors was essential; otherwise, there was no way to get the new word "out."

Harriet Monroe, just turned fifty, was a senior member of the Chicago literary group, a friend of Floyd Dell, Margy Currie, and Francis Hackett. A poet and playwright herself, she found it almost impossible to get her own poetry published. She abominated "American magazines" and felt that they all should "be exterminated in revenge for the damage they have done to American poetry in that they specialize in two or three tones. . . . They chase a popularity, express one or two moods, usually cheap complacency, or, elsewhere, stereotyped pity. Since the death of Whitman there has been no literary figure. . . ."

Although Monroe came from a prosperous, upper-class Chicago family (she was a close friend of the architect Louis Sullivan), she herself was not wealthy and made her living by teaching and free-lance journalism. Her solution to the indifference of the established literary journals was to start a poetry magazine. The first issue of *Poetry* appeared in 1912 and formally ushered in the poetry of the new age. Soon Ezra Pound was both a contributor and an adviser to *Poetry*. The magazine spawned a flotilla of "little" magazines and "reviews." Margaret Anderson started the *Little Review*. Emma Goldman's *Mother Earth* did not limit its poetry to that of social activism, although it gave preference to "political" poetry, as did the *Masses*. George Jean Nathan and H. L. Mencken started the *Smart Set,* and Van Wyck Brooks and Waldo Frank, as we have noted, edited the short-lived but influential *Seven Lively Arts*. The *Friday Literary Review,* edited by Hackett and Dell as a supplement to the *Chicago Evening Post,* was an important literary journal.

The critics were in their own way as essential to the new movement as the novelists and poets, and their influence was perhaps even more widely felt. The relation between Van Wyck Brooks and Waldo Frank, on the one hand, and Sherwood Anderson, on the other, is both typical and instructive. In addition to the Hapgoods, Hackett, Dell, Frank, Brooks, Mencken, and Nathan, Randolph Bourne and Harold Stearns had a wide influence in literary circles.

Bourne was born in Bloomfield, New Jersey in 1886, one of the few important literary figures of this era who was not either Midwestern or Jewish. He had a broad vision of a postwar nation, a "transnational America," the "first international nation," in which peoples of all the world would create a genuinely new global culture, thereby demonstrating their unity on a practical political level. Bourne, who died in the influenza epidemic of 1918, which also killed Willard Straight, anticipated Wyndham Lewis's vision of the American as the "cosmic man." Like Anderson, Hapgood, and many other Gentile Americans, Bourne was strongly drawn to Judaism and to American Jewish intellectuals like Lippmann and Frank and was, in fact, a much stronger supporter of Zionism than deracinated Jews like Berenson and Lippmann.

Harold Stearns was five years younger than Bourne and, like him, a small-town Easterner. Stearns was a kind of enfant terrible who appointed himself the scourge of liberal intellectuals and the leader of the expatriates.

While the prose writers of our era were making heroic efforts to free themselves from inherited literary conventions, the painters, inspired by the Postimpressionists and the Cubists, were ranging boldly through intoxicating new visual realms, finding in forms and colors a heretofore unimagined freedom. The poets, like the painters, broke through almost instantly. The poetry renaissance was just that: a rebirth of that muse in the American scene devoid, in large part, of the painful and protracted struggles of the writers of fiction.

The first of the poets of the new age, Edwin Arlington Robinson, was born in Maine in 1869 and attended Harvard for two years at great sacrifice to his family. He was a kind of poetic counterpart to the women short-story writers of New England, Alice Brown, Sarah Orne Jewett, and Mary Wilkins Freeman. He wrote his verse in the same minor, ironically affectionate key, telling of decaying families and diminished hopes in mythical Tilbury Town. Stifled by the provincialism of Gardiner, the small Maine town where he and his wife lived, the Robinsons moved to New York, where the only job the poet could find was as a timekeeper on a construction project.

Theodore Roosevelt, who admired Robinson's poetry and reviewed it in the *Outlook* in 1905, invited him and his wife to the White House and secured a clerkship for Robinson in the New York customs office, thus ensuring him a modest income for the period of Roosevelt's presidency and placing him in the company of Hawthorne and Melville as one of those American literary figures sustained at least for a time by a government sinecure. In *The Children of the Night,* containing poems written between 1890 and 1897, Robinson wrote the first of his brilliant vignettes of defeated small-town characters, anticipating by almost three decades Sherwood Anderson's Winesburg grotesques and providing a model for Edgar Lee Masters's Spoon River poems. The first poem in the book, somber and mysterious, struck what would become an increasingly familiar note over the years to come. It centers on John Evereldown, who "follows the women wherever they call. . . . So the clouds may come and the rain may fall,/ The shadows may creep and the dead men crawl,—/ But I follow the women wherever they call."

The second poem echoes the theme of "a call." This time it is Luke Havergal who waits at the "western gate" for a call, presumably from the woman he loves.

Many of Robinson's poems have a mood of persuasive sadness, an elegiac mourning for what is spent and gone. The House on the Hill is abandoned; its occupants are gone.

> They are all gone away,
>   The House is shut and still,
> There is nothing more to say.
>
> Through broken walls and gray
>   The winds blow bleak and shrill:
> They are all gone away.

Richard Cory, "clean favored, and imperially slim," who "glittered when he walked," is another of Robinson's unforgettable portraits. A "gentleman from sole to crown" and "richer than a king," Cory was admired and envied by the townsfolk of Tilbury Town.

> So on we worked, and waited for the light,
> And went without the meat, and cursed the bread;
> And Richard Cory, one calm summer night,
> Went home and put a bullet through his head.

There was Cliff Klingenhagen, who took on himself the troubles and sorrows of the town, and Charles Charville, who was "not so melancholy as it seemed,/ When once you knew him, for his mouth redeemed/ His insufficient eyes, forever sad. . . . His eyes were sorry, but his mouth was glad." When he was dead, his blank eyes spoke. "Then we heard him, every word."

Robinson's eulogy of Thomas Hood revealed the essence of the poet's own philosophy: "And there are woven with his jollities/ The nameless and eternal tragedies/ That render hope and hopelessness akin."

Reuben Bright was the town butcher. When he learned that his wife must die, he "shook with grief and fright." After she had died,

"He packed a lot of things that she had made/ Most mournfully away in an old chest/ Of hers, and put some chopped-up cedar boughs/ In with them, and tore down the slaughter-house."

We may take Robinson's eulogy of George Crabbe, the poet of Puritan England, as his own epitaph:

> Give him the darkest inch your shelf allows,
> Hide him in the lonely garrets, if you will,—
> But his hard, human pulse is throbbing still
> With the sure strength that fearless truth endows.
> In spite of all fine science disavows,
> Of his plain excellence and stubborn skill
> There yet remains what fashion cannot kill,
> Though years have thinned the laurel from his brows.

Robinson wrote steadily away until his death in 1935: sonnets; a cycle of Arthurian poems; his gallery of small-town figures—Shadrach O'Leary, "a poet—for a while"; Miniver Cheevy, who scorned the mundane life of Tilbury; Uncle Ananias, the town liar. The children of the town loved Ananias "All summer long for the same/ Perennial inspiration of his lies. . . . So to the sheltered end of many a year/ He charmed the seasons out with pageantry/ Wearing upon his forehead with no fear,/ The laurel of approved iniquity." Robinson belonged to or founded no school, though his experiments with unrhymed meters had a considerable influence on his younger contemporaries. A small, quiet, shy man, he came at last into his own, was honored, given awards and degrees eventually, and recognized as one of our finest and most enduring poets.

Robert Frost, the poet of rural New England, was born in San Francisco in 1874. His grandfather, William Prescott Frost, was a member of an old New England family and a cotton mill executive in the industrial town of Lawrence, Massachusetts. Frost's father, William Prescott Frost, Jr., was a graduate of Harvard who moved to San Francisco after his marriage to a young Scottish woman, Isabelle Moodie, to seek his fortune as a journalist. A restless and rather irresponsible young man, he died in 1885 at the age of thirty-four of tuberculosis. His widow returned to Massachusetts with Frost and his sister and found a position as head of a school near Salem, New Hampshire. Mrs. Frost stressed learning through the memorization of poetry, a pedagogical method which had a strong influence on her son, who was her pupil until he entered high school in Lawrence. There he met

Elinor Miriam White, the bright and pretty daughter of a Universalist minister. They were covaledictorians at their graduation in 1892 and had an "understanding."

Encouraged by his grandmother, Frost entered Dartmouth College but remained for less than a semester. He had already started writing poetry and was determined to become a poet. After a stint of teaching with his mother he worked for a time as a mill hand. It was during this time that he sold his first poem to the *Independent*, a magazine that had been edited by Henry Ward Beecher but now had a more secular and literary bent. Shortly after its publication in 1894 Frost and Elinor White became engaged. When she was graduated from the Universalist college that she was attending, the high school sweethearts were married, and both began teaching at Frost's mother's school. A year later the Frosts' first child was born, and Frost, with financial assistance from his grandfather, entered Harvard. He left Harvard after two years, shortly before his second child was born. The death of the Frosts' first child, a son, in 1900, was followed by the death of his mother from cancer. The double blow gave Frost's early poems a somber tone. He had by this time had a number of his poems published and was irrevocably committed to his craft. After his mother's death, finding that teaching palled, Frost persuaded his grandfather to put up the money to buy a farm and to subsidize his initial efforts to make a go of farming, of which, it might be said, he knew little or nothing. His grandfather acquiesced, and the Frosts found a farm in Derry, New Hampshire, that suited them, "thirty acres, rather run down and poor, but with orchards, fields, pasture, woodland and spring," as Frost wrote his skeptical grandfather.

"Shall I give you a year?" his grandfather replied. "Will you settle down if I give you a year to try this out?"

"Give me twenty" was Frost's rather impudent reply. The Frosts had hardly enough land to do more than play at farming, although Frost took up poultry to try to augment their minuscule income. He loved chickens and came to consider himself somewhat of an expert at their management; certainly he wrote the best (and perhaps the only) poem to a chicken: "The Blue Ribbon at Amesbury." The important thing was that he wrote poetry, although after six difficult years and the birth of four more children, one of whom died in infancy, he turned increasingly to teaching to make ends meet. The fact was the Frosts loved the farm but were less than enthusiastic about farming, a plight not unfamiliar to intellectuals before and since.

After his grandfather's death in 1912 Frost on a sudden and quixotic impulse decided to sell the farm and move his family to England, where the so-called Georgian poets, who included Thomas Hardy, Walter de la Mare, and John Masefield, were writing in a style that seemed compatible with the direction of his own work. It proved a fortunate move; as had been the case with so many other American writers, Frost found in England the support and encouragement, indeed the recognition that he had failed to get in the United States, in part because there was no similar "poetry establishment" in America. He soon found a publisher for his first book, A Boy's Will, which appeared in 1913; Frost was thirty-nine. The book was enthusiastically reviewed. Frost met Ezra Pound, who was acting as a kind of foreign agent for Harriet Monroe's Poetry, and Pound wrote a favorable review of A Boy's Will for that magazine, praising Frost as a writer who "has the good sense to speak naturally and to paint the thing, the thing as he sees it." An Englishwoman who visited the Frosts at their cottage in Herefordshire was impressed by their directness and naturalness. Frost was "friendly and undemonstrative . . . [and] his talk was shrewd and speculative. . . . His New England speech came readily and leisurely, and of all the writers of worth I have met, he spoke with the least sophistication." The Frosts did not live by the clock but largely out of doors. North of Boston followed A Boy's Will and also was widely praised.

Frost's first books of verse displayed a mature and confident talent. "The Pasture," which served as a kind of invitation to the reader of A Boy's Will, was hardly excelled as classical Frost:

> I'm going out to clean the pasture spring;
> I'll only stop to rake the leaves away
> (And wait to watch the water clear, I may):
> I shan't be gone long.—You come too.
>
> I'm going out to fetch the little calf
> That's standing by the mother. It's so young,
> It totters when she licks it with her tongue.
> I shan't be gone long.—You come too.

It is as perfect a lyric as our literature avows, and in its very artlessness it is the finest form of art with the natural tones of the voice speaking through it. Another example of Frost at his best, relating some simple rural act to the deeper rhythms of human existence, is

"To a Thawing Wind": "Burst into my narrow stall;/ Swing the picture on the wall;/ Run the rattling ages o'er;/ Scatter poems on the floor;/ Turn the poet out of door." "Mowing," "Going for Water," "The Tuft of Flowers" carry on the same mood. *North of Boston* opened with "Mending Wall," one of Frost's best-known poems, starting "Something there is that doesn't love a wall," and ending with the contradictory " 'Good fences make good neighbors.' "

The outbreak of the European War in 1914 persuaded the Frosts to return to the United States. There his reputation had, in part because of Pound's endorsement, preceded him. *North of Boston* had been published (in a minute edition to be sure), and an American edition of *A Boy's Will* followed in 1915. *Mountain Interval* was published in 1916, and it, too, opened with one of his most memorable poems, "The Road Not Taken": "Two roads diverged in a yellow wood,/ And sorry I could not travel both/ And be one traveler, long I stood/ And looked down one as far as I could/ To where it bent into the undergrowth;/ Then took the other, as just as fair. . . ."

As with Edwin Arlington Robinson, fame and recognition came finally to Frost—and far more abundantly. He had, in fact, accomplished a minor miracle. He had revived the old tradition of American nature (and popular) poetry that had begun with Philip Freneau and William Cullen Bryant and had been carried on by Whittier, Emerson, and Longfellow. Those poets shared an attitude toward nature. Nature, properly addressed and lovingly observed, was full of moral instruction. For all the noise and clamor of American life, of "getting ahead," of "making it," of coping with its manifold pressures and distractions, nature was the sovereign remedy. Frost was not interested in experiment or innovation except insofar as he had to use the most painstaking art to convey the cadences of the speaking voice. Like Pound and Eliot, from whom he differed in virtually every other respect, he was essentially apolitical and deeply conservative in his feeling for the tragic drama of existence. He thus belongs to the Classical-Christian Consciousness (he wrote that he was never radical when young for fear of being conservative when old; and elsewhere in his later years that he was "only more sure of everything he knew was true").

Ezra Pound was born in the town of Hailey, Idaho, in 1885. His father, Homer Pound, had come to Hailey on a political appointment by President Chester Arthur to take over the U.S. Land Office there. Pound's grandfather, Thaddeus Coleman Pound, had been an influential politician and owned extensive mining properties throughout the Rocky Mountain West. Pound was related to Henry Wadsworth Longfellow and could trace his ancestry back on both sides through a series of distinguished New England forebears and, on his grandmother's side, to some well-known horse thieves. From Hailey the Pounds moved to Philadelphia, where Homer Pound worked in the U.S. Mint and his son grew up attending private schools until he entered the University of Pennsylvania. According to Pound, he decided to become a poet at the age of fifteen. The only question that remained was how he was to achieve his goal. At the University of Pennsylvania, Pound concentrated on Greek and Latin as well as on the study of colonial American history. After two years he transferred to Hamilton College, a much smaller institution at Clinton, New York. There Pound studied German, French, and Italian. When William Carlos Williams met Pound in 1904, he discovered an immediate affinity for the rather eccentric young man. "Not one person in a thousand likes him," Williams noted. Williams found him "a brilliant talker and thinker," who, though he clearly wished to be liked, put people off with his odd mannerisms.

While Pound was a student at the University of Pennsylvania, he became the friend and, to a degree, the suitor of a sprightly young woman named Hilda Doolittle, whose father was professor of astronomy. It was to Hilda Doolittle that Pound gave his first handmade book of poetry, which he entitled *Hilda's Book*. The "book" contained the poem "The Tree," which revealed a poet already formed:

> I stood still and was a tree amid the wood,
> Knowing the truth of things unseen before;
> Of Daphne and the laurel bow
> And that god-feasting couple old
> That grew elm-oak amid the wold

The tree was an image he liked, and he tried it again in "A Girl":

> The tree has entered my hands,
> The sap has ascended my arms,
> The tree has grown in my breast
> Downward,
> The branches grow out of me, like arms.
> Tree you are,
> Moss you are,
> You are violets with the wind above them.
> A child—*so* high—you are;
> And all this is folly to the world.

Pound's poems were self-consciously and determinedly literary, full of classical allusions, of Italian or Latin words and phrases: "Your mind and you are our Sargasso Sea. . . . You are a person of some interest, one comes to you/ And takes strange gain away:/ Trophies fished up; some curious suggestion;/ Fact that leads nowhere; and a tale for two,/ Pregnant with mandrakes. . . ."

For a young man, scarcely finished his college training, to write a poem in praise of the medieval alchemist Paracelsus was somewhat daunting. Yet Pound had the unmistakable gift. "Night Litany" began:

> O dieu, purifiez nos coeurs!
> Purifiez nos coeurs!
> Yea the lines hast thou laid unto me
> in pleasant places,
> And the beauty of this thy Venice
> hast thou shown unto me
> Until is its loveliness become unto me
> a thing of tears.

Having traveled to England and Spain on a fellowship in "Romantics" in 1906 and 1907, Pound was impatient to return. But after a brief spell as teacher of comparative literature (he was the whole department) at Wabash College in Crawfordsville, Indiana, he was delighted to flee again to London, where he arrived with only £3 in his pocket. It was the beginning of his lifelong self-exile from his homeland. Although he returned to the United States, he extricated himself as soon as he could manage the finances.

While Pound was far too esoteric to become in any sense a popular poet, his self-assumed role as a kind of broker of modern poetry, his association with Harriet Monroe, and his tireless experiments with verse forms made him one of the most influential representatives of the new consciousness in modern literature. Although he fled America, there was always something about him of the small-town cracker-box philosopher. In his political ideas and in his infatuation with the era of the American Revolution (John Adams was his favorite Founding Father, and he wrote a long poem in praise of him), Pound was plainly on the conservative side—the Classical-Christian Consciousness, as we have termed it throughout this work.

Thomas Stearns Eliot was born in St. Louis, Missouri, in 1888, the son of parents steeped in the traditions of New England intellectualism. Eliot went as a matter of course to Harvard and did subsequent stints at the University of Paris and at Oxford. In 1914 he followed his friend Ezra Pound to Europe, although Eliot made his home in England, while Pound favored France and Italy. Like Pound, who was three years his senior, Eliot combined scholarship with poetry—that is, perhaps more accurately, he and Pound believed that a poet must be familiar with all the poetic forms and the principal languages in which they were expressed. They had, in consequence, little interest in or sympathy with the spirit of rebelliousness that characterized the work of such writers as Dreiser and Anderson or the yearning to articulate America. Poetry, as opposed to prose, was an instrument requiring the most painstaking craftsmanship and endless refinement. The fusion of the word and the image it was intended to evoke was an arduous discipline that should not even be essayed without a long apprenticeship and a knowledge approaching the universal. Certainly Pound and Eliot were as aware as their more socially conscious contemporaries of the need to create new forms of expression within the realm of poetry. Like Henry James, whom he resembled in many ways, Eliot could not stand the crudeness and vulgarity of the United States; even more distasteful to him was what seemed to him the creed of the Secular Democratic Consciousness, which ignored the tragedies and dilemmas of historic man in favor of a simple, if touching, faith in the innate goodness of the people and the inevitability of the triumph of socialism. Again like Pound and, of course, John Jay Chapman (who chose to stay home), Eliot partook of the Classical-Christian Consciousness. He did not tire of chiding the liberals and radicals. "The World," one of his characters says in an argument that is clearly Eliot's own, "is trying the experiment of attempting to form a civilized but non-Christian mentality. The experiment will fail; but we must be very patient in awaiting its collapse; meanwhile redeeming the time. . . ."

However all that may be, a great poet is as mysterious as a great painter. When Thomas Stearns Eliot wrote the opening lines of "The Love Song of J. Alfred Prufrock" in 1912, he ushered in a new era in poetry:

> Let us go then, you and I,
> When the evening is spread out against the sky
> Like a patient etherised upon a table;
> Let us go, through certain half-deserted streets,
> The muttering retreats
> Of restless nights in one-night cheap hotels
> And sawdust restaurants with oyster-shells:

Streets that follow like a tedious argument
Of insidious intent
To lead you to an overwhelming question . . .
Oh, do not ask, "What is it?"
Let us go and make our visit.

It would be a mistake to leave the realm of poetry without mention of one of the most eccentric figures of this era. Amy Lowell was born in Brookline, Massachusetts, in 1874, the newest member of the remarkable Lowell-Lawrence clan. James Russell Lowell was her great-uncle, and she remembered his aloof and forbidding presence from her childhood. Her brother A. Lawrence, eighteen years her senior, was to be Charles William Eliot's successor as president of Harvard, and his tenure lasted almost as long as Eliot's. An exuberant tomboy, Amy Lowell became the leader among a troop of cousins. Returning from a trip to California at the age of nine, she wrote a classic Boston poem:

The folks go
On the lake
In sailboat and barge.
But for all of its beauty
I'd rather go home,
To Boston,
Charles River,
And the State House's
Dome.

Through her brother Percival, an expert on Korean art and Japanese culture, Amy acquired a lifelong infatuation with Oriental culture, especially the art of Japan (one of her books of poetry was entitled *Pictures of the Floating World*). As she grew older, she grew stouter and more eccentric, collecting rare books and manuscripts and becoming a Keats scholar. She traveled through Europe, viewed the Sphinx, and ascended the cataracts of the Nile. Back in Boston, she had the nervous breakdown that was almost a requirement for women of her class and time. It lasted for nearly seven years, a period of incapacitating headaches and jangled nerves. When her formidable father died in 1900, the twenty-six-year-old Amy became the proprietress of the family mansion, Sevenel (for Seven Lowells), in Brookline, the manager of a fortune, and, before long, one of the famous hostesses and literary figures of New England. "The difficulty with American civilization," she wrote, "is that it is essentially vulgar in tone, not so much in manner as in essence. The theatres, the newspapers, the popular amusements, all show this. The few people with refined ideas and cultivated tastes can make no impression against this mass of Vulgarism. The tendency is not so much directly vicious as it is undermining and deteriorating. The cheap and tawdry exert their fatal influence throughout the whole national life." Amy Lowell set out to row against that current.

In 1902 the decisive event of Lowell's life occurred when she saw Eleonora Duse playing in *La Gioconda*. "The effect on me," she wrote, "was something tremendous. What really happened was that it revealed me to myself. . . . I just knew that I had got to express the sensations that Duse's acting gave me, somehow." She had always been interested in writing and had indeed written plays, short stories, and essays. She decided that poetry would be her medium. Eight years later she sent four sonnets to the editor of the *Atlantic Monthly*, Ellery Sedgwick, her cousin by marriage, who printed them all. Not long afterward she met the actress Ada Russell. Soon Lowell and Russell were familiar figures in Boston (indeed all over the world), driving about in Lowell's mulberry-colored Pierce Arrow with *two* chauffeurs in matching livery. They became, in the manner of so many independent-minded women, lifelong companions, traveling the world together and living together at Sevenel.

Encouraged by a meeting with Ezra Pound and by Pound's acceptance of one of her poems for his new magazine, *Des Imagistes*, Lowell cast her poetic lot with the new movement and became its principal advocate in the United States. Her first book of verse, *A Dome of Many-Colored Glass*, was followed by an aggressively imagist volume, *Sword Blades and Poppy Seeds*, in which she wrote:

> I have whetted my brain until it is like a Damascus blade,
> So keen it knicks off the floating fringes of passers by . . .
> My brain is curved like a scimitar
> And sighs at its cutting like a sickle mowing grass.

Her enemy, as she saw it, was what she and others called the Cosmic School of Poetry, which she, at least, identified with her uncle James Russell Lowell. In her view, it was inflated and moralistic. Imagist poetry should seek the exact word to evoke the "image." Smoking long manila cigars and lecturing and reading her poetry everywhere, Lowell wrote and published more than 600 poems, designed her own books, and produced an enormous life of Keats while undergoing four major operations and suffering from chronic gastritis, severe eyestrain, and high blood pressure. Huge and imperious, she dominated the literary life of Boston much as James Russell Lowell, so different in his notion of what constituted poetry, had done earlier. Carl Sandburg told a friend that "arguing with Amy was like arguing with a big blue wave."

Pictures of the Floating World, published in 1919 and referring, of course, to the world of geisha, demonstrated both the strength and the weakness of the imagist school. It had, rather incongruously, a quotation from Whitman as its frontispiece: "In the name of these States and in your and my name, the Past, And in the name of these States and in your and my name, the Present time."

"The Pond" read:

> Cold, wet leaves,
> Floating in moss-coloured water,
> And the croaking of frogs—
> Cracked bell-notes in the twilight.

"A Street":

> Under red umbrellas with cream-white centres,
> A procession of Geisha passes
> In front of the silk-shop of Matusuzaka-ya.

And "November":

> The vine leaves against the brick walls of my house
> Are rusty and broken.
> Dead leaves gather under the pine-trees,
> The brittle boughs of the lilac-bushes
> Sweep against the stars.
> And I sit under a lamp
> Trying to write down the emptiness of my heart.
> Even the cat will not stay with me,
> But prefers the rain
> Under the meagre shelter of a cellar window.

In a sense imagist poetry was too easy. The lines, reread too often, went slack; the form was not strict enough, and the emotion too fragile. It appeared that the fusion of passion and moral content was, after all, essential to poetry.

On the "popular" and political side, three poets remain to be considered. Edgar Lee Masters was born in Garnett, Kansas, in 1869 (he was the same age as Edwin Arlington Robinson) and grew up in a series of small towns in the Middle West. After a year at Knox College, in Galesburg, Illinois, Masters moved to Chicago, where he practiced law, espoused the Populist cause, and became a leader in the literary circles of that city, which revolved around Floyd Dell and Margy Currie. There it was almost as if the Chicago literary figures had launched a coordinated assault against the Midwestern small towns which had produced them. Masters decided to write a series of biographies of small-town figures, their images evoked by a visit to the burial grounds at mythical Spoon River. While he was considering the form his project might take, a friend lent him a Greek anthology of short poems, or epigrams, brief biographies of the notable and obscure dead. Masters was captivated by the form. He wrote his epitaph-biographies in the form of poems. The lives of his subjects form a grim collective portrait of defeated hopes, of forgotten lusts, of murders, suicides, and empty dreams. The opening poem of the *New Spoon River,* published ten years after the original, sets the tone for both works:

> Where is the hope of happiness,
> And where the faith in friends,
> And where the loyalty in love,
> And where the peace of plenty that never came,
> And where the sorrows that were of life,
> And the struggles that ceased not,
> And the laughter that turned to tears,
> And the tears scorched drying the dearth of days?—
> All, all are vanished in the Stillness of the Valley
> Beyond the Hill!

The most notable thing about *Spoon River Anthology* is undoubtedly the sensation that it caused when it was published in 1915, that remarkable year which, like 1854, saw so many powerful and original literary works of the new consciousness. Masters's book, while nearer prose than poetry, caused a sensation and was one of the few books of at least ostensible poetry to achieve best-seller status. The small town was in the process of becoming a national symbol for all that was narrow and provincial in American life.

Spoon River Anthology is hardly poetry or indeed literature, but it gives us a further insight into the American mind of this era when attention focused on the city as the hope of the future. Masters's book is, as much as anything else, a bitter indictment of the effects of an urban industrial society on the ancient values of the town. In its abashedly Populist flavor it recalled a better time and revived memories of the not so distant days when it seemed that the Midwest might redeem the country from the excesses of capitalism.

Another member of the Chicago literary circle was a young second-generation Swede, Carl Sandburg, son of a blacksmith, born in Galesburg, Illinois, in 1878. After serving in the Spanish-American War, Sandburg returned to Galesburg and there attended Lombard College, a Universalist institution that was considered dangerously close to free thought by its neighboring Presbyterian institution, Knox College. At Lombard the curriculum included the poetry of Robert Burns and the writings of Lester Ward and was supplemented by a series of visiting lecturers, among them Elbert Hubbard; Bob Ingersoll, the famous atheist; Booker T. Washington; Jacob Riis; and, most important, Eugene V. Debs, brought by the Socialist club. At Lombard Sandburg decided "I'm going to be a writer or a bum." Working first as a fireman to give him time to write and then as an editor for an obscure liberal journal, *Tomorrow,* Sandburg, perhaps unfortunately, read Whitman and decided to become the Whitman of the Middle West. He adopted the least fetching of Whitman's mannerisms, what we might call the poetry of the inventory, which consists of long lists of qualities or attributes. Sandburg's *Chicago Poems* brought him a degree of fame and placed him squarely with "Socialist poets" who saw their task as writing poetry for the people that would help hasten the day of the revolution. Sandburg's greatest appeal lay in the persona he created for himself as the spokesman for the Middle West. With a blunt, rugged face and a shock of hair as yellow as the sun-ripened wheat of his beloved Midwest, he was an ideal visual embodiment of the Populist-Socialist ideals he espoused.

One of the most appealing of the self-consciously popular poets imbued with the spirit of populism was Vachel Lindsay, born in Springfield, Illinois, in 1879. Lindsay attended Hiram College and then studied art in Chicago and New York. Beginning in 1905 and taking his inspiration from Johnny Appleseed, he began hoboing around the country, from one small town to another, offering to recite his poems in return for board and food. With a splendid flair for the dramatic, Lindsay "acted" his poems more than conventionally recited them. He picked themes that lent themselves to sonorous and dramatic renditions. When Harriet Monroe started *Poetry* in 1912, one of the first "new" poets to come to her attention was the disarming Lindsay. In the first issue of 1913 Monroe published "General William Booth Enters into Heaven" with its haunting refrain: "Are you washed in the blood of the Lamb?" The next year Lindsay received a generous accolade from the great William Butler Yeats, who, visiting Chicago at Monroe's invitation, called him "a fellow craftsman" and praised "General Booth . . . as a poem stripped bare of ornament," with "an earnest simplicity, a strange beauty." "The Congo" is perhaps Lindsay's most famous poem: "Fat black bucks in a wine-barrel room,/ Barrel-house kings, with feet unstable,/ Sagged and reeled and pounded on the table,/ Pounded on the table,/ Beat an empty barrel with the handle of a broom,/ Hard as they were able,/ Boom, boom, Boom. . . ."

Lindsay's deep social concerns are reflected in such poems as "The Leaden-Eyed":

> Let not young souls be smothered out before
> They do quaint deeds and fully flaunt their pride.
> It is the world's one crime its babes grow dull,
> Its poor are ox-like, limp and leaden-eyed.
> Not that they starve, but starve so dreamlessly,
> Not that they sow, but that they seldom reap,
> Not that they serve, but have no gods to serve,
> Not that they die, but that they die like sheep.

The poet Octavia Corneau was infatuated by Lindsay, "but I had to give him up," she wrote. "Vachel's idea of a date was riding tandem on a mule along the rim of the Grand Canyon in a driving rain singing 'Washed in the Blood of the Lamb.'"

We cannot propel Vachel Lindsay, appealing a personality as he is, into the ranks of our major poets, but he has a secure, if minor place, among the singers of America.

51

Four Women Writers

There were dozens of women novelists writing during this period, including most prominently Elinor Glyn, whose sexy romances scandalized respectable readers; Margaret Deland, who wrote in a vaguely Jamesian manner; and Marie Corelli, given to lurid romances in exotic settings. But four women rose well above the pack: Edith Wharton, Willa Cather, Ellen Glasgow, and the less well-known Gertrude Atherton. Moreover, each represented a different social and geographical segment of America—Wharton, the Eastern upper class; Cather, the frontier West; Glasgow, the South; and Atherton, the Far West.

Edith Wharton, née Newbold Jones, was born in 1862 to wealthy and socially prominent parents who divided their time between New York City and Great Barrington, Massachusetts. Although Great Barrington was a town of modest size, the Jones family had a secure place in New York City's aristocracy and moved easily in that city's social elite. Indeed, Edith Newbold Jones was the only major American writer, Henry James possibly excepted, to be born with a silver spoon in her mouth. (The James family, while socially and financially secure, was too eccentric to have a clearly defined place in New York society or to care to have one.) Edith Jones was a tireless reader and an accomplished linguist who wrote and spoke three or four languages and was well acquainted with the great nineteenth-century British and Continental writers. Educated by tutors and governesses in a predominantly masculine environment, she spent almost as much time abroad with her family as in New York. Their itinerary was that of the wealthy upperclass Americans whose European peregrinations we have already described. "My parents' ears were wounded by an unsuitable word as those of the musical are hurt by a false note . . ." Edith Wharton wrote. "This feeling for good English was more than reverence, and nearer: it was love."

Miss Jones, like many refined young women, early discovered a disposition for poetry and, influenced by the school of female short-story writers, tried her hand at that genre as well. When she was twenty-three, she became engaged to a charming, wealthy Bostonian, Edward Wharton. When Edith Jones, in a state of extreme anxiety about the sexual aspects of married life, plucked up the courage to mention that unmentionable subject to her mother, Mrs. Jones replied, "I never heard such a ridiculous question in my life."

"I'm afraid, Mamma—I want to know what will happen to me."

Mrs. Wharton looked disgusted. "You've seen enough pictures and statues in your life. Haven't you noticed that men are . . . made differently from women?"

The marriage was not consummated until three weeks after the wedding, and then it was an extremely traumatic experience for Edith. The young couple divided their time between handsome houses in New York City and, in the summers, Newport, Rhode Island. The household included an Alsatian housekeeper, a British butler, several maids, a cook, a carriageman, and three or four gardeners.

Edith Wharton had, besides a remarkable intelligence and a wit that confused the dull and conventional young men of her acquaintance, that absolute prerequisite for a nineteenth-century belle, a slim waist. In the early years of her marriage she, like such diverse figures as Charlotte Perkins Gilman and Jane Addams, suffered from periods of devastating depression. Like Gilman, she was overcome by weakness. She was hardly able to walk, could not read or write, and suffered from severe headaches, nausea, and loss of weight. She traveled to Philadelphia to take S. Weir Mitch's rest cure at his clinic, which involved complete isolation and daily massages for four months. Either therapy worked, or her natural vitality and high spirits reasserted themselves. She was able to complete the proofreading of her first book of short stories, *The Greater Inclination*. It was highly praised by a number of reviewers and had substantial sales for an unknown author, something more than 3,000 copies. While most of the stories were of the popular surprise ending type, several dealt with "modern problems" and displayed the wit and psychological insight that distinguished her work. In addition, they adumbrate the later novels.

In "Souls Related" Lydia Tillotson, a married woman, and her lover, Gannett, flee to an Italian resort for an illicit honeymoon. Lydia has found her life with her husband and mother-in-law in a handsome Fifth Avenue mansion unbearably confining. There "existence . . . had been reduced to a series of purely automatic acts. The moral atmosphere was as carefully screened and curtained as the house itself; Mrs. Tillotson senior dreaded ideas as much as a draught on her back. Prudent people liked an even temperature; and to do anything unexpected was as foolish as going out in the rain. One of the chief advantages of being rich was that one need not be exposed to unforeseen contingencies: by the use of ordinary firmness and common sense one could make sure of doing exactly the same thing every day at the same hour." Lydia's husband displays the same predictability, impressing her with "his punctuality at meals, and his elaborate precautions against burglars and contagious diseases." Into this world of paralyzing boredom comes a lively writer, critic, and intellectual-for-all-seasons named Gannett, who avows his love and whisks Lydia away. "Souls Related" is a brilliant examination of the consequences of Lydia's escape. Tillotson files for divorce, but Lydia has no desire to marry Gannett. She insists that since they have run away together, they must face honestly the meaning of their actions. Simply to marry would be to succumb tamely to convention, no less than a "vulgar fraud upon society—, and upon a society we despised and laughed at—this sneaking back into a position that we've voluntarily forfeited; don't you see what a cheap compromise it is? We neither of us believe in the abstract 'sacredness' of marriage; we both know that no ceremony is needed to consecrate our love for each other." The only reason to marry would be that they did not trust the enduringness of their love. Gannett is a bit disconcerted. He replies wryly, "I didn't know that we ran away to found a new system of ethics. I supposed it was because we loved each other." They quarrel over the issue; "they had reached that memorable point in every heart-history," Wharton wrote, "when, for the first time, the man seems obtuse and the woman irrational."

However, at the Italian resort where they have taken refuge, Lydia's principles desert her. She cannot face the complete social ostracism of the other guests, most of them English aristocrats, that must follow if it becomes known that she and Gannett are not married. She registers at the Hotel Bellosguardo as Mrs. Gannett. Her resolution further weakens when another woman guest confesses to a situation similar to Lydia's and begs her to keep her secret. It occurs to Lydia that she has escaped from one trap to thrust herself into another. "These people—the very prototypes," she tells Gannett, "of the bores you took me away from, with the same fenced-in view of life, the same keep-off-the-grass morality, the same little cautious virtues and the same frightened vices—well, I've clung to them. . . . Respectability! It was the one thing in life that I was sure I didn't care about, and it's grown so precious to me that I've stolen it because I couldn't get it in any other way. . . . I who used to fancy myself unconventional! I must have been born with a card-case in my hand." The principal function of marriage, she declares, is "to keep people away from each other. Sometimes I think that two people who love each other can be saved from madness only by the things that come between them—children, duties, visits, bores, relations—the things that protect married people from each other. . . . We've seen the nakedness of each other's souls."

Having said as much and having upbraided Gannett for what she instinctively felt was his psychological withdrawal from their relationship, Lydia slips away while her lover is still asleep. He awakens, realizes she is leaving, but feigns sleep and makes no effort to stop her. "At the last issue," he reflects, "he and she were two separate beings, not made one by the miracle of common forbearance, duties, abnegations, but bound together in a *noyade* of passion . . . that left them resisting yet clinging as they went down." At the end Lydia's resolution fails her. She turns back to Gannett, having, of course, no notion that he has been watching her from the bedroom window of the hotel. He begins to look "mechanically" at the train schedules for Paris. They will go on, presumably with soberer expectations.

Edith Wharton's first major effort in the novel form, *The Valley of Decision,* was a long historical novel set in eighteenth-century Italy. It appeared in 1902 and was followed by *The House of Mirth* three years later. *The House of Mirth* picked up the theme that she had explored in several stories included in *The Greater Inclination:* the narrow and confining life and the rigid formalities of society. In her words, "a frivolous society can acquire dramatic significance only through what its frivolity destroys. Its tragic implications lie in its power of debasing people and ideals." In the plainly autobiographical *House of Mirth,* Lily

Bart is frustrated in her efforts to develop her own character and her own talents by a society that has a vested interest in enforcing conformity. Thomas Wentworth Higginson, the friend and proponent of Emily Dickinson, at eighty-two the dean of American literary figures, declared that *The House of Mirth* stood "at the head of all American fiction, save Hawthorne alone."

Increasingly the Whartons spent time abroad, apparently feeling, as did so many of their class, that the United States was an impossible place in which to live. That was clearly the view of Edith Wharton's friend Henry James, who had chosen the life of an exile in England. Edward "Teddy" Wharton was a classic representative of his class, an agreeable, kindly, sensual man, rather self-important and extremely self-indulgent. More alarmingly he was subject to fits of depression and periods of unpredictable behavior.

Edith Wharton's unusual intelligence and penetrating wit went more and more into her writing, which was both an escape from the difficulties of her marriage and from the constraining circumstances of her social life and a profession pursued with devoted attention to the requirements of art. While to a modern reader Wharton treated sexual matters with the reserve characteristic of her age, her candor nonetheless alarmed some of the editors to whom she sent her work. One editor warned her, as she recalled, that no magazine would publish anything that could offend "a non-existent clergyman in the Mississippi valley. . . ." She was determined "from the first that I would never sacrifice my literary conscience to this ghostly censor."

Through the early years of her marriage her husband's friend and drinking companion Walter Berry, a graduate of Harvard and a man with sophisticated cultural tastes, encouraged and, to a degree, guided Wharton's literary progress. If Sarah Orne Jewett was the strongest influence on Willa Cather, the strongest literary influence on Edith Wharton seems to have been George Eliot. She wrote sympathetically (and almost prophetically) of George Eliot's long extramarital relationship with a married man, George Henry Lewes. Eliot, like Wharton, was a conservative in ethics. "She felt no call to found a new school of morals," Wharton wrote, in a sentence almost identical to the line of one of her characters in "Souls Related." A deep reverence for family ties, for the sanctities of tradition, the claims of slowly acquired convictions and slowly formed precedents, is revealed in every page of her books.

In 1911 Wharton published the book she is best known for, *Ethan*

Frome. Beside being a powerful and perfect, if deeply morbid, story, it is a brilliant *tour de force* since it tells the story of a doomed love in a New England town—Starkfield, Massachusetts—a world infinitely remote from that in which Wharton moved. Frome is one of those promising lads who fail to escape from the brutally repressive environment of their hometowns. He marries Zeena and finds himself anchored to the farming community. In the words of the town's chronicler, "Fust his father got a kick, out haying, and went soft in the brain. . . . Then got queer and dragged along for years as weak as a baby. . . . Sickness and trouble: that's what Ethan's had his plate full up with, ever since the first helping." Zeena herself is always "ailing" and querulous. When her sister Mattie comes to Starkfield, Ethan is drawn irresistibly to Mattie, so full of life and vitality. In contrast with her sister, not only is she "no fretter," but her delight in nature and her passionate temper match Ethan's. Soon it is clear they are in love. Zeena forces Mattie to leave Starkfield. On the night of her departure Ethan and Mattie go for a final, suicidal sled ride together. Frome apparently hopes to kill them both, but in a terrible crash they are seriously injured, and Mattie is permanently crippled. Frome recovers to live out his life with the two sisters, the three of them prisoners in the little farmhouse kitchen. Tragic as the story is, it has about it a perfection that few American works have achieved. It is, finally, about human relations from which we cannot escape. Edith Wharton had fled from the increasingly psychotic behavior of Teddy, her husband. They separated, but they had painful reunions. It is hard not to believe that the desperate triangle of Ethan, Zeena, and Mattie was related to the situation of Wharton's own marriage, from which, it seemed to her, there was no escape.

In fourteen years Edith Wharton had written sixteen books. After the publication of *Ethan Frome,* which had disappointing sales and a mildly favorable critical response, she sailed for Paris, to move, as they say, in the most aristocratic and sophisticated circles. There her life was one of hectic travel with a circle of close friends that included usually Walter Berry and Henry James and occasionally Bernard Berenson. One of her inimitable vignettes of American literary life is her account of Henry James's reading Walt Whitman's *Leaves of Grass* aloud. She agreed with James that Whitman was America's greatest poet.

When the war came, Edith Wharton threw herself with untiring energy into "war work." James, who had earlier found his friendship with her both stimulating and exhausting, wrote: "Her powers of devastation are ineffable, her repudiation of repose absolutely tragic. . . ." At the same time he found her, as she grew older, "more brilliant and able and interesting." Another friend said of her, "What she loved above all was *fun*—the farce of life in its wildest and subtlest surprises, and how· wild they could be, and how subtle, how blandly disguised, there was none like her to discover."

Even before she left for Europe, Wharton had begun a passionate love affair with an American journalist named Morton Fullerton, a Harvard-educated New Englander. Soon after they had met, Wharton was in love as she had never imagined she could be. Simply being in the same room with Fullerton was ecstasy. "This," she wrote in her diary, "must be what happy women feel." She wrote to him: "I should like to be to you, friend of my heart, like a touch of wings brushing by you in the darkness, or like the scent of an invisible garden, that one passes on an unknown road at night." They continued their affair in Paris, and after Edward Wharton had returned to the United States to consult doctors for *his* nervous depression, the romance between Edith Wharton and Morton Fullerton blossomed into a wildly sensual amour. She wrote a poem to commemorate their first physical intimacy:

> We watched, and felt the tides of time
> Coil round our hidden leafy place,
> Sweep on through changing race and clime
> And leave us at the heart of space.

The time of the flowering of her life had finally and wholly unexpectedly come. She wrote: "I have poured into it all my stored-up joy of living, all my sense of the beauty and mystery of the world, every impression of joy and loveliness, in sight or sound or touch."

It was ironic beyond the measure of mere fiction that Edith Wharton, who in "Souls Related" had so clearly perceived the pitfalls in extramarital unions, had to learn the lesson in real life. Her relationship with Fullerton gradually declined from its first high passion. She began to see him as he really was: a dedicated, apparently bisexual womanizer and something of an opportunist. She burst out to a friend, "Ah, the poverty, the miserable poverty, of any love that lies outside of marriage, of any love that is not a living together, a sharing of all."

In 1920 *The Age of Innocence* appeared. It was a brilliant study of upper-class New York life in the 1870s and 1880s. Ellen Olenska is a New York society woman who, having married Count Olenska, has run off with his secretary and is now in exile in New York, where she is forced to pay the price of defying convention. Young Newland Archer falls in love with Ellen. The tragedy of her marriage and her more cosmopolitan experience give him a glimpse of a larger and far more interesting existence, but she leaves him, secure and vaguely disappointed, in a conventional marriage. When they meet later, he tells her of his continuing love, adding, "You gave me my first glimpse of a real life, and at the same moment you asked me to go on with a sham one. It's beyond human enduring—that's all." She startles him by replying that she has had to endure it, too; she has loved him in return. But when he implores her to become his lover or to flee with him, Ellen Olenska echoes the words of Lydia Tillotson in "Souls Related," written twenty years earlier. It is not so easy to flee the conventions of society, loveless marriages, and failed hopes. "I know so many who've tried to find it; and, believe me, they all got out by mistake at wayside stations: at places like Boulogne, or Pisa, or Monte Carlo—and it wasn't all that different from the old world they'd left, but only rather smaller and dingier and more promiscuous."

So they return to the worlds that hold them—Ellen Olenska to what comfort she can derive from the artistic and intellectual circles of Europe and Newland Archer to the respectable social world of which he is a conspicuous ornament. They will live out their lives as best they can, sustained by the knowledge of the love they share and the fact that it has enhanced their respective lives as much by the sacrifice of it as by the love itself.

The novel is not only a brilliantly perceptive exploration of the old order, the older consciousness, and the stultifying character of upper-class life but also, somewhat paradoxically, a challenge to the easy notions of the modern age, the new consciousness that seems disposed to believe that relations can be put on and taken off like new garments, that nothing need be irreparably lost when old loves are put away and new loves taken on. Its success, like the success of the short story out of which it was born, lies in Wharton's ability to explore that tenuous borderline between convention and freedom, between sacrifice and indulgence.

The Age of Innocence was published when Wharton was fifty-eight. It won one of the early Pulitzer Prizes in literature and confirmed her reputation as a major literary figure, but the final measure of appreciation was withheld because, in the view at least of the contemporary critic Gore Vidal, she was a woman. Certainly Edith Wharton, whose life was as dramatic as any of her novels, took a narrow canvas, but on that she painted exceedingly well.

Willa Cather, born in Virginia in 1873, and thus eleven years Wharton's junior, moved with her family to Red Cloud, Nebraska, when she was a child. Red Cloud had been settled only a decade or so earlier, and its pioneer origins were everywhere evident. Most important to Cather, the town was a kind of microcosm of the rural, pioneer Middle West. It had been settled primarily by Scandinavians and Bohemians. There were also a scattering of French and German immigrants and a substantial element of older American families from the East. These contrasting cultural strains were to provide a major theme of Willa Cather's work. Red Cloud seemed to her hopelessly benighted—narrow, provincial, bigoted, hostile to all that was open and joyful. The only relief was provided by immigrants, especially the Bohemians and Germans, who brought with them a hint of the cultural riches of their homelands. Rejection of the cramped, inhibited life of the farm and town was Cather's first impulse; her goal was to escape by any means possible from that stifling environment where individual superiority or any deviation from the community's accepted values was distrusted and, more, feared and hated. The vital, highly regarded state university at Lincoln was her most accessible refuge.

Nebraska itself, in the years Cather was growing up, was a state full of social and intellectual ferment. Like Kansas, its sister to the south, Nebraska bore the unmistakable marks of its origin in the feverish days following the passage of the Kansas-Nebraska Act, which opened the Pandora's box of sectional bitterness that led directly to the Civil War. The adopted state of William Jennings Bryan, it was also a stronghold first of rural radicalism and later of populism. Although political issues remained outside Cather's literary realm, the electric atmosphere created by the events of the election year of 1892 clearly affected her.

Cather arrived in Lincoln with the half-formed intention of majoring in science and becoming a doctor, but she switched to literature under the influence of a professor of classics. Her remarkable intellectual gifts were immediately apparent to her teachers. In addition to excelling in her studies, she was soon serving as an editor of the campus literary journal and contributing pieces to the Lincoln newspaper. The

theater and the musical world became her ruling passions. Her reading
covered a wide range, from the great nineteenth-century French novelists, specifically Balzac and Flaubert, to the Pre-Raphaelites, the young
English poet A. E. Housman, whose rural lyrics exerted a strong influence on her, and, most important of all, Whitman. While we associate
the new consciousness with the great cities, the experience of Willa
Cather in Lincoln, Nebraska, serves to remind us that the Middle West
was really the seedbed of the new consciousness and that the state
universities of Wisconsin, Nebraska, Kansas, Iowa, and Michigan were
far more exciting intellectual centers than the older private institutions
of the East, Johns Hopkins excepted. In Lincoln, Cather's short hair
and mannish clothes proclaimed her a "new woman" in the making.

The theater and the opera—music in general—became for Cather,
as for many women of her generation, symbols of a freer, less inhibited
world. The gracelessness of American life might be redeemed by ascent
to the magic realm of art. She poured out a torrent of reviews of plays,
concerts, and operas. Her restless, omnivorous intelligence feasted on
every aspect of the artistic and literary world. Having escaped from
Red Cloud to Lincoln, she escaped from Lincoln to Pittsburgh to edit
a new magazine, *Home Monthly,* for which she wrote under a variety
of pen names. She had written poems and short stories since her early
years at the university. Now, with the stimulus of new friends, she
began to devote more time to serious writing. George Seibel, a fellow
journalist some years older than she, became her intellectual mentor.
He recalled her as "plump and dimpled, with dreamy eyes and an
eager mind." With the Seibels, Cather read aloud Alphonse Daudet,
Edmond Rostand's *Cyrano de Bergerac,* Alfred de Musset, and Paul
Verlaine. "Flaubert was our chief delight," Seibel wrote, "and Willa's
impeccable style was achieved by a sedulous study of this merciless
master. . . ." Soon Cather brought along her friend Dorothy Canfield
(later "Fisher"), whom she had known at Lincoln, where Canfield's
father had been chancellor of the university. To Canfield, Cather seemed
a marvel of emancipation. She lived by herself and, more important,
earned her own living. In the "wonderful, cosmopolitan talk" at the
Seibels', Canfield felt she had entered an exciting new world.

The Pittsburgh years were critical in Cather's development as a
writer and as a person. It was in the "Steel City" that she was surprised
by homesickness; Red Cloud began to tug at her heartstrings. But she
saw Sarah Bernhardt act and heard Emma Calve sing. She had lunch

with the famous Madame Helene Modjeska and dined with the Norwegian ambassador. And her short stories and poems were published with increasing regularity.

In 1900 her story "Eric Hermannson's Soul" appeared in *Cosmopolitan*. It is worth lingering over since the story foreshadows themes that were to characterize all of Cather's subsequent work. The story concerns a young man who has grown up in the small Nebraska community of Lone Star. He loves music, plays the fiddle with gusto, adores dancing, and takes a simple joy in life that alarms his more somber neighbors. His violin is "his only bridge into the kingdom of the soul," Cather wrote. He plays the fiddle for Lena Hanson, "whose name was a reproach throughout the Divide country where the women are usually too plain and too busy and too tired to depart from the ways of virtue." Lena knows "the strange language of flattery and idleness and mirth." The Free Gospelers have seized on the soul of Lone Star and do not rest until they have drawn a "redeemed" Eric Hermannson into their company, prevailing on him to smash his fiddle as a symbol of his emancipation from the devil. The night of Eric's conversion the Lone Star schoolhouse is filled with "poor exiles of all nations; men from the south and north, peasants from almost every country of Europe. . . . Honest men for the most part, but men with whom the World had dealt hardly; the failures of all countries, men sobered by toil and saddened by exile, who had been driven to fight for the dominion of an untoward soil, to sow where others should gather, the advance guard of a mighty civilization to be." For two years pious Eric has "kept the austere faith to which he had sworn himself . . . the sad history of those Norwegian exiles, transplanted in an arid soil and under a scorching sun, had repeated itself in his case. Toil and isolation had sobered him, and he grew more and more like the clods among which he labored."

A young woman, Margaret Elliot, comes from the East to Lone Star. She is, Cather wrote, "one of those women of whom there are so many in this day, when the old order, passing, giveth place to new; beautiful, talented, critical, unsatisfied, tired of the world at twenty-four." Eric and Margaret, the rough, untutored farm boy and the sophisticated Eastern woman, are drawn irresistibly to each other; they experience a transcendent moment at a dance where Eric escapes from his Free Gospel constraints, plays his fiddle, and makes ardent love to Margaret, believing he must pay in hell for his sin of passionate joy.

The main themes that Cather later developed are conspicuous in

"Eric Hermannson's Soul": the conflict and tension between the life of the rural town and that of the metropolis, the East, the glittering world of culture and wealth; exile; repression versus joy and delight in life; disappointed or impossible love; sophistication versus untutored naturalness, as well as of intellect versus emotion; the dreams and passions of youth (perhaps, finally, her principal theme) and the efforts of "society" to damp down and contain those dreams; and beyond that, the erosion of those dreams by life itself, primitive or sophisticated.

The Hermannson story received favorable attention, and Cather was encouraged to devote more of her time to her poetry and fiction and less to newspaper articles and reviews. She had secured a teaching position in a Pittsburgh high school when she met Isabelle McClung, the daughter of a judge. She formed immediately one of those intense feminine relations that came to characterize her life. McClung, rather to the alarm of her parents, insisted that Willa move into the large, comfortable McClung household.

In 1903 Cather published a volume of verse, *April Twilights*. For a young writer, barely turned thirty, it was a notable achievement. What is perhaps most surprising is her mastery of form and her infusion of form by passion. The best of the poems have that intensity of feeling that can hardly be feigned. Their most conspicuous themes are loss, decay, and death, all themes popular with young writers or at least with young poets and popular, moreover, with the literate public of the day. Another constant theme is love. But poetry did not give adequate range to the themes with which Cather wished to deal. Two years after *April Twilights*, she published a book of short stories— *The Troll Garden*—that marked her emergence as a major literary figure among her contemporaries.

Perhaps the grimmest story in *The Troll Garden* is "The Sculptor's Funeral." It is a tale of the funeral of a world-renowned sculptor, Harvey Merrick, whose body has been returned for burial to Sand City, the small Midwestern town where he was born and grew up. As the townspeople sit around discussing the deceased, all their hostility toward anyone who deviates from the narrow mores of the community pours out, and they recite a detailed inventory of "old Harve's" shortcomings according to the town's way of measuring things. "Where the old man made his mistake," one mourner declares, "was in sending the boy East to school. There was where he got his head full of traipsing to Paris and all such folly. What Harve needed, of all people, was a course in some first-class Kansas City business college." As the chorus of carping reminiscences rambles on, Merrick's boyhood friend Jim Laird, himself a bitter and defeated man, too much given to alcohol, breaks in angrily: "I've been with you gentlemen before when you've sat by the coffins of boys born and raised in this town; and, if I remember rightly, you were never any too well satisfied when you checked them up. What's the matter, anyhow? Why is it that reputable young men are scarce as millionaires in Sand City? It might almost seem to a stranger that something was the matter with your progressive town. Why did Ruben Sayer, the brightest young lawyer you ever turned out, after he had come home from the university as straight as a die, take to drinking and forge a check and shoot himself? Why was Mr. Thomas's son, here, shot in a gambling house? Why did young Adams burn his mill to beat the insurance companies and go to the pen? . . . I'll tell you why. Because you drummed nothing but money and knavery into their ears from the time they wore knickerbockers. . . . You wanted them to be successful rascals, they were only unsuccessful ones—that's all the difference . . . you hated Harvey Merrick more for winning out than you hated all the other boys who got under the wheels. . . . And we? Now that we've fought and lied and sweated and stolen and hated as only the disappointed strugglers in a bitter, dead little Western town know how to do, what have we got to show for it?" The real mystery was how a Harvey Merrick could have come out of such an environment. "It's not for me to say why," the lawyer concludes, "in the inscrutable wisdom of God, a genius should ever have been called from this place of hatred and bitter waters. . . ."

The most powerful piece in the collection is "A Wagner Matinée." The story is simple enough; the terrible cultural aridity of small-town life. The central figure, Aunt Georgiana, is based on Willa Cather's own beloved aunt, who had helped nourish her devotion to music as a child in Red Cloud. The narrator, a young man from a small Nebraska town, now living in Boston, receives a letter, delayed in the post, informing him that his aunt, having inherited a small legacy, is due to arrive in Boston for a visit. The narrator, who, as he notes, "owed to this woman most of the good that ever came my way in my boyhood," is shocked by her appearance. She wore ill-fitting false teeth, "and her skin was as yellow as a Mongolian's from constant exposure to a pitiless wind and to the alkaline water which hardens the most transparent cuticle into a sort of flexible leather." Recalling her love of music, the nephew decides to take her to a matinee of Wagner overtures. At the thrill of response to the opening bars of the *Tannhäuser Overture* her nephew realizes "that for her this broke a silence of thirty years; the inconceivable silence of the plains." He is overwhelmed by "the sense of the waste and wear we are so powerless to combat; and I saw the tall naked house on the prairie, black and grim as a wooden fortress; the black pond where I learned to swim, its margin pitted with sun-dried cattle tracks; the rain-gullied clay banks about the naked house, the four dwarf ash seedlings where the dish cloths were always hung to dry before the kitchen door."

His aunt seems dazed by the torrent of music. When the concert is over, she sits motionless. The audience files out. The musicians put away their music and gather up their instruments, "leaving the stage to the chairs and music stands, empty as a winter cornfield." When her nephew speaks to rouse her from her reverie, "she burst into tears and sobbed pleadingly. 'I don't want to go, Clark. I don't want to go!' "

Her nephew understood. "For her, just outside the door of the concert hall, lay the black pond with the cattle-tracked bluffs; the tall, unpainted house, with weather-curled boards; naked as a tower, the crooked-back ash seedlings where the dish-cloths hung to dry; the gaunt, moulting turkeys picking up refuse about the kitchen door."

The larger significance of *The Troll Garden* was that through it Cather freed herself of her bitterness toward Red Cloud. In subsequent stories and in her novels she continued to paint vivid pictures of rural and small-town life, and she continued to depict the towns' bigotry and repressiveness, but now there were redeeming touches, most strikingly the vitality and exuberance of recent immigrants. The newly arrived Bohemians embodied the richness of a European tradition conspicuous for its joy in life. The Nebraska landscape, bleak and bare as it was, became the heroine in her work, and in numerous lyrical passages she evoked it as powerfully as any American writer has evoked a landscape.

The most practical consequence of *The Troll Garden* was that Sam McClure, frenetic and prescient as ever, sought her out and invited her to become an editor of his magazine. As he had paid court to Ida Tarbell ten years earlier in Paris, so he courted Willa Cather in Pittsburgh. He had just suffered the mass defections of Tarbell, Steffens, Ray Stannard Baker, and several other of his prize editors, who, worn out by his mercurial and quixotic temperament, had resigned to start their own journal, the *American Magazine*. Suppressing her misgivings, Cather accepted what certainly was one of the most prestigious editorial positions in American journalism.

Assisted by McClure's patiently enduring wife, Harriet, Cather poured her remarkable energies into running *McClure's Magazine*. If worldly success was important to the young woman from Red Cloud, Nebraska, still in her mid-thirties, her job was the impressive measure of it. In the same period she formed what was to be a lifelong attachment to a young woman of equally emancipated views, Edith Lewis. Dorothy Canfield and Isabelle McClung continued to be close friends. In addition, Cather became a friend of Sarah Orne Jewett, whose stories of small-town New England life she greatly admired and whose work had influenced her own. Jewett, who was in her mid-fifties, frail and in poor health, took a keen interest in Cather's career as a writer. She was concerned that the younger woman would dull her talents by the grinding routines of journalism. ". . . if you don't keep guard and mature your force, and above all, [take] the time and quiet to perfect your work, you will be writing things not much better than you did five years ago," Jewett warned her. ". . . Your vivid and exciting companionship in the office must not be your audience, you must find your own quiet center of life, and write from that to the world that holds offices, and all society, all Bohemia; the city, the country—in short, you must write to the human heart. . . ."

The strain of Cather's job—she became managing editor of *McClure's* in 1908—and the conflict in her own mind about her future as a serious writer as opposed to a journalist came to a crisis in 1911, when what appears to have been a nervous breakdown forced her to take a much needed break. She chose a long vacation with her brother Douglas in Arizona. Her months there taught her, in the words of one of her characters, "the inevitable hardness of human life. No artist gets far who doesn't know that. And you can't realize it with your mind. You have to realize it in your body; deep. It's an animal sort of feeling. I sometimes think it's the strongest of all."

The following year, 1912, saw the publication of a short story, "The Bohemian Girl," that marked a critically important development in her career. It was clear after "The Bohemian Girl" that her major effort would be directed at the novel as a form and that the thematic framework would be the struggle of the young to express their passionate involvement in life, their dreams and ideals in the face of the indifference or the hostility of their neighbors. The rural community/ small town would still be in large measure the enemy, or perhaps the thesis, and the vital force of youthful dreams and ambitions would be the antithesis. But Cather realized that to give life and color to her own work, the community and especially the land itself could not be depicted in unrelievedly somber colors. In addition, her own thinking had changed. Every year her attachment to her own roots seemed to grow stronger. She was no longer simply the exile; she had become the reconciler. The narrowness and bigotry of the town had their counterparts in the city. The tension between the inhibitions of the town and the yearnings of its young men and women was a metaphor for a struggle in the American soul between a crass and unlovely materialism and those things—beauty represented both in nature and in art—that gave life whatever joy and meaning it had.

"Bohemian" became a talismanic word for Cather. New York City was full of self-proclaimed "bohemians," refugees from joyless small towns like Red Cloud, trying, often not particularly successfully, to live more vibrant, responsive lives in the cities and worshiping art. It occurred to Cather that the real Bohemians of Red Cloud were the prototypes, the irrepressible adventurers of the spirit.

The plot of "The Bohemian Girl" is simple, almost banal. Nils Erikson, who has prospered modestly in the world, comes back after many years to Sand River Valley, where he grew up, to visit his mother, Old Lady Erikson, who rather scandalizes the county by her independent ways, driving around the countryside in her car and caring for it as skillfully as a man would. When Nils inquires about his brothers, his mother recites their various marriages and enumerates the grandchildren, showing disapproval of her Bohemian daughter-in-law who is married to her son Olaf. "I never thought much of Bohemians," she says curtly; "always drinking." Yet Clara Vavrika, whose good-natured father, Joe, runs the Bohemian saloon, is one of the magnets that have drawn Nils back to Sand River Valley. She is the sullen and dissatisfied wife of the stolid, oafish Olaf. "There was never such a family for having nothing ever happen to them but dinner and threshing," she tells Nils when they meet. "I'd almost be willing to die, just to have a funeral."

Later Nils tells his disapproving mother that Joe Vavrika's bar was "the one jolly house in this country for a boy to go to. All the rest of you were working yourselves to death, and the houses were mostly a mess, full of babies and washing and flies." Sensing Clara's restlessness and dissatisfaction and, above all, her feeling of a lack of fulfillment among the passive, stolid Norwegian farmers, Nils challenges her to escape with him.

Clara leaves with Nils, to the thrilled dismay of the residents of Sand River Valley, and the two plot to help Nils's youngest brother,

Eric, a bright and imaginative boy, make his own escape. But Eric, fleeing on a train for Omaha and freedom, thinks of his mother's need for him, leaves the Omaha coach, and returns to Sand River. "I've come back, Mother," he says, appearing silently at the kitchen door.

"Very well," his mother replies.

"How about the milking?"

"It's been done hours ago."

So at the end there is a virtue in staying as well as in flight. Love which sacrifices freedom is as strong and necessary a value as freedom itself.

After her months in Arizona and the appearance of "The Bohemian Girl" the die was cast for Cather. She resigned from her editorial position to devote herself virtually full time to her writing.

O Pioneers!, published in 1913, was her first successful novel, and significantly it was dedicated to Sarah Orne Jewett, "in whose beautiful and delicate work there is the perfection that endures." *O Pioneers!* was a classic evocation of the desolate and beautiful landscape of the Sand Hill region of Nebraska, where Cather had grown up—the "wild land" she called it. As the novel opens, a little Swedish boy, Emil Bergson, is crying in the bitter wind, trying to retrieve his cat from a telephone pole. His sister, Alexandra, enlists her friend Carl Linstrum to rescue the animal. The cat rescued, Emil finds solace in playing with a little Bohemian girl, Marie Tovesky, who is visiting her uncle, Joe Tovesky, proprietor of the "Bohemian bar." Emil and Alexandra travel out across the wintry fields to their farm, where their father, John Bergson, lies dying, worn out by his fight to wrest a living from the intractable earth. He recalls the successive disasters that held him back: "One winter his cattle had perished in a blizzard. The next summer one of his plow horses broke its leg in a prairie-dog hole and had to be shot. Another summer he lost his hogs from cholera, and a valuable stallion died from a rattlesnake bite. Time and again his crops had failed. He had lost two boys . . . and there had been the cost of sickness and death. Now, when he had at last struggled out of debt, he was going to die himself. He was only forty-six. . . ." It seemed to him that the land was "like a horse that no one knows how to harness, that runs wild and kicks things to pieces."

After Bergson's death the full weight of the management of the farm falls on Alexandra, who, it turns out, has a gift for farming, for experimenting, trying new ways to make the land yield, if not a bounty, a fair living. When the less hardy farmers, deeply in debt and their spirits broken, "skin out," Alexandra buys up their lands. Finally, she is mistress of the land, rather than merely its servant. Viewing her wheat crop, she realizes the hold that the recalcitrant hills of the divide have upon her. "For the first time, perhaps, since that land emerged from the waters of the geologic ages, a human face was set toward it with love and yearning. It seemed beautiful to her, rich and strong and glorious. Her eyes drank in the breadth of it, until tears blinded her. Then the Genius of the Divide, the great, free spirit which breathes across it, must have bent lower than it ever bent to a human will before. The history of every country begins in the heart of a man or a woman."

Juxtaposed against the Swedish settlers, with their grim Protestant ethic of tireless and generally joyless labor, is the lively Bohemian community, represented by Marie, Emil's playmate. Carl Linstrum, who has been Alexandra Bergson's closest friend, escapes to New York, where he becomes an engraver rather than the artist he hoped to be. Returning to the divide country sixteen years later, he finds Alexandra presiding over thousands of acres of farmland, made productive by her resourceful management. Her brothers view the returnee with the barely suppressed hostility with which such communities viewed defectors. To Alexandra, delighted to see her old friend, Carl looks restless and unhappy, like "an overworked German professor off on his holiday." Alexandra reveals the story of her "success." She tells him, "The land did it. It had its own little joke. It pretended to be poor because nobody knew how to work it right; and then, all at once, it worked itself. It woke up out of its sleep and stretched itself, and it was so big, so rich, that we suddenly found we were rich, just from sitting still." Emil is the principal beneficiary of Alexandra Bergson's prosperity. "I'm sure it was to have sons like Emil, and to give them a chance, that father left the old country," Alexandra says. Emil was "just like an American boy." He had graduated from the state university. "He is going to have a chance, a whole chance. . . . And that, she reflected, was what she had worked for. She felt well satisfied with her life."

Carl, perversely, misses the "wild old beast" that was the divide country of his youth. Alexandra confesses to such occasional feelings. They talk about the old days and "those who are gone," their labors and their sacrifices, which brought so many of them to premature graves. "And now the old story has begun to write itself . . ." Carl says softly. "Isn't it queer: there are only two or three human stories, and they go on repeating themselves as fiercely as if they had never happened before; like larks in the country, that have been singing the same five notes over for thousands of years." The passage is one of Cather's most eloquent expressions of the enduringness and power of the classic forms of human life.

Alexandra senses that although Carl has prospered modestly, he is dissatisfied with his job and indeed with his life. He admits as much. His work as an engraver has been debased by cheap new methods of reproduction; he is on his way to Alaska to seek his fortune in partnership with a friend. "I'd rather have your freedom than my land," Alexandra protests.

"Freedom so often means that one isn't needed anywhere," Carl replies. "Here yo are an individual, you have background of your own, you would be missed. But off there in the cities there are thousands of rolling stones like me. We are all alike; we have no ties, we know nobody, we own nothing. When one of us dies, they scarcely know where to bury him. . . ."

"We pay a high rent, too, though we pay differently," Alexandra says. "We grow hard and heavy here. We don't move lightly and easily as you do, and our minds get stiff. If the world were no wider than my cornfields, if there were not something beside this, I wouldn't feel that it was much worth while to work. . . ."

When Carl asks Alexandra to marry him, her brothers object strenuously on the ground that Carl is just an adventurer, attracted by her landed wealth.

Emil, back from college, finds Marie Tovesky, his childhood playmate, in an impulsive and unhappy marriage with a fellow Bohemian, Frank Shabata. From this point the novel moves to its tragic and melodramatic denouement. Emil and Marie revive their old infatuation. Although they struggle against their mutual attraction, they succumb. Marie's jealous husband, Frank, finds them in each other's arms and shoots and kills them both. Disturbed by the resistance to her marriage, Alexandra has sent Carl off to Alaska, but the death of her brother brings them together again. They will marry, thus, in Cather's scheme of things, uniting the larger world that Carl has experienced with Alexandra's passion for the land. The old cycle that Carl spoke of earlier will repeat itself, with the difference that the hard, narrow life of the rural community will be enhanced by what he has brought back to it of the larger world. But Alexandra is clearly the dominant figure. "Fortunate country, that is one day to receive hearts like Alexandra's into its bosom, to give them out again in the yellow wheat, in the rustling corn, in the shining eyes of youth," Cather concluded.

O Pioneers! is perhaps Cather's most successful novel, though *My Ántonia* is better known. Certainly it is the clearest statement of her major themes: the power of the land; the tension between rural life and the world outside, specifically the city; escape from the hard, inhibited, dehumanizing character of small-town and farm life and the return of those who have fled, drawn back to the land as though to a magnet; the efforts of immigrants coming from less inhibited, more spontaneous cultures to infuse their spirit into the somber world of Midwestern Protestantism; and, finally, the passion and power (and tragedy) of youth, full of dreams that are doomed to frustration. "Money and office and success are the consolations of impotence," Cather wrote. "Fortune turns kind to such solid people and lets them suck their bone in peace. She flicks her whip upon flesh that is more alive, upon that stream of hungry boys and girls who tramp the streets of every city, recognizable by their pride and discontent, who are the Future, and who possess the treasure of creative power."

Two years after *O Pioneers!*, *The Song of the Lark* was published. It is the story of Thea Kronborg, who grows up in the town of Moonstone, Colorado, and becomes a famous and wealthy opera singer. The most rewarding part of a novel that is too long (almost 600 pages) is Cather's insight into both the world of music and the character of the performer. The first part of the novel describes the long, demanding apprenticeship required to develop Thea's natural gift into a major talent. The second part describes her life as a successful, indeed famous singer. What is the "secret" of the artist? one character in *The Song of the Lark* asks another, referring to Thea Kronborg's success. "Her secret? It is every artist's secret—passion. That is all. It is an open secret, and perfectly safe. Like heroism, it is inimitable in cheap materials." To the degree that Cather penetrates the psychology of the famous performer, the novel is powerfully realized, but the reader feels, finally, that the author has indulged herself rather excessively in her expertise in the operatic world.

My Ántonia followed *The Song of the Lark* by three years, appearing in 1918. In it Cather returned to the story of a rural Nebraska community that she had developed so successfully in *O Pioneers!* The narrator is Jim Burden, and the heroine is Ántonia Shimerda, the daughter of a Bohemian immigrant, a man who in the old country was a person of some position and cultivation but who is unable to cope with the harsh and demanding Nebraska frontier.

The principal power in *My Ántonia*, as in *O Pioneers!*, lies in the entirely convincing re-creation of daily life on the Nebraska frontier, the quietly recounted details of farm and household activity, and the interaction of the different immigrant settlers to each other. Ántonia's father dies, in Jim Burden's opinion, of homesickness, of the simple incapacity to cope with the harsh world around him. With her father dead, Ántonia must work like a farmhand to help support her mother and assist her older brother, Ambrosch, but she is bursting with life and vitality. "Her rapid footsteps shook her own floors, and she routed lassitude and indifference wherever she came. She could not be negative or perfunctory about anything." As she got older, Ántonia became the most prominent of a little band of country girls, looked down upon by the proper townsfolk, who thought them wild and poorly brought up and worried about their effect on their sons. As Jim Burden put it, "All the young men felt the attraction of the fine, well-set-up country girls who had come to town to earn a living, and, in nearly every case, to help the father struggle out of debt, or to make it possible for the younger children in the family to go to school. . . . Black Hawk boys looked forward to marrying Black Hawk girls, and living in a brand-new little house with best chairs that must not be sat upon, and hand-painted china that must not be used. . . . The country girls were considered a menace to the social order. Their beauty shone out too boldly against a conventional background."

The land itself is the book's truest heroine. To Burden/Cather the long, harsh winters revealed the true nature of the divide country. They said, "This is reality, whether you like it or not. All those frivolities of summer, the light and the shadow, the living mask of green that trembled over everything, they were lies, and this is what was underneath. This is the truth."

Despite the attraction Jim Burden feels for Ántonia, for her high spirits and zest for life, he goes off to the university at Lincoln, flirts with scholarship, and then goes on to Harvard. After graduation he comes back to visit Black Hawk and learns that a glib-talking railroad man has beguiled Ántonia with the promise of marriage, got her pregnant, and then abandoned her. She returns to Black Hawk, disgraced in the eyes of her neighbors, and proceeds with her indomitable spirit to work for a local farmer and to give birth to and rear a healthy, happy girl. Burden and Ántonia have a tender reunion before he departs for law school and a career that keeps him away from Black Hawk for some twenty years. Word reaches him that Ántonia has married a young Bohemian farmer and that they have a large brood of children. When he finally returns to Black Hawk, drawn back primarily by his love for Ántonia, he is startled to find how much she has aged, but her spirits flow as strongly as ever. "Whatever else was gone, Ántonia had not lost the fire of life, the same exuberant spirit burned unquenched with a deeper, richer humanity beneath it." What most impresses Burden is the feeling of happy, harmonious life in the family itself; "they leaned this way and that, and were not afraid to touch each other." He notes, "She was a battered woman now, not a lovely girl; but she still had something that fires the imagination, could stop one's breath for a moment by a look or gesture that somehow revealed the meaning in common things. She had only to stand in the orchard, to put her hand on a little crab tree and look up at the apples, to make you feel the goodness of planting and tending and harvesting at last. All the strong things of the heart came out in her body, that had been so tireless in serving generous emotions.

"It was no wonder that her sons stood tall and straight. She was a rich mine of life, like the founders of early races." It seems to Burden that he has come home at last to *his* Ántonia. For the future his life would be closely tied to theirs, her and her husband and their sons. "Now I understood that the same road was to bring us together again. Whatever we had missed, we possessed together the precious, the incommunicable past."

The novel ends on this quietly elegiac note: The "incommunicable past" is more powerful than the uncertain present, love endures, friendship endures, the land, tamed at last, endures, and joy flows from it to those who care for it in the true spirit.

The war which began for the United States in 1917 had its effect in Red Cloud as in every other community around the country. Willa Cather's young cousin Grosvenor Cather enlisted and died in France. As Claude Wheeler he became the hero of her darkest book, *One of Ours,* which appeared in 1922 and was dedicated to Cather's mother. The handsome and brilliant young Claude decides, while still a boy, that he must escape from Frankfort, a rural community in the Sand Hill country of Nebraska. Claude and his family are the first "native Americans" to be the central figures in a Cather novel. Claude's parents come from New England. His mother is a schoolteacher from Vermont; his father, Nat Wheeler, is, in contrast with his hustling neighbors, a large, impressive, easygoing man. "He had come to this part of Nebraska when the Indian and the buffalo were still about, remembered the grasshopper year and the big cyclone, had watched the farms emerge one by one from the great rolling page where once only the wind wrote its story. He had encouraged new settlers to take up homesteads, urged on courtships, lent young fellows the money to marry on, seen families grow and prosper; until he felt a little as if all this were his own enterprise . . . he liked every sort of human creature; he liked good people and honest people, and he liked rascals and hypocrites almost to the point of loving them."

Claude excels in school, and after a brief period at a stifling little denominational college in Lincoln he is allowed to transfer to the university, where his intellectual life blossoms and where he meets the cultivated and expressive German family the Erlichs. They open an intoxicating world to Claude, and he falls hopelessly in love with Mrs. Erlich, the mother of his university friends.

Although Claude has dreamed of escaping from Frankfort to a career in the larger world, he dutifully returns to help his father farm and becomes engaged to Enid Royce, a dedicated prohibitionist, who drives all over the state attending temperance meetings. Claude's closest woman friend in Frankfort, the schoolteacher Gladys Farmer, who marries Claude's successful and tightfisted brother Bayliss, dreads the marriage. "If he married Enid," she reflects, "that would be the end. He would go about strong and heavy . . . ; a big machine with the springs broken inside." Claude marries Enid nonetheless and discovers she is frigid. "Everything about a man's embrace was distasteful to Enid; something inflicted upon women, like the pain of childbirth,— for Eve's transgression perhaps. This repugnance was more than physical; she disliked ardour of any kind, even religious ardour." He is trapped in the town and trapped in his loveless marriage.

When the war comes, Claude, who, through his friends the Erlichs, has had great admiration for German culture, is dismayed. "He had always been taught that the German people were pre-eminent in the virtues Americans most admire; a month ago he would have said they had all the ideals a decent American boy would fight for. The invasion of Belgium was contradictory to the German character as he knew it in his friends and neighbours."

When Enid goes off to China to nurse her ill missionary sister, Claude, who has been working his father's farm, decides to enlist in the United States Army. The last half of the novel is a remarkable recreation of military life. The war brings a strange kind of fulfillment for Claude. He makes an excellent officer, courageous and regardful of his men. His life seems finally to have taken on a meaning and direction. When he is killed in the final offensive of the war, his mother mourns him as part of a lost world; it seems to her "as if the flood of meanness and greed had been held back just long enough for the boys to go over, and then swept down and engulfed everything that was left at home." In the sordidness, the self-seeking, and the repression at home there lay the seeds of a terrible disillusionment. Mrs. Wheeler comforts herself with the thought that her son "died believing his own country better than it was and France better than any country can ever be. And those were beautiful beliefs to die with. She realized that she would have dreaded his awakening, she sometimes even doubts whether he could have borne at all that last, desolating disappointment."

One of the most important sources of Claude Wheeler's war experiences were the letters of Victor Chapman, the aviator son of John Jay Chapman, who had died fighting with the Lafayette Escadrille. Cather was indeed indefatigable in searching out accounts of the American soldiers in France, and before she finished the novel, she and Edith Lewis visited the battlefields of France.

One of Ours was harshly criticized by many critics on the mistaken ground that it glorified war, but for the first time one of Cather's novels achieved the status of best seller and brought her substantial monetary rewards. It won the Pulitzer Prize in 1922, two years after Edith Wharton had won the same prize for *The Age of Innocence*.

In the flood of what we might call the literature of disillusion that followed the Treaty of Versailles, *One of Ours* is perhaps the most poignant. Willa Cather had more novels to write, but with the world she had made particularly her own, the farms and small towns of the Middle West, the divide, the Sand Hill country of Nebraska, she had already carved for herself a unique place in her country's enduring literature.

In much the same spirit as Edith Wharton, who toward the close of her life was strongly drawn to the Roman Catholic Church as she experienced it in France, Willa Cather joined her parents in becoming a confirmed member of the Episcopal Church in Nebraska.

Ellen Glasgow was born in 1873 (the same year as Willa Cather) in Richmond, Virginia. The Glasgows were of Scotch-Irish ancestry, and they had suffered, like every Southern family, from the devastating consequence of the War between the States, as Southerners preferred to call the Civil War. Ellen Glasgow was the youngest of nine children. The family was not a happy one. Her father was a remote and severe man. "His virtues," she wrote, "were more than Calvinistic; they were Roman. With complete integrity, and an abiding sense of responsibility, he gave his wife and children everything but the one thing they needed most, and that was love. Yet he was entirely unselfish, and in his long life . . . he never committed a pleasure." He had been impoverished by the war and the period of Reconstruction. In Richmond he ran an ironworks that, with the general recovery of the South, prospered enough to meet the needs of his large family.

Ellen Glasgow's earliest recollection was of terror—"a face without a body staring in at me, a vacant face, round, pallid, grotesque, malevolent." As a very young child her mother was the life-giving presence. To her, she wrote years later, she owed everything, "mental or physical." Glasgow was a distressingly frail and sickly child, "born without a skin," her black mammy, Lizzie, would exclaim in despair. Lizzie was even more important than her mother to Glasgow; she was her constant companion from the time she was three until she was seven. With her the delicate child lived "a life of wandering adventure." Lizzie was "endowed with an unusual intelligence, a high temper, and sprightly sense of humor." As a concession to her disposition toward nightmares and visions, Glasgow slept with her mother throughout her childhood.

When she was still a young child, the Glasgows moved to a large old house in Richmond, where Ellen Glasgow was to live for the rest of her life, aside from interludes in New York and Europe. "The many tragedies of my life, and fair measure at least of the happiness have come in this house," she wrote. "The fibers of my personality are interwoven, I feel, with some indestructible element of the place; and this element is superior to time and chance. . . ." When she was seven, her beloved Lizzie returned to the family, a few miles away, for whom she had earlier worked. It was Glasgow's first experience of loss, an experience that was to recur many times during her life. "It was," she wrote, "as if I could look ahead and see that the happiest time of my life was now over." The storytelling magic of Lizzie survived, and soon the seven-year-old child was including in her bedtime prayers the supplication "O God, let me write books! Please, God, let me write books!" From that time on there was never any doubt in her mind that "writing books" was to be her goal in life. Unhappy as Ellen Glasgow's childhood was, she found escape "from hostile circumstances—from school and fear and God altogether"—in the summer, when she roamed the fields of the family's farm outside Richmond. There she indulged to her heart's content in what became a lifelong infatuation with nature.

When Glasgow was ten years old, she was, in her words, "overtaken by a tragic occurrence which plunged my childhood into grief and anxiety, and profoundly affected, not only my mind and character, but my whole future life." Virtually overnight her mother was changed "from a source of radiant happiness into a chronic invalid, whose nervous equilibrium was permanently damaged." It seems to have been the kind of hysterical depression to which the young doctor Sigmund Freud was giving so much attention in Vienna. Ellen Glasgow's mother insisted that she and one of her sisters continue to sleep in her bedroom, and the two children "knew scarcely a night that was not broken by a sudden start of apprehension, or by a torment of pity and terror which was as physical as the turn of a screw in our flesh." The effects were felt throughout the family.

Glasgow herself suffered various nervous debilities—headaches and insomnia most commonly. She was able to attend school for only a few months each year, and she acquired such education as she had by her own voracious reading. Her frailty did not exclude her from the social life that was a kind of birthright of upper-class Southern girls. She was pretty and popular and loved to dance. At the University of Virginia, she recalled, "I won all the admiration and felt all the glorified sensations of a Southern belle in the Victorian age." Although she was, as a woman, not allowed to enroll at the university, she found a host of intellectual mentors, attracted by her intelligence and eagerness to learn. She read *Progress and Poverty* and developed a keen interest "in social history and in theories of economics," and already at work on a long novel, she waved aside the coming-out party at which young Richmond girls were formally introduced to society. When she was seventeen, she joined the City Mission to do social work, in the spirit of Jane Addams, and to observe at first hand the life of the poor. Soon she was a convert to socialism. Deeply affected by "the wrongs and general unfairness of what we call modern civilization," she dreamed of "running off to join some vague revolutionary movement."

Another severe trauma came with the sudden death of Glasgow's long-ailing mother and the effect of the loss on the family, especially on her father. Ellen Glasgow paid a kind of homage to her mother's memory by burning the manuscript of her novel, entitled *The Descendants,* and it was a year before she could resume her writing. She found some consolation in what she called "philosophical histories" that suggested a meaning in humanity's common experience. She went on to "German scientists" and to Darwin, Spencer, Kant, Fichte, and Schelling. Friedrich Nietzsche's *Thus Spake Zarathustra* proved the most powerful of all. She tried spiritualism and read, like revelation, William Lecky's *History of Rationalism*. When she looked back from the perspective of old age, it seemed to her that in her "own rebellious way, [she] was trying to find God, the God of Plotinus, or the God of St. Francis. . . . Something was wrong, I felt, in the mental state of the eighteen-nineties. I felt it, I knew it, though I could not say what it was. Ideas, like American fiction, had gone soft. In a world and a period that were simply waiting to be examined and interpreted, in terms of reality (by which I do not mean literary 'realism'), the literary mind had gone delirious over novels that dropped from the presses already mellowing before they were ripe. Critics and public alike rushed to devour incredible romances placed in impossible countries. . . . All America had dropped back into adolescence in fiction; but in the South there was not only adolescence to out grow, there was an insidious sentimental tradition to live down. . . . Southerners did not publish, did not write, did not read. Their appetite for information was Gargantuan but personal; it was either satisfied by oratory, or it was sated by gossip." She was determined to defy both those traditions: the "unripe" imagination that seemed to dominate the literary world and the dogged antiintellectualism of the South. She would write in a new vein; she would expose "the inherent falseness of much Southern tradition" and the mawkish sentimentality of American literature in general. She was determined to "write of all the harsher realities beneath manners, beneath social customs, beneath the poetry of the past, and the romantic nostalgia of the present. I would write," she told herself, "of an outcast, of an illegitimate 'poor white,' of a thinker, and of a radical socialist."

By the time she was eighteen, Glasgow had written two novels, one entitled *Sharp Realities*, the other, *The Descendant*, the first draft of which she had destroyed at her mother's death. She decided it was time for her to go to New York City and find a publisher. She had been urged to send her manuscripts to a "literary adviser" who advertised that he could help young writers find publishers for a fee. Glasgow sent him the manuscript of *Sharp Realities* and followed it to New York, where she discovered that the "adviser" had not read it and was interested only in seducing her. Glasgow fled and burned the novel, determined never to write again.

The novel that Ellen Glasgow picked up after she had recovered from what might be called the *Sharp Realities* episode dealt with the illegitimate son of a prostitute who is reared by a puritanical farm couple who never let him forget that his origins marked him as hopelessly inferior to "decent folk." Michael Akersham, fiercely ambitious and bitterly resentful of the indignities to which he has been subjected, escapes to New York, where he finds a job as editor of a radical journal. There he also meets the talented and independent young artist Rachel Gavin (who clearly represents Glasgow's image of herself). In their intense and difficult relationship each struggles not for dominance but for the preservation of self. The novel, as one might expect in the work of one so young, is full of talk—about politics, about love, about the conflict between science and religion, all topics that were vitally important to Glasgow herself. In the words of one character, "From our present state of inequalities and ignorance there is but one broad, upward way for humanity, a road that leads from the depths of sin and superstition to the cool heights of knowledge and demonstrable facts—there is such a road, and that road is Science. Without Science we would never have left the Middle Ages. Without Science we should still be trembling before a god in every breeze, preaching persecution and damnation as essential principles. There is but one salvation for mankind, and that is—" Here the speaker is interrupted by a voice that "shrieks 'Humanity!'" Another proposes religion, and a third wealth.

The novel ends with just that melodramatic twist so dear to the hearts of a predominantly feminine audience. Michael kills a fellow radical journalist in a blind rage, is arrested, and serves a prison term for manslaughter. Released, bitter and broken in health and spirit, he finds that Rachel, whom he deserted, is still waiting to love and care for him in his final illness.

What the novel appears, finally, to be about, the talk of contemporary issues aside, is the fact that as "modern" as Rachel is, and as deeply involved in her promising career as an artist, her feminine capacity for loving and caring for the man she loves is paramount.

Having finished her novel, Glasgow decided she had to make another assault on the New York publishing world. A friend of one of her unofficial teachers at the University of Virginia arranged a lunch at Delmonico's with Price Collier, a reader for the publishing house of Macmillan, who told her she looked as if she were no more than sixteen and should go home and get married. She informed Collier that she was a mature twenty-two. He would not even read her manuscript. It would only raise false hopes. There was no chance that Macmillan would publish it. She should produce babies rather than books.

Glasgow persevered, discovering, in the process that "the autocrats of American literature composed a self-centered group of benevolent old gentlemen in the Authors' Club" who decided in large part what was literature and what was not. Even though she could not read their novels, she "longed . . . to know these old gentlemen, who, however uninteresting in print, were at least 'literary,' " a state that seemed to her to approach bliss.

The Descendant was rescued from oblivion by the kindly intervention of the editor of a textbook publishing house who read it as a favor to Glasgow's University of Virginia professor and declared that nothing had moved him so much since he read Victor Hugo as a boy. Ellen Glasgow was overwhelmed. She had known "few of what we call the natural pleasures of childhood and girlhood. Fear and illness and heartbreak had pursued" her for as far back as she could remember. Now she was to be a published author.

When *The Descendant* was published anonymously, some critics attributed it to Harold Frederic, the well-known author of *The Damnation of Theron Ware*. It caused a minor sensation, especially when it was discovered that its author was a twenty-two-year-old Southern woman, but Glasgow was dissatisfied. She was shrewd enough to be conscious of the novel's serious shortcoming. "What I understood more and more" she wrote, "was that I needed a philosophy of fiction. I needed a technique of working. Above all I felt the supreme necessity of a prose style so pure and flexible that it could bend without breaking." In the midst of her perplexity she discovered Tolstoy's *War and Peace* and knew at once what was missing from her own work. "Life must use art; art must use life." She decided that she would take as her canvas the world she knew best, her own South, the South from which she had once longed to escape.

The Descendant was followed by *Phases of an Inferior Planet,* a title which promised more than the novel delivered. Despite her expressed intentions of dealing with life honestly and truly without sentiment, the book's sentimental romanticism was hardly exceeded by those writers she so scorned. Somewhat better was *The Battle-Ground,* which appeared in 1902, a typical novel of the Civil War. Filled with scenes of battle and of pillaging by Yankees, it is the story of Dandridge Montjoy, his heroism and his suffering in the war and his return to his childhood sweetheart, Betty Ambler. *The Battle-Ground* was a best seller and brought Ellen Glasgow enough money to afford a trip to England, where she visited Thomas Hardy and took in the literary sights.

The Voice of the People was the fruit of Glasgow's determination to break out of the existing conventions of the novel. Nick Burr is the son of a poor white who as a young boy rejected a life as a peanut farmer: "There ain't nothin' in peanut-raisin'. It's just farmin' fur crows. I'd ruther be a judge." Burr announces his ambition to Judge Bassett, an old Virginia aristocrat, who decides to help the boy realize it. The novel explores with considerable discernment and sympathy the relationship among the impoverished old aristocracy, the rising class of small farmers, and the freed slaves. Much of the book recounts old General Battle's desperately hard struggle to hold on to the shattered remains of the family plantation and take care of the numbers of people, black and white, who depend on him. Young Nicholas, with his sharp intelligence and restless ambition, is drawn to Eugenia Battle, daughter of the general, who reads Plato and shows other inappropriately intellectual inclinations, but they both come to accept the fact that despite their love for each other, the barrier of class is too high to surmount. Eugenia marries an equally ambitious young man of her own class, Dudley Webb, and single-minded Nicholas becomes first a successful lawyer and businessman and then a rapidly rising politician. At last Burr and Webb confront each other for control of the political apparatus of the state and the plum of the governorship. Burr wins the race, but he has never reconciled himself to losing Eugenia. As a governor he is exemplary, but on the eve of becoming his state's Senator he is shot and killed by a mob while trying to prevent the lynching of a black man accused of raping a white woman. *The Voice* marks a striking advance in style and power. Although the earlier novels had been enthusiastically reviewed, *The Voice* established Ellen Glasgow as a major American writer.

The Deliverance, published the same year as *The Voice of the People,* confirmed her status as an accomplished storyteller with her unique perspective. Like *The Voice,* the novel deals with the tension between the old order and the new. After the Civil War Bill Fletcher, the sharp and unscrupulous former overseer on the Blake plantation, wrests the ruined plantation from the Blake family and reduces young Christopher Blake to the status of a hired tobacco hand. The Blakes live a marginal existence economically, while the coarse and brutal Fletcher sends his daughter, Maria, off to a girls' finishing school. She returns very much the proper young lady, caught between the rough, aggressive world of her father and brothers and the decaying gentility of the Blakes.

Maria Fletcher and Christopher Blake fall passionately in love. Rather than betray a deathbed promise to his mother, Christopher renounces his love for Maria, who is superior to him in education, experience of the world, and sensitivity to nature but irredeemably inferior in social position. She marries a man of her class named Wyndham. Christopher Blake's revenge on Bill Fletcher is systematically to turn the latter's son Will against his father while making a drunkard and a ne'er-do-well of the young man. The drunken Will becomes involved in a violent scene with his father, kills him, and flees for help to Christopher, whom he considers his only friend. The remorseful Christopher confesses to the crime to protect Will and Maria. He is sentenced to prison for eight years on a charge of manslaughter, but before he has finished his term, Will confesses to the murder, and Christopher is free, free to marry Maria, whose husband has meanwhile conveniently died, as unwanted, unneeded, or wicked husbands are wont to do in all such romances.

Following the publication of *The Deliverance*, Glasgow, doubting her own powers as a novelist and depressed over her growing deafness, suffered a nervous collapse. "Science," she wrote, "had failed my body as ruinously as religion had failed my soul. Both quests, physical and spiritual, had ended in disillusionment. . . . It was then that I began to cultivate the ironic mood." She departed for Europe to try to recover her emotional equilibrium. "Though it is true that I was a born novelist," she wrote after the European trip, "it is true also that I flung myself into my work as desperately as a man might fling himself into a hopeless battle," to escape the "panic terror" that constantly stalked her. It was the time also of her great romance. She fell madly in love with a married man. When she looked back at it from the last years of her life, the whole episode still seemed "incredibly wild and romantic." It was, for her, "the one thing that has not passed," as fresh and vivid as "in the first moment of passion." An unsuspecting friend remarked that she had suddenly changed and blossomed "in a single spring." For seven years she lived "in an arrested pause between dreaming and waking. All reality was poured into . . . a solitary emotion."

The sublimation of the physical side of the relationship brought Glasgow a consuming mystical experience in which she felt at one with the soul of the universe. When her beloved died, Glasgow felt that she had received a gift of inestimable value in their love; it sustained her throughout her life.

In the years of her romance with the man she simply referred to as "Gerald," Glasgow wrote three novels. After his death she published *The Wheel of Life,* which she regarded, "from every point of view," as a failure. The novel concerns two devoted women friends, a common plot element in novels by woman writers. Gerty Bridewell is the pampered child of luxury. Her rich and indulgent husband treats her like a beautiful plaything, an adornment to his style of life. Perry Bridewell is a typical representative of his class and sex, "large, florid and impressive. . . . His life corresponded so evenly with his bodily impulses that the perfection of the adjustment had produced in him the amiable exterior of an animal that is never crossed. It was a case in which supreme selfishness exerted the effect of personality." Glasgow was at some pains to make it clear that Perry Bridewell is a type far more than an individual. He gives off "that appearance of ardent vitality which has appealed so strongly to the imagination of women."

Gerty Bridewell smokes six cigarettes a day and stays in bed till noon, signs of her general dissolution. Her closest friend is Laura Wilde, despite the fact that Laura's eccentric family, with its musical and literary tastes, is the antithesis of Gerty's hectic social milieu. Laura, determined to become a poet, lives a simple, Spartan life.

Even rough Perry Bridewell recognizes something peculiarly attractive about Laura: "She looks human, natural, real." He tells his highly artificial wife, "By Jove, she looks as if she were capable of big emotions—as if, too, you could like her without making love." He "felt suddenly that there were depths of consciousness which he had never sounded, vivid experiences which he had never glimpsed. 'She is different—but how is she different?' he asked himself. . . . Is she simply a bigger personality, or is she really more of a woman than any woman I have ever known?" That, of course, was really the heart of the matter for the woman writers. They all, to one degree or another, were devoted to the effort to establish the image of the new woman as "really more of a woman" than her predecessors.

Arnold Kemper is another handsome, self-indulgent male animal, and Laura is drawn irresistibly to him, although she is well aware of his reputation as a pursuer of women and *bon vivant:* He "had lived for the world and the world had repaid him." The struggle in Laura's soul is the struggle between her career as a writer and love—love, in this instance, represented by a man not too different in type from Perry Bridewell. Discovering that Kemper has betrayed her by resuming an old romance on the eve of their wedding, Laura flees, experiences all kinds of melodramatic horrors, and is reconciled with Gerty "in that intimate knowledge [between women] which is uttered without speech." She dedicates herself to her poetry and to work with poor children of the city. She feels a "love for the world—for all mankind." Now her happiness is the "happiness of freedom." She also discovers that she is in love with an old friend, a middle-aged editor, "a gaunt, scholarly man in his forties, with broad, singularly bony shoulders" and an "expression of kindly humour." If they marry, their marriage will be, it is implied, one of mature companionship and love ripened by suffering and experience. Both had come to understand "that all life is an evolution into the consciousness of God."

If *The Wheel of Life* is one of the less successful of Ellen Glasgow's novels, it is also the one in which, one suspects, she most plainly worked out her own relationship to the opposite sex. In this sense it is a novel of renunciation. Laura is Glasgow. Her rejection of Kemper, the healthy animal, and her rededication to her poetry and to the service of humanity corresponded to Gerald's death and Glasgow's commitment to the cause of women's suffrage. As she put it, she spoke "the first word ever uttered in Virginia in favor of votes for women." If that was somewhat of an exaggeration, it was true that no Virginian woman of Glasgow's prominence had spoken out so boldly, and it did start "an incredible storm of protest."

Almost a decade after Gerald's death, Ellen Glasgow gave her heart away again, this time to a rather charming but absurdly pompous and self-important Richmond character, whom she referred to as Harold. When he proved fickle, she tried, like a character in one of her novels, to kill herself. Increasingly she found refuge in England, where she enjoyed a literary celebrity never quite accorded her at home.

Glasglow's "war novel," *The Builders*, which appeared in 1919, was one of her lesser efforts. In it she dealt with the the effect of the war and the changes it brought about in a small Virginia town. "The world was changing—changing," and the heroine, young Caroline Meade, had to adapt to it. To an observer from another world, Glasgow wrote, the government of the United States might have appeared "a composite image of the time—sentimental, evasive of realities, idealistic in speech, and materialistic in purpose and action." But the challenge of the German enemy was a "challenge to the principles which are the foundation-stones of Western civilization. . . . The cause was the cause of humanity, therefore it was America's war."

The novel ends with a letter from a soldier friend of Caroline Meade's. The problem that faces the world, David Blackburn writes, is the relationship of the "individual citizen within the democracy, the national life with the international." Only America can solve it, and this must be the task of the "next generation or two . . . our chance of lasting services. . . . That is the only justification of the lives that have been sacrifices. America itself is in the process of changing from a mass of divergent groups, from a gathering of alien races, into a single people. . . . The war has forged us into a positive entity." The nation must achieve a balance between the "Northern belief in solidarity with the ardent Southern faith in personal independence and responsibility. . . . To see America avoid the pitfall of arbitrary power and the morass of visionary socialism; to see her lead the nations, not in the path of selfish conquest, but . . . toward the promised land of justice and liberty—this is a dream worth living for, and worth dying for. . . ."

The novel ends on the familiar note, in Glasgow's novels, of renunciation. Caroline Meade accepts the reality that her love for David Blackburn, who is married to a friend, must be sublimated to their respective duties. The sacrifice required of them is simply the reflection of the larger sacrifices required of all America if the nation is to play the role of unselfish leader in the world.

Gertrude Atherton had a life more romantic than any of her novels. Born in 1857 in San Francisco and thus the oldest of the four women writers, she spent her early years at her grandfather's ranch "down the peninsula." Her grandfather Stephen Franklin, who was the dominant figure in her life as long as he lived, was a descendant of Benjamin Franklin, known as the "handsomest of San Francisco's many handsome men," in the words of his granddaughter. He had lost a fortune and spent the latter part of his life as an executive of the Bank of California. His daughter, also named Gertrude, was by way of being a professional beauty, a much courted belle, whose major preoccupation was her appearance—"very beautiful, vivacious, flirtatious, fascinating, with a naturally brilliant mind and not an atom of common sense." One of her most ardent suitors was a Yankee named Thomas Horn, whom her family insisted she marry. He was, they declared, "the only man worth considering who wishes to marry you. He is rich now and will be richer. . . . Youth passes quickly . . . and only in youth has a woman the power to marry well." Gertrude Franklin was only nineteen; she wept and protested, but her parents were adamant, and she married Horn. They quarreled bitterly, and he took to drink. A divorce followed after three years of marriage, and San Francisco society was shocked; it was the first divorce in the city. The only substantial fruit of the marriage was their daughter, Gertrude, who was an angelic-looking blonde but was, by her own account, a little fiend. Meanwhile, her irresistible mother was again besieged by suitors. Gertrude Horn chose from the pack John Frederick Uhlhorne, scion of an old New York family of Dutch ancestry. He was aristocratic, handsome and, apparently wealthy. Young Gertrude Horn hated him, and he apparently reciprocated. It turned out that poor Uhlhorne was a worse husband than his predecessor; he was an alcoholic, a gambler, and a forger. Stephen Franklin put him on a ship bound for South America and forbade him to return to California.

Gertrude Horn was educated rather haphazardly at a series of private girls' schools in the San Francisco Bay area but most intensely and thoroughly by her grandfather, who told her, "You have naturally a bright mind, wayward as it is, and it is time to improve it. I wish you to become a well-read intellectual woman, and it is not too soon to begin. You will read aloud to me for two hours every night." What followed was a heavy diet of Washington Irving, supplemented by Adolphe Thiers's *History of the French Revolution,* David Hume's *History of England,* and *Jane Eyre.*

After word reached the Franklin family of John Uhlhorne's impoverished death in a New York hospital, the older Gertrude, thirty-four and still strikingly beautiful, was once more besieged by suitors. The younger Gertrude, doubtless considered a liability by her mother, who still hoped to make an advantageous marriage, and who was in any event wild and rebellious, was shipped off to stay with an aunt in Kentucky and attend a fashionable girls' school there. The experiment was not a success. The aunt gave up after a year and shipped her back to California, saying, as she kissed her good-bye, "You have your points, Gertrude, and I can't help liking you, but I am free to say that I was never so glad to see the last of anyone in my life. I think you are headed straight for the devil but I shall pray for you."

Her mother met her at the station in a buggy driven by a young man, George Atherton, whom the daughter disliked extremely. He was in exile from his wealthy and prominent family because he was paying court to the widow, fourteen years his senior. The young Gertrude was a strikingly attractive blonde, statuesque as they used to say, with a profile like that of the famous Gibson girl. Atherton shifted his attentions from the mother to the daughter and bedeviled her with proposals of marriage. "Handsome and magnetic" as he was, with "fine manners," Gertrude Horn thought him silly and egotistical; "he talked a good deal, although he never said anything," she wrote caustically. Finally, bored and depressed by the constant rain, she yielded to Atherton's importunings. They eloped.

The Athertons, who had been horrified at their son's pursuit of a twice-married (and once divorced) woman so many years older, apparently were relieved. In any event they accepted the daughter into their large, closely knit Catholic family, dominated by Mrs. Atherton, a grand Spanish lady who spoke little English. Faxon Dean Atherton, Gertrude Atherton's father-in-law, had been born in Dedham, Massachusetts. Seeking his fortune in Chile, he had met and married Dominga, and six of their seven children had been born in Valparaiso. The Atherton clan lived in Fair Oaks near Menlo Park in the home of the first Mexican governor of California. The setting was classic California, a low, rambling house set amid verdant gardens and palm tree–shaded lawns.

The younger Athertons' marriage was not a success. George Atherton had no business sense and failed in one venture after another, all financed by his father. A spectacular disaster was his effort to manage a 45,000-acre Spanish land grant at Milpitas. Dozens of poor Mexican families who had squatted on the land were evicted, a very painful episode which was used in one of Gertrude Atherton's novels, *Los Cerritos*.

Despite Atherton's lack of responsibility and his petty meanness with money, his bride felt he was "a decent sort on the whole. . . . Although he had an insane temper, [he] was invariably good-natured when there was nothing to provoke it." Bored and restless and angry at her husband's parsimoniousness, she decided to try her hand at writing. She had shown a flare for fiction in school, and her grandfather had encouraged her before her marriage. Like many young women in similar situations, she found that writing was virtually the only thing a young woman could do to make money. Writing was frowned on as a female activity by the respectable, especially if it resulted in publication; that was considered bad taste. Nonetheless, Gertrude Atherton set to work, to the intense irritation of her husband, who complained that she was failing to be properly attentive to him. Worst of all, she chose a thinly disguised family scandal as her topic, and though she published under a pseudonym, there was outrage in her family and in San Francisco society when word of her authorship leaked out.

George Atherton's business failures and his inability to hold a job meant that he was constantly around the house. It seemed to her "the worst trial I have yet been called upon to endure . . . having a husband continually on my hands. I couldn't talk to him," she added, "for he was interested in nothing but horses." As Gertrude Atherton continued writing pieces for the San Francisco literary journal the *Argonaut,* her husband complained constantly that she didn't love him and that he was going mad from the humiliation she had brought on him and the family by insisting on continuing her writing. The arrival of two children provided brief distractions, but the boy died of diphtheria when he was five and the girl's upbringing was closely supervised by the elder Mrs. Atherton and a squad of servants. Gertrude Atherton eventually forced her husband to move to San Francisco so that she could pursue her career as a journalist more actively, and she secretly rejoiced when he decided to sail to Chile to visit the scenes of his early childhood. When word arrived a few weeks later that he had died of a stomach hemorrhage, she had difficulty concealing her relief. She was free.

After the death of her husband Gertrude Atherton persuaded his extremely dubious mother to give her a small allowance and her blessing so that she could establish herself as an author in New York. There she found that publishers were too timid and conventional to accept manuscripts that seemed to them daring in subject matter and treatment. Atherton was also convinced that there was active prejudice against her as a Californian and as someone without proper credentials who was trying to crash the Eastern literary establishment and was, moreover, a woman. There were, to be sure, any number of popular women writers, but they had been approved and processed through William Dean Howells and the other ruling elders. Like Ellen Glasgow, Atherton believed that the influence of Howells was baneful, inhibiting the development of new ideas and new approaches to the writing of fiction. When she finally found a publisher bold enough to take *What Dream May Come* (his first and last publication), she was startled at the savagery of the attacks on the book and the intensely personal attacks on her. Part of that reaction, she suspected, was due to the fact that the publisher tried to exploit her Gibson girl blond beauty and youth.

The demoralized young author fled to Europe, first to England and then to Paris. The British, who have always been charmed by California and by handsome American women, received her warmly. She met George Moore (who had been recently denounced for writing "obscene literature"), Thomas Hardy, Henry James, and other literary lions, toothed and toothless. In France she took refuge in a convent and, drawing on the experience at the Atherton ranch at Milpitas, wrote *Los Cerritos*. It was her first "California" novel. Its subject is a romance between Carmelita, the vivid young niece of the famous bandit Joaquín Murieta, and the rich but jaded young man, Alexander Tremaine, who inherits the land on which Carmelita and her family and friends live and sets out to evict all the "squatters," among them Carmelita, "Nature's own child." Alexander Tremaine (he has "light cold blue eyes" with "latent power" and, on occasion "a humorous twinkle"; his hair, of course, is black) "had started in life with many ideals. He wished to be a reformer, a wise and self-abnegating statesman, a friend of the people, a swayer of the thoughts of men." All his ideals have fled when, armed with an inherited fortune, he finds that if he is to play a political role, he must use his money to bribe his way into power. He withdraws from politics "disheartened, worn out with futile anger. . . ." Retiring to New York, he is "aghast at the sleepless epidemic for wealth. . . . 'Money!' shrieked the flying trains as they plunged into the crowded, reeking districts of squalor. 'Money!' absently muttered the fur-wrapped man on the hotel steps as he waited for the bare-footed news-boy to give him change. 'Money!' sang the very air in endless echo." Still in search of an ideal worth committing himself to, Tremaine crosses to England, where he "plunged into the thick of Socialism." He attends meetings and engages in endless debates. He allows himself "to be buttonholed by every long-haired, illogical enthusiast who chose to spoil the shape of his coat. He read all the literature of the movement, calm, maniacal, practical and visionary." And then he gives it all up as a delusion and returns to California, where he marries a rich and beautiful young socialite. "Life and philosophy had taught him one great lesson—that personal happiness was the only good here below worth striving for."

Alexander Tremaine's wife pursues an idle existence at Menlo Park, trying in vain to extract some vital life from "that fashionable suburb's placid monotony and soporific physiology. . . . 'How I hate the place!'" she reflects. "'It is the Sleepy Hollow of California.'"

The plight of the impoverished Mexicans he is about to evict from his ranch stirs the dormant social conscience of Alexander Tremaine (as, of course, does the wild beauty of Carmelita). The Catholic padre gives him a lecture, reminding him that he cannot, despite his millions, escape responsibility for the social ills of the world. "Socialism is a failure," the padre tells Tremaine, "and the further it develops the deeper does it demonstrate its impotence. It will be a hundred years before Henry George is recognized as a great man. I see no present solution of a great and intricate problem but that the rich should realize their duty to the poor. . . ." Tremaine sees the light. Mrs. Tremaine is caught in a stampede of cattle and trampled to death, freeing Tremaine, after a suitable interval, to go to Carmelita; he kisses her "until the mountain reeled beneath them and the forest dinned in their ears. . . ." That was not the way people were supposed to kiss in 1890. Again the Eastern critics leaped on the novel. But the British were by and large delighted. The novel was certainly conventionally romantic, but Atherton described the California landscape—the redwood trees, the rolling hills, dotted with the twisted forms of live oaks, the purple hills—with considerable skill and wrote out of her knowledge of Spanish-American customs.

Increasingly her life and interests centered in England, which seemed to have an insatiable appetite for stories and novels dealing with California. She became a friend of John Sargent, the Whistlers, and the Pre-Raphaelites, among them Dante Gabriel Rossetti and Edward Burne-Jones. She even met Bret Harte, something of a literary lion in London, "a dapper dandified little man, who walked with short, mincing steps as if his patent leather shoes were too tight for him."

Convinced that her literary future was tied up with California, Atherton returned to San Francisco to visit her daughter in boarding school and her Atherton relatives. She traveled about the state, collecting material for future tales, and had a stormy friendship with Ambrose Bierce, who tried to kiss her by a pigsty. When she rebuffed him derisively, he called her "the most detestable little vixen I ever met in my life. . . ."

Since New York was still cold to her work, Atherton spent most of the next four years in England, plainly reveling in the literary life of London. There she wrote the better part of *Patience Sparhawk and Her Times*. It was by far her most ambitious effort to date, almost 500 pages in length (scaring off American publishers).

The story opens with two young women living at Monterey, California. Patience is a classic Yankee type, and her friend, Rosita, a representative of the region's Spanish culture. Rosita's "plump face was full of blood; her large, dark eyes were indolent and soft." Patience's mother is a drunkard. She had a mysterious past before she married the successful Yankee rancher John Sparhawk, now dead. Still beautiful, she compels masculine admiration despite her reputation for drink and careless behavior. As in *Los Cerritos,* much is made of the California landscape, this time the Carmel Valley, Point Lobos, and Monterey Bay. Patience flees from her dissolute mother to the home of a relative; there, like the young Gertrude, after whom she is plainly modeled, she becomes an indefatigable reader, who roams far afield from Balzac to Goethe to Hugo.

Patience falls in love with handsome, of course blue-eyed Beverly Peele. Their romance is similar to that of Gertrude and George Atherton. His spiritual coarseness, his pursuit of other women, and, above all, his intellectual limitations depress her. Their relationship grows first cold and then bitterly hostile. "Patience," he blurts out, "I do wish you'd give some of your attention to housekeeping and less to books." His aggressive, sexual passion for her she finds especially objectionable. "What sustained her was the hope that his passion would die a natural death, and that they would then go their diverse ways as other married people did. . . . Then she could enjoy her books, and he would permit her to spend the winters in New York, or in travel." Patience feels trapped in the marriage. In view of a woman's "uncertainty of support" and the scandal a divorce would cause, there seemed no way out.

When Patience tries to win the consent of her in-laws to a separation, they stonily refuse. Mr. Peele has no great regard for his son. "He has the cunning peculiar to the person of ugly disposition and limited mentality," he tells his daughter-in-law, but the thing that must be avoided at all costs is any breath of scandal.

In the midst of her dilemma Patience is interviewed by a young woman journalist because she has spoken out boldly against organized religion. The experience suggests a way out to Patience. She has strong intellectual interests, she has read widely; she herself will become a journalist and thereby escape Beverly. When her mother-in-law learns of Patience's resolution, she is furious. She will disgrace the family. "This girl is not one of us," she tells her son, "she never can be; for not to mention that we know nothing whatever of her family, she comes from that dreadful savage *new* Western country." Nonetheless, the determined Patience breaks free, finds a room in New York and a job with a newspaper as a reporter, and begins her "career." In the midst of her exciting new life, word comes that her husband is desperately ill and that the family doctor says only with Patience's return to nurse him will he have any chance to recover. She consents to return with the understanding that their marriage is over and she must be paid the wages of a nurse.

Soon after her return Beverly takes, by accident or intention, an overdose of morphine and dies during the night. Patience is charged with his murder. Beverly Peele's sister Honora perjures herself by declaring that she saw Patience pour the fatal dose into her brother's glass. Patience is convicted despite the best efforts of her lawyer, Gavan Bourke, and sentenced to be electrocuted. She has been strapped in the chair when Bourke arrives with a pardon. A Catholic priest had prevailed on Honora to admit that she lied. Bourke takes Patience in his arms.

Once again there was a hue and cry when the novel was published in the United States following its publication in Britain. A number of critics insisted that the topic was too gruesome. It was not appropriate material for a novel. Patience was, at heart, a faithless wife and immoral woman.

But England gave Atherton its collective literary heart. She was lionized and invited everywhere. She wrote *American Wives and English Husbands*. The heroine of the novel is Lee Tarleton, a young Virginian who spends part of her youth in Menlo Park and absorbs the larger and more expansive physical and psychological atmosphere of California. Her suitor is an English nobleman, Cecil Maundrell. When he asks her to marry him and come to England to be the mistress of the family estate, she joyfully consents. In sharp contrast with the relationship between Patience Sparhawk and Beverly Peele, Lee Tarleton's love for her husband grows stronger with the passing months, and he, so far as the duties of his parliamentary office permit, is thoughtful, attentive, and loving, the ideal husband. Nonetheless, Lee grows increasingly restive and homesick for California. Atherton's point seems to be that even an ideal marriage imposes intolerable constraints on an American wife. When friends visit from California, all her longing for the free and informal life asserts itself. "The great civilizations fascinate us," she tells an American friend "but they don't satisfy. . . . I'd like to put dynamite under the whole business, and then take Cecil and go and shoot bears with him in the Santa Lucia Mountains and sleep under the redwoods without so much as a tent." She becomes obsessed with the desire "to get away from her husband for a time and return to California—to that stupendous country of many parts where she had been Herself, where she had stood alone, where she had munched consecutively for twenty-one years those sweets of Individuality so dear to the American soul. . . ."

When she approaches Cecil with her proposal, he is dismayed. English wives do not behave so. They may take lovers or squander the family inheritance, but they do not abandon their husbands to go off on their own in the name of individuality. That is plainly an American aberration. But Lee is unshakable in her resolution, and Cecil nobly consents to let her go. Then a crisis arises in the family. He and his father are threatened with losing their estate. Lee decides that her place is with her husband.

The contrast between Patience Sparhawk and Lee Tarleton is instructive. There is, for one thing, the implication that American husbands are on the whole impossible. A decision to abandon one of them is, thus, less a matter of inner moral struggle than of the practical problems: how to support oneself, enduring the taint of scandal, etc. But suppose the husband is a perfect, in this instance English, husband. The conflict is still there, the feeling of limitation, of subordination to the will and life of another person, the suppression of one's own "individuality," as Lee Tarleton puts it. England is the land of tradition, of manners and formalities, of immutable codes of behavior; California is the land of vast spaces, of informality, above all, of individuality, where men and women can become "themselves."

Convinced that American reviewers had it in for her, she decided to publish *American Wives* anonymously in the United States. Whether for that reason or because the author made "American individuality" the real hero of her book, the critics were charmed. In addition, the story was also one of renunciation. As much as she longed for California, Lee Tarleton did not hesitate to do her duty as a faithful and loving wife when duty called. A leading British critic called the author of *American Wives* "the ablest woman writer of fiction now living."

Having lived in London for four years and, like so many other American writers, intending indeed to make her permanent home there, Atherton suddenly decided to return home. Her next topic would be a study of an American politician. The book was called *Senator North*, and it remained popular for years. In doing the research for *Senator North*, Atherton became fascinated by the character of Alexander Hamilton and decided that he would be her next subject. Publishers and editors did their best to discourage her. While it was true that for many Americans, Hamilton was second only to Washington as a hero, the public, she was told, was not interested in history. But Atherton was not to be dissuaded. For one thing she was determined to nail down once and for all the rumor that Hamilton was illegitimate, a rumor that Henry Cabot Lodge chose to ignore in his biography of Hamilton. Atherton sailed for the Caribbean island of St. Kitts, where Hamilton had been born, to examine court and parish records. There she established the essential facts and then visited St. Thomas, where Hamilton had lived during his youth. "I lived, breathed, slept in the past," she wrote, recalling the writing of the historical novel which she titled *The Conqueror*. "Every character of the period was a friend, acquaintance, or enemy, and I moved among them and listened to their voices."

The result was Atherton's most successful American book. Even the most obdurate of critics succumbed. The *New York Times* declared that *The Conqueror* held "more romance than nine-tenths of the imaginative fiction of the day, and more veracity than ninety-nine hundredths of the histories."

After the publication of *The Conqueror*, Munich became Atherton's home away from California, but the novels continued to appear year after year: *The Bell in the Fog*, dedicated to Henry James, in 1905; *Ancestors*, 1907; *Tower of Ivory* in 1910, to mention some of the better-known. The themes remained much the same, and if they seemed daring in the 1890s, by the second decade of the new century they were hardly to be distinguished from the great mass of romantic novels that poured off the presses year after year. Atherton's novels, originally considered too scandalous to be published, came in time to seem to the younger generation a symbol of all that was wrong with American popular literature. The young radical critic Harold Stearns wrote scathingly of her in 1919 as "that operatic soul who, from time to time, darts across the American horizon, like a comet running amuck, [and] really seems to believe that she is a great genius. . . ." He asked, "How can she help it when no one has ever effectively told her that she is not one?"

Few of Atherton's novels will bear reading today, but her own life, her preoccupation with the relationship between men and women, especially between husbands and wives, and her tireless advocacy of her home state make her a significant, if minor, literary figure. When we place her with her more original (or was it simply younger?) women authors—Edith Wharton, Willa Cather, and Ellen Glasgow—arresting comparisons appear.

As different as they were in temperaments and backgrounds, the four women writers whom we have considered here had much in common. If none of them was a feminist in the classic sense (Ellen Glasgow was the only active suffragist), they all shared a self-consciously feminine point of view. Three of them—Wharton, Glasgow, and Atherton—encountered strong resistance to embarking on careers as writers on the ground that such a career was unsuitable for women of their social position (in Glasgow's case, for a woman, period). In addition to approaching writing in a determinedly professional spirit (influenced largely by Henry James), they were women of remarkable cultivation, speaking a number of languages, well read in American and European letters and history. All were basically self-educated; Willa Cather, the Midwesterner, was the only college graduate. They were strongly oriented toward Europe, England especially, and traveled extensively abroad. Wharton and Atherton lived in Europe for years, Wharton for the latter part of her life. Moreover, they were highly critical of the manners and social mores of their countrymen and women. To Wharton the "American landscape" had "no foreground and the American mind no background," while Glasgow wrote: "Never . . . have I lost that sense of unreality, of insincerity, and of time-serving, in much, but by no means the greater part, of American culture." In line with their admiration for Old World culture, art and music are major themes in the work of all four women. Two wrote novels specifically about Wagnerian opera singers (Wagner and opera are the preferred form of musical expression). In addition to "The Wagner Matinée," one of Cather's most powerful short stories, *The Song of the Lark* is about Thea Kronborg's rise to stardom. Gertrude Atherton's *Tower of Ivory* is a long, turgid, wildly romantic novel about a rather disreputable American woman, Peggy Hill, who, cruelly misused by a succession of men, escapes to Bavaria, changes her name to Margarethe Styr, and enjoys a brilliant success as a singer of Wagnerian roles. She has "solved the greatest problem of woman's existence: she was quite happy and not because she had found the man of her heart, but because she had eliminated man from her existence altogether." When love is rekindled by an aristocratic young Engishman, John Oldham, Margarethe Styr, née Peggy Hill, commits suicide onstage in what must surely be the most lurid novelistic finale in American literature rather than ruin Oldham's life and her career by marrying him.

A major theme with all our authors was the stifling effect of social convention wedded to a puritanical sexual code, the brittleness and falsity of society. In *The Age of Innocence* Wharton wrote of the psychological destruction of a character: "It was the old New York way of taking life 'without effusion of blood'; the way of people who dreaded scandal more than disease, who placed decency above courage, and who considered that nothing was more ill-bred than 'scenes,' except the behavior of those who gave rise to them."

Escape was another major theme: escape from a bitterly unhappy marriage, from a confining environment—a repressive small-town atmosphere or an equally repressive social class—escape, most typically, to a big city (for the small-town characters) or to Europe for those who already live in big cities (Wharton and Atherton) and can't abide them. The theme of return was there as well. Wharton was particularly sensitive to the problems and complexities created as a consequence of trying to escape from a marriage; Cather, of the difficulty of escaping from the landscape that shaped youthful consciousness. Atherton's characters also wished to return (and often did) to the inexhaustibly potent California landscape. Indeed, all our writers were notably responsive to Nature with a capital *N;* Cather, Glasgow, and Atherton made landscapes an essential element in their stories. In *O Pioneers!* Cather wrote: "The great fact was the land itself, which seemed to overwhelm the little beginnings of human society that struggled in its somber wastes . . . the land wanted to be let alone, to preserve its own fierce strength, its peculiar, savage kind of beauty, its uninterrupted mournfulness."

Glasgow and Atherton were deeply concerned about the grim inequities of American life: the callous self-indulgence of the rich; the miserable and degrading poverty of the poor. Glasgow indeed embraced socialism in her younger days. Cather had less to say about social conditions than her sister authors. This was doubtless due to the fact that she deliberately focused on such timeless subjects as the life cycle of simple people. Moreover, she was inherently conservative in her own political views, and she took over as managing editor of *McClure's* in the period after the heyday of its startling exposés.

All four women were subject to terrible and disabling periods of depression. Glasgow and Atherton admitted to suicidal impulses or episodes, and suicide was a common event in Cather's stories. Glasgow wrote of being often "in the clutch of that wolfish terror" she had known since her "earliest memory," while Cather's biographer said that "she had to write to keep her sanity." They all plainly wrote to save their souls and doubtless their lives. Wharton certainly underwent periods of despair about her proper role in life—wife, social figure, or professional writer. When Wharton, Glasgow, and Atherton suffered most acutely from depression, they went abroad; Cather, by contrast, went to the Far West, Colorado, and Arizona, although she, too, traveled extensively in Europe.

They all were prodigious producers. Their combined output of novels, collections of short stories, and poems totals several hundred published works. Although Wharton was independently wealthy, the others made very good livings with their writings. Three won Pulitzer Prizes.

Most significantly, in their personal lives they all had experiences with men that ranged from merely discouraging to shattering. Edith Wharton's marriage was a long and finally excruciating disaster that she terminated, after years of anguished soul-searching, by divorce. Her affair with Morton Fullerton, while sexually fulfilling, was ultimately deeply disappointing. Walter Berry, a lifelong friend, was that classic undemanding, nonsexual male friend every American woman seemed to yearn for. Henry James was, of course, another, and Bernard Berenson as well.

Willa Cather seemed to have avoided strong emotional attachments with men, although when one reads *April Twilights*, it is difficult not to believe that she had had a very intense love affair with either a man or a woman. While masculine friendships—those with George Seibel and Sam McClure perhaps most notably—were important to her intellectually, her emotional life, at least after her college years in Lincoln, was reserved for other women—Isabelle McClung, Dorothy Canfield, and Edith Lewis.

Ellen Glasgow's infatuation with "Gerald" may well have been sustained for seven years by the fact that he was safely married. After his death and after what she considered her betrayal by his successor, "Harold," she attempted suicide.

Gertrude Atherton's marriage, like Wharton's, was a disaster, and once freed by her husband's timely death, she seems to never have been tempted to enter that perilous state again.

Considering these facts, it is not surprising that men (and marriage) did not appear in a very favorable light in the stories of our authors. American males were, commonly, clods or brutes or sometimes both. Their interests seldom extended beyond horses, sports in general, financial success, and the sexual pursuit of women. Arnold Kemper, the leading male figure in Ellen Glasgow's *The Wheel of Life,* was described as "robust, virile, sensual, with his dominant egotism and his pleasant affectations, half hero and half libertine." Gertrude Atherton's heroine Patience Sparhawk reflects, "Man is still a savage, a brute." Such lines abound. All males were not, of course, described in equally unflattering terms. Ellen Glasgow had a number of sympathetic males in her novels; Willa Cather, few. Gertrude Atherton's positive males were predominantly English, as in *American Wives and English Husbands.* With all our authors the sympathetic male figures were usually older men with, presumably, moderated sexual drives and strong artistic and intellectual interests. In some instances they were men who had been totally preoccupied with their ambitions but were now, in love, willing to have the aesthetic realm opened up to them by women.

Our authors plainly wanted male friends and "brothers," men who would share their more sophisticated cultural tastes with them, who would treat them as equals, and, perhaps above all, would make few sexual demands upon them. This desire, as expressed in their novels and stories, they shared with most of the popular novelists of the day.

If the men were, on the whole, such a poor lot, it is not surprising that marriage appeared in a bad light. There were even fewer successful marriages in the collective works of our writers than sympathetically drawn men. Many novels and short stories posed, directly or indirectly, the question of whether happy marriages were any longer possible in the modern age. Most of Cather's heroines either did not marry or married late in life in a kind of conditional spirit. In *The Song of the Lark,* Dr. Archie, a devoted sponsor of Thea Kronborg's musical career and himself the victim of a tragic marriage, says, "The whole question of a young man's marrying has looked pretty grave to me for a long while. How have they the courage to keep on doing it? . . . Such things used to go better than they do now, I believe. Seems to me all the married people I knew when I was a boy were happy enough." When he visits Thea Kronborg's dying mother, the same theme is repeated. "Bringing up a family is not all it's cracked up to be . . ." she declares. "The childen you don't especially need, you have always with you, like the poor. But the bright ones get away from you. They have their own way to make in the world. Seems like the brighter they are, the farther they go. I used to feel sorry that you had no family, doctor, but maybe you're as well off."

Another Cather character describes a woman's lot in the following words: "Torrid summers and freezing winters, labor and drudgery and ignorance, were the portion of their girlhood; a short wooing, a hasty, loveless marriage, unlimited maternity, thankless sons, premature age and ugliness were the dower of their womanhood." One of the older women in Glasgow's *The Wheel of Life* remarks; "It all comes very much to the same thing in the long run, and whether you begin by loving a man or hating him, after six months of marriage you can ask nothing better than to be able to regard him with Christian forbearance." Gerty Bridewell says, "I used to think that marriage meant rest, contentment, but now I know that it means a battle—all the time—every instant. I've never had one natural moment, I've never since the beginning been without a horrible suspicion—and I see now that I never shall be."

When marriage was endorsed at all, it was often endorsed in a decidedly backhanded manner. In Glasgow's *The Romance of a Plain Man* one male character advises a younger friend not to be a bachelor at all costs: "Find a good sensible woman who hasn't any opinions of her own, and you will be happy. But as you value your peace, don't fall in love with a woman who has any heathenish ideas in her head. When a woman once gets that maggot in her brain, she stops believing in gentleness and self-sacrifice, and by George, she ceases to be a woman." The husband, of course, has not thought of making sacrifices on his own account. Such behavior would be unsettling and unmasculine.

In the work of all our writers, women were the powerful and commanding figures. This is especially true, of course, in Willa Cather's novels, which give us a gallery of memorable women. However "new" or emancipated the women of these stories may be, they were capable of great love and yearned both to give and to receive it. Like Laura Wilde, the heroines were creatures "of divine mysteries, of exquisite surprises" with "luminous souls." But their fate was to get only "the mere husk," as one of the characters in Glasgow's *The Wheel of Life* puts it. They were not only bearers and creators of life but uniquely gifted in endowing it with joy and delight.

One of Edith Wharton's first literary efforts, entitled "The Fullness of Life," contains the paragraph "I sometimes thought that a woman's nature is like a great house full of rooms: there is the hall, through which everyone passes going in and out; the drawing room, where one receives formal visits, the sitting room, where members of the family come and go as they list; but beyond that, far, far beyond, are other rooms, the handles of those doors are never turned; no one knows the way to them, no one knows whither they lead; and in the innermost room, the holy of holies, the soul sits alone and waits for a footstep that never comes." It is perhaps the best enunciation of that feminine consciousness that our authors shared. Women, however sensitive, intelligent, loving, and self-sacrificing, lived perforce in a man's world, a world generally harsh and materialistic when it was not positively dangerous, a world indifferent to the ideals cherished by women. Men tramped through the "great house" of the woman's nature with clumsy, muddy boots and took her gifts—the ceremonies and furnishings of the house—for granted. But in the "innermost room" the woman's soul rested, lonely but invulnerable.

All our women were, at least by modern standards, highly romantic both in disposition and in the plots of their novels. Again, Cather aside, they had wildly romantic love affairs, licit and illicit, and love between men and women was a major element in many of their short stories and virtually all their novels. The intemperately sexual, sometimes madly aggressive, self-satisfied, promiscuous males who move through not only the novels of the women authors here considered but all the multitudinous novels produced by women writers of this period certainly bear little resemblance to the insecure and apprehensive American male described by Henry Adams who wanted "only love and doughnuts." Such men as our novelists described undoubtedly existed, but one suspects that they existed far more in the imaginations of the readers and writers of romantic novels than in the real world. What does seem beyond dispute is that our authors and most of their readers perceived men (and marriage) as highly problematical elements in American life. A major component in the feminine branch of the new consciousness was a persistent questioning of the ancient relationship between the sexes. Like so many other things in American life, it appeared to be in a highly uncertain state.

52

Recurrent Themes

Anxiety, which has been a theme throughout this work, remained
high in this period. Henry Adams wrote to Mabel La Farge:
"People are in a conspiracy to hide their troubles, but beneath the
surface they talk, only the anxieties are too close to be openly discussed. . . ." Few of the figures we have encountered in this volume
were immune to nervous—i.e., physical and mental—breakdown. So
far as we know their personal lives in any great detail, virtually all
suffered periods of incapacitating depression.

John Jay Chapman had the first of several nervous breakdowns
in law school. "The truth was," he wrote, "that I was oppressed with
the responsibilities of life, the dreaded hurdles, the fated race-course,
imaginative pressures, perhaps the inheritance of a Puritan's conscience, or the drive of a submerged ambition."

The new journalism, like virtually everything else in American
life, took its toll. Ray Stannard Baker, Lincoln Steffens, Finley Peter
Dunne, and Sam McClure himself suffered breakdowns and spells of
nervous exhaustion. In Baker's words, "for most of the members of
the staff, long continued overwork, nervous tension, and excitement
had begun to extort the price of high-flown ambition and swift success."

Baker returned from Germany in 1917 to a breakdown that drove him to the Arizona desert to recuperate.

The reasons for the anxiety were much the same as those observed almost a century earlier by Tocqueville and many other visitors to the United States and by native Americans like George Templeton Strong as well: anxiety over money, making a living, providing for one's "loved ones," avoiding the consequences of the panics and depressions that were a constant dark thread through American prosperity; too much strong coffee, too many cigarettes and/or cigars, too much liquor, cocaine, marijuana; too many sedatives and sleeping pills; the stress and strain of getting ahead; the loss of religious belief among the intellectual class and the general decline in the certainty of older religious convictions in the population as a whole. Finally, as we have seen, there was the devastating disillusionment that followed the conclusion of the World War.

Chapman deplored the effect of the fierce competition. "Almost every man who enters our society," he wrote, "joins it as a young man in need of money. His instincts are unsullied, his intellect is fresh and strong, but he must live. How comes it that the country is full of maimed human beings, of cynics and feeble good men, and outside of this no form of life except the diabolical intelligence of pure business? How to make yourself needed—it is the sycophant's problem; and why should we expect a young American to act differently from a young Spaniard at the Court of Philip the Second? He must get on. He goes into a law office, and if he is offended at its dishonest practices he cannot speak. He soon accepts them. Thereafter he cannot see them. He goes into a newspaper office, the same; a banker's, a merchant's, a dry-goods shop. What has happened to these fellows at the end of three years, that their minds seem to be drying up? I have seen many men I knew in college grow more and more uninteresting from year to year. Is there something in trade that desiccates and flattens out, that turns men into dried leaves at the age of forty? Certainly there is. It is not due to trade, but to intensity of self-seeking, combined with narrowness of occupation."

The prescribed remedies were, for the most part, familiar ones: temperance; hot baths; exercise (bicycling and camping were popular); rest cures; meditation; an improved diet of natural foods, stressing fruit juices and grains. Western resorts such as Estes Park, Colorado, and Pasadena and Santa Barbara in California became refuges for debilitated Easterners (everyone agreed that the pace of life in the East was much faster than that in the Middle or Far West). La Jolla, California, north of San Diego, became a refuge for artists and writers as well as for "health-seekers, idlers, golf-playing retired professional men, and merchants and farmers from the Middle West. It was our crowd," William Allen White wrote, briefly abandoning his family's summer refuge at Estes Park, Colorado.

Increasingly the wealthier and more adventuresome sought the services of an alienist, or, as they were coming to be called, psychiatrist. Sigmund Freud had lectured to an enthralled audience at Clark University in Worcester, Massachusetts, a leader in the disseminating of the discoveries of the newest "social science." Emma Goldman, who was lecturing in Vermont and had heard Freud in Vienna in 1896, made a side trip to hear him and wrote: "I was deeply impressed by the lucidity of his mind and simplicity of his delivery. Among the array of professors, looking stiff and important in their university caps and gowns, Sigmund Freud; in ordinary attire, unassuming, almost shrinking, stood out like a giant among pygmies." Carl Jung was also present, along with two of Freud's best-known pupils, Ernest Jones and his principal American advocate, A. A. Brill.

Frederic Howe consulted with a psychiatrist for the extreme depression that seized him after the war. As Eugen Rosenstock-Huessy had noted in his "The Crusade of the Star-Spangled Banner," written upon the entry of the United States into the war, America, "like France, and far more than France, was the land of 'psychology.'" For many intellectuals, psychology became the ruling passion, the putative key to unlocking the mysteries of the human psyche and healing the schizophrenic tendencies in American society that reflected or helped create that schizophrenia. Indeed, psychology became a kind of religion in the United States. It was, in a real sense, "made for America." The prominence of Freudian psychology has obscured the fact that the "science" was created, in large part, by William James, the "father of American psychology." It could be seen, in one perspective, as the descendant of Puritanism. The Puritans were constantly examining their innermost feelings to reassure themselves that they were being sufficiently pious and godly. Cotton Mather's often morbid reflections about his libido are the prototype of such self-examination.

By the end of the nineteenth century Henry Adams was complaining about the ubiquitousness of introspection among Americans of his class and generation. (Certainly, generation after generation, the Adamses were models of psychologizing.) Psychology had become a kind of omnium-gatherum, a compendious by-product of American individualism, for was it not the study of the emotional and mental states *of the individual?* The atomization of society and the anguish and anxiety that individuals experienced as a consequence produced a peculiar, if not unique, American science. And that science, once it had taken form, shaped, to a much greater degree than generally realized, not simply the individual's notion of himself and his relation to others but much larger questions. New Thought and Science of Mind sects—most strikingly Christian Science—were, in a manner of speaking, religions of psychology, which exhorted their members to take control of their lives by the "scientific" use of their minds.

Many Americans were obsessed by feelings of powerlessness. America was so vast, its geography so incomprehensible, the peoples who composed it so multifarious, its centers of power so inaccessible that "individuals" felt they were unable to affect the course of events or even to control their own destinies. Henry Adams wrote: "American society is a sort of flat fresh-water pond which absorbs silently, without reaction, anything that is thrown into it and its one merit is that it pretends to be nothing else. It does not cant. A few score of individuals,—counting women, perhaps a few hundred,—all more or less neurasthenic, try to create, and are desperate because society swallows passively whatever is thrown at it, but never even splashes when hit."

It was, in large part, to counteract such feelings of helplessness and "drift" that Walter Lippmann wrote *Drift and Mastery*. The challenge to Americans was to take control of the ship of state and steer it into the waters of social justice and political democracy. "Those who went before," he wrote, "inherited a conservatism and overthrew it; we inherit freedom and have to use it." Such archaic shibboleths as "the sanctity of property, the patriarchal family, hereditary caste, the dogma of sin, obedience to authority—the rock of ages, in brief, has been blasted for us. . . . The battle for us does not lie against a crusted prejudice, but against the chaos of a new freedom." This battle could be won by the application of scientific principles to the reordering of society. "Rightly understood," Lippmann wrote, "science is the culture under which people can live forward in the midst of complexity and treat life not as something given but as something to be shaped."

Drift and Mastery also announced Lippmann's formal divorce from socialism, which he dismissed as "a great citadel of dogma almost impervious to new ideas." He could not convince himself that "one policy, one party, one class, or one set of tactics, is as fertile as human need."

Americans, he wrote, were all "immigrants in the industrial world. . . . We are an uprooted people, newly arrived, and *nouveau riche.* . . . The modern man is not yet settled in his world. . . . The evidence is everywhere: the amusements of the city; the jokes that pass for jokes; the blare that stands for beauty, the folklore of Broadway, the feeble and apologetic pulpits, the cruel standards of success, raucous purity. We make love to ragtime and we die to it. We're blown hither and thither like litter before the wind." The new social sciences, especially Freudian psychology, offered hope that the problems of society might be "mastered." Lippmann developed the theme further in *A Preface to Politics* (1913). "Are you in your new book making much use of Freudian psychology?" he wrote to Graham Wallas, author of *Human Nature in Politics,* a book that had exerted a strong influence on Lippmann. "I have been studying it with a great deal of enthusiasm for several months now, and I feel about it as men might have felt about *The Origin of Species!* . . . [Its] political applications have hardly begun." Lippmann's book immediately became a text for generations of college students in introductory courses in government. One reviewer called it "The ablest book of its kind published during the last ten years." In it Lippmann showed a newly arrived-at skepticism about "the wisdom of the people" and called for a class of expert managers. "Instead of trying to crush badness," he wrote, "we must turn the power behind it to good account. . . . Instead of tabooing our instincts, we must direct them."

Class lines remained clearly drawn in the East, somewhat less so in the Middle West (St. Louis, Cincinnati, and Cleveland certainly maintained class lines). In the Far West, San Francisco and Portland, Oregon, had their own socialites. The upper class, by persistently deemphasizing the sexual side of the relations between young men and women, managed to keep control—that is to say, determine whom its offspring would marry or, perhaps more accurately, *whom they would not marry.* As we have noted in earlier volumes, the agencies of control were numerous and varied, and the penalties for disobedience were swift and certain—falling out of your "class." Churches, schools, and colleges, established and run by the upper class, helped maintain class lines.

Henry Adams was distressed at the number of marriages of his friends that broke up (or down), the most dramatic perhaps being that of Edith Wharton, whose husband became insane. Couples who divorced were dropped from the *Social Register,* or at least the "erring" party was dropped since all divorces had to be based on some verifiable sexual delinquency. (A divorce industry, which manufactured and recorded the sexual irregularities needed to obtain a divorce, flourished.) But "society" gave signs of losing the self-confidence, restraint, and morale on which its hegemony depended. Scandals, like the Stanford White–Harry Thaw affair, plagued it. A growing number of society marriages ended in divorce, often the consequence of some lurid sexual episode. Among the members of the younger generation, there were troubling suicides and breakdowns. "The rich and the highly educated are effete," Henry Adams complained. "They do nothing, produce nothing, and cannot even propagate. . . ." And to Mabel La Farge he wrote: "I am horrified by the selfishness of our world. We don't even curse each other heartily. A good hater is as rare as a good lover."

To John Jay Chapman the deaths of Julia Ward Howe and Sarah Whitman marked the end of an era when "society" sustained both manners and "taste." Whitman, in entertaining, mingled "old and young together," he noted, adding, "To do this is the first requisite of agreeable society, and the only way of civilizing the younger generation. Whenever the practice falls into disuse, the boys and girls will run to seed as they grow up. Young people are naturally barbarians; and unless they are furnished with examples of good manners they soon become negligent, unashamed and illiterate. . . . They would forget reading and writing, history, clothes, the multiplication table and how to tell time, if they were entirely abandoned by their elders." When Whitman died, Chapman wrote, "a whole society seemed to be suddenly extinguished. Vesuvius had covered the town of Boston, and we went about poking among the ashes to find each other in holes, corners and side streets."

The ratification of the Nineteenth Amendment, giving women the suffrage, so long anticipated and so long delayed, did nothing to resolve the debate on the proper role for women. That debate revolved around the treacherous issue of sex and, increasingly, the related issues of divorce and the disintegration of the family. The upper-class wives whose marriages ended in divorce or separation were a far cry from the Woodhull sisters and Angela Tilton Heywood. They were not advocates of free love or, with a few notable exceptions, crusaders for birth control. They were wealthy women of good birth, of "background," as the saying went, married to men of their own "class." They were equally far removed, in most instances, from the romantic new morality of Greenwich Village, where young women claimed control over their own bodies, often disdained marriage, and proclaimed the new sexual freedom (again very different from that of the serious-minded men and women of the seventies and eighties, the followers of Stephen Pearl Andrews and Moses Harman).

Sex, it seems safe to assume, was an important element in the dislocation of otherwise conventional marriages. Although the word was around that sexual experience might be very rewarding for married women as well as for men, the fact was that "nice" women were still expected to give no overt indications of sexuality. Uninhibited sexuality was something that middle- as well as upper-class men expected to experience exclusively with prostitutes and mistresses. There was, of course, plenty of suppressed sexuality in the air, in the elaborate and suggestive intricacies of women's clothes and in courtship rituals.

Henry Adams was the most shrewd and persistent observer of the opposite sex. The American woman, he wrote to Elizabeth Cameron, "has held nothing together, neither State nor Church, nor Society nor Family. . . . The enormous bigness and complexity of the problem crushes us all. . . . It worries me to see our women run away from the job. They think they improve themselves in Europe, but in reality they feel themselves helpless at home, and smothered by the multitude. You all run away just when you are making speed." It seemed to Adams that the issue was, in essence, no less than the future of the race. "Of all the movements of inertia, maternity and reproduction are the most typical," he wrote, "and women's property of moving in a constant line forever is ultimate, uniting history in its only unbroken and unbreakable sequence. Whatever else stops, the woman must go on reproducing . . . sex is a vital condition and race only a local one. . . . The woman seldom knows her own thought; she is as curious to understand herself as the man to understand her, and responds far more quickly than the man to a sudden idea. . . . Adams owed more to the American woman [he wrote] than to all the American men he had ever heard of and felt not the smallest call to defend his sex who seemed able to take care of themselves; but from the point of view of sex he felt much curiosity to know how far the woman was right, and, in pursuing this inquiry, he caught the trick of affirming that the woman was the superior." Yet, Adams insisted, in some essential and alarming way the American woman was a failure. "The cleverer the woman, the less she denied the failure. She was bitter at heart about it. She failed even to hold the family together, and her children ran away like chickens with their first feathers; her family was extinct like chivalry. . . . She might have her own way, without restraint or limit, but she knew not what to do with herself when free." Having reared a family, she found herself by the age of forty in a world "where nine men out of ten refused her request to be civilized, and the tenth bored her." While women like Mrs. Brooks Adams, Mrs. Henry Cabot Lodge, and Mrs. Cameron were far more than the "ornaments" of refined social life, "behind them, in every city, town, and farmhouse, were myriads of new types—or type-writers—telephone and telegraph girls, shop-clerks, factory-hands, running into millions of millions, and, as classes, unknown to themselves as to historians. Even the schoolmistresses were inarticulate. All these new women had been created since 1840. . . . Whatever they were, they were not content, as the ephemera proved; and they were hungry for illusions as ever in the fourth century of the Church. . . ." The problem cried out for solution; it was "the most vital of all problems of force. . . . It was surely true that, if her force were to be diverted from its axis, it must find a new field, and the family must pay for it. So far as she succeeded she must become sexless like the bees. . . . The Church had known more about women than science will ever know, and the historian who studied the sources of Christianity felt sometimes convinced that the Church had been made by the woman chiefly as her protest against man." Indeed, it seemed sometimes that the man had overthrown the church "chiefly because it was feminine," and after its overthrow "the woman had no refuge except such as the man created for himself. She was free; she had no illusions; she was sexless; she had discarded all that the male disliked; and although she secretly regretted the discard, she knew that she could not go backward. She must, like the man, marry machinery." So the final irony was that from at least one perspective, the "freedom" of women was no more than a phase which subjected her to the same disintegrative forces in American life—in the modern world—that her masculine counterpart suffered from acutely and that she was, in a sense, even less able to cope with.

Like his brother, Brooks Adams was obsessed with the effect of modern capitalism on American women. "Their whole relation to society is altered," he wrote. "From a religious sacrament marriage is metamorphosed into a civil contract; and as the obligations of maternity diminish, the relation of husband and wife resolves itself into a sort of business partnership, tending always to become more ephemeral." Divorce in the United States had become almost as common as in the days of Rome's decline and for many of the same reasons. "In many ways," Brooks Adams noted, "the female seems to serve as a vent for the energy of capital almost as well as men; in the higher planes of civilization they hold their property [in common], and, by means of money, wield a power not unlike Faustina's. If unmarried, the economic woman competes with the man on nearly equal terms, and everywhere, and in all ages, the result is not dissimilar. The stronger and more fortunate members of the sex have grown rich and bought social and political power."

Oswald Garrison Villard was confident that the gains for women far outweighed the losses. He wrote: "We see on every hand the new understanding that the private lives of individuals, where they do not affect public order or exploit victims of our capitalistic system, are their own affair; that morals and personal standards do change and change for the better; that individuals are not to be gravely punished and ostracized for life if they transgress what hoary tradition, selfish privilege, and hypocritical religionists declare to be the immovable *mores* of the hour." E. L. Godkin, the original editor of the *Nation,* had declared that a divorced woman should be "driven out of decent society." Villard, the sixth editor, had seen "the full acceptance in all circles of women known to have had children by men to whom they were not married, whom they never had any intention of marrying. . . . To me," he wrote, "this revolution means not license and debauchery but the emancipation of society from unbearably degrading chains of falsity, sanctimonious hypocrisy, stupid prudery, and deliberate disregard to truth and the realities of life. . . . Even youth may freely discuss the problems of sex not only without injury but on the whole immensely to its own benefit."

In the more advanced intellectual circles there was a disposition for emancipated women to place the blame for the muddled sexual situation (and virtually everything else) on men, a disposition Emma Goldman emphatically rejected. She resented "my sex's placing every evil at the door of the male. I pointed out," she wrote, "that if he were really as great a sinner as he was being painted by the ladies, women shared the responsibility with him. . . . Woman is naturally perverse," she argued; "from the very birth of her male child until he reaches a ripe age, the mother leaves nothing undone to keep him tied to her. Yet she hates to see him weak and she craves the manly man. She idolizes in him the very traits that help to enslave her—his strength, his egotism, and his exaggerated vanity. The inconsistencies of my sex keep the poor male dangling between the idol and the brute, the darling and the beast, the helpless child and the conqueror of worlds. It is really woman's inhumanity to man that makes him what he is."

Hutchins Hapgood's contribution to the debate was to write *The Story of a Lover,* a psychological study of his love for Neith and of the nature of love itself. It is a revealing essay, for it gives us more than a clue to the potency of the word "love" for Hapgood's generation of restless intellectuals. We have noted earlier that the notion of platonic nonsexual love, love between males of the same social class, had a peculiar power over the imaginations of such men as William James and Henry Adams. They and their friends addressed each other in their correspondence with terms of affection that would have brought a blush to the cheeks of earlier (and later) generations. James specifically devoted his life to the cultivation and expression of "loving affection." It was in some ways a religion, the religion of friendship. In that nonsexual love James and Adams and Chapman and their friends included women—typically the safely married wives of friends, nieces, female cousins, all male-female relationships in which the sexual aspects were muted or nonexistent. The next generation followed in those paths marked out by such eccentrics as Victoria Woodhull and her sister, Tennessee C., by Angela and Ezra Heywood, Moses Harman, and many others. Here sexual love became the metaphor for social reconciliation in a more direct and explicit way. What was, in effect, a new class—the intelligentsia—embraced it, embraced each other more or less indiscriminately. It was this intensely romantic spirit that Hapgood gave expression to in *The Story of a Lover.* "The philosophy of the proletarian," he wrote, was the starting point for the development of a richer notion of love. It was a kind of moral vantage point from which the believer could discern that all the fundamental institutions of the society were simply a "higher form of injustice and robbery and . . . see the criminal, the outcast and the disinherited by a new and wondering sympathy," a sympathy "which sees in the revolution the hope of a more vital art and literature, a deeper justice and a richer human existence. . . . Ideas of marriage and the love-relations in general were," in Hapgood's view, "affected like everything else by this far-reaching proletarian philosophy. To free love from convention and from the economic incubus seemed a profoundly moral need. The fear that the love of one's mistress was the indirect result of commercial necessity aroused a new variety of jealousy! In some strenuous lovers a strange passion was aroused—to break down all sex conventions in order to purify and strengthen the essential spiritual bond." Small wonder there were many failures. It was "a task for the gods."

Such questions were far less evident in the vast middle class that stretched across the country and had as its bastion the small town. There the sexual constraints embedded in the structure of the community and the churches gave support to the repressive mores of the community that punished any form of deviation. Hutchins Hapgood recalled that his only real companion in Alton, Illinois, was a mentally deranged boy. "None of the sane boys of my acquaintance," he wrote, "ever said anything at that time of any interest to me. Indeed, there was not another boy in the town, except my older brother, who really interested my imagination." Hapgood was the victim of periods of profound depression, he recalled. One of his few close friends was a boy named Ralph who shared some of his intellectual interests, but when Hapgood came back from college for a while "ill with 'nervous prostration,'" he found that Ralph had become plump and complacent. "The town had claimed him as its own. And he was content, that was the last straw." It was, in Hapgood's view, only the brave and persevering women, "and many existed in that dark little town," who redeemed it. The town was aesthetically barren. His father and mother, for example, never danced and disliked music. He could only see them as exiles "in the unfortunate town of Alton."

William Allen White painted a very different picture of Emporia, Kansas, in the early years of the new century. It was a town of some 10,000. There were only three automobiles in town. Horse-drawn transportation was the norm, and people prided themselves on their equipage, driving out on warm summer evenings with the family in a phaeton or buggy. A number of the more prosperous men in the town had prize trotting horses, which "they often drove themselves—doctors, lawyers, merchants, railroad men." There was a building with a swimming pool where the men of the town swam nude. Bridge-whist was the rage, and a few of the more daring went to the movies at the nickelodeon, "a freak entertainment," held in a vacant building with folding chairs for the audience. The opera house, on the other hand, was open three or four nights a week the year around, and a succession of lecturers, singers, touring theatrical companies occupied it. The wage scale in town ran from $2.50 for common labor to $5 a week for clerking.

The particular attention of the town focused on baseball. "Of a late summer afternoon, the town gathered at these games with noisy loyalty and great excitement, the women in their best big hats and high sleeves and wide skirts, the men in what were then called shirtwaists, tailless shirts gathered with a rubber string under the waist just inside and below the trouser top—quite fashionable and exciting."

White estimated that some 10 percent of the citizens of Emporia were "poor," or, as we would put it today, below the poverty line. But observing the poor families over the course of two generations, he noted that they made their way up the economic and social scale while many of the once prosperous families slid down.

Beatrice Webb and her husband, Sidney, the famous British Fabian socialists, attended a small-town Fourth of July celebration near San Francisco in 1898. There were "literary exercises" in a crowded hall. "These," Beatrice Webb wrote, "consisted of a plentiful supply of bad music, choruses, solos and orchestral overtures, all alike being refrains and varieties of the Star Spangled Banner; a welcoming speech from the Irish mayor and an oration from an Irish orator, a glowing tribute, to the 'Liberty, Independence and Free Institutions' of America." An elocutionist read the Declaration of Independence. "The note of the whole thing," Mrs. Webb wrote, "was the unique character of American institutions—the 'only Democracy in the world'—Americans being the chosen people who had, by their greatness of soul *discovered freedom,* and who were now to carry it to other races. . . . The *Declaration of Independence* was received with deafening applause as if the declaration had been made yesterday and sealed by the blood of the present generation. 'That all men are born free and equal,' was announced as a brand new revelation from heaven and received by the audience as if it were the basis of their existence." Beatrice Webb was struck with the thought that the same ritual was being repeated in every city and village in the United States. It made her realize "how French is American patriotic sentiment; how anxious to assure itself of the nation's glory and how swaddled up in abstract propositions which have long since lost their meaning."

Towns continued to lose ground to the cities. Their brightest and most ambitious youths headed for the bright lights and the intoxicating freedom of the metropolis. One consequence was that the long-existing gap between the city and the town grew wider with each passing decade. Money and its handmaid power remained firmly in the hands of the Eastern upper class. Of this we have seen numerous illustrations in earlier chapters of this volume. The Middle Western middle class had, primarily through the agency of the Progressive movement, made a determined assault on the Eastern centers of power, but they had been beaten back, and they clearly owed their defeat, in substantial degree, to their hero, Theodore Roosevelt, and the deep-seated hostility of the Eastern political and financial establishment, which in the last resort preferred to cling to its hegemony rather than accept its Midwestern allies as full partners in the task of reconstructing American society.

The "mother" and the "child" continued to be potent symbols, the first as the true bearer of the society's most central and enduring values, the second as "the hope of the future." George Creel's father was the typical "failed male," a drunkard and a nonprovider. His mother Creel adored. "If," he wrote, "I came to voting age with a passionate belief in equal suffrage, it was because I *knew* my mother had more character, brains, and competence than any man that ever lived. It was not only that she brought up three sons by her toil and sacrifice, imbuing them with some of her own indomitability and pride, but my father was ever a burden on her aching back. . . . Her rare understanding of childhood's intensities was another of Mother's gifts, and only God and His angels will ever know the sacrifices she made to give her boys the little pleasures that saved heartache. No matter how empty the family purse, she always managed to find a dime when a troupe came to the hall over the grocery store that went under the name of the Opera House." That was the classic American mother, celebrated in innumerably similar accounts by adoring sons. In the eve of Willard Straight's departure for France in 1918 he wrote to his eldest son: "You are blessed as no other children have been blessed in your mother. May your worship for her—for it will be with you as it is with me, reverence and real worship—guide you and lead you to treat all women with chivalry. Save yourself and tell Michael to save himself that you may go clean and unashamed to her who will be your wife and the mother some day of your children. There will be many temptations, but when they come, think of your mother."

As early as the 1820s and 1830s foreign travelers had commented on the disposition of American parents to indulge and feature their children, cheerfully accepting a juvenile rebelliousness and impudence that horrified Europeans. Arnold Bennett described the combination of "independence, . . . self-confidence, . . . adorable charm, and . . . neat sauciness" that characterized the attitude of an American daughter toward her father. The children regarded their parents with "an astonishing, amusing, exquisite, incomprehensible mixture of affection, admiration, trust, and rather tolerating scorn," he wrote. The parents, for their part, looked on their offspring with some uneasiness. Since they had always been considered to have a very special role as the putative rulers of America and the prospective creators of a vastly better and more prosperous society, parents felt obliged to do everything in their power, make every sacrifice, to bring out their offspring's natural goodness.

Ironically, it was the anarchists, ahead of their times in so many other respects, who set the style in child rearing and whose doctrines were, for the most part, reinforced by the teachings of John Dewey. If "irrational" and unscientific bourgeois methods of child rearing could be replaced by freer and more open, more "scientific" practices, they argued, a major step would have been taken in the reconstruction of society along anarchist lines. "No one," Emma Goldman wrote, "has yet fully realized the wealth of sympathy, kindness, and generosity hidden in the soul of the child. The effort of every true educator should be to unlock that treasure—to stimulate the child's impulses and call forth the best and noblest tendencies. . . . To build the man and woman of the future, to unshackle the soul of the child—what grander task . . . ?" The anarchists were convinced that the child, however rude or badly behaved, should never be checked or thwarted, and Hutchins Hapgood complained that he could not visit the homes of his married anarchist friends without being tormented by their "brats," who behaved "without correction or restraint. . . . Many years after my experiences with the results of libertarian education among the anarchists," he wrote, "I found the same phenomena existing among the respectable and rich uptown people whose Modern School borrowed of the anarchist idea."

American faith in education as the means of redeeming the world led, Arnold Bennett noted, to lavish outlays on schools. "A child is not a fool," he wrote; "a child is almost uncannily shrewd. And when it sees a splendid palace provided for it, when it sees money being showered upon hygienic devices for its comfort, even upon trifles for its distraction, when it sees brains all bent on discovering the best, nicest ways of dealing with its instincts, when it sees itself the center of a magnificent pageant, ritual, devotion, almost worship, it naturally lifts its chin, puts its shoulders back, steps out with a spring, and glances down confidently upon the whole world."

A Swedish feminist, Ellen Key, wrote a book published in the

United States in 1912 with a prophetic title: *The Century of the Child.* The child was thus the latest vessel of redemption. It superseded (or joined) the freed slave, the reformed drunkard, the emancipated woman, and the ennobled worker as the savior of America and, it was hoped, the world.

The American obsession with sports continued to be commented on by foreign visitors to the United States. There were two worlds of sports: the genteel upper-class world of amateur athletics, of tennis, golf, and polo most conspicuously, and the "national pastime" of professional baseball. With blacks excluded after their early prominence, the Irish and Germans predominated in baseball, demonstrating that professional sports was one of the most important, if not *the* most important, agency of assimilation for immigrant groups. In the 1921 World Series between the Giants and the Yankees, John McGraw, the famous manager of the Giants, was pitted against the equally famous Miller Huggins; such stars as Ryan, Kelly, Dolan, and Shea took the field with Frisch, Stengel, and E. Meusel for the Giants, and Hoyt, McNally, Quinn, Shawkey, Schang, Hoffman, Devomer, Roth, and R. Meusel played for the Yankees.

It was not just that baseball was an enticing avenue to fame and fortune, by means of which second-generation immigrant youths might escape the consequences of prejudice; it was, equally, that by becoming highly visible admired "stars," they helped change the perception of their "ethnic group," as we would say today.

Baseball was the quintessential American game. Mark Twain in 1889 called it "the very symbol, the outward and visible expression of the drive and push and rush and struggle of the raging, tearing booming 19th century," and a very different observer, Arnold Bennett, was equally eloquent on the subject, writing: "Its fame floats through as something prodigious, incomprehensible, romantic, and terrible." Carried off to a game by his enthusiastic American hosts, Bennett surrendered to the ambience, placing it "in broad dramatic quality—above cricket" and entering so far into the spirit of the occasion as to try chewing gum, finding the "singular substance . . . eternal and unconquerable."

Philosophers and historians as well as sportswriters have written learnedly on the peculiarly *American* character of baseball as a game. It is in ways the antithesis of its rival, football. Baseball is a game of doldrums interspersed with moments of intense drama. It is, after all, odd for a restless and impatient people to sit through two or three hours while pitchers throw balls (and strikes) past batters, at the end of which display the classic score is 1–0 or 2–1 and at which the no-hitter is the pinnacle of a pitcher's achievement. Since its "best" games are usually low-scoring affairs, the attraction of the sport is presumably aesthetic; it is perhaps closer to the dance than to the typical athletic endeavor. It is a game of nuances and subtleties, of strategy and finesse. It is also a primary democratic ritual. The spectators arrived, typically, by trolley or subway. They ate (and eat) prodigious amounts of indigestible food and hardly more potable liquids (baseball is ideally arranged for supplementary eating, which may be a substantial part of its charm).

Intercollegiate football, having recovered from its more murderous excesses in large part as a consequence of President Roosevelt's warning that a failure to moderate the mayhem would bring about the demise of the sport and imperil the morale of the Republic, was more popular than ever, but it was confined mainly to that very small portion of the population that enjoyed the benefits of higher education. Taking a cue from the British, Americans, as we have noted earlier, considered football a preeminent character builder. In the words of the famous sportswriter Grantland Rice:

> For when the one Great Scorer comes to write against your name
> He writes it not that you won or lost—
>   but how you played the game.

A landmark in collegiate football was the construction at New Haven in 1915 of the Yale Bowl, the first enclosed football stadium in the country. It soon had numerous imitators.

Attending a football game in a college town, Arnold Bennett found it "a psychological panorama whose genuineness can scarcely be doubted" (he thought baseball, by contrast, the result of a considerable degree of "self-hypnosis"). In the football hysteria, he noted, "the young men communicate the sacred contagion to their elders, and they also communicate it to the young women, who, in turn, communicate it to the . . . elders. . . ." What startled Bennett, besides the stream of casualties, was the fact that the injured players could be replaced (in contrast with rugby). It seemed to him less a game of amateurs than a "mimic battle," in which everything was subordinated to winning. "The desire to win, laudable and essential in itself, may by excessive indulgence," he wrote, "become a morbid obsession. . . . An enthusiast for American organization, I was nevertheless forced to conclude that here organization is being carried too far, outraging the sense of proportion and of general fitess." Bennett was also put off by "the almost military arrangements for shrieking the official yells." He pitied the "young men whose duty it was, by the aid of megaphones and of grotesque and undignified contortions, to encourage and even force spectators to emit in unison the complex noises which constitute the yell."

Class lines were as clearly drawn in the realm of sports as in other aspects of American life. Upper-class youths might play baseball in preparatory school and college, but they did not go on to play the sport professionally. The word "amateur" was a word not of denigration but of conscious superiority. Gentlemen did not play sports for money. Tennis and golf were confined to the cloistered preserves of private clubs. The same was true of sailing. Horse racing was a sport where swells mingled with the hoi polloi. But hunting and shooting and "camping" were again the pastimes of gentlemen and, to a modest degree, of gentlewomen. Theodore Roosevelt's "tennis cabinet" was a classic upper-crust institution made up of his peers. It was in these areas that "sports clothes" appeared and began to modify the stiff rectitude of Protestant attire, although women, who played tennis as soon as men did, wore long dresses and hats when they played until the great postwar emancipation in women's clothes (they still wore stockings, of course). The only consolation that John Jay Chapman found in America's "absurd fondness for sports" was that "it produces wonderful men's clothes. At the sacrifice of all reason art is produced as usual."

Upper-class women had participated in such sports as fox hunting, golf, and tennis as well as sailing almost since the inception of those sports. The crusade of Catharine Beecher for physical education for women had resulted in sports programs at all the women's colleges in the East and at most coeducational institutes, whether private colleges or state universities. Indeed, many of the academic positions open to women were in physical education and domestic economy, another of the Beecher sisters' crusades. Field hockey and soccer were popular women's sports by the turn of the century. Middle- and lower-class women lagged far behind. Working-class women were too busy working to have time or energy left for sports, and middle-class women, except the reform-minded, were still bound by notions of what kind of activity was appropriate for women. In addition, they seldom had access to golf courses (an upper-class monopoly) or equally restricted tennis courts.

The most sensational sports events of the era occurred in boxing, in the Olympics of 1912, and in baseball. They were, respectively, the match for the heavyweight boxing championship of the world between Jack Johnson, the first black man to hold the world championship, and Jim Jeffries, the former heavyweight champion, held at Reno, Nevada, in 1911; the spectacular triumphs of Jim Thorpe, a Sac and Fox Indian, in the Olympic decathlon and pentathlon, and the Black Sox scandal when members of the Chicago White Sox were convicted of taking bribes.

Jack Johnson had won the world title in Australia in 1908 by defeating a Canadian named Tommy Burns before 30,000 spectators, the largest audience for a boxing match to that time. Having a black American heavyweight boxing champion of the world was a devastating blow to most white Americans, and the sporting sheets became obsessed with the mission of finding "a great white hope," who would presumably restore the pride and honor of the white race by defeating the "black fiend." Johnson further inflamed public sentiment by marrying a series of white women. He was a superb fighter and athlete who made no compromise with white prejudices. He fought a series of white hopes, the most formidable being Stan Ketchel, the middleweight champion, who lasted twelve rounds. Johnson hit him so hard that it was an hour before Ketchel regained consciousness.

Jim Jeffries, who had retired as champion of the world six years earlier, was prevailed upon to redeem his race. Tex Rickard, who promoted the fight, raised a purse of $101,000, and Jack London was assigned by the *New York Herald* to cover the fight. London turned out a stream of color stories on the fighters and the fight: "Jeff Goes Fishing and Sees a Ball Game," "Actress Insane over Fight," etc. London began by calling it the "Fight of the Century" and ended by calling it the "Greatest Fight in History." Johnson, London pointed out, was "a Master Mouth Fighter," who kept up a stream of witty conversation with his opponents, his seconds, and ringside spectators and reporters during his bouts. It was Johnson, "the fighting boxer," against Jeffries, "the boxing fighter. Both are cool, both are experienced, both are terrible."

One of the most seriously discussed questions about Johnson prior to the fight was his alleged yellow streak. This yellow streak, students of the boxing craft declared, was a racial defect that was sure to manifest itself when Johnson faced a white fighter as formidable in appearance and reputation as Jeffries. Many authorities predicted that Johnson would simply be incapacitated by fear; Jeffries would win by default.

The fight took place on the Fourth of July, 1910, and London reported to the *Herald:* "Once again has Johnson sent down to defeat the chosen representative of the white race, and this time the greatest of them. And, as of old, it was play for Johnson. From the opening round to the closing round he never ceased his witty sallies, his exchanges of repartee with his opponent's seconds and with the audience. . . . Johnson played as usual. . . . And he played and fought a white man, in the white man's country, before a white man's audience. And the audience was a Jeffries audience. . . . The greatest battle of the century was a monologue delivered to twenty thousand spectators by a smiling negro [Johnson's smile was all the more infuriating to white spectators because he had all his teeth capped with gold], who was never in doubt and who was never serious for more than a moment at a time." The "yellow streak," London assured his readers, was "beyond a shadow of a doubt" not evident.

In New York word of Johnson's victory set off a race riot. The headlines of the *Herald* read: "Half a Dozen Dead [blacks, needless to say]; Crowds Attack Negroes; Reign of Terror Here; Africans Dragged from Street Cars and Attacked in Streets in Fury of Whites over Jeffries' Defeat. . . . Negroes Also Attacked and Lynchings Attempted in Philadelphia, Washington, Pittsburgh, Chattanooga, Atlanta, St. Louis and Many Other Points. Large Number of Victims Taken to Hospitals."

White anger was not appeased. Johnson was jailed on charges of violating the Mann Act by transporting a woman (white) across state lines, although he subsequently married her, and was forced to leave the country. Besides being arguably the greatest fighter in ring history, Johnson was an intelligent and well-read man whose favorite authors were Alexandre Dumas and Victor Hugo and who spoke and read three languages. His autobiography attests to his literacy and to his sense of humor, which was badly needed in his native land.

We have had ample evidence of the reactionary character of the American courts—state and Federal—and the chore boys of the corporations, the corporate lawyers. William Howard Taft himself complained to a friend in 1909 that "the condition of the Supreme Court is pitiable and yet those old fools hold on with a tenacity that is most discouraging." Still, when openings came during Taft's administration, he appointed two conservative Southerners and raised another, Edward White, to the chief justiceship. In the words of his biographer Henry Pringle, Taft felt that by the end of his term he had constructed a court that "would protect the Constitution from attacks by Roosevelt and other progressives."

Up to 1911 the Supreme Court intervened in fifty-nine cases involving the Fourteenth Amendment. Thirty-nine of these involved private corporations seeking the protection of a law intended to guard the rights of newly freed blacks. Only three concerned the civil rights of blacks. "The fourteenth amendment," the commissioners on industrial relations pointed out, "has not acted to secure or protect personal rights from State encroachment, but only to prevent encroachment on property rights."

Since capital "has now had, for more than one or even two generations," Brooks Adams wrote in 1913, "all the prizes of the law within its gift, this attitude of capital has had a profound effect upon shaping the American legal mind. . . . Quite honestly . . . the American lawyer has come to believe that a sheet of paper soiled with printers' ink and interpreted by half-a-dozen elderly gentlemen snugly dozing in armchairs, has some inherent marvellous virtue by which it can arrest the march of omnipotent Nature." Adams did not question that both capitalists and lawyers were "other than conscientious men." The point was: "What they do is think with specialized minds."

Adams traced the history of the Supreme Court from Washington's administration to its most recent decisions. He quoted Justice Harlan in the case of *United States* v. *American Tobacco Company.* "In short," Harlan had written in a minority opinion, "the Court now, by judicial legislation, in effect, amends an Act of Congress relating to a subject over which that department of the Government has exclusive cognizance."

As long as the courts retained their "present functions [of negative legislation]," Adams wrote, "no comprehensive administrative reform is possible. . . . American society must continue to degenerate until confusion supervenes, if our courts shall remain semipolitical chambers." Beatrice Webb, observing "the chaotic democracy of California," also noted that the State Supreme Court was busy declaring unconstitutional the laws passed by the legislature which they considered anticapitalistic. Anything which offended their "commonplace but hard headed minds" was, by that fact, unconstitutional.

The ubiquity of the corporation lawyer produced his antithesis, the anticorporation lawyer, a lawyer of reform sentiments. The most striking tactic of the new lawyers was to employ "sociology" as part of their briefs in defense of particular laws governing conditions of labor— laws often invalidated on the ground that they were an infringement of "property rights," meaning the right of an employer to set the terms of labor in a "free" negotiation with each individual employee (never with employees banded together to advance their own interests; that was commonly interpreted as conspiracy). When Florence Kelley's National Consumers' League hired Felix Frankfurter to defend the constitutionality of a District of Columbia law setting a minimum wage for women, Frankfurter, following the lead of Louis Brandeis, presented a "scholarly" study of some 1,000 pages, which described in detail the consequences of inadequate wages on the lives of particular women. The new law, like the new economics, was more interested in the practical consequences of laws than in finespun legal theories which in practice seemed to work invariably for the benefit of the rich and powerful and against the interests of the poor. Laws were not mere abstractions; they had consequences. These consequences either advanced or retarded the cause of social justice. If they retarded the spread of social justice, if they were prejudicial to workers, to women and children, to immigrants, to blacks, to the poor and powerless, the laws themselves were faulty, however splendid the philosophical musings from which they sprang, for the purpose of the law was, immemorially, to do justice.

Louis Brandeis was the pioneer in anticorporation law. Born in 1856, he was one of the first of a remarkable series of Jewish lawyers to attend the Harvard Law School, where he made the highest grades ever recorded there. Brandeis was an ally of Robert La Follette in 1911 in strengthening the Sherman Antitrust Act by the La Follette–Stanley antitrust bill. As the pioneer of the "Jewish band" Brandeis was always ready to give advice or lend a helping hand.

Felix Frankfurter was one of the most gifted and charming of Brandeis's protégés. Both he and his friend Morris Cohen were immigrants; Frankfurter had come from Vienna with his parents in 1894, while the Cohen family had arrived from Minsk two years earlier. They thus represented the two main currents of Jewish immigration— Frankfurter, the older, more established German (and Austrian) Jews, and Cohen, the influx of Eastern European Jews, predominantly Russian. Both lived as boys in the Jewish ghetto on the Lower East Side of New York City. Both went to City College of New York, which became almost a Jewish institution by virtue of the number of able young Jews who flocked there. Both went on to the Harvard Law School, where they compiled brilliant records. Neither was an Orthodox Jew or indeed a religious Jew. Like Walter Lippmann, who came from a much more prosperous Jewish family of third-generation Americans, Frankfurter and Cohen were strongly oriented toward the world of the upper-class Protestant establishment, although Frankfurter was an early and ardent Zionist. Henry Stimson, a disciple of Elihu Root, was appointed United States attorney for the Southern District of New York by Theodore Roosevelt. Stimson chose Frankfurter as his assistant, and Frankfurter absorbed from Stimson the Yankee spirit of public service and social reform, both of which were, to be sure, strong in his own tradition.

Meanwhile, Morris Cohen was attracting the attention of such men as Roscoe Pound, the experimentally minded new dean of the Harvard Law School, and Learned Hand, another member of the band of young upper-class men and women drawn into the Theodore Roosevelt orbit. Frankfurter secured his place in that company by marrying a bright Smith College graduate, Marion Denman, who had impeccable upper-class credentials (her father was a Congregational minister).

Harold Laski, the brilliant young English counterpart of Frankfurter and Cohen, who was teaching at the Harvard Law School, was one of the few guests present when the marriage ceremony was performed by Judge Benjamin Cardozo of the New York City Court of Appeals in the chambers of Learned Hand. The wedding marked a significant moment in American history. Marion Denman and Felix Frankfurter were not the first Gentile and Jew to marry in the United States. Charles Pancoast had courted a Jewish girl on the Missouri frontier in the 1840s. Southern Jews, usually converts to Episcopalianism, had married Gentile belles. But for a young woman of notably Protestant upper-class origins to marry a Jewish immigrant from New York's Lower East Side marked the breaking of two taboos, one racial and one class. Frankfurter's parents were more dismayed at the alliance than were Marion Denman's parents, who, as liberal Congregationalists, took the marriage in reasonably good spirit. Bride and groom belonged to the new world in which character and intelligence mattered more than the ancient barriers of race or religion. Moreover, Frankfurter, like Laski, Brandeis, and Lippmann, was to a large degree a deracinated Jew. He had shed with remarkable speed and ease the most conspicuous traits, mannerisms, and beliefs of his race. He was a new man in a new age.

Finally, there was the fact that the moment could also be taken as an episode in American legal history. The wedding and its location—in Learned Hand's office, with "new" Jewish lawyers—symbolized the emergence of a new breed of lawyer. There had been corporation lawyers in abundance for several generations, a large and, for the most part, rich fraternity, ready to do the bidding of their corporate chieftains, assiduous as courtiers, ingenious in evading the law, skilled in keeping their clients out of jail. They were, in the public mind, in the mind at least of farmers, state legislators of liberal persuasion, and striking workers against whom they so often secured injunctions, darker-hued villains than the tycoons whose interests they served. Advanced to the bench, they proved as tenacious in defense of the trusts and corporations as they had been as lawyers before the bar, and, by reason of their elevation, more effective, until it seemed to the reformers that they were met at every turn by the serried ranks of lawyers and judges, thwarting progress and doing so invariably in the name of the Constitution.

A fellow student of Frankfurter was Henry Moskowitz, whose wife, Belle Israels Moskowitz, outshone him as a welfare worker and authority on factory legislation. She became the guiding spirit in Al Smith's legislative program when he was elected governor of New York.

Still another of the fraternity of brilliant Jewish lawyers was Frederick Lehmann. Like Brandeis (he was three years older), Lehmann was a member of the older or pioneer generation. He had come to the United States as a child with his immigrant parents from Prussia. He had put down roots in the West, practicing law in Iowa and then in Missouri, where he became a leading figure in the bar and in the Republican Party. Taft made him United States solicitor general, but the Progressive-minded Lehmann was not entirely happy in his post. Frankfurter noted in his diary that at an informal meeting of lawyers in the attorney general's office Lehmann had replied to a scoffing comment about the recall of judges by bursting out that "crude, rude and ill-considered" as such a scheme might be, the fact was that "the legal profession, next to the press, have been [the] meanest, most selfish force in resisting just reforms and perpetuating . . . abuse [of the public] in administration of laws." He had no patience with the notion that the courts must be above criticism lest respect for law be undermined. Frankfurter, noting with approval Lehmann's outburst, added, "This sacrosanct notion of our judiciary must be hit whenever it can be effectively. . . . They [the courts and lawyers] have failed and failed wretchedly because by training and selfish interests they are a conservative and timid body of the community." Lehmann was also caustic about "intellectual leadership" divorced from moral principle, "pointing to selfish leadership of Southern oligarchy before war—the worst intellectual leadership the country has had."

Ernst Freund was, like Brandeis (he was eight years his junior), a second-generation German Jew who became professor of law at Columbia and who worked closely with liberal politicians first in New York State and later in Illinois, drafting uniform statutes for passage by state legislatures.

The emergence of Jews was not, of course, confined to the law, but in most other areas, notably in the academic world and in higher education generally, they encountered increasing prejudice and resistance. Anti-Jewish prejudice had somewhat the same source that it had in intellectual Jews like Bernard Berenson and Walter Lippmann: distaste for the alienness of the stream of lower-class Central European Jews, crowding first into the cities and then, most alarmingly, into Gentile resorts. At Atlantic City in 1919 John Jay Chapman deplored the ubiquitousness of "Judea—Israel—the Lost Tribes—lost no more! found—very much found, increased—multiplied—as the sands of the sea—Atlantic City—with the cliff dwellings of 10,000 souls each—a regurgitating with Hebrews—only Hebrews. Families of tens and dozens—grave old plodders, gay young friskers—angel Jews, siren Jewesses—puppy Jews—mastiff Jews—bulging matrons—spectacled blackfish—golden-haired Jewish Dianas—sable-eyed Jewish Pucks, Jewish Mirandas—Romeos and Juliets, Jew Caesars—only no Shylock. It is a Jewish menagerie of Israel." The only Christian was an elevator starter.

Finally, there is the matter of capitalism. In the Introduction to Volume Three of this work I wrote: " 'Capitalism' is not a word I am especially happy with, but since the United States is commonly denominated the world's leading 'capitalist nation,' we must engage it. . . . It presently claims . . . to be virtually synonymous with America, to embody the 'American way of life.' It has invaded and conquered its traditional adversary—agriculture—and has, beyond question, colored every aspect of American life from art to sports to food. It has done its best to turn the world into business. . . . So like it or not, we have to put business enterprise in all its various forms in the center of our history." I was somewhat disconcerted when the late Matthew Josephson, author of *The Robber Barons* and numerous other books on the villainies of nineteenth-century capitalists, objected strongly to my statement, which seemed to me a statement of fact rather than a hypothesis. But the problem of "capitalism" has grown in the course of this work rather than diminished. I titled Volume Six *The Rise of Industrial America* and gave considerable attention to that theme, a story familiar enough in general outline. It became evident to me in the course of doing research on the period covered by that volume that the war between capital and labor was the essential story. Moreover, the radicals and reformers turned out to be far more interesting individuals than the capitalists, if we except the first remarkable generation of inventor-capitalists like Alexander Graham Bell, George Westinghouse, George Pullman, Thomas Alva Edison, George Corliss, Andrew Carnegie, and their counterparts, who were the real originators of industrial capitalism in the United States. The consequence has been that the radicals and reformers have constantly threatened to run away with these latter volumes despite my, I fear, halfhearted efforts to restrain them. An extraordinarily compelling lot, vivid and powerful personalties, they demanded to be heard. The result has been a certain imbalance. The reader must remind himself or herself, and I perforce must remind myself, that the vast majority of Americans were in all these years busy earning livings, contending with a highly unstable economy that brought terrible panics and depressions every decade or so and produced, in consequence, a state of chronic anxiety in all those who had to work for a living or lived on inherited income. And that, of course, was virtually everybody. Making money was the basic preoccupation of a great many Americans. It was also true that industry and the money managers were by no means of one mind about how to proceed or where to deploy their vast economic power.

The Hegelian notion of a dialectic in history is a useful one (at least before it was taken over by Marx and turned into a dogma). Hegel posited in human affairs a thesis that was, in effect, the status quo, things as they were. This thesis was challenged by an antithesis, and out of an often desperate struggle for domination came, typically or ideally, a synthesis that contained elements of both thesis and antithesis. If we take this as a rough working principle in history, we can say that capitalism was the thesis in the years following the Civil War and that the efforts of the reformers and radicals of every stripe and denomination were the antithesis. It seems reasonable to say that once the thesis has been clearly established, it becomes the assumed or the given, and the center of interest shifts sharply to the antithesis, for it is the antithesis that carries the seeds of the future. It is the antithesis that is vigorous, active, creative, dramatic, that carries the vital currents of the new age. By this reading the prominence of the reformers/radicals in these volumes is not only understandable but inevitable.

The issue of capitalism not only persists but grows in importance during the period covered by this volume, in large part as a consequence of the seizure of power by the Bolsheviks in Russia; it is therefore imperative that we attempt to get a grip on this elusive word. We have encountered it so often with strongly negative connotations that it may be well to search out its most positive characteristics. There is, first of all, the fact that capitalism is a system of what we might call democratic production. Capitalists are not interested in producing what they think people *ought* to have (unless, of course, they can artificially *create* a demand for a product). They prosper by producing at a price people can afford to pay articles and services that people want. Capitalism does this with a degree of flexibility and responsiveness that cannot be equaled by any system in which "other" people decide what their compatriots want, or should want, or what is good for them. The fact that a substantial portion of what people want is, in the opinion of liberal and radical intellectuals, cheap, vulgar, ugly, or otherwise meretricious is beside the point. Capitalism is, if nothing else, responsive to people's desires, if not always to their needs. It is (or has been), moreover, remarkably adept at noncoercive methods of organizing human energies. That is to say, we do not *tell* people where they *must* work, although, to be sure, we often exert subtle pressures on them to work where we wish them to. For Arnold Bennett, the model of this capacity of American industrial capitalism to organize people for the distribution of things was a mail-order house he visited in Chicago.

The dazzled Bennett observed that the mail-order house sold "merely everything." He wrote: "Go into that house with money in your palm and ask for a fan or a pail or a fur-coat or a fountain-pen or a fiddle, and you will be requested to return home and write a letter about the proposed purchase. . . . On the day of my visit sixty thousand letters had been received, and every executable order contained in these was executed before closing time, by the co-ordinated efforts of over four thousand female employees and over three thousand males. The conception would make Europe dizzy." A machine "no bigger than a soup-plate" opened hundreds of envelopes at once. Bennett traced a letter from a woman in Wyoming, "a neat, earnest, harassed . . . woman," who "wanted all sorts of things and wanted them intensely." It seemed to him that there could be no hope that "that earnest, impatient woman in Wyoming should get precisely what she wanted." But the letter mysteriously disappeared, and soon packages for the woman of Wyoming and all her fellow yearners were rushing down "great shafts," being checked, packed, billed by 600 young women at 600 billing machines in "a fantastic aural nightmare." From there Bennett was conducted to the catalogue room, where printing presses were turning out "the most popular work of reference in the United States," a bulky book with an annual circulation of 5,500,000 copies. "For the first time," Bennett wrote, "I realized the true meaning of the word 'popularity'—and sighed. . . ." The mail-order house revealed to the visitor "all the daily domestic life of the small communities in the wilds of the West and Middle West, and in the wilds of the back streets of the great towns. . . . Here in a microcosm I thought I saw the simple reality of the backbone of all America, a symbol of the millions of the little plain people, who ultimately make possible the glory of the world-renowned streets and institutions in the dazzling cities. . . . I could see the whole little home and the whole life of the little home. . . . And afterward, as I wandered though the warehouses—pyramids of the same chair, cupboards full of the same cheap violin, stacks of the same album of music, acres of the same carpet and wallpaper, tons of the same gramophone, hundreds of tons of the same sewing machine and lawn-mower—I felt as if I had been made free of the secrets of every village in every State of the Union, and as if I had lived in every little house and cottage thereof all my life!" There was little or no sense of beauty "in those tremendous supplies of merchandise, but a lot of honesty, self-respect and ambition fulfilled." That is capitalism at its most potent and compelling.

Another demonstration of capitalism's capacity for providing things in abundance is the list of "luxuries" that David Houston, the secretary of the treasury in Wilson's postwar Cabinet, had drawn up by his staff. The list is an intriguing one both as an index to how Americans spent their money in the year 1919 and as a list of what were considered luxuries. Chewing gum—$50,000,000 —and candy—$1,000,000,000— were high on the list. Soft drinks accounted for $350,000,000, and ice cream for $250,000,000. Confections and "cereal beverages" totaled some $600,000,000, while cigarettes and cigars well exceeded $1,000,000,000 (if tobacco and snuff were added, the total was more than $2,300,000,000). Jewelry and watches "etc." accounted for $500,000,000, and "Perfumery and cosmetics," $750,000,000. "Admissions to places of amusement, $800,000,000"; "Pianos, organs, victrolas, etc." were a comparatively modest $250,000,000, while "Fur articles" were $300,000,000. Whereas Americans spent $1,500,000,000 on "Carpets, rugs, luxurious wearing apparel, etc.," "art works" accounted for only $25,000,000, and yachts a mere $1,000,000, as opposed to $8,000,000 for electric fans and $25,000,000 for sporting goods. "Luxurious service" soared to more than $3,000,000,000, as did "luxurious articles of food, etc." ($5,000,000,000); "other luxuries, including joyriding, pleasure resorts, races, etc." totaled another $3,000,000,000, while $2,000,000,000 went for "automobiles and parts." It occurred to Houston that "people who could chew $50,000,000 worth of chewing gum in one year could accomplish anything" (chewing gum was considered an outlet for nervous energy).

Houston's statistics are the kind that have been quoted by successive generations of Americans to prove that the United States is the greatest nation on earth *or* that capitalism is superior to socialism (or communism). Whether the production of "luxuries" in unprecedented quantities is the final measure of a nation's greatness might be challenged as an excessively materialistic standard. Some critics might be inclined to give more weight to what might be termed social justice, absence of class distinctions, and racial prejudice, devotion to peace, and similar humane values—which is not to say, of course, that the United States is without credentials in these areas as well.

The problem with capitalism, I suspect, is that its champions want to claim for it some inherent moral virtue. It is a very rough kind of economic system with many pre-, post-, and noncapitalist elements woven through it. It is clearly not "free enterprise" or "free competition." In its heyday and subsequently, it has done its level best, through trusts and various devices, legal and illegal, to suppress free competition and use the national government to advance its interests at the expense of workers and consumers—that is to say, the general public. The best thing that can be said for it is that it has worked, at least on the material level, to provide more people with more things than any other economic system. It has also done this, as its critics constantly remind us, at a considerable human cost. It is futile to argue about whether this cost was excessive. It has already in large part been paid. It should also be noted that capitalism, far from being the champion of individual liberties and the classic American freedoms—of speech, assembly, etc.—has done its best, wherever it was able, to suppress all criticism of it and prevent all measures designed to make it more responsible to its workers and more accountable to the public. It has done this in the name of what it claimed to be a sacred and inalienable right (which it invented) to use its property as it has seen fit. Much of this has fortunately changed, but only as the consequence of a long, bitter and often bloody "war," a word that neither capital nor labor hesitated to use to describe the true nature of "industrial relations" in the United States. Certainly we cannot escape the fact that the single-minded obsession of a substantial number of Americans with "getting ahead" by making money produced a whole new notion of what material well-being could be. The passion of Americans for entrepreneurial activity we neither can nor wish to scant; it is a natural human propensity, by no means limited to Americans. It was clearly the case that the character type produced by the Protestant Reformation, the geography, and, for a certainty, the political and social organization of American life gave free rein to such impulses and, furthermore, made them a kind of national ideal, lifting them from mere sordid desire for material gain to the status of quasi-religious principles.

Nor was the love of money necessarily the dominant motivation. American businessmen loved their businesses because of the sense of mastery they derived from combining techniques and technologies with human energies to produce a dazzling cornucopia of things. The human imagination had never before been applied to the material world so tirelessly and so extravagantly.

Far from being the classic "American" system, capitalism's principal virtue may well be that it is a *nonsystem*—a method of producing and distributing goods and services that is only mildly coercive, compared with the other leading brand. The problem is that some Americans have persisted in defending its faults—its failures and inequities and the disposition of many of its principal practitioners to exploit their workers and the general public—as the *essence of capitalism* and thereby done ordinary, grass-roots, run-of-the-mill capitalism a great disservice. Capitalists should get, in my view, no particular credit for doing what appears to come naturally to the species: pursuing their own selfish interests at the expense often of others. But neither should they be depicted as the incarnation of evil. They were; they existed;

they demonstrated remarkable creative capacities in developing, organizing, and utilizing the material world. The American businessman, Arnold Bennett wrote, "loves his business. It is not his toil, but his hobby, passion, vice, monomania—any virtuperative epithet you like to bestow upon it! He does not look forward to leaving in the evening; he lives most intensely when he is in the midst of his organization. His instincts are best appeased by the hourly excitements of a good scrimmaging commercial day. He needs these excitements as some natures need alcohol. . . ." This passion was, in Bennett's view, made overwhelmingly manifest by the opulence of the offices of successful businessmen, more luxurious than palaces, more richly embellished than temples. "Would a man enrich his office with rare woods and stuffs and marbles," he asked, "if it were not a temple?" The result was, of course, conspicuous impoverishment in other areas—the home; artistic and intellectual pursuits (only golf competed for their loyalties). "Could a man be happy long away from a hobby so entrancing [as his business], a toy so intricate and marvelous, a setting so splendid? Is it strange that, absorbed in that wonderful, satisfying hobby, he should make love with the nonchalance of an animal?" So perhaps if there was a uniquely "American" capitalism, it lay in this single-minded dedication of the man of business to his business: business as dream and fulfillment; business as the center of the universe, as the meaning and goal of life, indeed the object of a love more absorbing and compelling than erotic love. Radical journalists like Charles Edward Russell wrote contemptuously of the American passion for moneymaking. Most of the moneymakers Russell had known "were among the dullest of God's creatures and led lives flatter than a stove-lid." Arnold Bennett was perhaps closer to the mark in his description of the businessman living "most intensely when he is in the midst of his organization," in his office more luxurious than a palace. Bennett was also aware of the element of play in the activities of the American businessman. His business is both the object of his passion and a form of play in which the pyramiding of profits is clearly less important than the game itself.

But that single-mindedness, the passion of the American businessman for the game, is only a single part of the capitalist gestalt, albeit an important one. The word "capitalism" is, as we have seen, encrusted with a host of irrelevant notions. It is neither a system of government nor even a clearly defined economic system, but it is a curious jumble of obsolete shibboleths and practical operations, so that what really goes on in "capitalist America" has only a casual relationship to the notions of capitalism we hold in our minds. To descant upon the virtues of capitalism as opposed to socialism (rather than try to understand its true nature—which is to say, its strengths and weaknesses) is to obscure the truth and, more seriously, to muddy the waters of international politics to an alarming degree.

53

Conclusion

There are, finally, two dominant themes in this era. First, there was the dramatic intensification of the war between capital and labor that came to a climax with the succession to the presidency of Theodore Roosevelt and the subsequent rise of the Insurgent and/or Progressive Republicans in 1912. By then the era was more than half over, and the torch of reform passed to Woodrow Wilson, thereby demonstrating that it transcended party affiliations. The second major theme was the appearance of the United States on the stage of international politics. This began with Roosevelt's spectacular intervention in the Russo-Japanese War, perhaps the first "disinterested" act of modern diplomacy. Its second phase was, of course, the entry of the United States into the European War and Wilson's Fourteen Points.

In no other era of our history have two such dominating personalities virtually succeeded each other as presidents of the United States.

Roosevelt ushered in the era with a virtuoso performance unparalleled in the history of American presidents. His strenuous joy in life—his boundless enthusiasm for existence, for his office, for center stage in world history—was thoroughly compelling and probably, as his enemies insisted, somewhat mad. Not only did he vastly enlarge the powers of the presidency, but for all intents and purposes he re-created the office. Among his presidential predecessors, only Washington, Jefferson, and Jackson (Lincoln was a special case of what we might call delayed recognition) had had such a hold on the imaginations of their compatriots. He drew to him as a magnet draws filings the ablest and most idealistic young men and women in the nation and infused the entire Federal government with his energy and zeal. He was a meteor who flamed across the sky in a moment of dazzling brilliance and then flared out. There is no sadder story in our history than Theodore Roosevelt's decline into stridency and irrelevance, nor anything more touching than the fact that those who loved him loved him to the truly bitter end, when, full of futile rage, he was only an unhappy shadow of the real Roosevelt.

Charles Morris, a writer of books for "young people," as teenagers used to be called, wrote in 1910 a book entitled *The Marvelous Career of Theodore Roosevelt, Including What He Has Done and Stands For; His Early Life and Public Services; The Story of His African Trip; His Memorable Journey Through Europe; and His Enthusiastic Welcome Home.* Book Two of the four books the volume was divided into was headed "What Roosevelt Has Done and What He Stands For," and the chapter headings provide a convenient résumé of his admirers' view of the Colonel: "Good Citizenship and a Square Deal for All Men; Controlling the Corporations and Advancing the Reign of Law over That of Force and Fraud; Relations of Capital and Labor and the Arbitration of Labor Disputes; The Larger Good As Contrasted with the Demands of Expediency; The Conservation of Natural Resources and the Development of Public Works; National Defence and the Need of a Strong Army and Navy; Advocate of International Arbitration and World Peace; Hunter, Rancher, and Lover of Nature and Outdoor Life; Roosevelt as Scholar, Author and Orator; The Most Skilful Politician of the Century."

In a nation, among a people not conspicuous for unabashed spontaneity and simple delight in life, President Roosevelt, with his boundless and uninhibited enthusiasms and his remarkable energy, was irresistible, a kind of inspired magician, with, to be sure, a touch of the showman or trickster (charlatan, his enemies said). He suggested new possibilities and dimensions to life, "joy" enlivening "duty," work as play. An incorrigible moralizer (which, of course, appealed profoundly to the persistent moral stratum in American life), he made the moralizing go down all the easier by his talent for dramatization and improvisation. Someone called him pure act, but there was considerably more to the power he exercised over the imagination of his constituents, the American people. It is hard to resist the conviction that his father's "loving affection" (to use William James's phrase) gave him the confidence to be so completely himself that he could trust his instincts (they were not, of course, always right by any means). Clearly Roosevelt was one of those "new men," new human types that American life has been so prolific in, the surprising and unexpected product of a long and complex historical process. As uniquely "American" as Jackson and Lincoln, Roosevelt validated the creative potentialities inherent in the upper-class Eastern "gentlemen." At the moment when it seemed that the "democracy" was capable of responding only to mediocrity and that the "gentleman" was, at least politically, obsolete, Roosevelt demonstrated that the type was not only alive and well but capable of generating the kind of political excitement that the Republic had not known since the days of Andrew Jackson. In doing so, he gave the whole country a lift. John Jay Chapman, reconsidering Roosevelt's political career in 1919, wrote: "His genius, his personal power, was so very great that it polarized the minds of all who saw much of him. He was surrounded by adulators. I doubt whether he had a true friend, for his were dazed by him. . . . Roosevelt lived on earth in an apotheosis, flaming swords surrounded him always. One reason was the extreme ignorance about political matters in which his social friends were brought up." He "passed his entire life in this welter and yet became the most vital, most interesting, most important figure of his generation."

Oswald Garrison Villard, in his autobiography, confessed that the only way he could try to encompass Roosevelt was by a list of contrasting characteristics: "loyal and disloyal; intelligently honest and dishonest; truthful and lying; brave and (politically) cowardly; sincere and insincere; ingenuous and disingenuous; scrupulous and unscrupulous; unyielding and compromising; brilliant and commonplace . . . boyish and mature; an actor, a poseur, a passionately sincere advocate, amazingly deft and quick, highly beloved and deeply hated." The press "adored him for himself, because he created so much news, because he was so stimulating, so vital, so athletic. Moreover he took a deep interest in them, in their lives, their interests, their hobbies. He would talk birds with one until two A.M., horses with another, boats with a third. . . ."

For young men like the historian-to-be Samuel Eliot Morison, recently graduated from Harvard and contemplating rather gloomily the American political scene, Roosevelt's presidency was like a fresh breeze or, perhaps better, tornado, blowing away the old politics of cronyism, standpattism, and stubborn reaction. It was Felix Frankfurter's greatest regret that he had not been in Washington during Roosevelt's administration to experience at first hand "the surging, persuasive, dynamic personality of T.R." which "gave impetus and tone and passion to the government." He and his "stout loyal band of able men" had transmitted their vision and their energy to the whole country. He had been "a motive force instead of a ballast, a focuser and director."

If much of what Roosevelt did was more gesture than substance, the gesture was often of considerable importance. For instance, he gave at least the impression of astonishing accessibility. The fact that he reintroduced old-fashioned morality into presidential politics was not something that won him credit with the advocates of the new scientific approach to social and economic problems, but it added vastly to the dramatic side effects of his presidency, and these, we would argue, were as important in the long run as particular pieces of reform legislation.

All this was in a large measure secondary to his achievements in the realm of international politics. Although the present mode is to deplore his foreign policies and acts as ushering in the era of American imperialism, the fact is that he asserted the power and influence of the United States in world affairs in a remarkably skillful and relatively benign manner. His intervention in the Russo-Japanese war was a daring and imaginative act that announced the arrival of the United States as a world power. The morality of the Panama Canal deal aside, the building of it was another landmark in the expansion of American influence and, equally important, American trade, and it brought the United States into a new and important relationship with the Far East. Granted he was too ready to indulge in gunboat diplomacy in the Caribbean; his prescription of "speaking softly and carrying a big stick," for all its cynical realism, proved, in a fallen world, the penultimate basis of international politics. The fact that the "stick" today is too big to carry and too frightening to contemplate using should not obscure the soundness of the formula for the time in which it was enunciated.

Wilson closed the era Roosevelt had opened as the central actor in a world historical drama of incomprehensible vastness and complexity. A Virginian, Wilson was New England Puritanism/Calvinism revived. Austere, constipated, grimly moralistic (they both were moralistic for a certainty), he represented "the other half " of the American psyche, so to speak. The old Puritan zeal to remake the world burned in his breast. Certainly the will to dominate was in both men. Roosevelt wanted to do it in the traditional way, with battleships and soldiers—the "big stick," power politics of the conventional kind. Wilson wanted to dominate it by ideas, to make the United States "as a city upon a hill," the emancipator of mankind. All that pure personality, that charm as compelling as a magic potion could accomplish, Roosevelt accomplished. All that intellect and will could accomplish, Wilson accomplished.

Roosevelt was robust, if not stout; Wilson was the first thin President since Lincoln (there had been indeed only three other thin presidents—Jefferson, John Quincy Adams, and Jackson). Wilson, Calvinistic, if not a Calvinist, was the Puritan preacher/teacher reincarnated, a throwback to colonial New England. "Teddy," in his self-indulgent hedonism, in his infatuation with sports, with football, with hunting and boxing and the outdoor life in general, was in his psychic life a representative of the new consciousness. But Roosevelt's *ideas* were, for the most part, archaic in the extreme. Both men were pious, but Wilson scorned the simple moralisms that Roosevelt so tirelessly reiterated in his high-pitched voice. *His* relationship to God was at once more intimate and more reserved. With a mind perhaps overstocked with Burkean precepts and a corresponding and excessive reverence for British constitutionalism, Wilson was also deeply affected by George Herron's brand of Christian socialism, and while he was understandably reserved on the socialist issue, it greatly enlarged his ideas about the relationship of government to its citizens.

Both men saw life as pervaded by moral principles. To Roosevelt these were, in essence, the simple directives of *McGuffey's Readers:* Fear God and take your own part (the title of one of his books); be clean, manly, honest, and brave. Wilson's moral vision was more sophisticated, as befitted a professor. To put the matter succinctly, Roosevelt's personality looked forward while his mind looked back. With Wilson it was the reverse: His personality was thoroughly archaic; his intellect was far more "progressive" than that of his archrival.

Both men were spellbinding orators, but Roosevelt was a spellbinding orator of the William Jennings Bryan school. It was his assertion of commonplaces with irresistible gusto that captivated audiences. They could not always remember what he had said, but they felt marvelously uplifted. Read today, the speeches seem trite. But Wilson's speeches have that fusion of thought and emotion that makes for enduring utterance. "If style is the ultimate morality of mind," as Alfred North Whitehead put it, Wilson deserves to have his mind judged by his style, and the judgment must be that it was first-rate. Of all the presidents, only John Quincy Adams was his equal in that regard, and only Lincoln his superior. In the judgment of John Jay Chapman, Wilson was as "quotable" as Lincoln. Wherever his words came from, "they really come out of the brain of one hundred years of America."

There was a third remarkable personality of the era whose reputation was diminished by his failure to achieve the office that alone guarantees at least a modest degree of immortality. William Jennings Bryan was in many ways the most appealing of our three heroes, the most human, the politician closest to those famous "grass roots." Herbert Croly called him "amiable, winning, disinterested, courageous, enthusiastic, genuinely patriotic, and after a fashion, liberal in spirit . . . a Democrat of both Jeffersonian and Jacksonian tendencies . . . an advanced contemporary radical . . . more of a radical than any other political leader of similar prominence. . . ." He had, after all, "openly and unequivocally" advocated the public ownership of the railroads and proposed "Federal regulation of corporations . . . much more drastic than that of Mr. Roosevelt." William Allen White wrote: "I believe he was as honest and brave a man as I ever met, with a vast capacity for friendship. For his was an ardent nature. . . . I have never met a man with a kindlier face, with a gentler, more persuasive voice, nor with seemingly more profound ignorance about sophisticated, mundane matters. He was a twelve-year-old-boy in many things, yet a prophet far more discerning of the structure of the world that would be, and should be . . . than any of us"—Roosevelt or Wilson or La Follette.

With his Western manner, his simplicity and openness, his kindness and lack of pretense, Bryan won most people who knew him. When he became secretary of state, the State Department professionals were dismayed. To them he was a kind of political rube, an amusing specimen of *Politicus westernus,* the antithesis of the Harvard- or Yale-educated gentlemen who had so often occupied that office. But such, Florence Harriman wrote, "was the magnetism and power of the man" that when he took leave of the employees of the department, "they filed past him, many of them weeping. They couldn't but realize his thorough goodness and honesty of purpose." That he was weak on diplomatic protocol Mrs. Harriman conceded, but "he instinctively reads the thoughts of the common people, and has consistently for years fought to bring the government nearer to them. He is a prophet and evangelist, a blazer of trails, and lover of the heights."

One of the most striking characteristics of the time is that everything became political to a degree unequaled since the early days of the Republic (the Civil War, of course, excepted; the Civil War excepts everything). Art, literature, theology, economics, the relations between men and women, sex—all were political; all were involved in the creation of a new consciousness. Suddenly it seemed that the ancient, creaky, and discredited machinery of American politics might, after all, be cleaned, oiled, repaired, renovated, tuned up, and made, at long last, an instrument of the popular will of the "many" rather than the agent of the privileged and, worse, the unscrupulous "few."

One interpretation of the so-called Progressive Era has been that the upper classes, accustomed to running the country, and finding themselves displaced by middle- and lower-middle-class political hustlers, took up the Progressive cause in anger and frustration over their displacement. That is not the perspective of this volume. What we might call the rise of the gentleman-reformer was not an indication of loss of political power and influence by the upper class but rather an awakened determination on the part of many members of that class to play, for the first time since pre–Civil War days, a political role commensurate with their social standing and their education. Of course, it was more complicated since it supplemented (where it did not follow in the footsteps of) the efforts of small-town, middle-class, predominantly Midwestern and Western reformers. So it was both *an element in* and *a contributor to* the new consciousness that was taking shape. It was a far more an *action* than a *reaction,* a reaching for influence and power in a relatively disinterested spirit rather than an effort to retrieve power. It had, moreover, a substantial immigrant and working-class dimension and discovered its original impulse in the ancient Protestant Passion for the redemption of the world.

Index

FOR THE BEST IN PAPERBACKS, LOOK FOR THE

In every corner of the world, on every subject under the sun, Penguin represents quality and variety—the very best in publishing today.

For complete information about books available from Penguin—including Pelicans, Puffins, Peregrines, and Penguin Classics—and how to order them, write to us at the appropriate address below. Please note that for copyright reasons the selection of books varies from country to country.

In the United Kingdom: For a complete list of books available from Penguin in the U.K., please write to *Dept E.P., Penguin Books Ltd, Harmondsworth, Middlesex, UB7 0DA.*

In the United States: For a complete list of books available from Penguin in the U.S., please write to *Dept BA, Penguin*, Box 120, Bergenfield, New Jersey 07621-0120.

In Canada: For a complete list of books available from Penguin in Canada, please write to *Penguin Books Ltd, 2801 John Street, Markham, Ontario L3R 1B4.*

In Australia: For a complete list of books available from Penguin in Australia, please write to the *Marketing Department, Penguin Books Ltd, P.O. Box 257, Ringwood, Victoria 3134.*

In New Zealand: For a complete list of books available from Penguin in New Zealand, please write to the *Marketing Department, Penguin Books (NZ) Ltd, Private Bag, Takapuna, Auckland 9.*

In India: For a complete list of books available from Penguin, please write to *Penguin Overseas Ltd, 706 Eros Apartments, 56 Nehru Place, New Delhi, 110019.*

In Holland: For a complete list of books available from Penguin in Holland, please write to *Penguin Books Nederland B.V., Postbus 195, NL-1380AD Weesp, Netherlands.*

In Germany: For a complete list of books available from Penguin, please write to *Penguin Books Ltd, Friedrichstrasse 10-12, D-6000 Frankfurt Main 1, Federal Republic of Germany.*

In Spain: For a complete list of books available from Penguin in Spain, please write to *Longman, Penguin España, Calle San Nicolas 15, E-28013 Madrid, Spain.*

In Japan: For a complete list of books available from Penguin in Japan, please write to *Longman Penguin Japan Co Ltd, Yamaguchi Building, 2-12-9 Kanda Jimbocho, Chiyoda-Ku, Tokyo 101, Japan.*

FOR THE BEST IN HISTORY, LOOK FOR THE

FOR THE BEST IN HISTORY, LOOK FOR THE

☐ **THE FACE OF BATTLE**
John Keegan

In this study of three battles from three different centuries, John Keegan examines war from the fronts—conveying its reality for the participants at the "point of maximum danger."
366 pages   ISBN: 0-14-004897-9 $6.95

☐ **VIETNAM: A HISTORY**
Stanley Karnow

Stanley Karnow's monumental narrative—the first complete account of the Vietnam War—puts events and decisions of the day into sharp, clear focus. "This is history writing at its best."—*Chicago Sun-Times*
752 pages   ISBN: 0-14-007324-8 $12.95

☐ **MIRACLE AT MIDWAY**
Gordon W. Prange
with Donald M. Goldstein and Katherine V. Dillon

The best-selling sequel to *At Dawn We Slept* recounts the battles at Midway Island—events which marked the beginning of the end of the war in the Pacific.
470 pages   ISBN: 0-14-006814-7 $10.95

☐ **THE MASK OF COMMAND**
John Keegan

This provocative view of leadership examines the meaning of military heroism through four prototypes from history—Alexander the Great, Wellington, Grant, and Hitler—and proposes a fifth type of "post-heroic" leader for the nuclear age.
368 pages   ISBN: 0-14-011406-8 $7.95

☐ **THE SECOND OLDEST PROFESSION**
Spies and Spying in the Twentieth Century
Phillip Knightley

In this fascinating history and critique of espionage, Phillip Knightley explores the actions and missions of such noted spies as Mata Hari and Kim Philby, and organizations such as the CIA and the KGB.
436 pages   ISBN: 0-14-010655-3 $7.95

☐ **THE STORY OF ENGLISH**
Robert McCrum, William Cran, and Robert MacNeil

"Rarely has the English language been scanned so brightly and broadly in a single volume," writes the *San Francisco Chronicle* about this journey across time and space that explores the evolution of English from Anglo-Saxon Britain to Reagan's America.
384 pages   ISBN: 0-14-009435-0 $12.95